Frommer's

Great Britain

2nd Edition

by Darwin Porter & Danforth Prince

Here's what the critics say about Frommer's:

"Amazingly easy to use. Very portable, very complete."

—*Booklist*

"Detailed, accurate, and easy-to-read information for all price ranges."
—*Glamour Magazine*

"Hotel information is close to encyclopedic."

—*Des Moines Sunday Register*

"Frommer's Guides have a way of giving you a real feel for a place."
—*Knight Ridder Newspapers*

WILEY

Wiley Publishing, Inc.

About the Authors

A native of North Carolina, **Darwin Porter** was a bureau chief for the *Miami Herald* when he was 21 and was assigned to write the very first edition of a Frommer's guide devoted solely to one European country. Since then, he has written numerous best-selling Frommer's guides, notably to France, Italy, and Germany. In 1982, he was joined in his research efforts across England by **Danforth Prince,** formerly of the Paris bureau of the *New York Times,* who has traveled in and written extensively about England. Together, they are also the authors of *Frommer's London, Frommer's England, Frommer's England from $70 a Day,* and *Frommer's Scotland.*

Published by:

Wiley Publishing, Inc.

111 River St.
Hoboken, NJ 07030

ISBN 0-7645-3823-3
ISSN 1534-911X

Editor: Naomi P. Kraus
Production Editor: Ian Skinnari
Cartographer: Elizabeth Puhl
Photo Editor: Richard Fox
Production by Wiley Indianapolis Composition Services

For information on our other products and services or to obtain technical support, please contact our Customer Care Department within the U.S. at 800-762-2974, outside the U.S. at 317-572-3993 or fax 317-572-4002.

Wiley also publishes its books in a variety of electronic formats. Some content that appears in print may not be available in electronic formats.

Manufactured in the United States of America

5 4 3 2

Contents

10   Cambridge & Oxford   385

11   The Northwest & the Lake District   414

12   Yorkshire & Northumbria   448

13   Edinburgh & the Lothian Region   469

List of Maps

An Invitation to the Reader

In researching this book, we discovered many wonderful places—hotels, restaurants, shops, and more. We're sure you'll find others. Please tell us about them, so we can share the information with your fellow travelers in upcoming editions. If you were disappointed with a recommendation, we'd love to know that, too. Please write to:

Frommer's Great Britain, 2nd Edition
Wiley Publishing, Inc. • 111 River St. • Hoboken, NJ 07030

An Additional Note

Please be advised that travel information is subject to change at any time—and this is especially true of prices. We therefore suggest that you write or call ahead for confirmation when making your travel plans. The authors, editors, and publisher cannot be held responsible for the experiences of readers while traveling. Your safety is important to us, however, so we encourage you to stay alert and be aware of your surroundings. Keep a close eye on cameras, purses, and wallets, all favorite targets of thieves and pickpockets.

Frommer's Star Ratings, Icons & Abbreviations

Every hotel, restaurant, and attraction listing in this guide has been ranked for quality, value, service, amenities, and special features using a **star-rating system.** In country, state, and regional guides, we also rate towns and regions to help you narrow down your choices and budget your time accordingly. Hotels and restaurants are rated on a scale of zero (recommended) to three stars (exceptional). Attractions, shopping, nightlife, towns, and regions are rated according to the following scale: zero stars (recommended), one star (highly recommended), two stars (very highly recommended), and three stars (must-see).

In addition to the star-rating system, we also use **seven feature icons** that point you to the great deals, in-the-know advice, and unique experiences that separate travelers from tourists. Throughout the book, look for:

Finds	Special finds—those places only insiders know about
Fun Fact	Fun facts—details that make travelers more informed and their trips more fun
Kids	Best bets for kids, and advice for the whole family
Moments	Special moments—those experiences that memories are made of
Overrated	Places or experiences not worth your time or money
Tips	Insider tips—great ways to save time and money
Value	Great values—where to get the best deals

The following **abbreviations** are used for credit cards:

AE	American Express	DISC	Discover	V	Visa
DC	Diners Club	MC	MasterCard		

Frommers.com

Now that you have the guidebook to a great trip, visit our website at **www.frommers.com** for travel information on more than 3,000 destinations. With features updated regularly, we give you instant access to the most current trip-planning information available. At Frommers.com, you'll also find the best prices on airfares, accommodations, and car rentals—and you can even book travel online through our travel booking partners. At Frommers.com, you'll also find the following:

- Online updates to our most popular guidebooks
- Vacation sweepstakes and contest giveaways
- Newsletter highlighting the hottest travel trends
- Online travel message boards with featured travel discussions

What's New in Great Britain

The landscape of the three countries that make up Great Britain—England, Scotland, and Wales—is constantly shifting and being redefined at all times. In 2003, Britain distanced itself from Europe in two significant ways: it joined the U.S. in ousting Saddam Hussein in Iraq, and it reportedly has decided against adopting the euro, retaining the British pound sterling as its mode of currency. Here are some more of the latest developments:

SETTLING INTO LONDON Accommodations Prices go higher and higher, and still people arrive by the thousands checking in regardless of the cost.

The historic section of London known as Holborn now has a government-rated five-star hotel, the **Renaissance London Chancery Court,** 252 High Holborn, WC1 (© **020/7829-9888** and 020/829-9888), and already *The London Times* is hailing it as "one of the most exciting hotels in the world." This deluxe palace was refashioned from a landmark 1914 building in the financial district. On a more modest level, **New England,** 20 Saint George's Dr., SW1 (© **020/7834-1595**), has been completely refurbished and is today one of the finer choices in the Pimlico area around Victoria Station. The 19th-century exterior has been overhauled, and the interior brought completely up-to-date.

Dining The explosion of top-notch restaurants in London continues with the opening of **Club Gascon,** 57 West Smithfield, EC1 (© **020/7796-0600**), which brings a slice of southwestern France to London. This is the home of foie gras, Armagnac, and duck confit, each one delectably served at this domain of Chef Pascal Aussignac, a darling of London food critics.

At the British Museum, **The Court Restaurant,** Great Russell St., WC1 (© **020/7323-8978**), is previewing its affordable yet top-notch continental cuisine. The dining room overlooks the famous round Reading Room. You get culture and good food at the same address. TV chef and ex-Armani model Ed Baines is luring the *Sex and the City* crowd to his new Soho eatery, **Randall & Aubin,** 16 Brewer St., W1 (© **020/7287-4447**), which serves some of the district's best seafood dishes. His *soupe de poisson* or fish soup is acclaimed as Soho's best.

See chapter 4 for complete details.

EXPLORING LONDON The first major crossing over the Thames in a century, the wobbling **Millennium Bridge** is once again accepting foot passengers. The bridge closed after its opening at the millennium as it was feared unsafe. Now after 100 dampers and shock absorbers, the 1,050-foot span sees thousands of foot passengers cross it every day.

On the South Bank of the Thames, **London City Hall,** The Queen's Walk, SE1 (© **020/7983-4100**), has opened as the new office of the Lord Mayor. Visitors can explore the controversial structure, especially its rooftop gallery with panoramic views over London.

One of London's newest attractions is the **Dalí Universe,** County Hall, Riverside Building, South Bank, SE1 (© **020/7620-2720**). Featuring more than 500 works by the late Surrealist artist, this collection of Dalí is predictably filled with surprises ranging from his Mae West "lips sofa" to a monumental oil painting used in the Hitchcock movie, *Spellbound.*

At Windsor, site of the castle that is the favorite home of Queen Elizabeth II, the **Jubilee Gardens** are drawing thousands of visitors. The new, 2-acre gardens inside the castle's main entrance were created to honor the Queen's Jubilee.

On another front, her Majesty is selling her homemade jams and even her specially brewed beer at the **Windsor Farm Shop,** Datchet Rd., Old Windsor (© **01753/623800**). The queen also sells pheasants and partridges bagged in royal shoots.

See chapter 5 for more details.

SOUTHEAST ENGLAND Near the ancient battlefield of Battle, **Powder Mills Hotel,** Powder Mills Lane, Battle (© **01424/775511**), has opened to rave reviews. Set on 150 privately owned acres, this is one of the gems of the area. The historic property in the past attracted such visitors as the duke of Wellington.

In Brighton, called "London by the Sea," the **Brighton Museum & Art Gallery,** Royal Pavilion Gardens (© **01273/290900**), has opened across from the Royal Pavilion. Immediately, this has become one of the great cultural attractions of southeast England, with an eclectic collection of world art and artifacts.

See chapter 6 for more information.

THE SOUTH In the resort of Southsea, two early-20th-century homes have been combined to form the well-run **Westfield Hall,** 65 Festing Rd. (© **023/9282-6971**), outside Portsmouth. A family-run hotel, it's a most affordable choice. Bournemouth is hardly a citadel of haute cuisine, but with the opening of **The Grove Seafood Restaurant,** 79 Southbourne Grove (© **01202/566660**), it now has a superb place to eat. Serving the freshest seafood dishes in the area, the chefs cook dishes to order—so be prepared to wait.

See chapter 7 for further details.

THE WEST COUNTRY Generating the most excitement among the attractions of Bath, the **Thermae Bath Spa,** The Hetling Pump Room, Hot Bath St. (© **01225/780308**), is the only place in the U.K. where you can bathe in natural spring water. Health, leisure, architecture, history, and culture are combined at this new spa with its bubbling, mineral-rich waters.

In the cathedral city of Exeter, **Barcelona,** Magdalen St. (© **01392/281000**), is being hailed as the "designer hotel of the year." A former eye hospital has been cleverly recycled into a top-notch hotel whose rooms in part, evoke either the '30s or '60s. Its on-site Café Paradiso is arranged like a big-top circus.

See chapter 8 for more information.

SHAKESPEARE COUNTRY Harvard House, High St. (© **01789/204507**), in **Stratford-Upon-Avon** was the home of Katherine Rogers, mother of John Harvard, founder of Harvard University. Today the house has been turned into a Museum of British Pewter, tracing the use of pewter from the Roman era until modern times.

See chapter 9 for more details.

EDINBURGH One of the most elegant hotels of Edinburgh is the newly reopened **The Edinburgh Residence,** 7 Rothesay Terrace (© **01312/263380**), which coddles you in luxury in a series of town-house suites housed in a trio of beautifully restored Georgian buildings.

One of the most stylish hotels, **Point Hotel,** 34 Bread St. (© **01312/ 215555**), has opened in the shadow of the Edinburgh Castle. That fortress might be old, but this discovery is acclaimed by an architectural book as one of the 50 premier hotel designs in the world.

A hot new dining venue is **Howies,** 10–14 Victoria St. (© **01312/ 251721**), which is known for its first-rate Scottish cuisine and use of regional produce. Try their casserole of Scottish beef with wild mushrooms.

Beneath the City Chambers on the Royal Mile, **The Real Mary King's Close,** Writer's Court (© **0870/243- 0160**), is the city's latest attraction. It's a dug-out warren of long hidden streets where Edinburghers lived and worked for centuries.

For more details, see chapter 13.

THE BORDERS & GALLOWAY REGION

In the Kelso area in the Borders, the little **Edenwater House,** Ednam (off B6461; © **01573/ 224070**), is emerging as one of the finest places for a stopover in this region of southern Scotland. A former private manor house, it is increasingly acclaimed for serving some of the finest cuisine in the Borders as well.

See chapter 14 for more details.

GLASGOW

The historic Copthorne Hotel, erected in 1810 and famous for its role in World War II history, has re-emerged as the **Millennium Hotel Glasgow,** George Square (© **01413/326711**). Though completely modernized, the aura lives on here in its public rooms. Generating a lot of local press coverage, **Langs,** 2 Port Dundas (© **01413/331500**), is a hotel oddity for Glasgow in that it's decorated in a minimalist Japanese style and is trendy and contemporary, unlike many of the city's historic Victorian landmarks.

The Russians have invaded Glasgow with the opening of **Café Cossachok,** 10 King St. (© **01415/530733**) in Merchant City. Near the Tron Theatre, the chefs concentrate mainly on Russian cuisine but are also adept at turning out Armenian, Georgian, and Ukranian dishes. **Amaryllis,** at the swank Devonshire Gardens Hotel, 1 Devonshire Gardens (© **01413/ 373434**), has been taken over by Gordon Ramsay, England's most acclaimed chef, although he is of Scottish birth. Ramsay is not always here, of course, but his culinary concepts permeate the atmosphere.

The famous **Glasgow Art Gallery** has closed for renovation until 2006. In the meantime, many of its masterpieces are on display at the relatively little known **McLellan Galleries,** 20 Sauchiehall St. (© **01413/311854**), including a superb collection of Dutch and Italian Old Masters—everyone from Giorgione to Rembrandt.

See chapter 15 for more details.

CARDIFF & SOUTH WALES

The actor John Malkovich, along with investors, has opened **The Big Sleep Hotel,** Bute Terrace in Cardiff (© **029/2063-6363**). A rather dull office tower from the 1960s has been successfully converted into this chic yet affordable minimalist hotel. Sixteen kilometers (10 miles) west of the city, **Llanerch Vineyard,** Hensol (© **01443/225877**), has opened, offering country living in a farmhouse dating from 1848. It stands in a Vale of Glamorgan vineyard.

On the Cardiff restaurant front, **Da Castaldo,** 5 Romilly Crescent, Canton (© **029/2022-1905**), has opened, serving the best Italian cuisine in the Welsh capital. This popular bistro specializes in the robust cookery so beloved by the citizens of Naples.

See chapter 20 for more details.

1

The Best of Britain

Planning a trip to Britain can present you with a bewildering array of choices. We've scoured the country in search of the best places and experiences, and in this chapter we'll share our very personal and opinionated choices. We hope they'll give you some ideas and get you started.

1 Best British Experiences

- **Enjoying a Night at the Theater:** The torch passed down from Shakespeare is still burning brightly. Today, London's theater scene is acknowledged as the finest in the world. There are two major subsidized companies, the Royal Shakespeare Company, performing at the Barbican in London and at Stratford-upon-Avon, and the National Theatre on the South Bank. Fringe theater offers surprisingly good and often innovative productions staged in venues ranging from church cellars to the upstairs rooms of pubs.

- **Pub Crawling:** The pursuit of the pint takes on cultural significance in Britain. Ornate taps fill tankards and mugs in pubs that serve as the social heart of every village and town. Quaint signs for such names as the Red Lion or the White Swan dot the landscape and beckon you in—not only for the pint but also for the conviviality and perhaps even the food.

- **Motoring Through the Cotswolds:** If *driving* means going on a determined trip from one place to another, motoring is wandering at random, and there's no better place for it than the Cotswolds, located less than 100 miles west of London. Its rolling hills are peppered with ivy-covered inns and honey-colored stone cottages. See chapter 9.

- **Punting on the Cam:** This is Cantebridgian English for gliding along in a flat-bottom boat, a long pole pushed into the River Cam's shallow bed, as you watch the strolling students along the graveled walkways, and take in the picture-postcard vistas of green lawns along the water's edge. See chapter 10.

- **Touring Stately Homes:** Britain has hundreds of mansions open to visitors, some of them centuries old, and we'll tell you about dozens of them in the pages that lie ahead. The homes are often surrounded by beautiful gardens, and when the owners got fanciful, they added splashing fountains and miniature pagodas or temples.

- **Shopping for Antiques:** Whatever old treasure you're seeking, it can be found somewhere in Britain. We're talking Steiff teddy bears, a blunderbuss, an 1890 tinplate toy train, a first-edition English print from 1700, or the definitive Henry Harper grandfather clock. No one polishes up their antiques and curios quite as brightly as British dealers. From auction houses to quaint shops,

The Regions in Brief

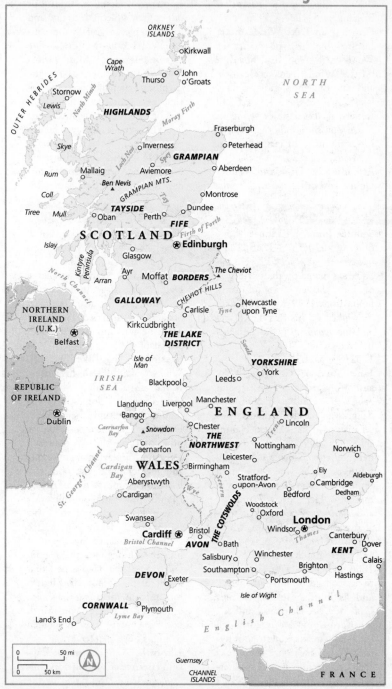

ORKNEY
ISLANDS
Kirkwall
Cape
Wrath
Thurso   John
o'Groats
NORTH
SEA
OUTER HEBRIDES
Stornow
Lewis
North Minch
HIGHLANDS
Moray Firth
Fraserburgh
Skye
Inverness   Peterhead
GRAMPIAN
Spey
Rum   Mallaig   Aberdeen
Aviemore
Ben Nevis
GRAMPIAN MTS.
Coll
Montrose
Tay
TAYSIDE   Dundee
Tiree   Mull   Oban   Perth
FIFE
SCOTLAND   Firth of Forth
Islay   Edinburgh
Glasgow
Kintyre
Peninsula   Ayr   Moffat   BORDERS   The Cheviot
North Channel   Arran   CHEVIOT HILLS
GALLOWAY   Carlisle   Tyne   Newcastle
upon Tyne
Kirkcudbright
NORTHERN
IRELAND
(U.K.)   THE LAKE
DISTRICT
Belfast   Isle of
Man   Swale   YORKSHIRE
IRISH   York
REPUBLIC   SEA   Leeds
OF IRELAND   Blackpool
Dublin   Llandudno   Liverpool   Manchester
Bangor   ENGLAND
Caernarfon   Snowdon   Chester   Trent   Lincoln
Bay   THE
NORTHWEST   Nottingham
Caernarfon   Norwich
Cardigan   Leicester
Bay   WALES   Birmingham   Ely
Aberystwyth   Stratford-   Cambridge   Aldeburgh
upon-Avon   Dedham
Cardigan   Wye   Bedford
Severn   Woodstock
Swansea   THE COTSWOLDS   Oxford
Cardiff   Bristol   London
St. George's Channel   AVON   Bath   Windsor   Thames
Bristol Channel   Canterbury
Salisbury   Winchester   KENT   Dover
DEVON   Southampton   Brighton   Calais
Exeter   Portsmouth   Hastings
CORNWALL   Plymouth   Isle of Wight
Land's End   Lyme Bay   English Channel

0   50 mi
0   50 km
Guernsey
CHANNEL
ISLANDS   FRANCE

from flea markets to country fairs, Britain, particularly Victorian Britain, is for sale.

- **Cruising on Lake Windermere:** Inspired by the lyric poetry of Wordsworth, you can board a boat at Windermere or Bowness and sail England's most famous lake. You'll see the Lake District's scenery, its tilled valleys lying in the shadow of forbidding peaks, as it was meant to be viewed—from the water. See chapter 11.
- **Attending a Highland Game:** Unlike any other sporting event,

a Highland Game in Scotland emphasizes clannish traditions rather than athletic dexterity, and the centerpiece is usually the exhibition of brute strength (tossing logs and the like). Most visitors show up for the men in kilts, the bagpipe playing, the pomp and circumstance, and the general celebration of all things Scottish. The best-known (and most widely televised) of the events is the **Braemar Royal Highland Gathering,** held near Balmoral Castle the first Saturday in September. See chapter 18.

2 The Best of Literary Britain

- **Samuel Johnson's House** (London; ℭ **020/7373-3745**): The backwater at No. 17 Gough Square, situated on the north side of Fleet Street, was Johnson's home from 1749 to 1758. Here he worked on his Rambler essays and his *Dictionary,* and here his beloved wife, "Tetty," died in 1752. See p. 163.
- **Jane Austen Country:** The author of *Pride and Prejudice* and *Sense and Sensibility* wrote of rural delights and a civilized society— set mainly in her beloved Hampshire. In 1809, she moved with her mother to Chawton, 50 miles south of Bath, where she lived until 1817. Her house is now a museum. Her novels *Persuasion* and *Northanger Abbey* are associated with the city of Bath, which she visited frequently in her youth and where she lived from 1801 to 1806. In her final year, she moved to 8 College St. in Winchester, and is buried in Winchester Cathedral. See chapters 7 and 8.
- **Stratford-upon-Avon:** Although the Bard remains a mysterious figure, the folks who live in touristy Stratford gleefully peddle his literary legacy. There is Shakespeare's

Birthplace, where the son of a glover was born on April 23, 1564. He died in Stratford on the same day, 52 years later. Anne Hathaway's cottage, in the hamlet of Shottery, is also popular; Shakespeare married Hathaway when he was only 18 years old. See chapter 9.
- **Grasmere** (The Lake District): William Wordsworth lived here with his sister, Dorothy, who commented on the "domestic slip of mountain" behind their home, Dove Cottage. The cottage itself is now part of the Wordsworth Museum, displaying manuscripts and memorabilia. The poet also lived for a time at nearby Rydal Mount, just north of Ambleside (one of his descendants still owns the property), where you can see gardens landscaped by the poet himself. Throughout the region, you'll find the landscapes that inspired this giant of English romanticism, including the shores of Ullswater, where Wordsworth saw his famous "host of golden daffodils." See chapter 11.
- **Haworth** (West Yorkshire): England's second major literary pilgrimage site is the home of the

Brontë Parsonage Museum. Here the famous Brontë sisters lived and spun their web of romance. Emily wrote *Wuthering Heights,* Charlotte, *Jane Eyre* and *Villette,* and even Anne wrote two novels, *The Tenant of Wildfell Hall* and *Agnes Grey,* although neither matches up to her sisters' work. See chapter 12.

- **Abbotsford House** (Melrose; ✆ **01896/752043**): In the Scottish Borders, this was the home that Sir Walter Scott, author of some of Britain's most memorable historical novels, built and lived in from 1812 until this death. In the Scottish baronial style, the mansion is filled with artifacts and mementos including his death mask. See p. 520.

- **Dylan Thomas Boathouse** (Laugharne, Wales; ✆ **01994/427420**): Ten miles east of Tenby in Wales, Swansea-born Dylan Thomas lived and worked. Later, of course, he was to be acclaimed as one of the great poets of the 20th century, but this "untidy wretch of a man" turned out his masterpieces in a modest little shack here. It's one of the most evocative literary shrines in Britain. See p. 715.

3 The Best of Legendary Britain

- **Stonehenge** (near Salisbury, Wiltshire): The most celebrated prehistoric monument in all of Europe, Stonehenge is some 5,000 years old. Despite the "definitive" books written on the subject, its original purpose remains a mystery. Was it an astronomical observatory for a sun-worshipping cult? The romantic theory that Stonehenge was "constructed by the druids" is nonsense, because it was completed before the druids reached Britain in the 3rd century B.C., but the legend still persists. See chapter 7.

- **Glastonbury Abbey** (Somerset): One of the great abbeys of England and once a center of culture and learning, Glastonbury quickly fell into ruins following the dissolution of the monasteries. One story about the abbey says that Jesus came here as a child with Joseph of Arimathea. According to another legend, King Arthur was buried at Glastonbury, which was the site of the fabled Avalon. Today, the abbey's large ruins are open to the public. See p. 302.

- **Tintagel** (Cornwall): On the windswept Cornish coast, the castle of Tintagel is said to have been the birthplace of King Arthur. The castle was actually built much later than the Arthurian legend, around 1150. But who wants to stand in the way of a good story? No one in Cornwall, that's for sure. Tintagel merrily touts the King Arthur legend—in town, you can order an Excaliburger! See chapter 8.

- **The Loch Ness Monster:** Scotland's most famous inhabitant and one of the country's greatest tourist attractions may not even exist! File that under "believe it or not." On any given day, you'll find visitors standing along the banks of Loch Ness waiting for Nessie to appear. Real or imagined, she's virtually the mascot of Scotland. See chapter 19.

4 The Best of Norman & Medieval Britain

- **Battle** (East Sussex): This is the site of the famous Battle of Hastings (fought on October 14, 1066), in which the Normans defeated King Harold's English army. A great commemorative abbey was built here by William the Conqueror, the high altar of its church erected over the spot where King Harold fell in battle. The abbey was destroyed at the time of the dissolution of the monasteries in 1538. A plaque identifies the place where the altar stood. Some ruins and buildings remain, about which Tennyson wrote, "O Garden, blossoming out of English blood." See chapter 6.

- **Hastings Castle** (Hastings, on the south coast of England): Now in ruins, this was the first of the Norman castles erected in England (ca. 1067). King John defortified the fortress in 1216. An audiovisual presentation of the castle's history—shown on the grounds—includes the famous battle of 1066. See p. 221.

- **Rye** (Sussex): Near the English Channel, and flourishing in the 13th century, this "Antient Cinque Port" was a smuggling center for centuries. Writer Louis Jennings once wrote, "Nothing more recent than a Cavalier's Cloak, Hat and Ruffles should be seen on the streets of Rye." It's one of England's best-preserved towns. See chapter 6.

- **Dunster Castle** (in the West Country): This castle, administered by the National Trust, was built on the site of a Norman castle granted to William de Mohun of Normandy by William the Conqueror shortly after his conquest of England. A 13th-century gateway remains from the original fortress. See p. 306.

- **Warwick Castle:** This is one of the major sights in the Midlands. Little remains of William the Conqueror's motte and bailey castle of 1068, but much of today's external structure remains unchanged from the mid-1300s. Today, Warwick Castle is the finest medieval castle in England, lying on a cliff overlooking the Avon. One of the best collections of medieval armor and weapons in Europe is housed behind its walls. See p. 357.

- **Dryburgh Abbey** (the Scottish Borders): Begun in 1150 against a meandering curve of the River Tweed, Dryburgh was once home to thousands of monks who transformed the surrounding forests into arable fields and drained many local swamps. The abbey's position astride the much-troubled border with England resulted in its destruction on three occasions (1322, 1385, and 1544), the last of which included the burning of the nearby village (Dryburgh) as well. Today, the red sandstone rocks are reminders of a long-ago monastic age. See p. 518.

- **Conwy Castle** (North Wales): Edward I ordered this masterpiece of medieval architecture constructed after he'd subdued the last native prince of Wales. Visitors today can tour the royal apartment where Edward brought his queen, Eleanor. The castle's eight towers command the estuary of the River Conwy. See p. 743.

5 The Best Museums

- **British Museum** (London): When Sir Hans Sloane died in 1753, he bequeathed to England his vast collection of art and antiquities for only £20,000 ($34,000). This formed the nucleus of the collection that would one day embrace everything from the Rosetta stone to the hotly contested Elgin marbles (Greece wants them back). It's all here—and much more—in one of the world's great museums. See p. 146.

- **National Gallery** (London): One of the world's greatest collections of Western art dazzles the eye. Every artist from da Vinci to Rembrandt to Picasso is represented here. The gallery is especially rich in works by Renaissance artists. See p. 148.

- **Tate Britain** (London): Two great national collections—some 10,000 works—call this gallery home. Sir Henry Tate, a sugar producer, started the nucleus of the collection with only 70 or so paintings. But the Tate has grown and was considerably enlarged when J. M. W. Turner bequeathed some 300 paintings and 19,000 watercolors to England on his death. See p. 147.

- **National Gallery of Scotland** (Edinburgh): This museum boasts a small but choice collection whose presence in Edinburgh is firmly entwined with the city's self-image as Scotland's cultural capital (Glaswegians will happily dispute that idea). Highlights include works by Velázquez, Zurbarán, Verrocchio, del Sarto, and Cézanne. See p. 498.

- **National Museum of Scotland** (Edinburgh): In 1998, the collections of the Royal Museum of Scotland and the National Museum of Antiquities were united into a coherent whole. Here you'll find everything you ever wanted to know about Scotland, from prehistory to the Industrial Age, as represented by the unsparing views of life in the Saltmarket District of Glasgow. It's all here, from a milk bottle once carried by Sean Connery when he was a milkman to a rock that's 2.9 billion years old from the Isle of South Uist. See p. 499.

- **Burrell Collection** (Glasgow): The contents of this collection were accumulated through the exclusive efforts of Sir William Burrell (1861–1958), an industrialist who devoted the last 50 years of his life to spending his fortune on art. Set in a postmodern building in a suburb of Glasgow, it's one of Scotland's most admired museums, with a strong focus on medieval art, 19th-century French paintings, and Chinese ceramics. See p. 560.

- **Hunterian Art Gallery** (Glasgow): This museum owns much of the artistic estate of James McNeill Whistler, as well as a re-creation of the home of Scotland's most famous designer, Charles Rennie Mackintosh. Grand oils are on display, including works by Whistler, Rubens, and Rembrandt, as well as one of the country's best collections of 19th-century Scottish paintings. See p. 561.

- **National Museum of Wales** (Cardiff): At this museum, the country's finest, you are carried through the panorama of the history of this little country from prehistoric times until the present. There are a lot of surprises along the way—for example, its collection of 18th-century porcelain is one of the finest in the world. See p. 689.

6 The Best Cathedrals

- **Westminster Abbey** (London): One of the world's greatest Anglo-French Gothic buildings has witnessed a parade of English history—from the crowning of William the Conqueror on Christmas Day 1066 to the funeral of Princess Diana in 1997.

With few exceptions, the kings and queens of England have all been crowned here, and many are buried here as well. See p. 143.

- **Canterbury Cathedral:** The object of countless pilgrimages, as described in Chaucer's *Canterbury Tales,* this cathedral replaced one that was destroyed by fire in 1067. A new cathedral, dedicated in 1130, was also destroyed by fire in 1174, when the present structure was built. Thomas à Becket, the archbishop of Canterbury, was murdered here, and his shrine was an important site for pilgrims until the Reformation. See p. 206.

- **Winchester Cathedral:** Construction of the cathedral that dominates this ancient city and capital of old Wessex began in 1079. In time, Winchester Cathedral became England's longest medieval cathedral, noted for its 12-bay nave. Many famous people are buried here, including Jane Austen. See p. 248.

- **Salisbury Cathedral:** The most stylistically unified of the cathedrals in England, this edifice was built between 1220 and 1265. The landmark spire—its most striking feature—was completed in 1325. Salisbury Cathedral epitomizes the Early English style of architecture. See p. 278.

- **York Minster:** The largest Gothic cathedral north of the Alps is also among the grandest, with incredible stained-glass windows. In fact, these windows combine to create the largest single surviving collection of medieval stained glass in England. Its unusual octagonal Chapter House has a late-15th-century choir screen by William Hyndeley. See p. 450.

- **Melrose Abbey** (The Borders): If it weren't for the abbey's location in the frequently devastated Borders, this would be one of the world's most spectacular ecclesiastical complexes. Founded in the 1100s, Melrose acquired vast wealth and was the target of its covetous enemies; it was burned and rebuilt several times before the Protestant takeover of Scotland. Today, this is one of the world's most beautiful ruins, a site immortalized by Robert Burns, who advised people to visit it only by moonlight. See p. 519.

- **Cathedral of St. Kentigern** (Glasgow): In the 7th century, St. Mungo built a wooden structure here, intending it as his headquarters and eventual tomb. It burned down but was rebuilt in the 1300s. St. Kentigern is mainland Scotland's only complete medieval cathedral, with a form based extensively on the pointed arch. In the 1600s, the Calvinists stripped it of anything hinting at papist idolatry, although a remarkable set of sculptures atop its stone nave screen, said to be unique in Scotland, still represent the seven deadly sins. See p. 563.

- **Dunfermline Abbey** (Fife): During the 1100s, in its role as Scotland's Westminster Abbey, Dunfermline became one of Europe's wealthiest churches. Three kings of Scotland were born here, and 22 members of the Scottish royal family were buried here. In the early 1800s, its ruined premises were partially restored to what you see today. Several years later, a different kind of benefactor, Andrew Carnegie, was born within the cathedral's shadow. See p. 598.

- **Llandaff Cathedral** (Llandaff, Wales): Begun under the Normans but added to the Middle Ages, this cathedral outside Cardiff makes a dramatic impression. From the 13th century, its west front is one of the best works of medieval art in Wales. That didn't prevent Cromwell's armies from using the edifice as a beer hall. See p. 689.

7 The Best Castles, Palaces & Historic Homes

- **Woburn Abbey:** A Cistercian abbey for 4 centuries and the seat of the dukes of Bedford, Woburn Abbey has been visited by everybody from Queen Victoria to Marilyn Monroe. You'll see Queen Victoria's bedroom and the Canaletto room, with its 21 perspectives of Venice. The grounds, even more popular than the house, include the Wild Animal Kingdom, the best zoological collection in England after the London Zoo. See p. 202.

- **Windsor Castle:** The largest inhabited stronghold in the world and England's largest castle, Windsor Castle has been a royal abode since William the Conqueror constructed a motte and bailey on the site 4 years after conquering England. Severely damaged by fire in 1992, the castle has been mainly restored. Its major attraction is the great Perpendicular Chapel of St. George's, begun by Edward IV. See p. 196.

- **Blenheim Palace** (Woodstock): England's answer to Versailles, this extravagant baroque palace was the home of the 11th duke of Marlborough as well as the birthplace of Sir Winston Churchill. Sir John Vanbrugh, of Castle Howard fame, designed the structure. Sarah, the duchess of Marlborough, wanted "a clean sweet house and garden be it ever so small." That she didn't get—the structure measures 255m (850 ft.) from end to end. Capability Brown designed the gardens. See p. 413.

- **Knole** (Kent): Begun in 1456 by the archbishop of Canterbury, Knole is celebrated for its 365 rooms (one for each day of the year), its 52 staircases (for each week of the year), and its 7 courts (for each day of the week). Knole, one of England's largest private houses and set in a 1,000-acre deer park, is a splendid example of Tudor architecture. See p. 225.

- **Penshurst Place** (Kent): One of England's most outstanding country homes, this mansion was the former residence of Elizabethan poet Sir Philip Sidney (1554–86). In its day, the house attracted literati, including Ben Jonson. The original 1346 hall has seen the subsequent addition of Tudor, Jacobean, and neo-Gothic wings. See p. 227.

- **Hever Castle & Gardens** (Kent): This was the childhood home of Anne Boleyn, second wife of Henry VIII and mother of Queen Elizabeth I. In 1903, American multimillionaire William Waldorf Astor, bought the castle, restored it, and landscaped the grounds. From the outside, it still looks like it did in Tudor times, with a moat and drawbridge protecting the castle. See p. 227.

- **Beaulieu Abbey-Palace House** (Beaulieu, in New Forest): The home of the first Lord Montagu, Palace House blends monastic Gothic architecture from the Middle Ages with Victorian trappings. Yet many visitors consider the property's National Motor Museum, with a collection of more than 250 antique automobiles, more fascinating than the house. See p. 262.

- **Harewood House & Bird Garden** (West Yorkshire): Edwin Lascelles began constructing this house in 1759, and his "pile" has been called an essay in Palladian architecture. The grand design involved some of the major talents of the day, including Robert Adam, Thomas Chippendale, and Capability Brown, who developed the grounds. A 4½-acre bird garden features exotic species from all over the world. See p. 460.

- **Castle Howard** (North Yorkshire): This was Sir John Vanbrugh's grand masterpiece and also the first building he ever designed. Many will recognize it as the principal location for *Brideshead Revisited*. A gilt-and-painted dome tops the striking entrance, and the park around Castle Howard is one of the most grandiose in Europe. See p. 459.

- **Edinburgh Castle:** Few other buildings symbolize the grandeur of an independent Scotland as clearly as this one. Begun around A.D. 1000 on a hilltop high above the rest of Edinburgh, it witnessed some of the bloodiest and most treacherous events in Scottish history, including its doomed 1573 defense by Scottish patriot Grange in the name of Mary Queen of Scots. See p. 492.

- **Palace of Holyroodhouse** (Edinburgh): Throughout the clan battles for independence from England, this palace served as a pawn between opposing forces being demolished and rebuilt at the whim of whomever held power at the time. In its changing fortunes, it has housed a strange assortment of monarchs involved in traumatic events: Mary Queen of Scots, Bonnie Prince Charlie, James VII (before his ascendancy to the throne), and French King Charles X (on his forced abdication after an 1830 revolution). The building's present form dates from the late 1600s, when it was

rebuilt in a dignified neo-Palladian style. Today, Holyroodhouse is one of Queen Elizabeth II's official residences. See p. 493.

- **Culzean Castle** (6.5km/4 miles west of Maybole): Designed for comfort and prestige, this castle was built in the late 1700s by Scotland's most celebrated architect, Robert Adam, as a replacement for a dark, dank, fortified tower that had stood for longer than anyone could remember. It was donated to the National Trust for Scotland just after World War II. A suite was granted to Dwight D. Eisenhower for his lifetime use, in gratitude for his role in staving off a foreign invasion of Britain. See p. 571.

- **Stirling Castle** (Stirling): Stirling is a triumph of Renaissance ornamentation, a startling contrast to the severe bulk of many other Scottish castles. Despite its beauty, after its completion in 1540 the castle was one of the most impregnable fortresses in the British Isles, thanks partly to its position on a rocky crag. See p. 614.

- **Scone Palace** (2 miles from Perth): As early as A.D. 900, Scottish kings were crowned here, on a lump of granite so permeated with ancient magic the English hauled it off to Westminster Abbey in the 13th century, where it remained until 1995. The building you see today was rebuilt in 1802 from ruins that incorporate a 1580 structure and stones laid during the dim early days of Scottish and Pictish union. See p. 638.

- **Glamis Castle** (Dundee): This castle's core was built for defense against rival clans during the 1400s, but over the centuries it evolved into a luxurious dwelling. The ghost of Lady Glamis, whom James V had burnt as a witch when she resisted his annexation of her castle, is said to haunt the property. It figured into the ambitions of Macbeth, thane of Glamis, as well. See p. 645.

- **Caernarfon Castle** (North Wales): This is as close as Wales comes to having a royal palace. It even impressed Dr. Samuel Johnson on a visit. It was here that the investiture of Charles as prince of Wales took place in 1969. Construction started in 1283 and proceeded rapidly, as 11 great towers and massive curtain walls were built to protect the castle's interior. See p. 735.

8 The Best Gardens

- **Royal Botanic (Kew) Gardens** (near London): A delight in any season. Everything from delicate exotics to common flowers and shrubs bloom in profusion in this 300-acre garden. It's all part of a vast lab dedicated to identifying plants from all parts of the globe and growing some for commercial purposes. An easy trip from London, Kew Gardens possesses the largest herbarium on earth. Fabled landscape architect Capability Brown helped lay out some of the grounds. See p. 167.

- **Sissinghurst Castle Garden** (Kent): A notorious literary couple, Vita Sackville-West and Harold Nicolson, created this garden in sunny Kent. Its flamboyant parentage, unusual landscaping (the grounds were laid between the surviving parts of an Elizabethan mansion), and location just 21 miles (34km) northeast of Cranbrook make it the most intriguing garden on London's doorstep. Overrun by tourists in summer, it's lovely in autumn, when the colors are at their dramatic best. See p. 228.

- **Stourhead** (near Shaftesbury): Outside of the Greater London area, this is the most famous garden in England. The birthplace of English landscape gardening, Stourhead is still the best-executed example of the taste for natural landscaping that swept England in the 1700s. The grounds have been compared to the painting of an old master such as Constable, but in 3-D. It's home to a wealth of flowering shrubs, trees, and beds upon beds of multihued blooms. Grottoes, bridges, and temples add to the allure. See p. 304.

- **Hidcote Manor Garden** (near Chipping Campden, in the Cotswolds): Just outside one of the Cotswolds' most charming towns lies this stunning garden, laid out around a stone-built manor house. It's the largest garden in the Cotswolds, and one of the most intriguing in all of Britain. The garden originally bloomed under Major Lawrence Johnstone, an American horticulturist who created it in 1907. He traveled the world and brought back specimens to plant here. See p. 382.

- **Royal Botanic Garden** (Edinburgh): Scotland's greatest garden lies only a mile from the center of Edinburgh, set on 70 acres of Eden. The rhododendrons, the world's greatest collection, are the major attraction, but winding paths lead through a series of lush landscapes. The main role of the garden is actually research into plant life. See p. 502.

9 The Best Luxury Hotels

- **Raffles Brown's Hotel** (London; ✆ **020/7493-6020**): All Chippendale and chintz, Brown's was launched by the former manservant to Lord Byron in 1837, and it's been going strong ever since. Today, it occupies 14 historic houses just off Berkeley Square, and coddles its well-heeled guests in luxury. See p. 103.

- **The Dorchester** (London; ✆ **800/ 727-9820** or 020/7629-8888): Acclaimed for decades as one of the world's great hotels, this citadel of luxury is owned by one of the richest men on earth, the sultan of Brunei. With such an owner, the hotel naturally drips with opulence. After a multimillion-pound restoration, "The Dorch" is more splendid than ever. The rooftop suites are dazzling, and the Promenade, the Grill Room, the Dorchester Bar, and the Oriental Room all deserve their acclaim. See p. 103.

- **Chewton Glen Hotel** (New Milton, Hampshire; ✆ **01425/ 275341**): On the fringe of New Forest between Lymington and Bournemouth, this hotel/health-and-country-club is the best place to stay in southwest England. Service, taste, and quality are its hallmarks. The health club has a stunning design, with a centerpiece swimming pool and 70 acres of manicured grounds. Guest rooms feature period furniture. See p. 263.

- **Ston Easton Park** (near Bath; ✆ **01761/241631**): This splendid 1740 Palladian house has been massively and magnificently restored. The hotel's gardens are reason enough to stay here, but the bedrooms, with Chippendale or Hepplewhite four-poster beds, are equally worthy. Check in here for a taste of 18th-century luxury. See p. 297.

- **Gidleigh Park Hotel** (Chagford, Devon; ✆ 01647/432367): Forty acres of grounds in the Teign valley surround a country-house

hotel that is the epitome of gracious living. Every detail suggests the best of rural life: the premier antiques, those big English sofas, and floral arrangements from the hotel's gardens. All that and it has a reputation for fine food unequaled in the area. See p. 317.

- **The Lygon Arms** (Broadway, Cotswolds; ✆ **01386/852255**): Dating from 1532, this fabled inn in the Cotswolds has hosted many famous guests—Charles I used to drop in, and even Oliver Cromwell spent a night here. Some of the inn's antiques are listed in *The Dictionary of English Furniture*. Request one of the nine rooms in the Tudor Wing that have tilted oak floors and wooden beams. Number 20, with its massive canopied bed, is our favorite. See p. 380.

- **Ettington Park Hotel** (Alderminster, south of Stratford-upon-Avon; ✆ **01789/450123**): From the plant-filled conservatory entrance, right up to the spacious, antiques-filled bedrooms, you know you're getting something special here. The house is refurbished every year, and guests can soak up old-England country-house living in the tasteful Victorian drawing room or the richly paneled library bar. See p. 352.

- **Howard Hotel** (Edinburgh; ✆ **01315/573500**): Three adjacent Georgian-style town houses in an upscale Edinburgh neighborhood have undergone millions of pounds' worth of renovations, creating the most alluring accommodations in a city filled with fine hotels. A restaurant in one of the cellars serves meals inspired by Scotland's traditions and ingredients. See p. 480.

- **Culloden House** (Inverness; ✆ 01463/790461): If you'd like to sleep where Bonnie Prince

Charlie did, head for this Adam-style Georgian mansion on 40 acres of parkland. Scottish tradition appears at every turn, from the grandly proportioned lounge to the sound of a bagpiper on the grounds. Several rooms have spa baths and antique four-posters. See p. 674.

- **One Devonshire Gardens** (Glasgow; ✆ 01413/392001): This is the best-groomed building in a neighborhood filled with similar sandstone-fronted town houses. Ring the doorbell, and an Edwardian-costumed maid will answer, curtsy, and usher you inside as if you're an extra in a Merchant-Ivory film. This re-creation of a high-bourgeois, very proper Scottish home from the early 1900s boasts antique furnishings and

discreetly concealed modern comforts. See p. 552.
- **Inverlochy Castle** (near Fort William; ✆ 01397/702177): This castle was built in 1863 by Lord Abinger in a style that set into stone the most high-blown hopes of Scottish Romantics. Today, lovers can follow the footsteps of Queen Victoria amid the frescoed walls of this Scottish baronial hideaway. See p. 662.
- **Bodysgallen Hall** (Llandudno, North Wales; ✆ 800-260-8338 in the U.S., or 01492/584466): One of Wales's greatest country-house hotels, this 17th-century mansion lies on 200 acres of gardens and parkland. Even though an antique, it oozes with modern comforts while retaining its charms in elegantly furnished suites. See p. 747.

10 The Best Moderately Priced Hotels

- **Hart House Hotel** (London; ✆ 020/7935-2288): This is a well preserved historic Georgian mansion once occupied by French aristocrats during the French revolution. It's been successfully converted into a well-run hotel, a blend of antique and modern. See p. 105.
- **Fielding Hotel** (London; ✆ 020/7836-8305): Named after the novelist Henry Fielding of *Tom Jones* fame, this hotel is one of the most eccentric in London. You'll either love it or hate it. Most guests love its cramped, quirky, quaint aura, and its location at Covent Garden is unbeatable. Everything is old-fashioned and traditional, but if you complain the bedrooms are too small, Smokey, the African gray parrot, will tell you off! See p. 109.
- **Howfield Manor** (west of Canterbury; ✆ 01227/738294): This former manor house outside the

cathedral city retains architectural treasures from its days as part of the Priory of St. Gregory. Bedrooms are divided between the original house and a new one. The manor is filled with character and has lots of details, such as solid oak pieces and exposed beams. See p. 211.
- **Caterham House** (Stratford-upon-Avon; ✆ 01789/267309): In Shakespeare's hometown, this little charmer was formed when two Georgian houses were restored and united into a seamless whole. Close to the Bard's birthplace, it is a family-run inn. See p. 351.
- **Mermaid Inn** (Rye; ✆ 01797/223065): England's most famous smugglers' inn, the Mermaid sheltered Elizabeth I on her visit to Rye in 1573. At the time of the queen's visit, the inn had already been operating for 150 years. Still going strong, it leans heavily on English romance—Old World furnishings, some four-poster

beds, and even a secret staircase. From its doorstep, the cobblestone streets of ancient Rye await exploration. See p. 219.

- **Easton Court Hotel** (Chagford; © **01647/433469**): This 1920s Tudor house was once a favorite of the literati, drawing such luminaries as Evelyn Waugh who wrote *Brideshead Revisited* here. It's a picture-postcard cliché of an English country house, built of stone under a thatch roof with log fires burning. There's even a walled-in flower garden. See p. 316.

- **Apsley House Hotel** (Bath; © **01225/336966**): Away from the city center on the road to Bristol, this 1830 house was supposedly constructed for the duke of Wellington. Its owners have restored it and created a period house of character with an ambience of subdued elegance. See p. 295.

- **Abbey Hotel** (Penzance; © **01736/366906**): Owned by Jean Shrimpton, a former international model, and her husband, Michael Cox, this small-scale hotel is charming and of high quality. Dating from 1660, it occupies the site of a 12th-century abbey overlooking Penzance Harbor. See p. 336.

- **The Judges Lodging** (York; © **01904/638733**): In the 19th century it was the home of a local judge. Today it's been turned into one of the best B&Bs in this historic cathedral city in northeast England. Fall asleep in a four-poster bed in the Prince Albert room—Queen Victoria's consort actually slept here once—and immerse yourself in England's past while still enjoying the comforts of today. See p. 454.

- **Kelvin Park Lorne Hotel** (Glasgow; © **01413/149955**): This charmer in the heart of the

residential West End was based on the designs of Charles Rennie Mackintosh, Scotland's most acclaimed designer. The bedrooms are contemporary but the public rooms evoke the aura of the 19th century. See p. 553.

- **Ednam House Hotel** (Kelso, Scotland; © **01573/224168**): In the Borders of Scotland, this 1761 Georgia house—called "that lovely place beside the river"—has been converted to a hotel of charm and grace with period furnishings. See p. 518.

- **Hunting Tower** (Perth; © **01738/583771**): This late-Victorian country house, lying a 10-minute drive from the city center, is for the discerning. A modern wing of comfortable rooms has been added, and taste and concern for guests' welfare permeate this discovery. See p. 636.

- **Polmaily House Hotel** (Drumnadrochit; © **01456/450343**): During your search for Nessie, the Loch Ness monster, you can find lodgings at this inn. The building dates from the 18th century and offers tasteful Edwardian-style living on an 18-acre farm of mixed gardens and woodland. See p. 670.

- **Cardiff Bay** (Cardiff, Wales; © **029/2047-5000**): In the heart of the restored waterfront along the bay of Cardiff, this is an elegant selection, evoking a modern cruise ship in its architectural style. The modern section is skillfully combined with a restored Victorian warehouse. See chapter 20.

- **Henllys Hotel** (The Old Courthouse, Betws-y-Coed, North Wales; © **01690/710534**): This is a luxurious B&B with the amenities of a small inn. It was converted from a Victorian magistrates court and is set in lovely gardens along the river. See p. 730.

11 The Best Restaurants

- **Gordon Ramsay at Claridge's** (London; ✆ 020/499-0099): In his new digs at London's most prestigious hotel, Claridge's, London's hottest chef is still reigning supreme and still dazzling *tout* London with his pots and pans. Everything he does bears an innovative twist, and though he's learned from past chefs, he's a total original. You'll want to adopt him and take him home. See p. 118.

- **Le Gavroche** (London; ✆ 020/7408-0881): Long known for its top-rate French cuisine, this stellar restaurant has risen to the top again following a bit of a slump in the 1990s. Go here for that grand meal and skip the trip to Paris (we don't really mean that). The menu options are a delight, with such tantalizing dishes as a cassoulet of snails with herb-seasoned frog legs. Naturally, the wine cellar is among London's finest. See p. 119.

- **The Carved Angel** (Dartmouth; ✆ 01803/832465): The elegant and airy Devon quayside setting is ideal for the inspired cuisine of Joyce Molyneux, doyenne of British chefs. Her imaginative and inventive technique is based on strong British tradition, but more and more, the flavors and aromas of Provence, Italy, and even Asia are appearing on the menus. A mandatory stop for foodies. See p. 325.

- **The Moody Goose** (Bath; ✆ 01225/466688): In this ancient spa city of highly competitive restaurants, this citadel of fine English cuisine has surfaced to the top. In an elegant Georgian terrace building, the chefs operate with a passion for fresh ingredients and food cooked to order—and they do so rather brilliantly. See p. 297.

- **Le Champignon Sauvage** (Cheltenham; ✆ 01242/573449): David Everitt-Matthias has awakened the sleepy taste buds of Cheltenham. Thoroughly imbued in the French classics, he also adds more modern and lighter touches to his table d'hôte menus, the finest at this old spa. Some dishes reach into the old English repertoire, including stuffed leg of wild rabbit served with black pudding and turnip sauerkraut. His desserts are acclaimed as the most luscious in England. See p. 363.

- **Le Manoir aux Quat' Saisons** (Great Milton, southeast of Oxford; ✆ 01844/278881): The country-house hotel and restaurant of self-taught chef Raymond Blanc have brought him a TV series, as well as cookbooks and a school of cuisine. Although still showing intensely French loyalties, the celebrated chef now roams the world for inspiration. A new lightness, inspired mainly by Japan and the Mediterranean, is more evident in his creations. More meatless dishes appear on the seasonal menu as well, although the classics remain. See p. 408.

- **Martin Wishart** (Edinburgh; ✆ 01315/5335571): This is Scotland's restaurant of the year, serving a modern French cuisine against a minimalist decor. The chef is hailed for knowing how to "marry" ingredients. See p. 491.

- **Pompadour Restaurant** (in the Caledonian Hotel, Edinburgh; ✆ 01312/228888): Named after the mistress of Louis XV, this dining room that opened in 1925 was once viewed as the only place in Edinburgh where you could find a decent meal. It's still serving them today, better than ever. Scottish specialties reign supreme at lunch, giving way in the evening to cuisine celebrating the Auld Alliance with France. Go for the multi-course tasting menu. See p. 486.

- **Cameron's** (Glasgow; ℃ **01412/ 045555**): This is the most glamorous restaurant in Glasgow's best hotel, and it also serves the finest cuisine, a modern Scottish version. The chef features market-fresh ingredients concentrating on the bounty of Scotland itself. See p. 555.
- **Ostlers Close** (Cupar, Fife; ℃ **01334/655574**): Chef Jimmy Graham is one of the finest in the St. Andrews area, and he's known to pick his own wild mushrooms. Golfers with discriminating palates flock to this modestly appointed place, which makes the best use of fish and seafood from the Fife coast and ducks from a local free-range supplier. Everything is accurately cooked and delectable. See p. 612.
- **Inverlochy Castle** (near Fort William; ℃ **01397/702177**): Cherubs cavort across frescoed ceilings and chandeliers drip with Venetian crystal in a dining room created in the 1870s for a mogul. A Relais & Châteaux member, Inverlochy is likely to draw aristocrats and movie stars with a cuisine focusing on flavor-filled and natural interpretations of Scottish delicacies (the Loch Fyne oysters with watercress-cream sauce, for example). See p. 665.
- **Walnut Tree Inn** (Abergavenny, South Wales; ℃ **01873/852797**). Dedicated foodies often drive all the way across South Wales to dine here, enjoying an unusual combination of kitchens—Welsh and Italian. One of the owners brought an 18th-century recipe for lasagna to Wales. The best of native Welsh produce is also featured. See p. 702.
- **Martins** (Llandudno, North Wales; ℃ **01492/870070**). This bright culinary beacon outshines everything else in the area, showcasing the talents of a superb chef, Martin James. The cuisine features locally caught seafood and market-fresh ingredients concocted into delicious results. See p. 750.

12 The Best Pubs

- **Salisbury** (London; ℃ **020/7836-5863**): Glittering cut-glass mirrors and old-fashioned banquettes, plus lighting fixtures of veiled bronze girls in flowing togas, re-create the Victorian gin-parlor atmosphere right in the heart of the West End. Theatergoers drop in for a homemade meat pie or a salad buffet before curtain time. See p. 194.
- **Grenadier** (London; ℃ **020/ 7235-3074**): Arguably London's most famous pub, and reputedly haunted, the Grenadier was once frequented by the duke of Wellington's officers on leave from fighting Napoleon. It pours the best Bloody Marys in town, and filet of beef Wellington is always a specialty. See p. 192.
- **The Ship Inn** (Exeter; ℃ **01392/ 272040**): Frequented by Sir Francis Drake and Sir Walter Raleigh, this pub on St. Martin's Lane near Exeter Cathedral is the most celebrated in Devon. It still provides tankards of real ale, the same drink swilled down by the likes of Sir John Hawkins. You can also eat here; portions are large, as in Elizabethan times. See p. 313.
- **The Turk's Head** (Penzance, Cornwall; ℃ **01736/363093**):

Dating from 1233, this durable local favorite is filled with artifacts and timeworn beams. Drinkers take their lagers into a summer garden or retreat inside to the snug chambers when the wind blows cold. See p. 337.

- **The Lamb Inn** (Burford; © **01993/823155**): This is our favorite place for a lager in all the Cotswolds. In a mellow old 15th-century house with thick stones and mullioned and leaded windows, it's a good place to spend the night, have a traditional English meal, or just have a beer. Snacks are served in the timeworn bars and lounges or in a garden in summer. See p. 368.

- **The Black Swan** (Stratford-upon-Avon; © **01789/297312**): This has been a popular hangout for Stratford players since the 18th century, and over the years we've spotted everybody from Peter O'Toole to Sir Laurence Olivier here having a drink. Locals affectionately call it "The Dirty Duck." In cool weather, an open fireplace blazes, and you can stick around if you wish and order the chef's specialty: honey-roasted duck. See p. 354.

- **Café Royal Circle Bar** (Edinburgh; © **01315/561884**): The Café Royal Circle stands out in a city famous for its pubs. This longtime favorite, boasting lots of atmosphere and Victorian trappings, attracts a sea of drinkers, locals as well as visitors. See p. 508.

- **Deacon Brodie's Tavern** (Edinburgh; © **01312/256531**): This is the best spot for a wee dram or a pint along Edinburgh's Royal Mile. It perpetuates the memory of Deacon Brodie, good citizen by day and robber by night, the prototype for Robert Louis Stevenson's *Dr. Jekyll and Mr. Hyde*. It's

been around since 1806 and has a cocktail lounge and a rowdy tavern. See p. 508.

- **Globe Inn** (Dumfries; © **01387/252335**): In the Borders, this was Robert Burn's favorite *howff* (small cozy room). Today, you can imbibe as he did in a pub that's been in business since 1610. He liked the place so much that he had a child with a barmaid. A small museum is devoted to Burns. See p. 534.

- **Corn Exchange** (Glasgow; © **01412/485380**): There was a time when it took a bit of courage or a foolish heart to enter a Glasgow pub. Those old days are long forgotten at this reliable pub in the center. In the mid-1800s, the Corn Exchange was here (hence the name), but today it's a watering hole with good drinks and modestly priced bar platters. See p. 571.

- **Dreel Tavern** (Anstruther; © **01333/310727**): Dreel is a 16th-century wood-and-stone coaching inn that was converted into a pub where old salts from the harbor and other locals gather to unwind on windy nights. Try the Orkney Dark Island on hand pump. Anstruther, 74km (46 miles) northeast of Edinburgh, is a gem of a Scottish seaside town and former fishing port. See p. 603.

- **Ship Inn** (Elie; © **01333/330246**): Down at the harbor in this little port town, the Ship Inn is one of the best places for a pint along the east coast. The building dates from 1788 and the pub from 1830. In summer, you can enjoy your pint outside with a view over the water, but on blustery winter days, the blazing fireplace is the attraction. Stick around for dinner—the menu ranges from pheasant to venison to fresh seafood, not your typical pub grub. See p. 604.

- **Angel Tavern** (Cardiff; ⓒ **029/2064-9200**): This is the local favorite, still charming and popular after all these years. Ales are drawn by hand-pumps from the cellars. See p. 699.

- **Griffin Inn** (Llyswen, South Wales; ⓒ **01874/754241**): In the 15th century it was a cider house. Today it's an inn frequented by fishermen casting into the River Wye. It was once voted Britain's "Pub of the Year," and it's just as good or better than ever. See p. 706.

13 The Best Websites for Great Britain

- **Britannia** (www.britannia.com): This expansive site is much more than a travel guide—it's chock-full of lively features, history and regional profiles, including sections on Wales and King Arthur.

- **Automobile Association–UK** (www.theaa.co.uk): This outstanding guide lists hundreds of places to stay, ranked by price and quality with apparently objective reviews. Many of the lodgings accept online bookings. You'll also find dining information with ratings based on food, service, atmosphere, and price. Many restaurants list typical meal prices and which credit cards are accepted.

- **Londontown.com: The Official Internet Site for London** (www.londontown.com): A fab site from the tourist board that will get you panting to start your trip. It lists events, accommodations, attractions, pubs and living it up after dark. Daily special features include discount offers. You can download mini-area maps, by Tube stop, attraction, theater, or street. And the editorial is written like a chat with a friend.

- **The 24 Hour Museum** (www.24hourmuseum.org.uk): This excellent website aims to promote Britain's thousands of museums, galleries, and heritage attractions—and, boy, does it do a good job. It is entertaining and downloads fast. You can search geographically or gear your holiday around one of its themed "trails" and tour Museums and the Macabre, Art Treasures of the North East, and so on.

- **Cathedrals of Britain** (www.cathedrals.org.uk): This well-designed site features dozens of cathedrals, organized by region. Each listing includes a couple of photos, advice for getting there, and history. You could surf here to plan an entire touring vacation.

- **English Heritage** (www.english-heritage.org.uk): Mouthwatering photographs and details of the hundreds of glorious historic castles, country houses, Roman sites, churches, abbeys, and ancient monuments cared for by this organization all over England. This is a must-visit website for pre-trip planning.

- **Travel Scotland** (www.travelscotland.co.uk): Produced in association with the Scottish Tourist Board, this lively site offers restaurant reviews, feature stories, sightseeing advice, and information on upcoming events.

- **Wales Cymru** (www.visitwales.com): The Welsh tourist bureau's website is loaded with information on accommodations, dining, special events, activities, and planning tips. The site also allows visitors to request brochures on outdoor activities, including golf, hiking, fishing, and cycling.

2

A Traveler's Guide to Great Britain's Art & Architecture

by Reid Bramblett

No single artist, period, or museum defines Great Britain's art and architecture. You can see the region's art in medieval illuminated manuscripts, Thomas Gainsborough portraits, and Damien Hirst's pickled cows, its architecture from Norman castles to Christopher Wren's Baroque St. Paul's Cathedral and towering postmodern skyscrapers. This chapter will help you make sense of it all.

1 Art 101

CELTIC & MEDIEVAL (CA. 800 B.C.–16TH CENTURY)

The Celts, mixed with plenty of Scandinavian and Dutch tribes of varying origins, ruled England until the Romans established rule there in A.D. 43. **Celtic art** survived mainly by (1) masquerading as carved swirls and decorations on the "Celtic crosses" peppering medieval cemeteries, and (2) shrinking down to decorate the borders of Bibles and Gospels. The latter, the art of **illuminated manuscript,** thrived on the British Isles during the Dark and Middle Ages. Diligent scholar-monks copied out Bibles, Gospels, holy treatises, historical chronicles, and sometimes pagan texts on vellum manuscripts, decorating the margins with colorful images, illustrations, or ornate, initial letters.

Important examples and artists of this period include:

- **Wilton Diptych, National Gallery, London.** The first truly important, truly British painting, this diptych (a painting on two hinged panels) was crafted in the late 1390s for Richard II by an unknown artist who mixed Italian and northern European influences.
- **Lindisfarne Gospels, British Library, London.** One of Europe's greatest illuminated manuscripts, this work was painted on the "Holy Isle" in the 7th century and now resides in the British Library.
- **Matthew Paris** (died 1259). A Benedictine monk who decorated his own writings, Paris put his significant artistic gifts to good use as the official St. Albans Abbey chronicler. Some of his works survive in London's **British Library** and Cambridge's **Corpus Christi College.**

THE RENAISSANCE & BAROQUE (16TH–18TH CENTURIES)

The **Renaissance** was more of a southern European movement, but Britain's museums contain many important old master paintings from Italy and Germany. Renaissance means "rebirth," in this case, the renewed use of classical styles and forms originating in ancient Greece and Rome. Artists strove for greater naturalism, using newly developed techniques, such as linear perspective. A few foreign Renaissance masters did come to work at the English courts and had an influence on some local artists, but significant Brits didn't emerge until the Baroque period.

The **Baroque,** a more decorative version of the Renaissance, mixes compositional complexity and explosions of dynamic fury, movement, color, and figures with an exaggeration of light and dark, called *chiaroscuro,* and a kind of superrealism based on using peasants as models. The **rococo** is Baroque art gone awry, frothy, and chaotic.

Significant artists of this period include:

- **Pietro Torrigiano** (1472–1528). An Italian Renaissance sculptor, Pietro had to flee Florence after breaking the nose of classmate Michelangelo. He ended up in London crafting elaborate tombs for the Tudors in **Westminster Abbey,** including Lady Margaret Beaufort, and Henry VII and Elizabeth of York. London's **Victoria and Albert Museum** preserves Pietro's terra-cotta bust of Henry VII.
- **Hans Holbein the Younger** (1497–1543). A German Renaissance master of penetrating portraits, Holbein the Younger cataloged many significant figures in 16th-century Europe. These include paintings of Henry VIII and the duke of Norfolk in **Castle Howard** outside York. More works can be found in London's **National Gallery** and **National Portrait Gallery, Windsor Castle,** and Edinburgh's **National Gallery.**
- **Anton Van Dyck** (1599–1641). This Belgian artist painted passels of royal portraits in the Baroque style for Charles I and other Stuarts, setting the tone for British portraiture for the next few centuries and earning himself a knighthood. You'll find his works in London's **National Portrait Gallery, National Gallery,** and **Wilton House,** with more in Oxford's **Ashmolean Museum.**
- **Joshua Reynolds** (1723–92). A fussy Baroque painter and first president of the Royal Academy of Arts, Reynolds was a firm believer in a painter's duty to celebrate history. Reynolds knew on which side his bread was buttered and spent much of his career casting his noble patrons as ancient gods in portrait compositions cribbed from old masters. You'll find his works in London's **National Gallery** and **Tate Britain,** Oxford's **Cathedral Hall,** and the **Aberdeen Art Gallery.**
- **Thomas Gainsborough** (1727–88). Although he was a classical/Baroque portraitist like his rival Reynolds, at least Gainsborough could be original. Too bad his tastes ran to rococo pastels, frothy feathered brushwork, and busy compositions. When not immortalizing noble patrons, such as Jonathan Buttell (better known as "Blue Boy"), he painted quite a collection of landscapes just for himself. His works grace the **Victoria Art Gallery** in Bath (where he first came to fame), London's **National Gallery** and **National Portrait Gallery,** Cambridge's **Fitzwilliam Museum,** Oxford's **Cathedral Hall** and **Ashmolean Museum,** and Edinburgh's **National Gallery.**

THE ROMANTICS

The Romantics felt the classically minded Renaissance and Baroque had gotten it wrong and that the Gothic Middle Ages was the place to be. They idealized the Romantic tales of chivalry, had a deep respect for nature, human rights, and the nobility of peasantry, and a suspicion of progress. Their paintings tended to be heroic, historic, dramatic, and beautiful. They were inspired by critic and art theorist **John Ruskin** (1819–1900), who traveled throughout northern Italy and was among the first to sing the praises of pre-Renaissance painting and Gothic architecture.

Significant artists of this period include:

- **William Blake** (1757–1827). Romantic archetype, Blake snubbed the stuffy Royal Academy to do his own engraving, prints, illustrations, poetry, and painting. He believed in divine inspiration, but it was the vengeful Old Testament God he channeled; his works are filled with melodrama, muscular figures, and sweeping lines. Modern angst-ridden Goth teens really dig his stuff. Judge for yourself at London's **Tate Britain,** Manchester's **Whitworth Art Gallery,** Edinburgh's **National Gallery,** and Glasgow's **Pollock House.**
- **John Constable** (1776–1837). Constable was a great British landscapist, whose scenes (especially those of happy, agricultural peasants) got more idealized with each passing year—while his compositions and brushwork became freer. You'll find his best stuff in London's **National Gallery** and **Victoria and Albert Museum.**
- **J. M. W. Turner** (1775–1851). Turner, called by some "the First Impressionist," was a prolific and multitalented artist whose mood-laden, freely brushed watercolor landscapes influenced Monet. The River Thames and London, where he lived and died, were frequent subjects. He bequeathed his collection of some 19,000 watercolors and 300 paintings to the people of Britain with the request that they be kept in one place. London's **Tate Britain** displays the largest number of Turner's works; others grace London's **National Gallery,** Cambridge's **Fitzwilliam Museum,** Manchester's **Whitworth Art Gallery,** Edinburgh's **National Gallery,** the **Glasgow Art Gallery & Museum,** and the **Aberdeen Art Gallery.**
- **Pre-Raphaelites** (1848–1870s). This "brotherhood" of painters declared that art had gone all wrong with Italian Renaissance painter Raphael (1483–1520) and set about to emulate the Italian painters who preceded him—though they were not actually looking at specific examples. Their symbolically imbued, sweetly idealized, hyper-realistic work depicts scenes from Romantic poetry and Shakespeare's work as much as from the Bible. There were seven founders and many followers, but the most important were Dante Rossetti, William Hunt, and John Millais; you can see work by all three at London's **Tate Britain,** Oxford's **Ashmolean Museum,** and Manchester's **City Art Gallery.**

THE 20TH CENTURY

The only artistic movement or era in which the Brits can claim a major stake is contemporary art, with many British artists bursting onto the international gallery scene just before and after World War II. Art of the last century often followed international schools or styles—no major ones truly originated in Britain—and artists tended to move in and out of styles over their careers. If anything, the greatest artists of this period strove for a unique, individual expression rather than adherence to a particular school.

In the examples below, "London" stands for the **Tate Modern** and "Edinburgh" for the **National Gallery of Modern Art,** the major modern art galleries in those cities. Important British artists of the 20th century include:

- **Henry Moore** (1898–1986). A sculptor, Moore saw himself as a sort of reincarnation of Michelangelo. He mined his marbles from the same quarries as the Renaissance master and let the stone itself dictate the flowing, abstract, surrealistic figures carved from it. He did a lot of public commissions and started working in bronze after the 1950s. The **Henry Moore Institute** in Leeds, where he studied, preserves his drawings and sculpture. You'll also find his work in London, Edinburgh, and in Cambridge's **Fitzwilliam Museum.**
- **Francis Bacon** (1909–92). A dark, brooding expressionist (a style that expresses the artist's inner thoughts and feelings), Bacon presented man's

foibles in formats, such as the triptych (a set of three panels, often hinged and used as an altarpiece), which were usually reserved for religious subjects. Find his works in London, Edinburgh, Manchester's **Whitworth Art Gallery,** and the **Aberdeen Art Gallery.**

- **Lucien Freud** (born 1922). Grandson of the noted psychiatrist, Freud painted portraits and marvelous nudes that live in a depressing world of thick paint, fluid lines, and harsh light. Admire some at London, Edinburgh, and Manchester's **Whitworth Art Gallery.**

- **David Hockney** (born 1937). The closest thing to a British Andy Warhol, Hockney employs a less pop arty style than the famous American—though Hockney does reference modern technologies and culture—and is much more playful with artistic traditions. His work resides in London and Edinburgh.

- **Damien Hirst** (born 1965). The guy who pickles cows, Hirst is a celebrity/artist whose work sets out to shock. He's a winner of Britain's Turner Prize, and his work is prominent in the collection of Charles Saatchi, whose **Saatchi Gallery** in London displays his holdings.

2 Architecture 101

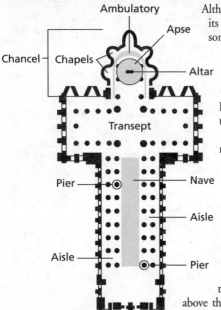

Church Floor Plan

Although each architectural era has its distinctive features, there are some elements, floor plans, and terms common to many. This commonality is particularly true of churches, large numbers of which were built in Europe from the Middle Ages through the 18th century.

From the Norman period on, most **churches** consist either of a single wide **aisle,** or a wide central **nave** flanked by two narrow, less tall aisles. The aisles are separated from the nave by a row of **columns,** or square stacks of masonry called **piers,** connected by **arches.** Sometimes—especially in the medieval Norman and Gothic eras—there is a second level to the nave, above these arches (and hence above the low roof over the aisles) punctuated by windows called a **clerestory.**

This main nave/aisle assemblage is usually crossed by a perpendicular corridor called a **transept** near the far, east end of the church so that the floor plan looks like a **Latin cross** (shaped like a crucifix). The shorter, east arm of the nave is called the **chancel;** it often houses the stalls of the **choir** and the **altar.** Some churches use a **rood screen** (so called because it supports a *rood,* the Saxon word for *crucifixion*) to separate the nave from the chancel. If the far end of the chancel is rounded off, we call it an **apse.** An **ambulatory** is a curving corridor outside the altar and choir area, separating it from the ring of smaller chapels radiating off the chancel and apse.

Some churches, especially after the Renaissance when mathematical proportion became important, were built on a **Greek cross** plan, each axis the same length like a giant "+."

It's worth pointing out that very few buildings (especially churches) were built in only one particular style. These massive structures often took centuries to complete, during which time tastes would change, and plans would be altered.

NORMAN (1066–1200)

Aside from a smattering of ancient sights—**preclassical** stone circles as at Stonehenge and Avebury, **Roman** ruins, such as the Bath spa and Hadrian's Wall—the oldest surviving architectural style in Britain dates to when the 1066 Norman conquest brought the Romanesque era to Britain, where it flourished as the **Norman** style.

Churches in this style were large, with a wide nave and aisles to fit the masses who came to hear mass and worship at the altars of various saints. But to support the weight of all that masonry, the walls had to be thick and solid (meaning they could be pierced only by a few small windows) resting on huge piers, giving Norman churches a dark, somber, mysterious, and often oppressive feeling.

IDENTIFIABLE FEATURES
- **Rounded arches.** These load-bearing architectural devices allowed the architects to open up wide naves and spaces, channeling all that weight of the stone walls and ceiling across the curve of the arch and down into the ground via the columns or pilasters.
- **Thick walls.**
- **Infrequent and small windows.**
- **Huge piers.** These load-bearing, vertical features resemble square stacks of masonry.
- **Chevrons.** These zigzagging decorations often surround a doorway or wrap around a column.

BEST EXAMPLES
- **White Tower, London** (1078). William the Conqueror's first building in Britain, White Tower, is the central keep of the Tower of London. The fortress-thick walls and rounded archways are textbook Norman.

White Tower

- **Cardiff Castle, Cardiff** (begun 1091). Originally built in the Norman style around Roman ruins (many are still incorporated into the design), the interior was restored in the 19th century by Victorian architect William Burges.
- **Conwy Castle, Conwy** (1283–89). Master James of Saint George designed this gritty, dark stone fortress in the Norman style (built after the introduction of the Gothic) for King Edward I.

GOTHIC (1150–1550)

The French Gothic style invaded England in the late 12th century, trading rounded arches for pointy ones—an engineering discovery that freed church architecture from the heavy, thick walls of Norman structures and allowed ceilings to soar, walls to thin, and windows to proliferate.

Instead of dark, somber, relatively unadorned Norman interiors that forced the eyes of the faithful toward the altar, where the priest stood droning on in Latin, the Gothic interior enticed the churchgoers' gaze upward to high ceilings filled with light. The priest still conducted mass in Latin, but now peasants could "read" the Gothic comic books of stained glass windows.

The squat, brooding exteriors of the Norman fortresses of God were replaced by graceful buttresses and soaring spires, which rose from town centers like beacons of religion.

The Gothic proper in Britain can be divided into three overlapping periods or styles: **early English** (1150–1300), **decorated** (1250–1370), and **perpendicular** (1350–1550). Though they share some identifiable features (see the next section), others are characteristic of the individual periods.

Gothic style proved hard to kill in Britain. Among its many revivals, it came back in the 17th century as **Laudian Gothic** in some Oxford and Cambridge buildings and in the 19th century as **Victorian Gothic revival,** discussed below.

IDENTIFIABLE FEATURES

- **Pointed arches** (all periods). The most significant development of the Gothic era was the discovery that pointed arches could carry far more weight than rounded ones.

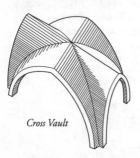

Cross Vault

- **Cross vaults** (all periods). Instead of being flat, the square patch of ceiling between four columns arches up to a point in the center, creating four sail shapes, sort of like the underside of a pyramid. The "X" separating these four sails is often reinforced with ridges called **ribbing.** As the Gothic progressed, four-sided cross-vaults became **fan vaults** (see below), and the spaces between the structural ribbing spanned with decorative **tracery** (see below).
- **Flying buttresses** (all periods). These freestanding exterior pillars connected by graceful, thin arms of stone help channel the weight of the building and its roof out and down into the ground. Not every Gothic church has evident buttresses.
- **Dogtooth molding** (early English). Bands of a repeated decoration of four triangle-shaped petals placed around a raised center.
- **Lancet windows** (early English). Tall, thin pointy windows, often in pairs or multiples, all set into a larger, elliptical pointy arch.

- **Tracery** (decorated and perpendicular). These delicate, lacy spider webs of carved stone often grace the pointy end of windows and the acute lower intersections of **cross vaults** (see above).
- **Fan vaults** (perpendicular). Lots of side-by-side, cone-shaped concave vaults springing from the same point, fan vaults are usually covered in **tracery** (see above).
- **An emphasis on horizontal and vertical lines** (perpendicular). What defines the perpendicular is its broad and rectilinear fashion, especially in the windows.

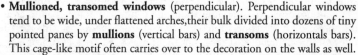

Fan Vault

- **Mullioned, transomed windows** (perpendicular). Perpendicular windows tend to be wide, under flattened arches,their bulk divided into dozens of tiny pointed panes by **mullions** (vertical bars) and **transoms** (horizontals bars). This cage-like motif often carries over to the decoration on the walls as well.
- **Stained glass** (all periods, but more common later). The multitude and size of Gothic windows allowed them to be filled with Bible stories and symbolism writ in the colorful patterns of stained glass.
- **Rose windows** (all periods). These huge circular windows, often appearing as the centerpieces of facades, are filled with elegant **tracery** (see above) and "petals" of stained glass.
- **Spires** (all periods). These pinnacles of masonry seem to defy gravity and reach toward heaven itself.
- **Gargoyles** (all periods). Disguised as wide-mouthed creatures or human heads, gargoyles are actually drain spouts.
- **Choir screen** (all periods). Serving as the inner wall of the ambulatory and outer wall of the choir section, choir screens are often decorated with carvings or tombs.

BEST EXAMPLES

- **Early English:** London's **Salisbury Cathedral** (1220–65) is almost unique in Europe for the speed with which it was built and the uniformity of its architecture (even if the spire was added 100 years later, they kept it early English). The first to use pointy arches was **Wells Cathedral** (1180–1321), with 300 statues on the original facade and some early stained glass.
- **Decorated: Exeter Cathedral** (1112–1206) has an elaborate Decorated facadeand fantastic nave vaulting.

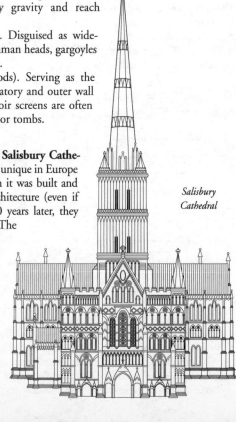

Salisbury Cathedral

- **Perpendicular: King's College Chapel** (1446–1515) at Cambridge has England's most magnificent fan vaulting, along with some fine stained glass. **Henry VII's Chapel** (1503–19) in London's Westminster Abbey is textbook perpendicular.
- **All styles:** The facade, nave, and chapter house of **York Minster** (1220–1480), which preserves the most medieval stained glass in Britain, are decorated, though the chancel is perpendicular, and the transepts survive from early English. Glasgow's **Cathedral of St. Kentigern,** Scotland's only complete medieval cathedral, covers all of the styles of the Gothic period and sports some of the finest Gothic detailing in Great Britain.

RENAISSANCE (1550–1650)

While the European Continent was experimenting with the Renaissance ideals of proportion, order, classical inspiration, and mathematical precision to create unified, balanced structures, England was still trundling along with the late **Tudor Gothic** perpendicular style (the Tudor use of red brick became a major feature of later Gothic revivals) in places such as Hampton Court Palace and Bath Abbey (great fan vaulting).

England's greatest Renaissance architect **Inigo Jones** (1573–1652) brought back from his Italian travels a fevered imagination full of the exactingly classical theories of **Palladianism,** as developed by **Andrea Palladio** (1508–80). However, most English architects at this time tempered the Renaissance style with a heavy dose of Gothic-like elements.

IDENTIFIABLE FEATURES

- **A sense of proportion.**
- **A reliance on symmetry.**
- **The use of classical orders.** This specifies three different column capitals: Corinthian, Ionic, and Doric.

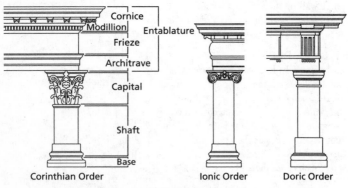

Classical Orders

BEST EXAMPLES

- **Stirling Castle, Stirling.** The palace of James the VI is an excellent example of the Renaissance style, then relatively unknown in Britain.
- **Robert Smythson** (1535–1614). This early Elizabethan-era architect was responsible for one of the greatest mansions of the period: **Longleat House** (1559–80), an elegant Wiltshire manse with a park designed by premier Renaissance landscape architect and garden designer **Capability Brown.**

- **Plas Mawr, Conwy** (1576–85). Built for a Welsh merchant, Plas Mawr is one of the finest surviving examples in Britain of an Elizabethan-era townhouse.
- **Inigo Jones** (1573–1652). Jones applied his theories of Palladianism to such edifices as **Queen's House** (1616–18 and 1629–35) in Greenwich; the **Queen's Chapel** (1623–25) in St. James's Palace and the **Banqueting House** (1619–22) in Whitehall, both in London; and the state rooms of Wiltshire's **Wilton House** (1603), where Shakespeare performed and D-Day was planned. Recently, London's **Shakespeare's Globe Theatre** dusted off one of his never-realized plans and used it to construct its new indoor theater annex.

BAROQUE (1650–1750)

Britain's greatest architect was **Christopher Wren** (1632–1723), a scientist and member of Parliament who got the job of rebuilding London after the Great Fire of 1666. He designed 53 replacement churches alone, plus the new St. Paul's Cathedral and numerous other projects. Other proponents of the Baroque were **John Vanbrugh** (1664–1726) and his mentor and frequent collaborator, **Nicholas Hawksmoor** (1661–1736), who sometimes worked in a more Palladian idiom.

IDENTIFIABLE FEATURES

- **Classical architecture rewritten with curves.** The Baroque is similar to Renaissance, but many of the right angles and ruler-straight lines are exchanged for curves of complex geometry and an interplay of concave and convex surfaces. The overall effect is to lighten the appearance of structures and to add some movement of line.
- **Complex decoration.** Unlike the sometimes severe designs of Renaissance and other classically inspired styles, the Baroque was often playful and apt to festoon structures with decorations intended to liven things up.

BEST EXAMPLES

- **St. Paul's Cathedral, London** (1676–1710). This cathedral is the crowning achievement of both the English Baroque and Christopher Wren himself. London's other main Wren attraction is the **Royal Naval College,** Greenwich (1696).
- **Queen's College, Sheldonian Theatre, and Radcliffe Camera, Oxford. Queen's College** is the only campus of Oxford constructed entirely in one style and includes a library by Hawksmoor. The **Sheldonian Theatre** (1664–69), an almost classically subdued rotunda showing little of later Baroque exuberance, was Wren's first crack at architecture. Compare this to the more Baroque **Radcliffe Camera** (1737–49), designed by James Gibbs (who influenced Thomas Jefferson).

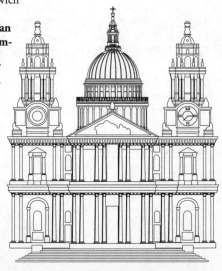

St. Paul's Cathedral

- **Blenheim Palace, Woodstock** (early 1700s). John Vanbrugh's crowning achievement, Blenheim Palace is a British Versailles surrounded by perhaps the best of Capability Brown's gardens.
- **Castle Howard, Yorkshire** (1699–1726). Another masterpiece by the team of Nicholas Hawksmoor and then-neophyte John Vanbrugh, Castle Howard became famous as a backdrop to *Brideshead Revisited*.

NEOCLASSICAL AND GREEK REVIVAL (1714–1837)

Many 18th-century architects cared little for the Baroque, and during the Georgian era (1714–1830) a restrained, simple **neoclassicism** reigned. A few interpretations developed, including a strict adherence to the precepts of Palladianism (see "Renaissance" above) and a more distilled vision as practiced by **Greek Revival** architect **John Soane** (1573–1637). Yet another version introduced by Scot **Robert Adam** (1728–92), a brilliant architect and decorator, was lighter and more gaily elegant than the others.

IDENTIFIABLE FEATURES

- **Mathematical proportion, symmetry, classical orders.** These classical ideals first rediscovered during Renaissance are the hallmark of every classically styled era.
- **Crescents and circuses.** The Georgians were famous for these seamless curving rows of identical stone townhouses with tall windows, each one simple yet elegant inside.
- **Open double-arm staircases.** This feature was a favorite of the neo-Palladians.

BEST EXAMPLES

- **Bath** (1727–75). Much of the city of Bath was made over in the 18th century, most famously by the father-and-son team of **John Woods Sr. and Jr.** (1704–54 and 1728–81, respectively). They were responsible, among others, for the **Royal Crescent** (1767–75), where you can visit one house's interior and lodge in another.

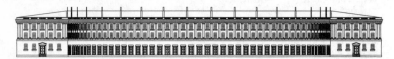

Royal Crescent

- **New Town, Edinburgh** (1767–1823). This urban expansion, chockablock with Georgian townhouses and mansions, is a monument to perfect town planning.
- **Mellarstain, Gordon.** This mansion in the Borders was designed by **William Adams** (1689–1748), Scotland's premier Palladian architect, and his better-known son, Robert Adams, whose picturesque, neoclassical designs and delicate, interior ornamentation influenced architects across Europe and in the United States.
- **John Soane's London sights.** The best Greek Revival building by Soane in London is his own idiosyncratic house (1812–13), now **Sir John Soane's Museum.** Of his most famous commission, the **Bank of England** (1732–34) in Bartholomew Lane, only the facade survived a 20th-century restructuring.

- **British Museum, London** (1823). Not the most important example of Greek Revival, the British Museum, by Robert and Sidney Smirke, is one that just about every visitor to England is bound to see.

VICTORIAN GOTHIC REVIVAL (1750–1900)
While neoclassicists were sticking to their guns in Bath and Edinburgh, the early Romantic movement swept up many others with rosy visions of the past. This imaginary perfect fairytale of the Middle Ages led to such creative developments as the pre-Raphaelite painters (see "The Romantics" earlier in this chapter) and Gothic Revival architects, who really got a head of steam under their movement during the Victorian era.

Gothic "Revival" is a bit misleading, as its practitioners usually applied their favorite Gothic features at random rather than faithfully re-creating a whole structure. Aside from this eclecticism, you can separate the revivals from the originals by age (Victorian buildings are several hundred years younger and tend to be in considerably better shape) and size (the revivals are often much larger).

IDENTIFIABLE FEATURES
- **Mishmash of Gothic features.** Look at the features described under Gothic above, and then imagine going on a shopping spree through them at random.
- **Eclecticism.** Few Victorians bothered with getting all the formal details of a particular Gothic era right (London's Palace of Westminster comes closest). They just wanted the overall effect to be pointy, busy with decorations, and terribly medieval.
- **Grand scale.** These buildings tend to be very large. This was usually accomplished by using Gothic only on the surface, with Industrial Age engineering underneath.

BEST EXAMPLES
- **Palace of Westminster (Houses of Parliament), London** (1835–52). Charles Barry (1795–1860) designed the wonderful British seat of government in a Gothic idiom that, more than most, sticks pretty faithfully to the old perpendicular period's style. His clock tower, usually called Big Ben after its biggest bell, has become an icon of London itself.

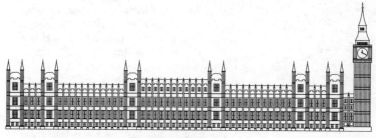

Palace of Westminster

- **St. Andrews Cathedral, Inverness** (1866–69). The castle offers a richly decorated example of Victorian architecture.
- **Albert Memorial, London** (1863–72). In 1861 Queen Victoria commissioned George Gilbert Scott (1880–1960) to build this massive Gothic canopy to memorialize her beloved husband.

- **Castle Coch, Cardiff** (1871). Built on the site of a 13th-century castle destroyed by fire, this fairy tale structure by William Burges (1827–81) contains vaulted ceilings, beautiful friezes, and a gloomy dungeon.

THE 20TH CENTURY

For the first half of the 20th century, Britain was too busy expanding into suburbs (in an architecturally uninteresting way) and fighting wars to pay much attention to architecture. The **Art Nouveau** movement only caught on in Glasgow with native son **Charles Rennie Mackintosh** (1868–1928). After the World War II Blitz, much of central London had to be rebuilt, but most of the new bank buildings and the like that went up in the city held to a functional school of architecture aptly named brutalism. It wasn't until the boom of the late 1970s and 1980s that **postmodern** architecture gave British architects a bold, new direction.

IDENTIFIABLE FEATURES

- **Art Nouveau.** Mackintosh combined native Scottish ideals with Art Nouveau's emphasis on craft, creating asymmetrical, curvaceous designs based on  the organic inspiration of plants and flowers. He produced his designs in wrought iron, stained glass, tile, and hand-painted wallpaper.
    - **Postmodern.** This style combines the skyscraper motif (basically, glass and steel as high as you can stack it) with a reliance on historical details. Like the Victorians, postmodernists recycled elements from architectural history, from classical to exotic.

BEST EXAMPLES

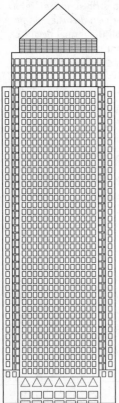

Canary Wharf Tower

- **Glasgow's Mackintosh buildings.** Most of the Art Nouveau movement in Britain stayed indoors as decor; it really only influenced architecture through Glaswegian Mackintosh. His **home and studio,** complete with furniture and architectural detains, is preserved on three levels at the Hunterian Art Gallery. He also designed the **Glasgow School of Art** (1907–9), **Queens Cross Church** (1897–99), and **Hill House** (1902–3) in nearby Helensburgh.
- **Lloyd's Building, London** (1978–86). Lloyd's is *the* British postmodern masterpiece by Richard Rogers (born 1933), who had a hand in Paris's funky Centre Pompidou.
- **Canary Wharf Tower, London** (1986). Britain's tallest building, by César Pelli (born 1926), is the postmodern centerpiece of the Canary Wharf office complex and commercial development.

3

Planning Your Trip to Great Britain

In the pages that follow, we'll outline the various regions of England and explain their appeal to visitors. You'll also find everything you need to know about the practicalities of planning your trip in advance: finding the best airfare, deciding when to go, figuring out British currency, and more.

1 The Regions in Brief

Great Britain is a widely varied island that is actually three countries in one—England, Scotland, and Wales. We'll highlight the main regions in each. To locate each region, see "The Regions in Brief" map on p. 5.

ENGLAND

London Some 7 million Londoners live in this mammoth metropolis, a parcel of land that's more than 1,577 sq. km (609 sq. miles). The City of London proper is merely 1 square mile, but the rest of the city is made up of separate villages, boroughs, and corporations. From London you can take the most important day trip out of the capital to Windsor Castle, Queen Elizabeth II's favorite residence.

The Southeast (Kent, Surrey, & Sussex) This is the land of Charles Lamb, Virginia Woolf, Sir Winston Churchill, and Henry James. Here are some of the nation's biggest attractions: **Brighton, Canterbury, Dover,** and dozens of country homes and castles—not only **Hever** and **Leeds Castles** but also **Chartwell,** the more modest abode where Churchill lived. In small villages, such as **Rye** in Sussex, you discover the charm of the southeast. Almost all of the Sussex shoreline is built up, and seaside towns, such as Hastings, are often tacky. In fact, although the area's major attraction is **Canterbury Cathedral,** the **Royal Pavilion at Brighton** rates as an outstanding, extravagant folly. Tea shops, antiques shops, pubs, and small inns abound in the area. Surrey is essentially a commuter suburb of London and is easily reached for day trips.

The South Southwest of London, these two counties possess two of England's greatest **cathedrals** (Winchester and Salisbury) and one of Europe's most significant prehistoric monuments, **Stonehenge.** But there are other reasons for visiting, too. Hampshire is bordered on its western side by the woodlands and heaths of **New Forest. Portsmouth and Southampton** loom large in naval heritage. In Wiltshire, you encounter the beginning of the **West Country,** with its scenic beauty and monuments— **Wilton House,** the 17th-century home of the earls of Pembroke Dorset, associated with Thomas Hardy, is a land of rolling downs, rocky headlands, well-kept villages, and rich farmlands.

The West Country This is southwest England, centering around the counties of **Somerset, Devon, and Cornwall.** Somerset of King Arthur and Camelot fame offers such magical towns as **Glastonbury.** Devon has both **Exmoor and Dartmoor,** and northern and southern coastlines peppered with such famous resorts as Lyme Regis and such villages as Clovelly. In Cornwall, you're never more than 20 miles from the rugged coastline, which ends at **Land's End.** Among the cities worth visiting in these counties are **Bath,** with its impressive Roman baths and Georgian architecture; **Plymouth,** departure point of the Mayflower; and **Wells,** site of a great cathedral.

Stratford-upon-Avon & the Cotswolds Warwickshire is Shakespeare country in the Midlands, the birthplace of the Industrial Revolution which made Britain the first industrialized country in the world. Its foremost tourist town is **Stratford-upon-Avon,** but also drawing visitors are **Warwick Castle,** one of England's great castles, and the ruins of **Kenilworth Castle.**

A wonderful region to tour, the **Cotswolds** are a bucolic land of honey-colored limestone villages where rural England unfolds before you like a storybook. In the Middle Ages, wool made the Cotswolders prosperous, but now they put out the welcome mat for visitors, with famously lovely inns and pubs. Start at **Burford,** the traditional gateway to the region, and continue on to **Bourton-on-the-Water, Lower and Upper Slaughter, Stow-on-the-Wold, Moreton-in-Marsh, Chipping Campden,** and **Broadway.** In the southern Cotswolds, one of our favorite villages is **Bibury,** with its cluster of former weavers' cottages, Arlington Row.

Cambridge & Oxford These, of course, are England's two great university cities. **Cambridge,** with its colleges and river, is the chief attraction of East Anglia. The most important museum is the Fitzwilliam in Cambridge, but visitors also flock to East Anglia for the scenery and its solitary beauty, fens, salt marshes, and villages of thatched cottages. The other great university is in the much larger and more industrialized city of **Oxford** lying in the Thames Valley. It's possible to visit here on a day trip from London.

Chester & the Lake District Stretching from Liverpool to the Scottish border, northwest England can be a bucolic delight if you steer clear of its industrial pockets. Most people come here to follow in the footsteps of such romantic poets as Wordsworth, who wrote of the beauty of the Lake District. But the walled city of **Chester** merits a stopover along the way. The literary Lakeland evokes memories of the Wordsworths, Samuel Taylor Coleridge, John Ruskin, and Beatrix Potter, among others. **Windermere** makes a good home base, but there are many others as well, including **Grasmere** and **Ambleside.** The Lake District contains some of England's most dramatic scenery.

Yorkshire & Northumbria Yorkshire will be familiar to fans of the Brontës and James Herriot. **York,** with its immense cathedral and medieval streets, is the city to visit. The whole area echoes the ancient border battles between the Scots and English. **Hadrian's Wall,** built by the Romans, is a highlight. Country homes abound; here you find **Harewood House** and **Castle Howard.**

SCOTLAND

Edinburgh & the Lothian Region This area includes not only the country's capital but also West Lothian, most of Midlothian, and East Lothian. Half medieval and half Georgian, **Edinburgh** is at its liveliest every

August at the International Arts Festival, but you can visit **Edinburgh Castle** and **Holyroodhouse** and walk the **Royal Mile** year-round. This is one of Europe's most beautiful capitals, and in 3 days you can do it royally, taking in the highlights of the Old Town and the New Town, which include some of the country's major museums. Edinburgh is surrounded by the major attractions of the Lothian region, which can be visited on day trips.

The Borders & Galloway Regions
Witness to a turbulent history, the Borders and Galloway regions between England and Scotland are rich in castle ruins and Gothic abbeys. Home of the cashmere sweater and the tweed suit, **the Borders** proved a rich mine for the fiction of Sir Walter Scott. Highlights are **Kelso,** which Scott found "the most beautiful," and **Melrose,** site of the ruined **Melrose Abbey** and Scott's former home of **Abbotsford.** Ancient monuments include **Dryburg Abbey,** Scott's burial place. At **Floors Castle,** outside Kelso, you can see one of the great mansions designed by William Adam.

Southwestern Scotland is known as **the Galloway region.** It incorporates much of the former stomping ground of Robert Burns and includes centers like **Dumfries, Castle Douglas,** and **Moffat.** Highlights are the artists' colony of **Kidcudbright,** the baronial **Threave Garden, Sweetheart Abbey** outside Dumfries (the ruins of a Cistercian abbey from 1273), and the **Burns Mausoleum** at Dumfries.

Glasgow & the Strathclyde Region
A true renaissance has come to the once-grimy industrial city of Glasgow, and we recommend that you spend at least 2 days in "the greatest surviving example of a Victorian city." Of course, part of the fun of going to Glasgow is enjoying meeting Glaswegians and, if only temporarily, becoming part of their life. But there are plenty of museums and galleries, too,

notably the **Burrell Collection,** a wealthy shipowner's gift of more than 8,000 items from the ancient world to the modern; the **Hunterian Art Gallery,** with its array of masterpieces by everybody from Rembrandt to Whistler; and the **Art Gallery and Museum at Kelvingrove,** home of Britain's finest civic collection of British and European paintings.

Glasgow is at the doorstep of one of the most historic regions of Scotland. You can explore Robert Burns country in the **Strathclyde** region, or visit a string of famous seaside resorts (including **Turnberry,** which boasts some of the country's greatest golf courses). An especially worthwhile destination in this region is **Culzean Castle,** overlooking the Firth of Clyde and designed by Robert Adam in the 18th century.

Argyll & the Southern Hebrides
Once the independent kingdom of Dalriada, the **Argyll Peninsula** of western Scotland is centered at **Oban,** a bustling port town and one of Scotland's leading coastal resorts. Ace attractions here are **Argyll Forest Park,** actually three forests—Benmore, Ardgartan, and Glenbranter—covering some 60,000 acres. You can also visit **Loch Awe,** a natural moat that protected the Campbells of Inveraray from their enemies to the north, and explore some of Scotland's most interesting islands, including the **Isle of Arran,** called "Scotland in miniature." The **Isle of Islay** is the southernmost of the Inner Hebrides, with lonely moors, lochs, tranquil bays, and windswept cliffs. The **Isle of Jura,** the fourth largest of the Inner Hebrides, is known for its red deer, and it was on this remote island that George Orwell wrote his masterpiece, *1984.* Finally, you can visit **Kintyre,** the longest peninsula in Scotland, more than 97km (60 miles) of beautiful scenery, sleepy villages, and sandy beaches.

Fife & the Central Highlands The "kingdom" of **Fife** is one of the most history-rich parts of Scotland, evocative of the era of romance and pageantry during the reign of the early Stuart kings. Its most enchanting stretch is a series of villages called **East Neuk.** Opening onto the North Sea, **St. Andrews,** the "Oxford of Scotland," is the capital of golf and boasts many great courses. The area is rich in castles and abbeys, notably **Dunfermline Abbey,** burial place of 22 royal personages, and **Falkland Palace and Gardens,** where Mary Queen of Scots came for hunting and hawking. You can also visit **Stirling,** dominated by its castle, where Mary Queen of Scots lived as an infant. **Loch Lomond,** largest of the Scottish lakes, is fabled for its "bonnie bonnie banks," and the **Trossachs** are perhaps the most beautiful area in Scotland, famed for their mountains and lakes.

Aberdeen, The Tayside, & Grampian Regions Carved from the old counties of Perth and Angus, **Tayside** takes its name from its major river, the Tay, running for 192km (119 miles). A lovely region, it's known for salmon and trout fishing. Major centers are **Perth,** former capital of Scotland, standing where the Highlands meet the Lowlands. The area abounds in castles and palaces, including **Glamis,** linked to British royalty for 10 centuries, and **Scone,** an art-filled palace from 1580. The great city of the north, **Aberdeen** is called Scotland's "granite city" and ranks third in population. It's the best center for touring "castle country." **Braemar** is known for its scenery as well as for being the site of every summer's Royal Highland Gathering, and **Balmoral Castle** at Ballater was the "beloved paradise" of Queen Victoria and still is a home to the royal family. Finally, you can follow the **Whisky Trail** to check out some of Scotland's most famous distilleries, including Glenlivet and Glenfiddich.

Inverness & the West Highlands Land of rugged glens and majestic mountain landscapes, the Highlands is one of the great meccas of the United Kingdom. The capital is **Inverness,** one of the oldest inhabited localities in Scotland, and another city of great interest is **Nairn,** old-time royal burgh and seaside resort. Ace attractions are **Loch Ness,** home of the legendary "Nessie," and **Cawdor Castle,** the most romantic in the Highlands, linked with Macbeth. The **Caledonian Canal,** launched in 1803, stretches for 97km (60 miles) of man-made canal, joining the natural lochs. As you proceed to the north you can visit the **Black Isle,** a historic peninsula, before heading for such far northern outposts as **Ullapool,** an 18th-century fishing village on the shores of Loch Broom (and for some, a gateway to the Outer Hebrides), and **John o' Groats,** the most distant point to which you can drive, near the northernmost point of mainland Britain, **Dunnet Head.**

WALES

Cardiff & South Wales The capital of Wales, **Cardiff,** is a large seaport on the tidal estuary of the River Taff. As the center of a small land mass, Wales, Cardiff admittedly can't be compared very well with London or Edinburgh, but it's a charmer in its own right. Newly restored, the capital invites with such attractions as that treasure trove, the **National Museum of Wales,** and **Cardiff Castle,** with all its rich architectural detail. If time remains, dip into **South Wales,** which isn't all remnants of the Industrial Revolution but is filled with beauty spots, such as the **Brecon Beacons National Park.** On the western side of Cardiff is the city of **Swanson,** opening onto Swansea Bay. This is Dylan Thomas country.

North Wales Even more rewarding in scenery than South Wales, North

Wales is a land of mountain peaks, spectacular estuaries, and rugged cliffs brooding over secluded coves, little rivers, valleys, and lakes. Its great towns and villages include **Betws-y-Coed, Llandudno,** and **Conwy,** along with such historic castles as **Harlech, Caernarfon,** and especially **Conwy Castle,** ordered built by Edward I and a masterpiece of medieval architecture. In this region, **Snowdonia National Park** covers 840 square miles of North Wales coastal areas and rugged hills.

2 Visitor Information

Before you go, you can obtain general information from **British Tourist Authority Offices:**

- In the United States: 551 Fifth Ave., Suite 701, New York, NY 10176-0799 (© **800/462-2748** or 212/986-2266; fax 212/986-1188).
- In Canada: 5915 Airport Rd., Mississagua, Toronto, ON L4V 1TI (© **888/VISIT-UK;** fax 905/405-1835).
- In Australia: Level 16, Gateway, 1 Macquarie Place, Sydney NSW 2000 (© **02/9377-4400;** fax 02/9377-4499).
- In New Zealand: P.O. Box 105-652, Aukland 1 (© **0800/700-741;** fax 09/377-6965).

For a full information package on London, write to the **London Tourist Board,** Glen House, Victoria, Stag Place, London SW1E 5LT (© **020/7932-2000**). You can also call the recorded message service, **Visitorcall** (© **0891/505490**), 24 hours a day. Various topics are listed; calls cost 50p (80¢) per minute.

You can usually pick up a copy of *Time Out,* the most up-to-date source for what's happening in London, at any international newsstand. You can also check it out online at **www.timeout.co.uk.**

If you're in London and are contemplating a trip north, you can visit the **Scottish Tourist Board,** 19 Cockspur St., London SW1 75BL (© **020/7930-8661**). In Scotland visit the **Edinburgh and Scotland Information Centre,** Waverley Market, 3 Princes St., Edinburgh EH2 2QP (© **01314/733800**).

Wales, like England and Scotland, has a number of regional tourist offices, but the **Wales Tourist Board** is at Brunel House, 2 Fitzalan Rd., Cardiff CF24 OUY (© **8701/211-251**). Detailed information is also available in London from the Wales Tourist Board, 12 Lower Regent St., London SW1 (© **020/7409-0969**).

WHAT'S ON THE WEB? The most useful site was created by a very knowledgeable source, the British Tourist Authority itself, with U.S. visitors targeted. A wealth of information is tapped at **www.travelbritain.org,** which lets you order brochures online, provides trip-planning hints, and even allows e-mail questions for prompt answers. All of Great Britain is covered.

Getting around London can be confusing, so you may want to visit **www.londontransport.co.uk** for up-to-the-minute info. For the latest on London's theater scene, consult **www.officiallondontheatre.co.uk.** At **www.multimap.com,** you can access detailed street maps of the whole United Kingdom—just key in the location or even just its postal code and a map of the area with the location circled will appear. For directions to specific places in London, consult **www.streetmap.co.uk.**

If you're surfing the web for accommodations, good browsing sites include **www.travelbritain.org** (site of the British Tourist Authority); **www.visitscotland.com** (site of the

Online Traveler's Toolbox

Veteran travelers usually carry some essential items to make their trips easier. Following is a selection of online tools to bookmark and use.

- **Visa ATM Locator** (www.visa.com), for locations of Plus ATMs worldwide, or **MasterCard ATM Locator** (www.mastercard.com), for locations of Cirrus ATMs worldwide.
- **Intellicast** (www.intellicast.com) and **Weather.com** (www.weather.com). Give weather forecasts for all 50 states and for cities around the world, including London.
- **Mapquest** (www.mapquest.com). This best of the mapping sites lets you choose a specific address or destination, and in seconds, it will return a map and detailed directions.
- **Universal Currency Converter** (www.xe.com/ucc). See what your dollar or pound is worth in more than 100 other countries.

Scotland Tourist Board); **www.visit wales.com** (site of the Wales Tourist Board), and **www.travelengland.org. uk** (official online guide to England).

3 Entry Requirements & Customs

ENTRY REQUIREMENTS

All U.S. citizens, Canadians, Australians, New Zealanders, and South Africans must have a passport with at least 2 months validity remaining. No visa is required. The immigration officer will also want proof of your intention to return to your point of origin (usually a round-trip ticket) and visible means of support while you're in Britain. If you're planning to fly from the United States or Canada to the United Kingdom and then on to a country that requires a visa (India, for example), you should secure that visa before you arrive in Britain.

Your valid driver's license and at least 1 year of driving experience is required to drive personal or rented cars.

For information on how to get a passport, go to the Fast Facts section of this chapter. For an up-to-date country-by-country listing of passport requirements around the world, go the "Foreign Entry Requirement" Web page of the U.S. State Department at **http://travel.state.gov/foreignentry reqs.html**.

CUSTOMS

For information on customs limits when entering Britain, **Non-EU Nationals** (including Americans) and **Citizens of the U.K.** can contact HM Customs & Excise at © **0845/010-9000** (from outside the U.K., 020/8929-0152), or consult their website at **www.hmce.gov.uk**.

WHAT YOU CAN TAKE HOME FROM BRITAIN

Returning **U.S. citizens** who have been away for at least 48 hours are allowed to bring back, once every 30 days, $800 worth of merchandise duty-free. You'll be charged a flat rate of 4% duty on the next $1,000 worth of purchases. Be sure to have your receipts handy. On mailed gifts, the duty-free limit is $100. With some exceptions, you cannot bring fresh fruits and vegetables into the United States. For specifics on what you can bring back, download the invaluable free pamphlet *Know Before You Go* online at **www.customs.gov**. (Click "Traveler Information," then "Know

Before You Go.") Or contact the **U.S. Customs Service**, 1300 Pennsylvania Ave. NW, Washington, DC 20229 (© **877/287-8867**) and request the pamphlet.

For a clear summary of **Canadian** rules, write for the booklet *I Declare*, issued by the **Canada Customs and Revenue Agency** (© **800/461-9999** in Canada, or 204/983-3500; www.ccra-adrc.gc.ca).

The duty-free allowance in **Australia** is A$400 or, for those under 18, A$200. A helpful brochure available from Australian consulates or Customs offices is *Know Before You Go*.

For more information, call the **Australian Customs Service** at © **1300/363-263**, or log on to **www.customs.gov.au**.

The duty-free allowance for **New Zealand** is NZ$700. Most customs questions are answered in a free pamphlet available at New Zealand consulates and Customs offices: *New Zealand Customs Guide for Travellers, Notice no. 4*. For more information, contact **New Zealand Customs,** The Customhouse, 17–21 Whitmore St., Box 2218, Wellington (© **04/473-6099** or 0800/428-786; www.customs.govt.nz).

4 Money

It's a good idea to exchange at least some money—just enough to cover airport incidentals and transportation to your hotel—before you leave home, so you can avoid lines at airport ATMs (automated teller machines). You can exchange money at your local American Express or Thomas Cook office, or your bank.

POUNDS & PENCE

Britain's decimal monetary system is based on the pound (£), which is made up of 100 pence (written as "p"). Pounds are also called "quid" by Britons. There are £1 and £2 coins, as well as coins of 50p, 20p, 10p, 5p, 2p, and 1p. Banknotes come in denominations of £5, £10, £20, and £50.

As a general guideline, the price conversions in this book have been computed at the rate of £1 = $1.60 (U.S.). Bear in mind, however, that exchange rates fluctuate daily.

ATMS

The easiest and best way to get cash away from home is from an ATM (automated teller machine). The **Cirrus** (© **800/424-7787**; www.mastercard.com) and **PLUS** (© **800/843-7587**; www.visa.com) networks span the globe; look at the back of your bank card to see which network you're on, then call or check online for ATM locations at your destination. Be sure you know your personal identification number (PIN) before you leave home and be sure to find out your daily withdrawal limit before you depart. Also keep in mind that many banks impose a fee every time a card is used at a different bank's ATM, and that fee can be higher for international transactions (up to $5 or more) than for domestic ones (where they're rarely more than $1.50). On top of this, the bank from which you withdraw cash

---

Regarding the U.S. Dollar, the British Pound & the Euro

You will not see Europe's newest currency, the euro (currently worth approximately $1.10), used in Great Britain, which steadfastly refuses to give up the British pound. As a result, all prices in this book are noted only in pounds and dollars at a rate of £1=$1.60. For up-to-the-minute exchange rates for all three currencies, check the currency converter website **www.xe.com/ucc**.

may charge its own fee. To compare banks' ATM fees within the U.S., use **www.bankrate.com**. For international withdrawal fees, ask your bank.

You can also get cash advances on your credit card at an ATM. Keep in mind that credit card companies try to protect themselves from theft by limiting the funds someone can withdraw outside their home country, so call your credit card company before you leave home.

TRAVELER'S CHECKS

These days, traveler's checks are less necessary than in the past because most cities have 24-hour ATMs that allow you to withdraw small amounts of cash as needed. However, keep in mind that you will likely be charged an ATM withdrawal fee if the bank is not your own, so if you're withdrawing money every day, you might be better off with traveler's checks—provided that you don't mind showing identification every time you want to cash one.

You can get traveler's checks at almost any bank. **American Express** traveler's checks are available over the phone by calling ⓒ **800/221-7282;** Amex gold and platinum cardholders who use this number are exempt from the 1% fee. **AAA** members can obtain checks without a fee at most AAA offices.

Visa offers traveler's checks at Citibank locations nationwide, as well as at several other banks. The service charge ranges between 1.5% and 2%. Call ⓒ **800/732-1322** for information. **MasterCard** also offers traveler's checks. Call ⓒ **800/223-9920** for a location near you.

Foreign currency traveler's checks can be useful when traveling to Great Britain; they're accepted at locations such as bed-and-breakfasts where dollar checks may not be, and they minimize the amount of math you have to do at your destination. **American Express, Visa,** and **MasterCard** all offer checks in British pounds.

If you choose to carry traveler's checks, be sure to keep a record of their serial numbers separate from your checks in the event that they are stolen or lost. You'll get a refund faster if you know the numbers.

CREDIT CARDS

Credit cards are a safe way to carry money, they provide a convenient record of all your expenses, and they generally offer good exchange rates. You can also withdraw cash advances from your credit cards at banks or ATMs, provided you know your PIN. If you've forgotten yours, or didn't even know you had one, call the number on the back of your credit card and ask the bank to send it to you. It usually takes 5 to 7 business days, though some banks will provide the number over the phone if you tell them your mother's maiden name or some other personal information. Your credit card company will likely charge a commission (1%–3%) on every foreign purchase you make, but don't sweat this small stuff; for most purchases, you'll still get the best deal with credit cards when you factor in things like ATM fees and higher traveler's check exchange rates.

Tips **Small Change**

When you change money, ask for some small bills or loose change. Petty cash will come in handy for tipping and public transportation. Consider keeping the change separate from your larger bills, so that it's readily accessible and you'll be less of a target for theft.

Places in England that accept credit cards take MasterCard and Visa and to a much lesser extent, American Express. Diners Club trails in a poor fourth position.

5 When to Go

THE WEATHER

Yes, it rains in England, but you'll rarely get a true downpour. It's heaviest in November (2½ in. on average). English temperatures can range from 30° to 110°F (-1°C–43°C), but they rarely drop below 35°F (1.6°C) or go above 78°F (25.5°C). Evenings are cool, even in summer. Note that the English, who consider chilliness wholesome, like to keep the thermostats about 10°F below the American comfort level. Hotels have central heating, but are usually kept just above the goose bump (in Britspeak, "goose pimple") margin.

Weather is of vital concern in Scotland. It can seriously affect your travel plans. The Lowlands usually have a moderate year-round temperature. In spring, the average temperature is 53°F (11.6°C), rising to about 65°F (18.3°C) in summer. By the time the crisp autumn has arrived, the temperatures have dropped to spring levels. In winter, the average temperature is 43°F (6°C). Temperatures in the north of Scotland are lower, especially in winter, and you should dress accordingly. It rains a lot in Scotland, but perhaps not as much as age-old myths would have it. The rainfall in Edinburgh is exactly the same as that in London. September can be the sunniest month.

Great Britain's Average Daytime Temperatures and Rainfall

	Jan	Feb	Mar	Apr	May	June	July	Aug	Sept	Oct	Nov	Dec
London												
Temp. (°F)	40	40	44	49	55	61	64	64	59	52	46	42
Temp. (°C)	4	4	7	9	13	16	18	18	15	11	8	6
Rainfall (in.)	2.1	1.6	1.5	1.5	1.8	1.8	2.2	2.3	1.9	2.2	2.5	1.9
Edinburgh												
Temp. (°F)	38	38	42	44	50	55	59	58	54	48	43	40
Temp. (°C)	3	3	6	7	10	13	15	14	12	9	6	4
Rainfall (in.)	2.2	1.6	1.9	1.5	2.0	2.0	2.5	2.7	2.5	2.4	2.5	2.4
Cardiff												
Temp. (°F)	40	40	43	46	52	57	61	61	57	52	45	42
Temp. (°C)	4	4	6	8	11	14	16	16	14	11	7	6
Rainfall (in.)	4.2	3.0	2.9	2.5	2.7	2.6	3.1	4.0	3.8	4.6	4.3	4.6

Wales enjoys a temperate climate, but there are variations in the time the seasons change from north to south, from seashore to mountains. For instance, spring comes a week or two earlier to Anglesey in the far northwest than in Snowdonia to its east. In winter, mild sea breezes blow around the southern and western coastal areas; winter can be hard in the mountains, and the peaks may be snow-capped until spring. It rains a lot in the hills and mountains, but, then, Wales has lots of bright, sunny days. In whatever section you plan to visit, it's best to take a light wrap or sweater even in summer, unless you're a hardy northerner from the United States or Canada.

WHEN YOU'LL FIND BARGAINS

The cheapest time to travel to Britain is in the off-season: that means from November 1 to December 12 and December 25 to March 14. In the last few years, the airlines have been offering irresistible fares during these periods. Weekday flights are cheaper than weekend fares (often by 10% or more).

Rates generally increase between March 14 and June 5 and in October, then hit their peak in the high travel seasons between June 6 and September 30 and December 13 and 24. July and August are also the months when most Britons take their own holidays, so besides the higher prices, you'll have to deal with crowds and limited availability of accommodations.

You can avoid crowds by planning trips for November or January through March. Sure, it may be rainy and cold—but Britain doesn't shut down when the tourists leave! In fact, the winter season includes some of London's best theater, opera, ballet, and classical music offerings and gives visitors a more honest view of British life. Additionally, many hotel prices

drop by 20%, and cheaper accommodations offer weekly rates (unheard of during peak travel times). By arriving after the winter holidays, you can also take advantage of post-Christmas sales to buy your fill of woolens, china, crystal, silver, fashion clothing, crafts, and curios.

In short, spring offers the countryside at its greenest; autumn brings the bright colors of the northern moorlands, and summer's warmer weather gives rise to the many outdoor music and theater festivals. But winter offers savings across the board and a chance to see Britons going about their everyday lives largely unhindered by tourist invasions.

HOLIDAYS

Britain observes New Year's Day, Good Friday, Easter Monday, May Day (1st Mon in May), spring and summer bank holidays (the last Mon in May and Aug, respectively), Christmas Day, and Boxing Day (Dec 26).

BRITISH CALENDAR OF EVENTS

January

Schroders London Boat Show, ExCel, Docklands, E16 XL (© **01784/223627;** www.boat shows.co.uk). This is the largest boat show in Europe. January 8 to January 18, 2004.

Charles I Commemoration, London. To mark the anniversary of the execution of King Charles I "in the name of freedom and democracy," hundreds of cavaliers march through central London in 17th-century dress, and prayers are said at Whitehall's Banqueting House. Last Sunday in January. Call © **020/8781-9500.**

Burns Night, Ayr (near his birthplace), Dumfries, and Edinburgh. Naturally, during the celebration to honor Robert Burns, there's much toasting with scotch and eating of haggis, whose arrival is announced by a bagpipe. For details, call ✆ **01292/443700** in Ayr, **01314/733800** in Edinburgh, or **01387/253862** in Dumfries. January 25.

February

Jorvik Festival, York. This 2-week festival celebrates this historic cathedral city's role as a Viking outpost. For more information, call ✆ **01904/621756.**

April

The Shakespeare Season, Stratford-upon-Avon. The Royal Shakespeare Company begins its annual season, presenting works by the Bard in his hometown, at the **Royal Shakespeare Theatre,** Waterside (✆ **01789/403403**). Tickets are available at the box office, or through such agents as **Keith Prowse** (✆ **800/669-8687**). April through January.

Edinburgh Folk Festival. For details on this feast of Scottish folk tunes held in various venues, call ✆ **01314/733800.** Generally first of April.

May

Brighton Festival. England's largest arts festival, with some 400 different cultural events. For information, write the **Brighton Tourist Information Centre,** 10 Bartholomew Sq., Sussex IJS 1EL (✆ **0906/711-2255;** www.visitbrighton.com). Most of May.

Glyndebourne Festival. One of England's major cultural events, this festival is centered at the 1,200-seat Glyndebourne Opera House in Sussex. Tickets, which cost anywhere from £15 to £150 ($24–$240), are available from **Glyndebourne Festival Opera Box Office,** Lewes, East Sussex BN8 5UU (✆ **01273/812321;** www.glyndebourne.com). Mid-April to late August.

Bath International Music Festival. One of Europe's most prestigious international festivals of music and the arts features as many as 1,000 performers at various venues in Bath. For information, contact the **Bath Festivals Trust,** 5–6 Broad St., Bath, Somerset BA1 5LJ (✆ **01225/462231**). May 19 to June 4.

Chelsea Flower Show, London. The best of British gardening, with plants and flowers of the season, is displayed at the Chelsea Royal Hospital. Contact the **Chelsea Show Ticket Office,** Shows Department, Royal Horticultural Society, Vincent Square, London SW1P 2PE (✆ **020/7649-1885**). Tickets are also available through **London Ticketmaster** (✆ **020/7344-4444**). Late May.

Chichester Festival Theatre. Some great classic and modern plays are presented at this West Sussex theater. For tickets and information, contact the **Festival Theatre,** Oaklands Park, West Sussex PO19 4AP (✆ **01243/781312**). The season runs from May to October.

Highland Games and Gatherings, at various venues throughout Scotland. More details are available from the Edinburgh and Scotland Information Centre (see "Visitor Information," earlier in this chapter). Early May to mid-September.

Pitlochry Festival Theatre, Pitlochry. Scotland's "theater in the hills" launches its season in mid-May. For details, call ✆ **01796/472215** or check out **www.pitlochry.org.uk.** May to October.

June

Trooping the Colour. This is the queen's official birthday parade, a quintessential British event, with exquisite pageantry and pomp as she inspects her regiments and takes their salute as they parade their colors before her at the Horse Guards Parade, Whitehall in London. Tickets for the parade and two reviews, held on preceding Saturdays, are allocated by ballot. Applicants must write between January 1 and the end of February, enclosing a self-addressed stamped envelope or International Reply Coupon to the **Ticket Office,** HQ Household Division, Horse Guards, Whitehall, London SW1A 2AX. The ballot is held in mid-March, and only successful applicants are informed in April. Tickets are free. The ceremony will be held on "A Day Designated in June." Call ✆ **020/ 7414-2271.**

Aldeburgh Festival of Music and the Arts. Composer Benjamin Britten launched this festival in 1948. For more details on the events and for the year-round program, contact the **Aldeburgh Foundation,** High Street, Aldeburgh, Suffolk IP15 5AX (✆ **01728/687110;** www.aldeburgh.co.uk). Two weeks from mid- to late June.

Royal Ascot Week. Although Ascot Racecourse is open year-round for guided tours, events, exhibitions, and conferences, there are 25 race days throughout the year, with the feature races being the Royal Meeting in June, Diamond Day in late July, and the Festival at Ascot in late September. For information, contact **Ascot Racecourse,** Ascot, Berkshire SL5 7JN (✆ **01344/ 622211;** www.ascot.co.uk).

The Exeter Festival. The town of Exeter in Devon, England, hosts more than 150 events celebrating classical music, ranging from concerts and opera to lectures. For more information, contact the **Exeter Festival Office** (✆ **01392/ 265200;** www.Exeter.gov.uk). Two weeks in mid-July.

Lawn Tennis Championships, Wimbledon. Ever since players took to the grass courts at Wimbledon outside London in 1877, this tournament has attracted quite a crowd, and there's still an excited hush at Centre Court and a certain thrill associated with being there.

Acquiring tickets and overnight lodgings during the annual tennis competitions at Wimbledon can be difficult to arrange independently. Two of several outfits that can book both hotel accommodations and tickets to the event include **Steve Furgal's International Tennis Tours,** 11808 Rancho Bernardo Rd., Suite 123-418, San Diego, CA 92128 (✆ **800/258-3664;** www. tours4tennis.com), and **Championship Tennis Tours,** 15221 Clubgate Dr., Suite 1058, Scottsdale, AZ 85254 (✆ **800/468-3664;** www. tennistours.com). Early bookings for the world's most famous tennis tournament are strongly advised. Tickets for the Centre and Number One courts are obtainable through a lottery. Write in from August to December to **All England Lawn Tennis Club,** P.O. Box 98, Church Road, Wimbledon, London SW19 5AE (✆ **020/8944-1066).** Outside court tickets are available daily, but be prepared to wait in line. Late June to early July.

City of London Festival. This annual art festival is held in venues throughout the city. Call ✆ **020/ 7377-0540** or see **www.colf.org** for information. June and July.

Ludlow Festival. This is one of England's major arts festivals, complete with an open-air Shakespeare performance within the Inner Bailey of Ludlow Castle. Concerts, lectures, readings, exhibitions, and workshops round out the offerings. From March onward, a schedule can be obtained from the box office. Write to **Ludlow Festival Box Office,** Castle Square, Ludlow, Shropshire SY8 1AY, enclosing a self-addressed stamped envelope, or call ✆ **01584/872150.** The box office is open daily beginning from late June to early July.

Selkirk Common Riding. Scotland's most elaborate display of horsemanship, celebrates Selkirk's losses in the 1560 Battle of Flodden—only one Selkirk soldier returned alive from the battle to warn the town before dropping dead in the marketplace. Some 400 horses and riders parade through the streets, and a young man is crowned at the sound of the cornet, representing the soldier who sounded the alarm. For details, call ✆ **01750/20054** in Selkirk. Mid-June.

July

Henley Royal Regatta, Henley, in Oxfordshire. This international rowing competition is the premier event on the English social calendar. For more information, call ✆ **01491/572153.** Early July.

Kenwood Lakeside Concerts. These annual concerts on the north side of Hampstead Heath in London have continued a British tradition of outdoor performances for nearly 50 years. Fireworks displays and laser shows enliven the premier musical performances. Concerts are held every Saturday from early July to late August. For more information call ✆ **020/8348-1286.**

The Proms, London. A night at "The Proms" (✆ **020/7589-8212;** www.bbc.co.uk/proms)—the annual Henry Wood promenade concerts at Royal Albert Hall—attracts music aficionados from around the world. Staged almost daily (except for a few Sun), these traditional concerts were launched in 1895 and are the principal summer engagements for the BBC

Symphony Orchestra. Cheering and clapping, Union Jacks on parade, banners and balloons—it's great summer fun. Mid-July to mid-September.

Glasgow International Jazz Festival. Jazz musicians from all over the world come together to perform at various venues around the city. For details, call ✆ **01412/044400** or surf over to **www.jazzfest.co.uk.** First week in July.

Aberystwyth Musical Festival. This is a pageant of cultural and sporting events in Aberystwyth, the cultural center of the western section of middle Wales. For more information, contact **Aberystwyth Arts Centre,** Penglais, Aberystwyth SW23 3DE (✆ **01970/623232;** www.aber.ac.uk). End of July.

Cardiff Festival. In venues across the Welsh capital, this festival is a celebration of pop, jazz, theater, street performances, funfairs, opera, comedies, and children's events. Most events are free and take place in public and open-air places. For more information, contact the **Cardiff Festival,** Health Park, Cardiff CF4 4EP (✆ **029/2087-2087;** www.Cardiff.gov.uk). Three weeks from July into August.

August

International Beatles Week, Liverpool. Tens of thousands of fans gather in Liverpool to celebrate the music of the Fab Four. There's a whole series of concerts from international cover bands, plus tributes, auctions, and tours. For information, contact Cavern City Tours at ✆ **0871/222-1963;** www.cavern-liverpool.co.uk or the Tourist Information Centre in Liverpool at ✆ **01517/095111.** August 24 to August 29.

Pontardawe International Music Festival, Wales. The little village of Pontardawe, lying 8 miles north of

Swansea, attracts some of the world's leading folk and rock musicians for its annual summer concert series. For more information, call © **01792/830200** or see **www. pontardawefestival.org.uk**. Mid-August.

World Pipe Band Championships, Glasgow. For this relatively new event, bagpipe bands from around the world gather on the park-like Glasgow Green in the city's East End. From 11am to about 6pm there's a virtual orgy of bagpiping, as kilted participants strut their stuff in musical and military precision. For details, call © **01412/044400** in Glasgow. Mid-August.

Edinburgh International Festival. Scotland's best-known festival is an "arts bonanza," drawing major talent from around the world, with more than 1,000 shows presented and 1 million tickets sold. Book, jazz, and film festivals are also staged at this time, but nothing tops the Military Tattoo against the backdrop of spotlit Edinburgh Castle. For details, contact the **Festival Society,** 21 Market St., Edinburgh, Scotland EH1 1BW (© **01314/732001**; www.eif.co.uk). Three weeks in August.

September

Horse of the Year Show, Wembley Arena, Wembley. Riders fly from every continent to join in this festive display of horsemanship (much appreciated by the queen). The British press calls it an "equine extravaganza." It's held at Wembley Arena, outside London. For more information, call © **020/8902-8833.** Late September to early October.

Ben Nevis Mountain Race, Fort William. A tradition since 1895, when it was established by a member of the MacFarlane clan, it assembles as many as 500 runners who compete for the coveted MacFarlane cup, a gold medal, and a prize of £50 ($85). Runners congregate at the base of Ben Nevis (Britain's highest peak) for registration at 11am and begin running at 2pm in a course that takes them up narrow footpaths to the summit and back. Bagpipes rise in crescendos at the beginning and end of the experience. For details, call © **01397/705184** or see **www.visitfort william.co.uk**. First Saturday in September.

Highland Games & Gathering in Braemar. The queen and many members of the royal family often show up for this annual event, with its massed bands, piping and dancing competitions, and performances of great strength by a tribe of gigantic men. For details, contact the tourist office in **Braemar,** The Mews, Mar Road, Braemar, Aberdeenshire, AB35 5YP (© **01339/741600**; www.braemargathering. org). First Saturday in September.

October

Opening of Parliament, London. Ever since the 17th century, when the English beheaded Charles I, British monarchs have been denied the right to enter the House of Commons. Instead, the monarch opens Parliament in the House of Lords, reading an official speech that is in fact written by the government. Queen Elizabeth II rides from Buckingham Palace to Westminster in a royal coach accompanied by the Yeoman of the Guard and the Household Cavalry. The public galleries are open on a first-come, first-served basis. Call © **020/7219-4272** or check out **www.parliament.uk**. Late October to mid-November.

November

Guy Fawkes Night, throughout England. This British celebration commemorates the anniversary of the "Gunpowder Plot," an attempt to blow up King James I and Parliament. Huge organized bonfires are lit throughout London, and Guy Fawkes, the plot's most famous conspirator, is burned in effigy. Check *Time Out* for locations. Early November.

Lord Mayor's Procession and Show, The City, London. The queen has to ask permission to enter the square mile in London called The City—and the right of refusal has been jealously guarded by London merchants since the 17th century. Suffice it to say that the lord mayor is a powerful character, and the procession from the Guildhall to the Royal Courts is appropriately impressive. You can watch the procession from the street; the banquet is by invitation only. Call © **020/7606-3030.** Second Saturday in November.

December

Hogmanay, Edinburgh. Hogmanay begins on New Year's Eve and merges into New Year's Day festivities. Events include a torchlight procession, a fire festival along Princes Street, a carnival, and a street theater spectacular. For details, call © **01314/733800.** December 31.

6 Travel Insurance

Since Britain for most of us is far from home, and a number of things could go wrong—lost luggage, trip cancellation, a medical emergency—consider the following types of insurance.

Check your existing insurance policies and credit-card coverage before you buy travel insurance. You may already be covered for lost luggage, canceled tickets or medical expenses. The cost of travel insurance varies widely, depending on the cost and length of your trip, your age, health, and the type of trip you're taking.

TRIP-CANCELLATION INSURANCE Trip-cancellation insurance helps you get your money back if you have to back out of a trip, if you have to go home early, or if your travel supplier goes bankrupt. Allowed reasons for cancellation can range from sickness to natural disasters to the State Department declaring your destination unsafe for travel. (Insurers usually won't cover vague fears, though, as many travelers discovered who tried to cancel their trips in Oct 2001 because they were wary of flying.) In this unstable world, trip-cancellation insurance is a good buy if you're getting tickets well in advance—who knows what the state of the world, or of your airline, will be in nine months? Insurance policy details vary, so read the fine print—and especially make sure that your airline or cruise line is on the list of carriers covered in case of bankruptcy. For information, contact one of the following insurers: **Access America** (© 866/807-3982; www.accessamerica.com); **Travel Guard International** (© 800/826-4919; www.travelguard.com); **Travel Insured International** (© 800/243-3174; www.travel insured.com); and **Travelex Insurance Services** (© 888/457-4602; www.travelex-insurance.com).

MEDICAL INSURANCE Most health insurance policies cover you if you get sick away from home—but check, particularly if you're insured by an HMO. With the exception of certain HMOs and Medicare/Medicaid, your medical insurance should cover medical treatment—even hospital care—overseas. However, most out-of-country hospitals make you pay your bills up front, and send you a refund after you've returned home and filed the necessary paperwork. And in a worst-case scenario, there's the high cost of emergency evacuation. If you require additional medical insurance, try **MEDEX International** (✆ **800/527-0218** or 410/453-6300; www.medexassist.com) or **Travel Assistance International** (✆ **800/821-2828;** www.travelassistance.com; for general information on services, call the company's Worldwide Assistance Services, Inc., at ✆ **800/777-8710**).

LOST-LUGGAGE INSURANCE
On international flights (including US portions of international trips), baggage is limited to approximately $9.07 per pound, up to approximately $635 per checked bag. If you plan to check items more valuable than the standard liability, see if your valuables are covered by your homeowner's policy, get baggage insurance as part of your comprehensive travel-insurance package, or buy Travel Guard's "BagTrak" product. Don't buy insurance at the airport, as it's usually overpriced. Be sure to take any valuables or irreplaceable items with you in your carry-on luggage, as many valuables (including books, money and electronics) aren't covered by airline policies.

If your luggage is lost, immediately file a lost-luggage claim at the airport, detailing the luggage contents. For most airlines, you must report delayed, damaged, or lost baggage within 4 hours of arrival. The airlines are required to deliver luggage, once found, directly to your house or destination free of charge.

7 Health & Safety

STAYING HEALTHY
The tap water in Great Britain is safe to drink, the milk is pasteurized, and health services are good.

The mad-cow crisis continues but at a very slow trot, and caution is still advised. (For example, it's been suggested that it's safer to eat British beef cut from the bone instead of on the bone.) The rare case or two of foot-and-mouth disease doesn't pose a threat to human beings. Unlike mad-cow disease, foot-and-mouth disease is not passed on from animals to people.

WHAT TO DO IF YOU GET SICK AWAY FROM HOME
If you need a doctor, your hotel can recommend one, or you can contact your embassy or consulate. Outside London, dial ✆ **100** and ask the operator for the local police, who will give you the name, address, and telephone number of a doctor in your area. *Note:* U.S. visitors who become ill while they're in England are eligible only for free *emergency* care. For other treatment, including follow-up care, you'll be asked to pay.

In most cases, your existing health plan will provide the coverage you need. But double-check; you may want to buy **travel medical insurance** instead. (See the section on insurance, above.) Bring your insurance ID card with you when you travel.

If you suffer from a chronic illness, consult your doctor before your departure. For conditions like epilepsy, diabetes, or heart problems, wear a **Medic Alert Identification Tag** (✆ 800/825-3785; www.medicalert.org), which will immediately alert doctors to your condition and give them access to your records through Medic Alert's 24-hour hot line.

Pack **prescription medications** in your carry-on luggage, and carry prescription medications in their original containers, with pharmacy labels—otherwise they won't make it through airport security. Also bring along copies of your prescriptions in case you lose your pills or run out. Don't forget an extra pair of contact lenses or prescription glasses. Carry the generic name of prescription medicines, in case a local pharmacist is unfamiliar with the brand name.

Contact the **International Association for Medical Assistance to Travelers (IAMAT)** (*①* 716/754-4883 or 416/652-0137; www.iamat.org) for tips on travel and health concerns in the countries you're visiting, and lists of local, English-speaking doctors. The United States **Centers for Disease Control and Prevention** (*①* 800/311-3435; www.cdc.gov) provides up-to-date information on necessary vaccines and health hazards by region or country.

STAYING SAFE

Britain is one of the safer destinations of the world, but the sensible precautions one would heed anywhere prevail, of course. Conceal your wallet or else hold onto your purse, and don't flaunt your wealth, be it jewelry or cash. In other words, do as your mother told you. Pickpockets are a major concern in the big cities, though violent crime is relatively rare, especially in the heart of London, which hasn't seen a Jack the Ripper in a long time. Even so, it is not wise to go walking in parks at night. King's Cross is a dangerous area at night, frequented by prostitutes or johns who would like to purchase their services. Unquestionably, the city with the most crime in the U.K. is Glasgow, which has a large drug problem, but even this city is safer than most comparable spots in the U.S. In rural Britain, you will be relatively safe, though if you watch a lot of murder mysteries on TV or read about them in paperback, there seem to be a lot of murders going on.

8 Specialized Travel Resources

TRAVELERS WITH DISABILITIES

Many British hotels, museums, restaurants, and sightseeing attractions have wheelchair ramps, less so in rural areas. Persons with disabilities are often granted special discounts at attractions and, in some cases, nightclubs. These are called "concessions" in Britain. It always pays to ask. Free information and advice is available from **Holiday Care,** Sunley House, 7th Floor, 4 Bedford Park, Croydon, Surrey CR0 2AP (*①* 0845/124-9971; www.holidaycare.org.uk).

Bookstores in London often carry *Access in London* (£7.95/$13), a publication listing facilities for persons with disabilities, among other things.

The transport system, cinemas, and theaters are still pretty much off-limits, but **Transport for London** does publish a leaflet called *Access to the Underground,* which gives details of elevators and ramps at individual Underground stations; call *①* 020/7918-3312. And the **London black cab** is perfectly suited for those in wheelchairs; the roomy interiors have plenty of room for maneuvering.

London's most visible organization for information about access to theaters, cinemas, galleries, museums, and restaurants is **Artsline,** 54 Chalton St., London NW1 1HS (*①* 020/7388-2227; fax 020/7383-2653; www.artsline.org.uk). It offers free information about wheelchair access, theaters with hearing aids, tourist attractions, and cinemas. Artsline will mail information to North America, but it's more helpful to contact Artsline once you arrive in London; the line is staffed Monday through Friday from 9:30am to 5:30pm.

An organization that cooperates closely with Artsline is **Tripscope,** The Courtyard, 4 Evelyn Rd., London W4

5JL (© **020/8580-7021;** www.just
mobility.co.uk), which offers advice
on travel in Britain and elsewhere for
persons with disabilities.

Information for travelers with disabilities going to Wales is available
from **Disability Wales,** Caerbragdy
Industrial Estate, Bedwas Road, Caerphilly, Mid Glamorgan CF8 3SL
(© **029/2088-7325;** www.dwac.
demon.co.uk). The staff can tell you
about facilities suitable in touring,
accommodations, restaurants, cafes,
pubs, public restrooms, attractions,
and other phases of hospitality to
make a trip pleasurable.

Many travel agencies offer customized tours and itineraries for travelers with disabilities. **Accessible
Journeys** (© **800/846-4537** or 610/
521-0339; www.disabilitytravel.com)
caters specifically to slow walkers and
wheelchair travelers and their families,
and offers several independent and
escorted tours to Great Britain.

Organizations that offer assistance
to travelers with disabilities include
the **Moss Rehab Hospital** (www.
mossresourcenet.org), which provides
a library of accessible-travel resources
online; and the **Society for Accessible
Travel and Hospitality** (© **212/
447-7284;** www.sath.org; annual
membership fees: $45 adults, $30 seniors and students), which offers a
wealth of travel resources for all types of
disabilities and informed recommendations on destinations, access guides,
travel agents, tour operators, vehicle
rentals, and companion services.

For more information specifically
targeted to travelers with disabilities,
the community website **iCan** (**www.
icanonline.net/channels/travel/
index.cfm**) has destination guides and
several regular columns on accessible
travel.

GAY & LESBIAN TRAVELERS

Britain has one of the most active gay
and lesbian scenes in the world, centered mainly around London. Gay

bars, restaurants, and centers are also
found in all large English cities,
notably Glasgow, Edinburgh, Bath,
Birmingham, Manchester, and especially Brighton.

You can pick up the latest edition of
Frommer's Gay & Lesbian Europe, at
your local bookstore; it covers the gay
scene in both London and Brighton.
Lesbian and Gay Switchboard
(© 020/7837-7324) is open 24 hours
a day, providing information about
gay-related activities in London or
advice in general. The **Bisexual
Helpline** (© 020/8569-7500) offers
useful information, but only on Tuesday and Wednesday from 7:30 to
9:30pm, and Saturday between
9:30am and noon. London's best gay-
oriented bookstore is **Gay's the Word,**
66 Marchmont St., WC1 (© **020/
7278-7654;** www.gaystheword.co.uk;
Tube: Russell Sq.), the largest such
store in Britain. The staff is friendly
and helpful and will offer advice about
the ever-changing scene in London.
At Gay's the Word as well as other gay-
friendly venues, you can find a number of publications, many free,
including the popular *Boyz.* Another
free publication is *Pink Paper* (with a
good lesbian section), and check out
9X, filled with data about new clubs.

Scotland doesn't boast much of a gay
scene. Gay-bashing happens, especially
in the grimy industrial sections of Glasgow, where neo-Nazi skinheads hang
out. Although it's a crime, it's rarely
punished. Open displays of affection
between same-sex couples will usually
invite scorn in rural Scotland.

In Scotland, bars, clubs, restaurants, and hotels catering to gays are
confined almost exclusively to Edinburgh, Glasgow, and Inverness. Call
the **Lothian Gay and Lesbian
Switchboard** at © 01315/564049 or
the **Glasgow Gay and Lesbian
Switchboard** at © 01418/470447
for information about local events.

The **International Gay & Lesbian Travel Association (IGLTA)** (𝄐 **800/ 448-8550** or 954/776-2626; www. iglta.org) is the trade association for the gay and lesbian travel industry and offers an online directory of gay- and lesbian-friendly travel businesses; go to their website and click on "Members."

Many agencies offer tours and travel itineraries specifically for gay and lesbian travelers. **Above and Beyond Tours** (𝄐 800/397-2681; www.abovebeyondtours.com) is the exclusive gay and lesbian tour operator for United Airlines. **Now, Voyager** (𝄐 **800/255-6951;** www.nowvoyager. com) is a well-known San Francisco–based gay-owned and -operated travel service.

SENIOR TRAVEL

Many discounts are available to seniors, though in England you often have to be a member of an association to get them. Public-transportation reductions, for example, are available only to holders of British Pension books. However, many attractions do offer discounts for seniors (women 60 or over and men 65 or over). Even if discounts aren't posted, ask if they're available. And make sure you carry ID showing your date of birth.

If you're over 60, you're eligible for special 10% discounts on **British Airways** through its Privileged Traveler program. You also qualify for reduced restrictions on APEX cancellations. Discounts are also granted for BA tours and for intra-Britain air tickets booked in North America. **British Rail** offers seniors discounted rates on first-class rail passes around Britain. See the "Getting There" section later in this chapter.

The British Tourist Authority puts out a booklet designed to assist seniors traveling in Great Britain. It offers tips on obtaining discounts on admission fees and rail fares, as well as touring ideas. *Britain: A Time to Travel,* can be obtained in the United States by calling the BTA at 𝄐 **877/899-8391,** Monday through Friday between 9am and 6pm EST. On the Web, surf over to **www.maturebritain.org**.

Members of **AARP** (formerly known as the American Association of Retired Persons), 601 E St. NW, Washington, DC 20049 (𝄐 **800/ 424-3410** or 202/434-2277; www. aarp.org), get discounts on hotels, airfares, and car rentals. AARP offers members a wide range of benefits, including *AARP: The Magazine* and a monthly newsletter. Anyone over 50 can join.

Many reliable agencies and organizations target the 50-plus market. **Elderhostel** (𝄐 **877/426-8056;** www.elderhostel.org) arranges study programs for those age 55 and over (and a spouse or companion of any age) in the U.S. and in more than 80 countries around the world. Most courses last 2 to 4 weeks, and many include airfare, accommodations in university dormitories or modest inns, meals, and tuition.

Recommended publications offering travel resources and discounts for seniors include: the quarterly magazine *Travel 50 & Beyond* (www.travel 50andbeyond.com); and *101 Tips for Mature Travelers,* available from Grand Circle Travel (𝄐 **800/221-2610** or 617/350-7500; www.gct. com).

FAMILY TRAVEL

If you have enough trouble getting your kids out of the house in the morning, dragging them thousands of miles away may seem like an insurmountable challenge. But family travel can be immensely rewarding, giving you new ways of seeing the world through smaller pairs of eyes.

On airlines, you must request a special menu for children at least 24 hours in advance. If baby food is required, however, bring your own and ask a flight attendant to warm it to the right temperature.

Arrange ahead of time for such necessities as a crib, bottle warmer, and a car seat (in England, small children aren't allowed to ride in the front seat).

If you're staying with friends in London, you can rent baby equipment from **Chelsea Baby Hire,** 108 Dorset Rd., SW19 3HD (*②* **020/8540-8830;** www.chelseababyhire.co.uk).

A recommendable London babysitting service is **Childminders** (*②* **020/7487-5040;** www.babysitter.co.uk). Babysitters can also be found for you at most hotels throughout Great Britain.

To find out what's on for kids while you're in London, pick up the leaflet *Where to Take Children,* published by the London Tourist Board. If you have specific questions, ring **Kidsline** (*②* **020/7487-5040;** www.kidsline.co.uk) Monday through Friday from 4 to 6pm and summer holidays from 9am to 4pm, or the **London Tourist Board's** special children's information lines (*②* **0891/505490)** for listings of special events and places to visit for children. The number is accessible in London at 50p (80¢) per minute.

Familyhostel (*②* **800/733-9753;** www.learn.unh.edu/familyhostel) takes the whole family, including kids ages 8 to 15, on moderately priced domestic and international learning vacations. Lectures, fields trips, and sightseeing are guided by a team of academics.

Look also for our "Kids" icon, indicating attractions, restaurants, or hotels and resorts that are especially family friendly. Be advised that some B&Bs in Great Britain will not accept young children as guests, so ask before you make a reservation.

You can find good family-oriented vacation advice on the Internet from sites such as the **Family Travel Network** (www.familytravelnetwork.com);

and **Traveling Internationally with Your Kids** (www.travelwithyourkids. com), a comprehensive site offering sound advice for long-distance and international travel with children.

STUDENT TRAVEL

If you're planning to travel outside the U.S., you'd be wise to arm yourself with an **International Student Identity Card (ISIC),** which offers substantial savings on rail passes, plane tickets, and entrance fees. It also provides you with basic health and life insurance and a 24-hour help line. The card is available for $22 from **STA Travel,** 86 Old Brompton Rd., London SW7 3LQ (*②* **800/781-4040** in the U.S.; www.statravel.com; Tube: South Kensington), the biggest student travel agency in the world. If you're no longer a student but are still under 26, you can get a **International Youth Travel Card (IYTC)** for the same price from the same people, which entitles you to some discounts (but not on museum admissions).

Travel CUTS (*②* **800/667-2887** or 416/614-2887; www.travelcuts. com) offers similar services for both Canadians and US residents. Irish students should turn to **USIT** (*②* **01/602-1600;** www.usitnow.ie).

The International Student House, 229 Great Portland St., W1W 5PN (*②* **020/7631-8310;** www.ish.org. uk), lies at the foot of Regent's Park across from the Tube stop for Great Portland Street. It's a beehive of activity, such as discos and film showings, and rents blandly furnished, institutional rooms for £33 ($53) single, £25 to £27 ($40–$42) per person double, £20 ($32) per person triple, and £18 ($29) per person in a dorm. Laundry facilities are available; a £10 ($16) key deposit is charged. Reserve way in advance.

University of London Student Union, Malet St., WC1E 7HY (*②* **020/7664-2000;** www.ululon.ac. uk; Tube: Goodge St. or Russell Sq.),

---

> **Tips** **Checking your E-mail in Great Britain**
>
> Travelers who want to check their e-mail and access the Internet in Great Britain have several options. The major cities all have cybercafes and the following directories should help you locate one in the city you're visiting: **www.cybercaptive.com**, **www.netcafeguide.com**, and **www.cybercafe. com**. Aside from formal cybercafes, most **youth hostels** nowadays have at least one computer you can get to the Internet on. And most **public libraries** across the world offer Internet access free or for a small charge. Avoid **hotel business centers**, which often charge exorbitant rates.
>
> To retrieve your e-mail, ask your **Internet Service Provider (ISP)** if it has a web-based interface tied to your existing e-mail account. If it doesn't, you may want to open a free, web-based e-mail account with **Yahoo! Mail** (mail.yahoo.com) or **Hotmail** (www.hotmail.com).

---

is the best place to go to learn about student activities in the Greater London area. The Union has a swimming pool, fitness center, gymnasium, general store, sports shop, ticket agency, banks, bars, inexpensive restaurants, venues for live events, an office of STA Travel, and many other facilities. It's open Monday through Thursday from 8:30am to 11pm, Friday from 8:30am to 1pm, Saturday from 9am to 2pm, and Sunday from 9:30am to 10:30pm. Bulletin boards provide a rundown on events; some you may be able to attend, others may be "closed door."

Two good publications aimed at student travelers are *Britain on a Budget,* and *UK—The Guide.* Both are published by the British Tourist Authority and can be obtained the United States by calling the BTA at ℂ **877/899-8391,** Mondays through Fridays between 9am and 6pm EST. On the Web, surf over to **www. budgetbritain.com**.

9 Planning Your Trip Online

SURFING FOR AIRFARES

The "big three" online travel agencies, **Expedia.com**, **Travelocity.com**, and **Orbitz.com**, sell most of the air tickets bought on the Internet. (Canadian travelers should try expedia.ca and Travelocity.ca; U.K. residents can go for expedia.co.uk and opodo.co.uk.) Each has different business deals with the airlines and may offer different fares on the same flights, so it's wise to shop around. Expedia and Travelocity will also send you **e-mail notification** when a cheap fare becomes available to your favorite destination. Of the smaller travel agency websites, **Side-Step** (www.sidestep.com) has gotten the best reviews from Frommer's authors. It's a browser add-on that purports to "search 140 sites at once," but in reality only beats competitors' fares as often as other sites do.

Also remember to check **airline websites,** especially those for low-fare carriers whose fares are often misreported or simply missing from travel agency websites. Even with major airlines, you can often shave a few bucks from a fare by booking directly through the airline and avoiding a travel agency's transaction fee. But you'll get these discounts only by **booking online:** Most airlines now offer online-only fares that even their phone agents know nothing about. For the websites of airlines that fly to and from your destination, go to "Getting There," below.

Frommers.com: The Complete Travel Resource

For an excellent travel-planning resource, we highly recommend Frommers.com (www.frommers.com). We're a little biased, of course, but we guarantee that you'll find the travel tips, reviews, monthly vacation giveaways, and online-booking capabilities thoroughly indispensable. Among the special features are our popular **Message Boards,** where Frommer's readers post queries and share advice (sometimes even our authors show up to answer questions); **Frommers.com Newsletter,** for the latest travel bargains and insider travel secrets; and **Frommer's Destinations Section,** where you'll get expert travel tips, hotel and dining recommendations, and advice on the sights to see for more than 3,000 destinations around the globe. When your research is done, the **Online Reservations System** (www.frommers.com/book_a_trip/) takes you to Frommer's preferred online partners for booking your vacation at affordable prices.

Great **last-minute deals** are available through free weekly e-mail services provided directly by the airlines. Most of these are announced on Tuesday or Wednesday and must be purchased online. Sign up for weekly e-mail alerts at airline websites or check mega-sites that compile comprehensive lists of last-minute specials, such as **Smarter Living** (smarterliving.com). For last-minute trips, **lastminute.com** in Europe often has better deals than the major-label sites.

If you're willing to give up some control over your flight details, use an **opaque fare service** such as **Priceline** (www.priceline.com; www.priceline.co.uk for Europeans) or **Hotwire** (www.hotwire.com). Both offer rockbottom prices in exchange for travel on a "mystery airline" at a mysterious time of day, often with a mysterious change of planes enroute. The mystery airlines are all major, well-known carriers. But your chances of getting a 6am or 11pm flight are pretty high. Hotwire tells you flight prices before you buy; Priceline usually has better deals than Hotwire, but you have to play their "name our price" game. If you're new at this, the helpful folks at **BiddingForTravel**

(www.biddingfortravel.com) do a good job of demystifying Priceline's prices. Priceline and Hotwire are great for flights between the U.S. and Europe, including England.

For much more about airfares and savvy air-travel tips and advice, pick up a copy of *Frommer's Fly Safe, Fly Smart* (Wiley Publishing).

SURFING FOR HOTELS

Of the "big three" sites, **Expedia** may be the best choice, thanks to its long list of special deals. **Travelocity** runs a close second. Hotel specialist sites **hotels.com** and **hoteldiscounts.com** are also reliable. An excellent free program, **TravelAxe** (www.travelaxe.net), can help you search multiple hotel sites at once, even ones you may never have heard of.

Priceline and Hotwire are even better for hotels than for airfares; with both, you're allowed to pick the neighborhood and quality level of your hotel before offering up your money. Priceline's hotel product covers a large number of hotels in Great Britain, though it's much better at getting five-star lodging for three-star prices than at finding anything at the bottom of the scale. *Note:* Hotwire overrates its hotels by one star—what Hotwire calls a four-star is a three-star anywhere else.

SURFING FOR RENTAL CARS

For booking rental cars online, the best deals are usually found at rental-car company websites, although all the major online travel agencies also offer rental-car reservations services. Priceline and Hotwire work well for rental cars, too; the only "mystery" is which major rental company you get, and for most travelers the difference between Hertz, Avis, and Budget is negligible.

10 Getting There

BY PLANE

British Airways (© 800/247-9297; www.britishairways.com) offers flights from 18 U.S. cities to Heathrow and Gatwick airports, as well as many others to Manchester, Birmingham, and Glasgow. Nearly every flight is nonstop. With more add-on options than any other airline, British Airways can make a visit to Britain cheaper than you might have expected. Ask about packages that include both airfare and discounted hotel accommodations in Britain.

Known for consistently offering excellent fares, **Virgin Atlantic Airways** (© 800/862-8621; www.virginatlantic.com) flies daily to either Heathrow or Gatwick from Boston; Newark, New Jersey; New York's JFK; Los Angeles; San Francisco; Washington's Dulles; Miami; and Orlando.

American Airlines (© 800/433-7300; www.aa.com) offers daily flights to Heathrow from half a dozen U.S. gateways—New York's JFK (six times daily), Newark (once daily), Chicago (three times daily), Boston (twice daily), and Miami and Los Angeles (each once daily).

Depending on the day and season, **Delta Air Lines** (© 800/241-4141; www.delta.com) runs either one or two daily nonstop flights between Atlanta and Gatwick. Delta also offers nonstop daily service from Cincinnati.

Northwest Airlines (© 800/225-2525 or 800/447-4747; www.nwa.com) flies nonstop from Minneapolis and Detroit to Gatwick, with connections possible from other cities, such as Boston or New York.

Continental Airlines (© 800/231-0856; www.continental.com) has daily flights to London from Houston and Newark.

United Airlines (© 800/241-6522; www.united.com) flies nonstop from New York's JFK and Chicago to Heathrow two or three times daily, depending on the season. United also offers nonstop service three times a day from Dulles Airport, near Washington, D.C., plus once-a-day service from Newark and Los Angeles, and twice-a-day service from San Francisco and Boston.

For travelers departing from Canada, **Air Canada** (© 888/247-2262 in the U.S., or 800/268-7240 in Canada; www.aircanada.ca) flies daily to London's Heathrow nonstop from Vancouver, Montreal, and Toronto. There are also frequent direct flights from Calgary and Ottawa. **British Airways** (© 800/247-9297) has direct flights from Toronto, Montreal, and Vancouver.

For travelers departing from Australia, **British Airways** (© 800/247-9297) has flights to London from Sydney, Melbourne, Perth, and Brisbane. **Qantas** (© 131313; www.qantas.com) offers flights from Australia to London's Heathrow. Direct flights depart from Sydney and Melbourne. Some have the bonus of free stopovers in Bangkok or Singapore.

Departing from New Zealand, **Air New Zealand** (© 800/262-1234) has direct flights to London from Auckland. These flights depart daily.

Short flights from Dublin to London are available through **British Airways** (© 800/247-9297), with four flights daily into London's Gatwick airport, and **Aer Lingus** (© 800/FLY-IRISH;** www.aerlingus.com), which flies into Heathrow. Short flights from Dublin to London are also available through **Ryan Air** (© 0870/156-9569;** www.ryanair.com) and **British Midland** (© 0870/607-0555;** www.flybmi.com).

Once in London, a visitor will find frequent flights available to Scotland. **British Airways** (© 0845/773-3377) flies from Heathrow to both Edinburgh and Glasgow, with frequent daily flights. **KLM UK** (© 0870/507-4077) flies from Stansted and London City airports to both Edinburgh and Glasgow daily. **Rynair** (© 0871/246-0000) flies from Stansted outside London to Prestwick on the west coast of Scotland, and **British Midland** (© 0870/607-0555) flies from Heathrow to both Edinburgh and Glasgow. To reach Wales from London, you can avail yourself of frequent rail links, especially between London and Cardiff.

A budget airline that's growing in popularity, **EasyJet** (© 0870/600-0000;** www.easyjet.com) offers service within Great Britain and from the Continent to London, Edinburgh, and several other U.K destinations.

GETTING THROUGH THE AIRPORT

With the federalization of airport security, security procedures at U.S. airports are more stable and consistent than ever. Generally, you'll be fine if you arrive at the airport **1 hour** before a domestic flight and **2 hours** before an international flight; if you show up late, tell an airline employee and he or she will probably whisk you to the front of the line.

Bring a **current, government-issued photo ID** such as a driver's license or passport, and if you've got an E-ticket, print out the **official confirmation page;** you'll need to show your confirmation at the security checkpoint, and your ID at the ticket counter or the gate. (Children under 18 do not need photo IDs for domestic flights, but the adults checking in with them need them.)

Security lines are getting shorter than they were during 2001 and 2002, but some doozies remain. If you have trouble standing for long periods of time, tell an airline employee; the airline will provide a wheelchair. Speed up security by **not wearing metal objects** such as big belt buckles or clanky earrings. If you've got metallic body parts, a note from your doctor can prevent a long chat with the security screeners. Keep in mind that only **ticketed passengers** are allowed past security, except for folks escorting disabled passengers or children.

Federalization has stabilized **what you can carry on** and **what you can't.** The general rule is that sharp things are out, nail clippers are okay, and food and beverages must be passed through the X-ray machine—but that security screeners can't make you drink from your coffee cup. Bring food in your carry-on rather than checking it, as explosive-detection machines used on checked luggage have been known to mistake food (especially chocolate, for some reason) for bombs. Travelers in the U.S. are allowed one carry-on bag, plus a "personal item" such as a purse, briefcase, or laptop bag. Carry-on hoarders can stuff all sorts of things into a laptop bag; as long as it has a laptop in it, it's still considered a personal item. The **Transportation Security Administration (TSA)** has issued a list of restricted items; check its website

(http://www.tsa.gov/public/index.
jsp) for details.

In 2003 the TSA will be phasing out
gate check-in at all U.S. airports. Passengers with E-tickets and without
checked bags can still beat the ticket-
counter lines by using **electronic
kiosks** or even **online check-in.** Ask
your airline which alternatives are available, and if you're using a kiosk, bring
the credit card you used to book the
ticket. If you're checking bags, you will
still be able to use most airlines' kiosks;
again call your airline for up-to-date
information. **Curbside check-in** is also
a good way to avoid lines, although a
few airlines still ban curbside check-in
entirely; call before you go.

FLYING FOR LESS:
TIPS FOR GETTING
THE BEST AIRFARE

Passengers sharing the same airplane
cabin rarely pay the same fare. Travelers who need to purchase tickets at the
last minute, change their itinerary at a
moment's notice, or fly one-way often
get stuck paying the premium rate.
Here are some ways to keep your airfare costs down.

- Passengers who can book their
  ticket **long in advance,** who can
  stay over Saturday night, or who
  fly midweek or **at less-trafficked
  hours** will pay a fraction of the
  full fare. If your schedule is flexible, say so, and ask if you can
  secure a cheaper fare by changing
  your flight plans.

- You can also save on airfares by
  keeping an eye out in local newspapers for **promotional specials**
  or **fare wars,** when airlines lower
  prices on their most popular
  routes. You rarely see fare wars
  offered for peak travel times, but if
  you can travel in the off-months,
  you may snag a bargain.

- Search **the Internet** for cheap
  fares (see "Planning Your Trip
  Online," earlier in this chapter).

- **Consolidators**, also known as
  bucket shops, are great sources for
  international tickets. Start by looking in Sunday newspaper travel
  sections. For less-developed destinations, small travel agents who
  cater to immigrant communities
  in large cities often have the best
  deals. *Beware:* Bucket shop tickets
  are usually nonrefundable or
  rigged with stiff cancellation
  penalties, often as high as 50% to
  75% of the ticket price, and some
  put you on charter airlines with
  questionable safety records. Several
  reliable consolidators are worldwide and available on the Net.
  STA Travel is now the world's
  leader in student travel, thanks to
  its purchase of Council Travel. It
  also offers good fares for travelers
  of all ages. **Flights.com** (© 800/
  TRAV-800;   www.flights.com)
  started in Europe and has excellent
  fares worldwide, but particularly
  to that continent. It also has "local"
  websites in 12 countries. **Fly-
  Cheap** (© 800/FLY-CHEAP;
  www.1800flycheap.com) is owned
  by package-holiday megalith
  MyTravel and so has especially
  good access to fares for sunny destinations. **Air Tickets Direct**
  (© 800/778-3447; www.airtickets
  direct.com) is based in Montreal
  and leverages the currently weak
  Canadian dollar for low fares.

- Join **frequent-flier clubs.** Accrue
  enough miles, and you'll be
  rewarded with free flights and elite
  status. It's free, and you'll get the
  best choice of seats, faster response
  to phone inquiries, and prompter
  service if your luggage is stolen,
  your flight is canceled or delayed,
  or if you want to change your seat.
  You don't need to fly to build frequent-flier miles—**frequent-flier
  credit cards** can provide thousands of miles for doing your
  everyday shopping.

- For many more tips about air travel, including a rundown of the major frequent-flier credit cards, pick up a copy of *Frommer's Fly Safe, Fly Smart* (Wiley Publishing, Inc.).

BY CAR FROM CONTINENTAL EUROPE

If you plan to transport a rented car between England and France, check in advance with the car-rental company about license and insurance requirements and additional drop-off charges before you begin.

The English Channel is crisscrossed with "drive-on, drive-off" car-ferry services, with many operating from Boulogne and Calais in France. From either of those ports, Sealink ferries will carry you, your luggage, and, if you like, your car. The most popular point of arrival along the English coast is Folkestone.

Taking a car beneath the Channel is more complicated and more expensive. Since the Channel Tunnel's opening, most passengers have opted to ride the train alone, without being accompanied by their car. The Eurostar trains, discussed below, carry passengers only; *Le Shuttle* trains carry freight cars, trucks, and passenger cars.

Count on at least £227 ($363) for a return ticket, but know that the cost of moving a car on Le Shuttle varies according to the season and day of the week. Frankly, it's a lot cheaper to transport your car across by conventional ferryboat, but if you insist, here's what you'll need to know: You'll negotiate both English and French customs as part of one combined process, usually on the English side of the Channel. You can remain within your vehicle even after you drive it onto a flatbed railway car during the 35-minute crossing. (For 19 min. of this crossing, you'll actually be underwater; if you want, you can leave the confines of your car and ride within a brightly lit, air-conditioned passenger car.) When the trip is over, you simply drive off the flatbed railway car and toward your destination. Total travel time between the French and English highway system is about 1 hour. As a means of speeding the flow of perishable goods across the Channel, the car and truck service usually operates 24 hours a day, at intervals that vary from 15 minutes to once an hour, depending on the time of day. Neither BritRail nor any of the agencies dealing with reservations for passenger trains through the Chunnel will reserve space for your car in advance, and considering the frequency of the traffic on the Chunnel, they're usually not necessary. For information about Le Shuttle car-rail service after you reach England, call © 0870/535-3535; www.eurotunnel.com.

Duty-free stores, restaurants, and service stations are available to travelers on both sides of the Channel. A bilingual staff is on hand to assist travelers at both the British and French terminals.

BY TRAIN FROM CONTINENTAL EUROPE

Britain's isolation from the rest of Europe led to the development of an independent railway network with different rules and regulations from those observed on the Continent. That's all changing now, but one big difference that may affect you still remains: If you're traveling to Britain from the Continent, *your Eurailpass will not be valid when you get there.*

In 1994, Queen Elizabeth and President François Mitterand officially opened the Channel Tunnel, or Chunnel, and the *Eurostar* express passenger train began twice-daily service between London and both Paris and Brussels—a 3-hour trip. The $15 billion tunnel, one of the great engineering feats of all time, is the first link between Britain and the Continent since the Ice Age.

So if you're coming to London from say, Rome, your Eurailpass will get you as far as the Chunnel. At that point you can cross the English Channel aboard the *Eurostar,* and you'll receive a discount on your ticket. Once in England, you must use a separate BritRail pass or purchase a direct ticket to continue on to your destination.

Rail Europe (© 800/848-7245 in the U.S.; 800/361-RAIL in Canada; fax 800/432-1329; www.raileurope. com) sells direct-service tickets on the Eurostar between Paris or Brussels and London. A one-way fare between Paris and London costs $279 in first class and $199 in second class.

In London, make reservations for **Eurostar** by calling © 0870/530-0003; in Paris, call © 01/44-51-06-02; and in the United States, it's © 800/EUROSTAR (www.eurostar. com). Eurostar trains arrive and depart from London's Waterloo Station, Paris's Gare du Nord, and Brussels's Central Station.

BY FERRY/HOVERCRAFT FROM CONTINENTAL EUROPE

P & O Ferries (© 800/677-8585 or 08705/202020; www.posl.com) operates car and passenger ferries between Dover and Calais, France (25 sailings a day; 75 min. each way).

By far the most popular route across the English Channel is between Calais and Dover. **HoverSpeed** (© 0870/5240241; www.hoverspeed.com) operates at least 12 hovercraft crossings daily; the trip takes 35 minutes. They also run a SeaCat (a catamaran propelled by jet engines) that takes slightly longer to make the crossing between Boulogne and Folkestone. The SeaCats

depart about four times a day on the 55-minute voyage.

Traveling by hovercraft or SeaCat cuts the time of your surface journey from the Continent to the United Kingdom. A hovercraft trip is definitely a fun adventure, because the vessel is technically "flying" over the water. A SeaCat crossing from Folkestone to Boulogne is longer in miles, but it is covered faster than conventional ferryboats making the Calais–Dover crossing. For reservations and information, call Hover-Speed (see above). For foot passengers, a typical adult fare, with a 5-day return policy, is £24 ($36) or half fare for children.

BY BUS

If you're traveling to London from elsewhere in the United Kingdom, consider purchasing a **Britexpress Card,** which entitles you to a 30% discount on National Express (England and Wales) and Caledonian Express (Scotland) buses. Contact a travel agent for details.

Bus connections to Britain from the continent are generally not very comfortable, though some lines are more convenient than others. One line with a relatively good reputation is **Eurolines,** 52 Grosvenor Gardens, London SW1W 0AU (© 020/7730-8235; www.eurolines.com). They book passage on buses traveling twice a day between London and Paris (9 hr.); three times a day from Amsterdam (12 hr.); three times a week from Munich (24 hr.); and three times a week from Stockholm (44 hr.). On the longer routes, which employ two alternating drivers, the bus proceeds almost without interruption, taking occasional breaks for meals.

11 Package Deals & Escorted Tours

Note: The best specialist in arranging travel to London and as well as Britain in general is the **London Travel**

Center (© 800/FLY-TDAY in the U.S.; www.londontravelcenter.com). This agency can handle all your travel needs between the United States and Britain, including all prices of air fares, hotels, and car rentals, even rail passes and travel insurance.

VACATION PACKAGES

Before you start your search for the lowest airfare, you may want to consider booking your flight as part of a travel package. Package tours are not the same thing as escorted tours. Package tours are simply a way to buy the airfare, accommodations, and other elements of your trip (such as car rentals, airport transfers, and sometimes even activities) at the same time and often at discounted prices—kind of like one-stop shopping. Packages are sold in bulk to tour operators—who resell them to the public at a cost that usually undercuts standard rates.

One good source of package deals is the airlines themselves. Most major airlines offer air/land packages, including **American Airlines Vacations** (ⓒ 800/321-2121; www.aavacations.com), **Delta Vacations** (ⓒ 800/221-6666; www.deltavacations.com), **Continental Airlines Vacations** (ⓒ 800/301-3800; www.coolvacations.com), and **United Vacations** (ⓒ 888/854-3899; www.unitedvacations.com). Great deals—probably the best of all the airline packagers—can often be found by booking a package tour through **Virgin Atlantic Airways** (ⓒ 800/862-8621; www.virgin.com).

Far and away, the most options are with **British Airways Holidays** (ⓒ 877/428-2228; www.british-airways.com). Its offerings within the British Isles are more comprehensive than those of its competitors and can be tailored to your specific interests and budget. For a free catalog and additional information, call British Airways before you book; some of the company's available options are contingent upon the purchase of a round-trip transatlantic air ticket.

Several big **online travel agencies**—Expedia, Travelocity, Orbitz, Site59,

and Lastminute.com—also do a brisk business in packages. If you're unsure about the pedigree of a smaller packager, check with the Better Business Bureau in the city where the company is based, or go online at **www.bbb.org**. If a packager won't tell you where it's based, don't fly with them.

Liberty Travel (ⓒ 888/271-1584 or 201/934-3888 to be connected with the agent closest to you; www.libertytravel.com), one of the biggest packagers in the Northeast, often runs a full-page ad in the Sunday papers. **American Express Travel** (ⓒ 800/941-2639; www.travelimpressions.com) is another option.

Travel packages are also listed in the travel section of your local Sunday newspaper. Or check ads in the national travel magazines such as *Arthur Frommer's Budget Travel Magazine, Travel & Leisure, National Geographic Traveler,* and *Condé Nast Traveler.*

Package tours can vary by leaps and bounds. Some offer a better class of hotels than others. Some offer the same hotels for lower prices. Some offer flights on scheduled airlines, while others book charters. Some limit your choice of accommodations and travel days. You are often required to make a large payment up front. On the plus side, packages can save you money, offering group prices but allowing for independent travel. Some even let you add on a few guided excursions or escorted day trips (also at prices lower than if you booked them yourself) without booking an entirely escorted tour.

Make sure, however, to look for **hidden expenses.** Ask whether airport departure fees and taxes, for example, are included in the total cost.

ESCORTED TOURS

Escorted tours are structured group tours, with a group leader. The price usually includes everything from airfare to hotels, meals, tours, admission costs, and local transportation.

Before you invest in an escorted tour, ask about the **cancellation policy:** Is a deposit required? Can they cancel the trip if they don't get enough people? Do you get a refund if they cancel? If *you* cancel? How late can you cancel if you are unable to go? When do you pay in full? *Note:* If you choose an escorted tour, think strongly about purchasing trip-cancellation insurance, especially if the tour operator asks you to pay up front. See "Travel Insurance," earlier in this chapter.

You'll also want to get a complete **schedule** of the trip to find out how much sightseeing is planned each day and whether enough time has been allotted for relaxing or wandering solo.

The **size** of the group is also important to know up front. Generally, the smaller the group, the more flexible the itinerary, and the less time you'll spend waiting for people to get on and off the bus. Find out the **demographics** of the group as well. What is the age range? What is the gender breakdown? Is this mostly a trip for couples or singles?

Discuss what is included in the **price**. You may have to pay for transportation to and from the airport. A box lunch may be included in an excursion, but drinks might cost extra. Tips may not be included. Find out if you will be charged if you decide to opt out of certain activities or meals.

Before you invest in a tour, get some answers. Ask about the **accommodation choices** and prices for each. If you need a certain type of room, ask for it; don't take whatever is thrown your way. Request a nonsmoking room, a room with a view, or whatever you fancy.

Finally, if you plan to travel alone, you'll need to know if a **single supplement** will be charged and if the company can match you up with a roommate.

TOUR OPERATORS

Abercrombie & Kent (✆ 800/323-7308; www.abercrombiekent.com) offers extremely upscale escorted tours that are loaded with luxury. Their most unusual conveyance is the *Royal Scotsman* train, which, for 1 night and 2 days, hauls participants along less frequently used railway spurs of Wiltshire, Somerset, and Devon within vintage railway cars that were fashionable around the turn of the 20th century. Prices begin at $890 per person, double occupancy, for lots of local color and spit-and-polish service. Tours emphasize visits to sites of historical interest.

In Edinburgh, passengers can board the luxury train and can enjoy either a 4-night Scotland tour, or a new 2-night tour of the east or west coasts of Scotland. The food rivals that served in the finest restaurants, and the package includes bus trips, tours of castles, manor houses, gardens, and historic sites, many of which are not open to the public. The train stops every evening in a quiet place to guarantee passengers a good night's sleep. Two-night tours begin at $2,450 per person for a twin or single cabin. Call for other tour information and departure times.

One of Abercrombie's top rivals is **Travcoa** (✆ 800/992-2003; www.travcoa.com), which offers upscale tours by deluxe motor coach through the countryside of England and Scotland. Tours last from 8 to 27 days, include at least 3 nights in London, usually at such citadels of glamour as The Dorchester, and come with meals and virtually every other aspect of a holiday included in the price. Don't expect cost savings here: Without airfare, rates range from $5,395 to $16,295 per person double occupancy.

Other contenders in the upscale package-tour business include **Maupintour** (✆ 800/255-4266; www.maupintour.com) and **Tauck**

World Discovery (© 800/468-2825; www.tauck.com).

But not all escorted tours are so pricey. Mostly older, British folks make up a large portion of the clientele of one of the United Kingdom's largest tour operators, **Wallace Arnold Holidays** (© 0208/686-2378; www.wallacearnold.com). Most of the company's tours last between 5 and 10 days, include lodgings at solid but not particularly extravagant hotels, most meals, and are reasonably priced from £239 ($382), without airfare.

U.S.-based **Trafalgar Tours** (© 800/854-0103; www.trafalgar tours.com), offers affordable packages with lodgings in unpretentious but comfortable hotels. It's one of Europe's largest tour operators. There may not be a lot of frills, but you can find 8-day itineraries priced from $760 per person, double occupancy, without airfare, that include stopovers in London, York, and Edinburgh; they also offer a comprehensive 16-day Best of Britain tour covering London, the Highlands, and Cardiff, among others for $1699 per person, double occupancy.

One of Trafalgar's leading competitors, known for roughly equivalent moderately priced tours through Britain, is **Globus & Cosmos Tours** (© 800/338-7092; www.globusand cosmos.com).

A fabulous way to see the lochs and far-flung islands of Scotland is by boat, and one company geared for this sort of travel is **Hebridean Island Cruises,** Acorn Park, Skipton, North Yorkshire BD23 2UE (© 800/659-2648 in the U.S. and Canada, or 01756/704704; www.hebridean.co. uk). The company operates the *Hebridean Princess,* a shallow-draft, much-refitted and retooled remake (1990) of an older vessel. Equipped with 30 staterooms and a crew of 38, it can carry up to 50 passengers in cozy circumstances to some of the most remote and inaccessible regions of Scotland. The ship is equipped with beach landing craft especially useful during explorations of the fragile ecosystems and bird life of the more remote islands.

From March to October, the company offers 12 itineraries that focus on nature and ecology or on the castles, gardens, and archaeology of Scotland. The tours and prices vary enormously depending on the date of travel but generally range from 4 to 10 nights and cost £900 to £12,500 ($1,440–$20,000). All meals and shore excursions are included, but liquor tabs at the well-stocked bar, wine at dinner, and gratuities are extra.

For more luxurious tours through the islands and lochs of Scotland, contact **Seabourn Cruise Line** (© 800/929-9595 or 305/463-3000; www. seabourn.com), which offers cruises aboard its top-of-the-line yacht *Seabourn Sun,* often as part of longer itineraries around the British Isles.

12 Special Interest Trips

BIKE TRIPS

If you're planning a bike trip on your own, you can take your two wheels on passenger trains in Britain if you pay a £5 ($8) extra charge. Brits have rediscovered the bicycle, and by 2005 a **National Cycle Network** will cover 12,880km (8,000 miles) throughout the country. The network will run from Dover in southeast England to

Inverness in the Highlands. Some 5,635km (3,500 miles)—known as the Millennium Route—opened in 2000.

Most routes cross old railway lines, canal towpaths, and riversides. Among the more popular routes are the **Sea-to-Sea Cycle Route,** a 225km (140-mile) path linking the Irish Sea with the North Sea across the Pennine Hills and into the north Lake District and the Durham Dales. The **Essex Cycle Route** covers 402km (250 miles) of countryside, going through some of England's most charming villages; the **Devon Coast-to-Coast Route** runs for 145km (90 miles) in southwest England, skirting the edge of Dartmoor; the West Country Way for 399km (248 miles) links the Cornish coast to Bath and Bristol; and the 161km (100 miles) **Severn and Thames Route** links two of Britain's major rivers.

For a free copy of "Britain for Cyclists," with information on these routes, call the **British Tourist Authority** at ⓒ **888/VISITUK** or contact the Cyclists Touring Club (see below).

The **Cyclists Touring Club,** Cotterell House, 69 Meadrow, Godalming, Surrey GU7 3H5 (ⓒ **0870/873-0060;** www.ctc.org.uk), can suggest routes and provide information. Memberships cost £27 ($43) a year.

FISHING

Fly-fishing was born in Britain, and it's an art form. An expert in leading programs for fly-fishermen eager to experience the cold, clear waters of Britain is **Rod & Reel Adventures,** 2294 Oakmont Way, Eugene, OR 97401 (ⓒ **800/356-6982;** 541/349-0777; www.rodreeladventures.com). Don't expect smooth salesmanship at this place, but if you persevere, someone at this company should be able to link you up with a local fishing guide who can lead you to local waters that are well stocked with trout, perch, grayling, sea bream, Atlantic salmon, and such lesser-known species as rudd and roach. Rod & Reel Adventures has contacts in the Lake District, Scotland, and the Norfolk Broads.

If you prefer to go it alone, contact the **British Salmon & Trout Association,** Fishmonger's Hall, London Bridge, London EC4R 9EL (ⓒ **020/7283-5838**), for information about British fishing regulations.

GOLF

Though the sport originated in Scotland, golf also has been around in England since Edward VII first began stamping over the greens of such courses as Royal Lytham & St. Annes, in England's northwest, or Royal St. Georges, near London.

The unyielding reality is that golf in England remains a clubby sport where some of the most prestigious courses are usually reserved exclusively for members. Rules at most English golf courses tend to be stricter in matters of dress code and protocol than their equivalents in the United States.

If, however, your heart is set on enjoying a round or two on the emerald-colored turf of England, **Golf International,** 14 E. 38th St., New York, NY 10016 (ⓒ **800/833-1389** or 212/986-9176; www.golfinternational.com), can open doors for you. Golf packages in England are arranged for anywhere from 7 to 14 days and can include as much or as little golf, on as many different courses, as a participant wants. Weeklong vacations, with hotels, breakfasts, car rentals, and greens fees included, range from $1,965 to $3,500 per person, double occupancy, airfare not included. Golf International also offers the best golf tours of Scotland and will guarantee its clients starting times at 40 or so of Scotland's most sought-after courses, including St. Andrews, Carnoustie, and Royal Troon.

Worthy competitors that operate on a less comprehensive scale than Golf International include **Adventures in Golf,** 11 Northeastern Blvd., Suite 360, Nashua, NH 03062 (ⓒ **603/882-8367;** www.adventures-in-golf.com); and **Jerry Quinlan's Celtic Golf,** 1129 Rte. 95, Cape May Courthouse, NJ 08210 (ⓒ **800/535-6148;** www.jqcelticgolf.com). Each of their tours is customized, and usually includes lodging in anything from simple guesthouses to five-star deluxe manor houses.

HIKING, WALKING & RAMBLING

In England and Wales alone, there are some 161,000km (100,000 miles) of trails and footpaths. The **Ramblers' Association,** Camelford House, 87–90 Albert Embankment, 2nd Floor, London SE1 7TW (© **020/ 7339-8500;** www.ramblers.org.uk), publishes an annual yearbook that lists some 2,500 bed-and-breakfasts near the trails; it costs £12 ($19). Send a check in British pounds for the yearbook if you plan to order before your trip; otherwise the yearbook can be purchased in England for £6 ($9.60).

Alternatively, you can join an organized hiking tour. **Wilderness Travel, Inc.,** 1102 Ninth St., Berkeley, CA 94710 (© **800/368-2794** or 510/558-2488; www.wildernesstravel. com), specializes in treks and inn-to-inn hiking tours, plus less strenuous walking tours of Cornwall and the Cotswolds that combine transportation with walking sessions of 3 hours or less.

English Lakeland Ramblers, 18 Stuyvesant Oval, Suite 1A, New York, NY 10009 (© **800/724-8801** or 212/505-1020; www.ramblers.com), offers 7- or 8-day walking tours for the average active person. On its Lake District tour, you'll stay and have your meals in a charming 17th-century country inn near Ambleside and Windermere. A minibus takes hikers and sightseers daily to trails and sightseeing points. Experts tell you about the area's culture and history and highlight its natural wonders. There are also tours of the Cotswolds and Scotland, as well as inn-to-inn tours and privately guided tours.

Other contenders include **Country Walkers,** P.O. Box 180, Waterbury, VT 05676 (© **800/464-9255** or 802/244-1387; www.countrywalkers.com). This company's "walking vacations"

lasts 5 to 7 days and tend to focus on such scenic areas as the Lake District, Cornwall, and the Cotswolds. These packages include overnight accommodations at well-respected, but not excessively luxurious, three-star hotels, and the occasional manor house; most meals; and a guide who's well versed in local paths, trails, and lore. About 6.5km to 19km (4–12 miles) are covered each day. Prices start at $2,098 per person, double occupancy, without airfare.

To explore the mountain activities of Wales's Snowdonia National Park, contact Bob Postings, **Ozanam Centre,** Tyn y Pwll, Tan-yr-allt, Caernarfon, in North Wales (© **01766/ 810909**). Bob and his skilled team specialize in walking the summits, rock climbing, kayaking, and rafting, among other activities.

HORSEBACK RIDING

You can learn to ride or brush up on your skills at **Eastern Equation,** a facility located on the Essex/Suffolk border. British Horse Society–certified instructors teach riders at a facility with a large indoor arena, a jumping course, and 30 horses and ponies of various sizes and abilities. Many trails go directly from the farm to the countryside. You can stay in a room with a private bath at the beautiful 16th-century farmhouse (subject to availability) or find accommodations in a comfortable nearby hotel. Contact **Cross Country International,** P.O. Box 1170, Millbrook, NY 12545 (© **800/828-8768;** www.equestrian vacations.com).

A number of American companies offer horseback-riding package tours of England. **Equitour,** P.O. Box 807, Dubois, WY 82513 (© **800/545-0019** or 307/455-3363; www.riding tours.com), is one such firm, specializing in package tours for riding enthusiasts who want to experience the horsey traditions of the land of foxes and hounds. Two types of tours can be arranged: stationary tours, with instruction in jumping and dressage, over a 7-day period at a stable beside the Bristol Channel or on the fields of Dartmoor; and "progressive" tours in Wales, with treks of 4 to 10 days. Most riders, eager to experience as wide a view of England as possible, opt for the latter, spending nights at different B&Bs or inns and lodging their mount at nearby stables. Accommodations are simple, and prices are kept deliberately low. A 6-day horseback excursion in Cumbria that includes use of a horse, guide services, overnight accommodations, and all meals costs around $1,625 per person, double occupancy.

The Welsh countryside lends itself to horseback riding, and the trekking terrain is tame enough that even beginners can join in the fun. The best outfitter for this is the **Llangenny Riding Centre** (✆ 01874/730871; www.pony9.force9.co.uk), which offers trekking through the Brecon Beacons National Park.

BEER & BREWERY TOURS

A Seattle-based company, **MIR Corporation,** 85 S. Washington St., Suite 210, Seattle, WA 98104 (✆ **800/424-7289**; www.mircorp.com), offers customized Brew Tasting and Brewery Tours, for groups of 10 or more, that include visits to such major breweries as Samuel Smith's and Young's, outside of London; the Caledonian brewery, outside of Edinburgh; and a host of lesser-known, family-owned breweries scattered throughout the countryside. Included are frequent opportunities to taste local brew at atmospheric pubs en route.

Don't expect demure sobriety during the course of this experience. Most participants quaff their first pint at least an hour before lunch and continue sampling the merchandise throughout the course of the day and evening. Call for prices, which are subject to change. Accommodations are in unpretentious moderate hotels and inns. Each tour is limited to 20 participants, and transport throughout is by train and motor coach.

UNIVERSITY STUDY PROGRAMS

You can study English literature at renowned universities such as Oxford and Cambridge during the week and then take weekend excursions to the countryside of Shakespeare, Austen, Dickens, and Hardy. While doing your coursework, you can live in dormitories with other students and dine in elaborate halls or the more intimate Fellows' clubs. Study programs in England are not limited to the liberal arts, or to high school or college students. Some programs are designed specifically for teachers and seniors (see "Senior Travel," on p. 51). For more information, contact organizations listed below.

Affiliated with Richmond College, in London, **American Institute For Foreign Study,** River Plaza, 9 W. Broad St., Stamford, CT 06902 (✆ **800/727-2437** or 203/399-5000; www.aifs.com), offers 4 weeks and up of traveling programs for high school students, and internships and academic programs for college students. There are also programs leading to the British equivalent of an MBA.

IIE (Institute of International Education), U.S. Student Programs Division, 809 United Nations Plaza, New York, NY 10017-3500 (✆ **800/445-0443** or 212/883-8200; www.iie.org), administers a variety of academic, training, and grant programs for the U.S. Information Agency (USIA), including Fulbright grants. It is especially helpful in arranging enrollments for U.S. students in summer school programs.

University Vacations, 3660 Bougainvillea Rd., Coconut Grove, FL 33133 (✆ **800/792-0100;**

www.universityvacations.com), offers upmarket liberal arts programs at Oxford and Cambridge universities. Courses usually last 7 to 12 days and combine lectures and excursions with dining in the intimate Fellows' Dining Rooms. Accommodations are in private rooms with available en-suite facilities in the medieval colleges. There are neither formal academic requirements nor pressure for examinations or written requirements. Its summer headquarters is Magdalen College, Oxford.

Worldwide Classrooms, P.O. Box 1166, Milwaukee, WI 53201 (**www.worldwide.edu**), offers a directory-like catalog of schools offering study abroad programs in England for $9.95.

13 Getting Around Britain

BY CAR

The British car-rental market is among the most competitive in Europe. Nevertheless, car rentals are often relatively expensive, unless you avail yourself of one of the promotional deals that are frequently offered by British Airways and others.

Because cars in Britain travel on the left side of the road, steering wheels are positioned on the "wrong" side of the vehicle. Keep in mind that most rental cars are manual, so be prepared to shift with your left hand; you'll pay more for an automatic—and make sure to request one when you reserve.

Most car-rental companies will accept your U.S. driver's license, provided you're 23 years old (21 in rare instances) and have had the license for more than a year. Many rental companies will grant discounts to clients who reserve their cars in advance (usually 48 hr.) through the toll-free reservations offices in the renter's home country. Rentals of a week or more are almost always less expensive per day than day rentals.

When you reserve a car, make sure you know the total price, including the 17.5% value-added tax (VAT).

Rentals are available through **Avis** (© 800/331-1084; www.avis.com), **British Airways** (© 800/AIRWAYS; www.british-airways.com), **Budget** (© 800/472-3325; www.budget.com), and **Hertz** (© 800/654-3001; www.hertz.com). **Kemwel Holiday Auto** (© 800/678-0678; www.kemwel.com) is among the cheapest and most reliable of the rental agencies. **Auto-Europe** (© 800/223-5555 in the U.S., or 0800/899-893 in London; www.autoeurope.com) acts as a wholesale company for rental agencies in Europe.

Car-rental rates vary even more than airline fares. The price you pay depends on the size of the car, where and when you pick it up and drop it off, length of the rental period, where and how far you drive it, whether you purchase insurance, and a host of other factors. A few key questions could save you hundreds of dollars, so make sure to ask about potential hidden costs, such a mileage charges, refueling costs (it's almost always cheaper if you fuel up the car before you return it), and drop-off fees if you do not return the car to the same location where you picked it up.

You should always inquire if special promotions are available when you make your reservation. If you're a member of an organization such as AARP or AAA, you may be entitled to a special discount.

Note: Unlike U.S. rentals, almost all rental cars in Great Britain have manual transmissions. If you need an automatic, be aware that you're going to pay extra for it.

RENTAL INSURANCE Before you drive off in a rental car, be sure you're insured. Hasty assumptions about your personal auto insurance or a rental agency's additional coverage could end up costing you tens of thousands of dollars—even if you are involved in an accident that was clearly the fault of another driver.

U.S. drivers who already have their own car insurance are usually covered in the United States for loss of or damage to a rental car and liability in case of injury to any other party involved in an accident. But coverage probably doesn't extend outside the United States. Be sure to find out whether you are covered in England, whether your policy extends to all persons who will be driving the rental car, how much liability is covered in case an outside party is injured in an accident, and whether the type of vehicle you are renting is included under your contract. (Rental trucks, sport utility vehicles, and luxury vehicles such as the Jaguar may not be covered.)

Most **major credit cards** provide some degree of coverage as well—provided they are used to pay for the rental. Terms vary widely, however, so be sure to call your credit-card company directly before you rent. But though they will cover damage to or theft of your rental, *credit cards will not cover liability* or the cost of injury to an outside party and/or damage to an outside party's vehicle. If you do not hold an insurance policy or if you are driving outside the United States, you may want to seriously consider purchasing additional liability insurance from your rental company. Be sure to check the terms, however: Some rental agencies only cover liability if the renter is not at fault.

Bear in mind that each credit-card company has its own peculiarities. Most American Express Optima cards, for instance, do not provide any insurance. American Express does not cover vehicles valued at over $50,000 when new, such as luxury vehicles or vehicles built on a truck chassis. Master-Card does not provide coverage for

loss, theft, or fire damage, and only covers collision if the rental period does not exceed 15 days. Call your own credit-card company for details.

DRIVING RULES & REQUIREMENTS
In Britain, *you drive on the left* and pass on the right. Road signs are clear and the international symbols are unmistakable.

You must present your passport and driver's license when you rent a car in Britain. No special British license is needed. It's a good idea to get a copy of the *British Highway Code,* available from almost any gas station or newsstand (called a "news stall" in Britain).

Warning: Pedestrian crossings are marked by striped lines (zebra striping) on the road; flashing lights near the curb indicate that drivers must stop and yield the right of way if a pedestrian has stepped out into the zebra zone to cross the street.

ROAD MAPS
The best road map is *The Ordinance Survey Motor Atlas of Great Britain,* whether you're trying to find the fastest route to Manchester or locate some obscure village. Revised annually, it's published by Temple Press and is available at most bookstores, including **Foyle, Ltd.,** 113 and 119 Charing Cross Rd., London WC2 H0EB (© **020/7440-3225**).

BREAKDOWNS
If you are a member of AAA in the United States, you are automatically eligible for the same roadside services you receive at home. Be sure to bring your membership card with you on your trip. In an emergency, call the Automobile Association of Great Britain's emergency road service (© **0800/085-2721**). If you are not a member of AAA, you may want to join one of England's two major auto clubs—the **Automobile Association (AA),** Carr Ellison House, William Armstrong Drive, New Castle-upon-Tyne NE4 7YA (© **0870/550-0600**); and the **Royal Automobile Club (RAC),** P.O. Box

700, Bristol, Somerset BS99 1RB (© **0870/572-2722**). Membership, which can be obtained through your car-rental agent, entitles you to free legal and technical advice on motoring matters, as well as a whole range of discounts on automobile products and services.

If your car breaks down on the highway, you can call for **24-hour breakdown service** from a roadside phone. The 24-hour number to call for **AA** is © **0800/085-2721;** for **RAC** it is © **0800/028-0829.** All superhighways (called motorways in Britain) have special emergency phones that are connected to police traffic units, and the police can contact either of the auto clubs on your behalf.

GASOLINE Called "petrol," gasoline is sold by the liter (4.2 liters to a gal.). Prices are much higher than in the States, and you'll probably have to serve yourself. In some remote areas, stations are few and far between, and many are closed on Sunday.

BY PLANE

British Airways (© **800/AIRWAYS**) flies to more than 20 cities outside London, including Manchester, Glasgow, and Edinburgh.

For passengers planning on visiting widely scattered destinations within the United Kingdom, perhaps with a side trip to a city on Europe's mainland, British Airways' **Europe Airpass** allows discounted travel in a continuous loop to between 3 and 12 cities anywhere on BA's European and domestic air routes. Passengers must end their journey at the same point they begin it and fly exclusively on BA flights. Such a ticket (for instance, from London to Paris, then to Manchester, and finally to London again) will cut the cost of each segment of the itinerary by about 40% to 50% over individually booked tickets. The pass is available for travel to about a dozen

of the most visited cities and regions of Britain, with discounted add-ons available to most of BA's destinations in Europe as well.

BA's Europe Airpass must be booked and paid for at least 7 days before a passenger's departure from North America. All sectors of the itinerary, including transatlantic passage from North America, must be booked simultaneously. Some changes are permitted in flight dates (but not in destinations) after the ticket is issued. Check with British Airways for full details and restrictions.

BY TRAIN

A Eurailpass is not valid in Great Britain, but there are several special passes offered by Britrail for train travel outside London. For railroad information, go to Rail Travel centers in the main London railway stations (Waterloo, King's Cross, Euston, and Paddington).

BritRail Passes allow unlimited travel in England, Scotland, and Wales on any British rail scheduled train over the whole of the network during the validity of the pass without restrictions. If you're traveling beyond London anywhere in the United Kingdom, and plan to hop on and off the train, consider purchasing a **BritRail Classic (aka Consecutive) Pass.** These passes allow you to travel for a consecutive number of days for a flat rate. In first class adults pay $285 for 4 days, $405 for 8 days, $609 for 15 days, $769 for 22 days, and $915 for 1 month. In second class, fares are $189 for 4 days, $269 for 8 days, $405 for 15 days, $515 for 22 days, and $609 for 1 month. Seniors (60 and over) qualify for discounts in first class travel and pay $245 for 4 days, $345 for 8 days, $519 for 15 days, $659 for 22 days, and $779 for 1 month of first class travel. Passengers under 26 qualify for a **Youth Pass:** $155 for 4 days, $219 for 8 days,

$285 for 15 days, $359 for 22 days, and $429 for 1 month. One child (5–15) can travel free with each adult or senior pass by requesting the **BritRail Family Pass** when buying the adult pass. Additional children pay half the regular adult fare.

A more versatile pass is the **BritRail FlexiPass** allowing you to travel when you want. It costs $519 for 8 days of travel in first class or $349 in standard class. Discounts are granted to seniors, and children (ages 5–15) pay half the adult fare.

If you plan to focus intensively on Scotland, a regular BritRail pass might not be adequate. The **Freedom of Scotland Travelpass** offers unlimited transportation on trains and most ferries throughout Scotland and discounts for bus travel. It includes access to obscure bus routes to almost forgotten hamlets, free rides on ferries operated by Caledonian MacBrayne, and discounted fares with P&O Scottish Lines. Their ferries connect to the Western Islands, the islands of the Clyde, and the historic Orkneys.

The Travelpass covers the entire Scottish rail network and is usable from Carlisle on the western border of England and Scotland and from Berwick-upon-Tweed on the eastern Scottish border. In addition, if you have to fly into London and want to go straight to Scotland from there, a reduced rate is available for a round-trip ticket between London and Edinburgh or Glasgow for Travelpass holders.

A pass, sold by Britrail in the U.S., costs $139 for 4 days; $179 for 8 days, and $219 for 12 days. When you validate the pass at the beginning of your journey, you'll get a complete packet of rail, bus, and ferry schedules. For more information on the pass, call **ScotRail** at © **0845/755-0033;** or surf over to **www.scotrail.co.uk**.

A **Freedom of Wales FlexiPass** is also offered through Britrail in the U.S. This economy pass offers two options—in an 8-day period you can travel any 4 days by rail and every day by bus for $89; or else in a 15-day period you can travel 7 days by rail and every day by bus for $149.

For more information on Britrail pass options and on rail vacation packages in England and the U.K., contact **BritRail** (© **866/BRITAIL** or 877/ 677-1066; www.britrail.net and www. BritainSecrets.com). You can download faxable order forms or order online using a BritRail Pass Shopping Cart feature (**www.britainontrack. com**).

BY BUS

In Britain, a long-distance touring bus is called a "coach," and "buses" are taken for local transportation. An efficient and frequent express motorcoach network—run by National Express and other independent operators—links most of Britain's towns and cities. Destinations off the main route can be easily reached by transferring to a local bus at a stop on the route. Tickets are relatively cheap, often half the price of rail fare, and it's usually cheaper to purchase a round-trip (or "return") ticket than two one-way fares separately.

Victoria Coach Station, on Buckingham Palace Road (© **020/ 77303466**), is the departure point for most large coach operators. The coach station is located just 2 blocks from Victoria Station. For credit-card sales (MasterCard and Visa only), call © **020/7730-3499** Monday through Saturday between 9am and 7pm. For cash purchases, get there at least 30 minutes before the coach departs.

National Express (© **020/7529-2000;** www.nationalexpressgroup. com) runs long-distance coaches that are equipped with reclining seats, toilets, and nonsmoking areas. The National Express ticket office at Victoria Station is open from 6am to 11pm.

Train Routes in Great Britain

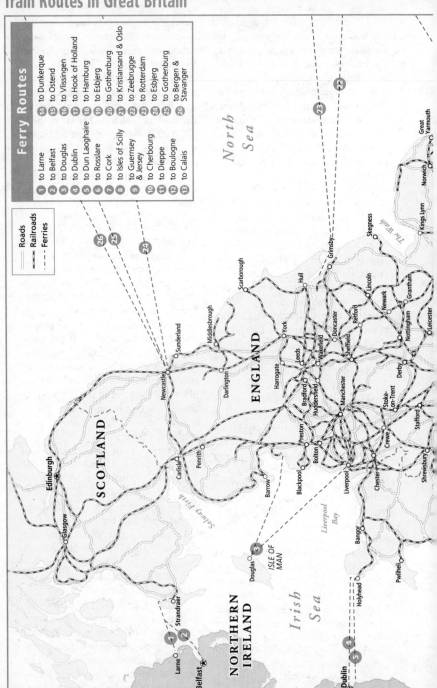

Ferry Routes

① to Larne
② to Belfast
③ to Douglas
④ to Dublin
⑤ to Dun Laoghaire
⑥ to Rosslare
⑦ to Cork
⑧ to Isles of Scilly
⑨ to Guernsey & Jersey
⑩ to Cherbourg
⑪ to Dieppe
⑫ to Boulogne
⑬ to Calais
⑭ to Dunkerque
⑮ to Ostend
⑯ to Vlissingen
⑰ to Hook of Holland
⑱ to Hamburg
⑲ to Esbjerg
⑳ to Gothenburg
㉑ to Kristiansand & Oslo
㉒ to Zeebrugge
㉓ to Rotterdam
㉔ to Esbjerg
㉕ to Gothenburg
㉖ to Bergen & Stavanger

Roads
Railroads
Ferries

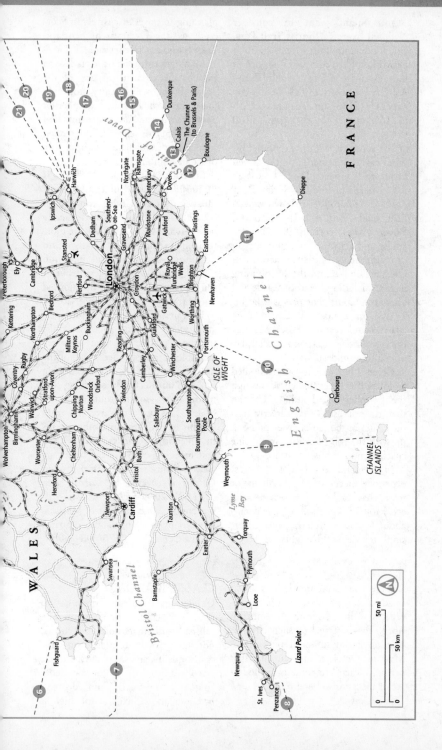

You might want to consider National Express's **Tourist Trail Pass,** which offers unlimited travel on their network. (This company's service is most extensive in England and Wales.) A 1-day pass costs £49 ($78), a 5-day pass £85 ($136), an 8-day pass, £135 ($216), and a 15-day pass, £190 ($304).

For journeys within a 56km (35-mile) radius of London, try the **Green Line** coach service, 23–27 Endsleigh Rd., Merstham Redhill, Surrey RH1 3LX (✆ **0870/608-7261;** www.green line.co.uk). With a 1-day **Diamond Rover Ticket,** costing £8 ($13) for adults and £5 ($8) for children, you can visit many of the attractions of Greater London and the surrounding region, including Windsor Castle and Hampton Court. The pass is valid for 1 day on almost all Green Line coaches and country buses Monday through Friday after 9am and all day on Saturday and Sunday.

Green Line has bus routes called Country Bus Lines that circle through the periphery of London. Though they do not usually go directly into the center of the capital, they do hook up with the routes of the Green Line coaches and red buses that do.

In Scotland, the bus is the least expensive means of travel. All major towns have a local bus service, and every tourist office will provide details about ½-day or full-day bus excursions to scenic highlights. If you're planning to travel extensively in Scotland, see the **Freedom of Scotland Travelpass,** described above.

Many adventurous travelers like to explore the country on one of the postal buses, which carry not only mail, but also a limited number of passengers to rural areas. Ask any local post office for details. A general timetable is available at the head post office in Edinburgh.

Scottish CityLink (✆ **08705/ 505050;** www.citylink.co.uk) offers most inter-city service throughout Scotland, and is the most frequently used service, of course. Buses are more frequent in and around Glasgow and Edinburgh, but as you head north into the Highlands, service is less frequent. On Sunday the operation functions at only a fraction of its regular service.

In Wales, 65 independent bus operators serve the little country. Public transport guides for local areas are available at tourist offices. One of the most important is **TrawsCambria** (✆ **08706/082608**), servicing the main north–south route through Wales. This bus will carry you from Cardiff to Holyhead and other points in the north of Wales, and BritRail and Freedom of Wales rail passes are valid on this run. The area around Cardiff is covered by **Cardiff Bus** (✆ **029/2039-6521;** www.cardiff bus.com). Most of North Wales is serviced by a regional bus company, **Arriva Cymru** (✆ 0870/608-2608).

14 Tips on Accommodations

Reserve your accommodations as far in advance as possible, even in the so-called slow months from November to April. Tourist travel to such cities as London and Edinburgh peaks from May to October, and during that period, it's hard to come by a moderate or inexpensive hotel room.

CLASSIFICATIONS

Unlike some countries, Britain has no rigid hotel classification system. The tourist board grades hotels by crowns, not stars. Hotels are judged on standards, quality, and hospitality, and are rated "approved," "commended," "highly commended," and "deluxe." Five crowns (deluxe) is the highest rating. A classification of "listed" (no crowns) refers to accommodations that are for the most part very modest.

In a five-crown hotel, all rooms must have a private bathroom; in a four-crown hotel, only 75% have them. In a one-crown hotel, buildings are required to have hot and cold running water in all rooms, but in "listed" hotels, hot and cold running water in rooms is not mandatory. Crown ratings are posted outside the buildings. However, the system is voluntary, and many hotels do not participate.

Many hotels, especially older ones, still lack private bathrooms for all rooms. Most, however, have hot and cold running water, and many have modern wings with all the amenities (and older sections that are less up to date). When making reservations, always ask what section of the hotel you'll be staying in.

All hotels once included in the room price a full English, Welsh, or Scottish breakfast of bacon and eggs, but today that is true for only some hotels. A continental breakfast of tea or coffee and toast is usually still included.

BED & BREAKFASTS

In towns, cities, and villages throughout Britain, homeowners take in paying guests. Watch for the familiar bed-and-breakfast (B&B) signs. Generally, these are modest family homes, but sometimes they may be built like small hotels, with as many as 15 rooms. If they're that big, they are more properly classified as guesthouses. B&Bs are the cheapest places you can stay in Britain and still be comfortable.

Hometours International (© 866/ 367-4668 or 865/690-8484; hometours@aol.com) will make bed-and-breakfast reservations in England, Scotland, and Wales. This is the only company to guarantee reservations for more than 400 locations in Britain. Accommodations are paid for in the United States in dollars, and prices start as low as $50 per person per night, though they can go as high as $100 per person in London. The company can also arrange for apartments in London or cottages in Great Britain that begin at $800 to $1,400 per week for a studio.

Reservations for bed-and-breakfast accommodations in London can also be made by writing (not calling) the **British Visitor Centre**, 1 Lower Regent St., London SW1 4PQ. Once in London, you can also visit their office (Tube: Piccadilly Circus).

In addition, Susan Opperman and Rosemary Lumb run **Bed and Breakfast Nationwide**, P.O. Box 2100, Clacton-on-Sea, Essex CO16 9BW, an agency specializing in privately owned bed-and-breakfasts all over Great Britain. Host homes range from small cottages to large manor houses, as well as working farms, and the prices vary accordingly. One thing you can be sure of is that owners have been specially selected for their wish to entertain visitors from overseas. Remember that these are private homes, so hotel-type services are not available. You will, however, be assured of a warm welcome, a comfortable bed, a hearty breakfast, and a glimpse of British life. For bookings in accommodations outside London, call © **01255/831235** daily between 9am and 6pm. Or check out their website at **www.bed andbreakfastnationwide.com**.

FARMHOUSES

In many parts of Britain, farmhouses have one, two, even four rooms set aside for paying guests, who usually arrive in the summer months. Farmhouses don't have the facilities of most guesthouses, but they have a rustic appeal and charm, especially for motorists, as they tend to lie off the beaten path. Prices are generally lower than bed-and-breakfasts or guesthouses, and sometimes you're offered some good country home cooking (at an extra charge) if you make arrangements in advance. The British Tourist Authority will provide a booklet, *Stay on a Farm,* or you can ask at local tourist offices.

Farm Stay UK (© 024/7669-6909; www.farmstayuk.co.uk) publishes an annual directory in early December that includes 1,000 farms and bed-and-breakfasts throughout the United Kingdom. The listings include quality ratings, the number of bedrooms, nearby attractions and activities, prices, and line drawings of each property. Also listed are any special details, such as rooms with four-poster beds or activities on the grounds (fishing, for example). Many farms are geared toward children, who can participate in light chores—gathering eggs or just tagging along—for an authentic farm experience. The prices range from £21 to £53 ($34–$85) a night and include an English breakfast and usually private facilities. (The higher prices are for stays at mansions and manor houses.)

Another option is self-catering accommodations, which are usually cottages or converted barns that cost from £165 to £510 ($264–$816) per week and include dishwashers and central heating. Each property is inspected annually. The majority of the properties, with the exception of those located in the mountains, are open year-round.

For a copy of the directory called *Stay on a Farm,* contact the **Farm Stay UK,** National Agricultural Centre, Stoneleigh Park, Warwickshire CV8 2LZ (© 024/7669-6909). It costs £3.95 ($6.30) for postage and may be purchased by credit card.

NATIONAL TRUST PROPERTIES

The National Trust of England, Wales, and Northern Ireland, 36 Queen Anne's Gate, London SW1H 9AS

(© 020/7222-9251; www.national trust.org.uk), is Britain's leading conservation organization. In addition to the many castles, forests, and gardens it maintains, the National Trust owns almost 300 houses and cottages in some of the most beautiful parts of England, Wales, and Northern Ireland. Some of these properties are in remote and rural locations; some have incomparable views of the coastline; and others stand in the heart of villages and ancient cities.

Most of these comfortable self-catering holiday accommodations are available for rental throughout the year. Examples include a simple former coast guard cottage in Northumbria, a 15th-century manor house in a hidden corner of the Cotswolds, and a superb choice of cottages in Devon and Cornwall. Houses can be booked for a week or more. Many can be booked for midweek or weekend breaks on short notice, particularly in autumn and winter. National Trust properties can sleep from 2 to 12 guests, and range in price from £170 ($272) per week for a small rental in winter to £1,705 ($2,728) per week for a larger property in peak season. Prices include value-added tax (VAT). Call © 01225/791199 for reservations.

Though anyone can book rentals in National Trust properties, it's worth mentioning the trust's U.S. affiliate, the **Royal Oak Foundation,** 26 Broadway, Suite 950, New York, NY 10004 (© 800/913-6565 or 212/480-2889; www.royal-oak.org), which publishes a full-color 350-page booklet that describes all National Trust holiday rental properties, their facilities, and prices. Copies cost $10 for nonmembers. Individual annual memberships are $50, and family memberships are $75. Benefits include free admission to all National Trust sites and properties open to the public, plus discounts on reservations at cottages and houses owned by them and discounted air and train travel.

HOLIDAY COTTAGES & VILLAGES

Throughout Britain, fully furnished studios, houses, cottages, "flats" (apartments), even trailers suitable for families or groups, can be rented by the month. From October to March, rents are sometimes reduced by 50%.

The British Tourist Authority and most tourist offices have lists available. The BTA's free *Apartments in London and Holiday Homes* lists rental agencies such as **At Home Abroad, Inc.,** 405 E. 56th St., Suite 6H, New York, NY 10022 (© **212/421-9165;** fax 212/752-1591; www.athomeabroadinc.com). Interested parties should write or fax a description of their needs; At Home Abroad will send listings at no charge.

British Travel International (© **800/327-6097** or 540/298-2232; www.britishtravel.com) represents between 8,000 and 10,000 rental properties in the United Kingdom, with rentals by the week (Sat–Sat), and requires a 50% payment at the time of booking. A catalog with pictures of their offerings is available for a $5 fee that is counted toward a deposit. They have everything from honey-colored, thatch-roofed cottages in the Cotswolds to apartments in a British university city. The company represents about 100 hotels in London whose rates are discounted by 5% to 50%, depending on the season and market conditions, and they have listings of some 4,000 bed-and-breakfast establishments.

Barclay International Group (**BIG;** 3 School St., Glen Cove, NY 11542; © **800/845-6636** or 516/759-5100; www.barclayweb.com) specializes in short-term apartment (flat) rentals in London and cottages in the British countryside. These rentals can be appropriate for families, groups of friends, or businesspeople traveling together and are sometimes less expensive than equivalent stays in hotels. Apartments, available for stays as short as 1 night (though you are charged a premium if your stay is shorter than 3 nights), are usually more luxurious than you'd imagine. Furnished with kitchens, they offer a low-cost alternative to restaurant meals. Apartments suitable for one or two occupants begin, during low season, at around $500 a week (including tax) and can go much higher for deluxe accommodations that offer many hotel-like features and amenities. For extended stays in the countryside, BIG has country cottages in such areas as the Cotswolds, the Lake District, and Oxford, as well as farther afield in Scotland and Wales. A big catalog of their offerings costs $10.

At the cheaper end of the spectrum, there's **Hoseasons Holidays,** Sunway House, Lowestoft, NR32 2LW (© **01502/502588;** www.hoseasons.co.uk), a reservations agent based in Suffolk (East Anglia). They arrange stopovers in at least 300 vacation villages throughout Britain. Though many are isolated in bucolic regions far from any of the sites covered within this guidebook, others lie within an hour's drive of Stratford-upon-Avon. Don't expect luxury or convenience: Vacation villages in England usually consist of a motley assortment of trailers, uninsulated bungalows, and/or mobile homes perched on cement blocks. They're intended as frugal escapes for claustrophobic urbanites with children. Such a place might not meet your expectations for a vacation in the English countryside (and a minimum stay of 3 nights is usually required), but it's hard to beat the rate. A 3-day sojourn begins from £87 ($139) per person, double occupancy.

CHAIN HOTELS

Many American chains, such as Best Western, Hilton, and Sheraton are found throughout Britain. In addition, Britain has a number of leading chains with which North American travelers are generally not familiar. **Travelodge** (© **0870/085-0950;** www.travelodge.co.uk) offers good quality modern budget accommodations across the U.K. with a family restaurant on site. **Swallow Hotels** (© **01914/194666;** www.swallow hotels.com) are modern government-rated four-crown hotels, most with leisure facilities. **Thistle Hotels** (© **0870/333-9292;** www.thistle hotels.com) is a well-regarded chain of upscale to moderate full-service hotels that caters to both business and leisure travelers. An exclusive chain of government-rated three-crown hotels is called **Malmaison** (© **01737/780200;** www.malmaison.com/html. htm). There's not a bad hotel in their post. **Premier Lodge** (© **0870/201-0203**) is a new chain of modern, moderately priced accommodations across

the U.K., each one featuring a licensed restaurant.

HOUSE SWAPPING

The market leader in home exchanges is **HomeLink International,** P.O. Box 47747, Tampa, FL 33647 (© **800/638-3841** or 813/975-9825; www. homelink.org), which costs $70 to join. This is the oldest, largest, and best home exchange holiday organization in the world. The series is called a "home from home," and so it is. The only trouble is, you've got to turn your own home over to a stranger.

A competitor is **Intervac U.S. & International,** 30 Corte San Fernando, Tiburon, CA 94159 (© **800/756-HOME** or 415/435-3497; www. intervacus.com). To hook up with this outfitter, you pay $65 annually. Intervac is also adept at securing a list of home exchanges throughout Great Britain.

15 Sightseeing Passes

Several passes can cut down considerably on entrance costs to the country's stately homes and gardens. If you plan to do extensive touring, you'll save a lot of pounds by using one of these passes instead of paying the relatively steep entrance fees on an attraction-by-attraction basis.

Listed below are three organizations that offer passes waiving admission charges to hundreds of historical properties located throughout the United Kingdom. Each is a good deal, as the money you'll save on visitation to just a few of the available sites will pay for the price of the pass.

The British National Trust offers members free entry to some 340 National Trust sites scattered throughout Britain. Focusing on gardens, castles, historic parks, abbeys, and ruins, sites include Chartwell, St. Michael's Mount, and Beatrix Potter's House. The membership fee includes a listing

of properties, maps, essential information for independent tours, and listings and reservations for holiday cottages located on the protected properties.

Individual memberships cost £33 ($52) annually, and family memberships, for up to seven people, run £60 ($96). Savings on admission charges, combined with discounts on holiday cottage reservations and British Air or BritRail travel, make this especially appealing. Visa and MasterCard are accepted.

Contact **The British National Trust,** 36 Queen Anne's Gate, London SW1H 9AS (© **020/7222-9251;** www.nationaltrust.org.uk), or **The Royal Oak Foundation,** 26 Broadway, Suite 950, New York, NY 10004 (© **800/913-6565** or 212/480-2889; www.royal-oak.org).

English Heritage (www.English-heritage.org.uk) sells 7- and 14-day

How to Get Your VAT Refund

To receive back a portion of the tax paid on purchases made in Britain, first ask the store personnel if they do VAT refunds and what their minimum purchase is. Once you've achieved this minimum, ask for the paperwork; the retailer will have to fill out a portion themselves. Several readers have reported that merchants have told them that they can get refund forms at the airport on their way out of the country. *This is not true.* You must get a refund form from the retailer (don't leave the store without one), and it must be completed by the retailer on the spot.

Fill out your portion of the form and present it, along with the goods, at the Customs office in the airport. Allow a half-hour to stand in line. *Remember:* You're required to show the goods at your time of departure, so don't pack them in your luggage and check it; put them in your carry-on instead.

Once you have the paperwork stamped by the officials, you have two choices: You can mail the papers and receive your refund in either a British check (no!) or a credit-card refund (yes!), or you can go directly to the Cash VAT Refund desk at the airport and get your refund in your hand, in cash. The bad news: If you accept cash other than sterling, you will lose money on the conversion rate. (If you plan on mailing your paperwork, try to remember to bring a stamp with you to the airport; if you forget, you can usually get stamps from stamp machines and/or the convenience stores in the terminal.)

Be advised that many stores charge a flat fee for processing your refund, so £3 to £5 may be automatically deducted from the refund you receive. But because the VAT in Britain is 17.5%, if you get back 15%, you're doing fine.

Note: If traveling to other countries within the European Union, you don't go through any of this in Britain. At your final destination, prior to departure from the European Union, you file for all your VAT refunds at one time.

passes and annual memberships, offering free admission to more than 300 historical sites in England, and half-price admission to more than 100 additional sites in Scotland, Wales, and the Isle of Man. (Admission to these additional sites is free for anyone who renews his or her annual membership after the first year.) Sites include Hadrian's Wall, Stonehenge, and Kenilworth Castle.

Also included are: free or reduced admission to 450 historic re-enactments and open-air summer concerts,

a handbook detailing all properties, a map, and, with the purchase of an annual membership, events and concerts diaries, and *Heritage Today,* a quarterly magazine.

A 7-day Overseas Visitor Pass runs £13.50 ($22) for an adult or £30 ($48) for a family of six or less. A child accompanied by an adult goes free. A 14-day pass is £17.50 ($28) for an adult (free for a child) or £38 ($61) for a family. Annual memberships are also available with rates of £31 ($50) for an adult, £20 ($32) for those between 16 and 21, and free for a child under 16, or else £55 ($88) for a family ticket. MasterCard and Visa are accepted.

For visitor passes and membership, contact **Customer Services, English Heritage,** 429 Oxford St., London W1R 2HD (© **020/7973-3434;** www.english-heritage.org.uk), or join directly at the site.

The Great British Heritage Pass, available from **BritRail,** allows entry to more than 500 public and privately owned historic properties, including Shakespeare's birthplace, Stonehenge, Windsor Castle, and Edinburgh Castle. Included in the price is *The Great British Heritage Gazetteer,* a brochure that lists the properties with maps and essential information.

A pass gains you entrance into private properties not otherwise approachable. A 7-day pass costs $54, a 15-day pass is available for $75, and a 1-month pass is $102. Passes are nonrefundable, and there is no discounted children's rate. A $10 handling fee is charged additionally for each ticket issued.

To order passes, contact **BritRail Travel International, Inc.,** 500 Mamaroneck Ave., Suite 314, Harrison, NY 10528; visit BritRail's British Travel Shop at 551 Fifth Ave. (at 45th St.), New York, NY 10176; or call © **800/677-8585.** Passes can also be ordered on the net at **www.britainon track.com.**

16 Recommended Books

GENERAL & HISTORY

Anthony Sampson's *The Changing Anatomy of Britain* (Random House) still gives great insight into the idiosyncrasies of the country's society, Winston Churchill's *History of the English-Speaking Peoples* (Dodd Mead) is a tour de force in four volumes, while *The Gathering Storm* (Houghton-Mifflin) captures Europe on the brink of World War II.

Britons: Forging the Nation (1707–1837) (Yale University Press), by Linda Colley, took more than a decade to finish. Ms. Colley takes the reader from the date of the Act of Union (formally joining Scotland and Wales to England) to the succession of the adolescent Victoria to the British throne.

In *A Writer's Britain* (Knopf), contemporary English author Margaret Drabble takes readers on a tour of the sacred and haunted literary landscapes of England, places that inspired Hardy, Woolf, Spenser, and Marvell.

Good historical overviews of Scotland, beginning with its earliest prehistory, are provided by Michael Jenner's *Scotland Through the Ages,*

Rosalind Mitchison's *A History of Scotland,* and *A New History of Scotland,* by W. Croft Dickinson and George S. Pryde. Also insightful, perhaps because of its authorship by a famous Scottish novelist, is Alistair Maclean's *Alistair Maclean Introduces Scotland.*

Dealing in detail with the famous personalities of the 16th century is Alison Plowden's *Elizabeth Tudor and Mary Stewart: Two Queens in One Isle.* Antonia Fraser's *Mary, Queen of Scots* is highly readable.

ART & ARCHITECTURE

For general reference, there's the huge multivolume *Oxford History of English Art* (Oxford University Press), and also the *Encyclopedia of British Art* (Thames Hudson), by David Bindman. *Painting in Britain 1530–1790* (Penguin), by Ellis Waterhouse, covers British art from the Tudor miniaturists to Gainsborough, Reynolds, and Hogarth, while *English Art, 1870–1940* (Oxford University Press), by Dennis Farr, covers the modern period.

On architecture, for sheer amusing, opinionated entertainment try John Betjeman's *Ghastly Good Taste—the*

Rise and Fall of English Architecture (St. Martin's Press). *A History of English Architecture* (Penguin), by Peter Kidson, Peter Murray, and Paul Thompson, covers the subject from Anglo-Saxon to modern times. Nikolaus Pevsner's *The Best Buildings of England: An Anthology* (Viking) and his *Outline of European Architecture* (Penguin) concentrate on the great periods of Tudor, Georgian, and Regency architecture. Mark Girouard has written several books on British architecture including *Life in the English Country House* (Yale University Press), a fascinating social/architectural history from the Middle Ages to the 20th century, with handsome illustrations. *Looking Up in London* by Jane Peyton (Wiley Academy) offers colorful photos of some of London's architectural features.

FICTION & BIOGRAPHY

Among English writers are found some of the greatest exponents of mystery and suspense novels from which a reader can get a good feel for English life both urban and rural. Agatha Christie, P. D. James, and Dorothy Sayers are a few of the familiar names, but the great London character is, of course, Sherlock Holmes of Baker Street, created by Sir Arthur Conan Doyle. Any of these writers will give pleasure and insight into your London experience.

Britain's literary heritage is so vast, it's hard to select particular titles, but here are a few favorites. Master storyteller Charles Dickens re-creates Victorian London in such books as *Oliver Twist, David Copperfield*, and his earlier satirical *Sketches by Boz.*

Edwardian London and the '20s and '30s is captured wonderfully in any of Evelyn Waugh's social satires and comedies; any work from the Bloomsbury group will also prove enlightening, such as Virginia Woolf's *Mrs. Dalloway*, which peers beneath the surface of the London scene. For a portrait of wartime London there's Elizabeth Bowen's *The Heat of the Day;* for an American slant on England and London there's Henry James's *The Awkward Age.*

Among 18th-century figures, there's a great biography of Samuel Johnson by his friend James Boswell, whose *Life of Samuel Johnson* (Modern Library College Editions) was first published in 1791. Antonia Fraser's *The Wives of Henry VIII* (Knopf), tells the sad story of the six women foolish enough to marry the Tudor king.

Another great Tudor monarch, Elizabeth I, emerges in a fully rounded portrait: *The Virgin Queen, Elizabeth I, Genius of the Golden Age* (Addison-Wesley), by Christopher Hibbert.

No woman—or man, for that matter—had greater influence on London than did Queen Victoria during her long reign (1837–1901). The Duchess of York (Prince Andrew's former wife, "Fergie") along with Benita Stoney, a professional researcher, captures the era in *Victoria and Albert: A Family Life at Osborne House* (Prentice Hall).

In *Elizabeth II, Portrait of a Monarch* (St. Martin's Press), Douglas Keay drew on interviews with Prince Philip and Prince Charles.

Dickens (Harper Perennial), by Peter Ackroyd, is a massive volume, tracing everything from the reception of the novelist's first book, *The Pickwick Papers,* to his scandalous desertion of his wife.

Burns: A Biography of Robert Burns, by James MacKay, is one of the best works devoted to Scotland's national poet (1759–96). The life of Burns is portrayed against the historical framework of 18th-century Scotland. A Burns scholar, MacKay defends the author of *Tam O'Shanter* and "Auld Lang Syne" against previously published charges that he was a drunkard and a rake.

Robert Louis Stevenson: A Biography, by Frank McLynn, maintains that the frail adventurer and author of *The Strange Case of Dr. Jekyll and Mr. Hyde* was Scotland's greatest writer. The book documents the tragic life of the writer who suffered from "bloody jack" (a hemorrhaging consumptive) and died at 44.

How Green Was My Valley, by Richard Llewellyn (Scribner Paperback Fiction) was the subject of a famous 1941 movie, starring Walter Pidgeon and Maureen O'Hara (still shown on The Late Show). This 1939 classic about growing up in a Welsh coal-mining village is endearing but not overly sentimental. No tale has ever captured the soul of the Welsh people like this long-time favorite.

 FAST FACTS: **Great Britain**

For information on London, refer to "Fast Facts: London," on p. 98; for Edinburgh, p. 475; and for Cardiff, p. 687.

Area Codes　The country code for Britain is **44**. The area code for London is **020**; for Edinburgh is **0131**; for Cardiff is **029**.

Business Hours　With many, many exceptions, business hours are Monday through Friday from 9am to 5pm. In general, stores are open Monday through Saturday from 9am to 5:30pm. In country towns, there is usually an early closing day (often on Wed or Thurs), when the shops close at 1pm.

Drugstores　In Britain, they're called "chemists." Every police station in the country has a list of emergency chemists. Dial ✆ **0** (zero) and ask the operator for the local police, who will give you the name of the one nearest you.

Electricity　British electricity is 240 volts AC (50 cycles), roughly twice the voltage in North America, which is 115 to 120 volts AC (60 cycles). American plugs don't fit British wall outlets. Always bring suitable transformers and/or adapters—if you plug an American appliance directly into a European electrical outlet without a transformer, you'll destroy your appliance and possibly start a fire. Tape recorders, VCRs, and other devices with motors intended to revolve at a fixed number of revolutions per minute probably won't work properly even with transformers. Many laptops can be used overseas without any problems, but check before you plug in.

Embassies & High Commissions　See "Fast Facts: London," on p. 98.

Emergencies　Dial ✆ **999** for police, fire, or ambulance. Give your name, address, and telephone number and state the nature of the emergency.

Legal Aid　The American Services section of the U.S. Consulate (see "Embassies & High Commissions," under "Fast Facts: London," in chapter 4) will give you advice if you run into trouble abroad. They can advise you of your rights and will even provide a list of attorneys (for which you'll have to pay if services are used). But they cannot interfere on your behalf in the legal processes of Great Britain. For questions about American citizens who are arrested abroad, including ways of getting money to them, telephone the **Citizens Emergency Center** of the Office of Special Consulate Services in Washington, D.C. (✆ **202/647-5225**).

Liquor Laws The legal drinking age is 18. Children under age 16 aren't allowed in pubs, except in certain rooms, and then only when accompanied by a parent or guardian. Don't drink and drive. Penalties are stiff.

In Britain, pubs can legally be open Monday through Saturday from 11am to 11pm, and on Sunday from noon to 10:30pm. Restaurants are also allowed to serve liquor during these hours, but only to people who are dining on the premises. The law allows 30 minutes for "drinking-up time." A meal, incidentally, is defined as "substantial refreshment." And you have to eat and drink sitting down. In hotels, liquor may be served from 11am to 11pm to both residents and nonresidents; after 11pm, only residents, according to the law, may be served.

Mail Post offices and subpost offices are open Monday through Friday from 9am to 5:30pm and Saturday from 9:30am to noon.

Sending an airmail letter to North America costs 45p (70¢) for 10 grams (.35 oz.), and postcards require a 40p (65¢) stamp. British mailboxes are painted red and carry a royal coat of arms. All post offices accept parcels for mailing, provided they are properly and securely wrapped.

Passports **For Residents of the United States:** Whether you're applying in person or by mail, you can download passport applications from the U.S. State Department website at **http://travel.state.gov**. For general information, call the **National Passport Agency** (© **202/647-0518**). To find your regional passport office, either check the U.S. State Department website or call the **National Passport Information Center** (© **900/225-5674**); the fee is 55¢ per minute for automated information and $1.50 per minute for operator-assisted calls.

For Residents of Canada: Passport applications are available at travel agencies throughout Canada or from the central **Passport Office,** Department of Foreign Affairs and International Trade, Ottawa, ON K1A 0G3 (© **800/567-6868**; www.dfait-maeci.gc.ca/passport).

For Residents of Ireland: You can apply for a 10-year passport at the **Passport Office,** Setanta Centre, Molesworth Street, Dublin 2 (© **01/ 671-1633**; www.irlgov.ie/iveagh). Those under age 18 and over 65 must apply for a 12€ 3-year passport. You can also apply at 1A South Mall, Cork (© **021/272-525**) or at most main post offices.

For Residents of Australia: You can pick up an application from your local post office or any branch of Passports Australia, but you must schedule an interview at the passport office to present your application materials. Call the **Australian Passport Information Service** at © **131-232**, or visit the government website at www.passports.gov.au.

For Residents of New Zealand: You can pick up a passport application at any New Zealand Passports Office or download it from their website. Contact the **Passports Office** at © **0800/225-050** in New Zealand or 04/474-8100, or log on to www.passports.govt.nz.

Pets It is illegal to bring pets to Great Britain—except with veterinary documents, and then most animals are subject to an outrageous 6-month quarantine.

Police Dial © **999** if the matter is serious. Losses, thefts, and other criminal matters should be reported to the police immediately.

Safety Stay in well-lit areas and out of questionable neighborhoods, especially at night. In Britain, most of the crime perpetrated against tourists involves pickpocketing and mugging. For more, see "Health & Safety" earlier in this chapter.

Taxes To encourage energy conservation, the British government levies a 25% tax on gasoline (petrol). There is also a 17.5% national value-added tax (VAT) that is added to all hotel and restaurant bills, and will be included in the price of many items you purchase. This can be refunded if you shop at stores that participate in the Retail Export Scheme (signs are posted in the window). See the box on "How to Get Your VAT Refund."

Telephone To call Britain from North America, dial ℂ **011** (international code), ℂ **44** (Britain's country code), the local area codes (usually three or four digits and found in every phone number we've given in this book), and the seven-digit local phone number. The local area codes found throughout this book all begin with "0"; you drop the "0" if you're calling from outside Britain, but you need to dial it along with the area code if you're calling from another city or town within Britain. For calls within the same city or town, the local number is all you need.

For **directory assistance** in London, dial ℂ **142**; for the rest of Britain, ℂ **192**.

There are three types of public pay phones: those taking only coins, those accepting only phonecards (called Cardphones), and those taking both phonecards and credit cards. At coin-operated phones, insert your coins before dialing. The minimum charge is 10p (15¢).

Phonecards are available in four values—£2 ($3.20), £4 ($6.40), £10 ($16), and £20 ($32)—and are reusable until the total value has expired. Cards can be purchased from newsstands and post offices. Finally, the credit-call pay phone operates on credit cards—Access (MasterCard), Visa, American Express, and Diners Club—and is most common at airports and large railway stations.

To make an international call from Britain, dial the international access code **(00),** then the country code, then the area code, and finally the local number. Or call through one of the following long-distance access codes: **AT&T USA Direct** (ℂ **0800/890-011), Canada Direct** (ℂ **0800/890-016), Australia** (ℂ **0800/890-061),** and **New Zealand** (ℂ **0800/890-064).** Common country codes are: USA and Canada, **1;** Australia, **61;** New Zealand, **64;** South Africa, **27.**

If you're calling **collect** or need the assistance of an international operator, dial ℂ **155.**

Caller, beware: Some hotels routinely add outrageous surcharges onto phone calls made from your room. Inquire before you call! It'll be a lot cheaper to use your own calling card number or to find a pay phone.

Time Britain follows Greenwich mean time (5 hr. ahead of Eastern Standard Time), with British summertime lasting (roughly) from the end of March to the end of October. Because of different daylight savings time practices in the two nations, there's a brief period (about a week) in autumn when Britain is only 4 hours ahead of New York, and a brief period in spring when it's 6 hours ahead of New York.

Tipping For cab drivers, add about 10% to 15% to the fare shown on the meter. However, if the driver personally loads or unloads your luggage, add something extra.

In hotels, porters receive 75p ($1.20) per bag, even if you have only one small suitcase. Hall porters are tipped only for special services. Maids receive £1 ($1.60) per day. In top-ranking hotels, the concierge will often submit a separate bill showing charges for newspapers and other items; if he or she has been particularly helpful, tip extra.

Hotels often add a service charge of 10% to 15% to most bills. In smaller B&B's, the tip is not likely to be included. Therefore, tip for special services such as the waiter who serves you breakfast. If several people have served you in a bed-and-breakfast, you may ask that 10% to 15% be added to the bill and divided among the staff.

In both restaurants and nightclubs, a 15% service charge is added to the bill, which is distributed among all the help. To that, add another 3% to 5%, depending on the service. Waiters in deluxe restaurants and nightclubs are accustomed to the extra 5%. Sommeliers (wine stewards) get about £1 ($1.60) per bottle of wine served. Tipping in pubs isn't common, but in wine bars, the server usually gets about 75p ($1.20) per round of drinks.

Barbers and hairdressers expect 10% to 15%. Tour guides expect £2 ($3.20), although it's not mandatory. Gas station attendants are rarely tipped, and theater ushers don't expect tips.

4

Settling into London

Europe's largest city is like a great wheel, with **Piccadilly Circus** at the hub and dozens of communities branching out from it. Because London is such a conglomeration of neighborhoods, each with its own personality, first-time visitors may well be confused until they get the hang of it.

You'll probably spend most of your time in the **West End**, where many attractions are located, and in the historic part of London known as **The City**, which includes the Tower of London. This chapter will help you get your bearings.

1 Orientation

ARRIVING
BY PLANE

London is served by four airports. The one you'll fly into will depend on your airline's point of departure.

LONDON HEATHROW AIRPORT   West of London in Hounslow (© **0870/000-0123** for flight information), Heathrow is one of the world's busiest airports. It has four terminals, each relatively self-contained. Terminal 4, the most modern, handles the long haul and transatlantic operations of British Airways. Most transatlantic flights on U.S.-based airlines arrive at Terminal 3. Terminals 1 and 2 receive the intra-European flights of several European airlines.

Getting to Central London from Heathrow   It takes 35 to 40 minutes by the Underground (Tube) and costs £3.70 ($5.90) to make the 24km (15-mile) trip from Heathrow to the center of London.. A taxi is likely to cost from £35 to £40 ($56–$64). For more information about Tube or bus connections, call © **020/7222-1234.**

The British Airport Authority now operates **Heathrow Express** (© **0845/ 600-1515** or 877/677-1066; www.heathrowexpress.com), a 100-mph train service running every 15 minutes daily from 5:10am until 11:40pm between Heathrow and Paddington Station in the center of London. Trips cost £13 ($21) each way in economy class, rising to £21 ($34) in first class. Children under 15 go for free (when accompanied by an adult). You can save £1 ($1.60) by booking online or by phone. The trip takes 15 minutes each way between Paddington and Terminals 1, 2, and 3, 23 minutes from Terminal 4. The trains have special areas for wheelchairs. From Paddington, passengers can connect to other trains and the Underground, or they can hail a taxi. You can buy tickets on the train or at self-service machines at Heathrow Airport (also available from travel agents).

At Paddington, a bus link, **Hotel Express,** takes passengers to a number of hotels in central London. Cost is £3 ($4.80) for adults, £2 ($3.20) for children 5 to 15, free for children under 5. The service has revolutionized travel to and from the airport, much to the regret of London cabbies. Hotel Express buses are clearly designated outside the station, with frequent departures throughout the day.

GATWICK AIRPORT   While Heathrow still dominates, more and more scheduled flights land at relatively remote **Gatwick** (✆ **01293/535353** for flight information), located some 40km (25 miles) south of London in West Sussex but only a 30-minute train ride away.

Getting to Central London from Gatwick   From Gatwick, the fastest way to get to London is via the **Gatwick Express trains** (✆ **0845/850-1530;** www. gatwickexpress.co.uk), which leave for Victoria Station in London every 15 minutes during the day and every hour at night. The one-way charge is £11 ($18) Express Class for adults, £18 ($28) for First Class, half price for children 5 to 15, free for children under 5.

A taxi from Gatwick to central London usually costs £60 to £75 ($96–$120). However, you must negotiate a fare with the driver before you enter the cab; the meter doesn't apply because Gatwick lies outside the Metropolitan Police District. For further transportation information, call ✆ **020/7222-1234.**

LONDON CITY AIRPORT   Located just 5km (3 miles) east of the bustling business community of Canary Wharf and 9.5km (6 miles) east of The City, London City Airport (✆ **020/7646-0000**) is served by 12 airlines (Air Engiadina, Air France, Air Jet, Air UK, Augsburg Airways, CityJet, Crossair, Denimair, Lufthansa, Malmö Aviation, Sabena, and VLM) that fly from 18 cities in western Europe and Scandinavia.

Getting to Central London from London City Airport   A blue-and-white bus charges £6 ($9.60) each way to take you from the airport to the Liverpool Street Station, where you can connect with rail or Underground transportation to almost any destination. The bus runs daily every 10 minutes during the hours the airport is open (approximately 6:50am–9:20pm and closed on Sat at 1pm).

A shuttle bus can take you to Canary Wharf, where trains from the Dockland Line Railway make frequent 10-minute runs to the heart of London's financial district, known as "The City." Here, passengers can catch the Underground from the Bank Tube stop.

In addition, London Transport bus no. 473 goes from The City Airport to East London, where you can board any Underground at the Plaistow Tube stop.

LONDON STANSTED AIRPORT   Located some 80km (50 miles) northeast of London's West End, **Stansted,** in Essex (✆ **0870/000-0303**), handles mostly flights to and from the European continent.

Getting to Central London from Stansted   From Stansted, your best bet to central London is the **Stansted Express train** (✆ 0845/850-0150; www.stansted express.com) to Liverpool Street Station, which runs every 15 minutes from 8am to 5pm, and every 30 minutes in the early mornings, evening weekdays, and weekends. It costs £13 ($21) for a standard ticket and £18 ($29) for business class and takes 42 minutes.

By bus, you can take the **A6 Airbus** (**www.gobycoach.com**), which runs regular departures 24 hours a day to both Victoria rail and coach stations, and costs £7.50 ($12). If you prefer the relative privacy of a taxi, you'll pay dearly for the privilege. For a ride to London's West End, they'll charge you from £45 ($72) for up to four passengers and from £100 ($160) for five or six passengers. Expect the ride to take around 75 minutes during normal traffic conditions, but beware of Friday afternoons when dense traffic may double your travel time. Our advice: Stick to the Express.

BY TRAIN

Each of London's train stations is connected to the city's vast bus and Underground network, and each has phones, restaurants, pubs, luggage storage areas, and London Regional Transport Information Centres.

If you're coming from France, the fastest way to get to London is by the **HoverSpeed** connection between Calais and Dover (see "By Ferry/Hovercraft from Continental Europe," under "Getting There," in chapter 3), where you can get a BritRail train into London. For one-stop travel, you can take the Chunnel train direct from Paris to Waterloo Station in London.

BY CAR

If you're taking a car ferry across the Channel, you can quickly connect with a motorway into London. *Remember to drive on the left.* London is encircled by a ring road, the M25. Determine which part of the city you wish to enter and follow the signs there.

Once you're in London, we don't recommend driving. Unfortunately, parking is scarce and expensive. Before you arrive in London, call your hotel and ask for advice on where to park your car.

VISITOR INFORMATION

The **British Travel Centre,** Rex House, 4–12 Lower Regent St., London SW1 4PQ (Tube: Piccadilly Circus), caters to walk-in visitors who need information about all parts of Britain. Telephone service has been suspended; you must show up in person and often wait in a lengthy line. On the premises, you'll find a British Rail ticket office, travel and theater ticket agencies, a hotel-booking service, a bookshop, and a souvenir shop. It's open Monday through Friday from 9am to 6:30pm, and Saturday and Sunday from 10am to 4pm, with extended hours on Saturday from June to September.

The London Tourist Board's **Tourist Information Centre,** Victoria Station Forecourt, SW1 (walk-ins only; no phone; Tube: Victoria Station), can help you with almost anything. The center deals chiefly with accommodations in all price categories and can handle the whole spectrum of travelers' questions. It also arranges tour ticket sales, theater reservations, and offers a wide selection of books and souvenirs. From Easter to October, the center is open daily from 8am to 7pm; from November to Easter, it's open Monday through Saturday from 8am to 6pm and Sunday from 9am to 4pm.

Tips **London Fights Gridlock with Pounds**

In a desperate move to ease traffic, gridlocked London has begun charging cars £5 to enter the most congested parts of Central London. The charge is in effect from 7am to 6:30pm Monday through Friday. A network of some 700 video cameras record license plates of vehicles moving into the zone. Traffic fees, at least according to the mayor (who rides the Tube), are expected to cut car usage by 10% to 15%.

How to pay? Londoners can pay online, over the phone, or at specially installed machines at newspaper shops, petrol stations, and food stores. Before renting a car to drive into Central London (not a good idea in the 1st place), check with your rental company about how the charges will apply to you.

The tourist board also has offices at **Heathrow** Terminals 1, 2, and 3, and on the Underground concourse at **Liverpool Street Railway Station.**

LONDON'S NEIGHBORHOODS IN BRIEF

The West End Neighborhoods

Mayfair Bounded by Piccadilly, Hyde Park, and Oxford and Regent streets, this is the most elegant, fashionable section of London, filled with luxury hotels, Georgian town houses, and swank shops. Grosvenor Square (pronounced *Grov*-nor) is nicknamed "Little America," home to the American embassy and a statue of Franklin D. Roosevelt; Berkeley Square (*Bark*-ley) was made famous by the song, "A Nightingale Sang in Berkeley Square." At least once you'll want to dip into this exclusive section. One curiosity of Mayfair is **Shepherd Market,** a tiny village of pubs, two-story inns, book and food stalls, and restaurants, sandwiched between Mayfair's greatness.

Marylebone All first-time visitors head to Marylebone (*Mar*-le-bone) to explore Madame Tussaud's waxworks or walk along Baker Street in the make-believe footsteps of Sherlock Holmes. The streets form a near-perfect grid, with major ones running north–south from Regent's Park toward Oxford Street. Marylebone Lane and High Street still retain some of their former village atmosphere, but this is otherwise a now rather anonymous area. At Regent's Park, you can visit Queen Mary's Gardens or, in summer, see Shakespeare performed in an open-air theater.

St. James's Often called "Royal London," St. James's is home to Elizabeth II, who lives at the neighborhood's most famous address, Buckingham Palace. The neighborhood begins at Piccadilly Circus and moves southwest, incorporating Pall Mall, The Mall, St. James's Park, and Green Park; it's "frightfully convenient," as the English say, enclosing many of London's leading department stores. Be sure to stop in at Fortnum & Mason, at 181 Piccadilly, the world's most luxurious grocery store.

Piccadilly Circus & Leicester Square **Piccadilly Circus** is the very heart and soul of London—its gaudy living room. The circus isn't Times Square yet, but its traffic, neon, and jostling crowds do nothing to make it fashionable. If you want a little more grandeur, retreat to the Regency promenade of exclusive shops, the Burlington Arcade, designed in 1819.

A bit more tawdry is **Leicester Square,** a center of theaters, restaurants, movie palaces, and nightlife. Once a chic address, it changed forever in the Victorian era when four towering entertainment halls were opened (even Queen Victoria saw a circus here). In time, the old palaces changed from stage to screen; three still show films.

Soho These densely packed streets in the heart of the West End are famous for a gloriously cosmopolitan mix of people and trades. A decade ago, much was heard about the decline of Soho, when the thriving sex industry threatened to engulf it. That destruction has now largely been halted. Respectable businesses have returned, and chic restaurants and shops prosper; it's now the heart of London's expanding gay colony. But Soho wouldn't be Soho without a few sex shops and porn theaters.

Soho starts at Piccadilly Circus and spreads out; it's basically bordered by Regent Street, Oxford

London at a Glance

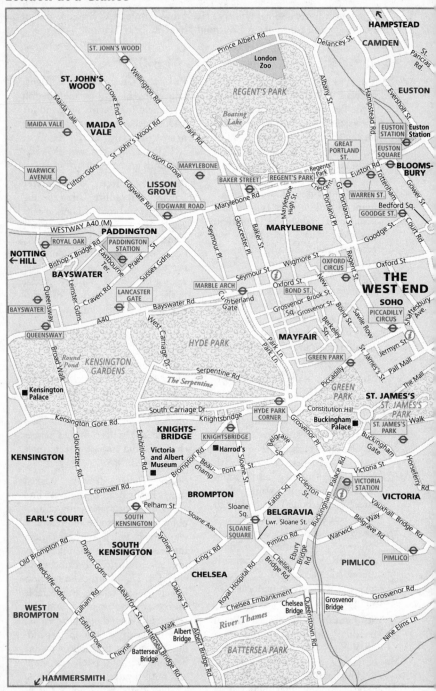

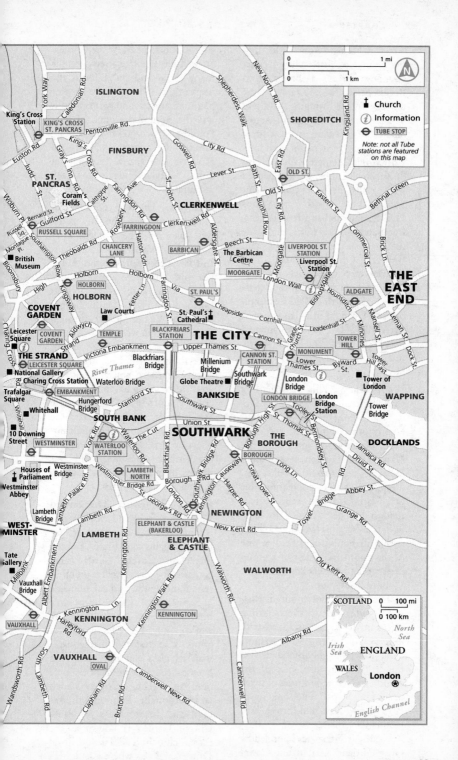

Street, Charing Cross Road, and the theaters of Shaftesbury Avenue. Carnaby Street, a block from Regent Street, was the center of the universe in the Swinging '60s, and appears to be rising again. Across Shaftesbury Avenue, a busy street lined with theaters, is London's **Chinatown,** centered on Gerrard Street: small, authentic, and packed with excellent restaurants. But Soho's heart—with marvelous French and Italian delicatessens, fine butchers, fish stores, and wine merchants—is farther north, on Brewer, Old Compton, and Berwick streets; Berwick is also a wonderful open-air fresh-food market. To the north of Old Compton Street, Dean, Frith, and Greek streets have fine little restaurants, pubs, and clubs. The British movie industry is centered in Wardour Street.

Bloomsbury This district, a world in itself, lies northeast of Piccadilly Circus, beyond Soho. It is, among other things, the academic heart of London; you'll find the University of London, several other colleges, and many bookstores. Despite its student population, this neighborhood is fairly staid. Its reputation has been fanned by such writers as Virginia Woolf, who lived within its bounds and became one of the unofficial leaders of a group of artists and writers known as "the Bloomsbury Group."

The heart of Bloomsbury is **Russell Square,** and the streets jutting off from the square are lined with hotels and B&Bs. Most visitors come to the neighborhood to visit the British Museum, one of the world's greatest repositories of treasures. The British TeleCom Tower (1964) on Cleveland Street is a familiar landmark.

Nearby is **Fitzrovia,** bounded by Great Portland, Oxford, and Gower streets, and reached by the Goodge Street Tube. Goodge Street, with its many shops and pubs, forms the heart of the "village." Once a major haunt of artists and writers—this was the stomping ground of Ezra Pound and George Orwell, among others—the bottom end of Fitzrovia is a virtual extension of Soho, with a cluster of Greek restaurants.

Holborn The old borough of Holborn, abutting The City to the west, takes in the heart of legal London—the city's barristers, solicitors, and law clerks call it home. A 14-year-old Dickens was once employed as a solicitor's clerk at Lincoln's Inn Fields. Old Bailey has stood for English justice through the years (Fagin went to the gallows from this site in *Oliver Twist*). Everything here seems steeped in history. Even as you're quenching your thirst with a half pint of bitter at the Viaduct Tavern, 126 Newgate St. (Tube: St. Paul's), you learn the pub was built over the notorious Newgate Prison (which specialized in death by pressing) and was named after the Holborn Viaduct, the world's first overpass.

Covent Garden & The Strand The flower, fruit, and "veg" market is long gone, but memories of Professor Higgins and Eliza Doolittle linger on. **Covent Garden** now contains the city's liveliest group of restaurants, pubs, and cafes outside of Soho, as well as some of the city's hippest shops—including the world's only Dr. Marten's Super Store. The restored marketplace, with its glass and iron roofs, has been called a "magnificent example of urban recycling." Covent Garden is traditionally London's theater area, and Inigo Jones's St. Paul's Covent Garden is known as the actors' church. The Theatre Royal Drury Lane was where Charles II's mistress Nell Gwynne made her debut in 1665.

Beginning at Trafalgar Square, **The Strand** runs east into Fleet Street and borders Covent Garden to the south. Flanked with theaters, shops, hotels, and restaurants, it runs parallel to the River Thames; to walk it is to follow the footsteps of Mark Twain, Henry Fielding, James Boswell, William Thackeray, and Sir Walter Raleigh. The Savoy Theatre helped make Gilbert and Sullivan household names.

Westminster The seat of the British government since the days of Edward the Confessor and dominated by the Houses of Parliament and Westminster Abbey, the area runs along the Thames to the east of St. James's Park. **Trafalgar Square,** at the area's northern end and one of the city's major landmarks, remains a testament to England's victory over Napoleon in 1805, and the paintings in its landmark **National Gallery** will restore your soul. Whitehall is the main thoroughfare, linking Trafalgar Square with Parliament Square. You can visit Churchill's Cabinet War Rooms and no. 10 Downing St., the world's most famous street address, home to Britain's prime minister. No visit is complete without seeing **Westminster Abbey,** one of the great Gothic churches in the world.

Westminster also encompasses **Victoria,** an area that takes its unofficial name from bustling Victoria Station, known as "the gateway to the Continent."

The City & Environs

The City When Londoners speak of "The City," they don't mean all of London; they mean the original square mile that's now the British version of Wall Street. The buildings of this district are known all over the world: the Bank of England, the London Stock Exchange, and the financially troubled Lloyd's of London. This was the origin of Londinium, as it was called by its Roman conquerors. Despite its age, The City doesn't easily reveal its past; much of it has been swept away by the Great Fire of 1666, the German bombs of 1940, the IRA bombs of the early 1990s, and the zeal of modern developers. Still, it retains its medieval character; landmarks include **St. Paul's Cathedral,** the masterpiece of Sir Christopher Wren, which stood virtually alone amongst the rubble after the Blitz.

London's journalistic hub since William Caxton printed the first book in English, **Fleet Street** has recently been abandoned by most of the London tabloids for the Docklands development across the river.

The City of London still prefers to function on its own, separate from the rest of the city; in keeping with its independence, it maintains its own **Information Centre** at St. Paul's Churchyard, EC4 (✆ **020/7332-1456**). It's open Monday through Friday from 9am to 5pm and Saturday from 9am to noon.

Docklands In the last 2 decades, this area—bordered roughly by Tower Bridge to the west and London City Airport and the Royal Docks to the east—has witnessed an ambitious redevelopment. Thames-side warehouses have been converted to Manhattan-style lofts, and the neighborhood has attracted many businesses, including most of the Fleet Street newspapers, museums, entertainment complexes, shops, and an ever-growing list of restaurants.

Canary Wharf, on the Isle of Dogs, is the heart of Docklands; a 240m (800-ft.) high tower designed by César Pelli, the tallest building in the United Kingdom, dominates this huge 71-acre site. The Piazza is lined with shops and restaurants. On the south side of the river at Surrey Docks, the Victorian warehouses of **Butler's Wharf** have been converted by Sir Terence Conran into offices, workshops, houses, shops, and restaurants; Butler's Wharf is also home to the Design Museum.

To get to Docklands, take the Underground to Tower Hill and pick up the **Docklands Light Railway** (© **0877/677-1066**), which operates Monday through Friday from 5:30am to 12:30am, with selected main routes now offering weekend service from 6am to midnight Saturday, and from 7:30am to 11:30pm Sunday.

The East End Traditionally one of London's poorest districts, it was nearly bombed out of existence by the Nazis. Hitler, in the words of one commentator at the time, created "instant urban renewal." The East End extends from the City Walls east encompassing Stepney, Bow, Poplar, West Ham, Canning Town, and other districts. The East End has always been filled with legend and lore. It's the home of the Cockney, London's most colorful character. To be a true Cockney, it's said that you must have been born "within the sound of Bow Bells," a reference to a church, St. Mary-le-Bow, rebuilt by Sir Christopher Wren in 1670. Many immigrants to London have found a home here.

South Bank Although not officially a district like Mayfair, South Bank is the setting today for the **South Bank Arts Centre,** now the largest arts center in Western Europe and still growing. Reached by Waterloo Bridge, it lies across the Thames from the Victoria Embankment. Culture buffs flock to its galleries and halls, including the National Theatre, Queen Elizabeth Hall, Royal Festival Hall, and the Hayward Gallery. It's also the setting of the National Film Theatre and the Museum of the Moving Image (MOMI). Neighborhoods nearby are Elephant & Castle and **Southwark,** home to the grand Southwark Cathedral. To get here, take the Tube to Waterloo Station.

Central London Beyond the West End

Knightsbridge One of London's most fashionable neighborhoods, Knightsbridge is a top residential and shopping district, just south of Hyde Park. **Harrods,** on Brompton Road, is its chief attraction. Right nearby, Beauchamp Place (*Beech*-am) is a Regency-era, boutique-lined little shopping street with a scattering of fashionable restaurants.

Belgravia South of Knightsbridge, this area has long been the aristocratic quarter of London, rivaling Mayfair in grandness. Although it reached the pinnacle of its prestige during the reign of Queen Victoria, it's still a chic address; the duke and duchess of Westminster, one of England's richest families, still live at Eaton Square. Its centerpiece is Belgrave Square, built between 1825 and 1835. When the town houses were built, the aristocrats followed—the duke of Connaught, the earl of Essex, even Queen Victoria's mother, the duchess of Kent. Chopin, on holiday in 1837, was appropriately impressed: "And the English! And the houses! And the palaces! And the pomp, and the carriages! Everything from soap to the razors is extraordinary."

Chelsea This stylish Thames-side district lies south of Belgravia. It begins at Sloane Square, where flower sellers hustle their flamboyant blooms year-round. The area has always been a favorite of writers and artists, including such names as Oscar Wilde (who was arrested here), George Eliot, James Whistler, J. M. W. Turner, Henry James, and Thomas Carlyle. Mick Jagger and Margaret Thatcher have been more recent residents, and the late Princess Diana and the "Sloane Rangers" of the 1980s gave it even more fame.

Its major boulevard is **King's Road,** where Mary Quant launched the miniskirt in the '60s and where the English punk look began. King's Road runs the entire length of Chelsea; it's at its liveliest on Saturday. The hip-hop of King's Road isn't typical of otherwise upmarket Chelsea, an elegant village filled with town houses and little mews dwellings that only successful stockbrokers and solicitors can afford to occupy.

On the Chelsea/Fulham border is **Chelsea Harbour,** a luxury development of apartments and restaurants with a private marina. You can spot its tall tower from far away; the golden ball on top moves up and down to indicate tide level.

Kensington This Royal Borough (W8) lies west of Kensington Gardens and Hyde Park and is traversed by two of London's major shopping streets, Kensington High Street and Kensington Church Street. Since 1689, when asthmatic William III fled Whitehall Palace for Nottingham House (where the air was fresher), the district has enjoyed royal associations. In time, Nottingham House became Kensington Palace, and the royals grabbed a chunk of Hyde Park to plant their roses. Queen Victoria was born here. "KP," as the royals say, was the home of Princess Diana and her two young princes for a time. Kensington Gardens is now open to the public.

Southeast of Kensington Gardens and Earl's Court, primarily residential **South Kensington** is often called "museumland" because it's dominated by a complex of museums and colleges—set upon land bought with the proceeds from Prince Albert's Great Exhibition, held in Hyde Park in 1851—that include the **Natural History Museum,** the **Victoria and Albert Museum,** and the **Science Museum;** nearby is **Royal Albert Hall.** South Kensington is also home to some fashionable restaurants and town-house hotels. One of the district's chief curiosities is the **Albert Memorial;** for sheer excess, the Victorian monument is unequaled in the world.

Earl's Court Earl's Court lies below Kensington, bordering the western half of Chelsea. For decades a staid residential district, Earl's Court now attracts a new and younger crowd (often gay), particularly at night, to its pubs, wine bars, and coffeehouses. It has long been a popular base for budget travelers (particularly Australians), thanks to its wealth of B&Bs and budget hotels, and its convenient access to central London: A 15-minute Tube ride will take you into the heart of Piccadilly, via either the District or Piccadilly lines.

Once regarded as the boondocks, nearby **West Brompton** is seen today as an extension of central London. It lies directly south of Earl's Court (take the Tube to West Brompton) and directly southeast of West Kensington. It also has many good restaurants, pubs, and taverns, as well as some budget hotels.

Notting Hill Increasingly fashionable Notting Hill is bounded on the north by Bayswater Road and on the east by Kensington. Hemmed in on the north by West

Way and on the west by the Shepherd's Bush ramp leading to the M40, it has many turn-of-the-20th-century mansions and small houses sitting on quiet, leafy streets, plus a growing number of hot restaurants and clubs. Gentrified in recent years, it's becoming an extension of central London.

On the north end, across Notting Hill, west of Bayswater, is the increasingly hip neighborhood known as **Notting Hill Gate;** its Portobello Road is home to one of London's most famous street markets. The area Tube stops are Notting Hill Gate, Holland Park, and Ladbroke Grove.

Nearby **Holland Park** is a stylish residential neighborhood visited chiefly by the chic guests of Halcyon Hotel, one of the grandest of London's small hotels.

Paddington & Bayswater Centering around Paddington Station, north of Kensington Gardens and Hyde Park, Paddington is one of the major centers in London, attracting budget travelers who fill up the B&Bs in Sussex Gardens and Norfolk Square. After the first railway was introduced in London in 1836, it was followed by a circle of sprawling railway termini, including **Paddington Station**, which spurred the growth of this middle-class area, now blighted in parts.

Just south of Paddington, north of Hyde Park, and abutting more fashionable Notting Hill to the west is **Bayswater,** a sort of unofficial area also filled with a large number of B&Bs attracting budget travelers. Inspired by Marylebone and elegant Mayfair, a relatively prosperous set of Victorian merchants built homes for their families in this area.

Farther Afield

Greenwich Some 6.5km (4 miles) from the city, Greenwich—ground zero for use in the reckoning of terrestrial longitudes—enjoyed its heyday under the Tudors. Henry VIII and both of his daughters, Mary I and Elizabeth I, were born here. Greenwich Palace, Henry's favorite, is long gone, though; today's visitors come to this lovely port village for nautical sights along the Thames, including the 1869 tea clipper *Cutty Sark.*

Hampstead This residential suburb of north London, beloved by Keats and Hogarth, is a favorite spot for weekending Londoners. Notables from Sigmund Freud to John Le Carré have lived here, and it remains one of the most desirable districts in the Greater London area to call home. Its centerpiece is **Hampstead Heath,** nearly 800 acres of rolling meadows and woodlands with panoramic views; it maintains its rural atmosphere though engulfed by cityscapes on all sides. The hilltop village is filled with cafes, tearooms, and restaurants, as well as pubs galore, some with historic pedigrees. Take the Northern Line to Hampstead Heath station.

Highgate With Hampstead, Highgate in north London is another choice residential area, particularly on or near Pond Square and along Hampstead High Street. Long a desirable place to live, Londoners used to flock to its taverns and pubs for "exercise and harmless merriment"; some still do. Today, most visitors come to see moody **Highgate Cemetery,** London's most famous cemetery, the final resting place of such famous figures as Karl Marx and George Eliot.

2 Getting Around

Remember that cars *drive on the left,* and vehicles have the right-of-way in London over pedestrians. Wherever you walk, always look both ways before stepping off a curb.

BY PUBLIC TRANSPORTATION

The London Underground and the city's buses operate on a common system of six fare zones. They radiate out in rings from the central zone 1, which is where most visitors spend the majority of their time. It covers an area from Aldgate East and Tower Gateway in the east to Notting Hill in the west, and from Waterloo in the south to Baker Street, Euston, and King's Cross in the north. To travel beyond these boundaries, you need at least a two-zone ticket. Note that all one-way, round-trip, and 1-day pass tickets are valid only on the day of purchase.

Tube and bus maps should be available at any Underground station. You can also download them before you travel from the excellent **London Transport (LT)** website at **www.londontransport.co.uk.** (You can also send away for a map by writing to **London Transport,** Travel Information Service, 55 Broadway, London SW1H 0BD.) **LT Information Centres** are at several major Tube stations: Euston, King's Cross, Oxford Circus, St. James's Park, Liverpool Street Station, and Piccadilly Circus, as well as the British Rail stations at Euston and Victoria and each terminal at Heathrow Airport. Most are open daily (some close Sun) from at least 9am to 5pm. A **24-hour information service** is also available (© **020/7222-1234**).

DISCOUNT PASSES If you plan to use public transportation a lot, investigate the range of fare discounts available. **Travelcards** offer unlimited use of buses, Underground, and British Rail services in Greater London for any period ranging from a day to a year. Travelcards are available from Underground ticket offices, Travel Information Centres, main post offices in the London area, and some newsstands. You need to bring a passport-size photo to purchase all but single-day and weekend Travelcards; you can take a photo at any of the instant photo booths in London's train stations. Children under age 5 generally travel free on the Tube and buses.

The **1-Day Travelcard** allows you to go anywhere throughout Greater London. For travel anywhere within zones 1 and 2, the cost is £5.10 ($8.15) for adults or £2 ($3.20) for children 5 to 15. The **Off-Peak 1-Day Travelcard,** which isn't valid until after 9:30am on weekdays (or on night buses), is even cheaper. For two zones, the cost is £4.10 ($6.55) for adults and £2 ($3.20) for children 5 to 15.

Weekend Travelcards are valid for 1 weekend, plus the Monday if it's a national holiday. They're not valid on night buses; travel anywhere within zones 1 and 2 all weekend costs £7.60 ($12) for adults or £3 ($4.80) for kids 5 to 15.

One-Week Travelcards cost adults £19.60 ($31) and children £8 ($13) for travel in zones 1 and 2.

The 1-day **Family Travelcard** allows as many journeys as you want on the Tube, buses (excluding night buses) displaying the London Transport bus sign, and even the Docklands Light Railway or any rail service within the travel zones designated on your ticket. The family card is valid Monday through Friday after 9:30am and all day on weekends and public holidays. It's available for families as small as two (one adult and one child) to as large as six (two adults and four children). Cost is £3.40 ($5.45) per adult and 80p ($1.30) per child.

Tips **Don't Leave Home Without It**

For another option for public transportation in London, make sure you buy a **London Visitor Travelcard** before you leave home. This card, which allows unlimited transport within all six zones of Greater London's Underground (as far as Heathrow) and bus network, as well as some discounts on London attractions, isn't available in the U.K. You don't even need a passport picture. A pass good for 3 consecutive days of travel is $32 for adults, $15 for children 5 to 15; for 4 consecutive days of travel, it's $43 for adults, $17 for children; and for 7 consecutive days of travel, it's $64 for adults, $27 for children. Contact **BritRail Travel International,** 500 Mamaroneck Ave., Suite 314, Harrison, NY 10528 (© **800/677-8585,** or 800/555-2748 in Canada; www.raileurope.com). It will take up to 21 days for the card to reach you at home.

You can also buy **Carnet** tickets, a booklet of 10 single Underground tickets valid for 12 months from the issue date. Carnet tickets are valid for travel only in zone 1 (Central London) and cost £11.50 ($18) for adults and £5 ($8) for children (up to 15). A book of Carnet tickets saves you £2.50 ($4) over the cost of 10 separate single tickets.

BY UNDERGROUND

The Underground, or Tube, is the fastest and easiest way to get around. All Tube stations are clearly marked with a red circle and blue crossbar. Routes are conveniently color-coded.

If you have British coins, you can get your ticket at a vending machine. Otherwise, buy it at the ticket office. You can transfer as many times as you like as long as you stay in the Underground. The flat fare for one trip within the Central zone is £1.60 ($2.55). Trips from the Central zone to destinations in the suburbs range from £1.60 to £3.70 ($2.55–$5.90) in most cases. It's also possible to purchase weekly passes (see "Discount Passes," above), going for £20 ($31) for adults or £7.90 ($13) for children in the Central zone, £28 ($45) for adults or £13 ($21) for children for all six zones.

Slide your ticket into the slot at the gate, and pick it up as it comes through on the other side and hold on to it—it must be presented when you exit the station at your destination. If you're caught without a valid ticket, you'll be fined £40 ($64) on the spot. If you owe extra money, you'll be asked to pay the difference by the attendant at the exit. The Tube runs roughly from 5am to 11:30pm. After that you must take a taxi or night bus to your destination. For information on the London Tube system, call the **London Underground** at © **020/7222-1234,** but expect to stay on hold for a good while before a live person comes on the line. Information is also available on **www.londontransport.co.uk.**

The long-running saga known as the Jubilee Line Extension is beginning to reach completion. This line, which once ended at Charing Cross, has been extended eastward to serve the growing suburbs of the southeast and the Docklands area. This east–west axis helps ease traffic on some of London's most hard-pressed underground lines. The line also makes it much easier to reach Greenwich.

BY BUS

The first thing you learn about London buses is that nobody just boards them. You "queue up"—that is, form a single-file line at the bus stop.

The comparably priced bus system is almost as good as the Underground and gives you better views of the city. To find out about current routes, pick up a free bus map at one of London Transport's Travel Information Centres, listed above. The map is available in person only, not by mail. You can also obtain a map at **www.londontransport.co.uk/buses**.

London still has some old-style Routemaster buses, with both driver and conductor. After you board, a conductor comes to your seat; you pay a fare based on your destination and receive a ticket in return. This bus is being phased out and replaced with buses that have only a driver; you pay the driver as you enter and you exit via a rear door. As with the Underground, fares vary according to distance traveled. Generally, bus fares are 70p to £1 ($1.10–$1.60), slightly less than Tube fares. If you travel for two or three stops, cost is £1.50 ($2.40). If you want your stop called out, simply ask the conductor or driver.

Buses generally run between about 5am and 11:30pm. A few night buses have special routes, running once an hour or so; most pass through Trafalgar Square. Keep in mind that night buses are often so crowded (especially on weekends) that they are unable to pick up passengers after a few stops. You may find yourself waiting a long time. Consider taking a taxi. Call the 24-hour **hot line** (© 020/7222-1234) for schedule and fare information.

BY TAXI

London cabs are among the most comfortable and best-designed in the world. You can pick one up either by heading for a cab rank or by hailing one in the street (the taxi is available if the yellow taxi sign on the roof is lighted); once it has stopped for you, a taxi is obliged to take you anywhere you want to go within 9.5km (6 miles) of the pickup point, provided it's within the metropolitan area. To **call a cab,** phone © 020/7272-0272 or 020/7253-5000.

The meter starts at £3.80 ($6.10), with increments of 20p (30¢) thereafter, based on distance or time. Each additional passenger is charged 40p (65¢). Passengers pay 10p (15¢) for each piece of luggage in the driver's compartment and any other item more than .6m (2 ft.) long. Surcharges are imposed after 8pm and on weekends and public holidays. All these tariffs include VAT. Fares usually increase annually. It's recommended that you tip 10% to 15% of the fare.

If you call for a cab, the meter starts running when the taxi receives instructions from the dispatcher, so you could find that the meter already reads a few pounds more than the initial drop of £3.80 ($6.10) when you step inside.

Minicabs are also available, and they're often useful when regular taxis are scarce or when the Tube stops running. These cabs are meterless, so you must negotiate the fare in advance. Unlike regular cabs, minicabs are forbidden by law to cruise for fares. They operate from sidewalk kiosks, such as those around Leicester Square. If you need to call one, try **Brunswick Chauffeurs/Abbey Cars** (© 020/8969-2555) in west London; **London Cabs, Ltd.** (© 020/8778-3000) in east London; or **Newname Minicars** (© 020/8472-1400) in south London. Minicab kiosks can be found near many Tube or BritRail stops, especially in outlying areas.

If you have a complaint about taxi service or if you leave something in a cab, contact the **Public Carriage Office,** 15 Penton St., N1 9PU (Tube: Angel Station). If it's a complaint, you must have the cab number, which is displayed in the passenger compartment. Call © 020/7230-1631 with complaints.

Cab sharing is permitted in London, as British law allows cabbies to carry two to five persons. Taxis accepting such riders display a notice on yellow plastic, with the words "Shared Taxi." Each of two riders sharing is charged 65% of the fare a lone passenger would be charged. Three persons pay 55%, four pay 45%, and five (the seating capacity of all new London cabs) pay 40% of the single-passenger fare.

BY CAR

Don't drive in congested London. It is easy to get around without a car, traffic and parking are nightmares, and—to top it all off—you'd have to drive from what you normally consider the passenger seat on the wrong side of the road. It all adds up to a big headache.

BY BICYCLE

One of the most popular bike-rental shops is **On Your Bike,** 52–54 Tooley St., London Bridge, SE1 (© **020/7378-6669;** Tube: London Bridge), open Monday through Friday from 8am to 7pm, and Saturday from 9:30am to 5:30pm. The first-class mountain bikes, with high seats and low-slung handlebars, cost £12 ($19) per day, £25 ($40) per weekend, or £60 ($96) per week, and require a £200 ($320) deposit on a credit card.

 FAST FACTS: **London**

American Express The main office is at 30–31 Haymarket, SW1 (© **020/ 7484-9600;** Tube: Piccadilly Circus). Full services are available Monday through Saturday from 9am to 6pm. On Sunday from 10am to 5pm, only the foreign-exchange bureau is open.

Area Codes London now has only one area code: **020.** Within the city limits, you don't need to dial it; use only the eight-digit number. If you're calling London from home before your trip, the country code for England is **44.** It must precede the London area code. When you're calling London from outside Britain, drop the "0" in front of the local area code.

Babysitters If your hotel can't recommend a sitter, call **Childminders,** 9 Paddington St. (© **020/7935-2049;** www.babysitter.co.uk; Tube: Baker St.). The rates are £7 ($11) per hour during the day and £6 to £8 ($9.60–$13) per hour at night, with a 4-hour minimum. Hotel guests pay a £12 ($18) booking fee each time they use a sitter. You must also pay reasonable transportation costs.

Currency Exchange See "Money," in chapter 3.

Dentists For dental emergencies, call **Eastman Dental Hospital** (© **020/ 7915-1000;** Tube: King's Cross).

Doctors In a medical emergency, call **999.** Some hotels also have doctors on call. **Medical Express,** 117A Harley St. (© **020/7499-1991;** Tube: Regent's Park), is a private British clinic. If you need a prescription filled, stop by, but to fill the British equivalent of a U.S. prescription, you'll sometimes have to pay a surcharge of £20 ($32) in addition to the cost of the medication. The clinic is open Monday through Friday from 9:30am to 5:30pm and Saturday from 9:30am to 2:30pm.

Embassies & High Commissions The **U.S. Embassy** is at 24 Grosvenor Sq., W1 (© **020/7499-9000;** Tube: Bond St.). However, for passport and visa information, go to the **U.S. Passport and Citizenship Unit,** 55–56 Upper

Brook St., London, W1 (℗ **020/7499-9000**, ext. 2563 or 2564; Tube: Marble Arch or Bond St.). Hours are Monday through Friday from 8:30am to 5:30pm. Passport and citizenship unit hours are Monday through Friday from 8:30 to 11:30am and Monday, Wednesday, and Friday from 2 to 4pm.

The **Canadian High Commission,** MacDonald House, 38 Grosvenor Sq., W1 (℗ **020/7258-6600;** Tube: Bond St.), handles visas for Canada. Hours are Monday through Friday from 8am to 4pm.

The **Australian High Commission** is at Australia House, The Strand, WC2 (℗ **020/7379-4334;** Tube: Charing Cross or Aldwych). Hours are Monday through Friday from 10am to 4pm.

The **New Zealand High Commission** is at New Zealand House, 80 Haymarket at Pall Mall, SW1 (℗ **020/7930-8422;** Tube: Charing Cross or Piccadilly Circus). Hours are Monday through Friday from 9am to 5pm.

The **Irish Embassy** is at 17 Grosvenor Place, SW1 (℗ **020/7235-2171;** Tube: Hyde Park Corner). Hours are Monday through Friday from 9:30am to 1pm and 2 to 5pm.

Emergencies In London, for police, fire, or an ambulance, dial ℗ **999.**

Hospitals The following offer emergency care in London, 24 hours a day, with the first treatment free under the National Health Service: **Royal Free Hospital,** Pond Street (℗ **020/7794-0500;** Tube: Belsize Park), and **University College Hospital,** Gower Street (℗ **020/7387-9300;** Tube: Warren St.). Many other London hospitals also have accident and emergency departments.

Hot Lines If you're in some sort of legal emergency, call **Release** (℗ **020/ 7729-9904**) 24 hours a day. The **Rape Crisis Line** (℗ **020/7837-1600** or 020/8572-0100) accepts calls after 6pm. **Samaritans,** 46 Marshall St. (℗ **020/ 7734-2800**), maintains a crisis hot line that helps with all kinds of trouble, even threatened suicides. From 9am to 9pm daily, a live attendant is on duty to handle emergencies; the rest of the time, a series of recorded messages tells callers other phone numbers and addresses where they can turn to for help. **Alcoholics Anonymous** (℗ **020/7833-0022**) answers its hot line daily from 10am to 10pm. The **AIDS** 24-hour hot line is ℗ **0800/567-123.**

Information See "Visitor Information," earlier in this chapter.

Maps If you plan on exploring London in any depth, you'll need a detailed street map with an index, not one of those superficial overviews given away at many hotels and tourist offices. The best ones are published by Falk, and they're available at most newsstands and nearly all bookstores. And no Londoner is without a *London A to Z,* the ultimate street-by-street reference, available at bookstores and newsstands everywhere. One good source for maps is **W & G Foyle, Ltd.,** 113–119 Charing Cross Rd., WC2 (℗ **020/7439-8501;** Tube: Leicester Square).

Police In an emergency, dial ℗ **999** (no coins are needed).

Telephone For **directory assistance** for London, dial ℗ **142;** for the rest of Britain, dial ℗ **192.** See also "Area Codes," above.

3 Where to Stay

Moving deeper into the 21st century, more than 10,000 hotel rooms have opened to the public from 2000 to 2003. That's good news for what had been an

London Accommodations

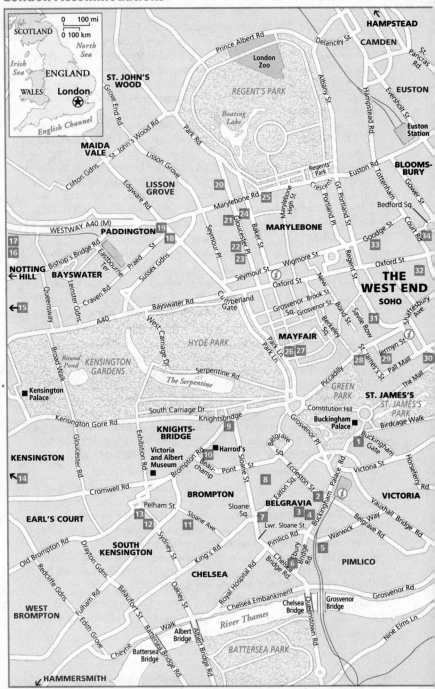

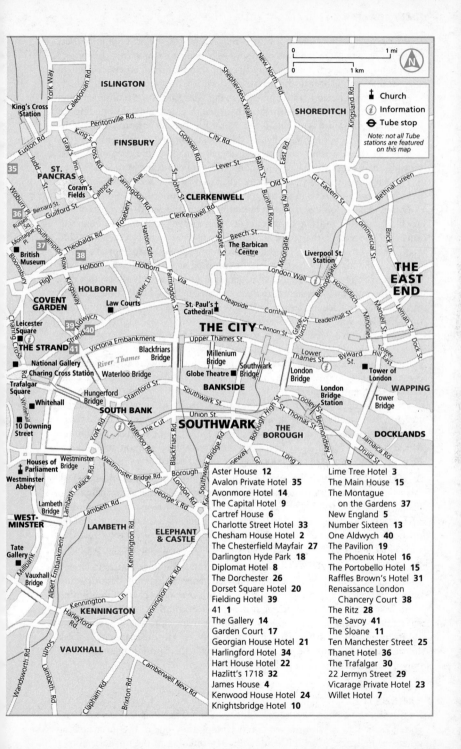

Aster House **12**
Avalon Private Hotel **35**
Avonmore Hotel **14**
The Capital Hotel **9**
Cartref House **6**
Charlotte Street Hotel **33**
Chesham House Hotel **2**
The Chesterfield Mayfair **27**
Darlington Hyde Park **18**
Diplomat Hotel **8**
The Dorchester **26**
Dorset Square Hotel **20**
Fielding Hotel **39**
41 **1**
The Gallery **14**
Garden Court **17**
Georgian House Hotel **21**
Harlingford Hotel **34**
Hart House Hotel **22**
Hazlitt's 1718 **32**
James House **4**
Kenwood House Hotel **24**
Knightsbridge Hotel **10**

Lime Tree Hotel **3**
The Main House **15**
The Montague
  on the Gardens **37**
New England **5**
Number Sixteen **13**
One Aldwych **40**
The Pavilion **19**
The Phoenix Hotel **16**
The Portobello Hotel **15**
Raffles Brown's Hotel **31**
Renaissance London
  Chancery Court **38**
The Ritz **28**
The Savoy **41**
The Sloane **11**
Ten Manchester Street **25**
Thanet Hotel **36**
The Trafalgar **30**
22 Jermyn Street **29**
Vicarage Private Hotel **23**
Willet Hotel **7**

overcrowded situation. The downside is that most of these hotels are in districts far from the city center and are of the no-frills budget chain variety. In spite of these bandbox modern horrors sprouting up, some hoteliers wisely decided to adapt former public or institutional buildings rather than start from scratch.

Another trend noted is a shift away from the West End as the traditional hotel stomping ground. Of course, the fact that there is a dearth of old buildings to turn into hotels in the West End is the reason for the shift toward such salubrious sections of London as Greenwich, the Docklands, and even The City.

With all the vast improvements and upgrades made at the turn of the 21st century, chances are you'll like your room. What you won't like is the price. Even if a hotel remains scruffy, London hoteliers have little embarrassment about jacking up prices. Hotels in all categories remain overpriced.

London boasts some of the most famous hotels in the world—temples of luxury like Claridge's and The Dorchester and more recent rivals like the Four Seasons. The problem is that there are too many of these high-priced hotels (and many cheap budget options) and not enough moderately priced options.

Even at the luxury level, you might be surprised at what you don't get. Many of the stately Victorian and Edwardian gems are so steeped in tradition that they lack many modern conveniences that are standard in other luxury hotels around the world. Some have modernized with a vengeance, but others retain amenities from the Boer War era. London does have some cutting-edge, chintz-free hotels that seem to have been flown in straight from Los Angeles—complete with high-end sound systems and gadget-filled marble bathrooms. However, these cutting-edge hotels are not necessarily superior; though they're streamlined and convenient, they frequently lack the personal service and spaciousness that characterize the grand old hotels.

It's also harder to get a hotel room, particularly an inexpensive one, during July and August. Inexpensive hotels are also tight in June, September, and October. If you arrive without a reservation, begin looking for a room as early in the day as possible. Many West End hotels have vacancies, even in peak season, between 9 and 11am, but by noon they are often booked.

A NOTE ABOUT PRICES   Unless otherwise noted, published prices are rack rates for rooms with a private bathroom. Many include breakfast (usually continental) and a 10% to 15% service charge. The British government also imposes a VAT (value-added tax) that adds 17.5% to your bill. This is not included in the prices quoted in the guide. Always ask for a better rate, particularly at the first-class and deluxe hotels (B&Bs generally charge a fixed rate). Parking rates are per night.

RATE REGULATIONS   All hotels, motels, inns, and guesthouses in Britain with four bedrooms or more (including self-catering accommodations) must display notices listing minimum and maximum overnight charges in a prominent place in the reception area or at the entrance, and prices must include any service charge and may include VAT. It must be made clear whether these items are included; if VAT isn't included, then it must be shown separately. If meals are included, this must be stated. If prices aren't standard for all rooms, then only the lowest and highest prices need be given.

HOLBORN
EXPENSIVE

Renaissance London Chancery Court ★★★   The *London Times* may have gotten carried away with the hype, proclaiming this "one of the most exciting hotels in the world," but this landmark 1914 building in the financial district has been stunningly transformed into a government-rated five-star hotel, retaining the grandeur of the past but boasting all the comforts and conveniences of today. The surprise hit of 2003, this is a seven-floor Edwardian monument with a marble staircase. The building has been used as a backdrop for such films as *Howard's End* and *The Saint* because filmmakers were drawn to its soaring archways and classical central courtyard. The interior of the hotel encases you in womb-like luxury. The glamorous and exceedingly comfortable rooms are all furnished and decorated in different hues of cream, red, and blue, with fine linens. The Italian marble bathrooms are about the most spacious in London. The best accommodations are on the sixth floor, opening onto a cozy interior courtyard hidden from the busy world outside.

252 High Holborn, WC1V 7EN ℰ 800/468-3571 in the U.S. or Canada, or 020/7829-9888. Fax 020/7829-9889. www.renaissancehotels.com. 356 units. £195 ($312) double; £270–£370 ($432–$592) suite. AE, DC, MC, V. Tube: Holborn. **Amenities:** Restaurant; cocktail lounge; luxurious spa; business center; 24-hr. room service; babysitting; laundry service; same-day dry cleaning. *In room:* A/C, TV w/pay movies, dataport, minibar, hair dryer, iron, safe.

MAYFAIR
VERY EXPENSIVE

The Dorchester ★★★ *Finds*   One of London's best hotels, it has all the elegance of its deluxe competitors, but without the upper-crust attitude that can verge on snobbery. Few hotels have the time-honored experience of "The Dorch," which has maintained a tradition of fine comfort and cuisine since it opened in 1931.

Breaking from the neoclassical tradition, the most ambitious architects of the era designed a building of reinforced concrete clothed in terrazzo slabs. Within you'll find a 1930s take on Regency motifs: The monumental arrangements of flowers and the elegance of the gilded-cage promenade seem appropriate for a diplomatic reception, yet they convey a kind of comfort in which guests from all over the world feel at ease.

The Dorchester boasts guest rooms outfitted with Irish linen sheets on comfortable beds, plus all the electronic gadgetry you'd expect, and double- and triple-glazed windows to keep out noise, along with plump armchairs, cherrywood furnishings, and, in many cases, four-poster beds piled high with pillows. The large bathrooms are equally stylish, with mottled Carrara marble and Lalique-style sconces, makeup mirrors and posh toiletries, and deep tubs. The best rooms offer views of Hyde Park.

53 Park Lane, London W1A 2HJ. ℰ 800/727-9820 in the U.S., or 020/7629-8888. Fax 020/7495-7342. www. dorchesterhotel.com. 248 units. £385 ($616) double; from £925 ($1,480) suite. AE, DC, MC, V. Parking £32 ($51). Tube: Hyde Park Corner or Marble Arch. **Amenities:** 3 restaurants; bar; health club; spa; concierge; tour desk; car-rental desk; courtesy car; business services center; small shopping arcade; 2 salons; 24-hr. room service; babysitting; laundry service; same-day dry cleaning. *In room:* A/C, TV/VCR, dataport, minibar, hair dryer, iron, safe.

Raffles Brown's Hotel ★★★   Almost every year a hotel sprouts up trying to evoke an English country-house ambience with Chippendale and chintz; this quintessential town-house hotel watches these competitors come and go, and it always comes out on top. Brown's was founded by James Brown, a former manservant to Lord Byron, who knew the tastes of well-bred gentlemen and wanted to create a dignified, club-like place for them. He opened its doors in 1837, the same year Queen Victoria took the throne.

Brown's occupies 14 historic houses just off Berkeley Square and its guest rooms vary considerably in decor, but all show restrained taste in decoration and appointments; even the washbasins are antiques. Accommodations range in size from small to extra spacious; some suites have four-poster beds. Bathrooms come in a variety of sizes, but they are beautifully equipped with robes, luxurious cosmetics, tubs, and showers.

30 Albemarle St., London W1S 4BP. ℂ 020/7493-6020. Fax 020/7493-9381. www.brownshotel.com. 118 units. £225–£320 ($360–$512) double; from £540 ($864) suite. AE, DC, MC, V. Off-site parking £40 ($64). Tube: Green Park. **Amenities:** 3 restaurants; bar; health club; concierge; courtesy car; business center; 24-hr. room service; laundry service; same-day dry cleaning. *In room:* A/C, TV/VCR (plus pay movies), dataport, minibar, hair dryer, safe.

EXPENSIVE

The Chesterfield Mayfair ★★   Just a short distance from Berkeley Square, the elegant Chesterfield serves up a traditional English atmosphere, and a lot more bang for the buck than you usually get in pricey Mayfair. The hotel, once home to the Earl of Chesterfield, still sports venerable features that evoke an air of nobility, including public rooms richly decorated in woods, antiques, fabrics, and marble. The secluded Library Lounge is a great place to relax, and the glassed-in conservatory is a good spot for tea; the sumptuously decorated restaurant is well regarded.

The guest rooms are generally not huge, but they are dramatically decorated and make excellent use of space—there's a ton of closet and counter space. The spotless marble bathrooms are similarly compact, but come with bathrobes and heated floors. For a more memorable experience, book one of the themed junior or executive suites. You'll get larger amounts of space, upgraded amenities (DVD players and umbrellas, for example), and theatrical decor schemes. Most have Jacuzzi tubs or separate tubs and power showers, and some have wholly separate sitting rooms. Some favorites include the Music Suite, with a lace canopy bed and pop-up TV; the Theatre Suite, which features a Jacuzzi and draperies that once hung in the Drury Lane theatre; and the lovely Garden Suite, with latticework headboard and a two-person Jacuzzi bath.

35 Charles St., London W1J 5EB. ℂ 877/955-1515 in the U.S. and Canada, or 020/7491-2622. Fax 020/7491-4793. www.chesterfieldmayfair.com. 110 units. £190–£260 ($304–$416) double; £250–£595 ($400–$950) suite. Special packages available. AE, DC, MC, V. Tube: Green Park. **Amenities:** 2 restaurants; bar; concierge; business services; 24-hr. room service; babysitting; laundry service; same-day dry cleaning. *In room:* A/C, TV w/pay movies, dataport, coffeemaker, hair dryer, iron, safe.

MARYLEBONE
EXPENSIVE

Dorset Square Hotel ★★★   Just steps away from Regent's Park, this is one of London's best and most stylish "house hotels," overlooking Thomas Lord's (the man who set up London's first private cricket club) first cricket pitch. Hot hoteliers Tim and Kit Kemp have furnished the interior of these two Georgian town houses with a comfy mix of antiques, reproductions, and chintz that makes you feel as if you're in an elegant private home. All of the impressive bedrooms are decorated in a personal, beautiful style—the Kemps are interior decorators known for their bold and daring taste. About half of the rooms are air-conditioned. Eight rooms feature crown-canopied beds, but all appointments are of a very high standard. The full marble bathrooms are exquisite, with robes, deluxe toiletries, and shower-tub combinations.

39–40 Dorset Sq., London NW1 6QN. ℂ 020/7723-7874. Fax 020/7724-3328. www.dorsetsquare.co.uk. 38 units. £140–£195 ($224–$312) double; from £240 ($384) suite. AE, MC, V. £32 ($51), free on weekends. Tube: Baker St. or Marylebone. **Amenities:** Restaurant; bar; 24-hr. room service; massage; babysitting; laundry service; same-day dry cleaning. *In room:* TV/VCR (plus pay movies), dataport, minibar, hair dryer, safe.

MODERATE

Hart House Hotel ★ *Kids*   Hart House is a long-enduring favorite with Frommer's readers. In the heart of the West End, this well-preserved historic building (one of a group of Georgian mansions occupied by exiled French nobles during the French Revolution) lies within easy walking distance of many theaters. The rooms—done in a combination of furnishings, ranging from Portobello antique to modern—are spick-and-span, each one with a different character. Favorites include no. 7, a triple with a big bathroom and shower. Ask for no. 11, on the top floor, if you'd like a brightly lit aerie. Housekeeping rates high marks here, and the bedrooms are comfortably appointed with chairs, an armoire, a desk, and a large chest of drawers. The shower-only bathrooms, although small, are efficiently organized. Hart House has long been known as a good, safe place for traveling families. Many of its rooms are triples. Larger families can avail themselves of special family accommodations with connecting rooms.

51 Gloucester Place, Portman Sq., London W1U 8JF. (© 020/7935-2288. Fax 020/7935-8516. www.harthouse. co.uk. 15 units. £85–£98 ($136–$157) double; £95–£130 ($152–$208) triple; £110–£150 ($176–$240) quad. Rates include English breakfast. AE, MC, V. Tube: Marble Arch or Baker St. **Amenities:** Babysitting; laundry service; dry cleaning. *In room:* TV, coffeemaker, hair dryer, iron, safe.

Ten Manchester Street ★ *Value*   Constructed in 1919 as a residence hall for nurses, this terraced redbrick building is now a smart town-house hotel. We like its location in Marylebone, close to those top shopping destinations, Bond and Regent streets, and near chic boutiques and numerous cafes and restaurants. The guest rooms are small but well designed, and are furnished with comfort in mind. Each room has a well-organized bathroom with tub and shower. There is the aura of a private home here, due to the inviting atmosphere and helpful staff.

10 Manchester St., London W1M 5PG. (© 020/7486-6669. Fax 020/7224-0348. 46 units. www.10manchester street.com. £120–£150 ($192–$240) double; £150–£195 ($240–$312) suite. Rates include continental breakfast. AE, DC, MC, V. Tube: Baker St. or Bond St. **Amenities:** Same-day dry cleaning. *In room:* TV, dataport, fridge, coffeemaker, hair dryer, iron.

INEXPENSIVE

Georgian House Hotel   Central London, which is filled with luxury hotels, suffers an acute lack of small, personally run places, but Georgian House fills this gap. It lies near Sherlock Holmes's Baker Street and is within walking distance of Oxford Street and Regent's Park. Run by the same family since 1973, the Georgian House has a dedicated staff and management intent on improving the hotel. We especially like the top-quality English breakfast served here, and the way that original architectural features were retained even as modern comforts were added. Rooms have private bathrooms, and there's an elevator to all floors. Bedrooms are neutral in style and the ground-floor rooms are the least preferred. Don't expect views from some of the back rooms, which open onto a wall.

87 Gloucester Place (Baker St.), London W1H 3PG. (© 020/7935-2211. Fax 020/7486-7535. www.london centralhotel.com. 19 units. £90 ($144) double; £100 ($160) triple; £130 ($208) family room. Rates include English breakfast. AE, MC, V. Tube: Baker St. *In room:* TV, coffeemaker.

Kenwood House Hotel   This 1812 Adam-style town house, run by Fairfiele Assets, is a historical landmark (the front balcony is said to be original) that has been converted into a small hotel. Guests gather in the mirrored lounge with its *antimacassars* (those small coverings on the backs and arms of chairs) in place, just as they were in Victoria's day. Most of the basically furnished bedrooms were upgraded and restored in 1993, and rooms in the front have double-glazed windows. Some rooms have private bathrooms with shower-units, and spick-and-span modern public bathrooms with showers are on every floor.

114 Gloucester Place, London W1H 3DB. © 020/7935-3473. Fax 020/7224-0582. www.kenwoodhousehotel. com. 19 units, 12 with bathroom. £58 ($93) double without bathroom, £68 ($109) double with bathroom; £78 ($125) triple with bathroom; £88 ($141) family room for 4 with bathroom. Rates include continental breakfast. AE, DC, MC, V. Parking £15 ($24). Tube: Baker St. **Amenities:** Babysitting. *In room:* TV, hair dryer, iron/ironing board.

ST. JAMES'S
VERY EXPENSIVE

The Ritz ★★★ Built in the French-Renaissance style and opened by César Ritz in 1906, this hotel, overlooking Green Park, is synonymous with luxury. Gold-leafed molding, marble columns, and potted palms abound, and a gold-leafed statue, *La Source,* adorns the fountain of the Palm Court. After a major restoration, the hotel is better than ever: Luxurious carpeting and air-conditioning have been installed, and an overall polishing has recaptured much of the Ritz's original splendor. The Belle Epoque guest rooms, each with its own character, are spacious and comfortable. Many rooms have marble fireplaces, elaborate gilded plasterwork, and a decor of soft pastel hues. A few rooms have their original brass beds and marble fireplaces. The bathrooms are elegantly appointed in either tile or marble and boast deep tubs with showers, robes, phones, and deluxe toiletries. Corner rooms are more grand and spacious.

The Ritz's **Ritz Palm Court** is still the most fashionable place in London for tea (p. 136). The **Ritz Restaurant,** one of the loveliest dining rooms in the world, has been restored to its original splendor.

150 Piccadilly, London W1J 9BR. © 877/748-9536 or 020/7493-8181. Fax 020/7493-2687. www.theritzlondon. com. 133 units. £365–£505 ($584–$808) double; from £785 ($1,256) suite. Children under 12 stay free in parent's room. AE, DC, MC, V. Parking £54 ($86). Tube: Green Park. **Amenities:** 2 restaurants (including the Palm Court); bar; exercise room; concierge; courtesy car; business services; 2 salons; 24-hr. room service; massage; babysitting; laundry service; same-day dry cleaning. *In room:* A/C, TV/VCR (plus pay movies), fax, dataport, mini-bar, hair dryer, safe.

22 Jermyn Street ★★★ This is London's premier town-house hotel, a bastion of elegance and discretion. Set behind a facade of gray stone with neoclassical details, this structure, only 50 yards from Piccadilly Circus, was built in 1870 for English gentlemen doing business in London. Since 1915, the Togna family has been in charge. After a radical renovation and reopening in 1990, 22 Jermyn revels in its role as a chic, upscale boutique hotel. It offers an interior filled with greenery, and the kind of art you might find in an elegant private home. The sixth floor features one of the best-equipped computer centers in London, which guests may use for free. This hotel doesn't have the bar or restaurant facilities of Stafford or Dukes, but its recently refurbished rooms are more richly appointed, done in traditional English style with fresh flowers and chintz. Beds are luxurious and bathrooms are clad in granite and contain deep tubs and showers, luxurious toiletries, and phones. If you like space, ask for one of the studios in the rear.

22 Jermyn St., London SW1Y 6HL. © 800/682-7808 in the U.S., or 020/7734-2353. Fax 020/7734-0750. www.22jermyn.com. 18 units. £210 ($336) double; from £346 ($554) suite. AE, DC, MC, V. Valet parking £35 ($56). Tube: Piccadilly Circus. **Amenities:** Access to nearby health club and spa; concierge; business services; 24-hr. room service; massage; babysitting; laundry service; same-day dry cleaning. *In room:* TV/VCR (plus pay movies), dataport, minibar, hair dryer, safe.

SOHO
EXPENSIVE

Charlotte Street Hotel ★★ *Finds*   In North Soho, a short walk from the heartbeat of Soho Square, this town house has been luxuriously converted into a high-end hotel that is London chic at its finest, possessing everything from a Los Angeles–style juice bar to a private screening room. The latter has made the hotel a hit with the movie, fashion, and media crowd, many of whom had never ventured to North Soho before. One local told us, "Charlotte Street is for those who'd like to imagine themselves in California." Midsize to spacious bedrooms have fresh modern English interiors and everything from two-line phones with voice mail to fax-modem points and fax outlets. Bathrooms are state of the art, designed in solid granite and oak with twin basins, walk-in showers, and even color TVs. Guests can relax in the elegant drawing room and library with a log-burning fireplace. The decor evokes memories of the fabled Bloomsbury set of Virginia Woolf.

15 Charlotte St., London W1P IRJ. ℂ 800/553-6674 in the U.S., or 020/7806-2000. Fax 020/7806-2002. www. firmdale.com. 52 units. £210–£240 ($336–$384) double; from £595 ($952) suite. AE, DC, MC, V. Tube: Tottenham Court. **Amenities:** Restaurant and long pewter bar; exercise room; concierge; 24-hr. room service; laundry service; same-day dry cleaning. *In room:* A/C, TV/VCR, fax, dataport, minibar, hair dryer, safe.

Hazlitt's 1718 ★★ *Finds*   This gem, housed in three historic homes on Soho Square, is one of London's best small hotels. Built in 1718, the hotel is named for William Hazlitt, who founded the Unitarian church in Boston and wrote four volumes on the life of his hero, Napoleon.

Hazlitt's is a favorite with artists, actors, and models. It's eclectic and filled with odds and ends picked up around the country at estate auctions. Some find its Georgian decor a bit spartan, but the 2,000 original prints hanging on the walls brighten it considerably. Many bedrooms have four-poster beds, and some bathrooms have their original claw-foot tubs (only one unit has a shower). Some of the floors dip and sway, and there's no elevator, but it's all part of the charm. It has just as much character as the Fielding Hotel (see below) but is a lot more comfortable. Some rooms are a bit small, but most are spacious, all with state-of-the-art appointments. Most bathrooms have 19th-century styling but up-to-date plumbing, with oversize tubs and old brass fittings; the showers, however, are mostly hand-held. Accommodations in the back are quieter but perhaps too dark, and only those on the top floor have air-conditioning. Swinging Soho is at your doorstep; the young, hip staff will be happy to direct you to the local hot spots.

6 Frith St., London W1V 5TZ. ℂ 020/7434-1771. Fax 020/7439-1524. www.hazlittshotel.com. 23 units. £195 ($312) double; £300 ($480) suite. AE, DC, MC, V. Tube: Leicester Sq. or Tottenham Court Rd. **Amenities:** 24-hr. room service; babysitting; laundry service; same-day dry cleaning. *In room:* A/C (some rooms), TV/VCR, dataport, minibar, hair dryer, safe.

BLOOMSBURY
EXPENSIVE

The Montague on the Gardens ★★   This hotel offers a winning combination of plush accommodations and exceptional service. The location is right across the street from the British Museum, and a short walk from the West End and the shopping on Oxford and Bond streets. One staff member aptly describes the Montague as a "country house hotel in the heart of London." The public rooms are meticulously (if not minimally) decorated in various woods, light fabrics, and antiques, conjuring the atmosphere of an expensive manor home.

Guest rooms are individually sized and decorated; most aren't huge, but all are cozy and spotless. The beds are most comfortable; some are four-posters and most sport half-canopies. Bi-level deluxe king rooms feature pullout couches and would be classified as suites in many other hotels. Rooms overlooking the garden offer the best views and are quiet, although guaranteeing one for your stay will cost you a bit more. *Note:* Always ask about discount rates when you book; the hotel usually offers a number of promotions throughout the year.

15 Montague St., London WC1B 5BJ. ✆ **877/955-1515** in the U.S. and Canada, or 020/7637-1001. Fax 020/7637-2516. www.redcarnationhotels.com. 104 units. £140–£238 ($224–$381) double; £245–£460 ($392–$736) suite. AE, DC, MC, V. Tube: Russell Sq. **Amenities:** Restaurant; 4 lounges; bar; health club; steam room; sauna; concierge; business center; 24-hr. room service; laundry service; dry cleaning. *In room:* A/C, TV w/pay movies, fax (in some rooms), beverage maker, hair dryer, iron, safe.

MODERATE

Harlingford Hotel *Value* This hotel is comprised of three town houses built in the 1820s and joined together around 1900 with a bewildering array of staircases and meandering hallways. Set in the heart of Bloomsbury, it's run by a management that seems genuinely concerned about the welfare of its guests, unlike the management at many of the neighboring hotel rivals. (They even distribute little mincemeat pies to their guests during the Christmas holidays.) Double-glazed windows cut down on the street noise, and all the bedrooms are comfortable and inviting. Shower-only bathrooms are small, however, since the house wasn't originally designed for them. The most comfortable rooms are on the second and third levels, but expect to climb some steep English stairs (there's no elevator). Avoid the rooms on ground level, as they are darker and have less security. You'll have use of the tennis courts in Cartwright Gardens.

61–63 Cartwright Gardens, London WC1H 9EL. ✆ **020/7387-1551.** Fax 020/7387-4616. www.holidaycity. com. 44 units. £95 ($152) double; £100 ($160) triple; £108 ($173) quad. Rates include English breakfast. AE, DC, MC, V. Tube: Russell Sq., King's Cross, or Euston. **Amenities:** Use of tennis courts in Cartwright Gardens. *In room:* TV, coffeemaker, hair dryer.

INEXPENSIVE

Avalon Private Hotel A bit of a comedown after the Harlingford (see above), this hotel is easier on the purse. One guidebook from Victoria's day claimed that the Bloomsbury neighborhood attracted "medical and other students of both sexes and several nationalities, American folk passing through London, literary persons 'up' for a week or two's reading in the British Museum, and Bohemians pure and simple." The same might be said for today's patrons of this hotel, which was built in 1807 as two Georgian houses in residential Cartwright Gardens. Guests have use of a semiprivate garden across the street with tennis courts. Top-floor rooms, often filled with students, are reached via steep stairs, but bedrooms on the lower levels have easier access. A professional decorator recently added many Victorian-inspired touches to the hotel, in addition to new carpeting, making it more inviting. The bedrooms were also recently renewed with new linens and fresh curtains. Private bathrooms with showers are extremely small. Most guests in rooms without bathrooms have to use the corridor bathrooms (four bedrooms to a bathroom), which are generally adequate and well maintained.

46–47 Cartwright Gardens, London WC1H 9EL. ✆ **020/7387-2366.** Fax 020/7387-5810. www.avalonhotel. co.uk. 27 units (5 with shower). £59 ($94) double without shower, £79 ($126) double with shower; £69 ($110) triple without shower, £89 ($142) triple with shower; £69 ($110) quad without shower, £99 ($158) quad with shower. Rates include English breakfast. AE, DC, MC, V. Tube: Russell Sq., King's Cross, or Euston. **Amenities:** Use of tennis courts in Cartwright Gardens; coin-op washers and dryers; same-day dry cleaning. *In room:* TV, dataport, coffeemaker, safe.

Thanet Hotel   Most of the myriad hotels around Russell Square become almost indistinguishable at some point, but the Thanet stands out. It no longer charges the same rates it did when it appeared in *England on $5 a Day*, but it's still a winning choice, and an affordable option close to the British Museum, the theater district, and Covent Garden. It's a landmark-status building on a quiet Georgian terrace between Russell and Bloomsbury squares. Although it has been restored many times, many original features remain. For the most part, the Orchard family (3rd-generation hoteliers) offers small, adequately furnished rooms. However, scattered throughout the hotel are some unacceptable bedrooms. One guest reported that the foot of her lumpy bed was higher than the head. Try to see the room before accepting it. This place is always full, so it must be doing something right, and indeed many of the bedrooms are fine. It depends largely on which rooms were most recently renovated—ask for those. All units are equipped with shower-only bathrooms that are very small but neatly maintained. Washbasins in the bathrooms must have been designed for Tiny Tim.

8 Bedford Place, London WC1B 5JA. ℂ 020/7636-2869. Fax 020/7323-6676. www.thanethotel.co.uk. 16 units. £90 ($144) double; £99 ($158) triple; £108 ($173) quad. Rates include English breakfast. AE, MC, V. Tube: Holborn or Russell Sq. *In room:* TV, dataport, coffeemaker, hair dryer.

COVENT GARDEN
VERY EXPENSIVE

One Aldwych ★★   Just east of Covent Garden, this government-rated five-star hotel occupies the classic-looking 1907 building that served as headquarters for the now defunct *Morning Post*. Before its conversion in 1998, all but a fraction of its interior was gutted and replaced with an artfully simple layout. Although a first-rate hostelry in every way, it lacks the cutting-edge chic of some of its trendier competitors. The bedrooms are sumptuous, decorated with elegant lines and rich colors and accessorized with raw silk curtains, deluxe furnishings and electrical outlets that can handle both North American and European electrical currents. Bathrooms boast full tubs and showers, plus luxurious toiletries.

1 Aldwych, London WC2B 4RH. ℂ 800/223-6800 in the U.S., or 020/7300-1000. Fax 020/7300-1001. www.onealdwych.co.uk. 105 units. £346–£423 ($554–$677) double; from £496 ($794) suite. AE, DC, MC, V. Parking £35 ($56). Tube: Temple. **Amenities:** 2 restaurants; 2 bars; indoor heated pool; state-of-the-art health club; spa; sauna; concierge; tour desk; courtesy car; 24-hr. room service; massage; babysitting; laundry service; same-day dry cleaning. *In room:* A/C, TV/VCR (plus pay movies), dataport, minibar, hair dryer, safe.

MODERATE

Fielding Hotel ★ *Finds*   One of London's more eccentric hotels, the Fielding is cramped, quirky, and quaint, and an enduring favorite. Luring media types, the hotel is named after novelist Henry Fielding of *Tom Jones* fame, who lived in Broad Court. It lies on a pedestrian street still lined with 19th-century gas lamps. The Royal Opera House is across the street, and the pubs, shops, and restaurants of lively Covent Garden are just beyond the front door. Rooms are small but charmingly old-fashioned and traditional. Some units are redecorated or at least "touched up" every year, though floors dip and sway, and the furnishings and fabrics, though clean, have known better times. The bathrooms, some with antiquated plumbing, are equipped with shower-tub combinations. But with a location like this, in the heart of London, the Fielding keeps guests coming back; in fact, many love the hotel's rickety charm.

4 Broad Ct., Bow St., London WC2B 5QZ. ℂ 020/7836-8305. Fax 020/7497-0064. www.the-fielding-hotel.co.uk. 24 units. £100–£115 ($160–$184) double; £130 ($208) suite. AE, DC, MC, V. Tube: Covent Garden. **Amenities:** Bar. *In room:* TV, coffeemaker.

ALONG THE STRAND
VERY EXPENSIVE

The Savoy ★★★ Although not as swank as The Dorchester, this London landmark is the premier hotel in the Strand/Covent Garden area. Richard D'Oyly Carte built it in 1889 as an annex to his nearby Savoy Theatre, where many Gilbert and Sullivan operettas were staged. Each room is individually decorated with color-coordinated accessories, solid and comfortable furniture, large closets, and an eclectic blend of antiques, such as gilt mirrors, Queen Anne chairs, and Victorian sofas. 48 units have their own sitting rooms. The hand-made beds—real luxury models—have top-of-the-line crisp linen clothing and other lavish appointments. Some bathrooms have shower stalls, but most have a combination shower and tub. Bathrooms are spacious, with deluxe toiletries. The suites overlooking the river are the most sought after, and for good reason— the vistas are the best in London. *Tip:* Ask for one of the newer rooms, with a view of the river, in what was formerly a storage space. They are among the best in the hotel, with views of the Thames and Parliament.

The Strand, London WC2R 0EU. ℂ 800/63-SAVOY in the U.S., or 020/7836-4343. Fax 020/7240-6040. www.the-savoy.co.uk. 263 units. £345–£425 ($552–$680) double; from £465 ($744) suite. AE, DC, MC, V. Parking £36 ($58). Tube: Charing Cross or Covent Garden. **Amenities:** 4 restaurants (including the celebrated Savoy Grill and the River Restaurant, which overlooks the Thames); bar; city's best health club; spa; concierge; business center; 24-hr. room service; laundry service; same-day dry cleaning. *In room:* A/C, TV/VCR, dataport, minibar, hair dryer, safe.

TRAFALGAR SQUARE
EXPENSIVE

The Trafalgar ★★ In the heart of landmark Trafalgar Square, this is Hilton's first boutique hotel in London. The facade of this 19th-century structure was preserved, while the guest rooms inside were refitted to modern standards. Because of the original architecture, many of the rooms are uniquely shaped and sometimes offer split-level layouts. Large windows open onto panoramic views of Trafalgar Square. The decor in the rooms is minimalist, and comfort is combined with simple luxury, including the deluxe tiled bathrooms with tub-and-shower combinations. The greatest view of London's cityscape is from the Hilton's rooftop garden.

Unusual for London, the bar, Rockwell, specializes in bourbon, with more than 100 brands. Jago is the hotel's organic produce restaurant, serving comfort food.

2 Spring Gardens, Trafalgar Square, London SW1A 2TS. ℂ 800/774-1500 in the U.S., or 020/7870-2900. Fax 020/7870-2911. www.hilton.com. 129 units. £179–£229 ($286–$366) double; from £380 ($608) suite. AE, DC, MC, V. Tube: Charing Cross. **Amenities:** 2 restaurants; bar; concierge; courtesy car; business services; 24-hr. room service; laundry service; same-day dry cleaning. *In room:* A/C, TV w/pay movies, dataport, minibar, hair dryer, safe.

WESTMINSTER/VICTORIA
EXPENSIVE

41 ★★★ *Finds* This relatively unknown but well-placed gem is a treasure worth seeking out, especially if you're looking for a touch of class. The property offers the intimate atmosphere of a private club combined with a level of personal service that's impossible to achieve at larger hotels. It's best suited to couples or those traveling alone—especially women, who will be made to feel comfortable. The cordial staff goes the extra mile to fulfill a guest's every wish. The surroundings match the stellar service. Public areas feature an abundance of mahogany, antiques, fresh flowers, and rich fabrics. Read, relax, or watch TV in the library-style lounge, where a complimentary continental breakfast, afternoon snacks, and evening canapés (all included in the room rate) are served each day.

Guest rooms are individually sized, but all feature elegant black-and-white color schemes, magnificent beds with handmade mattresses and Egyptian cotton linens, and "AV centers" that offer free Internet access and DVD/CD players. Most rooms have working fireplaces. The spotless marble bathrooms sport separate tubs and power showers (only one room has only a tub-shower combo), and feature Penhaligon toiletries. The bi-level junior suites toss in a separate seating area (good for families looking for extra space) and Jacuzzi tubs.

41 Buckingham Palace Road, London SW1W 0PS. ⓒ 877/955-1515 in the U.S. and Canada, or 020/7300-0041. Fax 020/7300-0141. www.41hotel.com. 174 units. £200 ($320) double; £400–£500 ($640–$800) suite. Rates include continental breakfast, afternoon snacks, and evening canapés. Extra person £45 ($72). Special Internet packages and discounts available. AE, DC, MC, V. Tube: Victoria. **Amenities:** Lounge; bar; access to nearby health club; concierge; business center, 24-hr. room service; laundry/dry cleaning. *In room:* A/C, TV, minibar, tea/coffeemaker, hair dryer, iron, safe.

MODERATE

Lime Tree Hotel   The Wales-born Davies family, longtime veterans of London's B&B business, have transformed a rundown guesthouse into a cost-conscious, cozy hotel for budget travelers. The simply furnished bedrooms are scattered over four floors of a brick town house; each has been recently refitted with new curtains and cupboards. The front rooms have small balconies overlooking Ebury Street; units in the back don't have balconies, but are quieter and feature views over the hotel's small rose garden. The Lime Tree's rooms tend to be larger than other hotel rooms offered at similar prices, and breakfasts are generous. Six rooms come with a tub-and-shower combo, the rest with shower only. Buckingham Palace, Westminster Abbey, and the Houses of Parliament are within easy reach, as is Harrods. Nearby is the popular Ebury Wine Bar.

135–137 Ebury St., London SW1W 9RA. ⓒ 020/7730-8191. Fax 020/7730-7865. www.limetreehotel.co.uk. 29 units. £115–£175 ($184–$280) double. Rates include English breakfast. AE, DC, MC, V. Tube: Victoria. *In room:* TV, hair dryer, safe.

New England   A family-run business, going strong for nearly a quarter of a century, this hotel shut down at the millennium for a complete overhaul. Today, it's better than ever and charges an affordable price. Its elegant 19th-century exterior conceals a completely bright and modern interior. The hotel is justly proud of its clientele of "repeats." On a corner in the Pimlico area, which forms part of the City of Westminster, the hotel is neat and clean and one of the most welcoming in the area. It's also one of the few hotels in the area with an elevator. Bathrooms have power showers, and rooms come with dataports.

20 Saint George's Dr., London SW1V 4BN. ⓒ 020/7834-1595. Fax 020/7834-9000. www.newenglandhotel. com. 25 units. £95–£99 ($152–$158) double; £119 ($190) triple; £135 ($216) quad. Rates include breakfast. AE, MC, V. Tube: Victoria. *In room:* TV, dataport, hair dryer.

INEXPENSIVE

Chesham House Hotel ★ *Value*   Just 5 minutes from Victoria Station, this hotel is often cited as one of the best B&Bs in London. Although Ebury Street is not as grand as it used to be, it's still prime London real estate. Thomas Wolfe stayed at no. 75 in 1930 while working on *Of Time and the River.* Chesham House consists of two brick Georgian buildings connected on the top floor and in the basement breakfast area. Outside is a pair of old-fashioned carriage lamps and window boxes, a facade that has won various prizes in local competitions. Livinia Sillars, the leaseholder, has decorated the bedrooms to create a warm, cozy ambience. Rooms without private bathrooms have hot and cold running water, with well-maintained and generous shared hallway bathrooms with showers.

64–66 Ebury St., London SW1W 9QD. © 020/7730-8513. Fax 020/7730-1845. www.chesham-house-hotel. com. 23 units, 3 with bathroom. £55 ($88) double without bathroom, £70 ($112) double with bathroom. Rates include English breakfast. AE, MC, V. Tube: Victoria. *In room:* TV, dataport, iron, no phone.

James House/Cartref House *(Kids* Hailed by many publications, including the *Los Angeles Times,* as one of the top 10 B&B choices in London, James House and Cartref House (across the street from each other) deserve their accolades. Each room is individually designed. Some of the large rooms have bunk beds that make them suitable for families. Clients in rooms with a private shower-only bathroom will find somewhat cramped quarters; corridor bathrooms are adequate and frequently refurbished. The English breakfast is so generous that you might end up skipping lunch. There's no elevator, but guests don't seem to mind. Both houses are nonsmoking. You're just a stone's throw from Buckingham Palace should the queen invite you over for tea. *Warning:* Whether or not you like this hotel will depend on your room assignment. Some accommodations are fine but several rooms (often when the other units are full) are hardly large enough to move around in. This is especially true of some third-floor units. Some "bathrooms" reminded us of those found on small ocean-going freighters. Ask before booking and request a larger room.

108 and 129 Ebury St., London SW1W 9QD. James House © **020/7730-7338**; Cartref House © **020/7730-6176.** Fax 020/7730-7338. www.jamesandcartref.co.uk. 19 units, 12 with bathroom. £70 ($112) double without bathroom, £85 ($136) double with bathroom; £135 ($216) quad with bathroom. Rates include English breakfast. AE, MC, V. Tube: Victoria. *In room:* TV, dataport, coffeemaker, hair dryer, no phone.

IN AND AROUND KNIGHTSBRIDGE
VERY EXPENSIVE

The Capital Hotel ★★★ We'd be delighted to check in here for the season. Only 50 yards from Harrods department store, this family-run town-house hotel is also at the doorstep of the shops of Knightsbridge and the "green lung" of Hyde Park. There are less than 40 bedrooms here, but you get many of the luxuries and services of a mammoth hotel. Warmth, intimacy, and an attention to detail are the hallmarks of this luxury oasis. Fabled designer Nina Campbell created the spacious bedrooms, furnishing them with luxurious fabrics, art, and antiques. David Linley, nephew of Her Majesty, also assisted in the design. Bathrooms with tubs and showers are luxurious. The liveried doorman standing outside has welcomed royalty, heads of state, and international celebrities to this hotel. For dining, you don't have far to go. The restaurant, directed by Chef Eric Chavot, has already achieved the distinction of two Michelin stars.

22–24 Basil St., London SW3 1AT. © 020/7589-5171. Fax 020/7225-0011. www.capitalhotel.co.uk. 48 units. £245–£315 ($392–$504) double; from £375 ($600) suite. AE, DC, MC, V. Tube: Knightsbridge. **Amenities:** Restaurant; bar; concierge; 24-hr. room service; babysitting; laundry service; same-day dry cleaning. *In room:* A/C, TV/VCR, dataport, minibar, hair dryer, safe in most units.

EXPENSIVE

Aster House ★★★ *(Value* This is the winner of the 2002 London Tourism Award for best B&B in London. It's just as good now as it was then. Within an easy walk of Kensington Palace, the late Princess Diana's home, and the museums of South Kensington, it is a friendly, inviting, and well-decorated lodging on a tree-lined street. The area surrounding the hotel, Sumner Place, looks like a Hollywood set depicting Victorian London. Aster House guests eat breakfast in a sunlit conservatory and can feed the ducks in the pond outside. Since the

B&B is a Victorian building spread across five floors, each unit is unique in size and shape. Rooms range from spacious, with a four-poster bed, to a Lilliputian special with a single bed. Some beds are draped with fabric tents for extra drama, and each room is individually decorated in the style of an English manor house bedroom. The small bathrooms are beautifully kept with showers ("the best in Europe," wrote one guest) or tubs and showers.

3 Sumner Place, London SW7 3EE. ℭ 020/7581-5888. Fax 020/7584-4925. www.asterhouse.com. £125–£160 ($200–$256) double. Rates include buffet breakfast. MC, V. Tube: South Kensington. Amenities: Laundry service; same-day dry cleaning. *In room:* A/C, TV, dataport, coffeemaker, hair dryer, safe.

Knightsbridge Hotel ★★★ *Value*   The Knightsbridge Hotel attracts visitors from all over the world seeking a small, comfortable hotel in a high-rent district. It's fabulously located, sandwiched between fashionable Beauchamp Place and Harrods, with many of the city's top theaters and museums close at hand. Built in the early 1800s as a private town house, this place sits on a tranquil, tree-lined square, free from traffic. Two of London's premier hoteliers, Kit and Tim Kemp, who have been celebrated for their upmarket boutique hotels, have gone more affordable with a revamp of this hotel in the heart of the shopping district. It's rare to get such *luxe* touches in a moderately priced London hotel. All the Kemp "cult classics" are found here, including granite-and-oak bathrooms, the Kemps' famed honor bar, and Frette linens. The hotel has become an instant hit. All the beautifully furnished rooms have shower-only private bathrooms clad in marble or tile. Most bedrooms are spacious and furnished with traditional English fabrics. The best rooms are nos. 311 and 312 at the rear, each with a pitched ceiling and a small sitting area. Bathrooms are clad in marble or tile.

10 Beaufort Gardens, London SW3 1PT. ℭ 020/7589-9271. Fax 020/7584-6355. www.firmdalehotels.com. 44 units. £155–£245 ($248–$392) double; from £325 ($520) suite. Rates include English or continental breakfast. AE, MC, V. Tube: Knightsbridge. **Amenities:** Bar; concierge; courtesy car; 24-hr. room service; laundry service; same-day dry cleaning. *In room:* TV w/pay movies (VCR in most rooms), dataport, minibar, hair dryer, safe.

IN CHELSEA
EXPENSIVE

The Sloane ★★   This "toff" (dandy) address, a redbrick Victorian-era town house that has been tastefully renovated in recent years, is located in Chelsea near Sloane Square. It combines valuable 19th-century antiques with modern comforts. Our favorite spot here is the rooftop terrace; with views opening onto Chelsea, it's ideal for a relaxing breakfast or drink. Bedrooms come in varying sizes, ranging from small to spacious, but all are opulently furnished with flouncy draperies, tasteful fabrics, and sumptuous beds. Many rooms have draped four-poster or canopied beds and, of course, antiques. The deluxe bathrooms have combination tub and shower, with chrome power showers, wall-width mirrors (in most rooms), and luxurious toiletries.

29–34 Draycott Place, London SW3 2SH. ℭ 800/324-9960 in the U.S., or 020/7581-5757. Fax 020/7584-1348. www.sloanehotel.com. 22 units. £195–£240 ($312–$384) double; £225 ($360) suite. AE, DC, MC, V. Tube: Sloane Sq. **Amenities:** Airport transportation (with prior arrangement); business services; 24-hr. room service; laundry service; same-day dry cleaning. *In room:* A/C, TV/VCR (plus pay movies), dataport, hair dryer, safe.

MODERATE

Willett Hotel ★ *Value*   On a tree-lined street leading off Sloane Square, this dignified Victorian town house lies in the heart of Chelsea. Named for the famous London architect William Willett, its stained glass and chandeliers reflect the opulence of the days when Prince Edward was on the throne. Under a mansard roof with bay windows, the hotel is a 5-minute walk from the shopping mecca of King's Road and close to such stores as Peter Jones, Harrods, and Harvey Nichols. Individually decorated bedrooms come in a wide range of sizes. All rooms have well-kept bathrooms, equipped with shower-tub combinations. Some rooms are first class, with swagged draperies, matching armchairs, and canopied beds. But a few of the twins are best left for Lilliputians.

32 Sloane Gardens, London SW1 8DJ. ℂ 020/7824-8415. Fax 020/7730-4830. www.eeh.co.uk. 19 units. £90–£155 ($144–$248) double. Rates include English breakfast. AE, DC, MC, V. Tube: Sloane Sq. **Amenities:** Bar; concierge; 24-hr. room service; laundry service; same-day dry cleaning. *In room:* A/C in most rooms, TV/VCR, dataport, coffeemaker, hair dryer, iron.

IN NEARBY BELGRAVIA
EXPENSIVE

Diplomat Hotel ⭑ *(Finds)*   Part of the Diplomat's charm is that it is a small and reasonably priced hotel located in an otherwise prohibitively expensive neighborhood. Only minutes from Harrods Department Store, it was built in 1882 as a private residence by noted architect Thomas Cubbitt. It's very well appointed and was completely overhauled in 2002 and 2003. The registration desk is framed by the sweep of a partially gilded circular staircase; above it, cherubs gaze down from a Regency-era chandelier. The staff is helpful, well mannered, and discreet. The high-ceilinged guest rooms are tastefully done in Victorian style. You get good—not grand—comfort here. Rooms are a bit small and usually furnished with twin beds. Bathroom, with shower stalls, are also small but well maintained.

2 Chesham St., London SW1X 8DT. ℂ 020/7235-1544. Fax 020/7259-6153. www.btinternet.com/~diplomat. hotel. 26 units. £125–£170 ($200–$272) double. Rates include English buffet breakfast. AE, DC, MC, V. Tube: Sloane Sq. or Knightsbridge. **Amenities:** Snack bar; nearby health club; business services; laundry service; same-day dry cleaning. *In room:* TV, dataport, coffeemaker, hair dryer, iron.

KENSINGTON
INEXPENSIVE

Vicarage Private Hotel ⭑ *(Kids)*   Owners Eileen and Martin Diviney enjoy a host of admirers on all continents. Their hotel is tops for old-fashioned English charm, affordable prices, and hospitality. Situated on a residential garden square close to Kensington High Street, not far from Portobello Road Market, this Victorian town house retains many original features. Individually furnished in country-house style, the bedrooms can accommodate up to four, making it a great place for families. If you want a little nest to hide away in, opt for the very private top-floor aerie (no. 19). Guests find the corridor shower-only bathrooms adequate and well maintained. Guests meet in a cozy sitting room for conversation and to watch the telly. As a thoughtful extra, hot drinks are available 24 hours a day. In the morning, a hearty English breakfast awaits.

10 Vicarage Gate, London W8 4AG. ℂ 020/7229-4030. Fax 020/7792-5989. www.londonvicaragehotel.com. 17 units, 8 with bathroom. £46 ($75) single without bathroom; £100 ($160) double with bathroom, £76 ($122) double without bathroom; £93 ($149) triple without bathroom; £100 ($160) family room for 4 without bathroom. Rates include English breakfast. No credit cards. Tube: High St. Kensington or Notting Hill Gate. *In room:* TV, coffeemaker, hair dryer (upon request), no phone.

SOUTH KENSINGTON
EXPENSIVE

Number Sixteen ⭑   This luxurious pension is composed of four early-Victorian town houses linked together. The scrupulously maintained front and rear gardens make this one of the most idyllic spots on the street. The rooms are decorated with an eclectic mix of English antiques and modern paintings, although some of the decor looks a little faded. Accommodations range from small to spacious and have themes such as tartan or maritime. The beds are comfortable, and bathrooms are tiled and outfitted with vanity mirrors, heated towel racks, and hand-held showers over small tubs. There's an honor-system bar in the library. On chilly days, a fire roars in the fireplace of the flowery drawing room, although some prefer the more masculine library. Breakfast can be served in your bedroom, in the conservatory or, if the weather's good, in the garden, with its bubbling fountain and fishpond.

16 Sumner Place, London SW7 3EG. © **800/592-5387** in the U.S., or 020/7589-5232. Fax 020/7584-8615. www.numbersixteenhotel.co.uk. 39 units. £150–£165 ($240–$264) double; £225 ($360) suite. Rates include continental breakfast. AE, DC, MC, V. Parking £25 ($40). Tube: South Kensington. **Amenities:** Access to nearby health club; 24-hr. room service; babysitting; laundry service; same-day dry cleaning. *In room:* TV/VCR, dataport, minibar, hair dryer, safe.

MODERATE

Avonmore Hotel ★ *(Finds* The recently refurbished Avonmore is easily accessible to West End theaters and shops, yet it's located in a quiet neighborhood, only 2 minutes from the West Kensington stop on the District Line. This privately owned place—a former National Award winner as the best private hotel in London—boasts wall-to-wall carpeting and radio alarms in each tastefully decorated room. All rooms have small shower-only bathrooms. The owner, Margaret McKenzie, provides lots of personal service. An English breakfast is served in a cheerful room, and a wide range of drinks are available in the cozy bar.

66 Avonmore Rd., London W14 8RS. © **020/7603-4296.** Fax 020/7603-4035. www.avonmorehotel.co.uk. 9 units. £105 ($168) double; £120 ($192) triple. Rates include English breakfast. AE, MC, V. Tube: West Kensington. **Amenities:** Bar; limited room service; laundry service; same-day dry cleaning. *In room:* TV, dataport, minibar, coffeemaker, hair dryer.

The Gallery ★ *(Finds* This is the place to go if you want to stay in an exclusive little town-house hotel but don't want to pay £300 a night for the privilege. Two splendid Georgian residences have been restored and converted into this remarkable hotel, which remains relatively unknown. The location is ideal, near the Victoria and Albert Museum, Royal Albert Hall, Harrods, Knightsbridge, and King's Road. Bedrooms are individually designed and decorated in Laura Ashley–style, with half-canopied beds and marble-tiled bathrooms with brass fittings and tub-and-shower combos. The junior suites have private roof terraces, minibars, Jacuzzis, and air-conditioning. A team of butlers takes care of everything. The lounge, with its mahogany paneling and moldings and deep colors, has the ambience of a private club. The drawing room beckons you to relax and read in a quiet corner. The Gallery Room displays works by known and unknown artists for sale.

8–10 Queensberry Place, London SW7 2EA. © **020/7915-0000.** Fax 020/7915-4400. www.eeh.co.uk. 36 units. £120–£145 ($192–$232) double; from £220 ($352) junior suite. Rates include buffet English breakfast. AE, DC, MC, V. Tube: South Kensington. **Amenities:** Bar; access to nearby health club; courtesy car; business center; babysitting; laundry service; same-day dry cleaning; 24-hr. butler service. *In room:* TV, dataport, coffeemaker, hair dryer, safe.

NOTTING HILL
EXPENSIVE

The Portobello Hotel ★ On an elegant Victorian terrace near Portobello Road, two 1850s-era town houses have been combined to form a quirky property that has its devotees. We remember these rooms when they looked better, but they still have plenty of character. Who knows what will show up in what nook? Perhaps a Chippendale, a claw-foot tub, or a round bed tucked under a gauze canopy. Try for no. 16, with a full-tester bed facing the garden. Some of the cheaper rooms are so tiny that they're basically garrets, but others have been combined into large doubles. Most of the small bathrooms have showers but no tubs. An elevator goes to the third floor; after that, it's the stairs. Since windows are not double-glazed, request a room in the quiet rear. Some rooms are air-conditioned. Service is erratic at best, but this is still a good choice.

22 Stanley Gardens, London W11 2NG. ℂ 020/7727-2777. Fax 020/7792-9641. www.portobello-hotel.co.uk. 24 units. £160–£260 ($256–$416) double; £320 ($512) suite. Rates include continental breakfast. AE, MC, V. Tube: Notting Hill Gate or Holland Park. **Amenities:** 24-hr. bar and restaurant in basement; business services; 24-hr. room service; laundry service; same-day dry cleaning. *In room:* A/C (some rooms), TV/VCR, dataport, minibar, hair dryer.

MODERATE

The Main House ★★ *Finds*   Each beautifully appointed room takes up a whole floor of this Victorian town house in Notting Hill, close to Portobello Road, the antiques markets, art galleries, and designer shops. Such attractions as Kensington Palace and Albert Hall are within walking distance. Russian princesses, Japanese pop stars, and Los Angeles film producers have already discovered this spot. Owner and creator Caroline Main is a former African explorer, Mayfair nightclub owner, and DJ. To furnish the house, she shopped "quirky" on Portobello Road, picking up gilded mirrors, watercolors of elegantly dressed 1930s women, and similar antiques. The ceilings are dramatically high, and the gleaming wood floors are swathed in animal skins. All rooms have freshly renewed private bathrooms with showers.

6 Colville Rd., London W11 2BP. ℂ 020/7221-9691. www.themainhouse.co.uk. 4 units. £90 ($144) double; £130 ($208) suite. MC, V. Tube: Notting Hill Gate. Parking: £4 ($6.40). Bus: 23, 27, 52, 94, or 328. **Amenities:** Reduced rate at nearby health club and spa; bike rental; courtesy car to and from point of arrival; limited room service; laundry service; same-day dry cleaning. *In room:* TV, dataport, hair dryer, safe.

PADDINGTON & BAYSWATER
EXPENSIVE

Darlington Hyde Park ★   Although it's not flashy and it lacks a full range of services, the Darlington Hyde Park is a winning choice for central London. Renovated and well-maintained rooms are decorated in an updated Victorian style: tasteful and neat, albeit a bit short on flair. They range from small to medium, and each is fitted with a tiny but adequate bathroom with a shower-tub combination. There is a happy blend of business people and vacationers. The in-room amenities are superior to those at other hotels along this street. Five bedrooms are nonsmoking. There is no bar, but guests are invited to BYOB and drink in the lounge. A number of neighboring restaurants cater room service for the hotel; they are listed in a restaurant book found in each room.

111–117 Sussex Gardens, London W2 2RU. ℂ 020/7460-8800. Fax 020/7460-8828. www.darlington hotel.co.uk. 40 units. £140 ($224) double; £155 ($248) family room; £160 ($256) suite. Rates include continental breakfast. AE, DC, MC, V. Tube: Paddington or Lancaster Gate. **Amenities:** Nearby health club; laundry service; same-day dry cleaning. *In room:* TV, dataport, hair dryer, safe.

London Elizabeth Hotel ★   This elegant Victorian town house is ideally situated, overlooking Hyde Park. Amid the buzz and excitement of central London, the hotel's atmosphere is an oasis of charm and refinement. Even before the hotel's recent £3 million restoration, it oozed character. Individually decorated rooms range from executive to deluxe and remind us of staying in an English country house. Deluxe rooms are fully air-conditioned, and some contain four-poster beds. Executive units usually contain one double or twin bed. Some rooms have special features such as Victorian antique fireplaces, and all contain first-rate bathrooms with showers and tubs. Suites are pictures of grand comfort and luxury—the Conservatory Suite boasts its own veranda, part of the house's original 1850 conservatory.

Lancaster Terrace, Hyde Park, London W2 3PF. © 020/7402-6641. Fax 020/7224-8900. www.londonelizabeth hotel.co.uk. 49 units. £115–£140 ($184–$224) double; £180–£250 ($288–$400) suite. AE, DC, MC, V. Parking £10 ($16). Tube: Lancaster Gate or Paddington. **Amenities:** Restaurant; bar; business services; 24-hr. room service; laundry service; same-day dry cleaning. *In room:* A/C, TV, dataport, hair dryer, iron.

MODERATE

The Pavilion *Finds*   Until the early 1990s, this was a rather ordinary-looking B&B. Then, a team of entrepreneurs with ties to the fashion industry took over and redecorated the rooms with sometimes-wacky themes, turning it into an idiosyncratic little hotel. The result is a theatrical and often outrageous decor that's appreciated by the many fashion models and music-industry folks who regularly make this their temporary home in London. Rooms are, regrettably, rather small, but each has a distinctive style. Examples include a kitschy 1970s room ("Honky-Tonk Afro"), an Oriental bordello themed room ("Enter the Dragon"), and even rooms with 19th-century ancestral themes. One Edwardian-style room, a gem of emerald brocade and velvet, is called "Green with Envy." Each contains tea-making facilities and small, but efficiently organized, bathrooms with excellent showers.

34–36 Sussex Gardens, London W2 1UL. © 020/7262-0905. Fax 020/7262-1324. www.eol.net.mt/pavilion. 29 units. £100 ($160) double; £120 ($190) triple. Rates include continental breakfast. AE, DC, MC, V. Parking £5 ($8). Tube: Edgware Rd. **Amenities:** Same-day dry cleaning. *In room:* TV, dataport, coffeemaker.

The Phoenix Hotel   This hotel, a member of the Best Western chain, occupies the entire south side of Kensington Garden Square, one of the most famous garden squares in Europe. Well situated in an ethnically mixed neighborhood, the Phoenix is composed of a series of 1854 town houses. The atmosphere is welcoming. Well-furnished bedrooms keep to a smart international standard, with a palette of muted tones. Everything is designed for comfort and ease, including the luggage racks. Bathrooms, most of which contain shower-tub combinations, are a bit small but well kept. The bar is a good place to unwind, and moderately priced meals are served in the downstairs cafe. Our biggest complaint? The public areas are too small for a hotel of this size.

1–8 Kensington Garden Sq., London W2 4BH. © 800/528-1234 in the U.S., or 020/7229-2494. Fax 020/7727-1419. www.phoenixhotel.co.uk. 125 units. £129 ($206) double; £145 ($232) suite; £185 ($296) family room. Rates include buffet breakfast. AE, DC, MC, V. Tube: Bayswater Station. **Amenities:** Cafe; bar; limited business services; 24-hr. room service; laundry services; same-day dry cleaning. *In room:* TV, dataport, hair dryer.

INEXPENSIVE

Garden Court   You'll find this hotel on a tranquil Victorian garden square in the heart of the city. Two private houses (dating from 1870) were combined to form one efficiently run hotel, located near such attractions as Kensington Palace, Hyde Park, and the Portobello Antiques Market. Each year, rooms are redecorated and refurbished, although an overall renovation plan seems to be lacking. Most accommodations are spacious, with good lighting, generous shelf and closet space, and comfortable furnishings. If you're in a room without a bathroom, you'll generally have to share with the occupants of only one other room. There are many homelike touches throughout the hotel, including ancestral portraits and silky flowers. Each room is individually decorated and "comfy"; it's like visiting your great-aunt. Rooms open onto the square in front or the gardens in the rear. Shower and tub bathrooms are installed in areas never intended for plumbing, so they tend to be very cramped. There is no elevator.

30–31 Kensington Gardens Sq., London W2 4BG. © 020/7229-2553. Fax 020/7727-2749. www.gardencourt hotel.co.uk. 34 units, 16 with bathroom. £58 ($93) double without bathroom, £88 ($141) double with bathroom; £72 ($115) triple without bathroom, £99 ($158) triple with bathroom. Rates include English breakfast. MC, V. Tube: Bayswater. **Amenities:** Coin-op washers and dryers. *In room:* TV, dataport, hair dryer.

4 Where to Dine

London is one of the great food capitals of the world. Both its veteran and upstart chefs have fanned out around the globe for culinary inspiration and have returned with innovative dishes, flavors, and ideas that London diners have never seen before—or at least not at such unprecedented rates. These chefs are pioneering a new style of cooking called "Modern British," which is forever changing yet comfortingly familiar in many ways. They've committed to centering their dishes around local ingredients from field, stream, and air, and have become daringly innovative with traditional recipes—too much so in the view of some critics, who don't like fresh mango over their blood pudding.

Traditional British cooking has made a comeback, too. The dishes that British mums have been forever feeding their reluctant families are fashionable again. Yes, we're talking British soul food: bangers and mash, Norfolk dumplings, nursery puddings, cottage pie—the works. This may be a rebellion against the excessive minimalism of the nouvelle cuisine that ran rampant over London in the 1980s, but who knows? Maybe it's just plain old nostalgia. Pigs' nose with parsley-and-onion sauce may not be your idea of cutting-edge cuisine, but Simpson's-in-the-Strand is serving it for breakfast.

If you want a lavish meal, London is a good place to eat it. Some of the world's top restaurants call the city home. For those who don't want to break the bank, we include many affordable restaurants where you can dine well. You'll find that London's food revolution has infiltrated every level of the dining scene—even the lowly pub has entered London's culinary sweepstakes. Believe the unthinkable: At certain pubs, you can now dine better than in many restaurants. In some, standard pub grub has given way to Modern British and Mediterranean-style fare; in others, oyster bars have taken hold.

TAXES & TIPPING   All restaurants and cafes are required to display the prices of their food and drink in a place visible from outside. Charges for service, as well as any minimums or cover charges, must also be made clear. The prices shown must include 17.5% VAT. Most restaurants add a 10% to 15% service charge to your bill, but check to make sure. If nothing has been added, leave a 10% to 15% tip. It is not considered rude to tip, so feel free to leave something extra if service was good.

MAYFAIR
VERY EXPENSIVE
Gordon Ramsay at Claridge's ✸✸✸ EUROPEAN   Gordon Ramsey is the hottest chef in London today. He now rules at the staid, traditional hotel of Claridge's, legendary since 1860 when Queen Victoria stopped by for tea with the Empress Eugenie. The famed Art Deco dining room still retains many of its original architectural features, but the cuisine is hardly the same. Most definitely Victoria wasn't served an *amuse-bouche* of pumpkin soup dribbled with truffle

Travel Tip: He who finds the best hotel deal has more to spend on facials involving knobbly vegetables.

Hello, the Roaming Gnome here. I've been nabbed from the garden and taken round the world. The people who took me are so terribly clever. They find the best offerings on Travelocity. For very little cha-ching. And that means I get to be pampered and exfoliated till I'm pink as a bunny's doodah.

travelocity®

1-888-TRAVELOCITY / travelocity.com / America Online Keyword: Travel

oil and studded with truffles. On a recent lunchtime visit, we were dazzled by a fixed-price menu (the only type served here) that wasn't outrageously priced.

Although the menu changes frequently, a memorable culinary highlight began with filets of baby red mullet on a juniper-flavored sauerkraut and went on to include a breast and confit leg of guinea fowl with vegetables and foie gras, finishing off with rum-baba with glazed oranges and crème fraîche. A three-course dinner was even more spectacular, featuring such delights as filet of sea bass rapped in fresh basil leaves and served with a caviar sauce, and roast Scottish baby lobster cooked slowly in lime butter and served with tomato couscous. The desserts are among our favorite in London, including the likes of a bread-and-butter brioche pudding with clotted-cream ice cream or a prune and Armagnac vanilla tart with *fromage blanc* in cream.

Brook St., W1. ✆ 020/7499-0099. Reservations required as far in advance as possible. Fixed-price lunch £25 ($40); fixed-price dinner £50 ($80). AE, DC, MC, V. Mon–Sat noon–3pm and 5:45–11pm; Sun 6–10:30pm. Tube: Bond St.

Le Gavroche ✰✰✰ CLASSICAL FRENCH Although challengers come and go, this luxurious dining room remains the number-one choice in London for classical French cuisine. It may have fallen off briefly in the early 1990s, but it's fighting its way back to stellar ranks. There's always something special coming out of the kitchen of Burgundy-born Michel Roux; the service is faultless and the ambience formally chic without being stuffy. The menu changes constantly, depending on the fresh produce that's available and the current inspiration of the chef. But it always remains classically French, though not of the "essentially old-fashioned bourgeois repertoire" that some critics suggest. Signature dishes have been honed over years of unswerving practice, including the soufflé Suissesse, papillote of smoked salmon (salmon cooked in a greased paper wrapper), or whole Bresse chicken with truffles and a Madeira cream sauce. Game is often served, depending on availability. New menu options include cassoulet of snails with frog thighs, seasoned with herbs; mousseline of lobster in champagne sauce; and filet of red snapper with caviar and oyster-stuffed tortellini.

43 Upper Brook St., W1. ✆ 020/7408-0881. Fax 020/7491-4387. Reservations required as far in advance as possible. Main courses £24–£45 ($38–$72); fixed-price lunch £40 ($64); menu exceptional £80 ($128) per person. AE, MC, V. Mon–Fri noon–2pm and 7–11pm. Tube: Marble Arch.

EXPENSIVE

The Square ✰✰✰ FRENCH Hip, chic, casual, sleek, and modern, The Square still doesn't scare Le Gavroche as a competitor for first place on London's dining circuit, but it is certainly a restaurant to visit on a serious London gastronomic tour. Chef Philip Howard delivers the goods at this excellent restaurant. You get immaculate food in a cosseting atmosphere with abstract modern art on the walls. Howard has a magic touch with pasta—it appears as a bulging roll of cannelloni stuffed with shredded trout and green leeks, and as ravioli of partridge on a pool of creamy game-flavored sauce with finely shredded cabbage. Surprise dishes await in every corner of the menu—for example, a tortellini of crab with a cappuccino of shellfish flavored with fresh basil. Roast foie gras is a dazzling appetizer. Fish is stunningly fresh, and the Bresse pigeon is as good as it is in its hometown in France. If you're a vegetarian, stay clear of this place, as many dishes are aimed at the true carnivore. For dessert, try the shortbread sandwich filled with strawberries and crème fraîche, and served with a velvety vanilla ice cream.

6–10 Bruton St., W1. ✆ 020/7495-7100. Reservations required. Fixed-price lunch £25–£30 ($40–$48); fixed-price dinner £55–£75 ($88–$120). AE, DC, MC, V. Mon–Fri noon–3pm; Mon–Sat 6:30–11pm. Tube: Bond St. or Green Park.

London Dining

HAMPSTEAD
CAMDEN
Prince Albert Rd.
Delancey St.
St. Pancras Rd.
London Zoo
Albany St.
Hampstead Rd.
EUSTON
REGENT'S PARK
Boating Lake
Euston Station
Lisson Grove
Regents Park
Euston Rd.
Tottenham
BLOOMS BURY
LISSON GROVE
Marylebone Rd.
Crescent
Gt. Portland St.
Gower St.
Bedford Sq.
Goodge St.
Park Rd.
Edgware Rd.
Gloucester Pl.
Baker St.
Marylebone High St.
Gt. Portland St.
Regent St.
MARYLEBONE
Court Rd.
THE WEST END
Sussex Gdns.
Seymour Pl.
Wigmore St.
Seymour St.
Oxford St.
New
SOHO
Bayswater Rd.
Cumberland Gate
Grosvenor Sq.
Brook St.
Bond St.
Savile Row
Shaftesbury Ave.
Grosvenor St.
West Carriage Dr.
HYDE PARK
Park Ln.
Park Ln.
Berkeley
MAYFAIR
Jermyn St.
St. James's St.
Pall Mall
The Serpentine
Serpentine Rd.
Piccadilly
GREEN PARK
The Mall
ST. JAMES'S
South Carriage Dr.
Knightsbridge
Constitution Hill
Grosvenor Pl.
Buckingham Palace
Birdcage Walk
ST. JAMES'S PARK
KNIGHTS-BRIDGE
Buckingham Gate
Victoria and Albert Museum
Harrod's
Brompton Rd.
Beauchamp
Pont
Sloane St.
Belgrave Sq.
Victoria St.
Buckingham Palace Rd.
Horseferry Rd.
VICTORIA
Pelham St.
BROMPTON
Sloane
Sloane Sq.
Eaton Sq.
Eccleston St.
BELGRAVIA
Lwr. Sloane St.
Vauxhall Bridge Rd.
Belgrave Rd.
Belgrave Way
Sloane Ave.
Sydney St.
King's Rd.
Pimlico Rd.
Ebury Bridge Rd.
Chelsea Bridge Rd.
Warwick
PIMLICO
CHELSEA
Royal Hospital Rd.
Oakley St.
Chelsea Embankment
Chelsea Bridge Rd.
Queenstown Rd.
Grosvenor Rd.
Grosvenor Bridge
Grosvenor Rd.
Walk
Albert Bridge
River Thames
Chelsea Bridge
Nine Elms Ln.
Battersea Bridge
Battersea Bridge Rd.
Albert Bridge Rd.
BATTERSEA PARK

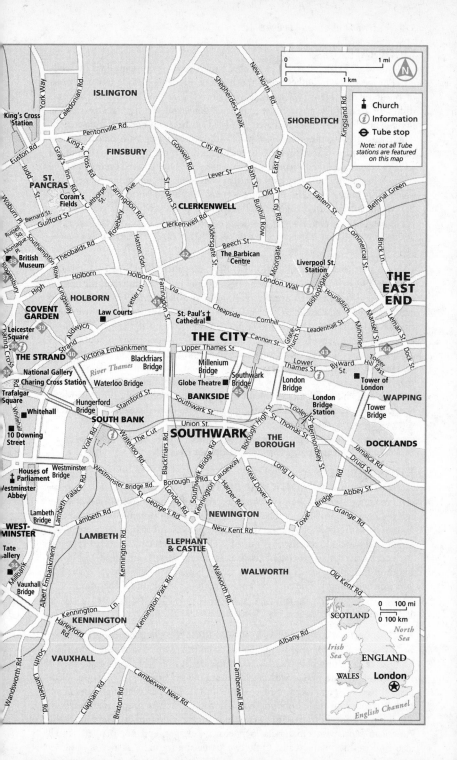

ISLINGTON

SHOREDITCH

King's Cross
Station

Pentonville Rd.

FINSBURY

City Rd.

THE
EAST
END

Euston Rd.

King's Cross Rd.

Goswell Rd.

Lever St.

Old St.

Gt. Eastern St.

Bethnal Green

ST.
PANCRAS

Coram's
Fields

CLERKENWELL

Beech St.

The Barbican
Centre

Liverpool St.
Station

Brick Ln.

Clerkenwell Rd.

Aldersgate St.

Moorgate

Bishopsgate

Commercial St.

Mansell St.

Leman St.

Dock St.

British
Museum

Theobalds Rd.

Holborn

Holborn

42

London Wall

Hounsditch

HOLBORN

Via.

Cheapside

Cornhill

Leadenhall St.

Minories

Tower
Hill East

44

COVENT
GARDEN

Law Courts

St. Paul's †
Cathedral

THE CITY

Grace Church St.

43

Byward
St.

Leicester
Square

39

Aldwych

Cannon St.

Upper Thames St.

Lower
Thames St.

Tower of
London

WAPPING

THE STRAND

35

40

Strand

Victoria Embankment

Blackfriars
Bridge

Millenium
Bridge

Southwark
Bridge

London
Bridge

Tower
Bridge

National Gallery
Charing Cross Station

River Thames

Waterloo Bridge

Globe Theatre ■

45

London
Bridge
Station

Trafalgar
Square

Hungerford
Bridge

Stamford St.

Southwark St.

BANKSIDE

Tooley St.

DOCKLANDS

Whitehall

SOUTH BANK

Union St.

SOUTHWARK

St. Thomas St.

Bermondsey St.

10 Downing
Street

Waterloo Rd.

The Cut

THE
BOROUGH

Long Ln.

Jamaica Rd.

Houses of
Parliament

Westminster
Bridge

York Rd.

Blackfriars Rd.

Borough High St.

Great Dover St.

Druid St.

Westminster
Abbey

Westminster Bridge Rd.

Southwark Bridge Rd.

Kennington Causeway

Harper Rd.

Tower Bridge Rd.

Abbey St.

Grange Rd.

WEST-
MINSTER

Lambeth
Bridge

Lambeth Rd.

Borough Rd.

London Rd.

St. George's Rd.

NEWINGTON

Old Kent Rd.

Tate
Gallery

34

LAMBETH

New Kent Rd.

Millbank

Vauxhall
Bridge

Kennington Rd.

ELEPHANT
& CASTLE

Walworth Rd.

WALWORTH

KENNINGTON

Kennington Park Rd.

Albany Rd.

VAUXHALL

Camberwell New Rd.

Clapham Rd.

Brixton Rd.

Camberwell Rd.

MODERATE

Greenhouse EUROPEAN   Head chef Paul Merrett is quite inspired by modern European food. Dishes from the heart of England include a roast breast of pheasant that Henry VIII would have loved. The produce is first-class and dishes are beautifully prepared, without ever destroying the natural flavor of the ingredients. Fine examples included pan-fried sea bass and breast of guinea fowl. The chef deftly handles essential flavors without interfering with them, as is the case with his filet of Scottish beef. To make this dish more interesting, though, he adds such wake-up-the-tastebuds sides as sautéed foie gras and red onion jam. The menu is backed up by a very large wine list with some 500 selections. Some of the delightfully sticky desserts, including a moist bread-and-butter pudding and a baked ginger loaf with orange marmalade, would please a Midlands granny.

27A Hays Mews, W1. © 020/7499-3331. Reservations required. Main courses £15–£30 ($24–$48). AE, DC, DISC, MC, V. Mon–Fri noon–2:30pm and 5:30–11pm; Sat 6:30–11pm. Closed Christmas and bank holidays. Tube: Green Park.

Langan's Brasserie TRADITIONAL BRITISH/FRENCH   In its heyday in the early 1980s, this was one of the hippest restaurants in London, and the upscale brasserie still welcomes an average of 700 diners a day. The 1976 brainchild of actor Michael Caine and chef Richard Shepherd, Langan's sprawls over two noisy floors filled with potted plants and ceiling fans that create a 1930s feel. The menu is "mostly English with a French influence" and includes spinach soufflé with anchovy sauce, quail eggs in a pastry case served with a sautéed hash of mushrooms and hollandaise sauce, and roast crispy duck with applesauce and sage-lemon stuffing. There's always a selection of English pub fare, including bangers and mash, and fish and chips. The dessert menu is a journey into nostalgia: bread-and-butter pudding, treacle tart with custard, apple pie with clotted cream . . . Wait, how did mango sorbet slip in here?

Stratton St., W1. © 020/7491-8822. Reservations recommended. Main courses £14–£19 ($22–$30). AE, DC, MC, V. Mon–Fri 12:15pm–midnight; Sat 7pm–midnight. Tube: Green Park.

INEXPENSIVE

The Granary *Value* TRADITIONAL BRITISH   This family-operated country-style restaurant serves a simple flavor-filled array of home-cooked dishes that are listed daily on a blackboard. These might include lamb casserole with mint and lemon; pan-fried cod; or avocado stuffed with prawns, spinach, and cheese. Vegetarian meals include mushrooms stuffed with mixed vegetables, stuffed eggplant with curry sauce, and vegetarian lasagna. Tempting desserts are bread-and-butter pudding and apple brown Betty (both served hot). The large portions guarantee you won't go hungry. The cooking is standard but quite good for the price.

39 Albemarle St., W1. © 020/7493-2978. Main courses £8.90–£9.90 ($14–$16). MC, V. Mon–Fri 11:30am–7:15pm; Sat 11:30am–3pm. Tube: Green Park.

Pizzeria Condotti ★ *Kids* ITALIAN/AMERICAN   On pizza, there can never be any agreement, but many aficionados claim this favorite of visiting American families is London's best (frankly, we think dozens of New York spots have it beat). Tastefully decorated with fresh flowers and art from the 1970s, this place just off Regent Street looks more costly than it is. The pizzas are light and crisp, and arrive at your table bubbling hot. They range from a simple margherita to the sublime King Edward with potato, four cheeses, and tomato. Dare to try the American Hot, with mozzarella, pepperoni, sausages, and hot peppers. You'll also find freshly made salads. Only two pastas are featured, savory versions of lasagna and cannelloni. The wine list is impressive and reasonable. Finish off with a scoop of creamy tartufo ice cream made with chocolate liqueur, perhaps evoking memories of Rome's Piazza Navona.

4 Mill St., W1. ℂ 020/7499-1308. Pizzas £7–£8.50 ($11–$14); pastas £8 ($13); salads £3.10–£9.75 ($4.95–$16). AE, DC, MC, V. Mon–Sat noon–midnight. Tube: Oxford Circus.

ST. JAMES'S
EXPENSIVE

L'Oranger ✮ FRENCH   This bistro-cum-brasserie occupies a high-ceilinged space in an affluent neighborhood near the bottom of St. James's Street. Amid paneling, burnt-orange and forest-green paint, patterned carpeting, immaculate linens, flowers, and a uniformed waitstaff, you'll appreciate the choreographed set fixed-price menus of executive chef Kamel Benamar. The clientele, who pundits frequently refer to as "people who have made it," have praised Benamar's arrangement of flavors. Depending on the chef's inspiration, the set menu may include foie gras poached in a red Pessac wine sauce; a pan-fried filet of sea bass with zucchini, tomatoes, basil, and a black-olive vinaigrette; or roast Bresse chicken with truffles. Starters may include a terrine of ham and tongue served with gherkins and parsley, bound with a layer of spinach and served on a bed of *choron* sauce, which is a tomato-enriched béarnaise. Only fixed-price menus are served here.

5 St. James's St., SW1A. ℂ 020/7839-3774. Reservations recommended. Fixed-price lunches £18–£23 ($29–$37); fixed-price dinner £45 ($72). AE, DC, MC, V. Mon–Fri noon–2pm; Mon–Sat 6:30–11pm. Tube: Green Park.

MODERATE

Greens Restaurant & Oyster Bar SEAFOOD/TRADITIONAL BRITISH Critics say it's a triumph of tradition over taste, but as far as seafood in London goes, this is a tried-and-true favorite, thanks to an excellent menu with moderately priced dishes, a central location, and a charming staff. This place has a cluttered entrance leading to a crowded bar where you can sip fine wines and, from September to April, enjoy oysters. In the faux-Dickensian dining room, you can choose from a long menu of fresh seafood dishes, which changes monthly depending on what is in season. The standard menu ranges from fish cakes with leaf spinach to whole Scottish lobster. For zesty starters, opt for the smoked haddock or the smoked duck salad. Desserts include bread-and-butter pudding. (**Note:** London has two different Duke streets; Greens is on the one in St. James's.)

36 Duke St., St. James's, SW1. ℂ 020/7930-4566. Reservations recommended. Main courses £12–£38 ($18–$61); most dishes are moderately priced. AE, DC, MC, V. Restaurant daily 11:30am–3pm; Mon–Sat 5:30–11pm. Oyster Bar Mon–Sat 11:30am–3pm and 5:30–11pm; Sun noon–3pm and 5:30–9pm. Tube: Green Park.

PICCADILLY CIRCUS & LEICESTER SQUARE
EXPENSIVE

Fung Shing ✮✮ CANTONESE   In a city where the competition is stiff, Fung Shing emerges as London's finest Cantonese restaurant. Firmly established as a culinary landmark, it dazzles with classic and nouvelle Cantonese dishes. Look for the seasonal specials. Some of the dishes may be a bit experimental, notably stir-fried fresh milk with scrambled egg white, but you'll feel right at home with the soft-shell crab sautéed in a light batter and served with tiny rings of red-hot chile and deep-fried garlic. Chinese gourmets come here for the fried intestines; you may prefer the hotpot of stewed duck with yam. The spicy sea bass and the stir-fried crispy chicken are worthy choices. There are some 150 dishes from which to choose and most are moderate in price.

15 Lisle St., WC2. ⓒ **020/7437-1539.** Reservations required. Main courses £10–£26 ($16–$42); fixed-price menus £26–£34 ($42–$54). AE, DC, MC, V. Daily noon–11:30pm. Tube: Leicester Sq.

MODERATE

The Ivy ⭐⭐ MODERN BRITISH/INTERNATIONAL   Effervescent and sophisticated, The Ivy is the dining choice of visiting theatrical luminaries and has been intimately associated with the theater district ever since it opened in 1911. With its ersatz 1930s look and tiny bar near the entrance, this place is fun, and hums with the energy of London's glamour scene. The kitchen has a solid appreciation for fresh ingredients and a talent for preparation. Favorite dishes include white asparagus with sea kale and truffle butter; seared scallops with spinach, sorrel, and bacon; and salmon fish cakes. You'll also find such English desserts as sticky toffee (sponge cake soaked in a thick caramelized syrup) and caramelized bread-and-butter pudding. Meals are served quite late to accommodate the post-theater crowd.

1–5 West St., WC2. ⓒ **020/7836-4751.** Reservations required. Main courses £9–£35 ($14–$56); Sat–Sun fixed-price 3-course lunch £18 ($29). AE, DC, MC, V. Daily noon–3pm and 5:30pm–midnight (last order). Tube: Leicester Sq.

Randall & Aubin ⭐ *Finds* SEAFOOD   If you walk past the sex boutiques of Soho, you'll stumble upon this real discovery. The restaurant's consultant is TV chef Ed Baines, an ex-Armani model who turned this former butcher shop into a cool, hip champagne-and-oyster bar. It's an ideal place to take a lover for a *Sex and the City* type of meal and some champagne or a bottle of wine. You're never rushed here. The impressive display of the night's shellfish goodies will lure you inside. Chances are you won't be disappointed. Loch Fyne oysters, lobster with chips, garlic langoustines, pan-fried fresh scallops—the parade of seafood we've sampled here has in each case been genuinely excellent. The fish soup is the best in Soho. You might want to sample one of the hors d'oeuvres such as delightful Japanese–style fish cakes or fresh Cornish crab. Yes, lotto winners can get their fix of Sevruga caviar here. For anyone who would prefer to eat meat (although we don't know why they would, considering the great seafood here), there is a limited array of dishes such as a perfectly spit-roasted chicken flavored with fresh herbs. The lemon tart with crème fraîche rounds off a perfect meal.

16 Brewer St., W1. ⓒ **020/7287-4447.** Reservations not accepted. Main courses £11–£19 ($17–$30). AE, DC, MC, V. Mon–Sat noon–11pm; Sun 4–10:30pm. Tube: Piccadilly Circus.

INEXPENSIVE

Brown's BRITISH/CONTINENTAL   The decor of this enormously popular restaurant is reminiscent of an Edwardian brasserie, with mirrors, dark wood trim, and cream-colored walls. The staff is attentive, hysterically busy, and high spirited. The most amazing thing about the restaurant is its size. It's a cavernous labyrinth of tables complemented by a bar whose (often single) clients tend to be good-looking, happy-go-lucky, and usually up for a chat. Expect well-prepared cuisine here, hauled out through the stand-up crowds to battered tables and bentwood chairs by an army of well-intentioned European staff. Menu items include traditional British favorites (salmon and fish cakes, or steak, mushroom, and Guinness pies); as well as continental dishes such as confit of duck on a bed of lentils with pancetta, or chicken filet in red pesto served with linguine and rocket. The site of the restaurant was originally conceived in 1787 as a magistrate's court. Today, the somber overtones of the court are gone, as the restaurant is usually awash with bubbly theatergoers either headed to or coming from a West End play.

82–94 St. Martins Lane, WC2. ☏ 020/7497-5050. Reservations recommended. Two-course set-price menu £11 ($18), available noon–6:30pm. Main courses £7.50–£14 ($12–$22). AE, DC, MC, V. Daily noon–11:30pm. Tube: Leicester Sq. or Covent Garden.

SOHO
EXPENSIVE

Alastair Little ✿ MODERN BRITISH/CONTINENTAL In an 1830 brick-fronted town house (which supposedly housed John Constable's art studio for a brief period), this informal, cozy restaurant is a pleasant place to enjoy a well-prepared lunch or dinner. Some critics claim that Alastair Little is the best chef in London, but lately he's been buried under the avalanche of new talent. Actually, Little is not often here; he spends a good deal of time at other enterprises. The talented James Rix is usually in charge. Style is modern European with a slant toward Italian. The menu changes daily. Starters might include a salad of winter leaves with crispy pork or chicken livers in Vin Santo (a sweet wine), flavored with fresh tomatoes and basil. The terrine of wild duck and foie gras is a surefire pleaser, as are such main-course delights as risotto with both flap and field mushrooms and salted cod with spicy chickpeas and greens. For dessert, you can select an array of British cheeses or order such classics as a pear-and-red-wine tart. Ever have olive oil cake? It's served here with a winter fruit compote.

49 Frith St., W1. ☏ 020/7734-5183. Reservations recommended. Fixed-price dinner £35 ($56); fixed-price 3-course lunch £27 ($43). AE, DC, MC, V. Mon–Fri noon–3pm; Mon–Sat 6–11pm. Tube: Leicester Sq. or Tottenham Court Rd.

MODERATE

Atlantic Bar & Grill ✿✿ MODERN BRITISH A titanic restaurant in a former Art Deco ballroom off Piccadilly Circus, this 160-seat locale draws a trendy crowd to London's heart. The restaurant is cosmopolitan, and it's one of the best choices for the after-theater crowd because it closes at 3am most nights. It doesn't attract celebrities as it did back in 1994, but it's still going strong. Chef Steve Carter is doing much to recapture the restaurant's mid-1990s chic. He turns out a new menu every 2 months, with emphasis on organic and homegrown produce, seafood, and meats. Many dishes are quite complicated and taste as good as they sound: swordfish dumplings with a salsa of plum tomatoes, fresh cilantro, sautéed shiitake, soy-infused ginger, and fresh wilted spinach.

For a starter, we recommend the smoked-chicken Caesar club salad. Also memorable is the loin of yellowfin tuna served with a wild parsley-and-eggplant relish and a roasted red bell pepper pesto. The desserts are purposefully unsophisticated: Rice pudding or poached pears are standards. If you're rushed, you can drop into Dick's Bar for a quick bite. The offerings at Dick's include everything from lamb burgers sparked with yogurt and fresh mint to Cashel blue cheese and pumpkin seeds on ciabatta bread. Most dishes are at the low end of the price scale.

20 Glasshouse St., W1. ☏ 020/7734-4888. Reservations required. Main courses £13–£22 ($20–$34); fixed-price 3-course lunch £16 ($26). AE, DC, MC, V. Mon–Fri noon–3pm; Mon–Sat 6pm–3am; Sun 6–10:30pm. Tube: Piccadilly Circus.

Bam-Bou ✿ VIETNAMESE/FRENCH London's best Vietnamese-inspired eatery is spread over a series of dining rooms, alcoves, and bars in a town house with tattered French colonial decor. A favorite of young London, the restaurant is so popular that you may have to wait for 30 minutes to an hour for a table. The smell of lime and lemon grass lures you to the table—this combination is married perfectly in the chicken in lemon grass dish. Equally worthy is the caramelized ginger chicken. Also try such delights as tempura of softshell crab, or crispy beef with papaya and crabmeat flavored with a lime dressing. Rock lobster and spring chicken hot-pot is an eternal favorite, as are the flavorful prawns with green herbs and coconut. Our favorite starter is spicy raw beef with aromatic basil, lime, and chile, or fried marinated squid. A winner for dessert is the dish of sweet banana rolls with chocolate sauce.

1 Percy St., W1. ⓒ 020/7323-9130. Reservations required. Main courses £8.50–£14 ($14–$22). AE, DC, MC, V. Mon–Fri noon–11:15pm; Sat 6–11:15pm. Tube: Tottenham Court Rd.

Deca ★★ *Finds* FRENCH   Deca's chef, Paul Rhodes, was head chef at Chez Nico at Grosvenor House when that restaurant was awarded three stars by Michelin. At this new brasserie-style restaurant, he works some of that same culinary magic, adding several innovative twists as well. His cooking is based upon sound French techniques and the lavish use of market-fresh ingredients. Tastes and textures come together in pleasing combinations, as characterized by the tender breast of chicken with wild mushrooms, and the breast of duck with honey and peppercorns. Freshness is the key to many dishes. The oysters are brought down from Loch Fyne in Scotland. The veal sweetbreads Pojarski have found many admirers.

23 Conduit St., W1. ⓒ 020/7493-7070. Reservations required. Main courses £12–£20 ($19–$32); fixed-price lunch £13 ($20). AE, DC, MC, V. Mon–Sat noon–3pm and 5:30–11pm. Tube: Oxford Circus.

INEXPENSIVE

Mildreds ★ *Finds* VEGETARIAN   Mildreds may sound like a 1940s Joan Crawford movie, but it's one of London's most enduring vegetarian and vegan dining spots. It was vegetarian long before such restaurants became trendy. Jane Muir and Diane Thomas worked in various restaurants together before opening their own place. Today they run a busy, bustling diner with casual, friendly service. Sometimes it's a bit crowded, and tables are shared. They do a mean series of delectable stir-fries. The ingredients in their dishes are naturally grown, and they strongly emphasize the best seasonal produce. The menu changes daily but always features an array of homemade soups, casseroles, and salads. Organic wines are served, and portions are very large. Save room for the desserts, especially the nutmeg-and-mascarpone ice cream or the chocolate, rum, and amaretto pudding.

45 Lexington St., W1. ⓒ 020/7494-1634. Reservations not accepted. Main courses £5.30–£7 ($8.50–$11). No credit cards. Mon–Sat noon–11pm. Tube: Tottenham Court Rd.

Veeraswamy *Value* INDIAN   The oldest Indian restaurant in England, originally established in the 1920s, Veeraswamy has been restyled and rejuvenated and is looking better than ever. Its menu has been redone, and today it serves some of the most affordable fixed-price menus in Central London, the heart of the city. Shunning the standard fare offered in most London-based Indian restaurants, Veeraswamy features authentic, freshly prepared dishes—the kind that would be served in a private Indian home. Try almost anything: spicy oysters, succulent Tandoori chicken, tender and flavorful lamb curry. One of our favorite dishes is the savory lamb with turnips from Kashmir, flavored with large black cardamons, powdered fennel, and a red chile powder, giving the dish a vivid red color.

Victory House, 99 Regent St., W1 ⓒ 020/7734-1401. Reservations recommended. Lunch and pre/posttheater menu £13–£15 ($20–$24). Sun menu £15 ($24). Lunch and dinner main courses £13–£22 ($21–$35). AE, DC, MC, V. Mon–Fri noon–2:30pm; Sat–Sun 12:30–3pm; daily 5:30–11pm. Tube: Picadilly Circus.

TRAFALGAR SQUARE
MODERATE

The Portrait Restaurant ☆ MODERN BRITISH   This rooftop restaurant is a sought-after dining ticket on the fifth floor of the National Portrait Gallery's Ondaatje Wing. Along with the view (Nelson's Column, the London Eye, Big Ben, and the like), you get superb meals. Patrons usually go for lunch, not knowing that the chefs also cook on Thursday and Friday nights. In spring, there's nothing finer than the green English asparagus. All the main courses are filled with flavor. The high quality of the produce really shines through in such dishes as the whole plaice cooked in shrimp butter, the pot-roasted shank of lamb served in its roasting juices, and especially the roast pheasant and foie gras. For your "pudding," nothing is finer than the chocolate tart with espresso ice cream. Chefs aren't afraid of simple preparations mainly because they are assured of the excellence of their products. The wine list features some organic choices.

In the National Portrait Gallery, Trafalgar Square, WC2. ℰ 020/7313-2490. Reservations recommended. Main courses £13–£18.50 ($21–$30). AE, DC, MC, V. Sat–Wed 11:45am–2:45pm; Thurs–Fri 5:30–8:30pm. Tube: Leicester Sq.

BLOOMSBURY
VERY EXPENSIVE

Pied-à-Terre ☆ FRENCH   This foodie heaven understates its decor in favor of an intense focus on its subtle, sophisticated cuisine. You'll dine in a strictly mini- malist room, where gray and pale pink walls complement metal furniture and focused lighting that reveals a collection of modern art. France is the inspiration for the impressive wine list and some of the cuisine. The menu changes with the seasons but might include braised snails with celeriac, garlic, and a morel-flavored cream sauce; roasted scallops with apple and puréed ginger; halibut filets with queen scallops and caramelized endive; roasted partridge with pear; and the house specialty, a ballotine (stuffed and rolled into a bundle) of duck confit. If you're not dining with a vegetarian, braised pigs' head is another specialty. Our favorite item on the menu? Sea bass with vichyssoise (a thick soup of potatoes, leeks and cream) and caviar sauce. The food is beautifully presented on hand-painted plates with lush patterns. Prix-fixe menus only.

34 Charlotte St., W1. ℰ 020/7636-1178. Reservations recommended. Fixed-price 3-course lunch £23–£35 ($37–$56); fixed-price 3-course dinner £45–£60 ($72–$96); 8-course tasting menu £55 ($88). AE, MC, V. Tues–Fri noon–2:30pm (last order); Mon–Sat 7–11pm. Closed last week of Dec and first week of Jan. Tube: Goodge St.

MODERATE

Townhouse Brasserie ☆ FRENCH/INTERNATIONAL   Near the British Museum, this Georgian town-house restaurant is one of Bloomsbury's new up- and-coming dining establishments. The ground floor is decorated with contem- porary art, while the upstairs is a traditional English dining room with an infusion of Peruvian art. The frequently changing menu is a culinary tour de force, drawing inspiration from around the world. Ingredients are fresh, and are deftly handled by a skilled kitchen staff. You may want to begin with cream of leek soup or sweet potato soup with basil. Then it's on to a delectable charcoal- grilled duck breast with an Asian-style salad or an especially pleasing fresh seafood pasta flavored with chives, thick cream, and white wine. Save room for one of the tempting desserts made fresh daily.

24 Coptic St., WC1. ℰ 020/7636-2731. Reservations recommended. Main courses £11–£18 ($18–$29). AE, DC, MC, V. Mon–Sat 11am–11pm; Sun 10am–6pm. Tube: Tottenham Court Rd. or Holborn.

Wagamama JAPANESE   This noodle joint, in a basement just off New Oxford Street, is noisy and overcrowded, and you'll have to wait in line for a table. It calls itself a "non-destination food station" and caters to some 1,200 customers a day. Many dishes are built around ramen noodles with your choice of chicken, beef, or salmon. Try the tasty gyoza, light dumplings filled with vegetables or chicken. Vegetarian dishes are available, but skip the so-called "Korean-style" dishes.

4 Streatham St., WC1. ✆ 020/7323-9223. Reservations not accepted. Main courses £5.50–£11 ($8.80–$18). AE, MC, V. Mon–Sat noon–11pm; Sun 12:30–10pm. Tube: Tottenham Court Rd.

INEXPENSIVE

The Court Restaurant ⭐ *Value* CONTINENTAL   Nothing in London brings culture and cuisine together quite as much as this gem of a restaurant on the second floor of the British Museum with views opening onto Norman Foster's millennium development, the Great Court. The restaurant overlooks the famous round Reading Room and nestles close to the spectacular glass-and-steel roof. For museum buffs, it's the perfect venue for morning coffee, hot or cold lunches, afternoon tea, or a dinner. A special feature is a cultural date, one of the museum's lecture, supper, and private view packages costing £45 ($72) per person. You must reserve for this date, however.

The chef, Alain Allard, got his training at the prestigious Savoy Hotel, and he turns out a succulent menu of familiar favorites such as coq au vin (chicken casserole in red wine), sesame-seed coated Scottish salmon, or savory lamb and mint sausages with a "mash" of parsnips. You can watch the cooks as they prepare the market-fresh dishes for the day. The most blissful ending to a meal here is the chocolate truffle cake, which is really pure cocoa. The museum even serves its own beer, and it can compete with the product of any brewery.

The British Museum, Great Russell St., WC1. ✆ 020/7323-8978. Reservations required. Main courses £8–£13 ($13–$21); 2-course fixed-price menu £11 ($17). AE, MC, V. Mon–Wed 11am–5pm; Thurs–Sat 11am–9pm; Sun 11am–5pm. Tube: Holborn, Tottenham Court Rd., or Goodge St.

COVENT GARDEN & THE STRAND
EXPENSIVE

Rules ⭐ TRADITIONAL BRITISH   If you're looking for London's most quintessentially British restaurant, eat here. London's oldest restaurant was established in 1798 as an oyster bar; today, the antler-filled Edwardian dining rooms exude nostalgia. You can order such classic dishes as Irish or Scottish oysters, jugged hare, and mussels. Game dishes are offered from mid-August to February or March, including wild Scottish salmon; wild sea trout; wild Highland red deer; and game birds like grouse, snipe, partridge, pheasant, and woodcock. As a finale, the "great puddings" continue to impress.

35 Maiden Lane, WC2. ✆ 020/7836-5314. Reservations recommended. Main courses £15–£20 ($24–$32). AE, DC, MC, V. Daily noon–11:30pm. Tube: Covent Garden.

Simpson's-in-the-Strand ⭐⭐ *Kids* TRADITIONAL AND MODERN BRITISH   Simpson's is more of an institution than a restaurant. Long a family favorite with lots of large tables, it has been in business since 1828. As a result of a recent £2 million renovation, it's now better than ever with its Adam paneling, crystal, and army of grandly formal waiters (to whom nouvelle cuisine means anything after Henry VIII) who serve traditional British fare.

Most diners agree that Simpson's serves the best roasts in London, an array that includes roast sirloin of beef, roast saddle of mutton with red-currant jelly, roast Aylesbury duckling, and steak, kidney, and mushroom pie. (Remember to tip the tailcoated carver.) For a pudding, you might order the treacle roll and custard or Stilton with vintage port. Simpson's also serves traditional breakfasts. The most popular one, is "The Ten Deadly Sins": a plate of sausage; fried egg; streaky and back bacon; black pudding; lambs' kidneys; bubble and squeak; baked beans; lambs' liver; and fried bread, mushrooms, and tomatoes. That will certainly fortify you for the day.

100 The Strand (next to the Savoy Hotel), WC2. **℃ 020/7836-9112.** Reservations required. Main courses £25–£30 ($40–$48); fixed-price pretheater dinner £16.50–£21 ($26–$34); breakfast from £15.95 ($26). AE, DC, MC, V. Mon–Fri 7:15–10:30am; Mon–Sat 12:15–2:30pm and 5:30–10:45pm; Sun 6–9pm. Tube: Charing Cross or Embankment.

MODERATE

Porter's English Restaurant ★★ *Kids* TRADITIONAL BRITISH The 7th Earl of Bradford serves "real English food at affordable prices." He succeeds notably—and not just because Lady Bradford turned over her carefully guarded recipe for banana-and-ginger steamed pudding. This comfortable, two-story restaurant is family friendly, informal, and lively. Porter's specializes in classic English pies, including Old English fish pie; lamb and apricot; ham, leek, and cheese; and, of course, bangers and mash. Main courses are so generous—and accompanied by vegetables and side dishes—that you hardly need appetizers. They have also added grilled English fare to the menu, with sirloin and lamb steaks and pork chops. The puddings, including bread-and-butter pudding or steamed syrup sponge, are served hot or cold, with whipped cream or custard. The bar does quite a few exotic cocktails, as well as beers, wine, or English mead. A traditional English tea is also served from 2:30 to 5:30pm for £4.75 ($7.60) per person. Who knows? You may even bump into his Lordship.

17 Henrietta St., WC2. **℃ 020/7836-6466.** Reservations recommended. Main courses £8.95–£12.95 ($14–$21); fixed-price menu £19.95 ($32). AE, DC, MC, V. Mon–Sat noon–11:30pm; Sun noon–10:30pm. Tube: Covent Garden or Leicester Sq.

WESTMINSTER/VICTORIA
EXPENSIVE

Rhodes in the Square ★★★ MODERN BRITISH In this discreet residential district, super-chef and media darling Gary Rhodes strikes again. Rhodes is known for taking traditional British cookery and giving it daring twists and new flavors. You can count on delightful surprises from this major talent. The glitterati can be seen nightly in the apartment-block-cum-hotel, sampling Rhodes' offerings in an elegant high-ceilinged room done in midnight blue. You never know what will be available—maybe a filet of lamb with a turnip and prune gratin. Start, perhaps, with chicken liver parfait with foie gras, and go on to an open omelet topped with chunky bits of lobster with a Thermidor sauce and cheese crust. Glazed duck served with bitter orange jus is how this dish is supposed to taste. For dessert, make your selection from the British "pudding" plate that offers everything from a lemon meringue tart to a simple seared carpaccio of pineapple, oozing with flavor. Only fixed-price menus are served.

Dolphin Sq., Chichester St., SW1. **℃ 020/7798-6767.** Reservations required. Fixed-price meals £31 ($49) for 2 courses, £37 ($58) for 3 courses. AE, DC, MC, V. Tues–Fri noon–2:30pm; Tues–Sat 7–10pm. Tube: Pimlico.

MODERATE

Tate Gallery Restaurant ★★ *Value* MODERN BRITISH This restaurant is particularly attractive to wine fanciers. It offers what may be the best bargains for superior wines anywhere in Britain. Bordeaux and burgundies are in abundance, and the management keeps the markup between 40% and 65%, rather than the 100% to 200% added in most restaurants. In fact, the prices here are lower than they are in most wine shops. Wine begins at £15 ($24) per bottle, or £3.85 ($6.15) per glass. Oenophiles frequently come for lunch. The restaurant offers an English menu that changes about every month. Dishes might include pheasant casserole, pan-fried skate with black butter and capers, and a selection of vegetarian dishes. One critic found the staff and diners as traditional "as a Gainsborough landscape." Access to the restaurant is through the museum's main entrance on Millbank.

Millbank, SW1. © 020/7887-8877. Reservations recommended. Main courses £11–£18 ($17–$29); fixed-price 2-course lunch £17 ($27); fixed-price 3-course lunch £20 ($31). AE, DC, MC, V. Mon–Sat noon–3pm; Sun noon–4pm. Tube: Pimlico. Bus: 77 or 88.

INEXPENSIVE

Jenny Lo's Teahouse CANTONESE/SZECHUAN   London's noodle dives don't get much better than this. Before its decline, Ken Lo's Memories of China offered the best Chinese dining in London. The late Ken Lo, whose grandfather was the Chinese ambassador to the Court of St. James, made his reputation as a cookbook author. Jenny Lo is Ken's daughter, and her father taught her many of his culinary secrets. Belgravia matrons and young professionals come here for perfectly prepared, reasonably priced fare. Ken Lo cookbooks contribute to the dining room decor of black refectory tables set with paper napkins and chopsticks. Opt for such fare as a vermicelli rice noodle dish (a large plate of noodles topped with grilled chicken breast and Chinese mushrooms) or white noodles with minced pork. Rounding out the menu are stuffed Peking dumplings, chile-garnished spicy prawns, and wonton soup with slithery dumplings. The black-bean-seafood noodle dish is a delight, as is the chili beef soup.

14 Eccleston St., SW1 9LT. © 020/7259-0399. Reservations not accepted. Main courses £5.50–£8 ($8.80–$13). No credit cards. Mon–Fri 11:30am–3pm; Sat noon–3pm; Mon–Sat 6–10pm. Tube: Victoria Station.

THE CITY
MODERATE

Café Spice Namaste ★★ INDIAN   This is our favorite Indian restaurant in London, where the competition is stiff. It's cheerfully housed in a landmark Victorian hall near Tower Bridge, just east of the Tower of London. The Parsi chef, Cyrus Todiwala, is a former resident of Goa (a Portuguese territory absorbed by India long ago), where he learned many of his culinary secrets. He concentrates on southern and northern Indian dishes with a strong Portuguese influence. Chicken and lamb are prepared a number of ways, from mild to spicy-hot. As a novelty, Todiwala occasionally even offers a menu of emu dishes; when marinated, the meat is rich and spicy and evocative of lamb. Emu is not the only dining oddity here. Ever have ostrich gizzard kebab, alligator tikka, or minced moose, bison, and blue boar? Many patrons journey here just for the complex chicken curry known as *xacutti*. Lambs' livers and kidneys are also cooked in the tandoor. A weekly specialty menu complements the long list of regional dishes. The homemade chutneys alone are worth the trip; our favorite is made with kiwi. All dishes come with fresh vegetables and Indian bread. With its exotic ingredients, often time-consuming preparation, impeccable service, warm hospitality, and spicy but subtle flavors, this is no Indian dive.

16 Prescot St., E1. © 020/7488-9242. Reservations required. Main courses £12–£15 ($19–$24). AE, DC, MC, V. Mon–Fri noon–3pm and 6:15–10:30pm; Sat 6:30–10:15pm. Tube: Tower Hill.

Club Gascon ★★ *Finds* FRENCH   This slice of Southwestern France serves such tasty treats as foie gras, Armagnac, and duck confit. Chef Pascal Aussignac is all the rage in London, ever since he opened his bistro next to the meat market in Smithfield. He dedicates his bistro to his favorite ingredient: foie gras. Foie gras appears in at least nine different incarnations on the menu, and most of the first-class ingredients are imported from France. His menu is uniquely divided into these categories—"The Salt Route," "Ocean," and "Kitchen Garden." The best way to dine here is to arrive in a party of four or five and share the small dishes, each harmoniously balanced and full of flavor. Each dish is accompanied by a carefully selected glass of wine. After a foie gras pig-out, proceed to such main courses as a heavenly quail served with pear and rosemary honey. A cassoulet of morels and truffles transforms a plain but perfectly cooked steak. To finish an absolutely elegant repast—dare we call it too rich—there is a selection of "puds," as the British say, ranging from strawberries with basil sorbet to a confit of rhubarb and sherry vinegar. If those don't interest you, opt for a moist almond tart with a biting shot of granny smith juice.

57 West Smithfield, EC1. ℂ 020/7796-0600. Reservations required. Fixed-price 5-course menu £35 ($56); main courses £7–£16 ($11–$26). AE, MC, V. Mon–Fri noon–2pm; Mon–Thurs 7–10pm; Sat 7–10:30pm. Tube: Barbican.

Poons in the City ★★ CHINESE   Since 1992, Poons has operated this branch in The City, less than a 5-minute walk from the Tower of London. The restaurant is modeled on the Luk Yew Tree House in Hong Kong. Main courses feature crispy aromatic duck, prawns with cashew nuts, and barbecued pork. Poons's famous *lap yuk soom* (like Cantonese tacos) includes finely chopped wind-dried bacon. Special dishes can be ordered on 24-hour notice. At the end of the L-shaped restaurant is an 80-seat fast-food area and take-out counter that's accessible from Mark Lane. The menu changes every 2 weeks.

2 Minster Pavement, Minster Court, Mincing Lane, EC3. ℂ 020/7626-0126. Reservations recommended for lunch. Fixed-price lunch and dinner £15–£31 ($24–$50); a la carte main courses £6–£10 ($9.60–$16); fast-food main dishes £5.50–£7 ($8.80–$11). AE, DC, MC, V. Mon–Fri noon–10:30pm. Tube: Tower Hill or Monument.

INEXPENSIVE

Ye Olde Cheshire Cheese *Kids* BRITISH   The foundation of this carefully preserved building was laid in the 13th century, and it holds the most famous of the old City chophouses and pubs. Established in 1667, it claims to be the spot where Dr. Samuel Johnson (who lived nearby) entertained admirers with his acerbic wit. Charles Dickens and other literary lions also patronized the place. Later, many of the ink-stained journalists and scandalmongers of 19th- and early-20th-century Fleet Street made it their watering hole. You'll find six bars and two dining rooms here. The house specialties include "Ye Famous Pudding" (steak, kidney, mushrooms, and game) and Scottish roast beef with Yorkshire pudding and horseradish sauce. Sandwiches, salads, and standby favorites such as steak and kidney pie are also available, as are dishes such as Dover sole. The Cheshire is the best and safest venue to introduce your children to a British pub.

Wine Office Court, 145 Fleet St., EC4. ℂ 020/7353-6170. Main courses £7.50–£10 ($12–$16). AE, DC, MC, V. Meals Mon–Fri noon–10pm; Sat noon–2:30pm and 6–10pm; Sun noon–2:30pm. Drinks and bar snacks daily 11:30am–11pm. Tube: St. Paul's or Blackfriars.

SOUTH BANK
MODERATE

Cantina Vinopolis ★ *Finds* MEDITERRANEAN   Not far from the re-created Globe Theatre of Shakespeare's heyday, this place has been called a "Walk-Through

Wine Atlas." In the revitalized Bankside area, south of the Thames near Southwark Cathedral, this bricked, walled, and high-vaulted brasserie was converted from long abandoned Victorian railway arches. Inside you can visit both the Vinopolis Wine Gallery and the Cantina Restaurant. Although many come here just to drink the wine, the food is prepared with quality ingredients (very fresh), and the menu is sensibly priced. Start with a bit of heaven like the pumpkin and Parmesan soup with a lime-flavored crème fraîche. Dishes are full of flavor and never overcooked. Squid fried in a crispy batter won us over along with its side dish, wasabi slaw. A rump of lamb was tender and perfectly flavored and served with a polenta cake. Many of the dishes have the good country taste of a trattoria you'd find in the countryside of Southern Italy. Naturally, the wine list is the biggest in the U.K.

1 Bank End, London Bridge, SE1. © 020/7940-8333. Reservations required. Main courses £14–£16 ($22–$26). MC, V. Mon–Sat noon–3pm and 6–10:45pm; Sun noon–3:45pm. Tube: London Bridge.

KNIGHTSBRIDGE
VERY EXPENSIVE

Zafferano ★★ ITALIAN   There's something honest and satisfying about this restaurant, where decor consists of little more than ochre-colored walls, immaculate linens, and a bevy of diligent staff members. A quick review of past clients includes Margaret Thatcher, Richard Gere, Princess Margaret, and Eric Clapton. The modernized interpretation of Italian cuisine features such dishes as ravioli of pheasant with black truffles, wild pigeon with garlic purée, sea bream with spinach and balsamic vinegar, and monkfish with almonds. Joan Collins claimed that the chefs produce culinary fireworks but found the bright lighting far too harsh. The owners pride themselves on one of the most esoteric and well-rounded collections of Italian wine in London: You'll find as many as 20 different vintages each of Brunello and Barolos and about a dozen vintages of Sassecaia.

15 Lowndes St., SW1. © 020/7235-5800. Reservations required. Set menus £29–£35 ($46–$56). AE, MC, V. Daily noon–2:30pm and 7–11pm. Tube: Knightsbridge.

INEXPENSIVE

Le Metro INTERNATIONAL   Located just around the corner from Harrods, Le Metro draws a fashionable crowd to its basement precincts. The place serves good, solid, reliable food prepared with flair. The menu changes frequently, but try the chargrilled salmon with pesto, or the confit of duck with butterbeans, garlic, and shallots if you can. You can order special wines by the glass.

28 Basil St., SW3. © 020/7589-6286. Main courses £7–£11 ($11–$18). AE, DC, MC, V. Mon–Sat 7:30am–11pm. Tube: Knightsbridge.

CHELSEA
VERY EXPENSIVE

Aubergine ★★ FRENCH   "Eggplant" is luring savvy diners down to the lower reaches of Chelsea where new chef Williams Drabble takes over from where the renowned Gordon Ramsay left off. Drabble, who earned his first Michelin star in 1998, has remained true to the style and ambience of this famous establishment. Although popular with celebrities, the restaurant remains unpretentious and refuses to pander to the whims of the rich and famous. (Madonna was once refused a late-night booking!)

Every dish is satisfyingly flavorsome, from warm salad of truffled vegetables with asparagus purée to roasted monkfish served with crushed new potatoes, roasted leeks, and red-wine sauce. Starters continue to charm and delight palates, ranging from ravioli of crab with mussels, chile, ginger, and coriander nage, to terrine of foie gras with confit of duck and pears poached in port. Also resting on your Villeroy & Boch aubergine plate might be mallard with a celeriac fondant or assiette of lamb with a thyme-scented jus. Another stunning main course is a tranche of sea bass with bouillabaisse potatoes. A new dish likely to catch your eye is roasted veal sweetbreads with caramelized onion purée and a casserole of flap mushrooms. There are only 14 tables, so bookings are imperative.

11 Park Walk, SW10. ✆ 020/7352-3449. Reservations required and accepted up to 4 weeks in advance. 3-course lunch £32 ($51); fixed-price 3-course dinner £50 ($80); menu gourmand £70 ($112). AE, DC, MC, V. Mon–Fri noon–2:15pm; Mon–Sat 7–10:30pm. Tube: South Kensington.

Front Page THAI   Front Page is favored by young professionals who like the atmosphere of wood paneling, wooden tables, and pews and benches. On cold nights, an open fire burns. The pub stands in a residential section of Chelsea and is a good place to go for a drink and some Thai pub grub. Check the chalkboard for the daily specials, which might include hot chicken salad and fish cakes.

35 Old Church St., SW3. ✆ 020/7352-0648. Main courses £6.75–£12 ($11–$19). AE, DC, DISC, MC, V. Restaurant Mon–Fri noon–2:30pm; Sat–Sun 12:30–3pm; Mon–Sat 7–11pm; Sun 7–10:30pm. Pub Mon–Sat 11am–11pm; Sun noon–10:30pm. Tube: Sloane Sq.

KENSINGTON & SOUTH KENSINGTON
EXPENSIVE
Launceston Place ☆ MODERN BRITISH   Launceston Place is in an almost village-like neighborhood where many Londoners would like to live, if only they could afford it. This stylish restaurant lies within a series of uncluttered Victorian parlors, the largest of which is illuminated by a skylight. Each room contains a collection of Victorian-era oils and watercolors, as well as contemporary paintings. The restaurant has been known for its new British cuisine since 1986. The menu changes every 6 weeks, but you're likely to be served such appetizers as smoked salmon with horseradish crème fraîche, goat cheese soufflé, or seared foie gras with lentils and vanilla dressing. For a main dish, perhaps it'll be roast partridge with bacon, onions, and parsnip mash, or grilled sea bass with tomato and basil cream.

1A Launceston Place, W8. ✆ 020/7937-6912. Reservations required. Main courses £14–£18 ($22–$29); fixed-price menu for lunch and early dinner until 8pm £16 ($25) for 2 courses, £19 ($30) for 3 courses. AE, DC, MC, V. Mon–Thurs and Sun noon–2:30pm; daily 7-11:30pm. Tube: Gloucester Rd. or High St. Kensington.

MODERATE
Blue Elephant ☆ THAI   This is the counterpart of the famous L'Eléphant Bleu restaurant in Brussels. Located in a converted factory building in West Brompton, the Blue Elephant has been all the rage since 1986. It remains the leading Thai restaurant in London, where the competition seems to grow daily. In an almost magical garden setting of tropical foliage, diners are treated to an array of MSG-free Thai dishes. You can begin with a "Floating Market" (shellfish in clear broth, flavored with chile paste and lemon grass), then go on to a splendid selection of main courses, for which many of the ingredients have been flown in from Thailand. We recommend the roasted duck curry served in a clay cooking pot.

3–6 Fulham Broadway, SW6. ✆ 020/7385-6595. Reservations required. Main courses £9–£18 ($14–$29); Royal Thai banquet £33–£37 ($53–$59); Sun buffet £22 ($35). AE, DC, MC, V. Mon–Fri and Sun noon–2:30pm; daily 7pm–midnight. Tube: Fulham Broadway.

INEXPENSIVE

Admiral Codrington ⭐ *Finds* ENGLISH/CONTINENTAL   Once a lowly pub, this stylish bar and restaurant is now all the rage. The exterior has been maintained, but the old "Cod," as it is affectionately known, has emerged to offer plush dining with a revitalized decor by Nina Campbell and a glass roof that rolls back on sunny days. The bartenders still offer a traditional pint, but the sophisticated menu features such delectable fare as linguine with zucchini, crab, and chile peppers, or rib-eye steak with slow-roasted tomatoes. Opt for the grilled breast of chicken salad with bean sprouts, apple, or cashews, or the perfectly grilled tuna with a couscous salad and eggplant "caviar."

17 Mossop St., SW3. ⏱ 020/7581-0005. Reservations recommended. Main courses £10–£15 ($16–$24). MC, V. Mon–Sat noon–11:30pm; Sun noon–11pm. Tube: South Kensington.

MARYLEBONE
EXPENSIVE

Assaggi ⭐⭐ *Finds* ITALIAN   Some of London's finest Italian cuisine is served in this room above a pub. This place is a real discovery, and completely unpretentious. The relatively simple menu highlights the creative, outstanding cookery. All the ingredients are fresh and deftly handled by a skilled kitchen staff. Simplicity and flavor reign throughout. The appetizers, such as smoked swordfish salad or beef carpaccio, are so truly sublime that you'll want to make a meal entirely of them. At least three freshly made pastas are featured nightly. The tortellini (pocket-shaped noodles filled with cheese) with pork and a zesty tomato sauce is especially delicious. For a main course, opt for such delights as the thick, juicy, tender grilled veal, flavored with fresh rosemary; or the grilled sea bass with braised fennel. Another savory choice is a plate of lamb cutlets (without any fat) with eggplant and a raisin salad. The chocolate truffle cake is the finest you'll find this side of northern Italy.

39 Chepstow Place, W2. ⏱ 020/7792-5501. Reservations required (as far in advance as possible). Main courses £16–£20 ($26–$32). AE, DC, MC, V. Mon–Fri 12:30–2:30pm and 7:30–11pm; Sat 1–11pm. Closed 2 weeks at Christmas. Tube: Notting Hill Gate.

MODERATE

Bush Bar & Grill ⭐ *Finds* MODERN BRITISH/FRENCH   Hip, lighthearted, and sought after by the quasi-celebrities of London's world of media and entertainment, this bar and brasserie was established in 2000 by the owners of two of the city's most desirable private clubs, Woody's and The Groucho Club. Both of these are membership-only venues in other parts of town. At the tables near you at this spinoff restaurant (not a members-only spot), you're likely to see members of those clubs plus celebs like Jerry Hall, Kate Moss, cookbook author Nigella Lawson, pop singer Kylie Minogue, and writers from such publications as *British Vogue* and *Tatler*. The setting was originally conceived as a milk-bottling plant, but since a team of decorators revamped it, it evokes an arts-conscious Manhattan bistro with a neo-industrial decor, exposed air ducts, and a busy kitchen that's open to view. Chefs here place an emphasis on organic produce, preparing dishes that include French onion soup, marinated mussels, rémoulade of celeriac, roasted rib of beef served with Béarnaise and french fries and prepared only for two diners sharing the meal, and roasted duck with mashed potatoes and black peppercorn sauce. Grilled squid, braised lamb shank, well-seasoned fish cakes, and a smoked haddock salad are some of the other delectable offerings.

45 Goldhawk Rd. ⏱ 020/8746-2111. Reservations required. Main courses £9.50–£17 ($15–$27); fixed-price menus, served lunch (Mon–Fri) and at dinner till 7:30pm £11–£12 ($17–$19); fixed-price lunch menu £11–£15 ($20–$24) (Sat and Sun). AE, MC, V. Mon–Sat noon–3pm and 7–10:30pm; Sun noon–4pm and 7-10:30pm. Tube: Goldhawk Road.

NOTTING HILL GATE
EXPENSIVE

Pharmacy Restaurant and Bar ✰ EUROPEAN   The theme of this medical-chic restaurant evokes all sorts of drug-related venues, from a harmless small-town pharmacy to a drug lord's secret stash of mind-altering pills. This ambiguity is appreciated by the arts-conscious crowd that flocks here, partly because they're interested in what Damien Hirst (*enfant terrible* of London's art world) has created, and partly because the place can be a lot of fun. You'll enter the street-level bar, where a drink menu lists lots of highly palatable martinis as well as a somewhat icky concoction known as a Cough Syrup (cherry liqueur, honey, and vodka that's shaken, not stirred, over ice). Bottles of pills; bar stools with seats shaped like aspirins; and painted representations of fire, water, air, and earth decorate the bar area. Upstairs in the restaurant, the pharmaceutical theme is less pronounced but subtly omnipresent. Menu items include trendy but comforting food items such as carpaccio of whitefish, chargrilled lamb, pan-fried cod in red wine with Jerusalem artichokes and shallots, and roast saddle of hare in pear sauce.

150 Notting Hill Gate, W11. ✆ 020/7221-2442. Reservations required Fri–Sat, strongly recommended other nights. Main courses £14–£20 ($22–$32). AE, DISC, MC, V. Daily noon–3pm and 7–10:30pm. Tube: Notting Hill Gate.

MODERATE

The Cow ✰ *Finds* MODERN BRITISH   You don't have to be a young fashion victim to enjoy the superb cuisine served here (although many of the diners are). Tom Conran (son of entrepreneur Sir Terence Conran) holds forth in this increasingly hip Notting Hill watering hole. It looks like an Irish pub, but the accents you'll hear are trustafarian rather than street-smart Dublin. With a pint of Fuller's or London Pride, you can linger over the modern European menu, which changes daily but is likely to include ox tongue poached in milk; mussels in curry and cream; or a mixed grill of lamb chops, calves' liver, and sweetbreads. The seafood selections are delectable. "The Cow Special"—a half-dozen Irish rock oysters with a pint of Guinness or a glass of wine for £10 ($16)—is the star of the show. A raw bar downstairs serves other fresh seafood choices. To finish, skip the filtered coffee served upstairs (it's wretched), and opt for an espresso downstairs.

89 Westbourne Park Rd., W2. ✆ 020/7221-0021. Reservations required. Main courses £14–£20 ($22–$32). MC, V. Mon–Sat 6–11pm; Sun 12:30–4pm (brunch) and 6:30–10:30pm; bar daily noon–midnight. Tube: Westbourne Grove.

INEXPENSIVE

Prince Bonaparte INTERNATIONAL   This offbeat restaurant serves great pub grub in what used to be a grungy boozer before Notting Hill Gate became fashionable. Now pretty young things show up, spilling onto the sidewalk when the evenings are warm. The pub is filled with mismatched furniture from schools and churches; and CDs of jazz and lazy blues fill the air, competing with the babble. It may seem at first that the staff doesn't have its act together, but once the food arrives, you won't care—the dishes served here are very good. The menu roams the world for inspiration: Moroccan chicken with couscous is as good or better than any you'll find in Marrakesh, and the seafood risotto is delicious. Roast lamb, tender and juicy, appears on the traditional Sunday menu. We recommend the London Pride or Grolsch to wash it all down.

80 Chepstow Rd., W2. ✆ 020/7313-9491. Reservations required. Main courses £8.50–£13 ($14–$21). AE, MC, V. Mon–Sat noon–11pm; Sun 12:30–10:30pm. Tube: Notting Hill Gate or Westbourne Park.

5 Afternoon Tea

Everyone should indulge in a formal afternoon tea at least once while in London. This relaxing, drawn-out, civilized affair usually consists of three courses, all elegantly served on delicate china: first, dainty finger sandwiches (with the crusts cut off, of course); then fresh-baked scones served with jam and deliciously decadent clotted cream (also known as Devonshire cream); and lastly, an array of bite-size sweets. All the while, an indulgent server keeps the pot of your choice fresh at hand. Sometimes ports or aperitif are on offer for your final course. A quintessential British experience; here are a few of our favorite places to indulge.

MAYFAIR

Claridge's ⭐ Claridge's teatime rituals have managed to persevere through the years with as much pomp and circumstance as the British Empire itself. The experience is never stuffy, though; you'll feel very welcome. Tea is served in the Reading Room. A portrait of Lady Claridge gazes from above as your choice from 17 kinds of tea is served ever so politely. The courses are served consecutively, including finger sandwiches with cheese savories, apple and raisin scones, and yummy pastries.

Brook St., W1. ℂ 020/7629-8860. Reservations recommended. Jacket and tie required for men after 6pm. High tea Mon–Fri £26 ($42), Sat–Sun £35 ($56) including champagne. AE, DC, MC, V. Daily 3–5:30pm. Tube: Bond St.

The Palm Court This is one of the great London favorites for tea. Restored to its former charm, the lounge has an atmosphere straight from 1927, with a domed yellow-and-white glass ceiling, *torchères,* and palms in Compton stoneware *jardinières.* A delightful afternoon repast that includes a long list of different teas is served daily against the background of live harp music.

In the Sheraton Park Lane Hotel, Piccadilly, W1. ℂ 020/7290-7328. Reservations recommended. Afternoon tea £19 ($30), with a glass of Park Lane champagne £25 ($40). AE, DC, MC, V. Daily 3–6pm. Tube: Hyde Park Corner or Green Park.

ST. JAMES'S

Ritz Palm Court ⭐⭐⭐ This is the most fashionable place in London to order afternoon tea—and the hardest to get into without reserving way in advance. The spectacular setting is straight out of *The Great Gatsby,* complete with marble steps and columns, and a baroque fountain. You can choose from a long list of teas served with delectable sandwiches and luscious pastries.

In The Ritz Hotel, Piccadilly, W1. ℂ 020/7493-8181. Reservations required at least 8 weeks in advance. Jeans and sneakers not accepted. Jacket and tie required for men. Afternoon tea £29 ($46). AE, DC, MC, V. 3 seatings daily at 1:30, 3:30 and 5:30pm. Tube: Green Park.

St. James Restaurant and The Fountain Restaurant This pair of tea salons functions as a culinary showplace for London's most prestigious grocery store, Fortnum & Mason. The more formal of the two, the St. James, on the store's fourth floor, is a pale green and beige homage to formal Edwardian taste. More rapid and less formal is The Fountain Restaurant, on the street level, where a sense of tradition and manners is very much a part of the dining experience, but in a less opulent setting. There is no longer an "official" afternoon tea at The Fountain, but you can order pots of tea plus food from an a la carte menu that includes sandwiches, scones and the like (£4.50–£12/$7.20–$19).

In Fortnum & Mason, 181 Piccadilly, W1. ℂ 020/7734-8040. St. James afternoon tea £19 ($30); high tea £21 ($33). The Fountain: a la carte menu £4.50-£12 ($7.20-$19). AE, DC, MC, V. St. James, Mon–Sat 3–5:30pm; The Fountain, Mon–Sat 3–6pm. Tube: Piccadilly Circus.

KNIGHTSBRIDGE

The Georgian Restaurant   For as long as anyone can remember, tea at Harrods has been a distinctive feature of Europe's most famous department store. A flood of visitors is gracefully herded into a high-volume but elegant room. Many come here for the ritual of the tea service, as staff members haul silver pots and trolleys laden with pastries and sandwiches through the cavernous dining hall. Most exotic is Betigala tea, a rare blend from China, similar to Lapsang Souchong.

On the 4th floor of Harrods, 87–135 Brompton Rd., SW1. ℂ 020/7225-6800. High tea £19 ($30) or £26 ($41) with Harrods champagne per person. AE, DC, MC, V. Mon–Sat 3:15–5:30pm (last order). Tube: Knightsbridge.

KENSINGTON

The Orangery ★ *Finds*   In its way, the Orangery is the most amazing place for afternoon tea in the world. Set 50 yards north of Kensington Palace, it occupies a long narrow garden pavilion built in 1704 by Queen Anne. In homage to her original intentions, rows of potted orange trees bask in sunlight from soaring windows, and tea is served amid Corinthian columns, ruddy-colored bricks, and a pair of Grinling Gibbons woodcarvings. There are even some urns and statuary that the royal family imported from Windsor Castle. The menu includes soups and sandwiches, with a salad and a portion of upscale potato chips known as kettle chips. The array of different teas is served with high style, accompanied by fresh scones with clotted cream and jam, and Belgian chocolate cake.

In the gardens of Kensington Palace, W8. ℂ 020/7376-0239. Reservations not accepted. Pot of tea only £1.75–£1.95 ($2.80–$3.10); summer cakes and puddings £2.95–£3.95 ($4.70–$6.30); sandwiches £5.95–£8.95 ($9.50–$14). MC, V. Daily 10am–6pm. Tube: High St. Kensington or Queensway.

5

Exploring London

London is more eclectic and electric than it's been in years. Some even think it's surpassed New York for sheer energy, outrageous fashion, trendy restaurants, and a nightlife that's second to none.

But we don't want to mislead. Although London is more open and dynamic than it's been since 1969, it's not one giant house party. There are problems here, as elsewhere, that all the trendy restaurants and pricey boutiques in the world cannot obliterate. The gulf between rich and poor continues to widen, and violent crime, once relatively rare, is on the rise.

Although the cool youth culture is grabbing headlines, it's not all there is to London these days. What makes the city so fascinating is its cultural diversity. It seems that half the world is flocking there, not just from the far-flung former colonies of the once great British empire, but also from Algeria, Argentina, China, and Senegal. These recent transplants are transforming a city once maligned as a drab, stuffy metropolis with their talent and new ideas. In the London of today, where everything's changing, only the queen appears the same. (After she's gone, even the House of Windsor may be in for a shake-up.)

In this chapter, we can explore only a fraction of what's exciting in London. We went in search of what's causing the hottest buzz in shopping and nightlife, but we also provide plenty of detail about London's time-tested treasures: ancient monuments, literary shrines, walking tours, Parliament debates, royal castles, waxworks, palaces, cathedrals, and royal parks.

SUGGESTED ITINERARIES

For the first-time visitor, the question is never what to do, but what to do *first*.

If You Have 1 Day

No first-time visitor should leave London without a visit to **Westminster Abbey,** with Poet's Corner and its royal tombs. Also see the **Changing of the Guard** at Buckingham Palace if it's on, and walk over to **10 Downing Street,** home of the prime minister. After lunch, walk over to see **Big Ben** and the **Houses of Parliament.** Dine at one of the little restaurants in **Covent Garden,** such as Porter's, owned by the earl of Bradford. Try one of its classic English pies (maybe lamb and apricot). For a pretheater drink,

head over to the ultimate Victorian pub, the Red Lion in Mayfair; it's the kind of place Oscar Wilde might have chosen for a brandy. If you're so inclined, head for a play—musical or drama—in the West End. London has the best English-language theater in the world, and the offerings are even greater than that of New York.

If You Have 2 Days

Day 1 Spend Day 1 as above.

Day 2 Devote a good part of the second day exploring the **British Museum,** one of the best museums in the world. Spend the afternoon visiting the **Tower of London** and seeing the **Crown Jewels** (expect slow-moving lines). Later, go to a really local place for dinner, such as Shepherd's in Westminster, where you'll be able to dine alongside MPs from the House of Commons. Perhaps you'll catch another play that evening or head for one of London's numerous nightclubs to dance the night away.

If You Have 3 Days

Days 1–2 Spend Days 1 and 2 as above.

Day 3 In the morning, visit the masterworks in the **National Gallery.** For a change of pace in the afternoon, head to **Madame Tussaud's** waxworks if you have kids in tow. Take a walking tour of **St. James's.** In the evening, take in a **West End** play or a performance at the **National Theatre** or Queen Elizabeth Hall at South Bank Centre.

If You Have 4 or 5 Days

Days 1–3 Spend Days 1, 2, and 3 as above.

Day 4 In the morning, head for **The City,** London's financial district.

Your major sightseeing goal here will be **St. Paul's Cathedral,** designed by Sir Christopher Wren. Take a walking tour of The City. In the afternoon, head for **King's Road** in Chelsea for some boutique hopping and to dine at one of Chelsea's many restaurants. Later that evening, take in a show at a **Soho** nightclub, such as Ronnie Scott's, which hosts some of the city's best jazz.

Day 5 Explore the **Victoria and Albert Museum** in the morning, then go to the **Tate Britain Gallery** for a look at some of its many masterpieces; have lunch at its restaurant, which offers some of the best values on wine in Britain. For a historic glimpse of the dark days of World War II, visit the **Cabinet War Rooms** at Clive Steps, where Churchill directed British operations in the war against the Nazis. Spend the evening at the theater.

Take in as many West End shows as you can manage during your evenings in London.

1 The Top Attractions

One of Britain's greatest private art collections, **The Saatchi Gallery** should have opened at County Hall by the time you read this. On London's South Bank, the new gallery stands right between the sites of the two Tate galleries: Tate Modern and Tate Britain. Devoted to modern, often very controversial and headline-grabbing art, the gallery focuses on the work of younger British artists, such as Damien Hirst. Ex-adman Charles Saatchi has amassed one of the largest independent collections of modern British and international art on the world.

Note: As a rule, and unless otherwise stated on the listings below, children's prices at London attractions apply to those age 16 and under. You must be 60 years of age or older to obtain available senior discounts at some attractions. For students to get available discounted admissions they must have a valid student ID card.

Tower of London ★★★ *Kids* This ancient fortress continues to pack in the crowds, largely because of its macabre associations with all the legendary figures who were imprisoned and/or executed here. There are more spooks to the square foot than in any other building in the whole of haunted Britain. Even today, centuries after the last head rolled on Tower Hill, a shivery atmosphere of impending doom lingers over the mighty walls. Plan on spending a lot of time here.

London Sights

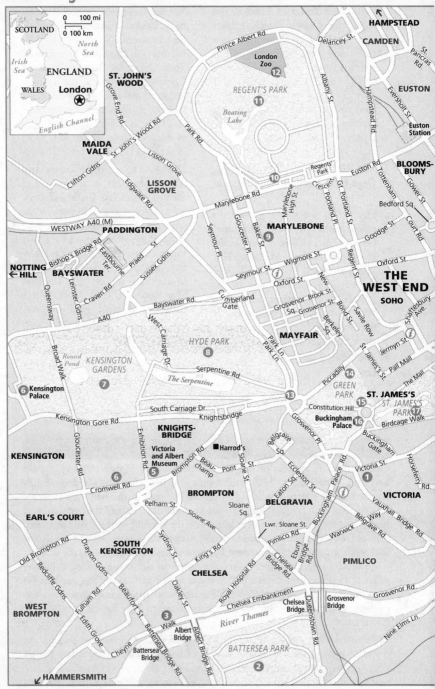

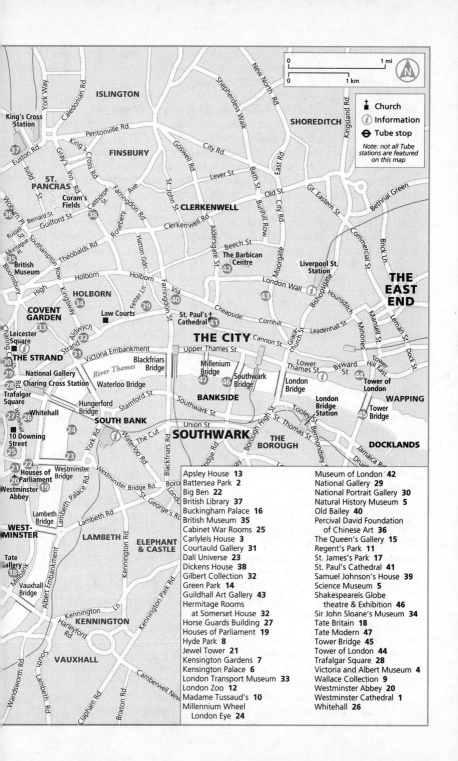

Church †
Information ⓘ
Tube stop ⊖
Note: not all Tube stations are featured on this map

King's Cross Station
ISLINGTON
SHOREDITCH
FINSBURY
ST. PANCRAS
Coram's Fields
CLERKENWELL
British Museum
The Barbican Centre 42
Liverpool St. Station
THE EAST END
HOLBORN
COVENT GARDEN
Law Courts
Sir John Sloane's Museum 34
Samuel Johnson's House 39
St. Paul's Cathedral 41
Guildhall Art Gallery 43
Leicester Square
THE STRAND
National Gallery
Charing Cross Station
Trafalgar Square
Whitehall
10 Downing Street
Waterloo Bridge
Hungerford Bridge
SOUTH BANK
THE CITY
Millenium Bridge 47
Southwark Bridge 46
BANKSIDE
London Bridge
London Bridge Station
WAPPING
Tower of London 44
Tower Bridge 45
DOCKLANDS
SOUTHWARK
THE BOROUGH
Houses of Parliament
Westminster Bridge
Westminster Abbey
WEST-MINSTER
Tate Gallery
Vauxhall Bridge
LAMBETH
ELEPHANT & CASTLE
KENNINGTON
VAUXHALL

Apsley House **13**
Battersea Park **2**
Big Ben **22**
British Library **37**
Buckingham Palace **16**
British Museum **35**
Cabinet War Rooms **25**
Carlyleís House **3**
Courtauld Gallery **31**
Dalí Universe **23**
Dickens House **38**
Gilbert Collection **32**
Green Park **14**
Guildhall Art Gallery **43**
Hermitage Rooms
  at Somerset House **32**
Horse Guards Building **27**
Houses of Parliament **19**
Hyde Park **8**
Jewel Tower **21**
Kensington Gardens **7**
Kensington Palace **6**
London Transport Museum **33**
London Zoo **12**
Madame Tussaud's **10**
Millennium Wheel
  London Eye **24**

Museum of London **42**
National Gallery **29**
National Portrait Gallery **30**
Natural History Museum **5**
Old Bailey **40**
Percival David Foundation
  of Chinese Art **36**
The Queen's Gallery **15**
Regent's Park **11**
St. James's Park **17**
St. Paul's Cathedral **41**
Samuel Johnson's House **39**
Science Museum **5**
Shakespeareís Globe
  theatre & Exhibition **46**
Sir John Sloane's Museum **34**
Tate Britain **18**
Tate Modern **47**
Tower Bridge **45**
Tower of London **44**
Trafalgar Square **28**
Victoria and Albert Museum **4**
Wallace Collection **9**
Westminster Abbey **20**
Westminster Cathedral **1**
Whitehall **26**

The tower is actually an intricately patterned compound of structures built over the ages for varying purposes, mostly as expressions of royal power. The oldest is the **White Tower,** begun by William the Conqueror in 1078 to keep London's native Saxon population in check. Later rulers added other towers, more walls, and fortified gates, until the building became something like a small town within a city. Until the reign of James I, the tower was also one of the royal residences. But above all, it was a prison for distinguished captives.

Every stone of the tower tells a story—usually a gory one. In the **Bloody Tower,** according to Shakespeare, the two little princes (the sons of Edward IV) were murdered by henchmen of Richard III. Attempts have been made by some historians to clear Richard's name, but he remains the chief suspect, and his deed caused him to lose the "hearts of the people" according to the *Chronicles of London* at the time.

Sir Walter Raleigh spent 13 years before his date with the executioner in Bloody Tower. On the walls of the **Beauchamp Tower,** you can still read the last messages scratched by despairing prisoners. Through **Traitors' Gate** passed such ill-fated, romantic figures as Robert Devereux, the second earl of Essex, a favorite of Elizabeth I. A plaque marks the eerie place at **Tower Green** where two wives of Henry VIII, Anne Boleyn and Catherine Howard, Sir Thomas More, and the 9-day queen, Lady Jane Grey, all lost their lives.

In the latest development here, the presumed prison cell of Sir Thomas More opened to the public in 2000. More left this cell in 1535 to face his executioner after he'd fallen out with Henry VIII over the monarch's desire to divorce Catherine of Aragon, the first of his six wives. In the lower part of the Bell Tower, More is believed to have lived here in this whitewashed cell during the last 14 months of his life, although some historians doubt this claim.

The tower, besides being a royal palace, fortress, and prison, was also an armory, a treasury, a menagerie, and in 1675 an astronomical observatory. Reopened in 1999, the White Tower holds the **Armouries,** which date from the reign of Henry VIII, as well as a display of instruments of torture and execution that recall some of the most ghastly moments in the tower's history. In the **Jewel House,** you'll find the tower's greatest attraction, the **Crown Jewels.** Here, some of the world's most precious stones are set into robes, swords, scepters, and crowns. The Imperial State Crown is the most famous crown on earth; made for Queen Victoria in 1837, it's worn today by Queen Elizabeth when she opens Parliament. Studded with some 3,000 jewels (mostly diamonds), it includes the Black Prince's Ruby, worn by Henry V at Agincourt. You'll have to stand in long lines to catch just a glimpse of the jewels as you and hundreds of others scroll by on moving sidewalks, but the wait is worth it.

A palace once inhabited by King Edward I in the late 1200s stands above Traitors' Gate. It's the only surviving medieval palace in Britain. Guides are dressed in period costumes. Reproductions of furniture and fittings, including Edward's throne, evoke the era, along with burning incense and candles.

Oh, yes—don't forget to look for the ravens. Six of them (plus two spares) are all registered as official tower residents. According to a legend, the Tower of London will stand as long as those black, ominous birds remain, so to be on the safe side, one of the wings of each raven is clipped.

One-hour guided tours of the entire compound are given by the Yeoman Warders (also known as "Beefeaters") every ½-hour, starting at 9:30am from the Middle Tower near the main entrance. The last guided walk starts about 3:30pm in summer, 2:30pm in winter, weather permitting.

You can attend the nightly **Ceremony of the Keys,** the ceremonial locking-up of the tower by the Yeoman Warders. For free tickets, write to the Ceremony of the Keys, Waterloo Block, Tower of London, London EC3N 4AB, and request a specific date, but also list alternative dates. At least 6 weeks' notice is required. All requests must be accompanied by a stamped, self-addressed envelope (British stamps only) or two International Reply Coupons. With ticket in hand, you'll be admitted by a Yeoman Warder at 9:35pm. Frankly, we think it's not worth the trouble to go through to see this rather cheesy ceremony, but we know some diehard Anglophiles who disagree with us.

Insider tip: The secret of avoiding the tower's notoriously long lines is to buy your ticket in a kiosk inside the Tube station before emerging above ground. Even so, choose a day other than Sunday if you can—crowds are at their worst then.

Tower Hill, EC3. © 020/7709-0765. www.hrp.org.uk. Admission £11.50 ($18) adults, £8.75 ($14) students and seniors, £7.50 ($12) children, free for children under 5, £34 ($54) family ticket for 5 (but no more than 2 adults). Mar–Oct Mon–Sat 9am–5pm, Sun 10am–5pm; Nov–Feb Tues–Sat 9am–4pm, Sun and Mon 10am–4pm. Tube: Tower Hill.

Westminster Abbey ★★★ With its square twin towers and superb archways, this Early English Gothic abbey is one of the greatest examples of ecclesiastical architecture on earth. But it's far more than that: It's the shrine of a nation, the symbol of everything Britain has stood for and stands for, the place in which most of its rulers were crowned and where many lie buried.

Nearly every figure in English history has left his or her mark on Westminster Abbey. Edward the Confessor founded the Benedictine abbey in 1065 on this spot, overlooking Parliament Square. The first English king crowned in the abbey was Harold in 1066. The man who defeated him at the Battle of Hastings the next year, William the Conqueror, was also crowned here. The coronation tradition has continued to the present day, broken only twice (by Edward V and Edward VIII). The essentially Early English Gothic structure existing today owes more to Henry III's plans than to those of any other sovereign, although many architects, including Wren, have contributed to the abbey.

Built on the site of the ancient lady chapel in the early 16th century, the **Henry VII Chapel** is one of the loveliest in Europe, with its fan vaulting, Knights of Bath banners, and Torrigiani-designed tomb of the king himself, over which hangs a 15th-century Vivarini painting, *Madonna and Child.* Also here, ironically buried in the same tomb, are Catholic Mary I and Protestant Elizabeth I (whose archrival, Mary Queen of Scots, is entombed on the other side of the Henry VII Chapel). At one end of the chapel, you can stand on Cromwell's memorial stone and view the **Royal Air Force chapel** and its Battle of Britain memorial window, unveiled in 1947 to honor the RAF.

You can also visit the most hallowed spot in the abbey, the **shrine of Edward the Confessor** (canonized in the 12th century). In the chapel is the Coronation Chair, made at the command of Edward I in 1300 to display the Stone of Scone. Scottish kings were once crowned on it (it has since been returned to Scotland).

When you enter the transept on the south side of the nave and see a statue of the Bard with one arm resting on a stack of books, you've arrived at **Poets' Corner.** Shakespeare himself is buried at Stratford-upon-Avon but resting here are Chaucer, Ben Jonson, Milton, Shelley, and many others; there's even an American, Henry Wadsworth Longfellow, as well as monuments to just about everybody: Chaucer, Shakespeare, "O Rare Ben Johnson" (his name misspelled), Samuel Johnson, George Eliot, Charles Dickens, and others. The most stylized monument is Sir Jacob Epstein's sculpted bust of William Blake. More recent tablets commemorate poet Dylan Thomas and Lord Laurence Olivier.

Statesmen and men of science—such as Benjamin Disraeli, Isaac Newton, and Charles Darwin—are also interred in the abbey or honored by monuments. Near the west door is the 1965 memorial to Sir Winston Churchill. In the vicinity of this memorial is the tomb of the **Unknown Soldier,** commemorating the British dead of World War I.

Although most of the abbey's statuary commemorates notable figures of the past, 10 new statues were unveiled in July 1998. Placed in the Gothic niches above the West Front door, these statues honor 10 modern-day martyrs drawn from every continent and religious denomination. The sculptures include Elizabeth of Russia, Janani Luwum, and Martin Luther King Jr., representatives of all those who have sacrificed their lives for their convictions.

Off the Cloisters, the **College Garden** is the oldest garden in England, under cultivation for more than 900 years. Established in the 11th century as the abbey's first infirmary garden, this was once a magnificent source of fruits, vegetables, and medicinal herbs. Five trees in the garden were planted in 1850 and continue to thrive today. Surrounded by high walls, flowering trees dot the lawns and park benches provide comfort where you can hardly hear the roar of passing traffic. It's open only on Tuesday and Thursday, April through September from 10am to 6pm and October through March from 10am to 4pm.

Insider tip: Far removed from the pomp and glory is the **Abbey Treasure Museum,** with a bag of oddities. They're displayed in the undercroft or crypt, part of the monastic buildings erected between 1066 and 1100. Here are royal effigies that were used instead of the real corpses for lying-in-state ceremonies because they smelled better. You'll see the almost lifelike effigy of Admiral Nelson (his mistress arranged his hair) and even that of Edward III, his lip warped by the stroke that felled him. Other oddities include a Middle English lease to Chaucer, the much-used sword of Henry VI, and the Essex Ring Elizabeth I gave to her favorite when she was feeling good about him.

On Sunday, the Royal Chapels are closed, but the rest of the church is open unless a service is being conducted. For times of services, phone the **Chapter Office** (𝄢 **020/7222-5152**). Up to six supertours of the abbey are conducted by the vergers Monday through Saturday, beginning at 10am and costing £3 ($4.50) per person.

Broad Sanctuary, SW1. 𝄢 **020/7654-4900.** www.westminster-abbey.org. Admission £6 ($9.60) adults; £3 ($4.80) for students, seniors, and children 11–18; free for children under 11; family ticket £12 ($19). Mon–Fri 9:30am–4:45pm; Sat 9am–2:45pm. Tube: Westminster or St. James's Park.

Houses of Parliament ★★

The Houses of Parliament, along with their trademark clock tower, are the ultimate symbol of London. They're the stronghold of Britain's democracy, the assemblies that effectively trimmed the sails of royal power. Both the House of Commons and the House of Lords are in the former royal Palace of Westminster, the king's residence until Henry VIII moved to Whitehall. The current Gothic Revival buildings date from 1840 and were designed by Charles Barry. (The earlier buildings were destroyed by fire in 1834.) Assisting Barry was Augustus Welby Pugin, who designed the paneled ceilings, tiled floors, stained glass, clocks, fireplaces, umbrella stands, and even the inkwells. There are more than 1,000 rooms and 2 miles of corridors.

The clock tower at the eastern end houses the world's most famous timepiece, and the international icon of London. **Big Ben** refers not to the clock tower

(**Finds** A Hidden Gem

Across the street from the Houses of Parliament is the **Jewel Tower** ⭐, Abingdon St. (© **020/7222-2219**), one of only two surviving buildings from the medieval palace of Westminster. It was constructed in 1365 as a place where Edward III could stash his treasure trove. The tower hosts an exhibition on the history of that governing body and makes for a great introduction to the inner workings of the British government. The video presentation on the top floor is especially informative. The tower is open daily: from 10am to 6pm April through September; from 10am to 4pm in October; and from 10am to 4pm November through March. Admission is £1.60 ($2.55) for adults, £1.20 ($1.90) for students and seniors, and 80p ($1.30) for children.

itself but to the largest bell in the chime, which weighs close to 14 tons and is named for the first commissioner of works. When the House of Commons is in session, the light above the clock is lit.

You may observe parliamentary debates from the **Stranger's Galleries** in both houses. Sessions usually begin in mid-October and run to the end of July, with recesses at Christmas and Easter. The debates in the House of Commons are often lively and controversial (seats are at a premium during crises). The chances of getting into the House of Lords when it's in session are generally better than for the more popular House of Commons, where even the queen isn't allowed.

For years London tabloids have portrayed members of the House of Lords as a bunch of "Monty Pythonesque upper-class twits," with one foreign secretary calling the House of Lords "medieval lumber." Today, under Tony Blair's Labour government, the House of Lords is being shaken up as peers are losing their hereditary posts. Panels are studying what to do with this largely useless house, its members often descendants of royal mistresses and ancient landowners.

Those who'd like to book a tour can do so, but it takes a bit of work. Both houses are open to the general public for guided tours only for a limited season in August and September. The palace is open Monday through Saturday from 9:30am with the last entry at 4:15pm during those times. All tour tickets cost £7 ($11) per person. You need to send a written request for tours to the Public Information Office, 1 Derby Gate, Westminster, London SW1A 2TT. The staff is prompt in replying but only if you include a stamped return address (international postage only). Tickets for postal delivery must be booked up to 3 days in advance of a visit when collected from the British Visitor Centre at 1 Regent St., SW1; tube: Piccadilly Circus. Tickets can also be booked through London's Ticketmaster (© **020/7344-9966;** www.ticketmaster.co.uk).

If you arrive just to attend a session, these are free. You line up at Stephen's Gate, heading to your left for the entrance into the Commons or to the right for the Lords. The London daily newspapers announce sessions of Parliament.

Insider tip: The hottest ticket and the most exciting time to visit is during "Prime Minister's Question Time" on Wednesday from 3 to 3:30pm, which must seem like hours to Tony Blair who is virtually on the hot seat. Blair holds his own admirably against any and all who are trying to embarrass him and his government.

Westminster Palace, Old Palace Yard, SW1. House of Commons © **020/7219-4272.** House of Lords © **020/ 7219-3107.** www.parliament.uk. Free admission. £7 ($11) for all tours (only during Aug and Sept). House of

Lords open mid-Oct to Aug Mon–Wed from 2:30pm, Thurs from 3pm, and sometimes Fri (check by phone). House of Commons open mid-Oct to Aug Mon 2:30–10:30pm, Tues–Wed 11:30am–7:30pm, Thurs 11:30am–6pm, Fri call ahead—not always open. Both houses are open for tours during July and Aug, from 9:30am–4:15pm. Join line at St. Stephen's entrance. Tube: Westminster.

British Museum ★★★ Set in scholarly Bloomsbury, this immense museum grew out of a private collection of manuscripts purchased in 1753 with the proceeds of a lottery. It grew and grew, fed by legacies, discoveries, and purchases, until it became one of the most comprehensive collections of art and artifacts in the world. It's utterly impossible to take in this museum in a day.

The overall storehouse splits basically into the national collections of antiquities; prints and drawings; coins, medals, banknotes; and ethnography. Even on a cursory first visit, be sure to see the Asian collections (the finest assembly of Islamic pottery outside the Islamic world), the Chinese porcelain, the Indian sculpture, and the prehistoric and Romano-British collections. Special treasures you might want to seek out on your first visit include the **Rosetta Stone,** whose discovery led to the deciphering of hieroglyphs, in the Egyptian Room; the **Elgin Marbles,** a priceless series of pediments, metopes, and friezes from the Parthenon in Athens, in the Duveen Gallery; and the legendary **Black Obelisk,** dating from around 860 B.C., in the Nimrud Gallery. Other treasures include the contents of Egyptian royal tombs (including mummies); fabulous arrays of 2,000-year-old jewelry, cosmetics, weapons, furniture, and tools; Babylonian astronomical instruments; and winged lions (in the Assyrian Transept) that once guarded Ashurnasirpal's palace at Nimrud. The exhibits change throughout the year, so if your heart is set on seeing a specific treasure, call ahead to make sure it's on display.

Insider tip: If you're a first-time visitor, you will, of course, want to concentrate on some of these fabled treasures previewed above. But what we do is duck into the British Museum several times on our visits to London, even if we have only an hour or two to see the less heralded but equally fascinating exhibits. These include wandering rooms 33 and 34 and 91 to 94 to take in the glory of the Orient, covering Taoism, Confucianism, and Buddhism. The Chinese collection is particularly strong. Sculpture from India is as fine as anything at the Victoria and Albert. The ethnography collection is increasingly being beefed up, especially the Mexican Gallery in room 33C, which traces that country's art from the 2nd millennium B.C. to the 16th century A.D. There's even a gallery in room 68, tracing the story of money.

In 2000, the "Great Court" project was completed. The inner courtyard is canopied by a lightweight, transparent roof transforming the area into a covered square; housing a Centre for Education, exhibition space, bookshops, and restaurants. The center of the Great Court features the Round Reading Room restored to its original decorative scheme.

Great Russell St., WC1. ☎ **020/7323-8299** or 020/7636-1555. www.thebritishmuseum.ac.uk. Free admission. Sat–Wed 10am–5:30pm; Thurs–Fri 10am–8:30pm. Tube: Holborn, Tottenham Court Rd., or Goodge St.

⎛Tips **Timesaver**

With 4km (2½ miles) of galleries, the British Museum is overwhelming. To get a handle on it, we recommend taking a 1½-hour overview tour for £7 ($11) Monday through Saturday at 10:30am and 1pm or Sunday at 11am, 1:30, 2:30, and 4pm. Afterwards, you can return to the galleries that most interest you.

Buckingham Palace ✿✿   This massive, graceful building is the official residence of the queen. The redbrick palace was built as a country house for the notoriously rakish duke of Buckingham. In 1762, it was bought by King George III, who needed room for his 15 children. It didn't become the official royal residence, though, until Queen Victoria took the throne; she preferred it to St. James's Palace. From George III's time, the building was continuously expanded and remodeled, faced with Portland stone, and twice bombed (during the Blitz). Located in a 40-acre garden, it's 108m (360 ft.) long and contains 600 rooms. You can tell whether the queen is at home by the Royal Standard flying at the masthead.

Since 1993, much of the palace has been open for tours during an 8-week period in August and September, when the royal family is usually vacationing outside London. Visitors can tour the State Room, the Grand Staircase, the Throne Room, and other areas designed by John Nash for George IV, as well as the huge Picture Gallery, which displays masterpieces by Van Dyck, Rembrandt, Rubens, and others. Admission charges help pay for repairs to Windsor Castle, badly damaged by fire in 1992. You have to buy a timed-entrance ticket on the same day you tour the palace. Tickets go on sale at 9am, but rather than lining up outside the gate at sunrise with other tourists—it's one of London's most popular attractions—book with credit card by calling ✆ 020/7766-7300 and save yourself a dreary morning.

Visitors are also allowed to stroll through the royal family's garden, along a 446m (1,485-ft.) walk on the south side of the grounds, with views of a lake and the usually off-limits west side of the palace. The garden is home to 30 types of birds, including the great crested grebe, plus 350 types of wildflowers.

Buckingham Palace's most famous spectacle is the vastly overrated **Changing of the Guard** (daily Apr–July and every other day the rest of the year). The new guard, marching behind a band, comes from either the Wellington or Chelsea Barracks and takes over from the old guard in the forecourt of the palace. The ceremony begins at 11:30am, though it's frequently canceled for bad weather, major state events, and other harder-to-fathom reasons—always check before you go. We like the changing of the guards at Horse Guards better (p. 154) where you can actually see the men marching and don't have to battle such tourist hordes. However, few first-time visitors can resist the Buckingham Palace changing of the guard. If you're one of them, arrive as early as 10:30am and claim territorial rights to a space directly in front of the palace. If you're not firmly anchored here, you'll miss much of the ceremony. Call ahead for times.

Insider's tip: You can avoid the long queues at Buckingham Palace by purchasing tickets before you go through **Global Tickets,** 234 West 44th St., Suite 1000, New York, NY 10034 (✆ **800/223-6108** or 212/332-2435). You'll have to pick the exact date on which you'd like to go. Visitors with disabilities can reserve tickets directly through the palace by calling ✆ **020/7930-5526.**

At end of The Mall (on the road running from Trafalgar Sq.). ✆ **020/7389-1377** or 020/7321-2233. www.royal. gov.uk. Palace tours £12 ($19) adults, £10 ($16) seniors, £6 ($9.60) children under 17. Changing of the Guard free. Palace open for tours Aug 6–Sept 28 daily 9:30am–4:15pm. Changing of the guard daily Apr–July at 11:30am, and every other day for the rest of the year at 11am. Tube: St. James's Park, Green Park, or Victoria.

Tate Britain ✿✿✿   Fronting the Thames near Vauxhall Bridge in Pimlico, the Tate looks like a smaller and more graceful relation of the British Museum. The most prestigious gallery in Britain, it houses the national collections covering British art from the 16th century to the present day, as well as an array of international artists. In spring of 2000, the Tate moved its collection of 20th- and 21st-century art to the **Tate Modern** (see below). This split helped open more space at the Tate Britain, but the collection here is still much too large to be displayed at once, so the works on view change from time to time.

The older works include some of the best of Gainsborough, Reynolds, Stubbs, Blake, and Constable. William Hogarth is well represented, particularly by his satirical *O the Roast Beef of Old England* (known as *The Gate of Calais*). The illustrations of William Blake, the incomparable mystical poet, for such works as *The Book of Job, The Divine Comedy,* and *Paradise Lost* are here. The **collection of works by J. M. W. Turner** ✦✦✦ is its largest collection of works by a single artist; Turner himself willed most of the paintings and watercolors here to the nation.

Also on display are the works of many major 19th- and 20th-century painters, including Paul Nash. In the modern collections are works by Matisse, Dalí, Modigliani, Munch, Bonnard, and Picasso. Truly remarkable are the several enormous abstract canvases by Mark Rothko, the group of paintings and sculptures by Giacometti, and the paintings of one of England's best-known modern artists, the late Francis Bacon. Sculptures by Henry Moore and Barbara Hepworth are also occasionally displayed.

Insider tip: Drop in to the Tate Gallery Shop for some of the best art books and high-quality printed postcards in London. As a whimsical touch, the gallery sells T-shirts with art masterpieces printed on them; it also stocks the town's best art posters. Invite your friends for tea at the Coffee Shop with its excellent cakes and pastries, or lunch at the Tate Gallery Restaurant (see p. 129).

Millbank, SW1. ✆ 020/7887-8000. www.tate.org.uk. Free admission; special exhibitions sometimes incur a charge varying from £3–£8.50 ($4.80–$14). Daily 10:30am–5:40pm. Tube: Vauxhall.

Tate Modern ✦✦✦   In a transformed Bankside Power Station in Southwark, this museum, which opened in 2000, draws some 2 million visitors a year to see the greatest collection of international 20th-century art in Britain. How would we rate the collection? At the same level of the Pompidou in Paris with a slight edge over New York's Guggenheim. Of course, New York's Museum of Modern Art remains in a class of its own. Tate Modern is also viewer friendly with eye-level hangings. All the big painting stars are here, a whole galaxy ranging from Dalí to Duchamp, from Giacometti to Matisse and Mondrian, from Picasso and Pollock to Rothko and Warhol. The Modern is also a gallery of 21st-century art, displaying new and exciting art recently created.

You can cross the Millennium Bridge, a pedestrian-only walk from the steps of St. Paul's, over the Thames to the new gallery. Instead of exhibiting art chronologically and by school, the Tate Modern, in a radical break from tradition, takes a thematic approach. This allows displays to cut across movements.

Bankside, SE1. ✆ 020/7887-8008. www.tate.org.uk. Free admission. Sun–Thurs 10am–6pm; Fri–Sat 10am–10pm. Tube: Southwark.

National Gallery ✦✦✦   This stately neoclassical building contains an unrivaled collection of Western art that spans 7 centuries—from the late 13th to the early 20th—and covers every great European school. For sheer skill of display and arrangement, it surpasses its counterparts in Paris, New York, Madrid, and Amsterdam.

The largest part of the collection is devoted to the Italians, including the Sienese, Venetian, and Florentine masters. On display are such works as Leonardo's *Virgin of the Rocks;* Titian's *Bacchus and Ariadne;* Giorgione's *Adoration of the Magi;*

and unforgettable canvases by Bellini, Veronese, Botticelli, and Tintoretto. Botticelli's *Venus and Mars* is eternally enchanting.

Of the early-Gothic works, the Wilton Diptych (French or English school, late 14th c.) is the rarest treasure; it depicts Richard II being introduced to the Madonna and Child by John the Baptist and the Saxon kings Edmund and Edward the Confessor.

Then there are the Spanish giants: El Greco's *Agony in the Garden* and portraits by Goya and Velázquez. The Flemish-Dutch school is represented by Brueghel, Jan van Eyck (his popular masterpiece, the *Arnolfini Portrait*), Vermeer, Rubens, and de Hooch; the Rembrandts include two of his immortal self-portraits. There's also an immense French Impressionist and post-Impressionist collection that includes works by Manet, Monet, Degas, Renoir, and Cézanne. Particularly charming is the peep-show cabinet by Hoogstraten in one of the Dutch rooms: It's like spying through a keyhole.

The National Gallery does have some fine 18th-century British masterpieces, including works by Hogarth, Gainsborough, Reynolds, Constable, and Turner.

Guided tours of the National Gallery are offered daily at 11:30am and 2:30pm. For those who want to enhance their experience, the Gallery Guide Soundtrack is available. A portable CD player provides audio information on paintings of your choice with the mere push of a button. Although this service is free, voluntary contributions are appreciated.

Insider tip: The National Gallery has a computer information center where you can design your own personal tour map. The computer room, located in the Micro Gallery, includes a dozen hands-on workstations. The online system lists 2,200 paintings and has background notes for each artwork. The program includes four indexes that are cross-referenced for your convenience. Using a touch-screen computer, you design your own personalized tour by selecting a maximum of 10 paintings you would like to view. Once you have made your choices, you print a personal tour map with your selections; this mapping service is free.

Northwest side of Trafalgar Sq., WC2. © 020/7747-2885. www.nationalgallery.org.uk. Free admission. Thurs–Tues 10am–6pm; Wed 10am–9pm. Tube: Charing Cross, Embankment, Leicester Sq., or Piccadilly Circus.

Kensington Palace ⚅   Once the residence of British monarchs, Kensington Palace hasn't been the official home of reigning kings since George II. It was acquired in 1689 by joint monarchs William III and Mary II as an escape from the damp royal rooms along the Thames. Since the end of the 18th century, the palace has been home to various members of the royal family, and the State Apartments are open for tours.

It was here, in 1837, that a young Victoria was roused from her sleep with the news that her uncle, William IV, had died and that she was now queen of England. You can view a nostalgic collection of Victoriana, including some of her memorabilia. In the apartments of Queen Mary II is a striking 17th-century writing cabinet inlaid with tortoiseshell. Paintings from the Royal Collection line the walls of the apartments. A rare 1750 lady's court dress and splendid examples of male court dress from the 18th century are on display in rooms adjacent to the State Apartments. The former apartment of the late Princess Margaret has opened to the public as an education center and an exhibition space for royal ceremonial dress. The palace was once also the home of Diana, Princess of Wales, and her two sons (Harry and William now live with their father at St. James's Palace), and is probably best known for the millions of flowers placed in front of it during the days following Diana's death.

Moments   Roses Are Red

One of the most enjoyable aspects of a spring visit to London is saunter-
ing through the free gardens of St. Paul's when the roses are in bloom.

Warning: You don't get to see the apartments where Princess Di lived or
where both Di and Charles lived until they separated.

Kensington Gardens are open daily to the public for leisurely strolls through
the manicured grounds and around the Round Pond. One of the most famous
sights is the controversial **Albert Memorial** ★★, a lasting tribute not only to
Victoria's consort but also to the questionable artistic taste of the Victorian era.
A wonderful afternoon tea is offered in The Orangery (p. 137).

The Broad Walk, Kensington Gardens, W8. © 020/7937-9561. www.hrp.org.uk. Admission £10 ($16) adults,
£7.50 ($12) seniors/students, £6.50 ($10) children, free under 5, £30 ($48) family. Mar–Oct daily 10am–6pm;
Nov–Feb daily 10am–5pm. Tube: Queensway or Notting Hill Gate; High St. Kensington on south side.

St. Paul's Cathedral ★★★   That St. Paul's survived World War II at all is a
miracle because it was badly hit twice during the early years of the bombardment
of London. But St. Paul's is accustomed to calamity, having been burned down
three times and destroyed once by invading Norsemen. It was during the Great
Fire of 1666 that the old St. Paul's was razed, making way for a new structure
designed by Sir Christopher Wren and built between 1675 and 1710. It's the
architectural genius's ultimate masterpiece.

The classical dome of St. Paul's dominates The City's square mile. The golden
cross atop it is 110m (365 ft.) above the ground; the golden ball on which the
cross rests measures 2m (6 ft.) in diameter yet looks like a marble from below.
Surrounding the interior of the dome is the Whispering Gallery, an acoustic
marvel in which the faintest whisper can be heard clearly on the opposite side—
so be careful of what you say. You can climb to the top of the dome for a spectacular 360-degree view of London.

Although the interior looks almost bare, it houses a vast number of monuments. The duke of Wellington (of Waterloo fame) is entombed here, as are
Lord Nelson and Sir Christopher Wren himself. At the east end of the cathedral
is the American Memorial Chapel, honoring the 28,000 U.S. service personnel
who lost their lives while stationed in Britain in World War II.

Guided tours last 1½ hours and include parts of the cathedral not open to the
general public. Tours run Monday through Saturday at 11, 11:30am, 1:30, and
2pm. Recorded tours lasting 45 minutes are available throughout the day.

St. Paul's is an Anglican cathedral with daily services at the following times:
matins at 7:30am Monday through Friday, 8:30am on Saturday; Holy Communion Monday through Saturday at 8am and 12:30pm; and evensong Monday
through Saturday at 5pm. On Sunday, Holy Communion is at 8 and 11:30am,
matins at 10:15am, and evensong at 3:15pm. Admission charges don't apply if
you're attending a service.

St. Paul's Churchyard, EC4. © 020/7236-4128. www.stpauls.co.uk. Cathedral and galleries £6 ($9.60)
adults, £3 ($4.80) children 6–16. Guided tours £2.50 ($4) adults, £2 ($3.20) students and seniors, £1 ($1.60)
children; recorded tours £3.50 ($5.60). Free for children 5 and under. Sightseeing Mon–Sat 8:30am–4pm; gal-
leries Mon–Sat 9:30am–4pm. No sightseeing Sun (services only). Tube: St. Paul's.

Victoria and Albert Museum ★★★   The Victoria and Albert (V&A) is the
greatest museum in the world devoted to the decorative arts. It's also one of the

liveliest and most imaginative museums in London—where else would you find the quintessential "little black dress" in the permanent collection?

The medieval holdings include such treasures as the Early English Gloucester Candlestick; the Byzantine Veroli Casket, with its ivory panels based on Greek plays; and the Syon Cope, a highly valued embroidery made in England in the early 14th century. An area devoted to Islamic art houses the Ardabil Carpet from 16th-century Persia.

The V&A houses the largest collection of Renaissance sculpture outside Italy. A highlight of the 16th-century collection is the marble group *Neptune with Triton* by Bernini. The cartoons by Raphael, which were conceived as designs for tapestries for the Sistine Chapel, are owned by the queen and are on display here. A most unusual, huge, and impressive exhibit is the Cast Courts, life-size plaster models of ancient and medieval statuary and architecture.

The museum has the greatest collection of Indian art outside India, plus Chinese and Japanese galleries as well. In complete contrast are suites of English furniture, metalwork, and ceramics, and a superb collection of portrait miniatures, including the one Hans Holbein the Younger made of Anne of Cleves for the benefit of Henry VIII, who was again casting around for a suitable wife.

The Dress Collection includes corsetry through the ages that's sure to make you wince. There's also a remarkable collection of musical instruments.

V&A has recently opened 15 new galleries—called **The British Galleries** ⭐⭐⭐ —unfolding the story of British design from 1500 to 1900. From Chippendale to Morris, all of the top British designers are featured in some 3,000 exhibits displayed. Star exhibits range from the 5m (17-ft.) high Melville Bed (1697) with its luxurious wild silk damask and red silk velvet hangings, to 19th-century classics such as furniture by Charles Rennie Mackintosh. One of the most prized possessions is the "Great Bed of Ware," mentioned in Shakespeare's *Twelfth Night,* and the wedding suite of James II. The interactive displays hold special interest. Learning about heraldry is far more interesting when you're designing your own coat-of-arms.

Insider's tip: As incongruous as it sounds, the museum hosts a jazz brunch on Sunday from 11am to 3pm. Some of the hottest jazz in the city accompanies a full English brunch for only £8.50 ($14). And don't miss the V&A's most bizarre gallery, "Fakes and Forgeries." The impostors here are amazingly authentic—in fact, we'd judge some of them as better than the old masters themselves.

Cromwell Rd., SW7. ✆ 020/7942-2000. www.vam.ac.uk. Free admission. Daily 10am–5:45pm (Wed until 10pm). Tube: South Kensington.

Trafalgar Square ⭐⭐   One of the landmark squares of London, Trafalgar Square (Tube: Charing Cross) honors one of England's great military heroes, Horatio Viscount Nelson (1758–1805), who died at the Battle of Trafalgar. Although he suffered from seasickness all his life, he went to sea at the age of 12 and was an admiral at the age of 39. Lord Nelson was a hero of the Battle of Calvi in 1794 where he lost an eye, the Battle of Santa Cruz in 1797 where he lost an arm, and the Battle of Trafalgar in 1805 where he lost his life.

The square today is dominated by a 145-foot granite column, the work of E. H. Baily in 1843. The column looks down Whitehall toward the Old Admiralty, where Lord Nelson's body lay in state. The figure of the naval hero towers 17 feet high, not bad for a man who stood 5 feet 4 inches in real life. The capital is of bronze cast from cannon recovered from the wreck of the *Royal George.* Queen Victoria's favorite animal painter, Sir Edward Landseer, added the four lions at the base of the column in 1868. The pools and fountains were not added until 1939, the last work of Sir Edwin Lutyens.

Political demonstrations still take place at the square and around the column, which has the most aggressive pigeons in London. The birds are part of a long feathery tradition, for this site was once used by Edward I (1239–1307) to keep his birds of prey. Richard II, who ruled from 1377 to 1399, kept goshawks and falcons here, too. By the time of Henry VII, who ruled from 1485 to 1509, the square was used as the site of the royal stables. Sir Charles Barry, who designed the Houses of Parliament, created the present square in the 1830s.

To the southeast of the square, at 36 Craven St., stands a house once occupied by Benjamin Franklin when he was a general of the Philadelphia Academy (1757–74). On the north side of the square rises the National Gallery, constructed in the 1830s. In front of the building is a copy of a statue of George Washington by J. A. Houdon.

National Portrait Gallery ★★   In a gallery of remarkable and unremarkable pictures (they're collected here for their notable subjects rather than their artistic quality), a few paintings tower over the rest, including Sir Joshua Reynolds's first portrait of Samuel Johnson ("a man of most dreadful appearance"). Among the best are Nicholas Hilliard's miniature of a handsome Sir Walter Raleigh and a full-length Elizabeth I, along with the Holbein cartoon of Henry VIII. A portrait of William Shakespeare (with a gold earring, no less) by an unknown artist bears the claim of being the "most authentic contemporary likeness" of its subject. One of the most famous pictures in the gallery is the group portrait of the Brontë sisters (Charlotte, Emily, and Anne) painted by their brother, Bramwell. An idealized portrait of Lord Byron by Thomas Phillips is also on display.

The galleries of Victorian and early-20th-century portraits were radically redesigned recently. Occupying the whole first floor, they display portraits from 1837 (when Victoria took the throne) to present day; later 20th-century portraiture includes major works by such artists as Warhol and Hambling. Some of the more flamboyant personalities of the past 2 centuries are on show: T. S. Eliot, Disraeli, Macmillan, Sir Richard Burton, Elizabeth Taylor, Baroness Thatcher, and our two favorites: G. F. Watts's famous portrait of his great actress wife, Ellen Terry, and Vanessa Bell's portrait of her sister, Virginia Woolf. The late Princess Diana is on the Royal Landing; this portrait seems to attract the most viewers.

In 2000, Queen Elizabeth opened the Ondaatje Wing of the gallery, granting the gallery more than 50% more exhibition space. The most intriguing of the new space is the splendid Tudor Gallery, opening with portraits of Richard III and Henry II, his conqueror in the Battle of Bosworth in 1485, as well as a portrait of Shakespeare that the gallery first acquired in 1856. Rooms lead through centuries of English monarchs, with some literary and artistic figures thrown in. A Balcony Gallery displays more recent figures whose fame has lasted longer than Warhol's predicted 15 minutes. This new wing certainly taps into the cult of the celebrity.

St. Martin's Place, WC2. ⓒ 020/7306-0055. www.npg.org.uk. Free admission; fee charged for certain temporary exhibitions. Mon–Wed 10am–6pm; Thurs–Fri 10am–9pm; Sat–Sun 10am–6pm. Tube: Charing Cross or Leicester Sq.

Tower Bridge ★★   This is one of the world's most celebrated landmarks and possibly the most photographed and painted bridge on earth. In spite of its medieval appearance, Tower Bridge was actually built in 1894.

Finds **Drake's Long Voyage**

As you're strolling along the riverside, you come upon the old dock of St. Mary Overie, SE1. Here to your delight is an exact replica of the *Golden Hinde,* in which Sir Francis Drake circumnavigated the globe. It's amazingly tiny for such an around-the-world voyage. But this actual ship has sailed around the world some two dozen times, exploring both oceans and the American coast. Visits are daily from 10am to 6pm, costing £3 ($4.80). For information, call © **020/7403-0123.**

In 1993, an exhibition opened inside the bridge to commemorate its century-old history; it takes you up the north tower to high-level walkways between the two towers with spectacular views of St. Paul's, the Tower of London, and the Houses of Parliament—a photographer's dream. You're then led down the south tower and on to the bridge's original engine room, with its Victorian boilers and steam-pumping engines that used to raise and lower the bridge for ships to pass. Exhibits in the bridge's towers use advanced technology, including animatronic characters, video, and computers to illustrate the history of the bridge. Admission to the **Tower Bridge Experience** (© **020/7403-3761;** www.towerbridge.org.uk) is £4.50 ($7.20) for adults and £3 ($4.80) for children 5 to 15, students, and seniors; family tickets start at £18.25 ($29); it's free for children 4 and under. Open daily from 9:30am to 6pm (last entrance 5pm). Closed Christmas Eve and Christmas Day.

At Tower Bridge, SE1. © 020/7403-3761. Tube: Tower Hill or London Bridge.

2 More Attractions

OFFICIAL LONDON

Whitehall ⚘, the seat of the British government, grew up on the grounds of Whitehall Palace and was turned into a royal residence by Henry VIII, who snatched it from its former occupant, Cardinal Wolsey. Whitehall extends south from Trafalgar Square to Parliament Square. Along it you'll find the Home Office, the Old Admiralty Building, and the Ministry of Defence.

Visitors today can see the **Cabinet War Rooms** ⚘, the bombproof bunker suite of rooms, just as they were when abandoned by Winston Churchill and the British government at the end of World War II. You can see the Map Room with its huge wall maps, the Atlantic map a mass of pinholes (each hole represents at least one convoy). Next door is Churchill's bedroom-cum-office, which has a bed and a desk with two BBC microphones on it for his famous speech broadcasts that stirred the nation.

The **Transatlantic Telephone Room,** its full title, is little more than a broom closet, but it housed the Bell Telephone Company's special scrambler phone, called *Sigsaly,* and it was where Churchill conferred with Roosevelt. Visitors are provided with a step-by-step personal sound guide, providing a detailed account of each room's function and history.

The entrance to the War Rooms is by Clive Steps at the end of King Charles Street, SW1 (© **020/7930-6961;** Tube: Westminster or St. James's), off Whitehall near Big Ben. Admission is £5.80 ($9.30) for adults, £4.20 ($6.70) for students and seniors, and free for children 16 and under. The rooms are open May through September daily from 9:30am to 6pm (last admission is 5:15pm); and October through April daily from 10am to 5:30pm; they're closed during Christmas holidays. Tube: Westminster or St. James's.

At the Cenotaph (honoring both world wars' dead), turn down unpretentious **Downing Street** to the modest little town house at no. 10, flanked by two bobbies. Walpole was the first prime minister to live here; Churchill was the most famous. But Margaret Thatcher was around longer than any of them.

Nearby, north of Downing Street, is the **Horse Guards Building** ⟨, Whitehall (✆ **020/7414-2396**; Tube: Westminster), now the headquarters of the horse guards of the Household Division and London District. There has been a guard change here since 1649, when the site was the entrance to the old Palace of Whitehall. You can watch the Queen's Life Guards ceremony at 11am Monday through Saturday (10:30am on Sun). You can also see the hourly smaller **change of the guard,** when mounted troopers are changed. And at 4pm, you can watch the evening inspection, when 10 unmounted troopers and two mounted troopers assemble in the courtyard.

Across the street is Inigo Jones's **Banqueting House,** Palace of Whitehall, Horse Guards Avenue (✆ **020/7515-5178;** Tube: Westminster), site of the execution of Charles I. William and Mary accepted the crown of England here, but they preferred to live at Kensington Palace. The **Banqueting House** was part of Whitehall Palace, which burned to the ground in 1698, but the ceremonial hall escaped razing. Its most notable feature today is an allegorical ceiling painted by Peter Paul Rubens. Admission to the Banqueting House is £4 ($6.40) for adults, £3 ($4.80) for seniors and students, £2.60 ($4.15) for children under 16, and free for children under 5. It's open Monday through Saturday from 10am to 5pm (last admission 4:30pm). Tube: Westminster, Charing Cross, or Embankment.

LEGAL LONDON

The smallest borough in London, bustling Holborn (pronounced *Ho*-burn) is often referred to as Legal London, home of the city's barristers, solicitors, and law clerks. It also embraces the university district of Bloomsbury. Holborn, which houses the ancient **Inns of Courts**—Gray's Inn, Lincoln's Inn, Middle Temple, and Inner Temple—was severely damaged during World War II bombing raids. The razed buildings were replaced with modern offices, but the borough still retains pockets of its former days.

⟨*Finds* **A City of Wine**

At **Vinopolis,** 1 Bank End, Park Street, SE1 (✆ **0870/241-4040;** www. vinopolis.co.uk), you can partake of London's largest selection of wine sold by the glass. On the South Bank, this "city of wine" lies in cavernous railway arches created in Victoria's era. The bacchanalian attraction was created at the cost of £23 million, in a multimedia format, so it seems as though you are journeying through some of the earth's most prestigious wine regions. You can even drive a Vespa through the Tuscan countryside or take a "flight" over the vineyards of Australia. The price of entrance includes free tastings of five premium wines, and an on-site shop sells almost any item related to the grape. The site also boasts a good restaurant (see Cantina Vinopolis on p. 131). Admission is £11.50 ($18) for adults, £5 ($8) for ages 5 to 14, and £10.50 ($17) for seniors.

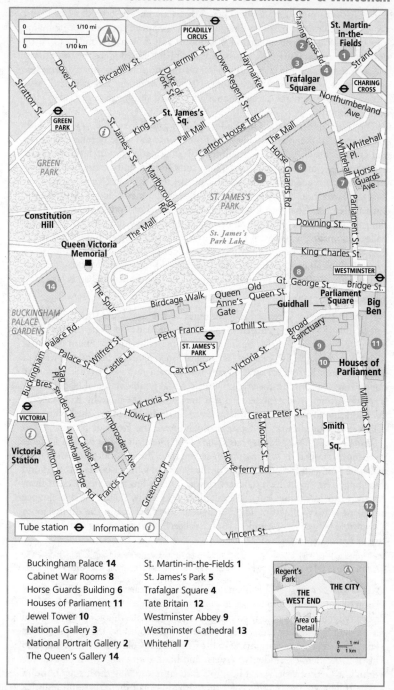

Official London: Westminster & Whitehall

0 1/10 mi
0 1/10 km

PICADILLY CIRCUS

St. Martin-in-the-Fields

Strand

CHARING CROSS

Trafalgar Square

Northumberland Ave.

Piccadilly St.

Dover St.

Stratton St.

Jermyn St.

Duke of York St.

Lower Regent St.

Haymarket

Charing Cross Rd.

GREEN PARK

King St.

St. James's St.

St. James's Sq.

Pall Mall

Carlton House Terr.

Marlborough Rd.

The Mall

Whitehall Pl.

Whitehall

Horse Guards Ave.

Parliament St.

GREEN PARK

ST. JAMES'S PARK

Horse Guards Rd.

The Mall

St. James's Park Lake

Downing St.

King Charles St.

Constitution Hill

Queen Victoria Memorial

The Spur

WESTMINSTER

Gt. George St.

Bridge St.

Parliament Square

Big Ben

BUCKINGHAM PALACE GARDENS

Birdcage Walk

Queen Anne's Gate

Old Queen St.

Guidhall

Buckingham Palace Rd.

Palace St.

Wilfred St.

Castle La.

Petty France

Tothill St.

Broad Sanctuary

ST. JAMES'S PARK

Caxton St.

Victoria St.

Houses of Parliament

Millbank St.

Stag Pl.

Bres senden Pl.

VICTORIA

Victoria St.

Howick Pl.

Great Peter St.

Monck St.

Smith Sq.

Victoria Station

Wilton Rd.

Vauxhall Bridge Rd.

Carlisle Pl.

Ambrosden Ave.

Francis St.

Greencoat Pl.

Horseferry Rd.

Vincent St.

Tube station ⊖ Information ⓘ

Buckingham Palace **14**
Cabinet War Rooms **8**
Horse Guards Building **6**
Houses of Parliament **11**
Jewel Tower **10**
National Gallery **3**
National Portrait Gallery **2**
The Queen's Gallery **14**

St. Martin-in-the-Fields **1**
St. James's Park **5**
Trafalgar Square **4**
Tate Britain **12**
Westminster Abbey **9**
Westminster Cathedral **13**
Whitehall **7**

Regent's Park

THE WEST END

THE CITY

Area of Detail

0 1 mi
0 1 km

At the 60 or more **Law Courts** presently in use on The Strand, all civil and some criminal cases are heard. Designed by G. E. Street, the neo-Gothic buildings (1874–82) have more than 1,000 rooms and 5.5km (3½ miles) of corridors. Sculptures of Christ, King Solomon, and King Alfred grace the front door; Moses is depicted at the back. Admission is free, and courts are open during sessions Monday through Friday from 10am to 4:30pm. No cameras, tape recorders, video cameras, or cellphones are allowed during sessions. Tube: Holborn or Temple.

The court known as the **Old Bailey,** on Newgate Street, EC4 (© **020/7248-3277**), replaced the infamous Newgate Prison, once the scene of public hangings and other forms of "public entertainment." It's fascinating to watch the bewigged barristers presenting their cases to the high court judges. Entry is strictly on a first-arrival basis, and guests line up outside. Courts 1 to 4, 17, and 18 are entered from Newgate Street, and the balance from Old Bailey (the street). To get here, take the Tube to Temple, Chancery Lane, or St. Paul's. Travel east on Fleet Street, which along the way becomes Ludgate Hill. Cross Ludgate Circus and turn left to the Old Bailey, a domed structure with the figure of Justice standing atop it. Admission is free; children under 14 are not admitted, and ages 14 to 16 must be accompanied by adult. No cameras or tape recorders are allowed. Hours are Monday through Friday from 10:30am to 1pm and 2 to 4pm. The best time to line up is 10am.

MORE MUSEUMS

Apsley House ✦   The former town house of the Iron Duke, the British general (1769–1852) who defeated Napoleon at the Battle of Waterloo and later became prime minister, this building was designed by Robert Adam and constructed in the late 18th century. Wellington once retreated behind the walls of Apsley House, fearing an attack from Englishmen outraged by his autocratic opposition to reform. In the vestibule is a colossal marble statue of Napoleon by Canova—ironic, to say the least; it was presented to the duke by King George IV. In addition to the famous *Waterseller of Seville* by Velázquez, the Wellington collection includes works by Correggio, Jan Steen, and Pieter de Hooch.

Insider's tip: Apsley House has some of the finest silver and porcelain pieces in Europe. Grateful to Wellington for saving their thrones, European monarchs endowed him with treasures. Head for the Plate and China Room on the ground floor first. The Sèvres Egyptian service was intended as a divorce present from Napoleon to Josephine, but she refused it. Eventually, Louis XVIII of France presented it to Wellington. The Portuguese Silver Service in the dining room was created between 1812 and 1816: It has been hailed as the single greatest artifact of Portuguese neoclassical silver.

149 Piccadilly, Hyde Park Corner, W1. © 020/7499-5676. www.apsleyhouse.org.uk. Admission £4.50 ($7.20) adults, £3 ($4.80) seniors, free for children under 18. Tues–Sun 11am–5pm. Tube: Hyde Park Corner.

British Library ✦✦   This is one of the world's greatest libraries, with a collection of some 12 million books, manuscripts, and other items, moved from the British Museum to its own home here in St. Pancras. In the new building, you get modernistic beauty rather than the fading glamour and the ghosts of Karl Marx, Thackeray, and Virginia Woolf of the famous old library at the British Museum. Academics, students, writers, and bookworms visit from all over the world. On a recent visit, we sat next to a student researching the history of pubs.

The bright, roomy interior is far more inviting than the rather dull redbrick exterior suggests. The most spectacular room is the Humanities Reading Room, constructed on three levels and with daylight filtered through the ceiling.

Value **Museum Discounts**

A tourist ticket provides admission to 60 attractions in and around London, plus a pocket guidebook (free travel on public transport is available
at an additional cost). **The London Pass** costs £26 ($42) for 1 day, £58 ($93)
for 3 days, or £91 ($146) for 6 days (children pay £16/$26, £37/$59, or
£50/$80), and includes free admission to St. Paul's Cathedral, HMS *Belfast,*
the Jewish Museum, the Tower of London, and many more. Go to
www.londonpass.com for more information.

The fascinating collection includes such items of historical and literary interest as two of the four surviving copies of the Magna Carta (1215), a Gutenberg
Bible, Nelson's last letter to Lady Hamilton, and the journals of Captain Cook.
Almost every major author—Dickens, Jane Austen, Charlotte Brontë, Keats,
and hundreds of others—is represented in the section devoted to English literature. Beneath Roubiliac's 1758 statue of Shakespeare stands a case of documents
relating to the Bard, including a mortgage bearing his signature and a copy of
the First Folio of 1623. There's also an unrivaled collection of philatelic items.

Visitors can also view the Diamond Sutra, dating from 868, said to be the
oldest surviving printed book. Using headphones set up around the room, you
can also hear thrilling audio snippets such as James Joyce reading a passage from
Finnegans Wake. Curiosities include the earliest known tape of a birdcall, dating
from 1889. Particularly intriguing is an exhibition called "Turning the Pages."
You can, for example, electronically read a complete Leonardo da Vinci note-
book, putting your hands on a special computer screen that flips from one page
to another. There is a copy of *The Canterbury Tales* from 1410, and even manuscripts from *Beowulf* (ca. 1000). Illuminated texts from some of the oldest
known Biblical displays include the *Codex Sinaitticus* and *Codex Alexandrius,*
3rd-century Greek gospels. In the Historical Documents section are epistles by
everybody from Henry VIII to Napoleon, from Elizabeth I to Churchill. In the
music displays, you can seek out works by Beethoven, Handel, Stravinsky, and
Lennon and McCartney. An entire day spent here will only scratch the surface.

Walking tours of the library are conducted Monday, Wednesday, and Friday
at 10:30am and 3pm, with an extra tour on Sunday at 11:15am and 3pm. The
cost of these tours are £7 ($11) for adults, £5.50 ($8.80) for students and seniors, and reservations are advised 3 weeks in advance.

96 Euston Rd., NW1. *©* 020/7412-7000. www.bl.uk. Free admission. Mon and Wed–Fri 9:30am–6pm; Tues
9:30am–8pm; Sat 9:30am–5pm. Tube: King's Cross/St. Pancras or Euston.

Courtauld Gallery   Although surprisingly little known, the Courtauld contains a fabulous wealth of paintings. It has one of the world's greatest collections
of Impressionist works outside Paris. There are French Impressionists and post-
Impressionists, with masterpieces by Monet, Manet, Degas, Renoir, Cézanne,
van Gogh, and Gauguin. The gallery also has a superb collection of old-master
paintings and drawings, including works by Rubens, Michelangelo, and Tiepolo;
early Italian paintings, ivories, and majolica; the Lee collection of old masters;
and early-20th-century English and French paintings, as well as 20th-century
British paintings.

Like the Frick Collection in New York, it's a superb display, a visual feast in a
jewel-like setting. We come here at least once every season to revisit one painting

in particular: Manet's exquisite *A Bar at the Folies-Bergère.* Many of the paintings are displayed without glass, giving the gallery a more intimate feeling than most.

Somerset House, The Strand, WC2. ℂ 020/7848-2526. www.courtauld.ac.uk. Admission £5 ($8) adults, £4 ($6.40) seniors and students, free for children under 18. Free admission Mon 10am–2pm. Daily 10am–6pm; last admission 5:15pm. Tube: Temple or Covent Garden.

Dalí Universe ✦ *Finds*   Next to the "London Eye," this exhibition is devoted to the remarkable Spanish artist Salvador Dalí (1904–1989), and is one of London's newest attractions. Featuring more than 500 works of art, including the Mae West Lips sofa, the exhibitions are divided into a trio of themed areas: Sensuality and Femininity, Religion and Mythology, and Dreams and Fantasy. Showcased are important Dalí sculptures, rare graphics, watercolors, and even furnishings and jewelry. You can feast on such surreal works as Dalí's monumental oil painting for the Hitchcock movie, *Spellbound,* or view a series of original watercolors and collages including the mystical Tarot Cards, and see the world's largest collection of rare Dalí graphics, illustrating themes from literature.

County Hall, Riverside Building, South Bank, SE1. ℂ 020/7620-2720. www.daliuniverse.com. Admission £8.50 ($14) adults, £6 ($9.60) students and seniors, £5 ($8) ages 5–16, and £22 ($35) family ticket. Open daily 10am–5:30pm. Tube: Waterloo.

Gilbert Collection ✦✦✦ *Finds*   In 2000, Somerset House became the permanent home for the Gilbert Collection of decorative arts, one of the most important bequests ever made to England. Sir Arthur Gilbert made his gift of decorative arts to the nation in 1996, at which time the value was estimated at £75 million ($120 million). The collection of some 800 objects in three fields (gold and silver, mosaics, and gold snuffboxes) is among the most distinguished in the world. The silver collection here is arguably better than the one at the V&A. The array of mosaics is among the most comprehensive ever gathered, with Roman and Florentine examples dating from the 16th to the 19th centuries. The gold and silver collection has exceptional breadth, ranging from the 15th to the 19th centuries, spanning India to South America. It is strong in masterpieces of great 18th-century silversmiths, such as Paul de Lamerie. Such exhibits as the Maharajah pieces, the "Gold Crown," and Catherine the Great's Royal Gates are fabulous. The gallery also displays one of the most representative collections of gold snuffboxes in the world, with some 200 examples, Some of the snuffboxes were owned by Louis XV, Frederick the Great, and Napoleon.

Somerset House, The Strand WC2. ℂ 020/7240-9400. Admission £5 ($8) adults, £4 ($6.40) seniors, free for under 18. Daily 10am–6pm. Tube: Temple.

Guildhall Art Gallery ✦   In 1999, Queen Elizabeth opened this £70 million ($112 million) gallery in The City, a continuation of the original gallery, launched in 1886, that was burned down in a severe air raid in May 1941. Many famous and much-loved pictures, which for years were known only through temporary exhibitions and reproductions, are once again available for the public to see in a permanent setting. The gallery can display only 250 of the 4,000 treasures it owns at a time. A curiosity is the huge double-height wall built to accommodate Britain's largest independent oil painting, John Singleton Copley's *The Defeat of the Floating Batteries at Gibraltar, September 1782.* The Corporation of London in The City owns these works and has been collecting them since the 17th century. The most popular art is in the Victorian collection, including such well-known favorites as Millais's *My First Sermon* and *My Second Sermon,* and Landseer's *The First Leap.* There is also a large landscape of Salisbury Cathedral by John Constable. Since World War II, all paintings acquired by the gallery have concentrated on London subjects.

Guildhall Yard, E.C. ℂ 020/7332-3700. www.guildhall-art-gallery.org.uk. Admission £2.50 ($4) adults, £1 ($1.60) children. Mon–Sat 10am–5pm; Sun noon–4pm. Tube: Bank, St. Paul's, Mansion House, or Moorgate.

Hermitage Rooms at Somerset House ⭐⭐⭐   This is a virtual branch of St. Petersburg's State Hermitage Museum, which owns a great deal of the treasure trove left over from the Czars, including possessions of art-collecting Catherine the Great. Now you don't have to go to Russia to see some of Europe's great treasures.

The rotating exhibitions will change, but you'll get to see such Czarist treasures as medals, jewelry, portraits, porcelain, clocks, and furniture. A rotating "visiting masterpiece" overshadows all the other collections. Some items that amused us on our first visit (and you are likely to see similar novelties) were a wig made entirely out of silver thread for Catherine the Great; a Wedgwood "Green Frog" table service; and two very rare Chinese silver filigree toilet sets. The rooms themselves have been designed in the style of the Winter Palace at St. Petersburg. *Note:* Because this exhibit attracts so much interest, tickets should be purchased in advance. Tickets are available from Ticketmaster at ℂ **020/7413-3398** (24 hr.). You can book online at **www.ticketmaster.co.uk**.

Strand, WC2. ℂ 020/7845-4600. www.hermitagerooms.com. Admission £6 ($9.60) adults, £5 ($8) students and seniors. Daily 10am–6pm. Tube: Temple, Covent Garden, or Charing Cross.

London Transport Museum ⭐ *Kids*   This splendidly restored Victorian building once housed the flower market. Now it's home to horse buses, motor buses, trams, trolley buses, railway vehicles, models, maps, posters, photographs, and audiovisual displays that trace 200 years of London transport history. The story is enlivened by several interactive video exhibits—you can put yourself in the driver's seat of a bus or Tube train. The fabulous gift shop sells a variety of London Transport souvenirs. Much to the glee of parents, the museum has added "kidzones"—interactive programs for children so that parents can enjoy the museum without having to entertain the kids.

The Piazza, Covent Garden, WC2. ℂ 020/7379-6344, or 020/7565-7299 for recorded info. www.ltmuseum. co.uk. Admission £5.95 ($9.50) adults, £4.50 ($7.20) students and seniors, free for children under 16 accompanied by an adult. Sat–Thurs 10am–6pm; Fri 11am–6pm (last entrance at 5:15pm). Tube: Covent Garden.

Madame Tussaud's ⭐ *Kids*   Madame Tussaud's is not so much a wax museum as an enclosed amusement park. A weird, moving, sometimes terrifying (to children) collage of exhibitions, panoramas, and stage settings, it manages to be most things to most people, most of the time.

Madame Tussaud attended the court of Versailles and learned her craft in France. She personally took the death masks from the guillotined heads of Louis XVI and Marie Antoinette (which you'll find among the exhibits). She moved her original museum from Paris to England in 1802. Her exhibition has been imitated in every part of the world, but never with the realism and imagination on hand here. Madame herself molded the features of Benjamin Franklin, whom she met in Paris. All the rest—from George Washington to John F. Kennedy, Mary Queen of Scots to Sylvester Stallone—have been subjects for the same painstaking (and often breathtaking) replication.

In the well-known Chamber of Horrors—a kind of underground dungeon—are all kinds of instruments of death, along with figures of their victims. The shadowy presence of Jack the Ripper lurks in the gloom as you walk through a Victorian London street. Present-day criminals are portrayed within the confines of prison. "The Spirit of London" is a musical ride that depicts 400 years of London's history, using special effects that include audio-animatronic figures that move and speak. Visitors take "time-taxis" that allow them to see and hear "Shakespeare" as he writes and speaks lines, be received by Queen Elizabeth I, and feel and smell the Great Fire of 1666 that destroyed London.

We've seen these changing exhibitions so many times over the years that we feel they're a bit cheesy, but we still remember the first time we were taken here as a kid. We thought it fascinating back then.

Insider's tip: To avoid the long lines, sometimes more than an hour in summer, call the waxworks in advance and reserve a ticket for fast pickup at the entrance. If you don't want to bother with that, be aggressive and form a group of nine people waiting in the queue. A group of nine or more can go in almost at once through the "group door." Otherwise, go when the gallery first opens or late in the afternoon when crowds have thinned.

Marylebone Rd., NW1. © **0870/400-3000.** www.madame-tussauds.com. Admission £15 ($24) adults, £12 ($19) seniors, £11 ($17) children ages 5–16, free for children under 5. Combination tickets including the new planetarium £17 ($27) adults, £14 ($22) seniors, £8 ($13) children under 16. Mon–Fri 10am–5:30pm; Sat–Sun 9:30am–5:30pm. Tube: Baker St.

Museum of London ★★   In the Barbican district near St. Paul's Cathedral, the Museum of London allows visitors to trace the city's history from prehistoric times to the postmodern era through relics, costumes, household effects, maps, and models. Anglo-Saxons, Vikings, Normans—they're all here, displayed on two floors around a central courtyard. The exhibits are arranged so that visitors can begin and end their chronological stroll through 250,000 years at the museum's main entrance, and exhibits have quick labels for museum sprinters, more extensive ones for those who want to study, and still more detail for scholars. It's an enriching experience for everybody—allow at least an hour for a full (but still quick) visit.

You'll see the death mask of Oliver Cromwell; the Great Fire of London in living color and sound; reconstructed Roman dining rooms with kitchen and utensils; cell doors from Newgate Prison, made famous by Charles Dickens; and an amazing shop counter with pre–World War II prices on the items. But the pièce de résistance is the lord mayor's coach, built in 1757 and weighing 3 tons. Still used each November in the Lord Mayor's Procession, this gilt-and-red horse-drawn vehicle is like a fairy-tale coach. Early in 2002, the museum unveiled its latest permanent gallery, occupying an entire floor. Called the World City Gallery, it examines through its exhibits life in London between 1789 and 1914, the beginning of World War I. Some 2,000 objects are on view.

Free lectures on London's history are often given during lunch hours; ask at the entrance hall if one will be given the day you're here. You can reach the museum, which overlooks London's Roman and medieval walls, by going up to the elevated pedestrian precinct at the corner of London Wall and Aldersgate, 5 minutes from St. Paul's.

150 London Wall, EC2. © **020/7600-3699.** www.museumoflondon.org.uk. Free admission. Mon–Sat 10am–5:50pm; Sun noon–5:50pm. Tube: St. Paul's or Barbican.

Natural History Museum ★★ *Kids*   This is the home of the national collections of living and fossil plants, animals, and minerals, with many magnificent specimens on display. The zoological displays are quite wonderful; though not up to the level of the Smithsonian in Washington, D.C., they're definitely worthwhile. Exciting exhibits designed to encourage people of all ages to learn about natural history include "Human Biology—An Exhibition of Ourselves," "Our Place in Evolution," "Creepy Crawlies," and "Discovering Mammals." The Mineral Gallery displays marvelous examples of crystals and gemstones. Visit the Meteorite Pavilion, which exhibits fragments of rock that have crashed into the earth, some from the farthest reaches of the galaxy. What attracts the most attention is the dinosaur exhibit, displaying 14 complete skeletons. The center of the show depicts a trio of full-size robotic Deinonychus enjoying a freshly killed Tenontosaurus.

The latest development here is the new Darwin Centre, with final completion scheduled for 2007, though there is already much on view. The center reveals the museum's scientific work with specimens, research, and outreach activities. Learn how specimens are collected today (ethical considerations as well) or about the alien habitat of the deep sea and the strange animals which inhabit its murky depths. Fourteen behind-the-scenes free tours (ages 10 and up only) are given of the museum daily; you should book immediately upon entering the museum if you're interested.

Cromwell Rd., SW7. ℂ 020/7942-5000. www.nhm.ac.uk. Free admission. Mon–Sat 10am–5:50pm; Sun 11am–5:50pm. Tube: South Kensington.

Percival David Foundation of Chinese Art ★

This foundation displays the greatest collection of Chinese ceramics outside China. Approximately 1,700 ceramic objects reflect Chinese court taste from the 10th to 18th centuries, and include many pieces of exceptional beauty. An extraordinary collection of stoneware from the Song (960–1279) and Yuan (1279–1368) dynasties includes examples of rare Ru and Guan wares. Among the justifiably famous blue-and-white porcelains are two unique temple vases, dated by inscription to A.D. 1351. A wide variety of polychrome wares is also represented; they include examples of the delicate doucai wares from the Chenghua period (1465–87) as well as a remarkable group of 18th-century porcelains.

53 Gordon Sq., WC1. ℂ 020/7387-3909. Free admission; donations encouraged. £5 ($8) per person for a guided tour of 10–20 people. Admission to the library must be arranged with the curator ahead of time. There is a charge for use of the library. Mon–Fri 10:30am–5pm. Tube: Russell Sq. or Euston Sq.

The Queen's Gallery ★★

The refurbished gallery at Buckingham Palace reopened to the public in 2002 in time for the Golden Jubilee celebration of Queen Elizabeth II. Visitors going through the Doric portico entrance will find three times as much space as before. A chapel for Queen Victoria in 1843, the 1831 building by John Nash was destroyed in an air raid in 1940. The gallery is dedicated to changing exhibitions of the wide-ranging treasure trove that forms the Royal Collection. Anticipate special exhibitions of paintings, prints, drawings, watercolors, furniture, porcelain, miniatures, enamels, jewelry, and other works of art. At any given time, expect to see such artistic peaks as Van Dyck's equestrian portrait of Charles I; the world-famous *Lady at the Virginal* by Vermeer; a dazzling array of gold snuffboxes, paintings by Monet from the collection of the late Queen Mother, personal jewelry, studies by Leonardo da Vinci; and even the recent and very controversial portrait of the present queen by Lucian Freud.

Buckingham Palace, SW1. ℂ 020/7321-2233. Admission £6.50 ($10) adults, £5 ($8) students and seniors, and £3 ($4.80) children 16 and under. Daily 10am–5:30pm. Tube: St. James's Park, Green Park, or Victoria.

Science Museum ★★★ Kids

This museum traces the development of science and industry and their influence on everyday life. These scientific collections are among the largest, most comprehensive, and most significant anywhere. On display is Stephenson's original rocket and the tiny prototype railroad engine; you can also see Whittle's original jet engine and the Apollo 10 space module. The King George III Collection of scientific instruments is the highlight of a gallery on science in the 18th century. Health Matters is a permanent gallery on modern medicine. The museum has two hands-on galleries, as well as working models and video displays.

Insider's tip: A large addition to this museum explores such topics as genetics, digital technology, and artificial intelligence. Four floors of a new Welcome Wing shelter half a dozen exhibition areas and a 450-seat IMAX theater. One exhibition explores everything from drug use in sports to how engineers observe sea life with robotic submarines. On an upper floor, visitors can learn how DNA was used to identify living relatives of the Bleadon Man, a 2,000-year-old Iron Age Man. On the third floor is the computer that Tim Berners-Lee used to design the World Wide Web outside Geneva, writing the first software for it in 1990.

Note: Marvelous interactive consoles are placed strategically in locations throughout the museum. These display special itineraries, including directions for getting to the various galleries for families, teens, adults, and those with special interests.

Exhibition Rd., SW7. ⓒ 0870/870-4868. www.sciencemuseum.org.uk. Free admission. Daily 10am–6pm. Tube: South Kensington. Closed Dec 24–26.

Sir John Soane's Museum ⭐   This is the former home of Sir John Soane (1753–1837), an architect who rebuilt the Bank of England (not the present structure). With his multiple levels, fool-the-eye mirrors, flying arches, and domes, Soane was a master of perspective and a genius of interior space (his picture gallery, for example, is filled with three times the number of paintings a room of similar dimensions would be likely to hold). William Hogarth's satirical series, *The Rake's Progress,* includes his much-reproduced *Orgy* and *The Election,* a satire on mid-18th-century politics. Soane also filled his house with paintings and classical sculpture. On display is the sarcophagus of Pharaoh Seti I, found in a burial chamber in the Valley of the Kings. Also exhibited are architectural drawings from the collection of 30,000 in the Soane Gallery.

13 Lincoln's Inn Fields, WC2. ⓒ 020/7405-2107. www.soane.org. Free admission (donations invited). Tues–Sat 10am–5pm; 1st Tues of each month 6–9pm. Tours given Sat at 2:30pm; £3 ($4.80) tickets distributed at 2pm, first-come, first-served (group tours by appointment only). Tube: Holborn.

Wallace Collection ⭐⭐ *Finds*   Located in a palatial setting (the modestly described "town house" of the late Lady Wallace), this collection is a contrasting array of art and armaments. The collection is evocative of the Frick Museum in New York and the Musée d'Jacque André in Paris. The art collection (mostly French) includes works by Watteau, Boucher, Fragonard, and Greuze, as well as such classics as Frans Hals's *Laughing Cavalier* and Rembrandt's portrait of his son Titus. The paintings of the Dutch, English, Spanish, and Italian schools are outstanding. The collection also contains important 18th-century French decorative art, including furniture from a number of royal palaces, Sèvres porcelain, and gold boxes. The European and Asian armaments, on the ground floor, are works of art in their own right: superb inlaid suits of armor, some obviously for parade rather than battle, with more businesslike swords, halberds, and magnificent Persian scimitars.

Manchester Sq., W1. ⓒ 020/7563-9500. www.the-wallace-collection.org.uk. Free admission. Mon–Sat 10am–5pm; Sun noon–5pm. Tube: Bond St. or Baker St.

LITERARY LANDMARKS

Carlyle's House   From 1834 to 1881, Thomas Carlyle, author of *The French Revolution*, and Jane Baillie Welsh Carlyle, his noted letter-writing wife, resided in this modest 1708 terraced house. Furnished essentially as it was in Carlyle's day, the house is located about ¾ of a block from the Thames, near the Chelsea Embankment along King's Road. The most interesting room is the not-so-soundproof "soundproof" study in the sky-lit attic. It's filled with Carlyle memorabilia—his books, a letter from Disraeli, personal effects, a writing chair, even his death mask.

24 Cheyne Row, SW3. © 020/7352-7087. Admission £3.60 ($5.75) adults, £1.80 ($2.90) children 5–16, free for children 4 and under. Wed–Sun 11am–5pm. Closed Nov–Mar. Tube: Sloane Sq.

Dickens House   In Bloomsbury stands the simple abode in which Charles Dickens wrote *Oliver Twist* and finished *The Pickwick Papers* (his American readers actually waited at the dock for the ship that brought in each new installment). The place is almost a shrine for a Dickens fan; it contains his study, manuscripts, and personal relics, as well as reconstructed interiors.

48 Doughty St., WC1. © 020/7405-2127. www.dickensmuseum.com. Admission £4 ($6.40) adults, £3 ($4.80) students, £2 ($3.20) children, £9 ($14) families. Mon–Sat 10am–5pm. Tube: Russell Sq.

Samuel Johnson's House ★★   Dr. Johnson and his copyists compiled a famous dictionary in this Queen Anne house, where the lexicographer, poet, essayist, and fiction writer lived from 1748 to 1759. Although Johnson also lived at Staple Inn in Holborn and at a number of other places, the Gough Square house is the only one of his residences remaining in London. The 17th-century building has been painstakingly restored, and it's well worth a visit.

17 Gough Sq., EC4. © 020/7353-3745. www.drjh.dircon.co.uk. Admission £4 ($6.40) adults, £3 ($4.80) students and seniors, £1 ($1.60) children. May–Sept Mon–Sat 11am–5:30pm; Oct–Apr Mon–Sat 11am–4:45pm. Tube: Blackfriars or Chancery Lane. Walk up New Bridge St. and turn left onto Fleet; Gough Sq. is tiny and hidden, north of Fleet St.

Shakespeare's Globe Theatre & Exhibition ★   A recent re-creation of what was probably the most important public theater ever built, it's on the exact site where many of Shakespeare's plays opened. The late American filmmaker, Sam Wanamaker, worked for some 20 years to raise funds to re-create the theater as it existed in Elizabethan times, thatched roof and all. A fascinating exhibit tells the story of the Globe's construction, using the material (including goat hair in the plaster), techniques, and craftsmanship of 400 years ago. The new Globe isn't an exact replica: It seats 1,500 patrons, not the 3,000 who regularly squeezed in during the early 1600s, and this thatched roof has been specially treated with a fire retardant. Guided tours offered throughout the day.

New Globe Walk, Southwark, SE1. © 020/7902-1400. www.shakespeares-globe.org. Admission £8 ($13) adults, £5.50 ($8.80) children 15 and under, £6.50 ($10) seniors and students. Oct–Apr daily 10am–5pm; May–Sept daily 9am–noon and 1–4pm. Tube: Mansion House or London Bridge.

HANGING "AROUND" IN LONDON

The world's largest observation wheel, the **Millennium Wheel London Eye** ★, Millennium Jubilee Gard (© **0870/500-0600;** www.londoneye.com), opened in February 2000. The fourth-tallest structure in London, it offers panoramic views that extend for some 40km (25 miles) if the weather's clear. Passengers are carried in 32 "pods" that make a complete revolution every half-hour. Along the way you see some of London's landmarks from a bird's-eye point of view.

Bloomsbury

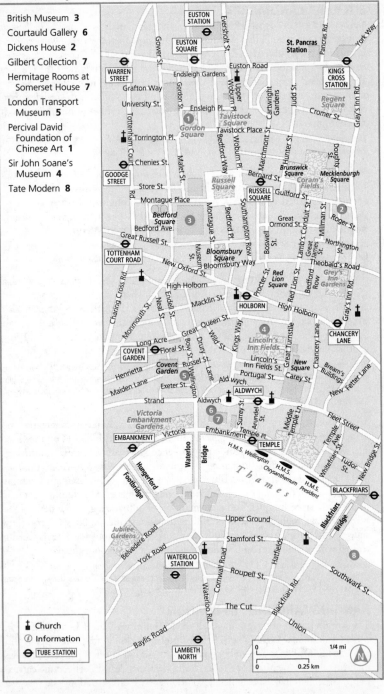

Built of steel by a European consortium, this eye was conceived and designed by London architects Julia Barfield and David Marks, who claimed inspiration from both the Statue of Liberty in New York and the Eiffel Tower in Paris. Some 2 million visitors are expected to ride the eye every year.

The eye lies close to Westminster Bridge (you can hardly miss it). Tickets for the ride are £11 ($18) for adults, £10 ($16) for seniors, and £5.50 ($8.80) for children. In May and September hours are Monday through Thursday from 9:30am to 8pm, Friday through Sunday from 9:30am to 9pm; June Monday through Thursday from 9:30am to 9pm; Friday through Sunday from 9:30am to 10pm; July and August from 9:30am to 10pm; October through April daily from 9:30am to 8pm. Tube: Embankment or Waterloo.

3 London's Parks & Gardens

London has the greatest system of parklands of any large city on the globe. Not as rigidly laid out as the parks of Paris, London's are maintained with a loving care and lavish artistry that puts their American equivalents to shame.

The largest of them—and one of the world's biggest—is **Hyde Park** ✪, W2. With the adjoining Kensington Gardens, it covers 636 acres of central London with velvety lawn interspersed with ponds, flowerbeds, and trees. Hyde Park was once a favorite deer-hunting ground of Henry VIII. Running through the width is a 41-acre lake known as the Serpentine. Rotten Row, a 2.5km (1½-mile) sand track, is reserved for horseback riding and on Sunday attracts some skilled equestrians.

At the northeastern corner of Hyde Park, near Marble Arch, is **Speaker's Corner** (**www.speakerscorner.net**), where anyone can speak. The only rules: You can't blaspheme, be obscene, or incite a riot. The tradition actually began in 1855—before the legal right to assembly was guaranteed in 1872—when a mob of 150,000 gathered to attack a proposed Sunday Trading Bill. Orators from all over Britain have been taking advantage of this spot ever since.

Lovely **Kensington Gardens,** W2, blending with Hyde Park, border on the grounds of Kensington Palace. These gardens are home to the celebrated statue of Peter Pan, with the bronze rabbits that toddlers are always trying to kidnap. The Albert Memorial is also here, and you'll recall the sea of flowers and tributes left here after the death of Diana, princess of Wales.

East of Hyde Park, across Piccadilly, stretch **Green Park** ✪ and **St. James's Park** ✪, W1, forming an almost-unbroken chain of landscaped beauty. This is an ideal area for picnics, and one that you'll find hard to believe was once a festering piece of swamp near a leper hospital. There is a romantic lake, stocked with a variety of ducks and pelicans, descendants of the pair that the Russian ambassador presented to Charles II in 1662.

Regent's Park ✪✪✪, NW1, covers most of the district by that name, north of Baker Street and Marylebone Road. Designed by the 18th-century genius John Nash to surround a palace of the prince regent that never materialized, this is the most classically beautiful of London's parks. The core is a rose garden planted around a small lake alive with waterfowl and spanned by humped Japanese bridges. The open-air theater and the London Zoo are here, and, as in all the local parks, there are hundreds of deck chairs on the lawns in which to sunbathe. The deck-chair attendants, who collect a small fee, are mostly college students on vacation.

The **London Zoo** ✪ (**© 020/7722-3333**) is more than 150 years old. Run by the Zoological Society of London, the 36-acre garden houses some 8,000 animals, including some of the rarest species on earth. It waned in popularity the last few years, but a recent campaign won the zoo corporate sponsorship that is funding a modernization program. Zoo admission is £10 ($16) for adults, £9 ($14) for children ages 4 to 14, and free for children under age 4. The zoo is open daily from 10am to 5:30pm (closes at 4pm Nov–Feb). You can watch the penguins or the denizens of the aquarium being fed their lunch daily at 2:30pm. Take the tube to Camden Town or bus no. 274 or Z2 in summer only.

Battersea Park, SW11 (© **020/8871-7530**), is a vast patch of woodland, lakes, and lawns on the south bank of the Thames, opposite Chelsea Embankment between Albert Bridge and Chelsea Bridge. Formerly known as Battersea Fields, the present park was laid out between 1852 and 1858 on an old dueling ground. The park, which measures 1km (¾ mile) on each of its four sides, has a lake for boating, a fenced-in deer park with wild birds, and fields for tennis and football (soccer). There's even a children's zoo. The park's architectural highlight is the Peace Pagoda, built of stone and wood. The park, open May through September daily from dawn until dusk, is not well serviced by public transportation. The nearest Tube is in Chelsea on the right bank (Sloane Square); from here it's a brisk 15-minute walk. If you prefer the bus, take no. 137 from the Sloane Square station, exiting at the first stop after the bus crosses the Thames.

Located about 6.5km (4 miles) north of the center of London, **Hampstead Heath,** an 800-acre expanse of high heath surrounded entirely by London, is a chain of continuous park, wood, and grassland. On a clear day you can see St. Paul's Cathedral and even the hills of Kent south of the Thames. For years, Londoners have come here to fly kites, sun worship, fish the ponds, swim, picnic, or jog. At the shore of Kenwood Lake, in the northern section, is a concert platform devoted to symphony performances on summer evenings. In the northeast corner, in Waterlow Park, ballets, operas, and comedies are staged at the Grass Theatre in June and July.

When the Underground came to **Hampstead Village** (Tube: Hampstead) in 1907, its attraction as a place to live became widely known, and writers, artists, architects, musicians, and scientists—some from The City—came to join earlier residents. D. H. Lawrence, Rabindranath Tagore, Percy Bysshe Shelley, and Robert Louis Stevenson once lived here; John Le Carré still does.

The Regency and Georgian houses in this village are just 20 minutes by Tube from Piccadilly Circus. Along Flask Walk, a pedestrian mall, is a palatable mix of historic pubs, toyshops, and chic boutiques. The original village, on the side of a hill, still has old roads, alleys, steps, courts, and groves to be strolled through.

See "Sights on the Outskirts," below, for details on Kew Gardens.

4 Sights on the Outskirts

HAMPTON COURT

Hampton Court Palace ✿✿✿   The 16th-century palace of Cardinal Wolsey can teach us a lesson: Don't try to outdo your boss, particularly if he happens to be Henry VIII. The rich cardinal did just that, and he eventually lost his fortune, power, prestige, and ended up giving his lavish palace to the Tudor monarch. Henry took over, even outdoing the Wolsey embellishments. The Tudor additions included the Anne Boleyn gateway, with its 16th-century astronomical clock that even tells the high-water mark at London Bridge. From Clock Court, you can see one of Henry's major contributions, the aptly named Great Hall, with its hammer-beam ceiling. Also added by Henry were the tiltyard (where jousting competitions were held), a tennis court, and a kitchen.

To judge from the movie *A Man for All Seasons,* Hampton Court had quite a retinue to feed. Cooking was done in the Great Kitchen. Henry cavorted through the various apartments with his wife of the moment—from Anne Boleyn to Catherine Parr (the latter reversed things and lived to bury her erstwhile spouse). Charles I was imprisoned here at one time and managed to temporarily escape his jailers.

Although the palace enjoyed prestige and pomp in Elizabethan days, it owes much of its present look to William and Mary—or rather to Sir Christopher Wren, who designed and had built the Northern or Lion Gates, intended to be the main entrance to the new parts of the palace. The fine wrought-iron screen at the south end of the south gardens was made by Jean Tijou around 1694 for William and Mary. You can parade through the apartments today, filled as they were with porcelain, furniture, paintings, and tapestries. The King's Dressing Room is graced with some of the best art, mainly paintings by old masters on loan from Queen Elizabeth II. Finally, be sure to inspect the royal chapel (Wolsey wouldn't recognize it). To confound yourself totally, you may want to get lost in the serpentine **shrubbery maze** in the garden, also the work of Wren.

The gardens—including the Great Vine, King's Privy Garden, Great Fountain Gardens, Tudor and Elizabethan Knot Gardens, Board Walk, Tiltyard, and Wilderness—are open daily year-round from 7am until dusk (but not later than 9pm) and can be visited free except for the Privy Garden. A garden cafe and restaurant is in the Tiltyard Gardens.

Hampton. ℂ 0870/752-7777. www.hrp.org.uk. Admission £11 ($18) adults, £8.25 ($13) students and seniors, £7.25 ($12) children 5–15, free for children under 5, family ticket £33 ($53). Gardens open year-round daily 7am–dusk (no later than 9pm), free admission to all except Privy Garden (admission £3/$4.80 adults, £2/$3.20 child) without palace ticket during summer months. Cloisters, courtyards, state apartments, great kitchen, cellars, and Hampton Court exhibition open Mar 30–Oct 26 Mon 10:15am–6pm; Tues–Sun 9:30am–6pm, last entry 5:15pm; Oct 27–Mar 29 Mon 10:15am–4:30pm, Tues–Sun 9:30am–6pm, last entry 5:15pm.

KEW ★★★

About 15km (9 miles) southwest of central London, Kew is home to one of the best-known botanical gardens in Europe. It's also the site of **Kew Palace** ★★, former residence of George III and Queen Charlotte. A dark redbrick structure, it is characterized by its Dutch gables. The house was constructed in 1631, and at its rear is the Queen's Garden in a very formal design and filled with plants thought to have grown here in the 17th century. The interior is very much an elegant country house of the time, fit for a king, but not as regal as Buckingham Palace. You get the feeling that someone could have actually lived here as you wander through the dining room, the breakfast room, and go upstairs to the Queen's drawing room where musical evenings were staged. The rooms are wallpapered with designs actually used at the time. Perhaps the most intriguing exhibits are little possessions once owned by royal occupants here—everything from snuffboxes to Prince Frederick's gambling debts. The most convenient way to get to Kew is to take the **District Line** Tube to the Kew Gardens stop, on the south bank of the Thames. Allow about 30 minutes.

Royal Botanic (Kew) Gardens ★★★   These world-famous gardens offer thousands of varieties of plants. But Kew is no mere pleasure garden—it's essentially a vast scientific research center that happens to be beautiful. The gardens, on a 300-acre site, encompass lakes, greenhouses, walks, pavilions, and museums, along with fine examples of the architecture of Sir William Chambers. Among the 50,000 plant species are notable collections of ferns, orchids, aquatic plants, cacti, mountain plants, palms, and tropical water lilies.

No matter what season you visit, Kew always has something to see, from the first spring flowers through to winter. Gigantic hothouses grow species of shrubs, blooms, and trees from every part of the globe, from the Arctic Circle to tropical rain forests. Attractions include a newly restored Japanese gateway in traditional landscaping, as well as exhibitions that vary with the season. The newest greenhouse, the Princess of Wales Conservatory (beyond the rock garden), encompasses 10 climatic zones, from arid to tropical; it has London's most thrilling collection of miniature orchids. The Marianne North Gallery (1882) is an absolute gem, paneled with 246 different types of wood that the intrepid Victorian artist collected on her world journeys; she also collected 832 paintings of exotic and tropical flora, all displayed on the walls. The Visitor Centre at Victoria Gate houses an exhibit telling the story of Kew, as well as a bookshop.

Kew. © 020/8940-1171. www.rbgkew.org.uk. Admission £7.50 ($12) adults, £5.50 ($8.80) students and seniors, free for children 16 and under. Daily 9:30am–5pm. Tube: District Line to Kew Gardens.

GREENWICH ★★★

When London overwhelms you, and you'd like to escape for a beautiful, sunny afternoon on the city's outskirts, make it Greenwich.

Greenwich mean time is the basis of standard time throughout most of the world, and Greenwich has been the zero point used in the reckoning of terrestrial longitudes since 1884. But this lovely village—the center of British seafaring when Britain ruled the seas—is also home of the Royal Naval College, the National Maritime Museum, and the Old Royal Observatory. In dry dock at Greenwich Pier is the clipper ship *Cutty Sark* (see "The Last of the Great Clipper Ships," below).

GETTING THERE   The fastest way to get to Greenwich is to take the tube in Central London to Waterloo Station, where you can take a fast train to Greenwich Station.

The Tube is for speed, taking only 15 minutes, but if you'd like to travel the 6.5km (4 miles) to Greenwich the way Henry VIII did, you still can. In fact, getting to Greenwich is still half the fun. The most appealing way involves boarding any of the frequent ferryboats that cruise along the Thames at intervals that vary from every half-hour (in summer) to every 45 minutes (in winter). Boats that depart from Westminster Pier (Tube: Westminster) are maintained by **Westminster Passenger Services, Ltd.** (© **020/7930-4097**). Boats that leave from Charing Cross Pier (Tube: Embankment) and Tower Pier (Tube: Tower Hill) are run by **Catamaran Cruises, Ltd.** (© **020/7987-1185**). Depending on the tides and the carrier you select, travel time varies from 50 to 75 minutes each way. Passage is £6 to £10 ($9.60–$16) round-trip for adults, £4 to £6 ($6.40–$9.60) round-trip for children 5 to 12; it's free for those under 5.

VISITOR INFORMATION   The **Greenwich Tourist Information Centre** is at 2 Cutty Sark Gardens (© **0870/608-2000**); open daily from 10am to 5pm. The Tourist Information Centre conducts **walking tours** of Greenwich's major

Whatever Became of the Millennium Dome?

Greenwich's much-maligned **Millennium Dome**, which struck out with visitors and locals alike, will be transformed into a 20,000-seat sports and music venue. The Dome is expected to become the "Madison Square Garden of Europe."

The Last of the Great Clipper Ships

Nearly 6.5km (4 miles) east of London, at Greenwich Pier, now in permanent dry dock, lies the last and ultimate word in sail power: the *Cutty Sark* ★★, King William Walk, Greenwich, SE10 (© **020/8858-3445**; www.cuttysark.org.uk; bus no. 177, 180, 188, or 199). Named after the witch in Robert Burns's poem "Tam O'Shanter," it was the greatest of the clipper ships that carried tea from China and wool from Australia in the most exciting ocean races ever sailed. The *Cutty Sark*'s record stood at a then unsurpassed 584km (363 miles) in 24 hours. Launched in Scotland in 1869, the sleek black three-master represented the final fighting run of canvas against steam. Although the age of the clippers was brief, they outpaced the steamers as long as wind filled their billowing mountain of sails. On board the *Cutty Sark* is a museum devoted to clipper lore. Admission is £3.95 ($6.30) for adults and £2.95 ($4.70) for children over 5, students, and seniors. A family ticket costs £9.80 ($16). It's open daily from 10am to 5pm, with last admission at 4:30pm.

sights. The tours cost £4.50 ($7.20), depart daily at 12:15 and 2:15pm, and last 1½ to 2 hours. Advance reservations aren't required, but you may want to phone in advance to find out any last-minute schedule changes.

SEEING THE SIGHTS

The **National Maritime Museum,** the **Old Royal Observatory,** and **Queen's House** stand together in a beautiful royal park, high on a hill overlooking the Thames. All three attractions are free to get into and open daily from 10am to 5pm. For more information, call © **020/8312-6608** or visit **www.nmm.ac.uk**.

From the days of early seafarers to 20th-century sea power, the **National Maritime Museum** ★★ illustrates the glory that was Britain at sea. The cannon, relics, ship models, and paintings tell the story of a thousand naval battles and a thousand victories, as well as the price of those battles. Look for some oddities here—everything from the dreaded cat-o'-nine-tails used to flog sailors until 1879 to Nelson's Trafalgar coat, with the fatal bullet hole in the left shoulder clearly visible. In time for the millennium, the museum spent £20 million ($32 million) in a massive expansion that added 16 new galleries devoted to British maritime history and improved visitor facilities.

Old Royal Observatory ★ is the original home of Greenwich mean time. It has the largest refracting telescope in the United Kingdom and a collection of historic timekeepers and astronomical instruments. You can stand astride the meridian and set your watch precisely by the falling time-ball. Sir Christopher Wren designed the Octagon Room. Here the first royal astronomer, Flamsteed, made his 30,000 observations that formed the basis of his *Historia Coelestis Britannica*. Edmond Halley, he of the eponymous Halley's Comet, succeeded him. In 1833, the ball on the tower was hung to enable shipmasters to set their chronometers accurately.

Designed by Inigo Jones, **Queen's House** ★★ (1616) is a fine example of this architect's innovative style. It's most famous for the cantilevered tulip staircase, the first of its kind. Carefully restored, the house contains a collection of royal and marine paintings and other objets d'art.

The Wernher Collection at Ranger's House ★★, Chesterfield Walk (② 020/ 8853-0035; www.English-heritage.org.uk), is a real find and one of the finest and most unusual 19th-century mixed-art collections in the world. Acquired by a German diamond dealer, Sir Julius Wernher, the collection contains some 650 exhibits, some dating as far back as 3 B.C. It's an eclectic mix of everything, including jewelry, bronzes, ivory, antiques, tapestries, porcelain pieces, and classic paintings. One salon is devoted to the biggest collection of Renaissance jewelry in Britain. Look also for the carved medieval, Byzantine, and Renaissance ivories along with Limoges enamels and Sèvres porcelain. The most unusual items are enameled skulls and a miniature coffin complete with 3-D skeleton. Don't expect everything to be beautiful. Wernher's taste was often bizarre. Admission is £4.50 ($7.20) adults, £3.50 ($5.60) seniors and students, £2.30 ($3.70) children, free for children under 5. Note that the museum is closed from December 23 to March 4.

Nearby is the **Royal Naval College** ★★, King William Walk, off Romney Road (② 020/8269-4747). Designed by Sir Christopher Wren in 1696, it occupies 4 blocks named after King Charles, Queen Anne, King William, and Queen Mary. Formerly, Greenwich Palace stood here from 1422 to 1640. It's worth stopping in to see the magnificent Painted Hall by Thornhill, where the body of Nelson lay in state in 1805, and the Georgian chapel of St. Peter and St. Paul. Open daily from 10am to 5pm; admission is free.

5 Organized Tours

BUS TOURS

For the first-timer, the quickest and most economical way to bring the big city into focus is to take a bus tour. One of the most popular is **The Original London Sightseeing Tour,** which passes by all the major sights in just about 1½ hours. The tour, which uses a traditional double-decker bus with live commentary by a guide, costs £15 ($24) for adults, £7.50 ($12) for children under 16, free for those under 5. The tour allows you to hop on or off the bus at any point in the tour at no extra charge. The tour plus admission to Madame Tussaud's is £30 ($48) for adults, £20 ($31) for children.

Departures are from convenient points within the city; you can choose your departure point when you buy your ticket. Tickets can be purchased on the bus or at a discount from any London Transport or London Tourist Board Information Centre. Most hotel concierges also sell tickets. For information or phone purchases, call ② 020/8877-1722. It's also possible to book online at **www.the originaltour.com**.

Big Bus Company Ltd., Waterside Way, London SW17 (② 020/8944-7810 or 0800/169-1365), operates a 2-hour tour in summer, departing frequently between 8:30am and 5pm daily from Marble Arch by Speakers Corner, Green Park by the Ritz Hotel, and Victoria Station (Buckingham Palace Rd. by the Royal Westminster Hotel). Tours cover the highlights—18 in all—ranging from the Houses of Parliament and Westminster Abbey to the Tower of London and Buckingham Palace (exterior looks only), accompanied by live commentary. The cost is £16 ($26) for adults, £6 ($9.60) for children. A 1-hour tour follows the same route but covers only 13 sights. Tickets are valid all day; you can hop on and off the bus as you wish.

WALKING TOURS

The Original London Walks, 87 Messina Ave., P.O. Box 1708, London NW6 4LW (② 020/7624-3978; http://london.walks.com), the oldest established walking-tour company in London, is run by an Anglo-American journalist/actor couple, David and Mary Tucker. Their hallmarks are variety, reliability, reasonably sized groups, and—above all—superb guides. The renowned crime historian Donald Rumbelow, the leading authority on Jack the Ripper and author of the classic guidebook *London Walks,* is a regular guide, as are several prominent actors (including classical actor Edward Petherbridge). Walks are regularly scheduled daily and cost £5 ($8) for adults, £4 ($6.40) for students and seniors; children under 15 go free. Call for schedule; no reservations needed.

Discovery Walks, 67 Chancery Lane, London WC2 (© **020/8530-8443;** www.Jack-the-Ripper-Walk.co.uk), are themed walks, led by Richard Jones, author of *Frommer's Memorable Walks in London.* **Stepping Out** (© **020/8881-2933;** www.walklon.ndirect.co.uk) offers a series of offbeat walks led by qualified historians. Tours generally cost £5 to £12 ($8–$19).

RIVER CRUISES

A trip up or down the river gives you an entirely different view of London from the one you get from land. You see how the city grew along and around the Thames and how many of its landmarks turn their faces toward the water. Several companies operate motor launches from the Westminster piers (Tube: Westminster), offering panoramic views of one of Europe's most historic waterways en route.

Westminster-Greenwich Thames Passenger Boat Service, Westminster Pier, Victoria Embankment, SW1 (© **020/7930-4097;** www.westminsterpier.co.uk), concerns itself only with downriver traffic from Westminster Pier to such destinations as Greenwich (see "Sights on the Outskirts," above). The most popular excursion departs for Greenwich (a 50-min. ride) at half-hour intervals between 10am and 4pm from April to October, and between 10:30am and 6pm from June to August; from November to March, boats depart from Westminster Pier at 30-minute intervals daily from 10:40am to 3:20pm. One-way fares are £6.30 ($10) for adults, £3.90 ($6.25) for children under 16, £5.20 ($8.30) for seniors. Round-trip fares are £7.80 ($12) for adults, £3.90 ($6.25) for children, £6.30 ($10) for seniors. A family ticket for two adults and up to three children under 15 costs £17 ($27) one-way, £20 ($32) round-trip.

Westminster Passenger Association (Upriver) Ltd., Westminster Pier, Victoria Embankment, SW1 (© **020/7930-2062** or 020/7930-4721; www.wpsa.co.uk), offers the only riverboat service upstream from Westminster Bridge to Kew, Richmond, and Hampton Court, with regular daily sailings from the Monday before Easter until the end of October on traditional riverboats, all with licensed bars. Trip time, one-way, can be as little as 1½ hours to Kew and between 2½ and 4 hours to Hampton Court, depending on the tide. Cruises from Westminster Pier to Hampton Court via Kew Gardens leave daily at 11, 11:15am, and noon. Round-trip tickets are £12 to £18 ($19–$29) for adults, £9 to £12 ($14–$19) for seniors, and £6 to £9 ($9.60–$14) for children ages 4 to 14; one child under 4 accompanied by an adult goes free.

6 Shopping

THE TOP SHOPPING STREETS & NEIGHBORHOODS

Several key streets offer some of London's best retail stores—or simply one of everything—compactly located in a niche or neighborhood so that you can just stroll and shop.

THE WEST END   The West End includes the Mayfair district and is home to the core of London's big-name shopping. Most of the department stores, designer shops, and multiples (chain stores) have their flagships in this area.

The key streets are **Oxford Street** for affordable shopping (start at Marble Arch Tube station if you're ambitious, or Bond St. station if you just want to see some of it) and **Regent Street,** which intersects Oxford Street at Oxford Circus (Tube: Oxford Circus).

While there are several branches of the private label department store **Marks & Spencer,** their Marble Arch store (on Oxford St.) is the flagship, and worth shopping for their high-quality goods. There's a grocery store in the basement and a home-furnishings department upstairs.

Regent Street has fancier shops—more upscale department stores (including the famed **Liberty of London**), multiples **(Laura Ashley),** and specialty dealers—and leads all the way to Piccadilly.

In between the two, parallel to Regent Street, is **Bond Street.** Divided into New and Old, Bond Street (Tube: Bond St.) also connects Piccadilly with Oxford Street and is synonymous with the luxury trade. Bond Street has had a recent revival and is the hot address for all the international designers; **Donna Karan** has not one, but two shops here. Many international hotshots have digs surrounding hers, from **Chanel** and **Ferragamo** to **Versace.**

Burlington Arcade (Tube: Piccadilly Circus), the famous glass-roofed, Regency-style passage leading off Piccadilly, looks like a period exhibition and is lined with intriguing shops and boutiques. The small, smart stores specialize in fashion, jewelry, Irish linen, cashmere, and more. If you linger in the arcade until 5:30pm, you can watch the beadles in their black-and-yellow livery and top hats ceremoniously put in place the iron grills that block off the arcade until 9am the next morning, at which time they just as ceremoniously remove them to mark the start of a new business day. Also at 5:30pm, a hand bell called the Burlington Bell is sounded, signaling the end of trading.

Just off Regent Street (actually tucked right behind it) is **Carnaby Street** (Tube: Oxford Circus), which is also having a comeback. While it no longer dominates the world of pacesetting fashion as it did in the 1960s, it's still fun to visit for teens who may need cheap souvenirs, a purple wig, or a little something in leather. A convenient branch of **Boots the Chemists** is also here.

For a total contrast, check out **Jermyn Street,** on the far side of Piccadilly, a tiny 2-block-long street devoted to high-end men's haberdashers and toiletries shops; many have been doing business for centuries. Several hold royal warrants, including **Turnball & Asser,** where HRH Prince Charles has his pj's made.

The West End leads to the theater district, and so two more shopping areas: the still-not-ready-for-prime-time **Soho,** where the sex shops are slowly being turned into cutting-edge designer shops; and **Covent Garden,** which is a masterpiece unto itself. The marketplace has eaten up the surrounding neighborhood so that even though the streets run a little higgledy-piggledy and you can easily get lost, it's fun to just wander and shop.

KNIGHTSBRIDGE & CHELSEA   This is the second-most famous of London's retail districts and the home of **Harrods** (Tube: Knightsbridge). A small street nearby, **Sloane Street,** is chockablock with designer shops; **Cheval Place,** in the opposite direction, is also lined with designer resale shops.

Walk toward Museum Row, and you'll soon find **Beauchamp Place** (pronounced *Bee*-cham; Tube: Knightsbridge). The street is only 1 block long, but it features the kinds of shops where young British aristos buy their clothing.

Tips **Shipping It Home**

You can ship purchases on your flight home by paying for excess baggage (rates vary with the airline), or you can have your package shipped independently. Independent operators are generally less expensive than the airlines. Try **London Baggage,** 120 Wilton Rd., Vigilant House, SW1V (© 020/7808-7166; Tube: Victoria), or **Burns International Facilities,** at Heathrow Airport Terminal 1 (© 020/8745-5301) and Terminal 4 (© 020/8745-6460). But remember, you can avoid the VAT up front only if you have the store ship directly to you. If you ship via excess baggage or London Baggage, you still have to pay the VAT up front and apply for a refund. See chapter 3 for more on claiming your VAT refund.

Head out at the **Harvey Nichols** end of Knightsbridge, away from Harrods, and shop your way through the designer stores on Sloane Street (**Hermès, Armani, Prada,** and the like), then walk past Sloane Square and you're in an altogether different neighborhood: King's Road.

King's Road (Tube: Sloane Sq.), the main street of Chelsea, which starts at Sloane Square, will forever remain a symbol of London in the Swinging Sixties. Today, the street is still frequented by young people, but with fewer Mohican haircuts, "Bovver boots," and Edwardian ball gowns than before. More and more, King's Road is a lineup of markets and "multistores," large or small conglomerations of indoor stands, stalls, and booths in one building or enclosure.

Chelsea doesn't begin and end with King's Road. If you choose to walk the other direction from Harrods, you connect to a part of Chelsea called **Brompton Cross,** another hip and hot area for designer shops made popular when Michelin House was rehabbed by Sir Terence Conran for **The Conran Shop.**

Also seek out **Walton Street,** a tiny little snake of a street running from Brompton Cross back toward the museums. About 2 blocks of this 3-block street are devoted to fairy-tale shops for m'lady where you can buy aromatherapy from **Jo Malone,** needlepoint, costume jewelry, or meet with your interior designer, who runs a small shop of objets d'art.

Finally, don't forget all those museums right there in the corner of the shopping streets. They all have great gift shops.

KENSINGTON & NOTTING HILL **Kensington High Street** is the new hangout of the classier breed of teen who has graduated from Carnaby Street and is ready for street chic. While a few staples of basic British fashion are on this strip, most of the stores feature items that stretch, are very, very short, or are very, very tight. The Tube station here is High Street Kensington.

From Kensington High Street, you can walk up **Kensington Church Street,** which, like Portobello Road, is one of the city's main shopping avenues for antiques. Kensington Church Street dead-ends into the Notting Hill Gate Tube station, which is where you would arrive for shopping on **Portobello Road.** The dealers and the weekend market are 2 blocks beyond.

THE DEPARTMENT STORES

Contrary to popular belief, Harrods is not the only department store in London. The British invented the department store, and they have lots of them—mostly in Mayfair, and each with its own customer profile.

Daks Simpson Piccadilly   Opened in 1936 as the home of DAKS clothing, Simpson's has been going strong ever since. It's known for menswear—its base-ment-level men's shoe department is a model of the way quality shoes should be fit-ted—as well as women's fashions, perfume, jewelry, and lingerie. Many of the clothes are lighthearted, carefully made, and well suited to casual elegance. Its Simp-son Collection rubs shoulders with international designer names such as Armani and Yves Saint Laurent. 34 Jermyn St., W1. © 020/7734-2002. Tube: Piccadilly Circus.

Fenwick of Bond Street   Fenwick (the "w" is silent), dating from 1891, is a stylish fashion store that offers an excellent collection of designer womenswear, ranging from moderately priced ready-to-wear items to more expensive designer fashions. A wide range of lingerie in all price ranges is also sold. 63 New Bond St., W1. © 020/7629-9161. Tube: Bond St.

Fortnum & Mason   The world's most elegant grocery store is a British tradi-tion dating back to 1707. This store exemplifies the elegance and style you would expect from an establishment with three royal warrants. Enter and be transported to another world of deep-red carpets, crystal chandeliers, spiraling wooden staircases, and unobtrusive, tail-coated assistants.

The grocery department is renowned for its impressive selection of the finest foods from around the world—the best champagne, the most scrumptious Bel-gian chocolates, and succulent Scottish smoked salmon. Wander through the four floors and inspect the bone china and crystal cut glass, find the perfect gift in the leather or stationery departments, or reflect on the changing history of furniture and ornaments in the antiques department. Dining choices include the recently refurbished **St. James Restaurant** and **The Fountain Restaurant** (for details on taking afternoon tea here, see chapter 4). After a £14 million ($22 million) development, Fortnum & Mason now offers exclusive and specialty ranges for the home, as well as beauty products and fashions for both women and men. 181 Piccadilly, W1. © 020/7734-8040. Tube: Piccadilly Circus.

Harrods   An institution as firmly entrenched in English life as Buckingham Palace and the Ascot Races, Harrods is an elaborate emporium and at times as fascinating as a museum. The sheer range, variety, and quality of merchandise are dazzling. If you visit only one store in all of England, make it Harrods, even if you're just looking.

The fifth floor is devoted to sports and leisure, with a wide range of equip-ment and attire. Toy Kingdom is on the fourth floor, along with children's wear. The Egyptian Hall, on the ground floor, sells crystal from Lalique and Baccarat, plus porcelain. You'll also find a men's grooming room, an enormous jewelry department, and a fashion-forward department for younger customers. In the basement, you'll find a bank, a theater-booking service, and a travel bureau. Harrods Shop for logo gifts is on the ground floor. When you're ready for a break, you have a choice of 18 restaurants and bars. Best of all are the Food Halls, stocked with a huge variety of foods and several cafes. Harrods began as a grocer in 1849, still the heart of the business. 87–135 Brompton Rd., Knightsbridge, SW1. © 020/7730-1234. Tube: Knightsbridge.

Liberty   This major British department store is celebrated for its Liberty Prints: top-echelon, carriage-trade fabrics, often in floral patterns, that are prized by decorators for the way they add a sense of English tradition to a room. The front part of the store on Regent Street isn't particularly distinctive, but don't be fooled: Some parts of the place have been restored to Tudor-style splendor that includes half-timbering and lots of interior paneling. Liberty houses six floors of fashion, china, and home furnishings, as well as the famous Liberty Print fashion fabrics, upholstery fabrics, scarves, ties, luggage, and gifts. 214–220 Regent St., W1. © 020/7734-1234. Tube: Oxford Circus.

SOME CLASSIC LONDON FAVORITES

ANTIQUES See also "The Markets," below. Portobello Road is really the prime hunting ground.

At the **Antiquarius Antiques Centre,** 131–141 King's Rd., SW3 (© 020/7969-1500; Tube: Sloane Sq.), more than 120 dealers offer specialized merchandise, such as antique and period jewelry, silver, first-edition books, boxes, clocks, prints, and paintings, with an occasional piece of antique furniture. You'll find a lot of items from the 1950s. Closed Sunday.

Alfie's Antique Market, 13–25 Church St., NW8 (© 020/7723-6066; Tube: Marylebone or Edgware Rd.), is the biggest and one of the best-stocked conglomerates of antiques dealers in London, all crammed into the premises of what was built before 1880 as a department store. It contains more than 370 stalls, showrooms, and workshops scattered over 35,000 square feet of floor space. Closed Sunday and Monday.

ARTS & CRAFTS Gabriel's Wharf, 56 Upper Ground, SE1 (© 020/7401-2255. Tube: Blackfriars, Southwark) is a South Bank complex of shops, restaurants and bars open Tuesday through Sunday from 11am to 6pm (dining and drinking establishments open later). Lying 2 minutes by foot from Oxo Tower Wharf, it is filled with some of the most skilled of London craftspeople, turning out original pieces of sculpture, jewelry, ceramics, art, and fashion. From food to fashion, from arts to crafts, it awaits you here. The place is a lot of fun at which to poke around.

BATH & BODY Branches of **The Body Shop** are seemingly everywhere. Check out the one at 375 Oxford St., W1 (© 020/7409-7868; Tube: Bond St.). Prices are much lower in the United Kingdom than in the United States.

Boots The Chemists has branches all over Britain. A convenient branch is at 490 Oxford St., W1C (© 020/7491-8545; Tube: Marble Arch). The house brands of beauty products are usually the best, be they Boots' products (try the cucumber facial scrub), Boots' versions of The Body Shop (two lines, Global and Naturalistic), or Boots' versions of Chanel makeup (called No. 7).

Stock up on essential oils, or perhaps dream pillows, candles, sachets of letters of the alphabet, and aromatherapy fans at **Culpeper the Herbalist,** 8 The Market, Covent Garden, WC2 (© 020/7379-6698). Another branch is in Mayfair at 21 Bruton St., W1 (© 020/7629-4559).

Floris, 89 Jermyn St., SW1 (© 020/7930-2885; Tube: Piccadilly Circus), stocks a variety of toilet articles and fragrances in floor-to-ceiling mahogany cabinets, which are architectural curiosities in their own right, dating from the Great Exhibition of 1851.

Lush, 11 The Piazza, Covent Garden (© 020/7240-4570; Tube: Covent Garden), sells the most intriguing handmade cosmetics in London. This outlet is always launching something new, such as its latest soap, "Rock Star," looking very pink and smelling like a Creamy Candy Bubble Bar. All products are made of fresh fruit and vegetables, the finest essential oils, and safe synthetics—no animal ingredients.

The Victorian perfumery called **Penhaligon's,** 41 Wellington St., WC2 (© 020/7836-2150, or 212/661-1300 for U.S. mail order; Tube: Covent Garden), offers a large selection of perfumes, after-shaves, soaps, and bath oils for women and men. Gifts include antique-silver scent bottles and leather traveling requisites.

FASHION, PART I: THE TRUE BRIT   Every internationally known designer worth his or her weight in shantung has a boutique in London, but the best buys are on the sturdy English styles that last forever.

The name **Burberry,** 18–22 Haymarket, SW1 (*©* 020/7930-3343; Tube: Piccadilly Circus), has been synonymous with raincoats ever since Edward VII publicly ordered his valet to "bring my Burberry" when the skies threatened. An impeccably trained staff sells the famous raincoats, along with excellent men's shirts, sportswear, knitwear, and accessories. Raincoats are available in women's sizes and styles as well. Prices are high, but you get quality and prestige.

The finest name in men's shirts, **Hilditch & Key,** 37 and 73 Jermyn St., SW1 (*©* 020/7734-4707; Tube: Piccadilly Circus or Green Park), has been in business since 1899. The two shops on this street both offer men's clothing (including a bespoke shirt service) and women's ready-made shirts. Hilditch also has an outstanding tie collection. Shirts go for half price during the twice-yearly sales. Men fly in from all over the world for them.

FASHION, PART II: THE CUTTING EDGE   Currently the most cutting-edge shopping street in London is **Conduit Street,** W1 in Mayfair (Tube: Oxford Circus). Once known for its dowdy display of international airline offices, it is now London's smartest street for fashion. Trendy shops are opening between Regent Street and the "blue chip" boutiques of New Bond Street even as we speak. Current stars include **Vivienne Westwood,** 44 Conduit St., W1 (*©* 020/7439-1109), who has overcome her punk origins to become the grande dame of English fashion. One of the most avant-garde, creative British designers, **Alexander McQueen,** 47 Conduit St., W1 (*©* 020/7734-2340), has moved in to give the neighborhood his blessing. No one pays more attention to fashion detail and craftsmanship than the celebrated McQueen.

Other famous designers with boutiques on Conduit Street include **Krizia,** 24 Conduit St., W1 (*©* 020/7491-4989); **Yohji Yamamoto,** 14–15 Conduit St., W1 (*©* 020/7491-4129); and **Issey Miyake,** 52 Conduit St., W1 (*©* 020/7851-4600).

The Library, 268 Brompton Rd., SW3 (*©* 020/7589-6569; Tube: South Kensington or Knightsbridge), in spite of its name, is a showcase for some of the best of the young designers for men. It's very cutting edge without dipping into the extremities of male fashion. The Library is famous for having introduced Helmut Lang to London, but now features such designers as Fabrizio del Carlo, Kostas Murkudis, or even Alexander McQueen.

FASHION, PART III: VINTAGE & SECONDHAND CLOTHING   A London institution since the 1940s, **Pandora,** 16–22 Cheval Place, SW7 (*©* 020/7589-5289; Tube: Knightsbridge), stands in fashionable Knightsbridge, a stone's throw from Harrods. Several times a week, chauffeurs drive up with bundles packed anonymously by the gentry of England. One woman voted best-dressed at Ascot several years ago was wearing a secondhand dress acquired here. Prices are generally one-third to one-half the retail value. Outfits are usually no more than two seasons old.

For the best in original street wear from the '50s, the '60s, and the '70s, **Pop Boutique,** 6 Monmouth St., WC2 (*©* 020/7497-5262; Tube: Covent Garden), is tops. Right next to the chic Covent Garden Hotel, it has fabulous vintage wear at affordable prices—leather jackets for £45 ($72), for example, the equivalent selling for $300 in New York.

Note: There's no value-added tax (VAT) refund on used clothing.

FILOFAX   All major department stores sell Filofax supplies, but the full range is carried in Filofax stores. Go to the main West End branch, **The Filofax Centre,** at 21 Conduit St., W1 (✆ **020/7499-0457;** Tube: Oxford Circus); it's larger and fancier than the Covent Garden branch at 69 Neal St. (✆ **020/ 7836-1977),** with the entire range of inserts and books and prices that will floor you: at least half off the U.S. going rate. They also have good sales; calendars for the next year go on sale very early in the previous year (about 10 months in advance).

FURNITURE   **David Linley Furniture,** 60 Pimlico Rd., SW1 (✆ **020/7730-7300;** Tube: Sloane Square). This is a showcase for the remarkable furniture of the Viscount Linley, a designer who bears a resemblance to his mother, the late Princess Margaret. He designs pieces of furniture of a complex nature, both in terms of design and structure. His Apsley House Desk, for example, is in French walnut with ebony and nickel-plated detailing, and contains secret drawers. The desk is rimmed with a miniature of the neoclassical Apsley House. The director at the Victoria and Albert Museum has predicted that Linley's furnishings and accessories will become the designs of the antiques of the future.

HOME DESIGN & HOUSEWARES   At the **Conran Shop,** Michelin House, 81 Fulham Rd., SW3 (✆ **020/7589-7401;** Tube: South Kensington), you'll find high style at reasonable prices from the man who invented it all for Britain: Sir Terence Conran. It's great for gifts, home furnishings, and tabletop knickknacks—or just for gawking.

MUSEUM SHOPS   Not only are the museums worth going to but so are their shops. The best museum shop in London is the **Victoria and Albert Gift Shop,** Cromwell Road, SW7 (✆ **020/7942-2667;** Tube: South Kensington). It sells cards, books, and the usual items, along with reproductions from the museum archives.

SHOES   Dr. Marten makes a brand of shoe that has become so popular that now an entire department store sells accessories, gifts, and even clothes: **Dr. Marten's Department Store,** 1–4 King St., WC2 (✆ **020/7497-1460;** Tube: Covent Garden). Teens come to worship here because ugly is beautiful and the prices are far better than they are in the United States or elsewhere in Europe.

TOYS   **Hamleys,** 188–196 Regent St., W1 (✆ **0870/333-2455;** Tube: Oxford Circus), is the finest toy shop in the world—more than 35,000 toys and games on seven floors of fun and magic. A huge selection is offered, including soft, cuddly stuffed animals, as well as dolls, radio-controlled cars, train sets, model kits, board games, outdoor toys, and computer games. A small branch is also at Covent Garden and another at Heathrow Airport.

THE MARKETS

THE WEST END   **Covent Garden Market** (✆ **020/7836-9136;** Tube: Covent Garden), the most famous market in all of England—possibly all of Europe—offers several different markets daily from 9am to 6:30pm (we think it's most fun to come on Sun, though it will be packed). George Bernard Shaw got his inspiration for *Pygmalion* here, where the character of Eliza Doolittle sold violets to wealthy operagoers. It can be a little confusing until you dive in and explore it all. **Apple Market** is the fun, bustling market in the courtyard where traders sell, well, everything. Many of the items are what the English call collectible nostalgia, including a wide array of glassware and ceramics, leather goods, toys, clothes, hats, and jewelry. Some merchandise is truly unusual. Many items are handmade, with some craftspeople selling their own wares—except on Mondays, when antiques dealers take over. Out back is **Jubilee Market** (© 020/ 7836-2139), also an antiques market on Mondays. Every other day, it's sort of a fancy hippie-ish market with cheap clothes and books. Out front are a few tents of cheap stuff, except on Monday.

The market itself (in the superbly restored hall) is one of the best shopping opportunities in London. Specialty shops sell fashions and herbs, gifts and toys, books and personalized dollhouses, hand-rolled cigars, and much, much more. You'll find bookshops and branches of famous stores **(Hamley's, The Body Shop)**, and prices are kept moderate.

St. Martin-in-the-Fields Market (Tube: Charing Cross) is good for teens and hipsters, who can make do with imports from India and South America, crafts, and some local football souvenirs. Located near Trafalgar Square and Covent Garden; hours are Monday through Saturday from 11am to 5pm, and Sunday from noon to 5pm.

NOTTING HILL **Portobello Market** (Tube: Notting Hill Gate) is a magnet for collectors of virtually anything. It's mainly a Saturday happening, from 6am to 5pm. You needn't be here at the crack of dawn; 9am is fine. Once known mainly for fruit and vegetables (still sold here throughout the week), in the past 4 decades Portobello has become synonymous with antiques. But don't take the stallholder's word for it that the fiddle he's holding is a genuine Stradivarius left to him in the will of his Italian great-uncle; it might just as well have been "nicked" from an East End pawnshop.

The market is divided into three major sections. The most crowded is the antiques section, running between Colville Road and Chepstow Villas to the south. (*Warning:* There's a great concentration of pickpockets in this area.) The second section (and the oldest part) is the "fruit and veg" market, lying between Westway and Colville Road. In the third and final section is a flea market, where Londoners sell bric-a-brac and lots of secondhand goods they didn't really want in the first place. But looking around still makes for interesting fun.

Note: Some 90 antiques and art shops along Portobello Road are open during the week when the street market is closed. This is actually a better time for the serious collector to shop because you'll get more attention from dealers, and you won't be distracted by the organ grinder.

SOUTH BANK Open on Fridays only, **New Caledonian Market** is commonly known as the **Bermondsey Market,** because of its location on the corner of Long Lane and Bermondsey Street (Tube: London Bridge, then bus no. 78, or walk down Bermondsey St.). The market is at the extreme east end, beginning at Tower Bridge Road. It's one of Europe's outstanding street markets for the number and quality of the antiques and other goods. The stalls are well known, and many dealers come into London from the country. Prices are generally lower here than at Portobello and the other markets. It gets under way at 5am—with the bargains gone by 9am—and closes at noon. Bring a "torch" (flashlight) if you go in the wee hours.

NORTH LONDON If it's Wednesday, it's time for **Camden Passage** (© 020/7359-0190; Tube: Northern Line to Angel) in Islington, where each

Wednesday and Saturday there's a very upscale antiques market. It starts in Camden Passage and then sprawls into the streets behind. It's on Wednesdays from 7am to 2pm, and Saturdays from 8am to 4pm.

7 London After Dark

Weekly publications, such as *Time Out* and *Where,* carry full entertainment listings, including information on restaurants and nightclubs. You'll also find listings in daily newspapers, notably the *Times* and the *Telegraph.*

THE THEATER

In London, you'll have a chance to see the world-renowned **English theater** on its home ground. Matinees are on Wednesday (Thurs at some theaters) and Saturday. Theaters are closed on Sunday. It's impossible to describe all of London's theaters in this space, so below are listed just a few from the treasure trove.

GETTING TICKETS

To see specific shows, especially hits, purchase your tickets in advance. The best method is to buy your tickets from the theater's box office, which you can do over the phone using a credit card. You'll pay the theater price and pick up the tickets the day of the show. You can also go to a reliable ticket agent (the greatest cluster is in Covent Garden), but you'll pay a fee, which varies depending on the show. You can also make theater reservations through ticket agents. In the case of hit shows, only brokers may be able to get you a seat, but you'll pay for the privilege. For tickets and information before you go, try **Global Tickets,** 234 West 44th St., Suite 1000, New York, NY 10036 (© **800/223-6108** or 212/398-1468; www.keithprowse.com). They also have offices in London at the **British Visitors Center,** 1 Regents St., W1 V1PJ (© **020/7014-8550**), or at the **Harrods** ticket desk, 87–135 Brompton Rd. (© **020/7589-9109**), located on the lower-ground floor opposite the British Airways desk. They'll mail tickets to your home, or fax you a confirmation and leave your tickets at the box office. Instant confirmations are available with special "overseas" rates for most shows. A booking and handling fee of up to 20% is added to the ticket price.

Another option is **Theatre Direct International (TDI;** © **800/334-8457,** U.S. only). TDI specializes in providing London fringe theater tickets, but they also have tickets to major productions, including those of the Royal National Theatre and Barbican. The service allows you to arrive in London with your tickets or to have them held for you at the box office.

London theater tickets are priced quite reasonably when compared with the United States. Prices vary greatly depending on the seat—from £18 to £70

Value Ticket Bargains

The **Society of London Theatre** (© **020/7577-6700**) operates a **TKTS booth** in Leicester Square, where tickets for many shows are available at half price, plus a £2.50 ($4) service charge. The booth now sells additional tickets the day of performances at 25% off and at full price for any of 55 theaters, including the English National Opera and the Royal Opera House. All major credit and debit cards are accepted. The TKTS booth also offers a limited number of seats for shows that are usually sold out. Hours are daily from noon to 6:30pm.

($29–$112). Sometimes gallery seats (the cheapest) are sold only on the day of the performance, so you'll have to head to the box office early in the day and return an hour before the performance to queue up, because they're not reserved seats.

Many of the major theaters offer reduced-price tickets to students on a stand-by basis, but not to the general public. When available, these tickets are sold 30 minutes prior to curtain. Line up early for popular shows, as standby tickets go fast and furious. Of course, you must have a valid student ID.

Warning: Beware of scalpers who hang out in front of theaters with hit shows. Many report that scalpers sell forged tickets, and their prices are outrageous.

THE MAJOR COMPANIES & THEATERS

Barbican Theatre—Royal Shakespeare Company The Barbican is the London home of the Royal Shakespeare Company, one of the world's finest theater companies. The core of its repertoire remains, of course, the plays of William Shakespeare. It also presents a wide-ranging program in its two theaters. Three productions are in repertory each week in the Barbican Theatre—a 2,000-seat main auditorium with excellent sight lines throughout, thanks to a raked orchestra. The Pit, a small studio space, is where the company's new writing is presented. The Royal Shakespeare Company performs both here and at Stratford-upon-Avon. It is in residence in London during the winter months; in the summer, it tours in England and abroad. For more information on the company and its current productions, check **www.rsc.org.uk**. In the Barbican Centre, Silk St., Barbican, EC2. © 020/7638-8891. Barbican Theatre £5–£35 ($8–$56). The Pit £7–£22 ($11–$35) matinees and evening performances. Box office daily 9am–8pm. Tube: Barbican or Moorgate.

Open-Air Theatre This outdoor theater is in Regent's Park; the setting is idyllic, and both seating and acoustics are excellent. Presentations are mainly of Shakespeare, usually in period costume. Its theater bar, the longest in London, serves both drink and food. In the case of a rained-out performance, tickets are given for another date. The season runs from June to mid-September, Monday through Saturday at 8pm, plus Wednesday, Thursday, and Saturday matinees at 2:30pm. Inner Circle, Regent's Park, NW1. © 020/7486-2431. http://openairtheatre.org/. Tickets £8.50–£25 ($14–$40). Tube: Baker St.

Royal Court Theatre This theater has always been a leader in producing provocative, cutting-edge, new drama. In the 1950s, it staged the plays of the angry young men, notably John Osborne's then-sensational *Look Back in Anger;* earlier it debuted the plays of George Bernard Shaw. A recent work was *The Beauty Queen of Leenane,* which won a Tony on Broadway. The theater is home to the English Stage Company, formed to promote serious stage writing. Sloane Sq., SW1. © 020/7565-5000. www.royalcourttheatre.com. Tickets from £7–£26 ($11–$42); call for the latest information. Box office 10am–6pm. Tube: Sloane Sq.

Royal National Theatre Home to one of the world's greatest stage companies, the Royal National Theatre is not one but three theaters—the Olivier, reminiscent of a Greek amphitheater with its open stage; the more traditional Lyttelton; and the Cottesloe, with its flexible stage and seating. The National presents the finest in world theater, from classic drama to award-winning new plays, including comedies, musicals, and shows for young people. A choice of at least six plays is offered at any one time. It's also a full-time theater center, with an amazing selection of bars, cafes, restaurants, free foyer music and exhibitions, short early-evening performances, bookshops, backstage tours, riverside walks, and terraces. You can have a three-course meal in Mezzanine, the National's restaurant; enjoy a light meal in the brasserie-style Terrace cafe; or have a snack in one of the coffee bars. South Bank, SE1. ℂ 020/7452-3400. www.nt-online.org. Tickets £10–£38 ($16–$61); midweek matinees, Sat matinees, and previews cost less. Tube: Waterloo, Embankment, or Charing Cross.

Shakespeare's Globe Theatre   In May 1997, the new Globe Theatre—a replica of the Elizabethan original, thatched roof and all—staged its first slate of plays (*Henry V* and *A Winter's Tale*) yards away from the site of the 16th-century theater where the Bard originally staged his work.

Productions vary in style and setting; not all are performed in Elizabethan costume. In keeping with the historic setting, no lighting is focused just on the stage, but floodlighting is used during evening performances to replicate daylight in the theater—Elizabethan performances took place in the afternoon. Theatergoers sit on wooden benches of yore—in thatch-roofed galleries, no less—but these days you can rent a cushion to make yourself more comfortable. About 500 "groundlings" can stand in the uncovered yard around the stage, just as they did when the Bard was here. Mark Rylane, the artistic director of the Globe, wanted the theater-going experience to be as authentic as possible—he told the press he'd be delighted if the audience threw fruit at the actors, as they did in Shakespeare's time.

From May to September, the company intends to hold performances Tuesday through Saturday at 2 and 7pm. There will be a limited winter schedule. In any season, the schedule may be affected by weather, because this is an outdoor theater. Performances last 2½ to 4 hours, depending on the play.

For details on the exhibition that tells the story of the painstaking re-creation of the Globe, as well as guided tours of the theater, see p. 163. New Globe Walk, Bankside, SE1. ℂ 020/7902-1400. Box office: 020/7401-9919. Tickets £5 ($8) for groundlings, £11–£27 ($18–$43) for gallery seats. Exhibition tickets £8 ($13) adults, £6 ($9.60) seniors and students, £5 ($8) ages 5–15. Tube: Mansion House or Blackfriars.

Theatre Royal Drury Lane   Drury Lane is one of London's oldest and most prestigious theaters, crammed with tradition—not all of it respectable. This, the fourth theater on this site, dates from 1812; the first was built in 1663. Nell Gwynne, the rough-tongued cockney lass who became Charles II's mistress, used to sell oranges under the long colonnade in front. Nearly every star of London theater has taken the stage here at some time. It has a wide-open repertoire but leans toward musicals, especially long-running hits. Guided tours of the backstage area and the front of the house are given most days at 2:15 and 4:45pm. Call ℂ 020/7494-5091 for more information. Catherine St., Covent Garden, WC2. ℂ 020/7494-5091. Tickets £8–£40 ($13–$64). Box office Mon–Sat 10am–8pm. Evening performances Mon–Sat 8pm; matinees Wed and Sat 3pm. Tube: Covent Garden.

THE REST OF THE PERFORMING ARTS SCENE

Currently, London supports five major orchestras—the **London Symphony,** the **Royal Philharmonic,** the **Philharmonia Orchestra,** the **BBC Symphony,** and the **BBC Philharmonic**—several choirs, and many smaller chamber groups and historic instrument ensembles. Look for the **London Sinfonietta,** the **English Chamber Orchestra,** and of course, the **Academy of St. Martin-in-the-Fields.** Performances are in the South Banks Arts Centre and the Barbican. Smaller recitals are at Wigmore Hall and St. John's Smith Square.

British Music Information Centre, 10 Stratford Place, W1 (ℂ 020/7499-8567; www.bmic.co.uk), is the city's clearinghouse and resource center for serious music. The center is open Monday through Friday from noon to 5pm and provides free telephone and walk-in information on current and upcoming events. Recitals featuring 20th-century British classical compositions cost up to £5 ($8) and are offered here weekly, usually on Tuesday and Thursday at 7:30pm; call ahead for day and time. Because capacity is limited to 40, you may want to check early. Take the Tube to Bond Street.

Barbican Centre   The largest art and exhibition center in Western Europe, the roomy and comfortable Barbican complex is a perfect setting for enjoying music and theater. Barbican Hall is the permanent home address of the **London Symphony Orchestra** as well as host to visiting orchestras and performers, from classical to jazz, folk, and world music.

In addition to the hall and the two Royal Shakespeare Company theatres, the Barbican Centre encompasses the Barbican Art Gallery, a showcase for visual arts; the Concourse Gallery and foyer exhibition spaces; Cinemas One and Two, which show recently released mainstream films and film series; the Barbican Library, a general lending library that places a strong emphasis on the arts; the Conservatory, one of London's largest plant houses; and restaurants, cafes, and bars. Silk St., The City, EC2. © 020/7638-8891. www.barbican.org.uk. Tickets £7–£40 ($11–$64). Box office daily 9am–8pm. Tube: Barbican or Moorgate.

English National Opera   Built in 1904 as a variety theater and converted into an opera house in 1968, the London Coliseum is the city's largest theater. One of two national opera companies, the English National Opera performs a wide range of works from classics to Gilbert and Sullivan to new and experimental works, staged with flair and imagination. All performances are in English. A repertory of 18 to 20 productions is presented 5 or 6 nights a week for 11 months of the year (dark in July). Although balcony seats are cheaper, many visitors seem to prefer the upper circle or dress circle. London Coliseum, St. Martin's Lane, WC2. © 020/7632-8300. www.eno.org. Tickets £6–£16 ($9.60–$26) balcony, £17–£61 ($27–$98) upper or dress circle or stalls; about 100 discount balcony tickets sold on the day of performance from 10am. Tube: Charing Cross or Leicester Sq.

Royal Albert Hall   Opened in 1871 and dedicated to the memory of Victoria's consort, Prince Albert, the circular building holds one of the world's most famous auditoriums. With a seating capacity of 5,200, it's a popular place to hear music by stars such as Eric Clapton and Tracy Chapman. Occasional sporting events (especially boxing) figure strongly here, too.

Since 1941, the hall has been the setting for the BBC Henry Wood Promenade Concerts, known as **"The Proms,"** a concert series that lasts for 8 weeks between mid-July and mid-September. The Proms have been a British tradition since 1895. Although most of the audience occupies reserved seats, true aficionados usually opt for standing room in the orchestra pit, which affords close-up views of the musicians performing on stage. Newly commissioned works are often premiered here. The final evening of The Proms is the most traditional; the rousing favorites "Jerusalem" or "Land of Hope and Glory" echo through the hall. For tickets, call Ticketmaster (© 020/7344-4444) directly. Kensington Gore, SW7 2AP. © 020/7589-8212. www.royalalberthall.com. Tickets £15–£50 ($24–$79), depending on the event. Box office daily 9am–9pm. Tube: South Kensington.

Royal Festival Hall   In the aftermath of World War II, the principal site of London's music scene shifted to the south bank of the Thames. Three of the most acoustically perfect concert halls in the world were erected between 1951 and 1964. They include Royal Festival Hall, the Queen Elizabeth Hall, and the Purcell Room. Together they hold more than 1,200 performances a year, including classical music, ballet, jazz, popular music, and contemporary dance. Royal Festival Hall, which opens daily at 10am, offers an extensive array of things to see and do, including free exhibitions in the foyers and free lunchtime music at 12:30pm. On Friday, Commuter Jazz in the foyer from 5:15 to 6:45pm is free. The Poetry Library is open from 11am to 8pm, and shops display a wide selection of books, records, and crafts. The Festival Buffet has a wide variety of food at reasonable prices, and bars dot the foyers. The People's Palace offers lunch and dinner with a panoramic view of the River Thames. Reservations by calling ℭ **020/7928-9999** are recommended. On the South Bank, SE1. ℭ **020/7960-4242.** Tickets £6–£55 ($9.60–$88). Box office daily 9am–8pm. Tube: Waterloo or Embankment.

The Royal Opera House—The Royal Ballet & the Royal Opera   The Royal Ballet and the Royal Opera make their home in a magnificently restored theater presenting world-class performances of opera and dance. Reopened in 1999, opera and ballet aficionados of yesterday hardly recognize the place, with its spectacular public spaces, including the Vilar Floral Hall, a rooftop restaurant, and bars and shops. The entire northeast corner of one of London's most famous public squares has been transformed, finally realizing Inigo Jones's original vision for this colonnaded piazza. Regular backstage tours are possible daily at 10:30am, 12:30, and 2:30pm (not on Sun or matinee days).

Performances of the Royal Opera are usually sung in the original language, but supertitles are projected, translating the libretto for the audience. The Royal Ballet, which compares favorably with the Kirov and the Paris Opera Ballet, performs a repertory with a tilt toward the classics, including works by its earlier choreographer/directors Sir Frederick Ashton and Sir Kenneth MacMillan. Bow St., Covent Garden, WC2. ℭ **020/7304-4000.** www.royalopera.org. Tickets £10–£155 ($16–$248). Box office daily 10am–8pm. Tube: Covent Garden.

Sadler's Wells Theatre   This premier venue for dance and opera occupies the site of a theater that was built in 1683, on the location of a well prized for the healing powers of its waters. In the early 1990s, the old-fashioned, turn-of-the-20th-century theater was demolished, and construction began on an innovative new design that was completed at the end of 1998. The original facade has been retained, but the interior has been completely revamped to create a stylish cutting-edge theater design. The new theater offers both traditional and experimental dance. Rosebery Ave., EC1. ℭ **020/7863-8000.** www.sadlers-wells.com. Tickets £9–£45 ($14–$72). Performances usually 8pm. Box office Mon–Sat 10am–8pm. Tube: Angel.

Wigmore Hall   An intimate auditorium, Wigmore Hall offers an excellent regular series of song recitals, piano and chamber music, early and baroque music, and jazz. A free list of the month's programs is available from Wigmore. A cafe-bar and restaurant are on the premises; a cold supper can be pre-ordered if you are attending a concert. 36 Wigmore St., W1. ℭ **020/7935-2141.** Tickets £10–£35 ($16–$56). Performances nightly, plus Sun Morning Coffee Concerts and Sun concerts at 11:30am or 4pm. Box office Mon–Sat 10am–8pm; Sun varies. Tube: Bond St. or Oxford Circus.

OUTSIDE CENTRAL LONDON

Kenwood Lakeside Concerts   These band and orchestral concerts on the north side of Hampstead Heath have been a British tradition for some 50 years. In recent years, laser shows and fireworks have added to a repertoire that includes everything from rousing versions of the *1812 Overture* to jazz and such operas as *Carmen*. The final concert of the season always features some of the Pomp and Circumstance marches of Sir Edward Elgar, everyone's favorite imperial composer. Music drifts across the lake to serenade wine-and-cheese parties on the grass. Kenwood, Hampstead Lane, Hampstead Heath, London NW3 7JR. © 020/7413-1443. Tickets for adults £10 ($16) for seats on the grass lawn, £12–£18 ($19–$29) for reserved deck chairs. Reductions of 12.5% for students and persons over 60. Every summer Sat at 7:30pm from July to early Sept. Tube: Golders Green or Archway, then bus no. 210.

THE CLUB & MUSIC SCENE
CABARET & COMEDY

The Comedy Store This is London's most visible showcase for established and rising comic talent. Inspired by comedy clubs in the United States, this club has given many comics their start. Today a number of them are established TV personalities. Even if their names are unfamiliar, you'll enjoy the spontaneity of live comedy performed before a British audience. Visitors must be 18 and older; dress is casual. Reserve through Ticketmaster (© **020/7344-4444**); the club opens 1½ hours before each show. *Insider's tip:* Go on Tuesday when the humor is more cutting edge and topical. 1A Oxendon St., off Piccadilly Circus, SW1. © 020/7344-0234. Cover £12–£15 ($19–$24). Tues–Sun from 6:30pm; Fri–Sat from 11:30pm. Tube: Leicester Sq. or Piccadilly Circus.

LIVE MUSIC

The Bull & Gate Outside central London, and smaller, cheaper, and often more animated and less touristy than many of its competitors, The Bull & Gate is the unofficial headquarters of London's pub rock scene. Indie and relatively unknown rock bands are often served up back to back by the half dozen in this somewhat-battered Victorian pub. If you like spilled beer, this is off-the-beaten-track London at its most authentic. The place operates pub hours, with music nightly from 9pm to midnight. 389 Kentish Town Rd., NW5. © 020/8806-8062. Cover £5 ($8). Tube: Kentish Town.

The Rock Garden A long-established performance site, The Rock Garden maintains a bar and a stage in the cellar, and a restaurant on the street level. The cellar, known as The Venue, has hosted such acts as Dire Straits, Police, and U2 before their rises to stardom. Today, bands vary widely, from promising up-and-comers to some that'll never be heard from again. Simple American-style fare is served in the restaurant. 6–7 The Piazza, Covent Garden, WC2. © 020/7240-3961. Cover £5–£15 ($8–$24); diners enter free. Mon–Thurs 5pm–3am; Fri and Sat 5pm–4am; Sun 5pm–2am. Bus: Any of the night buses that depart from Trafalgar Sq. Tube: Covent Garden.

Shepherd's Bush Empire In an old BBC television theater, with great acoustics, this is a major venue in London for big name pop and rock stars. Announcements appear in the local press. There's a capacity seating of 2,000. The box office is open Monday through Friday from noon to 5pm and Saturday from noon to 6pm. Shepherd's Bush Green, W12. © 020/8354-3300. Ticket prices vary according to show. Tube: Shepherd's Bush or Goldhawk Rd.

Sound Right in the very heart of London, this 700-seat venue books the big acts, everybody from Sinead O'Connor to Puff Daddy or the Spice Girls. This is really a music restaurant, one of the best of its type in London. The program is forever changing; call to see what's happening at the time of your visit. Swiss Centre at 10 Wardour St., Leicester Sq., W1. © 020/7287-1010. Tickets £8–£12 ($13–$19). Tube: Leicester Sq.

TRADITIONAL ENGLISH MUSIC

Cecil Sharpe House CSH was the focal point of the folk revival in the 1960s, and it continues to treasure and nurture the style. Here you'll find a whole range of traditional English music and dance. Call to see what's happening. 2 Regent's Park Rd., NW1. ℂ 020/7485-2206. Tickets £7–£8 ($11–$13). Box office Tues–Fri 9:30am–5:30pm. Tube: Camden Town.

JAZZ & BLUES

Ain't Nothing But Blues Bar   The club, which bills itself as the only true blues venue in town, features local acts and occasional touring American bands. On weekends, prepare to wait in line. From the Oxford Circus Tube stop, walk south on Regent Street, turn left on Great Marlborough Street, and then make a quick right on Kingly Street. 20 Kingly St., W1. ℂ 020/7287-0514. Cover Fri–Sat £4–£6 ($6.40–$9.60); free before 8:30pm. Mon–Thurs 6pm–1am; Fri–Sat 6pm–2am; Sun 7:30pm–midnight. Tube: Oxford Circus or Piccadilly Circus.

Jazz Café   Afro-Latin jazz fans are hip to this club hosting combos from around the globe. The weekends, described by one patron as "bumpy jazzy-funk nights," are the best time to decide for yourself what that means. Call ahead for listings, cover, and table reservations (when necessary); opening times can vary. 5 Parkway, NW1. ℂ 020/7916-6060. Cover £8–£20 ($13–$32). No charge to book a table, but you will have to order a meal. Tube: Parkway.

100 Club   Although less plush and expensive than some jazz clubs, 100 Club is a serious contender. Its cavalcade of bands includes the best British jazz musicians and some of their Yankee brethren. Rock, R&B, and blues are also on tap. 100 Oxford St., W1. ℂ 020/7636-0933. Cover £10–£12 ($16–$19); discounts available for club members. Mon–Thurs 7:30–11:30pm; Fri noon–3pm and 8:30pm–2am; Sat 7:30pm–1am; Sun 7:30–11:30pm. Tube: Tottenham Court Rd. or Oxford Circus.

Pizza Express   Don't let the name fool you: This restaurant-bar serves up some of the best jazz in London by mainstream artists. While enjoying a thin-crust Italian pizza, check out a local band or a visiting group, often from the United States. Although the club has been enlarged, it's important to reserve ahead of time. 10 Dean St., W1. ℂ 020/7439-8722. Cover £11–£20 ($18–$32). Daily noon–midnight, jazz from 9pm–midnight. Tube: Tottenham Court Rd.

Ronnie Scott's Club   Inquire about jazz in London and people immediately think of Ronnie Scott's, long the European vanguard for modern jazz. Located in the heart of Soho, only the best English and American combos, often fronted by a top-notch vocalist, are booked here. The programs inevitably make for an entire evening of cool jazz. In the Main Room, you can watch the show from the bar or sit at a table, from which you can order dinner. The Downstairs Bar is more intimate; among the regulars at your elbow may be some of the world's most talented musicians. On weekends, the separate Upstairs Room has a disco called Club Latino. 47 Frith St., W1. ℂ 020/7439-0747. Cover nonmember £15–£25 ($24–$40), member £5 ($8), Fri–Sat £10 ($16). Mon–Sat 8:30pm–3am. Tube: Leicester Sq. or Piccadilly Circus.

606 Club   Located in a discreet basement site in Chelsea, the 606 presents live music nightly. Predominantly a venue for modern jazz, style ranges from traditional to contemporary. Local musicians and some very big names play here, whether planned gigs or informal jam sessions after their shows elsewhere in town. This is actually a jazz supper club in the boondocks of Fulham; because of license requirements, patrons can only order alcohol with food. 90 Lots Rd., SW10. ℂ 020/7352-5953. Cover Mon–Thurs £6 ($9.60), Fri–Sat £8 ($13), Sun £7 ($11). Mon–Wed 7:30pm–1am; Thurs 8pm–1:30am; Fri–Sat 10pm–2am; Sun 8:30–11:30pm. Tube: Earl's Court.

DANCE, DISCO & ECLECTIC

Bar Rumba Despite its location on Shaftesbury Avenue, this Latin bar and club could be featured in a book of Underground London. A hush-hush address, it leans toward radical jazz fusion on some nights, phat funk on other occasions. The club boasts two full bars and a different musical theme every night; Tuesday and Wednesday are the only nights you probably won't have to queue at the door. Monday's "That's How It Is" showcase features jazz, hip-hop, and drum and bass; Friday's provides R&B and swing; and Saturday's "Garage City" buzzes with house and garage. On weeknights you have to be 18 and up; the age minimum is 21 on Saturday and Sunday. 36 Shaftesbury Ave., W1. © 020/7287-2715. Cover £3–£12 ($4.80–$19). Mon–Thurs 6pm–3:30am; Fri 6pm–4am; Sat 7pm–6am; Sun 8pm–1:30am. Tube: Piccadilly Circus.

Cargo Another watering hole in ultra-trendy Hoxton draws a smart urban crowd from more expensive West End flats. Its habitués assure us it's the place to go for a "wicked time" and great live bands. If not bands, then great DJs dominate the night. The joint is jumping by 9:30 nightly, because it has to close down at 1am because of its limited license. It's fun and funky, with two big arched rooms, fantastic acoustics, and a parade of videos. As to the patrons, the bartender characterized it just right: "We get the freaks and the normal people." Drinks are reasonably priced, as is the self-styled "street food." Kingsland Viaduct, 83 Rivington St., Shoreditch, EC2. © 020/7739-3440. Mon–Thurs noon–1:00am; Fri noon–3am; Sat 6pm–3am; Sun noon–midnight. Cover (after 10pm) £5–£9 ($8–$14.50), depending on the entertainment. Tube: Old Street.

The Cross In the backwaters of Kings Cross, this club has stayed hot since 1993. London hipsters come here for private parties thrown by Rough Trade Records or Red Or Dead, or just to dance in the space's cozy brick-lined vaults. It's always party time here. Call to find out who's performing. The Arches, Kings Cross Goods Yard, York Way, N1. © 020/7837-0828. Cover £8–£15 ($13–$24). Fri 11pm–5am; Sat 10pm–6am; Sun 11pm–5am. Tube: Kings Cross.

The End Better than ever after its recent enlargement, this club has a trio of large dance floors along with four bars and a chill-out area. Speaker walls blast you into orbit. The End is the best club in London for house and garage. It's real cutting edge, drawing both straight and gay London. "We can't tell the difference anymore," the club owner confessed, "and who cares anyway?" From its drinking fountain to its ritzy toilets, the club is alluring. Dress for glam and to be seen on the circuit. Some big names in London appear on weekends. 16A West Central St., WC1. © 020/7419-9199. Cover £4–£15 ($6.40–$24). Mon and Thurs 10pm–3am; Fri 10pm–5am; Sat 10pm–7am. Tube: Tottenham Court Rd.

Equinox Built in 1992 on the site of the London Empire, a dance emporium that has witnessed the changing styles of social dancing since the 1700s, the Equinox has established itself as a perennial favorite and frequently hosts the U.K.'s hottest talent. It contains nine bars, the largest dance floor in London, and a restaurant modeled after a 1950s American diner. With the exception of rave, virtually every kind of dance music is featured here, including dance hall, pop, rock, and Latin. The setting is lavishly illuminated with one of Europe's largest lighting rigs, and the crowd is as varied as London itself. Summer visitors can enjoy their theme nights, which are geared to entertaining a worldwide audience, including a once a month "Ibiza" foam party—you'll actually boogie the night away on a foam-covered floor. Leicester Sq., WC2. © 020/7437-1446. Cover £6–£12 ($9.60–$19), depending on the night of the week. Mon–Thurs 9pm–3am; Fri–Sat 9pm–4am. Tube: Leicester Sq.

Fabric   Still going strong since its opening in 1999, when other competitors have come and gone since, Fabric's main allure is its license for 24-hour music and dancing from Thursday to Sunday night. One of the most famous clubs in the increasingly trendy East London sector, it is said that when the owners power up its underfoot subwoofer, lights dim in London's East End. On some crazed nights, at least 2,500 members of young London, plus a medley of international visitors, crowd into this mammoth place. It has a trio of dance floors, bars wherever you look, unisex toilets, chill-out beds, and even a roof terrace. Live acts are presented every Friday, with DJs reigning on weekends. 77A Charterhouse St., EC1. ℭ 020/7336-8898. Cover £12–£15 ($19–$24). Fri 10pm–7am; Sat 10:30pm–7am; Sun 10pm–5am. Tube: Farringdon.

Hippodrome   Located near Leicester Square, the popular Hippodrome is London's grand old daddy of discos, a cavernous place with a great sound system and lights to match. It was Princess Di's favorite scene in her barhopping days. Tacky and touristy, the 'Drome is packed on weekends. Corner of Cranbourn St. and Charing Cross Rd., WC2. ℭ 020/7437-4311. Cover £8–£11 ($13–$18). Mon–Fri 9pm–3am; Sat 9pm–3:30am. Tube: Leicester Sq.

Limelight   Although opened in 1985, this large dance club—located inside a former Welsh chapel that dates to 1754—has only recently come into its own. The dance floors and bars share space with plenty of cool Gothic nooks and crannies. DJs spin the latest house music. 136 Shaftesbury Ave., WC1. ℭ 020/7434-0572. Cover £2–£12 ($3.20–$19). Mon–Thurs 10pm–3am; Fri–Sat 9pm–3:30am. Tube: Leicester Sq.

Ministry of Sound   Removed from the city center, this club-of-the-hour is still going strong after all these years. It remains hot, hot, hot. With a large bar and an even bigger sound system, it blasts garage and house music to energetic crowds that pack the two dance floors. If the stimulants in the rest of the club have gone to your head, you can chill in the cinema room. *Note:* The club's cover charge is stiff, and bouncers decide who is cool enough to enter, so leave the sneakers and denim at home and slip into your grooviest and most glamorous club wear. 103 Gaunt St., SE1. ℭ 020/7378-6528. Cover £12–£15 ($19–$24). Fri 10pm–5am; Sat 11pm–9am. Tube: Elephant & Castle.

Notting Hill Art Club   In one of the hippest nighttime venues in London, the action takes place in a no-frills basement in increasingly fashionable Notting Hill Gate. One habitué called it "the coolest night club on earth." Yes, that was Liam Gallagher you spotted dancing with Courtney Love. To justify the name of the club, art exhibitions are sometimes staged here. Most of the clients are under 35; other than that they come from the widest range of backgrounds— from Madonna wannabes to Bob Marley wannabes. The music is eclectic, varying from night to night—jazz improv, Latino salsa, hip-hop, indie, whatever. 21 Notting Hill Gate, W11. ℭ 020/7460-4459. Cover £3–£6 ($4.80–$9.60). Wed 6pm–1am; Sat 6pm–2am; Sun 4pm–1am. Tube: Notting Hill Gate.

Propaganda   This is one of the leading clubs of the West End lying in the vicinity of Oxford and Regent streets. It's a stylish rendezvous, drawing a crowd in their 20s and 30s to its plush precincts. The young Mick Jagger or aspirant Madonna of today might be seen lounging on one of the large white-covered sofas across from the sleek bar. Drinks are expensive, so be duly warned. Recorded music plays for dancing, and the weekends are especially busy. A supper club adjoins the joint and is open for most of the night. 201 Wardour St., W1. ℭ 020/7434-3820. Cover £5–£15 ($8–$24). Mon noon–1am; Tues–Sat noon–3am; Sun noon–midnight. Tube: Tottenham Court Rd. or Oxford Circus.

Scala This area of London is risky at night—so much so that the security staff at the club is happy to escort you to a taxi when you're leaving. In spite of its crime-ridden surroundings, this is a hot, happening venue for young London. A former movie theater has been converted into this successful club, where DJs spin the latest music and ramped balconies offer dancing on different tiers. The gigantic screen blows your mind with scintillating visuals. Some nights are theme oriented such as a long-running gay-mixed extravaganza called *Popstarz*. The music runs the range from garage to R&B to Latin salsa. Wear anything except on Saturday nights when caps and sportswear are forbidden. 275 Pentonville Rd., Kings Cross, N1. ℂ 020/7833-2022. Cover £8 ($13). Nightly 8pm–2am. Tube: Kings Cross.

The Velvet Room The Velvet Underground was a London staple for years. Times changed and the clientele grew up—hence The Velvet Room, a more mature setting that is luxurious but not stuffy. DJs Carl Cox and others spin favorite dance hits—more laid back to better represent the new theme. The Velvet Room hasn't sacrificed a shred of cool and still sets a standard for the next generation of Soho bar life. 143 Charing Cross Rd., WC2. ℂ 020/7439-4655. Cover £6–£10 ($9.60–$16). Wed–Thurs 10pm–3am; Fri–Sat 10pm–4am. Tube: Tottenham Court Rd.

Vibe Bar As more and more of hip London heads east, bypassing even Clerenwell for Hoxton, Vibe has been put on the map; *The Evening Standard* named it among the top five DJ bars in London. The paper compared it to an "expensively distressed pair of designer jeans." It's a nightspot operated by Truman Brewery. In summer the action overflows onto a courtyard. Patrons check their e-mail, lounge on comfortable couches, and listen to diverse music such as reggae, Latin, jazz, R&B, Northern Soul, African, or hip-hop. 91–95 Brick Lane, E1. ℂ 020/7428-0491. Cover: Free or £1–£2 ($1.60–$3.20) sometimes assessed after 6pm. Sun–Thurs noon–11pm; Fri–Sat noon–1am. Tube: Liverpool St.

Zoo Bar The owners spent millions of pounds outfitting this club in the slickest, flashiest, and most psychedelic decor in London. If you're looking for a true Euro nightlife experience replete with gorgeous *au pairs* and trendy Europeans, this is it. Zoo Bar upstairs is a menagerie of mosaic animals beneath a glassed-in ceiling dome. Downstairs, the music is intrusive enough to make conversation futile. Clients range from 18 to 35; androgyny is the look of choice. 3–18 Bear St., WC2. ℂ 020/7839-4188. Cover £6 ($9.60) after 11pm (Fri–Sat after 9pm). Mon–Sat 4pm–3:30am; Sun 4pm–12:30am. Tube: Leicester Sq.

THE GAY & LESBIAN SCENE

The most reliable source of information on gay clubs and activities is the **Lesbian and Gay Switchboard** (ℂ 020/7837-7324). The staff runs a 24-hour service for information on gay-friendly places and activities. *Time Out* also carries listings on such clubs. Also a good place for finding out what's hot and hip is **Prowler Soho,** 3–7 Brewer St., Soho, W1 (ℂ 020/7734-4031; Tube: Piccadilly Circus), the largest gay lifestyle store in London. (You can also buy anything from jewelry to CDs, books, fashion, and sex toys.) It's open until midnight on Friday and Saturday.

Admiral Duncan Gay men and their friends go here to drink and to have a good time but also to make a political statement. British tabloids shocked the world on April 30, 1999, when they revealed that this old pub had been bombed, with three people dying in the attack. Within 6 weeks, the pub defiantly reopened in the wake of such insane intolerance. We're happy to report it's back in business and better than ever; even nongays show up to show their support.

54 Old Compton St., W1. ✆ **020/7437-5300**. No cover. Mon–Sat noon–11pm; Sun noon–10:30pm. Tube: Piccadilly Circus.

Barcode   This is a very relaxed and friendly bar. With everything from skinheads to "pint-of-lager" types, it has very much a local atmosphere. "Code" is fairly male-dominated but does not object to women entering. 3–4 Archer St. W1. ✆ **020/7734-3342**. No cover. Daily 1pm–1am. Tube: Piccadilly Circus.

The Box   Adjacent to one of Covent Garden's best-known junctions, Seven Dials, this sophisticated Mediterranean-style bar attracts all types of men. In the afternoon, it is primarily a restaurant, serving meal-size salads, club sandwiches, and soups. Food service ends abruptly at 5:30pm, after which the place reveals its core: a cheerful, popular place of rendezvous for London's gay and counter-cultural crowds. The Box considers itself a "summer bar," throwing open doors and windows to a cluster of outdoor tables that attracts a crowd at the slightest hint of sunshine. 32–34 Monmouth St. (at Seven Dials), WC2. ✆ **020/7240-5828**. No cover. Mon–Sat 11am–11pm; Sun noon–10:30pm (cafe Mon–Sat 11am–5:30pm, Sun noon–6:30pm). Tube: Leicester Sq.

Candy Bar   The most popular lesbian bar in London at the moment, it has an extremely mixed clientele from butch to fem, from young to old. With a bar and a club downstairs, design is simple, with bright colors and lots of mirrors upstairs while darker and more flirtatious downstairs. Men are welcome as long as they are escorted by a woman. 4 Carlisle St., W1 ✆ **020/7494-4041**. Cover £3–£6 ($4.80–$9.60). Club hours Mon–Thurs 8pm–midnight; Fri–Sat 8pm–2am; Sun 7–11pm. Tube: Tottenham Court Rd.

The Edge   Few bars in London can rival the tolerance, humor, and sexual sophistication found here. The first two floors are done up with accessories that, like an English garden, change with the seasons. Dance music can be found on the high-energy and crowded lower floors. One reader claims the bartenders water down the drinks. Three menus are featured: a funky daytime menu, a cafe menu, and a late-night menu. Dancers hit the floors starting around 7:30pm. Clientele ranges from the flamboyantly gay to hetero pub-crawlers out for a night of slumming. 11 Soho Sq., W1. ✆ **020/7439-1313**. No cover. Mon–Sat 11am–1am; Sun noon–10:30pm. Tube: Tottenham Court Rd.

First Out   First Out prides itself on being London's first (est. 1986) all-gay coffee shop. Set in a 19th-century building whose wood panels have been painted the colors of the gay liberation rainbow, the bar offers an exclusively vegetarian menu. Cappuccino and whiskey are the preferred libations; curry dishes, potted pies in phyllo pastries, and salads are the foods of choice. Don't expect a raucous pickup scene—some clients come here with their grandmothers. Look for the bulletin board with leaflets and business cards of gay and gay-friendly entrepreneurs. 52 St. Giles High St., W1 ✆ **020/7240-8042**. No cover. Mon–Sat 10am–11pm; Sun 11am–10:30pm. Tube: Tottenham Court Rd.

G.A.Y.   The name notwithstanding, the clientele here is mixed, and on a Saturday night this could well be the most rollicking club in London. A mammoth place, this club draws a young crowd to dance at this pop extravaganza with its mirrored disco balls. Overheard recently: One young man asked another his sexual orientation. The reply: "Total confusion!" London Astoria, 157 Charing Cross Rd., WC2. ✆ **020/7734-9592**. Admission £10 ($16) Mon–Fri 10:30am–4am; Sat 10:30pm–5am. Tube: Tottenham Court Rd.

Heaven   This club in the vaulted cellars of Charing Cross Railway Station is a London landmark. Owned by the same investors who brought the world Virgin Atlantic Airways, Heaven is one of the biggest and best-established gay venues in Britain. Painted black and reminiscent of an air-raid shelter, the club is divided into at least four distinct areas, connected by a labyrinth of catwalk stairs and hallways. Each area has a different activity going on. Heaven also has theme nights, frequented at different times by gays, lesbians, or a mostly heterosexual crowd. Thursday in particular seems open to anything, but Saturday is gay only. The Arches, Villiers and Craven sts., WC2. ✆ 020/7930-2020. Cover £5–£15 ($8–$24). Mon and Wed 10:30pm–3am; Fri 10:30pm–6am; Sat 10:30pm–5am. Tube: Charing Cross or Embankment.

Ku Bar   The Happy Hour here lasts from noon to 9pm, and the bartenders assure us that their watering hole attracts "the tastiest men in London." Those bartenders also serve up some of the tastiest drinks. If you want a schnapps, they'll ask you if you want peach, melon, apple, lemon, or butterscotch. Come here for a fab time, to have a bash, and to cruise. 75 Charing Cross Rd., WC2. ✆ 020/7437-4303. Tube: Leicester Sq.

THE BAR & PUB SCENE
OUR FAVORITE BARS

American Bar   The bartender in this sophisticated gathering place is known for his special concoctions, "Savoy Affair" and "Prince of Wales," as well as what is reputedly the best martini in town. Monday through Saturday evenings, jazz piano is featured from 7 to 11pm. Near many West End theaters, the location is ideal for a pre- or posttheater drink. In The Savoy, The Strand, WC2. ✆ 020/7836-4343. Smart casual: No jeans, sneakers, T-shirts. Tube: Charing Cross, Covent Garden, or Embankment.

Beach Blanket Babylon   Go here for a hot singles bar that attracts a crowd in their 20s and 30s. This Portobello joint—named after a kitschy musical revue in San Francisco—is a huge pickup spot. The decor is a bit wacky, no doubt designed by an aspiring Salvador Dalí who decided to make it a fairy-tale grotto (or did he mean a medieval dungeon?). Close to the Portobello Market, Saturday and Sunday nights are the hot, crowded times to show up for bacchanalian revelry. 45 Ledbury Rd., W11. ✆ 020/7229-2907. Tube: Notting Hill Gate.

Cantaloupe   This bustling pub and restaurant is hailed as the bar that jump-started the increasingly fashionable Shoreditch scene. Business people leaving their jobs in The City mix with East End trendoids in the early evening at what has been called a "gastro pub/pre-club bar." Wooden tables and benches are found up front, although the Red Bar is more comfortable, as patrons lounge on Chesterfield chairs. The urban beat is courtesy of the house DJ. Its restaurant and tapas menus are first rate. 35–42 Charlotte Rd., Shoreditch, EC2. ✆ 020/7613-4411. Tube: Old St.

The Library   For one of London's poshest drinking retreats, head for this deluxe hotel with its high ceilings, leather chesterfields, respectable oil paintings, and grand windows. Its collection of ancient cognacs is unparalleled in London. In the Lanesborough Hotel, 1 Lanesborough Place, SW1. ✆ 020/7259-5599. Tube: Hyde Park Corner.

Lillie Langtry Bar   Next door to Langtry's Restaurant, this 1920s-style bar epitomizes the charm and elegance of the Edwardian era. Lillie Langtry, the turn-of-the-20th-century actress and society beauty (notorious as the mistress of Edward VII), once lived here. Oscar Wilde—arrested in this very hotel bar—is honored on the drinks menu by his favorite libation, the Hock and Seltzer. Sir John Betjeman's poem "The Arrest of Oscar Wilde at the Cadogan Hotel" tells the story. The Cadogan Cooler seems to be the most popular drink here. An

Finds **Drinks a la Americana**

Everybody's heard of the Hard Rock Cafe and Planet Hollywood, but the real news coming out of London is the sudden opening of so many American-theme bars. The best includes **Navajo Joe,** 34 King St., WC2 (✆ 020/7240-4008), which offers the largest tequila selection outside of Mexico and whose southwestern cuisine is already starting to win some restaurant awards. For the atmosphere of a different part of the American south, head for **Old Orleans,** corner of Wellington and Tavistock streets, WC2 (✆ 020/7497-2433), with its colorful cocktail bar and its rich decor from the old American South in its restaurant featuring Creole cuisine. Both are reached by taking the Tube to Covent Garden.

international menu is served in the adjoining restaurant. In the Cadogan Hotel, 75 Sloane St., SW1. ✆ 020/7235-7141. Tube: Sloane Sq. or Knightsbridge.

The Lobby Bar   This bar and the bar associated with the Axis restaurant are in London's newest five-star hotel. We advise that you check out the dramatic visuals of both before selecting your preferred nesting place for a drink or two. The Lobby Bar occupies what was built in 1907 as the very grand, very high-ceilinged reception area for one of London's premier newspapers. If that setting doesn't appeal to you, check out the travertine, hardwood, and leather-sheathed bar in the Axis restaurant. The Lobby Bar is open daily from 9am to 11pm; the Axis bar is open at hours that correspond to those of the restaurant. In the Hotel One Aldwych, 1 Aldwych, WC2. ✆ 020/7300-1000. Tube: Covent Garden.

The Mandarin Bar   No other bar in London showcases the art of the cocktail as artfully as this one. Designed by design-industry superstar Adam Tihany around a geometric theme of artfully backlit glass, it provides the kind of cool, hip, and confidently prosperous venue where men look attractive, women look fantastic, and cocktails are sublime. These are prepared without fuss behind frosted-glass panels, in a style akin to a holy rite at a pagan temple, then presented with tact and charm. There's live music every Monday through Saturday from 9pm till closing, and a leather-upholstered area off to the side, with a state-of-the-art air filtration system, for cigar smokers and their fans. In the Mandarin Oriental Hyde Park Hotel, 66 Knightsbridge, SW1. ✆ 020/7235-2000. Tube: Knightsbridge.

Match EC1   An epicenter of the fashionable set in London has put the *P* in partying in the once staid Clerkenwell district. High on the list for evening fun is Match, drawing a 20s to 30s crowd. Drinkers sit on elegant sofas or retreat to one of the cozy booths for a late bite. The bar claims to be the home of the Cosmopolitan, the cocktail that swept across the speakeasies of New York. The bartenders make some of the best drinks in London but warn you that "there is no such thing as a chocolate martini." 45–47 Clerkenwell Rd., EC1. ✆ 020/7250-4002. Tube: Farringdon.

The Met Bar   Very much the place to be seen, this has become the hottest bar in London. Mix with the elite of the fashion, TV, and the music world. A lot of American celebrities have been seen here, sipping on a martini, from Demi Moore to Courteney Cox. Despite the caliber of the clientele, the bar has managed to maintain a relaxed and unpretentious atmosphere. In the Metropolitan Hotel, 19 Old Park Lane, W1. ✆ 020/7447-1000. Members only and hotel guests. Tube: Hyde Park Corner.

The Phoenix Artist Club Want something so old it's new again? This is where Lord Laurence Olivier made his stage debut in 1930, although he couldn't stop giggling even though the play was drama. Live music is featured, but it's the hearty welcome, the good beer, and friendly patrons that make this "rediscovered" theater bar worth a detour. 1 Phoenix St., WC2. ℂ **020/7836-1077.** Tube: Tottenham Court Rd.

THE WORLD'S GREATEST PUB CRAWL
BELGRAVIA
Grenadier *Finds* Tucked away in a mews, the Grenadier is one of London's reputedly haunted pubs. Aside from the poltergeist, the basement houses the original bar and skittles alley used by the duke of Wellington's officers on leave from fighting Napoleon. The scarlet front door of the one-time officers' mess is guarded by a scarlet sentry box and shaded by a vine. The bar is nearly always crowded. Lunch and dinner are offered daily—even Sunday, when it's a tradition to drink Bloody Marys here. In stalls along the side, you can order good-tasting fare based on seasonal ingredients. Well-prepared dishes include pork Grenadier and chicken and Stilton roulade. Snacks such as fish and chips are available at the bar. 18 Wilton Row, SW1. ℂ **020/7235-3074.** Tube: Hyde Park Corner.

BLOOMSBURY
Museum Tavern Across the street from the British Museum, this pub (ca. 1703) retains most of its antique trappings: velvet, oak paneling, and cut glass. It lies right in the center of the University of London area and is popular with writers, publishers, and researchers from the museum. (Supposedly, Karl Marx wrote while dining in the pub.) Traditional English food is served: shepherd's pie, sausages cooked in English cider, turkey-and-ham pie, ploughman's lunch, and salads. Several English ales, cold lagers, cider, Guinness, wines, and spirits are available. Food and coffee are served all day; the pub gets crowded at lunchtime. 49 Great Russell St., WC1. ℂ **020/7242-8987.** Tube: Holborn or Tottenham Court Rd.

THE CITY
Bow Wine Vaults Bow Wine Vaults has existed since long before the wine-bar craze began in the 1970s. One of the most famous wine bars of London, it attracts cost-conscious diners and drinkers to its vaulted cellars for such traditional fare as deep-fried Camembert, lobster ravioli, and a mixed grill, along with fish. More elegant meals, served in the street-level dining room, include mussels in cider sauce, English wild mushrooms in puff pastry, beef Wellington, and steak with brown-butter sauce. Adjacent to the restaurant is a cocktail bar that's popular with City employees after work (open weekdays 11:30am–11pm). 10 Bow Chuchyard, EC4. ℂ **020/7248-1121.** Tube: Mansion House, Bank, or St. Paul's.

Jamaica Wine House Jamaica Wine House was one of the first coffeehouses in England and, reputedly, the Western world. For years, merchants and daring sea captains came here to transact deals over rum and coffee. Nowadays, the two-level house dispenses beer, ale, lager, and fine wines, among them a variety of ports. The oak-paneled bar is on the street level, attracting a jacket-and-tie crowd of investment bankers. You can order standard but filling dishes such as a ploughman's lunch and toasted sandwiches. St. Michael's Alley off Cornhill, EC3. ℂ **020/7929-6972.** Tube: Bank.

Ye Olde Cock Tavern Dating back to 1549, this tavern boasts a long line of literary patrons: Samuel Pepys mentioned the pub in his diaries, Dickens frequented it, and Tennyson referred to it in one of his poems (a copy of which is

framed and proudly displayed near the front entrance). It's one of the few buildings in London to have survived the Great Fire of 1666. At street level, you can
order a pint as well as bar food, steak-and-kidney pie, or a cold chicken-and-beef
plate with salad. At the Carvery upstairs, a meal includes a choice of appetizers,
followed by lamb, pork, beef, or turkey. 22 Fleet St., EC4. ℭ 020/7353-8570. Tube: Temple or Chancery Lane.

Ye Olde Watling   Ye Olde Watling was rebuilt after the Great Fire of 1666.
On the ground level is a mellow pub; upstairs is an intimate restaurant where,
under oak beams and at trestle tables, you can dine on simple English main
dishes for lunch. The menu varies daily, with such choices and reliable standbys
as fish and chips, lamb satay, lasagna, fish cakes, and usually a vegetarian dish.
All are served with two vegetables or salad, plus rice or potatoes. 29 Watling St., EC4.
ℭ 020/7653-9971. Tube: Mansion House.

COVENT GARDEN

Lamb & Flag   Dickens once hung out in this pub, and the room itself is little
changed from the days when he prowled this neighborhood. The pub has an
amazing and somewhat scandalous history. Dryden was almost killed by a band
of thugs outside its doors in December 1679; the pub gained the nickname the
"Bucket of Blood" during the Regency era (1811–20) because of the routine
bare-knuckled prizefights that broke out here. Tap beers include Courage Best
and Directors, Old Speckled Hen, John Smith's, and Wadworth's 6X. 33 Rose St.,
off Garrick St., WC2. ℭ 020/7497-9504. Tube: Leicester Sq.

Nag's Head   The Nag's Head is one of London's most famous Edwardian
pubs. In days of yore, patrons had to make their way through lorries of fruit and
flowers to drink here. But when the market moved, 300 years of British tradition faded away. Today, the pub is patronized mainly by young people. The draft
Guinness is very good. Lunch is typical pub grub: sandwiches, salads, pork
cooked in cider, and garlic prawns. The sandwich platters mentioned above are
served only during the lunch hour (noon–4pm); however, snacks are available in
the afternoon. 10 James St., WC2. ℭ 020/7836-4678. Tube: Covent Garden.

EAST END (WAPPING)

Prospect of Whitby   One of London's most historic pubs, it was founded in
the days of the Tudors, taking its name from a coal barge that made trips
between Yorkshire and London. Come here for a tot, noggin, or whatever it is
you drink and soak up its traditional pub atmosphere. It has quite a pedigree.
Dickens and Samuel Pepys used to drop in, and Turner came here for weeks at
a time studying views of the Thames. In the 17th century, the notorious Hanging Judge Jeffreys used to get drunk here while overseeing hangings he'd ordered
at the adjoining Execution Dock. Tables in the courtyard look out over river
views. You can order a Morlands Old Speckled Hen from a handpump, or a malt
whisky. 57 Wapping Wall, E1. ℭ 020/7481-1095. Mon–Fri 11:30am–3pm and 5:30–11pm; Sat
11:30am–11pm; Sun noon–10:30pm. Tube: Wapping.

HOLBORN

Cittie of Yorke   This pub boasts the longest bar in all of Britain, rafters
ascending to the heavens, and a long row of immense wine vats, all of which give
it the air of a great medieval hall—appropriate because a pub has existed at this
location since 1430. Samuel Smith's is on tap, and the bar offers novelties such
as chocolate-orange-flavored vodka. 22 High Holborn, WC1. ℭ 020/7242-7670. Tube:
Holborn or Chancery Lane.

KNIGHTSBRIDGE

Nag's Head This Nag's Head (not to be confused with the more renowned one at 10 James St.; see above) is snuggled on a back street a short walk from the Berkeley Hotel. Previously a jail dating from 1780, it's said to be the smallest pub in London, although others claim that distinction. In 1921, it was sold for £12 and 6p ($20). Have a drink up front or wander to the tiny little bar in the rear. For food, you might enjoy "real ale sausage" (made with pork and ale), shepherd's pie, or even the quiche of the day. This warm and cozy pub, with a welcoming staff, is patronized by a cosmopolitan clientele—newspaper people, musicians, and curious tourists. This pub touts itself as an "independent," or able to serve any "real ale" they choose because of their lack of affiliation. 53 Kinnerton St., SW1. (℄ 020/7235-1135. Tube: Hyde Park.

LEICESTER SQUARE

Salisbury *Finds* Salisbury's glittering cut-glass mirrors reflect the faces of English stage stars (and hopefuls) sitting around the curved buffet-style bar. A less prominent place to dine is the old-fashioned wall banquette with its copper-topped tables and Art Nouveau decor. The pub's specialty, home-cooked pies set out in a buffet cabinet with salads, is really quite good and inexpensive. 90 St. Martin's Lane, WC2. (℄ 020/7836-5863. Tube: Leicester Sq.

MAYFAIR

Shepherd's Tavern This pub is one of the focal points of the all-pedestrian shopping zone of Shepherd's Market. It's set amid a warren of narrow, cobble-covered streets behind Park Lane, in an 18th-century town house very similar to many of its neighbors. The street-level bar is cramped but congenial. Many of the regulars recall this tavern's popularity with the pilots of the Battle of Britain. Bar snacks include simple plates of shepherd's pie and fish and chips. More formal dining is available upstairs in the cozy, cedar-lined Georgian-style restaurant; the classic British menu probably hasn't changed much since the 1950s. You can always get Oxford ham or roast beef with Yorkshire pudding. 50 Hertford St., W1. (℄ 020/7499-3017. Tube: Green Park.

NOTTING HILL GATE

Ladbroke Arms Previously honored as London's "Dining Pub of the Year," Ladbroke Arms is that rare pub known for its food. A changing menu includes chicken breast stuffed with avocado and garlic steak in pink-peppercorn sauce. With background jazz and rotating art prints, the place strays a bit from a traditional pub environment, but it makes for a pleasant stop and a good meal. The excellent Eldridge Pope Royal is on tap, as well as John Smith's and Courage Directors, and several malt whiskies. 54 Ladbroke Rd., W11. (℄ 020/7727-6648. Tube: Notting Hill Gate.

ST. JAMES'S

Red Lion This little Victorian pub, with its early-1900s decorations and mirrors that are 150 years old, has been compared in spirit to Manet's painting *A Bar at the Folies-Bergère* (on display at the Courtauld Gallery). You can order pre-made sandwiches, but once they're gone you're out of luck. On Saturday, homemade fish and chips are also served. Wash down your meal with Ind Coope's fine ales or the house's special beer, Burton's, an unusual brew made of spring water from the Midlands town of Burton-on-Trent. 2 Duke of York St. (off Jermyn St.), SW1. (℄ 020/7321-0782. Tube: Piccadilly Circus.

SOHO

Dog & Duck   This snug little joint, a Soho landmark, is the most intimate pub in London. One former patron was author George Orwell, who came here to celebrate his sales of *Animal Farm* in the United States. A wide mixture of patrons of all ages and persuasions flock here, chatting amiably while ordering the delights of Tetley's LA or Timothy Taylor Landlord. Perhaps in autumn customers will ask for Addlestone's Cider. A lot of patrons head later for Ronnie Scott's Jazz Club, which is close by. If business warrants it, the cozy upstairs bar is opened. 18 Bateman St. (corner of Frith St.), W1. ℂ 020/7494-0697.

SOUTHWARK

George   Preserved by the National Trust, the existing structure here was built to replace the original pub, which was destroyed in the Great Fire. The pub's accolades date to 1598, when it was reviewed as a "faire inn for the receipt of travellers." No longer an inn, it's still a great place to enjoy Flowers Original, Boddington's, and London Pride Abbot on tap. Off 77 Borough High St., SE1. ℂ 020/ 7407-2056. Tube: Northern Line to London Bridge or Borough.

TRAFALGAR SQUARE

Sherlock Holmes   The Sherlock Holmes was the old gathering spot for the Baker Street Irregulars, a once-mighty clan of mystery lovers who met here to honor the genius of Sir Arthur Conan Doyle's most famous fictional character. Upstairs, you'll find a re-creation of the living room at 221B Baker Street and such "Holmesiana" as the serpent of *The Speckled Band* and the head of *The Hound of the Baskervilles.* In the upstairs dining room, you can order complete meals with wine. Try "Copper Beeches" (grilled butterfly chicken breasts with lemon and herbs). You select dessert from the trolley. Downstairs is mainly for drinking, but there's a good snack bar with cold meats, salads, cheeses, and wine and ales sold by the glass. 10 Northumberland St., WC1. ℂ 020/7930-2644. Tube: Charing Cross or Embankment.

8 Side Trips From London

There's much more to England than just London. But you could spend the best part of a year—or a lifetime—exploring *only* London, without risking either boredom or repetition. Still, we advise you to tear yourself away from Big Ben for at least a day or two, as the capital city is surrounded by some of the most memorable sports on earth.

WINDSOR & ETON ⊛
21 miles (34km) W of London

Were it not for the castle, Windsor may still be a charming Thames town to visit. But because it is the home of the best-known asset the royal family possesses, it is overrun in summer by tourists who all but obscure the town's charm.

The good news is that after the disastrous fire of 1992, Windsor Castle is restored, though some of the new designs for it have been called a "Gothic shocker" or "ghastly." If you visit, you can decide. And you won't be alone: Windsor Castle remains Britain's second-most-visited historic building, behind the Tower of London, attracting 1.2 million visitors a year.

ESSENTIALS
GETTING THERE   The train from Waterloo or Paddington Station in London makes the trip in 30 minutes (you'll have to transfer at Slough to the

Slough–Windsor shuttle train). With more than a dozen trains per day, the cost is £6.50 ($10) round-trip. Call **Thames Trains, Ltd.,** at © **0845/748-4950** for more information.

Green Line coaches (© **0870/608-7261**) nos. 700 and 702 from Hyde Park Corner in London take about 1½ hours, depending on the day of the week. A same-day round-trip costs £8 ($13). The bus drops you near the parish church, across the street from the castle.

If you're driving from London, take the M4 west.

VISITOR INFORMATION A **Tourist Information Centre** is located across from Windsor Castle on High Street (© **01753/743900;** www.windsor.gov.uk). An information booth is also in the Tourist Centre at Windsor Coach Park. Both are open Monday through Friday from 10am to 4pm, Saturday from 10am to 5pm.

CASTLE HILL SIGHTS

Windsor Castle ★★★   William the Conqueror first ordered a castle built on this location, and since his day it's been a fateful spot for English sovereigns: King John cooled his heels at Windsor while waiting to put his signature on the Magna Carta at nearby Runnymede; Charles I was imprisoned here before losing his head; Queen Bess did some renovations; Victoria mourned her beloved Albert, who died at the castle in 1861; the royal family rode out much of World War II behind its sheltering walls; and when Queen Elizabeth II is in residence, the royal standard flies. With 1,000 rooms, Windsor is the world's largest inhabited castle.

George IV's elegant **Semi-State Chambers** ★★ can only be visited from the end of September until the end of March. They were created by the king in the 1820s as part of a series of Royal Apartments designed for his personal use. Seriously damaged in 1992, they have been returned to their former glory, with lovely antiques, paintings, and decorative objects. The Crimson Drawing room is evocative of the king's flamboyant taste with gilt, crimson silk damask hangings, and sumptuous art works.

In November 1992, a fire swept through part of the castle, severely damaging it. The castle has since reopened, and its public rooms are available for viewing. It is recommended that you take a free guided tour of the castle grounds, including the romantic 2-acre **Jubilee Gardens.** Guides are very well informed and recapture the rich historical background of the castle.

In our opinion, the Windsor **Changing of the Guard** ★ is a much more exciting experience than the London exercises. The guard marches through the town whether the court is in residence or not, stopping the traffic as it wheels into the castle to the tunes of a full regimental band; when the queen is not here, a drum-and-pipe band is mustered. From April to July, the ceremony takes place Monday through Saturday at 11am. In winter, the guard is changed every 48 hours Monday through Saturday. It's best to call © **020/7321-2233** for a schedule.

Castle Hill. © 020/7321-2233. . Admission £11.50 ($18) adults, £6 ($9.60) children 16 and under, £29 ($46) family of 4. Mar–Oct daily 9:45am–5:15pm; Nov–Feb daily 9:45am–4:15pm. Last admission 1 hr. before closing. Closed for periods in Apr, June, and Dec when the royal family is in residence.

Queen Mary's Doll's House   A palace in perfect miniature, the Doll's House was given to Queen Mary in 1923 as a symbol of national goodwill. The house, designed by Sir Edwin Lutyens, was created on a scale of 1 to 12. It took 3 years to complete and involved the work of 1,500 tradesmen and artists. Every item is a miniature masterpiece; each room is exquisitely furnished, and every item is made exactly to scale. Working elevators stop on every floor, and there is running water in all five bathrooms.

Castle Hill. © **01753/831118** for recorded information. Admission is included in entrance to Windsor Castle. Mar–Oct daily 10am–4pm; Nov–Feb daily 10am–3pm. As with Windsor Castle, it's best to call ahead to confirm opening times.

St. George's Chapel ★★★   A gem of the Perpendicular style, this chapel shares the distinction with Westminster Abbey of being a pantheon of English monarchs (Victoria is a notable exception). The present St. George's was founded in the late 15th century by Edward IV on the site of the original Chapel of the Order of the Garter (Edward III, 1348). You first enter the nave, which contains the tomb of George V and Queen Mary, designed by Sir William Reid Dick. Off the nave in the Urswick Chapel, the Princess Charlotte memorial provides an ironic touch; if she had survived childbirth in 1817, she, and not her cousin Victoria, would have ruled the British empire. In the aisle are tombs of George VI and Edward IV. The Edward IV "Quire," with its imaginatively carved 15th-century choir stalls, evokes the pomp and pageantry of medieval days. In the center is a flat tomb, containing the vault of the beheaded Charles I, along with Henry VIII and his third wife, Jane Seymour. Finally, you may want to inspect the Prince Albert Memorial Chapel, reflecting the opulent tastes of the Victorian era.

Castle Hill. © **01753/848883**. Admission is included in entrance to Windsor Castle. Mon–Sat 9:45am–4:15pm. Closed Sun and for a few days in June, Nov, and Dec.

Windsor Farm Shop   Had any of the queen's jars of jam lately, maybe her homemade pork pie, or a bottle of her special brew? If not, head for this outlet on the edge of the royal estate, which sells produce from the queen's estates outside Windsor, including pheasants and partridges bagged at royal shoots. Much of the produce bears the seal of the Royal Farms. The meat counter is especially awesome, with its cooked hams and massive ribs of beef. The steak-and-ale pies are especially tasty. Stock up on the queen's vittles and head for a picnic in the area.

Datchet Rd., Old Windsor. © **01753/623800**. Free admission. Mon–Fri 9am–5pm; Sat 9–6pm; Sun 10am–4pm.

NEARBY ETON COLLEGE ★★

Eton is home of what is arguably the most famous public school (Americans would call it a private school) in the world. From Windsor Castle's ramparts, you can look down on the river and onto the famous playing fields of Eton.

To get there, take a train from Paddington Station, go by car, or take the Green Line bus to Windsor. By car, take the M4 to Exit 5 to go straight to Eton.

Insider's tip: Parking is likely to be a problem, so we advise turning off the M4 at Exit 6 to Windsor; you can park here and take an easy stroll past Windsor Castle and across the Thames bridge. Follow Eton High Street to the college.

Eton College (© **01753/671177**; www.etoncollege.com) was founded by 18-year-old Henry VI in 1440. Some of England's greatest men, notably the duke of Wellington, have played on these fields. Twenty prime ministers were educated here, as well as such literary figures as George Orwell, Aldous Huxley, Ian Fleming, and Percy Bysshe Shelley, who, during his years at Eton (1804–10), was called "Mad Shelley" or "Shelley the Atheist" by his fellow pupils. Prince William, second in line to the throne, was recently a student here. If it's open, take a look at the Perpendicular chapel, with its 15th-century paintings and reconstructed fan vaulting.

The history of Eton College since its inception in 1440 is depicted in the **Museum of Eton Life,** Eton College (© **01753/671177**), located in vaulted wine cellars under College Hall, which were originally used as a storehouse by the college's masters. The displays, ranging from formal to extremely informal, include a turn-of-the-20th-century boy's room, schoolbooks, and canes used by senior boys to apply punishment they felt needful to their juniors.

Admission to the school and museum is £3.70 ($5.90) for adults and £2 ($3.20) for children under 15. You can also take guided tours for £4.70 ($7.50). Eton College is open from March 22 to April 22 and June 28 to September 5, daily from 10:30am to 4:30pm; from April 23 to June 27 and September 3 to October 5, daily from 2 to 4:30pm. Call in advance; Eton may close for special occasions. These dates vary every year depending on term and holiday dates. It's best to call.

MORE TO DO IN & AROUND WINDSOR

The town of Windsor is largely Victorian, with lots of brick buildings and a few remnants of Georgian architecture. In and around the castle are two cobblestone streets, Church and Market, which have antiques shops, silversmiths, and pubs. After lunch or tea, you can stroll along the 5km (3-mile), aptly named **Long Walk.**

Savill Garden, Wick Lane, Englefield Green, Egham, and Surrey (© **01753/ 860222**) are all in **Windsor Great Park** ★, which is signposted from Windsor, Egham, and Ascot. Started in 1932, the 35-acre garden is one of the finest of its type in the northern hemisphere. The display starts in spring with rhododendrons, camellias, and daffodils beneath the trees; then throughout the summer are spectacular displays of flowers and shrubs presented in a natural and wild state. It's open daily year-round (except at Christmas) from 10am to 6pm (to 4pm in winter). Admission prices vary throughout the year: from November to March, £3.25 ($5.20) for adults, £2.75 ($4.40) for seniors; in April and May, £5.50 ($8.80) adults, £5 ($8) for seniors; and from June to October £4.50 ($7.20) adults, £4 ($6.40) for seniors. Children 5 and under are admitted free. The location is 8km (5 miles) from Windsor along the A30; turn off at Wick Road and follow the signs to the gardens. The nearest rail station is at Egham; from here you'll need to take a taxi a distance of 5km (3 miles). There's a licensed, self-service restaurant and gift shop on the premises.

Adjoining Savill Garden are the **Valley Gardens,** full of shrubs and trees in a series of wooded natural valleys running to the water. Open daily year-round, entrance to the gardens is free, though parking is £3 ($4.80) per vehicle.

On the B3022 Bracknell/Ascot Road, outside Windsor, **Legoland** (© **08705/ 040404;** www.lego.com/legoland), a 150-acre theme park, opened in 1996. Although a bit corny, it's fun for the entire family. Attractions, spread across five main activity centers, include Duplo Gardens, offering a boat ride, puppet theater, and water works, plus a Miniland, showing European cities or villages re-created

---

Finds **Where the Empress of India Rests**

Queen Victoria, who ruled an empire, including India, on which the sun never set, died on January 22, 1901, and was buried beside her beloved Prince Albert in a mausoleum at **Frogmore** (a private estate on the grounds of Windsor Castle), a mile from Windsor. The prince consort died in December 1861. The house, gardens, and mausoleum are open only a few days out of the year, usually in May and August, from around 10am to 6pm. The cost for adults is £6.60 ($11); seniors pay £5.50 ($8.80). Call © **01753/869898** for more details.

Moments Windsor from a Queen Victoria Carriage

You can take a 30-minute **carriage ride** up the sycamore-lined length of Windsor Castle's Long Walk. Horses with their carriages and drivers should be lined up beside the castle waiting for fares, charging from about £20 ($32) for up to four passengers.

---

in minute detail from millions of Lego bricks. Enchanted Forest has treasure trails, a castle, and animals created from Lego bricks. The latest attraction is Dragon Knight's Castle, taking you back to the days of knights and dragons and including a blazing dragon roller coaster. The park is open daily from 10am to 6pm from mid-March to October. Admission varies through the season, starting at £19 to £23 ($30–$37) for adults, £13 to £17 ($21–$27) for seniors, and £16 to £20 ($26–$32) for children 3 to 15 (free for children 2 and under).

Only 5km (3 miles) south of Windsor is **Runnymede,** the 188-acre meadow on the south side of the Thames, in Surrey, where it's believed that King John put his seal on the Great Charter after intense pressure from his feudal barons and lords. Today, Runnymede is also the site of the John F. Kennedy Memorial, an acre of English ground given to the United States by the people of Britain. The memorial, a large block of white stone, is hard to see from the road, but is clearly signposted and reached after a short walk. The pagoda that shelters it was placed here by the American Bar Association to acknowledge the fact that American law stems from the English system.

The historic site, to which there is free access all year, lies beside the Thames, 1km (½ mile) west of the hamlet of Old Windsor on the south side of the A308. If you're driving on the M25, exit at Junction 13. The nearest rail connection is at Egham, 1km (½ mile) away. Trains depart from London's Waterloo Station and take about 25 minutes.

BUS & BOAT TOURS, HORSE RIDES & GUIDED WALKS OF WINDSOR

The tourist office can put you in touch with a Blue Badge (official) guide to lead you on a **walking tour** of town. The cost depends upon the number of people and the length of the tour. Advance booking is essential.

Boat tours depart from Windsor's main embarkation point along Windsor Promenade, Barry Avenue, for a 45-minute round-trip to Boveney Lock. The cost is £4.20 ($6.70) for adults, half price for children. You can also take a 2-hour tour through the Boveney Lock and up past stately private riverside homes, the Bray Film Studios, Queens Eyot, and Monkey Island, for £6.60 ($11) for adults, half price for children. There's also a 45-minute tour from Runnymede on board the *Lucy Fisher,* a replica of a Victorian paddle steamer. You pass Magna Carta Island, among other sights. This tour costs £4.20 ($6.70) for adults, half price for children. In addition, longer tours between Maidenhead and Hampton Court are offered. The boats offer light refreshments and have a well-stocked bar, plus the decks are covered in case of an unexpected shower. Tours are operated by **French Brothers, Ltd.,** Clewer Boathouse, Clewer Court Road, Windsor (© 01753/851900).

WHERE TO STAY IN THE WINDSOR AREA

During the Ascot races and Windsor Horse Show, reservations are necessary far in advance.

The Castle Hotel ✦   In the shadow of Windsor Castle, on the main street, is this solid choice with a dignified Georgian facade. It was originally built in the 15th century to shelter the workers laboring on the town's foundations and royal buildings. The grounds behind the hotel once served as the stable yard for Windsor Castle, but now they contain a modern wing, where the bedrooms are much more sterile than those in the main building.

18 High St., Windsor, Berkshire SL4 1LJ. © **01753/851011.** Fax 01753/830244. www.macdonaldhotels.co.uk. 111 units. £140–£160 ($224–$256) double; £200–£250 ($320–$400) suite. Children 12 and under stay free in parent's room. AE, DC, MC, V. **Amenities:** 2 restaurants; bar; room service; laundry service. *In room:* TV, coffeemaker, hair dryer, safe, trouser press.

The Oakley Court Hotel ✦✦   Built beside the Thames (a 20-min. drive from Heathrow) by a Victorian industrialist, the Oakley Court is imbued with a sense of tradition. Today it's affiliated with the Queen's Moat House hotel chain. The building's jutting gables and bristling turrets have lent themselves to the filming of several horror movies, including *The Rocky Horror Picture Show* and *Dracula*. Last renovated in 1997, the hotel is a comfortable place to stay— far superior to choices in the heart of Windsor. Although the grandest public areas are in the main house, most rooms are in a trio of well-accessorized modern wings that ramble through the estate's 35 acres of parks and gardens. Some rooms offer four-poster beds and views of the River Thames.

Windsor Rd., Water Oakley, Windsor, Berkshire SL4 5UR. © **01753/609988.** Fax 01628/637011. www. moathousehotels.com. 118 units. £180 ($288) double (weekends with breakfast), £220 ($352) (Mon–Fri with breakfast). AE, DC, MC, V. Take the river road, A308, 5km (3 miles) from Windsor toward Maidenhead. **Amenities:** Restaurant; bar; gym with sauna/steam room; Jacuzzi; boat rentals; room service; babysitting; laundry service; dry cleaning. *In room:* A/C (most rooms), TV, minibar, hair dryer, safe, trouser press.

Royal Adelaide Hotel   This interesting Georgian building is located just opposite the famous Long Walk leading to Windsor Castle, a mere 5-minute-walk away. Named for Queen Adelaide, who visited the premises during her reign, thereby dubbing it "royal," all its well-furnished rooms are individually decorated and have recently been refurbished. Some of the rooms offer castle views.

46 King's Rd., Windsor, Berkshire SL4 2AG. © **01753/863916.** Fax 01753/830682. www.meridianleisure.com. 42 units. £99–£115 ($158–$184) double. Rates include English breakfast. AE, DC, MC, V. **Amenities:** Restaurant; bar; room service; babysitting. *In room:* TV, coffeemaker, safe, trouser press.

Sir Christopher Wren's House Hotel ✦   Designed by Christopher Wren in 1676 as his home, this former town house occupies a prime position on the Thames, just a 3-minute walk from the castle. Wren's oak-paneled former study is equipped with his Empire desk, a fireplace, and shield-back Hepplewhite chairs. The bay-windowed main drawing room opens onto a garden and a riverside flagstone terrace for after-dinner coffee and drinks. Rooms come in a wide range of sizes; some have fine old furniture and a full-canopied bed, others have a half-canopied bed. Several bedrooms overlook the river. Room no. 2, which was Wren's bedroom, is said to be haunted.

Thames St., Windsor, Berkshire SL4 1PX. © **01753/861354.** Fax 01753/860172. www.wrensgroup.com. 92 units. Mon–Thurs £200 ($320) double; Fri–Sun (including breakfast) £150–£170 ($240–$272) double. Daily £275 ($440) suite. AE, DC, MC, V. Parking £10 ($16). **Amenities:** Restaurant; bar; gym; sauna; concierge; secretarial services; room service; babysitting; laundry service; dry cleaning. *In room:* TV, coffeemaker, hair dryer, trouser press.

Ye Harte & Garter Hotel   On Castle Hill opposite Windsor Castle is the old Garter Inn. Named for the Knights of the Garter, and used as the setting for scenes in Shakespeare's *The Merry Wives of Windsor*, the Garter burned down in the 1800s and was rebuilt as part of one hostelry that included the Harte. From the front rooms, you can watch the guards marching up High Street every morning on their way to change the guard at the castle. The recently renovated rooms are comfortable and rather functionally furnished, though they vary greatly in size. More expensive are the Windsor rooms, which have front views and Jacuzzis.

31 High St., Windsor, Berkshire SL4 1PH. (C) 01753/863426. Fax 01753/830527. harteandgarter@windsor.com. 39 units. £125 ($200) double; £180 ($288) suite. AE, DC, MC, V. **Amenities:** 2 restaurants; bar; laundry service. *In room:* TV, coffeemaker, hair dryer, trouser press.

WHERE TO DINE IN WINDSOR & ETON

Many visitors prefer to dine in Eton; most of the restaurants and fast-food places along the main street of Windsor, in front of the castle, serve dreary food.

Antico ✪ ITALIAN   Eton's finest Italian restaurant, Antico serves Mediterranean food in a formal setting. People have been dining here for 200 years, though not from an Italian menu. On your way to the tiny bar, you pass a cold table, displaying hors d'oeuvres and cold meats. With many fish dishes, such as grilled fresh salmon, Dover sole, or sea bass, and a wide selection of pastas, the food is substantial and filling—a good value, but rarely exciting.

42 High St., Eton. (C) 01753/863977. Reservations strongly recommended. Main courses £11–£20 ($18–$32). AE, MC, V. Mon–Fri 12:30–2:30pm; Mon–Sat 7–10:30pm. Closed bank holidays.

Gilbey's Bar and Restaurant MODERN BRITISH/CONTINENTAL Just across the bridge from Windsor, this charming place is located on Eton's main street, among the antiques shops. Furnished with pinewood tables and simple chairs, a glassed-in conservatory is out back. A brigade of seven chefs turns out quite good modern British dishes. Begin with one of the well-prepared soups, or a smoked-salmon-and-artichoke tart. Main dishes include pan-fried skate wing with a champagne or chile and caper risotto. For dessert, try the delicious white and dark mousse with amaretto cream.

82–83 High St., Eton. (C) 01753/854921. Reservations recommended. Main courses £10–£15 ($16–$24). AE, DC, MC, V. Mon–Fri 12–2:30pm; Sat–Sun 12–3pm; Mon–Thurs 6–9:30pm; Fri–Sat 6–10:30pm; Sun 6–9:30pm.

House on the Bridge ENGLISH/INTERNATIONAL   This restaurant is in a charming redbrick and terra-cotta Victorian building, adjacent to the bridge and beside the river at the edge of Eton. Near the handful of outdoor tables is an almost vertical garden whose plants cascade into the Thames. Among the well-prepared main dishes are crispy duckling with Calvados and Seville oranges, and chateaubriand. Good ingredients go into the dishes, and the food, although traditionally based, has many modern touches.

71 High St., Eton. (C) 01753/860914. Reservations recommended. Main courses from £14 ($22); fixed-price meal £20 ($32) at lunch, £30 ($48) at dinner. AE, DC, MC, V. Daily noon–3pm; Mon–Sat 6–11pm.

The Oak Leaf Restaurant at the Oakley Court Hotel ✪✪ INTERNATIONAL   In the mid-1990s, this chic London restaurant, known for its delectable food and sophisticated clientele, moved from central London to this new setting beside the Thames. Today, under the supervision of chef Damien Bradley, the reincarnated Oak Leaf serves a modern cuisine that may include a parfait of duck livers with a confit of red onions and mandarin oranges, or a pavé (a type of pastry) of Scottish salmon with creamed leeks served with broad beans and a red-wine shallot sauce.

Windsor Rd., Water Oakley, Windsor. (C) 01753/609988. Reservations recommended. Table d'hôte lunch and dinner £30 ($47); main courses £17–£25 ($27–$40). AE, DC, MC, V. Daily 7–10am, noon–2pm, and 7–10pm.

Finds   Golf, Goldfinger & Posh Decadence

One of Europe's greatest hotels lies only 30 minutes from London's West End and in close proximity to Ascot and Windsor. It's **Stoke Park Club,** Park Rd., Stoke Poges, Buckinghamshire SL2 4PG (© **877/HOTELUK** in the U.S., or 01753/717171; www.stokeparkclub.com). Golfers from all over the world flock to the 27-hole golf course designed by celebrated architect Harry Shapland Colt. James Bond defeated Goldfinger on its 18th green in 1964. Each bedroom or suite is individually decorated with antiques, paintings, and original prints, and all bedrooms feature fireplaces. Double rooms range from £270 to £325 ($432–$520) per night, with suites costing from £390 ($624).

Strok's MODERN BRITISH/CONTINENTAL   This restaurant, located near the castle, is Windsor's most elegant and charming, possessing garden terraces, a conservatory, and a dining room designed a bit like a greenhouse. Chef Philip Wild selects an individual garnish to complement each well-prepared dish. For starters, try the tower of smoked salmon and asparagus. For a main course, enjoy the rosettes of spring lamb with beans, artichokes and an herb Yorkshire pudding, or a seafood platter of lobster, king prawns, crab, mussels, and shrimps. A variety of vegetarian dishes is also offered. At dinner, a pianist entertains.

In Sir Christopher Wren's House Hotel, Thames St., Windsor. © **01753/861354.** Main courses £15–£20 ($23–$32); fixed-price menu £24 ($38). AE, DC, MC, V. Daily 12:30–3pm and 6:30–10pm.

WOBURN ABBEY: ENGLAND'S GREAT GEORGIAN MANOR ★★★
44 miles (71km) N of London

Aside from Windsor Castle, the most visited attraction in the Home Counties is Woburn Abbey, which is so spectacular you should try to visit even if you have to miss all the other historic homes described in this chapter. The great 18th-century Georgian mansion has been the traditional seat of the dukes of Bedford for more than three centuries.

TOURING THE ESTATE

Woburn Abbey   In the 1950s, the present duke of Bedford opened Woburn Abbey to the public to pay off his debt of millions of pounds in inheritance taxes. In 1974, he turned the estate over to his son and daughter-in-law, the marquess and marchioness of Tavistock, who reluctantly took on the business of running the 75-room mansion. And what a business it is, drawing hundreds of thousands of visitors a year and employing over 300 people to staff the shops and grounds.

Its state apartments are rich in furniture, porcelain, tapestries, silver, and a valuable art collection, including paintings by Van Dyck, Holbein, Rembrandt, Gainsborough, and Reynolds. Of all the paintings, one of the most notable is the Armada Portrait of Elizabeth I. Her hand rests on the globe, as Philip's invincible armada perishes in the background.

Queen Victoria and Prince Albert visited Woburn Abbey in 1841; Victoria's Dressing Room displays a fine collection of 17th-century paintings from the Netherlands. Among the oddities and treasures at Woburn Abbey are a Grotto of Shells, a Sèvres dinner service (gift of Louis XV), and a chamber devoted to memorabilia of "The Flying Duchess," the wife of the 11th duke of Bedford, a remarkable woman who disappeared on a solo flight in 1937 (coincidentally, the same year as Amelia Earhart). The duchess was 72 years old at the time.

Today, Woburn Abbey is surrounded by a 3,000-acre deer park that includes the famous Père David deer herd, originally from China and saved from extinction at Woburn. The **Woburn Safari Park** has lions, tigers, giraffes, camels, monkeys, Przewalski's horses, bongos, elephants, and other animals.

1km (½ mile) from the village of Woburn, which is 21km (13 miles) southwest of Bedford. © 01525/290666. www.woburnabbey.co.uk. Admission £8.50 ($14) adults, £7.50 ($12) seniors, £4 ($6.40) children. House open late Mar to late Sept Mon–Sat 11am–4pm, Sun 11am–5pm; Oct and Jan to late Mar Sat–Sun and bank holidays 11am–4pm. Park open late Mar to late Sept daily 10am–5pm. In summer, travel agents can book you on organized coach tours out of London. Otherwise, if driving, take M1 north to Junction 12 or 13, where directions are signposted.

NEARBY SHOPPING & AFTERNOON TEA

In a wonderful old building, **Town Hall Antiques,** Market Place (© **01525/ 290950**), is a treasure trove of collectibles and antiques, including Early English porcelain and pieces from the 1940s. Some unusual commemorative items are also sold, such as an array of Victorian, Georgian, and Edwardian memorabilia. There's something here to suit a wide range of pocketbooks including clocks, Victorian jewelry, brass, copper, "kitchenalia," paintings (originals and reproductions), guns, and swords.

At teatime, head to **Copperfields,** Woburn (© **01525/290464**), inside a B&B with low-beamed ceilings that add to its intimacy and charm. A pot of tea with clotted cream and a cake is £3.95 ($6.30). Baked goods include scones, and chocolate, lemon, Victoria sponge, carrot, coffee, and fruitcakes, as well as daily specials. The tearoom is open Thursday through Tuesday, but it's a good idea to call on weekends between January and Easter as it may be closed if business is slow.

WHERE TO DINE

Paris House ★★ CONTINENTAL/FRENCH   This reconstructed timbered house stands in a park where you can see deer grazing. The black-and-white building originally stood in Paris, where it was constructed for the Great Exhibition of 1878, but it was torn down and transplanted, timber by timber, to Woburn. Since 1983, it has been the domain of Bedfordshire's finest chef, Peter Chandler, the first English apprentice of the legendary Roux brothers. Chandler has brought his own innovative touch to the dishes served here. He still regularly visits France for new ideas and is known for his use of the freshest of seasonal ingredients. Try his delectable marinated Cajun prawns, delicately spiced savory, or his duck confit in a black currant and orange sauce. The chef is rightly known for his *tulipe en fantaisie,* a sugar-fairy fantasy with fruit and ice cream.

Woburn Park (3.5km/2¼ miles southeast of Woburn on A4012). © 01525/290692. Reservations required. Fixed-price dinner £55 ($88); fixed-price lunch £30 ($48). AE, DC, MC, V. Tues–Sat noon–2pm and 7–10pm; Sun noon–2pm. Closed Feb.

6

Southeast England

Lying to the south and southeast of London are the shires (counties) of Kent, Surrey, and Sussex—fascinating areas within easy commuting distance of the capital.

In **Kent,** Canterbury is the major highlight and makes the best base for exploring the area. Dover, which is Britain's historic gateway to the Continent, is famed for its white cliffs and is another convenient option. This county is on the fringes of London, yet is far removed in spirit and scenery. Since the days of the Tudors, cherry blossoms have enlivened the fertile landscape. Orchards and hop fields abound, earning Kent the title of "the garden of England"—and in England, the competition's tough. Kent suffered severe destruction during World War II, as it was the alley over which the *Luftwaffe* flew in its blitz of London. But despite much devastation, it's still filled with interesting old towns and castles.

In fact, Kent boasts some of Europe's grandest mansions. If your time is limited, seek out the big four: **Knole,** one of the largest private houses of England and a great example of Tudor architecture; **Hever Castle,** dating from the end of the 13th century and a gift from Henry VIII to the "great Flanders mare," Anne of Cleves; **Penhurst Place,** a magnificent English Gothic mansion and one of the outstanding country houses of Britain; and lovely **Leeds Castle,** near Maidstone, dating from A.D. 857. Although it doesn't compare with these grand castles, Chartwell House also merits a visit because of the man who used to call it home: Sir Winston Churchill. For more advice on how to tour these homes, refer to "Kent's Country Houses, Castles & Gardens," later in this chapter.

With the continuing expansion of London's borders, it's a wonder that the tiny county of **Surrey** hasn't been gobbled up and turned into a sprawling suburb. Yet its countryside remains unspoiled, even though many people commute from homes here to jobs in London (you're only about 45 min. to an hour away).

If King Harold hadn't loved **Sussex** so much, the course of English history might have been changed forever. Had the brave Saxon waited longer in the north, he could have marshaled more adequate reinforcements before striking south to meet the Normans. But William the Conqueror's soldiers were ravaging the countryside he knew so well, and Harold rushed down to counter them.

Harold's enthusiasm for Sussex is understandable. The landscape rises and falls like waves. The county is known for its woodlands, from which came the timbers to build England's mighty fleet in days gone by. The shires lie south of London and Surrey, bordering Kent in the east, Hampshire in the west, and opening directly onto the English Channel, where the coast is dotted with seaside towns.

Like the other sections in the vulnerable south of England, Sussex was the setting of some of the most significant events in English history. Apart from the Norman landings at Hastings, the most life-changing transformation occurred in the 19th century, as middle-class Victorians flocked to the seashore, pumping new spirit into Brighton and even old Hastings.

The old towns and villages of Sussex, particularly Rye and Winchelsea, are far more intriguing than the seaside resorts. No Sussex village is lovelier than Alfriston (and the innkeepers know it, too); Arundel is noted for its castle; and the cathedral city of Chichester is a mecca for theater buffs. The old market town of Battle was the setting for the Battle of Hastings in 1066.

Where to base yourself in Sussex? The best option is **Brighton,** because it has a wide choice of hotels, restaurants, and nightclubs. There's more excitement here at "London by the Sea" than at Hastings. If you're seeking old-English charm and village life, head instead to Alfriston or Rye.

1 Canterbury ★★★

90km (56 miles) SE of London

Under the arch of the ancient West Gate journeyed Chaucer's knight, solicitor, nun, squire, parson, merchant, miller, and others—spinning tales. They were bound for the shrine of Thomas à Becket, archbishop of Canterbury, who was slain by four knights of Henry II on December 29, 1170. (The king later walked barefoot from Harbledown to the tomb of his former friend, where he allowed himself to be flogged in penance.) The shrine was finally torn down in 1538 by Henry VIII as part of his campaign to destroy the monasteries and graven images. But Canterbury, by then, had already become an attraction.

The medieval Kentish city on the River Stour is the ecclesiastical capital of England. The city was once completely walled, and many traces of its old fortifications remain. Canterbury was inhabited centuries before the birth of Jesus. Although its most famous incident was the murder of Becket, the medieval city witnessed other major events in English history, including Bloody Mary's order to burn nearly 40 victims at the stake. Richard the Lion-Hearted returned this way from crusading, and Charles II passed through on the way to claim his crown.

Canterbury pilgrims still continue to arrive today, except now they're called day-trippers and they overrun the city and its monuments. It's amazing that the central core of the city is as interesting and picture-perfect as it is, considering the enormous damage caused by the Nazi Blitz of 1941. The city has an active university life—mainly students from Kent—and an enormous number of pubs. And its High Street is filled with shoppers in from the country. We suggest exploring Canterbury in the early morning or the early evening, after the busloads have departed.

ESSENTIALS

GETTING THERE   There is frequent train service from Victoria, Charing Cross, Waterloo, and London Bridge stations. The journey takes 1½ hours. For rail information, call ⓒ **0845/748-4950.**

The bus from Victoria Coach Station takes 2 to 3 hours and leaves every ½ hour. For schedules, call ⓒ **0870/580-8080.**

If you're driving from London, take A2, then M2. Canterbury is signposted all the way. The city center is closed to cars, but it's only a short walk from several parking areas to the cathedral.

VISITOR INFORMATION   A few doors away from St. Margaret's Church, the **Canterbury Tourist Information Centre,** 34 St. Margaret's St., Canterbury

CT1 2TG (© **01227/378100**), is open daily from 10am to 4pm April through October, and daily from 9am to 5pm November through March.

GETTING AROUND BY BIKE　A call placed to **Byways Bicycle Hire,** 2 Admiralty Walk (© **01227/277397**), will get you a bike delivered to your hotel, but you must post a £50 ($80) deposit. Rentals are £10 ($16) per day. For the same deposit, you can also arrange rentals at **Downland Cycle Hire,** West Railway Station (© **01227/479543**), which charges £11 ($18) per day.

SEEING THE SIGHTS

Canterbury Cathedral ✹✹✹　The foundation of this splendid cathedral dates from A.D. 597, but the earliest part of the present building is the great Romanesque crypt built around A.D. 1100. The monastic "quire" erected on top of this at the same time was destroyed by fire in 1174, only 4 years after the murder of Thomas à Becket on a dark December evening in the northwest transept, which is still one of the most famous places of pilgrimage in Europe. The destroyed "quire" was immediately replaced by a magnificent early Gothic one, the first major expression of that architectural style in England.

The cathedral is noteworthy for its medieval tombs of royal personages, such as King Henry IV and Edward the Black Prince, as well as numerous archbishops. To the later Middle Ages belong the great 14th-century nave and the famous central "Bell Harry Tower." The cathedral stands on spacious precincts amid the remains of the buildings of the monastery—cloisters, chapter house, and Norman water tower—which have survived intact from Henry VIII's dissolution to the present day.

Becket's shrine was destroyed by the Tudor king, but the site of that tomb is in Trinity Chapel, near the high altar. The saint is said to have worked miracles, and the cathedral has some rare stained glass depicting those feats.

But the most miraculous event is that the windows escaped Henry VIII's agents of destruction as well as Hitler's bombs. The windows were removed as a precaution at the beginning of the war. During the war, a large area of Canterbury was flattened, but the main body of the church was unharmed. However, the cathedral library was damaged during a German air raid in 1942. The replacement windows of the cathedral were blown in, which proved the wisdom of having the medieval glass safely stored away.

11 The Precincts. © **01227/762862**. www.Canterbury-cathedral.org. Admission £4 ($6.40) adults, £3 ($4.80) students, seniors, and children. Guided tours, £3.50 ($5.60) adults, £2.50 ($4) students and seniors, £1.50 ($2.40) children, £6.50 ($10) family. Easter–Sept 30 Mon–Sat 9am–6:30pm; Oct 1–Easter Mon–Sat 9am–4:30pm; year-round Sun 12:30–2:30pm and 4:30–5:30pm.

OTHER ATTRACTIONS

Canterbury Roman Museum　This museum is located beneath street level and is constructed around actual archaeological excavations. Interactive computer shows and the actual handling of Roman artifacts bring the past to life for all ages. The Roman town of Durovernum Cantiacorum was established shortly after Emperor Claudius's invasion of the area in A.D. 43 and continued to flourish for nearly 400 years. Visitors can follow the archaeologists' detective work through an excavated Roman house site containing patterned mosaics that were discovered after the wartime bombing.

Butchery Lane. © **01227/785575**. Admission £2.60 ($4.15) adults, £1.65 ($2.65) students, seniors, and children, £6.80 ($11) family ticket. Year-round Mon–Sat 10am–5pm; June–Oct Sun 1:30–5pm. Last entry time is 4pm. Closed Christmas week and Good Friday.

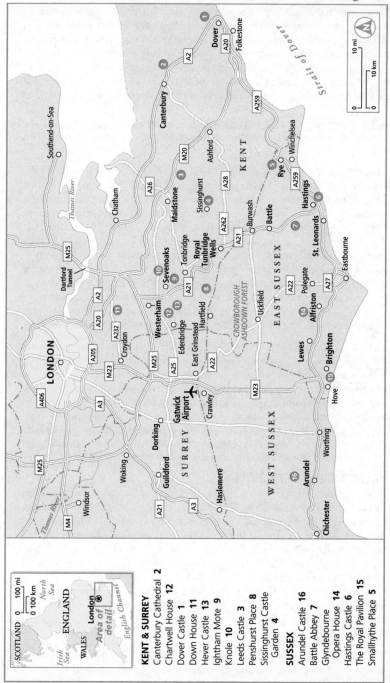

Museum of Canterbury   Set in the ancient Poor Priests' Hospital with its medieval interiors and soaring oak roofs, the museum features award-winning displays to showcase the best of the city's treasures and lead visitors through crucial moments that have shaped Canterbury's history. State-of-the-art video, computer, and hologram technology transport visitors back in time to such events as the Viking raids and the wartime Blitz. Collections include a huge display of pilgrim badges from medieval souvenir shops and the Rupert Bear Gallery.

Stour St. ✆ 01227/452747. Admission £3 ($4.80) adults, £2 ($3.20) students, seniors, and children. Year-round Mon–Sat 10:30am–5pm; June–Sept Sun 1:30–5pm. Last entry time is 4pm. Closed Christmas week and Good Friday.

St. Augustine's Abbey 🏛🏛   One of the most historic religious centers in the country, only its ruins remain, mostly at ground level. Augustine was buried here, along with other archbishops and Anglo-Saxon kings. Adjacent to the remains are the abbey buildings that were converted into a royal palace by Henry VIII and used briefly by several monarchs, including Elizabeth I and Charles I.

In an attempt to convert the Saxons, Pope Gregory I sent Augustine to England in 597. Ethelbert, the Saxon King, allowed Augustine and his followers to build a church outside the city walls, and it endured until Henry VIII tore it down. In its day, the abbey church rivaled the cathedral in size, and enough of the ruins remain to conjure the whole of the cloister, church, and refectory.

Corner of Lower Chantry Lane and Longport Rd. ✆ 01227/767345. Admission £3 ($4.80) adults, £3.30 ($5.30) students and seniors, £1.50 ($2.40) children. Apr–Sept daily 10am–6pm; Oct–Mar daily 10am–4pm.

The Canterbury Tales   One of the most visited museums in town re-creates the pilgrimages of Chaucerian England through a series of medieval tableaux. Visitors are handed headsets with earphones, which give oral recitations of five of Chaucer's *Canterbury Tales* and the murder of St. Thomas à Becket. Audiovisual aids bring famous characters to life, and stories of jealousy, pride, avarice, and love are recounted. A tour of all exhibits takes about 45 minutes.

23 St. Margaret's St. (off High St., near the cathedral). ✆ 01227/454888. Admission £6.50 ($10) adults, £5.50 ($8.80) seniors and students, £5 ($8) children 5–16, free for children 4 and under. Family ticket £20 ($32). Mar–Aug daily 10am–4:30pm; Sept–Oct daily 10am–5:30pm; Nov–Feb daily 10am–5pm.

WALKING & BOAT TOURS

From Easter to early November, daily guided tours of Canterbury are organized by the **Guild of Guides** (✆ 01227/459779), costing £3.20 ($5.10) for adults, £2.70 ($4.30) for students and children over age 14, and £20 ($32) for a family ticket. Meet at the Tourist Information Centre at 34 St. Margaret's St., in a pedestrian area near the cathedral, daily (including Sun) at 10am and 4:30pm. From the beginning of July to the end of August there's also a tour at 11:30am Monday through Saturday.

From just below the Weavers House, boats leave for ½-hour **trips on the river** with a commentary on the history of the buildings you pass. Umbrellas are provided to protect you against inclement weather.

HORSEBACK RIDING

The **Bursted Manor Riding Centre** in Pett Bottom (✆ 01227/830568) is open from 9am to dusk Tuesday through Sunday. The last lesson is at 7pm on weekdays and 6pm on Saturday and Sunday. A 1-hour group lesson or hack ride is available for £23 ($37). A Boxing Day hunt is open to the public.

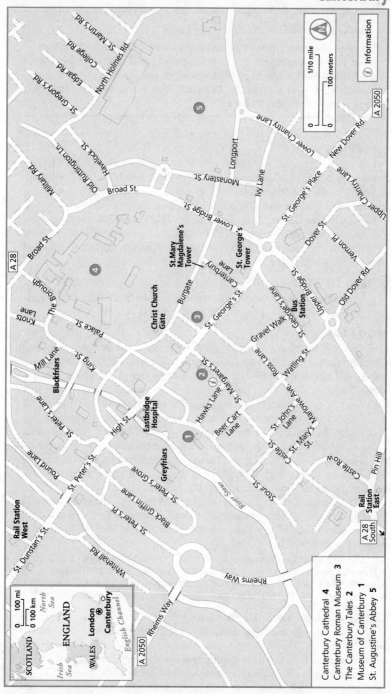

Canterbury

Canterbury Cathedral **4**
Canterbury Roman Museum **3**
The Canterbury Tales **2**
Museum of Canterbury **1**
St. Augustine's Abbey **5**

> **Finds** **A Stroll Down Medieval Lane**
>
> The most charming street in Canterbury is **Mercery Lane,** a bustling little street that still evokes the charm of Canterbury as it existed in the Middle Ages. A walk along this street also gives you the best views of the western towers of Canterbury Cathedral. You'll also have an equally good view of Christchurch Gate.

SHOPPING

Put on your tweed jacket and grab your pipe for a trip to a secondhand **Chaucer Bookshop,** 6 Beer Cart Lane (© **01227/453912; www.Chaucer-bookshop. co.uk**), with first editions (both old and modern), out-of-print books, special leather-bound editions, and a large selection of local history books.

At the **Chaucer Centre,** 22 St. Peter's St. (© **01227/470379**), *The Canterbury Tales* in book and tape formats join all things Chaucerian, including *Canterbury Tales* T-shirts, St. Justin jewelry from Cornwall, Ellesmere cards, and balls and plates for juggling.

WHERE TO STAY

In spite of all its fame as a tourist destination, Canterbury still lacks a really first-class hotel. What you get isn't bad, but it's not state of the art.

MODERATE

The Chaucer Hotel ☆   Located on a historic street, the recently refurbished Chaucer Hotel is in a Georgian house that stands a few minutes' walk from the cathedral. Comfortably furnished rooms lie at the end of a labyrinth of stairs, narrow hallways, and doors. (The hotel staff carries your luggage and parks your car.) The best rooms, with views over Canterbury rooftops and the cathedral, are nos. 60, 61, and 65. All rooms, however, are named in a wonderfully quirky way that honors former archbishops as well as some of Chaucer's racier pilgrims. Units range from midsize to most spacious, each chamber evoking a country inn. The most elegant room is no. 16, the honeymoon chamber with a Henry VIII–style four-poster bed. If you'd like to share a room with a ghost, book no. 62. Bathrooms are fairly large and have heated towel racks.

You can have a drink in the Pilgrim's Bar, with its Regency mantelpieces and French windows that open to outdoor terraces in summer. The hotel also has a good restaurant, the **63 Ivy Lane,** serving English meals until 9:30pm, and it provides room service.

63 Ivy Lane (off Lower Bridge St.), Canterbury, Kent CT1 1TU. © **888/892-0038** in the U.S. and Canada, or 01227/464427. Fax 01227/450397. www.mcdonaldhotels.co.uk. 42 units. £100–£120 ($160–$192) double. AE, DC, MC, V. **Amenities:** 2 restaurants; bar; secretarial services; room service; babysitting; laundry service; dry cleaning. *In room:* A/C, TV, minibar, coffeemaker, hair dryer, safe, trouser press.

County Hotel ☆   The leading hotel in Canterbury, it's been around since the closing years of Victoria's reign, with a recorded history going back to the end of the 12th century. The time-mellowed atmosphere is exemplified by the residents' lounge on the second floor, with its old timbers and carved antiques. The hotel is constantly refurbished. Its sumptuous suite is the best room in Canterbury. A dozen period rooms have either Georgian or Tudor four-poster beds; opt for these if available. Rooms have thoughtful extras, such as hospitality trays, fruit baskets, and mineral water. Beds are four-poster, half-tester, or carved oak. Bathrooms are tiled and well maintained.

High St., Canterbury, Kent CT1 2RX. ℂ **01227/766266.** Fax 01227/451512. www.macdonaldhotels.co.uk. 74 units. £100–£139 ($160–$222) double; £170 ($272) suite. AE, DC, MC, V. Parking £2.50 ($4). **Amenities:** Restaurant; bar; room service; babysitting; laundry service. *In room:* TV, coffeemaker, hair dryer, trouser press.

Ebury Hotel ★ *Value*   One of the finest B&Bs in Canterbury, this gabled Victorian house stands on 2 acres of gardens at the city's edge, easy walking distance from the city center. Built in 1850, it's composed of two separate houses that were joined several years ago; the management also rents flats on a weekly basis. The accommodations are roomy and pleasantly decorated. The rooms range from small to medium, each with traditional styling and a small bathroom, mainly with a tub and shower combination. Rooms are constantly being refurbished. *Note:* It's important to reserve in advance.

65–67 New Dover Rd., Canterbury, Kent CT1 3DX. ℂ **01227/768433.** Fax 01227/459187. www.ebury-hotel. co.uk. 15 units. £75–£85 ($120–$136) double; £85–£95 ($136–$152) triple; £95–£105 ($152–$168) quad. Rates include English breakfast. AE, MC, V. Closed Dec 14–Jan 16. Follow the signs to A2, Dover Rd., on left-hand side, south of the city. **Amenities:** Restaurant; bar; heated indoor pool; spa; room service; laundry service; dry cleaning. *In room:* TV, coffeemaker, hair dryer, iron, trouser press.

Howfield Manor ★★ *Finds*   Once part of the estate of the Priory of St. Gregory, this is one of the most charming country manors near Canterbury. It's not plush, but it's a good and reliable choice, with enough beams and private nooks to please the traditionalist. Set on 5 acres of rolling meadows, the house offers snug, attractive rooms with solid comfort. Rooms in the original house have more character (exposed beams), whereas rooms in the new wing are larger and furnished with solid oak pieces. All units offer comfortable beds. Bathrooms are small but well appointed, each with a shower stall.

Chartham Hatch (3km/2 miles from Canterbury along A28 Ashford Rd.), Canterbury, Kent CT4 7HQ. ℂ 01227/ 738294. Fax 01227/731535. www.howfield.invictanet.co.uk. 15 units. £100 ($159) double; £115 ($184) suite. Rates include English breakfast. AE, MC, V. Take A28 3.5km (2¼ miles) from Canterbury. **Amenities:** Restaurant; bar; room service; laundry service; dry cleaning. *In room:* TV, hair dryer, trouser press.

INEXPENSIVE

Cathedral Gate Hotel   For those who want to stay close to the cathedral and perhaps have a view of it, this is the choice. Built in 1438, adjoining Christchurch Gate and overlooking the Buttermarket, this former hospice was one of the first fashionable teahouses in England in the early 1600s, and the interior reveals many little architectural details of that century. Rooms are modestly furnished, with sloping floors and massive oak beams. You'll sleep better than the former pilgrims who often stopped over here, sometimes crowding in as many as six and eight in a bed. Rooms with bathroom have a shower stall; otherwise corridor bathrooms are adequate and you rarely have to wait in line for your turn at them.

36 Burgate, Canterbury, Kent CT1 2HA. ℂ **01227/464381.** Fax 01227/462800. www.cathgate.co.uk. 26 units, 13 with bathroom (shower only). £47–£56 ($74–$89) double without bathroom, £84 ($134) double with bathroom. Rates include continental breakfast. AE, DC, MC, V. **Amenities:** Restaurant; bar; room service. *In room:* TV, coffeemaker, hair dryer, trouser press.

Pointers Hotel   The O'Brien family welcome you to their well-run little hotel lying a 5-minute walk from "The high," with its attractions such as Canterbury Cathedral. The house (ca. 1740) overlooks the 10th-century Church of St. Dunstans. The hotel lies at the end of the London Road at the junction at St. Dunstans, and can be rather noisy because of traffic; however, double-glazing on the windows helps. This redbrick Georgian building offers well-maintained bedrooms, ranging from rather small to midsize, each with a private bathroom with shower. Travel light if you stay here—there is no elevator.

1 London Rd., Canterbury, Kent CT2 8LR. © 01227/456846. Fax 01227/452786. www.cantweb.co.uk/pointers. 12 units. £60–£75 ($96–$120) double; £85 ($136) family unit for 3. rates include breakfast. AE, DC, MC, V. Closed Dec 20 to mid-Jan. **Amenities:** Breakfast room. *In room:* TV, beverage maker.

A NEARBY PLACE TO STAY

The Old Coach House The inn stands halfway between Canterbury and Dover on the A2 (southbound), which makes it ideal for exploring, shopping, country walking, or horseback riding. A coaching inn in the 19th century, it is now run as a relaxed French country auberge by chef-patron Jean-Claude Rozard and his English wife, Julie. Rooms are a bit small, like a pub hotel, but each has a small bathroom with a shower stall.

Dover Rd., Barham, Kent. © 01227/831218. Fax 01227/831932. 10 units. £54 ($86) double; £95 ($152) suite. MC, V. **Amenities:** Restaurant; bar; babysitting. *In room:* TV, coffeemaker, hair dryer.

WHERE TO DINE

Duck Inn *(Finds* ENGLISH Once called the Woodsmen Arms, this restaurant is known as the Duck Inn because of its low door. (As you entered, the clientele would shout "Duck!") Set in the Pett Bottom valley in a 16th-century structure, it offers traditional English fare. Diners can sit outdoors in the English country garden in the summer. The menu posted on chalkboards changes weekly, though a few standard English favorites remain on a permanent basis. For main course, the menu may include game pies (in season), and some duck preparation is always on the menu.

Pett Bottom, near Bridge. © 01227/830354. Reservations recommended. Main courses £7–£12 ($11–$19). MC, V. Mon–Sat 11am–11pm; Sun noon–10:30pm. Drive 8km (5 miles) outside Canterbury near the village of Bridge on the road to Dover.

Old Well Restaurant CONTINENTAL At this country manor (see Howfield Manor, above), nonresidents and guests can enjoy a meal served in the chapel, dating from 1181. The old well can still be seen; monks drew their water here. Head chef James Wealinds and his brigade create a market-fresh cuisine that's prepared daily. The excellent food is backed up by a homey atmosphere, friendly service, and a well-chosen wine list. You may start with smoked haddock and parsley fish cake, and proceed to sirloin steak with red onion gravy. Arrive early to enjoy a drink in the Priory Bar, with its *trompe l'oeil* murals and a real "priesthole" (the bar staff will be delighted to explain what that means, just to get the conversation rolling).

At Howfield Manor, Chartham Hatch. © 01227/738294. Reservations recommended. Main courses £11–£18 ($18–$29); set menu £15 ($24). AE, MC, V. Daily noon–2pm and 7–9pm.

Sully's ★ ENGLISH/CONTINENTAL This restaurant is located in the city's most distinguished hotel (see County Hotel, above). Although the place is without windows and the decor is a bit dated (ca. 1965), the seating and comfort level

---

Fun Fact **The Spy Who Lived Here**

James Bond fans may be stirred by the Duck Inn's location; according to the film *You Only Live Twice,* 007 grew up next door to the Duck Inn in Pett Bottom before heading off to Her Majesty's Secret Service.

are first-rate. Considering the quality of the ingredients, the menu offers good value. You can always count on a selection of plain, traditional English dishes, but try one of the more imaginatively conceived platters instead. We recommend the grilled lemon sole or the roasted pheasant breast with kumquats served on lentils with caramelized apple and a mellow curry cream.

In the County Hotel, High St. ℂ **01227/766266.** Reservations recommended. Fixed-price lunch £10 ($16) for 2 courses; main courses £14–£18 ($22–$29). Fixed price dinner £24 ($38). AE, DC, MC, V. Daily 7–10am, 12:30–2pm, and 7–9pm.

Tuo e Mio ITALIAN   Tuo e Mio is a bastion of zesty Italian cookery. Signor R. P. M. Greggio, known locally as "Raphael," sets the style and plans the menu at his casual and long-standing bistro. Some dishes are standard, including the pastas, beef, and veal found on most Italian menus, but the daily specials have a certain flair, based on the freshest ingredients available on any given day. Try the fish dishes, including skate, which is regularly featured. A selection of reasonably priced Italian wines accompanies your meal.

16 The Borough. ℂ **01227/761471.** Reservations recommended, especially at lunch; call ℂ 01227/472362. Main courses £7.50–£16 ($12–$25); lunch £13 ($20). AE, DC, MC, V. Tues, Thurs, Sat noon–2:30pm and 7–10:45pm; Sun noon–2:30pm and 7–10pm. Closed the last 2 weeks in Aug and the last 2 weeks in Feb.

CANTERBURY AFTER DARK

Gulbenkian Theatre, University of Kent, Giles Lane (ℂ **01227/769075**), is open during school terms (except Cricket Week, the 1st week in Aug) and offers a potpourri of jazz and classical productions, dance, drama, comedy, and a mix of new and student productions. Check newspapers for schedules; tickets cost £3 to £16 ($4.80–$26).

   Marlowe, The Friars (ℂ **01227/787787**), is Canterbury's only commercial playhouse. It's open year-round and offers drama, jazz, and classical concerts, and contemporary and classical ballet. Tickets cost from £14 to £35 ($22–$56).

   A favorite local pub, **Alberry's Wine & Food Bar,** 38A St. Margaret's St. (ℂ **01227/452378**), offers live music, mostly jazz, played by local and student groups. Cover charge is £3 ($4.80). The menu offers affordable daily specials and light snacks at lunch and dinner.

   A laid-back student hangout, **The Cherry Tree,** 10 White Horse Lane (ℂ **01227/451266**), offers a wide selection of beers, including Bass Ale on draft, Cherry Tree ale, three traditional lagers, and four bitters. The atmosphere is clubby, filled with casual conversation. If you visit for lunch, you'll find a 32-item menu—the best pub menu in town—plus three types of ploughman's lunch. On Sundays it offers a traditional English roast for £5 ($8).

   Another good choice on your Canterbury pub-crawl is **The Flying Horse,** 1 Dover St. (ℂ **01227/463803**), which attracts a garrulous mix of young and old. This 16th-century pub bridges generations from oldsters to the hip student crowd. A weekly quiz night stirs the conversation.

2 The White Cliffs of Dover

122km (76 miles) SE of London; 135km (84 miles) NE of Brighton

In Victoria's day, Dover was popular as a seaside resort; today it's known as a port for cross-Channel car and passenger traffic between England and France (notably Calais). One of England's most vulnerable and easy-to-hit targets during World War II, repeated bombings destroyed much of its harbor. The opening of the Channel Tunnel (Chunnel) in 1994 renewed Dover's importance.

Unless you're on your way to France or want to use Dover as a base for exploring the surrounding countryside, you can skip a visit here. Dover has always been rather dull except for those white cliffs. Even its hotels are second-rate; many people prefer to stay in Folkestone, about 16km (10 miles) to the southwest.

ESSENTIALS

GETTING THERE Frequent trains run daily between Victoria Station or Charing Cross Station in London and Dover from 5am to 10pm. You arrive in Dover at Priory Station, off Folkestone Road. During the day, two trains per hour depart Canterbury East Station heading for Dover. For rail information, call © **08457/484950.**

Frequent buses leave throughout the day—daily from 7:30am to 11pm—from London's Victoria Coach Station bound for Dover. Call © **0870/580-8080** for schedules. Call the local bus station on Pencester Road (© **01304/240024**). Stagecoach East Kent provides daily bus service between Canterbury and Dover.

If you're driving from London, head first to Canterbury (see "Essentials," in section 1), then continue along A2 southeast until you reach Dover, on the coast.

VISITOR INFORMATION The Tourist Information Centre is on Old Town Gaol Street (© **01304/205108**). It's open Monday through Friday from 9am to 5:30pm, Saturday from 10am to 4pm; June, July and August daily from 9am to 5:30pmpm.

EXPLORING DOVER

You'll get your best view of the famous **white cliffs** if you're arriving at Dover by ferry or hovercraft from Calais. Otherwise, you could walk out to the end of the town's Prince of Wales pier, the largest of the town's western docks. The cliffs loom above you. Or you could drive 8km (5 miles) east of Dover to the pebble-covered beaches of the fishing hamlet of Deal. Here, a local fisherman might take you on an informal boat ride.

Deal Castle ⋆ Deal Castle is .5km (¼ mile) south of the Deal town center, 8km (5 miles) from Dover. A defensive fort built around 1540, it's the most spectacular example of the low, squat forts constructed by Henry VIII. Its 119 gun positions made it the most powerful of his defense forts. Centered around a circular keep surrounded by two rings of semicircle bastions, the castle was protected by an outer moat. The entrance was approached by a drawbridge with an iron gate. The castle was damaged by bombs during World War II but has been restored to its earlier form.

On the seafront. © **01304/372762.** Admission £3.20 ($5.10) adults, £2.60 ($4.15) seniors, £1.60 ($2.55) children. Apr–Sept daily 10am–6pm; Oct–Mar Wed–Sun 10am–4pm. Closed Dec 24–26.

Dover Castle ⋆⋆⋆ Rising nearly 120m (400 ft.) above the port is one of the oldest and best-known castles in England. Its keep was built at the command of Becket's fair-weather friend, Henry II, in the 12th century. The ancient castle was called back to active duty as late as World War II. The "Pharos" on the grounds is a lighthouse built by the Romans in the first half of the 1st century. The Romans first landed at nearby Deal in 54 B.C., but after 6 months they departed and didn't return until nearly 100 years later, in A.D. 43, when they stayed and occupied the country for 400 years. The castle houses a military museum and a film center, plus "Live and Let's Spy," an exhibition of World War II spying equipment.

Castle Hill. © **01304/211067.** Fax 01304/214739. Admission £8 ($13) adults, £4 ($6.40) children under 15, £6 ($9.60) seniors and students, £20 ($32) family. Apr–Sept daily 10am–6pm (last tour at 5pm); Oct daily 10am–6pm (last tour at 4pm); Nov–Mar daily 10am–4pm (last tour at 3pm). Bus: 90 bound for Deal.

Roman Painted House ★★   This 1,800-year-old Roman structure, called Britain's "buried Pompeii," has exceptionally well-preserved walls and an under-floor heating system. It's famous for its unique bacchic murals and has won four national awards for presentation. Brass rubbing is also offered. You'll find it in the town center near Market Square.

New St. ✆ **01304/203279**. Admission £2 ($3.20) adults, 80p ($1.30) seniors and children age 16 and under. Apr–Sept Tues–Sun 10am–5pm.

Secret War Time Tunnels ★ *Finds*   These secret tunnels, used during the evacuation of Dunkirk in 1940 and the Battle of Britain, can now be explored on a guided tour. The tunnels were originally excavated to house cannons to be used (if necessary) against an invasion by Napoleon. Some 60m (200 ft.) below ground, they were the headquarters of Operation Dynamo, when more than 300,000 troops from Dunkirk were evacuated. Once forbidden ground to all but those with the strongest security clearance, the networks of tunnels can now be toured. You can stand in the very room where Ramsey issued orders; experi-ence the trauma of life in an underground operating theater; and look out over the English Channel from the hidden, cliff-top balcony, just as Churchill did during the Battle of Britain.

Dover Castle, Castle Hill. ✆ **01304/211067** or 01304/201628. Admission £8 ($13) adults, £6 ($9.60) sen-iors, £4 ($6.40) children. Apr–Sept daily 10am–6pm; Oct–Mar daily 10am–4pm. Last tour leaves 1 hr. before castle closing time. Bus: 90 bound for Deal.

WHERE TO STAY

The Churchill   Dover's most consistently reliable hotel is this interconnected row of town houses built to overlook the English Channel in the 1830s. After World War I, the premises were transformed into a hotel, and in 1994 it was completely refurbished after being acquired by the Henley Lodge hotel chain. It offers a seafront balcony, a glass-enclosed front veranda, and tranquil rooms. Ranging from small to spacious, many bedrooms offer uninterrupted views of the coast of France. Eurotunnel travelers find the compact bathrooms with shower stalls comfortable. The hotel lies close to the eastern and western docks and the Hoverport for travel to and from France and Belgium.

Waterloo Crescent, Dover Waterfront, Dover, Kent CT17 9BP. ✆ **01304/203633**. Fax 01304/216320. www.churchill-hotel.com. 66 units. £62 ($99) double; £82 ($131) triple; £93 ($149) quad. AE, DC, MC, V. **Amenities:** Restaurant; bar; health club with sauna; salon; room service; laundry service; dry cleaning. *In room:* TV w/pay movies, dataport, minibar (in some rooms), coffeemaker, hair dryer, trouser press.

The Dovercourt Hotel   Situated 5km (3 miles) north of Dover's Center, within a semi-industrial maze of superhighways and greenbelts, the court was originally custom-built as a motel in the 1970s. Bedrooms are carefully posi-tioned so that most of them overlook lawns (and a view of the motorway), fields, and a children's playground next door. Each room is functional and comfortable; the tidy shower-only bathrooms are extremely compact.

Singledge Lane, Whitfield, near Dover CT16 3LF. ✆ **01304/821230**. Fax 01304/825576. www.dovercourt-hotel.com. 68 units. Mon–Thurs £69 ($110) double, Fri–Sun £59 ($94) double. AE, DC, MC, V. Free parking. Lies adjacent to the Whitifield exit of the A2 motorway. **Amenities:** Restaurant; bar; 24-hr. room service; laun-dry. *In room:* TV w/pay movies, coffeemaker, hair dryer, trouser press.

Wallett's Court ★ *Finds*   Surrounded by fields and gardens in a tiny hamlet 2.5km (1½ miles) east of Dover, this is our preferred stopover in the area. Rebuilt in the Jacobean style in the 1400s, it rests on a foundation dated from the time of the Norman Conquest of England. In 1975, members of the Oakley family bought the seriously dilapidated structure and restored it. The setting, near cliff tops overlooking the English Channel, is savored by bird-watchers and hill climbers. Each carefully restored bedroom features a different decorative theme, with the more expensive ones containing four-poster beds. Some lie within a barn that was comfortably converted into living quarters. Richly accessorized, each has a vivid Edwardian country-house motif and lots of mementos. Bathrooms, though small, are neatly organized; half have shower-tub combinations, the rest showers only.

West Cliffe, St. Margaret's at Cliffe, Dover, Kent CT15 6EW. © **01304/852424.** Fax 01304/853430. www.walletts court.com. 16 units. £90–£150 ($144–$240) double. Rates include English breakfast. AE, DC, MC, V. Closed Dec 24–27. Follow A258 for 2.5km (1½ miles) east from the center of Dover (signposted Deal). Wallett's Court is signposted off A258. **Amenities:** Restaurant; bar; indoor pool; tennis court; health club; spa; room service; babysitting; laundry service; dry cleaning. *In room:* TV, minibar, coffeemaker, hair dryer.

WHERE TO DINE

Topo Gigio *(Kids* ITALIAN   Established by an Italian entrepreneur from Vicenza, this restaurant is named after the most famous cartoon character in Italy, Topo Gigio, a Mickey Mouse look-alike. Located a short walk from Dover's market square in a setting accented with brick arches and a wood-burning pizza oven, it serves 15 types of pastas, 16 types of pizzas, and steak, chicken, veal, and fish dishes prepared Italian-style or any way you request. The restaurant's staff and clientele tend to be animated and energetic, which makes an outing here lighthearted and fun. The food's not gourmet, but it's satisfying and filling.

1–2 King St. © **01304/201048.** Reservations recommended on weekends. Pizzas £4.85–£7.60 ($7.75–$12); main courses £6–£15 ($9.60–$24). AE, DC, MC, V. Winter daily noon–2:30pm and 6:30–10:30pm; summer daily noon–10:30pm.

Wallett's Court *(★* BRITISH/INTERNATIONAL   One of the most appealing restaurants in the area lies within a half-timbered Jacobean-era manor house, grandly restored over 15 years by Chris Oakley and his family. Within a dining room that's exemplary for its sense of history, you can enjoy dishes such as leek and potato soup; a Kentish huntsman's platter (terrine of game served with apple jelly); salmon with a champagne and shallot sauce; or Scottish Angus beef with a wine and tarragon sauce. The menu changes every month, but meals are always relatively formal, well prepared, and in most cases, very appealing.

West Cliffe, St. Margaret's at Cliffe (in Wallett's Court hotel, see review above). © **01304/852424.** Reservations recommended. 3-course fixed-price dinner £35 ($56). AE, DC, MC, V. Sun–Fri noon–2pm; daily 7–9pm. Closed 1 week at Christmas.

3 The Ancient Seaport of Rye *(★(★*

100km (62 miles) SE of London

"Nothing more recent than a Cavalier's Cloak, Hat and Ruffles should be seen on the streets of Rye," said Louis Jennings. This ancient town, formerly an island, flourished in the 13th century. In its early days, **Rye** was a smuggling center, its residents sneaking in contraband from the marshes to stash away in little nooks.

But the sea receded from Rye, leaving it perched like a giant whale out of water, 3km (2 miles) from the Channel. Attacked several times by French fleets, Rye was practically razed in 1377. But it rebuilt itself successfully, in full Elizabethan panoply. When Queen Elizabeth I visited in 1573, she was so impressed that she bestowed upon the town the distinction of Royal Rye. This has long been considered a special place and over the years has attracted famous people, such as novelist Henry James.

Its narrow cobblestone streets twist and turn like a labyrinth and jumbled along them are buildings whose sagging roofs and crooked chimneys indicate the town's medieval origins. The town overflows with sites of architectural interest.

Neighboring Winchelsea has also witnessed the water's ebb. It traces its history from Edward I and has experienced many dramatic moments, such as sacking by the French. In the words of one 19th-century writer, Winchelsea is "a sunny dream of centuries ago." The finest sight of this dignified residential town is a badly damaged 14th-century church with a number of remarkable tombs.

ESSENTIALS

GETTING THERE   From London, the Southern Region Line offers trains south from Charing Cross or Cannon Street Station, with a change at Ashford, before continuing on to Rye. You can also go via Tunbridge Wells with a change in Hastings. Trains run every hour during the day, arriving at the Rye Train Station off Cinque Ports Street. The trip takes 1½ to 2 hours. Call ℂ **0845/748-4950** for schedules and information.

You'll need to take the train to get to Rye, but once there you'll find buses departing every hour on the hour for many destinations, including Hastings. Various bus schedules are posted on signs in the parking lot. For bus information on connections in the surrounding area, call ℂ **0870/608-2608.**

If you're driving from London, take M25, M26, and M20 east to Maidstone, going southeast along A20 to Ashford. At Ashford, continue south on A2070.

VISITOR INFORMATION   The **Rye Tourist Office** is in the Heritage Centre on the Strand Quay (ℂ **01797/226696**). It's open daily from March to the end of October from 9am to 5:30pm; November until February, Monday through Saturday from 10am to 4pm and Sunday from 10am to 2pm. The Heritage Centre houses a free exhibition and is also home to **Story of Rye,** a sound-and-light show depicting more than 700 years of Rye's history. Adults pay £2.50 ($4), seniors and students £1.50 ($2.40), and children £1 ($1.60).

EXPLORING THE AREA

In Rye, the old town's entrance is **Land Gate,** where a single lane of traffic passes between massive, 121m (40-ft.) high stone towers. The parapet of the gate has holes through which boiling oil used to be poured on unwelcome visitors, such as French raiding parties.

Rye has had potteries for centuries, and today is no exception, with a number of outlets in town. The best potteries include the **Rye Pottery,** Ferry Road (ℂ **01797/223038**); **Rye Tiles,** Wishward Street (ℂ **01797/223038**); **David Sharp Ceramics,** The Mint (ℂ **01797/222620**); and the **Cinque Ports Pottery,** Conduit Hill (ℂ **01797/222033**), where you can see the potters at work during the week. The town also abounds in antiques and collectibles shops and new and used bookstores.

Lamb House   Henry James lived at Lamb House from 1898 to 1916. Many James mementos are scattered throughout the house, which is set in a walled garden. Its previous owner joined the gold rush in North America but perished in the Klondike, and James was able to buy the freehold for a modest £2,000 ($3,200). Some of his well-known books were written here. In *English Hours,* James wrote: "There is not much room in the pavilion, but there is room for the hard-pressed table and tilted chair—there is room for a novelist and his friends."

West St. (at the top of Mermaid St.). ℂ 01892/890651. Admission £2.60 ($4.15) adults, £1.30 ($2.10) children. Wed and Sat 2–6pm. Closed Nov–Mar.

Rye Castle Museum   This stone fortification was constructed around 1250 by King Henry III to defend the coast against attack by the French. For 300 years it was the town jail but has long since been converted into a museum. In 1996, the medieval tower was restored.

Gungarden. ☎ **01797/226728.** Admission £2.90 ($4.65) adults, £2 ($3.20) students and seniors, £1.50 ($2.40) children, £5.95 ($9.50) family ticket. Apr–Oct daily 10:30am–1pm and 2:30–5pm; Nov–Mar Sat–Sun 10:30am–1pm and 2–3:30pm.

St. Mary's Parish Church   One notable historical site is the mid-12th-century church with its 16th-century clock flanked by two gilded cherubs (known as Quarter Boys because of their striking of the bells on the quarter-hour). The church is often referred to as "the cathedral of East Sussex" because of its expansive size and ornate beauty. If you're brave, you can climb a set of wooden stairs and ladders to the bell tower of the church for an impressive view.

Church Square. ☎ 01797/224935. Admission to tower £2 ($3.20) adults, £1 ($1.60) children. Contributions appreciated to enter the church. June–Aug daily 9am–7pm; off season daily 9am–5:30pm.

Smallhythe Place *(Finds)*   On the outskirts of Winchelsea, this was for 30 years the country house of Dame Ellen Terry, the English actress acclaimed for her Shakespearean roles, and who had a long theatrical association with Sir Henry Irving; she died in the house in 1928. This timber-framed structure, known as a "continuous-jetty house," was built in the first half of the 16th century and is filled with Terry memorabilia—playbills, props, makeup, and a striking display of costumes. An Elizabethan barn, adapted as a theater in 1929, is open for viewing on most days.

Smallhythe (on B2082 near Tenterden, about 9.5km/6 miles north of Rye). ☎ 01580/762334. Admission £3.40 ($5.45) adults, £1.70 ($2.70) children, £8.54 ($14) family ticket. Apr–Oct Sat–Wed 11am–5pm. Closed Good Friday. Take bus no. 312 from Tenterden or Rye.

WHERE TO STAY

Some of the best rooms in Rye are at the Benson Hotel on East Street; see "Where to Dine," below, for a review of its restaurant.

Durrant House Hotel   This beautiful Georgian house, restored in 2003, is set on a quiet residential street at the end of Market Street. The hotel's charm and character are enhanced by a cozy lounge with an arched, brick fireplace. The renowned artist Paul Nash lived next door until his death in 1946; in fact, his celebrated view, as seen in his painting *View of the Rother,* can be enjoyed from the River Room, a four-poster bedroom suite. Bedrooms range from small to medium in size; some of them are big enough for families, and others have four-poster beds. All rooms come with tidy bathrooms and shower units. At one time, the house was used as a relay station for carrier pigeons; these birds brought news of the victory at Waterloo.

Market St. (off High St.), Rye, E. Sussex TN31 3LA. ☎ 01797/223182. Fax 01797/226940. www.durrant house.com. 6 units. £68–£75 ($109–$120) double; £90 ($144) four-poster room. Rates include English breakfast. MC, V. **Amenities:** Lounge; babysitting. *In room:* TV, coffeemaker, hair dryer.

The George *(★)*   This coaching inn enjoys a long history dating from 1575. In the 18th century, it drew a diverse clientele: some traveling by horse-drawn carriage, others by boat between London and France. The half-timbered architecture charms a visitor like no other small inn in the region (except the Mermaid, which has even more of an antique atmosphere). Some of the timbers may be from the wreck of an English ship broken up in Rye Harbour after the defeat of the Spanish Armada. Bedrooms are snug and furnished in traditional English country-house style; each has a compact shower-only bathroom. Two accommodations are large enough for family use, though most units are a bit small. Five bedrooms are designated as nonsmoking.

High St., Rye, E. Sussex TN31 7JP. © **01797/222114.** Fax 01797/224065. £90 ($144) double; £110 ($176) suite. AE, DC, MC, V. **Amenities:** Restaurant; bar; room service; babysitting; laundry service; dry cleaning. *In room:* TV, minibar, coffeemaker, hair dryer, iron, safe, trouser press.

Mermaid Inn ★★ The Mermaid Inn is one of the most famous of the old smugglers' inns of England, known to that band of cutthroats, the real-life Hawkhurst Gang, as well as to Russell Thorndike's fictional character, Dr. Syn. (One of the rooms, in fact, is called Dr. Syn's Bedchamber, and is connected to the bar by a secret staircase, stowed away in the thickness of the wall.) This place, with its Elizabethan associations and traditional touches, remains one of the most romantic old-world inns in Sussex. The most sought-after rooms are in the building overlooking the cobblestone street. Five units have four-poster beds. The accommodations vary considerably in shape and size, some quite large, others a bit cramped, as befits a building of this age. Comfort is the keynote, regardless of room assignment. Six units are spacious enough for a small family. Bathrooms are compact but have good maintenance, some with both tub and shower.

Mermaid St. (between West St. and The Strand), Rye, E. Sussex TN31 7EY. © **01797/223065.** Fax 01797/225069. 31 units, 29 with private bathroom. £75–£95 ($120–$152) double with breakfast, £100–£125 ($160–$200) double with breakfast and dinner. Rates include English breakfast. AE, DC, MC, V. **Amenities:** Restaurant; bar; room service; babysitting; laundry service; dry cleaning. *In room:* A/C, TV, hair dryer.

White Vine House ★ *(Finds* The winner of several awards for the beauty of its small front garden and the quality of its restoration, this charming house dates from 1568. Restored from an almost derelict shell in 1987, and recently refurbished by its owners, the creeper-clad inn carefully maintains the Georgian detailing of the formal public rooms and the Tudor-style wall and ceiling beams of the antique bedrooms. The soft beds with fine linens are most comfortable, and the tiny shower bathrooms are tidily maintained.

High St., Rye, E. Sussex TN31 7JF. © **01797/224748.** Fax 01797/223599. 7 units. £80–£115 ($128–$184) double; £140 ($224) family room. Rates include English breakfast. AE, DC, MC, V. **Amenities:** Restaurant (breakfast only). *In room:* TV, coffeemaker, hair dryer.

WHERE TO DINE

Our preferred spot for teatime is the **Swan Cottage Tea Rooms,** 41 The Mint, High St. (© **01797/222423**), dating from 1420 and situated on the main street. This black-and-white half-timbered building is one of the most historic in town. We gravitate to the room in the rear because of its big brick fireplace. Delectable pastries and freshly made cakes await you along with a selection of teas, including Darjeeling, Earl Grey, Pure Assam, and others.

Flushing Inn ★ SEAFOOD/ENGLISH The best restaurant in Rye, this 16th-century inn has preserved the finest of the past, including a wall-size fresco dating from 1544 that depicts a menagerie of birds and heraldic beasts. A rear dining room overlooks a flower garden. A special feature is the Sea Food Lounge Bar, where sandwiches and plates of seafood are available. You can begin with the justifiably praised hors d'oeuvres—a fine selection of smoked fish and shellfish. Main dishes range from locally caught Rye Bay plaice to an old-fashioned loin of English lamb prepared with honey and lavender.

Besides lunch and dinner, gastronomic evenings are held at regular intervals between October and April. One of these specialty meals costs £65 ($104) per person, including your aperitif, wine, and after-dinner brandy. Fine wine evenings cost £60 to £70 ($96–$112) per person.

The owners have also constructed a luxurious accommodation known as the John Lester Suite within the 15th-century building. It costs £190 ($304) for two persons per night, which includes dinner and a full English champagne breakfast.

4–5 Market St. ℂ **01797/223292.** Reservations recommended. Fixed-price meal from £18 ($29) at lunch, £27–£37 ($43–$59) at dinner. AE, DC, MC, V. Wed–Mon noon–1:30pm; Wed–Sun 7–8:30pm. Closed first 2 weeks in Jan and first 2 weeks in June.

The Landgate Bistro MODERN BRITISH People come from miles around to dine in this pair of interconnected Georgian shops whose exteriors are covered with "mathematical tiles" (18th-century simulated brick, applied over stucco facades to save money). Inside, Toni Ferguson-Lees and her partner, Nick Parkin, offer savory modern British cuisine. Skillfully prepared dishes may include braised squid with white wine, tomatoes, and garlic; Dover sole; and grilled English lamb with butter beans, bacon, and fresh basil.

5–6 Landgate. ℂ **01797/222829.** Reservations required on weekends. Main courses £9.90–£13 ($16–$21); fixed-price menu Tues–Thurs £17 ($27). AE, DC, MC, V. Tues–Fri 7–9:30pm; Sat 7–10pm (closing time may vary).

4 1066 & All That: Hastings ⭐⭐⭐ & Battle ⭐⭐

Hastings: 72km (45 miles) SW of Dover; 101km (63 miles) SE of London. Battle: 55km (34 miles) NE of Brighton; 88km (55 miles) SE of London

The world has seen bigger skirmishes, but few are as well remembered as the Battle of Hastings in 1066. When William, Duke of Normandy, landed on the Sussex coast and lured King Harold (already fighting Vikings in Yorkshire) south to defeat, the destiny of the English-speaking people was changed forever.

The actual battle occurred at what is now Battle Abbey (13km/8 miles away), but the Norman duke used Hastings as his base of operations. You can visit the abbey, and then have a cup of tea in Battle's main square, and then you can be off, as the rich countryside of Sussex is much more intriguing than this sleepy market town.

Present-day Hastings is a little seedy and run-down. If you're seeking an English seaside resort, head for Brighton instead.

ESSENTIALS
GETTING THERE Daily trains run hourly from London's Victoria Station or Charing Cross to Hastings. The trip takes 1½ to 2 hours. The train station at Battle is a stop on the London–Hastings rail link. For rail information, call ℂ **08457/484950.**

Hastings is linked by bus to Maidstone, Folkestone, and Eastbourne, which has direct service with scheduled departures. **National Express** operates regular daily service from London's Victoria Coach Station. If you're in Rye or Hastings in summer, several frequent buses run to Battle. For information and schedules, call ℂ **020/7529-2000.**

If you're driving from the M25 ring road around London, head southeast to the coast and Hastings on A21. To get to Battle, cut south to Sevenoaks and continue along A21 to Battle via A2100.

VISITOR INFORMATION In Hastings, the **Hastings Information Centre** is at Queen's Square, Priory Meadow (ℂ **01424/781111**). It's open daily from 8:30am to 6:15pm.

In Battle, the **Tourist Information Centre** is at 88 High St. (© 01424/773721), and is open April through September daily from 10am to 6pm; off season Monday through Saturday from 10am to 4pm and on Sunday from 11am to 3pm.

EXPLORING THE HISTORIC SITES

Battle Abbey ★ *Kids*   King Harold, last of the Saxon kings, fought bravely here, not only for his kingdom but also for his life. As legend has it, he was killed by an arrow through the eye, and his body was dismembered. To commemorate the victory, William the Conqueror founded Battle Abbey; some of the construction stone was shipped from his lands at Caen in northern France.

During the Dissolution of the Monasteries from 1538 to 1539 by King Henry VIII, the church of the abbey was largely destroyed. Some buildings and ruins, however, remain in what Tennyson called "O Garden, blossoming out of English blood." The principal building still standing is the Abbot's House, which is leased to a private school for boys and girls and is open to the general public only during summer holidays. Of architectural interest is the gatehouse, which has octagonal towers and stands at the top of Market Square. All of the north Precinct Mall is still standing, and one of the most interesting sights of the ruins is the ancient Dorter Range, where the monks once slept.

The town of Battle flourished around the abbey; even though it has remained a medieval market town, many of the old half-timbered buildings have regrettably lost much of their original character because of stucco plastering carried out by past generations.

This is a great place for the kids. A themed play area is here, and at the gate, a daily activity sheet is distributed. You can relax with a picnic or stroll in the parkland that once formed the monastery grounds.

At the south end of Battle High St. (a 5-min. walk from the train station). © 01424/773792. Admission £5 ($8) adults, £2.50 ($4) children, £3.50 ($5.60) seniors and students, £11 ($18) family ticket. Apr–Sept daily 10am–6pm; Oct daily 10am–5pm; Nov–Mar daily 10am–4pm.

Hastings Castle ★★   In ruins now, the first of the Norman castles built in England sprouted on a western hill overlooking Hastings, around 1067. Precious little is left to remind us of the days when proud knights, imbued with a spirit of pomp and spectacle, wore bonnets and girdles. The fortress was defortified by King John in 1216 and was later used as a church. Owned by the Pelham dynasty from the latter 16th century to modern times, the ruins have been turned over to Hastings. There is now an audiovisual presentation of the castle's history, including the famous battle of 1066. From the mount, you'll have a good view of the coast and promenade.

Castle Hill Rd., West Hill. © 01424/781112. Admission £3.20 ($5.10) adults, £2.60 ($4.15) seniors and students, £2.10 ($3.35) children. Easter–Sept daily 10am–5pm; Oct–Easter daily 11am–3pm. Take the West Hill Cliff Railway from George St. to the castle for 80p ($1.30), 40p (65¢) for children.

SEASIDE AMUSEMENTS

Linked by a 5km (3-mile) promenade along the sea, Hastings and St. Leonards were given a considerable boost in the 19th century by Queen Victoria, who visited several times. Neither town enjoys such royal patronage today; instead, they do a thriving business with English families on vacation. Hastings and St. Leonards have the usual shops and English sea-resort amusements.

Smugglers Adventure   Here you can descend into the once-secret underground haunts of the smugglers of Hastings. In these chambers, where the smugglers stashed their booty away from Customs authorities, you can see an exhibition and museum, a video in a theater, and take a subterranean adventure walk with 50 life-size figures, along with dramatic sound and lighting effects.

St. Clements Caves, West Hill. © 01424/422964. Admission £5.50 ($8.80) adults, £3.65 ($5.85) children, £16 ($25) family. Apr–Sept daily 10am–5:30pm; Oct–Mar daily 11am–4:30pm. Take the West Cliff Railway from George St. to West Hill for 70p ($1.10) adults, 40p (65¢) for children.

WHERE TO STAY
IN HASTINGS

Beauport Park Hotel ⭐   This hotel has a cozy country-house aura and is more intimate and hospitable than The Royal Victoria (reviewed below). Originally the private estate of General Murray, former governor of Quebec, the building was destroyed by fire in 1923 and rebuilt in the old style. It's surrounded by beautiful gardens; the Italian-style grounds in the rear feature statuary and flowering shrubbery. Rooms range from midsize to large, and some are fitted with elegant four-poster beds. Nine bedrooms are set aside for nonsmokers. The self-contained Pine Lodge is equipped with a double, twin, children's room, living area, sauna, and kitchen.

Battle Rd. (A2100), Hastings, E. Sussex TN38 8EA. © 01424/851222. Fax 01424/852465. www.beauportpark hotel.co.uk. 26 units. £130 ($208) double; £155 ($248) Pine Lodge. Rates include English breakfast. AE, DC, MC, V. Bus: 4 or 5 from Hastings. Head 5.5km (3½ miles) northwest of Hastings, to the junction of A2100 and B2159. **Amenities:** 2 restaurants; bar; outdoor heated pool; tennis court; badminton court; croquet; room service; laundry service; dry cleaning. *In room:* TV, coffeemaker, hair dryer, trouser press.

The Royal Victoria   This seafront hotel, constructed in 1828, offers the most impressive architecture in town and the best accommodations in Hastings or St. Leonards. It has welcomed many famous visitors, including its namesake, Queen Victoria herself. Many of the elegant and comfortably appointed rooms have separate lounge areas and views of the English Channel and Beachy Head. Many of the bedrooms are extremely large; all of them look as if Laura Ashley traipsed through, as evoked by dozens of half-tester beds in English chintz. Some of the accommodations are large enough for families, and a number of them are duplexes. Some of the units are wheelchair accessible. Bathrooms are roomy and well maintained.

Marina, St. Leonards, Hastings, E. Sussex TN38 OBD. © 01424/445544. Fax 01424/721995. www.royalvictoria-hotel.co.uk. 56 units. £130 ($208) double. Children 15 and under stay free in parent's room. Rates include English breakfast. AE, DC, MC, V. **Amenities:** Restaurant; 3 bars; room service; laundry service; dry cleaning. *In room:* TV, dataport, coffeemaker, hair dryer, iron, safe, trouser press.

IN BATTLE

Powder Mills Hotel ⭐ *Finds*   Near Battle Abbey and adjacent to the fabled battlefield of 1066, this restored Georgian house sits on 150 acres. On-site was a thriving gunpowder industry, which operated for two centuries beginning in 1676. The name of the hotel honors that long ago tradition. Privately owned by Douglas and Julie Cowpland, the property has attracted such distinguished guests as the duke of Wellington. It's also said to be haunted by a lady dressed in white. Bedrooms are spacious and tastefully furnished, mostly with antiques and various period pieces. Some rooms offer four-poster beds; all come with a well-maintained private bathroom with tub or shower. Grace notes include log fires on winter evenings, a drawing room, a music room, and the Orangery Restaurant with its colonial-style wicker seating.

Powder Mills Lane, Battle, E. Sussex TN33 OSP. © 01424/775511. Fax 01424/774540. http://members.aol. com/powdc. 35 units. £105–£135 ($168–$216) double; £175 ($280) suite. Rates include English breakfast. AE, DC, MC, V. **Amenities:** Restaurant; bar; outdoor pool; fishing; room service; babysitting; laundry service. *In room:* TV, beverage maker, hair dryer, trouser press.

WHERE TO DINE

Victoria's Tea Room (D-Day's)   Courthouse Street in Hasting's Old Town has attracted as many as 17 antiques stores in recent years, creating a kind of mecca for antiques buyers. Their hub and centerpiece, and site of endless cups of up to 20 varieties of tea, is this combination tearoom and antiques store. The owners, D-Day White (who was born on the day of the famous invasion in Normandy) and Beverly, have transformed their 18th-century premises into the coziest tearoom in town and filled its nether regions with an intriguing collection of period furniture and "collectible junk" that includes everything from Victorian sideboards to gas masks from World War I. The place is especially appealing when the wind and rain blow in from the Channel.

19 Courthouse St., Hastings Old Town. ℂ 01424/465205. Cream teas £2.50 ($4); sandwiches £2–£3 ($3.20–$4.80). No credit cards. Mon–Thurs and Sat 10am–4:30 or 5pm; Sun noon–4:30pm.

5 Kent's Country Houses, Castles & Gardens

Many of England's finest country houses, castles, and gardens are in Kent, where you'll find the palace of Knole, a premier example of English Tudor-style architecture; Hever Castle, the childhood home of Anne Boleyn and later the home of William Waldorf Astor; Leeds Castle, a spectacular castle with ties to America; and Penshurst Place, a stately home that was a literary salon of sorts during the first half of the 17th century. Kent also has a bevy of homes that once belonged to famous men but have since been turned into intriguing museums, such as Chartwell, where Sir Winston Churchill lived for many years, and Down House, where Charles Darwin wrote *On the Origin of Species.* Here you can amble down the same path the naturalist trod every evening.

It would take at least a week to see all of these historic properties—more time than most visitors have. When you make your choices, keep in mind that Knole, Hever, Penshurst, Leeds, and Chartwell are the most deserving of your attention.

We have found the guided tours to some of Kent's more popular stately homes too rushed and too expensive to recommend. Each attraction can be toured far more reasonably on your own. Because public transportation into and around Kent can be awkward, we advise driving from London, especially if you plan to visit more than one place in a day. Accordingly, this section is organized as you may drive it from London. However, if it's possible to get to an attraction via public transportation, we include that information in the individual listings below.

If you only have a day, you may want to confine your time to Chartwell, former home of Winston Churchill; and Knole, one of England's largest private estates with a vast complex of courtyards and buildings. You need an entire second day to visit Leeds Castle and Hever Castle. Leeds allows morning visits (most castles and country homes in Kent can only be visited in the afternoon), so you can see Leeds in the morning, then tour Hever Castle that afternoon.

If you have more time for castle hopping, visit Canterbury Cathedral on the morning of your third day, then tour Penshurst Place in the afternoon. (See the "Canterbury" section earlier in this chapter for details on Canterbury.) Penshurst is one of the finest Elizabethan houses in England, and its Baron's Hall is one of the greatest interiors to have survived from the Middle Ages.

Two other notable attractions are Sissinghurst Castle Garden and Ightham Mote, a National Trust property dating from 1340. They are open afternoons during the week, and mornings Saturday and Sunday.

Chartwell ⍟ Sir Winston Churchill's home from 1922 until his death, though not as grand as his birthplace (Blenheim Palace; p. 413), Chartwell has preserved its rooms as the Conservative politician left them—maps, documents, photographs, pictures, personal mementos, and all. Two rooms display gifts that the prime minister received from people all over the world. A selection of many of his well-known uniforms includes his famous "siren-suits" and hats. Many of Churchill's paintings are displayed in a garden studio. You can see the garden walls that the prime minister built with his own hands and the pond where he sat to feed the Golden Orfe. A restaurant on the grounds serves food from 10:30am to 5pm on days when the house is open.

Near the town of Edenbridge. ⏱ **01732/868381.** Admission to house, garden, and studio £6.50 ($10) adults, £3.25 ($5.20) children, £16 ($26) family. Late Mar to early Nov Wed–Sun 11am–5pm; July–Aug Tues–Sun 11am–5pm. If driving from London, head east on M25, taking the exit to Westerham. Drive 3km (2 miles) south of Westerham on B2026 and follow the signs.

Down House Here stands the final residence of the famous naturalist Charles Darwin. In 1842, on moving in, he wrote, "House ugly, looks neither old nor new." Nevertheless, he lived there "in happy contentment" until his death in 1882. The drawing room, dining room, billiards room, and old study have been restored to the way they were when Darwin was working on his famous (and still controversial) book *On the Origin of Species,* first published in 1859. The garden retains its original landscaping and a glass house, beyond which lies the Sand Walk or "Thinking Path," where Darwin took his daily solitary walk.

On Luxted Rd., in Downe. ⏱ **01689/859119.** Admission £6.30 ($10) adults, £4.50 ($7.20) students and seniors, £3 ($4.80) children. Apr–Oct daily 10am–6pm; Nov–Mar Wed–Sun 10am–4pm. Closed Dec 24–26. From Westerham, get on A233 and drive 8.8km (5½ miles) south of Bromley to the village of Downe. Down House is .4km (¼ mile) southeast of the village. From London's Victoria Station, take a train (available daily) to Bromley South, then go by bus no. 146 (Mon–Sat only) to Downe or to Orpington by bus no. R2.

Groombridge Place Gardens These formal gardens, with a vineyard and woodland walks, date from the 17th century. Part of the complex includes an Enchanted Forest, an ancient woodland in which the artist Ivan Hicks designed a series of "interactive" gardens, using natural objects, native wild flowers, mirrors, and glass to create a mysterious, surreal ambience. The White Rose Garden is compared favorably to that at fabled Sissinghurst. The English Knot Garden is based on paneling in the drawing room of an English country house. In the Fern Valley, huge Jurassic plants are as old as time. At the center is Groombridge Place, built on the site of a 12th-century castle and one of the most beautiful moated manor houses in England. Sir Christopher Wren, or so it is believed, helped with the architecture. The palace was built in 1662 by one of the courtiers to King Charles II, Philip Packer. Sir Arthur Conan Doyle was a regular visitor to the house to take part in séances, and the manor was the setting for the Sherlock Holmes mystery, *The Valley of Fear.*

Groombridge. ⏱ **08192/861444.** www.groombridge.co.uk. Admission £8.30 ($13) adults, £7.50 ($12) seniors, £6.80 ($11) children 3–12, £28 ($44) family ticket. Apr–Oct daily 9am–6pm.

Ightham Mote ⍟ Dating from 1340, Ightham Mote was extensively remodeled in the early 16th century, and remodeling is still going on. The chapel, with its painted ceiling, timbered outer wall, and ornate chimneys, reflects the Tudor period. You'll cross a stone bridge over a moat to its central courtyard. From the Great Hall, known for its magnificent windows, a Jacobean staircase leads to the old chapel on the first floor, where you go through the solarium, which has an oriel window, to the Tudor chapel.

Unlike many other ancient houses in England that have been occupied by the same family for centuries, Ightham Mote passed from owner to owner, with each family leaving its mark on the place. When the last private owner, an American who was responsible for a lot of the restoration, died, he bequeathed the house to the National Trust, which chose to keep the Robinson Library laid out as it was in a 1960 edition of *Homes & Gardens*.

C **01732/810378.** Admission £6 ($9.60) adults, £3 ($4.80) children, £15 ($24) family. Sun–Mon and Wed–Fri 10am–5:30pm. Closed Nov–Mar. Drive 9.5km (6 miles) east of Sevenoaks on A25 to the small village of Ivy Hatch; the estate is 4km (2½ miles) south of Ightham; it's also signposted from A227.

Knole ★★ Begun in the mid–15th century by Thomas Bourchier, archbishop of Canterbury, and set in a 1,000-acre deer park, Knole is one of the largest private houses in England and is one of the finest examples of pure English Tudor-style architecture.

Henry VIII liberated the former archbishop's palace from the church in 1537. He spent considerable sums of money on Knole, but history records only one visit (in 1541) after extracting the place from the reluctant Archbishop Cranmer. It was a royal palace until Queen Elizabeth I granted it to Thomas Sackville, first earl of Dorset, whose descendants have lived here ever since. (Virginia Woolf, often a guest of the Sackvilles, used Knole as the setting for her novel *Orlando*.)

The house covers 7 acres and has 365 rooms, 52 staircases, and 7 courts. The elaborate paneling and plasterwork provide a background for the 17th- and 18th-century tapestries and rugs, Elizabethan and Jacobean furniture, and collection of family portraits. If you want to see a bed that's to die for, check out the state bed of James II in the King's Bedroom.

8km (5 miles) north of Tonbridge, at the Tonbridge end of the town of Sevenoaks. *C* **01732/462100.** www.nationaltrust.org.uk. Admission to house £5.60 ($8.95) adults, £2.75 ($4.40) children, £13.75 ($22) family. Admission to gardens £2 ($3.20) adults, £1 ($1.60) children. House open late Mar to early Nov Wed–Sun 11am–4pm; Good Friday and bank holiday Mon 11am–4pm. Gardens open only 1st Wed of the month in May–Sept 11am–4pm; last admission at 3pm. Park is open daily to pedestrians and open to cars only when the house is open. To reach Knole from Chartwell, drive north to Westerham, pick up A25, and head east for 13km (8 miles). Frequent train service is available from London (about every 30 min.) to Sevenoaks, and then you can take the connecting hourly bus service, a taxi, or walk the remaining 2.5km (1½ miles) to Knole.

Squerryes Court Built in 1681, and owned by the Warde family for 250 years, this still-occupied manor house has pictures and relics of General Wolfe's family. A house on this site was occupied by the de Squerie family from 1216 until the mid–15th century. The family restored the formal gardens, dotting the banks surrounding the lake with spring bulbs, herbaceous borders, and old roses to retain its beauty year-round, and returned the rooms to their original uses. You can enjoy the fine collection of Old Master paintings from the Italian, 17th-century Dutch, and 18th-century English schools, along with antiques, porcelain, and tapestries, all acquired or commissioned by the family in the 18th century. The military hero received his commission on the grounds of the house—the spot is marked by a cenotaph.

.8km (½ mile) west of the center of Westerham (10 min. from Exit 6 or Exit 5 on the M25). *C* **01959/562345.** www.squerryes.co.uk. Admission to house and grounds £4.80 ($7.70) adults, £4.10 ($6.55) seniors and students, £2.60 ($4.15) children under age 14. Grounds only £3.20 ($5.10) adults, £2.70 ($4.30) seniors, £1.60 ($2.55) children under age 14. End of Apr 1–Sept 30 Wed and Sat–Sun, grounds are open noon–5:30pm, house 1:30–5:30pm. Take A25 just west of Westerham and follow the signs.

TOURING LEEDS CASTLE: "THE LOVELIEST IN THE WORLD"

Once described by Lord Conway as the loveliest castle in the world, **Leeds Castle** ★★★ (© 01622/765400) dates from A.D. 857. Originally constructed of wood, it was rebuilt in 1119 in its present stone structure on two small islands in the middle of the lake; it was an almost impregnable fortress before the importation of gunpowder. Henry VIII converted it to a royal palace.

The castle has strong ties to America through the sixth Lord Fairfax who, as well as owning the castle, owned 5 million acres in Virginia and was a close friend and mentor of the young George Washington. The last private owner, the Hon. Lady Baillie, who restored the castle with a superb collection of fine art, furniture, and tapestries, bequeathed it to the Leeds Castle Foundation. Since then, the royal apartments, known as *Les Chambres de la Reine* (the queen's chambers), in the Gloriette, the oldest part of the castle, have been open to the public. The Gloriette, the last stronghold against attack, dates from Norman and Plantagenet times, with later additions by Henry VIII.

Within the surrounding parkland is a wildwood garden and duckery where rare swans, geese, and ducks abound. The redesigned aviaries contain a superb collection of birds, including parakeets and cockatoos. Dog lovers will enjoy the Dog Collar Museum at the gatehouse, which features a unique collection of collars dating from the Middle Ages. A nine-hole golf course is open to the public. The Culpepper Garden is a delightful English country flower garden. Beyond are the castle greenhouses, with the maze centered on a beautiful underground grotto and the vineyard recorded in the *Domesday Book*. It is once again producing Leeds Castle English white wine.

From March to October, the park is open daily from 10am to 5pm; the castle, daily from 11am to 5:30pm. From November to February, the park is open daily from 10am to 3pm; the castle, daily from 10:15am to 3:30pm. The castle and grounds are closed on the last Saturday in June and the first Saturday in July before open-air concerts. Admission to the castle and grounds is £11 to £12 ($18–$19) for adults and £7.50 to £8.50 ($12–$14) for children. Students and seniors pay £9.50 to £10.50 ($15–$17). A family ticket costs £32 ($51). Car parking is free, with a free ride on a fully accessible minibus available for those who cannot manage the 1km (½-mile) or so walk from the parking area to the castle.

Trains run frequently from London's Victoria Station to Maidstone. Buses run weekdays from London's Victoria Coach Station to Maidstone, 58km (36 miles) to the southeast. If you're driving, from London's ring road, continue east along M26 and M20. The castle is 6.5km (4 miles) east of Maidstone at the junction of the A20 and the M20 London–Folkestone roads.

Snacks, salads, cream teas, and hot meals are offered daily at a number of places on the estate, including Fairfax Hall, a restored 17th-century tithe barn, and the Terrace Restaurant, which provides a full range of hot and cold meals.

Kentish Evenings are presented in Fairfax Hall on the first Saturday of the month throughout the year (except in Aug), starting at 7pm with a cocktail

---

Finds **Feathery Friends on the Endangered List**

Hurried visitors overlook the Aviary at Leeds Castle, but it's really special. Opened by Princess Alexandra in 1988, it houses a collection of more than 100 rare species of birds. It aims not only at conservation but also at successful breeding—to reintroduce endangered species into their original habitats.

reception, then a private guided tour of the castle. Guests feast on a five-course banquet, starting with smoked salmon mousse, followed by broth and roast beef carved at the table, plus seasonal vegetables. A half bottle of wine is included in the overall price of £49 ($78) per person. During the meal, musicians play appropriate music for the surroundings and the occasion. Advance reservations are required and can be made by calling the castle. Kentish Evenings finish at 12:30am, so it's best to stay overnight nearby.

Instead of driving back late at night, you can spend the night at **Grangemoor/Grange Park,** 4–8 St. Michael's Rd. (off Tonbridge Rd.), Maidstone, Kent ME16 8BS (© **01622/677623;** fax 01622/678246), which are two buildings facing each other across the street. Grangemoor is the main accommodation, with 38 well-furnished rooms, each with private bathroom, phone, and TV. The cost is £55 ($88) for a double, Monday through Thursday, and £54 ($86) on other nights, including an English breakfast. Across the street, Grange Park has only 12 rooms but is similarly furnished, renting for £54 to £55 ($86–$88) a night, including an English breakfast. Both places are located in a tranquil residential area that's close to the center of Maidstone. A Tudor-style bar and restaurant offers a three-course meal for £17 ($26). Children are welcome in both the bar and restaurant area.

MORE KENT ATTRACTIONS

Hever Castle & Gardens ★★   Hever Castle dates from 1270, when the massive gatehouse, the outer walls, and the moat were first constructed. Some 200 years later, the Bullen (or Boleyn) family added a comfortable Tudor dwelling house inside the walls. Hever Castle was the childhood home of Anne Boleyn, the second wife of Henry VIII and mother of Queen Elizabeth I.

In 1903, William Waldorf Astor acquired the estate and invested time, money, and imagination in restoring the castle, building the Tudor Village, and creating the gardens and lakes. The Astor family's contribution to Hever's rich history can be appreciated through the castle's collections of furniture, paintings, and objets d'art, as well as the quality of its workmanship, particularly in the wood carving and plasterwork.

The gardens are ablaze with color throughout most of the year. The spectacular Italian Garden contains statuary and sculpture dating from Roman to Renaissance times. The formal gardens include a walled Rose Garden, fine topiary work, and a maze. There's a 35-acre lake and many streams, cascades, and fountains.

© **01732/865224.** www.hevercastle.co.uk. Admission to castle and gardens £8.40 ($13) adults, £7.10 ($11) seniors and students, £4.60 ($7.35) children ages 5–14. Family ticket (2 adults, 2 children) £21 ($34). Garden only £6.70 ($11) adults, £5.70 ($9.10) seniors and students, £4.40 ($7.05) children ages 5–14, family ticket £18 ($28), free for children 4 and under. Gardens daily 11am–6pm; castle daily noon–6pm, closes at 4pm Mar and Nov. Closed Dec–Feb. Follow the signs northwest of Royal Tonbridge Wells; it's 5km (3 miles) southeast of Edenbridge, midway between Sevenoaks and East Grinstead, and 30 min. from Exit 6 of M25.

Penshurst Place ★★   Stately Penshurst Place is one of Britain's outstanding country houses, as well as one of England's greatest defended manor houses, standing in a peaceful rural setting that has changed little over the centuries. In 1338, Sir John de Pulteney, four times lord mayor of London, built the manor house whose Great Hall still forms the heart of Penshurst. The boy king, Edward VI, presented the house to Sir William Sidney, and it has remained in that family ever since. In the first half of the 17th century, Penshurst was known as a center of literature and attracted such personages as Ben Jonson, who was inspired by the estate to write one of his greatest poems.

The Nether Gallery, below the **Long Gallery** with its suite of ebony-and-ivory furniture from Goa, houses the Sidney family collection of armor. You can also see the splendid state dining room. In the Stable Wing is a toy museum, with playthings from past generations. On the grounds are nature and farm trails plus an adventure playground for children.

9.5km (6 miles) west of Tonbridge. ℂ **01892/870307.** www.penshurstplace.com. Admission to house and grounds £6.50 ($10) adults, £6 ($9.60) seniors and students, £4.50 ($7.20) children 5–16. Grounds only £5 ($8) adults, £4.50 ($7.20) seniors and students, £4 ($6.40) children 5–16, free for children 4 and under. Apr–Oct daily, house noon–5:30pm, grounds 10:30am–6pm. Closed Nov–Feb. From M25 Junction follow A21 to Tonbridge, leaving at the Tonbridge (North) exit; then follow the brown tourist signs. The nearest mainline station is Tonbridge.

Sissinghurst Castle Garden ⭐⭐   These spectacular gardens, which are situated between surviving parts of an Elizabethan mansion, were created by one of England's most famous and dedicated gardeners, Bloomsbury writer Vita Sackville-West, and her husband, Harold Nicolson. In spring, the garden is resplendent with flowering bulbs and daffodils in the orchard.

The white garden reaches its peak in June. The large herb garden, a skillful montage that reflects her profound plant knowledge, has something to show all summer long, and the cottage garden, with its flowering bulbs, is at its finest in the fall. Meals are available in the Granary Restaurant. The garden area is flat, so it is wheelchair accessible; however, only two wheelchairs are allowed at a time.

ℂ **01580/715330.** www.nationaltrust.org.uk. Admission £6.50 ($10) adults, £2 ($3.20) children, family ticket £16 ($26). Apr–Oct Mon–Tues and Fri 11am–6:30pm; Sat–Sun 10am–6:30pm. The garden is 85km (53 miles) southeast of London and 24km (15 miles) south of Maidstone. It's most often approached from Leeds Castle, which is 6.5km (4 miles) east of Maidstone at the junction of A20 and M20 London–Folkestone roads. From this junction, head south on B2163 and A274 through Headcorn. Follow the signposts to Sissinghurst.

6 Chichester

50km (31 miles) W of Brighton; 111km (69 miles) SW of London

Chichester might have been just a market town if the Chichester Festival Theatre had not been born there. One of the oldest Roman cities in England, Chichester draws a crowd from all over the world for its theater presentations. Although it lacks other attractions besides theater, the town makes a good base for exploring a history-rich part of southern England.

ESSENTIALS

GETTING THERE   Trains depart for Chichester from London's Victoria Station once every hour during the day. The trip takes 1½ hours. However, if you visit Chichester to attend the theater, plan to stay over—the last train back to London is at 9pm. For rail information, call ℂ **0845/722-5225.**

Buses leave from London's Victoria Coach Station once a day. For schedules, call ℂ **0870/580-8080.**

If you're driving from London's ring road, head south on A3, turning onto A286 for Chichester.

VISITOR INFORMATION   The **Tourist Information Centre,** 29A South St. (ℂ **01243/775888**), is open Monday through Saturday from 9:15am to 5:15pm, and from May to September, also on Sunday from 10am to 4pm.

THE CHICHESTER FESTIVAL THEATRE ⭐

Only a 5-minute walk from the Chichester Cathedral and the old Market Cross, the 1,400-seat theater, with its apron stage, stands on the edge of Oaklands Park. It opened in 1962, and its first director was none other than Lord Laurence

---

⌐Finds Bosham: A Hidden Surprise

In addition to the sights listed below, you might want to stop in nearby **Bosham,** which is primarily a sailing resort and one of the most charming villages in West Sussex. It's 6.5km (4 miles) west of Chichester on the A259, and there's a good bus service between the two towns. Bosham was the site where Christianity was first established on the Sussex coast. The Danish king, Canute, made it one of the seats of his North Sea empire, and it was the home of a manor (now gone) of the last of England's Saxon kings. Harold sailed from here to France on a journey that finally culminated in the invasion of England by William the Conqueror in 1066.

Bosham's little **church** was depicted in the Bayeux Tapestry. Its graveyard overlooks the boats, and the church is filled with ship models and relics, showing the villagers' link to the sea. A daughter of King Canute is buried inside. Near the harbor, it is reached by a narrow lane.

Olivier. Its reputation has grown steadily, pumping new vigor and life into the former walled city, although originally many irate locals felt the city money could have been better spent on a swimming pool instead of a theater.

Chichester Festival Theatre, built in the 1960s, offers plays and musicals during the summer (May–Sept), and in the winter and spring months, orchestras, jazz, opera, theater, ballet, and a Christmas show for the entire family.

The **Minerva,** built in the late 1980s, is a multifunctional cultural center that includes a theater plus dining and drinking facilities. The Minerva Studio Theatre and the Chichester Festival Theatre are managed by the same board of governors but show different programs and different plays.

Theater reservations made over the telephone will be held for a maximum of 4 days (call ✆ **01243/781312**). It's better to mail inquiries and checks to the Box Office, Chichester Festival Theatre, Oaklands Park, Chichester, West Sussex PO19 4AP. MasterCard, Visa, and American Express are accepted. Season ticket prices range from £9 to £30 ($14–$48).

A RACE TRACK

One of the most famous sports-car-racing courses in the world, **Goodwood Motor Circuit** (✆ **01243/755055**), reopened in 1998 near Chichester. It has been restored to its look 50 years ago. The course became dangerous for faster cars and was retired as an active track in the 1960s, as the 4km (2½-mile) circuit was never modernized. Now, that is part of its charm, offering a chance to relive the days when courageous drivers raced Jaguars or Ferraris on tracks enveloped by cornfields and hay bales. The course is now used for special exhibition races featuring historic sports cars from the '50s and '60s. The track can be reached by taking the A3 to Milford and the A283 to Petwork, then the A285 to Halnaker, following the signposts from there. Call to see if any exhibitions are being staged during your visit to the area.

Roman Palace   This is what remains of the largest Roman residence yet discovered in Britain. Built around A.D. 75 in villa style, it has many mosaic-floored rooms and even an under-floor heating system. The gardens have been restored to their original 1st-century plan. The story of the site is told both by an audiovisual program and by text in the museum. Guided tours are offered twice a day. (See what an archaeological dig in July 1996 unearthed.)

North of A259, off Salthill Rd. (signposted from Fishbourne; 2.5km/1½ miles from Chichester). ℭ **01243/785859.** Admission £5 ($8) adults, £2.60 ($4.15) children, £12.90 ($21) family ticket. Mar–Oct daily 10am–5pm (to 6pm in Aug); Feb and Nov to mid-Dec daily 10am–4pm; mid-Dec to Jan Sat–Sun 10am–4pm. Buses stop regularly at the bottom of Salthill Rd., and the museum is within a 10-min. walk of British Rail's station at Fishbourne.

Weald & the Downland Open Air Museum In the beautiful Sussex countryside, historic buildings, saved from destruction, are reconstructed on a 40-acre downland site. The structures show the development of traditional building from medieval times to the 19th century, in the weald and downland area of southeast England. Exhibits include a Tudor market hall, a working water mill producing stone-ground flour, a blacksmith's forge, plumbers' and carpenters' workshops, a toll cottage, a charcoal burner's camp, and a 19th-century village school. A "new" reception area with shops and offices is set in Longport House, a 16th-century building rescued from the site of the Channel Tunnel.

At Singleton, 9.5km (6 miles) north of Chichester on A286 (the London Rd.). ℭ **01243/811363.** www.weald down.co.uk. Admission £7 ($11) adults, £6.50 ($10) seniors, £4 ($6.40) students and children 5–15, family ticket £19 ($30). Mar–Oct daily 10:30am–6pm; Nov–Feb Wed and Sat–Sun 10:30am–4pm. MC, V. Bus: 60 from Chichester.

WHERE TO STAY IN THE AREA

Forge Hotel ⊀ (Finds) This is a typical 17th-century brick and flint cottage set on well-landscaped grounds with the South Downs Way only a short distance to the north. The cottage has been meticulously restored, with beautiful interiors of tasteful decoration and homelike touches such as fresh flowers and mineral water. Each bedroom comes with a private bathroom with shower. You'll have to negotiate steep stairs to some of the rooms, but one ground-floor room is suitable for those with mobility impairments. The owner Neil Rusbridget is also a chef, preparing "house party" menus.

Chilgrove, Chicester, W. Sussex PO1B 9HX. 4 units. ℭ **01243/535333.** £69 ($110) double. AE, MC, V. www. forgehotel.com. **Amenities:** Restaurant; bar; room service. *In room:* TV, hair dryer.

Marriott Goodwood Park Hotel & Country Club ⋆⋆ This is the most upmarket hotel in the area. Goodwood House was the home to the dukes of Richmond for more than 300 years. The hotel now located on these grounds was built in the 1786 style of the original Goodwood House. Bedrooms have been refurbished and upgraded, and easily qualify as the best in the area. Some of the rooms open onto panoramic views, and 66 accommodations are set aside for nonsmokers. Each bathroom is equipped with an efficient shower.

Goodwood, Chichester PO18 0QB. ℭ **800/228-9290** in the U.S., or 01243/775537. Fax 01243/520120. www. marriott.com. 94 units. £119–£210 ($190–$336) double; £210 ($336) suite. Rates include breakfast. AE, DC, MC, V. **Amenities:** 2 restaurants; 3 bars; indoor pool; 18-hole golf course; 2 tennis courts; health club with sauna; Jacuzzi; concierge; 24-hr. room service; babysitting; laundry service; dry cleaning. *In room:* TV, dataport, minibar, coffeemaker, hair dryer, iron, safe, trouser press.

Millstream Hotel Bosham Lane The Millstream, built in the 1700s to provide food and accommodation for travelers through Sussex from other parts of England, is 8km (5 miles) south of Chichester. The hotel is in the hamlet of Bosham, with its beautiful harbor. Behind a facade of weathered yellow bricks, the hotel exudes a sense of history. The rooms, modern in style, have recently been redecorated and upgraded.

Bosham Line, Chichester, W. Sussex PO18 8HL. ℭ **01243/573234.** Fax 01243/573459. www.millstream-hotel.co.uk. 35 units. £125–£139 ($200–$222) double. Rates include English breakfast. Double room and half board available for £138 ($221) weekdays, £160 ($256) Sat–Sun. AE, DC, MC, V. Bus: Bosham bus from Chichester. Take the road to the village of Bosham and its harbor, off A27. **Amenities:** Restaurant; bar; room service; babysitting; laundry service; dry cleaning. *In room:* TV, dataport, coffeemaker, hair dryer, iron, safe, trouser press.

Ship Hotel   A classic Georgian building, the Ship is only a few minutes' walk from Chichester Cathedral, Chichester Festival Theatre, and many fine antiques shops. Built as a private house in 1790 for Adm. Sir George Murray, it retains an air of elegance and comfort. A grand Adam staircase leads from its main entrance to the bedrooms, which are named after historic ships. All of the rooms have bathrooms with shower-tub combinations and have recently been refurbished. Some rooms have four-poster beds; others are specially designated for families.

North St., Chichester, W. Sussex PO19 1NH. © **01243/778000.** Fax 01243/788000. www.shiphotel.com. 38 units. £79–£99 ($126–$158) double. Rate includes English breakfast. AE, DC, MC, V. **Amenities:** Restaurant; bar; room service; laundry service; dry cleaning. *In room:* TV, dataport, coffeemaker, hair dryer, iron, trouser press.

The Spread Eagle Hotel ★★ *Finds*   This 1430 inn, and the market town of Midhurst, are so steeped in history that the room you sleep in and the pavement you walk on probably have a thousand tales to tell. The rooms here are medieval in character, with beams, small mullioned windows, and unexpected corners. The most elegant have four-poster antique beds, fireplaces, and 500-year-old wall paneling. Most rooms have a shower-and-tub combination; the four rooms in the Market House annex across from the main hotel have showers only. The eagle in the lounge is the actual one from the back of Hermann Göring's chair in the Reichstag. It was acquired for its apt illustration of the hotel's name.

South St., Midhurst, W. Sussex GU29 9NH. © **01730/816911.** Fax 01730/815668. www.hshotels.co.uk/ spread/spreadeagle-main.htm. 39 units. £135–£225 ($216–$360) double; £225 ($360) suite. Rates include English breakfast. AE, DC, MC, V. Midhurst bus from Chichester. **Amenities:** Restaurant; bar; indoor pool; health spa with sauna and steam room; gym; salon; room service; laundry service; dry cleaning. *In room:* TV, dataport, coffeemaker, hair dryer.

WHERE TO DINE IN THE AREA

Comme ça ★ FRENCH   This is the best French restaurant in town—in fact, the best restaurant, period. The unpretentious decor blends old Victorian and Edwardian prints with objets d'art. The theme continues in the new garden room leading through French doors to an enclosed patio and garden. In summer, you'll want to dine out here, although in winter, a log fire in the inglenook fireplace welcomes you to the bar.

Try delights of the field, river, and forest such as baked fresh Scottish salmon or roasted breasts of pigeons served with Armagnac and tarragon sauce. Only the finest-quality ingredients are used. All menus have vegetarian dishes, and special dietary requirements can also be catered to.

67 Broyle Rd. (a 10-min. walk from the town center). © **01243/788724.** Reservations required. Tues–Sun main courses £13–£15 ($21–$24), 2-course lunch £16 ($26), 3-course lunch £19 ($30). MC, V. Tues–Sun 12:15–2pm; Tues–Sat 6–9:30pm.

White Horse ENGLISH/FRENCH   The wine cellar at this informally elegant country restaurant is one of the most comprehensive in Britain, partly because of the careful attention the owners pay to the details of their 18th-century inn, whose patina has been burnished every day since it was built in 1765. The menu is heavy on local game in season, bought from people known by the owners. Menu choices include roast breast of pheasant on a bed of celeriac purée and roast lamb in a reduced sauce.

1 High St., Chilgrove. © **01243/535219.** Reservations required on weekends. Main courses £9.50–£25 ($15–$40). AE, MC, V. Tues–Sun noon–2pm and 7–10pm. Closed Dec 25–26. Head 10km (6½ miles) north of Chichester on B2141 to Petersfield.

7 Arundel ★ ★

34km (21 miles) W of Brighton; 93km (58 miles) SW of London

The small town of Arundel in West Sussex nestles at the foot of one of England's most spectacular castles. Without the castle, it would be just another English market town. The town was once an Arun River port, and its residents enjoyed the prosperity of considerable trade and commerce. Today, however, buses filled with tourists have replaced the harbor traffic.

ESSENTIALS

GETTING THERE   Trains leave hourly during the day from London's Victoria Station. The trip takes 1¼ hours. For rail information, call ℂ **0845/748-4950.**

Most bus connections are through Littlehampton, opening onto the English Channel west of Brighton. From Littlehampton, you can leave the coastal road by taking bus no. 11, which runs between Littlehampton and Arundel hourly during the day. If you're dependent on public transportation, the Tourist Information Centre (see below) keeps an update on the possibilities.

If you're driving from London, follow the signs to Gatwick Airport and from there head south toward the coast along A29.

VISITOR INFORMATION   The **Tourist Information Centre,** 61 High St. (ℂ **01903/882268**), is open April through October, Monday through Friday from 9am to 5pm and on weekends from 10am to 5pm; off season Monday through Friday from 10am to 2:30pm and weekends from 10am to 2:30pm.

SEEING THE SIGHTS

Arundel Castle ★★   The ancestral home of the dukes of Norfolk, Arundel Castle is a much-restored mansion of considerable importance. Its legend is associated with some of the great families of England—the Fitzalans and the powerful Howards of Norfolk. This castle received worldwide exposure when it was chosen as the backdrop for *The Madness of King George* (it was "pretending" to be Windsor Castle in the film).

Arundel Castle has suffered destruction over the years, particularly during the civil war, when Cromwell's troops stormed its walls, perhaps in retaliation for the 14th earl of Arundel's (Thomas Howard) sizable contribution to Charles I. In the early 18th century, the castle had to be virtually rebuilt, and in late Victorian times it was remodeled and extensively restored again. Today it's filled with a valuable collection of antiques, along with an assortment of paintings by old masters, such as Van Dyck and Gainsborough.

Surrounding the castle, in the center off High Street, is a 1,100-acre park whose scenic highlight is Swanbourne Lake.

Mill Rd. ℂ 01903/883136. www.arundelcastle.org. Admission £9 ($14) adults, £7 ($11) seniors and students, £5.50 ($8.80) children 5–15, free for children 4 and under. Family ticket £25 ($39). Apr–Oct Sun–Fri noon–5pm; last admission 4:30pm. Closed Nov–Mar.

Arundel Cathedral   A Roman Catholic cathedral, the Cathedral of Our Lady and St. Philip Howard stands at the highest point in town. A. J. Hansom, inventor of the Hansom taxi, built it for the 15th duke of Norfolk. However, it was not consecrated as a cathedral until 1965. The interior includes the shrine of St. Philip Howard, featuring Sussex wrought-iron work.

On the street level, adjacent to rooms housing the tourist information office, is the **Heritage of Arundel Museum.** It displays memorabilia, antique costumes, and historic documents relating to the history of Arundel and its famous castle.

London Rd. ✆ **01903/882297**. www.arundelcathedral.org. Free admission, but donations appreciated. Daily 9:30am–dusk. From the town center, continue west from High St.

WHERE TO STAY IN THE AREA

Amberley Castle Hotel ★★ *Finds*   The best place for food and lodging is near the village of Amberley. Joy and Martin Cummings offer accommodations in a 14th-century castle with sections dating from the 12th century. Elizabeth I held the lease on this castle from 1588 to 1603, and Cromwell's forces attacked it during the civil war. Charles II visited the castle on two occasions. Each of the sumptuous rooms, all doubles, is named after a castle in Sussex; each has a generously sized private Jacuzzi bathroom with luxury toiletries and bathrobes. All rooms also have a video library. Bedrooms are the ultimate in English country-house luxury; you can choose from four-poster, twin four-poster, or brass double beds.

Amberley, near Arundel, W. Sussex BN18 9ND. ✆ **800/525-4800** in the U.S., or 01798/831992. Fax 01798/831998. www.amberleycastle.co.uk. 19 units. £155–£340 ($248–$544) double; £295–£325 ($472–$520) suite. AE, DC, MC, V. Take B2139 north of Arundel; the hotel is 2.5km (1½ miles) southwest of Amberley. **Amenities:** 2 restaurants; bike rental; concierge; room service; massage; dry cleaning. *In room:* TV/VCR, minibar, coffeemaker, hair dryer, trouser press.

Hilton Avisford Park ★   This is not your usual Hilton Hotel. Set in 89 acres of gardens and lovely parkland, it opens onto England's South Downs. Once it was the home of Baronet Montagu, admiral and friend of Lord Nelson. Now successfully converted into a hotel, it is completely modernized but still keeps some of the allure of its original construction. Bedrooms come in a range of styles, sizes, and designs, and are handsomely laid out each with a tiled bathroom. The hotel is also the best equipped in the area, especially if sports are part of your vacation. There is a first-class restaurant on-site.

Yapton Lane, Walberton, Arundel, W. Sussex BN18 9JJ. ✆ **01243/551215**. Fax 01243/552485. www.arundel.hilton.com. 139 units. Summer £210–£230 ($336–$368) double, £260 ($416) suite; off season £108–£128 ($173–$205) double, £158 ($253) suite. Lies 4.8km (3 miles) west of Arundel on B2132 (off A27). **Amenities:** Restaurant; bar; indoor pool; golf course; tennis court; fitness room; business center; room service; babysitting; laundry service. *In room:* TV w/pay movies, dataport, hair dryer, iron.

Norfolk Arms   A former coaching inn, the Norfolk Arms is on the main street just a short walk from the castle. It's the best place to stay if you want to be in the market town itself. The lounges and dining room are in the typically English country-inn style. The hotel has been restored with many modern amenities blending with the old architecture. The bedrooms are handsomely maintained and furnished, each with personal touches. Rooms vary considerably in size, from small to spacious; bathrooms are small. Some rooms lie in a separate modern wing overlooking the courtyard. Four bedrooms are large enough for small families.

22 High St., Arundel, W. Sussex BN18 9AD. ✆ **01903/882101**. Fax 01903/884275. www.forestdale.com. 34 units. £115–£125 ($184–$200) double. Children under 14 stay free when sharing room with two paying adults. Rates include breakfast. AE, DC, MC, V. **Amenities:** Restaurant; 2 bars; room service; laundry service. *In room:* TV, coffeemaker, hair dryer, trouser press.

Portreeves Acre   This modern, two-story house built by a local architect lies within a stone's throw of the ancient castle and rail station. Today the glass-and-brick edifice is the property of Charles and Pat Rogers. Double guest rooms are on the ground floor and have views of the flowering acre in back. Each bedroom is well organized and includes a small bathroom with a shower stall. The property is bordered on one side by the River Arun.

2 Causeway, Arundel, W. Sussex BN18 9JJ. ℂ 01903/883277. 3 units. £50 ($80) double. Rates include English breakfast. No credit cards. *In room:* TV, coffeemaker.

WHERE TO DINE

China Palace BEIJING/SZECHUAN   The most prominent Chinese restaurant in the region, it has an elaborately carved 17th-century ceiling imported by a former owner from a palace in Italy. Interior decorations include the artfully draped sails from a Chinese junk. It's located across the road from the crenellated fortifications surrounding Arundel's castle. The Beijing and Szechuan cuisine includes such classic dishes as Peking duck, king prawns Kung Po, and lobster with fresh ginger and spring onions.

67 High St. ℂ 01903/883702. Reservations recommended on weekends. Main courses £7–£8 ($11–$13); fixed-price 3-course dinner for 2 £37 ($59). AE, MC, V. Daily noon–2:15pm and 6pm–midnight.

Queens Room Restaurant ★★ ENGLISH/CONTINENTAL   No contest: The best cuisine around Arundel is served at the Amberley Castle Hotel (see above). The chef has raided England's culinary past for inspiration but gives his dishes modern interpretations. We especially admire his use of natural ingredients from the area—wild Southdown rabbit, lavender, lemon thyme, and nettles. The menu changes frequently, though the special menu of the day is always alluring. The gourmet Castle Cuisine menu is worth driving across Sussex to enjoy. One recent menu included poached halibut with smoky soy broth and roasted guinea fowl with sweet potato fondant. The intermediate course was a quince-and-gin water-rice. (Where else can you find that?) Desserts such as a warm gratin of orange and dark chocolate with Grand Marnier sabayon make a perfect finish. The staff is attentive and friendly, yet warmly informal, and there's a well-chosen wine list.

In the Amberley Castle Hotel, Amberley, near Arundel. ℂ 01798/831992. Reservations required. 3-course fixed-price dinner £36–£45 ($58–$72); 2-course lunch £16 ($25). AE, DC, MC, V. Daily noon–2pm and 7–9:30pm.

8 Brighton: London by the Sea ★★

84km (52 miles) S of London

Brighton was one of the first of the great seaside resorts of Europe. The Prince of Wales (later George IV), the original swinger who was to shape so much of its destiny, arrived in 1783; his presence and patronage gave it immediate status.

Fashionable dandies from London, including Beau Brummell, turned up. The construction business boomed as Brighton blossomed with charming and attractive town houses and well-planned squares and crescents. From the Prince Regent's title came the voguish word *Regency,* which was to characterize an era, but more specifically refers to the period between 1811 and 1820. Under Victoria, and despite the fact that she cut off her presence, Brighton continued to flourish.

But earlier in this century, as the English began to discover more glamorous spots on the Continent, Brighton lost much of its old *joie de vivre.* People began to call it "tatty," and it began to feature the usual run of fun-fair-type English seaside amusements. However, that state of affairs changed long ago, owing largely to the huge number of Londoners who moved in (some of whom now

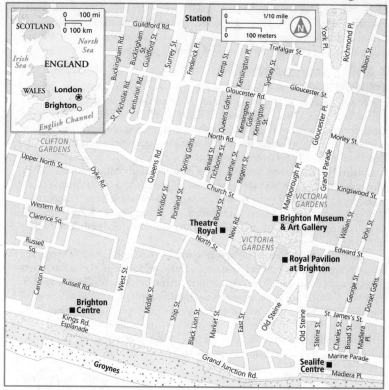

commute); the invasion has made Brighton increasingly lighthearted and sophisticated today. It now attracts a fair number of gay vacationers, and a beach east of town has been set aside for nude bathers (Britain's first such venture).

ESSENTIALS

GETTING THERE   Fast trains (41 a day) leave from Victoria or London Bridge Station and make the trip from London in 55 minutes. For rail information, call ℱ **0345/484950.** Buses from London's Victoria Coach Station take around 2 hours.

If you're driving, M23 (signposted from central London) leads to A23, which takes you into Brighton.

VISITOR INFORMATION   At the **Tourist Information Centre,** 10 Bartholomew Sq. (ℱ **0906/711-2555;** http://tourism.brighton.co.uk), opposite the town hall, you can make hotel reservations, reserve tickets for National Express coaches, and pick up a list of current events. It's open Monday through Friday from 9am to 5pm, and Saturday from 10am to 4pm. From March to October also open on Sundays from 10am to 4pm.

GETTING AROUND   The **Brighton Borough Transport** serves both Brighton and Hove with frequent and efficient service. Local fares are only £1 ($1.60), and free maps giving the company's routes are available at the Tourist Information Centre (see above). You can also call the company directly at ℱ **01273/886200.**

SPECIAL EVENTS   If you're here in May, the international **Brighton Festival,** the largest arts festival in England, features drama, literature, visual art, dance, and concerts ranging from classical to rock. A festival program is available annually in February for those who want to plan ahead.

A ROYAL AMUSEMENT

The Royal Pavilion at Brighton ★★★   Among royal residences in Europe, the Royal Pavilion at Brighton, a John Nash version of an Indian Moghul's palace, is unique. Ornate and exotic, it has been subjected over the years to the most devastating wit of English satirists and pundits, but today we can examine it more objectively as one of the most outstanding examples of the oriental tendencies of England's romantic movement.

Originally a farmhouse, a neoclassical villa was built on the site in 1787 by Henry Holland, but it no more resembled its present appearance than a caterpillar does a butterfly. By the time Nash had transformed it from a simple classical villa into an oriental fantasy, the prince regent had become King George IV, and the king and one of his mistresses, Lady Conyngham, lived in the palace until 1827.

A decade passed before Victoria, then queen, arrived in Brighton. Though she was to bring Albert and the children on a number of occasions, the monarch and Brighton just didn't mix. The very air of the resort seemed too flippant for her. By 1845, Victoria began packing, and the royal furniture was carted off. Its royal owners gone, the Pavilion was in serious peril of being torn down when, by a narrow vote, Brightonians agreed to purchase it. Gradually it was restored to its former splendor, enhanced in no small part by the return of much of its original furniture, including many items on loan from the queen. A new exhibit tours the Royal Pavilion Gardens.

Of exceptional interest is the domed **Banqueting Room,** with a chandelier of bronze dragons supporting lily-like glass globes. In the Great Kitchen, with its old revolving spits, is a collection of Wellington's pots and pans from his town house at Hyde Park Corner. In the **State Apartments,** particularly the domed salon, dragons wink at you, serpents entwine, and lacquered doors shine. The Music Room, with its scalloped ceiling, is a fantasy of water lilies, flying dragons, reptilian paintings, bamboo, silk, and satin.

In the first-floor gallery, look for Nash's views of the Pavilion in its elegant heyday. Other attractions include **Queen Victoria's Apartments,** beautifully re-created, and the impressively restored **South Galleries,** breakfast rooms for George IV's guests. Refreshments are available in the Queen Adelaide Tea Room, which has a balcony overlooking the Royal Pavilion Gardens.

🕐 01273/290900. www.royalpavilion.org.uk. Admission £5.80 ($9.30) adults, £4 ($6.40) seniors and students, £3.40 ($5.45) children ages 5–15, £15 ($24) family ticket, free for children 5 and under. Apr–Sept daily 9:30am–5:45pm; Oct–Mar daily 10am–5:15pm. Closed Dec 25–26.

OTHER ATTRACTIONS

Brighton Museum & Art Gallery ★   After a £10 million ($16 million) redevelopment, one of the great cultural attractions in the southeast of England has opened. In Victorian buildings opposite the Royal Pavilion, the museum is devoted to an eclectic collection of world art and artifacts, ranging from Salvador Dalí's "Mae West's Lips Sofa" to costumes worn at King George IV's coronation in 1821. Employing all the latest museum interpretative techniques, the museum is one of the most user-friendly outside London. The central gallery displays 20th-century decorative art, including furniture by Philippe Starck, works by Lalique and Bugatti, and a host of other luminaries. You'll see everything from Henry Willett's collection of 2,000 pieces of innovative porcelain to Shiro Kuramata's "How High the Moon Chair" from 1986 (it was inspired by the Duke Ellington jazz standard). The "Fashion & Style" Gallery draws upon Brighton's extensive collections of period costumes over the centuries. In the museum's World Art Collection, you'll find some 15,000 objects collected from the Americas, Africa, Asia, and the Pacific, ranging from Vietnamese water puppets to a black basalt George Washington bust by Wedgwood.

Royal Pavilion Gardens. © 01273/290900. Free admission. Tues 10am–7pm; Wed–Sat 10am–5pm; Sun 2–5pm.

SEASIDE AMUSEMENTS & ACTIVE PURSUITS

The beaches at Brighton aren't sandy; they're pebbly, and unfortunately, the waters are polluted. So, instead of swimming, most visitors to Brighton sunbathe, promenade along the boardwalk, play video arcade games, drink in local pubs and "caffs," and generally enjoy the sea air. Beachfront areas are more for the promenade crowd, which often consists of gay men and women.

Brighton is also the site of Britain's first officially designated clothing-optional beach, located a short walk west of the Brighton Marina. Local signs refer to it as simply "Nudist Beach." Telescombe Beach, mostly frequented by gay men and lesbians, lies 7.2km (4½ miles) to the east of the Palace Pier.

You can't miss the **Palace Pier,** a somewhat battered late Victorian iron structure jutting seaward toward France. Built between 1889 and 1899 and renovated during the early 1990s, it's lined with somewhat tacky concessions and a late-night crowd that's a bit more sinister than the one that frequents it during the day.

If you want to rent or charter a boat, stop by the **Brighton Marina,** at the intersection of A259 and King's Cliff Parade (© **01483/417782**). There's good fishing at the marina as well, but the breakwaters near Hove may be better because there aren't as many boats or swimmers in that area.

One of the best and most challenging 18-hole golf courses around is the **East Brighton Golf Club,** Roedean Road (© **01273/604838**). A less challenging 18-hole course is the **Hollingbury Park Golf Club,** Ditching Road (© **01273/ 552010**). Buses from the **Old Steine** are available to both courses.

An indoor pool, diving pool, learner's pool, solarium, and water slide are all available daily at the **Prince Regent Swimming Complex,** Church St. (© **01273/685692**).

If you enjoy wagering on the horses, the **Brighton Races** are held frequently between April and October at the **Brighton Racecourse,** Race Hill (© **01273/ 603580**). An admission fee of £8 to £15 ($13–$24) is charged.

SHOPPING

Mall rats head for **Churchill Square,** Brighton's spacious shopping center, which has major chain stores. The shopping center runs from Western Road to North Street (about 3.2km/2 miles long) and offers many inexpensive shops and stalls with great buys on everything from antiques to woolens. On Saturdays, there are many more antiques exhibits and sidewalk stalls.

Regent Arcade, which is located between East Street, Bartholomew Square, and Market Street, sells artwork, jewelry, and other gift items, as well as high-fashion clothing.

Everyone raves about the shopping on **The Lanes,** although you may find them too quaint. The Lanes are a close-knit section of alleyways off North Street in Brighton's Old Town; many of the present shops were formerly fishers' cottages.

The shopping is mostly for tourists, and, while you may fall for a few photo ops, you'll find that the nearby **North Laine**—between the Lanes and the train station—is the area for up-and-coming talent and for alternative retail. Just wander along a street called Kensington Gardens to get the whole effect. There are innumerable shops located in the Lanes that carry antique books and jewelry, and many boutiques are found in converted backyards on Duke Lane just off Ship Street. In the center of the Lanes is Brighton Square, which is ideal for relaxing or for people-watching near the fountain on one of the benches or from a cafe-bar.

On Sunday, Brighton has a good **flea market** in the parking lot of the train station. On the first Tuesday of each month there's the **Brighton Racecourse Antiques and Collectors Fair** (9am–3pm) with about 300 stalls.

There are many stores to visit at the Brighton Marina. **Leave It to Jeeves** (© **01273/818585**) has old photographs of the local area, illustrations, prints, and a complete framing service.

In addition to its malls and shopping complexes, Brighton also abounds in specialty shops. One of our favorites is the finest gift shop in Brighton, **The Pavilion Shop,** 425 Pavillion Building, Brighton (© **01273/292798**), next door to the Royal Pavilion. Here you can purchase many gift and home-furnishing items in the style of the design schools that created the look (from Regency to Victorian) at the Royal Pavilion. Also available are books, jams, needlepoint kits, notebooks, pencils, stencil kits, and other souvenirs. The latest British designers for women are showcased at a fashionable store, **Pussy,** 3A Kensington Gardens (© **01273/604861**).

WHERE TO STAY

Gay travelers should refer to "Brighton's Gay Scene," later in this section, for a selection of gay-friendly accommodations.

VERY EXPENSIVE

The Grand ✦✦✦   Brighton's premier hotel, the original Grand was constructed in 1864 and entertained some of the most eminent Victorians and Edwardians. This landmark was massively damaged in a 1984 terrorist attack directed at Margaret Thatcher and other key figures in the British government. Mrs. Thatcher narrowly escaped, though several of her colleagues were killed; entire sections of the hotel looked as if they had been hit by an air raid. The incident gave the present owners, De Vere Hotels, the challenge to create a new Grand, and frankly, the new one is better than the old. It's the most elegant Georgian re-creation in town.

You enter via a glassed-in conservatory and register in a grandiose public room, with soaring ceilings and elaborate moldings. The rooms, of a very high standard, are generally spacious with many extras, including hospitality trays and Sony Playstations. The sea-view rooms have minibars, and new beds and furniture; the deluxe rooms offer separate sitting rooms and views of the English Channel. "Romantic rooms" offer double whirlpool baths, and some rooms are equipped with additional facilities for travelers with disabilities. All standard rooms have been refurbished with new bathrooms.

King's Rd., Brighton, E. Sussex BN1 1FW. © 01273/224300. Fax 01273/224321. www.grandbrighton.co.uk. 200 units. £240–£345 ($384–$552) double; from £650 ($1,040) suite. Rates include English breakfast. AE, DC, MC, V. Parking £14 ($22). Bus: 1, 2, or 3. **Amenities:** Restaurant; bar; pool; spa with sauna; salon; room service; babysitting; laundry service; dry cleaning. *In room:* TV, minibar, coffeemaker, hair dryer, safe, trouser press.

Finds **Shelley's House: A Bygone Era**

One of the most exclusive hotels in England, **Alexander House,** Turners Hill, West Sussex RH10 4QD (© **01342/714914;** fax 01342/717328; www. alexanderhouse.co.uk), evokes a bygone era yet is imbued with modern comforts. Although secluded on its own grounds, it is hardly remote, lying just a 15-minute drive from Gatwick Airport and only 19km (12 miles) east of Brighton. In the 17th century the estate was owned by the family of the famous poet Percy Bysshe Shelley. All 15 guest rooms and 6 luxurious suites are designed with utter poshness—one four-poster was a gift of Napoleon, for example. Set on 135 acres of private gardens and parkland, the hotel also offers an award-winning restaurant known for its classic French and English cuisine. In a double the price is £185 ($296) or from £265 to £310 ($424–$496) in a suite.

Leave the M23 motorway at junction 10 and follow the signs for East Grinstead. At the second roundabout follow the signs for Turners Hill (B2028). Once in Turners Hill Village, turn left at the crossroads (B2110) to East Grinstead and Alexander House is on the left-hand side after approximately 2.4km (1½ miles).

Hilton Brighton Metropole ⭐ Originally built in 1889, with a handful of its rooms housed in a postwar addition, the Brighton Metropole is the largest hotel in Brighton and one of the city's top three or four hotels (though not as grand as the Grand). This hotel, with a central seafront location, often hosts big conferences. The recently refurbished rooms are comfortable and generous in size with roomy sitting areas. The spacious bathrooms include faux marble vanities.

106 King's Rd., Brighton, E. Sussex BN1 2FU. © **01273/775432.** Fax 01273/207764. www.stakis.co.uk. 334 units. £150–£230 ($240–$368) double; £210–£470 ($336–$752) suite. Rates include English breakfast. AE, DC, MC, V. Parking £7.50 ($12). Bus: 1, 2, or 3. **Amenities:** Restaurant; bar; pool; spa; room service; babysitting; laundry service; dry cleaning. *In room:* TV, dataport, minibar (in suites), coffeemaker, hair dryer, trouser press.

Old Ship Hotel ⭐ First used as an inn in 1559, this hotel, a favorite among conference groups, is the largest and best of Brighton's middle-priced choices. The place is proud of its pedigree and was once the site of royal gatherings and society balls. Most of the hotel's structure dates from the 1880s; despite many subsequent modernizations, it retains a sense of its old-time late Victorian origins. Nearly two-thirds of the rooms are nicely furnished, with modern bathrooms containing shower-tub combinations; the rest are still somewhat dowdy. The east wing has the most smartly furnished rooms. This may be Brighton's oldest hotel, but it has managed to stay abreast of the times in comfort. Try to stay for more than 1 night; prices drop if you do.

King's Rd., Brighton, E. Sussex BN1 1NR. © **01273/329001.** Fax 01273/820718. www.paramount-hotels. co.uk. 152 units. £175 ($280) double; £280 ($448) suite. Children under 12 stay free in parent's room. Rates include English breakfast. AE, DC, MC, V. Parking £15 ($24). Bus: 1, 2, or 3. **Amenities:** Restaurant; bar; room service; babysitting; dry cleaning. *In room:* TV, coffeemaker, hair dryer, iron, safe, trouser press.

Thistle Brighton ⭐⭐ This relatively modern hotel is one of the finest in the south of England, topped in Brighton only by the Grand. Rising from the seafront, just minutes from the Royal Pavilion, it has been luxuriously designed for maximum comfort. Rooms tend to be large but are often blandly decorated in a sort of international modern style. Each is exceptionally comfortable, with small sitting areas and long desks. Tile bathrooms come with shower-tub combinations, deluxe toiletries, and even rubber ducks to play with in your bath.

King's Rd., Brighton, E. Sussex BN1 2GS. © **01273/206700.** Fax 01273/820692. www.thistlehotels.com. 208 units. £125–£240 ($200–$384) double; £210–£314 ($336–$502) suite. Children under 17 stay free in parent's room. AE, DC, MC, V. Bus: 1, 2, or 3. **Amenities:** Restaurant; 2 bars; indoor pool; health club with spa; 24-hr. room service; babysitting; laundry service; dry cleaning. *In room:* A/C, TV, dataport, minibar, coffeemaker, iron, hair dryer, safe, trouser press.

MODERATE

Blanch House ★ *(Finds)* Is it a hotel or is it theater? This small hotel in a restored Georgian building is known for its very theatricalized theme rooms, ranging from Moroccan to "Snowstorm" to our favorite "The Decadence Suite." For those who got off on the movie of the same name, there is always "Boogie Nights." Either queen- or king-size beds have been installed, and each accommodation comes with a well-maintained private bathroom with shower. The bar is one of the hippest in Brighton where the competition is severe, and the on-site restaurant is a gastronomic delight with such offerings as seared pigeon breast with grilled salsify and butternut squash and a fresh pea and mint risotto with honeyed parsnip "pearls."

17 Atlingworth St., Brighton, E. Sussex BN2 1PL. © **01273/603504.** Fax 01273/689813. www.blanch house.co.uk. 12 units. £125–£150 ($200–$240) double; £250 ($400) suite. Rates include breakfast. MC, V. **Amenities:** Restaurant; bar. *In room:* TV, hair dryer, iron.

Nineteen ★ *(Finds)* Only a few minutes' walk from the beach, this rather stunning urban hotel lies close to the Brighton Pier. It's located in Kemptown, a rapidly gentrified and up-and-coming section of Brighton. The hotel is an oasis of pure white, its bedrooms filled with works by contemporary local artists. This artwork is all that breaks the pure white, that and slatted silver blinds and glass beds illuminated by blue lighting. That same subtle blue lighting bathes the rooms in a lovely glow. Everything here is as modern as tomorrow, including the state-of-the-art bathrooms. The comfortable beds are supported on glass brick platforms. Guests are invited to use the cellar kitchen to make their own snacks.

19 Broad St., Brighton, E. Sussex BN2 1TJ. © **01273/675529.** Fax 01273/675531. www.hotelnineteen.co.uk. 7 units. £95–£150 ($152–$240) double. Rates include breakfast. Minimum of 2 nights required for weekend bookings. MC, V. **Amenities:** Breakfast room; bar; room service. *In room:* TV, beverage maker, hair dryer.

Topps Hotel This cream-colored hotel enjoys a diagonal view of the sea from its position beside the sloping lawn of Regency Square. Each room is differently shaped and individually furnished. In 2000, the owners began a gradual refurbishment of all bedrooms. Except for the singles, most rooms have a fireplace. All units have well-kept bathrooms. Try for a room with a four-poster bed and private balcony opening to a view of the sea.

17 Regency Sq., Brighton, E. Sussex BN1 2FG. © **01273/729334.** Fax 01273/203679. toppshotel@aol.com. 15 units. £75–£84 ($120–$134) double. Rates include English breakfast. AE, DC, MC, V. Parking £9.20–£11 ($14–$16). Bus: 1, 2, 3, 5, or 6. **Amenities:** Room service; laundry service. *In room:* TV, minibar, coffeemaker, hair dryer, iron, safe, trouser press.

INEXPENSIVE

Paskins Hotel This well-run eco-friendly hotel is a short walk from the Palace Pier and Royal Pavilion. Rates depend on plumbing and furnishings, the most expensive units fitted with four-poster beds. Bedrooms are individually decorated with contemporary styling. Bathrooms, compact but tidily maintained, have shower stalls. Recent upgrading has made this one of the more charming B&Bs in Brighton. A friendly, informal atmosphere prevails; the freshly cooked award-winning English breakfast (vegetarians are specially catered to), served in a cozy room, is one of the best in town.

19 Charlotte St., Brighton, E. Sussex BN2 1AG. ℂ **01273/601203.** Fax 01273/621973. www.paskins.co.uk. 19 units, 16 with shower. £50–£65 ($80–$104) double without shower, £80–£95 ($128–$152) double with shower, £120 ($192) double with 4-poster bed. Children 10 and under sharing with 2 adults are charged £10 ($16). Rates include English breakfast. AE, DC, MC, V. Bus: 7 or 52. **Amenities:** Lounge. *In room:* TV, dataport, coffeemaker, hair dryer, trouser press.

Regency Hotel   This typical 1820 Regency town house, once the home of Jane, dowager duchess of Marlborough, and great-grandmother of Sir Winston Churchill, is a skillfully converted family-managed hotel with licensed bar and modern comforts. Many rooms enjoy window views across the square and out to the sea. Bedrooms are nonsmoking, though you can smoke in the lounge bar. Rooms come in a variety of shapes and sizes, but each is well furnished with such extras as bedside radios. Bathrooms are small but adequate, each with a shower stall. The Regency Suite has a half-tester bed (1840) and antique furniture, along with a huge bow window dressed with ceiling-to-floor swagged curtains and a balcony facing the sea and West Pier. The Regency is only a few minutes' walk from the Conference Center and an hour by train or car from Gatwick Airport.

28 Regency Sq., Brighton, E. Sussex BN1 2FH. ℂ **01273/202690.** Fax 01273/220438. www.regency brighton.co.uk. 13 units, 9 with shower, 1 suite with bathroom. £85 ($136) double without shower, £95 ($152) double with shower; £150 ($240) Regency suite with bathroom. Rates include English breakfast. AE, DC, MC, V. Parking £12 ($19). Bus: 1, 2, 3, 5, or 6. **Amenities:** Bar; lounge; room service; laundry service. *In room:* TV, coffeemaker, hair dryer.

IN NEARBY HOVE

The Dudley   Near the seafront in Hove, the Dudley is just a few blocks from the resort's bronze statue of Queen Victoria. Going up marble steps, you register within view of 18th-century antiques and oil portraits of Edwardian-era debutantes. The large, high-ceilinged public rooms emphasize the deeply comfortable chairs and the chandeliers. The bedrooms offer tall windows and conservatively stylish furniture. Bedrooms are usually midsize with walnut furnishings and brass lamps. Bathrooms are well appointed with a bidet, baths with marble basins, and heated towel racks. The hotel is currently renovating and upgrading some of its bedrooms and public areas.

Lansdowns Place, Hove, Brighton, E. Sussex BN3 1HQ. ℂ **01273/736266.** Fax 01273/729802. www.the dudleyhotel.co.uk. 72 units. £90–£100 ($144–$160) double. AE, DC, MC, V. Bus: 2 or 5. **Amenities:** Restaurant; bar; 24-hr. room service; babysitting; laundry service; dry cleaning. *In room:* TV, coffeemaker, hair dryer, iron, trouser press.

WHERE TO DINE

The **Mock Turtle Tea Shop,** 4 Pool Valley (ℂ **01273/327380**), is a small but busy tearoom that has many locals stopping by to gossip and take their tea. It offers only a few sandwiches, but the varieties of cakes, flapjacks, tea breads, and light, fluffy scones with homemade preserves are dead-on. Everything is made fresh daily. The most popular item is the scones with strawberry preserves or whipped cream. It also serves a wide variety of good teas.

EXPENSIVE

China Garden BEIJING/CANTONESE   The menu at the China Garden is large and satisfying. It may not be ready for London, and it's certainly pricey, but it's the brightest in town, with many classic dishes deftly handled by the kitchen staff. Dim sum (a popular luncheon choice) is offered only until 4pm. Try crispy sliced pork Szechuan-style, or Peking roast duck with pancakes.

88 Preston St. (in the town center off Western Rd.). ℭ **01273/325124.** Reservations recommended. Main courses £18–£35 ($29–$56); fixed-price menu from £18 ($29). AE, DC, MC, V. Mon–Tues noon–11pm; Wed–Sun noon–11:30pm. Closed Dec 25–26.

Old Ship Hotel Restaurant ENGLISH   A longtime favorite, the Old Ship Hotel Restaurant, in the center of town, enjoys an ideal location on the waterfront. When possible, locally caught fish is on the menu, from Dover sole to pan-fried red bream filet. Try such dishes as Magret duck breast, served sliced with shallot and orange confit and juniper and red currant jus. Vegetables that accompany the main dishes are always fresh and cooked "new style." Sometimes local dishes such as turkey from Sussex appear on the menu, but with a French sauce. The wine list is excellent. Stop in the adjoining pub for a before- or after-dinner drink.

In the Old Ship Hotel, King's Rd. ℭ **01273/329001.** Reservations recommended. Main courses £8–£13 ($13–$20). AE, DC, MC, V. Sun–Fri 12:30–2:30pm; daily 6–9:45pm. Bus: 1, 2, or 3.

One Paston Place ✸ FRENCH   Mark (the chef) and Nicole Emmerson offer a wisely limited menu based on the freshest of ingredients available at the market. You may begin with a delectable almond-coated quail and parsnip pancake, then move on to a savory anchovy-studded sea bass with grilled stuffed squid and a lemon-and-basil couscous. Vegetarian dishes are available on request. For dessert, try the sumptuous almond and amaretto soufflé with apricot coulis.

1 Paston Place (near the waterfront off King's Cliff). ℭ **01273/606933.** www.onepastonplace.co.uk. Reservations required. Main courses £21–£23 ($34–$37); fixed-price 2-course lunch £17 ($26); fixed-price 3-course lunch £21–£23 ($34–$37). AE, DC, MC, V. Tues–Sat 12:30–1:45pm and 7:30–9:45pm. Closed 2 weeks in Jan and 2 weeks in Aug.

MODERATE

English's Oyster Bar and Seafood Restaurant SEAFOOD   This popular seafood restaurant occupies a trio of very old fishermen's cottages. Owned and operated by the same family since the end of World War II, it sits in the center of town, near Brighton's bus station. For years, diners have enjoyed native oysters on the half shell, a hot seafood platter with hollandaise sauce and garlic butter, fried Dover sole, and fresh, locally caught plaice. The upstairs dining area incorporates murals depicting Edwardian dinner and theater scenes. In summer, guests can dine alfresco on the terrace.

29–31 East St. ℭ **01273/327980.** www.englishs.co.uk. Reservations recommended. Main courses £10–£20 ($16–$32). Weekly price-fixed menu £4–£10 ($6.40–$16). AE, DC, MC, V. Mon–Sat noon–10pm; Sun 12:30–9:30pm.

INEXPENSIVE

Brighton Rock Beach House ✸ *(Finds)*   Brighton grows hipper and hipper, the latest rage being a take on a Cape Cod beach bar, the type that JFK Jr. might have dropped in on in days of yore. This gay-friendly spot was inspired by the U.S. travels of its owner, Neil Woodcock. At this light, spacious, and airy bar, drinks are consumed at a glass-topped bar covering sand, driftwood, shells, and pebbles. The lunch also has a New England spin. Savor those old favorites such as a creamy clam chowder, a Boston meatloaf, a vegetable hotpot, and—get this—a savory lobster cheesecake. For dessert, the chef leaves Cape Cod heading south for a Key lime pie. The bar even has its own transport cafe: an old Jeep parked outside with a table in the back where patrons can sit and sip their drinks.

6 Rock Place. (C) 01273/601139. Reservations not needed. Main courses £6–£12 ($9.60–$19). Mon–Sat noon–11pm; Sun noon–10:30pm. Food daily 1–4pm.

Terre à Terre ★★ *Finds* VEGETARIAN/VEGAN   The finest vegetarian restaurant on the south coast of England, this is a truly outstanding choice even if you're a carnivore. You dine in a trio of spacious rooms in vivid colors, and everything has a bustling brasserie aura. Cooks roam the world for inspiration in the preparation of their delectable dishes. Sushi, couscous, pizza—it's all here and does it ever taste good, especially the selection of tapas. To give you an idea of what to expect, select as an appetizer a perfectly textured baked Spanish custard with a deliciously crisp and caramelized topping, adorned with a well-ripened passion fruit. Breads are Italian, and the house wine is organic French. Children's meals are available.

71 East St. (C) 01273/729051. Reservations recommended. Main courses £11–£12 ($17–$19). AE, DC, MC, V. Tues–Sun noon–10:30pm; Mon 6–10:30pm.

BRIGHTON AFTER DARK

Brighton offers lots of entertainment options. You can find out what's happening by picking up the local entertainment monthly, the *Punter,* and by looking for *What's On,* a single sheet of weekly events posted throughout the town.

There are two theaters that offer drama throughout the year: the **Theatre Royal,** New Road ((C) **01273/328488**), which has pre-London shows, and the **Gardner Arts Center** ((C) **01273/685861**), a modern theater-in-the-round, located on the campus of Sussex University, a few miles northeast of town in Falmer. Bigger concerts are held at **Brighton Centre,** Russell Road ((C) **0870/ 900-9100**), a 5,000-seat facility featuring mainly pop-music shows.

Nightclubs also abound. Cover charges range from free admission (most often on early or midweek nights) to £10 ($16), so call the clubs to see about admission fees and updates in their nightly schedules, which often vary from week to week or season to season.

The smartly dressed can find their groove at **Steamers,** King's Road ((C) **01273/775432**), located in the Metropole Hotel, which insists on stylish casual attire. **Creation,** West Street ((C) **01273/321628**), is a popular club that features Gay Night on Monday, and **The Escape Club,** 10 Marine Parade ((C) **01273/606906**), home to both gay and straight dancers, has two floors for dancing, and offers different music styles on different nights of the week.

One of the best hunting grounds for dance clubs is **Kingswest,** a King's Road complex that houses two clubs featuring a blend of techno, house, and disco. **Event II** ((C) **01273/732627**) sports more than £1 million worth of lighting and dance-floor gadgetry.

Gloucester, Gloucester Plaza ((C) **01273/699068**), has a variety of music through the week, from '70s and '80s music to alternative and groove. For a change of pace, visit **Casablanca,** Middle Street ((C) **01273/321817**), which features jazz with an international flavor.

Pubs are a good place to kick off the evening, especially the **Colonnade Bar,** New Road ((C) **01273/328728**), which has been serving drinks for more than

100 years. The pub gets a lot of theater business because of its proximity to the Theatre Royal. **Cricketers,** Black Lion Street (© **01273/329472**), is worth a stop because it's Brighton's oldest pub, parts of which date from 1549. Drinking lures them to **Fortune of War,** 157 King's Rd. (© **01273/205065**).

H. J. O'Neils, 27 Ship St. (© **01273/827621**), is an authentic Irish pub located at the top of the Lanes. A stop here will fortify you with traditional Irish pub grub, a creamy pint of Guinness, and a sound track of folk music. Of course, they make the best Irish stew in town.

BRIGHTON'S GAY SCENE

After London, Brighton has the most active gay scene in England. Aside from vacationers, it's home to gay retirees and executives who commute into central London by train. The town has always had a reputation for tolerance and humor, and according to the jaded owners of some of the town's 20 or so gay bars, there are more drag queens living within the local Regency town houses than virtually anywhere else in England.

But the gay scene here is a lot less glittery than in London. And don't assume that the south of England is as chic as the south of France. Its international reputation is growing, but despite that, gay Brighton remains thoroughly English, and at times, even a bit dowdy.

GAY-FRIENDLY PLACES TO STAY

Coward's Guest House   Originally built in 1807, this five-story Regency-era house is extremely well maintained. Inside, Jerry and his partner, Cyril (a cousin of the late playwright and bon vivant Noël Coward), welcome only gay men of all degrees of flamboyance. Don't expect any frills in the conservative, standard rooms, like those you may find in any modern hotel in Britain. It offers very few extras, though a number of gay bars and watering holes lie nearby.

12 Upper Rock Gardens, Brighton BN2 1QE. © 01273/692677. 8 units, 2 with shower. £55–£70 ($88–$112) double. Rates include full English breakfast. MC, V. *In room:* TV, coffeemaker.

New Europe   Hands-down, this is the largest, busiest, and most fun gay hotel in Brighton. First, it's a bona fide hotel, not a B&B as most of Brighton's other gay-friendly lodgings are. Unlike many of its competitors, it welcomes women, though very few of them tend to be comfortable. Because of the high jinks and raucousness that can float up from the bars below, rooms can be noisy, but are nonetheless comfortable, clean, and unfrilly. All units have well-kept bathrooms with showers. The staff is happy to camp it up for you before your arrival (adding balloons, champagne, flowers, and streamers), for a fee.

31–32 Marine Parade, Brighton BN2 1TR. © 01273/624462. Fax 01273/624575. www.legendsbar.co.uk. 30 units. £50–£70 ($80–$112) double. Rates include breakfast. AE, DC, MC, V. **Amenities:** 2 bars. *In room:* TV, coffeemaker.

GAY NIGHTLIFE

A complete, up-to-date roster of the local gay bars is available in any copy of **G-Scene** magazine (© **01273/749947**), distributed free in gay hotels and bars throughout the south of England.

See also "Brighton After Dark," above, for a few popular dance clubs.

Doctor Brighton's Bar, 16 Kings Rd., The Seafront (© **01273/328765**), is the largest and most consistently reliable choice. The staff expends great energy on welcoming all members of the gay community into its premises. In their words, "We get everyone from 18-year-old designer queens to 50-year-old leather queens, and they, along with all their friends and relatives, are welcome."

Originally built around 1750, with a checkered past that includes stints as a smuggler's haven and an abortion clinic, it also has more history, and more of the feel of an old-time Victorian pub than any of its competitors. It's open Monday through Saturday from 11am to 11pm, Sunday from noon to 10:30pm. Because there's no real lesbian bar in town, gay women tend to congregate at Doctor Brighton's.

Two of the town's busiest and most flamboyant gay bars, **Legends** and **Schwarz,** lie within the previously recommended New Europe Hotel. The one with the longer hours is Legends, a pubby, clubby bar with a view of the sea that's open to the public daily from noon to 11pm, and to residents of the New Europe Hotel and their guests to 5am. Legends features cross-dressing cabarets three times a week (Tues and Thurs at 9pm, Sun afternoons at 2:30pm), when tweedy-looking English matrons and diaphanous Edwardian vamps are portrayed with loads of tongue-in-cheek satire and humor. Schwarz is a cellar-level denim-and-leather joint that does everything it can to encourage its patrons to wear some kind of uniform. Schwarz is open only Friday and Saturday from 10pm to 2am, and charges a £4 to £6 ($6.40–$9.60) cover.

The Marlborough, 4 Princes St. (© **01273/570028**), has been a staple on the scene for years. Set across from the Royal Pavilion, this is a Victorian-style pub with a cabaret theater on its second floor. It remains popular with the gay and, to a lesser degree, straight communities. A changing roster of lesbian performance art and both gay and straight cabaret are presented in the second-floor theater.

7

The South

You're in Hampshire and Dorset, two shires jealously guarded by the English as special rural treasures. Everybody knows of Southampton and Bournemouth, but less known is the hilly countryside farther inland. You can travel through endless lanes and discover tiny villages and thatched cottages untouched by the industrial invasion.

Jane Austen wrote of Hampshire's firmly middle-class inhabitants, all doggedly convinced that Hampshire was the greatest place on earth. Her six novels, including *Pride and Prejudice* and *Sense and Sensibility,* earned her a permanent place among the pantheon of 19th-century writers and unexpected popularity among modern film directors and producers. Her books provide an insight into the manners and mores of the English who soon established a powerful empire. You can visit her grave in **Winchester Cathedral** and the house where she lived, **Chawton Cottage.**

Hampshire encompasses the South Downs, the Isle of Wight (Victoria's favorite retreat), and the naval city of **Portsmouth.** More than 90,000 acres of the New Forest were preserved by William the Conqueror as a private hunting ground, and even today this vast woodland and heath is ideal for walking and exploring. Although Hampshire is filled with many places of interest, for our purposes we've concentrated on two major areas: **Southampton,** for convenience, and **Winchester,** for history.

Dorset is Thomas Hardy country. Some of its towns and villages, although altered considerably, are still recognizable from his descriptions. "The last of the great Victorians," as he was called, died in 1928 at age 88. His tomb occupies a position of honor in Westminster Abbey.

One of England's smallest shires, Dorset encompasses the old seaport of **Poole** in the east and **Lyme Regis** (known to Jane Austen) in the west. Dorset is a southwestern county and borders the English Channel. It's known for its cows, and Dorset butter is served at many an afternoon tea. This is mainly a land of farms and pastures, with plenty of sandy heaths and chalky downs.

The most prominent tourist center of Dorset is the Victorian seaside resort of **Bournemouth.** If you don't stay here, you can try a number of Dorset's other seaports, villages, and country towns; we mostly stick to the areas along the impressive coastline. Dorset, as the frugal English might tell you, is full of bargains.

Where to stay? You'll find the most hotels, but not the greatest charm, at the seaside resort of Bournemouth. (More intriguing than Bournemouth is the much smaller Lyme Regis, with its famed seaside promenade, the Cobb, a favorite of Jane Austen and a setting for *The French Lieutenant's Woman.*) If you're interested in things maritime, opt for Portsmouth, the premier port of the south and the home of HMS *Victory,* Nelson's flagship. For the history buff and Jane Austen fans, it's Winchester, the ancient capital of England, with a cathedral built by William the Conqueror. Winchester also makes a good base for exploring the countryside.

The best beaches are at Bournemouth, set among pines with sandy beaches and fine coastal views, and Chesil Beach, a 32km (20-mile) long bank of shingle running from Abbottsbury to the Isle of Portland—great for beachcombing. However, the most natural spectacle is New Forest itself, 375 sq. km (145 sq. miles) of heath and woodland, once the hunting ground of Norman kings.

Most people agree that the West Country, a loose geographical term, begins at **Salisbury,** with its Early English cathedral that has a 123m (404-ft.) pinnacle. Nearby is **Stonehenge,** England's oldest prehistoric monument. (Both Stonehenge and Salisbury are in Wiltshire.) When you cross into Wiltshire, you'll be entering a country of chalky, grassy uplands and rolling plains. Much of the shire is agricultural, and a large part is pastureland.

1 Winchester ★ ★

116km (72 miles) SW of London; 19km (12 miles) N of Southampton

The most historic city in all of Hampshire, Winchester is big on legends, because it's associated with King Arthur and the Knights of the Round Table. In the Great Hall, which is all that remains of Winchester Castle, a round oak table, with space for King Arthur and his 24 knights, is attached to the wall, but all that spells is undocumented romance. What is known, however, is that when the Saxons ruled the ancient kingdom of Wessex, Winchester was the capital.

The city is also linked with King Alfred, who is believed to have been crowned here and is honored today by a statue. The Danish conqueror Canute came this way, too, as did the king he ousted, Ethelred the Unready (Canute got his wife, Emma, in the bargain).

Of course, Winchester is a mecca for Jane Austen fans. You can visit her grave in Winchester Cathedral (Emma Thompson did, while working on her adapted screenplay of *Sense and Sensibility*), as well as Chawton Cottage, Jane Austen's house, which is 24km (15 miles) east of Winchester.

Its past glory but a memory, Winchester is essentially a market town today, lying on the downs along the Itchen River. Although Winchester hypes its ancient past, the modern world has arrived, as evidenced by the fast food, reggae music, and the cheap retail-clothing stores that mar its otherwise perfect High Street.

ESSENTIALS

GETTING THERE   Frequent daily train service runs from London's Waterloo Station to Winchester. The trip takes 1½ hours. For rail information, call ✆ 0845/748-4950. Arrivals are at Winchester Station, Station Hill, northwest of the city center. **National Express** buses leaving from London's Victoria Coach Station depart regularly for Winchester during the day. The trip takes 2 hours. Call ✆ 020/7529-2000 for schedules and information.

If you're driving, from Southampton drive north on the A335; from London, take the M3 motorway southwest.

VISITOR INFORMATION   The **Tourist Information Centre,** at the Winchester Guildhall, The Broadway (✆ 01962/840500; www.visitwinchester. com), is open from 10am to 5pm Monday through Saturday. Beginning in May and lasting through October, guided walking tours are conducted for £3 ($4.80)

per person, departing from this tourist center. Hours are October through May, Monday through Saturday from 10am to 5pm; June through September, Monday through Saturday from 9:30am to 6pm and Sunday from 11am to 4pm.

EXPLORING THE AREA

The Hospital of St. Cross ★★ The hospital was founded in 1132 and is the oldest charitable institution in the entire country. It was established by Henri du Blois, the grandson of William the Conqueror, as a link for social care and to supply life's necessities to the local poor and famished travelers. It continues the tradition of providing refreshments to visitors. Simply stop at the Porter's Lodge for a Wayfarer's Dole and you'll receive some bread and ale. St. Cross is set in the beautiful scenery that inspired Keats and Trollope, and is still the home of 25 brothers, whose residence is on one side of the historic landmark.

Cross Rd. ☏ **01962/851375.** Admissions £2 ($3.20). May–Sept daily 9:30am–5pm; off season daily 10:30am–3:30pm.

Winchester Cathedral ★★★ For centuries, this has been one of the great churches of England. The present building, the longest medieval cathedral in Britain, dates from 1079, and its Norman heritage is still evident. When a Saxon church stood on this spot, St. Swithun, bishop of Winchester and tutor to young King Alfred, suggested modestly that he be buried outside. Following his subsequent indoor burial, it rained for 40 days. The legend lives on: Just ask a resident of Winchester what will happen if it rains on St. Swithun's Day, July 15, and you'll get a prediction of rain for 40 days.

In the present building, the nave, with its two aisles, is most impressive, as are the *chantries* (chapels), the *reredos* (late-15th-century ornamental screens), and the elaborately carved choir stalls. Jane Austen is buried here; her grave is marked with a commemorative plaque. There are also chests containing the bones of many Saxon kings and the remains of the Viking conqueror Canute and his wife, Emma, in the presbytery. The son of William the Conqueror, William Rufus (who reigned as William II), was also buried at the cathedral.

The library houses Bishop Morley's 17th-century book collection and an exhibition room contains the 12th-century Winchester Bible. The Triforium shows sculpture, woodwork, and metalwork from 11 centuries and affords magnificent views over the rest of the cathedral.

The Close. ☏ **01962/857200.** Free admission to the cathedral, but £3.50 ($5.60) donation requested. Admission to library and Triforium Gallery £1 ($1.60) adults, 50p (80¢) children. Free guided tours year-round 10am–3pm hourly. Crypt is often flooded during winter, but part may be seen from a viewing platform. Library and Triforium Gallery Easter–Oct Mon 2–4:30pm, Tues–Sat 11am–4:30pm; Nov–Dec Wed and Sat 11am–3:30pm; Jan–Easter Sat 11am–3:30pm.

Winchester College ★ Winchester College was founded by William of Wykeham, bishop of Winchester and chancellor to Richard II, and was first occupied in 1394. Its buildings have been in continuous use for 600 years. The structures vary from Victorian Tudor Gothic to the more modern trimmings of the New Hall designed in 1961. The Chapel Hall, kitchens, and the Founder's Cloister all date back to the 14th century. In the 17th century buildings were added on the south side, including a schoolroom constructed between 1683 and 1687.

73 Kings Gate. ☏ **01962/621209.** . Admission £2.50 ($4). Mon–Sat 10am–noon; Mon, Wed, Fri and Sun 2–3:15pm.

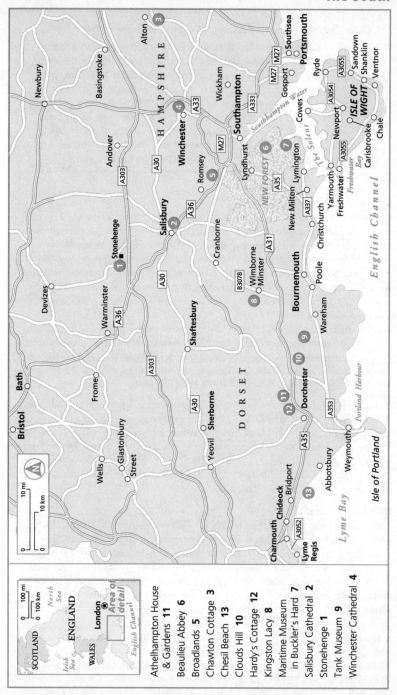

The South

Alton

Newbury

Basingstoke

H A M P S H I R E

Wickham

Andover

A303

A30

Winchester **4** A33

Southampton

Southsea
Portsmouth

M27 M27 Gosport

Ryde

A3055 Sandown
Shanklin
Ventnor

ISLE OF
WIGHT

Newport
A3054

Carisbrooke
Chale

Stonehenge

A36

Salisbury **2**

A36

Cranborne

Romsey **5**

M27

Lyndhurst

NEW FOREST **6** **7**

A35

New Milton Lymington

A337

Christchurch

Cowes

A3055 Freshwater

Yarmouth
Freshwater
Bay

The Solent

Southhampton Water

English Channel

Devizes

Warminster

A36

A30

A303

Shaftesbury

Wimborne
Minster **8**

B3078

A31

Bournemouth

Poole

Wareham

Portland Harbour

Bath

Frome

A303

Sherborne

A30

D O R S E T

9

10

11 Dorchester

12

A353

A35

Weymouth

Isle of Portland

Bristol

Glastonbury

Wells Street

Yeovil

Charmouth Chidsock

Bridport

Abbotsbury

Lyme Bay

13

A3052

Lyme
Regis

10 mi
10 km

N

SCOTLAND

ENGLAND

WALES

London
*Area of
detail*

North
Sea

Irish
Sea

English Channel

100 mi
100 km

Athelhampton House
& Gardens **11**

Beaulieu Abbey **6**

Broadlands **5**

Chawton Cottage **3**

Chesil Beach **13**

Clouds Hill **10**

Hardy's Cottage **12**

Kingston Lacy **8**

Maritime Museum
in Buckler's Hard **7**

Salisbury Cathedral **2**

Stonehenge **1**

Tank Museum **9**

Winchester Cathedral **4**

249

Finds **Rambling and Fishing the South Downs Way**

For a day of rambling through the countryside, try strolling part of **South Downs Way,** a 159km (99-mile) trail from Winchester to Eastbourne; **Clarendon Way,** a 38km (24-mile) path from Winchester to Salisbury; or **Itchen Way,** a beautiful riverside trail from near Cheriton to Southampton.

If you prefer casting your rod to a ramble, Winchester and the surrounding area is by far one of the best places to fish in all of England, especially for trout. Try your hand at any of the nearby rivers including the Rivers Itchen, Test, Meon, Dever, and Avon. The Tourist Information Centre (see above) will provide complete details on the best spots.

OUTSIDE OF WINCHESTER

Chawton Cottage ★   You can see where Jane Austen spent the last 7½ years of her life, her most productive period. In the unpretentious but pleasant cottage is the table on which she penned new versions of three of her books and wrote three more, including *Emma.* You can also see the rector's George III mahogany bookcase and a silhouette likeness of the Reverend Austen presenting his son to the Knights. In this cottage, Jane Austen became ill in 1816 with what would have been diagnosed by the middle of the 19th century as Addison's disease. She died in July 1817.

The grounds feature an attractive garden where you can picnic and an old bake house with Austen's donkey cart. A bookshop stocks new and secondhand books.

Chawton. © **01420/83262.** Admission £4 ($6.40) adults, £3 ($4.80) students and seniors, 50p (80¢) children 8–18. Mar–Nov daily 11am–4pm; Dec–Feb Sat–Sun 11am–4pm. Closed Dec 25–26. 1.5km (1 mile) southwest of Alton off A31 and B3006, 24km (15 miles) east of Winchester.

SHOPPING   Fill up those empty suitcases you brought over at **Cadogan,** 30–31 The Square (© **01962/877399**). They've got an upscale and stylish selection of British clothing for both men and women. For a unique piece of jewelry by one of the most acclaimed designers of today, stroll into **Carol Darby Jewellery,** 23 Little Minster St. (© **01962/867671**). The oldest book dealer in town is **P&G Wells,** 11 College St. (© **01926/852016**) with new releases and secondhand fiction and nonfiction.

WHERE TO STAY

Lainston House ★★★   The beauty of this fine, restored William-and-Mary redbrick manor house strikes visitors as they approach via a long, curving, tree-lined drive. It's situated on 63 acres of rolling land and linked with the name Lainston in the *Domesday Book.* Elegance is keynote inside the stately main house, where panoramically big suites are located. Other rooms, less spacious but also comfortable and harmoniously furnished, are in a nearby 1990 annex. Bathrooms are well equipped, with robes, and deluxe toiletries; some have two-person tubs and separate tubs and showers. The better units have large dressing areas and walk-in closets. The latest block of beautifully appointed rooms is a series of six converted stables.

Sparsholt, Winchester, Hampshire SO21 2LT. © **01962/863588.** Fax 01962/776672. www.exclusivehotels. co.uk. 50 units. £155–£325 ($248–$520) double; £500 ($800) suite. AE, DC, MC, V. Take B3420 2.5km (1½ miles) northwest of Winchester. **Amenities:** Restaurant; bar; 2 tennis courts; health club; concierge; room service; babysitting; laundry service; dry cleaning. *In room:* TV, minibar, hair dryer, safe, trouser press.

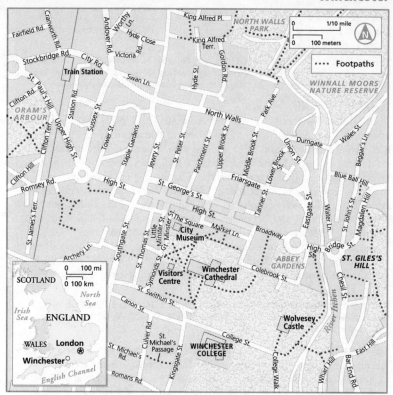

The Winchester Royal Hotel

This fine hotel is a comfortable choice. Built at the end of the 17th century as a private house, it was used by Belgian nuns as a convent for 50 years before being turned into a hotel, quickly becoming the center of the city's social life. Only a few minutes' walk from the cathedral, it still enjoys a secluded position. A modern extension overlooks gardens, and all rooms have traditional English styling. Bedrooms in the main house are more traditional than those in the modern wing, but each accommodation is well appointed. All rooms have well-kept bathrooms.

St. Peter St., Winchester, Hampshire SO23 8BS. ⓒ **800/528-1234** in the U.S., or 01962/840840. Fax 01962/841582. www.marstonhotels.com. 75 units. £132 ($211) double; £182 ($291) suite. Rates include English breakfast. AE, DC, MC, V. **Amenities:** Restaurant; bar; room service; babysitting; laundry service; dry cleaning. *In room:* TV, coffeemaker, hair dryer, trouser press.

Wykeham Arms ★ *Finds*

Our longtime favorite in Winchester, it lies behind a 200-year-old brick facade in the historic center of town, near the cathedral. Rooms are traditionally furnished with antiques or reproductions and such touches as fresh flowers and baskets of potpourri. Most of the bedrooms are a bit small but attractively appointed. Six rooms were recently added in a 16th-century building that faces the original hotel. The annex has the most luxurious accommodations; the rooms are more spacious. The large modern bathrooms are well equipped. A large suite with cozy fire-warmed sitting room and upstairs bedroom is also available. Overlooking the Winchester College Chapel, these rooms have the same amenities as the original rooms. *Note:* The hotel does not accept children under 14 as guests.

75 Kingsgate St., Winchester, Hampshire SO23 9PE. © **01962/853834.** Fax 01962/854411. 14 units. £90 ($144) double in original building; £98 ($156) double in extension; £120 ($192) suite. Rates include English breakfast. AE, DC, MC, V. **Amenities:** Restaurant; bar. *In room:* TV, minibar, coffeemaker, hair dryer.

WHERE TO DINE

Hotel du Vin & Bistro ⭐ *Value* ENGLISH/CONTINENTAL   This inn offers both food and lodging, bringing a touch of chic to Winchester. It's a town-house hotel that dates from 1715 and has a walled garden. Gerard Basset and Robin Hutson learned their lessons well at exclusive Chewton Glen (p. 263) before embarking on their own enterprise. The chef, Gareth Longhurst, delivers the finest food in Winchester today. The bistro food is excellent and a good value. The menu always features regional ingredients: Try the Torbay sole filet served with spinach and potato galette, with a mushroom, white-wine, and cream sauce. Basset has collected the finest wine list in the county.

You can stay overnight in one of 23 rooms decorated with a wine theme. The comfortable rooms have good beds, antiques, TVs, and state-of-the-art bathrooms with shower-tub combination, costing from £105 to £205 ($168–$328).

14 Southgate St., Winchester, Hampshire SO23 9EF. © **01962/841414.** Fax 01962/842458. www.hotel duvin.com. Reservations recommended. Main courses £15–£16 ($23–$26). AE, DC, MC, V. Daily noon–1:45pm and 7–9:45pm.

Old Chesil Rectory ⭐⭐⭐ MODERN ENGLISH   One of the finest restaurants in Hampshire, the 15th-century building, restored over the years, is aglow with half-timbered architecture and whitewashed panels. Philip and Catherine Storey love white; white candles, white flowers, and white table linen create a lovely mood for dining. The kitchen turns out refined versions of classic English dishes, made lighter for more modern and discerning palates. The menu is adjusted seasonally to take advantage of regional produce. For example, a perfectly flavored and delicately balanced wild mushroom risotto appears in autumn, and a fresh asparagus greets the spring. Ever had Jerusalem artichoke soup with smoked haddock? It's addictive, and you'll want the recipe. Philip believes in "weddings" in the kitchen—for example, veal loin is mated with liver or pork with classic black pudding. Roasted brill with wild mushrooms and onion compote is one of the most richly textured dishes we've enjoyed here. Desserts are made here, including such offerings as chocolate tart with coffee anglaise.

1 Chesil St. © **01962/851555.** Reservations required. Fixed-price lunch £18 ($29) for 2 courses, £22 ($35) for 3 courses; fixed-price dinner £35 ($56) for 2 courses, £40 ($64) for 3 courses. DC, MC, V. Tues–Sat noon–3pm and 7pm–midnight.

WINCHESTER AFTER DARK

The place to go is **The Porthouse,** Upper Brook Street (© **01962/869397**), a pub-cum-nightclub, sprawling across three floors. Different nights have different themes, from karaoke to retro music from the 1960s to the 1980s. On Friday, the 25-plus crowd takes over. The only cover, ranging from £3 to £5 ($4.80–$8), is charged on Thursday, Friday, and Saturday nights after 9pm. A ground-floor pub offers lunch.

2 Portsmouth ⋆ & Southsea

121km (75 miles) SW of London; 31km (19 miles) SE of Southampton

Virginia, New Hampshire, and even Ohio may have a Portsmouth, but the fore-runner of them all is the old port and naval base on the Hampshire coast, seat of the British navy for 500 years. German bombers in World War II leveled the city, hitting about 90% of its buildings. But the seaport was rebuilt admirably and now aggressively promotes its military attractions. It draws visitors inter-ested in the nautical history of England as well as World War II buffs.

Its maritime associations are known around the world. From Sally Port, the most interesting district in the Old Town, countless naval heroes have embarked to fight England's battles. That was certainly true on June 6, 1944, when Allied troops set sail to invade occupied France.

Southsea, adjoining Portsmouth, is a popular seaside resort with fine sands, lush gardens, bright lights, and a host of vacation attractions. Many historic monuments can be seen along the stretches of open space, where you can walk on the Clarence Esplanade, look out on the Solent Channel, and view the busy shipping activities of Portsmouth Harbour.

ESSENTIALS

GETTING THERE Trains from London's Waterloo Station stop at Portsmouth and Southsea Station frequently throughout the day. The trip takes 2½ hours. Call ℭ **0845/748-4950.**

National Express coaches operating out of London's Victoria Coach Station make the run to Portsmouth and Southsea every 2 hours during the day. The trip takes 2 hours and 45 minutes. Call ℭ **020/7529-2000** for information and schedules.

If you're driving from London's ring road, drive south on A3.

VISITOR INFORMATION The **Tourist Information Centre,** at The Hard in Portsmouth (ℭ **02392/826722**), is open daily April through September from 9:30am to 5:15pm, and October through March daily from 9:30am to 5:15pm.

EXPLORING PORTSMOUTH & SOUTHSEA

You might want to begin your tour on the Southsea front, where you can see a number of **naval monuments.** These include the big anchor from Nelson's ship *Victory,* plus a commemoration of the officers and men of HMS *Shannon* for heroism in the Indian mutiny. An obelisk with a naval crown honors the mem-ory of the crew of HMS *Chesapeake,* and a massive column, the Royal Naval Memorial, honors those lost at sea in the two world wars. A shaft is also dedi-cated to men killed in the Crimean War. There are also commemorations of those who fell victim to yellow fever in Queen Victoria's service in Sierra Leone and Jamaica.

MARITIME ATTRACTIONS IN PORTSMOUTH

You can buy a ticket that admits you to four attractions: HMS *Victory,* the *Mary Rose,* the HMS *Warrior 1860,* and the Royal Naval Museum. It costs £13.75 ($22) for adults, £11 ($18) for seniors, and £8.90 ($14) for children ages 5 to 16.

HMS *Victory* ★★★ Of major interest is Lord Nelson's flagship, a 104-gun, first-rate ship that is the oldest commissioned warship in the world, launched

May 7, 1765. It earned its fame on October 21, 1805, in the Battle of Trafalgar, when the English scored a victory over the combined Spanish and French fleets. It was in this battle that Lord Nelson lost his life. The flagship, after being taken to Gibraltar for repairs, returned to Portsmouth with Nelson's body on board (he was later buried at St. Paul's in London).

1–7 College Rd., in Portsmouth Naval Base. ⓒ 023/9286-1533. www.flagship.org.uk. See above for admission prices. Apr–Oct daily 10am–5:30pm; Nov–Mar daily 10am–5pm. Closed Dec 25. Use the entrance to the Portsmouth Naval Base through Victory Gate and follow the signs.

The Mary Rose Ship Hall and Exhibition ⚝

The *Mary Rose,* flagship of the fleet of King Henry VIII's wooden men-of-war, sank in the Solent Channel in 1545 in full view of the king. In 1982, Prince Charles watched the *Mary Rose* break the water's surface after more than 4 centuries on the ocean floor, not exactly in shipshape condition, but surprisingly well preserved nonetheless. Now the remains are on view, but the hull must be kept permanently wet.

The hull and more than 20,000 items brought up by divers constitute one of England's major archaeological discoveries. On display are the almost-complete equipment of the ship's barber-surgeon, with cabin saws, knives, ointments, and plaster all ready for use; long bows and arrows, some still in shooting order; carpenters' tools; leather jackets; and some fine lace and silk. Close to the Ship Hall is the *Mary Rose* Exhibition, where artifacts recovered from the ship are stored, featuring an audiovisual theater and spectacular two-deck reconstruction of a segment of the ship, including the original guns. A display with sound effects recalls the sinking of the vessel.

College Rd., Portsmouth Naval Base. ⓒ 023/9275-0521. www.flagship.org.uk. See above for admission prices. Apr–Oct daily 10am–5:30pm; Nov–Mar daily 10am–5pm. Closed Dec 25. Use the entrance to the Portsmouth Naval Base through Victory Gate and follow the signs.

Royal Naval Museum ⚝

The museum is next to Nelson's flagship, HMS *Victory,* and the *Mary Rose,* in the heart of Portsmouth's historic naval dockyard. The only museum in Britain devoted exclusively to the general history of the Royal Navy, it houses relics of Nelson and his associates, together with unique collections of ship models, naval ceramics, figureheads, medals, uniforms, weapons, and other memorabilia. Special displays feature "The Rise of the Royal Navy" and "HMS *Victory* and the Campaign of Trafalgar."

In the dockyard, Portsmouth Naval Base. ⓒ 023/9272-7562. See above for admission prices. Apr–Oct daily 10am–5:30pm; Nov–Mar daily 10am–5pm.

Royal Navy Submarine Museum

Cross Portsmouth Harbour by one of the ferries that bustles back and forth all day to Gosport. Some departures go directly from the station pontoon to HMS *Alliance* for a visit to the submarine museum, which traces the history of underwater warfare and life from the earliest days to the present nuclear age. Within the refurbished historical and nuclear galleries, the principal exhibit is HMS *Alliance,* and after a brief audiovisual presentation, visitors are guided through the boat by ex-submariners. Midget submarines, not all of them English, including an X-craft, can be seen outside the museum.

Haslar Jetty Rd., Gosport. ⓒ 023/9252-9217. www.rnsubmus.co.uk. Admission £4 ($6.40) adults, £2.75 ($4.40) children and seniors, £11 ($18) family. Apr–Oct daily 10am–5:30pm; Nov–Mar daily 10am–4:30pm. Last tour 1 hr. before closing. Closed Dec 25. Bus: 19. Ferry: From The Hard in Portsmouth to Gosport.

MORE ATTRACTIONS

Charles Dickens's Birthplace Museum

The 1804 small terrace house, in which the famous novelist was born in 1812 and lived for a short time, has been

restored and furnished to illustrate the middle-class taste of the southwestern counties of the early 19th century.

393 Old Commercial Rd. (near the center of Portsmouth, off Mile End Rd./M275 and off Kingston Rd.). ✆ **023/9282-7261.** Admission £2.50 ($4) adults, £1.80 ($2.90) seniors, £1.50 ($2.40) students, free for children 12 and under. Daily 10am–5:30pm. Closed Nov–Mar.

D-Day Museum   Next door to Southsea Castle, this museum, devoted to the Normandy landings, displays the Overlord Embroidery, which shows the complete story of Operation Overlord. The appliquéd embroidery, believed to be the largest of its kind (82m/272 ft. long and 1m/3 ft. high), was designed by Sandra Lawrence and took 20 women of the Royal School of Needlework 5 years to complete. A special audiovisual program includes displays such as reconstructions of various stages of the mission. You'll see a Sherman tank in working order, jeeps, field guns, and even a DUKW (popularly called a Duck), an incredibly useful amphibious truck that operates on land and sea.

Clarence Esplanade (on the seafront), Southsea. ✆ **023/9282-7261.** www.ddaymuseum.co.uk. Admission £5 ($8) adults, £3.75 ($6) seniors, £3 ($4.80) children and students, £13 ($21) family, free for children under 5. Apr–Sept 10am–5:30pm; Oct–Mar 10am–5pm. Closed Dec 24–26.

Portchester Castle   On a spit of land on the northern side of Portsmouth Harbour are the remains of this castle, plus a Norman church. Built in the late 12th century by King Henry II, the castle is set inside the impressive walls of a 3rd-century Roman fort built as a defense against Saxon pirates when this was

---

Finds The Best Walks, The Best Picnics

Southsea Common, between the coast and houses of the area, known in the 13th century as Froddington Heath and used for army bivouacs, is a picnic and play area today. Walks can be taken along Ladies' Mile if you tend to shy away from the common's tennis courts, skateboard and roller-skating rinks, and other activities.

---

the northwestern frontier of the declining Roman Empire. By the end of the 14th century, Richard II had modernized the castle and had made it a secure small palace. Among the ruins are the hall, kitchen, and great chamber of this palace.

On the south side of Portchester off A27 (between Portsmouth and Southampton, near Fareham). © 023/9237-8291. Admission £3 ($4.80) adults, £2.30 ($3.70) seniors, £1.50 ($2.40) children 5–15, free for children 4 and under. Apr–Oct daily 10am–6pm; Nov–Mar daily 10am–4pm.

Southsea Castle A fortress built of stones from Beaulieu Abbey in 1545 as part of King Henry VIII's coastal defense plan, the castle is now a museum. Exhibits trace the development of Portsmouth as a military stronghold, as well as the naval history and the archaeology of the area. The castle is in the center of Southsea near the D-Day Museum.

Clarence Esplanade, Southsea. © 023/9282-7261. www.southseacastle.co.uk. Admission £2.50 ($4) adults, £1.80 ($2.90) seniors, £1.50 ($2.40) students and children ages 13–18, £6.50 ($10) family, free for children 12 and under. Apr–Sept daily 10am–5:30pm. Closed Nov–March.

WHERE TO STAY

Portsmouth Marriott Located a short walk from the ferryboat terminal for ships arriving from Le Havre and Cherbourg in France, this 7-story building towers above everything in its district. Originally built as a Holiday Inn in 1980, Marriott acquired it in 1992, and refurbished it in 1997. The bedrooms, comfortable and modern, have the aura of a quality motel. All the small bathrooms come with plenty of toiletries.

North Harbour, Cosham (3km/2 miles southeast of Portsmouth's center, at the junction of A3 and M27), Portsmouth, Hampshire PO6 4SH. © 800/228-9290 in the U.S. and Canada, or 023/9238-3151. Fax 0870/400-7385. www.marriott.com. 172 units. £78–£150 ($125–$240) double. AE, DC, MC, V. Take the bus marked Cosham from Portsmouth's center. **Amenities:** Restaurant; bar; pool; health club; spa bath; sauna; solarium; room service; laundry service; dry cleaning. *In room:* A/C, TV, dataport, minibar, coffeemaker, hair dryer, safe, trouser press.

Royal Beach Hotel The balconied Victorian facade of this hotel, directly east of Southside Common, rises above the boulevard running beside the sea. Restored by its owners, the hotel's interior decor ranges from contemporary to full-curtained traditional, depending on the room. However, it doesn't stack up with the nearby Marriott. Each of the bedrooms has been renovated with built-in furniture. The bathrooms are small but well maintained.

South Parade, Southsea, Portsmouth, Hampshire PO4 ORN. © 023/9273-1281. Fax 023/9281-7572. www.royalbeachhotel.co.uk. 115 units. £80 ($128) double; £150 ($240) suite. Rates include English breakfast. Children under 6 stay free in parent's room. AE, DC, MC, V. **Amenities:** Restaurant; bar; room service; laundry service; dry cleaning. *In room:* TV, coffeemaker, hair dryer, safe, trouser press.

Westfield Hall *Finds* In the resort of Southsea, two early-20th-century homes near the water have been turned into a hotel with a certain charm and character. One of the most inviting and most comfortable of the little family-run hotels in the area, this highly commendable establishment offers a warm welcome and beautifully maintained and comfortably furnished bedrooms, each with a full bath with tub or shower or else a private shower only. Many accommodations are graced with large bay windows. Guests enjoy the use of three lounges.

65 Festing Rd., Southsea, Portsmouth, Hampshire PO4 0NQ. © 023/9282-6971. Fax 023/9287-0200. 25 units. £78–£90 ($125–$144) double. AE, DC, MC, V. **Amenities:** Restaurant. *In room:* TV, dataport, coffeemaker, hair dryer.

IN NEARBY WICKHAM

The Old House Hotel ★ *Finds*   A handsome early Georgian (1715) structure, the Old House is surrounded by low, medieval timber structures around the square. The hotel has undergone a classic refurbishment, giving it the look of a proud English country house. The paneled rooms on the ground and first floors of the hotel contrast with the beamed bedrooms on the upper floors, once the servants' quarters. All nine bedrooms have period furniture, many pieces original antiques. All the prettily decorated bedrooms have warm, comfortable beds.

The Square, Wickham, Fareham, Hampshire PO17 5JG. © 01329/833049. Fax 01329/833672. 9 units. £90 ($144) double. Rates include continental breakfast. AE, MC, V. Bus no. 69 from Fareham. Head 14km (9 miles) west from Portsmouth on M27; exit at number 10. The village is 3km (2 miles) north of the junction of B2177 and A32. **Amenities:** Restaurant; bar; guest lounge. *In room:* TV, coffeemaker.

WHERE TO DINE

Bistro Montparnasse ★ BRITISH/FRENCH   Serving the best food in the area, this bistro offers a welcoming atmosphere and background music to get you in the mood. Fresh produce is delicately prepared in the well-rounded selection of dishes here. The cooking is familiar fare but well executed. Although the menu changes, you might try the roast rack of lamb with a walnut and herb crust. Homemade breads and fresh fish, caught locally, are the specialties.

103 Palmerston Rd., Southsea. © 023/9281-6754. Reservations recommended. 2-course lunch £14 ($22); 3-course lunch £18 ($29); 2-course dinner £20 ($32); 3-course dinner £26 ($41). MC, V. Tues–Sat noon–2pm and 7–10pm. Southsea bus. Follow the signs to the D-Day Museum, and at the museum turn left and go to the next intersection; the restaurant is on the right.

3 Southampton

140km (87 miles) SW of London; 259km (161 miles) E of Plymouth

For many North Americans, England's number-one passenger port, home base for the soon-to-be-retired *QE2* and the brand new *Queen Mary II,* is the gateway to Britain. Southampton is a city of sterile, wide boulevards, parks, and dreary shopping centers. During World War II, some 31.5 million men set out from here (in World War I, more than twice that number), and Southampton was repeatedly bombed, destroying its old character. Today, the rather shoddy downtown section represents what happens when a city's architectural focus is timeliness rather than grace. There's not much to see in the city itself, but there's a lot on the outskirts. If you're spending time in Southampton between ships, you may want to explore some of the major sights of Hampshire nearby (New Forest, Winchester, the Isle of Wight, and Bournemouth, in neighboring Dorset).

Its supremacy as a port dates from Saxon times when the Danish conqueror Canute was proclaimed king here in 1017. Southampton was especially important to the Normans and helped them keep in touch with their homeland. Its denizens were responsible for bringing in the bubonic plague, which wiped out a quarter of the English population in the mid–14th century. On the Western Esplanade is a memorial tower to the Pilgrims, who set out on their voyage to the New World from Southampton on August 15, 1620. Both the *Mayflower* and the *Speedwell* sailed from here but were forced by storm damages to put in at Plymouth, where the *Speedwell* was abandoned.

In the spring of 1912, the "unsinkable" White Star liner, the 46,000-ton *Titanic,* sailed from Southampton on its maiden voyage. Shortly before midnight on April 14, while steaming at 22 knots, the great ship collided with an iceberg and sank to the bottom of the icy Atlantic. The sinking of the *Titanic,* subject of the Oscar-winning box office smash of 1997, is one of the greatest disasters in maritime history, as 1,513 people perished.

ESSENTIALS

GETTING THERE Trains depart from London's Waterloo Station several times daily. The trip takes just over an hour. Call ✆ **0845/722-5225.**

National Express operates buses on hourly departures from London's Victoria Coach Station. The trip takes 2½ hours. Call ✆ **020/7529-2000** for information and schedules.

If you're driving, take M3 southwest from London.

VISITOR INFORMATION The **Tourist Information Centre,** 9 Civic Centre Rd. (✆ **023/8022-1106**), is open Monday through Wednesday and Friday and Saturday from 9am to 5pm, and Thursday from 10am to 5pm; closed Good Friday and Easter Monday, Christmas, December 26, and New Year's Day.

EXPLORING SOUTHAMPTON

Ocean Village and the town quay on Southampton's waterfront are bustling with activity and are filled with shops, restaurants, and entertainment possibilities.

West Quay Retail Park, the first phase of Southampton's £250 million ($400 million) Esplanade development, has become a major hub for shoppers. The central shopping area is pedestrian-only, and tree- and shrub-filled planters provide a backdrop for summer flowers and hanging baskets. You can sit and listen to the *buskers* (street entertainers) or perhaps watch the world parade from one of the nearby restaurants or pavement cafes. For a vast array of shops, try the **Town Quay** (✆ **023/8023-4397**), the **Canutes Pavilion** at Ocean Village (✆ **023/8022-8353**), or **Southampton Market** (✆ **023/8061-6181**).

The most intriguing shopping on the outskirts is at the **Whitchurch Silk Mill,** 28 Winchester St., Whitchurch (✆ **01256/892065**). Admission is £3.75 ($6) for adults, £3.25 ($5.20) for seniors, £1.75 ($2.80) for children, and £9 ($14) for a family ticket. Visitors flock to this working mill, located in colorful surroundings on the River Test. Historic looms weave silk here as in the olden days, and visitors can observe water-wheel-powered machinery, warping, and winding. The gift shop sells silk on the roll, ties, scarves, handkerchiefs, jewelry, and souvenirs. Hours are Tuesday through Sunday from 10:30am to 5pm.

Value **Those Shoes Are Made for Walking**

City tour guides offer a wide range of **free guided walks** and regular **city bus tours.** Free guided walks of the town are offered throughout the year on Sunday and Monday at 10:30am and June through September twice daily at 10:30am and 2:30pm. Tours start at Bargate. For details of various boat or bus trips that might be offered at the time of your visit, check with the tourist office.

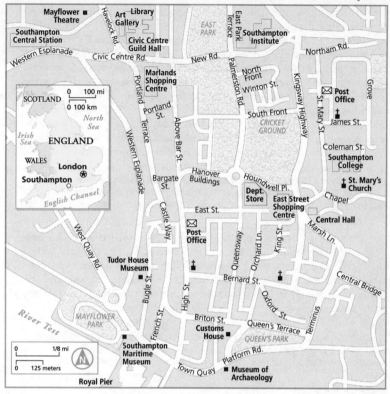

Southampton Maritime Museum

Southampton Maritime Museum   This museum is housed in an impressive 14th-century stone warehouse with a magnificent timber ceiling. Its exhibits trace the history of Southampton, including a model of the docks as they looked at their peak in the 1930s. Also displayed are artifacts from some of the great ocean liners whose home port was Southampton.

The most famous of these liners was the fabled *Titanic,* which was partially built in Southampton and sailed from this port on its fateful, fatal voyage. James Cameron's box office smash has increased traffic to the relatively small *Titanic* exhibit at the museum. It features photographs of the crew (many of whom were from Southampton) and passengers, as well as letters from passengers, Capt. Edward Smith's sword, and a video with a dated interview with the fallen captain plus modern interviews with survivors.

The Wool House, Town Quay. *Ⓒ* **023/8022-3941.** Free admission. Apr–Sept Tues–Fri 10am–1pm, Sat 10am–1pm and 2–4pm, Sun 2–5pm; Oct–Mar Tues–Sat 10am–4pm, Sun 2–4pm. Closed bank holiday Mon, Christmas, and Boxing Day.

WHERE TO STAY

Finding a place to stay right in Southampton isn't as important as it used to be. Very few ships now arrive, and the places to stay just outside the city are generally better. For more choices in the area, refer to "Where to Stay Around The New Forest," below.

De Vere Grand Harbour Hotel ★★ If you must stay in town and you can afford it, this is the most comfortable place to be. Completed in 1994, the five-story structure, sheathed in granite and possessing a dramatically tilted glass facade, is the most exciting hotel to open in Southampton since World War II. Some 30 of the brightly painted bedrooms have air-conditioning. Most of the bathrooms are filled with luxuries, including tubs, separate walk-in showers, and granite vanities. Bathroom extras include both hand-held and overhead showers, and robes and rubber ducks in the executive rooms only. Bedrooms range from midsize to spacious, with a pair of armchairs and traditional polished wood surfaces, plus snug beds. Some rooms offer balconies; some have waterfront views. About nine of the rooms are equipped for persons with limited mobility.

W. Quay Rd., Southampton, Hampshire SO15 1AG. ℭ 023/8063-3033. Fax 023/8063-3066. www.devere grandharbour.co.uk. 172 units. £185–£215 ($296–$344) double; £330 ($528) suite. Rates include English breakfast. AE, DC, MC, V. **Amenities:** 2 restaurants; 2 bars; pool; health club; spa bath; steam room; sauna; room service; babysitting; laundry service; dry cleaning. *In room:* TV, minibar, coffeemaker, hair dryer, safe, trouser press.

The Dolphin ★ If you want tradition, this is your best choice. This bow-windowed Georgian coaching house in the center of the city was Jane Austen's choice, and Thackeray's, too. Even Queen Victoria visited via her horse-drawn carriage. The rooms vary widely in size but are generally spacious and well equipped. Bedrooms are being refurbished as part of an ongoing restoration program. Three rooms are large enough for families. Each unit comes with a bathroom, which for the most part contain shower-tub combinations.

35 High St., Southampton, Hampshire SO14 2HN. ℭ 023/8033-9955. Fax 023/8033-3650. 73 units. £80 ($128) double; £90 ($144) suite. Children under 16 stay free in parent's room. AE, DC, MC, V. Bus: 2, 6, or 8. **Amenities:** Restaurant; bar; room service; laundry service; dry cleaning. *In room:* TV, coffeemaker, hair dryer, trouser press.

WHERE TO DINE

Ennio's ITALIAN This is the best restaurant in Southampton, but in this gastronomic wasteland that's not saying much. Scottish-born architect John Geddes designed Ennio's as a warehouse and boatyard. At the time, the sea came up to its foundations, and boats could unload their cargoes directly into its cavernous interior. Today, though the exterior is rustic and weathered, its interior is stylish. The restaurant's wine cellar, with 600-year-old walls, once part of the medieval wall that ringed Southampton, has an extensive list of Italian wines as well as some French and New World labels. Meals feature typical pastas, as well as farm-fresh venison. Freshly caught fish are listed daily on a blackboard. The restaurant, informal wine bar, and brasserie are much favored by local businesspeople at lunch and by relatively informal diners in the evening.

Town Quay Rd. ℭ 023/8022-1159. Reservations recommended. Main courses £8.50–£15 ($14–$24). AE, MC, V. Mon–Sat noon–2pm and 6:30–10:30pm. Bus: 2, 6, or 8.

Langleys Bistro CONTINENTAL/BRITISH Since its establishment in 1994, this restaurant continues to grow in popularity. It deserves its local fame. In these tastefully decorated precincts, you get a relaxed bistro ambience with posters and mirrors of Southampton's heyday in the steamship era decorating the walls. The location is convenient, lying near Southampton's dockland. Under the whir of summer ceiling fans, you can peruse the menu. Dishes come in generous portions, and chefs show a certain skill. Roasted sea bass filets appear enticingly on a bed of green beans topped with prawns and toasted almonds. One of the best poultry dishes is a breast of chicken married to some intriguing flavors such as fresh tarragon, shallots, and West Country ham. The chefs also turn out premiere Scottish filet of beef with a Roquefort and bacon sauce or else with wild mushrooms and cognac. The staff has a small bar area for an aperitif, where you can also sample some of the finest cognacs, ports, and champagne.

10–11 Bedrord Place. ⓒ 023/8022-4551. Reservations required. Main courses £13–£17 ($21–$26); 2-course set lunch £13 ($21); 3-course set lunch £17 ($27); 2-course set dinner £17 ($27); 3-course set dinner £21 ($33). AE, DC, MC, V. Mon–Fri noon–2pm; Mon–Sat 6:30–10:30pm.

The Red Lion ✦ ENGLISH   One of the few architectural jewels to have survived World War II, this pub traces its roots to the 13th century (as a Norman cellar), but its Henry V Court Room, with high ceilings and rafters, is from Tudor times. The room was the scene of the trial of the earl of Cambridge and his accomplices, Thomas Grey and Lord Scrope, who were condemned to death for plotting against the life of the king in 1415. Today, the Court Room is adorned with coats-of-arms of the noblemen who were peers of the condemned trio. The Red Lion is a fascinating place for a drink and a chat. Typical pub snacks are served in the bar, whereas in the somewhat more formal restaurant section, the well-seasoned specialties include an array of steaks (including sirloin), stews, roasts, and fish platters.

55 High St. ⓒ 023/8033-3595. Main courses £6.50–£13 ($10–$21); pub snacks £3–£4.95 ($4.80–$7.90). MC, V. Daily 11am–2:30pm and 7–9:30pm. Pub: Daily noon–11:30pm. Bus: 1, 2, 6, or 8.

A SIDE TRIP TO BROADLANDS: HOME OF THE LATE EARL OF MOUNTBATTEN

Broadlands ✦   Broadlands was the home of the late Earl Mountbatten of Burma, who was assassinated in 1979. Earl Mountbatten, who has been called "the last war hero," lent the house to his nephew, Prince Philip, and Princess Elizabeth as a honeymoon haven in 1947, and in 1981, Prince Charles and Princess Diana spent the first nights of their honeymoon here.

Broadlands is now owned by Lord Romsey, Earl Mountbatten's eldest grandson, who has created a fine exhibition and audiovisual show that depicts the highlights of his grandfather's brilliant career as a sailor and statesman. The house, originally linked to Romsey Abbey, was transformed into an elegant Palladian mansion by Capability Brown and Henry Holland. Brown landscaped the parkland and grounds.

13km (8 miles) northwest of Southampton in Romsey, on A31. ⓒ 01794/505010. www.broadlands.net. Admission £5.95 ($9.50) adults, £4.95 ($7.90) students and seniors, £3.95 ($6.30) children 12–16, free for children under 12. June 10–Sept 1 daily noon–5:30pm.

4 The New Forest ✦/✦

153km (95 miles) SW of London; 16km (10 miles) W of Southampton

Encompassing about 92,000 acres, the New Forest is a large tract created by William the Conqueror, who laid out the limits of this then-private hunting preserve. Successful poachers faced the executioner if they were caught, and those who hunted but missed had their hands severed. Henry VIII loved to hunt deer in the New Forest, but he also saw an opportunity to build up the British naval fleet by supplying oak and other hard timbers to the boatyards at Buckler's Hard on the Beaulieu River.

Today, you can visit the old shipyards and also the museum, with its fine models of men-of-war, pictures of the old yard, and dioramas showing the building of these ships, their construction, and their launching. It took 2,000 trees to construct one man-of-war. A motorway cuts through the area, and the once-thick forest has groves of oak trees separated by wide tracts of common land that's grazed by ponies and cows, hummocked with heather and gorse, and frequented by rabbits. But away from the main roads, where signs warn of wild ponies and deer, you'll find a private world of peace and quiet.

ESSENTIALS

GETTING THERE   On the train, go to Southampton (see "Essentials," in section 3), where rail connections can be made to a few centers in the New Forest. Where the train leaves off, bus connections can be made to all the towns and many villages. Southampton and Lymington have the best bus connections to New Forest villages.

If you're driving, head west from Southampton on A35.

VISITOR INFORMATION   The information office is at the **New Forest Visitor Centre,** Main Car Park, Lyndhurst (© **023/8028-2269**), which is open daily from 10am to 6pm April through September, and daily from 10am to 5pm October through March.

SEEING THE SIGHTS

Beaulieu Abbey-Palace House 🌟🌟   The abbey and house, as well as the National Motor Museum, are on the property of Lord Montagu of Beaulieu (pronounced *Bew*-ley). A Cistercian abbey was founded on this spot in 1204, and you can explore its ruins. The Palace House, surrounded by gardens, was the gatehouse of the abbey before it was converted into a private residence in 1538.

National Motor Museum 🌟🌟, one of the best and most comprehensive automotive museums in the world, with more than 250 vehicles, is on the grounds and is open to the public. Famous autos include four land-speed record holders, among them Donald Campbell's Bluebird. The collection was built around Lord Montagu's family collection of vintage cars. A special feature is called "Wheels." In a darkened environment, visitors travel in specially designed "pods" that carry up to two adults and one child along a silent electric track. Moving at a predetermined but variable speed, each pod can rotate almost 360 degrees. Seated in these, you'll view displays (with sound and visual effects) spanning 100 years of motor development without the fatigue of standing in line. For further information, contact the visitor reception manager at the John Montagu Building (© **01590/612345**).

Beaulieu, on B3056 in the New Forest (8km/5 miles southeast of Lyndhurst and 23km/14 miles west of Southampton). © **01590/612345**. www.beaulieu.co.uk. Admission £12 ($19) adults, £10 ($16) seniors and students, £6.95 ($11) children 4–16, free for children 3 and under, £34 ($54) family (2 adults and up to 3 children). May–Sept daily 10am–6pm; Oct–Apr daily 10am–5pm. Closed Dec 25. Buses run from the Lymington bus station Mon–Sat; Sun you'll need a taxi or car.

Maritime Museum 🌟   Buckler's Hard, a historic 18th-century village 4km (2½ miles) from Beaulieu on the banks of the River Beaulieu, is where ships for Nelson's fleet were built, including the admiral's favorite, *Agamemnon,* as well as *Eurylus* and *Swiftsure.* The Maritime Museum highlights the village's shipbuilding history as well as Henry Adams, master shipbuilder; Nelson's favorite ship; Buckler's Hard and Trafalgar; and models of Sir Francis Chichester's yachts and items of his equipment. The cottage exhibits re-create 18th-century life in Buckler's Hard—stroll through the New Inn of 1793 and a shipwright's cottage of the same period or look in on the family of a poor laborer.

The walk back to Beaulieu, 4km (2½ miles) on the riverbank, is well marked through the woodlands. During the summer, you can take a 20-minute cruise on the River Beaulieu in the present *Swiftsure,* an all-weather catamaran cruiser.

Buckler's Hard. © **01590/616203.** Admission £5 ($8) adults, £4.50 ($7.20) students, seniors, and children. Easter–Sept daily 10am–5pm; Oct–Easter daily 11am–4pm.

WHERE TO STAY AROUND THE NEW FOREST

Balmer Lawn Hotel ★ *Kids* This hotel lies about a 10-minute walk from Brockenhurst's center in a woodland location. Built as a private home during the 17th century, it was later enlarged into an imposing hunting lodge. During World War II, it was a military hospital. (In the past decade, many overnight guests have spotted the ghost of one of the white-coated doctors with his stethoscope, roaming the hotel's 1st floor.) The hotel has a pleasant and humorous staff (which refers to the ghost as "Dr. Eric"). A good range of bedrooms, in all shapes and sizes, all have an individual character; bathrooms are small. Request a room with a view of the forest. There are three family bedrooms, and children up to 16 stay free in their parent's room.

Lyndhurst Rd., Brockenhurst, Hampshire SO42 7ZB. © **01590/623116.** Fax 01590/623864. www.blh.co.uk. 55 units. £80 ($128) double. Rates include English breakfast. AE, DC, MC, V. Take A337 (Lyndhurst–Lymington Rd.) about 1km (½ mile) outside Brockenhurst. **Amenities:** Restaurant; bar; 2 pools (1 indoor; 1 outdoor); tennis court; health club; Jacuzzi; sauna; room service; laundry service; dry cleaning; 2 squash courts. *In room:* TV, coffeemaker, hair dryer, trouser press.

Carey's Manor ★ This manor house dates from Charles II, who used to come here when it was a hunting lodge. Greatly expanded in 1888, the building became a country hotel in the 1930s. Much improved in recent years, the old house is still filled with character, possessing mellow, timeworn paneling and a carved oak staircase. Each bedroom, whether in the restored main building or in the garden wing, has a bathroom with a shower-tub combination and bathrobes. Most rooms have balconies. Six rooms contain an old-fashioned four-poster bed, but whether your room does or not, it will still have a firm bed offering cozy comfort. *Note:* Children under 10 are not accepted as guests.

Lyndhurst Rd., Brockenhurst, Hampshire SO42 7RH. © **01590/623551.** Fax 01590/622799. www. careysmanor.co.uk. 79 units. £149–£179 ($238–$286) double; £199–£219 ($318–$350) suite. Rates include English breakfast. AE, DC, MC, V. From the town center, head toward Lyndhurst on A337. **Amenities:** Restaurant; bar; pool; health club; sauna; solarium; salon; room service; laundry service; dry cleaning. *In room:* TV, coffeemaker, hair dryer, trouser press.

Chewton Glen Hotel ★★★ *Finds* A gracious country house on the fringe of the New Forest, Chewton Glen, within easy reach of Southampton and Bournemouth, is the finest place to stay in southwest England (with princely rates to match). In the old house, the magnificent staircase leads to well-furnished double rooms opening onto views of the spacious grounds. In the new wing, you will find yourself on the ground level, with French doors opening onto your own private patio. Accommodations vary widely, coming in different shapes, sizes, and periods, but each is equipped with a double or twin bed. Attic accommodations and some of the newly refurbished rooms contain air conditioners. The best accommodations are the "Croquet Lawn Rooms," as they open onto the greens and have big private balconies or terraces. The bathrooms in all rooms are luxurious, with hair dryers, deluxe toiletries, and separate power showers in large stalls. Log fires burn and fresh flowers add fragrance; the garden sweeps down to a stream and then to rhododendron woods.

Christchurch Rd., New Milton, Hampshire BH25 6QS. ℂ **01425/275341.** Fax 01425/283045. www.chewton glen.com. 59 units. £305–£365 ($488–$584) double; £505–£720 ($808–$1,152) suite. AE, DC, MC, V. After leaving the village of Walkford, follow signs off A35 (New Milton–Christchurch Rd.), through parkland. **Amenities:** Restaurant; bar; 2 pools; 9-hole golf course; 4 tennis courts; health club, Jacuzzi; sauna; room service, laundry service; dry cleaning. *In room:* TV, minibar, hair dryer, safe, trouser press.

Country House Hotel New Park Manor ★

This former royal hunting lodge, dating from the days of William the Conqueror and a favorite of Charles II, is the only hotel in the New Forest itself. Although it's now a modern country hotel, the original rooms have been preserved, including such features as beams and in some rooms open log fires. Since its purchase in 1998 by the Countess von Essen, the hotel has been much improved, and each room is individually furnished and has a small bathroom. A romantic honeymoon suite comes complete with a four-poster bed. Most rooms have a view overlooking the forest.

Lyndhurst Rd., Brockenhurst, Hampshire SO42 7QH. ℂ **01590/623467.** Fax 01590/622268. www.newpark manorhotel.co.uk. 24 units. £110–£190 ($176–$304) double. Rates include English breakfast. AE, DC, MC, V. Head 3km (2 miles) north off A337 (Lyndhurst-Brockenhurst Rd.) toward the New Forest Show Ground. **Amenities:** Restaurant; bar; limited room service; babysitting; laundry service; dry cleaning; horseback riding. *In room:* TV, coffeemaker, hair dryer, trouser press.

The Crown Hotel

Though the present building is only 100 years old, a hostelry has been here on the main street of the New Forest village of Lyndhurst for centuries. For generations, it has been a favorite of visitors to the New Forest, who delight in its gardens, where afternoon tea is served, or its roaring fireplace in winter. Bedrooms are most inviting; each is furnished in the classic tradition of an English country house, with features such as four-poster beds in many cases. Some rooms are more modern, with padded headboards and fine furnishings. A few of the superior rooms can accommodate families. The small bathrooms are modern and well appointed.

9 High St., Lyndhurst, Hampshire SO43 7NF. ℂ **023/8028-2922.** Fax 023/8028-2751. www.crownhotel-lyndhurst.co.uk. 38 units. £135 ($216) double; £175 ($280) suite. Rates include English breakfast. Children under 16 stay free in parent's room. AE, DC, MC, V. Bus: 56 or 56A. Exit M27 at Junction 1 and drive 5km (3 miles) due south. **Amenities:** Restaurant; bar; room service; babysitting (by arrangement); laundry service; dry cleaning. *In room:* TV, dataport, coffeemaker, hair dryer, trouser press.

Master Builders House Hotel ★★

This hotel is located about 4km (2½ miles) south of Beaulieu, in the historic maritime village of Buckler's Hard. This 17th-century redbrick building was once the home of master shipbuilder Henry Adams, who incorporated many of his shipbuilding techniques into the construction of this lovely old house. Views from some of the bedrooms overlook the grass-covered slipways that, centuries ago, were used to ease newly built ocean vessels into the calm waters of the nearby river.

Most of the hotel's comfortable and conservatively decorated accommodations are in a modern wing, built after World War II. If you like the creaky floorboards and charm of old-world England, opt for one of the six old-fashioned bedrooms in the main house. If you want a greater number of luxuries and more space, select a room in the purpose-built annex; these are plainer but better equipped. Bedrooms vary in size and shape; most are equipped with king-size beds and contain such thoughtful touches as mineral water and bathrobes. Bathrooms are small but offer luxury toiletries, tubs, and power showers.

Buckler's Hard, Beaulieu, Hampshire SO42 7XB. ℂ **01590/616253.** Fax 01590/616297. www.themaster builders.co.uk. 25 units. £165–£215 ($264–$344) double. Rates include English breakfast. Half board £200–£255 ($320–$408) double. AE, MC, V. **Amenities:** Restaurant; bar; room service; laundry service; dry cleaning. *In room:* TV, hair dryer.

Montagu Arms ★★ This hotel has an interesting history; it was built in the 1700s to supply food and drink to the laborers who hauled salt from the nearby marshes to other parts of England. The garden walls were constructed with stones salvaged from Beaulieu Abbey after it was demolished by Henry VIII. The hexagonal column supporting a fountain in the hotel's central courtyard is one of six salvaged, according to legend, from the ruined abbey's nave. Bedrooms are individually decorated in an English country-house tradition, come in a range of shapes and sizes, and have extras including a trouser press and a writing desk. Many units contain a traditional four-poster bed. The small bathrooms are beautifully maintained.

Palace Lane, Beaulieu, Hampshire, SO42 7ZL. © **01590/612324.** Fax 01590/612188. www.montaguarms hotel.co.uk. 24 units. £145–£168 ($232–$269) double; £170–£210 ($272–$336) suite. Rates include English breakfast. £20 per extra person in room. AE, DC, MC, V. **Amenities:** 2 restaurants; 2 bars; room service; laundry service; dry cleaning. *In room:* TV, hair dryer, trouser press.

WHERE TO DINE

Simply Poussin ★ FRENCH/ENGLISH Serving the best food in the area, this restaurant is located in what was originally a 19th-century stable and workshop. To reach it, pass beneath the arched alleyway (located midway between nos. 49 and 55 Brookley Rd.) and enter the stylishly simple premises directed by English-born chef Alexander Aitken and his wife, Caroline.

Amid a decor accented with framed 19th-century poems and illustrations celebrating poultry, the staff offers fish and game dishes, with ingredients usually fresh from the nearby New Forest. Try "Fruits of the New Forest," individually cooked portions of pigeon, wild rabbit, hare, and venison, encased in puff pastry and served with game sauce. Dessert choices change seasonally but usually include lemon tart with lime sorbet or passion fruit soufflé.

The Courtyard, at the rear of 49–55 Brookley Rd., Brockenhurst. © **01590/623063.** Reservations recommended 1 month in advance on weekends. 2-course lunch £10 ($16); 3-course lunch £15 ($24); 2-course dinner £15 ($24); 3-course dinner £20 ($32). MC, V. Tues–Sat noon–2pm and 7–10pm.

5 Bournemouth ★

167km (104 miles) SW of London; 24km (15 miles) W of the Isle of Wight

The south-coast resort at the doorstep of the New Forest didn't just happen: It was carefully planned and executed—a true city in a garden. Flower-filled, park-dotted Bournemouth is filled with an abundance of architecture inherited from those arbiters of taste, Victoria and her son Edward. (The resort was founded back in Victoria's day, when sea bathing became an institution.) Bournemouth's most distinguished feature is its *chines* (narrow, shrub-filled, steep-sided ravines) along the coastline.

Bournemouth, along with neighboring Poole and Christchurch, forms the largest urban area in the south of England. It makes a good base for exploring a historically rich part of England; on its outskirts are the New Forest, Salisbury, Winchester, and the Isle of Wight.

ESSENTIALS

GETTING THERE An express train from London's Waterloo Station to Bournemouth takes 2½ hours, with frequent service throughout the day. For schedules and information, call © **0845/748-4950.** Arrivals are at the Bournemouth Rail Station, on Holden Surst Road.

Buses leave London's Waterloo Station every 2 hours during the day, heading for Bournemouth. The trip takes 2½ hours. Call ℂ **0870/580-8080** for information and schedules.

If you're driving, take M3 southwest from London to Winchester, then A31 and A338 south to Bournemouth.

VISITOR INFORMATION   The **information office** is at Westover Road (ℂ **01202/451731**). From May to September, it's open Monday through Saturday from 9am to 5:30pm, Sunday from 10am to 5:30pm; from September to May, hours are Monday through Saturday from 9:30am to 5:30pm.

EXPLORING THE AREA

The resort's amusements are varied. At the **Pavilion Theatre,** you can see West End–type productions from London. The **Bournemouth Symphony Orchestra** is justly famous in Europe. There's the usual run of golf courses, band concerts, variety shows, and dancing.

And of course, this seaside resort has a spectacular beach—11km (7 miles) of uninterrupted sand stretching from Hengistbury Head to Alum Chine. Most of it is known simply as **Bournemouth Beach,** although its western edge, when it crosses over into the municipality of Poole, is called **Sandbanks Beach.** Beach access is free, and a pair of blue flags will indicate where the water's fine for swimming. The flags also signify the highest standards of cleanliness, management, and facilities. A health-conscious, nonsmoking zone now exists at Durley Chine, East Beach, and Fisherman's Walk. Fourteen full-time lifeguards patrol the shore and the water; they are helped by three volunteer corps during the busiest summer months. The promenade is traffic-free during the summer. There are two piers, one at Boscombe and the other at Bournemouth.

Amenities at the beach include beach bungalows, freshwater showers, seafront bistros and cafes, boat trips, rowboats, pedalos, Jet Skis, and windsurfers. Cruises run in the summer from Bournemouth Pier to the Isle of Wight.

The traffic-free town center with its wide avenues is elegant but by no means stuffy. Entertainers perform on the corners of streets that are lined with boutiques, cafes, street furniture, and plenty of meeting places. Specialized shopping is found mainly in the suburbs—Pokesdown for antiques and collectibles, Westbourne for individual designer fashion and home accessories. Victorian shopping arcades can be found in both Westbourne and Boscombe.

Tank Museum   Aficionados of military history should head to this installation maintained by the British military. Among the dozens of rare and historic armed vehicles are exhibitions and memorabilia on the life of T. E. Lawrence (Lawrence of Arabia).

In the village and army base of Bovington Camp. ℂ **01929/405096.** www.tankmuseum.co.uk. Admission £7.50 ($12) adults, £5 ($8) children 5–16, £6.50 ($10) seniors, £21 ($34) family. Daily 10am–5pm.

Moments **The "Green Lungs" of Bournemouth**

About a sixth of Bournemouth's nearly 12,000 acres consists of green parks and flowerbeds such as the **Pavilion Rock Garden,** which is perfect for a stroll. The total effect, especially in spring, is striking and helps explain Bournemouth's continuing popularity with the garden-loving English.

Finds **Exploring Nearby Wareham**

This historic little town on the Frome River 3km (2 miles) west of Bournemouth is an excellent center for touring the South Dorset coast and the Purbeck Hills. See the remains of early Anglo-Saxon and Roman town walls, plus the Saxon church of St. Martin, with its effigy of T. E. Lawrence (Lawrence of Arabia), who died in a motorcycle crash in 1935. His former home, **Clouds Hill** (*C* **01929/405616**), lies 11km (7 miles) west of Wareham (1.5km/1 mile north of Bovington Camp) and is extremely small. It's open only from April to October Thursday through Sunday from noon to 5pm, and bank holiday Mondays from noon to 5pm. Admission is £2.60 ($4.15), free for children 4 and under.

POOLE & CHRISTCHURCH 🧚

True history buffs usually head 8km (5 miles) west to Poole, or 8km (5 miles) east to Christchurch, both of which predated Bournemouth by thousands of years. Both have large but shallow harbors, which were favored by the ancient Romans.

Christchurch Priory Church   The present monastic church was begun in 1094 on a site where a church has been since A.D. 700. It is famous for the "Miraculous Beam," Norman nave and turret, monks' quire with its Jesse reredos and misericords, Lady Chapel, chantries, 15th-century bell tower, and St. Michael's loft, once a school but now a museum.

Quay Rd., Christchurch. *C* **01202/485804.** Admission £1.50 ($2.40) adults, £1 ($1.60) children. Mon–Sat 9:30am–5pm; Sun 2:15–5pm.

Red House Museum   This museum occupies a redbrick building originally constructed in 1764 as a workhouse. In 1951, a civic-minded resident donated his extensive collection of archaeological and cultural artifacts to form the basis of the town's most visible public monument. An art gallery on the premises sells paintings, and exhibits showcase the region's cultural and social history.

Quay Rd., Christchurch. *C* **01202/482860.** Admission £1.50 ($2.40) adults, 80p ($1.30) seniors and children. Tues–Sat 10am–5pm; Sun 2–5pm.

Waterfront Museum   This museum celebrates the nautical influences that made the region great, with exhibits about the effects of seafaring commerce since the days of the ancient Romans.

High St., Poole. *C* **01202/262600.** Free admission. Apr–Oct Mon–Sat 10am–5pm, Sun noon–5pm; Nov–Mar Mon–Sat 10am–3pm, Sun noon–3pm.

WHERE TO STAY
VERY EXPENSIVE

Bournemouth Highcliff Marriott ★★★   This 1888 cliffside hotel is one of the best in Bournemouth, rivaled only by the Carlton and Royal Bath. The high-ceilinged interior has been tastefully renovated. A funicular elevator takes guests from the hotel to the seaside promenade. Many bedrooms have beautiful views of the sea. Each is traditionally furnished in elegant English style and is located in the main building or in coast-guard cottages built in 1912. Rooms are generally spacious, with midsize bathrooms.

105 St. Michael's Rd., W. Cliff, Bournemouth, Dorset BH2 5DU. ✆ **01202/557702.** Fax 01202/293155. www. marriotthotels.com/bohbm. 157 units. £156 ($250) double; from £216 ($346) suite. Rates include English breakfast. AE, DC, MC, V. **Amenities:** Restaurant; bar; 2 pools (1 indoor, 1 outdoor); tennis court; health club; sauna; solarium; 24-hr. room service; babysitting; laundry service; dry cleaning. *In room:* A/C, TV w/pay movies, minibar, coffeemaker, hair dryer, iron/ironing board.

Carlton Hotel ★★★   More of a resort than an ordinary hotel, the Carlton sits atop a seaside cliff lined with private homes and other hotels. This Edwardian pile, with panoramic views, is the best place to stay in Bournemouth. It exudes a 1920s aura, with rather opulent public rooms. Extensively renovated, most bedrooms are spacious and open onto panoramic views of the sea. Regardless of your room assignment, expect Bournemouth's ultimate in comfort. Many of the soothing rooms have marbled wallpaper, mottled mirrors, and armchairs. Bathrooms are generous in size.

Meyrick Rd., E. Overcliff, Bournemouth, Dorset BH1 3DN. ✆ **01202/552011.** Fax 01202/299573. www.book menzies.com. 73 units. £85–£145 ($136–$232) double; from £230 ($368) suite. AE, DC, MC, V. **Amenities:** Restaurant; bar; 2 heated pools (1 outdoor, 1 indoor); health club; spa; Jacuzzi; sauna; 24-hr. room service; babysitting; laundry service; dry cleaning. *In room:* TV, minibar, coffeemaker, hair dryer, trouser press.

Norfolk Royale Hotel ★★   One of the oldest and most prestigious hotels in town, a few blocks from the seafront and central shopping area, it recently underwent a major £5 million ($8 million) renovation program, restoring it to its former Edwardian elegance, with a two-tier, cast-iron veranda. Nevertheless, we think it still plays second fiddle to both the Carlton and the Royal Bath. It exudes the atmosphere of a country estate, with formal entrance, rear garden, and fountain shaded by trees. Rooms and suites have been luxuriously appointed with the styles of the period blending with modern comforts. Bathrooms are of good size; a few suites have whirlpool tubs.

Richmond Hill, Bournemouth, Dorset BH2 6EN. ✆ **01202/551521.** Fax 01202/229729. www.englishrose hotels.co.uk. 95 units. £150 ($240) double; £198 ($317) suite. Rates include breakfast. Children up to the age of 12 stay free in parent's room. AE, MC, V. **Amenities:** Restaurant; bar; pool; Jacuzzi; sauna; room service; babysitting; laundry service; dry cleaning. *In room:* TV, minibar, coffeemaker, hair dryer, trouser press.

Royal Bath Hotel ★★★   This early Victorian version of a French château, with towers and bay windows looking out over the bay and Purbeck Hill, dates from June 28, 1838, the very day of Victoria's coronation. After the adolescent Prince of Wales (later Edward VII) stayed here, the hotel added "Royal" to its name. Over the years, it has attracted notables from Oscar Wilde to Rudolf Nureyev to the great prime minister, Disraeli. In luxury and style, it is in a neck-and-neck race with the Carlton. It's located in a 3-acre garden where cliff-top panoramas open onto the sea. The mostly spacious bedrooms are furnished with a certain English style and grace, and the larger rooms have sitting areas. Most bedrooms have been recently refurbished, and the bathrooms are luxurious and come with Neutrogena bath products; superior rooms also offer bathrobes and slippers.

Bath Rd., Bournemouth, Dorset BH1 2EW. ✆ **01202/555555.** Fax 01202/554158. www.devereroyalbath. co.uk. 140 units. £170–£215 ($272–$344) double; £255 ($408) junior suite; £320 ($512) twin/double suite. Rates include English breakfast. AE, DC, MC, V. Parking £8.50 ($14). **Amenities:** 2 restaurants; bar; indoor pool; health spa; Jacuzzi; sauna; room service; babysitting; laundry service; dry cleaning. *In room:* TV w/pay movies, minibar, coffeemaker, hair dryer, iron/ironing board.

EXPENSIVE

Langtry Manor Hotel ★ *Finds*   A much more atmospheric choice and run with a more personal touch than the Carlton and Norfolk Royale, the Red House, as this hotel was originally called, was built in 1877 for Lillie Langtry, a gift from Edward VII to his favorite mistress. The house has all sorts of reminders of its illustrious inhabitants, including initials scratched on a window-pane and carvings on a beam of the entrance hall. On the half-landing is the peephole through which the prince could scrutinize the assembled company before coming down to dine, and one fireplace bears his initials. The bedrooms, each a double, range from ordinary twins to the Lillie Langtry Suite, Lillie's own room, with a four-poster bed and a double heart-shaped bathtub; or you can rent the Edward VII Suite, furnished as it was when His Royal Highness lived in this spacious room with a working fireplace and a cast-iron bathtub in the Edwardian-style bathroom. All bathrooms are tiled and beautifully maintained; some have Jacuzzis.

26 Derby Rd. (north of Christchurch Rd., A35), E. Cliff, Bournemouth, Dorset BH1 3QB. ℂ 01202/553887. Fax 01202/290115. www.langtrymanor.com. 28 units. £140 ($223) double; £180 ($287) suite for 2. Rates include English breakfast. AE, MC, V. **Amenities:** Restaurant; bar; room service; dry cleaning. *In room:* TV/VCR, dataport, minibar, hair dryer.

The Mansion House ★ *Finds*   In nearby Poole, this is a real discovery, an 18th-century town house for those seeking charm and atmosphere. The neoclassical detailing and fan-shaped windows are the pride and well-maintained joy of the owners. Graciously furnished bedrooms provide plenty of quiet, well-decorated corners for relaxation and offer homey touches such as mineral water. The building has been extended to provide roomy and inviting accommodations, each individually decorated according to various themes (Oriental, Georgian, French, and so on) with comfortable furnishings. Two rooms have four-poster beds; two are suitable for families. Most bathrooms have a tub-and-shower combination.

7–11 Thames St., Poole (6.5km/4 miles west of Bournemouth), Dorset BH15 1JN. ℂ 01202/685666. Fax 01202/665709. www.themansionhouse.co.uk. 32 units. Mon–Thurs £125 ($200) double, £140 ($224) suite. Fri–Sun £120 ($192) double, £140 ($224) suite. Rates include English breakfast. AE, DC, MC, V. **Amenities:** 2 restaurants; 2 bars; room service; babysitting. *In room:* TV, hair dryer.

The Priory Hotel   This hotel lies 3km (2 miles) west of Bournemouth in Wareham, beside the River Frame and near the village church. It has a well-tended garden adorned by old trees. Inside, a paneled bar and a lounge filled with antiques open onto views of the lawn. Rooms are individually decorated (often with fine antiques) and offer much comfort, including such items as mineral water, fruit, and bathrobes; some feature four-poster beds. Some accommodations are in a well-crafted annex. Most of the small bathrooms contain a tub-and-shower combination; a few have Jacuzzis. *Note:* Children under 8 are not permitted as guests, and those over 8 are charged full price.

Church Green, Wareham, Dorset BH20 4ND. ℂ 01929/551666. Fax 01929/554519. www.theprioryhotel. co.uk. 18 units. £175–£235 ($280–$376) double; £325 ($520) suite. Rates include English breakfast. DC, MC, V. **Amenities:** 2 restaurants; bar; room service; laundry service; dry cleaning. *In room:* TV, minibar (some), hair dryer.

INEXPENSIVE

Sunnydene   This Victorian private hotel is in a substantial gabled house on a tree-lined road between the Central Station and Bournemouth Bay. Rooms are carpeted and centrally heated. Hot and cold running water is in all the bedrooms, and seven have a small bathroom equipped with a shower stall. Otherwise, corridor bathrooms are adequate and frequently refreshed so that they'll be inviting for the next guest. All the beds offer much comfort, but not a lot of frills. The hotel is licensed, and drinks and other refreshments are served in the sun lounge.

11 Spencer Rd., Bournemouth, Dorset BH1 3TE. ℰ **01202/552281.** 10 units, 8 with bathroom. £46 ($74) double without bathroom, £52 ($83) double with bathroom. Rates include breakfast. No credit cards. Bus: 121 or 124. **Amenities:** Bar; sun lounge. *In room:* TV, coffeemaker, no phone.

Westcliff Hotel *(Value)* This hotel is a 5-minute walk from the town center, near Durley Chine, and was once the luxurious south-coast home of the duke of Westminster, who had it built in 1876. Now run by the Blissert family, the hotel draws lots of repeat business. All rooms are comfortably furnished and well maintained; some have four-posters. As befits a former private home, bedrooms come in various shapes and sizes, but each is fitted with a good bed plus a small bathroom with a shower. There's a large garden and a parking area.

27 Chine Crescent, W. Cliff, Bournemouth, Dorset BH2 5LB. ℰ **01202/551062.** Fax 01202/315377. www. newwestcliffhotel.co.uk. 53 units. £58–£84 ($93–$134) double. Rates include English breakfast. Half board £34–£49 ($54–$78) per person. MC, V. **Amenities:** Restaurant; 2 bars; indoor heated pool; Jacuzzi; sauna; solarium; theater area with surround-sound cinema. *In room:* TV, coffeemaker, hair dryer, trouser press.

WHERE TO DINE

The Grove Seafood Restaurant ★★ *(Finds)* SEAFOOD In a bistro atmosphere, Paul and Tina Collins serve some of the finest and freshest seafood dishes in the area. Look to the blackboard for a daily list of the fish specials, but know that you won't necessarily be limited to the fruits of the sea, as they also prepare meat dishes almost equally as well. A relaxed, almost family-like atmosphere prevails, although the service is very professional. Paul cooks the dishes to order, so be prepared to wait. The soup of the day might be potato and fennel, although you might also opt for a tian of crab stacked on top of a chunky guacamole served with a tangy mango salsa. We like Paul's blend of classical French and modern British cuisine, as exemplified by his filet of trout on a bed of watercress mash with a tomato compote. Grilled sardines come lightly sprinkled with fresh basil and lemon with a light dusting of olive oil with roasted Mediterranean vegetables served on a polenta bruschetta. The steamed mussels are delectably seasoned with fresh ginger, lime, and coriander.

79 Southbourne Grove. ℰ **01202/566660.** Reservations required. Main courses £9.95–£15 ($16–$24); 3-course Sun lunch £9.95 ($16); fixed-price dinner £13 ($20) for 2 courses, £15 ($24) for 3 courses. AE, MC, V. Tues–Sun noon–1:30pm; Thurs–Sat 7–10pm.

Oscar's ★ FRENCH Sporting Oscar Wilde mementos, this restaurant is located cliffside, with panoramic sea views. The chef, John Wood, presents a la carte dishes as well as fixed-price menus. The excellent appetizers may include a terrine of salmon scallops and king prawns with a saffron and basil jelly. The imaginative main courses may include filet of steamed bass with sesame crust, cucumber noodles, mussels and lemon-grass jus; or Dorset lamb enhanced with zucchini duxelle bay-flavored jus, and dauphinoise of celeriac and potatoes.

In the Royal Bath Hotel, Bath Rd. ℰ **01202/555555.** Reservations required. Main courses £20–£28 ($31–$45) fixed-price meal, £20 ($31) at lunch, £37 ($59) at dinner. AE, DC, MC, V. Daily 12:30–2pm and 7:30–10pm.

Saint Michel *(Kids)* BRITISH/FRENCH This brasserie-style restaurant and bar offers some of the best Anglo-French cookery in the area. With a traditional decor, it is warm and inviting. And its chefs don't muck up the ingredients with a lot of fancy sauces. Food is relatively straightforward, but preparation is right on target. You may order, for example, grilled calves' liver with bacon or something more imaginative—a twice-baked Finnan haddock soufflé. They also have an excellent roast duck with glazed apples; sea bass with pesto sauce is another worthy choice. Family friendly, the restaurant offers service that is gracious, and the opportunity to dine inexpensively at the bar.

In the Swallow Highcliff Hotel, 105 St. Michael's Rd., W. Cliff. ℭ **01202/315716.** Reservations recommended. Main courses £15–£17 ($24–$27); fixed-price lunch £16 ($26). DC, MC, V. Sun–Fri noon–2pm; Mon–Sat 7–9:30pm.

BOURNEMOUTH AFTER DARK

A choice of major art venues offers great performances throughout the year. **International Centre's Windsor Hall** hosts leading performers from London, the **Pavilion** puts on West End musicals as well as dancing with live music, and the **Winter Gardens,** the original home and favorite performance space of the world-famous Bournemouth Symphony Orchestra, offer regular concerts. Program and ticket information for all three of these venues is available by calling ℭ **01202/456456.**

EN ROUTE TO DORCHESTER: A 17TH-CENTURY MANSION

Kingston Lacy   An imposing 17th-century mansion set on 250 acres of wooded park, Kingston Lacy was the home of the Bankes family for more than 300 years. They entertained such distinguished guests as King Edward VII, Kaiser Wilhelm, Thomas Hardy, and George V. The house displays a magnificent collection of artwork by Rubens, Titian, and Van Dyck, as well as an important collection of Egyptian artifacts. The present structure replaced Corfe Castle, the Bankes family home that was destroyed in the civil war. During her husband's absence while performing duties as chief justice to King Charles I, Lady Bankes led the defense of the castle, withstanding two sieges before being forced to surrender to Cromwell's forces in 1646 because of the actions of a treacherous follower. The keys to Corfe Castle hang in the library at Kingston Lacy.

At Wimborne Minster, on B3082 (Wimborne–Blandford Rd.), 2.5km (1½ miles) west of Wimborne. ℭ 01202/ 883402. Admission to the house, garden, and park £6.80 ($11) adults, £3.40 ($5.45) children, £18 ($29) family ticket. Garden only £3.50 ($5.60) adults, £1.75 ($2.80) children. Sat–Wed noon–5:30pm; park daily 10:30am–6pm. Closed Jan–Feb.

6 Dorchester: Hardy's Home ✶

190km (120 miles) SW of London; 43km (27 miles) W of Bournemouth

Thomas Hardy, in his 1886 novel *The Mayor of Casterbridge,* gave Dorchester literary fame. Actually, Dorchester was notable even in Roman times, when Maumbury Rings, the best Roman amphitheater in Britain, was filled with the sounds of 12,000 spectators screaming for the blood of the gladiators. Today it's a sleepy market town that seems to go to bed right after dinner.

ESSENTIALS

GETTING THERE   Trains run from London's Waterloo Station each hour during the day. The trip takes 2½ hours. For rail information, call ℭ **0845/ 722-5225.** Dorchester has two train stations, the South Station at Station Approach and the West Station on Great Western Road. For information about both, call ℭ **0845/748-4950.**

Several **National Express** coaches a day depart from London's Victoria Coach Station heading for Dorchester. The trip takes 3 hours. Call ℭ **020/7529-2000** for information and schedules.

If you're driving from London, take M3 southwest, but near the end take A30 toward Salisbury where you connect with A354 for the final approach to Dorchester.

VISITOR INFORMATION   The **Tourist Information Centre** is at Unit 11, Antelope Walk (© **01305/267992**). It's open from April to October, Monday through Saturday from 9am to 5pm; from May to September (also Sunday from 10am to 3pm); and from November to March, Monday through Saturday from 9am to 4pm.

SEEING THE SIGHTS

Athelhampton House & Gardens ★★   This is one of England's great medieval houses and the most beautiful and historic in the south, lying a mile east of Puddletown. Thomas Hardy mentioned it in some of his writings but called it Athelhall. It was begun during the reign of Edward IV on the legendary site of King Athelstan's palace. A family home for over 500 years, it's noted for its 15th-century Great Hall, Tudor great chamber, state bedroom, and King's Room.

In 1992, a dozen of the house's rooms were damaged by an accidental fire caused by faulty wiring in the attic. Skilled craftspeople, however, have restored all the magnificent interiors.

Insider's tip: Though many visitors come to see the house, the gardens are even more inspiring. Dating from 1891, they are full of vistas, and their beauty is enhanced by the River Piddle flowing through and by fountains. These walled gardens, winners of the HHA/Christies garden of the year award, contain the famous topiary pyramids and two pavilions designed by Inigo Jones. You'll see fine collections of tulips and magnolias, roses, and lilies, and also a 15th-century dovecote. Yes, they were often visited by Thomas Hardy.

On A35, 8km (5 miles) east of Dorchester. © **01305/848363**. www.athelhampton.co.uk. Admission £7 ($11) adults, £6.30 ($10) seniors, £4.95 ($7.90) students. Mar–Oct Sun–Fri 10:30am–5pm; Nov–Feb Sun 10:30am–5pm. Take the Dorchester–Bournemouth Rd. (A35) east of Dorchester for 8km (5 miles).

Hardy's Cottage   Thomas Hardy was born in 1840 at Higher Bockhampton. His home, now a National Trust property, may be visited by appointment. Approach the cottage on foot—it's a 10-minute walk—after parking your vehicle in the space provided in the woods. Write in advance to Hardy's Cottage, Higher Bockhampton, Dorchester, Dorset DT2 8QJ, England, or call the number below.

Higher Bockhampton (5km/3 miles northeast of Dorchester and 1km/½ mile south of Blandford Road/A35. © **01305/262366**. Admission £2.80 ($4.50). Sun–Thurs 11am–5pm. Closed Nov–Mar.

WHERE TO STAY & DINE IN & AROUND DORCHESTER

Kings Arms Hotel   In business for over 3 centuries, the Kings Arms offers great bow windows above the porch and a swinging sign hanging over the road,

---

⌐Finds **In Search of Hardy's Heart**

One mile east of Dorchester is **Stinsford Church,** where Hardy's heart is buried. Hardy was christened in this church, and his death wish was to be entombed here. But because he was such a towering figure in English literature at the time of his death, his estate agreed to have him buried at Westminster Abbey. In partial deference to his wishes though, his heart was donated to Stinsford Church.

To get to the church, officially called the Church of St. Michael, follow the signs from Dorchester for the Kingston Maurward Agricultural College, then just before the entrance gates to the college, turn right, following the signs toward the Stinsford Church.

Finds   Time Out for an Old-Fashioned Cuppa

The best place for tea in this bustling market town is the **Potters,** 19 Durngate St. (© **01305/260312**), with a blue-and-white interior and a small herb-and-flower garden out back with several tables. A proper sit-down tea is served for £3.50 ($5.60). You can also order freshly made sandwiches, cakes, scones, and pastries.

---

a legacy of its days as a coaching inn. It's still the best place to stay within Dorchester's center, though superior lodgings are on the outskirts. An archway leads to the courtyard and parking area at the back of the hotel. All rooms are comfortably furnished; most are small to medium in size and have been modernized while retaining a traditional English aura. The shower-only bathrooms are tiled and rather cramped.

30 High East St., Dorchester, Dorset DT1 1HF. © **01305/265353.** Fax 01305/260269. 33 units. £48 ($76) double; £149 ($238) suite. AE, MC, V. **Amenities:** Restaurant; bar. *In room:* TV, coffeemaker, hair dryer, trouser press.

Summer Lodge ★★   In this country-house hotel 24km (15 miles) north of Dorchester, resident owners Nigel and Margaret Corbett provide care, courtesy, and comfort. Once home to heirs of the earls of Ilchester, the house, in the village of Evershot, stands on 4 acres of secluded gardens. Evershot appears as Evershed in *Tess of the D'Urbervilles,* and author Thomas Hardy (that name again) designed a wing of the house. More recently, Summer Lodge hosted many stars of the locally filmed *Sense and Sensibility,* including Emma Thompson.

In this relaxed, informal atmosphere, bedrooms have views either of the garden or over village rooftops to fields beyond. The hotel is regularly redecorated and recarpeted, and a new kitchen has been added. Bedrooms are individually decorated and have many comforts, as reflected by such extras as hot-water bottles, fresh flowers, and racks of magazines. Most of the bathrooms have a tub-and-shower combination. Though centrally heated, the hotel offers log fires in winter. Guests can sit around the fire in a convivial atmosphere.

Summer Lane, Evershot, Dorset DT2 0JR. © **01935/83424.** Fax 01935/83005. www.summerlodgehotel. com. 18 units. £215–£420 ($344–$672) double. Rates include English breakfast, afternoon tea, and 5-course dinner and newspaper. AE, DC, MC, V. Head north from Dorchester on A37. **Amenities:** Restaurant; bar; pool; tennis court; room service; babysitting; laundry service; croquet lawn. *In room:* TV, coffeemaker, hair dryer.

Yalbury Cottage Hotel and Restaurant ★ *Finds*   This thatch-roofed cottage with inglenooks and beamed ceilings is in a small country village within walking distance of Thomas Hardy's cottage and Stinsford Church. The cottage is some 300 years old and was once home to a local shepherd and the keeper of the water meadows. A mile to the north is Thorncombe Wood (home to badgers, deer, and many species of birds), offering a pleasant stroll and a chance to see Hardy's birthplace, which is tucked in under the edge of the woods. The bedrooms overlook the English country garden beyond, reflecting a mood of tranquillity, and have pinewood furniture in the English cottage style. Bedrooms received considerable refurbishing in 2002 and are now more comfortable than ever. Bathrooms are well appointed and clad in tiles, each with a tub and shower.

Lower Bockhampton, near Dorchester, Dorset DT2 8PZ. ② **01305/262382.** Fax 01305/266412. www.
smoothhound.co.uk/hotels/yalbury. 8 units. £90 ($144) double. Rates include half board. MC, V. Head 3km
(2 miles) east of Dorchester (A35) and watch for signs to Lower Bockhampton. **Amenities:** Restaurant; room
service; babysitting; laundry service. *In room:* TV, coffeemaker, hair dryer.

7 Dorset's Coastal Towns ⭑⭑: Chideock, Charmouth & Lyme Regis

Chideock and Charmouth: 253km (157 miles) SW of London; 1.5km (1 mile) W of Bridport. Lyme Regis: 258km
(160 miles) SW of London; 40km (25 miles) W of Dorchester

Chideock is a charming village hamlet of thatched houses with a dairy farm in
the center. About a mile from the coast, it's a gem of a place for overnight
stopovers and is even better for longer stays. You may be tempted to explore the
countryside and the rolling hills.

On Lyme Bay, Charmouth, like Chideock, is another winner. A village of
Georgian houses and thatched cottages, Charmouth provides some of the most
dramatic coastal scenery in West Dorset. The village is west of Golden Cap,
which, according to adventurers who measure such things, is the highest cliff
along the coast of southern England.

Also on Lyme Bay, near the Devonshire border, the resort of Lyme Regis is
one of the most attractive centers along the south coast. For those who shun big,
commercial resorts, Lyme Regis is ideal—it's a true English coastal town but
with a mild climate. Seagulls fly overhead, the streets are steep and winding, and
walks along Cobb Beach are brisk. The views, particularly of the craft in the harbor, are so photogenic that John Fowles, a longtime resident of the town,
selected it as the site for the 1980 filming of his novel *The French Lieutenant's
Woman.*

During its heyday, the town was a major seaport. Later, Lyme developed into
a small spa, including among its visitors Jane Austen. She wrote her final novel,
Persuasion (published posthumously and based partly on the town's life), after
staying here in 1803 and 1804.

ESSENTIALS

GETTING THERE   The nearest train connection to Chideock and Charmouth is Dorchester (see "Essentials," in the Dorchester section, above). Buses
run frequently throughout the day, west from both Dorchester and Bridport.

To get to Lyme Regis, take the London–Exeter train, getting off at Axminster
and continuing the rest of the way by bus. For rail information, call ② **0845/
748-4950.** Bus no. 31 runs from Axminster to Lyme Regis (one coach per hour
during the day). There's also **National Express** bus service (no. 705) that runs
daily in summer at 9:50am from Exeter to Lyme Regis, taking 1¾ hours. Call
② **0870/580-8080** for schedules and information.

If you're driving to Chideock and Charmouth from Bridport, continue west
along A35. To get to Lyme Regis from Bridport, continue west along A35, cutting south to the coast at the junction with A3070.

VISITOR INFORMATION   In Lyme Regis, the **Tourist Information Centre,** at Guildhall Cottage, Church Street (② **01297/442138**), is open November through March, Monday through Friday from 10am to 4pm and Saturday
from 10am to 2pm; in April, daily from 10am to 5pm; May through September, Monday through Friday from 10am to 4pm and Saturday and Sunday from
10am to 5pm; and October, daily from 10am to 5pm.

EXPLORING THE TOWNS

Chideock and Charmouth are the most beautiful villages in Dorset. It's fun to stroll though them to see the well-kept cottages, well-manicured gardens, and an occasional 18th- or 19th-century church. Charmouth, more than Chideock, boasts a small-scale collection of unusual antiques shops. Both villages are less than a mile from the western edge of Chesil Beach, one of the Hampshire coast's most famous (and longest) beaches. Although it's covered with shingle (sharp rocks), and hard on your feet if you go sunbathing, the beach nonetheless provides 8km (5 miles) of sweeping views toward France.

Another famous building is **The Guildhall,** Bridge Street (call the tourist office for information), whose Mary and John Wing (built in 1620) houses the completed sections of an enormous tapestry woven by local women. Depicting Britain's colonization of North America, it's composed of a series of 3.5m-by-1m (11-ft.-by-4-ft.) sections, each of which took a team of local women 2 years to weave. Admission is free, but if anyone wants to add a stitch to the final tapestry as a kind of charitable donation, it costs £1.50 ($2.40). It's open Monday through Friday from 10am to 4pm, but only if someone is working on the tapestry.

The surrounding area is a fascinating place for botanists and zoologists because of the predominance of blue Lias, a sedimentary rock well suited to the formation of fossils. In 1810, Mary Anning (at the age of 11) discovered one of the first articulated ichthyosaur skeletons. She went on to become one of the first professional fossilists in England. Books outlining walks in the area and the regions where fossils can be studied are available at the local information bureau.

WHERE TO STAY & DINE
IN CHIDEOCK & CHARMOUTH

Chideock House Hotel ★★ *Finds*   In a village of winners, this 15th-century thatched house is the prettiest. The house was used by the Roundheads in 1645, and ghosts of the village martyrs still haunt it, because their trial was held here. Located near the road, behind a protective stone wall, the house has a garden in back; a driveway leads to a large parking area. The beamed lounge, recently face-lifted, has two fireplaces, one an Adam fireplace with a wood-burning blaze on cool days. Bedrooms are individually decorated and vary in size; superior rooms have dressing gowns and toiletries. Each has a small bathroom.

Moments   Following the Town Crier

Today in Lyme Regis, one of the town's most visible characters is **Richard J. Fox,** three-time world champion Town Crier who, though retired, still does **guided walks.** Famed for his declamatory delivery of official (and sometimes irreverent) proclamations, he followed a 1,000-year-old tradition of newscasting. Dressed as Thomas Payne, a dragoon who died in Lyme Regis in 1644 during the civil war, Mr. Fox leads visitors on a 1½-hour walk around the town every Tuesday and Thursday at 2:30pm, beginning at The Guildhall (mentioned above). No reservations are necessary, and the price is £3 ($4.80) for adults and £2 ($3.20) for children. He can be reached on the premises of **Mister Fox,** 17 Haye St. (© **01297/443568** or 01297/445097). This shop sells such wares as woodcrafts and shells and is open daily from 10am to 5pm (open until 6:30pm in summer).

Main St., Chideock, Dorset DT6 6JN. © **01297/489242.** Fax 01297/489184. www.chideockhousehotel.com. 8 units, all with bathroom. £60–£80 ($96–$128) double. Rates include English breakfast. £105–£125 ($168–$200) double with half board. AE, MC, V. Bus: no. 31 from Bridport. **Amenities:** Restaurant; bar. *In room:* TV, coffeemaker, hair dryer.

White House ✦   The White House is the best place to stay in Charmouth. This Regency home, with its period architecture and bow doors, is well preserved and tastefully furnished. Ian and Liz Simpson took this place, constructed in 1827, and made it comfortable, with touches such as electric kettles in their handsomely furnished bedrooms. Rooms range in size from small to medium and include such extras as complimentary decanters of sherry and homemade shortbread. Bathrooms are small.

2 Hillside, The Street, Charmouth, Dorset DT6 6PJ. © **01297/560411.** Fax 01297/560702. 9 units. £128 ($205) double. Rates include English breakfast and 5-course table d'hôte. MC, V. Closed Nov–Jan, but open for New Year's Day. Bus: no. 31 from Bridport. **Amenities:** Restaurant; bar; room service; laundry service; dry cleaning. *In room:* TV, coffeemaker, hair dryer.

IN LYME REGIS

Hotel Alexandra ✦   Built in 1735, this hotel is situated on a hill about 5 minutes from the center of Lyme Regis. Today, it has the best bedrooms and amenities of any inn in town, although it lacks the personal charm of Kersbrook Hotel (see below). In bedrooms once occupied by such "blue bloods" as Dowager Countess Poulett or Duc du Stacpoole, you sleep in grand comfort in the handsome beds. Most rooms command superb sea views over Lyme Regis and the Cobb. Expect such extras as thermostatic heating, along with small but beautifully maintained private baths. It's been discreetly modernized around its original character.

Pound St., Lyme Regis, Dorset DT7 3HZ. © **01297/442010.** Fax 01297/443229. www.hotelalexandra.co.uk. 25 units. £75–£130 ($120–$208) double. Rates include English breakfast. DC, MC, V. **Amenities:** Restaurant; bar, room service, laundry service; dry cleaning. *In room:* TV, coffeemaker, hair dryer.

Kersbrook Hotel ✦ *(Finds*   Built of stone in 1790, and crowned by a thatch roof, the Kersbrook sits on a ledge above the village (which provides a panoramic view of the coast), on 1½ acres of gardens landscaped according to the original 18th-century plans. The public rooms have been refurnished with antique furniture, re-creating old-world charm with modern facilities. All of the small to medium-sized bedrooms have a certain 17th-century charm, with furnishings ranging from antique to contemporary. Rooms are comfortable, and the tidy bathrooms have showers.

Pound Rd., Lyme Regis, Dorset DT7 3HX. © and fax **01297/442596.** www.lymeregis.com/kersbrook-hotel. 10 units. £65 ($104) double. Rates include breakfast. AE, MC, V. Closed Dec–Jan. **Amenities:** Bar; breakfast room. *In room:* TV, coffeemaker, hair dryer, iron/ironing board.

Royal Lion *(Kids*   This former coaching inn dates to 1610, growing throughout the years to incorporate oak-paneled bars, lounges, and comfortably up-to-date bedrooms. Situated in the center of town on a hillside climbing up from the sea, the hotel features country-inspired furnishings and such venerable antiques as the half-tester bed regularly used by Edward VII when he was Prince of Wales. Bedrooms are divided between the main house, where the traditionally furnished rooms have more character and fireplaces, and a modern wing, where rooms have contemporary furnishings and the added advantage of a private terrace with sea view. Bathrooms are small, each with a shower. Children are warmly welcomed and some of the hotel's family rooms have bunk beds.

Broad St., Lyme Regis, Dorset DT7 3QF. ⓒ **01297/445622.** Fax 01297/445859. www.royallionhotel.com. 30 units. £74–£92 ($118–$147) double with breakfast, £98–£118 ($157–$189) double with breakfast and dinner. AE, DC, MC, V. **Amenities:** Restaurant; bar; lounge; pool; Jacuzzi; sauna; game room. *In room:* TV, coffeemaker.

8 Salisbury ★★

144km (90 miles) SW of London; 85km (53 miles) SE of Bristol

Long before you've even entered Salisbury, the spire of its cathedral will come into view—just as John Constable captured it on canvas. The 121m (404-ft.) pinnacle of the Early English and Gothic cathedral is the tallest in England.

Salisbury, or New Sarum, lies in the valley of the Avon River. Filled with Tudor inns and tearooms, it is the only true city in Wiltshire. It's an excellent base for visitors anxious to explore Stonehenge or Avebury, and, unfortunately, they tend to visit the cathedral and then rush on their way. But the old market town is an interesting destination in its own right, and if you choose to linger here for a day or two, you'll find that its pub-to-citizen ratio is perhaps the highest in the country.

ESSENTIALS

GETTING THERE   **Network Express trains** depart for Salisbury hourly from Waterloo Station in London; the trip takes 1½ hours. Sprinter trains offer fast, efficient service every hour from Portsmouth, Bristol, and South Wales. Also, direct rail service is available from Exeter, Plymouth, Brighton, and Reading. For rail information, call ⓒ **0845/748-4950** in the United Kingdom.

If you're driving from London, head west on M3 to the end of the run, continuing the rest of the way on A30.

Three **National Express** buses per day run from London, Monday through Friday. On Saturday and Sunday, three buses depart Victoria Coach Station for Salisbury. The trip takes 2½ hours. Call ⓒ **020/7529-2000** for schedules and information.

VISITOR INFORMATION   The **Tourist Information Centre** is at Fish Row (ⓒ **01722/334956**), and is open October through April, Monday through Saturday from 9:30am to 5pm; in May, Monday through Saturday from 9:30am to 5pm and Sunday from 10:30am to 4:30pm; in June and September, Monday through Saturday from 9:30am to 6pm and Sunday from 10:30am to 4:30pm; and in July and August, Monday through Saturday from 9:30am to 7pm and Sunday from 10:30am to 5pm.

SPECIAL EVENTS   The Salisbury **St. George's Spring Festival** in April is a traditional medieval celebration of the city's patron saint. You can witness St. George slaying the dragon in the Wiltshire mummers play and see acrobats and fireworks. For information, call the Tourist Information Centre (see above).

With spring comes the annual **Salisbury Festival** (ⓒ **01722/332241** for the box office). The city drapes itself in banners, and street theater—traditional and unexpected—is offered everywhere. There are also symphony and chamber music concerts in Salisbury Cathedral, children's events, and much more. It takes place from mid-May to the beginning of June.

At the end of July, you can see **The Salisbury Garden and Flower Show,** Hudson's Field (ⓒ **01189/478996**). This is a treat for gardening enthusiasts: There's a floral marquee packed with Chelsea exhibits, as well as display gardens created especially for the event. But there's plenty more for the rest of the family, including specialty food tastings, antiques and crafts sales, and a vintage and classic car show.

EXPLORING SALISBURY

You can easily see Salisbury by foot, either on your own or by taking a guided daytime or evening walk sponsored by the **Tourist Information Centre** (see above). Tickets are £2.50 ($4) for adults and £1 ($1.60) for children.

Mompesson House ⭐   This is one of the most distinguished houses in the area. Built by Charles Mompesson in 1701, while he was a member of Parliament for Old Sarum, it is a beautiful example of the Queen Anne style and is well known for its fine plasterwork ceilings and paneling. It also houses a collection of 18th-century drinking glasses. Visitors can wander through a garden and order a snack in the garden tearoom.

Cathedral Close. (✆ **01722/335659.** Admission £3.90 ($6.25) adults, £1.95 ($3.10) children under 18. Apr–Oct Sat–Wed 11am–5pm.

Old Sarum ⭐   Believed to have been an Iron Age fortification, Old Sarum was used again by the Saxons and flourished as a walled town into the Middle Ages. The Normans built a cathedral and a castle here; parts of the old cathedral were taken down to build the city of New Sarum (Salisbury).

3km (2 miles) north of Salisbury off A345 on Castle Rd. (✆ **01722/335398.** Admission £2 ($3.20) adults, £1.50 ($2.40) seniors, £1 ($1.60) children. Apr–Sept daily 10am–5pm; Oct daily 10am–5pm; Nov–Mar daily 10am–5pm. Bus nos. 3, 5, 6, 7, 8, and 9 run every 20 minutes during the day from the Salisbury bus station.

Salisbury Cathedral ⭐⭐⭐   You'll find no better example of the Early English, or pointed, architectural style than Salisbury Cathedral. Construction on this magnificent building began as early as 1220 and took only 45 years to complete. (Most of Europe's grandest cathedrals took 3 centuries to build.) Salisbury Cathedral is one of the most homogenous of all the great European cathedrals.

The cathedral's 13th-century octagonal chapter house possesses one of the four surviving original texts of the Magna Carta, along with treasures from the diocese of Salisbury and manuscripts and artifacts belonging to the cathedral. The cloisters enhance the cathedral's beauty, along with an exceptionally large close. There are at least 75 buildings in the compound, some from the early 18th century and others from much earlier.

Insider tip: The 121m (404-ft.) spire was one of the tallest structures in the world when it was completed in 1315. In its day, it was far more advanced technology than the world's tallest skyscrapers. Amazingly, the spire was not part of the original design; it was conceived and added some 30 years after the rest. The name of the master mason is lost to history. Sir Christopher Wren in 1668 expressed alarm at the tilt of the spire, but no further shift has since been measured. The whole ensemble is still standing; if you trust towering architecture from 700 years ago, you can explore the tower on guided visits Monday through Saturday from 11am to 2pm (extra tours in summer depending on demand). The cost of the tour is £3 ($4.80).

(✆ **01722/555120.** . Suggested donation £3.50 ($5.60) adults, £2.50 ($4) students and seniors, £2 ($3.20) children, £8 ($13) family ticket. Jan–May and Sept–Dec Mon–Sat 7:15am–6:15pm; June–Aug Mon–Sat 7:15am–8:15pm. Sun year-round 7:15am–6:15pm.

The Royal Gloucestershire, Berkshire, and Wiltshire Regiment (Salisbury) Museum—Redcoats in the Wardrobe   The elegant house in which the museum's collections are displayed dates from 1254 and contains exhibits covering 3 centuries of military history. Visitors can relax in the garden leading to the River Somerset (with views made famous by Constable) and enjoy homemade fare from the Redcoats Tea Rooms.

The Wardrobe, 58 The Close, Salisbury, Wiltshire. ✆ **01722/414536.** www.thewardrobe.org.uk. Admission £2.50 ($4) adults, £2 ($3.20) seniors, 75p ($1.20) children, £5 ($8) family ticket. Feb–Mar and Nov to mid-Dec Tues–Sun 10am–5pm; Apr–Oct daily 10am–5pm.

Wilton House ★★   The home of the earls of Pembroke is in the town of Wilton. It dates from the 16th century but has undergone numerous alterations, most recently in Victoria's day, and is noted for its 17th-century staterooms, designed by celebrated architect Inigo Jones. Shakespeare's troupe is said to have entertained here, and Eisenhower and his advisers prepared here for the D-Day landings at Normandy, with only the Van Dyck paintings as silent witnesses.

The house is filled with beautifully maintained furnishings and world-class art, including paintings by Rubens, Brueghel, and Reynolds. You can visit a reconstructed Tudor kitchen and Victorian laundry plus "The Wareham Bears," a unique collection of some 200 miniature dressed teddy bears.

On the 21-acre estate are giant cedars of Lebanon trees, the oldest of which were planted in 1630, as well as rose and water gardens, riverside and woodland walks, and a huge adventure playground for children.

5km (3 miles) west of Salisbury on A36. ✆ **01722/746720.** www.wiltonhouse.com. Admission £9.25 ($15) adults, £7.50 ($12) seniors, £5 ($8) children 5–15, £22 ($35) family ticket, free for children under 5. Price inclusive of grounds. Easter–Oct daily 10:30am–5:30pm (last entrance at 4:30pm).

WHERE TO STAY
EXPENSIVE

The Beadles ★★ *Finds*   A traditional modern Georgian house with antique furnishings and a view of the cathedral, The Beadles offers unobstructed views of the beautiful Wiltshire countryside from its 1-acre gardens. It's situated in a small, unspoiled English village, 13km (8 miles) from Salisbury, which offers excellent access to Stonehenge, Wilton House, the New Forest, and the rambling moors of Thomas Hardy country. Even the road to Winchester is an ancient Roman byway. Furnished tastefully, this nonsmoking household contains rooms with twins or doubles, each with a full private bathroom. Owners David and Anne Yuille-Baddeley delight in providing information on the area.

Middleton, Middle Winterslow, near Salisbury, Wiltshire SP5 1QS. ✆ **01980/862922.** Fax 01980/863565. www.guestaccom.co.uk/754.htm. 3 units. £60 ($96) double. Rates include English breakfast. MC, V. Turn off A30 at Pheasant Inn to Middle Winterslow. Enter the village, make the first right, turn right again, and it's the first right after "Trevano." **Amenities:** Dining room; tour services. *In room:* TV, coffeemaker, hair dryer, trouser press.

Grasmere House ★ *Kids*   Grasmere House stands near the confluence of the Nadder and Avon rivers on 1½ acres of grounds. Constructed in 1896 for Salisbury merchants, the house still suggests a family home. The original architectural features were retained as much as possible, including a "calling box" for servants in the dining room. A conservatory bar overlooks the cathedral, as do three luxurious rooms. Four rooms are in the original house, with the remainder in a new wing. Each room has a distinctive character and often opens onto a scenic view. Two rooms are suitable for guests with disabilities. Two accommodations are large enough for families and the hotel welcomes young children. Each bathroom is well maintained and most have shower-and-tub combinations.

70 Harnham Rd., Salisbury, Wiltshire SP2 8JN. ✆ **01722/338388.** Fax 01722/333710. www.grasmere hotel.com. 20 units. £95–£155 ($152–$248) double. Rates include English breakfast. AE, DC, MC, V. Take A3094 2.5km (1½ miles) from town center. **Amenities:** Restaurant; bar; room service; babysitting; laundry service; dry cleaning. *In room:* TV, coffeemaker, hair dryer, trouser press.

Red Lion Hotel ✶ *Value*   In business since the 1300s, the Red Lion continues to accommodate wayfarers from London on their way to the West Country. This Best Western–affiliated hotel no longer reigns supreme in town—we prefer the White Hart and The Rose and Crown—but it's a fine choice and somewhat more affordable than those two. Cross under its arch into a courtyard with a hanging, much-photographed creeper, a red lion, and a half-timbered facade, and you'll be transported back to an earlier era.

The antiques-filled hotel is noted for its unique clock collection, which includes a skeleton organ clock in the reception hall. Each small to medium-sized bedroom is individually furnished and tastefully decorated. Two units are spacious enough for families, and the most expensive rooms have four-poster beds.

4 Milford St., Salisbury, Wiltshire SP1 2AN. ☎ **800/528-1234** in the U.S., or 01722/323334. Fax 01722/ 325756. www.the-redlion.co.uk. 52 units. £110 ($176) double; £130 ($208) suite. AE, DC, MC, V. **Amenities:** Restaurant; bar; room service; laundry service; dry cleaning. *In room:* TV, coffeemaker, hair dryer.

The Rose and Crown ✶✶✶   This half-timbered, 13th-century gem stands with its feet almost in the River Avon; beyond the water, you can see the tall spire of the cathedral. Because of its tranquil location, it's our top choice. From here, you can easily walk over the arched stone bridge to the center of Salisbury in 10 minutes. Old trees shade the lawns and gardens between the inn and the river, and chairs are set out so that you can enjoy the view and count the swans. The inn has both a new and an old wing. The new wing is modern, but the old wing is more appealing, with its sloping ceilings and antique fireplaces and furniture. Bedrooms in the main house range from small to medium in size, though those in the new wing are more spacious and better designed.

Harnham Rd., Salisbury, Wiltshire SP2 8JQ. ☎ **01722/399955**. Fax 01722/339816. 28 units. £118 ($189) double. AE, DC, MC, V. Take A3094 2.5km (1½ miles) from the center of town. **Amenities:** Restaurant; 2 bars; room service; laundry service; dry cleaning. *In room:* TV, coffeemaker, hair dryer, trouser press.

White Hart ✶   Combining the best of old and new, the White Hart is a Salisbury landmark from Georgian times. Its classic facade is intact, with tall columns crowning a life-size hart. The older accommodations are traditional, and a new section has been added in the rear, opening onto a large parking area. All units were refurbished in 1995. New-wing units are tastefully decorated; although rooms in the main building have more style and character, many of these are quite small. Bathrooms are a bit small. You can enjoy a before-dinner drink, followed by a meal of modern English fare, in the White Hart Restaurant.

1 St. John St., Salisbury, Wiltshire SP1 2SD. ☎ **01722/327476**. Fax 01722/412761. www.macdonald hotels.co.uk. 68 units. £111–£148 ($178–$237) double. AE, DC, MC, V. **Amenities:** Restaurant; bar; room service; laundry service. *In room:* TV, coffeemaker.

INEXPENSIVE

Cricket Field House Hotel ✶ *Finds*   This snug B&B takes its name from the cricket field it overlooks. The original structure was a gamekeeper's cottage that has been handsomely converted. In its own large garden, the family-run house is comfortably furnished and modernized. Rooms are in both the main house and an equally good pavilion annex. Each unit is decorated and furnished individually, and has a small but neatly kept shower-only bathroom.

Wilton Rd., Salisbury, Wiltshire SP2 9NS. ☎ **01722/322595**. www.cricketfieldhousehotel.co.uk. 14 units. £60–£80 ($96–$128) double. Rates include English breakfast. AE, MC, V. Lies on the A36, 3km (2 miles) west of Salisbury. **Amenities:** Restaurant for guests only. *In room:* TV, coffeemaker, hair dryer, trouser press.

Fun Fact Sleuthing After Miss Marple

Thirteen kilometers (8 miles) east of Salisbury is the little village of **Nether Wallop** (not to be confused with Over Wallop or Middle Wallop, also in the same vicinity). Agatha Christie fans should note that it's the fictitious town of St. Mary Mead, Miss Marple's home, in the PBS *Miss Marple* mysteries. It's 19km (12 miles) from Stonehenge and 16km (10 miles) from Winchester, on a country road between the A343 and the A30.

Wyndham Park Lodge   From this appealing Victorian 1880 house, it's an easy walk to the heart of Salisbury and its cathedral, and about a 5-minute walk to a swimming pool and the bus station. The small to midsize rooms are comfortably furnished with Victorian and Edwardian antiques. They have either one double or two twin beds. Only one unit has a tub-and-shower combination, the rest have efficient showers. Reservations are recommended.

51 Wyndham Rd., Salisbury, Wiltshire SP1 3AB. ⓒ **01722/416517.** Fax 01722/328851. www.wyndham parklodge.co.uk. 4 units. £42–£46 ($67–$74) double; £60–£66 ($96–$106) family room for 3. Rates include English breakfast. MC, V. **Amenities:** Breakfast room. *In room:* TV, coffeemaker, hair dryer.

A CHOICE IN NEARBY DINTON

Howard's House ★ *(finds)*   Housed in a 17th-century dower house that has been added to over the years and set in a medieval hamlet, this property is the most appealing small hotel and restaurant in the area. Much care is lavished on the decor here, with fresh flowers in every public room and bedroom. Most bedrooms are spacious in size, and one room is large enough for a family. All units contain well-kept bathrooms with shower-tub combinations; some rooms have four-poster beds. The hotel has attractive gardens, and on chilly nights, log fires burn. *Tip:* Even if you don't stay here, consider stopping by for a wonderful three-course dinner (call to reserve a table first) in the hotel's restaurant.

Teffont Evias, near Salisbury, Wiltshire SP3 5RJ. ⓒ **01722/716392.** Fax 01722/716820. www.howards househotel.com. 9 units. £145–£165 ($232–$264) double. Rates include English breakfast. AE, DC, MC, V. Leave Salisbury on the A36 until you reach a roundabout. Take the first left leading to the A30. On the A30, continue for 5km (3 miles) coming to the turnoff (B3089) for Barford Saint-Martin. Continue for 6.5km (4 miles) on this secondary road to the town of Teffont Evias, where the hotel is signposted. **Amenities:** Restaurant; bar; room service. *In room:* TV, hair dryer.

WHERE TO DINE

The best restaurant is not in Salisbury itself but on the outskirts—at Howard's House at Teffont Evias (see below). See also "Salisbury After Dark," below, for a selection of pubs offering affordable fare.

Foodies should stop in at **David Brown Food Hall & Tea Rooms,** 31 Catherine St. (ⓒ **01722/329363**). It carries the finest fresh foods—meats, cheeses, breads, and other baked goods—making it a terrific place to put together a picnic.

Harper's Restaurant ENGLISH/INTERNATIONAL   The chef-owner of this place prides himself on specializing in homemade and wholesome "real food." The pleasantly decorated restaurant is on the second floor of a redbrick building at the back end of Salisbury's largest parking lot, in the center of town. In the same all-purpose dining room, you can order from two different menus, one with affordable bistro-style platters, including beefsteak casserole with "herbey dumplings." A longer menu, listing items that take a bit more time to prepare, includes all-vegetarian pasta diavolo, or spareribs with french fries and rice.

6–7 Ox Row, Market Sq. ℂ 01722/333118. Reservations recommended. Main courses £6.50–£14 ($10–$22); 2-course fixed-price meal £7.20–£11 ($12–$18) at lunch and dinner. AE, DC, MC, V. Mon–Sat noon–2pm; daily 6–9:30pm (10pm on Sat). Closed Sun Oct–May.

Howard's House Hotel Restaurant ✦ INTERNATIONAL   If you'd like to dine in one of the loveliest places in the area, and enjoy a refined cuisine at the same time, leave Salisbury and head for this previously recommended hotel. It's a 14km (9-mile) drive to Teffort Evias but well worth the trip. The village itself is one of the most beautiful in Wiltshire.

The elegantly appointed restaurant showcases a finely honed cuisine prepared with first-class ingredients such as mallard duck or local pheasant. The menu changes daily but is likely to feature such delights as home-smoked filet of salmon in a saffron sauce with a side dish of steamed leeks. We like the use of red-onion marmalade with some of the dishes such as the pan-seared calves' liver, which also comes with honey-roasted parsnips. Desserts would surely please the most exacting, including a chilled mango mousse with marinated strawberries.

Teffont Evias, near Salisbury. ℂ 01722/716392. Reservations required. Main courses £14–£20 ($22–$32); fixed-price menu £24 ($38). AE, DC, MC, V. Daily 7:30–9pm; Sun noon–2pm. For directions, see the Howard's House listing in the "Where to Stay" section above.

LXIX ✦ MODERN ENGLISH   Close to the Salisbury Cathedral, this is the finest dining room within the city itself. It's awakened the sleepy tastebuds of Salisbury, which has suffered for decades without a really good first-class restaurant. In a stylish contemporary interior, a modern English but French inspired cuisine is served. Ingredients are adjusted on the menu to take advantage of the changing seasons. Try, for example, roasted sea bass with a "mash" of spinach served in a velvety smooth and chive-laced white butter sauce. One excellent dish is Angus beef served with foie gras and very thick potatoes cooked like french fries. A more delicate offering, but one equally good is *mille feuille,* "a thousand leaves," in this case, puff pastry filled with wild mushrooms and toasted peanuts. Smoked river eel adds an exotic touch to the menu.

69 New St. ℂ 01722/340000. Reservations not required. Main courses £6.90–£13 ($11–$21). AE, DC, MC, V. Mon–Sat noon–3pm and 6–11pm. Closed last week in Dec, 1st week in Jan.

Salisbury Haunch of Venison ENGLISH   Right in the heart of Salisbury, this creaky-timbered chophouse (it dates back to 1320) serves excellent dishes, especially English roasts and grills. Stick to its specialties and you'll rarely go wrong. Begin with a tasty warm salad of venison sausages with garlic croutons, and then follow with the time-honored roast haunch of venison with parsnips and juniper berries. Other classic English dishes are served as well, including grilled Barnsley lamb chops with "bubble and squeak" (cabbage and potatoes).

1 Minster St. ℂ 01722/322024. Main courses £8.25–£14 ($13–$22); bar platters for lunches, light suppers, and snacks £5–£8 ($8–$13). MC, V. Daily noon–2pm; Mon–Sat 6–9pm. Pub Mon–Sat 11am–11pm; Sun noon–3pm and 7–10:30pm. Closed Christmas and Easter.

SALISBURY AFTER DARK

The **Salisbury Playhouse,** Malthouse Lane (ℂ 01722/320117, or 01722/ 320333 for the box office), produces some of the finest theater in the region. Food and drink are available from the bar and restaurant to complete your evening's entertainment.

The City Hall, Malthouse Lane (© 01722/334432, or 01722/327676 for the box office), has a program of events to suit most tastes and ages in comfortable surroundings. A thriving entertainment center, it attracts many of the national touring shows in addition to local amateur events, exhibitions, and sales, thus providing good entertainment at a reasonable price.

The Salisbury Arts Center, Bedwin Street (© 01722/321744), housed within the former St. Edmund's Church, offers a wide range of performing and visual arts. A typical program contains a broad mix of music, contemporary and classic theater, and dance performances, plus cabaret, comedy, and family shows. Regular workshops are available for all ages in arts, crafts, theater, and dance. The lively cafe/bar is a pleasant meeting place.

Many a Salisbury pub crawl begins at the Haunch of Venison (see above). Another good pub is The Pheasant on Salt Lane, near the bus station (© 01722/320675), which attracts locals as well as visitors on their way to Stonehenge. Snacks, ploughman's lunches, and hot pub grub, including meat pies, are served all day. It's all washed down with a goodly assortment of ales. To cap the night, head for the Avon Brewery Inn, 75 Castle St. (© 01722/327280), which is decorated like a Victorian saloon from the gay 1890s, and has an idyllic garden setting overlooking the River Avon. It offers some of the tastiest and most affordable food in town.

9 Prehistoric Britain: Stonehenge ★★★ & Avebury ★★

Stonehenge ★★★ This huge circle of lintels and megalithic pillars, believed to be approximately 5,000 years old, is the most important prehistoric monument in Britain.

Some visitors are disappointed when they see that Stonehenge is nothing more than concentric circles of stones. But perhaps they don't understand that Stonehenge represents an amazing engineering feat, because many of the boulders, the bluestones in particular, were moved many miles (perhaps from southern Wales) to this site.

The widely held view of 18th- and 19th-century romantics that Stonehenge was the work of the druids is without foundation. The boulders, many weighing several tons, are believed to have predated the arrival in Britain of the Celtic culture. Recent excavations continue to bring new evidence to bear on the origin and purpose of Stonehenge. Controversy surrounds the prehistoric site, especially since the publication of *Stonehenge Decoded* by Gerald S. Hawkins and John B. White, which maintains that Stonehenge was an astronomical observatory— that is, a Neolithic "computing machine" capable of predicting eclipses.

Your ticket permits you to go inside the fence surrounding the site that protects the stones from vandals and souvenir hunters. You can go all the way up to a short rope barrier, about 15m (50 ft.) from the stones.

A full circular tour around Stonehenge is possible. A modular walkway was introduced to cross the archaeologically important avenue, the area that runs between the Heel Stone and the main circle of stones. This enables visitors to complete a full circuit of the stones and to see one of the best views of a completed section of Stonehenge as they pass by. This is an excellent addition to the informative audio tour.

Wilts & Dorset (© 01722/336855) runs several buses daily (depending on demand) from Salisbury to Stonehenge, as well as buses from the Salisbury train

---

Finds Biking to Stonehenge

If you'd like to bike out to Stonehenge, go to **Hayball's Cycle Shop,** 26–30 Winchester St. (© **01722/411378**), which rents mountain bikes for £9 ($14) per day. For an extra £2.50 ($4), you can keep the bike overnight. A £25 ($40) deposit is required. A 7-day rental is £65 ($104). Hours are daily from 9am to 5pm.

---

station to Stonehenge. The bus trip to Stonehenge takes 40 minutes, and a round-trip ticket costs £5.50 ($8.80) for adults and £2.75 ($4.40) for children ages 5 to 14 (free for ages 4 and under).

At the junction of A303 and A344/A360. © **01980/623108** for information. Admission £4.40 ($7.05) adults, £3.30 ($5.30) seniors and students, £2.30 ($3.70) children, £11 ($18) family ticket. June–Aug daily 9:30am–7pm; Mar 16–May and Sept–Oct 15 daily 9am–5pm; Oct 16–Mar 15 daily 9:30am–4pm. If you're driving, head north on Castle Rd. from the center of Salisbury. At the first roundabout (traffic circle), take the exit toward Amesbury (A345) and Old Sarum. Continue along this road for 13km (8 miles) and then turn left onto A303 in the direction of Exeter. You'll see signs for Stonehenge, leading you up A344 to the right. It's 3km (2 miles) west of Amesbury.

Avebury ★★ One of the largest prehistoric sites in Europe, Avebury lies on the Kennet River, 11km (7 miles) west of Marlborough and 32km (20 miles) north of Stonehenge. Some visitors say visiting Avebury, in contrast to Stonehenge, is a more organic experience—you can walk right up and around the stones, as there's no fence keeping you away. Also, the site isn't mobbed with tour buses.

Visitors can walk around the 28-acre site at Avebury, winding in and out of the circle of more than 100 stones, some weighing up to 50 tons. The stones are made of sarsen, a sandstone found in Wiltshire. Inside this large circle are two smaller ones, each with about 30 stones standing upright. Native Neolithic tribes are believed to have built these circles.

Wilts & Dorset (© **01722/336855**) has two buses (nos. 5 and 6) that run between the Salisbury bus station and Avebury, three times a day from Monday through Saturday and twice daily on Sunday. The one-way trip takes 1 hour and 40 minutes. Round-trip tickets are £5.50 ($8.80) adults and £2.75 ($4.40) children ages 5 to 14 (free for ages 4 and under).

Also here is the **Alexander Keiller Museum** (© **01672/539250**), which houses one of Britain's most important archaeological collections, including material from excavations at Windmill Hill and Avebury, and artifacts from other prehistoric digs at West Kennet, Long Barrow, Silbury Hill, West Kennet Avenue, and the Sanctuary. The museum is open April through October daily from 10am to 6pm, November through March from 10am to 4pm. Admission is £4 ($6.40) for adults and £2 ($3.20) for children.

On A361 between Swindon and Devizes (1.6km/1mile from the A4 London–Bath road). The closest rail station is at Swindon, 12 miles (19km) away, which is served by the main rail line from London to Bath. For rail information, call © **0845/748-4950**. A limited bus service (no. 49) runs from Swindon to Devizes through Avebury.

8

The West Country

For our look at the "West Countree," we move into the southwestern historic shires of England. Once you reach this area of pastoral woodland, London seems far removed.

Somerset has some of the most beautiful scenery in England. The undulating limestone hills of Mendip and the irresistible Quantocks are especially lovely in spring and fall. Somerset opens onto the Bristol Channel, with Minehead serving as its chief resort. The shire is rich in legend and history, possessing particularly fanciful associations with King Arthur and Queen Guinevere, Camelot, and Alfred the Great. Its villages are noted for the tall towers of their parish churches.

Somerset also encompasses the territory around the old port of Bristol and the old Roman city of **Bath,** known for its abbey and spa water, lying beside the River Avon.

Glastonbury, with its once-great abbey that is now a ruined sanctuary, may be one of Britain's oldest inhabited sites. The greatest natural spectacle in the area is **Exmoor National Park,** once an English royal hunting preserve, stretching for 265 square miles on the north coast of Devon and Somerset. There are also many terrific country houses and palaces in this region. The other two major attractions, **Longleat House** and the fabled gardens at **Stourhead,** can be visited in a busy day while you're based at Bath.

The British approach sunny **Devon** with the same kind of excitement normally reserved for hopping over to the Continent. Especially along the coastline—the English Riviera—the names of the seaports, villages, and resorts are synonymous with holidays in the sun: Torquay, Clovelly, Lynton-Lynmouth. Devon is a land of jagged coasts—the red cliffs in the south face the English Channel. In South Devon, the coast from which Drake and Raleigh set sail, tranquillity prevails, and on the bay-studded coastline of North Devon, pirates and smugglers found haven.

Along the south coast, the best bases from which you can explore the region are Exeter, Plymouth, and Torquay. The area's most charming village (with very limited accommodations) is Clovelly. The greatest natural spectacle is **Dartmoor National Park,** northeast of Plymouth, a landscape of gorges and moors filled with gorse and purple heather—home of the Dartmoor pony.

The ancient duchy of **Cornwall** is in the extreme southwestern part of England, often called "the toe." This peninsula is a virtual island—culturally if not geographically. Encircled by coastline, it abounds in rugged cliffs, hidden bays, fishing villages, sandy beaches, and sheltered coves where smuggling was once rampant. Although many of the little seaports with hillside cottages resemble towns along the Mediterranean, Cornwall retains its own distinctive flavor.

The ancient land had its own language until about 250 years ago, and some of the old words (*pol* for pool, *tre* for house) still survive. The Cornish dialect is more easily understood by the Welsh than by those who speak the Queen's English.

We suggest basing yourself at one of the smaller fishing villages, such as East or West Looe, Polperro, Mousehole, or Portloe, where you'll experience the true charm of the duchy. Many of the villages, such as St. Ives, are artists' colonies. Except for St. Ives and Port Isaac, some of the most interesting places lie on the southern coast, often called the Cornish Riviera. However, the north coast has its own peculiar charm as well. The majestic coastline is studded with fishing villages and hidden coves for swimming, with Penzance and St. Ives serving as the major meccas. A little further west is Land's End, where England actually comes to an end.

1 Bath: Britain's Most Historic Spa Town ★★★

185km (115 miles) W of London; 21km (13 miles) SE of Bristol

In 1702, Queen Anne made the trek from London to the mineral springs of **Bath,** thereby launching a fad that was to make the city the most celebrated spa in England.

The most famous name connected with Bath was the 18th-century dandy Beau Nash, who cut a striking figure as he made his way across the city, with all the plumage of a bird of paradise. This polished arbiter of taste and manners made dueling déclassé. While dispensing (at a price) trinkets to the courtiers and aspirant gentlemen of his day, Beau was carted around in a sedan chair.

The 18th-century architects John Wood the Elder and his son provided a proper backdrop for Nash's considerable social talents. These architects designed a city of stone from the nearby hills, a feat so substantial and lasting that Bath today is the most harmoniously laid-out city in England. During Georgian times, this city, on a bend of the River Avon, was to attract a following of leading political and literary figures, such as Dickens, Thackeray, Nelson, and Pitt. Canadians may already know that General Wolfe lived on Trim Street, and Australians may want to visit the house at 19 Bennett St., where their founding father, Admiral Phillip, lived. Even Henry Fielding came this way, observing in *Tom Jones* that the ladies of Bath "endeavour to appear as ugly as possible in the morning, in order to set off that beauty which they intend to show you in the evening."

And even before its Queen Anne, Georgian, and Victorian popularity, Bath was known to the Romans as Aquae Sulis. The foreign legions founded their baths here (which you can visit today) to ease their rheumatism in the curative mineral springs.

Remarkable restoration and careful planning have ensured that Bath retains its handsome look today. The city suffered devastating destruction from the infamous Baedeker air raids of 1942, when Luftwaffe pilots seemed more intent on bombing historical buildings than in hitting any military target.

After undergoing major restoration in the postwar era, Bath today has somewhat of a museum look, with the attendant gift shops. Its parks, museums, and architecture continue to draw hordes of visitors, and because of this massive tourist invasion, prices remain high. It's one of the high points of the West Country and a good base for exploring Avebury.

ESSENTIALS

GETTING THERE   Trains leave London's Paddington Station bound for Bath once every ½ hour during the day. The trip takes about 1½ hours. For rail information, call ☎ **0845/748-4950.**

One **National Express** coach leaves London's Victoria Coach Station every 2 hours during the day. The trip takes 3½ hours. Coaches also leave Bristol bound for Bath and make the trip in 40 minutes. For schedules and information, call © **020/7529-2000.**

Drive west on M4 to the junction with A4, on which you continue west to Bath.

VISITOR INFORMATION   The **Bath Tourist Information Centre** is at Abbey Chambers, Abbey Church Yard (© **01225/477101;** www.visitbath.co. uk), next to Bath Abbey. It's open June through September, Monday through Saturday from 9:30am to 6pm, Sunday from 10am to 4pm; off season, Monday through Saturday from 9:30am to 5pm and Sunday from 10am to 4pm.

GETTING AROUND   One of the best ways to explore Bath is by bike. Rentals are available at **Avon Valley Cycle Shop** (© **01225/442442**), behind the train station. It's open daily from 9am to 5:30pm, charging £14 ($22) per day, and about £50 ($80) per week, depending on the bike. A bond of £300 ($480) can be put on a credit card.

SPECIAL EVENTS   Bath's graceful Georgian architecture provides the setting for one of Europe's most prestigious international festivals of music and the arts, the **Bath International Music Festival.** For 17 days in late May and early June each year, the city is filled with more than 1,000 performers. The festival focuses on classical music, jazz, new music, and the contemporary visual arts, with orchestras, soloists, and artists from all over the world. In addition to the main music and art program, there are walks, tours, and talks, plus free street entertainment, a free Festival Club, and opening-night celebrations with fireworks. For detailed information, contact the **Bath Festivals Box Office,** 2 Church St., Abbey Green, Bath BA1 1NL (© **01225/463362**).

SEEING THE SIGHTS

You'll want to stroll around to see some of the buildings, crescents, and squares in town. The **North Parade** (where Goldsmith lived) and the **South Parade** (where English novelist and diarist Frances Burney once resided) represent harmony, and are the work of John Wood the Elder. He also designed beautiful **Queen Square,** where both Jane Austen and Wordsworth once lived. Also of interest is **The Circus** ★★★, built in 1754, as well as the shop-lined **Pulteney Bridge,** designed by Robert Adam and often compared to the Ponte Vecchio of Florence.

The younger John Wood designed the **Royal Crescent** ★★★, an elegant half-moon row of town houses (copied by Astor architects for their colonnade in New York City in the 1830s). At **No. 1 Royal Crescent** (© **01225/428126**), the interior has been redecorated and furnished by the Bath Preservation Trust to look as it might have toward the end of the 18th century. The house is located at one end of Bath's most magnificent crescent, west of the Circus. Admission is £4 ($6.40) for adults and £3.50 ($5.60) for children, seniors, and students; a family ticket is £10 ($16). Open from mid-February to October, Tuesday through Sunday from 10:30am to 5pm, and November, Tuesday through Sunday from 10:30am to 4pm (last admission 30 min. before closing); closed Good Friday.

Free 1¾-hour walking tours are conducted throughout the year by **The Mayor's Honorary Society** (© **01225/477786**). Tours depart from outside the Roman Baths Monday through Friday at 10:30am and 2pm, Sunday at 2:30pm, and May through September, Tuesday, Friday, and Saturday at 7pm.

To tour Bath by bus, you can choose among several tour companies. Among the best is **Patrick Driscoll,** Elmsleigh, Bathampton (© **01225/462010**), with tours that are more personalized than most.

Bath's newest attraction, the **Jane Austen Centre,** 40 Gay St. (© **01225/443000**), is located in a Georgian town house on an elegant street where Miss Austen once lived. Exhibits and a video convey a sense of what life was like in Bath during the Regency period. The center is open Monday through Saturday from 10am to 5pm and Sunday from 10:30am to 5:30pm. Admission is £4.45 ($7.10) for adults, £3.65 ($5.85) seniors and students, and £2.45 ($3.90) children.

River Avon boat cruises depart from a pier adjacent to the Pulteney Bridge (directly across the water from the Parade Gardens). Cruises last 1 hour and are priced £6 ($9.60) for adults, and £2.50 ($4) for children. They're offered from Easter to October via two boats maintained by **The Boating Station** (© **01225/466407**).

The American Museum 🏛️🏛️   Some 4km (2½ miles) outside Bath, get an idea of what life was like in America prior to the mid-1800s. The first American museum established outside the U.S., it sits proudly on extensive grounds high above the Somerset Valley. Among the authentic exhibits shipped over from the States are a New Mexico room, a Conestoga wagon, the dining room of a New York town house of the early 19th century, and (on the grounds) a copy of Washington's flower garden at Mount Vernon. Throughout the summer, the museum hosts various special events, from displays of Native American dancing to very realistic re-enactments of the Civil War.

Claverton Manor, Bathwick Hill. © **01225/460503.** www.americanmuseum.org. Admission £6 ($9.60) adults, £5.50 ($8.80) students and seniors, £3.50 ($5.60) children 5–16, free for 4 and under. Late Mar to Nov Tues–Sun 2–5pm for the museum, Tues–Fri 1–6pm and Sat–Sun noon–6pm for the garden. Bus: 18.

Bath Abbey 🏛️   Built on the site of a much larger Norman cathedral, the present-day abbey is a fine example of the late Perpendicular style. When Queen Elizabeth I came to Bath in 1574, she ordered a national fund to be set up to restore the abbey. The west front is the sculptural embodiment of a Jacob's Ladder dream of a 15th-century bishop. When you go inside and see its many windows, you'll understand why the abbey is called the "Lantern of the West." Note the superb fan vaulting with its scalloped effect. Beau Nash was buried in the nave and is honored by a simple monument totally out of keeping with his flamboyant character. The Bath Abbey Heritage Vaults opened in 1994 on the south

---

⌒**Value** A Discount Pass Option for Bath

The **Bath Pass** is a new discount card that provides admission to 30 attractions in and around Bath and nearby Bristol; transportation, restaurant, and shopping discounts; and a pocket guidebook. If you spend a full day or two in the Bath/Bristol area (not a particularly hard thing to do), you're almost guaranteed to save money by using the pass. The Bath Pass costs £22 ($35) for 1 day, £29 ($46) for 2 days, or £39 ($62) for 3 days (children pay £25/$40) and includes free admission to the Roman Baths and Pump Room, the Museum of Costumes and Assembly Rooms, and much more. For more information, call © **01664/500107** or head online to **www.bathpass.com.**

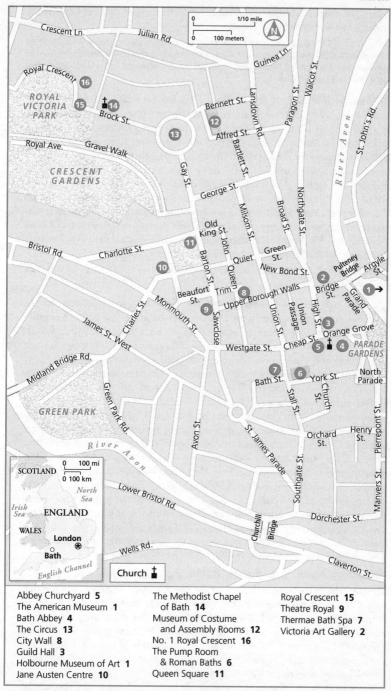

Bath

| 0 | 1/10 mile |
| 0 | 100 meters |

Crescent Ln.

Julian Rd.

Guinea Ln.

Royal Crescent **16**

ROYAL VICTORIA PARK **15** † **14** Brock St.

Bennett St.

Lansdown Rd.

Paragon St.

Walcot St.

River Avon

St. John's Rd.

12

Alfred St.

13

Bartlett St.

Gay St.

George St.

Royal Ave.

Gravel Walk

CRESCENT GARDENS

Milsom St.

Broad St.

Northgate St.

Old King St.

John St.

11

Green St.

Bristol Rd.

Charlotte St.

Quiet

New Bond St.

2 Pulteney Bridge

Argyle St.

10

Barton St.

Queen St.

Beaufort St.

Trim **8**

Upper Borough Walls

Bridge St.

High St.

1 →

Grand Parade

Charles St.

Monmouth St.

Sawclose

9

Union St.

Union Passage

3

Cheap St.

Orange Grove

James St. West

Westgate St.

5 † **4**

PARADE GARDENS

Midland Bridge Rd.

Green Park Rd.

7

Bath St.

6

York St.

Church St.

Stall St.

North Parade

GREEN PARK

River Avon

Avon St.

St. James Parade

Orchard St.

Henry St.

Pierrepont St.

Manvers St.

SCOTLAND

North Sea

Irish Sea

ENGLAND

WALES

London ✶

Bath

English Channel

| 0 | 100 mi |
| 0 | 100 km |

Lower Bristol Rd.

Southgate St.

Churchill Bridge

Dorchester St.

Wells Rd.

Claverton St.

Church †

Abbey Churchyard **5**
The American Museum **1**
Bath Abbey **4**
The Circus **13**
City Wall **8**
Guild Hall **3**
Holbourne Museum of Art **1**
Jane Austen Centre **10**

The Methodist Chapel
of Bath **14**
Museum of Costume
and Assembly Rooms **12**
No. 1 Royal Crescent **16**
The Pump Room
& Roman Baths **6**
Queen Square **11**

Royal Crescent **15**
Theatre Royal **9**
Thermae Bath Spa **7**
Victoria Art Gallery **2**

side of the abbey. This subterranean exhibition traces the history of Christianity at the abbey site since Saxon times.

Orange Grove. ℂ **01225/422462.** www.bathabbey.org. £2.50 ($4) donation requested. Admission to the Heritage Vaults £2.50 ($4) adults, £1.50 ($2.40) students, children, and seniors. Abbey Apr–Oct Mon–Sat 9am–6pm; Nov–Mar Mon–Sat 9am–4:30pm; year-round Sun 1–2:30pm and 4:30–5:30pm. The Heritage Vaults year-round Mon–Sat 10am–4pm.

Holbourne Museum of Art ★ *Finds*   This has been called, quite accurately, "one of the most perfect small museums of Europe." It was constructed in 1796 as a building in which to entertain guests to Sydney Gardens, the luminaries including Jane Austen. It was converted into a museum at the turn of the 20th century to display a collection of Sir William Holburne's treasures, such as a bronze nude favored by Louis XIV, along with some of the finest Renaissance majolica in England. Also on display are works illuminating the glittering society of 18th-century Bath at its pinnacle, including masterpieces by Thomas Gainsborough, such as *The Byam Family,* on indefinite loan. Other choice tidbits from this treasure trove include the lovely portrait of *The Reverend Carter Thelwall and His Family* by Stubbs, and such surprising exhibits as a Steinway piano used by Rachmaninoff for rehearsals of his music.

Great Pulteney St. ℂ **01225/466669.** Admission £3.50 ($5.60). Mid-Feb to mid-Dec Tues–Sat 10am–5pm, Sun 2:30–5:30pm.

Museum of Costume and Assembly Rooms ★★   Operated by the National Trust and housed in an 18th-century building, the grand **Assembly Rooms** played host to dances, recitals, and tea parties. Damaged in World War II, the elegant rooms have been gloriously restored and look much as they did when Jane Austen and Thomas Gainsborough attended society events here.

Housed in the same building, the **Museum of Costume** sports one of the best collections of fashion and costume in Europe. A fascinating audio tour escorts visitors through the history of fashion—including accessories, lingerie, and shoes—from the 16th century to the present day. Highlights include a 17th-century "silver tissue" dress; an ultra-restricting whalebone corset; an original suit from Christian Dior's legendary "New Look" collection; and the ultra-sheer Versace dress made famous—or infamous—by actress Jennifer Lopez. The museum is also famous for its "Dress of the Year" collection, which highlights notable ideas in contemporary style. Only 2,000 of the museum's 30,000 items are on display at any one time, but exhibits change frequently and special themed collections are often presented. Plan on spending at least an hour or two.

Bennett St. ℂ **01225/477785.** www.museumofcostume.co.uk. Admission £5.50 ($8.80) adult, £4.50 ($7.20) seniors and students, £3.75 ($6) children age 6 and over, £15 ($24) family ticket. Admission includes free audio tour. Daily 10am–5pm. Last admission 4:30pm. Closed December 25–26.

The Pump Room ★ **& Roman Baths** ★★   Founded in A.D. 75 by the Romans, the baths were dedicated to the goddess Sulis Minerva; in their day, they were an engineering feat. Even today, they're among the finest Roman remains in the country, and they are still fed by Britain's most famous hot-spring water. After centuries of decay, the original baths were rediscovered during Queen Victoria's reign. The site of the Temple of Sulis Minerva has been excavated and is now open to view. The museum displays many interesting objects from Victorian and recent digs (look for the head of Minerva).

Coffee, lunch, and tea, usually with music from the Pump Room Trio, can be enjoyed in the 18th-century pump room, overlooking the hot springs. You can also find a drinking fountain with hot mineral water that tastes horrible.

In the Bath Abbey churchyard. © 01225/477785. www.romanbaths.co.uk. Admission £8.50 ($14) adults,
£4.50 ($7.20) children, £22 ($35) family ticket. Apr–Sept daily 9am–6pm; Oct–Mar Mon–Sat 9am–5pm.

Theatre Royal Bath   Theatre Royal, located next to the new Seven Dials
development, was restored in 1982 and refurbished with plush seats, red carpets,
and a painted proscenium arch and ceiling; it is now the most beautiful theater
in Britain. It has 940 seats, with a small pit and grand tiers rising to the upper
circle. Despite all the work, Theatre Royal has no company, depending upon
touring shows to fill the house during the 8-week theater season each summer.
Beneath the theater, reached from the back of the stalls or by a side door, are the
theater vaults, where you will find a bar in one with stone walls. The next vault
has a restaurant, serving an array of dishes from soup to light a la carte meals.

A studio theater at the rear of the main building opened in 1996. The theater
publishes a list of forthcoming events; its repertoire includes West End shows,
among other offerings.

Sawclose. © 01225/448844. www.theatreroyal.org.uk. Tickets £10–£25 ($15–$38). Box office Mon–Sat
10am–8pm; Sun noon–8pm. Shows Mon–Wed at 7:30pm; Thurs–Sat at 8pm; Wed and Sat matinees at
2:30pm.

Thermae Bath Spa ★★   This is the only place in the U.K. where you can
bathe in natural, hot spring water. Used for thousands of years, the restored
baths are in operation for the first time since 1978. Health, leisure, architecture,
history, and culture are all combined here at these bubbling, mineral-rich waters.
Five impressive heritage buildings, including the sacred Cross Bath, have been
restored for one of Europe's most remarkable spas. Not all the buildings are old;
a stunning new glass-and-stone building was designed by international architects. Facilities include indoor and outdoor thermal spa bathing, steam rooms,
massage and treatment rooms, a restaurant, and a visitor center.

One of the most eye-catching parts of the new spa is an open-air, rooftop
pool, from which bathers can gaze out over the skyline of the city. Because of its
naturally hot water, the rooftop pool is open all year. The location is set in the
center of the city, just 31m (100 ft.) from the Roman Baths. The steam rooms
are particularly impressive, with 4 circular glass pods, a "waterfall" shower, foot-
baths, an open-air terrace, and a solarium. A dozen wet treatment rooms feature
such luxuries as hydrotherapy, hay and herbal wraps, a Vichy shower, mud treatments, and shiatsu/watsu.

The Hetling Pump Room, Hot Bath St. © 01225/780308. Admission: £17 ($27) for 2-hr. session, £23 ($37)
for 4-hr. session, £35 ($56) for all-day ticket. Daily 9am–10pm.

Victoria Art Gallery   This relatively unknown gallery showcases the area's
best collection of British and European art from the 15th century to the present. Most of the works are on display in the sumptuous Victorian Upper Gallery.
The collection includes paintings by artists who have lived and worked in the
Bath area, including Gainsborough. Singled out for special attention is the
art of Walter Richard Sickert (1860–1942) now that he has been "outed" as the
real Jack the Ripper in Patricia Cornwell's bestseller, *Portrait of a Killer: Jack the
Ripper—Case Closed*. In the two large modern galleries downstairs, special exhibitions are shown. These exhibitions change every six to eight weeks, and are
likely to feature displays ranging from cartoons to boat sculpture.

Bridge St. © 01225/477233. www.victoriagal.org.uk. Free admission. Tues–Fri 10am–5:30pm; Sat
10am–5pm.

OUTDOOR PURSUITS

GOLF   The 18-hole **Bath Golf Club,** at North Road (© **01225/463834**), charges £29 ($46) per round on weekdays and £35 ($56) on Saturday and Sunday. There are no golf carts. The club is open to visitors with established handicap certificates or letters of introduction from their own club. Before playing, call © **01225/466953** for the best tee times. To get to Bath Golf Club, take A36 (Warminster Rd.) out of Bath. Turn right onto North Road, signposted Golf Club, University, and American Museum.

Another 18-hole course is the **Lansdown Golf Club,** Lansdown (© **01225/422138**), with greens fees of £22 ($35) weekdays, £28 ($45) weekends. Visitors are accepted only with a handicap certificate from their own club. Call © **01225/420242** to book tee times in advance. To get to Lansdown Golf Club, take Lansdown Road out of Bath toward the racecourse and Lansdown Park-and-Ride. At the edge of the city, pass the Park-and-Ride and the Blathway Arms; the Golf Club is on the left-hand side.

A nine-hole public course is the **Entry Hill Golf Course,** Entry Hill (© **01225/834248**), with greens fees of £6.85 ($11). The cost for 18 holes is £11 ($17). Golfers need proper golf shoes or trainers. Club rentals are available. Call to reserve tee times. To get to Entry Hill Golf Course, take A367 south of Bath along Wellsway. Turn left at the sign for Entry Hill Golf Course.

HORSEBACK RIDING   The Wellow Trekking Centre, in Wellow, near Bath (© **01225/834376**), is open daily from 9:30am to 4pm. One-hour rides cost £18 ($29), 2-hour rides are £30 ($48) .

TENNIS   There are public outdoor hard courts at **Royal Victoria Park, Sydney Gardens,** and **Alice Park.** Courts are open year-round till sunset; rates are £2.50 ($4) per person per hour. They also offer indoor courts that stay open until 10pm for £11 ($18) per court per hour. All courts are centrally located and marked on the city map available from the Tourist Information Centre at Abbey Chambers. For racquet and ball rentals or more information, contact **Excel Tennis** (© **01225/425066**).

SHOPPING

Bath is loaded with markets and fairs, antiques centers, and small shops. There are literally hundreds of opportunities to buy (and ship) anything you want (including the famous spa waters, which are for sale by the bottle). Prices are traditionally less than in London but more than in the British boonies.

The whole city is basically one long, slightly uphill shopping area. It's not defined by one Main Street, as are so many British towns—if you arrive by train, don't be put off by the lack of scenery. Within 2 blocks are several shopping streets. The single best day to visit, if you are a serious shopper intent on hitting the flea markets, is Wednesday.

The Bartlett Street Antiques Centre, Bartlett Street (© **01225/466689**), encompasses 60 dealers and 160 showcases displaying furniture, silver, antique jewelry, paintings, toys, military items, and collectibles. Another option is the **Great Western Antiques Centre,** Bartlett Street (© **01225/425450**), with 30 dealers. Here you can find costumes, costume jewelry, trains and other railway items, lace and linens, porcelain and glass, music boxes, canes, and much more.

Walcot Reclamation, 108 Walcot St. (© **01225/444404**), is Bath's salvage yard. This sprawling and appealingly dusty storeroom of 19th-century architectural remnants is set .5km (¼ mile) northeast of the town center. Its 6,096-sq.-m

(20,000-sq.-ft.) warehouse offers pieces from demolished homes, schools, hospitals, and factories throughout south England. Mantelpieces, panels, columns, and architectural ornaments are each departmentalized into historical eras. Items range from a complete, dismantled 1937 Georgian library crafted from Honduran mahogany to objects costing around £10 ($16) each. Anything can be shipped by a battery of artisans who are trained in adapting antique fittings for modern homes.

The largest purveyor of antique coins and stamps in Bath, **The Bath Stamp & Coin Shop,** 12–13 Pulteney Bridge (© **01225/463073**), offers hundreds of odd and unusual numismatics. Part of the inventory is devoted to Roman coins, some of which were unearthed in archaeological excavations at Roman sites near Bath.

Near Bath Abbey, the **Beaux Arts Gallery,** 13 York St. (© **01225/464850**), is the largest and most important gallery of contemporary art in Bath, specializing in well-known British artists, including Ray Richardson, John Bellany, and Nicola Bealing. Closely linked to the London art scene, the gallery occupies a pair of interconnected, stone-fronted Georgian houses. Its ½-dozen showrooms exhibit objects beginning at £30 ($48) .

The very upscale **Rossiter's,** 38–41 Broad St. (© **01225/462227**), sells very traditional English tableware and home decor items. They'll ship anywhere in the world. Look especially for the display of Moorcraft ginger jars, vases, and clocks, as well as the Floris perfumes.

Whittard of Chelsea, 14 Union Passage (© **01225/483529**), is the most charming and unusual tea emporium in Bath. Inside, you'll find strainers, traditional table and tea services (plus a large selection of offbeat teapot designs), tea biscuits, tea cozies, tea caddies, and teas from all parts of what used to be the empire. Looking for a fabulously exotic tea to wow your friends with back home? How about monkey-picked oolong—a Chinese tea made from plants so inaccessible their leaves can only be gathered by trained monkeys!

WHERE TO STAY
VERY EXPENSIVE

Bath Priory ★★★   Converted from one of Bath's Georgian houses in 1969, the Priory is situated on 2 acres of formal and award-winning gardens with manicured lawns and flowerbeds. The hotel reopened in the spring of 1997, vastly refurbished and more inviting than ever. The rooms are furnished with antiques; our personal favorite is Clivia (all rooms are named after flowers or shrubs), a nicely appointed duplex in a circular turret. Rooms range from medium in size to spacious deluxe units, the latter with views, large sitting areas, and generous dressing areas. Each has a lovely old English bed, often a half-tester; bathrooms are beautifully kept and come with a set of deluxe toiletries.

Weston Rd., Bath, Somerset BA1 2XT. © **01225/331922.** Fax 01225/448276. www.thebathpriory.co.uk. 28 units. £345 ($552) standard double; £315 ($504) deluxe room. Rates include English breakfast and dinner. AE, DC, MC, V. **Amenities:** Restaurant; bar; 2 pools; health club; Jacuzzi; sauna; concierge; room service; babysitting; laundry service; dry cleaning; croquet lawn. *In room:* A/C, TV, hair dryer.

Bath Spa Hotel ★★★   This stunning restored 19th-century mansion is a 10-minute walk from the center of Bath. Behind a facade of Bath stone, it lies at the end of a tree-lined drive on 7 acres of landscaped grounds, with a Victorian grotto and a Grecian temple. In its long history, it served many purposes (once as a hostel for nurses) before being returned to its original grandeur. The hotel uses log fireplaces, elaborate moldings, and oak paneling to create country-house charm. The rooms are handsomely furnished, and most of them are spacious. Most beds are doubles, and some even offer an old-fashioned four-poster. The marble bathrooms are among the city's finest, each with long tubs, hand-held showers, and deluxe toiletries.

Sydney Rd. (east of the city, off A36), Bath, Somerset BA2 6JF. © **01225/444424.** Fax 01225/444006. www.bathspahotel.com. 102 units. Sun–Thurs £290 ($464) double; Fri–Sat £300 ($480) double; weeklong £315–£355 ($504–$568) suite for 2. AE, DC, MC, V. **Amenities:** 2 restaurants; bar; pool; tennis court; health spa; children's nursery; room service; salon; laundry service; valet. *In room:* TV, minibar, coffeemaker, hair dryer, safe, trouser press.

The Queensberry Hotel ★   A gem of a hotel, this early Georgian-era town house has been beautifully restored by Stephen and Penny Ross. In our view, it is now among the finest places to stay in a city where the competition for restored town-house hotels is fierce. The marquis of Queensberry commissioned John Wood the Younger to build this house in 1772. Rooms—often spacious but usually medium in size—are delightful, each tastefully decorated with antique furniture and such thoughtful extras as fresh flowers. Bathrooms are well kept and equipped with good showers.

Russel St., Bath, Somerset BA1 2QF. © **800/323-5463** in the U.S., or 01225/447928. Fax 01225/446065. www.bathqueensberry.com. 29 units. £120–£225 ($192–$360) double. Rates include continental breakfast. MC, V. Free parking. **Amenities:** Restaurant; bar; room service; laundry service; dry cleaning. *In room:* TV, hair dryer.

Royal Crescent Hotel ★★★ *Finds*   This special place stands proudly in the center of the famed Royal Crescent. Long regarded as Bath's premier hotel (before the arrival of the even better Bath Spa), it has attracted the rich and famous. The bedrooms, including the Jane Austen Suite, are lavishly furnished with such amenities as four-poster beds and marble tubs. Each room is individually designed and offers such comforts as bottled mineral water, fruit plates, and other special touches. Bedrooms, generally quite spacious, are elaborately decked out with thick wool carpeting, silk wall coverings, and antiques, each with a superb and rather sumptuous bed. Bathrooms are equally luxurious with deluxe toiletries and robes.

15–16 Royal Crescent, Bath, Somerset BA1 2LS. © **888/295-4710** in the U.S., or 01225/823333. Fax 01225/ 339401. www.royalcrescent.co.uk. 45 units. £240–£340 ($384–$544) double; from £486 ($778) suite. AE, DC, MC, V. **Amenities:** Restaurant; bar; health club; Jacuzzi; steam room; concierge; car-rental desk; room service; babysitting; laundry service; dry cleaning. *In room:* TV, minibar, hair dryer, safe.

EXPENSIVE

The Francis on the Square ★   An integral part of Queen Square, the Francis is an example of 18th-century taste and style, but we find it too commercial and touristy. Originally consisting of six private residences dating from 1729, the Francis was opened as a private hotel by Emily Francis in 1884 and has offered guests first-class service for more than 100 years. Many of the well-furnished and traditionally styled bedrooms overlook Queen Square, named in honor of George II's consort, Caroline. Rooms range in size from rather small to medium, with either twin or double beds. Accommodations in the older building have more charm, especially the upper floor.

Queen Sq., Bath, Somerset BA1 2HH. © **888/892-0038** in the U.S. and Canada, or 0870/400-8223. Fax 01225/319715. 95 units. £150 ($240) double; £210 ($336) suite. AE, DC, MC, V. **Amenities:** Restaurant; bar; room service; laundry service; dry cleaning. *In room:* TV, hair dryer.

MODERATE

Pratt's Hotel ⭑ Once the home of Sir Walter Scott, Pratt's dates from the heady days of Beau Nash. Functioning as a hotel since 1791, it has become part of the legend and lore of Bath. Several elegant terraced Georgian town houses were joined together to form this complex with a very traditional British atmosphere. Rooms are individually designed, and as is typical of a converted private home, bedrooms range from small to spacious (the larger ones are on the lower floors). Regardless of their dimensions, the rooms are furnished in a comfortable though utilitarian style, with small but efficiently organized shower-only bathrooms.

S. Parade, Bath, Somerset BA2 4AB. ⓒ 01225/460441. Fax 01225/448807. www.forestdale.com. 46 units. £125–£160 ($200–$256) double. Children under 15 sharing a room with 2 adults stay free. Rates include English breakfast. AE, DC, MC, V. Parking £10 ($16). **Amenities:** Restaurant; bar; room service; babysitting; laundry service; dry cleaning. *In room:* TV, coffeemaker, hair dryer, trouser press.

INEXPENSIVE

Apsley House Hotel ⭑⭑ *(Finds)* This charming and stately building, just 1.5km (1 mile) west of the center of Bath, dates from 1830, during the reign of William IV. In 1994, new owners refurbished the hotel, filling it with country-house chintzes and a collection of antiques borrowed from the showrooms of an antiques store they own. (Some furniture in the hotel is for sale.) Style and comfort are the keynote here, and all the relatively spacious bedrooms are inviting, appointed with plush beds and tidy shower-only bathrooms.

141 Newbridge Hill, Bath, Somerset BA1 3PT. ⓒ 01225/336966. Fax 01225/425462. www.apsley-house.co.uk. 9 units. £75–£140 ($120–$224) double; £120–£140 ($192–$224) suite. Rates include English breakfast. AE, MC, V. Take A4 to Upper Bristol Rd., fork right at the traffic signals into Newbridge Hill, and turn left at Apsley Rd. **Amenities:** Bar; room service; babysitting. *In room:* TV, coffeemaker, hair dryer.

Badminton Villa Located about a kilometer (½-mile) south of the city center, this house dates back to 1883. Constructed of honey-colored blocks of Bath stone, it lies on a hillside with sweeping views over the world-famous architecture of Bath. In 1992, John and Sue Barton transformed it from a villa in disrepair to one of the most charming small hotels in Bath. Furnishings are an eclectic but unpretentious mix of objects gathered by the Burtons during their travels. The small to medium-sized bedrooms feature double-glazed windows and new carpeting throughout. Bathrooms have a tub or an upgraded shower. There's also a three-tiered garden with patio.

10 Upper Oldfield Park, Bath, Somerset BA2 3JZ. ⓒ 01225/426347. Fax 01225/420393. www.s-h-systems.co.uk/hotels/badmintn.html. 5 units. £70 ($112) double; £75–£85 ($120–$136) triple. Rates include English breakfast. MC, V. Bus: 14. **Amenities:** Breakfast room; guest lounge. *In room:* TV, coffeemaker, hair dryer.

Duke's Hotel A short walk from the heart of Bath, this 1780 building is fresher than ever following a complete restoration in 2001. Many of the original Georgian features, including cornices and moldings, have been retained. Rooms, ranging from small to medium, are exceedingly comfortable. All of the bathrooms are small but efficiently arranged and offer bathrobes. Guests can relax in a refined drawing room or patronize the cozy bar overlooking a garden. The entire setting has been called a "perfect *Masterpiece Theatre* take on Britain," with a fire burning in the grate.

53–54 Great Pulteney St., Bath, Somerset BA2 4DN. ⓒ 01225/787960. Fax 01225/787961. www.dukes-bath.co.uk. 18 units. £125–£145 ($200–$232) double; £195–£235 ($312–$376) family room. Rates include continental breakfast. MC, V. Bus: 18. **Amenities:** Restaurant; bar; room service; babysitting; laundry service; dry cleaning. *In room:* TV, hair dryer.

Laura Place Hotel   Built in 1789, this hotel hides behind a stone facade, and it lies within a 2-minute walk of the Roman Baths and Bath Abbey. This very formal hotel has been skillfully decorated with antique furniture and fabrics evocative of the 18th century. The bedrooms here are exceedingly cozy in the best tradition of an English B&B. Baths are small, usually with a shower stall instead of a tub, but have adequate shelf space. *Note:* The hotel closes in the winter months (times vary according to year).

3 Laura Place, Great Pulteney St., Bath, Somerset BA2 4BH. © 01225/463815. Fax 01225/310222. 8 units. £70–£92 ($112–$147) double; £115 ($184) family suite. Rates include English breakfast. AE, MC, V. Free parking. Bus: 18 or 19. **Amenities:** Breakfast room. *In room:* TV, coffeemaker, hair dryer.

Number Ninety Three   This small, well-run guesthouse is a traditional, British-style B&B. The small to midsize bedrooms have soft, cozy beds, and the owners undertake a continuing program of maintenance and redecoration in the slower or winter months. Bathrooms are small with a shower stall. The elegant Victorian house serves a traditional English breakfast, and it is within easy walking distance from the city center and the rail and National Bus stations. Its owner is a mine of local information. The entire property is nonsmoking.

93 Wells Rd., Bath, Somerset BA2 3AN. © 01225/317977. 4 units. £45–£65 ($72–$104) double; £60–£81 ($96–$130) triple. Rates include English breakfast. No credit cards. Free parking. Bus: 3, 13, 14, 17, or 23; ask for Lower Wells Rd. stop. **Amenities:** Breakfast room. *In room:* TV, coffeemaker, hair dryer.

Sydney Gardens Hotel   This spot is reminiscent of the letters of Jane Austen, who wrote to friends about long walks she enjoyed in Sydney Gardens, a public park just outside the city center, a 15- to 20-minute walk away. In 1852, this Italianate Victorian villa was constructed of gray stone on a lot immediately adjacent to the gardens. Three rooms have twin beds; the other three have 1.5m (5-ft.) wide double beds. Each accommodation is individually decorated with an English country-house charm. A footpath runs beside a canal for leisurely strolls. The entire property is nonsmoking.

Sydney Rd., Bath, Somerset BA2 6NT. © 01225/464818. Fax 01225/484347. www.sydneygardens.co.uk. 6 units. £80 ($128) double. Rates include English breakfast. AE, MC, V. **Amenities:** Breakfast room. *In room:* TV, coffeemaker, hair dryer.

Tasburgh House Hotel   Set about 1.5km (1 mile) east of Bath center, amid 7 acres of parks and gardens, this spacious Victorian country house dates from 1890. The redbrick structure contains a large glassed-in conservatory, stained-glass windows, and antiques. Bedrooms are tastefully decorated, often with half-tester beds, and most have sweeping panoramic views. Four rooms have four-poster beds. All the bathrooms are excellent, and five of them are equipped with a tub-and-shower combination, the rest with shower only. Since there is no air-conditioning, windows have to be opened on hot summer nights, which will subject you to a lot of traffic noise. The Avon and Kennet Canal runs along the rear of the property, and guests enjoy summer walks along the adjacent towpath. Smoking is not permitted anywhere on the property.

Warminster Rd., Bath, Somerset BA2 6SH. © 01225/425096. www.bathtasburgh.co.uk. 12 units. £85–£120 ($136–$192) double; £110 ($176) triple; £140 ($224) quad. Rates include English breakfast. AE, DC, MC, V. Bus: 4. **Amenities:** Restaurant; bar; room service; laundry service; dry cleaning. *In room:* TV, coffeemaker, hair dryer.

IN NEARBY HINTON CHARTERHOUSE

Homewood Park ★★   This small, family-run hotel, set on 10 acres of grounds, dates back to the 18th century. Overlooking the Limpley Stoke Valley, it's a large Victorian house with grounds adjoining the 13th-century ruin of

Hinton Priory. You can play croquet in the garden. Riding and golfing are available nearby, and beautiful walks in the Limpley Stoke Valley lure guests. Each of the small to midsize rooms is luxuriously decorated and most overlook the award-winning gardens and grounds or offer views of the valley.

Hinton Charterhouse, Bath, Somerset BA2 7TB. ℂ 01225/723731. Fax 01225/723820. www.homewood park.com. 19 units. £145–£265 ($232–$424) double; £265 ($424) suite. Rates include English breakfast. AE, DC, MC, V. Take A36 (Bath–Warminster Rd.) 9.5km (6 miles) south of Bath. **Amenities:** Restaurant; bar; pool; room service; babysitting; laundry service; dry cleaning. In room: TV, hair dryer.

IN NEARBY STON EASTON

Ston Easton Park ★★★ (Finds)   This is one of the great country hotels of England. From the moment you pass a group of stone outbuildings and century-old beeches set on a 30-acre park, you know you've come to a very special place. The mansion was created in the mid-1700s from the shell of an Elizabethan house; in 1793, Sir Humphry Repton designed the landscape. In 1977, after many years of neglect, Peter and Christine Smedley acquired the property and poured money, love, and labor into its restoration.

The tasteful rooms are filled with flowers and antiques, and feature spacious, sumptuous beds. A gardener's cottage was artfully upgraded from a utilitarian building to contain a pair of intensely decorated and very glamorous suites. In addition to the cottage suite, plus the "standard and deluxe" rooms of the main house, you'll find half a dozen "state rooms," four of which have four-poster beds, and all of which contain lavish but genteel decor. Bathrooms are equally luxurious with deluxe toiletries.

Ston Easton, Somerset BA3 4DF. ℂ 01761/241631. Fax 01761/241377. www.stoneaston.co.uk. 24 units, 1 cottage suite, 7 state rooms. £185–£345 ($296–$552) double; from £750 ($1,200) 3-room cottage suite; £345 ($552) state room. AE, DC, MC, V. Lies 19km (12 miles) south of Bath; follow A39 south to the signposted turnoff to the hamlet of Ston Easton. **Amenities:** Restaurant; room service; babysitting; laundry service; dry cleaning. In room: TV, hair dryer, safe.

WHERE TO DINE

The best place for afternoon tea is **The Pump Room & Roman Baths** (see "Seeing the Sights," earlier in this chapter). Another choice, just a 1-minute walk from the Abbey Church and Roman Baths, is **Sally Lunn's House,** 4 North Parade Passage (ℂ 01225/461634), where visitors have been eating for more than 600 years. For £5 ($8) you can get the Fantastic Sally Lunn Cream Tea, which includes toasted and buttered scones served with strawberry jam and clotted cream, along with your choice of tea or coffee.

Café Retro, York Street (ℂ 01225/339347), serves a variety of teas and coffees. You can order a pot of tea for £1.20 ($1.90), or a large cappuccino for £1.70 ($2.70) and add a tea cake, scone, or crumpet for £1.20 ($1.90).

EXPENSIVE

The Moody Goose ★★★ ENGLISH   In a highly competitive city, this "bird" serves the finest and most refined cuisine. In an elegant, landmarked Georgian terrace in the center of the city, the restaurant has two cozy dining rooms and a little bar. The kitchen has an absolute passion for fresh ingredients and food cooked to order, and the chefs believe in using produce grown as near home as possible, though the Angus beef comes in from Scotland, and the fresh fish from the coasts of Cornwall and Devon. Natural flavors are appreciated here and not smothered in sauces. Even the breads, ice creams, and petits fours are homemade. The kitchen team is expert at chargrilling.

Launch your repast with such temptations as pan-fried veal sweetbreads with a salad of pink grapefruit and walnuts or a brown trout confit in puff pastry. For a main dish, be dazzled with whole roasted quail with braised chicory and roasted apple, roasted rump of lamb, or poached filet of halibut with fresh clams. We're especially fond of the desserts, particularly a fresh rhubarb cheesecake.

7A Kingsmead Sq. ℂ **01225/466688.** Reservations required. Main courses £18–£20 ($29–$31); fixed-price lunch £18 ($28); fixed-price dinner £25 ($40). AE, DC, MC, V. Mon–Sat noon–1:30pm and 6–9:30pm.

MODERATE

Beaujolais *Kids* FRENCH   This is the best-known bistro in Bath, maintaining its old regulars while attracting new admirers every year. Diners are drawn to the honest fare and good value. The house wines are modestly priced. Begin with grilled monkfish served with a creamy white sauce, then follow up with roast partridge or duck confit. Also served is a wide variety of vegetarian dishes, one of which is a mushroom and spinach combination. One area of the restaurant is reserved for nonsmokers. Persons with disabilities will appreciate the wheelchair access, and parents can order special helpings for children.

5 Chapel Row, Queen Sq. ℂ **01225/423417.** Reservations recommended. 2- and 3-course lunches £13–£17 ($20–$27); dinner main courses £12–£18 ($19–$28). AE, MC, V. Mon–Sat noon–2:30pm and 6–10pm; Sun 6–10pm.

The Hole in the Wall ★ MODERN ENGLISH/FRENCH   This much-renovated Georgian town house is owned by Gunna and Christopher Chown, whose successful restaurant in Wales has received critical acclaim. Menu choices change according to the inspiration of the chef and the availability of ingredients. Begin with such delights as a foie gras and duck-liver terrine with pistachio and red-onion marmalade. Proceed to a tasty breast of free-range chicken with wild mushrooms and leeks; or pan-fried filets of red mullet with a yellow pepper sauce. Desserts are often a surprise—say, rhubarb parfait with a confit of ginger.

16 George St. ℂ **01225/425242.** Reservations recommended for weekdays and required Sat. Main courses £9.50–£17 ($15–$27); 2-course lunch £11 ($18); 3-course dinner £20 ($31). AE, MC, V. Mon–Sat noon–2pm and 6–9:30pm.

The Olive Tree MODERN ENGLISH/MEDITERRANEAN   Stephen and Penny Ross operate one of the most sophisticated little restaurants in Bath. Stephen uses the best local produce, with an emphasis on freshness. The menu is changed to reflect the season, with game and fish being the specialties. You might begin with grilled scallops with noodles and pine nuts, or Provençal fish soup with rouille and croutons. Then you could proceed to grilled Aberdeen Angus rump filet, creamed onions, and rosemary in a red-wine-and-peppercorn jus. Stephen is also known for his desserts, which are likely to include such treats as a hot chocolate soufflé or an apricot and almond tart.

In the Queensberry Hotel, Russel St. ℂ **01225/447928.** Reservations highly recommended. Main courses £17–£18 ($26–$29); 3-course fixed-price lunch £16 ($25); 3-course fixed-price dinner £26 ($42). MC, V. Mon–Sat noon–2pm and 7–10pm; Sun 7–9:30pm.

Popjoy's Restaurant MODERN BRITISH/CONTINENTAL   Two sprawling dining rooms on separate floors are in this Georgian home (ca. 1720) where Beau Nash and his mistress, Julianna Popjoy, once entertained friends and set the fashions of the day. Inventiveness and solid technique go into many of the dishes. The food is unpretentious and generally quite satisfying. The starters are always imaginative and good tasting, as exemplified by the guinea fowl and wood pigeon terrine with cranberry jam and brandy-soaked prunes. Equally excellent is the smoked-fish plate with oak-smoked salmon, tuna, trout, and egg with fresh horseradish served with a glass of iced Smirnoff Black label. A certain exoticism appears in the oven-roasted Barbary duck breast with a wild bramble and cherry marmalade, or the stir-fried shiitake mushrooms, pak-choi, zucchini, and roasted almonds on sun-dried tomatoes blinis with spicy sour cream and chick peas.

Sawclose. ℂ **01225/460494.** www.popjoys.co.uk. Reservations recommended. Main courses £18–£22 ($28–$35); 3-course fixed-price lunch £16 ($25). AE, DC, MC, V. Mon–Sat noon–2pm and 6–11pm.

INEXPENSIVE

The Moon and Sixpence INTERNATIONAL   One of the leading restaurants and wine bars of Bath, The Moon and Sixpence occupies a stone structure east of Queen Square. The food may not be as good as that served at more acclaimed choices, including The Hole in the Wall, but the value is unbeatable. At lunch, a large cold buffet with a selection of hot dishes is featured in the wine bar section. In the upstairs restaurant overlooking the bar, full service is offered. Main courses may include filet of lamb with caramelized garlic or roast breast of duck with Chinese vegetables. Look for the daily specials on the continental menu.

6A Broad St. ℂ **01225/460962.** Reservations recommended. Main courses £14–£15 ($22–$23); fixed-price lunch £7.50 ($12); fixed-price dinner £20–£25 ($33–$40). AE, MC, V. Daily noon–2:30pm; Mon–Thurs 5:30–10:30pm; Fri–Sat 5:30–11pm; Sun 6–10:30pm.

Woods ⟨Value⟩ MODERN ENGLISH/FRENCH/ASIAN   Named after John Wood the Younger, architect of Bath's famous Assembly Room, which lies across the street, this restaurant is run by horseracing enthusiast David Price and his French-born wife, Claude. A fixed-price menu is printed on paper, whereas the seasonal array of a la carte items is chalked onto a frequently changing blackboard. Good bets include the pear and parsnip soup or chicken cooked with mushrooms, red wine, and tarragon.

9–13 Alfred St. ℂ **01225/314812.** Reservations recommended. Main courses £9.50–£18 ($15–$29); fixed-price lunch £10 ($15); fixed-price dinner £25 ($40). MC, V. Mon–Sat noon–2:30pm and 6–10:30pm.

BATH AFTER DARK

To gain a very different perspective of Bath, you may want to take the **Bizarre Bath Walking Tour** (ℂ **01225/335124**), a 1½-hour improvisational tour of the streets during which the tour guides pull pranks, tell jokes, and behave in a humorously annoying manner toward tour-goers and unsuspecting residents alike. It's a seasonal affair, running nightly at 8pm from Easter to September. No reservations are necessary; just show up, ready for anything, at the Huntsman Inn at North Parade Passage. The cost of the tour is £5 ($8), £4 ($6.40) for students and children.

After your walk, you may need a drink, or may want to check out the local club and music scene. At **The Bell,** 103 Walcot St. (ℂ **01225/460426**), music ranges from jazz and country to reggae and blues on Monday and Wednesday nights and Sunday at lunch. On music nights, the band performs in the center of the long, narrow 400-year-old room.

The two-story **Hat and Feather,** 14 London St. (ℂ **01225/425672**), has live musicians or DJs playing funk, reggae, or dance music nightly.

2 Wells ⟨★⟨★ & the Caves of Mendip ⟨★

198km (123 miles) SW of London; 34km (21 miles) SW of Bath

To the south of the Mendip Hills, the cathedral town of Wells is a medieval gem. Wells was a vital link in the Saxon kingdom of Wessex—important long before the arrival of William the Conqueror. Once the seat of a bishopric, it was eventually toppled from its ecclesiastical hegemony by the rival city of Bath. But the subsequent loss of prestige has paid off handsomely for Wells today: After experiencing the pinnacle of prestige, it fell into a slumber—and much of its old look was preserved.

Many visitors come only for the afternoon or morning, look at the cathedral, then press on to Bath for the evening. But though it's rather sleepy, Wells's old inns make a tranquil stopover.

ESSENTIALS

GETTING THERE   Wells has good bus connections with surrounding towns and cities. Take the train to Bath (see "Essentials," under "Bath: Britain's Most Historic Spa Town ," earlier in this chapter) and continue the rest of the way by Badgerline bus no. 175. Departures are every hour Monday through Saturday and every 2 hours on Sunday. Both nos. 376 and 378 buses run between Bristol and Glastonbury every hour daily. Call ✆ **01179/553231** for bus schedules and information.

If you're driving, take M4 west from London, cutting south on A4 toward Bath and continuing along A39 into Wells.

VISITOR INFORMATION   The **Tourist Information Centre** is at the Town Hall, Market Place (✆ **01749/672552**), and is open daily November through March from 10am to 4pm and April through October from 9:30am to 5:30pm.

SEEING THE SIGHTS

After a visit to the cathedral, walk along its cloisters to the moat-surrounded **Bishop's Palace.** The Great Hall, built in the 13th century, is in ruins. Finally, the street known as the **Vicars' Close** is one of the most beautifully preserved streets in Europe.

Easily reached by heading west out of Wells, the caves of Mendip are two exciting natural attractions: the great caves of Cheddar and Wookey Hole; see below.

Cheddar Showcaves & Gorge ★★   A short distance from Bath, Bristol, and Wells is the village of Cheddar, home of cheddar cheese. It lies at the foot of Cheddar Gorge, within which lie the Cheddar Caves, underground caverns with impressive formations. The caves are more than a million years old, including Gough's Cave, with its cathedral-like caverns, and Cox's Cave, with its calcite sculptures and brilliant colors. The Crystal Quest is a dark walk "fantasy adventure" taking you deep underground, and in the Cheddar Gorge Heritage Centre, you'll find a 9,000-year-old skeleton. You can also climb Jacob's Ladder for cliff-top walks and Pavey's Lookout Tower for views over Somerset—on a clear day you may even see Wales.

Adults and children over 12 years of age can book an Adventure Caving expedition for £12.50 ($20), which includes overalls, helmets, and lamps. Other attractions include local craftspeople at work, ranging from the glass blower to the sweets maker, plus the Cheddar Cheese & Cider Depot.

Cheddar, Somerset. ✆ 01934/742343. www.cheddarcaves.co.uk. Admission £8.90 ($14) adults, £5.90 ($9.45) children 5–15, free for 4 and under. Easter–Sept daily 10am–5pm; Oct–Easter daily 10:30am–4:30pm. Closed Dec 24–25. From A38 or M5, cut onto A371 to Cheddar.

Wells Cathedral ★★★   Begun in the 12th century, this is a well-preserved example of Early English architecture. The medieval sculpture (six tiers of statues recently restored) of its west front is without equal. The western facade was completed in the mid–13th century. The landmark central tower was erected in the 14th century, with the fan vaulting attached later. The inverted arches were added to strengthen the top-heavy structure.

Much of the stained glass dates from the 14th century. The fan-vaulted Lady Chapel, also from the 14th century, is in the Decorated style. To the north is the vaulted chapter house, built in the 13th century and recently restored. Look also for a medieval astronomical clock in the north transept.

In the center of town, Chain Gate. (C) 01749/674483. www.wellscathedral.org.uk. Free admission but donations appreciated: £4.50 ($7.20) adults, £3 ($4.80) seniors, £1.50 ($2.40) students and children. Apr–Oct daily 7am–7pm; Nov–Mar daily 7am–6:15pm.

Wookey Hole Caves & Paper Mill ⚜ Just 3km (2 miles) from Wells, you'll first come upon the source of the Axe River. In the first chamber of the caves, as legend has it, is the Witch of Wookey turned to stone. These caves are believed to have been inhabited by prehistoric people at least 60,000 years ago. A tunnel, opened in 1975, leads to the chambers unknown in early times, and previously accessible only to divers.

Leaving the caves, follow a canal path to the mill, where paper has been made by hand since the 17th century. Here, the best-quality handmade paper is made by skilled workers according to the tradition of their ancient craft. Also in the mill are "hands-on vats," where visitors can try their hand at making a sheet of paper, and an Edwardian Penny Pier Arcade where you can exchange new pennies for old ones to play the original machines. Other attractions include the Magical Mirror Maze and an enclosed passage of multiple image mirrors.

Wookey Hole, near Wells. (C) 01749/672243. www.wookey.co.uk. 2-hr. tour £8.80 ($14) adults, £5.50 ($8.80) children 16 and under. Apr–Oct daily 10am–5:30pm; Nov–Mar daily 10:30am–4:30pm. Closed Dec 17–25. Follow the signs from the center of Wells for 3km (2 miles). Bus no. 172 from Wells.

WHERE TO STAY

The Crown ⚜ This is one of the oldest and most historic hotels in the area, a tradition for overnighting since medieval times. William Penn was thrown in jail here in 1695. The charge? Preaching without a license. The landmark status building lies at the medieval Market Place in the heart of Wells, overlooking the splendid cathedral. The building still retains much of its 15th-century character, although the bedrooms are completely up-to-date—in fact, furnished with a Nordic contemporary style. For more tradition, ask for one of a quartet of rooms graced with four-posters. Each unit comes with a well-maintained private bathroom with shower. Lunch or dinner can be enjoyed in either the Penn Bar, named in honor of that "jailbird," or else Anton's Bistrot, the latter named after the well-known cartoonist and former resident whose work was featured in *Punch* magazine. Some of his original drawings line the walls of the hotel.

Market Place, Wells, Somerset BA5 2RP. (C) 01749/673457. Fax 01749/679792. www.crownatwells.co.uk. 15 units. £60–£70 ($96–$112) double; £90 ($144) suite. AE, MC, V. **Amenities:** Restaurant; pub; babysitting. *In room:* TV, coffeemaker, hair dryer, iron, trouser press, no phone.

The Swan Hotel ⚜ Set behind a stucco facade on one of the town's main streets, this place was originally built in the 15th century as a coaching inn. Today, facing the west front of Wells Cathedral, it is the best of the inns within the town's central core. Rooms vary in style and size; a third of them have four-poster beds. Bathrooms are small. The spacious and elegant public rooms stretch out to the left and right of the entrance. Both ends have a blazing and baronial fireplace and beamed ceilings.

Moments   Glastonbury Abbey

Glastonbury, just 9.5km (6 miles) southwest of Wells, is England's New Age center, where Christian spirituality blends with Druidic beliefs. Though it's no more than a ruined sanctuary today, **Glastonbury Abbey** ★★ was once one of the wealthiest and most prestigious monasteries in England. It provides Glastonbury's claim to historical greatness, an assertion augmented by legendary links to such figures as Joseph of Arimathea, King Arthur, Queen Guinevere, and St. Patrick.

It is said that Joseph of Arimathea journeyed to what was then the Isle of Avalon with the Holy Grail in his possession. According to tradition, he buried the chalice at the foot of the conical Glastonbury Tor, and a stream of blood burst forth. You can scale this more than 500-foot-high hill today, on which rests a 15th-century tower.

Joseph, so it goes, erected a church of wattle in Glastonbury. (The town, in fact, may have had the oldest church in England, as excavations have shown.) And at one point, the saint is said to have leaned against his staff, which was immediately transformed into a fully blossoming tree; a cutting alleged to have survived from the Holy Thorn can be seen on the abbey grounds today—it blooms at Christmastime. Some historians have traced this particular story back to Tudor times.

Another famous chapter in the story, popularized by Tennyson in the Victorian era, holds that King Arthur and Queen Guinevere were buried on the abbey grounds. In 1191, the monks dug up the skeletons of two bodies on the south side of the Lady Chapel, said to be those of the king and queen. In 1278, in the presence of Edward I, the bodies were removed and transferred to a black marble tomb in the choir. Both the burial spot and the shrine are marked today.

11 Sadler St., Wells, Somerset BA5 2RX. ⓒ **800/528-1234** in the U.S. and Canada, or 01749/836300. Fax 01749/836301. www.bhere.co.uk. 50 units. £110–£135 ($176–$216) double. Rates include English breakfast. AE, DC, MC, V. **Amenities:** Restaurant; bar; room service. *In room:* TV, hair dryer, coffeemaker, trouser press.

White Hart Opposite the cathedral, this is the best located hotel in Wells. A former coaching inn, it dates from the 15th century. The Swan is more comfortable and remarkable, but the White Hart is an enduring favorite nonetheless. The creaky old bedrooms lie in the main house, or you can live in more modern surroundings in a converted stable block where horses and coaches from London were housed in olden times. Each bedroom is comfortably and tastefully furnished. Even if you're not staying here, drop in for a drink at the pub or a meal in the beamed restaurant. A fixed-price dinner is offered or you can order from a brasserie-style menu.

Sadler St., Wells, Somerset BA5 2RR. ⓒ **01749/672056.** Fax 01749/671074. www.whitehart-wells.co.uk. 16 units. £86 ($138) double. Rates include English breakfast. AE, MC, V. **Amenities:** Restaurant; room service; laundry service; dry cleaning. *In room:* TV.

WHERE TO DINE

Ritcher's FRENCH   This eatery occupies a 16th-century stone cottage whose entrance lies behind a wrought-iron gate and a tile-covered passageway running

A large Benedictine Abbey of St. Mary grew out of the early wattle church. St. Dunstan, who was born nearby, was the abbot in the 10th century and later became archbishop of Canterbury. Edmund, Edgar, and Edmund "Ironside," three early English kings, were buried at the abbey.

In 1184, a fire destroyed most of the abbey and its vast treasures. It was eventually rebuilt, after much difficulty, only to be dissolved by Henry VIII. Its last abbot, Richard Whiting, was hanged at Glastonbury Tor. Like the Roman forum, the abbey was used as a stone quarry for years.

Today, you can visit the ruins of the chapel, linked by an early English "Galilee" to the nave of the abbey. The best-preserved building on the grounds is a 14th-century octagonal Abbot's Kitchen, where oxen were once roasted whole to feed the wealthier pilgrims.

For information on the abbey, call ℂ **01458/832267** or surf over to **www.glastonburyabbey.com**. Admission costs £3.50 ($5.60) adults, £3 ($4.80) students and seniors, £1.50 ($2.40) children age 5–16 years, and £8 ($13) for a family ticket. The abbey is open daily from 10am to 5pm.

Glastonbury is easily reached from London's Paddington Station by rail (ℂ **0845/748-4950**, for information). One **National Express** bus a day (no. 403) leaves London's Victoria Coach Station at 6:30pm and arrives in Glastonbury at 10pm. For more information and schedules, call ℂ **020/7529-2000**. If you're driving, take M4 west from London, then cut south on A4 via Bath to Glastonbury.

beneath another building near the cathedral. The best dining in town, Ritcher's has a likable bistro on the ground floor and a more formal restaurant one floor above street level. Both charge the same prices and offer the same cuisine. Menu items include turkey and venison pies, fresh asparagus, and a modernized version of salade niçoise served with raspberry vinaigrette. Featured also is a saddle of lamb roasted with garlic-and-herb crust and Beaujolais sauce, or slices of Scottish salmon glazed with freshwater prawns in a Chablis-flavored cream sauce. Pan-fried guinea fowl with truffles and mushrooms is one of our favorite dishes. The chefs don't pull off every dish, but do take care and concern with the cuisine.

5 Sadler St. ℂ 01749/679085. Reservations recommended in restaurant. 2-course fixed-price lunch £8.95 ($14); 3-course fixed-price lunch £11 ($18); 2-course fixed-price dinner £20 ($31); 3-course fixed-price dinner £23 ($37). MC, V. Bistro: Daily noon–2pm and 7–9:30pm.

3 Longleat House ✸✸✸ & Stourhead Gardens ✸✸✸

If you're driving, you can visit both Longleat and Stourhead in 1 busy day. Follow the directions to Longleat given below, then drive 9.5km (6 miles) down B3092 to Stourton, a village just off the highway, 5km (3 miles) northwest of Mere (A303), to reach Stourhead.

Longleat House and Safari Park ★★★ A magnificent Elizabethan house built in the early Renaissance style, Longleat House was owned by the seventh marquess of Bath. On first glimpse it's romantic enough, but once you've been inside, it's hard not to be dazzled by the lofty rooms and their exquisite paintings and furnishings.

From the Elizabethan Great Hall and the library to the State Rooms and the grand staircase, the house is filled with all manner of beautiful things. The walls of the State Dining Room are adorned with fine tapestries and paintings, whereas the room itself has displays of silver and plate. The library represents the finest private collection in the country. The Victorian kitchens are open, offering a glimpse of life "below the stairs" in a well-ordered country home. Various exhibitions are mounted in the stable yard.

Adjoining Longleat House is **Longleat Safari Park.** The park hosts several species of magnificent and endangered wild animals, including rhinoceros and elephants, which are free to roam these bucolic surroundings. Here you can walk among giraffes, zebras, camels, and llamas, and view lions and tigers, as well as England's only white tiger, from your car. You can also ride on a safari boat around the park's lake to see gorillas and to feed sea lions. You can see the park by train for a railway adventure, or visit the tropical butterfly garden.

The park provides plenty of theme park–like thrills as well, including an Adventure Castle, a *Doctor Who* exhibition, and the world's longest maze, **The Maze of Love.** Commissioned by the marquess of Bath and designed by Graham Burgess, the maze was inspired by the Garden of Love in Villandry, France, and Botticelli's painting *Primavera.* It lies between Longleat House and the Orangery, and at first appears to be a traditional parterre with gravel paths and small leafed box hedging; it's only on closer examination that its amorous shapes become apparent. The most obvious ones are the four giant hearts and a pair of women's lips, but there are many more. Love's symbolic flower, the rose, has been planted in the beds, and climbing roses trail over the heart-shaped arches. More than 1,300 rose bushes have been planted with names that enhance the symbolic story: First Kiss, Eve, Seduction, and more.

Warminster, Wiltshire. ℂ **01985/844400.** www.longleat.co.uk. Admission to Longleat House £9 ($14) adults, £6 ($9.60) children. Safari Park £9 ($14) adults, £6 ($9.60) children. Special exhibitions and rides require separate admission tickets. Passport tickets for all attractions £16 ($26) adults, £13 ($21) seniors and children.4–14. House open daily 10am–5:30pm. Park open Apr–Nov 2 daily 10am–6pm (last cars admitted at 5pm or sunset). From Bath, take the train to Warminster; then take a taxi to Longleat (about 10 min.). Driving from Bath, take A36 south to Warminster; then follow the signposts to Longleat House.

Stourhead ★★★ In a country of superlative gardens and gardeners, Stourhead is the most fabled. It's certainly the most celebrated example of 18th-century English landscape gardening. More than that, it's a delightful place to wander— among its trees, flowers, and colorful shrubs, bridges, grottos, and temples are tucked away, almost-hidden. Although Stourhead is a garden for all seasons, it is at its most idyllic in summer when rhododendrons are in full bloom.

A Palladian house, Stourhead was built in the 18th century by the Hoare banking family, who created 100 acres of prime 18th-century landscaped gardens, complete with classical temples, lakes, and grottos. Henry Hoare II (1705–85), known as "Henry the Magnificent," contributed greatly to the development of the landscape of this magnificent estate.

The Temple of Flora was the first building in the garden, designed by the architect Henry Flitcroft in 1744. The wooden seats are copies of those placed near the altar where images of pagan gods were laid. Marble busts of Marcus Aurelius and Alexander the Great can be seen in the niches on the wall.

The Grotto, constructed in 1748, is lined with tufa, a water-worn limestone deposit. The springs of the Stour flow through the cold bath where a lead copy of the sleeping Ariadne lies. In a cave beyond her, the white lead statue of the River God is seen dispensing justice to the waves and nymphs who inhabit his stream.

The Pantheon was built in 1753 to house Rysbrack's statues of Hercules and Flora and other classical figures. The temple was originally heated through brass grilles. The nearby Iron Bridge replaced a wooden one in 1860.

In 1765, Flitcroft built the **Temple of Apollo,** the route that takes the visitor over the public road via a rock-work bridge constructed in the 1760s. The Apollo Temple is copied from a round temple excavated at Baalbec: The statues that used to be in the niches are now on the roof of Stourhead House. The Turf Bridge was copied from Palladio's bridge in Vicenza.

The **Bristol High Cross** dates from the early 15th century and commemorates the monarchs who benefited the city of Bristol. It was removed from Bristol and set up by Henry Hoare at Stourhead in 1765.

The house at Stourhead, designed by Colen Campbell, a leader in the Palladian revival, was built for Henry Hoare I between 1721 and 1725. It closely resembles the villas Palladio built for wealthy Venetians. The magnificent interior hosts an outstanding library and picture gallery and a wealth of paintings, art treasures, and Chippendale furniture.

The three fine redbrick-walled terraces were built in the early 19th century to supply cut flowers, fresh fruit, salads, and vegetables to the mansion house. They were in use up to the deaths of Sir Henry and Lady Alda Hoare in 1947.

The lower combined an herbaceous garden with a peach and vine house. The pool was part of an irrigation system fed by rainwater from the greenhouses and stable yard.

Henry Hoare II's 18th-century redbrick folly, **Alfred's Tower,** is another feature at Stourhead. It sits 48m (160 ft.) above the borders of Wiltshire, Somerset, and Dorset and has 221 steps. **The Obelisk** was built between 1839 and 1840 of Bath stone and replaced the original of Chilmark stone constructed by William Privet for Henry Hoare in 1746.

The plant center is situated near the entrance to the main parking lot in part of the Old Glebe Farm—a small estate dairy farm. A working farm until the early 1970s, it's now a place where visitors buy plants they've just seen in the garden.

Lunches and suppers are served at the **Spread Eagle Inn,** near the garden entrance. Boxes are available to order for picnics in the grounds and garden. The Spread Eagle is noted for dinner, as well as for its Sunday lunches in the autumn, winter, and spring. A self-service buffet is available in the Village Hall tearoom.

(C) 01747/841152. Mar–Oct, admission for garden or house £5.10 ($8.15) adults, £2.90 ($4.65) children; off season garden only, £3.95 ($6.30) adults, £1.90 ($3.05) children. Fri–Tues 9am–7pm (or until dusk). Last admission is at 4:30pm. A direct bus from Bath runs only on the 1st Sat of each month. Getting to Stourhead by public transportation is very difficult if you don't have a car. You can take the train from Bath to Frome, a 30-min. trip. From here it's still 10 miles away. Most visitors take a taxi from Frome to Stourhead. A direct bus from Bath runs only on the first Sat of each month.

4 Dunster ✶✶ & Exmoor National Park ✶✶

296km (184 miles) W of London; 5km (3 miles) SE of Minehead

The village of Dunster, in Somerset, lies near the eastern edge of Exmoor National Park. It grew up around the original Dunster Castle, constructed as a fortress for the de Mohun family, whose progenitor came to England with William the Conqueror. The village, about 6.4km (4 miles) from the Cistercian monastery at Cleeve, has an ancient priory church and dovecote, a 17th-century gabled yarn market, and little cobbled streets dotted with whitewashed cottages.

ESSENTIALS

GETTING THERE   The best route by rail is to travel to Minehead via Taunton, which is easily reached on the main London–Penzance line from Paddington Station in London. For rail information, call ✆ **0845/748-4950**. From Minehead, you have to take a taxi or bus to reach Dunster.

At Taunton, you can take one of the seven **Southern National** coaches (no. 28) (✆ **01823/272033**), leaving hourly Monday through Saturday; there is only one bus on Sunday. Trip time is 1 hour and 10 minutes. Buses (no. 38 or 39) from Minehead stop in Dunster Village at the rate of one per hour, but only from June to September. Off-season visitors must take a taxi.

If you're driving from London, head west along M4, cutting south at the junction with M5 until you reach the junction with A39, going west to Minehead. Before your final approach to Minehead, cut south to Dunster along A396.

VISITOR INFORMATION   Dunster doesn't have an official tourist office, but **Exmoor National Park Visitor Centre** is at Dunster Steep (✆ **01643/ 821835**), 3km (2 miles) east of Minehead. It's open Easter to October daily from 10am to 5pm, plus limited hours in winter (call ahead).

EXPLORING THE AREA

Dunster Castle ✸✸   Dunster Castle is on a *tor* (high hill), from which you can see Bristol Channel. It stands on the site of a Norman castle granted to William de Mohun of Normandy by William the Conqueror shortly after the conquest of England. The 13th-century gateway, built by the de Mohuns, is all that remains of the original fortress. In 1376, the castle and its lands were bought by Lady Elizabeth Luttrell; her family owned it until it was given to the National Trust in 1976, together with 30 acres of surrounding parkland.

The first castle was largely demolished during the civil war. The present Dunster Castle is a Jacobean house constructed in the lower ward of the original fortifications in 1620, then rebuilt in 1870 to look like a castle. From the terraced walks and gardens, you'll have good views of Exmoor and the Quantock Hills.

Some outstanding artifacts within include the 17th-century panels of embossed painted and gilded leather depicting the story of Antony and Cleopatra, and a remarkable allegorical 16th-century portrait of Sir John Luttrell (shown wading naked through the sea with a female figure of peace and a wrecked ship in the background). The 17th-century plasterwork ceilings of the dining room and the finely carved staircase balustrade of cavorting huntsmen, hounds, and stags are also noteworthy.

On A396 (just off A39). ✆ **01643/821314**. Admission to castle and grounds £6.40 ($10) adults, £3.20 ($5.10) children, family ticket £16 ($26); to grounds only £3.50 ($5.60) adults, £1.50 ($2.40) children, family ticket £8 ($13). Castle Apr–Sept Sat–Wed 11am–5pm; Oct Sat–Wed 11am–4pm. Grounds Jan–Mar and Oct–Dec daily 11am–4pm; Apr–Sept daily 10am–5pm. Take bus no. 28 or 39 from Minehead.

Exmoor National Park ✸✸   Between Somerset and Devon, along the northern coast of England's southwest peninsula, is Exmoor National Park, an unspoiled plateau of lonely moors. One of the most cherished national parks in Britain, it includes the wooded valleys of the rivers Exe and Barle, the Brendon Hills, a sweeping stretch of rocky coastline, and such sleepy but charming villages as **Culbone, Selworthy, Parracombe,** and **Allerford.** Bisected by a network of heavily eroded channels for brooks and streams, the park is distinctive for lichen-covered trees, gray-green grasses, gorse, and heather. The moors reach their highest point at Dunkery Beacon, 512m (1,707 ft.) above sea level.

Exmoor National Park is one of the smallest in Britain, yet it contains one of the most beautiful coastlines in England. Softly contoured, without the dramatic peaks and valleys of other national parks, the terrain is composed mostly of primeval layering of sandstone slate. Although noteworthy for its scarcity of trees, the terrain encompasses a limited handful of very old oak groves, which are studied by forestry experts for their growth patterns.

On clear days, the coast of South Wales, 32km (20 miles) away, can be spotted across the estuary of the Bristol Channel. The wildlife that thrives on the park's rain-soaked terrain includes a breed of wild pony (the Exmoor pony), whose bloodlines can be traced from ancient species.

Although the park boasts more than 1,127km (700 miles) of walking paths, most visitors stay on the **coastal trail** that winds around the bays and inlets of England's southwestern peninsula or along some of the shorter **riverside trails.**

The park's administrative headquarters is located in a 19th-century workhouse in the village of Dulverton, in Somerset, near the park's southern edge, where you can pick up the *Exmoor Visitor* brochure, listing events, guided walks, and visitor information. A program of walking tours is offered at least five times a week. Themes include Woodland Walks, Moorland Walks, Bird-Watching Excursions, and Deer Spottings. Most of the tours last from 4 to 6 hours, and all are free, with an invitation to donate. Wear sturdy shoes and rain gear.

Dulverton, Somerset TA22 9EX. © **01398/323841.** Visitor center open daily between Easter and end of Oct, 10am–5pm; 10:30am–3pm through the winter.

NEARBY SIGHTS

Coleridge Cottage   The hamlet of Nether Stowey is on the A39, north of Taunton, across the Quantock Hills to the east of Exmoor. The cottage is at the west end of Nether Stowey on the south side of the A39. Here you can visit the home of Samuel Taylor Coleridge, where he penned "The Rime of the Ancient Mariner." During his 1797 to 1800 sojourn here, he and his friends, William Wordsworth and sister Dorothy, enjoyed exploring the Quantock woods. The parlor and reading room of his National Trust property are open to visitors.

35 Lime St., Nether Stowey, near Bridgwater. © **01278/732662.** Admission £3 ($4.80) adults, £1.50 ($2.40) children. Apr 1–Oct 1 Tues–Thurs and Sun 2–5pm. From Minehead, follow A39 east about 48km (30 miles), following the signs to Bridgwater. About 13km (8 miles) from Bridgwater, turn right, following signs to Nether Stowey.

Combe Sydenham Hall ⭐   This hall was the home of Elizabeth Sydenham, wife of Sir Francis Drake, and it stands on the ruins of monastic buildings that were associated with nearby Cleeve Abbey. Here you can see a cannonball that legend says halted the wedding of Lady Elizabeth to a rival suitor in 1585. The gardens include Lady Elizabeth's Walk, which circles ponds originally laid out when the knight was courting his bride-to-be. The valley ponds fed by spring water are full of rainbow trout (ask about getting fly-fishing lessons). You can also take a woodland walk to Long Meadow, with its host of wildflowers. Also to be seen are a deserted hamlet, whose population reputedly was wiped out by the Black Death, and a historic corn mill. In the hall's tearoom, smoked trout and paté are produced on oak chips, as in days of yore, and there is a shop, working bakery, and parking lot.

Monksilver. ℂ **01984/656284**. Admission £5.50 ($8.80) adults, £2.30 ($3.70) children. Country Park, Easter–Sept Sun–Fri 9am–5pm; courtroom and gardens, May–Sept at 1:30pm for guided tours only, Mon and Wed–Thurs. From Dunster, drive on A39, following signs pointing to Watchet and/or Bridgwater. On the right, you'll see a minor zoo, Tropiquaria, at which you turn right and follow the signs pointing to Combe Sydenham.

WHERE TO STAY & DINE IN THE AREA

Curdon Mill *Finds*   Situated on 200 acres 12km (5 miles) northeast of Dunster, this guesthouse, a former mill, sports a 100-year-old water wheel made by the local ironworks. Daphne and Richard Criddle own this place, offering home-style food and accommodations. The individually decorated rooms are small to midsize. The small bathrooms are well maintained.

Vellow, Williton, Somerset, TA4 4LS. ℂ **01984/656522**. Fax 01984/656606. www.s-h-systems.co.uk/hotels/curdonmill.html. 6 units (with tub or shower). £70 ($112) double. Rates include English breakfast. AE, MC, V. **Amenities:** Restaurant; bar; pool; room service; laundry service; dry cleaning. *In room:* TV, coffeemaker, hair dryer.

Luttrell Arms ★★ *Kids*   A hostelry for weary travelers has been on this site for more than 600 years. Simply the best choice around, this hotel is the outgrowth of a guesthouse the Cistercian abbots at Cleeve had built in the village of Dunster. It was named for the Luttrell lords of the manor, who bought Dunster Castle and the property attached to it in the 14th century. It has, of course, been updated with modern amenities, but from its stone porch to the 15th-century Gothic hall with hammer-beam roof, it still retains a feeling of antiquity. Bedrooms range in size and are attractively decorated in keeping with the hotel's long history; five of them have four-poster beds. Rooms in a section called the "Latches" are cottage-like in style, with tight stairways and narrow corridors. One room is big enough for use by a family, and nine of the bedrooms are non-smoking. Baths are small but have a shower-and-tub combination.

32–36 High St., Dunster, Somerset TA24 6SG. ℂ **01643/821555**. Fax 01643/821567. www.luttrellarms.co.uk. 28 units. £120–£142 ($192–$227) double. Dinner, B&B rates, Mar–June and Sept–Oct £70–£89 ($112–$142) per person per night; July–Sept £90 ($144) per person per night; Oct–Feb £75–£89 ($120–$142) per person per night. 2-night minimum stay required for the Oct–Feb rate. AE, DC, MC, V. **Amenities:** 2 restaurants; bar; room service; babysitting. *In room:* TV, coffeemaker, hair dryer.

5 Exeter ★★

324km (201 miles) SW of London; 74km (46 miles) NE of Plymouth

Exeter was a Roman city founded in the 1st century A.D. on the banks of the River Exe. Two centuries later it was encircled by a mighty stone wall, traces of which remain today. Conquerors and would-be conquerors, especially Vikings, stormed the fortress in later centuries; none was more notable than William the Conqueror, who brought Exeter to its knees.

Under the Tudors, the city grew and prospered. Sir Walter Raleigh and Sir Francis Drake were two of the striking figures who strolled through Exeter's streets. In May 1942, the Germans bombed Exeter, destroying many of its architectural treasures. The town was rebuilt, but the new, impersonal-looking shops and offices can't replace the Georgian crescents and the black-and-white-timbered buildings with their plastered walls. Fortunately, much was spared, and Exeter still has its Gothic cathedral, a renowned university, some museums, and several historic houses.

Exeter is a good base for exploring both Dartmoor and Exmoor National Parks, two of the finest England has to offer. It's also a good place to spend a day—there's a lot to do in what's left of the city's old core.

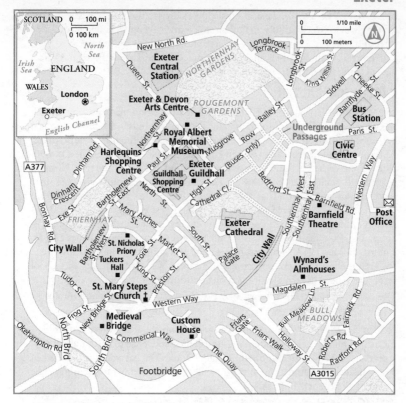

ESSENTIALS

GETTING THERE **Exeter Airport** (℗ 01392/367433) serves the south-west, offering both charter and scheduled flights. Lying 12km (5 miles) east of the historic center of Exeter, it has scheduled flights to and from Belfast (only in summer), Jersey, Dublin (Mar–Oct), and the Isles of Scilly, but no direct flights from London.

Trains from London's Paddington Station depart every hour during the day. The trip takes 2½ hours. For rail information, call ℗ **0845/748-4950** in the United Kingdom. Trains also run every 20 minutes during the day between Exeter and Plymouth; the trip takes 1 hour. Trains often arrive at Exeter St. David's Station at St. David's Hill.

A **National Express** coach departs from London's Victoria Coach Station every 2 hours during the day; the trip takes 4 hours. You can also take bus no. 38 or 39 between Plymouth and Exeter. During the day two coaches depart per hour for the 1-hour trip. For information and schedules, call ℗ **020/7529-2000**.

If you're driving from London, take M4 west, cutting south to Exeter on M5 (junction near Bristol).

VISITOR INFORMATION The **Tourist Information Centre** is at the Civic Centre, Paris Street (℗ **01392/265700**; fax 01392/265260). It's open Monday through Saturday from 9am to 5pm, and from July to August, Monday through Saturday from 9am to 5pm and Sunday from 10am to 4pm.

SPECIAL EVENTS   A classical music lover's dream, the **Exeter Festival,** held for the first two weeks in July, includes more than 150 events, ranging from concerts and opera to lectures. Festival dates and offerings vary from year to year, and more information is available by contacting the **Exeter Festival Office,** Civic Center (© **01392/265200;** www.exeter.gov.uk).

EXPLORING EXETER

Exeter Cathedral ★★   The Roman II Augusta Legion made its camp on the site where the Cathedral Church of Saint Peter now stands in Exeter. It has been occupied by Britons, Saxons, Danes, and Normans. The English Saint Boniface, who converted northern Germany to Christianity, was trained here in A.D. 690. The present cathedral structure was begun around 1112, and the twin Norman towers still stand. Between the towers runs the longest uninterrupted true Gothic vault in the world, at a height of 20m (66 ft.) and a length of 91m (300 ft.). It was completed in 1369 and is the finest existing example of decorated Gothic architecture. The Puritans destroyed the cathedral cloisters in 1655, and a German bomb finished off the twin Chapels of St. James and St. Thomas in May 1942. Now restored, it's one of the prettiest churches anywhere. Its famous choir sings evensong every day except Wednesday during the school term. On school holidays, visiting choirs perform.

1 The Cloisters. © **01392/255573.** Free admission, though a donation of £3 ($4.80) is requested of adults. Mon–Sat 7:30am–5:15pm; Sun 7:30am–7:30pm.

Exeter Guildhall   This colonnaded building on the main street is the oldest municipal building in the kingdom—the earliest reference to the guildhall is in a deed from 1160. The Tudor front that straddles the pavement was added in 1593. Inside you'll find a fine display of silver, plus a number of paintings. The ancient hall is paneled in oak.

High St. © **01392/665500.** Free admission. Mon–Fri 10am–1pm and 2–4pm. It's best to call before visiting.

Powderham Castle ★   This private house is occupied by the countess and earl of Devon, who let Ismail Merchant and James Ivory use their home as a setting for *The Remains of the Day,* starring Anthony Hopkins and Emma Thompson. It was built in the late 14th century by Sir Philip Courtenay, sixth son of the second earl of Devon, and his wife, Margaret, granddaughter of Edward I. Their magnificent tomb is in the south transept of Exeter Cathedral.

The castle has many family portraits and fine furniture, including a remarkable clock that plays full tunes at 4, 8pm, and midnight; some 17th-century tapestries; and a chair used by William III for his first council of state at Newton Abbot. The chapel dates from the 15th century, with hand-hewn roof timbers and carved pew ends.

Moments **A Relic from William the Conqueror**

Just off "The High," at the top of Castle Street, stands an impressive **Norman gatehouse** from William the Conqueror's castle. Although only the house and walls survive, the view from here and the surrounding gardens is panoramic. Stand here for a moment and contemplate all the invasions that have assaulted Exeter, from the Romans to the Nazi bombers of World War II.

In Powderham, Kenton. © **01626/890243**. www.powderham.co.uk. Admission £6.90 ($11) adults, £6.40 ($10) seniors, £3.90 ($6.25) children 5–17, free for children 4 and under, family ticket £18 ($28). Easter–Oct Sun–Fri 10am–5:30pm. Take the A379 Dawlish Rd. 13km (8 miles) south of Exeter; the castle is signposted.

Underground Passages The Underground Passages, accessible from High Street, were built to carry the medieval water supply into the city. By entering the new underground interpretation center, visitors can view a video and exhibition before taking a guided tour.

Boots Corner, off High St. © **01392/665887**. Admission £3.75 ($6) adults, £2.75 ($4.40) children, £11 ($18) family ticket. June–Sept Mon–Sat 10am–5pm; Oct–May Tues–Fri noon–5pm, Sat 10am–5pm.

SHOPPING

Exeter has long been famous for its silver. If you seek, ye shall find old Exeter silver, especially spoons, sold in local stores. **Burfords,** 17 Guildhall, Queen St. (© **01392/254901**), sells modern silver and jewelry.

You can find a number of antiques dealers in Exeter. At least six are on the Quay off Western Way. **The Quay Gallery Antiques Emporium** (© **01392/213283**) houses 10 dealers who sell furniture, porcelain, metalware, and other collectibles. **The Antique Centre** on the Quay (© **01392/493501**) has 20 dealers.

The Edinburgh Woolen Mill, 23 Cathedral Yard (© **01392/412318**), carries a large selection of woolen goods, including kilts, Arran jumpers, tartan travel rugs, and quality wool suits for women and trousers for men.

A daily market on Sidwell Street is Exeter's version of an American flea market.

WHERE TO STAY
EXPENSIVE

The Thistle Hotel Exeter Although its history is far less impressive than that of the Royal Clarence Hotel (see below), this great, old-fashioned, rambling Victorian hotel (which was renovated fairly recently) is also a traditional choice for those who want to stay in the center of town. Its small to medium bedrooms are comfortably furnished in a modern style. Units come with well-maintained private bathrooms.

Queen St. (opposite the central train station), Exeter, Devon EX4 3SP. © **01392/254982**. Fax 01392/420928. www.thistlehotels.com/exeter. 90 units. £136 ($218) double; £181–£203 ($290–$325) suite. AE, DC, MC, V. **Amenities:** Restaurant; bar; room service; laundry service. *In room:* A/C, TV, coffeemaker, hair dryer.

MODERATE

Barcelona *(Finds)* When it opened, Britain's *Good Hotel Guide* hailed this winning choice as "designer hotel of the year." A former hospital devoted to the treatment of eye problems, this hip, modern, and rather tony hotel was created from an old redbrick pile. The big corridors used for wheeling patients and the giant elevators are still here, but everything else is new. Many adornments and artifacts from past decades, notably the '30s and '60s, have been put in place, giving the hotel a distinctive look. The bedrooms are rather luxurious, each tastefully furnished and equipped with first-class aquamarine bathrooms with showers. Expect bold spreads and carpets in geometric patterns, large windows, and the original parquet floors, along with such conveniences as cordless phones and CD players.

Magadalen St., Exeter, Devon EX2 4HY. © **01392/281000**. Fax 01392/281001. www.hotelbarcelona-uk.com. 46 units. £85–£105 ($136–$168) double. Children stay free in parent's room. AE, MC, V. **Amenities:** Restaurant; bar. *In room:* TV/VCR, dataport, beverage maker, hair dryer.

Buckerell Lodge Hotel *(Kids)* This country house originated in the 12th century, but it has been altered and changed beyond recognition over the years. The exterior is a symmetrical and severely dignified building with a Regency feel. Often hosting business travelers, it's also a tourist favorite, especially in summer. The bedrooms, in a range of styles and sizes, are well decorated and nicely equipped. The best rooms are the executive accommodations in the main house, though most bedrooms are in a more sterile modern addition. Two units are large enough to accommodate families.

Topsham Rd., Exeter, Devon EX2 4SQ. © **800/528-1234** in the U.S. and Canada, or 01392/221111. Fax 01392/491111. www.corushotels.com. 53 units. £99–£125 ($158–$200) double. AE, DC, MC, V. Bus: S, T, or R. Take B3182 1.5km (1 mile) southeast, off Junction 30 of M5. **Amenities:** Restaurant; bar; room service; laundry service; dry cleaning. *In room:* TV, coffeemaker, hair dryer, trouser press.

Gipsy Hill *Kids*   This late-Victorian country house stands on the eastern edge of the city and is close to the airport. (It's especially convenient if you're driving, as it's within easy reach of the M5 Junction 30.) Bedrooms, ranging from small to medium, are comfortably appointed; some have four-poster beds. Five accommodations are large enough for families. Bedrooms have more tradition and ambience in the main house, and the other 17 rooms are located in an annex.

Gipsy Hill Lane, via Pinn Lane, Monkerton, Exeter, Devon EX1 3RN. © **01392/465252.** Fax 01392/464302. www.gipsyhillhotel.co.uk. 37 units. £90–£125 ($144–$200) double. Rates include English breakfast. AE, DC, MC, V. Bus: T. **Amenities:** Restaurant; bar; room service; babysitting. *In room:* TV, coffeemaker, hair dryer, trouser press.

Royal Clarence Hotel ★ *Kids*   This hotel offers far more tradition and style than the sometimes better rated and more recently built Southgate at Southernhay East, or the Thistle on Queen Street. It dates from 1769 and escaped the Nazi blitz. Just a step away from the cathedral, it offers individually furnished rooms in Tudor, Georgian, or Victorian styling. Five rooms are large enough for families; some rooms have four-poster beds.

Cathedral Yard, Exeter, Devon EX1 1HD. © **01392/319955.** Fax 01392/439423. www.regalhotels.co.uk/royal clarence. 56 units. £60–£80 ($96–$128) double; from £135 ($216) suite. AE, DC, MC, V. **Amenities:** 2 restaurants; 2 bars; room service; laundry service; dry cleaning. *In room:* A/C, TV, coffeemaker, hair dryer, safe, trouser press.

St. Olaves Court Hotel ★   This is our favorite place to stay in town. The location is ideal, within a short walk of the cathedral—you can hear the church bells. A Georgian mansion, it was constructed in 1827 by a rich merchant as a home. The house has been discreetly furnished, in part with antiques. Each of the bedrooms, last renovated in 2001, is tastefully decorated; some have four-poster beds.

Mary Arches St. (off High St.), Exeter, Devon EX4 3AZ. © **800/544-9993** in the U.S., or 01392/217736. Fax 01392/413054. www.olaves.co.uk. 15 units. Mon–Thurs £75–£95 ($120–$152) double; £100–£145 ($160–$232) suite. Rates include continental breakfast. MC, V. **Amenities:** Restaurant; bar; concierge; room service. *In room:* TV, coffeemaker, hair dryer.

White Hart Hotel   In the center of town, this inn, a coaching inn in the 15th century, is one of the oldest in the city. Oliver Cromwell stabled his horses here. The hotel is a mass of polished wood, slate floors, oak beams, and gleaming brass and copper. The rooms, which combine old and new, are housed in either the old wing or a more impersonal modern one. Some units are deluxe. Six rooms are large enough for families.

65–66 South St., Exeter, Devon EX1 1EE. © **01392/279897.** Fax 01392/250159. 54 units. Mon–Thurs £69 ($110) double; Fri–Sun £49 ($78) double. Family rooms Mon–Thurs £89 ($142), Fri–Sun £69 ($110). Rates include English breakfast. AE, DC, MC, V. **Amenities:** 2 restaurants; bar; room service; laundry service. *In room:* TV, coffeemaker, hair dryer, trouser press.

INEXPENSIVE

Claremont   This Regency-style 1840 town house is in a quiet residential area, close to the center of town. The rooms, much like those you would find in a private home, are well kept and tastefully decorated. Each room has a small bathroom with a shower unit (some have tubs). Kathy and Tony Gray, who run the property, assist visitors in many ways.

36 Wonford Rd., Exeter, Devon EX2 4LD. (C) **01392/426448.** 4 units. £44 ($70) double; £70 ($112) suite for 4. Rates include continental breakfast. No credit cards. Bus: H. **Amenities:** Breakfast room. *In room:* TV, coffeemaker, hair dryer.

Lea-Dene (*Value*)   This Victorian-style 1930 guesthouse is built of redbrick and set in a southern suburb of Exeter, a 10- to 15-minute walk from the town center. It contains many original details. The small to midsize rooms are simply but comfortably furnished and have recently been improved. You're given a set of towels, which you can use in one of the corridor shower-only bathrooms with other guests. For within Exeter, the cost of staying here is a good value. Owners Karen and Chris Rogers offer a hearty breakfast.

34 Alphington Rd. (A377), St. Thomas, Exeter, Devon EX2 8HN. (C) **01392/257257.** Fax 01392/427952. 11 units, none with bathroom. £42 ($67) double; £60 ($96) family room. DC, MC, V. Rates include English breakfast. Blue minibus D from the center. *In room:* TV, coffeemaker.

Park View Hotel   This hotel lies near the heart of town and the train station. A landmark Georgian house, it offers comfortably but plainly furnished rooms, ranging in size from small to medium. The decor is regularly upgraded. Rooms with private bathroom usually have a shower (only two have a tub-and-shower combination). The public bathrooms available to other guests are convenient and well maintained. Guests take their breakfast in a cozy room opening onto the hotel's garden. Breakfast is the only meal served, but the staff will prepare a packed lunch for touring.

8 Howell Rd., Exeter, Devon EX4 4LG. (C) **01392/271772.** Fax 01392/253047. 12 units, 11 with bathroom. £45 ($72) double without bathroom, £50 ($80) double with bathroom. Rates include English breakfast. AE, MC, V. *In room:* TV, coffeemaker.

WHERE TO DINE

Michael Caines at Royal Clarence ★★ FRENCH   Exeter at long last offers a restaurant worthy of itself, with an aura of smart, sophisticated brasserie. Try to get a table near one of the bay windows overlooking the cathedral. As is obvious by the name, Michael Caines, a skilled chef, is in charge of the overall operation. Excellent, not deluxe, raw materials are purchased and turned into an impressive array of dishes beautifully prepared and served. The dishes we've sampled have been filled with flavor and perfectly spiced, as in appetizers such as a terrine of game and winter vegetables with truffle vinaigrette. Main dishes are likely to feature braised turbot with roasted red onions and mussels in a saffron sauce. Desserts are worth saving room for, especially banana parfait in a chocolate and lime coulis.

Cathedral Yard. (C) **01392/310031.** Reservations required. Main courses £16–£23 ($26–$37). AE, DC, MC, V. Daily noon–2:30pm and 7–10pm.

The Ship Inn (*Finds*) ENGLISH   Often visited by Sir Francis Drake, Sir Walter Raleigh, and Sir John Hawkins, this restaurant still provides tankards of real ale, lager, and stout. A large selection of snacks is offered in the bar every day, whereas the restaurant upstairs provides more substantial English fare. At either lunch or dinner, you can order French onion soup, whole grilled lemon sole, five different steaks, and more. Portions are large, as in Elizabethan times.

St. Martin's Lane. (*C*) **01392/272040.** Reservations recommended. Restaurant main courses £4–£7 ($6.40–$11). Pub platters £2.35–£7 ($3.75–$11). MC, V. Restaurant Mon–Fri noon–2:30pm and 6–9pm; Sat–Sun noon–2:30pm.

EXETER AFTER DARK

Exeter is a lively university town offering an abundance of classical concerts and theater productions, as well as clubs and pubs. For information concerning cultural events and theaters, the **Exeter Arts Booking and Information Centre,** Princesshay ((*C*) **01392/211080**), open daily from 9:30am to 5:30pm, provides a monthly brochure of upcoming events and sells tickets.

An abundance of concerts, opera, dance, and film can be found year-round at the **Exeter & Devon Arts Centre,** Bradninch Place, Gandy St. ((*C*) **01392/ 667080**), and Exeter University's **Northcott Theatre,** Stocker Road ((*C*) **01392/ 256182**), which is also home to a professional theater company.

On the club scene, head to **Volts,** The Quay ((*C*) **01392/211347;** info line 01392/435820), a two-story club featuring funk, soul, dance, and alternative tunes on the first floor, and The Hot House, playing classic pop music on the second floor. The crowd here is young, and there's a full bar and fast food available. The cover charge varies from free to £3 ($4.80).

Attracting a more diverse crowd, **The Warehouse/Boxes Disco & Boogies,** Commercial Road ((*C*) **01392/259292**), is another split club, with different musical styles featured throughout the week. The cover charge varies from free to £5 ($8) before 11pm, and £6 ($9.60) afterward, which gets you into all three clubs on Thursday and Saturday. Warehouse is only open on Fridays and Boxes is only open on Wednesdays.

Pubs vary from the ancient and haunted to haunts of folk-music fans, with the **Turks Head,** High Street ((*C*) **01392/256680**), offering a bit of local color, since it's housed in a 600-year-old dungeon allegedly haunted by the Turks who were tortured and killed here. The first two floors are unchanged from that bygone era, but the top three floors were turned into the existing pub more than 450 years ago. It was a favorite hangout and scribbling spot of Charles Dickens, whose favorite chair is still on display. Today, it's a lively pub with a computerized jukebox and a fast-food menu. There is a DJ on weekends.

Well House Tavern, Cathedral Close ((*C*) **01392/319953**), is part of the Royal Clarence Hotel. It's housed in a building believed to have been constructed in the 14th century, although the Roman well in the basement predates that estimate. It, too, is said to be haunted—only the ghost here, affectionately called Alice, is said to be good-spirited when she appears in her flowing white dress. Join Alice and the other regulars for a pint or a light meal.

Featuring a great view of the canal, **Double Locks,** Canal Banks ((*C*) **01392/ 256947**), welcomes a varied crowd, largely students. It features live music (jazz, rock, and blues) with no cover charge 2 or 4 evenings a week (Thurs, Fri, and Sun), and you can get traditional pub grub to go with your pint. Although spaciously spread through a Georgian mansion, the **Imperial Pub,** New North Road ((*C*) **01392/434050**), is friendly to frugal travelers, with the cheapest brand-name beer in town, starting at £1.45 ($2.30), and a fast-food menu.

6 Dartmoor National Park ⁄★⁄★

343km (213 miles) SW of London; 21km (13 miles) W of Exeter

This national park lies northeast of Plymouth, stretching from Tavistock and Okehampton on the west to near Exeter in the east, a granite mass that sometimes rises to a height of 600m (2,000 ft.) above sea level. The landscape offers vistas of gorges with rushing water, gorse, and purple heather ranged over by Dartmoor ponies—a foreboding landscape for experienced walkers only.

In Dartmoor, you'll find 805km (500 miles) of foot- and bridle paths and more than 90,000 acres of common land with public access. The country is rough, and on the high moor you should always make sure you have good maps, a compass, and suitable clothing and shoes.

ESSENTIALS

GETTING THERE   Take the train down from London to Exeter (see "Essentials," in section 5), then use local buses to connect you with the various villages of Dartmoor.

Transmoor Link, a public transport bus service, usually operates throughout the summer and is an ideal way to get onto the moor. Information on the Transmoor Link and on the bus link between various towns and villages on Dartmoor is available from the **Transport Coordination Centre** (© **01392/ 382800**).

If you're driving, Exeter is the most easily reached gateway. From here, continue west on B3212 to such centers of Dartmoor as Easton, Chagford, Moretonhampstead, and North Bovey. From these smaller towns, tiny roads—often not really big enough for two cars—cut deeper into the moor.

VISITOR INFORMATION   The main source of information is the **Dartmoor National Park Tourist Information Centre,** Town Hall, Bedford Square, Tavistock (© **01822/612938**). It will book accommodations within a 80km (50-mile) radius for free. It's open April through October daily from 9:30am to 5pm. From November to March, it's open on Monday, Tuesday, Friday, and Saturday from 10am to 4pm.

EXPLORING THE MOORS

This region is as rich in myth and legend as anywhere else in Britain. Crisscrossed by about 805km (500 miles) of bridle paths and hiking trails and covering about 953 sq. km (368 sq. miles) (180 of which make up the Dartmoor National Park), the moors rest on a granite base with numerous rocky outcroppings.

The Dartmoor National Park Authority (DNPA) runs **guided walks** of varying difficulty, ranging from 1½ to 6 hours for a trek of some 14km to 19km (9–12 miles). All you have to do is turn up suitably clad at your selected starting point. Details are available from DNP information centers or from the **Dartmoor National Park Authority,** High Moorland Visitor Centre, Tavistock Road, Princetown (near Yelverton) PL20 6QF (© **01822/890414**). Guided tours cost £3 ($4.80) for a 2-hour walk, £4 ($6.40) for a 3-hour walk, £4.50 ($7.20) for a 4-hour walk, and £5 ($8) for a 6-hour walk. These prices are subsidized by the national parks services.

Throughout the area are stables where you can arrange for a day's trek across the moors. For **horseback riding** on Dartmoor, there are too many establishments to list. All are licensed, and you are accompanied by an experienced rider/ guide. The moor can be dangerous because sudden fogs descend on treacherous marshlands without warning. Prices are around £11 ($18) per hour. Most riding stables are listed in a useful free publication, *The Dartmoor Visitor,* which also provides details on guided walks, places to go, accommodations, local events, and articles about the national park. *The Dartmoor Visitor* is obtainable from DNP information centers and tourist information centers or by mail. Send an International Reply Coupon to the DNPA headquarters (address above).

CHAGFORD: A GOOD BASE FOR EXPLORING THE PARK ✷
351km (218 miles) SW of London; 21km (13 miles) W of Exeter; 32km (20 miles) NW of Torquay

One hundred and eighty meters (600 ft.) above sea level, Chagford is an ancient town; with moors all around, it's a good base from which to explore north Dartmoor. Chagford overlooks the Teign River in its deep valley and is itself overlooked by the high granite tors. There's good fishing in the Teign. From Chagford, the most popular excursion is to Postbridge, a village with a prehistoric clapper bridge.

Surrounded by moors, romantic Chagford is one of the best bases for exploring the often forlorn but romantic north Dartmoor. It's also Sir Francis Drake country.

To get here, take a train to Exeter (see "Essentials," in section 5), and then catch a local bus to Chagford (Transmoor Link National Express bus no. 82). If you're driving from Exeter, drive west on A30, then south on A382 to Chagford.

EXPLORING THE TOWN
Castle Drogo ✷ This massive granite castle, in the hamlet of Drewsteignton some 27km (17 miles) west of Exeter, was designed and built between 1910 and 1930 by architect Sir Edwin Lutyens, then at the height of his powers, for his client, Julius Drewe. It was the last private country house built in the United Kingdom on a grand scale. Though constructed of granite and castellated and turreted like a medieval castle from the age of chivalry, it was never intended to be a military stronghold. The castle occupies a bleak but dramatic position high above the River Teign, with views sweeping out over the moors.

The tour covers an elegant series of formal rooms designed in the tradition of the Edwardian age. Two restaurants and a buffet-style tearoom are on premises.

Insider's tip: The castle is so overpowering it's easy to forget the secluded gardens. But they are wonderful, including a sunken lawn enclosed by raised walkways, a circular croquet lawn (sets are available for rent), geometrically shaped yew hedges, and a children's playroom based on a 1930s residence.

6.5km (4 miles) northeast of Chagford and 9.5km (6 miles) south of the Exeter–Okehampton Rd. (A30). ✆ 01647/433306. Admission (castle and grounds) £5.90 ($9.45) adults, £2.95 ($4.70) children. Grounds only £2.90 ($4.65) adults, £1.45 ($2.30) children. Apr–Oct Wed–Sun 11am–5:30pm; grounds daily 10:30am–dusk. Take A30 and follow the signs.

Sir Francis Drake's House ✷ Constructed in 1278, Sir Francis Drake's House was originally a Cistercian monastery. The monastery was dissolved in 1539 and became the country seat of sailors Sir Richard Grenville and, later, Sir Francis Drake. The house remained in the Drake family until 1946, when the abbey and grounds were given to the National Trust. The abbey is now a museum, with exhibits including Drake's drum, banners, and other artifacts. There is also an audiovisual presentation about the history of the house.

Buckland Abbey, Yelverton. ✆ 01822/853607. Admission £5 ($8) adults, £2.50 ($4) children. Apr–Oct Fri–Wed 10:30am–5:30pm; Nov–Mar Sat–Sun 2–5pm. Last admission 45 min. before closing. Go 5km (3 miles) west of Yelverton off A386.

WHERE TO STAY & DINE
Easton Court Hotel ✷ *Finds* Established in the 1920s, this Tudor house is a longtime favorite of the literati and theatrical celebrities. Best known as the place where Evelyn Waugh wrote *Brideshead Revisited,* the atmosphere here is very English country house: ancient stone house with thatched roof, inglenook where log fires burn, and high-walled flower garden. Bedrooms are snug and comfortable, ranging in size from small to medium. Rooms are appointed with

---

Moments **A Cuppa & an Homage to Lorna Doone**

When it's teatime, drop in at **Whiddons,** High Street (© **01647/433406**), decorated with fresh flowers in summer. They have freshly baked scones and delectable cucumber sandwiches. After tea, drop in at the Church of St. Michael nearby, where a spurned lover killed Mary Whiddon on her wedding day (later fictionalized in R. D. Blackmore's classic *Lorna Doone*).

---

comfortable beds and excellent mattresses upon which the greats of yesteryear slept; some have four-posters. Most rooms open onto views; all but two bathrooms have shower-tub combinations and the rest have showers only.

Easton Cross, Chagford, Devon TQ13 8JL. © 01647/433469. Fax 01647/433654. www.Easton.co.uk. 5 units. £50–£65 ($80–$104) double. Rates include English breakfast. MC, V. Take A382 2.5km (1½ miles) northeast of Chagford. Bus no. 359 from Exeter. **Amenities:** Guest lounge. *In room:* TV, coffeemaker, hair dryer.

Gidleigh Park Hotel ★★★ This Tudor-style hotel, a Relais & Châteaux member, is country house supreme, the finest and most elegant place to stay in the Dartmoor area. The hotel lies in the Teign Valley, opening onto panoramic vistas of the Meldon and Nattadon Hills. Its American owners, Kay and Paul Henderson, have renovated and refurnished the house with flair and imagination. Most of the bedrooms are on the second floor and are reached by a grand staircase. Bedrooms are roomy and furnished in the most elegant English country-house tradition. Half-canopies usually crown the sumptuous English beds, and each well-appointed bathroom has Crabtree & Evelyn toiletries and Frette bathrobes. The hotel has a two-bedroom thatched cottage with two bathrooms across the river, 315m (350 yd.) from the hotel, available for two to four people.

Gidleigh Park (3km/2 miles outside town), Chagford, Devon TQ13 8HH. © 01647/432367. Fax 01647/432574. www.gidleigh.com. 14 units, 1 cottage. £435–£565 ($696–$904) double; £565 ($904) cottage for 2; £765 ($1,224) cottage for 4. Rates include English breakfast, morning tea, and dinner. AE, DC, MC, V. To get here from Chagford Sq., turn right onto Mill St. at Lloyds Bank. After 135m (150 yd.), turn right and go down the hill to the crossroads. Cross straight over onto Holy St., following the lane passing Holy St. Manor on your right and shifting into low gear to negotiate 2 sharp bends on a steep hill. Over Leigh Bridge, make a sharp right turn into Gidleigh Park. A 1km (½-mile) drive will bring you to the hotel. **Amenities:** Restaurant; bar; putting green; tennis court; babysitting; laundry service; bowling green; croquet lawn. *In room:* TV, hair dryer.

OTHER TOWNS IN & AROUND DARTMOOR

Some 21km (13 miles) west of Exeter, the peaceful little town of **Moreton-hampstead** is perched on the edge of Dartmoor. Moretonhampstead contains an old market cross and several 17th-century colonnaded almshouses.

The much-visited Dartmoor village of **Widecombe-in-the-Moor** is only 11km (7 miles) from Moretonhampstead. The fame of the village of Widecombe-in-the-Moor stems from an old folk song about Tom Pearce and his gray mare, listing the men who were supposed to be on their way to Widecombe Fair when they met with disaster. Widecombe also has a parish church worth visiting. Called the **Cathedral of the Moor,** with a roster of vicars beginning in 1253, the house of worship in a green valley is surrounded by legends. When the building was restored, a wall plate was found bearing the badge of Richard II (1377–99), the figure of a white hart. The town is very disappointing, tacky, and unkempt in spite of its fame.

The market town of **Okehampton** owes its existence to the Norman castle built by Baldwin de Bryonis, sheriff of Devon, under orders from his uncle,

William the Conqueror, in 1068, just 2 years after the conquest. The Courtenay family lived here for many generations until Henry VIII beheaded one of them and dismantled the castle in 1538.

Museum of Dartmoor Life, at the Dartmoor Centre, 3 West St., Oke-hampton (✆ **01837/52295;** www.museumofdartmoorlife.eclipse.co.uk), is housed in an old mill with a water wheel and is part of the Dartmoor Centre, a group of attractions around an old courtyard. Also here are working craft studios, a Victorian cottage tearoom, and a tourist information center. Museum displays cover all aspects of Dartmoor's history from prehistoric times, including some old vehicles—a Devon box wagon of 1875 and a 1922 Bullnose Morris motorcar. There's a reconstructed cider press, and a blacksmith. The museum is open from October to Easter, Monday through Friday from 10am to 4pm, and from Easter to October, Monday through Saturday from 11am to 4:30pm. It also opens on Sunday June through September from 10am to 5pm. Admission is £2 ($3.20) for adults, £1.80 ($2.90) for seniors, £1 ($1.60) for children, and £5.60 ($8.95) for a family ticket (two adults, two children).

Let yourself drift back in time to the days when craftspeople were the lifeblood of thriving communities. Basket weavers, wood turners, and potters are among the traditional crafters that can still be seen throughout the area. Indulge yourself with some genuine Devon pieces of craftsmanship. In the Dartmoor National Park in West Devon, you'll find that **The Yelverton Paperweight Centre,** Leg O'Mutton (✆ **01822/854250**), presents an impressive display of more than 800 glass paperweights for sale along with paintings of Dartmoor scenes.

For an interesting outdoor shop, **The Kountry Kit,** 22–23 West St., Tavistock (✆ **01822/613089**), carries all the best names in gear and outerwear. It also is a clearinghouse of name-brand seconds.

WHERE TO STAY & DINE IN THE AREA

The Castle Inn A 12th-century structure next to Lydford Castle, this inn lies midway between Okehampton and Tavistock. With its pink facade and row of rose trellises, it is the hub of the village. The owners have maintained the character of the roomy old rustic lounge. One room, the Snug, has a group of high-backed oak benches arranged in a circle. Bedrooms are not large but are attractively furnished, often with mahogany and marble Victorian pieces. Half the bathrooms have showers only, the rest a tub-and-shower combination.

Lydford, near Okehampton (1.5km/1 mile off A386), Devon EX20 4BH. ✆ **01822/820241.** Fax 01822/820454. 7 units. £65–£80 ($104–$128) double. Special Country Breaks (any 2 nights): £90 ($144), including breakfast. MC, V. **Amenities:** Restaurant; bar. *In room:* TV, coffeemaker.

Cherrybrook Hotel This is a small family-run hotel in the center of the Dartmoor National Park, on the high moor but within easy driving distance of Exeter and Plymouth. It was built in the early 19th century by a prince regent's friend who received permission to enclose a large area of the Dartmoor forest for farming. The lounge and bar with their beamed ceilings and slate floors are a reminder of those times. Andy and Margaret Duncan rent small to medium-sized rooms with a traditional decor, often with a granite fireplace. A different group of bedrooms is redecorated each year. Bathrooms contain a shower stall.

On B3212 between Postbridge and Two Bridges, Yelverton, Devon PL20 6SP. ✆/fax **01822/880260.** www.cherrybrook-hotel.co.uk. 7 units. £100 ($160) double. Rates include English breakfast and dinner. No credit cards. Closed Dec 22–Jan 2. **Amenities:** Restaurant; bar. *In room:* TV, coffeemaker, hair dryer.

Holne Chase Hotel ⚘ *Kids*   The hotel is a white-gabled country house, 5km (3 miles) northwest of the center of town, within sight of trout- and salmon-fishing waters. You can catch your lunch and take it back to the kitchen to be cooked. Though the mood of the moor predominates, Holne Chase is surrounded by trees, lawns, and pastures—a perfect setting for walks along the Dart. The house is furnished in period style; a stable block has been converted into four sporting lodges. Rooms come in various shapes, sizes, and styles; some have their original fireplaces and four-poster beds, ideal for a romantic interlude. If assigned a room in the stable, don't be disappointed, as they are really delightful split-level suites. All the comforts of English country living are found here. Seven rooms are large enough for families.

Two Bridges Rd., Ashburton, near Newton Abbot (off the main Ashburton–Princetown Rd., between the Holne Bridge and New Bridge), Devon TQ13 7NS. © **01364/631471.** Fax 01364/631453. www.holne-chase.co.uk. 16 units. £130–£150 ($208–$240) double; from £170 ($272) suite. Rates include English breakfast. Discount packages available. MC, V. **Amenities:** Restaurant; bar; room service; babysitting; laundry service. *In room:* TV, coffeemaker, hair dryer.

Lewtrenchard Manor   On the northwest edges of Dartmoor, near the popular touring center of Okehampton, this is a 17th-century English house with a certain charm and grace. It was at one time the residence of the Victorian hymn writer, the Rev. Sabine Baring Gould (hardly a household name today). It is set in a garden so lovely it is open to the general public as part of the National Gardens Scheme. Lovely walks are possible in several directions. As is typical of its time, the house features oak paneling, leaded windows, beautifully detailed ceilings, and antiques. Rooms come in various shapes and sizes, but each is exceedingly comfortable.

Lewdown, Devon EX20 4PN. © **01566/783256.** Fax 01566/783332. www.lewtrenchard.co.uk. 9 units. £130 ($208) double; £195 ($312) suite. Rates include English breakfast. AE, DC, MC, V. **Amenities:** Restaurant; bar; room service; laundry service. *In room:* TV, hair dryer.

7 Torquay: The English Riviera ⋆

359km (223 miles) SW of London; 37km (23 miles) SE of Exeter

In 1968, the towns of Torquay, Paignton, and Brixham joined to form "the English Riviera" as part of a plan to turn the area into one of the super three-in-one resorts of Europe. The area today—the birthplace of mystery writer Agatha Christie—opens onto 35km (22 miles) of coastline and 18 beaches. Palm trees even grow here!

Torquay is set against a backdrop of the red cliffs of Devon, with many sheltered pebbly coves. With its parks and gardens, including numerous subtropical plants, it's often compared to the Mediterranean. At night, concerts, productions from the West End, vaudeville shows, and ballroom dancing keep the vacationers and many honeymooners entertained.

ESSENTIALS

GETTING THERE   The nearest connection is Exeter Airport (see "Essentials," in section 5), 40 minutes away. Frequent trains run throughout the day from London's Paddington Station to Torquay, whose station is at the town center on the seafront. The trip takes 2½ hours. For rail information, call © **0845/ 748-4950.**

National Express coach links from London's Victoria Coach Station leave every 2 hours during the day for Torquay. For information and schedules, call © **020/7529-2000.**

If you're driving from Exeter, head west on A38, veering south at the junction with A380.

VISITORS INFORMATION   The **Tourist Information Centre,** at Vaughan Parade (✆ **01803/297428**), is open Monday through Thursday from 8:40am to 5:15pm and Friday from 9:40am to 4:15pm.

PALM TREES & AGATHA CHRISTIE

This resort region is known for offering one of the balmiest climates in Britain. It's so temperate because of its exposure to the Gulf Stream; subtropical plants such as palm trees and succulents thrive.

Oldway Mansion   You'll see the conspicuous consumption of England's Gilded Age here. The mansion was built in 1874 by Isaac Merritt Singer, founder of the sewing-machine empire. His son, Paris, enhanced its decor, massive Ionic portico, and 17 acres of Italianate gardens. The mansion's eclectic decor includes a scaled-down version of the Hall of Mirrors in the Palace of Versailles. During its Jazz Age heyday, Oldway served as a rehearsal space and performance venue for Isadora Duncan, who was having a not terribly discreet affair with Paris.

Torbay Rd., in Preston, near Paignton (a short drive south of the center of Torquay on the main Paignton–Torquay Rd.). ✆ **01803/207933.** Tours available Easter–Oct 9am–1pm for £1 ($1.60). Free admission without guided tour. Apr–Oct daily 9am–5pm; Nov–Mar Mon–Fri 9am–5pm.

Torre Abbey   Originally built as a monastery in 1196, then converted into a private home in the 16th century, it has long been associated with Torquay's leading citizens. Today, the Torquay Town Council maintains it as a museum. The museum features a room outfitted in a close approximation of **Agatha Christie's private study.** After the mystery writer's death, her family donated for display her Remington typewriter, many of her original manuscripts, an oil portrait of Ms. Christie as a young woman, family photographs, and more.

Kings Dr. (.5km/¼ mile east of Torquay's center). ✆ **01803/293593.** Admission £3.25 ($5.20) adults, £1.70 ($2.70) children. Easter or Apr 1 (whichever is earlier) to Oct 31 daily 9:30am–6pm.

WHERE TO STAY
EXPENSIVE

The Imperial ★★★ *Finds*   This leading five-star hotel in the West Country dates from the 1860s, but a major refurbishing has kept it abreast of the times and way ahead of its competition. It sits on 5½ acres of subtropical gardens opening onto rocky cliffs, with views of the Channel. You'll follow the example of some of the characters of Agatha Christie if you check in here. She called it the Esplanade in *The Rajah's Emerald,* the Castle in *Partners in Crime,* and the Majestic in *Peril at End House.* Inside is a world of soaring ceilings, marble columns, and ornate plasterwork—enough to make a former visitor, Edward VII,

---

(*Fun Fact* **Looking for Fawlty Towers?**

Fans of the British comedy *Fawlty Towers,* the television series that made Torquay and the English Riviera known the world over, may be disappointed to learn that it wasn't filmed in Torquay at all, but rather in one of the Home Counties closer to London. Regardless, Torquay continues to be identified with the series, inspired by John Cleese's sojourn in Torquay during one of his tours of duty with the Monty Python team.

> **Fun Fact Under the Sheltering Palms on the Riviera**
>
> Three seaside towns—Torquay, Brixham, and Paignton—combine to form the longest sweep of beachfront in Britain. This almost continuous sweep of sandy beach opening onto calm waters has earned the title "the English Riviera." The Gulf Stream climate allows for subtropical vegetation, and the palm trees imported from Australia in the 19th century still make for a Riviera-like backdrop.

feel at home. Rooms are studies in grand living, with beautiful reproduction pieces, striped wallpaper and upholstered seating. Many have private balconies suspended high above a view that encompasses offshore islands with black rocks and sheer sides. Bathrooms are grandly appointed with deluxe toiletries.

Park Hill Rd., Torquay, Devon TQ1 2DG. ✆ **800/225-5843** in the U.S. and Canada, or 01803/294301. Fax 01803/298293. www.paramount-hotels.co.uk. 152 units. £190 ($304) double; from £180–£300 ($288–$480) suite. Rates include English breakfast, use of sporting facilities, and dancing in the ballroom Mon–Sat. AE, DC, MC, V. Garage parking £5 ($8); free parking lot. **Amenities:** 2 restaurants; bar; 2 heated pools (indoor, outdoor); 2 tennis courts; 2 squash courts; health club with sauna; concierge; room service; laundry service; dry cleaning. *In room:* TV, minibar, coffeemaker, hair dryer, safe, trouser press.

Orestone Manor ✮ Sometimes the best way to enjoy a bustling seaside resort is from afar, nestled in a country home. Orestone Manor is in nearby Maidencombe, a small village north of Torquay. In one of the loveliest valleys in South Devon, this gabled manor house, constructed in the early 19th century as a private home, enjoys a tranquil rural setting, situated on 2 acres of well-landscaped gardens. All of the bedrooms are handsomely furnished. The gable rooms are a bit small but some offer sea views; all the superior rooms have sea views and complimentary sherry. Because this was once a country lodge, all the bedrooms have an individual character and aren't just square boxes. Some of the good-sized bathrooms have claw-foot tubs with separate walk-in showers.

Rockhouse Lane, Maidencombe, Torquay, Devon TQ1 4SX. ✆ **01803/328098.** Fax 01803/328336. www. orestone.co.uk. 12 units. £110–£180 ($176–$288) double. Rates include English breakfast. Winter discounts available. AE, DC, MC, V. Closed 2 weeks in Jan. Drive 5.5km (3½ miles) north of Torquay on A379. Free parking. **Amenities:** Restaurant; bar; pool; room service; babysitting; laundry service; dry cleaning. *In room:* TV, coffeemaker, hair dryer, safe.

Palace Hotel ✮ In Torquay, only the Imperial is better. This 1921 hotel was built when life was experienced on a grand scale, an attitude reflected by spacious public rooms with molded ceilings and columns. With its recent improvements, the hotel has entered the 21st century in a premier position. Luxurious through and through, the bedrooms are well furnished, each with a well-maintained bathroom. The hotel occupies 25 choice acres of real estate in Torquay, sweeping down to Anstey's Cove.

Babbacombe Rd., Babbacombe, Torquay, Devon TQ1 3TG. ✆ **01803/200200.** Fax 01803/299899. www. palacetorquay.co.uk. 141 units. £142–£280 ($227–$448) double; £236 ($378) suite for 2. Rates include English breakfast. AE, DC, MC, V. Parking £5 ($8) for garage spaces. Bus: 32. From the town center take B3199 east. **Amenities:** Restaurant; 2 bars; 2 pools (heated indoor; outdoor); 9-hole golf course; 6 tennis courts; 2 squash courts; sauna; room service; babysitting; laundry service; dry cleaning. *In room:* TV, minibar, coffeemaker, hair dryer, trouser press.

INEXPENSIVE

Colindale This hotel is a good choice, about as central as you'd want. It opens onto King's Garden, a 5-minute walk from Corbyn Beach and a 3-minute walk from the railway station. Rooms are cozily furnished, in a range of sizes and shapes, each in a Victorian style. Rooms come with a private shower (one has a bath). Colindale is one of a row of attached brick Victorian houses, with gables and chimneys.

20 Rathmore Rd., Chelston, Torquay, Devon TQ2 6NY. © **01803/293947.** www.colindalehotel.co.uk. 8 units. £50–£56 ($80–$90) double. Rates include English breakfast. MC, V. Free parking. **Amenities:** Breakfast room; bar. *In room:* TV, coffeemaker, hair dryer.

Craig Court Hotel *Value*   This hotel is in a large Victorian mansion with a southern exposure that lies a short walk from the heart of town. Owner Ann Box's modernized rooms, many with private facilities, offer excellent value. Bedrooms tend to be small and cozy, each with a compact private bathroom with a shower. In addition to enjoying the good, wholesome food served here, guests can also make use of a lounge or an intimate bar opening onto the grounds.

10 Ash Hill Rd., Castle Circus, Torquay, Devon TQ1 3HZ. © **01803/294400.** Fax 01803/212525. www.craig courthotel.co.uk. £41–£47 ($66–$75) double. Rates include English breakfast. Special packages available. No credit cards. Take St. Marychurch Rd. (signposted St. Marychurch, Babbacombe) from Castle Circus (the town hall), make the 1st right onto Ash Hill Rd., go 180m (200 yd.), and the hotel is on the right. **Amenities:** Restaurant; bar. *In room:* TV, coffeemaker, hair dryer.

Fairmount House Hotel *★* *Finds*   Standing on a perch overlooking the Cockington Valley, this little haven of tranquillity is far removed from the bustle of the resort, lying in the residential valley of Chelston, on the periphery of Torquay. A converted Victorian building has been turned into a winning little B&B, with its gardens facing south. Torquay Harbour is within easy reach, and the sea is less than .6km (1 mile) away. The family home, complete with cellars and servants' quarters, dates from the turn of the 20th century. For an inglorious period in the 1950s, it was turned into apartments, but after its restoration its original character has been returned. The aura is more of a large family home than a hotel. A highlight is the Victorian Conservatory Bar, with French doors opening onto the suntrap patio. Bedrooms are midsize and tastefully furnished, each with a well-maintained private bathroom with shower. Two garden rooms have a tub and shower. An evening dinner can be arranged in advance.

Herbert Rd., Chelston, Torquay, S. Devon TQ2 6RW. © **01803/605446.** Fax 01803/605446. www.smooth hound.co.uk/hotels/fairmoun.html. £60–£62 ($96–$99) double. Rates include breakfast. MC, V. **Amenities:** Restaurant. *In room:* TV, beverage maker, hair dryer, no phone.

WHERE TO DINE

Capers Restaurant *★* INTERNATIONAL   This intimate, French-style bistro lies at Lisbourne Square, just off the main artery, Babbacombe Road. Torquay is not renowned for its dining, but this serious little restaurant is a bright note in a culinary wasteland. Families are among the regular patrons. The chef-owner, Robert Llewellyn, shops for the freshest of regional produce, when available, and serves locally caught fish and shellfish. A selection of vegetarian dishes is also available. The sauces that go with the fish are a perfect match to the catch of the day, as in the green peppercorn sauce that is zestily served with the monkfish or the caper sauce coming with the perfectly poached skate.

7 Lisbourne Sq. © **01803/291177.** Reservations required. Main courses £11–£18 ($18–$29). AE, MC, V. Tues–Fri noon–2pm; Mon–Sat 7–10pm. Closed 1 week in Aug.

Mulberry House *★* *Value* ENGLISH   Lesley Cooper is an inspired cook, and she'll feed you well in her little dining room, seating some two dozen diners at midday. The restaurant is situated in one of Torquay's Victorian villas, facing a patio of plants and flowers, with outside tables for summer lunches. Vegetarians will find comfort here, and others can feast on Lesley's smoked ham rissoles, honey-roasted chicken, or grilled natural fried filets of sole with tartar sauce. Traditional roasts draw the Sunday crowds. The choice is wisely limited so that everything served will be fresh.

You can even stay here in one of three bedrooms, each comfortably furnished and well kept, with private bathrooms. Bed-and-breakfast rates, from £30 ($48) per person daily, make this one of the best bargains of the whole area.

1 Scarborough Rd., Torquay, Devon TQ2 5UJ. ℂ 01803/213639. Reservations required. Main courses £9.50–£13 ($15–$20); 3-course meal £18–£25 ($28–$40). No credit cards. Fri–Sun noon–2pm; Wed–Sat 7:30–9:30pm. From the Sea Front, turn up Belgrave Rd.; Scarborough Rd. is the 1st right. Bus: 32.

TORQUAY AFTER DARK

Seven theaters in town, all open year-round, offer everything from Gilbert and Sullivan and tributes to Sinatra and Nat King Cole to Marine Band concerts and comedy shows. Among the most active are the **Palace Theatre,** Palace Avenue, Paignton (ℂ **01803/665800**); and the **Princess Theatre,** Torbay Road (ℂ **08702/414120**).

Fifteen area nightclubs cater to everyone from teenyboppers to the gay scene, but dancing rules the town, and there's virtually nowhere to catch live club acts. Among the better dance clubs are **Claires,** Torwood Street (ℂ **01803/292079**), for its Thursday-, Friday- and Saturday-night house music, with a cover charge varying from £3 to £7 ($4.80–$11), depending on the DJ; and the **Monastery,** Torwood Gardens Road (ℂ **01803/292929**), on Saturday, the only night this club opens its doors. You can get your fill of hip-hop and electronica here as the dancing starts at midnight and doesn't end until 7am. The cover charge is £5 ($8).

8 Dartmouth ✶✶

380km (236 miles) SW of London; 56km (35 miles) SE of Exeter

At the mouth of the Dart River, this ancient seaport is the home of the Royal Naval College. Traditionally linked to England's maritime greatness, Dartmouth sent out the young midshipmen who saw to it that "Britannia ruled the waves." You can take a river steamer up the Dart to Totnes (book at the kiosk at the harbor); the scenery along the way is panoramic, as the Dart is Devon's most beautiful river. Dartmouth's 15th-century castle was built during the reign of Edward IV. The town's most noted architectural feature is the Butter Walk, which lies below Tudor houses. The Flemish influence in some of the houses is pronounced.

ESSENTIALS

GETTING THERE   Dartmouth is not easily reached by public transport. Trains run to Totnes and Paignton. One bus a day runs from Totnes to Dartmouth. Call ℂ **0870/608-2608** for schedules.

If you're driving from Exeter, take the A38 southwest, cutting southeast to Totnes on the A381; then follow the A381 to the junction with the B3207.

VISITOR INFORMATION   The **Tourist Information Centre** is at the Engine House, Mayors Avenue (ℂ **01803/834224**), and is open April through October, Monday through Saturday from 9:30am to 5pm and Sunday from 10am to 4pm (off season Mon–Sat 9:30am–4:30pm).

EXPLORING DARTMOUTH

Many visitors come to Dartmouth for the bracing salt air and a chance to explore the surrounding marshlands, which are rich in bird life and natural beauty. The historic monuments here are steeped in much of the legend and lore of channel life and historic Devon.

The town's most historic and interesting church is **St. Petrox,** on Castle Road, a 17th-century Anglican monument with an ivy-draped graveyard whose tombstones evoke the sorrows of Dartmouth's maritime past. The church is open daily from 7am to dusk.

It's also worth walking through the waterfront neighborhood known as **Bayard's Cove,** a cobbled, half-timbered neighborhood that's quite charming. Set near the end of Lower Street, it prospered during the 1600s thanks to its ship-repair services. In 1620 its quays were the site for repairs of the Pilgrims' historic ships, the *Speedwell* and the *Mayflower,* just after their departure from Plymouth.

Dartmouth Castle Originally built during the 15th century, the castle was later outfitted with artillery and employed by the Victorians as a coastal defense station. A tour of its bulky ramparts and somber interiors provides insight into the changing nature of warfare throughout the centuries, and you'll see sweeping views of the surrounding coast and flatlands.

Castle Rd. (1km/½ mile south of the town center). © **01803/833588.** Admission £3.30 ($5.30) adults, £1.70 ($2.70) children. Apr–Sept daily 10am–6pm; Oct daily 10am–5pm; Nov–Mar Wed–Sun 10am–4pm.

Dartmouth Museum This is the region's most interesting maritime museum, focusing on the British Empire's military might of the 18th century. Built between 1635 and 1640, it's set amid an interconnected row of 17th-century buildings—The Butter Walk—whose overhanging, stilt-supported facade was originally designed to provide shade for the butter, milk, and cream sold there by local milkmaids. Today, the complex houses the museum, as well as shops selling wines, baked goods, and more.

In the Butter Walk. © **01803/832923.** Admission £1.50 ($2.40) adults, £1 ($1.60) seniors, 50p (80¢) children. Mar–Oct Mon–Sat 11am–5pm; Nov–Feb Mon–Sat noon–3pm.

WHERE TO STAY

Dart Marina Hotel ✸ This hotel sits at the edge of its own marina, within a 3-minute walk from the center of town. It was originally built as a clubhouse for local yachties late in the 19th century and was then enlarged and transformed into a hotel just before World War II. It does not have as much charm or character as the Royal Castle. The bar, the new riverside terrace, and each bedroom afford a view of yachts bobbing at anchor in the Dart River; 14 bedrooms have private balconies. The superior rooms also sport sofa beds, making them a good bet for families.

Sandquay, Dartmouth, Devon TQ6 9PH. © **01803/832580.** Fax 01803/835040. www.dartmarinahotel.com. 49 units. £135–£178 ($216–$285) double; £159–£203 ($254–$325) suite for 2. Rates include half board. MC, V. **Amenities:** Restaurant; bar; room service. *In room:* TV, coffeemaker, hair dryer, trouser press.

Royal Castle Hotel ✸ *(Kids)* A coaching inn on the town quay since 1639, this is the leading choice. The Royal Castle has hosted Sir Francis Drake, Queen Victoria, Charles II, and Edward VII. Horse-drawn carriages (as late as 1910) dispatched passengers in a carriageway, now an enclosed reception hall. The glassed-in courtyard, with its winding wooden staircase, has the original coaching horn and a set of 20 antique spring bells connected to the bedrooms. Three rooms open off the covered courtyard, and the rambling corridors display antiques. River-view rooms are the most sought after. All units have been recently restored and have central heating. Three rooms are air-conditioned, and eight units offer a Jacuzzi. Five rooms contain a four-poster bed, and each is individually decorated, although all reflect the age of the building. Four accommodations are large enough for families. All but four of the well-kept bathrooms have shower-tub combinations; the rest have showers only.

11 The Quay, Dartmouth, Devon TQ6 9PS. ⓒ **01803/833033.** Fax 01803/835445. www.royalcastle.co.uk. 25 units. £77.95–£94.95 ($125–$152) double. Rates include English breakfast. AE, MC, V. **Amenities:** Restaurant; 2 bars; room service; babysitting; laundry service; dry cleaning. *In room:* A/C, TV, coffeemaker, hair dryer, safe.

WHERE TO DINE

The Carved Angel ⭐⭐ CONTINENTAL   The best restaurant in town, the stylishly simple Carved Angel is on the riverfront. The building's half-timbered, heavily carved facade rises opposite the harbor. Inside, there's a statue of a carved angel (hence the name).

The cooking is both innovative and interesting, more akin to the creative cuisine of the Continent than to the traditional cookery of England. Appetizers range from crawfish bisque to chicken liver parfait with red-onion confit and toasted brioche. Main dishes include roasted salt cod with bacon, leeks, and olives and pan-fried local sea bass served with a shellfish ravioli and braised fennel. It's worth saving room for the kumquat bavarois with poached rhubarb in ginger syrup.

2 S. Embankment. ⓒ **01803/832465.** Reservations recommended. 4-course fixed-price lunch £24 ($38); 5-course fixed-price dinner £40 ($63). MC, V. Tues–Sun noon–2:30pm; Mon–Sat 7–9:30pm.

Carved Angel Café *Value* ENGLISH   The low-budget cafe and brasserie is associated with the upscale and pricey The Carved Angel; you are guaranteed a well-prepared, fairly priced meal in an environment reeking of bucolic charm and traditional English wholesomeness. Menu items are listed on a blackboard and change every day according to the seasonality of the ingredients and the inspiration of the chef. Good cooking is the rule here, as evoked by such dishes as chicken and mushroom casserole and such desserts as lemon-flavored cheesecake. Soups are rich and nutritious, and at least three traditional "puddings" are always available for dessert. The restaurant is fully licensed.

7 Foss St. ⓒ **01803/834842.** Reservations not necessary. Lunch main courses £5.50–£7 ($8.80–$11); dinner main courses £6–£12 ($9.60–$19). AE, DC, MC, V. Dec–Mar Tues–Sat 9am–5pm; Apr–Nov Mon–Thurs 9am–5pm, Fri–Sat 9am–5pm and 7–9pm.

Horn of Plenty ⭐ INTERNATIONAL   As you drive from Tavistock to Callington, a small sign points north along a leafy drive to a solid Regency house where the owners operate what the French call a restaurant *avec chambres*. It was built by the duke of Bedford in the early 1800s as a private home. After a day of touring the country, guests enjoy well-prepared dinners at this award-winning restaurant, which may include terrine of duck foie gras with sweet-and-sour leeks as an appetizer, followed by the fresh fish of the day. Our party of three recently enjoyed such specialties as lightly coated medallion of beef, roast loin of venison, and an especially delectable grilled sea bass in a lobster-flavored sauce. Even though all meals are fixed-price arrangements, there is a choice in each category.

You can stay in one of the spacious, warm, and elegant bedrooms (10 in all) that have been installed over the old stables of the house. With a full English breakfast included, doubles range from £130 to £200 ($208–$320). All accommodations have TVs, beverage makers, phones, and well-stocked minibars.

In the Tamar View House, Gulworthy, Tavistock, Devon PL19 8JD. (℃ **01822/832528. www.thehornofplenty. co.uk.** Reservations recommended. Fixed-price lunch £19 ($30); potluck menu Mon £24 ($38); fixed-price dinner (Tues–Sun) £40 ($63). AE, MC, V. Tues–Sun noon–2pm; daily 7–9pm. Closed Dec 24–26. Drive 5km (3 miles) west of Tavistock on A390.

A FAVORITE LOCAL PUB

Just a 2-minute walk from Bayard's Cove is one of our favorite pubs, **The Cherub,** 13 Higher St. (℃ **01803/832571**). It was originally built in 1380 as the harbormaster's house. Today this charming pub is a great place to drink and dine on simple traditional British platters and bar snacks. There's a more formal dining room upstairs that serves a number of fish dishes, steaks, lamb, and duck.

9 Plymouth *★★*

390km (242 miles) SW of London; 259km (161 miles) SW of Southampton

The historic seaport of Plymouth is more romantic in legend than in reality. But this was not always so—during World War II, greater Plymouth lost at least 75,000 buildings to Nazi bombs. The heart of present-day Plymouth, including the municipal civic center on the Royal Parade, has been entirely rebuilt; however, the way it was rebuilt is the subject of much controversy.

For the old part of town, you must go to the Elizabethan section, known as **The Barbican,** and walk along the quay in the footsteps of Sir Francis Drake (once the mayor of Plymouth). From here, in 1577, Drake set sail on his round-the-world voyage. The Barbican also holds special interest for visitors from the United States as the final departure point of the Pilgrims in 1620. The two ships, *Mayflower* and *Speedwell,* that sailed from Southampton in August of that year put into Plymouth after suffering storm damage. The *Speedwell* was abandoned as unseaworthy; the *Mayflower* made the trip to the New World alone.

ESSENTIALS

GETTING THERE Plymouth Airport lies 6.4km (4 miles) from the center of the city. **Brymon Airways** (℃ **01752/204090**) has direct service from the London airports, Heathrow and Gatwick, to Plymouth.

Frequent trains run from London's Paddington Station to Plymouth in 3¼ to 4 hours. For rail information, call ℃ **0845/748-4950** in the U.K. The **Plymouth Train Station** lies on North Road, north of the Plymouth Center. Western National Bus no. 83/84 runs from the station to the heart of Plymouth.

National Express has frequent daily bus service between London's Victoria Coach Station and Plymouth. The trip takes 4½ hours. Call ℃ **0870/580-8080** for schedules and information.

If you're driving from London, take M4 west to the junction with M5 going south to Exeter. From Exeter, head southwest on A38 to Plymouth.

VISITOR INFORMATION The **Tourist Information Centre** is at the Island House, The Barbican (℃ **01752/304049**). A second information center, **Plymouth Discovery Centre,** is at Crabtree Marsh Mills, Plymouth (℃ **01752/ 266030**). Both are open from Easter to October Monday through Saturday from 9am to 5pm and Sunday from 10am to 4pm, and from November to Easter Monday through Friday from 9am to 5pm and Saturday from 10am to 4pm.

SEEING THE SIGHTS

To commemorate the spot from which the *Mayflower* sailed for the New World, a white archway, erected in 1934 and capped with the flags of Great Britain and the United States, stands at the base of Plymouth's West Pier, on the Barbican. Incorporating a granite monument that was erected in 1891, the site is referred to as both the *Mayflower* **Steps** and the **Memorial Gateway.**

The **Barbican** is a mass of narrow streets, old houses, and quayside shops selling antiques, brass work, old prints, and books. It's a perfect place for strolling and browsing through shops at your leisure.

Fishing boats still unload their catches at the wharves, and passenger-carrying ferryboats run short harbor cruises. A trip includes views of Drake's Island in the sound, the dockyards, naval vessels, and The Hoe from the water. A cruise of Plymouth Harbour costs £5 ($8) for adults and £2.50 ($4) for children. A family ticket costs £11 ($18). Departures are February through November, with cruises leaving every ½ hour from 10am to 4pm daily. These **Plymouth Boat Cruises** are booked at 8 Anderton Rise, Millbrook, Torpoint (© **01752/ 822797**).

New Street Gallery   This gallery specializes in contemporary arts and crafts, with changing exhibitions of paintings and ceramics by local artists. It's a 5-minute walk from the town center in Plymouth's historic Barbican, near the *Mayflower* Steps.

38 New St., The Barbican. © **01752/221450**. Free admission. Mon noon–4pm; Tues–Sat 10am–8pm. Bus: 39.

Plymouth Gin Distillery   These premises, one of Plymouth's oldest surviving buildings, were where the Pilgrims met before sailing for the New World. Plymouth Gin has been produced here for 200 years on a historic site that dates from a Dominican monastery built in 1425. There are public guided tours. A Plymouth Gin shop is on the premises.

Black Friars Distillery, 60 Southside St. © **01752/665292**. Admission £2.75 ($4.40) adults, £2.25 ($3.60) children ages 10–18, free for children ages 9 and under. Jan–Feb Mon–Sat 10:30am–5pm; Mar–Dec 10am–4pm. Closed Christmas–Easter. Bus: 54.

Prysten House   Built in 1490 as a town house close to St. Andrew's Church, this is now a church house and working museum. Reconstructed in the 1930s with American help, it displays a model of Plymouth in 1620 and tapestries depicting the colonization of America. At the entrance is the gravestone of the captain of the U.S. brig *Argus,* who died on August 15, 1813, after a battle in the English Channel.

Finewell St. © **01752/661414**. Admission 70p ($1.10) adults, 30p (50¢) children. Mon–Sat 9:30am–6:30pm.

WHERE TO STAY

Astor Hotel   This appealing and completely restored hotel is better than ever following massive improvements in 2001 to its structure, once the private home of a sea captain during the Victorian era. The best rooms are the so-called executive suites with four-poster beds, and even better are the Bridal Suites with both four-posters and a Jacuzzi. Even the mostly midsize standard rooms are exceedingly comfortable. All rooms have a private bathroom with shower or tub. You don't need to leave the premises at night as there is a cozy lounge bar and a first-class restaurant serving both a traditional British and an international cuisine.

Finds King Arthur's Legendary Lair

On a wild stretch of the Atlantic coast 49 miles northwest of Plymouth, **Tintagel Castle** ★ is forever linked with the legends of King Arthur, Lancelot, and Merlin. So compelling was this legend that medieval writers treated it as a tale of chivalry, even though the real Arthur, if he lived, probably did so around the time of the Roman or Saxon invasions. (Some scholars have speculated that if Arthur existed at all, he might have been not a king but a warlord; his reign may have lasted 3 decades, leading native Britons who were fighting off the Saxon invasion.)

Despite its universal adoption throughout Europe, it was in Wales and southern England that the legend initially developed and blossomed. The story was polished and given a literary form for the first time by Geoffrey of Monmouth around 1135. Combining Celtic myth and Christian and classical symbolism (usually without crediting his sources), Geoffrey forged a fictional history of Britain whose form, shape, and elevated values were centered around the mythical King Arthur. Dozens of other storytellers embellished the written and oral versions of the tale.

The Arthurian legend has captured the imagination of the British people like no other. Arthur supposedly still lies sleeping, ready to rise and save Britain in its greatest need. The version of the legend by Sir Thomas Malory has become the classic, but there were many others: Edmund Spenser's in the Tudor period; John Milton's in the 17th century; Tennyson's, William Morris's, and Swinburne's in the Victorian age; and T. H. White's and C. S. Lewis's in the 20th century, not to mention the many film treatments.

14–22 Elliott St., The Hoe, Plymouth, Devon PL1 2PS. ② **01752/225511.** Fax 01752/251994. www.astor hotel.co.uk. 64 units. £65–£95 ($104–$152) double; £120 ($192) executive suite; £250 ($400) bridal suite. Rates include English breakfast. AE, DC, MC, V. Free parking overnight, £3.50 ($5.60) permit parking nearby. **Amenities:** Restaurant; 2 bars; room service; laundry service. *In room:* TV, coffeemaker, trouser press.

Duke of Cornwall Hotel ★ *Kids*   This hotel is a Victorian Gothic building that survived World War II bombings. Constructed in 1863, it was regarded by Sir John Betjeman as the finest example of Victorian architecture in Plymouth. The refurbished bedrooms are comfortable and well maintained. Four rooms contain antique four-poster beds; six units are large enough for families.

Millbay Rd., Plymouth, Devon PL1 3LG. ② **01752/275850.** Fax 01752/275854. www.duke.activehotels. com/TUK. 70 units. £104 ($166) double. Rates include English breakfast. AE, MC, V. **Amenities:** Restaurant (p. 330); bar; 24-hr. room service; laundry service; dry cleaning. *In room:* TV, coffeemaker, hair dryer, trouser press.

Holiday Inn Plymouth   This nine-story hotel, built in 1970, is situated on a hilltop above the bay and hosts an equal number of business and leisure travelers. The hotel has comfortable rooms, all but a dozen of which face the sea. Most rooms are a bit small, but bathrooms have adequate shelf space and a shower-tub combination. Ten executive rooms offer more space and upgraded amenities.

The legend of King Arthur gained considerable credibility in August 1998 when a stone bearing a Latin inscription referring to King Arthur was uncovered at the ancient ruined castle in Tintagel, where he was supposed to have been born. The piece of slate, 35cm (14 in.) by 25cm (10 in.), was found in a drain at the castle. For Arthur fans this is the find of a lifetime and is all that is needed to verify the existence of the king.

The 13th-century ruins of the castle that stand here—built on the foundations of a Celtic monastery from the 6th century—are popularly known as King Arthur's Castle. They stand 91m (300 ft.) above the sea on a rocky promontory, and to get to them you must take a long, steep, tortuous walk from the parking lot. In summer, many visitors make the ascent to Arthur's Lair, up 100 rock-cut steps. You can also visit Merlin's Cave at low tide.

One bus a day travels from Plymouth to Tintagel, at 4:20pm, but it takes twice the time (2 hr.) required for a private car (which only takes about 50 min.), because the bus stops at dozens of small hamlets along the way. For bus schedule information, call ✆ **01209/719988**.

The castle is .8km (½ mile) northwest of Tintagel. It's open from March 24 to July 13 from 10am to 6pm; from July 14 to August 27 from 10am to 7pm (later on Wed evenings); from August 28 to September 30 from 10am to 6pm; October from 10am to 5pm; November through March daily from 10am to 4pm. Admission is £3 ($4.80) for adults, £2.30 ($3.70) for students and seniors, and £1.50 ($2.40) for children. For information, call ✆ **01840/770328**.

Cliff Rd., The Hoe, Plymouth, Devon PL1 3DL. ✆ **0870/400-9064**. Fax 01752/660974. www.holiday-inn.com. 112 units. £99–£124 ($158–$198) double. Weekend break rate (including dinner and breakfast) £80 ($128) per person. AE, DC, MC, V. **Amenities:** Restaurant; bar; room service; laundry service; dry cleaning. *In room:* TV, dataport, minibar, coffeemaker, hair dryer, trouser press.

Novotel Plymouth *(Kids)* Novotel Plymouth, a 10-minute drive from the town center beside the A38, is convenient if you're driving and also if you're traveling with children. With landscaped gardens and plenty of parking, it offers an ample number of soundproof rooms. Bedrooms are a bit small and the compact bathrooms are motel standard with a shower-tub combination. Two children under 16 sharing a room with their parents also receive free breakfast. ***Note:*** The hotel has a couple of rooms designed to accommodate the mobility impaired.

Marsh Mills, Plymouth, Devon PL6 8NH. ✆ **800/221-4542** in the U.S., or 01752/221422. Fax 01752/223922. www.novotel.com. 100 units. £67–£82 ($107–$131) double. Children 16 or under stay free in parent's room. AE, DC, MC, V. Bus: 21 or 51. **Amenities:** Restaurant; bar; pool (May–Sept); room service (6am–midnight); laundry service. *In room:* TV, coffeemaker, hair dryer.

Plymouth Hoe Moat House Hotel *✿* One of the most distinguished hotels in the West Country, overlooking the harbor and The Hoe, the Plymouth Moat

House is a midget high-rise. It is the town's finest address, superior to the long-standing Duke of Cornwall. The good-sized rooms are well furnished with long double beds, and have wide picture windows, and compact bathrooms. The decor is tasteful, and the overall atmosphere is casual and comfortable.

Armada Way, Plymouth, Devon PL1 2HJ. ℂ **01752/639988.** Fax 01752/673816. www.moathousehotels. com. 211 units. £140–£170 ($224–$272) double. AE, DC, MC, V. Parking £3.50 ($5.60) for duration of stay. **Amenities:** Restaurant; 2 bars; pool; health club; spa; salon; room service; babysitting; laundry service; dry cleaning. *In room:* A/C, TV, minibar in executive rooms, coffeemaker, hair dryer, safe, trouser press.

WHERE TO DINE

The Plymouth Arts Centre Restaurant, 38 Looe St. (ℂ **01752/202616**), offers one of the most filling and down-home vegetarian meals in town. Prices range from £2.30 to £4.10 ($3.70–$6.55), and it's also ideal for a snack. You can even see a movie downstairs if you'd like. Food is served Monday from 10am to 2pm and Tuesday through Saturday from 10am to 8:30pm.

Chez Nous ✿✿ FRENCH   The most distinguished restaurant in Plymouth is Chez Nous, situated directly off Western Approach. Owner and chef Jacques Marchal borrows heavily from the past but also expresses his creative talent. His type of cooking is called *la cuisine spontanée*—using fresh produce that changes with the seasons. Look for the specials of the day on the chalkboard menu. Accompanied by a classic and predominantly French wine list, the food is likely to include scallops steamed with ginger, bouillabaisse, and duck breast on a bed of lentils. Fish, generally, is the preferred main dish to order here. Fresh, quality ingredients are a hallmark of the cuisine.

13 Frankfort Gate. ℂ **01752/266793.** Reservations required. Fixed-price lunch and dinner £35 ($56). AE, DC, V. Tues–Fri 12:30–2pm; Tues–Sat 7–10:30pm. Closed Sept and first 3 weeks in Feb.

Duke of Cornwall Hotel Restaurant ✿ MODERN BRITISH   It's not quite up to the level of Chez Nous, but other than that strong competition, this land-mark hotel dining room is one of the finest in the area. Lit by a Victorian chandelier, your menu is illuminated in an elegant setting. Traditional and classic favorites are included on the menu, but the taste is definitely contemporary English. High-quality ingredients are seriously and professionally cooked. "West Countree" favorites appear including a perfectly roasted loin of pork with a sage-flavored fruit stuffing. Or else you might prefer loin of lamb cooked in the wok with tempura vegetables. Fresh fish and fine meats go into the dishes. For dessert, you can opt for the old-fashioned Treacle tart and custard which tastes as good as it always did. Service is first-class, and there's also a good wine list.

Millbay Rd. ℂ **01752/275850.** Reservations recommended. Main courses £10–£15 ($16–$24). Fixed-price dinner £20 ($31). AE, DC, MC, V. Daily 7–10pm.

Finds **Follow the Fleet and Follow the Fish**

Watching the fresh fish land on the Plymouth pier, we trailed it to the first restaurant where it was headed. The chef came out to inspect the catch of the day and purchased it on sight. The restaurant discovery turned out to be **Piermaster's,** 33 Southside St., right at the Barbican (ℂ **01752/229345**). The decor's your typical seaside nautical joint, but the fish dishes served at wooden tables are excellent. And they're certainly fresh.

Finds A Side Trip to Clovelly

Just 386km (240 miles) south of London, Clovelly is the most charming of all Devon villages and one of the main attractions of the West Country. Starting at a great height, the village cascades down the mountainside. Its narrow, cobblestone High Street makes driving impossible. You park your car at the top and make the trip on foot; supplies are carried down by donkeys. Every step of the way provides views of tiny cottages, with their terraces of flowers lining the main street. The village fleet is sheltered at the stone quay at the bottom.

The major sight of Clovelly is Clovelly itself. Charles Kingsley once wrote, "It is as if the place had stood still while all the world had been rushing and rumbling past it." The price of entry to the village (see below) includes a guided tour of a fisherman's cottage as it would have been at the end of the 1800s. For the same price, you can also visit the **Kingsley Exhibition.** Author of *Westward Ho!* and *Water Babies,* Kingsley lived in Clovelly while his father was curate at the church. This exhibition traces the story of his life.

Right down below the Kingsley Exhibition—and our shopping note for the town—is a **craft gallery** where you have a chance to see and buy a wide variety of works by local artists and craftspeople. Once you've reached the end, you can sit and relax on the quay, taking in the views and absorbing Clovelly's unique atmosphere from this tiny, beautifully restored 14th-century quay.

Once you've worked your way to the bottom, how are you supposed to get back up? Those in good shape will climb all the way back up the impossibly steep cobbled streets to the top and the parking lot. For those who can't make the climb up the slippery incline, go to the rear of the Red Lion Inn and queue up for a Land Rover. In summer, the line is often long, but considering the alternative, it's worth the wait.

To avoid the tourist crowd, stay out of Clovelly from around 11am until teatime. When the midday congestion here is at its height, visit nearby villages, such as Bucks Mills (5km/3 miles to the east) and Hartland Quay (6.5km/4 miles to the west). If you want to stay in town for the night, the **Red Lion Inn,** The Quay, (© **01237/431237**), is the best in town and offers small, comfortable rooms with spectacular views of the sea for £65 to £75 ($103–$120) double.

When you arrive in town, go to the **Clovelly Visitor Centre** (© **01237/431781**), where you'll pay £3.50 ($5.60) for the cost of parking, use of facilities, entrance to the village, and an audiovisual theater admission, offering a multiprojector show tracing the story of Clovelly back to 2000 B.C. It's open Monday through Saturday from 9am to 5:30pm April through June, daily from 10am to 4pm November through March, and daily from 9am to 6pm July through September.

To drive to Clovelly from London, head west on M4, cutting south at the junction with M5. At the junction near Bridgwater, continue west along A39 toward Lynton. A39 runs all the way to the signposted turnoff for Clovelly. If you don't have a car, contact the Clovelly Visitor Centre for other transportation options.

10 The Fishing Villages of Looe & Polperro ⟨★⟩

Looe: 425km (264 miles) SW of London; 32km (20 miles) W of Plymouth. Polperro: 463km (271 miles) SW of London; 9.5km (6 miles) SW of Looe; 42km (26 miles) W of Plymouth

The ancient twin towns of East and West Looe are connected by a seven-arched stone bridge that spans the River Looe. Houses on the hills are stacked one on top of the other in terrace fashion. In each fishing village you can find good accommodations.

The old fishing village of Polperro is reached by a steep descent from the top of a hill from the main road leading to Polperro. You can take the 7km (4½-mile) cliff walk from Looe to Polperro, but the less adventurous will want to drive. However, in July and August you're not allowed to take cars into town unless you have a hotel reservation, to prevent traffic bottlenecks. There's a large parking area, which charges according to the length of your stay. For those unable to walk, a horse-drawn bus will take visitors to the town center.

Fishing and sailing are two of the major sports in the area, and the sandy coves, as well as **East Looe Beach,** are spots for sea bathing. Beyond the towns are cliff paths and chalky downs worth a ramble. Looe is noted for its shark fishing, but you may prefer simply walking the narrow, crooked medieval streets of East Looe, with its old harbor and 17th-century guildhall.

Polperro is one of the most handsome villages in Cornwall, and parts of it hark back to the 17th century. The village is surrounded by cliffs.

ESSENTIALS

GETTING THERE   Daily trains run from Plymouth to Looe, and rail connections can also be made from Exeter (Devon) and Bristol (Avon). Most visitors drive to Polperro, but the nearest main-line station is at Liskeard, less than 4½ hours from London's Paddington Station, with a branch line to Looe. Taxis meet incoming trains to take visitors to the various little villages in the area. For rail information in the area, call ⓒ **0845/748-4950.**

Local bus companies have various routings from Plymouth into Looe. Ask at the Tourist Information Centre in Plymouth for a schedule (see the section on Plymouth above). You can take a local bus to Polperro from Liskeard or Looe.

If you're driving to Looe from Plymouth, take A38 west, then B3253. To get to Polperro, follow A387 southwest from Looe.

VISITOR INFORMATION   The **Tourist Information Centre** is at the Guildhall, Fore Street (ⓒ **01503/262072**), and is open in summer only, daily from 10am to 2pm, and in winter on Saturdays only from 10am to 2pm.

WHERE TO STAY & DINE IN & AROUND LOOE

Barclay House   A family-operated, country-house hotel on the edge of town at the entrance to Looe, it's about a 5-minute walk from the harbor and the center of the resort and stands on a wooded hillside surrounded by 6 acres of private woodlands overlooking the Looe River Valley. Units are spacious and fitted with soft twin or king-size beds. Rooms have small bathrooms, usually with a tub-and-shower combination.

St. Martin's Rd. (the main Plymouth–Looe Rd., B3253), E. Looe, Cornwall PL13 1LP. ⓒ **01503/262929.** Fax 01503/262632. www.barclayhouse.co.uk. 11 units, 8 cottages. £90–£120 ($144–$192) double; £250–£1,100 ($400–$1,760) cottage per week. Rates include English breakfast. AE, MC, V. **Amenities:** Restaurant; bar; pool; concierge; room service (8am–11pm); babysitting. *In room:* TV, coffeemaker, hair dryer.

Fieldhead Hotel *(Kids)*   The Fieldhead, built in 1896 as a private home, is now one of the area's best hotels. Commanding a view of the sea, it is situated on

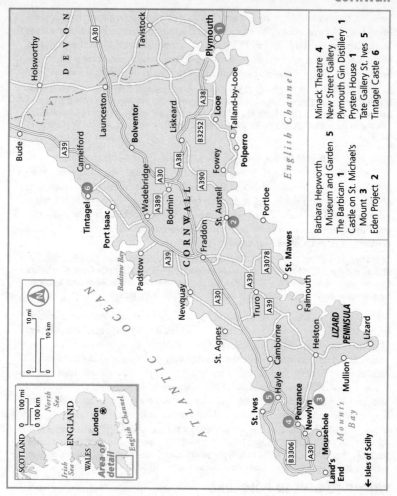

2 acres of gardens. The rooms have a high standard of traditional furnishings and are continually maintained. Rooms are warm and inviting; most of them open onto panoramic views of St. George's Island and the bay. Some rooms have balconies. *Note:* Families like not only the kid-friendly management here, but also the location in a garden setting where even young children can play in safety. This is also one of the few hotels in the area with a pool.

Portuan Rd., Hannafore, W. Looe, Cornwall PL13 2DR. ☎ **01503/262689.** Fax 01503/264114. **www.field headhotel.co.uk.** 16 units. £58–£190 ($93–$304) double. Rates include English breakfast. MC, V. **Amenities:** Restaurant; bar; pool; room service; laundry service. *In room:* TV, coffeemaker, hair dryer, trouser press.

Klymiarven ⭐ *Kids* This is the finest place to stay in the area, a family-run hotel perched on the East Cliff with panoramic views of the harbor some 450m (500 yd.) below. The original cellars of the building date from the 17th century; the present manor house was built in the early 1800s. An old tunnel discovered on the site was probably used by smugglers. A sun deck has been installed between the pool and the restaurant. All the roomy bedrooms are handsomely furnished. On the second floor is a series of family rooms with stunning views. In the new wing (built in the 1950s) are another attractive six bedrooms. The kitchen prepares an excellent three-course table d'hôte. The restaurant is renowned for its steaks, using grass-fed Hereford steers or Angus beef from Scotland.

Barbican Hill, East Looe, PL13 1BH. ℂ **01503/262333.** www.klymiarven.co.uk. 15 units. £55–£72 ($88–$115) per person. Rates include half board. Children 7 and under stay free, ages 8 to 12 £14 ($22), and 12 and over pay half price of the B&B rate. MC, V. Closed Jan. Lies 3km (2 miles) from Looe by A387 off B3253 (can also be reached by foot from the harbor). **Amenities:** Restaurant; bar; pool. *In room:* TV, coffeemaker, hair dryer.

Talland Bay Hotel ★   A country house dating from the 16th century, situated on 2½ acres, this hotel is the domain of George and Mary Granville, who will direct you to local beaches and the croquet lawn. Its rectangular swimming pool is ringed with flagstones and a semitropical garden. Views from the tastefully furnished bedrooms—last refurbished in 1995—include the sea and rocky coastline. Some bedrooms are in a comfortable annex. All rooms come with a private bathroom and shower combination.

Talland-by-Looe, Cornwall PL13 2JB. ℂ **01503/272667.** Fax 01503/272940. www.tallandbayhotel.co.uk. 22 units. Nov–Apr £140–£190 ($224–$304) double; May–Oct £170–£220 ($272–$352) double. Rates include English breakfast and dinner. MC, V. Take A387 6.5km (4 miles) southwest of Looe. **Amenities:** Restaurant; bar; pool; room service (8:30am–9:30pm). *In room:* TV, coffeemaker, hair dryer, safe.

Well House ★ *Kids*   Well House is one of those *restaurants avec chambres* found occasionally in the West Country, and it's one of the best. Located 5km (3 miles) from Liskeard, it has 5 acres of gardens opening onto vistas of the Looe Valley. It offers beautifully furnished bedrooms, with many thoughtful extras, such as fresh flowers. Two beautiful terrace rooms are at the garden level.

Most rooms have a twin bed or else a large double. Families are welcomed into extra-large rooms; especially popular is the hotel's family suite with one large double bedroom plus a twin-bedded unit as well.

St. Keyne, Liskeard, Cornwall PL14 4RN. ℂ **01579/342001.** Fax 01579/343891. www.wellhouse.co.uk. 9 units. £115–£170 ($184–$272) double; £185–£205 ($296–$328) family room. Rates include English breakfast. MC, V. From Liskeard, take B3254 to St. Keyne, 5km (3 miles) away. **Amenities:** Restaurant; bar; pool; tennis court; room service (7:30am–11pm); croquet lawn. *In room:* TV, hair dryer, safe.

WHERE TO DINE IN POLPERRO

The Kitchen SEAFOOD   This pink cottage halfway to the harbor from the parking area was once a wagon-builder's shop. Now a restaurant offering good English cooking, everything is homemade from fresh ingredients. The menu changes seasonally and features local fresh fish. Typical dishes include Fowey sea trout with lemon-and-herb butter and breast of duckling with blueberry-and-Drambuie sauce. Many vegetarian dishes are offered as main courses.

Fish na Bridge. ℂ **01503/272780.** Reservations required. Main courses £13–£18 ($21–$29). MC, V. Daily 7–9:30pm. Closed Oct–Easter.

Nelson's Restaurant SEAFOOD   Situated in the lower reaches of Polperro, near the spot where the local river meets the sea, this is the only structure in town specifically built as a restaurant. It features succulent preparations of regional fish and shellfish that arrive fresh from local fishing boats. The menu changes daily, but usually includes fresh crab, Dover sole, fresh lobster, and many other exotic fish. Fresh meat, poultry, and game, all from local suppliers, are also available and are prepared exceedingly well. A lower deck features a cafe-bar and bistro. A comprehensive wine list boasts some fine vintages.

Saxon Bridge. ℂ **01503/272366**. Reservations advised. Main courses £6.50–£20 ($10–$32); 2-course table d'hôte lunch or dinner £14 ($22). AE, MC, V. Tues–Sun 6:30pm–last customer; Thurs, Fri, and Sun 10:30am–2pm. Closed mid-Jan to mid-Feb.

11 Penzance ⭐

451km (°80 miles) SW of London; 124km (77 miles) SW of Plymouth

Th: little harbor town, which Gilbert and Sullivan made famous, is at the end of che Cornish Riviera. It's noted for its moderate climate (it's one of the first towns in England to blossom with spring flowers), and for the summer throngs that descend for fishing, sailing, and swimming. Overlooking Mount's Bay, Penzance is graced in places with subtropical plants including palm trees.

Those characters in *The Pirates of Penzance* were not entirely fictional. The town was raided by Barbary pirates, destroyed in part by Cromwell's troops, sacked and burned by the Spaniards, and bombed by the Germans. In spite of its turbulent past, it offers tranquil resort living today.

The most westerly town in England, Penzance makes a good base for exploring Land's End; the Lizard peninsula; St. Michael's Mount; the old fishing ports and artists' colonies of St. Ives, Newlyn, and Mousehole; and even the Isles of Scilly.

ESSENTIALS

GETTING THERE   Ten express trains depart daily from Paddington Station in London for Penzance. The trip takes 5½ hours. Call ℂ **0845/748-4950.**

The **Rapide,** run by National Express from Victoria Coach Station in London (ℂ **020/7529-2000**), costs £30.50 ($49) for the one-way trip from London, which takes about 8½ hours. The buses have toilets and reclining seats, and a hostess dispenses coffee, tea, and sandwiches.

Drive southwest across Cornwall on A30 all the way to Penzance.

VISITOR INFORMATION   The **Tourist Information Centre** is on Station Road (ℂ **01736/362207**). It's open from the end of May to September, Monday through Friday from 9am to 5:30pm, Saturday from 10am to 5pm, and Sunday from 10am to 1pm; from October to May, hours are Monday through Friday from 9am to 5pm and Saturday from 10am to 1pm.

SEEING THE SIGHTS AROUND PENZANCE

Castle on St. Michael's Mount ⭐   Rising about 75m (250 ft.) from the sea, St. Michael's Mount is topped by a part medieval, part 17th-century castle. It's 5km (3 miles) east of Penzance and is reached at low tide by a causeway. At high tide, the mount becomes an island, reached only by motor launch from Marazion. In winter, you can go over only when the causeway is dry.

A Benedictine monastery, the gift of Edward the Confessor, stood on this spot in the 11th century. The castle now has a collection of armor and antique furniture. A tea garden is on the island, as well as a National Trust restaurant, both open in summer. The steps up to the castle are steep and rough, so wear sturdy shoes. To avoid disappointment, call the number listed below to check on the tides, especially during winter.

On St. Michael's Mount, Mount's Bay. ℂ **01736/710507**. Admission £4.80 ($7.70) adults, £2.40 ($3.85) children, £13 ($21) family ticket. Apr–Oct Mon–Fri 10:30am–5:30pm (open weekends in summer); Nov–Mar Mon, Wed, and Fri by conducted tour only, which leaves at 11am, noon, 2, and 3pm, weather and tide permitting. Bus no. 2 or 2A from Penzance to Marazion, the town opposite St. Michael's Mount. Parking £1.50 ($2.40).

Minack Theatre   One of the most unusual theaters in southern England, this open-air amphitheater was cut from the side of a rocky Cornish hill near the

---

Finds   A Fishing Village & Artists' Colony

From Penzance, a promenade leads to Newlyn, another fishing village of infinite charm on Mount's Bay. In fact, its much-painted harbor seems to have more fishing craft than Penzance. Stanhope Forbes founded an art school in Newlyn, and in recent years, the village has achieved a growing reputation for its artists' colony, attracting both serious painters and Sunday sketchers. From Penzance, the old fishing cottages and crooked lanes of Newlyn are reached by bus.

---

village of Porthcurno, 14km (9 miles) southwest of Penzance. Its legendary creator was Rowena Cade, an arts enthusiast and noted eccentric, who began work on the theater after World War I by physically carting off much of the granite from her chosen hillside. On the premises, an exhibition hall showcases her life and accomplishments. She died a very old woman in the 1980s, confident of the enduring appeal of her theater to visitors from around the world.

Up to 750 visitors at a time can sit directly on grass- or rock-covered ledges, sometimes on cushions if they're available, within sight lines of both the actors and a sweeping view out over the ocean. Experienced theatergoers sometimes bring raincoats for protection against the occasional drizzle. Theatrical events are staged by repertory theater companies that travel throughout Britain and performances are likely to include everything from Shakespeare to musical comedy.

Porthcurno. © 01736/810694. www.minack.com. Theater tickets £7 ($11) adults, £3.50 ($5.60) children; tour tickets £2.50 ($4) adults, £1.80 ($2.90) seniors, £1 ($1.60) children. Exhibition hall, Oct–Mar daily 10am–4pm; Apr–Sept 9:30am–6pm. Performances end of May to mid-Sept, matinees Wed and Fri at 2pm, evening shows Mon–Fri at 8pm. Leave Penzance on A30 heading toward Land's End; after 5km (3 miles), bear left onto B3283 and follow the signs to Porthcurno.

WHERE TO STAY

Abbey Hotel ★★   This charming, small-scale hotel occupies a stone-sided house that was erected in 1660 on the site of a 12th-century abbey that was demolished by Henry VIII. On a narrow side street on raised terraces that overlook the panorama of Penzance Harbour, behind the hotel is a medieval walled garden that was part of the original abbey. The hotel has been considerably upgraded, with new baths, showers, and beds. Bedrooms are stylishly furnished with English country-house flair. Bathrooms have either a shower stall or tub-and-shower combination. The owners, Michael and Jean Cox, bring vitality, style, and charm to the hotel business. Mrs. Cox is the former international model Jean Shrimpton.

Abbey St., Penzance, Cornwall TR18 4AR. © 01736/366906. Fax 01736/351163. www.abbey-hotel.co.uk. 6 units. Low season £84–£124 ($134–$198) double, £140–£180 ($224–$288) suite. High season £105–£175 ($168–$280) double, £175–£225 ($280–$360) suite. Rates include English breakfast. AE, MC, V. **Amenities:** Restaurant; bar; laundry service. *In room:* TV, coffeemaker, hair dryer.

The Georgian House ★ *Value*   This former home of the mayors of Penzance, reputedly haunted by the ghost of a Mrs. Baines who owned it hundreds of years ago, has been completely renovated into an intimate hotel. The bright, cozy rooms each contain a small private bathroom with a shower stall and tub. The Abbey is better, but this one is quite good, too.

20 Chapel St., Penzance, Cornwall TR18 4AW. ©/fax 01736/365664. 11 units. £46 ($74) double. Rates include English breakfast. AE, MC, V. **Amenities:** Restaurant; bar. *In room:* TV, coffeemaker, hair dryer.

Tarbert Hotel This dignified granite-and-stucco house lies about a 2-minute walk northwest of the town center. Some of the small to midsize rooms retain original high ceilings and elaborate cove moldings. Each room has comfortable furniture and a well-kept shower-only bathroom. Recent improvements include a new reception area, a completely refurbished bar and lounge, and a sun patio.

11–12 Clarence St., Penzance, Cornwall TR18 2NU. © 01736/363758. Fax 01736/331336. www.tarbert-hotel.co.uk. 12 units. £64–£68 ($102–$109) double. Rates include English breakfast. AE, MC, V. Closed Jan 5–Feb 15. **Amenities:** Restaurant; bar; laundry service. *In room:* TV, coffeemaker, hair dryer, safe.

WHERE TO DINE

The Nelson Bar, in the Union Hotel on Chapel Street in Penzance (© 01736/ 362319), is known for its robust pub grub and collection of Nelsoniana. It's the spot where the admiral's death at Trafalgar was first revealed to the English people. Lunch and dinner are served Monday through Saturday.

Harris's Restaurant ⭐ FRENCH/ENGLISH Down a narrow cobblestone street off Market Jew Street, this warm, candlelit place has a relaxed atmosphere and is your best bet for a meal. A beacon of light against the culinary bleakness of Penzance, Harris's offers dining in two small rooms. The seasonally adjusted menu emphasizes local produce, including seafood and game. Dishes may include roast wild venison with caraway seeds, or John Dory in a bed of fresh spinach with a white-wine and saffron sauce.

46 New St. © 01736/364408. Reservations recommended. Main courses £15–£23 ($23–$36). AE, MC, V. Mon–Sat noon–2pm and 7–10pm. Closed 3 weeks in winter.

The Turk's Head ⭐⭐ ENGLISH/INTERNATIONAL Dating from 1233, this inn, said to be the oldest in Penzance, serves the finest food of any pub in town. In summer, drinkers overflow into the garden. Inside, the inn is decorated in a mellow style, as befits its age, with flatirons and other artifacts hanging from its timeworn beams. Meals include fishermen's pie, local seafood, and chicken curry, and prime quality steaks including rib-eye. See the chalkboards for the daily specials.

49 Chapel St. © 01736/363093. Main courses £5–£12 ($8–$19); bar snacks £2.95–£5 ($4.70–$8). AE, MC, V. Daily 11am–3pm and 5:30–11pm (bar daily 11am–3pm and 5:30–11pm). From the rail station, turn left just past Lloyd's Bank.

12 Mousehole ⭐ & Land's End ⭐

Mousehole: 5km (3 miles) S of Penzance, 3km (2 miles) S of Newlyn; Land's End: 14km (9 miles) W of Penzance

Reached by traveling through some of Cornwall's most beautiful countryside, Land's End is literally the end of Britain. The natural grandeur of the place has been somewhat marred by theme park–type amusements, but the view of the sea crashing against rocks remains undiminished. If you want to stay in the area, you can find accommodations in Mousehole, a lovely Cornish fishing village. If you visit in July and August, you'll need reservations far in advance, as Mousehole doesn't have enough bedrooms to accommodate the summer hordes.

GETTING THERE

From London, journey first to Penzance (see "Penzance" above), then take a local bus for the rest of the journey (bus A to Mousehole and bus no. 1 to Land's End). There is frequent service throughout the day.

If you're driving from Penzance, take the B3315 south.

Cornwall's Geodesic Domed Eden

At first you think some space ship filled with aliens has invaded sleepy old Cornwall. A second look reveals one of England's newest and most dramatic attractions, the **Eden Project,** Bodelva, St. Austell (② **01726/ 811911;** www.edenproject.com), a 48km (30-mile) drive west of Plymouth. This sprawling attraction presents plants from the world over, including the major climates, on 125 acres of a former clay quarry. One of the two conservatories is nearly 4 acres in dimension, reaching 54m (180 ft.) high, housing tropical plants from some of the world's rainforests, including the Amazon. The smaller dome, covering 1½ acres, grows plants from everywhere from California to South Africa. A roofless biome houses plants that thrive in the Cornish climate, including species from everywhere from India to Chile. The site takes in a small lake and offers a 2,300-seat amphitheater where special shows are staged. Within this biome is also a giant global garden planted in a crater. The crater is totally hidden from view until you walk through the visitor center, which is on the lip of the pit—very James Bondian.

Open from late March to late October, daily from 10am to 6pm, and from November to late March, daily from 10am to 4:30pm. Admission is £9.80 ($16) for adults, £7.50 ($12) for seniors, £5 ($8) for students, £4 ($6.40) for children 5 to 15, or £23 ($37) for a family ticket. The project lies 9.5km (6 miles) from the St. Austell train station, to which it is linked by frequent buses.

MOUSEHOLE

The Cornish fishing village of Mousehole (pronounced *Mou*-sel) attracts hordes of tourists, who, fortunately, haven't changed it too much. The cottages still sit close to the harbor wall; the fishers still bring in the day's catch; the salts sit around smoking tobacco, talking about the good old days; and the lanes are as narrow as ever. About the most exciting thing to happen here was the arrival in the late 16th century of the Spanish galleons, whose sailors sacked and burned the village. In a sheltered cove of Mount's Bay, Mousehole today has developed as the nucleus of an artists' colony.

WHERE TO STAY & DINE IN THE AREA

Carn Du Hotel   Twin bay windows gaze over the top of the village onto the harbor with its bobbing fishing vessels. The hotel's rooms (all doubles or twins) offer much comfort. Five rooms were recently redecorated. Most units have a shower stall, though two come with a tub-and-shower combination. The owners will arrange sporting options for active vacationers but won't mind if you prefer to sit and relax.

Raginnis Hill, Mousehole, Cornwall TR19 6SS. ②/fax **01736/731233.** 7 units. £60–£76 ($96–$122) double. Rates include English breakfast. AE, MC, V. Take B3315 from Newlyn past the village of Sheffield (2.5km/ 1½ miles) and bear left toward Castallack; after a few hundred yd., turn left to Mousehole, which is signposted; coming down the hill, the Carn Du is on the left facing the sea. **Amenities:** Restaurant; bar. *In room:* TV, coffeemaker, safe.

Lamorna Cove Hotel   Near one of the most perfect coves in Cornwall, this hotel lies only 8km (5 miles) south of Penzance, but is seemingly inaccessible down a winding, narrow road. The hotel was skillfully terraced, after months of blasting, into a series of rocky ledges that drop down to the sea. A rocky garden clings to the cliff sides. The cozy, small to midsize bedrooms have sea views. Each is furnished in a lovely old-fashioned way, and all rooms have showers.

Lamorna Cove, Penzance, Cornwall TR19 6XH. *(C)* **01736/731411.** www.lamorncove.com. 12 units. £120–£175 ($192–$280) per person double. Rates include VAT. AE, MC, V. Take a taxi from Penzance. **Amenities:** Restaurant; bar; laundry service. *In room:* TV, coffeemaker, hair dryer, trouser press.

The Ship Inn   This charming pub is located on the harbor in this fishing village. The exterior has a stone facade, and the interior has retained much of the original rustic charm with its black beams and paneling, granite floors, built-in wall benches, and, of course, a nautical motif decorating the bars. The rooms, offering views of the harbor and the bay, have window seats. The rooms are simply furnished and tend to be small but are cozy, each with a compact bathroom with a shower stall.

S. Cliff, Mousehole, Penzance, Cornwall TR19 6QX. *(C)* **01736/731234.** 8 units. £55 ($88) double. Rates include English breakfast. MC, V. **Amenities:** Restaurant; 2 bars. *In room:* TV, coffeemaker, hair dryer.

LAND'S END ✷
Craggy Land's End is where England comes to an end. America's coast is 5,299km (3,291 miles) west of the rugged rocks that tumble into the sea beneath Land's End. Some enjoyable cliff walks and panoramic views are available here.

WHERE TO STAY & DINE
Land's End Hotel   This hotel is situated behind a white facade in a complex of buildings rising from the rugged landscape at the end of the main A30 road, the very tip of England. The hotel has a panoramic cliff-top position and is exposed to the wind and sea spray. The rooms are attractively furnished and well maintained. Rooms range from small to spacious, especially the premier or family rooms. Three contain four-poster beds and offer sea views. Some rooms are reserved for nonsmokers. Bathrooms are small but have adequate shelf space.

Land's End, Sennen, Cornwall TR19 7AA. *(C)* **01736/871844.** Fax 01736/871599. 33 units. £96–£126 ($154–$202) double. Rates include breakfast. AE, MC, V. **Amenities:** Restaurant; bar; room service. *In room:* TV, coffeemaker, hair dryer, trouser press.

13 The Artists' Colony of St. Ives ✷/✷
514km (319 miles) SW of London; 34km (21 miles) NE of Land's End; 16km (10 miles) NE of Penzance

This north-coast fishing village, with its sandy beaches, narrow streets, and well-kept cottages, is England's most famous artists' colony. The artists settled in many years ago and have integrated with the fishers and their families. They've been here long enough to have developed several schools or "splits," and they almost never overlap—except in the pubs. The old battle continues between the followers of the representational and the devotees of the abstract in art, with each group recruiting young artists all the time. In addition, there are the potters, weavers, and other craftspeople—all working, exhibiting, and selling in this area.

St. Ives becomes virtually impossible to visit in August, when you're likely to be trampled underfoot by busloads of tourists, mostly the English themselves. However, in spring and early fall the pace is much more relaxed.

ESSENTIALS

GETTING THERE   There is frequent service throughout the day between London's Paddington Station and the rail terminal at St. Ives. The trip takes 8 hours and 20 minutes. Call © **0845/748-4950** for schedules and information.

Several coaches a day run from London's Victoria Coach Station to St. Ives. The trip takes 7 hours. Call © **0870/580-8080** for schedules and information.

If you're driving, take A30 across Cornwall, heading northwest at the junction with B3306, heading to St. Ives on the coast. During the summer, many streets in the center of town are closed to vehicles. You may want to leave your car in the Lelant Saltings Car Park, 5km (3 miles) from St. Ives on A3074, and take the regular train service into town, an 11-minute journey. Departures are every ½ hour. It's free to all car passengers and drivers, and the parking charge is £8 to £11 ($13–$17) per day. You can also use the large Trenwith Car Park, close to the town center, for £1.50 ($2.40) and then walk down to the shops and harbor or take a bus that costs 40p (65¢) per person.

VISITOR INFORMATION   The **Tourist Information Centre** is at the Guildhall, Street-an-Pol (© **01736/796297**). From January to mid-May and September through December, hours are Monday through Thursday from 9am to 5pm and Saturday from 10am to 4pm. From mid-May to August, hours are Monday through Saturday from 9am to 6pm and Sunday from 10am to 4pm.

SEEING THE SIGHTS

Barbara Hepworth Museum and Garden ✦   Dame Barbara Hepworth lived at Trewyn from 1949 until her death in 1975 at the age of 72. In her will she asked that her working studio be turned into a museum where future visitors could see where she lived and created her world-famous sculpture. Today, the museum and garden are virtually just as she left them. On display are about 47 sculptures and drawings, covering the period from 1928 to 1974, as well as photographs, documents, and other Hepworth memorabilia. You can also visit her workshops, housing a selection of tools and some unfinished carvings.

Barnoon Hill. © 01736/796226. Admission £4 ($6.40) adults, £2 ($3.20) students, free for seniors and children under 18. Mar–Oct daily 10am–5:30pm; Nov–Feb Tues–Sun 10am–4:30pm.

Tate Gallery St. Ives ✦✦   This branch of London's famous Tate Gallery exhibits changing groups of work from the Tate Gallery's preeminent collection of St. Ives painting and sculpture, dating from about 1925 to 1975. The gallery is administered jointly with the Barbara Hepworth Museum (see above). The collection includes works by artists associated with St. Ives, including Alfred Wallis, Ben Nicholson, Barbara Hepworth, Naum Gabo, Peter Lanyon, Terry Frost, Patrick Heron, and Roger Hilton. All artists shown here had a decisive effect on the development of painting in the United Kingdom in the second half of the 20th century. About 100 works are on display at all times.

Boasting dramatic sea views, the museum occupies a spectacular site overlooking Porthmear Beach, close to the home of Alfred Wallis and to the studios used by many of the St. Ives artists.

Porthmear Beach. © 01736/796226. www.tate.org.uk. Admission £4.25 ($6.80) adults, £2.50 ($4) students, free for seniors and children under 18. Mar–Oct daily 10am–5:30pm; Nov–Feb Tues–Sun 10am–4:30pm. Closes occasionally to change displays; call for dates.

WHERE TO STAY

Garrack Hotel and Restaurant ✔️*Value*   This small vine-covered hotel, once a private home, commands a panoramic view of St. Ives and Porthmear Beach from its 2-acre knoll at the head of a narrow lane. One of the friendliest and most efficiently run mid-priced hotels on the entire coast, its rooms are furnished in a warm, homey manner. Most units are midsize, but two rooms are large enough to accommodate families; one is suitable for persons with disabilities. The small bathrooms are well maintained.

Burthallan Lane, Higher Ayr, St. Ives, Cornwall TR26 3AA. ℭ 01736/796199. Fax 01736/798955. www. garrack.com. 18 units. Low season £70–£126 ($112–$202) double; high season £114–£162 ($182–$259) double. Rates include English breakfast. AE, DC, MC, V. Take B3306 to the outskirts of St. Ives; after passing a gas station on the left, take the 3rd road left toward Portmeor Beach and Ayr and after 180m (200 yd.) look for the hotel sign. **Amenities:** Restaurant; 2 bars; pool; health club; spa; car-rental desk; room service; laundry service. *In room:* TV, coffeemaker, hair dryer.

Pedn-Olva Hotel The panoramic view of the bay afforded from its restaurant and most rooms is the outstanding feature of this establishment. It was built in the 1870s as the home of the paymaster for the local mines, before being transformed into a hotel in the 1930s. The rooms are furnished in a modern style, with comfortable twin or double beds. Seven of the rooms are in a less desirable annex where the chambers are more sterile and lack the character of the main building. Five rooms are large enough for families. There are sun terraces with lounges, umbrellas, and a swimming pool for those who don't want to walk down the rocky path to Porthminster Beach. If you crave solitude, however, scramble down the rocks to sunbathe just above the gentle rise and fall of the sea.

The Warren, St. Ives, Cornwall TR26 2EA. ℭ 01736/796222. Fax 01736/797710. www.westcountryhotel-rooms.co.uk. 30 units. From £55–£68 ($88–$109) per person. Rates include English breakfast. Half board £65–£82 ($104–$131) per person. MC, V. Parking £3 ($4.80). **Amenities:** Restaurant; bar; pool. *In room:* TV, coffeemaker, hair dryer.

Porthminster Hotel ⭐ This leading Cornish Riviera resort, the town's best address, stands on the main road into town amid a beautiful garden and within easy walking distance of Porthminster Beach. Large and imposing, the Porthminster is a traditional choice for visitors to St. Ives. With its 1894 Victorian architecture, it's warm and inviting. The spacious rooms are well furnished, although with a bland decor. All units have well-maintained bathrooms with mainly shower-tub combinations. Over the years the bedrooms have been considerably upgraded, and the standard of comfort is high here.

The Terrace, St. Ives, Cornwall TR26 2BN. ℭ 01736/795221. Fax 01736/797043. www.porthminster-hotel. co.uk. 43 units. £62–£77 ($99–$123) per person. Rates include half board. AE, DC, MC, V. **Amenities:** Restaurant; bar; 2 pools; sauna; limited room service; laundry service. *In room:* TV, coffeemaker, hair dryer.

WHERE TO DINE

Garrack Hotel and Restaurant ENGLISH/INTERNATIONAL The dining room at the Garrack Hotel produces excellent cuisine and, whenever possible, uses fresh ingredients from their own garden. The hotel dining room, which is open to nonguests, offers a set dinner, plus a cold buffet or snacks at the bar. The menu features some of the best English dishes, such as roast shoulder of lamb with mint sauce, plus a wide sampling of continental fare, perhaps including a roast roulade of salmon with sesame crust and a cucumber sauce. Live lobsters swim in the seawater tank—until they're removed for preparation and cooked to order. Cheese and dessert trolleys are at your service.

In the Garrack Hotel, Burthallan Lane, Higher Ayr. ℭ 01736/796199. Fax 01736/798955. Reservations recommended. Main courses £8.75–£18 ($14–$28); fixed-price 4-course dinner £25 ($39). AE, DC, MC, V. Daily 7–9pm. Frequent minibus service.

Shakespeare Country & the Heart of England

After London, Shakespeare country is the most popular destination in England for North Americans. Many who don't recognize the county name, Warwickshire, know its foremost tourist town, **Stratford-upon-Avon,** birthplace of William Shakespeare and one of the great meccas for writers, readers, and playgoers from around the world.

Shakespeare's hometown is the best center for touring this part of England. You'll want to take in some theater while in Stratford-upon-Avon and branch out for day trips—notably to Warwick Castle in nearby Warwick.

Lying between Oxford and the River Severn, about a 2-hour drive west of London, the pastoral **Cotswolds** occupy a stretch of grassy limestone hills, deep ravines, and barren plateaus known as *wolds,* Old English for "God's high open land." Ancient villages with names like Stow-on-the-Wold and Moreton-in-Marsh dot this bucolic area, most of which is in Gloucestershire, with portions in Oxfordshire, Wiltshire, and Worcestershire.

Made rich by wool from their sheep, the landowners here invested in some of the finest domestic architecture in Europe, distinctively built of honey-brown Cotswold stone. The gentry didn't neglect their spiritual duties, for some of the simplest Cotswold hamlets have churches that, in style and architectural detail, seem far beyond their modest means.

You'll really want to rent a car and drive through the Cotswolds at your own pace. This way, you can spend hours viewing the land of winding goat paths, rolling hills, and sleepy hamlets. One of the reasons to visit the Cotswolds is to take advantage of its natural beauty. Play a round of golf on a scenic course, go fishing, or, better yet, take a ramble across a meadow where sheep graze or alongside a fast-flowing stream.

Mobbed by tourists, Broadway, with its 16th-century stone houses and cottages, is justifiably the most popular base for touring this area, but we suggest you also head for Bibury, or other small villages to capture the true charm of the Cotswolds. You'll find the widest range of hotels and facilities in Cheltenham, once one of England's most fashionable spas, with a wealth of Regency architecture.

1 Stratford-upon-Avon ★★

147km (91 miles) NW of London; 64km (40 miles) NW of Oxford; 13km (8 miles) S of Warwick

Crowds of tourists overrun this market town on the Avon River during the summer. In fact, today, **Stratford** aggressively hustles its Shakespeare connection—everybody seems to be in business to make a buck off the Bard. However, the throngs dwindle in winter, when you can at least walk on the streets and seek out the places of genuine historic interest.

Aside from the historic sites, the major draw for visitors is the **Royal Shakespeare Theatre,** where Britain's foremost actors perform during a long season that lasts from early April until late January. Other than the theater, Stratford is rather devoid of any rich cultural life, and you may want to rush back to London after you've seen the literary pilgrimage sights and watched a production of *Hamlet.* But Stratford-upon-Avon is also a good center for trips to Warwick Castle (see later in this chapter).

ESSENTIALS

GETTING THERE   The journey from London's Paddington Station to Stratford-upon-Avon takes about 2 hours and a round-trip ticket costs £23 ($37). For schedules and information, call ✆ **0845/748-4950.** The train station at Stratford is on Alcester Road. On Sundays from October to May, it is closed, so you'll have to rely on the bus.

Eight **National Express** buses a day leave from London's Victoria Station, with a trip time of 3¼ hours. A single-day round-trip ticket costs £13 ($21) except Friday when the price is £20 ($32). For schedules and information, call ✆ **020/7529-2000.**

If you're driving from London, take the M40 toward Oxford and continue to Stratford-upon-Avon on the A34.

VISITOR INFORMATION   The **Tourist Information Centre,** Bridgefoot, Stratford-upon-Avon, Warwickshire, CV37 6GW (✆ **01789/293127;** www.shakespeare-country.co.uk), provides any details you may wish to know about the Shakespeare houses and properties and will assist in booking rooms (see "Where to Stay," below). Call and ask for a copy of their free *Shakespeare Country Holiday* guide. They also operate an American Express currency-exchange office. It's open from April 1 through October, Monday through Saturday from 9am to 6pm and Sunday from 10:30am to 4:30pm; from November to March, Monday through Saturday from 9am to 5pm, and Sunday from 10am to 4pm.

To contact **Shakespeare Birthplace Trust,** which administers many of the attractions, call the Shakespeare Centre (✆ **01789/204016;** www.shakespeare.org.uk).

THE ROYAL SHAKESPEARE THEATRE

On the banks of the Avon, the **Royal Shakespeare Theatre,** Waterside, Stratford-upon-Avon CV37 6BB (✆ **01789/403404**), is a major showcase for the Royal Shakespeare Company and seats 1,500 patrons. The theater's season runs from November to September and typically features five Shakespearean plays. The company has some of the finest actors on the British stage.

You usually need **ticket reservations,** with two successive booking periods, each one opening about 2 months in advance. You can pick these up from a North American or English travel agent. A small number of tickets are always held for sale on the day of a performance, but it may be too late to get a good seat if you wait until you arrive in Stratford. Tickets can be booked through **Global Tickets** (✆ **800/223-6108** in North America, or 020/7014-8550 in London), or **Keith Prowse** (✆ **800/669-8687** in North America, or 870/840-1111 in London). Both will add a service charge.

You can also call the **theater box office** directly (✆ **01789/403403**) and charge your tickets. The box office is open Monday through Saturday from 9:30am to 8pm, although it closes at 6pm on days when there are no performances. Seat prices range from £8 to £50 ($13–$80). You can make a credit-card reservation and pick up your tickets on the performance day, but you must cancel at least 2 full weeks in advance to get a refund.

Opened in 1986, the **Swan Theatre** is architecturally connected to the back of its older counterpart and shares the same box office, address, and phone number. It seats 430 on three sides of the stage, as in an Elizabethan playhouse, an appropriate design for plays by Shakespeare and his contemporaries. The Swan presents a repertoire of about five plays each season, with tickets ranging from £10 to £30 ($16–$48).

The latest addition is **Summerhouse,** a 350-seat theater lying on Waterside between the Royal Shakespeare Theatre and Bancroft Gardens. Open from May to October, this is a different theater from the rest in that it is used for varied entertainment from music concerts to fashion and children's shows, even stand-up comedy. Information about its offerings and tickets (which vary in price) can be obtained through the Royal Shakespeare Theatre (see above).

An addition to the Royal Shakespeare complex is **The Other Place,** a small, starkly minimalist theater located on Southern Lane, about 270m (900 ft.) from its counterparts. It was redesigned in 1996 as an experimental workshop theater without a permanent stage; seats can be radically repositioned (or removed completely) throughout the theater. A recent example was a "promenade production" of *Julius Caesar,* in which the actors spent the whole play moving freely among a stand-up audience. Tickets are sold at the complex's main box office and generally range from £13 to £24 ($21–$38) each.

Within the Swan Theatre is a **painting gallery,** which has a basic collection of portraits of famous actors and scenes from Shakespeare's plays by 18th- and 19th-century artists. It also operates as a base for **guided tours** with lively running commentary through the world-famous theaters. Guided tours are conducted at 1:30 and 5:30pm, and four times every Sunday afternoon, production schedules permitting. Tours cost £4 ($6.40) for adults and £3 ($4.80) for students, seniors, or children. Call ahead for tour scheduling, which is subject to change.

SEEING THE SIGHTS

Besides the attractions on the periphery of Stratford, many Elizabethan and Jacobean buildings are in town, a number of them administered by the **Shakespeare Birthplace Trust** (✆ **01789/204016**). One ticket—costing £13 ($21) adults, £12 ($19) for seniors and students, and £6 ($9.60) for children—lets you visit the five most important sights. You can also buy a family ticket to all five sights (good for two adults and three children) for £29 ($46)—a good deal. Pick up the ticket if you're planning to do much sightseeing (obtainable at your first stopover at any one of the Trust properties).

Guided tours of Stratford-upon-Avon leave from near the **Guide Friday Tourism Centre,** Civic Hall, Rother Street (✆ **01789/294466**). In summer, open-top double-decker buses depart every 15 minutes daily from 10am to 6pm. You can take a 1-hour ride without stops, or you can get off at any or all of the town's five Shakespeare properties. Though the bus stops are clearly marked along the historic route, the most logical starting point is the sidewalk in front of the Pen & Parchment Pub, at the bottom of Bridge Street. Tour tickets are valid all day so you can hop on and off the buses as many times as you want. The tours cost £8.50 ($14) for adults, £7 ($11) for seniors or students, and £3 ($4.80) for children under 12. A family ticket sells for £18 ($29), and children under 5 go free.

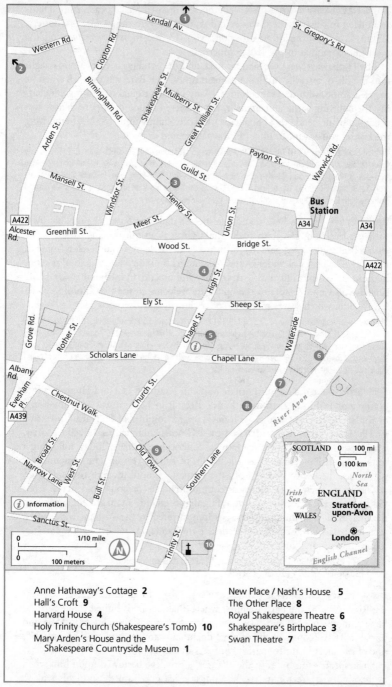

Kendall Av.

St. Gregory's Rd.

Western Rd.

Clopton Rd.

Shakespeare St.

Mulberry St.

Great William St.

Payton St.

Warwick Rd.

Birmingham Rd.

Arden St.

Mansell St.

Guild St.

Windsor St.

Henley St.

Bus Station

A34

A34

A422
Alcester Rd.

Greenhill St.

Meer St.

Union St.

Wood St.

Bridge St.

A422

High St.

Ely St.

Sheep St.

Grove Rd.

Rother St.

Chapel St.

Waterside

Scholars Lane

Chapel Lane

Albany Rd.

Chestnut Walk

Church St.

River Avon

Evesham Pl.

A439

Broad St.

West St.

Bull St.

Old Town

Southern Lane

Narrow Lane

i Information

Sanctus St.

Trinity St.

| 0 | 1/10 mile |
| 0 | 100 meters |

N

SCOTLAND | 0 | 100 mi |
| 0 | 100 km |

North Sea

Irish Sea

ENGLAND

Stratford-upon-Avon

WALES

London

English Channel

Anne Hathaway's Cottage **2**
Hall's Croft **9**
Harvard House **4**
Holy Trinity Church (Shakespeare's Tomb) **10**
Mary Arden's House and the
  Shakespeare Countryside Museum **1**

New Place / Nash's House **5**
The Other Place **8**
Royal Shakespeare Theatre **6**
Shakespeare's Birthplace **3**
Swan Theatre **7**

Anne Hathaway's Cottage ⭐ Before she married Shakespeare, Anne Hathaway lived in this thatched, wattle-and-daub cottage in the hamlet of Shottery, 1.5km (1 mile) from Stratford-upon-Avon. It's the most interesting and the most photographed of the Trust properties.

The Hathaways were yeoman farmers, and the cottage provides a rare insight into the life of a family in Shakespearean times. The Bard was only 18 when he married Anne, who was much older. Many of the original furnishings, including the courting settle and utensils, are preserved inside the house, which was occupied by descendants of Shakespeare's wife's family until 1892. After visiting the house, you'll want to linger in the garden and orchard.

Cottage Lane, Shottery. ℭ **01789/292100.** Admission £5 ($8) adults, £4 ($6.40) children, £29 ($46) family ticket (2 adults, 3 children) for all 5 Shakespeare-related houses. Nov–Mar daily 10am–4pm; Apr–May Mon–Sat 9:30am–5pm, Sun 10am–5pm; June–Aug Mon–Sat 9am–5pm, Sun 9:30am–5pm; Sept–Oct Mon–Sat 9:30am–5pm, Sun 10am–5pm. Closed Dec 23–26. Take a bus from Bridge St. or walk via a marked pathway from Evesham Place in Stratford across the meadow to Shottery.

Hall's Croft It was here that Shakespeare's daughter Susanna probably lived with her husband, Dr. John Hall. Hall's Croft is an outstanding Tudor house with a beautiful walled garden, furnished in the style of a middle-class home of the time. Dr. Hall was widely respected, and he built up a large medical practice in the area. Exhibits illustrating the theory and practice of medicine in Dr. Hall's time are on view. Visitors to the house are welcome to use the adjoining Hall's Croft Club, which serves morning coffee, lunch, and afternoon tea.

Old Town (near Holy Trinity Church). ℭ **01789/292107.** Admission £3.50 ($5.60) adults, £1.70 ($2.70) children, £20 ($32) family ticket (2 adults, 3 children) for all 5 Shakespeare-related houses. Nov–Mar daily 11am–4pm; Apr–May daily 11am–5pm; June–Aug Mon–Sat 9:30am–5pm, Sun 10am–5pm; Sept–Oct daily 11am–5pm. Closed Dec 23–26. To reach Hall's Croft, walk west from High St., which becomes Chapel St. and Church St. At the intersection with Old Town, go left.

Harvard House The most ornate home in Stratford, Harvard House is a fine example of an Elizabethan town house. Rebuilt in 1596, it was once the home of Katherine Rogers, mother of John Harvard, founder of Harvard University. In 1909, the house was purchased by a Chicago millionaire, Edward Morris, who presented it as a gift to the famous American university. Today, following a restoration, it has reopened as a Museum of British Pewter. The museum displays trace the use of pewter from the Roman era until modern times. Pewter, as you learn, used to be the most common choice for household items. Even kiddie toys were made from pewter. Highlights include a tankard engraved with the images of William and Mary; a teapot inspired by the Portland Vase, and a rare bell-based Elizabethan candlestick. Two "hands-on" activities allow children to examine original items.

High St. ℭ **01789/204507.** £1.50 ($2.40) adults, 50p (80¢) children. May–Nov Tues–Sat and bank holiday Mon 11:30am–4:30pm, Sun 10:30am–4:30pm.

Holy Trinity Church (Shakespeare's Tomb) In an attractive setting near the River Avon is the parish church where Shakespeare is buried ("and curst be he who moves my bones"). The Parish Register records his baptism in 1564 and burial in 1616 (copies of the original documents are on display). The church is one of the most beautiful parish churches in England.

Shakespeare's tomb lies in the chancel, a privilege bestowed upon him when he became a lay rector in 1605. Alongside his grave are those of his widow, Anne, and other members of his family. You can also see the graves of Susanna, his daughter, and those of Thomas Nash and Dr. John Hall. Nearby on the north wall is a bust of Shakespeare that was erected approximately 7 years after his death—within the lifetime of his widow and many of his friends.

Old Town. ✆ **01789/266316.** Church, free; Shakespeare's tomb, donation £1 ($1.60) adults, 50p (80¢) students. Apr–Oct Mon–Sat 8:30am–6pm, Sun 12:30–5pm; Mar Mon–Sat 9am–5pm, Sun 12:30–5pm; winter Mon–Sat 9am–4pm, Sun 12:30–5pm. Walk 4 min. past the Royal Shakespeare Theatre with the river on your left.

Mary Arden's House & the Shakespeare Countryside Museum ⭐

So what if millions of visitors have been tricked into thinking this timber-framed farmhouse with its old stone dovecote and various outbuildings was the girlhood home of Shakespeare's mother, Mary Arden? It's still one of the most intriguing sights outside Stratford, even if local historian, Dr. Nat Alcock, discovered in 2000 that the actual childhood home of Arden was the dull looking brick-built farmhouse, Glebe Farm, next door. It was all the trick of an 18th-century tour guide, John Jordan, who decided Glebe Farm was too unimpressive to be the home of the Bard's mother, so he told tourists it was this farmstead instead. Actually the so-called Mary Arden's House wasn't constructed until the late 16th century, a little late to be her home. Nonetheless, visit it anyway as it contains country furniture and domestic utensils. In the barns, stable, cowshed, and farmyard is an extensive collection of farming implements illustrating life and work in the local countryside from Shakespeare's time to the present.

Wilmcote. ✆ **01789/204016.** Admission £5.50 ($8.80) adults, £5 ($8) students and seniors, £2.50 ($4) children, family ticket £13.50 ($22). Nov–Mar Mon–Sat 10am–4pm, Sun 10:30am–4pm; Apr and May Mon–Sat 10am–5pm, Sun 10:30am–5pm; June–Aug Mon–Sat 9:30am–5pm, Sun 10am–5pm; Sept–Oct Mon–Sat 10am–5pm, Sun 10:30am–5pm. Closed Dec 23–26. Take A3400 (Birmingham) for 5.5km (3½ miles).

New Place/Nash's House

Shakespeare retired to New Place in 1610 (a prosperous man by the standards of his day) and died here 6 years later. Regrettably, the house was torn down, so only the garden remains. A mulberry tree planted by the Bard was so popular with latter-day visitors to Stratford that the garden's owner chopped it down. The mulberry tree that grows here today is said to have been planted from a cutting of the original tree. You enter the gardens through Nash's House (Thomas Nash married Elizabeth Hall, a granddaughter of the poet). Nash's House has 16th-century period rooms and an exhibition illustrating the history of Stratford. The popular Knott Garden adjoins the site and represents the style of a fashionable Elizabethan garden.

Chapel St. ✆ **01789/204016.** Admission £3.50 ($5.60) adults, £3 ($4.80) seniors and students, £1.70 ($2.70) children, £29 ($46) family ticket (2 adults, 3 children) for all 5 Shakespeare-related houses. Nov–Mar daily 11am–4pm; Apr and May daily 11am–5pm; June–Aug Mon–Sat 9:30am–5pm, Sun 10am–5pm; Sept and Oct daily 11am–5pm. Closed Dec 23–26. Walk west down High St.; Chapel St. is a continuation of High St.

Shakespeare's Birthplace ⭐

The son of a glover and *whittawer* (leather worker), the Bard was born on St. George's day, April 23, 1564, and died on the same date 52 years later. Filled with Shakespeare memorabilia, including a portrait and furnishings of the writer's time, the Trust property is a half-timbered structure, dating from the early 16th century. The house was bought by public donors in 1847 and preserved as a national shrine. You can visit the living room, the bedroom where Shakespeare was probably born, a fully equipped kitchen of the period (look for the "babyminder"), and a Shakespeare Museum, illustrating his life and times. Later, you can walk through the garden. You won't be alone: It's estimated that some 660,000 visitors pass through the house annually.

Built next door to commemorate the 400th anniversary of the Bard's birth, the modern **Shakespeare Centre** serves both as the administrative headquarters of the Birthplace Trust and as a library and study center. An extension houses a visitor center, which acts as a reception area for those coming to the birthplace.

Henley St. (in the town center near the post office, close to Union St.). (✆ **01789/204016.** Admission £6.50 ($10) adults, £5.50 ($8.80) students and seniors, £2.50 ($4) children, £29 ($46) family ticket (2 adults, 3 children) for all 5 Shakespeare-related houses. Nov–Mar Mon–Sat 10am–4pm, Sun 10:30am–4pm; Apr and May Mon–Sat 10am–4pm, Sun 10:30am–5pm; June–Aug Mon–Sat 9am–5pm, Sun 9:30am–5pm; Sept and Oct Mon–Sat 10am–5pm, Sun 10:30am–5pm. Closed Dec 23–26.

The Royal Shakespeare Theatre Summer House   This is a brass-rubbing center, where medieval and Tudor brasses illustrate the knights and ladies, scholars, merchants, and priests of a bygone era. The Stratford collection includes a large assortment of exact replicas of brasses. Entrance is free, but visitors are charged depending on which brass they choose to rub. According to size, the cost ranges from £1 ($1.60) to make a rubbing of a small brass, to a maximum of £19 ($30) for a rubbing of the largest.

Avonbank Gardens. (✆ **01789/297671.** Free admission. May–Oct daily 10am–6pm; Nov–Feb Sat–Sun 11am–4pm; Mar–Apr daily 10am–5pm.

SHOPPING

Among the many tacky tourist traps are some quality shops, including the ones described below.

Set within an antique house with ceiling beams, **The Shakespeare Bookshop,** 39 Henley St., across from the Shakespeare Birthplace Centre ((✆ **01789/ 292176**), is the region's premier source for textbooks and academic treatises on the Bard and his works. It specializes in books for every level of expertise on Shakespearean studies, from picture books for junior high school students to weighty tomes geared to anyone pursuing a Ph.D. in literature.

The largest shop of its kind in the Midlands, **Arbour Antiques, Ltd.,** Poets Arbour, off Sheep Street ((✆ **01789/293453**), sells antique weapons from Britain, Europe, and India. If you've always hankered after a full suit of armor, this place can sell you one.

Everything in the **Pickwick Gallery,** 32 Henley St. ((✆ **01789/294861**), is a well-crafted work of art produced by copper or steel engraving plates, or printed by means of a carved wooden block. Hundreds of botanical prints, landscapes, and renderings of artfully arranged ruins, each suitable for framing, can be purchased. Topographical maps of regions of the United Kingdom are also available if you're planning on doing any serious hiking.

At **The National Trust Shop,** 45 Wood St. ((✆ **01789/262197**), you'll find textbooks and guidebooks describing esoteric places in the environs of Stratford, descriptions of National Trust properties throughout England, stationery, books, china, pewter, and toiletries.

WHERE TO STAY

During the long theater season, you'll need reservations way in advance. The **Tourist Information Centre** ((✆ **01789/293127;** part of the national "Book-a-Bed-Ahead" service) will help find an accommodation for you in the price range you're seeking. The fee for room reservations is 10% of your first night's stay (B&B rate only), which is deductible from your final bill.

VERY EXPENSIVE

Welcombe Hotel ★★★   For a formal, historic hotel, there is none better in Stratford. The Welcombe is rivaled only by Ettington Park at Alderminster (see below). One of England's great Jacobean country houses, it's a 10-minute ride from the heart of Stratford-upon-Avon. Situated on 157 acres of grounds, its keynote feature is an 18-hole golf course. Guests gather for afternoon tea or drinks on the rear terrace, with its Italian-style garden and steps leading down to flowerbeds. The public rooms are heroic in size, with high mullioned windows providing views of the park. Regular bedrooms—some seemingly big enough for tennis matches—are luxuriously furnished; however, those in the garden wing, while comfortable, are small. The accommodations most recently refurbished and up-to-date are found in the Trevelyan and Garden wings. The rooms with the greatest character of old England are found in the main house. Many of the bedrooms have four-poster beds. The bathrooms are clad in marble or else tiled and offer deluxe toiletries and bathrobes.

Warwick Rd., Stratford-upon-Avon, Warwickshire CV37 ONR. (℃ **01789/295252.** Fax 01789/414666. www. welcombe.co.uk. 64 units. £185–£275 ($296–$440) double; £275–£350 ($440–$560) suite. Rates include English breakfast. AE, DC, MC, V. Take A439 2km (1½ miles) northeast of the town center. **Amenities:** Restaurant; bar; golf course; tennis court; room service; laundry service; dry cleaning. In room: TV, coffeemaker, hair dryer, iron.

EXPENSIVE

Alveston Manor Hotel ★★   This black-and-white timbered manor is perfect for theatergoers; it's just a 2-minute walk from the River Avon. The Welcombe and Ettington Park may have cornered the deluxe trade, but the Alveston, along with the Shakespeare (see below), are the most atmospheric choices in town. Mentioned in the *Domesday Book,* the building predates the arrival of William the Conqueror and has everything from an Elizabethan gazebo to Queen Anne windows. The 19 rooms in the manor house will appeal to those who appreciate old slanted floors, overhead beams, and antique furnishings; some have half-tester beds. Other accommodations—full of tour groups—are in a 3-decades-old motel-like wing. Furnishings here are fresher, but the ambience is lacking. Most bathrooms include a shower and tub. The lounges are in the manor; there's a view of the centuries-old tree at the top of the garden—said to have been the background for the first presentation of *A Midsummer Night's Dream.*

Clopton Bridge (off B4066), Stratford-upon-Avon, Warwickshire CV37 7HP. (℃ **800/225-5843** in the U.S. and Canada, or 0845/758-5593. Fax 01789/414095. www.heritage-hotels.co.uk. 114 units. £145–£160 ($232–$256) double; £230 ($368) suite. AE, DC, MC, V. **Amenities:** Restaurant; bar; room service; babysitting; laundry service; dry cleaning. In room: TV, minibar, coffeemaker, hair dryer.

Shakespeare Hotel ★★   Filled with historical associations, the original core of this hotel, dating from the 1400s, has seen many additions in its long life. Quieter and plusher than the Falcon (see below), it is equaled in the central core of Stratford only by Alveston Manor. Residents relax in the post-and-timber-studded public rooms, within sight of fireplaces and playbills from 19th-century productions of Shakespeare's plays. Bedrooms are named in honor of noteworthy actors, Shakespeare's plays, or Shakespearean characters. The oldest are capped with hewn timbers, and all have modern comforts. Even the newer accommodations are at least 40 to 50 years old and have rose-and-thistle patterns carved into many of their exposed timbers. Bathrooms range in size, but each is adequate and well appointed.

Chapel St., Stratford-upon-Avon, Warwickshire CV37 6ER. (℃ **800/225-5843** in the U.S. and Canada, or 0870/400-8182 or 01789/294771. Fax 01789/415411. www.macdonaldhotels.co.uk. 74 units. £136–£162 ($218–$259) double; £216–£240 ($346–$384) suite. Children up to 16 stay free in parent's room. AE, DC, MC, V. **Amenities:** Restaurant; bar; room service; laundry service. In room: AC, TV, minibar, coffeemaker, iron, hair dryer.

Stratford Moat House ⭐   The Moat House stands on 5 acres of landscaped lawns on the banks of the River Avon near Clopton Bridge. Although lacking the charm of the Alveston Manor or the Shakespeare, this modern hotel offers fine amenities and facilities. It is one of the flagships of the Queen's Moat House, a British hotel chain, and was built in the early 1970s and last renovated in 1995. The hotel hosts many conferences, so don't expect to have the place to yourself. Every bedroom has a high standard of comfort; bathrooms offer generous shelf space and large mirrors.

Bridgefoot, Stratford-upon-Avon, Warwickshire CV37 6YR. ℂ **01789/279988**. Fax 01789/298589. www. moathousehotels.com. 251 units. £120 ($192) double; £200 ($320) suite. AE, DC, MC, V. **Amenities:** 2 restaurants; 2 bars; heated indoor pool; spa; sauna; room service; laundry service. *In room:* TV, coffeemaker, hair dryer, trouser press.

Thistle Stratford-upon-Avon ⭐   Theatergoers flock here, because the hotel is across the street from the main entrance of the Royal Shakespeare and Swan theaters. The Thistle chain completely refurbished the interior after buying the hotel in 1993. Its redbrick main section dates from the Regency period, although over the years a handful of adjacent buildings were included and an uninspired modern extension added. Today, the interior has a lounge and bar; a dining room with bay windows; a covered garden terrace; and comfortable but narrow bedrooms. Most rooms are graced with a two- or four-poster bed. The small bathrooms are adequate and come with a shower or tub.

44 Waterside, Stratford-upon-Avon, Warwickshire CV37 6BA. ℂ **0870/333-9146**. Fax 0870/333-9246. www. stratford-upon-avon.co.uk/thistle.htm. 63 units. £73–£179 ($117–$286) double. AE, DC, MC, V. **Amenities:** Restaurant; bar; room service; babysitting; laundry service; dry cleaning. *In room:* TV, coffeemaker, hair dryer, trouser press.

MODERATE

Falcon   Located in the heart of Stratford, the Falcon blends the very old and the very new. The inn was licensed a quarter of a century after Shakespeare's death. A 1970s bedroom extension is connected to its rear by a glass passageway. The recently upgraded bedrooms in the mellowed part have oak beams, diamond leaded-glass windows, some antique furnishings, and good reproductions. Each room is comfortable and clean, but there is not enough soundproofing to drown out the BBC on your next-door neighbor's telly. Rooms in the newer section are also comfortable but are more sterile in tone. Carved headboards crown fine beds. The small bathrooms come with shower stalls. Some are rather unsightly with brown linoleum floors and plastic tub enclosures. The comfortable lounges, also recently upgraded, are some of the finest in the Midlands.

Chapel St., Stratford-upon-Avon, Warwickshire CV37 6HA. ℂ **01789/279953**. Fax 01789/414260. www. regalhotels.co.uk. 84 units. £80–£125 ($128–$200) double; from £140 ($224) suite. AE, DC, MC, V. **Amenities:** Restaurant; 2 bars; room service. *In room:* TV, coffeemaker, hair dryer.

Grosvenor House Hotel   A pair of Georgian town houses, built in 1832 and 1843, respectively, join to form this hotel, which is one of the second-tier choices of Stratford on equal footing with the Thistle (see above). Situated in the center of town, with lawns and gardens to the rear, it is a short stroll from the intersection of Bridge Street and Waterside, allowing easy access to the River Avon, Bancroft Gardens, and the Royal Shakespeare Theatre. All small to mid-size bedrooms are nicely furnished and comfortable. Bathrooms are compact but well maintained, most with a shower-tub combination.

12–14 Warwick Rd., Stratford-upon-Avon, Warwickshire CV37 6YT. ✆ **01789/269213.** Fax 01789/266087. 67 units. £95 ($152) double. AE, MC, V. **Amenities:** Restaurant; bar; free pass to nearby recreation center; room service; babysitting; laundry service. *In room:* TV, coffeemaker, hair dryer, trouser press.

The White Swan ⭐ This cozy, intimate hotel is one of the most atmospheric in Stratford and is, in fact, the oldest building here. In business for more than a century before Shakespeare appeared on the scene, it competes successfully with the Falcon in offering an ancient atmosphere. The gabled medieval front would present the Bard with no surprises, but the modern comforts inside would surely astonish him, even though many of the rooms have been preserved. Bedrooms are comfortable but generally lack style. Except for an occasional four-poster or half-canopy bed, most are twins or doubles. Bathrooms are compact with shower stalls.

Rother St., Stratford-upon-Avon, Warwickshire CV37 6NH. ✆ **01789/297022.** Fax 01789/268773. www. e-travelguide.info/whiteswan. 41 units. £88 ($141) double. Children up to 16 stay half-price in parent's room. Rates include English breakfast. AE, DC, MC, V. **Amenities:** Restaurant; bar; limited room service. *In room:* TV, coffeemaker, hair dryer, trouser press.

INEXPENSIVE

Caterham House ⭐ *Finds* A B&B full of charm and character was created when two Georgian houses were melded to form a cohesive building, lying a 10-minute walk from the Royal Shakespeare Theatre. The building dates from 1830, and it's been handsomely restored, with a conservatory style sitting room with an eclectic grouping of furnishings. The owner, Dominique Maury, and his wife, Olive, are among the most helpful hosts in town.

Bedrooms are small to midsize, each one individually decorated, often with antiques. The bathrooms with shower—one with tub—even have an occasional antique as well. Bedrooms are in the French country style, evoking the roots of Shakespeare-loving Frenchman Dominique. Most units are in the main building, with two extra accommodations in converted cottages that have been cleverly incorporated into the main hotel. Their breakfast, where homemade jam is served in jars, is one of the best in town.

58 Rother St., Stratford-upon-Avon, Warwickshire CV37 6LT. ✆ **01789/267309.** Fax 01789/414836. www. charmingsmallhotels.co.uk. 10 units. £82–£89 ($131–$142). MC, V. **Amenities:** Breakfast lounge; bar. *In room:* TV, hair dryer.

Sequoia House This hotel opens onto its own beautiful garden on ¾ of an acre across the Avon opposite the theater, conveniently located for visiting the major Shakespeare properties of the National Trust. Renovation has vastly improved the house, which was created from two late-Victorian buildings. In its price range, bedrooms are some of the most comfortable in town, with upholstered chairs and desk space. Bathrooms are small but tidy; the superior rooms have baths, the rest have showers only. Guests gather in a lounge that has a licensed bar and an open Victorian fireplace. The hotel also has a private parking area.

51–53 Shipston Rd., Stratford-upon-Avon, Warwickshire CV37 7LN. ✆ **01789/268852.** Fax 01789/414559. www.stratford-upon-avon.co.uk/sequoia.htm. 23 units. £79–£89 ($126–$142) double. Rates include English breakfast. AE, DC, MC, V. **Amenities:** Bar; limited room service. *In room:* TV, coffeemaker, hair dryer.

Stratheden Hotel A short walk north of the Royal Shakespeare Theatre, the Stratheden Hotel is tucked away in a desirable location. Built in 1673, and currently the oldest remaining brick building in the town center, it has a tiny rear garden and top-floor rooms with slanted, beamed ceilings. Under the ownership of the Wells family for the past quarter century, it has improved again in both decor and comfort with the addition of fresh paint, new curtains, and good beds. Most of the small bathrooms have a shower stall though a few have baths.

5 Chapel St., Stratford-upon-Avon, Warwickshire CV37 6EP. ©/fax **01789/297119.** www.ukstay.com/warwick/stratheden. 9 units. £66–£72 ($106–$115) double. Rates include full English breakfast. AE, MC, V. **Amenities:** Breakfast room. *In room:* TV.

Victoria Spa Lodge   This B&B is old-fashioned and atmospheric and still going strong. Opened in 1837, the year Queen Victoria ascended to the throne, this was the first establishment to be given her name. This lodge was originally a spa frequented by the queen's eldest daughter, Princess Vicky. The accommodating hosts offer tastefully decorated, comfortable bedrooms. The small bathrooms have shower stalls only. The entire property is nonsmoking.

Bishopton Lane (2.5km/1½ miles north of the town center where A3400 intersects A46), Stratford-upon-Avon, Warwickshire CV37 9QY. © **01789/267985.** Fax 01789/204728. www.stratford-upon-avon.co.uk/victoriaspa.htm. 7 units. £65 ($104) double; £80 ($128) for 3; £100 ($160) for 5-person family suite. Rates include English breakfast. MC, V. *In room:* TV, coffeemaker, hair dryer.

NEARBY PLACES TO STAY

Ettington Park Hotel ✸✸✸   This Victorian Gothic mansion has a history that spans over 9 centuries and is one of the most sumptuous retreats in Shakespeare Country. The land is a legacy of the Shirley family, whose 12th-century burial chapel is near the hotel. Like a grand private home, the hotel boasts baronial fireplaces, a conservatory, and a charming staff. Adam ceilings, stone carvings, and ornate staircases have been beautifully restored. A new wing, assembled with the same stone and neo-Gothic carving of the original house, stretches toward a Renaissance-style arbor entwined with vines. In the spacious and elegant bedrooms, the most modern comforts are concealed behind antique facades. The best units are deluxe doubles, which are larger than the standard units and open onto garden views. Some rooms are fitted with old-fashioned four-posters. Bathrooms have Victorian-style tiling, robes, and deluxe toiletries. Stay clear of the bookcase in the library; the ghost is very temperamental.

Alderminster, near Stratford-upon-Avon, Warwickshire CV37 8BU. © **01789/450123.** Fax 01789/450472. www.ettingtonpark.co.uk. 48 units. £100–£150 ($160–$240) double; £185–£335 ($296–$536) suite. Rates include English breakfast. AE, DC, MC, V. Drive 8km (5 miles) south along A3400 just past Alderminster, then take 2nd left (signposted) into Ettington Park. **Amenities:** Restaurant; bar; indoor pool; tennis court; Jacuzzi; sauna; room service; laundry service; horseback riding. *In room:* TV, coffeemaker, hair dryer, iron, trouser press.

Mary Arden Inn ✸ *(Finds)*   This is an escapist's retreat for those who want to avoid the hordes descending on Stratford. Shakespeare's mother, Mary Arden, lived in the tiny village of Wilmcote, some 5.5km (3½ miles) northwest of Stratford. Actually an upgraded village pub-hotel, this place offers not only appealing and well-furnished bedrooms at moderate prices but also good meals. The inn is relatively unpretentious and offers a welcome respite from the hordes in the center of Stratford. All of the rooms were upgraded in 2002, and offer a variety of amenities ranging from CD players to the complete works of Shakespeare. Some of the rooms are quite small, others more midsize. Bathrooms are very small with a minimum of shelf space and a shower stall. The Romeo and Juliet Suite features a four-poster bed and a Jacuzzi tub.

The Green, Wilmcote, Stratford-upon-Avon, Warwickshire CV37 9XJ. © **01789/267030.** Fax 01789/204875. www.oldenglish.co.uk. 11 units. £80 ($128) double; £100 ($160) suite. Rates include English breakfast. AE, MC, V. Take A3400 5.5km (3½ miles) northwest of Stratford. **Amenities:** Restaurant; bar. *In room:* TV, coffeemaker, hair dryer, iron.

WHERE TO DINE

After visiting the birthplace of Shakespeare, pop across the street for tea at **Brasserie,** Henley Street (© **01789/295261**). This airy tearoom is tremendously popular, but the very attentive staff more than compensates for the throngs of patrons that grace its doors. Choose from an array of tea blends, cream teas, and various gateaux, pastries, and tea cakes—all freshly baked in its own kitchen.

EXPENSIVE TO MODERATE

Desports ✹✹ ECLECTIC/INTERNATIONAL   At last Stratford boasts a restaurant worth writing home about. In the town center between the Shakespeare Centre and Market Place, Desports was installed in a 16th-century building. Here Paul Desport and his wife, Julie, offer good food in what had been a gastronomic wasteland in England (except for our recommendations, of course!). Extremely professional cooking, vivid use of spices, imaginative menus, and reasonable prices attract a never-ending stream of visitors and locals alike. We like how Paul experiments with Asian flavors and spices and always gets the balance right. Is this the Stratford of yore, you ask, as you taste the aromatic pumpkin and Cerny cheese tagliatelle with almond pesto, tomato, and candied eggplant? Even such English classics as bubble and squeak (cabbage and potatoes) are given added zest by an orange Dubonnet sauce.

13–14 Meer St. © **01789/269304.** Main courses £12–£18 ($19–$29); fixed-price 2-course lunch £20 ($32), 3-course £24 ($38). AE, DC, MC, V. Tues–Sat noon–2pm and 5:45–10:30pm.

Lambs ✹ CONTINENTAL/ENGLISH   A stone's throw from the Royal Shakespeare Theatre, this cafe-bistro is housed in a building dating back to 1547 (and with connections to Lewis Carroll). For a quick light meal or pretheater dinner, it's ideal. The menu changes monthly. Begin with a tomato-and-mozzarella salad, perhaps Scottish smoked salmon or a pasta, then follow with pan-fried filet of beef with roasted shallots or grilled filet of monkfish with an avocado-and-tomato-salsa. The chef takes chances (no doubt inspired by trips to the Continent), and it's a nice departure from the bland tearoom food served for decades in Stratford.

12 Sheep St. © **01789/292554.** Reservations required Sat night. Main courses £8.50–£16 ($14–$26); fixed-price menu £12 ($18) for 2 courses, £15 ($23) for 3. MC, V. Mon–Sat noon–2pm and 5–7pm; Sun 7–10pm.

The Quarto's Restaurant ✹ FRENCH/ITALIAN/ENGLISH   This restaurant enjoys the best location in town—in the theater itself, with glass walls providing an unobstructed view of swans on the Avon. You can purchase an intermission snack feast of smoked salmon and champagne, or dine by flickering candlelight after the performance. Many dishes, such as apple-and-parsnip soup, are definitely old English; others reflect a continental touch, such as fried polenta with filets of pigeon and bacon. For your main course, you may select Dover sole, pheasant suprême, or roast loin of pork. Homemade crème brûlée is an old-time favorite. The theater lobby has a special phone for reservations.

In the Royal Shakespeare Theatre, Waterside. © **01789/403415.** Reservations required. Matinee lunch £16 ($26); dinner £14–£20 ($22–$32). AE, MC, V. Thurs and Sat noon–2:30pm; Mon–Sat 5:30pm–midnight.

Thai Boathouse ✹ THAI   The only restaurant set on the Avon, this charming choice is reached by crossing Clopton Bridge toward Oxford and Banbury. The second-floor dining room opens onto vistas of the river. This restaurant, originally established 4 decades ago in Bangkok, has brought spice and zest to

Stratford's lazy restaurant scene. The decor comes from Thailand itself, with elephants, woodcarvings, and Buddhas. Seasonal specialties such as wild duck and pheasant are a special feature of the menu. Fresh produce, great skill in the kitchen, and exquisite presentations are the hallmarks of this restaurant. Sample a selection of authentic Thai appetizers before going on to such a delectable main course as fresh sea bass in lemon grass. One of our favorites is their lamb in a yellow curry with potatoes, onions, and cashew nuts.

Swan's Nest Lane. ℂ 01789/297733. Reservations recommended. Fixed-price menus £21–£26 ($34–$42). Main courses £5.50–£12 ($8.80–$19). MC, V. Sun–Fri noon–2:30pm; daily 5:30–10:30pm.

INEXPENSIVE

Hussain's INDIAN   This restaurant has many admirers—it's one of the brighter spots on the bleak culinary landscape hereabouts. The owner has chosen a well-trained and alert staff that welcomes guests and advises them about special dishes. You can select from an array of northern Indian dishes, many from the tandoor, plus various curries with lamb or prawn. Offering a 10% discount on pre- and posttheater dinners, Hussain's is across from the Shakespeare Hotel and historic New Place.

6A Chapel St. ℂ 01789/267506. Reservations recommended. Main courses £5.45–£12 ($8.70–$19). AE, MC, V. Thurs–Sun 12:30–2:30pm; daily 5pm–midnight.

Russons INTERNATIONAL   Because the theater is a short stroll away, this is a great place for a pre-show meal. The restaurant is housed in a 400-year-old building and the two simply furnished dining rooms both feature inglenook fireplaces. The menu changes regularly to reflect the availability of seasonal ingredients. Fresh seafood is the specialty here. Daily specials are posted on a blackboard and include rack of lamb, guinea fowl, and numerous vegetarian dishes. Finish with one of the delicious homemade desserts.

8 Church St. ℂ 01789/268822. Reservations required. Main courses £7.95–£16 ($13–$26). AE, MC, V. Tues–Sat 11:30am–1:30pm and 5:30–10pm.

A GOOD PLACE FOR A PINT

The Black Swan ("The Dirty Duck") ★★ ENGLISH   Affectionately known as The Dirty Duck, this has been a popular hangout for Stratford players since the 18th century. The wall is lined with autographed photos of its many famous patrons. Typical English grills, among other dishes, are featured in the Dirty Duck Grill Room, though no one has ever accused it of serving the best food in Stratford. You'll have a choice of a dozen appetizers, most of which would make a meal in themselves. In fair weather, you can have drinks in the front garden and watch the swans glide by on the Avon.

Waterside. ℂ 01789/297312. Reservations required for dining. Main courses £8–£15 ($13–$24); bar snacks £5–£7.25 ($8–$12). AE, DC, MC, V (in the restaurant only). Daily 11am–11pm.

2 Warwick: England's Finest Medieval Castle ★★★

148km (92 miles) NW of London; 13km (8 miles) NE of Stratford-upon-Avon

Most visitors come to this town just to see **Warwick Castle,** the finest medieval castle in England, but the historic center of ancient Warwick has a lot more to offer.

Warwick cites Ethelfleda, daughter of Alfred the Great, as its founder. But most of its history is associated with the earls of Warwick, a title created by the son of William the Conqueror in 1088. The story of those earls—the Beaumonts,

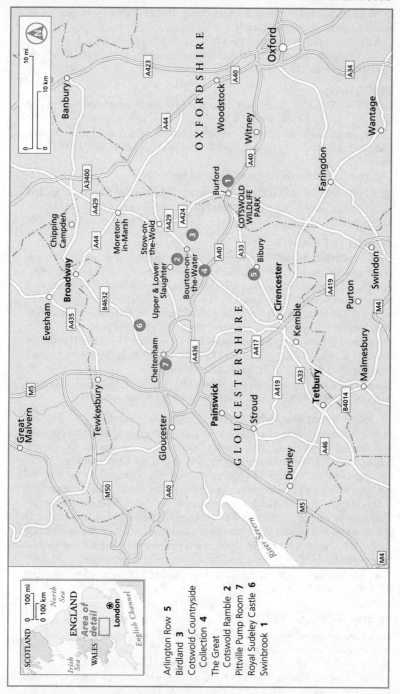

The Cotswolds

the Beauchamps (such figures as "Kingmaker" Richard Neville)—makes for an exciting episode in English history.

A devastating fire swept through the heart of Warwick in 1694, but a number of Elizabethan and medieval buildings still survive, along with some fine Georgian structures from a later date.

ESSENTIALS

GETTING THERE Trains run frequently between Stratford-upon-Avon and Warwick. Call ☎ **0845/748-4950** for schedules and information.

One **Stagecoach** bus per hour departs Stratford-upon-Avon during the day. The trip takes 15 to 20 minutes. Call the tourist office (☎ **01789/293127**) for schedules.

Take A46 if you're driving from Stratford-upon-Avon.

VISITOR INFORMATION The **Tourist Information Centre** is at The Court House, Jury Street (☎ **01926/492212**), and is open daily from 9:30am to 4:30pm; closed from December 24 to December 26 and January 1.

SEEING THE SIGHTS

Lord Leycester Hospital The great fire also spared this group of half-timbered almshouses at the West Gate. The buildings were erected around 1400, and the hospital was founded in 1571 by Robert Dudley, earl of Leicester, as a home for old soldiers. It's still used by ex-service personnel and their spouses. On top of the West Gate is the attractive little chapel of St. James, dating from the 12th century but renovated many times since. Closed to the public since 1903, the gardens in back of the hospital were recently restored. Nathaniel Hawthorne wrote of his visits to the gardens in 1855 and 1857; the gardens were restored based on the observations he made in his writings.

High St. ☎ 01926/491422. Admission £3.20 ($5.10) adults, £2.70 ($4.30) students and seniors, £2.20 ($3.50) children. Easter–Oct Tues–Sun 10am–5pm; Nov–Easter Tues–Sun 10am–4pm.

St. John's House Museum At Coten End, not far from the castle gates, this early-17th-century house has exhibits on Victorian domestic life. A schoolroom is furnished with original 19th-century furniture and equipment. During the school term, Warwickshire children dress in period costumes and learn Victorian-style lessons. Groups of children also use the Victorian parlor and the kitchen. Because it's impossible to display more than a small number of items at a time, a study room is available where you can see objects from the reserve collections. The costume collection is a particularly fine one, and visitors can study the drawings and photos that make up the costume catalog. These facilities are available by appointment only. Upstairs is a military museum, tracing the history of the Royal Warwickshire Regiment from 1674 to the present.

St. John's, at the crossroads of the main Warwick–Leamington Rd. (A425/A429) and the Coventry Rd. (A429). ☎ 01926/412021. Free admission. Tues–Sat (and bank holidays) 10am–5:30pm; Easter–Sept Sun 2:30–5pm.

St. Mary's Church Destroyed in part by the fire of 1694, this church, with rebuilt battlemented tower and nave, is among the finest examples of late-17th- and early-18th-century architecture. The Beauchamp Chapel, spared from the flames, encases the Purbeck marble tomb of Richard Beauchamp, a well-known earl of Warwick who died in 1439 and is commemorated by a gilded bronze effigy. Even more powerful than King Henry V, Beauchamp has a tomb that's one of the finest remaining examples of the Perpendicular Gothic style from the mid–15th century. The tomb of Robert Dudley, earl of Leicester, a favorite of

Elizabeth I, is against the north wall. The Perpendicular Gothic choir dates from the 14th century; the Norman crypt and chapter house are from the 11th century.

Church St. ☎ **01926/403940.** www.saintmaryschurch.co.uk. Free admission; donations accepted. Apr–Sept daily 10am–6pm; Oct–Mar daily 10am–4pm. All buses to Warwick stop at Old Sq.

Warwick Castle ★★   Perched on a rocky cliff above the River Avon in the town center, a stately late-17th-century mansion is surrounded by a magnificent 14th-century fortress, the finest medieval castle in England. Even 3 hours may not be enough time to see everything. Surrounded by gardens, lawns, and woodland, where peacocks roam freely, and skirted by the Avon, Warwick Castle was described by Sir Walter Scott in 1828 as "that fairest monument of ancient and chivalrous splendor which yet remains uninjured by time."

Ethelfleda, daughter of Alfred the Great, built the first significant fortifications here in 914. William the Conqueror ordered the construction of a motte-and-bailey castle in 1068, 2 years after the Norman Conquest. The mound is all that remains today of the Norman castle, which Simon de Montfort sacked in the Barons' War of 1264.

The Beauchamp family, the most illustrious medieval earls of Warwick, is responsible for the appearance of the castle today; much of the external structure remains unchanged from the mid–14th century. When the castle was granted to Sir Fulke Greville by James I in 1604, he spent £20,000 ($32,000, an enormous sum in those days) converting the existing castle buildings into a luxurious mansion. The Grevilles have held the earl of Warwick title since 1759.

The staterooms and Great Hall house fine collections of paintings, furniture, arms, and armor. The armory, dungeon, torture chamber, ghost tower, clock tower, and Guy's tower create a vivid picture of the castle's turbulent past and its important role in the history of England.

The private apartments of Lord Brooke and his family, who in recent years sold the castle to Tussaud's Group, are open to visitors. They house a display of a carefully reconstructed Royal Weekend House Party of 1898. The major rooms contain wax portraits of important figures of the time, including a young Winston Churchill. In the Kenilworth bedroom, a likeness of the Prince of Wales, later King Edward VII, reads a letter. The duchess of Marlborough prepares for her bath in the red bedroom. Among the most life-like of the figures is a uniformed maid bending over to test the temperature of the water running into a bathtub.

You can also see the Victorian rose garden, a re-creation of an original design from 1868 by Robert Marnock. Near the rose garden is a Victorian alpine rockery and water garden.

☎ **0870/442-2000.** www.warwick-castle.co.uk. Admission £12.50 ($20) adults, £7.50 ($12) children 4–16, £9 ($14) seniors, free for children 4 and under, £32 ($51) family ticket. Apr–Sept daily 10am–6pm; Oct–Mar daily 10am–5pm. Closed Christmas Day.

WHERE TO STAY

Many people prefer to stay in Warwick and commute to Stratford-upon-Avon, though the accommodations here are not as special as those at Stratford.

The Glebe at Barford ★ *Finds*   This 1820s rectory to the Church of St. Peter has been welcoming wayfarers to either Stratford-upon-Avon or Warwick since it was successfully converted into a small country-house hotel in 1948. The church still stands adjacent to the hotel's grounds. In recent years much redecorating and many modern facilities have been added, including the Cedars Conservatory Restaurant looking out onto the gardens. A small swimming pool with hydro jets has been added as well. Each of the bedrooms has been individually designed, with either a tented ceiling, a four-poster, or a coronet-style bed. All the first-class bathrooms come with extras such as heated towel racks. The hotel lies only a 10-minute drive from the center of Warwick, and we suggest that motorists stay here instead of the center of town.

Church St., Barford, Warwickshire CV35 8BS. © **01926/624218.** Fax 01926/624171. www.glebehotel.co.uk. 39 units. £118–£128 ($189–$205) double; £148 ($237) family unit; £150 ($240) Shakespeare Suite (with Jacuzzi corner bathroom). AE, DC, MC, V. **Amenities:** Restaurant; bar; heated indoor pool; fitness center; steam room; hot tub; sauna. *In room:* TV, beverage maker.

Hilton National Warwick/Stratford ☆

Though outside of town, the Hilton is the best choice in the area. Lying at the junction of a network of highways, it's popular with business travelers and hosts many conferences for local companies. But tourists also find that its comfort and easy-to-find location make it a good base for touring Warwick and the surrounding regions. It's a low-rise modern design with a series of interconnected bars, lounges, and public areas. Room furnishings are bland but comfortable. All units have well-kept bathrooms.

Warwick Bypass (A429 Stratford Rd.), Warwick, Warwickshire CV34 6RE. © **800/445-8667** in the U.S. and Canada, or 01926/499555. Fax 01926/410020. 181 units. £90–£175 ($144–$280) double. AE, DC, MC, V. Take A429 3km (2 miles) south of Warwick (11km/7 miles north of Stratford-upon-Avon). Junction 15 off M40 from London. **Amenities:** Restaurant; bar; pool; exercise room; sauna; 24-hr. room service; babysitting; laundry service; dry cleaning. *In room:* TV, coffeemaker, hair dryer, trouser press.

Lord Leycester Hotel (Calotels)

This affordable choice lies within walking distance of the castle and the other historic buildings of Warwick. In 1726, this manor house belonged to Lord Archer of Umberslade; in 1926, it was finally turned into this modest hotel. The rooms are small but offer reasonable comfort for the price with decent double or twin beds. Bathrooms are also small with a shower stall. A large parking lot is at the rear of the hotel.

17 Jury St., Warwick, Warwickshire CV34 4EJ. © **01926/491481.** Fax 01926/491561. 51 units. £75–£90 ($120–$144) double. Rates include English breakfast. AE, DC, MC, V. **Amenities:** 2 restaurants; bar; room service. *In room:* TV, coffeemaker, hair dryer, trouser press.

Tudor House Inn & Restaurant

At the edge of town, on the main road from Stratford-upon-Avon to Warwick Castle, is a 1472 timbered inn. It's one of the few buildings to escape the fire that destroyed High Street in 1694. Off the central hall are two large rooms, each of which could be the setting for an Elizabethan play. All the simply furnished bedrooms have washbasins, and two contain doors only one meter (4 ft.) high. Bathrooms are compact. In the corner of the lounge is an open turning staircase.

90–92 West St. (opposite the main Warwick Castle car park, 1km/½ mile south of town on A429), Warwick, Warwickshire CV34 6AW. © **01926/495447.** Fax 01926/492948. www.thetudorhouse.co.uk. 9 units, 5 with bathroom. £65–£75 ($104–$120) double. Rates include English breakfast. AE, MC, V. **Amenities:** Restaurant; bar. *In room:* TV, hair dryer, coffeemaker, iron.

WHERE TO DINE

When you're ready to take a break from sightseeing, it's hard to beat the ancient ambience of tea at **Brethren's Kitchen,** Lord Leycester Hospital (© **01926/491422**). This tearoom is part of a 16th-century hospital the earl established in the year 1571. It has cool stone floors and wonderful exposed oak beams. Indian, Chinese, and herbal teas are all available, as well as scones with fresh cream, sponge cake, and fruit cake. Closed February and Mondays, but open on bank holidays.

Moments   Biking & Hiking Through the Cotswolds

Biking the country roads of the Cotswolds is one of the best ways to experience the quiet beauty of the area. **Country Lanes,** 9 Shaftesbury St., Fordingbridge, Hampshire SP6 1JF (© **01425/655022**), offers visitors that opportunity.

The company rents 21-speed bicycles fully equipped with mudguards, a water bottle, lock and key, a rear carrier rack, and, of course, safety helmets.

Its recommended day trips are self-guided, so you can ride at your own pace. You'll get an easy-to-follow route sheet. As you explore, you'll pass manor farms and pretty cottages of honey-colored stone. Several villages are also along the path, and the Hidcote Manor Garden is a perfect spot to relax if your legs tire of pedaling. The 10-, 20-, or 28-mile trips all end at the Café Dijon. Here, you'll be served afternoon tea in the garden. The £25 ($40) price includes everything mentioned above. Advanced booking is essential; call © **01608/650065** to reserve by credit card.

This is also one of the most famous regions of England for hiking. With such a large area in which to ramble, it's a good idea to know where you are (and aren't) welcome. The **Cotswold Voluntary Wardens Service,** Shire Hall, Gloucester (© **01451/862000**), offers free brochures highlighting trails and paths.

The Wayfarers, 172 Bellevue Ave., Newport, RI 02840 (© **800/249-4620;** www.thewayfarers.com), sponsors about 10 Cotswold walks a year from May to October. The cost of a 1-week tour is $2,499 per person, including all meals and snacks, first-class accommodations with private bathroom along the route, and admission to attractions.

If you'd like to walk and explore on your own without a guide, you can get data from the **Cheltenham Tourist Information Centre** (© **01242/522878**). The center sells a Cotswold Way map.

Fanshaw's Restaurant BRITISH/FRENCH   In the heart of Warwick, at the edge of the city's commercial center, this restaurant occupies a late-Victorian building enlivened by flowered window boxes. Inside are only 32 seats in a well-maintained, rather flouncy dining room lined with mirrors. A well-trained staff serves food from a menu that changes every 2 months, but usually includes sirloin steak; filet of beef Wellington, with a red-wine and shallot sauce; and breast of pheasant with a shiitake and oyster mushroom brandy sauce. Especially elegant and usually offered during game season is a brace of quail with a hazelnut and apricot stuffing.

22 Market Place. © 01926/410590. Reservations recommended. Fixed-price menus £19 ($30). AE, MC, V. Mon–Sat 6:30–10pm.

Findon's Restaurant MODERN BRITISH   The building is authentically Georgian, constructed in 1700. You'll dine surrounded by original stone floors and cupboards, within a setting for only 43 diners to dine in snug comfort. Michael Findon, owner and sometime chef, works hard at orchestrating a blend of traditional and modern British cuisine. The set menus include such dishes as a sauté of pigeon breast with red wine and celery, followed by a suprême of cod with lemon and prawn butter and deep-fried parsley. A la carte meals may include pave of beef with basil crust and game jus or filet of sea bass with a fumet of lime. Consider a lunchtime visit to this place, when a two-course "plat du jour" includes soup of the day followed by such platters as venison sausages with a mustard sauce and fresh vegetables (or a suitable vegetarian substitute), all for only £5 ($8)—a great deal .

7 Old Sq. Warwick ℭ **01926/411755.** Reservations recommended. Main courses £11–£19 ($18–$30); fixed-price lunch £9.95 ($16). AE, DC, MC, V. Mon–Fri noon–2pm; Mon–Sat 7–9:30pm.

Vanilla (Value BRITISH It's the Castle that draws you to Warwick, not the cuisine, but this bistro is notable for serving affordable food that is both good-tasting and prepared with fresh ingredients. Launch your repast with a freshly made soup of the day or else something classic such as Parma ham and melon with a honey-and-mustard dressing. We recently dined very well on Gressingham duck breast, which was interestingly served with a fricassée of haricot vert and mushrooms. Our dinner companions preferred the roast cod, which came with buttery leeks, and the grilled Scottish rib-eye steak with wild mushrooms, roasted garlic, and a Claret jus. Save room for one of the old-fashioned desserts such as a vanilla crème brûlée with walnut shortbread or the warm dark chocolate tart with clotted cream.

6 Jury St. ℭ **01926/498930.** Reservations recommended. Main courses £11–£15 ($17–$24). 2-course lunch £10.50 ($17); 3-course lunch £14 ($22). Sun 2-course lunch £15 ($24), 3-course lunch £17 ($27). Sun 2-course dinner £19 ($30), 3-course dinner £23 ($36). AE, MC, V. Tues–Sat 11am–2pm and 6:30–10pm; Sun 11:30am–6pm.

3 Cheltenham (★

159km (99 miles) NW of London; 14km (9 miles) NE of Gloucester; 69km (43 miles) W of Oxford

Legend has it that the Cheltenham villagers discovered a mineral spring by chance when they noticed pigeons drinking from a spring and observed how healthy they were (the pigeon has been incorporated into the town's crest). King George III arrived in 1788 and launched the town's career as a spa.

Cheltenham today remains one of England's most fashionable spas, and many visitors come just to see its gardens from spring to autumn. The architecture is mainly Regency, with lots of ironwork, balconies, and verandas. Attractive parks and open spaces of greenery make the town especially inviting. The main street, the Promenade, has been called the most beautiful thoroughfare in Britain. Rather similar are Lansdowne Place and Montpellier Parade (with caryatids separating its stores, Montpellier Walk is one of England's most interesting shopping centers).

ESSENTIALS

GETTING THERE Twenty-one trains depart daily from London's Paddington Station for the 2¼-hour trip. You may have to change trains at Bristol or Swindon. For schedules and information, call ℭ **0845/748-4950.** Trains between Cheltenham and Bristol take only an hour, with continuing service to Bath.

National Express offers nine buses daily from London's Victoria Coach Station to Cheltenham. The ride takes about 2½ hours. For schedules and information, call ℭ **020/7529-2000.**

If you're driving from London, head northwest on the M40 to Oxford, continuing along the A40 to Cheltenham.

VISITOR INFORMATION   The **Tourist Information Centre,** 77 Promenade (*©* **01242/522878**), is open September through June, Monday through Saturday from 9:30am to 5:15pm.

SPECIAL EVENTS   The **International Festival of Music** and the **Festival of Literature** take place each year in July and October, respectively, and attract internationally acclaimed performers and orchestras.

EXPLORING THE TOWN

Cheltenham Art Gallery & Museum   This gallery houses one of the foremost collections of the Arts and Crafts movement, notably the fine furniture of William Morris and his followers. One section is devoted to Edward Wilson, Cheltenham's native son, who died with Captain Scott in the Antarctic in 1912. The gallery is located near Royal Crescent and the Coach Station.

Clarence St. *©* **01242/237431.** Free admission. Mon–Sat 10am–5:20pm; Sun 2–4:30pm. Closed bank holidays.

Everyman Theatre   Cheltenham is the cultural center of the Cotswolds, a role solidified by the Everyman Theatre. Designed in the 1890s as an opera house by Frank Matcham, Victorian England's leading theater architect, it retains its ornate cornices, sculpted ceilings, and plush velvets despite extensive renovations to its stage and lighting facilities. The theater has begun to attract some of England's top dramatic companies. Shakespeare, musicals, comedies, and other genres are performed in the small (658 seats) but charming hall.

Regent St. *©* **01242/572573.** Admission £5–£25 ($8–$40), depending on the event. Box office on performance days Mon–Sat 9:30am–8:30pm.

Pittville Pump Room   Cheltenham Waters are the only natural, consumable alkaline waters in Great Britain and are still taken at one of the spa's finest Regency buildings. The Pittville Pump Room is open Sundays from the end of May until the end of September for a host of activities, including lunch, afternoon cream teas, live classical music, landau carriage rides around the city, and brass bands playing in Pittville Park.

East Approach Dr., Pittville Park. *©* **01242/523852.** Free admission. Year-round Wed–Mon 10am–4pm. From the town center, take Portland St. and Evesham Rd.

SHOPPING

The different quarters that make up Cheltenham's shopping district turn shopping into an unusually organized event. Start in the **Montpellier quarter** for individual boutiques and craft and specialty shops. Then, continue to the nearby **Suffolk quarter** to find most of the town's antiques stores.

And an enjoyable short stroll to the **Promenade** takes you by stores featuring attractive clothing and shoes, as well as several bookstores. From the Promenade, take Regent Street to **High Street,** which is mostly pedestrian-only, and you'll find several brand-name department stores in the **Beechwood Shopping Centre.**

The **weekly market** is in the Henrietta Street car park on Thursday. Weather permitting, market is open from 9am to 4pm.

The **Courtyard,** on Montpellier Street in the heart of the Montpellier quarter, has become an award-winning shopping mall that offers a fun blend of shops specializing in unique fashion, furniture, and gift items. A good mix of restaurants, cafes, and wine bars rounds out the mall. **Hoopers** (*©* **01242/527505**) is a quality department store devoted to designer clothes for men and women. It also has a perfumery, hair and beauty salon, and fully air-conditioned restaurant.

Cavendish House, the Promenade (© **01242/521300**), is a long-established shopping landmark, housing two restaurants, a salon, an immense cosmetic and jewelry hall, and departments devoted to fine fashion, housewares, and furniture.

HITTING THE LINKS

Cotswold Hills Golf Club, Ullenwood, Cheltenham (© **01242/515263**), is open year-round. The only requirements at this par-71 golf course are a reasonable standard of play, your own clubs, and no jeans or sneakers. Greens fees on weekdays are £32 ($51) for 18 holes or unlimited play; £37 ($59) for 18 holes or unlimited play on Saturday and Sunday.

Tewkesbury Park Golf and Country Club, Lincoln Green Lane, Tewkesbury, 19km (12 miles) north of Cheltenham (© **01684/295405** or 01684/272320), is a par-73 course requiring a reasonable standard of play, a golf bag, and no jeans, sneakers, or club sharing. Clubs are available for rent for £10 ($16). Greens fees for 18 holes are £15 to £20 ($24–$32) Monday through Thursday and £26 to £32 ($42–$51) Friday through Sunday.

Gloucestershire Golf and Country Club, Matson Lane, Gloucester (© **01452/411331** or 01452/525653), is a par-70 course that requires a reasonable standard of play and disallows jeans and sneakers, though tailored shorts are okay. Eighteen holes costs £16 to £25 ($26–$40) weekdays, and £20 to £30 ($32–$48) Saturday and Sunday.

WHERE TO STAY

The Greenway ★★ An elegant and beautifully furnished former Elizabethan manor house in a garden setting, this is an ivy-clad Cotswold showpiece. Restored with sensitivity, Greenway rents rooms in both its main house and a converted coach house. Bedrooms, midsize to spacious, are rather sumptuously outfitted. Bathrooms have deluxe toiletries, combination tub and shower, and bathrobes. This is the best English country-house living in the area.

Shurdington, near Cheltenham, Gloucestershire GL51 4UG. © 800/543-4135 in the U.S., or 01242/862352. Fax 01242/862780. www.the-greenway.co.uk. 21 units. £140–£240 ($224–$384) double. Rates include English breakfast. AE, DC, MC, V. Take A46 less than 6.5km (4 miles) southwest of Cheltenham. **Amenities:** Restaurant; bar; concierge; car-rental desk; limited room service; laundry service; dry cleaning. *In room:* TV, hair dryer, iron/ironing board.

Hotel de la Bere and Country Club This 16th-century Cotswold-stone building stands near the Cheltenham racecourse and has been owned by the de la Bere family for 3 centuries. They converted it into a hotel in 1972 and have made every effort to ensure that it retains its original charm. All rooms are furnished to preserve their individual character, and 20 rooms have recently been refurbished. Five rooms have double four-poster beds. Bathrooms come with shower-tub combinations.

Southam, Cheltenham, Gloucestershire GL52 3NH. © 01242/545454. Fax 01242/236016. www.regalhotels. co.uk/delabere. 57 units. £110 ($176) double. Half board (2-night minimum required) Mon–Thurs £55 ($88) per person, Fri–Sun £48 ($77) per person. AE, DC, MC, V. Take B4632 5km (3 miles) northeast of town. **Amenities:** Restaurant; bar; outdoor heated pool; 5 tennis courts; health club; sauna; concierge; car-rental desk; room service; laundry service; dry cleaning. *In room:* TV, coffeemaker, hair dryer, trouser press.

Kandinsky ★ This Georgian inn has been dramatically modernized and is today a stylish stopover in this rather staid spa town. Fashionable teak designer furnishings decorate the modern accommodations, which are both tasteful and comfortable with attractive little bathrooms with showers. Large potted plants and a choice of antiques grace the public bedrooms and throw rugs cover many of the floors. The on-site Café Paradiso serves the best antipasti in town, along with other continental offerings; it's like a cool 1950s bar where entertainment is often presented.

Bayshill Rd., Montpellier, Cheltenham, Gloucestershire GL50 3AS. ℭ **01242/527788.** Fax 01242/226412. www.aliaskandinsky.com. 48 units. £89–£115 ($142–$184) double; £150 ($240) suite. AE, DC, MC, V. **Amenities:** Restaurant; bar; cafe/night club. *In room:* TV/VCR, dataports, CD players.

Lawn Hotel Built in 1830 with a stucco exterior, this elegant landmark Regency house lies just inside the iron gates leading to Pittville Park and the Pump Room. Owned by the Millier family, it offers nonsmoking, pleasantly decorated rooms, and is the only vegetarian/vegan hotel in the city. Each room has a small bathroom with a shower stall and adequate shelf space. The hotel is convenient to the town center and its Promenade, about a 10-minute walk away.

5 Pittville Lawn, Cheltenham, Gloucestershire GL52 2BE. ℭ/fax **01242/526638.** 6 units. £108–£158 ($173–$253) double; £158 ($253) suite. Rates include continental breakfast. No credit cards. Bus: 1A, 2A, or 3A. **Amenities:** Restaurant; bar; room service; laundry service. *In room:* TV, coffeemaker, hair dryer.

Lypiatt House ★ *Value* This beautifully restored Victorian home stands in the Montpellier area, the most fashionable part of Cheltenham. A hotel of ambience and character, it offers a large elegant drawing room with a colonial-style conservatory with an "honesty bar." The bedrooms are beautifully furnished and of generous size, each with a well-equipped bathroom with private shower. The friendly owners are the most helpful in town. You might use this B&B as your base for touring the Cotswolds.

Lypiatt Rd., Cheltenham, Gloucestershire GL50 2QW. ℭ **01242/224994.** Fax 01242/224996. www.lypiatt. co.uk. 10 units. £70–£90 ($112–$144) double. Rates include English breakfast. AE, MC, V. **Amenities:** Bar; laundry service. *In room:* TV, coffeemaker.

On the Park ★★ Opened in 1991, in what was formerly an 1830s private villa, this is one of the most talked-about hotels in town. It is located among similar terraced buildings in the once-prominent village of Pittville Spa, 1km (½ mile) north of Cheltenham's town center. Owned and operated by Darryl Gregory, who undertook most of the Regency-inspired interior design, it has received several awards. Each bedroom is named after a prominent 19th-century visitor who came here shortly after the villa was built. Comfortable and high-ceilinged, the rooms have stylish accessories and a tasteful assortment of antique and reproduction furniture. Bedrooms are beautifully appointed, with thoughtful extras such as sherry and mineral water. Bathrooms are laudable and roomy; each has deluxe toiletries and some have Jacuzzis.

Evesham Rd., Cheltenham, Gloucestershire GL52 2AH. ℭ **01242/518898.** Fax 01242/511526. www. hotelonthepark.co.uk. 12 units. £108–£148 ($173–$237) double; from £134–£158 ($214–$253) suite. AE, DC, MC, V. **Amenities:** Restaurant; bar; room service. *In room:* TV, coffeemaker, hair dryer.

WHERE TO DINE

Le Champignon Sauvage ★★★ FRENCH This is among the culinary highlights of the Cotswolds. David Everitt-Matthias, a chef of considerable talent, limits the selection of dishes each evening for better quality control. Some evenings, his imagination roams a bit, so dining here is usually a pleasant surprise. You may begin with light cauliflower soup flavored with cumin. Main courses may include braised lamb dumplings with roasted carrots and shallots. Matthias was recently named dessert chef of the year in England, so be sure to try one of the acclaimed sweet treats. Choices include iced licorice parfait with damson sorbet, and baked caramel cheesecake with caramelized banana.

24–26 Suffolk Rd. (℗ **01242/573449.** Reservations required. 2-course fixed-price lunch £17 ($26); 3-course fixed-price lunch £20 ($32); 2-course fixed-price dinner Tues–Fri £35 ($56); 3-course fixed-price dinner Tues–Fri £42 ($67). AE, DC, MC, V. Tues–Sat 12:30–1:30pm and 7:30–9pm.

Le Petit Blanc ⚘ FRENCH   Already a bit of a dining legend in Oxford, this offspring has invaded Cheltenham and is waking up the sleepy taste buds of the old-fashioned spa. Under the guidance of master chef Raymond Blanc, a local chef, Stephen Nash, is rather inspired in a brasserie mode with brushed steel tables, bench seating, and a hip staff. Knowledgeable and attentive, the staff presents you with beautifully prepared food based on the day's freshest and the best from the market. You might start with something classical, such as Oxford sausages with onion gravy and chips, or something more modern, perhaps salmon niçoise flavored with a mustard and pesto. Superb in every way is the sautéed asparagus with rocket and balsamic dressing. For a main dish, opt for a roast monkfish wrapped in Parma ham and served with pesto noodles that are "divine," in the words of one diner. Save room for the pineapple and kirsch parfait with a thin layer of meringue and a side helping of mango coulis.

In the Queen's Hotel. The Promenade. (℗ **01242/266800.** Reservations required. Main courses £9.95–£16 ($16–$26); fixed-price lunch or dinner £12.50–£15 ($20–$24) for 2 and 3 courses. AE, DC, MC, V. Daily noon–3pm; Mon–Sat 6–10:30pm; Sun 6–10pm.

CHELTENHAM AFTER DARK

The major venue for entertainment is the **Everyman Theatre** (see above), which is the premier sightseeing attraction of Cheltenham. But there's a lot more theater at the **Playhouse,** Bath Road (℗ **01242/522852**), with new local, amateur productions of drama, comedy, dance, and opera being staged at the dizzying pace of every 2 weeks. Tickets are £5 to £10 ($8–$16).

Choose your groove at **Chemistry,** St. James Square (℗ **01242/527700**); open on Monday, Thursday, Friday, and Saturday nights from 9pm to 2am. Cover ranges from £2 to £5 ($3.20–$8) after 10pm, depending on the night.

A SIDE TRIP TO ROYAL SUDELEY CASTLE

Royal Sudeley Castle and Gardens ⚘   This 15th-century structure is one of England's finer stately homes. It has a rich history that begins in Saxon times, when the village was the capital of the Mercian kings. Later, Catherine Parr, the sixth wife of Henry VIII, lived and died here. Her tomb is in a chapel on the grounds, which include a host of formal gardens like the Queen's Garden, now planted with old-world roses and dating to the time of Catherine Parr. While exploring the gardens, you're sure to see the waterfowl and flamboyant peacocks that call Sudeley home. For the past 30 years, Lady Ashcombe, an American by birth, has owned the castle and welcomed visitors from the world over. The castle houses many works of art by Constable, Turner, Rubens, and Van Dyck, among others, and has several permanent exhibitions, magnificent furniture and glass, and many artifacts from the castle's past. In the area to the right of the keep, as you enter the castle, workshops are devoted to talented local artisans who continue to use traditional techniques to produce stained glass, textiles, wood and leather articles, and marbled paper.

In the village of Winchcombe (9.5km/6 miles northeast of Cheltenham). (℗ **01242/602308.** www.sudeley castle.co.uk. Admission £6.70 ($11) adults, £5.50 ($8.80) seniors, £3.70 ($5.90) children 5–15 years, £19 ($30) family ticket. Apr–Oct daily 10:30am–4:30pm. From Cheltenham, take the regular bus to Winchcombe and get off at Abbey Terrace. Then, walk the short distance along the road to the castle. If you're driving, take B4632 north out of Cheltenham, through Prestbury, and up Cleve Hill to Abbey Terrace, where you can drive right up to the castle.

4 Bibury ✷

138km (86 miles) W of London; 48km (30 miles) W of Oxford; 42km (26 miles) E of Gloucester

On the road from Burford to Cirencester, Bibury is one of the loveliest spots in the Cotswolds. In fact, the utopian romancer of Victoria's day, poet William Morris, called it England's most beautiful village. In the Cotswolds, it is matched only by Painswick for its scenic village beauty and purity. Both villages are still unspoiled by modern intrusions.

GETTING THERE
About five trains per day depart London's Paddington Station for the 1-hour-10-minute trip to Kemble, the nearest station, 21km (13 miles) south of Bibury. Some will require an easy change of train in Swindon (the connecting train waits across the tracks). For information, call ✆ **0845/748-4950.** No buses run from Kemble to Bibury, but most hotels will arrange transportation if you ask in advance.

Five buses leave London's Victoria Coach Station daily for Cirencester, 11km (7 miles) from Bibury. For information, call ✆ **0870/580-8080.** With no connecting buses into Bibury, local hotels will send a car, and taxis are available.

If driving from London, take the M4 to Exit 15, head toward Cirencester, then follow the A33 (on some maps this is still designated as the B4425) to Bibury.

EXPLORING THE TOWN
On the banks of the tiny Coln River, Bibury is noted for **Arlington Row,** a group of 17th-century gabled cottages protected by the National Trust. Originally built for weavers, these houses are its biggest and most-photographed attraction, but it's rude to peer into the windows, as many do, because people still live here.

To get a view of something a bit out of the ordinary for the Cotswolds, check out **St. Mary's Parish Church.** As the story goes, the wool merchants who had the power and money in the area were rebuilding the churches. However, they did not finish the restoration to St. Mary's, and, as a result, much of the original Roman-style architecture has been left intact. The 14th-century Decorated-style windows have even survived the years. This is an often-overlooked treasure.

WHERE TO STAY & DINE
Bibury Court Hotel ✷ *Finds*   You can feel the history when you stay at this Jacobean manor house, built by Sir Thomas Sackville in 1633 (parts of it date from Tudor times). Sackville, an illegitimate son of the first Earl of Dorset, launched a family dynasty. His family occupied the house for several generations. Through the female line it passed to the Cresswells, who, eventually, owing to a disputed will and years of litigation, sold the house in the last century to Lord Sherborne. (Charles Dickens is said to have written *Bleak House* with this case in mind.) The house was a residence until it was turned into a hotel in 1968.

You enter the 8 acres of grounds through a large gateway, and the lawn extends to the Coln River. The structure is built of Cotswold stone, with many gables, huge chimneys, and a formal graveled entryway. Many rooms have four-poster beds, original oak paneling, and antiques. Bedrooms are furnished in old English style but have modern comforts, plus bathrooms with a shower-and-tub combination (one has a shower stall instead).

Bibury, Gloucestershire GL7 5NT. ℂ **01285/740337.** Fax 01285/740660. www.biburycourt.co.uk. 18 units. £130–£200 ($208–$320) double; £200 ($320) suite. Rates include continental breakfast and VAT. AE, DC, MC, V. **Amenities:** 2 restaurants; bar; room service; croquet lawn. *In room:* TV, coffeemaker, hair dryer, iron.

The Swan ★★ Well managed, upscale, and discreet, this hotel and restaurant is the finest in the village. It originated as a riverside cottage in the 1300s, was greatly expanded throughout the centuries, and received its latest enlargement and refurbishment in the early 1990s. Owners Alex and Liz Furtek outfitted parts of the interior in a cozily overstuffed mode reminiscent of the World War II era. There's an elegant bar and wood-burning fireplaces. An automatic *pianola* (player piano) provides music in the lobby. The bedrooms are outfitted with antique furniture and an individualized decor. Each contains an elegant bed— some are four-posters—with soft linens and a beautifully maintained bathroom with bathrobes and deluxe toiletries. Some bathrooms have Jacuzzi tubs. One accommodation is large enough for a family.

Bibury, Gloucestershire GL7 5NW. ℂ **01285/740695.** Fax 01285/740473. www.swanhotel.co.uk. 20 units. £180–£260 ($288–$416) double. Rates include English breakfast. AE, MC, V. **Amenities:** 2 restaurants; bar; room service; laundry service. *In room:* TV, hair dryer, coffeemaker, iron, trouser press.

5 Burford ⌒

122km (76 miles) NW of London; 32km (20 miles) W of Oxford

Built of Cotswold stone and serving as a gateway to the area, the unspoiled medieval town of Burford is largely famous for its Norman church (ca. 1116) and its High Street lined with coaching inns. Burford was one of the last of the great wool centers, the industry bleating out its last breath during Queen Victoria's day. Be sure to photograph the bridge across the Windrush River where Queen Elizabeth I once stood. As the antiques shops along High Street will testify, Burford today is definitely equipped for tourists.

The River Windrush, which toward Burford is flanked by willows through meadows, passes beneath the packhorse bridge and goes around the church and away through more meadows. Strolling along its banks is one of the most delightful experiences in the Cotswolds.

ESSENTIALS
GETTING THERE Many trains depart from London's Paddington Station to Oxford, a 45-minute trip. For information, call ℂ **0845/748-4950.** From Oxford, passengers walk a short distance to the entrance of the Taylor Institute, from which about three or four buses per day make the 30-minute run to Burford.

A **National Express** bus runs from London's Victoria Coach Station to Burford several times a day, with many stops along the way. It's a 2-hour ride. For schedules and information, call ℂ **020/7529-2000.**

If you're driving from Oxford, head west on the A40 to Burford.

VISITOR INFORMATION The **Tourist Information Centre** is at the Old Brewery on Sheep Street (ℂ **01993/823558**) and is open November through February, Monday through Saturday from 10am to 4:30pm; and March and April and in October, Monday through Saturday from 9:30am to 5:30pm; May through September Sunday from 10:30am to 3pm.

SEEING THE SIGHTS

Approaching Burford from the south, you'll experience one of the finest views of any ancient market town in the country. The main street sweeps down to the River Windrush, past an extraordinary collection of houses of various styles and ages. Burford's ancient packhorse bridge is still doing duty at the bottom of the hill. The hills opposite provide a frame of fields and trees and, with luck, panoramic skies.

Although the wool trade has long since vanished, most of Burford remains unchanged in appearance, with its old houses in the High Street and nearby side streets. Nearly all are built of local stone. Like many Cotswold towns, Burford has a Sheep Street, with many fine stone-built houses covered with roofs of Stonesfield slate. Burford Church (ca. 1175) is almost cathedral-like in proportion. It was enlarged throughout succeeding centuries until the decline of the wool trade. Little has changed here since about 1500.

Traders and vendors still set up their stalls under the Tolsey on Friday, where from the 12th century the guild has collected tolls from anyone wishing to trade in the town. It still stands at the corner of Sheep Street. On the upper floor is the minor Tolsey Museum, where you can see a medieval seal bearing Burford's insignia, the "rampant cat."

Three kilometers (2 miles) south of Burford on A361 lies the **Cotswold Wildlife Park** (© **01993/823006**). The 120 acres of gardens and forests around this Victorian manor house have been transformed into a jungle of sorts, with a Noah's Ark consortium of animals ranging from voracious ants to rare Asiatic lions. Children can romp around the farmyard and the adventure playground. A narrow-gauge railway runs from April to October, and there are extensive picnic areas plus a cafeteria. Hours are Easter through September daily from 10am to 7pm; off season daily from 10am to 5pm. Admission is £7.50 ($12) for adults, £5 ($8) for seniors and children 3 to 16, and free for children 2 and under.

And before you leave Burford, we suggest a slight detour to **Swinbrook,** a pretty village by the Windrush River immediately to the east. It's best known as the one-time home of the fabled Mitford sisters. Visit the local parish church to see the grave of writer Nancy Mitford and the impressive tiered monuments to the Fettiplace family.

On High Street in Burford, you'll find several antiques shops, including **Manfred Schotten Antiques,** The Crypt, 109 High St. (© **01993/822302**). Sporting antiques and collectibles, they also carry library and club furniture. **Jonathan Fyson Antiques,** 50–52 High St. (© **01993/823204**), carries English and continental furniture and porcelain, glass, and brass items. On Cheltenham Road, **Gateway Antiques** (© **01993/823678**) has a variety of items displayed in large showrooms. English pottery, metalware, and furniture dominate the inventory. Unique arts and crafts items and interesting decorative objects are fun to browse through, even if you don't buy.

WHERE TO STAY

Bay Tree Hotel ★★   This is the best and most atmospheric of Burford's many interesting old inns. The house was built for Sir Lawrence Tanfield, the unpopular lord chief baron of the Exchequer to Elizabeth I. The house has oak-paneled rooms with stone fireplaces, and a high-beamed hall with a minstrel's gallery. Twentieth-century comforts have been discreetly installed in the tastefully furnished rooms, some of which have four-poster beds. Some of the accommodations are in a comfortable annex, though the chambers in the main building—nine in all—have more character. Try to get a room overlooking the terraced gardens at the rear of the house. Each unit comes with a midsize bathroom, often with both tub and shower.

12–14 Sheep St., Burford, Oxfordshire OX18 4LW. © **01993/822791.** Fax 01993/823008. www.cotswold-inns-hotels.co.uk. 21 units. £155–£195 ($248–$312) double; £205–£270 ($328–$432) suite. Rates include English breakfast. AE, DC, MC, V. **Amenities:** Restaurant; bar; room service; babysitting; laundry service; dry cleaning. *In room:* TV, coffeemaker, hair dryer, trouser press.

Golden Pheasant Hotel ⭐   This inn is housed in what was once the 15th-century home of a prosperous wool merchant. It began serving food and drink in the 1730s when it was used both to brew and serve beer. Today, it's one of the best places to stay in town (though it lacks the rich furnishings of the best, the Bay Tree Hotel). Like many of its neighbors, the Golden Pheasant is capped with a slate roof and fronted with hand-chiseled stones. The cozy accommodations come in a range of sizes, many a bit small, and one room has a four-poster bed. Each, though, is stylishly appointed with period furniture. One room is large enough for a family; all but one come with a shower-and-tub combination (one has a shower stall).

91 High St., Burford, Oxfordshire OX18 4QA. © **01993/823223.** Fax 01993/822621. 12 units. £95–£100 ($152–$160) double. Rates include English breakfast. AE, MC, V. **Amenities:** Restaurant; bar. *In room:* TV, coffeemaker, hair dryer, iron, trouser press.

The Lamb Inn ⭐⭐   This thoroughly Cotswold house solidly built in 1430 offers thick stones, mullioned and leaded windows, many chimneys and gables, and a slate roof now mossy with age. Vying with the Bay Tree in antique furnishings, it opens onto a stone-paved rear garden, with a rose-lined walk and a shaded lawn. The bedrooms are a mixture of today's comforts and antiques. Rooms vary in size, and most have a compact bathroom with a tub-and-shower combination (one has a shower stall). The public living rooms have heavy oak beams, stone floors, window seats, Oriental rugs, and fine antiques.

Sheep St., Burford, Oxfordshire OX18 4LR. © **01993/823155.** Fax 01993/822228. 15 units. £125–£160 ($200–$256) double. Rates include English breakfast. MC, V. **Amenities:** Restaurant; bar; room service; laundry service. *In room:* TV, hair dryer.

WHERE TO DINE

After you've browsed through the antiques shops, head to **Burford House** (© **01993/823151**) for tea. This old Cotswold favorite serves daily from 8am to 5pm. Freshly baked goods, including flans, scones, cakes, and muffins, will tempt you.

Lamb Inn Restaurant ENGLISH/CONTINENTAL   A meal in this pretty pillared restaurant is the perfect way to cap off a visit to Burford. Good pub lunches dominate the agenda at midday; dinners are formal, candlelit affairs. The evening menu is beautifully cooked and served. You may begin with cream of broccoli and blue cheese soup before moving on to rack of lamb with parsnip, sage, and a port sauce, or medallions of venison with sautéed red cabbage and a beetroot coriander sauce. The pub here attracts folks from all walks of life. They seem to adore its mellow atmosphere and charm. Guinness, cider, and a carefully chosen collection of ales, including a local brew, Wadworth, are on tap.

Sheep St. © **01993/823155.** Reservations recommended for dinner. 2-course fixed-price menu £24.50 ($39); 3-course fixed-price menu £29.50 ($47); Sun lunch £22 ($35). MC, V. Mon–Sat noon–2pm; Sun 12:45–1:30pm; daily 7–9pm.

6 Bourton-on-the-Water ⭐

137km (85 miles) NW of London; 58km (36 miles) NW of Oxford

Its fans define it as the quintessential Cotswold village, with a history going back to the Celts. Residents fiercely protect the heritage of 15th- and 16th-century architecture, even though their town is singled out for practically every bus tour that rolls through the Cotswolds. Populated in Anglo-Saxon times, Burton-on-the-Water developed into a strategic outpost along the ancient Roman road, Fosse Way, that traversed Britain from the North Sea to St. George's Channel. During the Middle Ages, its prosperity came from wool, which was shipped all over Europe. During the Industrial Revolution when the greatest profits lay in finished textiles, it became a backwater as a producer of raw wool—albeit with the happy result (for us) that it was never "modernized," and its traditional appearance was preserved.

You'll feel like Gulliver traveling to Lilliput when you arrive in this scenic Cotswold village on the banks of the Windrush River. Its mellow stone houses, its village greens on the banks of the water, and its bridges have earned it the title of "Venice of the Cotswolds." Don't expect gondoliers, however. This makes a good stopover, if not for the night, at least as a place to enjoy a lunch and a rest along the riverbanks. Afterward, you can take a peek inside St. Lawrence's Church in the center of the village. Built on the site of a Roman temple, it has a crypt from 1120 and a tower dating back to 1784.

GETTING THERE

Trains run from London's Paddington Station to nearby Moreton-in-Marsh, a trip of 2 hours. For schedules and information, call ✆ **0845/748-4950.** From here, take a Pulhams Bus Company coach 6 miles to Bourton-on-the-Water. Trains also run from London to Cheltenham and Kingham; while somewhat more distant than Moreton-in-Marsh, both have bus connections to Bourton-on-the-Water.

National Express buses run from Victoria Coach Station in London to both Cheltenham and Stow-on-the-Wold. For schedules and information, call ✆ **020/7529-2000.** Pulhams Bus Company operates about four buses per day from both towns to Bourton-on-the-Water.

If you're driving from Oxford, head west on A40 to the junction with A429 (Fosse Way). Take it northeast to Bourton-on-the-Water.

LILLIPUT, THE BIRDS, VINTAGE CARS & MORE

Within the town are a handful of minor museums, each of which was established from idiosyncratic collections amassed over the years by local residents. They include the **Bourton Model Railway Exhibition and Toy Shop** (✆ **01451/820686**) and **Birdland,** described below.

After you've seen them, stop by the quaint little tearoom called **Small Talk,** on High Street (✆ **01451/821596**). It's full of dainty lace and fine china and appetizing scones and pastries. Sit at a table overlooking the water and enjoy a pot of tea and some good conversation.

Birdland   This handsomely designed attraction sits on 8½ acres of field and forests on the banks of River Windrush, about a mile east of Bourton-on-the-Water. It houses about 1,200 birds representing 361 species, many on exhibition for the first time. Included is the largest and most varied collection of penguins in any zoo, with glass-walled tanks that allow observers to appreciate their agile underwater movements. There's also an enviable collection of hummingbirds. Birdland has a picnic area and a children's playground in a wooded copse.

Rissington Rd. ℭ **01451/820480.** Admission £4.60 ($6.90) adults, £3.60 ($5.40) seniors, £2.60 ($4.15) children 4–14, £13 ($21) family ticket, free for children under 4. Apr–Oct daily 10am–6pm; Nov–Mar daily 10am–4pm.

Cotswold Motor Museum   This museum is actually in a historic water mill from the 1700s. It has fun displays of cars, bikes, caravans from the 1920s, toys, and the largest collection of advertising signs in Europe. Visitors can also see village shops from the past.

The Old Mill. ℭ **01451/821255.** Admission £2.50 ($4) adults, £1.75 ($2.80) children. Feb–Nov daily 10am–6pm.

Cotswold Perfumery   This permanent perfume exhibition details the history of the perfume industry and also focuses on its production. You'll find an audiovisual show in a "smelly vision" theater, a perfume quiz, a perfume garden full of plants grown exclusively for their fragrance, and a genealogy chart that can be used by visitors to select their own personal perfume. Perfumes are made on the premises and sold in the shop.

Victoria St. ℭ **01451/820698.** Admission £2 ($3.20) adults, £1.75 ($2.80) children and seniors. Mon–Sat 9:30am–5pm; Sun 10:30am–5pm. Closed Dec 25–26.

The Model Village at the Old New Inn   Beginning in the 1930s, a local hotelier, Mr. Morris, whiled away some of the doldrums of the Great Depression by constructing a scale model (1:9) of Bourton-on-the-Water as a testimony to its architectural charms. This isn't a tiny and cramped display set behind glass—the model is big enough that you can walk through this near-perfect and most realistic model village.

High St. ℭ **01451/820467.** Admission £2.75 ($4.40) adults, £2.50 ($4) seniors, £2 ($3.20) children. Daily 9am–6pm or dusk in summer; daily 10am–4pm in winter.

WHERE TO STAY & DINE

Chester House Hotel   This 300-year-old Cotswold-stone house, built on the banks of the Windrush River, is conveniently located in the center of town. The main building and its adjoining row of stables were converted into this comfortable hotel; the stables were completely renovated and turned into small to midsize bedrooms. Bathrooms are small and compact but with adequate shelf space; most of them have a tub-and-shower combination.

Victoria St., Bourton-on-the-Water, Cheltenham, Gloucestershire GL54 2BU. ℭ **01451/820286.** Fax 01451/820471. 22 units. £59–£100 ($94–$160) double. Rates include continental or English breakfast. AE, DC, MC, V. Closed mid-Dec to early Feb. **Amenities:** 2 restaurants; 2 bars; room service; laundry service; dry cleaning. *In room:* TV, coffeemaker.

Dial House Hotel ✮   Our top choice in town, this 1698 house is constructed from yellow Cotswold stone and stands in the heart of the village center. Mr. and Mrs. Adrian Campbell-Howard, your hosts, offer not only a nostalgic retreat but some of the best cuisine in the area.

Set on 1½ acres of manicured gardens, the house overlooks the River Windrush. Each room has an individual character, and some boast four-poster beds. Two of the rooms, as charming as those in the main building, are in a converted coach house. All rooms have well-kept bathrooms with shower units and Penhaligons toiletries.

Moments The Great Cotswold Ramble

A walking tour between the villages of Upper and Lower Slaughter, with an optional extension to Bourton-on-the-Water, is one of the most memorable in England. A mile each way between the Slaughters, or 4km (2½ miles) from Upper Slaughter to Bourton-on-the-Water, the walk can take 2 to 4 hours.

The architecture of Upper and Lower Slaughter is so unusual that you're likely to remember this easy hike for many years. You'll also avoid some of the traffic that taxes the nerves and goodwill of local residents during peak season. En route, you're likely to glimpse the waterfowl that inhabit the rivers, streams, and millponds that criss-cross this much-praised region.

A well-worn footpath known as **Warden's Way** meanders beside the edge of the swift-moving River Eye. From its well-marked beginning in Upper Slaughter's central car park, the path passes sheep grazing in meadows, antique houses crafted from local honey-colored stone, stately trees arching over ancient millponds, and footbridges that have endured centuries of foot traffic and rain.

The rushing river powers a historic mill on the northwestern edge of Lower Slaughter. In quiet eddies, you'll see ample numbers of water-fowl and birds, such as wild ducks, gray wagtails, mute swans, coots, and Canada geese.

Most visitors turn around at Lower Slaughter, but Warden's Way continues another 2.5km (1½ miles) to Bourton-on-the-Water by fol-lowing the Fosse Way, route of an ancient Roman footpath. Most of it, from Lower Slaughter to Bourton-on-the-Water, is covered by tarmac; it's closed to cars, but ideal for walking or biking. You're legally required to close each of the several gates that stretch across the footpath.

Warden's Way will introduce you to Bourton-on-the-Water through the hamlet's northern edges. The first landmark you'll see will be the tower of St. Lawrence's Anglican Church. From the base of the church, walk south along The Avenue (one of the hamlet's main streets) and end your Cotswold ramble on the Village Green, directly in front of the War Memorial.

You can follow this route in reverse, but parking is more plentiful in Upper Slaughter than in Lower Slaughter.

Log fires burn on chilly nights, and there are two small dining rooms, one with an inglenook fireplace. Under oak beams and on flagstone floors, candlelit dinners consist of modern British fare, the best local game, and fish. Try pink salmon fish cakes with a pink champagne sauce or medallions of pork with a pis-tachio and apricot stuffing. Nonresidents can dine here but should call first for a reservation.

The Chestnuts, High St., Bourton-on-the-Water, Gloucestershire GL54 2AN. © 01451/822244. Fax 01451/810126. www.dialhousehotel.com. 14 units. £110–£150 ($176–$240) double. Rates include English break-fast. MC, V. **Amenities:** 2 restaurants; bar; limited room service; croquet lawn. *In room:* TV, coffeemaker, hair dryer.

The Old Manse Hotel ★ (Finds) An architectural gem, this hotel sits in the center of town by the river that wanders through the village green. Built of Cotswold stone in 1748, with chimneys, dormers, and small-paned windows, it has been modernized inside. Rooms are midsize and cozy, like those you'd find in your favorite great aunt's home. Small shower bathrooms have adequate shelf space.

Victoria St., Bourton-on-the-Water, Cheltenham, Gloucestershire GL54 2BX. © **01451/820082.** Fax 01451/ 810381. 15 units. £100–£130 ($160–$208) double. Rates include English breakfast. AE, MC, V. **Amenities:** Restaurant; bar; room service; laundry service; dry cleaning. In room: TV, coffeemaker, hair dryer, iron, trouser press.

Old New Inn The Old New Inn is a landmark in the village. On the main street, overlooking the river, it's a good example of Queen Anne design (the miniature model village in its garden is reviewed above). Hungry or tired travelers are drawn to old-fashioned comforts and cuisine of this most English inn. Rooms are comfortable, with homey furnishings and soft beds. Some rooms are spacious, especially if they have a four-poster bed, but most are small and lie in a cottage annex. Bathrooms have shower stalls and adequate shelf space.

High St., Bourton-on-the-Water, Cheltenham, Gloucestershire GL54 2AF. © **01451/820467.** Fax 01451/ 810236. www.theoldnewinn.co.uk. 9 units. £76 ($122) double. Rates include English breakfast. MC, V. **Amenities:** Restaurant; 3 bars; laundry service; dry cleaning. In room: TV, minibar, hair dryer, coffeemaker.

7 Upper & Lower Slaughter

Midway between Bourton-on-the-Water and Stow-on-the-Wold are two of the prettiest villages in the Cotswolds: Upper and Lower Slaughter. Don't be put off by the name—"Slaughter" is actually a corruption of *de Sclotre,* the name of the original Norman landowner. Houses here are constructed of honey-colored Cotswold stone, and a stream meanders right through the street, providing a home for free-wandering ducks, which beg scraps from kindly passersby. Upper Slaughter has a fine example of a 17th-century Cotswold manor house.

The **Old Mill,** in Lower Slaughter (© **01451/820052**), is a sturdy 19th-century stone structure built on the River Eye with the sole purpose of grinding out flour. The river still turns the massive water wheel that powers this Victorian flour mill today. Visitors can enjoy an ice-cream parlor and tearoom while visiting the mill.

GETTING THERE

Lower Slaughter and Stow-on-the-Wold are 6.4km (4 miles) apart. From Stow, take A429 (the Main Fosse Way) and follow signs to Cirencester and Bourton-on-the-Water. Turn off the highway when you see signs to Upper and Lower Slaughter. The road will then divide, and you can pick which hamlet you want to head to.

WHERE TO STAY & DINE

Lords of the Manor Hotel ★★★ A 17th-century house set on several acres of rolling fields, the Lords of the Manor offers gardens with a stream featuring brown trout. A quintessentially British hotel of great style and amenities, it's a showplace. It may be modernized, but it successfully maintains the quiet country-house atmosphere of 300 years ago. Half the rooms are in a converted old barn and granary, and many have lovely views. Each has a high standard of comfort and elegant beds with sumptuous linens. The deluxe bathrooms are well appointed.

Upper Slaughter, near Cheltenham, Gloucestershire GL54 2JD. © 01451/820243. Fax 01451/820696. www.lordsofthemanor.com. 27 units. £149–£199 ($238–$318) standard double; £299–£349 ($478–$558) old rectory bedrooms; £249–£399 ($398–$638) suite. AE, DC, MC, V. Take A429 29km (18 miles) north of Cheltenham. **Amenities:** Restaurant; bar; limited room service; babysitting; laundry service. *In room:* TV, minibar, hair dryer, safe.

Lower Slaughter Manor ★★★   This hotel dates from 1658 when it was owned by Sir George Whitmore, high sheriff of Gloucestershire. It remained in the same family until 1964 when it was sold as a private residence. Today, it's one of the great inns of the Cotswolds, though its charms are matched in every way by Lords of the Manor. Standing on its own private grounds, it has spacious and sumptuously furnished rooms, some with four-poster beds. Bedrooms in the main building have more old English character, although those in the annex are equally comfortable and include the same luxuries. Each room is equipped with a beautifully maintained bathroom; some have tubs with separate shower units and twin sinks, the rest have tub-and-shower combinations.

Lower Slaughter, near Cheltenham, Gloucestershire GL54 2HP. © 01451/820456. Fax 01451/822150. www.lowerslaughter.co.uk. 16 units. £220–£395 ($352–$632) double. Rates include English breakfast. AE, DC, MC, V. Take A429 turnoff at the sign for The Slaughters, and drive 1km (½ mile); manor is on right as you enter the village. No children under 12. **Amenities:** Restaurant; lounge; tennis court; room service; laundry service; dry cleaning. *In room:* TV, hair dryer.

8 Stow-on-the-Wold ✦

14km (9 miles) SE of Broadway; 16km (10 miles) S of Chipping Campden; 6.5km (4 miles) S of Moreton-in-Marsh; 34km (21 miles) S of Stratford-upon-Avon

As you pass along through Shakespeare's "high wild hills and rough uneven ways," you arrive at Stow-on-the-Wold, its very name evoking the elusive spirit of the Cotswolds, one of the greatest sheep-rearing districts of England. Lying 240m (800 ft.) above sea level, it stands on a plateau where "the cold winds blow," or so goes the old saying. This town prospered when Cotswold wool was demanded the world over. Stow-on-the-Wold may not be the cognoscenti's favorite—Chipping Campden takes that honor—but it's even more delightful as it has a real Cotswold town atmosphere.

The town lies smack in the middle of the Fosse Way, one of the Roman trunk roads that cut a swath through Britain. Kings have passed through here, including Edward VI, son of Henry VIII, and they've bestowed their approval on the town. Stagecoaches stopped off here for the night on their way to Cheltenham.

A 14th-century cross stands in the large Market Square, where you can still see the stocks where "offenders" in the past were jeered at and punished by the townspeople who threw rotten eggs at them. The final battle between the Roundheads and the Royalists took place outside Stow-on-the-Wold, and mean old Cromwell incarcerated 1,500 Royalist troops in St. Edward's Market Square.

The square today teems with pubs and outdoor cafes. But leave the square at some point and wander at leisure along some of the narrowest alleyways in Britain. When the summer crowds get you down, head in almost any direction from Stow to surrounding villages that look like sets from a Merchant and Ivory film.

ESSENTIALS
GETTING THERE   Several trains run daily from London's Paddington Station to Moreton-in-Marsh (see below). For schedules and information, call © 0845/748-4950. From Moreton-in-Marsh, Pulhams Bus Company makes the 10-minute ride to Stow-on-the-Wold.

National Express buses also run daily from London's Victoria Coach Station to Moreton-in-Marsh, where you can catch a Pulhams Bus Company coach to Stow-on-the-Wold. For schedules and information, call ✆ **020/7529-2000.** Several Pulhams coaches also run daily to Stow-on-the-Wold from Cheltenham.

If driving from Oxford, take the A40 west to the junction with the A424, near Burford. Head northwest along the A424 to Stow-on-the-Wold.

VISITOR INFORMATION The **Tourist Information Centre** is at Hollis House, The Square (✆ **01451/831082**). It's open Easter through October, Monday through Saturday from 9:30am to 5:30pm, Sunday from 9am to 5pm; from November to mid-February, Monday through Saturday from 9:30am to 4:30pm; and from mid-February to Easter, Monday through Saturday from 9:30am to 5pm.

ANTIQUES HEAVEN

Don't be fooled by the village's sleepy, country-bucolic setting: Stow-on-the-Wold has developed over the last 20 years into the antiques-buyer's highlight of Britain and has at least 60 merchandisers scattered throughout the village and its environs.

Set within four show rooms inside an 18th-century building on the town's main square, **Anthony Preston Antiques, Ltd.,** The Square (✆ **01451/831586**), specializes in English and French furniture, including some very large pieces, such as bookcases, and decorative objects that include paperweights, lamps, paintings on silk, and small objects designed to add a glossy accent to carefully contrived interior decors.

Located on Church Street, **Baggott Church Street, Ltd.** (✆ **01451/830370**), is the smaller, and perhaps more intricately decorated, of two shops founded and maintained by a well-regarded local antiques merchant, Duncan ("Jack") Baggott, a frequent denizen at estate sales of country houses throughout Britain. The shop contains four show rooms loaded with furniture and paintings from the 17th to the 19th centuries.

More eclectic and wide-ranging is Baggott's second shop, **Woolcomber House,** on Sheep Street (✆ **01451/830662**). Among the largest retail outlets in the Cotswolds, it contains about 17 rooms that during the 16th century functioned as a coaching inn, but today are lavishly decorated, each according to a particular era of English decorative history.

Covering about ½ block in the heart of town, **Huntington's Antiques Ltd.,** Church Street (✆ **01451/830842**), contains one of the largest stocks of quality antiques in England. Wander at will through 10 ground-floor rooms, then climb to the second floor where a long gallery and a quartet of additional show rooms bulge with refectory tables, unusual cupboards, and all kinds of finds.

WHERE TO STAY & DINE

Fosse Manor Hotel Though lacking the charm of the Grapevine (see below), Fosse Manor is at least the second best in town, even more inviting than the Stow Lodge. The hotel lies near the site of an ancient Roman road that used to bisect England. Its stone walls and neo-Gothic gables are almost concealed by strands of ivy. From some of the high stone-sided windows, you can enjoy a view of a landscaped garden with a sunken lily pond and old-fashioned sundial. Inside, the interior is conservatively modern, with homey bedrooms. Some are large enough for a family; others have a four-poster bed. Six bedrooms, equal in comfort to the main building, are located in a converted coach house on the grounds. Bathrooms are small but well organized, most with a shower-tub combination.

Fosse Way, Stow-on-the-Wold, Cheltenham, Gloucestershire GL54 1JX. © **01451/830354.** Fax 01451/ 832486. www.fossemanor.co.uk. 22 units. £61 ($98) per person per night double. Rates include English breakfast. Half board £78 ($125) per person per night. Children under 10 stay free when sharing with paying adult. AE, MC, V. Take A429 2km (1¼ miles) south of Stow-on-the-Wold. **Amenities:** Restaurant; bar; room service; babysitting; laundry service; dry cleaning. In room: TV, coffeemaker, hair dryer, trouser press.

The Grapevine Hotel ★ Value
Facing the village green, The Grapevine mixes urban sophistication with reasonable prices, rural charm, and intimacy. It's the best inn in town, although it doesn't have the charm and grace of Wyck Hill House on the outskirts (see below). It was named after the ancient vine whose tendrils shade and shelter the beautiful conservatory restaurant. Many of the bedrooms have recently been redecorated, and each varies in size—some quite small—but comfort is the keynote here. Ten rooms are in a comfortably appointed annex and lack the character of the rooms in the main building. Some rooms offer four-poster beds. Each unit comes with a small bathroom, most with a tub-and-shower combination.

Sheep St., Stow-on-the-Wold, Cheltenham, Gloucestershire GL54 1AU. © **800/528-1234** in the U.S. and Canada, or 01451/830344. Fax 01451/832278. www.vines.co.uk. 22 units. £130–£150 ($208–$240) per person. Rates include breakfast. "Bargain Breaks" (2-night minimum): £160–£180 ($256–$288) per person, including half board. AE, DC, MC, V. Free parking. **Amenities:** Restaurant; bar; room service; laundry service; dry cleaning. In room: TV, coffeemaker, hair dryer.

Stow Lodge Hotel
Stow Lodge dominates the marketplace but is set back far enough to avoid too much noise. Its gardens, honeysuckle growing over the stone walls, diamond-shaped windows, gables, and many chimneys capture the best of country living, even though you're right in the heart of town. The ample, well-furnished rooms vary in size; one has a four-poster bed. The main building has more character, though some equally comfortable rooms are in a converted coach house (most on the ground floor). Room nos. 17 and 18—the smallest in the hotel—share a private bathroom. Bathrooms are small but adequate. Children under 5 are not welcome.

The Square, Stow-on-the-Wold, Cheltenham, Gloucestershire GL54 1AB. © **01451/830485.** Fax 01451/ 831671. www.stowlodge.com. 21 units. £98–£115 ($157–$184) double. 2-night minimum stay on Sat-Sun. Rates include English breakfast. MC, V. **Amenities:** Restaurant; bar; room service; laundry service. In room: TV, coffeemaker, hair dryer.

Wyck Hill House ★★★
This is sleepy old Stow's pocket of posh. Parts of this otherwise Victorian country house on 100 acres of grounds and gardens date from 1720, when its stone walls were first erected. It was discovered in the course of recent restoration that one wing of the manor house rests on the foundations of a Roman villa. Today, it is the showcase country inn of this area. The opulent interior adheres to 18th-century authenticity with room after room leading to paneled libraries and Adam sitting rooms. The well-furnished bedrooms are in the main hotel, in the coach-house annex, or in the orangery. Some rooms offer four-poster beds and views of the surrounding countryside. Bathrooms are state of the art; some have Jacuzzi tubs with separate showers.

Burford Rd., Stow-on-the-Wold, Cheltenham, Gloucestershire GL54 1HY. © **01451/831936.** Fax 01451/ 832243. www.wrensgroup.com. 32 units. £85–£135 ($136–$216) per person double; £135 ($216) per person suite. Children under 12 are charged £30 per night when sharing their parent's room. Rates include English breakfast. AE, MC, V. Drive 4km (2½ miles) south of Stow-on-the-Wold on A424. **Amenities:** Restaurant; bar; room service; laundry service; croquet lawn. In room: TV, coffeemaker, hair dryer, trouser press.

9 Moreton-in-Marsh ⟨★

134km (83 miles) NW of London; 6.5km (4 miles) N of Stow-on-the-Wold; 11km (7 miles) S of Chipping Campden; 27km (17 miles) S of Stratford-upon-Avon

This is no swampland as the name implies. Marsh derives from an old word meaning "border," so you won't be wading through wetlands to get here. Moreton is a real Cotswold market town that is at its most bustling on Tuesday morning when farmers and craftspeople who live in the surrounding area flood the town to sell their wares and produce. Some of the scenes that take place then are evocative of the classic film, *Brigadoon.*

An important stopover along the old Roman road, Fosse Way, as well as an important layover for the night for stagecoach passengers, Moreton-in-Marsh has one of the widest High streets in the Cotswolds. Roman legions trudged through here centuries ago, but today visitors and antiques shops have replaced them.

The town is still filled with records of its past, including a Market Hall on High Street, built in Victorian Tudor style in 1887, and Curfew Tower on Oxford Street dating from the 17th century. Its bell was rung daily until the late 19th century.

For a fascinating lesson on birds of prey, stop by the **Cotswold Falconry Centre,** Batsford Park (② **01386/701043**). These great birds are flown daily by experienced falconers for visitors to see firsthand the remarkable speed and agility of eagles, hawks, owls, and falcons. It's open daily from February 15 to November 30 from 10:30am to 5pm. Flying displays are daily at 11:30am, 1:30, 3, and 4:30pm. Admission is £4 ($6.40) for adults and £2.50 ($4) for children 4 to 14 (free for kids 3 and under).

GETTING THERE

Trains run from London's Paddington Station to Moreton-in-Marsh, a nearly 2-hour trip. For schedules and information, call ② **0845/748-4950.**

National Express buses run from London's Victoria Coach Station to Moreton-in-Marsh daily. For schedules and information, call ② **020/7529-2000.**

If you're driving from Stow-on-the-Wold (see above), take the A429 north.

WHERE TO STAY

Bell Inn ⟨*Value* This is a coaching inn from the 1700s. It has been well restored and is now a traditional and welcoming Cotswold inn for those desiring both a meal and a bed for the night. In summer guests can enjoy a pint or two in the old courtyard or join the locals in the large bar. Even if you're passing through Moreton just for the day, the bar is ideal for filling, affordable English food. Their specialty is a traditional ploughman's lunch with English Stilton and home-cooked ham, along with a chicken-liver-and-wild-mushroom paté, crusty bread, a salad, a pickle, and an apple, all at £4.95 ($7.90). Under beamed ceilings, bedrooms are comfortably and tastefully furnished in an old English styling, each with a small bathroom with shower. *Note:* The hotel publicizes that it caters to those with disabilities and while there are no entrance ramps, the entrance door is wide and there are some specially equipped bathrooms.

High St., Moreton-in-Marsh, Gloucestershire GL56 0AE. ② **01608/651688.** Fax 01608/652195. www. bellinncotswold.com. 5 units. £85 ($136) double; £90 ($144) for 3. Rates include English breakfast. **Amenities:** Restaurant; pub. *In room:* TV, beverage maker, no phone.

The Falkland Arms ⟨★ ⟨*Finds* Immerse yourself in ye olde England with a meal or an overnight at this historic Cotswold village dating back to the 1500s when it was known as the Hore & Groom. Many English inns claim to be "unspoiled," but this mellow old place actually is. You can smoke a clay pipe here, as many of the regulars do, and even purchase snuff as in olden days. The timeworn pub has the most awesome collection of jugs and mugs in the area, and they're displayed hanging from the oak beams. The original settle along with flagstone floors and an inglenook fireplace make this a warm, inviting place—that and the extensive range of malt whiskies. An on-site restaurant (reservations essential) offers an imaginative menu daily based on market-fresh ingredients.

A spiral stone staircase leads to the cozy accommodations, with brass steads and white covers. Rooms are beautifully furnished and look out over the countryside and the village green. Each comes with a well-kept bathroom with shower.

Great Tew, Oxfordshire OX7 4DB. (© **01608/683653**. www.falklandarms.org.uk. 6 units. £65 ($104) double. Rates include breakfast. AE, MC, V. Lies 7.4km (12 miles) east of Moreton-in-Marsh. Take A44 to Chipping Norton, then follow A361 to B4022. **Amenities:** Restaurant; pub. *In room:* No phone.

Manor House Hotel ⭐
The town's best hotel, the Manor House comes complete with its own ghost, a secret passage, and a moot room used centuries ago by local merchants to settle arguments over wool exchanges. On the main street, it's a formal yet gracious house, and its rear portions reveal varying architectural periods of design. Inside are many living rooms, one especially intimate with leather chairs and a fireplace-within-a-fireplace, ideal for drinks and swapping "bump-in-the-night" stories. The cozy rooms are tastefully furnished, often with antiques or fine reproductions. Many have fine old desks set in front of window ledges, with a view of the garden and ornamental pond.

High St., Moreton-in-Marsh, Gloucestershire GL56 0LJ. (© **01608/650501**. Fax 01608/651481. www. cotswold-inns-hotels.co.uk. 38 units, 1 family suite. £125–£170 ($200–$272) double; £170–£215 ($272–$344) suite. Rates include English breakfast. AE, MC, V. **Amenities:** Restaurant; bar; indoor pool; Jacuzzi; room service; babysitting; laundry service; dry cleaning. *In room:* TV, coffeemaker, hair dryer, iron, safe, trouser press.

Redesdale Arms
Though the Manor House is better appointed and more comfortable, this is one of the largest and best-preserved coaching inns in Gloucestershire. Originally established around 1774 as the Unicorn Hotel, it functioned around 1840 as an important link in the Bath–Lincoln stagecoach routes, offering food and accommodations to both humans and horses during the arduous journey. Since then, the inn has been considerably upgraded, with modernized and comfortably furnished bedrooms, but much of the old-fashioned charm remains intact. The small to midsize bedrooms are appointed with either twin or double beds. Each room has a compact bathroom with a shower stall.

High St., Moreton-in-Marsh, Gloucestershire GL56 0AW. (© **01608/650308**. Fax 01608/651843. www. redesdalearms.com. 14 units. £85 ($136) per person double. Rates include breakfast. MC, V. **Amenities:** Restaurant; bar; room service; laundry service; dry cleaning. *In room:* TV, coffeemaker, hair dryer, iron, trouser press.

The White Hart Royal Hotel
A mellow old Cotswold inn graced by Charles I in 1644, the White Hart provides modern amenities without compromising the personality of yesteryear. It long ago ceased being the town's premier inn but is still a comfortable place to spend the night. The well-furnished rooms all have a few antiques mixed with basic 20th-century pieces. Much of the original character of the bedrooms remains intact, but you get comfort here, not a lot of style. Each unit is fitted with a small, shower-only bathroom.

High St., Moreton-in-Marsh, Gloucestershire GL56 0BA. (© **01608/650731**. Fax 01608/650880. 19 units. £85–£90 ($136–$144) double. Rates include English breakfast. AE, MC, V. **Amenities:** Restaurant; bar; laundry service; dry cleaning. *In room:* TV, coffeemaker.

WHERE TO DINE

All of the establishments above have good restaurants, especially if you want to dine in town. The Manor House Hotel and Redesdale Arms are particularly recommended for dining. The best restaurant outside is found at The Falkland Arms.

10 Broadway ★★

24km (15 miles) SW of Stratford-upon-Avon; 150km (93 miles) NW of London; 24km (15 miles) NE of Cheltenham

This is the showcase village of the Cotswolds. If you don't mind the coach tours of summer, this is the most attractive spot to anchor into for the night. Many of the prime attractions of the Cotswolds, including Shakespeare Country, are close at hand. Flanked by honey-colored stone buildings, its High Street is a gem, remarkable for its harmonious style and design from a point overlooking the lovely Vale of Evesham.

Don't come here seeking a lot of museums and attractions. Show-stopping Broadway is its own attraction. When you see wisteria and cordoned fruit trees covering 17th-century cottages, fronted by immaculately maintained gardens, you'll understand why Henry James found it "delicious to be in Broadway."

ESSENTIALS

GETTING THERE   Rail connections are possible from London's Paddington Station via Oxford. The nearest railway stations are at Moreton-in-Marsh (11km/7 miles away) or at Evesham (8km/5 miles away). For schedules and information, call ✆ **0845/748-4950.** Frequent buses arrive from Evesham, but you have to take a taxi from Moreton.

One **National Express** coach departs daily from London's Victoria Coach Station to Broadway, a 2½-hour ride. For schedules and information, call ✆ **020/7529-2000.**

If you're driving from Oxford, head west on the A40, then take the A434 to Woodstock, Chipping Norton, and Moreton-in-Marsh.

VISITOR INFORMATION   The **Tourist Information Centre** is at 1 Cotswold Court (✆ **01386/852937**), open February through December, Monday through Saturday from 10am to 1pm and 2 to 5pm.

SEEING THE SIGHTS

The **High Street** is one of the most beautiful in England—perhaps the most beautiful. Many of its striking facades date from 1620 or a century or two later. The most famous facade is that of the **Lygon Arms,** High Street (✆ **01386/852255**), a venerable old inn. It has been serving wayfarers since 1532, and it stands on its own 3 acres of formal gardens. Even if you're not staying here, you may want to visit for a meal or a drink.

You may also seek out **St. Eadurgha's Church,** a place of Christian worship for more than 1,000 years. It's located just outside Broadway on Snowshill Road and is open most days, though with no set visiting hours. If it's closed at the time of your visit, a note on the porch door will tell you what house to go to for the key. Occasional Sunday services are held here.

Also along the street you can visit the **Broadway Magic Experience,** 76 High St. (✆ **01386/858323**), a showcase shop for teddy bear and doll artisans. The site is also the setting for a unique museum displaying hundreds of antique and collectors' teddy bears, toys, and dolls. This 18th-century stone shop offers a historical look at the world of teddy bears, ranging from Steiff to Pooh. Hours are

Tuesday through Sunday from 10am to 5pm. Admission is £2.50 ($4) for adults, and £1.75 ($2.80) for children under 14 and seniors, £7 ($11) for family ticket.

On the outskirts of Broadway stands the **Broadway Tower Country Park** on Broadway Hill (℃ **01386/852390**), a "folly" created by the fanciful mind of the sixth Earl of Coventry. Today, you can climb this tower on a clear day for a panoramic vista of 12 shires. It's the most sweeping view in the Cotswolds. The tower is open from early April to late October daily from 10:30am to 5pm. Admission is £4 ($6.40) for adults, and £3 ($4.80) for children. You can also bring the makings for a picnic here and spread it out for your lunch in designated areas.

South of Broadway, a final attraction is **Snowshill Manor,** at Snowshill (℃ **01386/852410**), a house that dates mainly from the 17th century. It was once owned by an eccentric, Charles Paget Wade, who collected virtually everything he could between 1900 and 1951. Queen Mary once remarked that Wade himself was the most remarkable artifact among his entire flea market. You'll find a little bit of everything here: Flemish tapestries, toys, lacquer cabinets, narwhal tusks, mousetraps, and cuckoo clocks—a glorious mess, like a giant attic of the 20th century. The property, owned by the National Trust, is open April through October, Wednesday through Sunday from noon to 5pm, and Monday in July and August. Admission is £6.40 ($10) per person or £16 ($26) for a family ticket.

WHERE TO STAY

The Broadway ★★   On the village green and one of the most colorful places in Broadway, this converted 15th-century house keeps its old-world charm while providing modern comforts. The recently refurbished rooms are tastefully and comfortably furnished. One room has a four-poster bed. Some guests seek out the more private bedrooms on the ground floor of a separate building, with its direct access to the garden. All but one room has a tub-and-shower combination.

The Green, Broadway, Worcestershire WR12 7AA. ℃ **01386/852401.** Fax 01386/853879. www.cotswold-inns-hotels.co.uk. 20 units. £119 ($190) double. Rates include English breakfast. AE, DC, MC, V. **Amenities:** Restaurant; bar; room service; laundry service. *In room:* TV, coffeemaker, hair dryer.

Buckland Manor Hotel ★★★   The Lygon Arms (see below) reigned supreme in Broadway for so long that people thought it had squatters' rights to the title of top inn in town, both for food and lodging. But along came Buckland Manor on the town's outskirts, topping The Lygon Arms in every way, especially in cuisine. This imposing slate-roofed manor house is ringed with fences of Cotswold stone. The core of the manor house was erected in the 13th century, with wings added in succeeding centuries. The Oak Room, with a four-poster bed and burnished paneling, occupies what used to be a private library. Leaded windows in the room overlook gardens and grazing land with Highland cattle and Jacob sheep. Some of the large bedrooms have four-poster beds and fireplaces, but all come with sumptuous beds. All rooms contain such luxuries as fresh fruit and flowers, bathrobes, and luxury toiletries. Each of the oversize bathrooms contains at least one antique, as well as carpeting. The bathrooms with shower-tub combinations use water drawn from the hotel's own spring.

Buckland, near Broadway, Worcestershire WR12 7LY. ℃ **01386/852626.** Fax 01386/853557. www.buckland manor.com. 13 units. £225–£360 ($360–$576) double. Rates include early morning tea and English breakfast. AE, DC, MC, V. Take B4632 about 3km (2 miles) south of Broadway, into Gloucestershire. No children under 12. **Amenities:** Restaurant; bar; heated pool; putting green; tennis court; room service; laundry service; dry cleaning; croquet lawn. *In room:* TV, hair dryer.

Dormy House ★   This manor house, high on a hill above the village, boasts views in all directions. Its panoramic position has made it a favorite place whether you're seeking a meal, afternoon tea, or lodgings. Halfway between Broadway and Chipping Campden, it was created from a sheep farm. The owners transformed it, furnishing the 17th-century farmhouse with a few antiques, good soft beds, shower-tub combinations, and full central heating; they also extended these luxuries to an old adjoining timbered barn, converted into studio rooms with open-beamed ceilings. Some rooms have four-poster beds. Bowls of fresh flowers adorn tables and alcoves throughout the hotel.

Willersey Hill, Broadway, Worcestershire WR12 7LF. ℂ **01386/852711.** Fax 01386/858636. www.dormy house.co.uk. 49 units. £155–£165 ($248–$264) double; £190 ($304) 4-poster room; £200 ($320) suite. Rates include English breakfast. AE, DC, MC, V. Closed Dec 24–27. Take A44 3km (2 miles) southeast of Broadway. **Amenities:** Restaurant; bar; putting green; sauna; room service; babysitting; laundry service; croquet lawn. *In room:* TV, coffeemaker, hair dryer, trouser press.

The Lygon Arms ★★★   Despite the challenge of Buckland Manor, this many-gabled structure with mullioned windows still basks in its reputation as one of the great old English inns. It opens onto a private rear garden, with 3 acres of lawns, trees, borders of flowers, stone walls with roses, and nooks for tea or sherry. The oldest portions date from 1532 or earlier, and additions have been made many times since then. King Charles I reputedly drank with his friends in one of the oak-lined chambers, and later, his enemy Oliver Cromwell slept here the night before the Battle of Worcester. Today, many but not all of the bedrooms are in the antique style; a new wing offers more of a 20th-century feel. Each room is furnished with a sumptuously comfortable bed. Bathrooms are kept in prime condition; most have both tub and shower, and all sport bathrobes and Floris toiletries. Some rooms are available for mobility-impaired travelers.

High St., Broadway, Worcestershire WR12 7DU. ℂ **01386/852255.** Fax 01386/858611. www.savoy-group.co.uk/lygon. 69 units. £265–£355 ($424–$568) double; from £395–£495 ($632–$792) suite. Value-added tax (VAT) extra. Rates include continental breakfast. AE, MC, V. **Amenities:** 2 restaurants; bar; pool; health club; sauna; room service; massage; laundry service. *In room:* TV, dataport, minibar, coffeemaker, hair dryer, iron, safe, trouser press.

Olive Branch Guest House *Value*   In the heart of an expensive village, this is a terrific bargain. The house, dating from the 16th century, retains its old Cotswold architectural features. Behind the house is a large-walled English garden and parking area. Guests are given a discount for purchases at the owners' attached antiques shop. Furnishings are basic, but comfortable, and the bathrooms are tiny with a tub or shower. One family room can accommodate up to four people and one room has a four-poster bed.

78 High St., Broadway, Worcestershire WR12 7AJ. ℂ **01386/853440.** Fax 01386/859070. www.theolive branch-broadway.com. 8 units, 7 with bathroom. £60–£75 ($96–$120) double with bathroom. Rates include English breakfast. MC, V. *In room:* TV, coffeemaker, hair dryer.

WHERE TO DINE

The best place in Broadway for a cup of tea is **Tisanes,** The Green (ℂ **01386/852112**). The shop offers perfectly blended teas with a variety of sandwiches and salads.

The Tapestry Restaurant ★ MODERN BRITISH   Set 3km (2 miles) from the center of Broadway, beside the highway to Moreton-in-Marsh and Oxford, this is one of the most charming and well-managed restaurants in the region. Elegant, though not as formal and stuffy as some competitors, the setting is as pastoral as a painting by Constable. You'll dine in a room ringed with Cotswold stone (with areas for smokers) or in an adjacent glass-sided conservatory (no smoking here).

Chef Alan Cutler turns out an intelligent and interesting cuisine. You may order an appetizer of fine slices of Parma ham with tomato and basil dressing, or a salad of avocado and pear; followed by roast rib of prime Scottish beef with a confit of shallots and a red-wine sauce; and a dessert of hot vanilla soufflé with a warm dark chocolate sauce. The cellar houses a superb collection of wines.

In Dormy House, off A44, Willersey Hill, Broadway. ✆ **01386/852711.** Reservations recommended. Fixed-price Sun lunch £21 ($33); dinner main courses £19–£25 ($30–$40); fixed-price dinner £35 ($56); gourmet 6-course fixed-price dinner £38 ($60). AE, DC, MC, V. Daily 7–9:30pm; Sun noon–2pm.

11 Chipping Campden ⟨★⟩⟨★⟩

58km (36 miles) NW of Oxford; 19km (12 miles) S of Stratford-upon-Avon; 150km (93 miles) NW of London

The wool merchants have long departed, but the architectural legacy of honey-colored stone cottages—financed by their fleecy "white gold"—remains to delight the visitor today. Try to tie in a stopover here as you rush from Oxford to Stratford-upon-Avon.

On the northern edge of the Cotswolds, Chipping Camden opens onto the dreamy Vale of Evesham that you've seen depicted in a thousand postcards. Except for the heavy traffic in summer, the main street still looks as it did centuries ago—in fact, the noted British historian G. M. Trevelyan called it "the most beautiful village street now left in the island." And so it is even today. You can tie in a visit here on the same day you visit Broadway (see above), lying 6.5km (4 miles) to the west.

Arriving through beautiful Cotswold landscapes—called "seductive" by some—you come upon this country town, whose landmark is the soaring tower of the Church of St. James. You'll see it for miles around. Constructed in the Perpendicular style by the town's wool merchants in the 15th century, it is one of the finest churches in the Cotswolds.

The town's long High Street is curved like Oxford's, and it's lined with stone houses dating from the 16th century. A hundred years later Chipping Campden was one of the richest wool towns of England. The Campden Trust, a determined group of dedicated conservationists, has preserved the town the way it should be.

Of special interest is the Silk Mill, Sheep Street, open Monday through Saturday from 9am to 5pm. The Guild of Handicrafts was established here in 1902, practicing such skills as bookbinding and cabinetmaking. It folded in 1920 but has been revived today with a series of craft workshops.

ESSENTIALS

GETTING THERE   Trains depart from London's Paddington Station for Moreton-in-Marsh, a 1½- to 2-hour trip. For schedules and information, call ✆ **0845/748-4950.** A bus operated by Castleway's travels the 7 miles from Moreton-in-Marsh to Chipping Campden five times a day. Many visitors opt for a taxi from Moreton-in-Marsh to Chipping Campden.

The largest and most important nearby bus depot is Cheltenham, which receives service several times a day from London's Victoria Coach Station. For schedules and information, call ✆ **020/7529-2000.** From Cheltenham, **Barry's Coaches** are infrequent and uncertain, departing three times per week at most. Call Gloucester Coach Station (✆ **01452/527516**) for details.

If you're driving from Oxford, take A40 west to the junction with A424. Follow it northwest, passing by Stow-on-the-Wold. The route becomes A44 until you reach the junction with B4081, which you take northeast to Chipping Campden.

VISITOR INFORMATION The **Tourist Information Centre** is at the Old Police Station, High Street (℡ **01386/841206**). It's open daily from 10am to 5pm.

SEEING THE SIGHTS

In 1907, American horticulturist Major Lawrence Johnstone created **Hidcote Manor Garden** ★★, 6.5km (4 miles) northeast of Chipping Campden and 14km (9 miles) south of Stratford-upon-Avon (℡ **01386/438333**). Set on 10 acres, this masterpiece is composed of small gardens, or rooms, that are separated by a variety of hedges, old roses, rare shrubs, trees, and herbaceous borders. April through October, the garden is open Monday, Wednesday, Saturday, and Sunday from 10:30am to 6:30pm. During June and July, the garden is also open on Thursday from 10:30am to 5:30pm. Last admission is at 5pm or 1 hour before sunset. Admission is £5.90 ($9.45) for adults, £2.90 ($4.65) for children, and £14.50 ($23) family ticket.

SHOPPING

The poet, artist, and craftsman William Morris (1834–96) called the Cotswold countryside home for most of his life. The worldwide Arts and Crafts movement he led in the late 19th century still inspires artists and craftspeople in this area.

At the studio of **D. I. Hart Silversmiths,** The Guild, The Silk Mill, Sheep Street (℡ **01386/841100**), silver is expertly smithed by descendants of George Hart, an original member of the Guild of Handicrafts, in the original Ashbee workshop. **Robert Welch Studio Shop,** Lower High Street (℡ **01386/840522**), is where Robert Welch has been crafting silverware, stainless steel, and cutlery for more than 40 years. **Martin Gotrel,** The Square (℡ **01386/841360**), designs and makes fine contemporary and traditional jewelry.

Campden Needlecraft Centre, High Street (℡ **01386/840583**), is widely known as one of the leading specialist embroidery shops in England with an interesting selection of embroidery and canvas work as well as fabrics and threads. If antiques and antiques-hunting are your passion, visit **School House Antiques,** High Street (℡ **01386/841474**), or **The Barn Antiques Centre,** Long Marston on the Stratford-upon-Avon Road (℡ **01789/721399**). For new, secondhand, and antiquarian books, look up **Campden Bookshop,** High Street (℡ **01386/840944**), or **Draycott Books,** 2 Sheep St. (℡ **01386/841392**).

WHERE TO STAY

Charingworth Manor Hotel ★★★ In nearby Charingworth, this elegant country home is the showpiece of the area, more luxurious than Cotswold House in town. A manor has stood on this spot since the time of the *Domesday*

(*Moments* **The Play's the Thing**

In summer, Shakespeare is performed on the Theatre Lawn at Manor Garden in Chipping Campden; there is no more memorable experience in the Cotswolds than watching *A Midsummer's Night Dream* performed here on a balmy evening in July.

Book. The present Tudor-Jacobean house, in honey-colored stone with slate roofs, has 55 acres of grounds. In the 1930s, it hosted such illustrious guests as T. S. Eliot. Its old-world charm has been preserved, in spite of modernization. Each spacious room is luxuriously furnished with antiques and English fabrics. Many of the period rooms have four-poster beds. The bathrooms are state of the art. Guests can also wander through a well-manicured garden.

Charingworth, near Chipping Campden, Gloucestershire GL55 6NS. (© **01386/593555.** Fax 01386/593353. 26 units. £130–£275 ($208–$440) double. Rates include English breakfast and dinner. AE, DC, MC, V. Take B4035 5km (3¼ miles) east of Chipping Campden. **Amenities:** Restaurant; bar; indoor heated pool; tennis court; gym; sauna; room service; laundry service; billiards room. *In room:* TV, coffeemaker, hair dryer, iron, safe, trouser press.

Cotswold House Hotel ★★   This is the best place to stay in town. A stately, formal Regency house dating from 1800, right in the heart of the village opposite the old wool market, Cotswold House sits amid 1½ acres of tended, walled gardens with shaded seating. Note the fine winding Regency staircase in the reception hall. The hotel has seen a number of improvements, including the addition of the exclusive and private Old Grammar School Suite, furnished with antiques and paintings, and ideal for a honeymoon retreat. All the bedrooms were refurbished in 2002–2003 with such luxuries as Hypnos beds and crisp Frette linen, along with Hermès bath products in the spacious bathrooms. Many guests prefer one of the more secluded Garden Cottages, each beautifully furnished, with more luxurious appointments than the main house bedrooms.

The Square, Chipping Campden, Gloucestershire GL55 6AN. (© **01386/840330.** Fax 01386/840310. www. cotswoldhouse.com. 20 units. £175–£395 ($280–$632) double; £275 ($440) 4-poster bed. Rates include English breakfast. AE, MC, V. **Amenities:** 2 restaurants; bar; room service; babysitting; laundry service. *In room:* TV/DVD, minibar, hair dryer, coffeemaker, iron, trouser press.

Noel Arms Hotel   Long before more elegant country houses came along, this old coaching inn was famous, and it still is, with a history going back to the 14th century. Charles II rested here in 1651 after his defeat at the Battle of Worcester. Tradition is kept alive in the decor, which includes fine antiques, muskets, swords, and shields. Twelve rooms date from the 14th century; the others, comfortably furnished and well appointed, are housed in a modern wing built of Cotswold stone. Those bedrooms in the older part of the hotel are the most stylish—one has an exquisitely carved four-poster bed—although comfort is perhaps better in the more modern annex, where the units are more spacious. All the bathrooms, though small, are neatly organized and come with a tub and shower for the most part.

High St., Chipping Campden, Gloucestershire GL55 6AT. (© **01386/840317.** Fax 01386/841136. www. cotswold-inns-hotels.co.uk. 26 units. £115–£140 ($184–$224) double. Rates include English breakfast. AE, DC, MC, V. **Amenities:** Restaurant; bar; room service; laundry service. *In room:* TV, coffeemaker, hair dryer, trouser press.

WHERE TO DINE

Traditionally one dined at the grand old inns of the town, and that is still possible. However, today there is a choice outside the hotels.

Malt House ★★ BRITISH   In the little hamlet bordering Chipping Camden, this classic Cotswold cottage has a well-manicured garden set against a backdrop of orchards. With its paneled walls, exposed beams, and leaded windows, it's a Cotswold cliché. Its fixed-price dinner is the finest in the area, with three selections per course offered. The menu is based on the best produce in any given season. Some veggies and herbs are grown in the house's garden. All dishes have flavor and are deftly handled, especially the seared duck breast with red onion marmalade or the pan-fried filet of Scottish salmon with gnocchi. The risotto with marinated artichokes is rich and creamy, and the filet of beef comes on a bed of wilted spinach and shallots. Save room for the rich desserts, including a chocolate fondant with homemade vanilla ice cream.

The inn also rents seven beautifully furnished bedrooms, costing £119 ($190) a night. To reach it, take the B4081 south of Chipping Campden for 2km (1¼ miles).

Broad Campden, GL55 6UU Gloucestershire. ⓒ **01386/840295.** Fax 01386/841334. www.a1tourism.com/uk/malthse.html. Fixed-price dinner £33 ($52). AE, MC, V. Thurs–Mon 7:30–9pm.

10

Cambridge & Oxford

It would be a shame to visit England without exploring at least one of its famous university towns. Not all of us can go to both Oxford and Cambridge, England's two greatest university cities, so which should you choose if you're pressed for time and can spare only a day out of London? We'd opt for Cambridge over Oxford because Cambridge more closely lives up to the image of what an English university town is like.

Although the university dominates central **Oxford,** it is also an industrial city known for its motor industry. Its 120,000 permanent residents seem to keep to themselves and go about their lives, trying to evade the thousands of tourists descending on their inner core. Oxford has some of England's greatest architecture, some excellent museums, and student pubs that are better than its restaurants. On an ideal itinerary it should not be crossed off the list.

Then there is **Cambridge.** It's really an agricultural market town, a more tranquil and secluded place, set just at the doorstep of the Fens, a vast area just north of the city that's a strange but fascinating terrain of reclaimed marshland and quaking bogs. In addition to its architecture and university, Cambridge allows you to preview the life of East Anglia, still one of the country's bucolic landscapes as painted by John Constable.

Unlike the city of Oxford, Cambridge is more compact and can be more easily walked and explored on a rushed day trip. You can go punting on the River Cam; explore "the Backs," that green swathe of land straddling the river, and walk the .8km (½-mile) parade of colleges from Magdalene to Peterhouse. Not bad for a day's outing. You may so fall in love with English university towns that you'll decide to stay in England for that extra day so you can take in Oxford after all.

1 Cambridge: Town & Gown ⋆⋆⋆

89km (55 miles) N of London; 129km (80 miles) NE of Oxford

The university town of Cambridge is a gem with many facets: the Bridge of Sighs; spires and turrets; drooping willows; dusty secondhand bookshops; carol-singing on Christmas Eve in King's College Chapel; dancing until sunrise at the May balls; the sound of Elizabethan madrigals; narrow lanes, where Darwin, Newton, and Cromwell once walked; the "Backs," where the lawns of the colleges sweep down to the Cam River; the tattered black robe of a hurrying upperclassman flying in the wind.

Along with Oxford, Cambridge is one of Britain's ancient seats of learning. In many ways their stories are similar, particularly the age-old conflict between town and gown. As far as the locals are concerned, alumni such as Isaac Newton, John Milton, and Virginia Woolf aren't from yesterday. Cambridge continues to graduate many famous scientists, including noted physicist Stephen Hawking, author of *A Brief History of Time.*

In the 1990s, Cambridge became known as a high-tech outpost, or "a silicon fen," if you will. More and more high-tech ventures are installing themselves here to produce new software—thousands of start-up companies producing £3 billion ($3.8 billion) a year in revenues. Even Bill Gates, in 1997, decided to finance an £80 million ($128 million) research center here, claiming that Cambridge was becoming "a world center of advanced technology."

ESSENTIALS

GETTING THERE   Trains depart frequently from London's Liverpool Street and King's Cross stations, arriving an hour later. For inquiries, call (C) **0845/ 748-4950.** An off-peak, same-day round-trip is £16 ($25). A peak-time, same-day round-trip is £18 ($29). An off-peak, longer stay round-trip (up to a 5-day period) is £25 ($39).

National Express buses run hourly between London's Victoria Coach Station for the 2-hour trip to Drummer Street Station in Cambridge. A one-way or same-day round-trip costs £8 ($13). If you'd like to return in a day or two, the cost is £14 ($22). For schedules and information, call (C) **020/7529-2000.**

If you're driving from London, head north on the M11.

VISITOR INFORMATION   The **Cambridge Tourist Information Centre,** Wheeler Street ((C) **01223/322640;** www.cambridge.gov.uk/leisure/index.htm), is in back of the Guildhall. The center has a wide range of information, including data on public transportation in the area and on different sightseeing attractions. From April to October, hours are Monday through Saturday from 10am to 6pm and Sunday from 11am to 4pm. In July and August, the office is open daily from 10am to 7pm. From November to March, hours are daily from 10am to 5:30pm.

A tourist reception center for Cambridge and Cambridgeshire is operated by Guide Friday Ltd. at Cambridge Railway Station ((C) **01223/362444**). The center, on the concourse of the railway station, sells brochures and maps. Also available is a full range of tourist services, including accommodations booking. Open in summer daily from 8:45am to 7pm (closes at 5pm off-season). Guided tours of Cambridge leave the center daily.

GETTING AROUND   The center of Cambridge is made for pedestrians, so leave your car at one of the many parking lots (they get more expensive as you approach the city center) and stroll to some of the colleges spread throughout the city. Follow the courtyards through to the Backs (the college lawns) and walk through to Trinity (where Prince Charles studied) and St. John's College, including the Bridge of Sighs.

Next to walking, the most popular way of getting around is bicycling. **City Cycle Hire** ((C) **01223/293030**), has bicycles for rent for £6 ($9.60) for 3 hours, £6 ($9.60) per day, or £13 ($21) per week. A deposit of £25 ($40) is required. Call their number to reserve a bike. At that time you'll be told the address at which to pick up the cycle. Open daily in summer from 9am to 6pm; off-season Monday through Saturday from 9am to 5:30pm.

Stagecoach Cambus, 100 Cowley Rd. ((C) **0870/608-2608**), services the Cambridge area with a network of buses, with fares ranging in price from 60p to £1.80 (95¢–$2.90). The local tourist office has bus schedules.

SPECIAL EVENTS   Cambridge has an artistic bent that peaks from the end of June to the end of July during **Camfest** ((C) **01223/359547**), a visual and performing arts festival. Event tickets are generally between £5 and £12 ($8–$19).

Cambridge

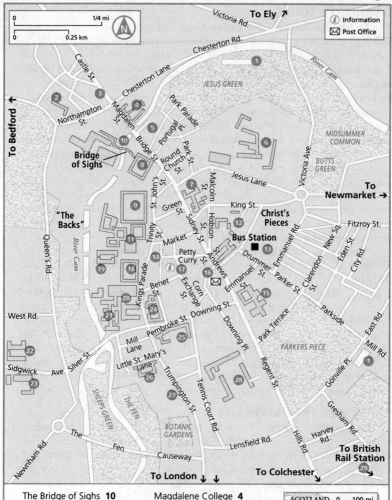

ORGANIZED TOURS

The **Cambridge Tourist Information Centre** (see above) sponsors two-hour walking tours, taking in the highlights of the university city, costing £7.25 ($12) for adults or £4.25 ($6.80) for children. Call for opening times.

For an informative spin on Cambridge, join in on one of the **Guided Walking Tours** given by a Cambridge Blue Badge Guide (© **01223/322640**). Two-hour walking tours leave the Tourist Information Centre (see above) and wind through the streets of historic Cambridge, visiting at least one of the colleges and the famous Backs. From mid-June to August, drama tours are conducted, during which participants may see various costumed characters walk in and out of the tour. Henry VIII, Queen Elizabeth I, Sir Isaac Newton, and others help breathe life into the history of Cambridge during the drama tours. Regular tours are given from April to mid-June, daily at 11:30am and 1:30pm; from mid-June to September, daily at 11:30am, and at 1:30 and 2:30pm; October through March, daily at 1:30pm and Saturday at 11:30am. Drama tours are offered July and August daily at 6:30pm. Admission for regular tours is £7.85 ($13) per person and for drama tours is £4.50 ($7.20) per person.

In addition to its visitor information services (see "Essentials," above), **Guide Friday Ltd.,** on the concourse of Cambridge Railway Station (© **01223/362444**), offers daily guided tours of Cambridge via open-top, double-decker buses. In summer, they depart every 15 minutes from 9:30am to 4pm. Departures are curtailed off season depending on demand. The tour can be a 1-hour ride, or you can get off at any of the many stops and rejoin the tour whenever you wish. Tickets are valid all day. The fare is £7.50 ($12) for adults, £5.50 ($8.80) for senior citizens and students, £3 ($4.80) for children age 6 to 12, and free for kids age 5 and under. A family ticket for £18 ($29) covers two adults and up to three children. Office hours are daily from 8:45am to 7pm in summer and from 9:30am to 5pm during off season.

EXPLORING THE UNIVERSITY

Oxford University predates Cambridge, but by the early 13th century, scholars began coming here, too. Eventually, Cambridge won partial recognition from Henry III, rising or falling with the approval of subsequent English monarchs. Cambridge consists of 31 colleges for both men and women. All colleges are closed for exams from mid-April until the end of June.

The following listing is only a sample of some of the more interesting colleges. If you're planning to be in Cambridge a while, you might also want to visit **Magdalene College,** on Magdalene Street, founded in 1542; **Pembroke College,** on Trumpington Street, founded in 1347; **Christ's College,** on St. Andrew's Street, founded in 1505; and **Corpus Christi College,** on Trumpington Street, which dates from 1352.

KING'S COLLEGE ★★ The adolescent Henry VI founded King's College on King's Parade (© **01223/331212**) in 1441. Most of its buildings today are from the 19th century, but its crowning glory, the **Perpendicular King's College Chapel** ★★★, dates from the Middle Ages and is one of England's architectural gems. Its most characteristic features are the magnificent fan vaulting, all of stone, and the great windows, most of which were fashioned by Flemish artisans between 1517 and 1531. The stained glass portrays biblical scenes in hues of red, blue, and amber. The chapel also houses Rubens's *The Adoration of the Magi.* The rood screen is from the early 16th century. *Insider tip:* For a classic view of the chapel, you can admire the architectural complex from the rear, which would be ideal for a picnic along the river. E. M. Forster came here to contemplate scenes for his novel *Maurice*.

The chapel is open during vacation time, Monday through Friday from 9:30am to 3:30pm, Saturday from 9:30am to 3:15pm, and on Sunday from 11:15am to 2:15pm and 5 to 5:30pm. During the term, the public is welcome to attend choral services Monday through Saturday at 5:30pm and on Sunday at 10:30am and 3:30pm. During the school vacations, the chapel is open to visitors Monday through Saturday from 9:30am to 4:30pm and on Sunday from 10am to 5pm; it is closed from December 23 to January 1. It may be closed at other times for recording sessions, broadcasts, and concerts.

There is an exhibition in the seven northern side chapels showing why and how the chapel was built. Admission to the college and chapel, including the exhibition, is £3.50 ($5.60) for adults, £2.50 ($4) for students and children age 12 to 17, and free for children under age 12.

PETERHOUSE This college, on Trumpington Street (© **01223/338200;** www.pet.cam.ac.uk), is the oldest Cambridge college, founded in 1284 by Hugh de Balsham, the bishop of Ely. Of the original buildings, only the hall remains, but this was restored in the 19th century and now boasts stained-glass windows by William Morris. Old Court, constructed in the 15th century, was renovated in 1754; the chapel dates from 1632. Ask permission to enter at the porter's lodge. *Insider tip:* Almost sadly neglected, the Little Church of St. Mary's next door was the college chapel until 1632. Pay it the honor of a visit.

EMMANUEL COLLEGE On St. Andrew's Street, Emmanuel (© **01223/ 334274;** www.emma.cam.ac.uk) was founded in 1584 by Sir Walter Mildmay, a chancellor of the exchequer to Elizabeth I. You can take a nice stroll around its attractive gardens and visit the chapel designed by Sir Christopher Wren and consecrated in 1677. Both the chapel and college are open daily from 9am to 6pm (closed during exam time). *Insider tip:* Harvard men and women, and those who love them, can look for a memorial window in Wren's chapel dedicated to John Harvard, an alumnus of Emmanuel who lent his name to that *other* university in Cambridge, Massachusetts.

QUEENS' COLLEGE ✪ On Queens' Lane, Queens' College (© **01223/ 335511;** www.quns.cam.ac.uk) is the loveliest of Cambridge's colleges. Dating from 1448, it was founded by two English queens, one the wife of Henry VI, the other the wife of Edward IV. Its second cloister is the most interesting, flanked by the early-16th-century President's Lodge. Admission is £1.50 ($2.40); free for children under age 12 accompanied by parents. A printed guide is issued. From November until March 19, hours are daily from 1:45 to 4:30pm;

Moments Punting on the Cam

Punting on the River Cam in a wood-built, flat-bottomed boat (which looks somewhat like a Venetian gondola) is a traditional pursuit of students and visitors to Cambridge. Downstream, you pass along the ivy-covered Backs of the colleges, their lush gardens sweeping down to the Cam.

People sprawl along the banks of the Cam on a summer day to judge and tease you as you maneuver your punt with a pole about 4.5m (15 ft.) long. The river's floor is muddy, and many a student has lost a pole in the riverbed shaded by the willows. If your pole gets stuck, it's better to leave it sticking in the mud instead of risking a plunge into the river.

About 3km (2 miles) upriver lies Grantchester, immortalized by Rupert Brooke. Literary types flock to Grantchester, which can be reached by punting or by taking the path following the River Granta for less than an hour to Grantchester Meadows (the town lies about a mile from the meadows). When the town clock stopped for repairs in 1985, its hands were left frozen "for all time" at 10 minutes to 3, in honor of Brooke's famed sonnet "The Soldier."

After so much activity, you're bound to get hungry or thirsty, so head to **The Green Man,** 59 High St. (© **01223/841178**), a 400-year-old inn named in honor of Robin Hood, where a crackling fire warms you in cold weather, and summer features a back beer garden, leading off toward the river, where your punt is waiting to take you back to Cambridge.

Scudamore's Boatyards, Granta Place (© **01223/359750**), by the Anchor Pub, has been in business since 1910. Punts and rowboats rent for £10 ($16) per hour. A £50 ($80) cash or credit-card deposit is required. There is a maximum of six persons per punt. It is open year-round (although Mar to late Oct is the high season) daily from 9am until dusk. You may prefer a chauffeur, in which case there is a minimum cost of £35 to £40 ($56–$64) for two people and £8 ($13) per person after that.

Cambridge Punt Company, working out of The Anchor Pub, Silver Street (© **01223/359750**), is recommended for its 45-minute punt tours. A guide (usually a Cambridge student) dressed in a straw boater hat will both punt and give running commentary to groups of between one and six persons. Tours cost a minimum of £50 ($80) for two, £10 ($16) for each extra adult, and £5 ($8) for children ages 5 to 12. Kids ages 4 and under ride free. The Anchor Pub's service staff can call a guide over to your table. If you want to row yourself along the Cam, "unchauffeured" boats rent for £12 to £14 ($19–$22) per hour. The company is open daily from 9am to dusk, although everyone packs up if it rains or if the winds get too high.

from March 20 to May 15, Monday through Friday from 1:45 to 4:30pm, Saturday and Sunday from 10am to 4:45pm; closed from May 17 to June 19. From June 20 to September 19, Monday through Friday from 10am to 4:30pm,

Saturday and Sunday from 10am to 4:45pm; from September 20 to October 31, Monday through Friday from 1:45 to 4:30pm, Saturday and Sunday from 10am to 4:45pm. Entry and exit is by the old porter's lodge in Queens' Lane only. The old hall and chapel are usually open to the public when not in use.

ST. JOHN'S COLLEGE ★★★   On St. John's Street, this college (© **01223/ 338600;** www.joh.cam.ac.uk) was founded in 1511 by Lady Margaret Beaufort, mother of Henry VII. A few years earlier she had founded Christ's College. Before her intervention, an old hospital had stood on the site of St. John's. The impressive gateway bears the Tudor coat of arms, and Second Court is a fine example of late Tudor brickwork. Its best-known feature is the **Bridge of Sighs** crossing the Cam, built in the 19th century and patterned after the bridge in Venice. It connects the older part of the college with New Court, a Gothic Revival on the opposite bank with an outstanding view of the famous Backs. The Bridge of Sighs is closed to visitors but can be seen from the neighboring Kitchen Bridge. The college is open from March to October daily from 9:30am to 5:30pm. Admission is £2 ($3.20) for adults and £1.50 ($2.40) for children. Visitors are welcome to attend choral services in the chapel. *Insider's tip:* The Bridge of Sighs links the old college with an architectural "folly" of the 19th century, the elaborate New Court, which is a crenellated neo-Gothic fantasy. It's adorned with a "riot" of pinnacles and a main cupola. Students call it "the wedding cake."

TRINITY COLLEGE ★★   On Trinity Street, Trinity College (not to be con-fused with Trinity Hall) is the largest college in Cambridge. It was founded in 1546 by Henry VIII, who consolidated a number of smaller colleges that had existed on the site. The courtyard is the most spacious in Cambridge, built when Thomas Nevile was master. Sir Christopher Wren designed the library. For entry to the college, apply at the Great Gate, or call © **01223/338400** for informa-tion. There is a charge of £2 ($3.20) from March to November. *Insider tip:* What's fun to do here is to contemplate what has gone on before you arrived. Pause at Nevile's Court, where Isaac Newton first calculated the speed of sound. Take in the delicate fountain of the Great Court where Lord Byron used to bathe naked with his pet bear. Why a bear? The university forbade students from hav-ing a dog, but there was no proviso for bears. Through the same courtyard years later walked Vladimir Nabokov, undoubtedly dreaming of that sexy little pubes-cent he would later immortalize as *Lolita.*

(*Moments* Cambridge's Most Bucolic Spot

The Grove at Queens' College fronts the west bank of the River Cam on the north side of the bridge. It's a riot of blossoms in spring. The walk along the riverbank reveals the best view of King's College but ends at a small branch channel in the river. Beyond the lawn on the other side of the river, the high stone wall dividing the two colleges is the last remain-ing fragment of a Carmelite monastery dissolved in 1538. Here's your best chance to relax a bit from a hectic day of sightseeing. From Queens' Col-lege wide green lawns lead down to the Backs, where you may want to go punting. Take in Mathematical Bridge, which is best viewed from the Silver Street road bridge, dating from 1902. Right by this bridge, stop off at the old pub, the Anchor, and contemplate what life would have been like if you'd attended Cambridge.

CAMBRIDGE'S OTHER ATTRACTIONS

The Fitzwilliam Museum ★★ One of the finest museums in Britain is worth the trip here. Though it features temporary exhibitions, its permanent collections are noted for their antiquities from ancient Egypt, Greece, and Rome. The Applied Arts section features English and European pottery and glass, along with furniture, clocks, fans, and armor; Chinese jades; ceramics from Japan and Korea; plus rugs and samplers. The museum is also noted for its rare-coin collection. Many rare printed books and illuminated manuscripts, both literary and musical, are also on display.

But the best we've saved for last: The paintings include masterpieces by Simone Martini, Domenico Veneziano, Titian, Veronese, Rubens, Van Dyck, Canaletto, Hogarth, Gainsborough, Constable, Monet, Degas, Renoir, Cézanne, and Picasso. There is also a fine collection of other 20th-century art, miniatures, drawings, watercolors, and prints.

Insider's tip: Occasional musical events, including evening concerts, and some of the best lectures in England are staged here throughout the year. For more details, call ℂ **01223/332900.**

Trumpington St., near Peterhouse. ℂ **01223/332900.** www.fitzmuseum.cam.ac.uk. Free admission, donations appreciated. Tues–Sat 10am–5pm; Sun 2:15–5pm. Guided tours £3 ($4.80) per person, Sun 2:45pm. Closed Jan 1, Good Friday, May Day, and Dec 24–31.

Great St. Mary's Cambridge's central church was built on the site of an 11th-century church, but the present building dates largely from 1478. It was closely associated with events of the Reformation. The cloth that covered the hearse of King Henry VII is on display in the church. There is a fine view of Cambridge from the top of the tower.

King's Parade. ℂ **01223/741716.** Admission to tower £2 ($3.20) adults, £1 ($1.60) children. Tower Mon–Sat 10am–5pm; Sun noon–4:30pm. Church daily 9am–6pm.

SHOPPING

Forage around the shops lining St. John's Street, Trinity Street, King's Parade, and Trumpington Street.

Check out **English Teddy Bear Company,** 1 King's Parade (ℂ **01223/ 300908**), which sells teddy bears handmade in cottages all over the United Kingdom—a real British souvenir.

Primavera, 10 King's Parade (ℂ **01223/357708**), is a showplace of British crafts, featuring pottery, glass, ceramics, jewelry, ironwork, and fabric crafts ranging from ties to wall hangings. Be sure to explore its basement exhibition of paintings and craft items.

Another well-defined shopping district is comprised of Bridge Street, Sidney Street, St. Andrew's Street, and Regent Street. Particularly worth noting in this area is **James Pringle Weavers,** 11 Bridge St. (ℂ **01223/361534**), a Scottish haven. You'll find a mind-boggling array of Scottish tartans, kilts, tweeds, fine knitwear, Scottish food, and, of course, postcards.

A posh area of extremely chic, small, and exclusive shops runs between Market Square and Trinity Street and is called **Rose Crescent.** Here, you can buy leather goods, smart women's clothing, and fine hats, as well as jewelry and a host of very expensive gift items.

Cambridge's pedestrian shopping district runs between Market Square and St. Andrew's Street and is known as the Lion Yard. **Culpepper the Herbalists,** 25 Lion Yard (ℂ **01223/367370**), carries a complete herbal line that includes everything from extracts of plants to jellies, honeys, teas, cosmetics, bath products, pillows, and potpourri.

If you're a book lover, Cambridge's bookstores will truly delight you. **Heffers of Cambridge** is a huge book, stationery, and music store with six branches, all of which can be contacted through its central phone number (© **01223/568568**). The main store, at 20 Trinity St., carries academic books; the children's book shop is at 30 Trinity St.; the stationery store can be found at 19 Sydney St.; Heffers's paperback and video shop is at 31 St. Andrews St.; its art-and-graphics shop has an address of 15–21 King St.; and the music store at 19 Trinity St. features classical and popular cassettes, CDs, and choral college music. Heffers also has a shop in the mall at Grafton Centre that carries new fiction and nonfiction titles.

G. David, 16 St. Edward's Passage (© **01223/354619**), hawks secondhand books, publishers' overruns at reduced prices, and antiquarian books. **Dillons,** 22 Sydney St. (© **01223/351688**), deals exclusively in new books on a variety of subjects. **The Haunted Bookshop,** 9 St. Edward's Passage (© **01223/312913**), specializes in out-of-print children's books and first editions.

WHERE TO STAY
VERY EXPENSIVE

Cambridge Garden House Moat House ★★   This modern hotel, the best in Cambridge, sits between the riverbank and a cobblestone street in the oldest part of town, a short stroll from the principal colleges. (Because of its riverside location, we prefer it over its nearest competitor, the University Arms, which is in the center of town.) It offers ample parking. You can rent punts at a boatyard next door. Visitors can relax on comfortable sofas and chairs in the bars and lounge. The soundproof bedrooms have glass-topped nightstands, adequate desk space, and private balconies. The expensive units (premium rooms) are very spacious with large sitting areas with face-to-face sofas. The river-view rooms are the most desirable. Bathrooms are large.

Overlooking the river and gardens, the hotel's restaurant, called simply "The Restaurant," offers fixed-price and a la carte menus, including vegetarian meals. The Riverside Lounge provides light meals, accompanied in the evening by piano music. The hotel has a series of outdoor terraces where drinks and afternoon tea are served in nice weather.

Granta Place, Mill Lane, Cambridge, Cambridgeshire CB2 1RT. © 01223/259988. Fax 01223/316605. www. moathousehotels.com. 120 units. £200–£255 ($320–$408) double. AE, DC, MC, V. **Amenities:** Restaurant; bar; pool; health club; Jacuzzi; sauna; business center; 24-hr. room service; laundry service; dry cleaning. *In room:* TV, minibar, coffeemaker, hair dryer, safe.

EXPENSIVE

De Vere University Arms Hotel ★   This 1834 hotel maintains much of its antique charm and many original architectural features despite modernization over the years. The only real rival in town to the Garden House, it lacks the river location and timeworn Edwardian elegance of the former. Near the city center and the university, it offers suitable bedrooms. Rooms range from small to mid-size, each with bedside controls; the premium rooms also have slippers and robes. Forty bedrooms were refurbished in 2001; eight have four-poster beds. Rooms in front are smaller but more up-to-date and have double-glazed windows. Each room comes with a king-size or twin beds, and bathrooms have a shower-and-tub combo (except the single rooms, which have showers only). Three rooms are suitable for families.

Regent St., Cambridge, Cambridgeshire CB2 1AD. © **01223/351241.** Fax 01223/315256. www.devere online.co.uk. 118 units. £160–£220 ($256–$352) double; £350 ($560) suite. Rates include English breakfast. AE, DC, MC, V. Parking £8 ($13). Bus: 1. **Amenities:** Restaurant; bar; room service; babysitting; dry cleaning; laundry service. *In room:* TV, minibar, coffeemaker, hair dryer, iron/ironing board.

MODERATE

Arundel House Hotel   The Arundel enjoys a great location. Until recently, it consisted of six identical Victorian row houses, connected many years ago. In 1994, after two additional row houses were purchased from the university, the hotel was enlarged and upgraded into the current well-maintained place. Rooms overlooking the River Cam and Jesus Green cost more than those facing the other way; and with no elevator, rooms on lower floors go for more than those upstairs. Regardless of location, all rooms are clean and comfortable, fitted with king-size or twin beds, plus compact bathrooms with shower-tub combinations. With a bar and restaurant (see "Where to Dine," below) and a garden with outdoor tables for drinks in warm weather, the Arundel offers the best dining of any hotel in town.

53 Chesterton Rd., Cambridge, Cambridgeshire CB4 3AN. © **01223/367701.** Fax 01223/367721. www. arundelhousehotels.co.uk. 105 units. £85–£215 ($136–$344) double. Rates include continental breakfast. AE, DC, MC, V. Bus: 1 or 3. **Amenities:** Restaurant; bar; laundry. *In room:* A/C, TV, coffeemaker, hair dryer.

Cambridgeshire Moat House   This place, a more affordable member of the same chain that manages the Cambridge Garden House Moat House (reviewed above), offers the best sports facilities in the Cambridge area. Built around 1977, it has comfortable bedrooms with nice views, a putting green, and an 18-hole championship golf course where greens fees range from £15 to £30 ($23–$45). There's a restaurant in the hotel, although the food is just standard stuff. Meals are also served daily in the bar.

Huntingdon Rd., Bar Hill, Cambridge, Cambridgeshire CB3 8EU. © **01954/249988.** Fax 01954/780010. www.moathousehotels.com. 134 units. £130–£160 ($208–$256) double. Children 15 and under stay free in parent's room. AE, DC, MC, V. Take A14 9km (5½ miles) northwest of the town center. **Amenities:** Restaurant; bar; indoor heated pool; golf course; gym; sauna; laundry service; dry cleaning. *In room:* TV, coffeemaker, hair dryer, trouser press.

Gonville Hotel   A 5-minute walk from the center of town, this hotel and its grounds are opposite Parker's Piece. The Gonville has been much improved in recent years. It's not unlike a country house, with shade trees and a formal car entry, and it attracts businesspeople as well as tourists. The recently refurbished rooms are comfortable and furnished in a modern style. The compact bathrooms contain shower-tub combinations. The restaurant is air-conditioned.

Gonville Place, Cambridge, Cambridgeshire CB1 1LY. © **800/528-1234** in the U.S. and Canada, or 01223/ 366611. Fax 01223/315470. www.gonvillehotel.co.uk. 78 units. £120 ($192) double. AE, DC, MC, V. **Amenities:** Restaurant; bar; room service; laundry service; dry cleaning. *In room:* TV, coffeemaker, hair dryer, iron/ironing board.

Holiday Inn Cambridge   Located a short walk from a small artificial lake, which the bedrooms overlook, this modern two-story hotel is vaguely influenced by the designs of nearby country houses. Like the Moat House, it emphasizes leisure facilities (though it doesn't offer golf), and of the two, it has better bedrooms. There's a grassy courtyard partially enclosed by the hotel's wings. Peak-ceilinged public rooms are furnished with scattered clusters of sofas and chairs. The small yet comfortable bedrooms have large windows with pleasant views. The bathrooms are compact. The restaurant has reproductions of paintings created by Sir Winston Churchill.

Lakeview, Bridge Rd., Lakeview Bridge, Impington, Cambridge, Cambridgeshire CB4 9PH. (②) 800/225-5843 in the U.S. and Canada, or 0870/400-9015. Fax 01223/233426. 165 units. £160 ($256) double. AE, DC, MC, V. Bus: 104, 105, or 106. Drive 3km (2 miles) north of Cambridge on B1049 (Histon Rd.) to A45 intersection. **Amenities:** Restaurant; bar; indoor heated pool; health club; Jacuzzi; sauna; room service; babysitting; laundry service; dry cleaning. *In room:* TV, minibar, hair dryer, safe.

Regent Hotel   This is one of the nicest of the reasonably priced small hotels in Cambridge. Right in the city center, overlooking Parker's Piece, the house was built in the 1840s as the original site of Newham College. It became a hotel when the college outgrew its quarters. *Note:* The hotel is currently closed as it undergoes major renovation and refurbishment. It is scheduled to reopen sometime in late 2003.

41 Regent St., Cambridge, Cambridgeshire CB2 1AB. (②) 01223/351470. Fax 01223/566562. www.regent hotel.co.uk. 25 units. £90 ($144) double. Rates include continental breakfast. AE, DC, MC, V. **Amenities:** Bar. *In room:* TV, hair dryer.

INEXPENSIVE

Hamilton Hotel *(Value*   One of the better and more reasonably priced of the small hotels of Cambridge, this redbrick establishment lies about a mile northeast of the city center, close to the River Cam. Well-run and modestly accessorized, the hotel stands on a busy highway, but there's a parking area out back. The well-furnished bedrooms contain reasonably comfortable twin or double beds. Bathrooms are compact with shower stalls. The hotel has a small, traditionally styled licensed bar, offering standard pub food and snacks.

156 Chesterton Rd., Cambridge, Cambridgeshire CB4 1DA. (②) 01223/365664. Fax 01223/314866. www. hamiltonhotelcambridge.co.uk. 26 units, 21 with bathroom. £50 ($80) double without bathroom, £65 ($104) double with bathroom. Rates include English breakfast. AE, DC, MC, V. Bus: 3 or 3A. **Amenities:** Bar. *In room:* No phone.

Regency Guest House   In a desirable location near the town center, overlooking the verdant city park known as Parker's Piece, this hotel dates from 1850. Set behind a stone facade, and similar in design to many of its neighbors, it offers small bedrooms with 1950s-style retro furniture. The rooms are painted about every 6 months and have a bright, fresh look. Most of the rooms are small, and the beds are reasonably comfortable. Those rooms with compact bathrooms contain a shower.

7 Regent Terrace, Cambridge, Cambridgeshire CB2 1AA. (②) 01223/329626. Fax 01223/301567. www.guest-house.demon.co.uk. 8 units, 3 with bathroom. £65 ($104) double without bathroom, £75 ($120) double with bathroom. Rates include continental breakfast. No credit cards. Bus: 5. *In room:* TV, coffeemaker.

WHERE TO DINE

Drop down into the cozy **Rainbow Vegetarian Bistro,** King's Parade, across from King's College (② **01223/321551**), for coffee, a slice of fresh-baked cake or a meal from its selection of whole-food and vegetarian offerings. A main course lunch or dinner goes for only £6.95 to £7.95 ($11–$13); if you're around for breakfast, an omelet is just £5.65 ($9.05). Open Monday through Saturday from 11am to 10:30pm. The cafe lies at the end of a lily-lined path.

VERY EXPENSIVE

Midsummer House ★★ *Finds* MEDITERRANEAN   Located in an Edwardian-era cottage near the River Cam, the Midsummer House is a real find. We prefer to dine in the elegant conservatory, but you can also find a smartly laid table upstairs. The fixed-price menus are wisely limited, and quality control and high standards are much in evidence here. Daniel Clifford is the master chef, and he has created such specialties as filet of beef Rossini with braised winter vegetables and sauce Perigourdine; and roast squab pigeon, pomme Anna, tart tatin of onions, caramelized endives, and jus of morels.

Midsummer Common. 🕐 **01223/369299.** Reservations required. 3-course lunch £26 ($42); 3-course fixed-price dinner £45 ($72). AE, MC, V. Tues–Sat noon–2pm and 7–10pm; Sun noon–2pm.

MODERATE

Arundel House Restaurant 🕸 FRENCH/BRITISH/VEGETARIAN One of the best and most acclaimed restaurants in Cambridge is in a hotel overlooking the River Cam and Jesus Green, a short walk from the city center. Winner of many awards, it's noted not only for its excellence and use of fresh produce, but also for its good value. The decor is warmly inviting with Sanderson curtains, Louis XV–upholstered chairs, and spacious tables. The menu changes frequently, and you can dine both a la carte or from the set menu. Perhaps you'll begin with a homemade golden-pea-and-ham soup or a white-rum-and-passion-fruit cocktail. Fish choices include plaice or salmon; try the pork-and-pigeon casserole or the Japanese-style braised lamb.

53 Chesterton Rd. 🕐 **01223/367701.** Reservations required. Main courses £10–£16 ($16–$26); fixed-price lunch £18 ($29); fixed-price dinner £19 ($30). AE, DC, MC, V. Daily 12:30–2pm and 6:30–9:30pm. Bus: 3 or 5.

Browns 🕸 *Value* ENGLISH/CONTINENTAL With a neoclassical colonnade in front, Browns has all the grandeur of the Edwardian era, but inside, it's the most lighthearted restaurant in the city, with wicker chairs, high ceilings, pre–World War I woodwork, and a long bar covered with bottles of wine. The extensive bill of continually varied fare includes pasta, scores of fresh salads, several selections of meat and fish (from charcoal-grilled leg of lamb with rosemary to fresh fish in season), hot sandwiches, and the chef's daily specials posted on a blackboard. If you drop by in the afternoon, you can also order thick milkshakes or natural fruit juices. In fair weather, there's outdoor seating.

23 Trumpington St. (5 min. from King's College and opposite the Fitzwilliam Museum). 🕐 **01223/461655.** Main courses £8–£15 ($13–$24). AE, MC, V. Mon–Sat noon–11:30pm; Sun noon–10:30pm. Bus: 2.

Twenty Two 🕸 ENGLISH/CONTINENTAL One of the best in Cambridge, this restaurant is located in a quiet district near Jesus Green, and is a secret jealously guarded by the locals. The homelike but elegant Victorian dining room offers an ever-changing fixed-price menu based on fresh market produce. Owners David Carter and Louise Crompton use time-tested recipes along with their own inspirations, offering creations such as white onion soup with toasted goat's cheese or sautéed breast of chicken on braised celery with thyme jus.

22 Chesterton Rd. 🕐 **01223/351880.** Reservations required. Fixed-price menu £25 ($40). AE, MC, V. Tues–Sat 7–9:30pm.

INEXPENSIVE

Cambridge Arms ENGLISH This no-nonsense pub in the center of town bustles with atmosphere and dispenses endless platters of food to clients over the bar's countertop. Favorites include the chef's daily specials, grilled steaks, vegetarian meals, and an array of both hot and cold dishes.

The pub was recently refurbished and now is a music-oriented theme pub. Guitars and various music paraphernalia adorn the walls.

4 King St. 🕐 **01223/505015.** Bar snacks £3–£7 ($4.80–$11). MC, V. Mon–Thurs noon–3pm; Fri–Sun noon–4:30pm. Pub Mon–Sat 11am–11pm; Sun noon–10:30pm.

Charlie Chan CHINESE   Most people agree this is the finest Chinese restaurant in Cambridge, and so do we. We've always found Charlie Chan reliable and capable, which is remarkable given its huge menu. Downstairs is a long corridor-like restaurant, with pristine decor. The ambience is more lush in the Blue Lagoon upstairs. Most of the dishes here are inspired by the traditional cuisine of Beijing. The specialties we've most enjoyed include an aromatic and crispy duck, lemon chicken, and prawn with garlic and ginger.

14 Regent St. ⓒ 01223/361763. Reservations recommended. Main courses £5.80–£16 ($9.30–$26); fixed-price menus £15–£36 ($24–$58). AE, MC, V. Daily noon–5pm and 6–11pm.

The Green Man ENGLISH   Named in honor of Robin Hood, this 400-year-old inn is the most popular pub for outings from Cambridge. It's located on A604, 3km (2 miles) south of Cambridge in the hamlet of Grantchester, made famous by poet Rupert Brooke (see "Punting on the Cam," on p. 390). Even if you haven't heard of Brooke, you may enjoy a late afternoon wandering through the old church and then heading, as everybody does, to the Green Man. In winter, a crackling fire welcomes the weary, but in summer it's more tempting to retreat to the beer garden, from which you can stroll to the edge of the River Cam. Place your order at the counter; a server will bring your food to your table. The fare ranges from fish cakes in a Thai curry sauce to chicken Kiev and even traditional English pies and bangers and mash, as well as various vegetarian choices.

59 High St., Grantchester. ⓒ 01223/841178. Reservations recommended. Main courses £6.95–£9.95 ($11–$16). MC, V. Mon–Fri 11:30am–2:30pm and 5:30–11pm; Sat 11:30am–11pm; Sun noon–10:30pm. Pub Mon–Sat noon–3pm and 6–9pm; Sun noon–10:30pm. Bus: 118 from Cambridge.

CAMBRIDGE AFTER DARK

You can take in a production where Emma Thompson and other well-known thespians got their start at **The Amateur Dramatic Club,** Park Street near Jesus Lane (ⓒ01223/359547; box office 01223/503333). It presents two student productions nightly, Tuesday through Saturday, with the main show tending toward classic and modern drama or opera, and the late show being of a comic or experimental nature. The theater is open 50 weeks a year, closing in August and September, and tickets run from £3 to £8 ($4.80–$13).

Then there's the most popular Cantabrigian activity: the **pub crawl.** There are too many pubs in the city to list them all here, but you might as well start at Cambridge's oldest pub, the **Pickerel,** on Bridge Street (ⓒ 01223/355068), which dates from 1432. English pubs don't get more traditional than this. If the ceiling beams or floorboards groan occasionally—well, they've certainly earned the right over the years. Real ales on tap include Bulmer's Traditional Cider, Old Speckled Hen, or Theakston's 6X, Old Peculiar, and Best Bitter. **The Maypole,** Portugal Place at Park Street (ⓒ 01223/352999), is the local hangout for actors when they're not in the nearby ADC Theatre. It's known for cocktails instead of ales, but you can get a Tetley's 6X or Castle Eden anyway.

The Eagle, Benet Street off King's Parade (ⓒ 01223/505020), will be forever famous as the place where Nobel laureates James Watson and Francis Crick first announced their discovery of the DNA double helix. Real ales include Icebreaker and local brewery Greene King's Abbott, so make your order and raise a pint to the wonders of modern science.

To meet up with current Cambridge students, join the locals at the **Anchor,** Silver Street (ⓒ 01223/353554), or **Tap and Spiel (The Mill),** Mill Lane, off Silver Street Bridge (ⓒ 01223/357026), for a pint of Greene King's IPA or

Abbott. The crowd at the Anchor spills out onto the bridge in fair weather, whereas the Tap and Spiel's clientele lay claim to the entire riverside park.

There's also musical entertainment to be had, and you can find out who's playing by checking out flyers posted around town, or reading the *Varsity.* **The Corn Exchange,** Wheeler Street and Corn Exchange (© **01223/357851**), hosts everything from classical concerts to bigger-name rock shows. **The Graduate**, 16 Chesterton Rd. (© **01223/301416**), a pub located in a former movie theater, has live music or DJs on Friday and Saturday, with no cover charge.

Entertainment in some form can be found nightly at **The Junction,** Clifton Road, near the train station (© **01223/511511**), where an eclectic mix of acts take to the stage weeknights to perform all genres of music, comedy, and theater, and DJs take over on the weekend. Cover charges vary from £7 to £13 ($11–$21), depending on the event.

5th Avenue, Lion Yard (© **01223/364222**), a second-story club, has a huge dance floor and plays everything from house to the latest pop hits, Monday through Saturday from 9pm until 2am. Sometimes they even DJ the old-fashioned way, by taking requests. The cover charge ranges from £3 to £8 ($4.80–$13), depending on what night you're here.

SIDE TRIPS FROM CAMBRIDGE
A GLIMPSE OF WARTIME BRITAIN

Imperial War Museum ⊛   At a former Battle of Britain station and U.S. Eighth Air Force base in World War II, you'll find a huge collection of historic civil and military aircraft from both world wars, including the only B-29 Superfortress in Europe. Other exhibits include midget submarines, tanks, and field artillery pieces, as well as a historical display on the U.S. Eighth Air Force.

In the summer of 1997, Elizabeth II opened the American Air Museum here as part of the larger complex. It houses Europe's finest collection of historic American combat aircraft and is the largest precast concrete structure in Europe. Aircraft on show range from a World War I biplane to the giant B-52 jet bomber. A number of them are dramatically suspended from the ceiling as if in flight.

Duxford, on A505, at Junction 10 of M11. © 01223/835000. Admission £8.50 ($14) adults, £6.50 ($10) seniors, £4.50 ($7.20) children over 16 and students, free for children under 16. Mid-Mar to Oct daily 10am–6pm; Nov to mid-Mar daily 10am–4pm. Closed Dec 24–26. Bus: Cambus no. 103 from Drummer St. Station in Cambridge. By car, take M11 to Junction 10, 13km (8 miles) south of Cambridge.

2 Oxford: The City of Dreaming Spires ⭑⭑

87km (54 miles) NW of London; 87km (54 miles) SE of Coventry

A walk down the long sweep of the High, one of the most striking streets in England; a mug of cider in one of the old student pubs; the sound of May Day dawn when choristers sing in Latin from Magdalen Tower; students in traditional gowns whizzing past on rickety bikes; towers and spires rising majestically; nude swimming at Parson's Pleasure; the roar of a cannon launching the bumping races; a tiny, dusty bookstall where you can pick up a valuable first edition—all that is Oxford, home of one of the greatest universities in the world.

Romantic Oxford is still here, but to get to it, you'll also have to experience the bustling and crowded city that is also Oxford. You may be surprised by the never-ending stream of polluting buses and the fast-flowing pedestrian traffic— the city core feels more like London than once-sleepy Oxford. Surrounding the university are suburbs that keep growing, and not in a particularly attractive manner.

Oxford

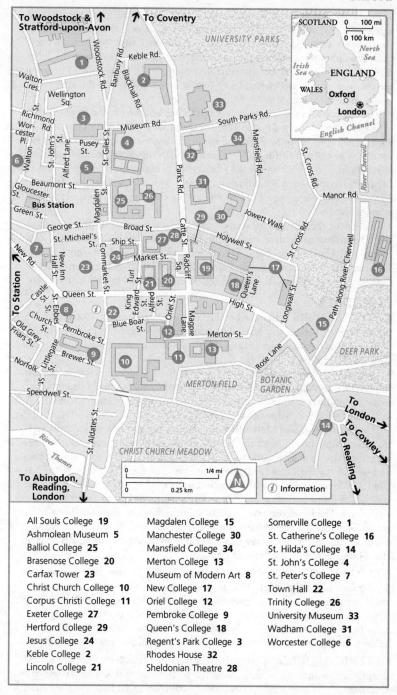

To Woodstock &
Stratford-upon-Avon

To Coventry

UNIVERSITY PARKS

Walton
Cres.
Wellington
Sq.

Richmond
Rd.
Worcester
Pl.

Walton

Gloucester
St.

Bus Station

Green St.

George St.

St. Michael's

New Inn
Hall St.

To Station

Castle
St.

Church
St.

Old
Friars

Grey
St.

Norfolk
St.

Littlegate

Speedwell St.

To Abingdon,
Reading,
London

Woodstock Rd.

Banbury Rd.

Keble Rd.

Blackhall Rd.

St. John's

St.

Alfred Lane

Pusey
St.

St. Giles St.

Museum Rd.

Beaumont St.

Magdalen St.

Broad St.

Ship St.

Cornmarket St.

Market St.

Turl
St.

King
Edward
St.

St.
Alfred
St.

Oriel St.

Blue Boar
St.

Brewer St.

Pembroke St.

Queen St.

St. Aldates St.

CHRIST CHURCH MEADOW

Parks Rd.

South Parks Rd.

Mansfield Rd.

St. Cross Rd.

Manor Rd.

Jowett Walk

Catte St.

Holywell St.

Radcliff
Sq.

Queen's
Lane

High St.

Merton St.

Magpie
Lane

MERTON FIELD

Rose Lane

BOTANIC
GARDEN

Longwall St.

Path along River Cherwell

River Cherwell

DEER PARK

To
London
To Cowley
To Reading

River
Thames

To Station

0   1/4 mi

0   0.25 km

N

ℹ Information

All Souls College 19
Ashmolean Museum 5
Balliol College 25
Brasenose College 20
Carfax Tower 23
Christ Church College 10
Corpus Christi College 11
Exeter College 27
Hertford College 29
Jesus College 24
Keble College 2
Lincoln College 21

Magdalen College 15
Manchester College 30
Mansfield College 34
Merton College 13
Museum of Modern Art 8
New College 17
Oriel College 12
Pembroke College 9
Queen's College 18
Regent's Park College 3
Rhodes House 32
Sheldonian Theatre 28

Somerville College 1
St. Catherine's College 16
St. Hilda's College 14
St. John's College 4
St. Peter's College 7
Town Hall 22
Trinity College 26
University Museum 33
Wadham College 31
Worcester College 6

At any time of the year, you can enjoy a tour of the colleges, many of which represent a peak in England's architectural history, as well as a valley of Victorian contributions. The Oxford Tourist Information Centre (see below) offers guided walking tours daily throughout the year. Just don't mention the other place (Cambridge), and you shouldn't have any trouble. Comparisons between the two universities are inevitable: Oxford is better known for the arts, Cambridge more for the sciences.

The city predates the university—in fact, it was a Saxon town in the early part of the 10th century. By the 12th century, Oxford was growing in reputation as a seat of learning, eclipsing Paris, and the first colleges were founded in the 13th century. The story of Oxford is filled with conflicts too complex and detailed to elaborate here. Suffice it to say the relationship between town and gown wasn't as peaceful as it is today. Riots often flared, and both sides were guilty of abuses. Nowadays, the young people of Oxford take out their aggressiveness in sporting competitions.

Ultimately, the test of a great university lies in the caliber of people it turns out. Oxford can name-drop a mouthful: Roger Bacon, Sir Walter Raleigh, John Donne, Sir Christopher Wren, Samuel Johnson, William Penn, John Wesley, William Pitt, Matthew Arnold, Lewis Carroll, Harold Macmillan, Graham Greene, A. E. Housman, T. E. Lawrence, Margaret Thatcher, and many others.

ESSENTIALS

GETTING THERE   Trains from Paddington Station reach Oxford in 1½ hours. Five trains run every hour. A cheap, same-day round-trip ticket costs £16 ($26); a 5-day round-trip ticket is £19 ($30). For more information, call ✆ 0345/484950.

Oxford CityLink provides coach service from London's Victoria Station (✆ 0870/580-8080) to the Oxford Bus Station. Coaches usually depart about every 30 minutes during the day; the trip takes approximately 1¾ hours. A same-day round-trip ticket costs £10 ($16).

If you're driving, take M40 west from London and just follow the signs. Traffic and parking are a disaster in Oxford, and not just during rush hours. However, there are four large park-and-ride parking lots on the north, south, east, and west of the city's ring road, all well marked. Parking is free at all times, but from 9:30am on and all day Saturday, you pay £2 ($3.20) for a bus ride into the city, which drops you off at St. Aldate's Cornmarket or Queen Street to see the city center. The buses run every 8 to 10 minutes in each direction. There is no service on Sunday. The parking lots are on the Woodstock road near the Peartree traffic circle, on the Botley road toward Farringdon, on the Abingdon road in the southeast, and on A40 toward London.

VISITOR INFORMATION   The **Oxford Tourist Information Centre** is at 15–16 Broad St. (✆ 01865/726871). The center sells a comprehensive range of maps, brochures, and souvenir items, as well as the famous Oxford University T-shirt. It provides hotel-booking services for £3 ($4.80). Guided walking tours leave from the center daily (see below). Open Monday through Saturday from 9:30am to 5pm and Sunday and bank holidays in summer from 10am to 3:30pm.

GETTING AROUND   Competition thrives in Oxford transportation, and the public benefits with swift, clean service by two companies. The **Oxford Bus Company,** 395 Cowley Rd. (✆ 01865/785400), has green Park and Ride buses that leave from four parking lots in the city using the north–south or east–west

---

(*Fun Fact*   **The Smoking Man**

A famous recent alumnus of Oxford's University College was William Jefferson Clinton, the Rhodes scholar who did not inhale here. If you'd like to see where America's former president lived, you can walk over to 46 Leckford Road.

---

routes. A round-trip costs £1.70 ($2.70). Its CityLink buses are blue and travel to London, Heathrow, and Gatwick. The company's red CityLink buses cover 15 routes in all suburbs, with a day pass allowing unlimited travel for £2.70 ($4.30). Weekly and monthly passes are available. The competition, **Stagecoach,** Unit 4, Horsepath, Cowley (© **01865/772250**), uses blue-and-cream minibuses and blue-and-orange coaches. City buses leave from Queen Street in Oxford center. Explorer passes cost £5.50 ($8.80). Abington Road buses are marked "Wantage," and Iffley Road buses are labeled "Rose Hill."

TOURS OF OXFORD

The best way to get a running commentary on the important sights is to take a 2-hour **walking tour** through the city and the major colleges. The tours leave daily from the Oxford Information Centre at 11am and 2pm. Tours costs £6.50 ($10) for adults and £3 ($4.80) for children; the tours do not include New College or Christ Church.

The **Oxford Story,** 6 Broad St. (© **01865/790055**), is a concise and entertaining audiovisual ride through the campus. It explains the structure of the colleges and highlights architectural and historical features. Visitors are also filled in on the general background of the colleges and the antics of some of the famous people who have passed through the University's portals. In July and August the audiovisual presentation is daily from 9:30am to 5pm. From September to December Monday through Saturday from 10am to 4:30pm, Sunday from 11am to 4:30pm, and January through June Monday through Saturday from 10am to 4:30pm, Sunday from 11am to 4:30pm. Admission is £7 ($11) for adults and £5.50 ($8.80) for seniors, students, and children. A family ticket for two adults and two children is £21 ($33).

For a good orientation, hour-long, open-top bus tours around Oxford are available from **Guide Friday,** whose office is at the railway station (© **01865/790522**). Buses leave every 20 minutes daily; in summer, buses leave every 5 to 10 minutes. Tickets are good for the day. Tours begin at 9:30am on winter weekends, 9:30am Monday through Friday. In summer, tours begin at 9:30am. The cost is £9 ($14) adults, £7 ($11) students and seniors, £3 ($4.80) children 5 to 12 years old, free for children under age 5. Tickets can be purchased from the driver.

The **Tourist Information Centre,** Old School Building, Gloucester Green (© **01865/726871**), offers a ghost tour that explores Oxford's ghoulish and gory past. The office also has a number of walking tours, with the ghost tour available Friday and Saturday evenings July through October. It begins at 7pm, ends at 8:30pm, and covers the dark alleyways around the ancient schools. The cost is £5.85 ($9.35) for adults and £3 ($4.80) children; tickets are available at the office during the day. Day tours begin at 10am daily, including Christmas, even for one person.

Moments   A Nostalgic Walk

Our favorite pastime here is to take **Addison's Walk** through the water meadows. The stroll is named after a former Oxford alumnus, Joseph Addison, the 18th-century essayist and playwright noted for his contributions to *The Spectator* and *The Tatler*.

EXPLORING OXFORD UNIVERSITY

Many Americans arriving at Oxford ask, "Where's the campus?" If a local looks amused when answering, it's because Oxford University is, in fact, made up of 35 colleges sprinkled throughout the town. To tour all of these would be a formidable task. It's best to focus on just a handful of the better-known colleges.

A word of warning: The main business of a university is, of course, to educate, and this function at Oxford has been severely hampered by the number of visitors who disturb the academic work of the university. So visiting is restricted to certain hours and small groups of six or fewer. Furthermore, there are areas where visitors are not allowed at all, but the tourist office will be happy to advise you when and where you may take in the sights of this great institution.

AN OVERVIEW   For a bird's-eye view of the city and colleges, climb **Carfax Tower** ⊛, located in the center of the city. This structure is distinguished by its clock and figures that strike on the quarter-hour. Carfax Tower is all that remains from St. Martin's Church, where William Shakespeare once stood as godfather for William Davenant, who also became a successful playwright. A church stood on this site from 1032 until 1896. The tower used to be higher, but after 1340 it was lowered, following complaints from the university to Edward III that townspeople threw stones and fired arrows at students during town-and-gown disputes. Admission is £1.50 ($2.40) for adults, £1 ($1.60) for children. The tower is open year-round, except for from Christmas Eve to January 1. April through October, hours are from 10am to 5pm daily. Off-season hours are Monday through Saturday from 10am to 3:30pm. Children under 5 are not admitted. For information, call ℂ **01865/792653.**

CHRIST CHURCH ✪✪   Begun by Cardinal Wolsey as Cardinal College in 1525, Christ Church (ℂ **01865/276150;** www.chch.ox.ac.uk), known as the House, was founded by Henry VIII in 1546. Facing St. Aldate's Street, Christ Church has the largest quadrangle of any college in Oxford. Tom Tower houses Great Tom, an 18,000-pound bell. It rings at 9:05pm nightly, signaling the closing of the college gates. The 101 times it peals originally signified the number of students in residence at the time the college was founded. Although the student body has grown significantly, Oxford traditions live forever. There are some interesting portraits in the 16th-century Great Hall, including works by Gainsborough and Reynolds. There's also a separate portrait gallery.

The college chapel was constructed over a period of centuries, beginning in the 12th century. (Incidentally, it's not only the college chapel but also the cathedral of the diocese of Oxford.) The cathedral's most distinguishing features are its Norman pillars and the vaulting of the choir, dating from the 15th century. In the center of the great quadrangle is a statue of Mercury mounted in the center of a fishpond. The college and cathedral can be visited between 9am and 5:30pm, though times vary. It's best to call before you visit. The entrance fee is £3 ($4.80) for adults and £2 ($3.20) for children.

Insider tip: Almost overlooked by the average visitor is an unheralded little gem known as **Christ Church Picture Gallery,** entered through the Canterbury Quad. Here you come across a stunning collection of old masters, mainly from the Dutch, Flemish, and Italian school, including works by Michelangelo and Leonardo da Vinci. Open from April to September, Monday through Saturday from 10:30am to 1pm and 2 to 5:30pm (closes at 4:30pm Oct–Mar). Admission is £2 ($3.20) for adults or £1 ($1.60) for seniors and students.

MAGDALEN COLLEGE   Pronounced *Maud*-lin, Magdalen College, High Street (© **01865/276000;** www.magd.ox.ac.uk), was founded in 1458 by William of Waynflete, bishop of Winchester and later chancellor of England. Its alumni range from Wolsey to Wilde. Opposite the botanic garden, the oldest in England, is the bell tower, where the choristers sing in Latin at dawn on May Day. Charles I, his days numbered, watched the oncoming Roundheads from this tower. Visit the 15th-century chapel, in spite of many of its latter-day trappings. Ask when the hall and other places of special interest are open. The grounds of Magdalen are the most extensive of any Oxford college; there's even a deer park. You can visit all year-round between 1pm and dusk daily. Admission is £3 ($4.80).

MERTON COLLEGE ★★   Founded in 1264, Merton College, Merton Street (© **01865/276310;** www.merton.ox.ac.uk), is among the three oldest colleges at the university. It stands near Corpus Christi College on Merton Street, the sole survivor of Oxford's medieval cobbled streets. Merton College is noted for its library (which was closed at press time), built between 1371 and 1379 and said to be the oldest college library in England. Though a tradition once kept some of its most valuable books chained, now only one book is secured in that manner to illustrate that historical custom. One of the library's treasures is an astrolabe (an astronomical instrument used for measuring the altitude of the sun and stars) thought to have belonged to Chaucer. You pay £1 ($1.60) to visit the ancient library as well as the Max Beerbohm Room (the satirical English caricaturist who died in 1956). The library and college are open Monday through Friday from 2 to 4pm, and Saturday and Sunday from 10am to 4pm. It's closed for 1 week at Easter and Christmas and on weekends during the winter.

NEW COLLEGE   New College, Holywell St. (© **01865/279555**), was founded in 1379 by William of Wykeham, bishop of Winchester and later lord chancellor of England. His college at Winchester supplied a constant stream of students. The first quadrangle, dating from before the end of the 14th century, was the initial quadrangle to be built in Oxford and formed the architectural design for the other colleges. In the antechapel is Sir Jacob Epstein's remarkable modern sculpture of Lazarus and a fine El Greco painting of St. James. One of the treasures of the college is a crosier (pastoral staff of a bishop) belonging to the founding father. The college (entered at New College Lane) can be visited

---

(*Finds* **A Quiet Oasis**

Though ignored by the average visitor, the **Botanic Gardens** opposite Magdalen were first planted in 1621 on the site of a Jewish graveyard from the early Middle Ages. Bounded by a curve of the Cherwell, they still stand today and are the best place in Oxford to escape the invading hordes. Open daily from noon to 4pm; admission is £2 ($3.20).

Moments **Punting the River Cherwell**

Punting on the River Cherwell remains the favorite outdoor pastime in Oxford. At Punt Station, **Cherwell Boathouse,** Bardwell Road (© **01865/ 515978;** www.cherwellboathouse.co.uk), you can rent a punt (flat-bottom boat maneuvered by a long pole and a small oar) for £10 to £12 ($16–$19) per hour, plus a £50 to £60 ($80–$96) deposit. Similar charges are made for punt rentals at Magdalen Bridge Boathouse. Punts are rented from mid-March to mid-October, daily from 10am until dusk. Hours of operation seem to be rather informal, however, and you're not always guaranteed that someone will be here to rent you a boat, even if the punt itself is available.

---

from Easter to October daily between 11am and 5pm; off season daily between 2 and 4pm. Admission is 50p to £2 (80¢–$3.20) (depending on what is open) from Easter to October and free off season.

Insider tips: In the beautiful garden of the college, you can stroll among the remains of the old city wall and the mound. It's an evocative, romantic site. New College is also known for its "notorious gargoyles." Check them out at the bell tower, decorated with Seven Virtues on one side and Seven Deadly Sins on the other. The virtues are just as grotesque as the deadly sins.

THE OLD BODLEIAN LIBRARY ★★ This famed library on Catte Street (© **01865/277224;** www.bodley.ox.ac.uk) was launched in 1602, initially funded by Sir Thomas Bodley. It is home to some 50,000 manuscripts and more than 5 million books. Over the years the library has expanded from the Old Library complex to other buildings, including the Radcliffe Camera next door. The easiest way to visit the library is by taking a guided tour, leaving from the Divinity School across the street from the main entrance. In summer there are four tours Monday through Friday, and two on Saturday; in winter, two tours leave per day. Call for specific times.

SHOPPING

Golden Cross, an arcade of first-class shops and boutiques, lies between Cornmarket Street and the Covered Market (or between High St. and Market St.). Parts of the colorful gallery date from the 12th century. Many buildings remain from the medieval era, along with some 15th- and 17th-century structures. The market also has a reputation as the Covent Garden of Oxford, where live entertainment takes place on Saturday mornings in summer. In the arcade shops you'll find a diverse selection of merchandise, including handmade Belgian chocolates, specialty gifts, clothing for both women and men, and luxury leather goods.

In its way, **Alice's Shop,** 83 St. Aldate's (© **01865/723793**), played an important role in English literature. Set within a 15th-century building that has housed some kind of shop since 1820, it functioned as a general store (selling brooms, hardware, and the like) during the period that Lewis Carroll, at the time a professor of mathematics at Christ Church College, was composing *Alice in Wonderland.* It is believed to have been the model for important settings within the book. Today, the place is a favorite stopover of Lewis Carroll fans from as far away as Japan, who gobble up commemorative pencils, chess sets, party favors, bookmarks, and in rare cases, original editions of some of Carroll's works.

The **Bodleian Library Shop,** Old School's Quadrangle, Radcliffe Square, Broad Street (© **01865/277216**), specializes in Oxford souvenirs, from books and paperweights to Oxford banners and coffee mugs.

Castell & Son (The Varsity Shop), 13 Broad St. (© **01865/244000**; www.varsityshop.co.uk), is the best outlet in Oxford for clothing emblazoned with the Oxford logo or heraldic symbol. Choices include both whimsical and dead-on-serious neckties, hats, T-shirts, sweatshirts, pens, bookmarks, beer and coffee mugs, and cuff links. It's commercialized Oxford, but it's still got a sense of relative dignity and style.

WHERE TO STAY IN & AROUND OXFORD

Accommodations in Oxford are limited, although recently, motels have sprouted on the outskirts—a good development for those wanting modern amenities. In addition, if you've got a car, you may want to consider country houses or small B&Bs on the outskirts of town; they're the best choices in the area if you don't mind commuting.

Bedrooms, albeit expensive ones, are also provided at Le Manoir aux Quat' Saisons (reviewed under "Where to Dine," below).

The **Oxford Tourist Information Centre,** Gloucester Green, behind the bus bays (© **01865/726871**), operates a year-round room-booking service for a £3 ($4.80) fee, plus a 10% refundable deposit. If you'd like to seek lodgings on your own, the center has a list of accommodations, maps, and guidebooks.

VERY EXPENSIVE

Old Parsonage Hotel ★★ This extensively renovated hotel, near St. Giles Church and Keble College, is so old it looks like an extension of one of the ancient colleges. Originally a 13th-century hospital, it was restored in the early 17th century. In the 20th century, a modern wing was added, and in 1991 it was completely renovated and made into a first-rate hotel. This intimate old hotel is filled with hidden charms such as tiny gardens in its courtyard and on its roof terrace. In this tranquil area of Oxford, you feel like you're living at one of the colleges yourself. The rooms are individually designed but not large; all the units have bathrooms with shower-tub combinations and each of them open onto the private gardens; 10 of them are on the ground floor.

1 Banbury Rd., Oxford OX2 6NN. © **01865/310210**. Fax 01865/311262. www.oxford-hotels-restaurants.co.uk. 30 units. £133–£168 ($213–$269) double; £193 ($309) suite. AE, DC, MC, V. Bus: 7. **Amenities:** Restaurant; bar; room service; laundry service; dry cleaning. *In room:* TV, dataport, hair dryer, safe, trouser press.

The Randolph ★ Since 1864, the Randolph has overlooked St. Giles, the Ashmolean Museum, and the Cornmarket. The hotel is an example of how historic surroundings can be combined with modern conveniences to make for elegant accommodations. The lounges, though modernized, are cavernous enough for dozens of separate and intimate conversational groupings. The furnishings are traditional. Some rooms are quite large; others are a bit cramped. All rooms have well-maintained bathrooms. The double-glazing on the windows appears inadequate to keep out the noise of midtown traffic. In this price range, we'd opt first for the more stylish and intimate Old Parsonage before checking in here.

Beaumont St., Oxford, Oxfordshire OX1 2LN. © **800/225-5843** in the U.S. and Canada, or 0870/400-8200. Fax 01865/791678. www.macdonaldhotels.co.uk. 114 units. £120–£195 ($192–$312) double; from £355–£600 ($568–$960) suite. AE, DC, MC, V. Parking £22 ($35). Bus: 7. **Amenities:** Restaurant; 2 bars; concierge; room service; babysitting; laundry service; dry cleaning. *In room:* TV, dataport, coffeemaker, hair dryer, iron.

Studley Priory Hotel ★★★ The Studley Priory Hotel, the best country-house hotel in Oxford, may be remembered by fans of the movie *A Man for All Seasons*. The former Benedictine priory, a hotel since 1961, was used in background shots as the private residence of Sir Thomas More. It's a stunning example of Elizabethan architecture, though it originally dates from the 12th century. Located on 13 acres of wooded grounds and occupied for around 300 years by the Croke family, the manor is 11km (7 miles) from Oxford. It's built of stone in the manorial style, with large halls, long bedroom wings, and gables with mullioned windows. The rooms are very large and the furnishings tasteful. Bed sizes range from a standard double to a master four-poster if you want to feel like Henry VIII. Little extras include a beverage tray with homemade crackers. Other than a suite, the best accommodations are the "master doubles," furnished in 16th-century style with antiques. Getting here is a bit complicated, so arm yourself with a good map when you strike out from Oxford.

Horton-cum-Studley, Oxfordshire OX33 1AZ. © **800/525-4800** in the U.S. and Canada, or 01865/351203. Fax 01865/351613. www.studley-priory.co.uk. 18 units. £165–£175 ($264–$280) double; £275 ($440) suite. Rates include English breakfast. AE, DC, MC, V. From Oxford, drive to the end of Banbury Rd. At the traffic circle, take the 3rd exit (toward London). Go about 5.5km (3½ miles). At the next traffic circle, take the 1st exit (signposted Horton-cum-Studley) and travel 7km (4½ miles). Go through the estate and stay on the same road until you come to "staggered crossroads." Go straight across, signposted Horton-cum-Studley, 4km (2½ miles). This road brings you right into the village; the hotel is at the top of the hill on the right-hand side. **Amenities:** Restaurant; bar; tennis court; room service; babysitting; laundry service; dry cleaning. *In room:* TV, coffeemaker, hair dryer, trouser press.

EXPENSIVE

Eastgate Hotel ★ The Eastgate, built on the site of a 1600s structure, stands within walking distance of Oxford College and the city center. Recently refurbished, it offers modern facilities while somewhat retaining the atmosphere of an English country house. The bedrooms are well worn but still cozy and range in size from small to medium. The bathrooms have minimum space but are equipped with shower-tub combinations.

23 Merton St., The High St., Oxford, Oxfordshire, OX1 4BE. © **0870/400-8201.** Fax 01865/791681. www.macdonaldhotels.co.uk. 64 units. £160 ($256) double; £180 ($288) suite. AE, DC, MC, V. Bus: 3, 4, 7, or 52. **Amenities:** Restaurant; bar; room service; babysitting; laundry service; dry cleaning. *In room:* A/C, TV, coffeemaker, hair dryer, trouser press.

Old Bank Hotel ★★★ The first hotel created in the center of Oxford in 135 years, the Old Bank opened late in 1999, and immediately surpassed the traditional favorite, the Randolph, in style and amenities. Located on Oxford's main street and surrounded by some of its oldest colleges and sights, the building dates back to the 18th century and was indeed once a bank. The hotel currently features a collection of 20th-century British art handpicked by the owners. Bedrooms are comfortably and elegantly appointed, often opening onto views. A combination of velvet and shantung silk-trimmed linen bedcovers give the accommodations added style. Each unit includes a well-kept bathroom with terra-cotta or marble tiles.

92–94 High St., Oxford OX1 4BN. © **01865/799599.** Fax 01865/799598. www.oxford-hotels-restaurants.co.uk. 42 units. £160–£235 ($256–$376) double; from £265–£320 ($424–$512) suite. AE, DC, MC, V. Bus: 7. **Amenities:** Restaurant; bar; concierge; room service; babysitting; laundry service; dry cleaning. *In room:* A/C, TV, dataport, coffeemaker, hair dryer, CD player.

Weston Manor ★★ Ideal as a center for touring the district (Blenheim Palace is only 8km/5 miles away), this 13-acre manor is owned and run by the Osborn family. It has existed since the 11th century; portions of the present building date from the 14th and 16th centuries. The estate is the ancestral home of the earls of Abingdon and Berkshire. It was also an abbey until Henry VIII abolished the abbeys and assumed ownership of the property. Of course, there are ghosts: Mad Maude, the naughty nun who was burned at the stake for her "indecent and immoral" behavior, returns to haunt the Oak rooms. Prince Rupert, during the English Civil War, hid from Cromwell's soldiers in one of the fireplaces, eventually escaping in drag as a "maiden of the milk bucket."

The reception lounge is dominated by a Tudor fireplace and a long refectory table. Most of the rooms are spacious and furnished with antiques (often four-poster beds), old dressing tables, and chests. Bedrooms are divided between the main house and a former coach that was skillfully converted into well-equipped guest rooms. Regardless of location, each bedroom is first-rate with extremely comfortable beds and fine linen, plus modernized bathrooms with adequate shelf space and a shower-tub combination. Half of the bedrooms are set aside for nonsmokers.

Weston-on-the-Green, Oxfordshire OX25 3QL. © **01869/350621.** Fax 01869/350901. www.westonmanor. co.uk. 35 units. £154 ($246) double; £215–£225 ($344–$360) suite. Rates include English breakfast. AE, DC, MC, V. Drive 9.5km (6 miles) north of Oxford on A34. **Amenities:** Restaurant; bar; pool; room service; laundry service; dry cleaning. *In room:* A/C, TV, dataport, coffeemaker, hair dryer, trouser press.

MODERATE

The Oxford Hotel   This is a good choice if you have a car; it's 3km (2 miles) north of the city center, and hidden from traffic at the junction of A40 and A34. It attracts a lot of business travelers, but also visitors, and is a good base for exploring not only Oxford but also the Cotswolds, which are within easy reach. The M40 motorway is just a 13km (8-mile) drive away. Rooms are motel-like, with modern, contemporary furnishings that are comfortable and spacious, but as of this writing, the hotel is undergoing extensive refurbishing and upgrading. Some bedrooms are set aside for nonsmokers. The shower-only bathrooms are nothing special but are well maintained.

Godstow Rd., Wolvercote Roundabout, Oxford, Oxfordshire OX2 8AL. © **01865/489988.** Fax 01865/ 310259. www.paramount-hotels.co.uk. 168 units. £159–£179 ($254–$286) double. AE, DC, MC, V. Bus: 6. **Amenities:** Restaurant; bar; pool; 2 squash courts; spa; room service; laundry service; dry cleaning. *In room:* A/C, TV, dataport, coffeemaker, hair dryer, safe, trouser press.

INEXPENSIVE

Dial House *Value*   Three kilometers (2 miles) east of the heart of Oxford, beside the main highway leading to London, is this country-style house, originally built between 1924 and 1927. In its conversion to a guest hotel, much of the original architecture of the once-private home has been retained and most of the individually designed furnished units open onto an attractive garden. Graced with mock Tudor half-timbering and a prominent blue-faced sundial (from which it derives its name), it has cozy and recently renovated rooms. Bathrooms are small, and most of them have a shower only, but a few offer a combination tub and shower. The owners, the Morris family, serve only breakfast in their bright dining room. The entire property is nonsmoking.

25 London Rd., Headington, Oxford, Oxfordshire OX3 7RE. ©/fax **01865/760743.** www.oxfordcity.co.uk/ accom/dialhouse. 8 units. £65–£70 ($104–$112) double. AE, MC, V. Bus: 2, 2A, 7, 7A, or 22. *In room:* TV, coffeemaker, hair dryer, safe, no phone.

Tilbury Lodge Private Hotel *Kids*   On a quiet country lane about 3km (2 miles) west of the center of Oxford, this small hotel is less than a mile from the railway station, where hotel staff will pick you up to save you the walk. Eddie and Eileen Trafford accommodate guests in their well-furnished and comfortable rooms. Each of the individually sized rooms is immaculately kept and furnished in a traditional English style with wood furnishings, excellent beds, rugs, and wall art to give each accommodation a homelike touch. The most expensive room has a four-poster bed; there is a also a room suitable for families. Bathrooms, although tiny, are well kept, usually with a shower. The guesthouse also has a Jacuzzi and welcomes children. *Note:* Like similar accommodations at Dial House, Tilbury Lodge offers a tranquil location on a country lane right outside the bustle of town. Many use it as a base for exploring not only Oxford, but the Cotswolds, Blenheim Palace, Stratford-upon-Avon, and even Bath. Because of the ample street parking, you can leave your car here and go by bus into the center.

5 Tilbury Lane, Eynsham Rd., Botley, Oxford, Oxfordshire OX2 9NB. ℭ **01865/862138.** Fax 01865/863700. 9 units. £66–£75 ($106–$120) double. Rates include English breakfast. MC, V. Bus: 4A, 4B, or 100. **Amenities:** Jacuzzi. *In room:* TV, coffeemaker, hair dryer.

WHERE TO DINE
VERY EXPENSIVE

Le Manoir aux Quat' Saisons ★★★ MODERN FRENCH   Some 19km (12 miles) southeast of Oxford, Le Manoir aux Quat' Saisons offers the finest cuisine in the Midlands. The gray- and honey-colored stone manor house was originally built by a Norman nobleman in the early 1300s, and over the years has attracted many famous visitors. Today, the restaurant's connection with France has been masterfully revived by the Gallic owner and chef, Raymond Blanc. His reputation for comfort and cuisine attracts guests from as far away as London.

You can enjoy such creative treats as roasted squab and foie gras ravioli with wild mushrooms; roasted grouse in a blackberry-and-red-wine sauce; or a truly delectable roasted breast of Barbary hen duck with figs and fennel seeds and a pan-fried foie gras. Each dish is an exercise in studied perfection.

Accommodations are also available here. The gabled house was built in the 1500s and improved and enlarged in 1908. Each very pricey room—rates are £265 to £855 ($424–$1,368) for a double—is decorated boudoir-style with luxurious beds and linens, ruffled canopies, and high-quality antique reproductions, plus deluxe bathrooms with thick towels and a hair dryer.

Great Milton, Oxfordshire. ℭ **800/845-4274** in the U.S., or 01844/278881. Fax 01844/278847. www.manoir. com. Reservations required. Main courses £26–£38 ($42–$61); lunch menu du jour £45 ($72); lunch or dinner menu gourmand £95 ($152). AE, DC, MC, V. Daily noon–2:30pm and 7–9:15pm. Take Exit 7 off M40 and head along A329 toward Wallingford; look for signs for Great American Milton Manor about a mile after.

EXPENSIVE

Cherwell Boathouse Restaurant ★ FRENCH/MODERN ENGLISH   An Oxford landmark on the River Cherwell, it's owned by Anthony Verdin, assisted by a young crew. With an intriguing fixed-price menu, the cooks change the fare every 2 weeks to take advantage of the availability of fresh vegetables, fish, and meat. There is a very reasonable, even exciting, wine list. The kitchen is often cited for its "sensible combinations" of ingredients, as reflected quite well by its cream of artichoke and celery soup for a starter, or its shellfish terrine with a velvety chive-flavored crème fraîche. The success of the main dishes is founded on savory treats such as a pink and juicy breast of pigeon matched with a salad of smoked bacon on which tantalizing dribbles of raspberry dressing have been dropped. Children are charged half price, but this isn't a particularly good place to take them. In summer, the restaurant also serves on the terrace. Enjoy such starters as warm salad of pigeon breast or toasted pine nuts and cranberry dressing. For a main course, you may opt for grilled filet of salmon with artichoke mash or a bubble and squeak. For dessert, indulge on the lemon and almond roulade. The style is sophisticated yet understated, with a heavy reliance on quality ingredients that are cooked in such a way that natural flavors are always preserved.

Bardwell Rd. ✆ **01865/552746.** www.cherwellboathouse.co.uk. Reservations recommended. Fixed-price dinner from £22 ($34); Sun lunch £22 ($34); Mon–Fri lunch £20 ($31). AE, DC, MC, V. Mon–Sun noon–2:30pm and 6:30–10pm. Closed Dec 24–30. Bus: Banbury Road.

Restaurant Elizabeth ★ FRENCH/CONTINENTAL Named after its original owner, a matriarch who founded this stone-sided house opposite Christ Church College in the 1930s, today, you're likely to find a well-trained staff from Spain, serving beautifully presented dishes in the French style. The larger of the two dining rooms displays reproductions of paintings by Goya and Velázquez and exudes a restrained dignity; the smaller room is devoted to *Alice in Wonderland* designs inspired by Lewis Carroll. Dishes are based on the use of fine produce prepared with a skilled culinary technique, as exemplified by filet of salmon sautéed in butter and cooked with a white-wine sauce or the grilled filet steak in a Madeira-flavored mushroom sauce. Breast of chicken is cooked in butter and delectably served in a creamy cognac and white-wine sauce.

82 St. Aldate's St. ✆ **01865/242230.** Reservations recommended. Main courses £14–£33 ($22–$53); fixed-price lunch £16 ($26). AE, DC, MC, V. Tues–Sat 12:30–2:30pm and 6:30–11pm; Sun 7–10:30pm. Closed Good Friday and Christmas week. Bus: 7.

MODERATE

Gee's Restaurant ★ MEDITERRANEAN/INTERNATIONAL This restaurant, in a spacious Victorian glass conservatory, was converted from what for 80 years was the leading florist of Oxford. Its original features were retained by the owners, the Old Parsonage Hotel (see above), who have turned it into one of the most nostalgic and delightful places to dine in the city. Open since 1984, it has come more into fashion under a new chef. From students to professors, clients are mixed, but all enjoy a well-chosen list of offerings that ranges from succulent pastas to chargrilled steaks, from fresh fish to crisp salads. The confit of duck is a savory choice, enhanced by Savoy cabbage, smoked bacon, and herb-roasted potatoes. Count on a freshly made soup and such Mediterranean-inspired salads as roast pepper, French beans, and olives. Always reliable is Scottish prime rib-eye steak with mushrooms and shoestring "chips."

61 Banbury Rd. ✆ **01865/553540.** Reservations recommended. Fixed-price lunch £9.50 ($15); main courses £10–£19 ($16–$30). AE, MC, V. Daily noon–2:30pm and 6–11pm.

Le Petit Blanc ★ FRENCH/MEDITERRANEAN The biggest culinary news in Oxford is the return of Raymond Blanc with another Le Petit Blanc. (A previous one proved disappointing.) Monsieur Blanc is a wiser restaurateur now, and this buzzing brasserie is doing just fine. A former piano shop has been converted into a stylish place offering a menu that promises something for every palate. Here you can get a taste of the famous chef's creations without the high prices of his famed Le Manoir aux Quat' Saisons. The menu is more straightforward here, with a large emphasis on fresh ingredients.

The food is wholesome and delicious, based on authentic provincial French cuisine, complemented by Mediterranean and Asian accents. We recently took delight in an appetizer, deep-fried goat's cheese with an olive tapenade, French beans, and tomato chutney, followed by a perfectly roasted John Dory with a coriander dressing. For other main courses, the braised rabbit with sweet-onion tarte tatin and flap mushrooms, or the Oxford sausage with parsley mash,

Madeira, and sweet-onion sauce are superb. The desserts are first-rate, especially the raspberry soufflé.

71–72 Walton St. ✆ **01865/510999.** Reservations recommended. Main courses £10–£15 ($16–$24); fixed-price lunch £15 ($24). AE, DC, MC, V. Mon–Sat noon–3:30pm and 6–11pm; Sun 12:30–3pm and 6:30–10:30pm.

INEXPENSIVE

Al-Shami LEBANESE   Bearing the archaic name for the city of Damascus, this Lebanese restaurant has two separate dining rooms: One with blessings from the Koran stenciled in calligraphic patterns under the coves; the other with pale beige walls and lots of wood paneling. Expect a clientele of local residents, with fewer students than you might expect, and a formally dressed, Arabic- and English-speaking staff wearing black trousers, bow ties, and white vests. Many diners don't go beyond the appetizers, because they comprise more than 35 delectable hot and cold selections—everything from falafel to a salad made with lamb's brains. Charcoal-grilled chopped lamb, chicken, or fish constitute most of the main-dish selections. In between, guests nibble on raw vegetables. Desserts are chosen from the trolley, and vegetarian meals are also available.

25 Walton Crescent. ✆ **01865/310066.** Reservations recommended. Main courses £5.75–£12 ($9.20–$19); fixed-price menu £15 ($24). MC, V. Daily noon–midnight.

Browns _Value_ ENGLISH/CONTINENTAL   Oxford's busiest and most bustling English brasserie suits all groups, from babies to undergraduates to grandmas. A 10-minute walk north of the town center, it occupies the premises of five Victorian shops whose walls were removed to create one large, echoing, and very popular space. A thriving bar trade (where lots of people seem to order Pimms) makes the place an evening destination in its own right.

A young and enthusiastic staff serves traditional English cuisine. Your meal might include meat pies, hot salads, burgers, pastas, steaks, or poultry. Afternoon tea here is a justly celebrated Oxford institution. Reservations are not accepted, so if you want to avoid a delay, arrive here during off-peak dining hours.

5–11 Woodstock Rd. ✆ **01865/511995.** Main courses £6–£15 ($9.60–$24). MC, V. Mon–Sat 11am–11:30pm; Sun 11:30am–11:30pm. Bus: 2 or 7.

OXFORD AFTER DARK
THE PERFORMING ARTS

Highly acclaimed orchestras playing in truly lovely settings mark the Music at Oxford series at the **Oxford Playhouse Theatre,** Beaumont Street (✆ **01865/ 305305;** www.oxfordplayhouse.com). The autumn season runs from mid-September to December, the winter season from January to April, the spring-summer season from May to early July. Tickets range from £9–£24 ($14–$38). Classical music is performed by outstanding groups such as the European Union Chamber Orchestra, the Canterbury Musical Society, the Bournemouth Symphony, and the Guild Hall String Ensemble of London. All performances are held in the Sheldonian Theatre, a particularly attractive site, designed by Sir Christopher Wren, with paintings on the ceiling.

The Apollo, George Street (✆ **01865/243041** for ticket reservations), is Oxford's primary theater. Tickets are £6.50 to £50 ($10–$79). A continuous run of comedy, ballet, drama, opera, and even rock contributes to the variety. The Welsh National Opera often performs, and The Glyndebourne Touring Opera appears regularly. Advance booking is recommended, though some shows may have tickets the week of the performance. Don't try for tickets for popular shows on the same day.

Finds Pubs with a Pedigree

Every college town the world over has a fair number of bars, but few can boast local watering holes with such atmosphere and history as Oxford.

A short block from The High, overlooking the north side of Christ Church College, the **Bear Inn,** on Alfred Street (© **01865/728164**), is an Oxford landmark, built in the 13th century and mentioned time and time again in English literature. The Bear brings together a wide variety of people in a relaxed way. You may talk with a raja from India, a university don, or a titled gentleman who's the latest in a line of owners that goes back more than 700 years. Some former owners developed an astonishing habit: clipping neckties. Around the lounge bar you'll see the remains of thousands of ties, which have been labeled with their owners' names.

Even older than the Bear is the **Turf Tavern,** 7 Bath Place (off Holywell St.; © **01865/243235**), on a very narrow passageway near the Bodleian Library. The pub is reached via St. Helen's Passage, which stretches between Holywell Street and New College Lane. (You'll probably get lost, but any student worth his beer can direct you.) Thomas Hardy used the place as the setting for *Jude the Obscure.* It was "the local" of the future U.S. president, Bill Clinton, during his student days at Oxford. In warm weather, you can choose a table in any of the three separate gardens that radiate outward from the pub's central core. For wintertime warmth, braziers are lighted in the courtyard and in the gardens. A food counter set behind a glass case displays the day's fare—salads, soups, sandwiches, and so on. Local ales (including one named Headbanger, with a relatively high alcohol content) are served, as well as a range of wines.

Just outside of town, hidden away some 4km (2½ miles) north of Oxford, the **Trout Inn,** 195 Godstow Rd., Wolvercote (© **01865/302071**), is a private world where you can get ale and beer and standard fare. Have your drink in one of the historic rooms, with their settles (wooden benches), brass, and old prints, or go out in sunny weather to sit on a stone wall. On the grounds are peacocks, ducks, swans, and herons that live in and around the river and an adjacent weir pool; they'll join you if you're handing out crumbs. Take an arched stone bridge, architecture with wildly pitched roofs and gables, add the Thames River, and you have the Trout. The Smoking Room, the original 12th-century part, complements the inn's relatively "new" 16th-century bars. Daily specials are featured. Hot meals are served all day in the restaurant; salads are featured in summer, and there are grills in winter. On your way there and back, look for the view of Oxford from the bridge. Take bus no. 6A, 6B, or 6C to Wolvercote, then walk 1km (½ mile); it's also fun to bike here from Oxford.

At the **Oxford Playhouse,** performances range from Shakespeare to modern comedy and drama. Tickets are £9 to £24 ($14–$38). They are open most nights year-round, except some Sundays and the week after Christmas.

Insider tip: For some of the best productions in England, with some of the most talented actors, ask at the tourist office about summer performances in some of the college gardens. These used to be student productions, but increasingly are being taken over by professional companies. There are two Shakespeare troupes as well as other groups. Ticket costs are significantly less here than you'd find for a comparable experience elsewhere.

THE CLUBS: BLUES, JAZZ & "CELTIC ROCK"

As a sign of the times, **Freud,** Walton Street at Great Clarendon Street (© **01865/ 311171**), has turned a 19th-century church, stained-glass windows and all, into a jazz and folk club with an expansive array of drink choices. The cover charge is £4.50 ($7.20) after 10pm on Friday and Saturday.

Old Fire Station, 40 George St. (© **01865/794494**), covers all the bases, including live entertainment, a bar, theater, art museum, and a new science museum called Curiosity, with a light show and other exhibits. The restaurant, open daily at noon, serves breakfast until 9pm, with free coffee, tea, and toast. Music cover charges begin at 9pm and are £6 to £8 ($9.60–$13) nightly. Offerings change nightly but include 1970s disco, blues, jazz, and local bands.

Zodiac, 190 Crowley Rd. (© **01865/726336**), presents everything from easy listening to "Celtic rock." The cover varies from £4 to £11 ($6.40–$18) depending on the group featured. It's usually open from about 7:30pm to 2am Monday through Friday; 9pm to 2am Saturday; closed Sunday. The club's ownership is shared by some major English bands, and local and big-name bands are featured along with DJs, so call ahead to be sure of what you're getting.

THE PUB SCENE

Note: These places are all good choices for affordable meals, too.

The Head of the River, Abingdon Road at Folly Bridge, near the Westgate Centre Mall (© **01865/721600**), is operated by Fuller Smith and Turner, a family brewery. It's a lively place where they offer true traditional ales and lagers, along with very good sturdy fare. In summer, guests sit by the river and can rent a punt or a boat with an engine. Twelve rooms, all with baths and overlooking the river, are available for £78 to £95 ($125–$152) in summer, including breakfast, newspaper, and parking.

At **The Eagle and Child,** 49 Saint Giles St. (© **01865/310154**), literary history suffuses the dim, paneled alcoves and promotes a sedate atmosphere. For at least a quarter of a century, it was frequented by the likes of C. S. Lewis and J. R. R. Tolkien. In fact, *The Chronicles of Narnia* and *The Hobbit* were first read aloud at this pub. Known as the "Bird and Baby," this hallowed ground still welcomes the local dons, and the food is good. It's a settled, quiet place to read the newspapers and listen to classical music on CDs.

The King's Arms, 40 Holywell St. (© **01865/242369**), hosts a mix of students, gays, and professors. One of the best places in town to strike up a conversation, the pub, owned by Young's Brewery, features six of the company's ales along with lagers and bitters that change periodically.

3 Woodstock & Blenheim Palace

100km (62 miles) NW of London; 13km (8 miles) NW of Oxford

The small country town of Woodstock, the birthplace in 1330 of the Black Prince, the ill-fated son of King Edward III, lies on the edge of the Cotswolds. Some of the stone houses here were constructed when Woodstock was the site of a royal palace. This palace had so suffered the ravages of time that its remains were demolished when Blenheim Palace was built. Woodstock was once the seat of a flourishing glove industry.

ESSENTIALS
GETTING THERE   Take the train to Oxford (see "Essentials," in section 2). The Gloucester Green bus (no. 20) leaves Oxford about every 12 minutes during the day. The trip takes just over ½ hour. Call **Stagecoach** at © **01865/ 772250** for details. If you're driving, take A44 from Oxford.

VISITOR INFORMATION   The **Tourist Information Centre** is on Hensington Road (© **01993/813276**), open Tuesday through Saturday from 10am to 4:30pm, and on Sunday 2 to 4:30pm year-round.

ONE OF ENGLAND'S MOST MAGNIFICENT PALACES
Blenheim Palace ★★★   The extravagantly baroque Blenheim Palace is England's answer to Versailles. Blenheim is the home of the 11th duke of Marlborough, a descendant of John Churchill, the first duke, who was an on-again, off-again favorite of Queen Anne's. In his day (1650–1722), the first duke became the supreme military figure in Europe. Fighting on the Danube near a village named Blenheim, Churchill defeated the forces of Louis XIV, and the lavish palace of Blenheim was built for the duke as a gift from the queen. It was designed by Sir John Vanbrugh, who was also the architect of Castle Howard; the landscaping was created by Capability Brown. The palace is loaded with riches: antiques, porcelain, oil paintings, tapestries, and chinoisserie.

North Americans know Blenheim as the birthplace of Sir Winston Churchill. The room in which he was born is included in the palace tour, as is the Churchill exhibition, four rooms of letters, books, photographs, and other relics. Today, the former prime minister lies buried in Bladon Churchyard, near the palace.

Insider tip: The **Marlborough Maze,** 549m (1,800 ft.) from the palace, is the largest symbolic hedge maze on earth, with an herb and lavender garden, a butterfly house, and inflatable castles for children. Also, be sure to look for the castle's gift shops, tucked away in an old palace dairy. Here you can purchase a wide range of souvenirs, handicrafts, and even locally made preserves.

© **01993/811091.** www.blenheimpalace.com. Admission £10 ($16) adults, £8 ($13) seniors and children 16–17, £5 ($8) children 5–15, free for children under age 5. Family ticket £26 ($42). Daily 9am–5pm. Last admission 4:45pm. Closed Nov to mid-Mar.

TWO FAVORITE LOCAL PUBS
Star Inn, 22 Market Place (© **01993/811373**) has three locally brewed real ales from which to choose: Tetley's, Wadworth's 6X, and Marston's Pedigree. You can enjoy the requisite bar munchies as well as full dinners. The management boasts that its half-shoulder of lamb is the most tender around because of the slow cooking process. You can also pick and choose from a hot and cold buffet that features salads and sandwich fixings.

King's Head is tucked away at 11 Park Lane (© **01993/812164**) in Woodstock. Tourists seem to like the "potato pub," as the locals call it, though it's a bit hard to find. The name comes from the wide variety of stuffed potato skins that the pub serves. Enjoy these with a real ale; the owners are sure to have a different specialty ale every month. If you come for dinner, a three-course meal, which may include fish, ribs, or homemade lasagna, costs from £6 to £10.50 ($9.60–$17).

11

The Northwest & the Lake District

Most visitors rush through the industry-laden Northwest in their hurry to get to the Lake District, but the region—home to **Chester, Liverpool,** and **Manchester**—is worth a look. The walled city of Chester is by far the most interesting stop, even more so than Liverpool, former home of the Beatles.

Chester lies in the county of Cheshire, world-renowned for its cheese. For centuries, the county was primarily agricultural, but it's being increasingly built up. Because it borders rebellious Wales, Cheshire has had a turbulent history. Try to plan at least a night's stopover here before heading on to the Lake District itself.

The **Lake District,** one of the most beautiful parts of Great Britain, is actually quite small, measuring about 35 miles wide. Most of the district is in Cumbria, although it begins in the northern part of Lancashire.

Bordering Scotland, the far-north-western part of the shire is generally divided geographically into three segments: the Pennines, dominating the eastern sector (loftiest point at Cross Fell, nearly 914m/3,000 ft. high); the Valley of Eden; and the lakes and secluded valleys of the west, which are by far the most interesting.

So beautifully described by the romantic poets, the area enjoys many literary associations with William Wordsworth, Samuel Taylor Coleridge, Charlotte Brontë, Charles Lamb, Percy Bysshe Shelley, John Keats, Alfred Lord Tennyson, and Matthew Arnold. In Queen Victoria's day, the Lake District was one of England's most popular summer retreats.

The largest town is Carlisle, up by the Scotland border, which is a possible base for exploring **Hadrian's Wall**—but for now, we will concentrate on the district's lovely lakeside villages. **Windermere** is the best base for exploring the Lake District.

1 Manchester: Gateway to the North ★

325km (202 miles) NW of London; 138km (86 miles) N of Birmingham; 56km (35 miles) E of Liverpool

The second-largest city in England, **Manchester** is becoming increasingly important, as major airlines now fly here from North America, making the city a gateway to northern England. In recent years, Manchester has made great strides to shake its image as an industrial wasteland. Although chimneys still spike the skyline, they no longer make the metropolitan sky an ash-filled canopy. Abandoned warehouses are being renovated to provide sleek new loft apartments for yuppies. Rustic factory equipment turns up in museums rather than piling up in salvage yards. Even the old Victorian architecture has been given a face-lift.

The once-dreary Manchester Docklands, evoking a painting of L. S. Lowry, has a spiffy new life following a £250 million ($400 million) restoration. It's

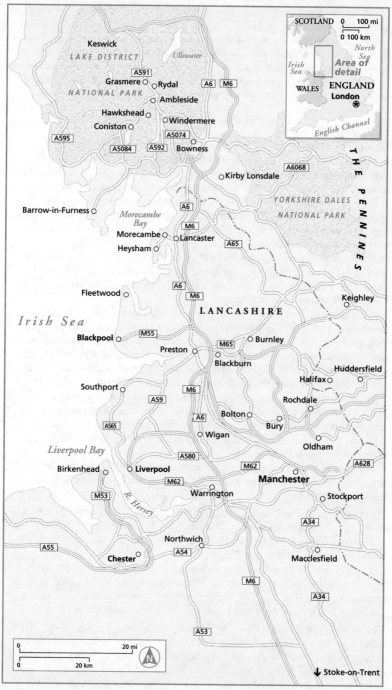

The Northwest

called simply "the Lowry," and the complex is filled with theaters, shops, galleries, and restaurants. Part of the restoration was financed by Britain's National Lottery. A plaza provides space for up to 10,000 at outdoor performances. In 2002, Manchester hosted the Commonwealth games, and as a result the city upgraded its transportation and leisure facilities, including the building of a new 70,000-seat stadium. The overall effect of the city's renovation is a gritty kind of charm, although we think you'll find your time better spent in Chester (see later in this chapter).

ESSENTIALS

GETTING THERE By Plane More and more North Americans are flying directly to Manchester to begin their explorations of the United Kingdom. **British Airways** (© 800/247-9297 in the U.S. and Canada, or 08457/222111 in the U.K.; www.british-airways.co.uk) has daily flights departing New York's JFK airport for Manchester at 6:30pm, arriving after 7 hours in the air. You can also fly from BA's many North American gateways nonstop to London, and from here take the almost shuttle-like service from either Gatwick or Heathrow airports to Manchester, a 50-minute flight.

American Airlines (© 800/433-7300 in the U.S. and Canada; www.aa.com) offers a daily nonstop flight to Manchester from Chicago's O'Hare Airport that departs at 6:40pm, arriving the following morning. American also flies from London's Heathrow back to Chicago.

Manchester is also served by flights from the Continent. For example, **Lufthansa** (© 800/645-3880; www.lufthansa.com) has frequent nonstop flights each week between Frankfurt and Manchester, depending on the season. Flight time is 1 hour and 45 minutes. For airport information, call © **01614/993322.**

Manchester's airport, 24km (15 miles) south of the town center, is served by both public transportation and a motorway network. The **Airport Link,** a modern aboveground train, connects the airport terminal to the Piccadilly Railway Station downtown in Manchester. Trains leave every 15 minutes from 5:15 to 10:10pm, sometimes through the night. The ride takes 25 minutes. Direct rail lines link the airport to surrounding northern destinations, such as Edinburgh, Liverpool, and Windermere.

Bus nos. 44 and 105 run between the airport and Piccadilly Gardens Bus Station every 15 minutes (hourly during the evenings and on Sun). The bus ride takes 55 minutes.

By Train, Bus & Car Trains from London's Euston Station travel directly to Manchester (© **0845/748-4950**). The trip takes 2½ to 3 hours.

National Express (© **020/7529-2000**) buses serve the Manchester region from London's Victoria Coach Station.

If you're driving from London to Manchester, go north on the M1 and the M6. At junction 21A, go east on the M62, which becomes the M602 as you enter Manchester. The trip from London to Manchester usually takes from 3 to 3½ hours, but it could be longer because of traffic and construction.

VISITOR INFORMATION The **Manchester Visitor Centre,** Town Hall Extension, Lloyd Street (© **01612/343157;** www.manchester.gov.uk/visitor centre), is open Monday through Saturday from 10am to 5:30pm and Sunday and bank holidays from 10:30am to 4pm. To reach it, take the Metrolink tram to St. Peter's Square. Especially useful is a series of four free pamphlets with information on accommodations, dining, city attractions, and cultural/entertainment options.

GETTING AROUND   It's not a good idea to try to hoof it in Manchester. It's better to take the bus and Metrolink. Timetables, bus routes, fare information, and a copy of a helpful leaflet, the *Passenger's Guide,* are available from **The Kiosk,** a general information booth within the Piccadilly Gardens Bus Station, Market Street (✆ **01612/287811**), open daily from 8am to 8pm.

Buses begin running within Manchester at 6am and operate in full force until 11pm, then continue with limited routes until 3am. Tickets are sold at a kiosk at Piccadilly Gardens Bus Station. A day pass, the **Wayfarer** (✆ **01612/ 287811**), costs £3.30 ($5.30) and is valid for a complete day of public bus travel. Another source of bus information is **Stagecoach** (✆ **01612/733377**).

Metrolink (✆ **01612/052000**) streetcars connect the bus stations and provide a useful north–south conduit. Self-service ticket machines dispense zone-based fares. The streetcars operate Monday through Saturday from 6am to 11:30pm, and on Sunday from 7am to 10:30pm. They are wheelchair accessible.

SEEING THE SIGHTS

The Lowry ★   At the newly restored docklands area, the Lowry, the industrial city landscapes of the artist L. S. Lowry (1887–1976) are showcased as never before. Lowry depicted the horror of the industrial north of England, before it disappeared forever. His matchstick people are dwarfed by the smokestacks and viaducts in his paintings. Lowry's paintings, as seen here, imposed a vision on a grim and gloomy urban sprawl. Lowry found a cohesion and lyric beauty in these industrial landscapes. His best-known paintings are from 1905 to 1925. The artist was especially fond of depicting the crudeness of capitalism, forcing workers into box-like row houses, as railroads nearby rattled across viaducts belching smoke.

The Lowry. ✆ **01618/762000.** Free admission. Sun–Wed 11am–5pm; Thurs–Fri 11am–7pm; Sat 11am–7:30pm. Bus: 51, 52, 71, 73, or M11.

Manchester Art Gallery ★★   Following an extensive expansion and rejuvenation, this gallery today is the proud owner of one of the best and most prestigious art collections in the north of England. Literally doubled in size, the new gallery displays works that are wide-ranging—from the pre-Raphaelites to old Dutch masters, from the land- and seascapes of Turner to Lowry's industrial panoramas.

Designed by Sir Charles Barry, this gallery has been a landmark since 1882. Today's fine collection is also noted for its paintings by Ford Madox Brown, Holman Hunt, and its bevy of 18th- and early-19th-century art, including High Victorian, Edwardian, and British modern. A highlight for us is the magnificent collection of Turner watercolors.

The gallery's decorative art collection is one of the finest outside London, especially in its 17th- and 18th-century pieces, its metalwork, and porcelain. The silver, in particular the Assheton Bennett collection, is especially distinguished.

If you're here between Easter and September, consider a visit to **Heaton Hall** (✆ **01617/731231**), the museum's annex, 6.5km (4 miles) to the east. It's the centerpiece of 650 acres of rolling parkland, and accessible via the Metrolink tram (get off at Heaton Park). Built of York stone in 1772, and filled with furniture and decorative art of the 18th and 19th centuries, it is open only between Easter and September. Opening hours may vary, however they are generally Thursday through Sunday from 10am to 5:30pm. Call the Visitor Centre to confirm. Admission is free.

Mosley St. ✆ **01612/358888.** www.cityartgalleries.org.uk. Free admission. Daily 10am–5pm.

Moments Winding Your Way Through Beatles Land

Liverpool, a great shipping port and industrial center 56km (35 miles) west of Manchester is best known as the home of Beatlemania. The Fab Four launched their careers here, and fans are always stopping in to see where it all began. At the end of August and running into the first couple of days of September, the annual **International Beatles Week** attracts about 100,000 fans to Liverpool for a 7-day celebration highlighted by concerts from bands from Argentina to Sweden (with such names as Lenny Pane, Wings over Liverpool, and the Beats). You can hear the news today at the Sgt. Pepper concert, and take in many other Beatles tributes, auctions, and tours.

If you'd like a Beatles-related bus tour, **Cavern City Tours** (✆ 01512/ 369091; www.cavern-liverpool.co.uk) presents a daily 2-hour Magical Mystery Tour, departing from Albert Dock at 2:20pm and from Roe Street at 2:30pm. This bus tour covers the most famous attractions associated with the Beatles. Tickets cost £11 ($18) and are sold at the **Tourist Information Centre** at the Atlantic Pavilion, Albert Dock (✆ 01517/088854), and at the Tourist Information Centre in the City Centre: **Queen's Square Centre,** Roe Street (✆ 01517/093285).

In the Britannia Pavilion at Albert Dock, you can visit **"The Beatles Story"** (✆ 01517/091963), a museum housing memorabilia of the famous group, including a yellow submarine with live fish swimming past the portholes. It's open Monday through Friday from 10am to 5pm, Saturday and Sunday from 10am to 6pm. From Easter to September, it's open daily from 10am to 6pm. Admission is £7.95 ($13) for adults and £5.45 ($8.70) for children and students, and a family ticket is £19 ($30).

The **McCartney House,** 20 Forthlin Rd., Allerton 16 (✆ 01517/ 088574 for booking; 0870/900-0256 for information; www.spekehall. org.uk/beatles.htm), where Paul lived before his meteoric rise to superstardom, has been purchased by the National Trust and restored to its original 1950s appearance, complete with the patterned brown

Manchester Cathedral ✰   Originally just a medieval parish in 1421, Manchester achieved cathedral status in 1847 with the creation of the new diocese. The cathedral's nave, the widest of its kind in Britain, is formed by six bays, as is the choir. The choir stall features unique 16th-century misericord seats—caricatures of medieval life. The choir screen is a wood carving from the same era. Carel Weight provides her 20th-century canvas rendition of the beatitudes, and there's also a sculpture by typographer Eric Gill.

Victoria St. ✆ 01618/332220. www.dws.ndirect.co.uk/mc.htm. Free admission. Daily 8am–6pm.

Manchester Town Hall ✰   Alfred Waterhouse designed this neo-Gothic structure that first opened in 1877, and extensions were added just before World War II. The tower rises nearly 90m (300 ft.) above the town. The Great Hall and its signature hammer-beam roof houses 12 pre-Raphaelite murals by Ford Madox Brown, commissioned between 1852 and 1856. The paintings chronicle sofa and armchair where Paul and John scribbled out their first songs. The house is only open to the public through tours organized by the National Trust. Six tours a day depart from Speak Hall, The Walk. Groups are limited to 14 people at any one time. Admission costs £5.50 ($8.80) for adults and £2.80 ($4.50) for children. The house's opening times vary, so call before you arrive. Book well in advance.

Everyone's curious about **Penny Lane** and **Strawberry Field**. Actually, the Beatles' song about Penny Lane didn't refer to the small lane itself, but to the area at the top of the lane called Smithdown Place. John Lennon lived nearby and attended school in the area. Today, this is a bustling thoroughfare for taxis and buses—hardly a place for nostalgic memories.

To reach Penny Lane and the area referred to, head north of Sefton Park. From the park, Green Bank Lane leads into Penny Lane itself, and at the junction of Allerton Road and Smithdown Road stands the Penny Lane Tramsheds. This is John Lennon country—or what's left of it.

Only the most diehard fans will want to make the journey to **Strawberry Field** along Beaconsfield Road, which is reached by taking Menlove Avenue east of the center. Today, you can stand at the iron gates and look in at a children's home run by the Salvation Army. As a child John played on the grounds, and in 1970, he donated a large sum of money to the home. A garden party held every summer here was attended by John.

Because these sights are hard to reach by public transport and lie outside the center, you may want to take one of the Cavern City Tours (see above), which feature both Strawberry Field and Penny Lane.

It's a 45-minute train ride (© **0845/748-4950** for schedules and information) from Manchester to Liverpool. **National Express** buses depart Manchester every hour for the 1-hour trip to Liverpool. For schedules and information, call © **020/7529-2000.**

the town's storied past, from the 1st-century Roman occupation to the Industrial Revolution of the 19th century.

Albert Square. © **01612/343157.** Free admission. Mon–Fri and Sun 8am–5pm. Closed Dec 25–26 and New Year's Day. Guided tours 2nd and 4th Wed at 2pm.

The Pump House People's History Museum   Few other museums in Europe catalog and commemorate the social history of the working class as carefully and with as much objectivity as this one. The museum began to take shape in 1990 when this was designated as the archive of Britain's communist party. Despite the fact that every exhibit is carefully couched in apolitical terms, it remains the most controversial museum in the Midlands. Of special note are exhibitions that describe the 1819 Peterloo Massacre of trade union activists by government forces and the ongoing struggles of the coal miners of Yorkshire in their fight for higher wages and better working conditions.

Left Bank, Bridge St. ℂ **01618/396061.** www.nmlhweb.org. Admission £1 ($1.60) adults Sat–Thurs, free Fri; free for students, seniors, and children. Tues–Sun 11am–4:30pm. Tram: Metrolink to St. Peter's Sq.

Whitworth Art Gallery   Whitworth was originally established in 1889 with a bequest to the city from a wealthy industrialist. The gallery was opened to the public in 1908. Behind the magnificent redbrick facade lies a light and spacious interior. The gallery is one of the richest research sources in England for antique patterns of wallpaper and textiles and the weaving techniques that produced them. It also features a superb collection of 18th- and 19th-century watercolors on display, including many by Turner.

At the University of Manchester, on Oxford Rd., near the corner of Denmark Rd. ℂ **01612/757450.** www. whitworth.man.ac.uk. Free admission. Mon–Sat 10am–5pm; Sun 2–5pm. Metrolink to St. Peter's Sq., then bus 41, 42, or 45.

WHERE TO STAY
EXPENSIVE TO MODERATE

Etrop Grange Hotel ⭐   This is the most historic of the many hotels near Manchester Airport. Originally built of redbrick in 1760, with a modern wing added in the late 1980s in the same architectural style as the original bedrooms, it lies only a couple of minutes drive east of the airport. Don't expect lush meadows and views of fen and forest: The setting is one of sprawling parking lots and industrial-looking warehouses. But inside you'll find open fireplaces, ornate chandeliers, Edwardian windows, and many of the architectural features of the building's original construction. Bedrooms are often small but comfortably appointed; many have antique beds, but all beds are ensconced in brass or else canopied. Black-and-white tiled bathrooms have brass fittings and toiletries and are equipped with antique-style tubs without showers or else stalls with cascading showerheads. The gem here is a series of four-poster master bedrooms with sitting areas and bathrooms fitted with whirlpool tubs.

Thorley Lane, Manchester Airport M90 4EG. ℂ **01614/990500.** Fax 01614/990790. www.corushotels.com. 64 units. £109–£149 ($174–$238) double; £180 ($288) suite. AE, DC, MC, V. **Amenities:** Restaurant; bar; 24-hr. room service; laundry service; dry cleaning. *In room:* TV, coffeemaker, hair dryer, iron.

Hilton Manchester Airport ⭐   This is the best of the many modern hotels that flank Manchester's airport. Built during the mid-1980s, it features conservative but modern bedrooms with soundproof windows. Plush carpets and pickled pine furnishings are inviting, and padded headboards back the comfortable beds. Bathrooms have adequate shelf space, plus a combination pseudo-marble tub and shower. The 60 more expensive "Plaza Club" rooms feature a wider assortment of perks and amenities than the less expensive accommodations.

Outwood Lane (near Junction 5 of M56), Manchester Airport, Manchester M90 4WP. ℂ **800/445-8667** in the U.S. and Canada, or 01614/353000. Fax 01614/353040. www.hilton.com. 223 units. £130–£155 ($208–$248) double; from £325–£400 ($520–$640) suite. AE, DC, MC, V. **Amenities:** Restaurant; bar; pool; health club; shuttle service; business center; room service; laundry service; dry cleaning. *In room:* TV, dataport, mini-bar, coffeemaker, hair dryer, trouser press.

Le Meridien Victoria & Albert Hotel ⭐⭐⭐ *Finds*   One of the most unusual hotels in Britain occupies a renovated brick-sided pair of warehouses, originally conceived in 1843 to store bales of cotton being barged along the nearby Irwell River and the Manchester Ship Canal to looms and mills throughout the Midlands. About a decade ago, Granada TV transformed the then-decrepit buildings into lodgings for their out-of-town guests, and a showcase for many of their creative ideas.

Bedrooms drip with the authenticity and charm of the Victorian age. Each has exposed brick walls, massive ceiling beams, an individualized shape and themed decor, and in many cases, the ornate cast-iron columns of its earlier warehouse manifestation. Each room carries the name of a Granada TV show or series, all instantly recognizable to millions of Brits. Rooms are well equipped, most often with one double bed, and the bathrooms have such touches as yellow ducks ready to float in the tubs with you. The best and most spacious accommodations, the Sovereign Rooms, and offer extra amenities such as bathrobes and slippers. Some rooms on the third floor are rented to women only for security reasons.

Water St., Castlefield, Manchester M3 4JQ. ℂ **01618/321188.** Fax 01618/342484. www.lemeridien-hotels. com. 158 units. £180 ($288) double; from £280 ($448) suite. Rates include full English breakfast Fri–Sun only. AE, DC, MC, V. **Amenities:** Restaurant; bar; room service; laundry service; dry cleaning. *In room:* A/C, TV w/pay movies, minibar, coffeemaker, hair dryer, iron, safe, trouser press.

The Lowry Hotel ★★★ Sexy and sinuous, this new, government-rated five-star hotel (rare in this part of England) is part of the new Chapel Wharf development. The windows of the bedrooms open onto a modern footbridge linking this once blighted industrial zone to the heart of town. The glass edifice exudes a sense of airy, spacious luxury living. The Lowry offers exceptionally comfortable bedrooms with deluxe furnishings and state-of-the-art marble bathrooms. The sleek design was directed by Olga Polizzi, who has helped redefine chic in the U.K. Polizzi's trademarks are wedge-wood paneling, built-in furniture, and floor-to-ceiling windows. Many patrons visit just to sample the international cuisine of The River Room Marco Pierre White, offering brasserie-style dishes overlooking the river.

50 Deadmans Place, Chapel Wharf. ℂ **01618/274000.** Fax 0161/827-4001. www.thelowryhotel.com. 164 units. £209–£259 ($334–$414) double; from £435 ($696) suite. AE, DC, MC, V. **Amenities:** Restaurant; bar; indoor pool; fitness center; spa; sauna; steam room; business center; salon. *In room:* TV, minibar, hair dryer, safe, trouser press.

Malmaison ★ *Finds* This is one of the best examples in Manchester of combining old architectural features with the new. Behind an Edwardian facade, a dramatic and strikingly modern design reigns, enough of a statement that pop stars visiting from London often stop off here. In the heart of the city, only a minute's walk from Piccadilly Station, individually designed and "modern-as-tomorrow" bedrooms await you. The accommodations are quite stunning in red, black, and ivory. Expect great big beds, CD players, and very contemporary bathrooms with power showers.

Piccadilly, Manchester M1 3AQ. ℂ **01612/781000.** Fax 0161/278-1002. www.malmaison.com. 167 units. £115–£125 ($184–$200) double; from £160 ($256) suite. AE, DC, MC, V. **Amenities:** Restaurant; bar; health club; spa; sauna; steam room; business center. *In room:* TV, dataport, hair dryer.

INEXPENSIVE

Kempton House Hotel A large Victorian house located 4km (2½ miles) south of the city center, this hotel offers basic, centrally located accommodations at a reasonable rate. You don't get much in the way of grand comfort in the rather smallish rooms here, but you do get a good bed for the night at a reasonable rate. Rooms that contain private plumbing will have a shower stall. Those who must share a bathroom will find the corridor bathrooms adequate, and you rarely have to wait in line. Several buses go by the hotel on a regular basis.

400 Wilbraham Rd., Chorlton-Cum-Hardy M21 0UH. *C*/fax **01618/818766.** www.thekempton.co.uk. 10 units, 7 with bathroom. £50–£55 ($80–$88) double with bathroom. Rates include English breakfast. MC, V. **Amenities:** Bar. *In room:* TV, coffeemaker.

WHERE TO DINE
EXPENSIVE

Juniper ★★★ ECLECTIC   Many of Britain's good food guides quite rightly hail this winning choice as one of the country's finest restaurants. It lies 13km (8 miles) outside Manchester. The chef, Paul Kitching, is often cited for "the menu's playful way with ingredients." In some cases, that could mean bad news. Not so with the offerings of Kitching, whose signature dishes include roast saddle of Cumbrian hare with foie gras, watercress, yogurt, spices, sugared cashews, and melon syrup juice. We sampled the concoction and found it quite wonderful. The setting isn't glamorous—in a parade of shops—but the food certainly is, especially the seafood, such as Dover sole filets served with preserved lemon and parsley in a creamy broth. For starters, try such divine concoctions as pieces of chicken breast, red pepper, carrots, and mushrooms bound together in a light jelly and topped with an intense tomato custard. By now, you surely have gotten the point: expect dishes you possibly have never tried before. Ever had chocolate mayonnaise? For dessert, we endorse the locally famed lemon tart with rosemary sorbet.

21 The Downs, Altrincham, Greater Manchester. *C* **01619/294008.** Reservations required. Main courses £15–£18 ($24–$29). AE, MC, V. Tues–Fri noon–2pm; Mon–Sat 7–9:30pm (until 10pm Fri–Sat).

The Lincoln ★ BRITISH/INTERNATIONAL   One of the best of the city center restaurants, The Lincoln continues to win new friends since its opening. Fine wine, excellent ingredients, affordable platters, and an imaginative menu have combined to form a winning combination. The chef, Ashley Clarke, is a whiz in the kitchen, concocting delightful dishes that not only look good in presentation, but are good. The menu changes weekly, but you can generally count on such delights as roast rib-eye of beef with Yorkshire pudding; and the market fish of the day. Also anticipate seasonal delights such as oven-roasted breast of wood pigeon.

1 Lincoln Sq. *C* **01618/349000.** Reservations required. Set lunch £13 ($20) for 2 courses, £15 ($23) for 3 courses; Sun lunch £17 ($27); main courses £14–£24 ($22–$38). AE, MC, V. Sun–Fri noon–3pm; Mon–Sat 6–10:30pm (11pm Fri–Sat).

Market Restaurant ENGLISH   Few other restaurants capitalize as successfully on a sense of old-fashioned English nostalgia as this one. Set in the heart of town, it promotes itself with an allegiance to very fresh ingredients, and a slightly dowdy but homelike decor that hasn't changed very much since the beginning of World War II. About a third of the dishes are vegetarian; others include smoked breast of duck with chicory, orange, and olive salad; filet of beef with horseradish pancakes and Madeira-based gravy; and a dessert specialty they refer to as a pistachio pavlova crafted with bananas, passionfruit, and whipped Jersey cream. The rhubarb crumble ice cream served with a compote of ice cream is as delicious as it is British.

19 Edge St. or 104 High St. *C* **01618/343743.** Reservations recommended. Main courses £12–£16 ($19–$26). AE, DC, MC, V. Wed–Fri 6–9:30pm; Sat 7–9:30pm. Tram: Metrolink to Piccadilly or Victoria Station (best to take a taxi).

Moss Nook FRENCH   This restaurant, named after the village where it is located, is a favorite local choice for an upscale dinner. The setting, complete with red suede wallpaper, hefty cutlery, and elaborate table settings, is rather formal and heavy. The service is professional but warm and friendly. Menu choices include everything from the standard to the exotically imaginative—breast of duckling can be served in an orange sauce or with red-currant-and-elderflower dressing. Especially good is a soufflé of Swiss cheese with chives and red-pepper sauce or halibut with scallops prepared in a parsley sauce.

Ringway Rd., Moss Nook, 1km (¾ mile) from the Manchester Airport. ⓒ 01614/374778. Reservations recommended. 5-course set lunch £20 ($31); 7-course set dinner £37 ($58); main courses £20–£28 ($31–$45). AE, MC, V. Tues–Fri noon–1:30pm (last order); Tues–Sat 7–9:30pm (last order).

MODERATE

The Lowry Restaurant ✿ MODERN BRITISH   Steven Saunders is one of England's best-known chefs. His latest offering is installed at The Lowry museum (see p. 417) in Manchester's restored dockland area. In an avant-garde split-level dining area, you can select a table with views over the quay. You can take comfort here in knowing that you'll be served market-fresh ingredients prepared with skill and flair by a well-trained staff. Most dishes are light and totally in step with the tenets of modern British cookery. A recently sampled main course was a first for us—hot *vichyssoise* (leek-and-potato soup) with Gorgonzola and truffle oil. Other delights on the ever-changing menu include a chargrilled rib-eye steak or a breast of herb-infused chicken with a lemon and herb risotto. From the tuna carpaccio with mango salsa and soy dressing, to such puddings as bread and butter with orange custard, the food here is colorful, fresh, and honest.

Pier 8, Salford Quays. ⓒ 01618/762121. Reservations recommended. Main courses £7.95–£14 ($13–$22); 2-course fixed-price lunch £11–£14 ($18–$22); fixed-price pretheater dinner 5:15–7:30pm £14–£18 ($22–$29). Daily noon–3pm and 5–10pm. Bus: 51, 52, 71, 73, or M11.

Mr. Thomas's Chophouse TRADITIONAL BRITISH   This mellow Manchester pub is also the city's oldest restaurant, established in 1872. Tall and thin, the building is squeezed into a narrow plot of land. The structure itself is a good example of the British Art Nouveau style in the ceramic cladding on the exterior and the provision of green tiles inside. Under brown ceilings, guests dine at tables placed on the checkerboard floors. Real ales are very popular here, including Boddingtons and Timothy Taylor's. The most traditional British food served in the city center is offered here at lunch, including dishes such as braised oxtail with cabbage and dumplings, and steak-and-kidney pudding. We recently dined on a very good pan-fried plaice with mushy peas. The French onion soup is the favorite starter of local diners, and it's always reliable.

52 Cross St. ⓒ 01618/322245. Reservations not needed. Main courses £9–£12 ($14–$19). AE, DC, MC, V. Mon–Sat 10:30am–3pm (bar serves till 11pm).

Simply Heathcote's ✿ BRITISH   The chef and owner, Paul Heathcote of Lancaster, has been hailed by many critics as the "cook of the North." His contemporary menu of old favorites and imaginative new dishes are well showcased in this Manchester outlet. The large dining room, decorated in a minimalist style, draws a wide range of patrons from families to soccer hoodlums. Think of this as a British brasserie with not much style, especially the windows without curtains. Obviously Martha Stewart has not been through here. But the food more than compensates. Look for such "oop Norf" favorites as black pudding with ham hock, calves' liver on creamy mash, strawberry trifle, bread-and-butter pudding, baked custard with scented rose water, and (our favorite) breast of Goosnargh duckling with gnocchi and foie gras butter.

Elliot House, Jackson's Row, Deansgate. ⓒ 01618/353534. Reservations recommended. Main courses £9.50–£15 ($15–$24); 2-course set menu £14 ($22); 3-course set menu £16 ($25). AE, DC, MC, V. Daily 11:45am–2:30pm and 5:30–10pm.

Moments Going to Market

Here in the north, markets are a tradition and offer a chance to jump in and barter with the locals. Tourists tend to steer clear of them, so this is a great chance for a really authentic experience.

Although markets tend to sell everyday items and foodstuff, some stalls are devoted to flea-market goods and "antiques." Market days vary throughout the region, but you're bound to find at least one in full swing each day of the work week. Two good ones in Manchester are Arndale Market and Market Hall.

Yang Sing *Finds* CANTONESE   Manchester's large population of Asian immigrants consider Yang Sing their favorite restaurant, as proven by the cacophony of languages spoken within its basement dining room. It's loud but efficient, with a fast turnover of tables. Dim sum, those delicate dumplings, are served in a blissful array of choices from a pair of oversize carts in the dining room's center. Menu items cover the gamut of the Cantonese repertoire.

In 1996, Yang Sing began offering a street-level "steamboat restaurant," where containers of bubbling broth are brought to your table accompanied with an assortment of raw chicken, fish, chopped vegetables, and beef. Use your chopsticks to dunk the tidbits into the hot broth (think of it as a Chinese version of a Swiss fondue).

34 Princess St. ℂ 01612/362200. Reservations required. Main courses £8.60–£12 ($14–$20). AE, MC, V. Mon–Fri noon–11:30pm; Sat–Sun noon–9:30pm. Metrolink tram to Piccadilly.

INEXPENSIVE

Cafe Istanbul TURKISH   This restaurant evokes an old Marlene Dietrich flick on the late, late show but is in fact the most savory spot for Turkish cuisine in Manchester. Decorated in a vague Mediterranean style, it draws a hip, young crowd, many who have traveled abroad and are in search of those exotic flavors discovered in their travels. The selection of *meze* (Turkish appetizers) alone is worth the trek here, and the wine list is extensive but without price gouging. Try any of the lamb kebabs (the house specialty) or the grilled seafood.

79 Bridge St. ℂ 01618/339942. Reservations recommended. Main courses £9.50–£13 ($15–$21). MC, V. Daily noon–3pm and 5–11pm.

Dimitri's GREEK   This bistro is a warm and friendly place, like the Greeks themselves. In the city center, it's so popular, especially with a young crowd, that you should call a day in advance for a table. Greek delicacies are the way to go, though Spanish and Italian dishes, including a tapas bar, are dished out nightly. Dimitri's also serves up some of the best veggie dishes in Manchester. On weekends, sit at the bar with a savory blend of Greek coffee and listen to a live jazz band.

1 Campfield Arcade. ℂ 01618/393319. Reservations recommended. Main courses £7–£12 ($11–$19). AE, MC, V. Mon–Sat 11am–midnight; Sun 11am–11:30pm.

MANCHESTER CLUB SCENE

Above all else, Manchester is known for its recent contributions to pop music. From the Smiths and New Order to Oasis and the Stone Roses, the "Manchester sound" has been known throughout the world for over a decade. Yet surprisingly enough, live music went by the wayside in the early 1990s, and clubs were in short supply until they started making a steady comeback in the last couple of years.

Bar 38, 10 Canal St. (© **01612/366005**), is known for its design, with artwork displayed on the bright orange glow of the walls. On weekends DJs play house and disco for the young crowd of all sexual persuasions. Sometimes a live funk band provides the hottest show in town. The club lies a 2-minute walk west of the town center, and the bar serves tasty tapas.

The Attic, 50 New Wakefield (© **01612/366071**), just southwest of the town center, offers the best of both worlds. Downstairs is a relaxing pub aptly named Thirsty Scholar, with a lot of gorgeous guys and dolls. Upstairs you descend into the funk/soul chaos of a club, The Attic, drawing a hip young crowd to dance and drink.

South, 4A King St. (© **01618/317756**), is a small industrial-style club. A 10-minute walk north of Piccadilly Gardens, this club has a sophisticated young aura, with '60s and '70s music on Friday and a hot house DJ on Saturday.

Dry Bar, 28–30 Old Oldham St. (© **01612/369840**), was launched by the band New Order and Factory Records. A lot of young, hip media people are drawn here to this "stretch" bar with its ultra-modern industrial steel look. A 5-minute walk north of the town center, it features live music every weekend and on some weekdays, too, ranging from Hip-Hop to Acid Jazz. Surprisingly, the food dished out here is inspired by Jamaica, including authentic jerk chicken.

The Roadhouse, Newton Street (© **01612/281789**), the hottest small venue in Manchester, hosts bands up to 7 nights a week. Monday through Saturday check out **Band on the Wall,** 25 Swan St. at Oak Street (© **01618/326625**), where live rock, blues, jazz, and reggae can be heard. For edgier music, check the stage at **Star & Garter,** Farefield Street (© **01612/736726**), on Wednesday through Friday, when harder rock and hard-core acts will get in your face.

Dance clubs here are still going strong. Just stroll through the Castlefield district on a weekend night and check out all the bars featuring a DJ. Located in the old three-story headquarters of Factory Records, **Industry,** 112–116 Princess St. (© **01612/735422**), offers up techno and disco to a mostly gay crowd.

2 The Walled City of Chester ★★

333km (207 miles) NW of London; 31km (19 miles) S of Liverpool; 147km (91 miles) NW of Birmingham

A Roman legion founded Chester on the Dee River in the 1st century A.D. It reached its pinnacle as a bustling port in the 13th and 14th centuries but declined following the gradual silting up of the river. The walls of other medieval cities of England were either torn down or badly fragmented, but Chester still has 3km (2 miles) of fortified city walls intact. The main entrance into Chester is Eastgate, which dates only from the 18th century. Within the walls are half-timbered houses and shops, although not all of them date from Tudor days. Chester is unusual in that some of its builders used black-and-white timbered facades even during the Georgian and Victorian eras.

Chester today has aged gracefully and is a lovely old place to visit, if you don't mind the summer crowds that overrun it. It has far more charm and intimacy then either Liverpool or Manchester and is one of the most interesting medieval cities in England.

ESSENTIALS

GETTING THERE   About 21 trains depart London's Euston Station every hour daily for the 2½-hour trip to Chester. Trains also run every hour between Liverpool and Chester, a 45-minute ride. For schedules and information, call ℭ 0845/748-4950.

A **National Express** bus runs every hour between Birmingham and Chester; the trip takes 2 hours. The same bus line also offers service between Liverpool and Chester. It's also possible to catch a National Express coach from London's Victoria Coach Station to Chester. For schedules and information, call ℭ 020/ 7529-2000.

If you're driving from London, head north on the M1, then take the M6 at the junction near Coventry. Continue northwest to the junction with the A54, which leads west to Chester.

VISITOR INFORMATION   The **Tourist Information Centre** is at the Town Hall, Northgate Street (ℭ 01244/402385). It offers a hotel-reservation service as well as information. Arrangements can also be made for coach tours or walking tours of Chester (including a ghost-hunter tour). It's open May through October Monday through Saturday from 9am to 5:30pm and Sunday from 10am to 4pm; off season, Monday through Saturday from 10am to 5:30pm.

SPECIAL EVENTS   The last 2 weeks of July are an active time in Chester, as the **Chester Summer Music Festival** (ℭ 01244/320700 or 01244/341200; Mon–Fri 9am–5:30pm, Sat 10am–4pm) hosts orchestras and other classical performers from around Britain in lunch concerts, with tickets averaging £6 ($9.60); small indoor evening concerts, where tickets cost between £6 and £30 ($9.60–$48). For additional information about the music festival, you can also write to the Chester Summer Music Festival Office, 8 Abbey Sq., Chester CH1 2HU.

Occurring simultaneously, the **Chester Fringe Festival** (ℭ 01244/321497) focuses on other musical genres, offering Latin, rock, Cajun, folk, and jazz concerts. Ticket prices vary widely, depending on the performer.

SEEING THE SIGHTS

In a big Victorian building opposite the Roman amphitheater, the largest uncovered amphitheater in Britain, the **Chester Visitor Centre,** Vicars Lane (ℭ 01244/ 351609), offers a number of services to visitors. A visit to a life-size Victorian street, complete with sounds and smells, helps your appreciation of Chester. The center has a gift shop and a licensed restaurant serving meals and snacks. Admission is free, and the center is open May through October, Monday through Saturday from 9am to 6:30pm, and Sunday from 10am to 4pm; November through April, Monday through Saturday 10am to 5pm, and Sunday from 10am to 4pm. Guided walking tours of the city depart daily at 10:30am in the winter and at 10:30am and 2pm in the summer.

To the accompaniment of a hand bell, the **town crier** appears at the City Cross—the junction of Watergate, Northgate, and Bridge streets—from April to September at noon and 3pm Tuesday through Saturday to shout news about sales, exhibitions, and attractions in the city.

In the center of town, you'll see the much-photographed **Eastgate clock.** Climb the nearby stairs and walk along the top of the **city wall** for a view down on Chester. Passing through centuries of English history, you'll go by a cricket field, see the River Dee, formerly a major trade artery, and get a look at many

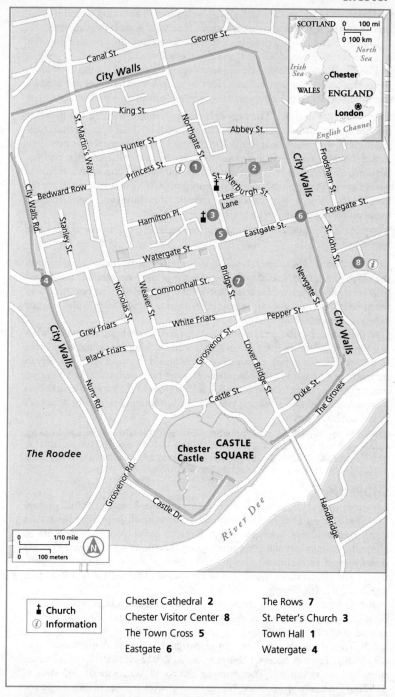

Chester

SCOTLAND 0   100 mi
0   100 km

North Sea

Irish Sea

WALES   **ENGLAND**

○ **Chester**

⊛ **London**

English Channel

George St.

Canal St.

City Walls

King St.

St. Martin's Way

Hunter St.

Princess St.

Bedward Row

Northgate St.

Abbey St.

St. Werburgh St.

Lee Lane

City Walls

Frodsham St.

Foregate St.

Hamilton Pl.

Eastgate St.

Watergate St.

City Walls Rd.

Stanley St.

Nicholas St.

Weaver St.

Commonhall St.

Bridge St.

Newgate St.

St. John St.

Grey Friars

White Friars

Grosvenor St.

Pepper St.

Black Friars

Nuns Rd.

Lower Bridge St.

Castle St.

Duke St.

The Groves

The Roodee

Grosvenor Rd.

Castle Dr.

Chester Castle

CASTLE SQUARE

River Dee

HandBridge

0   1/10 mile
0   100 meters

N

‡ Church
ⓘ Information

Chester Cathedral **2**
Chester Visitor Center **8**
The Town Cross **5**
Eastgate **6**

The Rows **7**
St. Peter's Church **3**
Town Hall **1**
Watergate **4**

18th-century buildings. The wall also goes past some Roman ruins, and it's possible to leave the walkway to explore them. The walk is charming and free.

Eastgate Street is now a pedestrian way, and musicians often perform for your pleasure beside St. Peter's Church and the Town Cross.

The Rows 😊😊 are double-decker layers of shops, one tier on the street level, the others stacked on top and connected by a footway. The upper tier is like a continuous galleried balcony—walking in the rain is never a problem here.

Chester Cathedral ⭐   The present building, founded in 1092 as a Benedictine abbey, was made an Anglican cathedral church in 1541. Many architectural restorations were carried out in the 19th century, but older parts have been preserved. Notable features include the fine range of monastic buildings, particularly the cloisters and refectory, the chapter house, and the superb medieval wood carving in the choir (especially the misericords). Also worth seeing are the long south transept with its various chapels, the consistory court, and the medieval roof bosses in the Lady Chapel.

St. Werburgh St. ℂ **01244/324756.** www.chestercathedral.org.uk. £3 ($4.80) donation suggested. Daily 9am–5pm.

Chester Zoo ⭐ *Kids*   The Chester Zoo is the largest repository of animals in the north of England. It is also the site of some of the most carefully manicured gardens in the region—110 acres that feature unusual shrubs, rare trees, and warm-weather displays of carpet bedding with as many as 160,000 plants timed to bloom simultaneously.

Many rare and endangered animal species breed freely here; the zoo is particularly renowned for the most successful colonies of chimpanzees and orangutans in Europe. The water bus, a popular observation aid that operates exclusively in summer, allows you to observe hundreds of water birds that make their home on the park's lake. There's also a monorail, which stops at the extreme eastern and western ends of the zoo, making visits less tiring. Youngsters love the Monkey's Island exhibit.

Off A41, Upton-by-Chester, 3km (2 miles) north of the town center. ℂ **01244/380280.** www.chesterzoo.org. Admission £11 ($17) adults, £8.50 ($14) seniors and children 3–15. Family ticket £36 ($58). Monorail £1.80 ($2.90) adults, £1.40 ($2.25) children. Free for kids under 3. Opens daily 10am; closing times vary, call for details. Closed Dec 25. From Chester's center, head north along Liverpool Rd.

SHOPPING

For stores with character and low prices, explore **the Rows,** a network of double-layered streets and sidewalks with an assortment of shops. The Rows runs along Bridge Street, Watergate Street, Eastgate Street, and Northgate Street. Shopping upstairs is much more adventurous than down on the street. Thriving stores operate in this traffic-free paradise: tobacco shops, restaurants, department stores, china shops, jewelers, and antiques dealers. For the best look, take a walk on arcaded Watergate Street.

Another shopping area to check out is **Cheshire Oaks,** a huge retail village of 60 shops, mainly clothing, perfume, and shoe outlet stores. Cheshire Oaks is located about 13km (8 miles) north of Chester on M53.

Chester has a large concentration of antiques and craft shops. Some better ones include **Lowe & Sons,** 11 Bridge St. Row (ℂ **01244/325850**), with antique silver and estate jewelry; **The Antique Shop,** 40 Watergate St. (ℂ **01244/316286**), specializing in brass, copper, and pewter items; **Adam's Antiques,** 65 Watergate Row (ℂ **01244/319421**), focusing on 18th- and 19th-century antiques; and **City Road Emporium,** 32 City Rd. (© **01244/329959**), a cluster of eight antique dealers in a three-story 18th-century grain-storage building.

Weekly antiques shows and auctions are held on Thursday at the Guildhall in Chester. Call the **Tourist Information Board** in Chester at © **01244/402111.**

One of the better shops for jewelry is **Boodle and Dunthorne,** 52 Eastgate St. (© **01244/326666**). Since the days of George III, **Brown's of Chester,** 34–40 Eastgate Road (© **01244/350001**), has carried women's fashions, perfumes, menswear, and children's clothes.

WHERE TO STAY
VERY EXPENSIVE

Chester Grosvenor Hotel ✦✦✦ This fine, half-timbered, five-story building in the heart of Chester is one of the most luxurious hotels in northern England, a reputation well deserved. Owned and named after the family of the dukes of Westminster, its origin can be traced from the reign of Queen Elizabeth I. Started as a Tudor inn, it became a political headquarters in Hanoverian days, was later transformed into a glittering mecca for the Regency and Victorian set, and continued to be a social center during the Edwardian era. It's hosted its share of royalty, including Prince Albert, Princess Diana, and Prince Rainier.

The high-ceilinged, marble-floored foyer of the hotel, with its 200-year-old chandelier, carved wooden staircase, and antiques, sets the tone. Each large, well-furnished bedroom is individually styled, with silks from France and handmade furnishings from Italy. Amenities include huge closets, CD players, and double-glazed windows. Some of the bathrooms are marble, but, regrettably, others are still a sorry sight with white laminate and linoleum. Each comes with heated towel racks, Floris toiletries, and bathrobes.

Eastgate, Chester, Cheshire CH1 1LT. © 01244/324024. Fax 01244/313246. www.chestergrosvenor.co.uk. 80 units. £210–£235 ($336–$376) double; £400–£525 ($640–$840) suite. Weekend rates include breakfast. Children under 15 stay free in parent's room. AE, DC, MC, V. **Amenities:** 2 restaurants; 2 bars; health club; sauna; business center; 24-hr. room service; laundry service. In room: A/C, TV, minibar, coffeemaker, hair dryer, iron, safe, trouser press.

EXPENSIVE

Crabwall Manor ✦✦ Chester's premier country-house hotel, the imposing crenellated Crabwall Manor traces its origins from the 16th century, though most of the present building dates from the early 1800s. It has a more peaceful location than the Chester Grosvenor, though it lacks the facilities and the top-notch service of its more highly rated competitor. Standing amid 11 acres of private grounds and gardens, the capably managed hotel rents quite large, well-furnished bedrooms. Some rooms have four-poster beds. The bathrooms are first-class; most have bidets and separate showers. Relax in the full-service spa after working out in the hotel's aerobics studio.

Parkgate Rd., Mollington, Chester, Cheshire CH1 6NE. © 01244/851666. Fax 01244/851400. www. marstonhotels.com. 48 units. £150–£175 ($240–$280) double; £225 ($360) suite. Weekend rates include breakfast. Children under 16 stay free when sharing room with 2 paying adults. AE, DC, MC, V. Bus: 22 or 23. Take A540 3.5km (2¼ miles) northwest of Chester. **Amenities:** Restaurant; bar; indoor pool; health club; Jacuzzi; sauna; room service; babysitting; laundry service; dry cleaning. In room: A/C, TV, coffeemaker, hair dryer, iron, trouser press.

MODERATE

Blossoms Hotel This hotel enjoys an ideal location in the very heart of Chester. Blossoms Hotel has been in business since the mid–17th century, though the present structure was rebuilt late in Victoria's day. An old open staircase in the reception room helps set the tone here, but otherwise the public rooms are uninspired. Bedrooms are fitted with dark wood pieces and firm beds—some of them four-posters—and many rooms have recently been refurbished. The beautiful bathrooms are carpeted and offer luxury toiletries and generous shelf space; most have a tub-and-shower combination.

St. John's St., Chester, Cheshire CH1 1HL. ℰ **01244/323186.** Fax 01244/346433. 64 units. £120 ($192) double; £135 ($216) suite. AE, DC, MC, V. **Amenities:** Restaurant; bar; room service; laundry service; dry cleaning. *In room:* TV, coffeemaker, hair dryer, trouser press.

Green Bough Hotel & Olive Tree Restaurant ✿✿✿   The North West Tourist Board named this Victorian house best small hotel of the year in 2002. Hoteliers Janice and Philip Martin have turned this establishment into the most exclusive small luxury hotel in Chester, both for cuisine and accommodations. Each bedroom has been restored and beautifully furnished, each individually designed with elegant fabrics, beautiful wallpapers, Italian tiles, and antique cast iron or carved wooden beds. A Roman-themed junior suite boasts a four-poster dating from 1890 and draped in *eau-de-nil voiles*. There is also a Louis XV carved wooden antique bed in the French-themed master suite. Each unit comes with a well-equipped private bathroom with tub and shower. Delightful on-site facilities feature the Champagne Lounge Bar and the award-winning Olive Tree Restaurant, known for serving imaginatively conceived local produce. Smoking is not permitted anywhere on the hotel premises.

60 Hoole Rd., Chester CH2 3NL. ℰ **01244/326241.** Fax 01244/325265. www.greenbough.co.uk/. 16 units. £105–£125 ($168–$200) double; £145–£225 ($232–$360) suite. Rates include English breakfast. AE, DC, MC, V. **Amenities:** Restaurant; bar; room service; laundry service. *In room:* TV, beverage maker, hair dryer.

Mollington Banastre ✿ *(Kids*   This Victorian mansion is a gabled house surrounded by gardens. It has been successfully converted into one of the leading country-house hotels in Cheshire, now affiliated with the Best Western reservation system. Rooms have comfortable doubles or twin beds; eight are spacious enough for families and two have four-poster beds. Each comes with a shower or tub-and-shower combination. It's not the most opulent choice in town, but it's a great value for the money.

Parkgate Rd., Chester, Cheshire CH1 6NN. ℰ **800/528-1234** in the U.S. and Canada, or 01244/851471. Fax 01244/851165. www.mollingtonbanastrehotel.com. 63 units. £105–£150 ($168–$240) double. Children 15 and under stay free in parent's room. Rates include breakfast. AE, DC, MC, V. Take A540 3km (2 miles) northwest of the center of Chester. Or take Junction 16 of M56 and continue for 2.5km (1½ miles). **Amenities:** 2 restaurants; bar, coffee shop; indoor pool; health club; sauna; salon; room service; laundry service; dry cleaning. *In room:* TV, minibar, coffeemaker, hair dryer, trouser press.

Rowton Hall Hotel   This stately home stands on the site of the Battle of Rowton Moor, which was fought in 1643 between the Roundheads and the Cavaliers. Built in 1779, with a wing added later, the house has an 8-acre garden, with a formal driveway entrance. Rowton Hall has comfortable traditional and contemporary furnishings. The better and more stylish luxury rooms are in the old house and offer amenities such as bathrobes. An adjoining wing contains more sterile and uninspired units, which some readers have complained about. Regardless of room assignment, each has a comfortable bed; four rooms are large enough for families. The shower-only bathrooms are small.

Whitchurch Rd., Rowton, Chester, Cheshire CH3 6AD. ℰ **01244/335262.** Fax 01244/335464. www.rowton hallhotel.co.uk. 38 units. £90–£150 ($144–$240) double; £150 ($240) junior suite; £200 ($320) suite. Rates include English or continental breakfast. AE, DC, MC, V. Take A41 3km (2 miles) from the center of Chester. **Amenities:** Restaurant; 2 bars; pool; 2 tennis courts; health club; room service; laundry service. *In room:* TV, coffeemaker, hair dryer, iron, safe.

WHERE TO DINE

Arkle Restaurant ★★★ (Finds) BRITISH/CONTINENTAL   Arkle is the premier restaurant in this part of England. The 45-seat formal, gourmet restaurant has a superb *chef de cuisine* and a talented 40-strong team that uses the freshest ingredients to create modern British and continental dishes prepared with subtle touches and a certain lightness. Main courses include langoustine ravioli, and Welsh black beef filet topped with fresh horseradish. Desserts are equally luscious and tempting. Arkle has an award-winning cheese selection and a choice of at least six unique breads daily.

In the Chester Grosvenor Hotel, Eastgate. © 01244/324024. Reservations required. 2-course fixed-price menu £45 ($72); 3-course fixed-price menu £52 ($83); fixed-price menu gourmand £60 ($96). AE, DC, MC, V. Tues–Sun noon–2:30pm; Tues–Sat 7–9:30pm.

Elliot's Restaurant BRITISH   In the heart of Chester, this family-run old English restaurant buys local produce and the best of regional products. It is concerned with free-range, organic, and natural products that it fashions into good-tasting and time-tested recipes. All vegetables are steam-cooked and served crisp. The abbreviated lunch menu includes a homemade soup of the day with freshly made bread, a selection of both hot and cold sandwiches, a cheese platter (a choice of four British cheeses), and daily specials posted on the board. For appetizers at night, select such delights as a seafood cocktail or venison sausages. Main dishes evoke England at its best, including a traditional roast beef dinner with Yorkshire pudding or free-range turkey pie flavored with fresh herbs. Vegetarian dishes are also served. Homemade pies make an excellent dessert.

2 Abbey Green, off Northgate St. © 01244/329932. Reservations not needed. Lunch specials £5.95–£8.95 ($9.50–$14); dinner main courses £8.50–£16 ($14–$26). MC, V. Daily noon–11pm.

La Brasserie (Value) ENGLISH/FRENCH   This is perhaps the best all-around dining choice in Chester for convenience, price, and quality. In a delightful Art Nouveau setting, the Brasserie offers an extensive a la carte menu to suit most tastes and pocketbooks. You get robust flavors and hearty ingredients. Main dishes include fried fish cakes with a hot Greek salad and crumbled feta; baked chicken with potato pancakes and garlic cheese; and other hearty brasserie food.

In the Chester Grosvenor Hotel, Eastgate St. © 01244/324024. Main courses £9.75–£25 ($16–$40). AE, DC, MC, V. Mon–Sat 7am–10:30pm; Sun 7am–10pm.

CHESTER AFTER DARK

If you want to relax in a pub, grab a pint of Marston's at the **Olde Custom House,** Watergate Street (© **01244/324435**), a 17th-century customhouse with many original features still intact. The **Pied Bull,** Northgate Street (© **01244/ 325829**), is an 18th-century coaching inn where you can still eat, drink, or rent a room. Real ales on tap include Flowers, and Greenall's Bitter and Traditional. At **Ye Olde King's Head,** Lower Bridge Street (© **01244/324855**), ales are not the only spirits you may encounter. This B&B pub, built in 1622, is said to be haunted by three ghosts: a crying woman and baby in room no. 6, and the ghostly initials "ST" that appear in steam on the bathroom mirror of room no. 4. If you prefer your spirits in a glass, stick to the pub, where you can sip on a Boddington's Bitter, or Greenall's Original or Local.

Live Irish music and atmosphere can be sampled at **The Red Lion,** 59 Northgate St. (© **01244/321750**), where you can hear traditional music on Wednesday and Sunday nights for the price of a pint of Guinness. **Alexandre's,** Rufus Court off Northgate Street (© **01244/340005**), offers more varied entertainment.

3 Kendal

435km (270 miles) NW of London; 103km (64 miles) NW of Bradford; 116km (72 miles) NW of Leeds; 14km (9 miles) SE of Windermere

The River Kent winds its way through a rich valley of limestone hills and cliffs, known as "fells," and down through the "Auld Grey Town" of Kendal, whose moniker refers to the large number of gray stone houses found in and about the town. Many visitors to the Lake District simply pass through Kendal on their way to more attractive destinations—the town is a gateway rather than a true stopping place. It's never depended entirely on the tourist dollar. This fact should not deter you, however, from taking a bit of time to discover some of this market town's more intriguing areas.

Kendal contains the ruins of a castle where Catherine Parr, the last wife of Henry VIII, was allegedly born. Recent speculation about her actual birthplace has led to a clouding of the historical record. Even if she wasn't born here, it is still said that she most likely lived at the castle at some time in her life. Among other historic sites, Kendal has a 13th-century parish church that merits a visit.

Today, Kendal is famous for its mint cake and its surrounding limestone fells, which offer excellent vistas of the area and make for great hikes.

ESSENTIALS

GETTING THERE   Trains from London's Euston Station do not go directly to Kendal; seven daily trains arrive in Oxenholme, about 2.5km (1½ miles) away. From here, you'll be able to take a cab or board one of the local trains that leave approximately every hour to Kendal proper (total trip time: 3½ hr.). For train schedules and information, call © **0845/748-4950.**

To get to Kendal from London by bus, take one of the three daily National Express buses (trip time: 7 hr.). For schedules and information, call **National Express** at © **020/7529-2000.**

If you're driving, follow the M1 out of London, then the M6 to Kendal (trip time: 5 hr.).

VISITOR INFORMATION   The **Tourist Information Centre of Kendal,** Town Hall, Highgate (© **01539/725758**), is open September through December and March through June, Monday through Saturday from 9am to 5pm and Sunday from 10am to 4pm; January and February Monday through Saturday from 9am to 5pm; July and August Monday through Saturday from 9am to 6pm and Sunday from 10am to 5pm.

SEEING THE SIGHTS

Abbot Hall Art Gallery   The Georgian elegance of Kendal's Abbot Hall Art Gallery has created an ideal setting for its display of fine art. Paintings by the town's famous son, 18th-century portrait painter George Romney, fill the walls of rooms furnished by Gillows of Lancaster. A major display of work by 20th-century British artists such as Graham Sutherland, John Piper, and Ben Nicholson is on permanent display. Visitors can see the region through the eyes of the many painters who have been inspired by the landscapes in another of the gallery's permanent exhibitions housed in the Peter Scott Gallery.

Kirkland. © 01539/722464. www.abbothall.org.uk. Admission £3.75 ($6) adults, £1.75 ($2.80) children, £9.50 ($15) family ticket. Apr to late Oct Mon–Sat 10:30am–5pm; Mid-Feb to Mar and Nov to late Dec Mon–Sat 10:30am–4pm.

Kendal Museum   One of England's oldest museums takes visitors on a journey of discovery from Roman times to the present. A natural history section

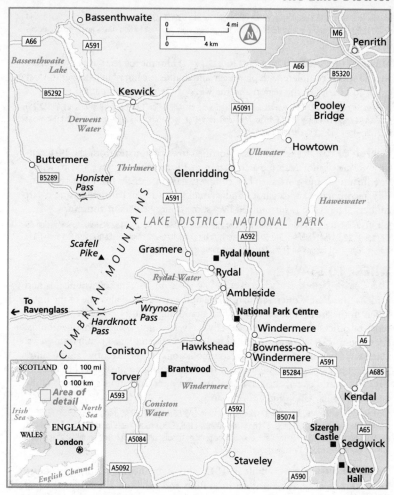

includes a nature trail from mountaintop to lakeside, on which visitors are brought face to face with many of the inhabitants of the area. The World Wildlife Gallery displays a vast collection of exotic animals. One of the exhibitions introduces visitors to the fell-tops' best-known visitor, Alfred Wainwright, who walked, talked, and wrote with a passion and flair about the region. Wainwright worked diligently until his death in 1991.

Station Rd. ☎ **01539/721374.** www.kendalmuseum.org.uk. Admission £3.50 ($5.60) adults, £1.75 ($2.80) children, £9 ($14) family. Mid-Feb to Mar and Nov–Dec 24 Mon–Sat 10:30am–4pm; Apr–Oct Mon–Sat 10:30am–5pm. Closed Dec 24 to mid-Feb.

Levens Hall   This Elizabethan mansion was constructed in the 1500s by James Bellingham. Today, the house is filled with Jacobean furniture and there's a fascinating collection of steam engines outside on the grounds. . The estate also has a **topiary garden** ★★ dating from 1692, with a host of yews and box hedges clipped into a variety of intriguing shapes.

Levens Park, Levens (6.5km/4 miles south of Kendal). ℂ **01539/560321.** www.levenshall.co.uk. Admission £7 ($11) for house and gardens; £5.50 ($8.80) for gardens only. Apr–Oct 14 Sun–Thurs noon–5pm (gardens open at 10am).

Museum of Lakeland Life and Industry   From the re-creation of a Victorian Kendal street, complete with pharmacy and market, visitors can discover the lost crafts and trades of the region and the ways of life that accompanied them.

Kirkland. ℂ **01539/722464.** www.lakelandmuseum.org.uk. Admission £2.75 ($4.40) adults, £1.40 ($2.25) children, £7 ($11) family. Mid-Feb to Mar and Nov–Dec Mon–Sat 10:30am–5pm; Apr–Oct Mon–Sat 10:30am–4pm. Closed Jan to mid-Feb.

Sizergh Castle   The castle has a fortified tower that dates from the 14th century. Inside, visitors can see a collection of Elizabethan carvings and paneling, fine furniture, and portraits. The complete garden, largely from the 18th century, incorporates a rock garden and a famous planting of hardy ferns and dwarf conifers. The castle is surrounded by a show of fiery colors in autumn.

5.5km (3½ miles) south of Kendal (northwest of interchange A590/591). ℂ **01539/560070.** Admission £5 ($8) adults, £2.50 ($4) children, £12.50 ($20) family ticket (2 adults and 2 children). Late Apr to Oct Sun–Thurs 1:30–5:30pm (last admission 5pm). The shop and gardens open at 12:30pm.

WHERE TO STAY

The Castle Green Hotel in Kendal ✰   Set on 14 acres of woodlands and gardens, this Best Western affiliate is one of the newest and also one of the finest hotels in the area. Though it looks like a rambling country estate, it was once a series of offices that have been cleverly converted into comfortable bedrooms. Each room is stylish and well furnished, many opening onto panoramic views. The best, albeit most expensive, accommodations are the executive studio suites with a lot of extra space. Guests enjoy free membership in the hotel's health club. **Tip:** The Castle Green also has one of the best pubs, Alexander's, and one of the best restaurants, Guesthouse, in the area.

Signposted from the M6, Junction 37. Kendal, Cumbria LA9 6BH. ℂ **01539/734000.** Fax 01539/735522. www.castlegreen.co.uk. 100 units. £118 ($189) double; £158 ($253) suite. Rates include English breakfast. AE, DC, MC, V. **Amenities:** Restaurant; pub; indoor pool; gym; solarium; steam room; aerobics; salon; room service; laundry. *In room:* TV, coffeemaker, hair dryer.

Garden House Hotel   Built in 1812, this is an inviting Georgian country house. It was once a convent for local nuns and has been a hotel for the past 30 years or so. It's nestled in 2 acres of walled garden and green pastureland, and is perfectly serene. Some guest rooms have fireplaces; one has a four-poster bed. Each tiled bathroom, quite compact, comes with a tub-and-shower combination. The public areas include a somewhat formal sitting room, an informal lounge and bar with lots of seating, an elegant breakfast room with a dark mahogany fireplace, and a restaurant conservatory.

Fowling Lane, Kendal, Cumbria LA9 6PH. ℂ **01539/731131.** Fax 01539/740064. www.gardenhousehotel. co.uk. 11 units. £79 ($126) double; £85 ($136) for 4-poster bed. £5 ($7.50) extra bed. Rates include English breakfast. MC, V. **Amenities:** Restaurant; bar; putting green; limited room service; limited laundry service; croquet lawn. *In room:* TV, coffeemaker, hair dryer, trouser press.

WHERE TO DINE

Déjà Vu FRENCH (TRADITIONAL AND MODERN)   The interior of this small and cozy French cabaret is inspired by one of van Gogh's landscape paintings. People come for good food and a fun time. A wide range of appetizers evoke a taste of Paris, featuring fresh scallops mille feuille with a basil cream sauce, or filet of venison with a red-wine and raspberry sauce. Follow with such mains as fresh monkfish filet on eggplant with a basil and fennel sauce, or Aberdeen Angus filet of beef with a port and pink peppercorn mousse. Desserts feature many classic French favorites, including the delicious peach tartlet.

124 Stricklandgate. © **01539/724843.** Reservations recommended. Main courses £9.50–£15 ($15–$24). AE, DC, MC, V. Mon–Sat 5:30–10pm; Fri–Sat noon–2pm.

Moon INTERNATIONAL   This bistro cooks up the best food in Kendal. Set in a building that's more than 250 years old and was once a grocery store, the dining room offers patrons a close, friendly, and informal environment. The food is interesting without being gimmicky. The owners take pride in offering market-fresh ingredients when available. Main courses include a lamb shank with either a mustard and Soya sauce or a cream, leek, and white-wine sauce; or for vegetarians, goat's cheese, red pepper, and mango wrapped in filo pastry with an apple, gooseberry, and honey sauce.

129 Highgate. © **01539/729254.** Main courses £8.75–£13.75 ($14–$22). MC, V. Tues–Sun 6–10pm; winter Wed–Sun 6–10pm.

Punch Bowl Inn ★★ *Finds* BRITISH   This is one of the best pubs for dining in the Lake District. The quality food is prepared and supervised by Steven Doherty, formerly executive chef for the Roux brothers, who are acclaimed as the finest chefs in Britain. Top-notch cuisine is served in a 17th-century coaching inn lying in the Lyth Valley, with black painted timbers, log fires, and walls covered with pictures of local artists. An Old World atmosphere permeates the restaurant with its low ceilings, beams, and open log fires. On summer evenings al fresco dining is enjoyed on the patio. The starters here may change your idea of pub grub forever, particularly if you sample the oven-baked beetroot tart with crumbled goat's cheese and honey or the fresh seared sea bass on pesto potatoes. For a main course, we suggest you dig into the sliced roasted chump of Cumbrian fell-bred lamb with oyster mushrooms. For dessert, the chocolate and ginger tart with homemade honey ice cream will make you want to return the following night.

The inn also rents three simply furnished bedrooms, with tub or shower, each with beverage maker, TV, and hair dryer. The cost is £60 ($96) in a double with an English breakfast.

Crosthwaite, near Kendal. © **01539/568237.** Reservations recommended. Main courses £12–£14 ($19–$22). MC, V. Tues–Sun 11:30am–2pm; Tues–Sat 7–8:30pm.

KENDAL AFTER DARK

One of the best entertainment centers in the Lake District is the **Brewery Arts Centre,** Highgate (© **01539/725133**), which includes two cinemas, a theater, the Green Room restaurant, two café bars, and other venues in a converted brewery. The box office for all attractions is open Monday through Saturday from 10am to 8:30pm and Sunday from 11am to 8:30pm.

4 Windermere & Bowness ★★

441km (274 miles) NW of London; 16km (10 miles) NW of Kendal; 89km (55 miles) N of Liverpool

The largest lake in England is Windermere, whose eastern shore washes up on the town of Bowness (or Bowness-on-Windermere), with the town of Windermere 2.5km (1½ miles) away. From either town, you can climb **Orrest Head** in less than an hour for a panoramic view of the Lakeland. From that vantage point, you can even view **Scafell Pike,** rising to a height of 978m (3,210 ft.)—it's the tallest peak in all of England.

ESSENTIALS

GETTING THERE Trains to Windermere meet the main line at Oxenholme for connections to both Scotland and London. Information about rail services in the area can be obtained by calling the railway information line at ℂ 0845/ 748-4950. Frequent connections are possible throughout the day. To get to Bowness and its ferry pier from Windermere, turn left from the rail terminal and cross the center of Windermere until you reach New Road, which eventually changes its name to Lake Road before it approaches the outskirts of Bowness. It's about a 20-minute walk downhill. The CMS Lakeland Experience bus also runs from the Windermere Station to Bowness every 20 minutes.

The **National Express** bus link, originating at London's Victoria Coach Station, serves Windermere, with good connections also to Preston, Manchester, and Birmingham. For schedules and information, call ℂ 020/7529-2000. Local buses operated mainly by **Stagecoach** (ℂ 0870/608-2608) go to Kendal, Ambleside, Grasmere, and Keswick. Call for information on various routings within the Lake District.

If you're driving from London, head north on the M1 and M6 past Liverpool until you reach the A685 junction heading west to Kendal. From Kendal, A591 continues west to Windermere.

VISITOR INFORMATION The **Tourist Information Centre** at Windermere is on Victoria Street (ℂ 01539/446499).

EXPLORING THE AREA

There is regular **steamer service** around **Windermere,** the largest of the lakes, about 17km (11 miles) long. It's also possible to take a steamer on Coniston Water, a small lake that Wordsworth called "a broken spoke sticking in the rim." Coniston Water is a smaller and less heavily traveled lake than Windermere.

Launch and steamer cruises depart from Bowness daily throughout the year operated by **Windermere Lake Cruises Ltd.** (ℂ 01539/443360; www. windermere-lakecruises.co.uk). Service is available from Bowness to Ambleside and to Lakeside at rates ranging from £5.80 to £10 ($9.30–$16) for adults and £2.90 to £5 ($4.65–$8)for children. There is a 45-minute Island Cruise for £4.50 ($7.20) for adults and £2.25 ($3.60) for children.

At Lakeside, you can ride a steam train to Haverthwaite. A combination boat/train ticket is £4.50 ($7.20) for adults and £2 ($3.20) for children. An attraction at Lakeside, near Newby Bridge, is the **Aquarium of the Lakes** (ℂ 01539/530153; www.aquariumofthelakes.co.uk), with an exhibit of fish and wildlife. The aquarium is open daily from 9am to 4pm November through March, and from 9am to 5pm April through October. Combination boat/admission tickets are £14 ($23) for adults, £8.15 ($13) for children, and £43 ($69) for a family ticket from Ambleside; and £11 ($17) for adults, £6 ($9.60) for children, and £33 ($54) for a family ticket from Bowness. Aquarium-only admission is £5.75 ($9.20) for adults, £3.75 ($6) for children, and £17 ($27) for a family ticket (two adults and two children).

Directly south of Windermere, **Bowness** is an attractive old lakeside town with lots of interesting architecture, much of it dating from Queen Victoria's day. This has been an important center for boating and fishing for a long time, and you can rent boats of all descriptions to explore the lake.

Windermere Steamboat Centre This museum houses the finest collection of steamboats in the world. Important examples of these elegant Victorian and Edwardian vessels have been preserved in working order. The steamboats are

Moments **Walks & Rambles**

Driving in the wilds of this scenic shire is fine for a start, but the best way to take in its beauty is by walking. Pack some good waterproof hiking boots and a lightweight rain jacket—even if you set out on a nice morning, you need to be prepared for changing conditions and sunny days are few. When the mist starts to fall, do as the locals do and head for the nearest inn or pub, where you can drop in and warm yourself beside an open fireplace.

If you want to make hiking in the Lake District a focus of your entire vacation, you may prefer an organized outing. **Countrywide Holidays, Miry Lane, Wigan, Lancashire, WN3 4AG (© 01942/823430;** www. countrywidewalking.com), has offered walking and special-interest vacations for more than 100 years. Safe and sociable guided walks are led by experienced guides for all ages and abilities. It's ideal for independent walkers, with boot-drying rooms provided. They have four comfortable, informal, and welcoming guesthouses set in beautiful Lakeland locations.

exhibited in a unique wet dock where they are moored in their natural lakeside setting. The fine display of touring and racing motorboats in the dry dock links the heyday of steam with some of the most famous names of powerboat racing and the record-breaking attempts on Windermere, including Sir Henry Segrave's world water-speed record set in 1930.

All the boats have intriguing stories, including the veteran SL *Dolly,* built around 1850 and probably the oldest mechanically driven boat in the world. The vessel was raised from the lakebed of Ullswater in 1962 and, following restoration, ran for 10 years with its original boiler. The *Dolly* is still steamed on special occasions.

The SL *Swallow* (1911) is steamed most days; visitors can make a 50-minute trip on the lake at a cost of £5 ($8) for adults and £2.50 ($4) for children, with the crew serving tea or coffee made using the Windermere steam kettle.

Rayrigg Rd. © **01539/445565.** www.steamboat.co.uk. Admission £3.50 ($5.60) adults, £2 ($3.20) children, £8.50 ($14) family ticket. Daily 10am–5pm. Closed Nov to mid-Mar.

The World of Beatrix Potter   This exhibit uses the latest technology to tell the story of Beatrix Potter's fascinating life. A video wall and special film describe how her tales came to be written and how she became a pioneering Lakeland farmer and conservationist. There is also a shop with a wealth of top-quality Beatrix Potter merchandise, from Wedgwood ceramics to soft toys. It's mobbed on summer weekends; try to come at any other time.

The Old Laundry, Bowness-on-Windermere. © **01539/488444.** www.hop-skip-jump.com. Admission £3.75 ($6) adults, £2.50 ($4) children. Easter–Oct daily 10am–5:30pm; rest of year daily 10am–4:30pm. Take A591 to Lake Rd. and follow the signs.

WHERE TO STAY
VERY EXPENSIVE
Holbeck Ghyll ★★★   This is the most tranquil oasis in the area and offers the most refined cuisine. Overlooking Lake Windermere, this country-house hotel

Lake District National Park

Despite the reverence with which the English treat the Lake District, it required an act of Parliament in 1951 to protect its natural beauty. Sprawling over 1,424 sq. km (885 sq. miles) of hills, eroded mountains, forests, and lakes, the **Lake District National Park** ★★★ is the largest and one of the most popular national parks in the United Kingdom, with 14 million visitors a year. Its scenery and literary references (Wordsworth, Beatrix Potter, John Ruskin, and Samuel Taylor Coleridge were among its most ardent fans) add an academic gloss to one of the most idealized regions of Britain. Lured by descriptions from the romantic lake poets, visitors arrive to take in the mountains, wildlife, flora, fauna, and secluded waterfalls. Much of the area is privately owned, but landowners work with national park officers to preserve the landscape and its 2,898km (1,800 miles) of footpaths.

Alas, the park's popularity is now one of its major drawbacks. Hordes of weekend tourists descend, especially in summertime and on bank-holiday weekends. During mild weather in midsummer, Windermere, Keswick, and Ambleside are likely to be among the most crowded towns of their size in England. But despite the crowds, great efforts are made to maintain the trails that radiate in a network throughout the district. Rigid building codes manage to accommodate the scores of tourist-industry facilities, while preserving the purity of a landscape that includes more than 100 lakes and countless numbers of grazing sheep.

Before setting out to explore the lake, stop in at the **National Park Visitor Centre** (℃ **01539/446601**), located on the lakeshore at Brockhole, on the A591 between Windermere and Ambleside. It can be reached by bus or by one of the lake launches from Windermere. Here, you can pick up useful information and explore 30 acres of landscaped

was once a 19th-century hunting lodge owned by Lord Lonsdale, one of the richest men in Britain, and has a high price tag but offers a lot for the money. An inglenook fireplace welcomes visitors. The most elaborate room is a honeymoon and anniversary room that has a four-poster bed and a bathroom with a spa bath for two. But each unit is fitted with a luxury bed, often crowned by a canopy or a padded headboard. Rooms are individually designed, coming in various shapes and sizes, and most of them open onto a view of the lake. Six rooms are in a separate nonsmoking lodge added in 1998, and these are even finer than the rooms in the main building. Lodge rooms are interconnecting with panoramic lake views, individual balcony or patio areas, fresh flowers, and CD players; four units have kitchenettes. Luxurious bathrooms have separate shower cubicles, as well as a tub. Children under 8 are not welcome in the restaurant.

Holbeck Lane (on A591 5.5km/3½ miles northwest of town center), Windermere, Cumbria LA23 1LU. ℃ 01539/432375. Fax 01539/434743. www.holbeckghyll.com. 21 units. £100–£135 ($160–$216) per person double; from £135 ($216) per person suite. Rates with English breakfast and dinner. Children under 17 stay for half price when sharing parent's room. AE, DC, MC, V. **Amenities:** Restaurant; bar; putting green; tennis court; spa; room service (8am–11pm); laundry service; croquet lawn. *In room:* TV, kitchenette (4 rooms only) coffeemaker, hair dryer, trouser press.

gardens and parklands; lake cruises, exhibitions, and film shows are also offered. Lunches and teas are served in Gaddums tearooms, which offer terrace seating. Admission is free, except for special events staged here. Parking costs £3.50 ($5.60) for 3 hours or £4 ($6.40) for a full day.

When setting out anywhere in the Lake District, it's wise to take adequate clothing and equipment, including food and drink. Weather conditions can change rapidly in this area, and in the high fells it can be substantially different from that found at lower levels. A weather line (© 01768/775757) provides the latest conditions.

Tourist information offices within the park are richly stocked with maps and suggestions for several dozen bracing rambles—perhaps a 6.4km (4-mile) loop around the town of Windermere; a long (11km/ 7-mile) or short (5.6km/3½-mile) hike between Ambleside and Grasmere; or a boat ride from Windermere to the southern edge of the town's lake, followed by a trek northward along the lake's scenic western shore. Regardless of the itinerary you select, you'll spot frequent green-and-white signs, or their older equivalents in varnished pine with Adirondack-style routed letters, announcing footpath to . . .

Be aware before you go that the Lake District receives more rainfall than any other district of England, and that sturdy walking shoes and rain gear are essential. Hiking after dark is not recommended under any circumstances.

Any tourist information office within the park can provide leaflets describing treks through the park. The **Windermere Tourist Information Centre,** Victoria Street, Windermere, Cumbria LA23 1AD (© **01539/ 446499),** is especially helpful.

Langdale Chase Hotel ★★   A grand old lakeside house, this hotel resembles a villa on Italy's Lake Como. It has better rooms than Miller Howe (see below), though the food is not as good. The bedrooms contain excellent furniture, and many were recently refurbished. Most of the bedrooms open onto panoramic views of the lake. Five bedrooms are in a converted cottage on the grounds, and these are equal in comfort to those units in the main building. Another bedroom lies over the boathouse on the lake, and this one is often requested. Bathrooms are tiled and have adequate shelf space. The interior of the Victorian stone château, with its many gables, balconies, large mullioned windows, and terraces, is a treasure trove of antiques. The main lounge hall looks like a setting for one of those English drawing-room comedies. On the walls are distinctive paintings, mostly Italian primitives, though one is alleged to be a Van Dyck.

On A591 (3km/2 miles north of town, toward Ambleside), Windermere, Cumbria LA23 1LW. © **01539/ 432201.** Fax 01539/432604. www.langdalechase.co.uk. 27 units. £80–£125 ($128–$200) per person double. Rates include breakfast and dinner. AE, DC, MC, V. Bus: 555. **Amenities:** Restaurant; bar; 24-hr. room service; babysitting; laundry service; croquet lawn. *In room:* TV, coffeemaker, hair dryer.

Lindeth Fell Hotel ★   High above the town is this traditional large Lakeland house, built of stone and brick in 1907. Many of its rooms overlook the handsome gardens and the lake. The owners, the Kennedys, run the place more like a country house than a hotel, achieving an atmosphere of comfort in pleasingly furnished surroundings. Bedrooms open onto beautiful views, especially on the lakeside of the house; many are quite spacious, others are snug, but all have comfortable beds. The shower-only bathrooms are neatly kept.

Lyth Valley Rd. (on A5074 1.5km/1 mile south of Bowness), Bowness-on-Windermere, Cumbria LA23 3JP. © 01539/443286. Fax 01539/447455. www.lindethfell.co.uk. 14 units. £160–£190 ($256–$304) double. Rates include breakfast and dinner. MC, V. Closed Jan–Feb 14. **Amenities:** Restaurant; bar; putting green; room service (8am–10:30pm); laundry service; croquet lawn. *In room:* TV, coffeemaker, hair dryer, trouser press.

The Linthwaite House Hotel ✦   This hotel, built in 1900, is surrounded by woodlands and gardens, with a panoramic view of Lake Windermere, Bell Isle, and the distant mountains. The bedrooms are beautifully decorated and offer many amenities, including bathrobes and satellite TVs. As befits its former role as an Edwardian gentleman's house, this hotel offers individually decorated bedrooms that come in various shapes and sizes. All are fitted with sumptuously comfortable beds.

Crook Rd., Bowness-on-Windermere, Cumbria LA23 3JA. © 01539/488600. Fax 01539/488601. www. linthwaite.com. 26 units. £100–£298 ($160–$477) double. Rates include English breakfast. AE, DC, MC, V. **Amenities:** Restaurant; bar; complimentary use of nearby spa; room service; laundry service. *In room:* TV, coffeemaker, hair dryer, trouser press.

Miller Howe Hotel ✦✦   International guests come to this inn, which bears the unique imprint of its creator, former actor John Tovey, who treats his guests as if they had been invited to a house party. His country estate overlooks Lake Windermere (with views of the Langdale Pikes) and offers stylish accommodations and exquisite cuisine. The house was built in 1916 in the Edwardian style, sitting on 4½ acres of statue-dotted garden and parkland. The large, graciously furnished rooms have names (not numbers), and each is supplied with binoculars to help guests fully enjoy the view; other amenities include CD players and umbrellas. Beds are sumptuous, often canopy-draped, each with colorful spreads, soft comfortable mattresses, and padded headboards. Four rooms have Jacuzzis. There are even copies of *Punch* from the 1890s.

Rayrigg Rd. (on A592 between Windermere and Bowness), Windermere, Cumbria LA23 1EY. © 01539/ 442536. Fax 01539/445664. www.millerhowe.com. 16 units. Winter £80–£135 ($128–$216) per person per night; high season £93–£175 ($149–$280) per person per night. Rates include English breakfast and 6-course dinner. AE, MC, V. **Amenities:** Restaurant; 3 lounges; conservatory room; room service; laundry service; croquet lawn. *In room:* TV, hair dryer, trouser press.

MODERATE

Cedar Manor ✦   One of the most desirable country-house hotels in the area is Cedar Manor, which just completed a renovation in 2003. Originally built in 1860, with gables and chimneys, it was the summer getaway home for a wealthy industrialist from Manchester. But since those times, it has been converted into a small hotel of exceptional merit, with well-furnished bedrooms. Each of the spacious bedrooms is individually designed and well maintained; some have canopied or four-poster beds. Bathrooms are small and compact, most with tub-and-shower combinations. The hotel takes its name from a cedar tree, perhaps from India, which has grown in the garden for some 2 centuries.

Ambleside Rd. (A591), Windermere, Cumbria LA23 1AX. © 01539/443192. Fax 01539/445970. www.cedar manor.co.uk. 11 units. £60–£140 ($96–$224) double. Rates include breakfast. MC, V. **Amenities:** Restaurant; lounge; complimentary use of nearby health club; room service (8am–11pm); laundry service. *In room:* TV, coffeemaker, hair dryer.

Lindeth Howe *Kids*   This is a country house in a scenic position above Lake Windermere, with 6 acres of garden. Part stone and part red brick, with a roof of green Westmoreland slate, the house was built for a wealthy mill owner in 1879, but its most famous owner was Beatrix Potter, who installed her mother here while she lived across the lake at Sawrey. The present owner, John A. Tiscornia, has furnished it in fine style. Nine of the bedrooms have lake views and are comfortably furnished. Three rooms have handsome four-poster beds, and some rooms have spa bathrooms. Three rooms are large enough for families. Most rooms have shower-tub combinations in the bathrooms.

Longtail Hill, Storrs Park, Bowness-on-Windermere, Cumbria LA23 3JF. ℭ 01539/445759. Fax 01539/446368. www.lindeth-howe.co.uk. 36 units. £50–£75 ($80–$120) per person double with breakfast, £75–£98 ($120–$157) per person double with breakfast and dinner. AE, MC, V. Take B5284 south of Bowness. **Amenities:** Restaurant; bar; indoor pool; health club; sauna; room service (8am–8pm); laundry service. *In room:* TV, dataport, hair dryer, trouser press.

INEXPENSIVE

Beaumont Hotel   This stone-sided Lakeland villa, originally built in the 1850s, is on a quiet residential street about a minute's walk from Windermere's commercial center. Mr. and Mrs. James C. Casey massively upgraded what had been a rather dowdy interior. Each of the bedrooms is named after one of the characters in the Beatrix Potter sagas (our favorite is Jemima PuddleDuck) and contains either some kind of elaborate canopy or a four-poster bed, fitted with a quality mattress. All the accommodations have recently been refurbished, with new showers, carpets, and curtains. The entire property is nonsmoking and children under 10 are not accepted.

Holly Rd., Windermere, Cumbria LA23 2AF. ℭ/fax 01539/447075. www.lakesbeaumont.co.uk. 10 units. £60–£100 ($96–$160) double. Rates include English breakfast. MC, V. *In room:* TV, coffeemaker, hair dryer.

Fir Trees ★ *Value*   This is one of the finest guesthouses in Windermere. It's very well run, essentially providing hotel-like standards at B&B prices. Opposite St. John's Church, halfway between the villages of Bowness and Windermere, Fir Trees is a Victorian house furnished with antiques. Proprietors Mark and Jill Drinkall offer a warm welcome and rent beautifully maintained bedrooms. The attractive tiled bathrooms are each equipped with a shower (some have shower-and-tub combinations). Some units are large enough for families; a few have four-poster beds. The Drinkalls can provide their guests with detailed information on restaurants, country pubs, or where to go and what to see.

Lake Rd., Windermere, Cumbria LA23 2EQ. ℭ and fax 01539/442272. www.fir-trees.com. 9 units. £56–£64 ($90–$102) double. Rates include English breakfast. MC, V. No smoking. **Amenities:** Free use of nearby health club. *In room:* TV, coffeemaker, hair dryer.

WHERE TO DINE

Miller Howe Café ★★ INTERNATIONAL   Owned by Ian and Annette Dutton, this charming little cafe lies at the back of a shop that is known as one of the largest retailers of "creative kitchenware" in Britain. Amid a very modern decor, clients place their food orders at a countertop, and then wait until waitresses bring the dishes to their tables. The cuisine draws upon culinary traditions from around the world and includes such dishes as diced and curried beef in a spicy sauce, filet of salmon with a fresh garden herb sauce, crispy salad bowl with an orange and honey vinaigrette, and breast of chicken served in a red-wine gravy. The restaurant is adjacent to the town's railway station.

Lakeland Limited, Station Precinct. ℭ 01539/446732. Main courses £6.95–£8.95 ($11–$14). MC, V. Mon–Fri 9am–6pm; Sat 9am–5pm; Sun 10:30am–4pm.

Porthole Eating House FRENCH/ITALIAN/ENGLISH   In a white-painted Lakeland house near the center of town, this restaurant, owned and operated by Gianni and Judy Barten for the last quarter of a century, serves French, English, and Italian cuisine inspired by Italian-born Gianni. Amid a decor enhanced by rows of wine and liqueur bottles and nautical accessories, you can enjoy well-flavored specialties that change with the seasons. Examples include lobster-and-crab bisque; vegetarian lasagna made with mixed vegetables, fresh herbs, and a fresh tomato coulis and basil sauce; and filet of beef lightly grilled and served with a reduction of butter, fresh herbs, and a touch of white wine.

3 Ash St. ⓒ 01539/442793. Reservations recommended. Main courses £11–£17 ($18–$27). AE, DC, MC, V. Sun and Thurs–Fri noon–2pm; Wed–Mon 6:30–10pm.

FAVORITE LOCAL PUBS

Drive a short distance south of Windermere to Cartmel Fell, situated between A592 and A5074, and you'll find a pub-lover's dream. The **Mason Arms,** Strawberry Bank (ⓒ **01539/568486**), is a Jacobean pub with original oak paneling and flagstone floors. There's sturdy, comfortable wooden furniture spread through a series of five rooms in which you can wander or settle. The outside garden, attractive in its own right, offers a dramatic view of the Winster Valley beyond. The pub offers so many beers that it has a 24-page catalog to help you order, plus a creative, reasonable menu that includes several tasty vegetarian options. Beer prices start at £2 ($3.20).

Southeast of the village, off the A5074 in Crosthwaithe, the **Punch Bowl** (ⓒ **01539/568237**) is a 16th-century pub; the central room features a high-beamed ceiling with upper minstrel galleries on two sides. Outdoors, a stepped terrace on the hillside offers a tranquil retreat. Theakston's Best Bitter, Jennings Cumberland, and Cocker Hoop are available on tap.

A popular 17th-century pub, **The Queens Head,** on the A592 north of Windermere (ⓒ **01539/432174**), uses a gigantic Elizabethan four-poster bed as its serving counter, and has an eclectic mix of antiques strewn in with basic bar furnishings. There are 14 rooms in which you can settle with a pint of Mitchell's Lancaster Bomber, Tetley's, or Boddington's.

Established in 1612, the **Hole in t' Wall,** Lowside (ⓒ **01539/443488**), is the oldest pub in Bowness, a real treasure for its character and friendliness. The barroom is decorated with a hodgepodge of antiquated farming tools, and there's a large slate fireplace lending warmth on winter days plus a good selection of real ales on tap. The menu is determined daily, and there's real ingenuity illustrated in an eclectic mix of vegetarian, seafood, and local game dishes. A small flagstone terrace in the front offers lingering on warmer days and evenings.

5 Ambleside & Rydal

448km (278 miles) NW of London; 23km (14 miles) NW of Kendal; 6.5km (4 miles) N of Windermere

An idyllic retreat, Ambleside is just a small village, but it's one of the major places to stay in the Lake District, attracting pony trekkers, hikers, and rock climbers. It's wonderful in warm weather, and even through late autumn, when it's fashionable to sport a mackintosh. Ambleside is perched at the north end of Lake Windermere.

Between Ambleside and Wordsworth's former retreat at Grasmere is Rydal, a small village on one of the smallest lakes, Rydal Water. The village is noted for its sheep-dog trials at the end of summer. It's 2.5km (1½ miles) north of Ambleside on A591.

ESSENTIALS

GETTING THERE   Take a train to Windermere (see earlier in this chapter), then continue the rest of the way by bus.

Stagecoach Cumberland (© 0870/608-2608) has hourly bus service from Grasmere and Keswick (see below) and from Windermere. All these buses into Ambleside are labeled either no. 555 or 557.

If you're driving from Windermere, continue northwest on A591.

VISITOR INFORMATION   The **Tourist Information Centre** is at Market Cross Central Building, in Ambleside (© 01539/432582), and is open daily from 9am to 5pm.

EXPLORING THE AREA

Lakeland Safari Tours, 23 Fisherbeck Park, Ambleside (© 01539/433904; www.lakesafari.co.uk), helps you discover the Lakeland's hidden beauty, heritage, and traditions. The owner, a qualified Blue Badge Guide, provides an exciting selection of full-day and half-day safaris in his luxury six-seat vehicle. A half-day safari is £22 ($35) per person; a daylong trek is £33 ($53) per person.

Rydal Mount ★   This was the home of William Wordsworth from 1813 until his death in 1850. Part of the house was built as a farmer's lake cottage around 1575. A descendant of Wordsworth now owns the property, which displays numerous portraits, furniture, and family possessions, as well as mementos and the poet's books. The 4½-acre garden, landscaped by Wordsworth, is filled with rare trees, shrubs, and other features of interest.

Off A591, 2.5km (1½ miles) north of Ambleside. © 01539/433002. Admission house and garden £4 ($6.40) adults, £3.25 ($5.20) seniors and students, £1.50 ($2.40) children ages 5–16, free for kids 4 and under. Mar–Oct daily 9:30am–5pm; Nov–Feb Wed–Mon 10am–4pm.

WHERE TO STAY & DINE
EXPENSIVE

Kirkstone Foot ★   This country house is one of the finest places to stay in the area. There's the main 17th-century manor house plus several apartments for rent in the surrounding park-like grounds. The original building is encircled by a well-tended lawn, whereas the interior is cozily furnished with overstuffed chairs and English paneling. The comfortable accommodations—11 in the main house and 16 in the less desirable outlying units—are tastefully decorated. The rooms facing the front are the most sought after. One room is spacious enough for families.

Kirkstone Pass Rd., Ambleside, Cumbria LA22 9EH. © 01539/432232. Fax 01539/432805. www.kirkstone foot.co.uk. 27 units. £160–£405 ($256–$648) double. Rates include English breakfast. MC, V. Take Rydal Rd. north, turning right onto Kirkstone Pass Rd. **Amenities:** Restaurant; bar; room service; babysitting; laundry service. *In room:* TV, coffeemaker, hair dryer.

Rothay Manor ★★ *Kids*   At this spot, which is reminiscent of a French country inn, the stars are the cuisine, the well-chosen French and American wines, and comfortable, centrally heated bedrooms and suites. It's our top choice in an area where the competition is stiff in the country-house race. Most bedrooms have shuttered French doors opening onto a sun balcony and a mountain view (two are wheelchair accessible). Throughout the estate you'll find an eclectic combination of antiques (some Georgian blended harmoniously with Victorian), flowers, and enticing armchairs.

The manor is a great place for families, renting both family rooms and family suites (big enough for a brood of six), and also providing cots free. "Baby-listening" devices are available, and there's a children's "high tea" served around

6 to 6:30pm, which is really a dinner, with burgers, fish sticks, pizzas, and the like. A children's play park is nearby.

Rothay Bridge, Ambleside, Cumbria LA22 0EH. (✆ **01539/433605**. Fax 01539/433607. www.rothaymanor. co.uk. 17 units. £130–£150 ($208–$240) double; £175 ($280) suite. Rates include English breakfast. AE, DC, MC, V. Take A593 1km (½ mile) south of Ambleside. **Amenities:** Restaurant; bar; room service (7:30am–10:30pm); babysitting; laundry service. *In room:* TV, coffeemaker, hair dryer.

Wateredge Inn ★   This is a winning little choice with an idyllic lakeside setting. The center of this hotel was formed long ago from two 17th-century fishing cottages. Wateredge was, in fact, listed as a lodging house as early as 1873, and further additions were made in the early 1900s. Situated in a beautiful garden overlooking Lake Windermere, the hotel also serves some of the best food in the area. Public rooms have many little nooks for reading and conversation. However, on sunny days guests prefer to relax in the chairs on the lawn. The rooms vary in size and appointments; some are spacious, others much smaller. Furnishings are continually renewed and upgraded as the need arises. Most of the tiled bathrooms come with a tub-and-shower combination; the Windermere room has a two-person tub with a separate walk-in shower.

Borrans Rd. (on A591, 1.5km/1 mile south of Ambleside), Waterhead, Ambleside, Cumbria LA22 0EP. (✆ **01539/432332**. Fax 01539/431878. www.wateredgeinn.co.uk. 21 units. £70–£120 ($112–$192) double. Rates include English breakfast. AE, MC, V. Closed early Jan. **Amenities:** Restaurant; bar; nearby health club. *In room:* TV, coffeemaker, hair dryer.

MODERATE TO INEXPENSIVE

Glen Rothay Hotel   Built in the 17th century as a wayfarer's inn, this hotel adjoins Dora's Field, immortalized by Wordsworth. Set back from the highway, it has a stucco-and-flagstone facade. Inside, the place has been modernized, but original details remain, including beamed ceilings and paneling. The comfortable bedrooms upstairs are tastefully furnished. Most rooms have twin or double beds, but a couple offer four-posters. The tiled bathrooms are small and compact, each with a shower.

On A591, Rydal, Ambleside, Cumbria LA22 9LR. (✆ **01539/434500**. Fax 01539/431079. www.theglenrothay. com. 8 units. £60 ($96) double; from £120 ($192) suite for 2. Rates include English breakfast and dinner. MC, V. On A591 2.5km (1½ miles) northwest of Ambleside. **Amenities:** Restaurant; bar; room service. *In room:* TV, coffeemaker, hair dryer.

Queens Hotel   In the heart of this area is the Queens, an old-fashioned family-run hotel where guests are housed and fed well. It began as a private home in the Victorian era and was later transformed into a hotel, with some restoration completed in 1992. Bedrooms are a bit smallish but reasonably comfortable, and the small bathrooms have shower stalls and tubs.

Market Place, Ambleside, Cumbria LA22 9BU. (✆ **01539/432206**. Fax 01539/432721. 26 units. Sun–Thurs £60–£70 ($96–$112) double; Fri–Sat £62–£72 ($99–$115) double (for 2-night minimum stay). AE, MC, V. **Amenities:** 2 restaurants; 2 bars. *In room:* TV, coffeemaker, hair dryer.

Riverside Hotel ★   Secluded on a quiet lane, this is a small country hotel formed by combining three adjoining riverside houses dating from the 1820s. It has the solid slate-block walls and slate roof common to Cumbria and, despite its peaceful location, lies a few minutes' walk from the center of Ambleside. Each of the painstakingly decorated rooms is comfortably furnished—one features a four-poster bed, and two suites have a Jacuzzi. One room is large enough for families.

Near Rothay Bridge, Under Loughrigg, Ambleside, Cumbria LA22 9LJ. (✆ **01539/432395**. Fax 01539/442041. www.riverside-at-ambleside.co.uk. 6 units. £58–£78 ($93–$125) double. Rates include breakfast. MC, V. Closed two weeks in Dec. From Windermere on A591, take the left fork at Waterhead toward Coniston. Follow

Coniston Rd. for about 1.5km (1 mile) until you come to the junction at Rothay Bridge. Turn left across the bridge and then immediately make a sharp right along the small lane signposted Under Loughrigg. **Amenities:** Access to nearby health club. *In room:* TV, coffeemaker, hair dryer.

Riverside Lodge Country House *Value* This early-Georgian house is set on a riverbank, a short walk from the town center, near the foot of Loughrigg Fell, on 3 acres of grounds. The property is run by Alan and Gillian Rhone. The lodge has some beamed ceilings and offers well-furnished bedrooms, some with river views. The charming bedrooms have been refurbished to a high standard, each with a tiled compact bathroom containing a shower. The breakfast room overlooks the river, and there's an intimate lounge with an open fire.

Near Rothay Bridge, Ambleside, Cumbria LA22 0EH. *©* **01539/434208.** Fax 01539/431884. www.riverside lodge.co.uk. 5 units. £27–£35 ($43–$56) per person per night. Rates include English breakfast. MC, V. From Ambleside, take A593, which crosses Rothay Bridge. **Amenities:** Dining room; lounge.

WHERE TO DINE

Glass House ✯ MODERN BRITISH/MEDITERRANEAN In the early 1990s, the owners of this popular restaurant renovated what had originally been built in the 1400s as a water-driven mill for the crushing of wheat into flour. Today, you'll find a split-level combination of medieval and postmodern architecture, with big sunny windows, interior views of the mill's original cogs and gears, lots of oaken interior trim, and on the buildings outside, a moss-covered, full-scale replica of the original water wheel. Menu items are more sophisticated and elegant than what's served by any of its competitors. Examples include a locally smoked, braised lamb shank in a red-wine sauce; a delectable grilled red snapper with a crushed potato cake; and a tantalizing warm feta cheese and polenta tart with rocket, French beans, beetroot, and fig-based salsa.

Rydal Rd. *©* **01539/432137.** Reservations recommended. Main courses £11–£19 ($18–$30). MC, V. Wed–Mon noon–2pm and 6:30–10pm.

WHERE TO SHARE A PINT

The friendliest pub in Ambleside is the **Golden Rule,** Smithy Brow (*©* **01539/ 433363**), named for the brass yardstick mounted over the bar. There's a country hunt theme in the barroom, which features comfortable leather furniture and cast-iron tables. You can step into one side room and throw darts, or go into the other for a quiet, contemplative pint. Behind the bar, a small but colorful garden provides a serene setting in warm weather. There's inexpensive pub grub if you get hungry.

Located 3 miles west of town, off the A593 in Little Langdale, **Three Shires** (*©* **01539/437215**), a stone-built pub with a stripped timber-and-flagstone interior, offers stunning views of the valley and wooded hills. You can get good pub grub here, as well as a pint of Black Sheep Bitter, Ruddles County, or Websters Yorkshire. Malt whiskies are well represented.

6 Grasmere ✯✯

454km (282 miles) NW of London; 29km (18 miles) NW of Kendal; 69km (43 miles) S of Carlisle

On a lake of the same name, **Grasmere** was the home of Wordsworth from 1799 to 1808. He called this area "the loveliest spot that man hath ever known."

ESSENTIALS

GETTING THERE Take a train to Windermere (see earlier in this chapter) and continue the rest of the way by bus.

Cumberland Motor Services (© 0870/608-2608) runs hourly bus service to Grasmere from Windermere (see earlier in this chapter). Buses running in either direction are marked no. 555 or 557.

If you're driving from Windermere (see earlier in this chapter), continue northwest along A591.

VISITOR INFORMATION The summer-only **Tourist Information Centre** is on Red Bank Road (© 01539/435245) and is open April through October daily from 9:30am to 5:30pm; and November through March Friday, Saturday, and Sunday only from 10am to 3:30pm.

A LITERARY LANDMARK

Afternoon tea is served in the **Dove Cottage Tearoom and Restaurant** (© 01539/435268). A good selection of open sandwiches, scones, cake, and tea breads is offered along with Darjeeling, Assam, Earl Grey, and herbal teas. The tearoom is open daily from 10am to 5pm and the restaurant from 6:30 to 9pm Wednesday through Sunday.

Dove Cottage/The Wordsworth Museum ✦ Wordsworth lived with his writer-and-diarist sister, Dorothy, at Dove Cottage, which is now part of the Wordsworth Museum and administered by the Wordsworth Trust. Wordsworth, the poet laureate, died in the spring of 1850 and was buried in the graveyard of the village church at Grasmere. Another tenant of Dove Cottage was Thomas De Quincey (*Confessions of an English Opium Eater*). The Wordsworth Museum houses manuscripts, paintings, and memorabilia. There are also various special exhibitions throughout the year that explore the art and literature of English romanticism.

On A591, south of the village of Grasmere on the road to Kendal. © 01539/435544. www.wordsworth. org.uk. Admission to both Dove Cottage and the adjoining museum £5.80 ($9.30) adults, £2.60 ($4.15) children. Daily 9:30am–5:30pm. Closed Dec 24–26 and Jan 6–Feb 2.

WHERE TO STAY & DINE
VERY EXPENSIVE

White Moss House ✦ This 1730 Lakeland cottage, once owned by Wordsworth, overlooks the lake and the fells. You'll be welcomed here by Peter and Susan Dixon, who will pamper you with morning tea in bed, turn down your bedcovers at night, and cater to your culinary preferences. The rooms are individually decorated, comfortably furnished, and well heated in nippy weather. All the bathrooms are well appointed, each with shower. There's also Brockstone, their cottage annex, a 5-minute drive along the road, where two, three, or four guests can be accommodated comfortably in utter peace.

On A591 (2.5km/1½ miles south of town), Rydal Water, Grasmere, Cumbria LA22 9SE. © 01539/435295. Fax 01539/435516. www.whitemoss.com. 6 units. £138–£178 ($221–$285) double. Rates include breakfast and dinner. AE, MC, V. Closed Dec–Jan. **Amenities:** Restaurant; bar; access to nearby health club; room service; laundry service; dry cleaning. *In room:* TV, coffeemaker, hair dryer, trouser press.

Wordsworth Hotel ✦✦ This choice, located in the heart of the village, is situated in a 3-acre garden next to the churchyard where Wordsworth is buried. An old stone Lakeland house that was once the hunting lodge of the earl of Cadogan, the Wordsworth has been completely refurbished to provide luxuriously appointed bedrooms with views of the fells, as well as modern bathrooms. Three rooms have four-poster beds. The original master bedroom contains a Victorian bathroom with a brass towel rail and polished pipes and taps. Bedrooms come with character and comfort, and the canopied beds are rather sumptuous. Three rooms are spacious enough for families. All contain beautifully maintained bathrooms with combination tub and shower; the suites have Jacuzzis.

Grasmere, Cumbria LA22 9SW. ℂ **01539/435592.** Fax 01539/435765. www.grasmere-hotels.co.uk. 37 units. £250 ($400) double; from £330 ($528) suite. Rates include English breakfast and dinner. AE, DC, MC, V. Turn left on A591 at the Grasmere Village sign and follow the road over the bridge, past the church, and around an S-bend; the Wordsworth is on the right. **Amenities:** Restaurant; bar; heated indoor pool; exercise room; sauna; 24-hr. room service; laundry service. *In room:* TV, coffeemaker, hair dryer, trouser press.

EXPENSIVE TO MODERATE

Grasmere Red Lion Hotel ⭐ *Kids*   This 200-year-old coaching inn is only a short stroll from Wordsworth's Dove Cottage, and it's assumed that the poet often stopped here for a meal, drink, or to warm himself by the fire. Recently refurbished, the hotel offers comfortably furnished bedrooms, half with Jacuzzis in the bathrooms. In 1999, the hotel opened eight rather snug new bedrooms. The older rooms are fine as well, each fitted with firm mattresses. Four rooms are spacious enough for families and offer bunk beds. Each room comes with a well-maintained bathroom with adequate shelf space and a shower.

Red Lion Sq., Grasmere, Cumbria LA22 9SS. ℂ **0800/WESTERN** or 01539/435456. Fax 01539/435579. www. hotelgrasmere.uk.com. 47 units. Sun–Thurs £99 ($158) double; Fri–Sat £109 ($174) double. Rates include English breakfast. AE, DC, MC, V. **Amenities:** Restaurant; 2 bars; exercise room; Jacuzzi; sauna; room service (8am–9pm); laundry service. *In room:* TV, coffeemaker, hair dryer, trouser press.

Swan Hotel   This is one of the best moderately priced choices in the area. Sir Walter Scott used to slip in for a secret drink early in the morning, and Wordsworth mentioned the place in "The Waggoner." In fact, the poet's wooden chair is in one of the rooms. Many bedrooms are in a modern wing, added in 1975, that fits gracefully onto the building's older core (only the shell of the original 1650 building remains). Bedrooms are comfortably furnished, each with a twin or double bed (one room has a four-poster bed). Bathrooms are midsize, and most have a combination tub and shower.

On A591 (on the road to Keswick, 1km/½ mile outside Grasmere), Grasmere, Cumbria LA22 9RF. ℂ **800/ 225-5843** in the U.S. and Canada, or 01539/435551. Fax 01539/435741. 38 units. £130–£180 ($208–$288) double. Apr–Aug leisure-break packages available Fri–Sun, £82 ($131) per person. Rates include breakfast and dinner. AE, DC, MC, V. **Amenities:** Restaurant; bar; room service (9:30am–10pm); laundry service. *In room:* TV, dataport, coffeemaker, hair dryer, trouser press.

INEXPENSIVE

Riversdale *Value*   This lovely old house, built in 1830 of traditional Lakeland stone, is situated on the outskirts of the village of Grasmere along the banks of the River Rothay. The bedrooms are tastefully decorated and offer every comfort, including hospitality trays, as well as views of the surrounding fells. Bedrooms, most often midsize, have quality furnishings. Each unit has a small bathroom; two have tub-and-shower combinations and the other a shower only. The staff has a wealth of information on day trips, whether by car or hiking. The delightful breakfasts offered here are served in a dining room overlooking Silver How and the fells beyond Easdale Tarn.

Grasmere, Cumbria LA22 9RQ. ℂ 01539/435619. www.riversdalegrasmere.co.uk. 3 units. £46–£56 ($74– $90) double. Rates include English breakfast. No credit cards. Drive 16km (10 miles) north of Windermere along A591 (signposted to Keswick), then turn left by the Swan Hotel. In 360m (1,200 ft.), you'll find the inn on the left side of the road facing the river. *In room:* Coffeemaker, hair dryer, no phone.

12

Yorkshire & Northumbria

Yorkshire, known to readers of *Wuthering Heights* and *All Creatures Great and Small,* embraces both the moors of North Yorkshire and the dales.

Across this vast region came the Romans, the Anglo-Saxons, the Vikings, the monks of the Middle Ages, kings of England, lords of the manor, craftspeople, hill farmers, and wool growers, all leaving their own mark. You can still see Roman roads and pavements, great abbeys and castles, stately homes, open-air museums, and craft centers, along with parish churches, old villages, and cathedrals.

Some cities and towns still carry the taint of the Industrial Revolution, but there's also wild and remote beauty to be found—limestone crags, caverns along the Pennines, mountainous uplands, rolling hills, chalk land wolds, heather-covered moorlands, broad vales, and tumbling streams. Yorkshire offers not only beautiful inland scenery but also 160km (100 miles) of shoreline, with rocky headlands, cliffs, and sandy bays, rock pools, sheltered coves, fishing villages, bird sanctuaries, former smugglers' dens, and yachting havens. In summer, the moors in **North York Moors National Park** bloom with purple heather. You can hike along the 110-mile (165km) **Cleveland Way National Trail,** encircling the park.

Yorkshire's most visited city is the walled city of **York. York Minster,** part of the cathedral circuit, is noted for its 100 stained-glass windows. In West Yorkshire is the literary shrine of **Haworth,** the home of the Brontës.

On the way north to Hadrian's Wall, we suggest you spend the night in the ancient cathedral city of **Durham.** This great medieval city is among the most dramatically sited and most interesting in the north.

Northumbria is made up of the counties of Northumberland, Cleveland, and Durham. The Saxons, who came to northern England centuries ago, carved out this kingdom, which at the time stretched from the Firth of Forth in Scotland to the banks of the Humber in Yorkshire. Vast tracts of that ancient kingdom remain natural and unspoiled. Again, this slice of England has more than its share of industrial towns, but you should explore the wild hills and open spaces and cross the dales of the eastern Pennines.

The whole area evokes ancient battles and bloody border raids. Many visitors tend to rush a visit here or skip it altogether, but we suggest that you at least venture to see **Hadrian's Wall,** a Roman structure that was one of the wonders of the Western world. The finest stretch of the wall lies within the **Northumberland National Park,** between the stony North Tyne River and the county boundary at Gilsland. About 64km (40 miles) of the 241km (150-mile) Pennine Way meanders through the park; the **Pennine Way** is one of Britain's most challenging hiking paths.

1 York ⋆⋆⋆

327km (203 miles) N of London; 42km (26 miles) NE of Leeds; 142km (88 miles) N of Nottingham

Few cities in England are as rich in history as York. It is still encircled by its 13th- and 14th-century city walls, about 4km (2½ miles) long, with four gates. One of these, Micklegate, once grimly greeted visitors coming up from the south with the severed heads of traitors. To this day, you can walk on the footpath of the medieval walls.

The crowning achievement of York is its minster, or cathedral, which makes the city an ecclesiastical center equaled only by Canterbury. It can easily be seen on a drive up to Edinburgh. Or, after visiting Cambridge, you can make a swing through the great cathedral cities of Ely, Lincoln, York, and Ripon.

There was a Roman York (Hadrian came this way), then a Saxon York, a Danish York, a Norman York (William the Conqueror slept here), a medieval York, a Georgian York, and a Victorian York (the center of a flourishing rail business). Today, a large amount of 18th-century York remains, including Richard Boyle's restored Assembly Rooms.

At some point in your exploration, you may want to visit the Shambles; once the meat-butchering center of York, it dates from before the Norman Conquest. The messy business is gone now, but the ancient street survives, filled today with jewelry stores, cafes, and buildings that huddle so closely together that you can practically stand in the middle of the pavement, arms outstretched, and touch the houses on both sides of the street.

ESSENTIALS

GETTING THERE   British Midland flights arrive at **Leeds/Bradford Airport,** a 50-minute flight from London's Heathrow Airport. For schedules and fares, call the airline at ✆ **0870/607-0555.** Connecting buses at the airport take you east and the rest of the distance to York.

From London's King's Cross Station, York-bound trains leave every 30 minutes. The trip takes 2 hours. For schedules and information, call ✆ **0845/748-4950.**

Four **National Express** buses depart daily from London's Victoria Coach Station for the 4½-hour trip to York. For schedules and information, call ✆ **0870/580-8080.**

If you're driving from London, head north on M1, cutting northeast below Leeds at the junction with A64, heading east to York.

VISITOR INFORMATION   The **Tourist Information Centre** at De Grey Rooms, Exhibition Square (✆ **01904/621756**), is open in winter Monday through Saturday from 9am to 5pm and Sunday from 10am to 4pm; summer hours are Monday through Saturday from 9am to 6pm and Sunday from 10am to 5pm.

SEEING THE SIGHTS

The best way to see York is to go to Exhibition Square (opposite the Tourist Information Centre), where a volunteer guide will take you on a **free 2-hour walking tour** of the city. You'll learn about history and lore through numerous intriguing stories. Tours are given April through October, daily at 10:15am and 2:15pm, plus 7pm from June to August; from November to March, a daily tour is given at 10:15am. Groups can book by prior arrangement by contacting the

Association of Volunteer Guides, De Grey Rooms, Exhibition Square, York YO1 2HB (© **01904/640780**).

York Minster ★★★ One of the great cathedrals of the world, York Minster traces its origins from the early 7th century; the present building, however, dates from the 13th century. Like the cathedral at Lincoln, York Minster is characterized by three towers built in the 15th century. The central tower is lantern-shaped in the Perpendicular style, and from the top of the tower on a clear day there are panoramic views of York and the Vale of York. The climb up a stone spiral staircase is steep and not recommended for very elderly or very young visitors or anyone with a heart condition or breathing difficulties.

The outstanding characteristic of the cathedral is its **stained glass** ★★★ from the Middle Ages, in glorious Angelico blues, ruby reds, forest greens, and honey-colored ambers. See especially the Great East Window, the work of a 15th-century Coventry-based glass painter. In the north transept is an architectural gem of the mid–13th century: the Five Sisters Window, with its five lancets in grisaille glass. The late-15th-century choir screen in its Octagonal Chapter House has an impressive lineup of historical figures—everybody from William the Conqueror to the overthrown Henry VI.

At a reception desk near the entrance to the minster, groups can arrange a guide, if one is available. Conducted tours are free but donations toward the upkeep of the cathedral are requested.

At the converging point of Deangate, Duncombe Place, Minster Yard, and Petergate. © **01904/557216;** www.yorkminster.org Admission to Chapter House is free (a £3.50 ($5.60) donation is suggested); crypt, foundations, and treasury £3.80 ($6.10) adults, £1.50 ($2.40) children. Chapter House, foundations, treasury, and tower Mon–Sat 10am–6:30pm; Sun 1–6pm (closing time in winter 4:30pm). Crypt Mon–Fri 10am–4:30pm; Sat 10am–3:30pm; Sun 1–3:30pm. Call ahead to verify times, as they are subject to change.

Treasurer's House The Treasurer's House lies on a site where a continuous succession of buildings has stood since Roman times. The main part of the house, built in 1620, was refurbished by Yorkshire industrialist Frank Green at the turn of the 20th century; he used this elegant town house to display his collection of 17th- and 18th-century furniture, glass, and china. An audiovisual program and exhibit explain the work of the medieval treasures and the subsequent fascinating history of the house. It has an attractive small garden in the shadow of York Minster.

Minster Yard. © **01904/624247**. Admission £3.80 ($6.10), £2 ($3.20) children, £9.50 ($15) family ticket. Sat–Thurs 11am–4:30pm. Closed Nov–Mar.

⌒*Tips* **A Medieval Meal**

Check out **St. William's Restaurant** at the front of St. William's Cottage (© **01904/634830**), close to the east end of the minster. This splendid timbered building provides a setting daily for coffee, an affordable lunch, or tea. Here you can get tasty quiches, homemade soups, and luscious desserts. And if you can arrange for a party of 35 or more, you can have a medieval banquet staged on your behalf, complete with minstrels, jesters, and jugglers. One way to do this is to post a notice at your hotel and get people to sign up and invite their newly made acquaintances. In 1 day our party swelled to nearly 50, and we were regally fed and entertained.

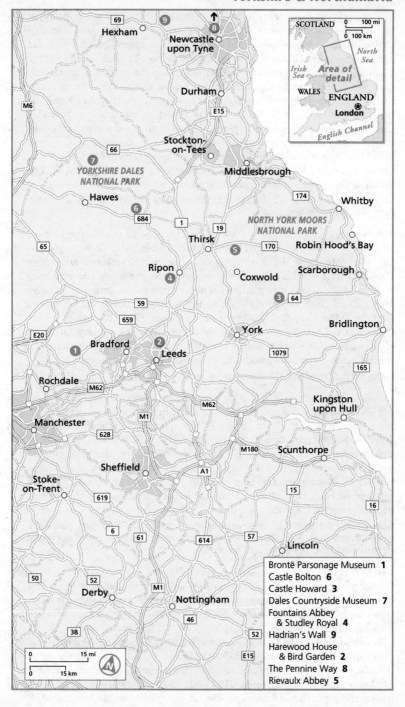

Yorkshire & Northumbria

SCOTLAND

0   100 mi

0   100 km

North
Sea

Irish
Sea

Area of
detail

WALES   ENGLAND

⊛ London

English Channel

69   Hexham

9

8 ↑

Newcastle
upon Tyne

Durham

E15

M6

66

Stockton-
on-Tees

7

YORKSHIRE DALES
NATIONAL PARK

Middlesbrough

Hawes

6

684

65

1

19

Thirsk

174   Whitby

NORTH YORK MOORS
NATIONAL PARK

170   Robin Hood's Bay

5

Ripon

4

59

Coxwold

Scarborough

3   64

659

E20

Bradford

2

Leeds

York

1079

Bridlington

165

1

Rochdale

M62

M62

Kingston
upon Hull

Manchester

628

M1

Stoke-
on-Trent

619

Sheffield

A1

M180   Scunthorpe

15

16

6

61

614

57

Lincoln

50

52   Derby

M1

Nottingham

46

52

38

E15

0   15 mi

0   15 km

Brontë Parsonage Museum **1**

Castle Bolton **6**

Castle Howard **3**

Dales Countryside Museum **7**

Fountains Abbey
& Studley Royal **4**

Hadrian's Wall **9**

Harewood House
& Bird Garden **2**

The Pennine Way **8**

Rievaulx Abbey **5**

York Castle Museum ✦ On the site of York's Castle, this is one of the finest folk museums in the country. Its unique feature is a re-creation of a Victorian cobbled street, Kirkgate, named for the museum's founder, Dr. John Kirk. He acquired his large collection while visiting his patients in rural Yorkshire at the beginning of the 20th century. The period rooms range from a neoclassical Georgian dining room to an overstuffed and heavily adorned Victorian parlor to the 1953 sitting room with a brand-new television set purchased to watch the coronation of Elizabeth II. In the Debtors' Prison, former prison cells display craft workshops. There is also a superb collection of arms and armor. In the Costume Gallery, displays are changed regularly to reflect the collection's variety. Half Moon Court is an Edwardian street, with a gypsy caravan and a pub (sorry, the bar's closed!). During the summer, you can visit a water mill on the bank of the River Foss. Allow at least 2 hours for your museum visit.

The Eye of York off Tower St. (?) **01904/653611.** Admission £6 ($9.60) adults, £3.50 ($5.60) children. Easter–Nov daily 9:30am–5pm.

National Railway Museum ✦✦✦ The first national museum to be built outside London, it has attracted millions of train buffs. Adapted from an original steam-locomotive depot, the museum gives visitors a chance to see how Queen Victoria traveled in luxury, and to look under and inside steam locomotives. In addition, there's a collection of railway memorabilia, including an early-19th-century clock and penny machine for purchasing tickets on the railway platform. More than 40 locomotives are on display. One, the *Agenoria,* dates from 1829 and is a contemporary of Stephenson's well-known *Rocket.* Of several royal coaches, the most interesting is Queen Victoria's Royal Saloon; it's like a small hotel, with polished wood, silk, brocade, and silver accessories.

Leeman York Rd. (?) **01904/621261.** www.nrm.org.uk. Free admission. Daily 10am–6pm. Closed Dec 24–26.

Jorvik Viking Centre ✦ This Viking city, discovered many feet below present ground level, was reconstructed as it stood in 948, and underwent major refurbishment in 2001. In a "time car," you travel back through the ages to 1067, when Normans sacked the city, and then you ride slowly through the street market peopled by faithfully modeled Vikings. You also go through a house where a family lived and down to the river to see the ship chandlers at work and a Norwegian cargo ship unloading. At the end of the ride, you pass through the Finds Hut, where thousands of artifacts are displayed. The time car departs at regular intervals.

Coppergate. (?) **01904/643211.** www.jorvik-viking-centre.co.uk. Admission £6.95 ($11) adults, £5.10 ($8.15) children 5–15, £6.10 ($9.75) seniors and students, family ticket £22 ($35). Rates may change depending on the event. Apr–Oct daily 10am–5pm; Nov–Mar daily 10am–4:30pm.

SHOPPING

Several of the main areas to explore include **Gillygate** for antiques dealers, **St. Mary's Square** and its **Coppergate** pedestrian mall for name brands and chain stores, and **Newgate Marketplace** for local vendors selling a variety of wares Monday through Saturday.

Several specialty shops that have ideal gift items include **Maxwell and Kennedy,** 79 Low Petergate ((?) **01904/610034**), a candy store specializing in both Belgian chocolate and Cambridge Wells dark, milk, and white chocolate; **Mulberry Hall,** 17 Stonegate ((?) **01904/620736**), housed in a medieval house from 1436, with 16 showrooms on three floors devoted to the best in British and European porcelain, fine china, crystal, and some antiques; and **Wooden**

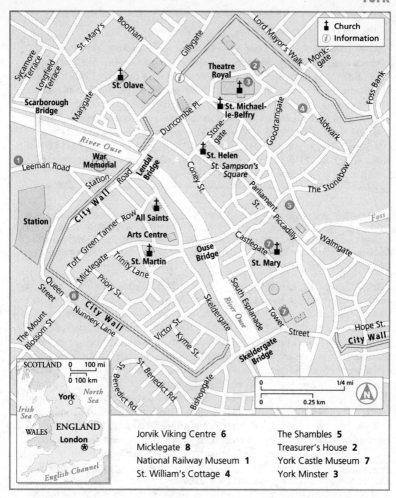

Church
Information

Lord Mayor's Walk
Monkgate
Bootham
St. Mary's
Gillygate
Theatre Royal
St. Olave
Scarborough Bridge
Sycamore Terrace
Longfield Terrace
Duncombe Pl.
St. Michael-le-Belfry
Margate
Stonegate
Goodramgate
Aldwark
Foss Bank
River Ouse
Leeman Road
War Memorial
St. Helen
St. Sampson's Square
The Stonebow
Station Road
Lendal Bridge
Coney St.
Parliament St.
Foss
Station
City Wall
All Saints
Piccadilly
Walmgate
Toft Green
Tanner Row
Arts Centre
Castlegate
St. Mary
Ouse Bridge
St. Martin
Micklegate
Trinity Lane
Priory St.
Queen Street
City Wall
Nunnery Lane
South Esplanade
River Ouse
Tower Street
Hope St.
City Wall
The Mount
Blossom St.
Victor St.
Kyme St.
Skeldergate
Skeldergate Bridge
St. Benedict Rd.
Bishopgate

SCOTLAND   0   100 mi
0   100 km
York   North Sea
Irish Sea
WALES   ENGLAND
London
English Channel

0   1/4 mi
0   0.25 km

Jorvik Viking Centre **6**
Micklegate **8**
National Railway Museum **1**
St. William's Cottage **4**

The Shambles **5**
Treasurer's House **2**
York Castle Museum **7**
York Minster **3**

Horse, 9 Goodramgate (© **01904/626012**), featuring an eclectic mixture of ethnic items such as shirts, tops, jewelry, cushions, rugs, and throws from Africa, India, China, and Mexico.

WHERE TO STAY
EXPENSIVE

Dean Court Hotel   This 1850 building lies right beneath the towers of the minster. It was originally constructed to provide housing for the clergy of York Minster and then converted to a hotel after World War I. This Best Western affiliate may not be the most atmospheric choice in York, but recent refurbishments have vastly improved the accommodations. The very comfortable rooms offer quality linens on the beds and small but well-kept bathrooms. The Superior and Deluxe rooms offer more space and such extras as bathrobes, mineral water, and fresh fruit. Two rooms are spacious enough for use by families.

Moments Is York Haunted?

After London, York has been the site of more beheadings, medieval tortures, and human anguish than any other city in Britain. Psychics and mystics insist that dozens of lost souls wander among the city's historic core reliving the traumatic moments of their earthly lives. Ghost walks are held every evening in York, allegedly England's most haunted city.

Several outfits conduct these tours, but the most charming one, **"The Ghost Hunt of York"** (© **01904/608700;** www.ghosthunt.co.uk), leaves at 7:30pm every night from The Shambles. The 1-hour tour costs £3 ($4.80) for adults and £2 ($3.20) for children. Be prepared for lively commentary and more ghoulishness than you may expect.

Duncombe Place, York, N. Yorkshire YO1 7EF. © **800/528-1234** in the U.S., or 01904/625082. Fax 01904/ 620305. www.deancourt-york.co.uk. 39 units. £115–£170 ($184–$272) double; £15 ($23) children under 17 in parent's room. Rates include English breakfast. AE, DC, MC, V. Parking £5 ($8) for 3–4 nights. **Amenities:** Restaurant; bar; room service; babysitting; laundry service; dry cleaning. *In room:* TV, coffeemaker, hair dryer, trouser press.

Middlethorpe Hall Hotel ★★★   Set on a 26-acre park, this hotel is on the outskirts of York, near the racecourse and away from the traffic. It's clearly York's leading hotel. Built in 1699, the stately, redbrick William-and-Mary country house was purchased by Historic House Hotels and beautifully restored, both inside and out. Fresh flowers are displayed profusely and lots of antiques create the ambience of a classic manor house. The rooms are located in the main house and restored outbuildings. Accommodations in the annex (a converted stable block), have slightly less drama and flair, though you can enjoy greater privacy there. Rooms have such niceties as homemade cookies and bottles of mineral water, as well as bathrobes. All the bedrooms, from decorations to antiques and fine pictures, have been styled to evoke the aura of a country house, though all the modern comforts have been installed as well. Each bedroom is decorated individually with four-poster beds or padded or canopied headboards.

Bishopthorpe Rd. (on A64, 2.5km/1½ miles south of town), York, N. Yorkshire YO23 2GB. © **800/260-8338** in the U.S., or 01904/641241. Fax 01904/620176. www.middlethorpe.com. 30 units. £140–£155 ($224–$248) double; £295–£360 ($472–$576) suite. MC, V. **Amenities:** 2 restaurants; bar; concierge; room service; laundry service; dry cleaning. *In room:* TV, hair dryer, trouser press.

York Moat House ★   Within the ancient city walls, this modern hotel overlooks the River Ouse and is the leading hotel within the center of York. Built in the 1970s, the hotel is the largest in town and is conveniently located for sightseeing. Many of the well-furnished and modern bedrooms have views looking toward the minster. Ten rooms are spacious enough for families.

North St., York, N. Yorkshire YO1 6JF. © **01904/459988.** Fax 01904/641793. www.moathousehotels.com. 200 units. £150 ($240) double; £210 ($336) suite. Rates include English breakfast. AE, DC, MC, V. Parking £6 ($9.60). **Amenities:** Restaurant; 2 bars; health club; sauna; room service; laundry service; dry cleaning. *In room:* TV, coffeemaker, hair dryer, trouser press.

MODERATE

The Judges Lodging ★ *Finds*   The earliest historical fact about this charming house is that it was the home of a certain Dr. Wintringham in 1711. It is listed as having been a judges' lodging at the beginning of the 19th century. To get to your room, you'll climb a circular wooden staircase, the only one of its type in the United Kingdom. Four bedrooms have four-poster beds. If you want to spoil yourself, book the large Prince Albert room, a twin-bedded room with three large windows overlooking the minster (Prince Albert actually slept in the room once). Bedrooms, ranging from small to midsize, have been thoughtfully renovated, many with antiques, four-poster beds, tiled bathrooms, and open fireplaces. Many rooms have a view of York Minster.

9 Lendal, York, N. Yorkshire YO1 8AQ. *(* 01904/638733. Fax 01904/679947. www.judgeslodgings.com. 14 units. £100–£150 ($160–$240) double. Rates include English breakfast. AE, MC, V. **Amenities:** Restaurant; bar; room service; babysitting; laundry service. *In room:* TV, coffeemaker, hair dryer.

Mount Royale Hotel *⋆*   A short walk west of York's city walls, in a neighborhood known as The Mount, this hotel is the personal statement of two generations of the Oxtaby family. They work hard to create a friendly, homey atmosphere. The main house was built as a private home in 1833, though several years ago the owners merged a neighboring house of the same era into the original core. Accommodations and public rooms are furnished with both modern pieces and antiques. Garden suites have private terraces leading to the garden. Bathrooms are small but well organized.

119 The Mount, York, N. Yorkshire YO2 2DA. *(* 01904/628856. Fax 01904/611171. www.mountroyale. co.uk. 23 units. £95–£100 ($152–$160) double; £150 ($240) suite. Rates include English breakfast. AE, DC, MC, V. **Amenities:** Restaurant; bar; pool; room service (6am–10pm); laundry service. *In room:* TV, coffeemaker, hair dryer, trouser press.

INEXPENSIVE

Beechwood Close Hotel   Beechwood is a large house that is surrounded by trees, a garden with a putting green, and a parking area. Mr. and Mrs. Blythe run the small hotel, which offers comfortable bedrooms with tasteful furnishings. Each small bathroom is well maintained; most have a tub-and-shower combination. The hotel is a 15-minute walk to the minster, either by road or along the river.

19 Shipton Rd. (on A19 north of the city), Clifton, York, N. Yorkshire YO30 5RE. *(* 01904/658378. Fax 01904/647124. www.beechwood-close.co.uk. 14 units. £80 ($128) double. Rates include English breakfast. AE, DC, MC, V. **Amenities:** Restaurant; bar; room service; laundry service. *In room:* TV, coffeemaker, hair dryer, iron/ironing board.

Cottage Hotel *Value*   About a 10-minute walk north of York Minster, this hotel comprises two refurbished and extended Victorian houses overlooking the village green of Clifton. The hotel offers cozy, small bedrooms with simple furnishings. Three rooms have four-poster beds. Each comes with a well-maintained bathroom with a shower stall and tub. Some 400-year-old timbers rescued from the demolition of a medieval building in one of the city's historic streets (Micklegate) grace the restaurant and bar, which does a thriving business in its own right.

3 Clifton Green, York, N. Yorkshire YO3 6LH. *(* 01904/643711. Fax 01904/611230. 25 units. £70–£80 ($112–$128) double. Rates include English breakfast. MC, V. Free parking. **Amenities:** Restaurant; bar. *In room:* TV, coffeemaker, hair dryer.

Heworth Court   Just a 10- to 15-minute walk east of the city center is this three-story redbrick Victorian structure (many of its bedrooms are located in a modern extension added during the 1980s). The rooms are agreeably furnished, and some open onto the courtyard. Each comes with a comfortable bed, plus a compact bathroom with a shower stall (some have tubs).

76 Heworth Green, York, N. Yorkshire YO3 7TQ. © **01904/425156.** Fax 01904/415290. www.heworth.co.uk. 28 units. £96–£111 ($154–$178) double. Rates include English breakfast. Free parking. AE, DC, MC, V. Take the A1036 to the east side of the city. **Amenities:** Restaurant; bar; laundry service. *In room:* TV, coffeemaker, hair dryer.

WHERE TO DINE

Oscar's Wine Bar & Bistro, 8A Little Stonegate (© **01904/652002**), offers heaping plates of meats and salads, attracting a young crowd (often because of the inexpensive beer). There's a courtyard and a large menu. It's open Monday through Saturday from 11:30am to 11pm, Sunday from 11am to 10:30pm.

The best place for afternoon tea is **Betty's Café & Tea Rooms,** 6–8 St. Helen's Sq. (© **01904/659142**). We also recommend **St. William's College Restaurant,** 3 College St. (© **01904/634830**), and **Theatre Royal Café Bar,** St. Leonard's Place (© **01904/632596**).

The Ivy/The Seafood Bar/The Brasserie ⭐ FRENCH/ENGLISH A 10-minute walk west of York Minster, this dining complex is the most appealing in town. It is within an ivy-covered Regency town house that's also a 30-room hotel.

The least formal venue is The Brasserie, a paneled, candlelit hideaway in the cellar. The hearty menu items include steaks, fish, and ale. It's the most crowded of the complex's three restaurants.

On the ground level, The Ivy restaurant and The Seafood Bar are set adjacent to one another. Cuisine is more upscale than that in the cellar and includes dishes such as a whole grilled Dover sole.

A few steps away, The Seafood Bar has a great *trompe l'oeil* panoramic mural of York's Racecourse, complete with views of the city's skyline. The menu here features mostly seafood prepared in many ways. Examples include grilled sea scallops, with sesame, soya, and a spring onion dressing.

In the Grange Hotel, 1 Clifton (off Bootham Rd.), York, N. Yorkshire YO30 6AA. © 01904/644744. Fax 01904/612453. Reservations recommended in The Ivy and The Seafood Bar; not necessary in The Brasserie. Fixed-price 3-course menu in The Ivy £28 ($45); main courses in The Seafood Bar £15–£24 ($24–$38); main courses in The Brasserie £8–£16 ($13–$26). AE, DC, MC, V. The Ivy Sun noon–2pm; Mon–Sat 7–9:30pm. The Seafood Bar Tues–Sat 7–10pm. The Brasserie Mon–Thurs 6–10pm; Fri–Sat 6–10:30pm; Sun 7–10pm.

Kites INTERNATIONAL About a 5-minute walk from the minster, this restaurant is in the heart of York, on a small street near Stonegate (walk up a narrow staircase to the 2nd floor). This is a simple York bistro where the food is good and the atmosphere and service are unpretentious. Kites' many fans are attracted to its eclectic brand of cooking. One recipe might have been a dish served in the Middle Ages in England (perhaps with adaptations); the next might come from Thailand. Meals may feature trout, game, tuna, or pork depending on what the hunters and gatherers return with. Fondues, fresh salads, and vegetarian meals are also available.

13 Grape Lane. © 01904/641750. Reservations required. Main courses £12–£17 ($18–$27). AE, DC, DISC, MC, V. Mon–Sat noon–2pm and 6:30–10:30pm.

Melton's Restaurant 🅺🆒 CONTINENTAL/ENGLISH Some local food critics claim that Michael and Lucy Hjort serve the finest food in York, though we give that honor to The Ivy. Their small and unpretentious restaurant is approximately 1.5km (1 mile) from the heart of the city. Mr. Hjort trained with the famous Roux brothers of Le Gavroche in London, but he doesn't charge their astronomical prices. His cuisine reflects his own imprint.

In what has always been known as a culinary backwater town, the Hjorts have created some excitement with this family-friendly place. Their menu changes frequently but could include roast monkfish with tiger prawns and eggplant "caviar"; roast venison with mixed vegetables such as kale and parsnips; and roast confit of duck. Vegetarian meals are available, and children are welcome.

7 Scarcroft Rd. ⓒ 01904/634341. Reservations required. Main courses £13–£18 ($20–$28); fixed-price menu (available on limited basis) £17 ($27). MC, V. Tues–Sat noon–2pm; Mon–Sat 5:30–10pm. Closed 1 week in early Aug and Dec 24–Jan 14.

19 Grape Lane ENGLISH   In the heart of York, on a cobbled lane off Peter-gate, this restaurant occupies two floors of a timbered building with a wealth of its original features. With such a name, you would expect a very British restau-rant, and it is, but with a very contemporary touch. You can begin with a Jamaican cocktail, which is their own blend of poached salmon, banana, prawns, and pineapple served with a spiced mayonnaise; follow with filets of trout stuffed with crabmeat and wrapped in lettuce leaves. The menus are wisely lim-ited to about 10 main courses, so that every dish will be fresh. The cooking is kept simple, without excessive adornment. The wine list is ever growing, and service is thoughtful and considerate.

19 Grape Lane. ⓒ 01904/636366. Reservations recommended for dinner. Main courses £7–£16 ($11–$26). AE, MC, V. Tues–Sat noon–2pm and 6–10pm.

A YORK PUB CRAWL

One of the city's oldest inns, **The Black Swan,** Peaseholme Green (ⓒ **01904/ 686911**), is a fine, timbered, frame house that was once the home of the lord mayor of York in 1417; the mother of Gen. James Wolfe of Quebec also lived here. You can enjoy pub meals in front of a log fire in a brick inglenook. There are fish and chips, burgers, and steak. This is one of York's "musical pubs," featur-ing live folk music on Thursday, with a small cover charge starting at £4 ($6.40).

Situated at the base of the Ouse Bridge, a few steps from the edge of the river, the 16th-century **Kings Arms Public House,** King's Staith (ⓒ **01904/ 659435**), is boisterous and fun. A historic monument in its own right, it's filled with charm and character and has the ceiling beams, paneling, and weathered brickwork you'd expect. In summer, rows of outdoor tables are placed beside the river. Your hosts serve a full range of draft and bottled beers, the most popular of which (Samuel Smith's) is still brewed in Tadcaster, only 16km (10 miles) away. The ghost walk we recommend leaves here every night at 8pm (see p. 454).

On a pedestrian street in Old York, **Ye Olde Starre Inne,** 40 Stonegate (ⓒ **01904/623063**), dates from 1644 and is York's oldest licensed pub. An inn (of one kind or another) has stood on this spot since 900. In a pub said to be haunted by an old woman, a little girl, and a cat, you enter into an atmosphere of cast-iron tables, an open fireplace, oak Victorian settles, and time-blackened beams. Recently, the owners have added a year-round glassed-in garden, so guests can enjoy the plants and the view of the minster from their tables year-round.

2 Haworth: Home of the Brontës ★★

72km (45 miles) SW of York; 34km (21 miles) W of Leeds

Haworth, a village on the high moor of the Pennines, is famous as the home of the Brontës and the most visited literary shrine in England after Stratford-upon-Avon.

ESSENTIALS

GETTING THERE   To reach Haworth by rail, take the Arriva Train from Leeds City Station to Keighley (it leaves approximately every 30 min.). Change trains at Keighley and take the Keighley and Worth Valley Railway to Haworth and Oxenhope. Train services operate every weekend year-round, with 7 to 12 departures. From late June to September, trains also run four times a day Monday through Friday. For general inquiries, call © **01535/645214;** for a 24-hour timetable, dial the tourist office (© **01535/642329**).

Keighley & District Bus Co., offers bus service between Keighley and Haworth. Bus nos. 663, 664, and 665 will get you there. For information, call © **01535/642329.**

If you're driving from York, head west toward Leeds on A64 approaching the A6120 Ring Road to Shipley; then take A650 to Keighley, and finally link up with the B6142 south to Haworth.

VISITOR INFORMATION   The **Tourist Information Centre** is at 2–4 West Lane in Haworth (© **01535/642329**). It's open April through October daily from 9:30am to 5:30pm; November through March daily from 9:30am to 5pm (closed December 24–26).

LITERARY LANDMARKS

Anne Brontë wrote two novels, *The Tenant of Wildfell Hall* and *Agnes Grey;* Charlotte wrote two masterpieces, *Jane Eyre* and *Villette,* which depicted her experiences as a teacher, as well as several other novels; and Emily is the author of *Wuthering Heights,* a novel of passion and haunting melancholy. Charlotte and Emily are buried in the family vault under the **Church of St. Michael.**

While in Haworth, you'll want to visit the **Brontë Weaving Shed,** Townend Mill (© **01535/646217**). The shop is not far from the Brontë Parsonage and features the famous Brontë tweed, which combines browns, greens, and oranges to evoke the look of the local countryside.

Brontë Parsonage Museum ✶   The parsonage where the Brontë family lived has been preserved as this museum, which houses their furniture, personal treasures, pictures, books, and manuscripts. The stone-sided parsonage, originally built near the top of the village in 1777, was assigned for the course of his lifetime as the residence of the Brontës' father, Patrick, the Perpetual Curator of the Church of St. Michael and All Angel's Church. Regrettably, the church tended by the Brontës was demolished in 1870; it was rebuilt in its present form the same year. The parsonage contains a walled garden very similar to the one cultivated by the Brontës, five bedrooms, and a collection of family furniture (some bought with proceeds from Charlotte's literary success), as well as personal effects, pictures and paintings, and original manuscripts. It also contains the largest archive of family correspondence in the world.

The museum is maintained by a professional staff selected by the Brontë Society, an organization established in 1893 to perpetuate the memory and legacy of Britain's most famous literary family. Contributions to the society are welcomed. The museum tends to be extremely crowded in July and August.

Church St. © 01535/642323. www.bronte.org.uk. Admission £4.80 ($7.70) adults, £3.50 ($5.60) seniors and students, £1.50 ($2.40) children 5–16, free for children under age 5, £11 ($17) family ticket (2 adults and 3 children). Oct–Mar daily 10am–5:30pm; Apr–Sept daily 11am–5:30pm. Closed mid–Jan to early Feb and at Christmas time.

WHERE TO STAY

Old White Lion Hotel   At the top of a cobblestone street, this hotel is dates from 1700 when it was built with a solid stone roof. It's almost next door to the church where the Reverend Brontë preached, as well as the parsonage where the family lived. Paul and Christopher Bradford welcome visitors to their warm, cheerful, and comfortable hotel. Though full of old-world charm, all rooms are completely up-to-date. Room size varies considerably, but each room is attractively furnished and has a comfortable bed and a small bathroom, most with shower-tub combinations. Two rooms are large enough for families.

6–10 West Lane, Haworth near Keighley, W. Yorkshire BD22 8DU. (C) 01535/642313. Fax 01535/646222. www.oldwhitelionhotel.com. 14 units. £65 ($104) double. Rates include English breakfast. AE, DC, MC, V. **Amenities:** Restaurant; bar; room service. *In room:* TV, coffeemaker, hair dryer.

WHERE TO DINE

Weaver's Restaurant ★ *Value* MODERN BRITISH   The best restaurant in the Brontë hometown, this spot is British to the core. In an inviting, informal atmosphere, it serves excellent food made with fresh ingredients. Jane and Colin Rushworth are quite talented in the kitchen. Dinners may include such classic dishes as slow-cooked Yorkshire lamb. If available, try one of the Gressingham ducks, which are widely praised in the United Kingdom. For dessert, try a British cheese or one of the homemade delicacies. The restaurant is likely to be closed for vacation for a certain period each summer, so call in advance to check. They also rent four bedrooms of high caliber that cost £75 ($120) for a double.

15 West Lane. (C) 01535/643822. Reservations recommended. Main courses £10–£17 ($15–$26); 3-course fixed-price dinner £12 ($19). AE, DC, MC, V. Tues–Sat 6:30–9:30pm.

3 Yorkshire's Country Houses, Castles & More

Yorkshire's battle-scarred castles, Gothic abbeys, and great country manor houses (from all periods) are unrivaled anywhere in Britain. Here are some of the highlights.

IN NORTH YORKSHIRE

Castle Howard ★★   In its dramatic setting of lakes, fountains, and extensive gardens, Castle Howard, the 18th-century palace designed by Sir John Vanbrugh, is undoubtedly the finest private residence in Yorkshire. This was the first major achievement of the architect who later created the lavish Blenheim Palace near Oxford. The Yorkshire palace was begun in 1699 for the third earl of Carlisle, Charles Howard.

The striking facade is topped by a painted and gilded dome, which reaches more than 24m (80 ft.) into the air. The interior boasts a 58m (192-ft.) long gallery, as well as a chapel with magnificent stained-glass windows by the 19th-century artist Sir Edward Burne-Jones. Besides the collections of antique furniture and sculpture, the castle has many important paintings, including a portrait of Henry VIII by Holbein and works by Rubens, Reynolds, and Gainsborough.

The seemingly endless grounds, including two rose gardens, also offer the visitor some memorable sights, including the domed Temple of the Four Winds, by Vanbrugh, and the richly designed family mausoleum, by Hawksmoor.

Malton (24km/15 miles northeast of York, 5km/3 miles off A64). (C) 01653/648333. www.castlehoward. co.uk. Admission £9 ($14) adults, £8 ($13) seniors and students, £6 ($9.60) children 4–16. Feb to late Nov, grounds daily 10am–5pm, house daily 11am–4:30pm (during winter, call to verify times).

Fountains Abbey & Studley Royal ★★★   On the banks of the Silver Skell, the abbey was founded by Cistercian monks in 1132 and is the largest monastic ruin in Britain. In 1987, it was awarded World Heritage status. The ruins provide the focal point of the 18th-century landscape garden at Studley Royal, one of the few surviving examples of a Georgian green garden. It's known for its conservation work in the water gardens, ornamental temples, follies, and vistas. The garden is bounded at its northern edge by a lake and 400 acres of deer park.

At Fountains, 6.5km (4 miles) southwest of Ripon off B6265. ℭ 01765/608888. www.fountainsabbey. org.uk. Admission £4.80 ($7.70) adults, £2.50 ($4) children, £12 ($19) family. Oct–Mar daily 10am–4pm; Apr–Sept daily 10am–6pm. Closed Dec 24–25, Fri in Nov–Jan. It's best to drive, though it can be reached from York by public transportation. From York, take bus no. 143 leaving from the York Hall Station to Ripon, 37km (23 miles) to the northwest (A59, A1, and B6265 lead to Ripon). From Ripon, it will be necessary to take a taxi 6.5km (4 miles) to the southwest, though some prefer to take the scenic walk.

IN WEST YORKSHIRE

Harewood House & Bird Garden ★★ _Kids_   Thirty-five kilometers (22 miles) west of York, the home of the earl and countess of Harewood is one of England's great 18th-century houses. It has always been owned by the Lascelles family. The fine Adam interior has superb ceilings and plasterwork and furniture made especially for Harewood by Thomas Chippendale. There are also important collections of English and Italian paintings and Sèvres and Chinese porcelain.

The gardens, designed by Capability Brown, include terraces, lakeside and woodland walks, and a 4½-acre bird garden with exotic species from all over the world, including penguins, macaws, flamingos, and snowy owls. Other facilities include an art gallery, shops, a restaurant, and cafeteria. Parking is free, and there is a picnic area, plus an adventure playground for the children.

At the junction of A61 and A659, midway between Leeds and Harrogate, at Harewood Village. ℭ 01132/886331. www.harewood.org. House, grounds, bird garden, and the terrace gallery £9.50 ($15) adults, £7.75 ($12) seniors, £5.25 ($8.40) children, family ticket £32 ($51). Grounds only £6.75 ($11) adults, £5.75 ($9.20) seniors, £4.25 ($6.80) children 15 and under, family ticket £21 ($34). House, bird garden, and adventure playground Mar–Oct daily 11am–4:30pm. Nov–Dec Terrace gallery 11am–5pm, garden and grounds 10am–4pm, bird garden 10am–3pm. From York, head west along B1224 toward Wetherby and follow the signs to Harewood from there.

4 Yorkshire Dales National Park ★

The national park consists of some 1,813 sq. km (700 sq. miles) of water-carved country. In the dales you'll find dramatic white limestone crags, roads and fields bordered by dry-stone walls, fast-running rivers, isolated sheep farms, and clusters of sandstone cottages.

Malhamdale receives more visitors annually than any dale in Yorkshire. Two of the most interesting historic attractions are the 12th-century ruins of Bolton Priory and the 14th-century Castle Bolton, to the north in Wensleydale.

Richmond, the most frequently copied town name in the world, stands at the head of the dales and, like Hawes (see below), is a good center for touring the surrounding countryside.

EXPLORING THE DALES

For orientation purposes, head first for **Grassington,** 16km (10 miles) north of Skipton and 40km (25 miles) west of Ripon. Constructed around a cobbled marketplace, this is a stone-built village that's ideal for exploring Upper Wharfedale, one of the most scenic parts of the Dales. In fact, the Dales Way footpath passes right through the heart of the village.

Drop in to the **National Park Centre,** Colvend, Hebdon Road (℗ **01756/ 752774**), which is open April through October daily from 9:30am to 5:15pm. November through March, hours are Monday from 11am to 1pm, Wednesday and Friday from 11am to 4pm, and Saturday and Sunday from 10am to 4pm. Maps, bus schedules through the dales, and a choice of guidebooks is available here to help you navigate your way. If you'd like a more in-depth look than what you can do on your own, you can arrange for a qualified guide who knows the most beautiful places and can point out the most interesting geological and botanical features of the wilderness.

Sixteen kilometers (10 miles) west of Grassington (reached along the B6265), **Malham** is a great place to set out on a hike in summer. Branching out from here, you can set out to explore some of the most remarkable limestone formations in Britain. First, it's best to stop in for maps and information at the **National Park Centre** (℗ **01729/830363**), which is open from Easter to October daily from 9:30am to 5pm; off season, only Saturday and Sunday from 10am to 4pm. Amazingly, this village of 200 or so souls receives half a million visitors annually. May or September is the time to come; the hordes descend June through August.

The scenery in this area has been extolled by no less an authority than Wordsworth, and has been painted by Turner. A trio of scenic destinations, **Malham Cove, Malham Tarn,** and **Gordale Scar,** can be explored on a circular walk of 13km (8 miles) that takes most hikers about 5 hours. If your time (and your stamina) is more limited, you can take a circular walk from the heart of the village to Malham Cove and Gordale Scar in about 2 hours. At least try to walk 1.5km (1 mile) north of the village to Malham Cove, a large natural rock amphitheater. Gordale Scar is a deep natural chasm between overhanging limestone cliffs, and Malham Tarn is a lake in a desolate location.

Another interesting center, **Kettlewell,** lies 13km (8 miles) northwest of Malham and 9.6km (6 miles) north of Grassington. This is the main village in the Upper Wharfedale and is a good base for hiking through the local hills and valleys, which look straight out of *Wuthering Heights.* Narrow pack bridges and riverside walks characterize the region, and signs point the way to **The Dales Way** hiking path.

After Kettlewell, you can drive for 6.5km (4 miles) on B6160 to the hamlet of **Buckden,** the last village in the Upper Wharfedale. Once here, follow the sign to **Kidstone Pass,** still staying on B6160. At Aysgarth, the river plummets over a series of waterfalls. This is one of the dramatic scenic highlights of the Yorkshire Dales.

MASHAM: A ROOM IN A CASTLE

For luxury lovers, the little village of Masham makes the best base—certainly the most luxurious—for exploring the Yorkshire Dales. Swinton Parks stands at the gateway to the Dales.

Swinton Park ★★★   If you weren't born in an aristocrat's vine-covered castle, you can stay here and have the experience after all. Mark Cunliffe-Lister, nephew of the Earl and Countess of Swinton, along with his wife, Felicity, have converted this historic manor into a luxury hotel, one of our preferred stopovers in the northeast of England. Set in 200 acres of parkland, lakes, and gardens, this family estate is a good base for exploring the Yorkshire Dales National Park, lying 52km (32 miles) northwest of York. Even with a pedigree going back to the 1500s, the castle is up to date with a spa and fitness area in a conservatory. There is also a bar in the family museum and a private cinema, even a Victorian game room. Each of the spacious and beautifully designed bedrooms is individually designed, taking the theme of a Yorkshire dale, castle, abbey, or town. The Harrogate Room, for example, opens toward the south with a view of the lake and a deer park. Romantics book into the turret room, which is on two floors and reached by one of Yorkshire's steepest staircases. The beautifully restored bathrooms come with tub and shower. Rooms and suites are assigned based on your royal rank, with knights and barons paying the cheapest tariff, the most expensive tabs being assessed from dukes and earls. The hotel's superb restaurant, Samuel's, serves a modern British cuisine with an emphasis on game. In its heyday, many famous guests came here, including Prime Minister Harold Macmillan, even crooner Bing Crosby.

Swinton Park, Masham, N. Yorkshire HG4 4JH. (℗ **01765/680900**. Fax 01765/680901. www.stinton park.com. 20 units. £100–£250 ($160–$400) double; suites from £275 ($440). Rates include Yorkshire breakfast. **Amenities:** Restaurant; bar; fitness center; spa; room service; laundry service; babysitting; dry cleaning. *In room:* TV, coffeemaker, iron/ironing board, trouser press.

HAWES: A BASE FOR EXPLORING YORKSHIRE DALES NATIONAL PARK

About 105km (65 miles) northwest of York, on A684, Hawes is the natural center of Yorkshire Dales National Park and a good place to stay. On the Pennine Way, it's England's highest market town and the capital of Wensleydale, which is famous for its cheese. There are rail connections from York taking you to Garsdale, which is 8km (5 miles) from Hawes. From Garsdale, bus connections will take you into Hawes.

While you're there, you might want to check out the **Dales Countryside Museum,** Station Yard (the old train station; (℗ **01969/667494**), which traces folk life in the Dales, a story of 10,000 years of human history. Peat cutting and cheese making, among other occupations, are depicted. The museum is open April through October daily from 10am to 5pm. Winter opening hours vary; you'll have to check locally. Admission is £3.50 ($5.60) for adults and £2.50 ($4) for children, students, and seniors.

WHERE TO STAY

Cockett's Hotel & Restaurant   This is an atmospheric choice, still sporting many remnants of its construction in 1668. In case you need reminding, the date of its construction is carved into one of its lintels. Set in the center of town, it's a two-story, slate-roofed, stone cottage whose front yard is almost entirely covered with flagstones. Rooms are done in an old-world style with exposed wooden beams; they're snug, cozy, and well maintained, some with a small shower-only bathroom, and some with tubs. Two rooms have four-poster beds.

Market Place, Hawes, North Yorkshire DL8 3RD. (℗ **01969/667312**. Fax 01969/667162. www.cocketts.co.uk. 8 units. £59–£69 ($94–$110) double. Rates include English breakfast. MC, V. **Amenities:** Restaurant; bar. *In room:* TV, coffeemaker, hair dryer, trouser press.

Simonstone Hall   Just north of Hawes, you can stay and dine at Simonstone Hall. Constructed in 1733, this building has been restored and converted into a comfortable, family-run, country-house hotel with a helpful young staff. It's the former home of the earls of Wharncliffe. Both the public rooms and the bedrooms are ideal for relaxation and comfort. Most bedrooms are spacious, and all are furnished tastefully with antiques. Each comes with a quality bed and a shower-only bathroom.

2.5km (1½ miles) north of Hawes on the road signposted to Muker, Hawes, North Yorkshire DL8 3RD. © 01969/667255. Fax 01969/667741. www.simonstonehall.co.uk. 18 units. £100–£170 ($160–$272) per person double. Rates include breakfast. AE, MC, V. **Amenities:** Restaurant; bar; room service; laundry service. *In room:* TV, coffeemaker, hair dryer.

5 North York Moors National Park ✦

The moors, on the other side of the Vale of York, have a wild beauty all their own, quite different from that of the dales. This rather barren moorland blossoms in summer with purple heather. Bounded on the east by the North Sea, it embraces 1435 sq. km (554 sq. miles), which have been preserved as a national park.

If you're looking for a hot, sunny beach vacation where the warm water beckons, the North Yorkshire Coast isn't for you—the climate here is cool because of the brisk waters of the North Sea. Even the summer months aren't very hot. Many Britons do visit North Yorkshire for beach vacations, however, so you will find a beach town atmosphere along the coast. Brightly colored stalls line the seafront, and the people seem to be a bit more relaxed than their inland counterparts.

The beauty and history of the area are the real reasons to visit North Yorkshire. The national park is perfect for solitary strolls and peaceful drives. For remnants of the area's exciting days of smugglers and brave explorers, visitors can follow the **Captain Cook Heritage Trail** along the coast. The fishing industry is still very much alive in the area, although the whaling ships of yesteryear have been anchored and the fishmongers now concentrate on smaller trappings.

Because the park sprawls over such a large area, you can access it from five or six different gateways. Most visitors enter it from the side closest to York, by following either the A19 north via the hamlet of **Thirsk,** or by detouring to the northeast along the A64 and entering via **Scarborough.** You can also get in through **Helmsley,** where the park's administrative headquarters are located; just follow the roads from York that are signposted Helmsley. Gateways along the park's northern edges, which are less convenient to York, include the villages of **Whitby** (accessible via A171), and **Stokesley** (accessible via A19).

For information on accommodations and transportation before you go, contact **North York Moors National Park,** The Old Vicarage, Bondgate, Helmsley, York YO62 5BP (© **01439/770657**). Advice, specialized guidebooks, maps, and information can be obtained at the **Sutton Bank Visitor Centre,** Sutton Bank, near Thirsk, North Yorkshire YO7 2EK (© **01845/597426**). Another well-inventoried information source is **The Moors Centre,** Danby Lodge, Lodge Lane, Danby, near Whitby YO21 2NB (© **01439/772737**).

EXPLORING THE MOORS

Bounded by the Cleveland and Hambleton hills, the moors are dotted with early burial grounds and ancient stone crosses. **Pickering** and **Northallerton,** both market towns, serve as gateways to the moors.

The North York Moors will always be associated with doomed trysts between unlucky lovers and with ghosts who wander vengefully across the rugged plateaus of their lonely and windswept surfaces. Although the earth is relatively fertile in the river valleys, the thin, rocky soil of the heather-clad uplands has been scorned by local farmers as wasteland, suitable only for sheep grazing and healthy (but melancholy) rambles. During the 19th century, a handful of manor houses were built on their lonely promontories by moguls of the Industrial

Revolution, but not until 1953 was the 1435-sq.-km (554-sq.-mile) district designated the North York Moors National Park.

Encompassing England's largest expanse of moorland, the park is famous for the diversity of heathers, which thrive between the sandstone outcroppings of the uplands. If you visit between October and February, you may see smoldering fires across the landscape—deliberately controlled attempts by shepherds and farmers to burn the omnipresent heather back to stubs. Repeated in age-old cycles every 15 years, the blazes encourage the heather's renewal with new growth for the uncounted thousands of sheep that thrive in the district.

Although public bridle and footpaths take you to all corners of the moors, there are two especially noteworthy, clearly demarcated trails that make up the most comprehensive moor walks in Europe. The shorter of the two is the **Lyle Wake Walk,** a 64km (40-mile) east–west trek that connects the hamlets of Osmotherly and Ravenscar. It traces the rugged path established by 18th-century coffin bearers. The longer trek (the **Cleveland Walk**) is a 177km (110-mile) circumnavigation of the national park's perimeter. A good section of it skirts the edge of the Yorkshire coastline; other stretches take climbers up and down a series of steep fells in the park's interior.

Don't even consider an ambitious moor trek without good shoes, a compass, an ordinance survey map, and a detailed park guidebook. With descriptions of geologically interesting sites, safety warnings, and listings of inns and farmhouses (haunted or otherwise) offering overnight stays, they sell for less than £4 ($6.40) each at any local tourist office.

The isolation and the beauty of the landscape attracted the founders of **three great abbeys:** Rievaulx near Helmsley, Byland Abbey near the village of Wass, and Ampleforth Abbey. Nearby is **Coxwold,** one of the most attractive villages in the moors. The Cistercian Rievaulx and Byland abbeys are in ruins, but the Benedictine Ampleforth still functions as a monastery and well-known Roman Catholic boys' school. Although many of its buildings date from the 19th and 20th centuries, they also contain earlier artifacts.

BASING YOURSELF IN THIRSK

You can drive through the moorland while based in York, but if you'd like to be closer to the moors, there are places to stay in and around the national park.

The old market town of Thirsk, in the Vale of Mowbray, 39km (24 miles) north of York on the A19, is near the western fringe of the park. It has a fine parish church, but what makes it such a popular stopover is its association with the late James Herriot (1916–95), author of *All Creatures Great and Small.* Mr. Herriot used to practice veterinary medicine in Thirsk. You can drop in at a visitor center, **The World of James Herriot,** 23 Kirkgate (© **01845/524234**), which is dedicated to his life and to veterinary science. The Kirkgate surgery where he practiced from 1930 until his death in 1995 and the house next door have been transformed into *The Herriot Experience.* You can view the surgery and see various exhibitions and displays on veterinary science. Open daily from Easter to September from 10am to 5pm, and from October to Easter from 11am to 4pm. Admission is £4.50 ($7.20) adults, £3.20 ($5.10) children 5 to 16.

6 Hexham, Hadrian's Wall ✶✶ & the Pennine Way

489km (304 miles) N of London; 60km (37 miles) E of Carlisle; 34km (21 miles) W of Newcastle upon Tyne

Above the Tyne River, the historic old market town of Hexham has narrow streets, an old market square, a fine abbey church, and a moot hall. It makes a good base for exploring Hadrian's Wall and the Roman supply base of Corsto-pitum at Corbridge-on-Tyne, the ancient capital of Northumberland. The tourist office has lots of information on the wall, whether you're hiking, driving, camping, or picnicking.

ESSENTIALS

GETTING THERE   Take one of the many daily trains from London's King's Cross Station to Newcastle upon Tyne. At Newcastle, change trains and take one in the direction of Carlisle. The fifth or sixth (depending on the schedule) stop after Newcastle will be Hexham. For schedules and information, call *C* **0845/748-4950.**

Hexham lies 23km (14 miles) southeast of Hadrian's Wall. If you are prima-rily interested in the wall (rather than in Hexham), get off the Carlisle-bound train at the second stop (Bardon Mill) or at the third stop (Haltwhistle), which are 6.4km (4 miles) and 4km (2½ miles), respectively, from the wall. At either of these hamlets, you can take a taxi to whichever part of the wall you care to visit. Taxis line up readily at the railway station in Hexham, but less often at the other villages. If you get off at one of the above-mentioned villages and don't see a taxi, call *C* **01434/321064** and a local taxi will come to get you. Many visi-tors ask their taxi drivers to return at a prearranged time (which they gladly do) to pick them up after their excursion on the windy ridges near the wall.

National Express coaches to Newcastle and Carlisle connect with Northum-bria bus service no. 685. Trip time to Hexham from Carlisle is about 1½ hours and from Newcastle about 1 hour. For schedules and information, call *C* **020/7529-2000.** Local bus services connect Hexham with North Tynedale and the North Pennines.

If you're driving from Newcastle upon Tyne, head west on A69 until you see the cutoff south to Hexham.

VISITOR INFORMATION   The **Tourist Information Centre** at Hexham is at the Wentworth Car Park (*C* **01434/652220**). It's open from Easter to Sep-tember Monday through Saturday from 9am to 6pm, and Sunday from 10am to 5pm; November through March, Monday through Saturday from 9am to 5pm.

HADRIAN'S WALL & ITS FORTRESSES

Hadrian's Wall ★★, which extends for 118km (73 miles) across the north of England, from the North Sea to the Irish Sea, is particularly interesting for a stretch of 16km (10 miles) west of Housesteads, which lies 4km (2¾ miles) northeast of Bardon Mill on B6318. Only the lower courses of the wall have been preserved intact; the rest were reconstructed in the 19th century using orig-inal stones. From the wall, there are incomparable views north to the Cheviot Hills along the Scottish border and south to the Durham moors.

The wall was built in A.D. 122 after the visit of the emperor Hadrian, who was inspecting far frontiers of the Roman Empire and wanted to construct a dra-matic line between the empire and the barbarians. Legionnaires were ordered to build a wall across the width of the island of Britain, stretching 118km (73 miles), beginning at the North Sea and ending at the Irish Sea.

The wall is one of Europe's top Roman ruins. The western end can be reached from Carlisle, which also has an interesting museum of Roman artifacts; the eastern end can be reached from Newcastle upon Tyne (where some remains can be seen on the city outskirts; there's also a nice museum at the university).

From early May to late September, the Tynedale Council and Northumberland National Park run a **bus service** that visits every important site along the wall, then turns around in the village of Haltwhistle and returns to Hexham. Buses depart from a point near the railway station in Hexham five times a day. Call ☎ **01434/652220** for more information. The cost is £5 ($8) for adults, £2.50 ($4) for children, and £10 ($16) for a family ticket. Many visitors take one bus out, then return on a subsequent bus, 2, 4, or 6 hours later. Every Sunday, a national-park warden leads a 2½-hour walking tour of the wall, in connection with the bus service. The Hexham tourist office (see "Visitor Information," above) will provide further details. You can find more information about Hadrian's Wall at the website, **www.hadrians-wall.org**.

Housesteads Fort and Museum ★★ Along the wall are several Roman forts, the largest and most well preserved of which was called *Vercovicium* by the Romans. This substantially excavated fort, on a dramatic site, contains the only visible example of a Roman hospital in Britain.

5km (3 miles) northeast of Bardon Mill on B6318. ☎ **01434/344363.** Admission £3.10 ($4.95) adults, £2.30 ($3.70) seniors and students, £1.60 ($2.55) children 5–16. Apr–Sept daily 10am–6pm; Oct–Nov daily 10am–5pm; Dec–Mar daily 10am–4pm. Closed Dec 25–26 and Jan 1.

Roman Army Museum ★ Close to the village of Greenhead, the Roman Army Museum traces the influence of Rome from its early beginnings to the expansion of the empire, with emphasis on the role of the Roman army and the garrisons of Hadrian's Wall. A barracks room depicts army living conditions. Realistic life-size figures make this a strikingly visual museum experience.

Within easy walking distance of the Roman Army Museum is one of the most imposing and high-standing sections of Hadrian's Wall, **Walltown Crags;** the height of the wall and magnificent views to the north and south are impressive.

At the junction of A69 and B6318, 29km (18 miles) west of Hexham. ☎ **01697/747485.** www. vindolanda.com. Admission £3.10 ($4.95) adults, £2.70 ($4.30) seniors and students, £2.10 ($3.35) children. Late Feb and Nov 10am–4pm; Mar and Oct 10am–5pm; Apr and Sept 10am–5:30pm; May–June 10am–6pm; July–Aug 10am–6:30pm.

Vindolanda This is another well-preserved fort south of the wall, the last of eight successive forts to be built on this site. An excavated civilian settlement outside the fort has an interesting museum of artifacts of everyday Roman life.

Just west of Housesteads, on a minor road 2km (1¼ miles) southeast of Twice Brewed off B6318. ☎ **01434/344277.** www.vindolanda.com. Admission £3.90 ($6.25) adults, £3.30 ($5.30) seniors and students, £2.80 ($4.50) children. Jan 25–Nov daily 10am–4pm. Closed Dec–Jan 24.

HIKING THE PENNINE WAY IN NORTHUMBERLAND NATIONAL PARK

Northumberland National Park, established in 1956, encompasses the borderlands that were a buffer zone between the warring English and Scots during the 13th and 14th centuries. Today, the park comprises almost 643 sq. km (400 sq. miles) of the least-populated area in England and is noted for its rugged landscape and associations with the northern frontier of the ancient Roman Empire.

Touching on the border with Scotland, the park covers some of the most tortured geology in England, the Cheviot Hills, whose surfaces have been wrinkled by volcanic pressures, inundated with sea water, scoured and gouged by glaciers, silted over by rivers, and thrust upward in a complicated series of geological events. Much of the heather-sheathed terrain here is used for sheep grazing; woolly balls of fluff adorn hillsides ravaged by high winds and frequent rain.

Northumberland Park includes the remains of Hadrian's Wall, one of the most impressive classical ruins of northern Europe. Footpaths run alongside it and there are a variety of walks in the country to the north and south of the monument. One of the most challenging hiking paths in Britain, the **Pennine Way** ★★, snakes up the backbone of the park. The 129km (80 miles) of the 403km (250-mile) path that are in the park are clearly marked; one of the most worthwhile (and safest) hikes is between Bellingham and the Hamlet of Riding Wood.

A map of the trails, priced at 50p (80¢), can be purchased for these and other hiking trails at almost any local tourist office in the district. There are **National Park Centres** at Once Brewed (✆ **01434/344396**), Rothbury (✆ **01669/620414**), and Ingram (✆ **01665/578248**). The Head Office is at Eastburn, South Park, Hexham, Northumberland NE46 1BS (✆ **01434/605555**; www. nnpa.org.uk).

NEARBY PLACES TO STAY & DINE

Anchor Hotel   This is the social center of the village. Ideally situated for visitors to the wall and its surroundings, between Haltwhistle (14km/9 miles away) and Hexham (11km/7 miles), this riverside village pub was once a coaching inn on the route from Newcastle to Carlisle. The building, which was constructed in 1700 near the edge of the North Tyne River (which still flows within a few feet of its foundations), sits in the heart of the tiny village of Haydon Bridge. The cozy bar is a local hangout. In the country dining room, wholesome evening meals are served. The bedrooms are comfortably furnished, albeit a bit small, and each comes with a cozy bed. Bathrooms are also small with shower stalls (some have tubs).

John Martin St. (on A69, 11km/7 miles west of Hexham), Haydon Bridge, Northumberland NE47 6AB. ✆ 01434/684227. Fax 01434/684586. 10 units. £55–£60 ($88–$96) double. Rates include English breakfast. AE, MC, V. **Amenities:** Restaurant; bar. *In room:* TV, coffeemaker, hair dryer, iron/ironing board.

George Hotel   Standing on the banks of the Tyne, this country hotel opens onto gardens leading to the riverbank. It's a convenient base for visiting Hadrian's Wall. The hotel dates from the 18th century, when the original structure was built of Roman stone. It has been extensively refurbished to a high standard, and all bedrooms are comfortably furnished and well equipped. Bathrooms are a bit cramped.

Chollerford, Humshaugh, near Hexham, Northumberland NE46 4EW. ✆ 01434/681611. Fax 01434/681727. 47 units. £120 ($192) double. Rate includes English breakfast. AE, DC, MC, V. Take A6079 8km (5 miles) north of Hexham. **Amenities:** Restaurant; bar; health club; room service; laundry service. *In room:* TV, coffeemaker, hair dryer, iron/ironing board, trouser press.

Hadrian Hotel   Ideal for a stopover along Hadrian's Wall, the Hadrian lies on the only street of the hamlet of Wall, 5.5km (3½ miles) north of Hexham. It's an ivy-covered, 18th-century building erected of stones gathered long ago from the site of the ancient wall. The owners have carefully refurbished the place. Each recently renovated bedroom is attractive, and all the rooms have been modernized and offer comfortable double or twin beds. Three rooms have a tub only. One room has a shower only, and two rooms have neither bath nor shower. The hotel has a private garden and a beer garden that serves as a warm-weather extension of its pub.

Wall, near Hexham, Northumberland NE46 4EE. ✆ 01434/681232. Fax 01434/681512. 6 units. £55 ($88) double. Rates include English breakfast. MC, V. **Amenities:** Restaurant; 2 bars; laundry service. *In room:* TV, coffeemaker, hair dryer.

Langley Castle Hotel ★ *Finds*   To experience a stately home, we recommend this hotel located on 10 acres of woodlands at the edge of Northumberland National Park, southwest of Haydon Bridge and about 11km (7 miles) west of Hexham. It's the only medieval fortified castle home in England that receives paying guests. The castle, built in 1350, was largely uninhabited after being damaged in 1400 during an English and Scottish war, until it was purchased in the late 19th century by Cadwallader Bates, a historian, who spent the rest of his life carefully restoring the property to its original beauty. Medieval features here include the 14th-century spiral staircase, stained-glass windows, huge open fireplaces, 2m (7-ft.) thick walls, and many turrets. The luxuriously appointed bedrooms vary in size; some have whirlpools or saunas in the bathrooms. An adjacent building has extra accommodations, including four new suites, as well as a small conference room with a view of the castle. The hotel has an elegant drawing room, with an adjoining oak-paneled bar.

Langley-on-Tyne, Hexham, Northumberland NE47 5LU. © 01434/688888. Fax 01434/684019. www.langley castle.com. 18 units. £105 ($168) double; £209 ($334) suite. Rates include English breakfast. AE, DC, MC, V. From Hexham, go west on A69 to Haydon Bridge, then head south on A686 for 3km (2 miles). **Amenities:** Restaurant; bar; gift shop; room service (8am–10pm); babysitting; laundry service. *In room:* TV, coffeemaker, hair dryer, iron/ironing board, trouser press.

13

Edinburgh &
the Lothian Region

Edinburgh (pronounced *Edin*-burra) has been called one of Europe's fairest cities, the Athens of the North, and the gateway to central Scotland. You can use it as a base for excursions to the Borders, the Trossachs (Scotland's Lake District), the silver waters of Loch Lomond, and the Kingdom of Fife on the opposite shore of the Firth of Forth.

Edinburgh is filled with historic and literary association: John Knox, Mary Queen of Scots, Robert Louis Stevenson, Sir Arthur Conan Doyle (creator of Sherlock Holmes and Dr. Watson), Alexander Graham Bell, Sir Walter Scott, and Bonnie Prince Charlie are all part of its past.

In modern times, the city has become famous as the scene of the ever-growing **Edinburgh International Festival,** with an action-packed list of cultural events. But remember the treasures of this ancient seat of Scottish royalty are available all year—in fact, when the festival-hoppers have gone home, the pace is more relaxed, the prices are lower, and the people themselves, under less pressure, return to their traditional hospitable nature.

Built on extinct volcanoes atop an inlet from the North Sea (the Firth of Forth) and enveloped by rolling hills, lakes *(lochs),* and forests, Edinburgh is a city made for walking. Its Old Town and its New Town sport elegant streets, cobbled alleys, lovely squares, and enough circuses and crescents to rival Bath in England; from every hilltop another panoramic view unfolds. Edinburgh's sunsets are spectacularly romantic—Scots call the fading evening light the "gloaming."

Edinburgh was once the cultural capital of the north, but it has lost that position to Glasgow. However, the lively capital is trying its best to regain its old reputation. In fact, if you could visit only two cities in all of Great Britain, we'd say make it London first and Edinburgh second. But you may want to budget some time for side trips, too. Notable attractions on the doorstep of Edinburgh are the royal burgh of Linlithgow, where Mary Queen of Scots was born at **Linlithgow Palace;** the port of **North Berwick** (today a holiday resort); and lovely **Dirleton,** with its 13th-century castle ruins.

1 Essentials

ARRIVING

BY PLANE   Edinburgh is about an hour's flying time from London, 633km (393 miles) south. **Edinburgh Airport** (© 01313/331000) is 10km (6 miles) west of the center, receiving flights from within the British Isles and the rest of Europe. Before heading into town, you might want to stop at the **information and accommodation desk** (© 01314/733800); it's open Monday through

Saturday from 8am to 8pm and Sunday from 9am to 4:30pm. A double-decker Airlink bus makes the trip from the airport to the city center every 15 minutes, letting you off near Waverley Bridge, between the Old Town and the New Town; the fare is £3.30 ($5.30) one-way or £5 ($8) round-trip, and the trip takes about 25 minutes. A taxi into the city will cost £12 ($19) or more, depending on traffic, and the ride will be about 25 minutes.

BY TRAIN   InterCity trains link London with Edinburgh and are fast and efficient, providing both restaurant and bar service as well as air-conditioning. Trains from London's Kings Cross Station arrive in Edinburgh at **Waverley Station,** at the east end of Princes Street (© **0845/748-4950** in London for rail info). Trains depart London every hour or so, taking about 4½ hours and costing about £41 to £91 ($65–$145) one-way. Overnight trains have a sleeper berth, which you can rent for an extra £35 ($56). Taxis and buses are right outside the station in Edinburgh.

BY BUS   The least expensive way to go from London to Edinburgh is by bus, but it's an 8-hour journey. Nevertheless, it'll get you there for only about £27 ($43) one-way or £38 ($61) round-trip. Scottish CityLink coaches depart from London's Victoria Coach Station, delivering you to Edinburgh's **St. Andrew Square Bus Station,** St. Andrew Square (© **0870/580-8080** for information).

BY CAR   Edinburgh is 74km (46 miles) east of Glasgow and 169km (105 miles) north of Newcastle-upon-Tyne in England. No express motorway links London and Edinburgh. The M1 from London takes you part of the way north, but you'll have to come into Edinburgh along secondary roads: A68 or A7 from the southeast, A1 from the east, or A702 from the north. The A71 or A8 comes in from the west, A8 connecting with M8 just west of Edinburgh; A90 comes down from the north over the Forth Road Bridge. Allow 8 hours or more for the drive north from London.

VISITOR INFORMATION

The **Edinburgh & Scotland Information Centre,** Waverley Shopping Centre, 3 Princes St., at the corner of Princes Street and Waverley Bridge (© **01314/ 733800;** www.edinburgh.org; bus: 3, 69, or 331), can give you sightseeing info and also help find lodgings. The center sells bus tours, theater tickets, and souvenirs of Edinburgh. July and August, hours are Monday through Saturday from 8am to 8pm and Sunday from 8am to 4:30pm. There's also an **information and accommodations desk** at Edinburgh airport (see above).

CITY LAYOUT

Edinburgh is divided into an Old Town and a New Town. Chances are, you'll find lodgings in the New Town and visit the Old Town only for dining, drinking, shopping, and sightseeing.

The **New Town,** with its world-famous **Princes Street,** came about in the 18th century in the Golden Age of Edinburgh. Everybody from Robert Burns to James Boswell visited in that era. The first building went up here in 1767, and by the end of the century classical squares, streets, and town houses had been added. Princes Street runs straight for about a mile; the street is known for its shopping and also for its beauty, as it opens onto the Princes Street Gardens with panoramic views of the Old Town.

North of and running parallel to Princes Street is the New Town's second great street, **George Street.** It begins at Charlotte Square and runs east to St.

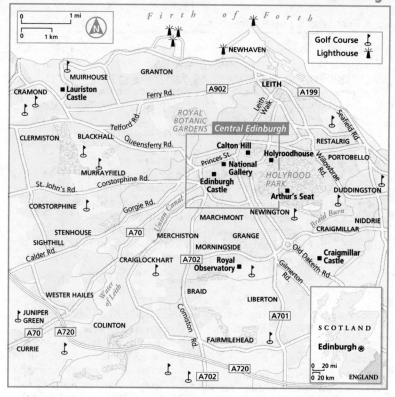

Andrew Square. Directly north of George Street is another impressive thoroughfare, **Queen Street,** opening onto Queen Street Gardens on its north side. You'll also hear a lot about **Rose Street,** directly north of Princes Street—it boasts more pubs per square block than any other place in Scotland and is filled with shops and restaurants.

Seemingly everyone has heard of the **Royal Mile,** the main thoroughfare of the **Old Town,** beginning at Edinburgh Castle and running all the way to the Palace of Holyroodhouse. This single street bears four names along its length: Castlehill, Lawnmarket, High Street, and Canongate. A famous street to the south of the castle (you have to descend to it) is **Grassmarket,** where convicted criminals were hung on the dreaded gallows that stood there.

Discovering Edinburgh's many hidden lanes and branching out to some of its interesting satellite communities is one of the pleasures of coming here.

THE NEIGHBORHOODS IN BRIEF

Old Town This area is where Edinburgh began. Its backbone is the **Royal Mile,** a medieval thoroughfare stretching for about 1.6km (1 mile) from Edinburgh Castle running downhill to the Palace of Holyroodhouse. It's composed of four connected streets: Castlehill, Lawnmarket, High Street, and Canongate (once a separate burgh). "This is perhaps the largest, longest, and finest street for buildings and number of

> *Tips*   **Finding an Address**
>
> Edinburgh's streets often follow no pattern whatsoever, and both names and house numbers seem to have been created purposely to confuse. First, the city is checkered with innumerable squares, terraces, circuses, wynds, and closes, which will jut into or cross or overlap or interrupt whatever street you're trying to follow, usually without the slightest warning.
>
> Then the house numbers run in sequences of odds or evens or run clockwise or counterclockwise as the wind blows. That is, when they exist at all. Many establishments don't use street numbers. (This is even truer when you leave Edinburgh and go to a provincial town.) Even though a road might run for a mile, some buildings on the street will be numbered and others will say only "Kings Road" or whatever, giving no number. Before heading out, you should get a detailed map of Edinburgh and ask for a location to be pinpointed; locals are generally glad to assist a bewildered foreigner. If you're looking for an address, try to get the name of the nearest cross street.

inhabitants in the world," or so wrote English author Daniel Defoe. The same might be said of the street today.

New Town   Lying below Old Town, New Town burst into full bloom between 1766 and 1840 and became one of the largest Georgian developments in the world. It takes in most of the northern half of the heart of the city, covering some 790 acres. With about 25,000 citizens living within its boundaries, it's the largest conservation area in all Britain. New Town is made up of a network of squares, streets, terraces, and circuses, reaching from Haymarket in the west to Abbeyhill in the east. New Town also goes from Canonmills on the northern perimeter down to Princes Street, its main artery, along the southern tier.

Marchmont   About a mile south of High Street, the suburb of Marchmont borders a public park, the Meadows. It was constructed between 1869 and 1914 as a massive building program of new housing for people who could no longer afford to live in New Town.

Bruntsfield   This suburb to the west is named for Bruntsfield Links. Now a residential district of moderate-income families, it was the ground on which James IV gathered the Scottish army he marched to defeat at Flodden in 1513. Plague victims were once brought here for burial; now suburban gardens have grown over those graves. Many low-cost B&Bs are found in this area.

Churchill   Churchill is known as "holy corner" because of the wide array of Scottish churches within its borders at the junctions of Colinton, Chamberlain, and Bruntsfield roads. These churches are primarily for local worshipers and are not of artistic interest. Many famous Scots have lived in this district, including Jane Welsh Carlyle and George Meikle Kemp, the architect who created the Scott Monument on Princes Street.

Leith   The Port of Leith lies only a few miles north of Princes Street and is the city's major harbor, opening onto the Firth of Forth. The area is currently going through a gentrification process, and many visitors come here for the restaurants and pubs, many of which specialize in seafood. The port isn't what it used to be in terms of maritime might; its glory days were back when stevedores unloaded cargoes by hand. Leith was once a bitter rival of Edinburgh, but now, as one resident put it, "We're just another bloody part of Auld Reekie [local name for Edinburgh]."

Newhaven   The fishing village adjacent to Leith, Newhaven was once known as Our Lady's Port of Grace. Founded in the 1400s, this former little fishing harbor with its bustling fish market was greatly altered in the 1960s. Many of its "bow-tows" (a nickname for closely knit, clannish residents) were uprooted, like the Leithers, in a major gentrification program. Now many of the old houses of the fisherfolk have been restored, and the fishwife no longer goes from door to door hawking fish—she'd gut and fillet the fish right on your doorstep if you asked her—from her basket (known as a creel). Newhaven's harbor is now mostly filled with pleasure craft instead of fishing boats. If your time is limited, you can skip this area, as its attractions are limited.

2 Getting Around

Because of its narrow lanes, wynds, and closes, you can explore the Old Town in any depth only on foot. Edinburgh is fairly convenient for the visitor who likes to walk, as most of the attractions are along the Royal Mile or Princes Street or on one of the major streets of the New Town.

BY BUS

The bus will probably be your chief method of transport. The fare you pay depends on the distance you ride, with the **minimum fare** 80p ($1.30) for 3 stages or less and the **maximum fare** £1 ($1.60) for 4 or more stages. (A stage isn't a stop but a distance of about ½ a mile with a number of stops.) Children ages 5 to 15 are charged a flat rate of 50p (80¢), but teenagers ages 13 to 15 must carry a **teen card** (available where bus tickets are sold—see below) as proof of age, and children ages 4 and under ride free. Exact change is required if you're paying your fare on the bus.

A **family ticket** for two adults and four children goes for £6 ($9.60) a day and another for £1.60 ($2.55) operates from 6:30pm onward. The **Edinburgh Day Saver Ticket** allows 1 day of unlimited travel on city buses at a cost of £1.50 to £2.50 ($2.40–$4) adults and £1.80 ($2.90) children.

For daily commuters or die-hard Scottish enthusiasts, a **RideCard** season ticket allows unlimited travel on all buses. For adults, the price is £11 ($18) for 1 week and £33 ($53) for 4 weeks; tickets for children cost £7 ($11) for 1 week and £21 ($34) for 4 weeks. Travel must begin on Sunday.

Tips **Look Both Ways**

Remember, you're in Great Britain, and cars drive on the left. Always look *both* ways before stepping off a curb. Lots of new arrivals practically commit suicide when crossing the street because they forget which way to look for traffic.

You can get these tickets and further information in the city center at the **Waverley Bridge Transport Office,** Waverley Bridge (© **01315/544494;** bus: 3 or 31), open Monday through Saturday from 6:30am to 6pm and Sunday from 9:30am to 5pm, or at the Hanover Street office (bus: 3 or 31), open Monday through Saturday from 6:30am to 6pm. For details on timetables, call © **01315/556363.**

BY TAXI

You can hail a taxi or pick one up at a taxi stand. Meters begin at £2 ($3.20) and increase £2 ($3.20) every 1 kilometer (⅔ mile). Taxi ranks are at Hanover Street, North St. Andrew Street, Waverley Station, Haymarket Station, and Lauriston Place. Fares are displayed in the front of the taxi and charges posted, including extra charges for night drivers or destinations outside the city limits, and a call-out is charged at 60p (95¢). You can also call a taxi. Try **City Cabs** at © **01312/ 281211** or **Central Radio Taxis** at © **01312/292468.**

BY CAR

Don't think about driving in Edinburgh—it's a tricky business, even for natives. A car, however, is great for touring the countryside around the city or for heading onward. Most companies will accept your U.S. or Canadian driver's license, provided you've held it for more than a year and are over age 21.

RENTALS Many companies grant discounts to people who reserve in advance before leaving home (see "By Car," under "Getting Around Britain" in chapter 3, "Planning Your Trip to Great Britain").

Most of the major car-rental companies maintain offices at the Edinburgh airport should you want to rent a car on the spot. Call **Avis** (© **01313/331866**), **Hertz** (© **01313/443260**), or **Europcar** (© **01313/332588**).

PARKING It's expensive and difficult to find. Metered parking is available, but you'll need the right change and have to watch out for traffic wardens who issue tickets. Some zones are marked PERMIT HOLDERS ONLY. Don't park in them unless you have a permit as a local resident—your vehicle will be towed if you do. A yellow line along the curb indicates NO PARKING.

Major **parking lots** (car parks) are at Castle Terrace, a large multistory car park convenient for Edinburgh Castle and the west end of Princes Street; at Lothian Road, a surface car park near the west end of Princes Street; at St. John Hill, a surface car park convenient to the Royal Mile, the west end of Princes Street, and Waverley Station; and at St. James Centre (entrance from York Place), a multistory car park close to the east end of Princes Street.

BY BICYCLE

You can rent bikes by the day or the week from a number of outfits. Nevertheless, bicycling isn't a good idea for most visitors because the city is constructed on a series of high ridges and terraces.

You may, however, want to rent a bike for exploring the flatter countryside around the city. Try **Central Cycle Hire,** 13 Lochrin Place (© **01312/286333;** bus: 10), off Home Street in Tollcross, near the Cameo Cinema. Depending on the type of bike, charges range from £15 ($24) per day. A deposit of £100 ($160) is imposed. June through September, the shop is open Monday through Saturday from 9:30am to 6pm and Sunday from noon to 7pm; October through May, hours are Monday through Saturday from 10am to 5:30pm.

FAST FACTS: Edinburgh

American Express The office in Edinburgh is at 139 Princes St. (℃ **01312/ 257881;** bus: 3, 39, or 69), 5 blocks from Waverley Station. It's open Monday through Friday from 9am to 5:30pm and Saturday from 9am to 4pm; on Wednesday, the office opens at 9:30am.

Babysitting The most reliable services are provided by **Guardians Baby Sitting Service,** 39 Rabelston Garden (℃ **01313/374150).**

Business Hours In Edinburgh, **banks** are usually open Monday through Friday from 9:15am to 4:45pm. **Shops** are generally open Monday through Saturday from 10am to 5:30 or 6pm; on Thursday stores are open to 8pm. **Offices** are open Monday through Friday from 9am to 5pm.

Currency Exchange The **Clydesdale Bank** operates a bureau de change of at 5 Waverley Bridge and at Waverley Market.

Dentist If you have a dental emergency, go to the **Edinburgh Dental Institute,** 39 Lauriston Place (℃ **01315/364900;** bus: 23 or 41), open Monday through Friday from 9am to 3pm.

Doctor You can seek help from the **Edinburgh Royal Infirmary,** 1 Lauriston Place (℃ **01315/361000;** bus: 23 or 41). Medical attention is available 24 hours.

Drugstores There are no 24-hour drugstores (called chemists or pharmacies) in Edinburgh. The major drugstore is **Boots,** 48 Shandwick Place (℃ **01312/256757;** bus: 3 or 31), open Monday through Friday from 8am to 9pm, Saturday from 8am to 7pm, and Sunday from 10am to 4pm.

Embassies/Consulates The Consulate of the **United States** is at 3 Regent Terrace (℃ **01315/568315;** bus: 26, 85, or 86), which is an extension of Princes Street beyond Nelson's Monument. All the other embassies are in London.

Emergencies Call ℃ **999** in an emergency to summon the police, an ambulance, or firefighters.

Hospital The most convenient is the **Edinburgh Royal Infirmary,** 1 Lauriston Place (℃ **01315/361000;** bus: 23 or 41).

Internet Access You can check your e-mail or send messages at the **International Telecom Centre,** 52 High St. (℃ **01315/597114),** along the Royal Mile. Rates are £1 ($1.60) for 15 minutes. Open daily from 9am to 10pm. Take bus no. 1 or 6.

Luggage/Storage/Lockers You can store luggage in lockers at **Waverley Station,** at Waverley Bridge (℃ **01315/502333),** open Monday through Saturday from 7am to 11pm and Sunday from 8am to 11pm.

Newspapers & Magazines Published since 1817, the *Scotsman* is a quality daily newspaper. Along with national and international news, it's strong on the arts. Among magazines, the field isn't outstanding, except for the *Edinburgh Review,* published quarterly by the University Press, which is mainly a cultural journal.

Police See "Emergencies," above.

Post Office The **Edinburgh Branch Post Office**, St. James's Centre, is open Monday through Friday from 9am to 5:30pm and Saturday from 9am to 6pm. For postal information and customer service, call © **0845/722-3344.**

Restrooms These are found at rail stations, terminals, restaurants, hotels, pubs, and department stores. Don't hesitate to use the system of public toilets, often marked wc, at strategic corners and squares throughout the city. They're perfectly safe and clean but likely to be closed late in the evening.

Safety Edinburgh is generally safer than Glasgow—in fact, it's one of Europe's safest capitals for a visitor to stroll at any time of day or night. But that doesn't mean crimes, especially muggings, don't occur. They do, largely because of Edinburgh's shockingly large drug problem.

Taxes A 17.5% **value-added tax (VAT)** is included in the price of all goods and services in Edinburgh, as elsewhere in Britain. (To find out how to get a VAT refund, see the box in chapter 3.) There are no special city taxes. Quoted hotel prices generally include this tax.

Weather For weather forecasts and road conditions, call © **0845/300-0300.** This number also provides data about weather information for Lothian, the Borders, Tayside, and Fife.

3 Where to Stay

Edinburgh offers a full range of accommodations throughout the year. However, it should come as no surprise that during the 3-week period of the Edinburgh International Festival in August, the hotels fill up; so if you're coming at that time, be sure to reserve far in advance.

The **Edinburgh & Scotland Information Centre,** Waverley Shopping Centre, 3 Princes St., at the corner of Princes Street and Waverley Bridge (© **01314/ 733800;** www.edinburgh.org; bus: 3, 7, 14, 31, or 69), compiles a lengthy list of small hotels, guesthouses, and private homes providing a bed-and-breakfast for as little as £18 ($29) per person. A £3 ($4.80) booking fee and a 10% deposit are charged. Allow about 4 weeks' notice, especially during summer and during the festival weeks. Hours are Monday through Saturday from 9am to 8pm and Sunday from 10am to 8pm; May, June, and September, hours are Monday through Saturday from 8am to 7pm and Sunday from 9am to 5pm; October through April, hours are Monday through Saturday from 9am to 6pm and Sunday from 10am to 6pm.

There's also an **information and accommodations desk** at Edinburgh Airport (see "Essentials," earlier in the chapter).

IN OR NEAR THE CENTER
VERY EXPENSIVE

Balmoral Hotel ★★★ *(Finds* This legendary establishment was originally opened in 1902 as the largest, grandest, and most impressive hotel in the north of Britain. Its soaring clock tower is a city landmark. Furnished with reproduction pieces, the guest rooms are distinguished, conservative, and rather large, a graceful reminder of Edwardian sprawl with a contemporary twist. Many benefit from rounded or oversize windows with views overlooking the city or Edinburgh Castle, and other Victorian/Edwardian quirks that were originally designed as part of the hotel's charm. The marble bathrooms feature deep tubs.

Princes St., Edinburgh, Lothian EH2 2EQ. ℭ **800/225-5843** in the U.S., or 01315/562414. Fax 01315/573747. www.thebalmoralhotel.com. 188 units. £220 ($352) double; from £450 ($720) suite. AE, DC, MC, V. Valet parking £15 ($24). Bus: 50. **Amenities:** 2 restaurants; bar; indoor pool; health club; spa; room service. *In room:* A/C, TV, minibar, hair dryer, safe.

Caledonian Hilton Hotel ✿✿✿ "The Caley" is Edinburgh's most visible hotel, with commanding views over Edinburgh Castle and the Princes Street Gardens. It's built of Dumfriesshire stone, a form of deep red sandstone used in only three other buildings in town. The pastel-colored public areas are reminiscent of Edwardian splendor. Rooms are conservatively but individually styled with reproduction furniture, and are often exceptionally spacious. Fifth-floor rooms are the smallest. Although the accommodations are comparable to other first-class hotels in Edinburgh, the Caledonian lacks the leisure facilities of its major competitor, the Balmoral.

Princes St., Edinburgh EH1 2AB. ℭ **01312/228888.** Fax 01312/228889. www.hilton.com. 249 units. £275–£380 ($440–$608) double; from £340 ($544) suite. Children ages 15 and under stay free in parent's room. AE, DC, MC, V. Parking £8 ($13). Bus: 33. **Amenities:** 2 restaurants; bar; pool; gym; room service; laundry service; dry cleaning. *In room:* TV, minibar, hair dryer, safe.

EXPENSIVE

The Bonham ✿✿ One of Edinburgh's newest and most stylish hotels occupies a trio of regency town houses. Rooms are outfitted in an urban and very hip blend of old and new. The decor combines ancient vases, Art Nouveau objects, marble busts, contemporary art—an eclectic but tasteful mix. Each has a high ceiling, along with a unique decorative theme. Each accommodation has eTV Interactive, a communications and entertainment system with a keyboard hooked up to the Internet and built-in DVD and CD players; it's the first setup of its kind in Scotland.

35 Drumsheugh Gardens, Edinburgh EH3 7RN. ℭ **01312/266050.** Fax 01312/266080. www.thebonham.com. 48 units. £190–£235 ($304–$376) double; £335 ($536) suite. Rates include continental breakfast. AE, DC, MC, V. Bus: 23 or 27. **Amenities:** Restaurant; 24-hr. room service. *In room:* TV/DVD, dataport, minibar, hair dryer, coffeemaker, iron, trouser press.

Carlton Highland Hotel ✿✿ The Paramount investment group substantially improved this landmark hotel with an influx of £8 million ($13 million) when it recently acquired it. Some bedrooms were done away with to make the rooms larger and more comfortable, and brand new bathrooms were installed. Furnishings are tasteful with a subdued modern simplicity and guests will find all of the modern conveniences. In spite of its overhaul, some of the architectural charm of 1900—back when it was a department store—still remains. Offering more facilities than the landmark Caledonian, the Carlton is known for its top-notch service and both formal and informal dining venues.

19 North Bridge, Edinburgh, Lothian EH1 1SD. ℭ **01315/567277.** Fax 01315/562691. www.paramounthotels.co.uk. 189 units. £180–£195 ($288–$312) executive double. Children ages 14 and under stay free in parent's room. AE, DC, MC, V. Parking £6 ($9.60). Bus: 55 or 80. **Amenities:** Restaurant; bar; indoor pool; 2 squash courts; gym and aerobics studio; whirlpool; solarium; 24-hr. room service. *In room:* TV, dataport, minibar, hair dryer, coffeemaker, iron, safe.

Channings Hotel ✿✿ Five Edwardian terrace houses combine to create this hotel 7 blocks north of Dean Village in a tranquil residential area. It maintains the atmosphere of a Scottish country house, with oak paneling, ornate fireplaces, molded ceilings, and antiques. Rooms are outfitted in a modern yet elegant style; some have four-poster beds and others have two-person tubs in the bathrooms. Front units have views of a cobblestone street. Back units are quieter, and

Edinburgh Accommodations & Dining

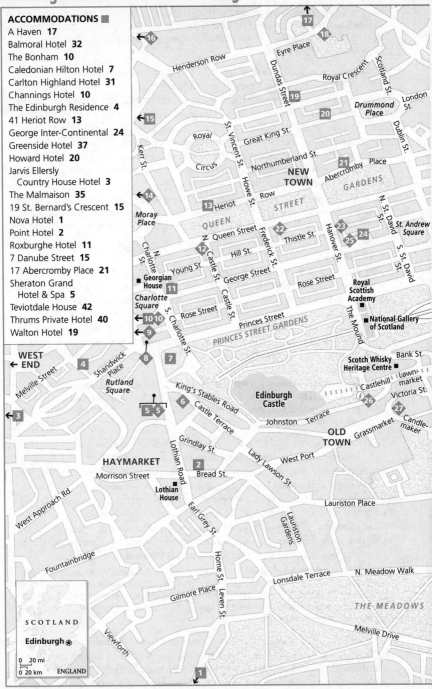

ACCOMMODATIONS ■
A Haven **17**
Balmoral Hotel **32**
The Bonham **10**
Caledonian Hilton Hotel **7**
Carlton Highland Hotel **31**
Channings Hotel **10**
The Edinburgh Residence **4**
41 Heriot Row **13**
George Inter-Continental **24**
Greenside Hotel **37**
Howard Hotel **20**
Jarvis Ellersly
 Country House Hotel **3**
The Malmaison **35**
19 St. Bernard's Crescent **15**
Nova Hotel **1**
Point Hotel **2**
Roxburghe Hotel **11**
7 Danube Street **15**
17 Abercromby Place **21**
Sheraton Grand
 Hotel & Spa **5**
Teviotdale House **42**
Thrums Private Hotel **40**
Walton Hotel **19**

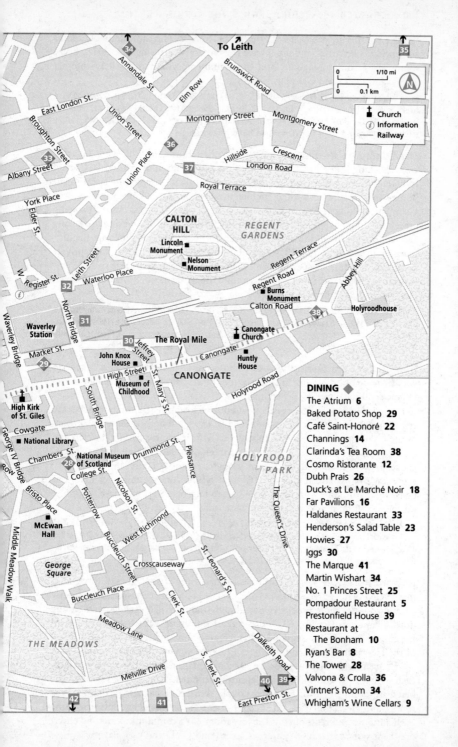

To Leith

Brunswick Road

Annandale St.
Elm Row
East London St.
Union Street
Broughton Street
Montgomery Street
Montgomery Street

| 34 | | 35 |

| 0 | 1/10 mi |
| 0 | 0.1 km |

† Church
ⓘ Information
— Railway

Albany Street
Union Place
Hillside Crescent
London Road

| 33 | | 36 |
| 37 |

York Place
Royal Terrace

Elder St.
W. Register St.
Leith Street
North Bridge

CALTON HILL
Lincoln Monument
Nelson Monument

REGENT GARDENS

Regent Terrace
Abbey Hill

Waterloo Place
Regent Road
Burns Monument
Calton Road

| 32 |

Waverley Station

| 31 |
| 30 |

Jeffrey Street
Canongate
† Canongate Church
Huntly House
Holyroodhouse

| 38 |

The Royal Mile

John Knox House
High Street
St. Mary's St.
CANONGATE
Museum of Childhood
Holyrood Road

Market St.

| 29 |

Waverley Bridge

† High Kirk of St. Giles

Cowgate
National Library

South Bridge

Chambers St.
National Museum of Scotland
College St.
Drummond St.

| 28 |

HOLYROOD PARK

George IV Bridge
Bristo Place
Potterrow
Nicolson St.
Pleasance

McEwan Hall

West Richmond

George Square

Buccleuch Street
Crosscauseway

St. Leonard's St.

The Queen's Drive

Buccleuch Place

Middle Meadow Walk

Clerk St.

Meadow Lane

THE MEADOWS

Melville Drive

S. Clerk St.

Dalkeith Road

| 40 | 39 |

| 42 | | 41 |

East Preston St.

DINING ◆

The Atrium **6**
Baked Potato Shop **29**
Café Saint-Honoré **22**
Channings **14**
Clarinda's Tea Room **38**
Cosmo Ristorante **12**
Dubh Prais **26**
Duck's at Le Marché Noir **18**
Far Pavilions **16**
Haldanes Restaurant **33**
Henderson's Salad Table **23**
Howies **27**
Iggs **30**
The Marque **41**
Martin Wishart **34**
No. 1 Princes Street **25**
Pompadour Restaurant **5**
Prestonfield House **39**
Restaurant at
  The Bonham **10**
Ryan's Bar **8**
The Tower **28**
Valvona & Crolla **36**
Vintner's Room **34**
Whigham's Wine Cellars **9**

standard rooms are a bit cheaper but much smaller. The most desirable rooms are labeled "Executive" and often have bay windows and wingback chairs. Every room has a communications and entertainment system that offers Internet access, and DVD and CD players.

South Learmonth Gardens 15, Edinburgh EH4 1EZ. ⓒ **01313/152226.** Fax 01313/329631. www.channings. co.uk. 48 units. £170 ($272) double; £250 ($400). Rates include breakfast. Children ages 14 and under £25 ($40) extra. AE, DC, MC, V. Bus: 18, 19, 41, or 81. **Amenities:** 2 restaurants; bar; 24-hr. room service; laundry service; dry cleaning. *In room:* TV/DVD, dataport, hair dryer, coffeemaker, iron.

The Edinburgh Residence ★★★   If Robert Burns, who liked his luxuries, were checking into a hotel in Edinburgh today, he no doubt would be booked in here. It's one of the finest luxury hotels in Scotland, a series of elegant townhouse suites installed in a trio of architecturally beautiful and sensitively restored Georgian buildings. As you enter, grand staircases and classic wood paneling greet you. A stay here is like finding lodging in an elegant town house from long ago, although with all the modern conveniences. Accommodations are the ultimate in local comfort, with a trio of classic suites having their own private entrances. All units are spacious, and even the smallest are the same size as a tennis court. The Grand Suites and Townhouse Apartments offer sofa or pull-down beds that can accommodate extra people.

7 Rothesay Terrace, Edinburgh EH3 7RY. ⓒ **01312/263380.** Fax 01312/263381. www.theedinburghresidence. com. 29 units. £150–£265 ($240–$424) suite; £260–£395 ($416–$632) apt. Rates include continental breakfast. AE, MC, V. Free parking. Bus: 19 or 37. **Amenities:** Meals (24-hr. room service only); honesty bar in the drawing room. *In room:* TV/DVD, minibar, hair dryer, iron/ironing board, microwave, CD player.

George Inter-Continental ★★★   This is one of the three so-called Victorian *grandes dames* of Edinburgh. It lacks the style of the Balmoral, but maintains a lead in grace and style over the Caledonian.

Designed by famed Robert Adam and only yards from St. Andrew Square, the city's financial center, the George opened in 1755 and housed the trading room of the Caledonian Insurance Company in 1845. It became a hotel in 1950 and a new wing was added in 1972. The public rooms have retained the style, elegance, and old-fashioned comfort of those in a country house. In various sizes, the guest rooms have undergone frequent refurbishments and offer luxurious beds, and bathrooms with robes. The best rooms, opening onto views, are those on the fourth floor and above in the new wing.

19–21 George St., Edinburgh EH2 2PB. ⓒ **800/327-0200** in the U.S., or 01312/251251. Fax 01312/265644. www.interconti.com. 195 units. £190–£275 ($304–$440) double; from £460 ($736) suite. AE, DC, MC, V. Bus: 41 or 42. **Amenities:** 2 restaurants; bar; nearby gym; 24-hr. room service; babysitting; laundry service; dry cleaning. *In room:* TV w/pay movies, minibar, hair dryer, safe.

Howard Hotel ★★ *(Finds*   This oasis of charm and class—actually, three landmark Georgian terrace houses (ca. 1770–1825) that have been cleverly combined—is a more expensive and slightly more refined version of its sibling hotel Channings (see above), and is one of Edinburgh's finest hotels. Some of the aura of a private house remains in each of the buildings. Service is a hallmark of the Howard, with a dedicated butler tending to your needs, even unpacking your luggage should you so desire. Accommodations are midsize to spacious, each individually and somewhat elegantly decorated. The hotel has some of the best bathrooms in town, featuring double showers or Jacuzzis in many of the rooms, and Floris toiletries. The decor is a mix of traditional and modern, using both antiques and reproductions. Every room has a communications and entertainment system that offers Internet access, and DVD and CD players.

34 Great King St., Edinburgh EH3 6QH. ☎ **01315/573500.** Fax 01315/576515. www.thehoward.com. 18 units. £180–£275 ($288–$440) double; £270–£475 ($432–$760) suite. Rates include breakfast. AE, DC, MC, V. Bus: 13, 23, 27, or C5. **Amenities:** Bar; 24-hr. room service; access to nearby fitness center; babysitting; laundry service; dry cleaning. *In room:* TV/DVD, dataport, hair dryer.

Roxburghe Hotel ⋆   Originally a stately Robert Adam town house, the hotel stands on a tree-filled square that's a short walk from Princes Street. In 1999, it opened a new wing, more than doubling the original size of the hotel. The old wing maintains a traditional atmosphere with ornate ceilings and woodwork, antique furnishings, and tall arched windows. The new wing offers top hotel comfort, completely contemporary styling, and up-to-date furnishings.

38 Charlotte Square, Edinburgh EH2 4HG.☎ **01312/405500.** Fax 01312/202518. www.macdonaldhotels. co.uk. 197 units. £90–£190 ($144–$304) double; from £200 ($320) suite. Children ages 13 and under stay free in parent's room. AE, DC, MC, V. Parking £8.50 ($14). Bus: 100. **Amenities:** 2 restaurants; 2 bars; pool; gym; sauna; 24-hr. room service; babysitting; laundry service; dry cleaning. *In room:* TV, minibar, coffeemaker, hair dryer, safe.

Sheraton Grand Hotel & Spa ⋆⋆   This elegant hotel, in a postmodern complex on a former railway siding, a short walk from Princes Street, is the most appealing modern hotel in the capital. If you seek Victorian grandeur, make it the Caledonian. But if you'd like to be in the "new Edinburgh" (a financial center called the Exchange), then make it the Sheraton Grand. The hotel has more of international flavor than its rival, the Balmoral. And, if luxurious pampering is your aim, the hotel's One Spa has been acclaimed as one of the best in Britain.

The Sheraton still pays homage to Scotland in its excessive use of tartans to cover everything. Rooms may lack character, but they are exceedingly comfortable, with Queen Anne cherrywood reproductions and bathrooms with robes and slippers. The best units are called "Castle View," and they are on the top three floors.

1 Festival Sq., Edinburgh, Lothian EH3 9SR. ☎ **800/325-3535** in the U.S. and Canada, or 01312/299131. Fax 01312/284510. www.sheraton.com 260 units. June–Sept £190–£260 ($304–$416) double; from £300 ($480) suite. Off season £115 ($184) double, £215 ($344) suite. Children ages 16 and under stay free in parent's room. AE, DC, MC, V. Bus: 4, 15, or 44. **Amenities:** 4 restaurants; 2 bars; indoor heated pool; "One" health club; spa; 24-hr. room service; laundry service; dry cleaning. *In room:* A/C, TV w/pay movies, dataport, minibar, hair dryer, safe, trouser press.

MODERATE

41 Heriot Row ⋆ *Finds*   This stone-fronted town house dates from 1817. Today, it's the home of Scottish-French Erlend and Hélène Clouston, who make an event out of breakfasts and are especially proud of the fenced-in-rectangular park across the street (guests can gain access to it); its decorative pond is said to have inspired Robert Louis Stevenson while he was writing *Treasure Island*. A highlight of the house is the impressive wide hallway, at one end of which rises a baronial light-flooded staircase. The furnishings are attractive and upscale, with unusual paintings and prints, exposed flagstone floors, and antique rugs and furnishings. The guest rooms have brass headboards and unusual books, some by writer/journalist Erlend.

41 Heriot Row, Edinburgh EH3 6ES. ☎/fax **01312/253113.** www.edinburghaccommodation.org.uk. 2 units. £95–£110 ($152–$176) double with bathroom. No credit cards. Bus: 4. **Amenities:** Breakfast room. *In room:* No phone.

19 St. Bernard's Crescent   One of the city's most appealing guest houses occupies the grand home of William Balfour, owner of Edinburgh's Theatre School of Dance and Drama. It was built as an architectural showplace in the early 1800s by the son of Sir Henry Raeburn, one of Scotland's most prominent portraitists. It has grand Doric pillars, a magnificent sandstone staircase that pivots upward around a circular stairwell, and a distinguished collection of 18th- and 19th-century furniture. Guests enjoy access to the salons and sitting rooms (site of a grand piano). The guest rooms are midsize and comfortably appointed, often with four-poster beds, and have shower-only bathrooms. You'll feel as if you're visiting the house of your favorite aunt. Smoking is not permitted.

19 St. Bernard's Crescent, Edinburgh EH4 1NR. ℂ/fax **01313/326162**. balfourwm@aol.com. 3 units. £100 ($160) double. Rates include continental or full Scottish breakfast. MC, V. Bus: 24 or 34. **Amenities:** Breakfast room. *In room:* TV, coffeemaker, hair dryer, iron/ironing board, no phone.

Point Hotel   With one of the most dramatic contemporary interiors of any hotel in Edinburgh, this is a stylish place in the shadow of Edinburgh Castle. The decor has appeared in a book detailing the 50 premier hotel designs in the world, with a great emphasis on color and innovation, including a black stone floor at the front that's marked by "dusty footprints." In one place red neon spots blue walls in different shades of brilliant light to create an optical fantasy. Sometimes for a dramatic minimalist effect, a lone armchair and sofa will occupy 1,000 square feet of space. Bedrooms are attractively furnished. Most of the guest rooms offer views of the castle; however, those in the rear do not, so be duly warned. If you like stainless steel, laser projections, and chrome instead of Scottish antiques, this might be an address for you. Standard rooms are a bit small; the Executive rooms offer king-size beds and are more comfortable and spacious.

34 Bread St., Edinburgh EH3 9AF. ℂ **01312/215555**. Fax 01312/219929. 136 units. Summer £105–£160 ($168–$256) double, £350 ($560) suite; off season £68–£88 ($109–$141) double, £115 ($184) suite. Rates include English breakfast. AE, DC, MC, V. Bus: 4 or 31. **Amenities:** Restaurant; bar; room service; laundry service; dry cleaning. *In room:* TV, hair dryer, iron.

17 Abercromby Place ⭑   Eirlys Lloyd runs this fine B&B, a 5-minute walk north of Princes Street. The five-story gray stone terrace house was home in the 1820s to William Playfair, who designed many of Edinburgh's most visible landmarks, including the Royal Scottish Academy and Surgeon Hall of the Royal College of Surgeons. Rooms vary in size, but all are acceptable with king- or queen-size beds. Two rooms are in what was originally conceived as a mews house (living quarters adapted from stables). The entire property is nonsmoking.

17 Abercromby Place, Edinburgh EH3 6LB. ℂ **01315/578036**. Fax 01315/583453. www.abercromby house.com. 10 units. £90–£130 ($144–$208) double. Rates include breakfast. MC, V. Free parking. Bus: 15 or 100. **Amenities:** Meals arranged. *In room:* TV, dataport, coffeemaker, hair dryer.

INEXPENSIVE

A Haven *(Kids)*   This semi-detached 1862 Victorian house is a 15-minute walk or 5-minute bus ride north of the rail station. Rooms are of various sizes (the biggest on the 2nd floor). Some in back overlook the Firth of Forth, and those in the front open onto views of Arthur's Seat. Moira and Ronnie Murdock extend a Scottish welcome in this family-type place, and often advise guests about sightseeing. Two well-decorated rooms with marble bathrooms are located in a lodge at the back of the house. Cots and family rooms are available and children can play in the park opposite the hotel.

180 Ferry Rd., Edinburgh EH6 4NS. ℂ **01315/546559**. Fax 01315/545252. www.a-haven.co.uk. 14 units. £50–£100 ($80–$160) double. Rates include breakfast. AE, MC, V. Free parking. Bus: 1, 6, 7, 25, C3, 17, 14A, or 25A. **Amenities:** Bar; babysitting; laundry service; dry cleaning. *In room:* TV, coffeemaker, hair dryer, trouser press.

Greenside Hotel   This 1786 Georgian house is furnished with antiques to give it the right spirit. There are singles, doubles, twins, and three family rooms, all centrally heated and all with private bathrooms with showers. Rooms, last refurbished in 1998, open onto views of a private garden or the Firth of Forth and are so large that 10 of them contain a double bed and two singles.

9 Royal Terrace, Edinburgh EH7 5AB. ℂ/fax **01315/570022**. www.townhousehotels.co.uk 15 units. £46–£92 ($74–$147) double. Rates include breakfast. AE, DC, MC, V. Bus: 4, 15, or 44. **Amenities:** Meals arranged; bar; lounge area. *In room:* TV, coffeemaker, hair dryer.

7 Danube Street ✦ This B&B is in Stockbridge, a quiet, stylish residential neighborhood a 10-minute walk north of the city center. It's the 1825 home of Fiona Mitchell-Rose and her husband, Colin. The establishment is proud of its charmingly decorated rooms that reflect Fiona's experience as a decorator in London. Rooms look out onto the sloping garden. The most desirable has a four-poster bed, a tub-shower combo, and direct garden access. The remaining shower-only bathrooms have perfumed soaps and shampoos, adapters, and nail files. You're likely to meet your hosts and other guests in the formal dining room in the morning, where the lavish breakfast is inspired by Scotland's old-fashioned agrarian tradition. The entire house is nonsmoking.

7 Danube St., Edinburgh EH4 1NN. ℂ **01313/322755**. Fax 01313/433648. www.aboutedinburgh.com/ danube.html. 5 units. £90–£110 ($144–$176) double. Rates include breakfast. MC, V. Free parking nearby. Bus: 28. **Amenities:** Babysitting; laundry service; complimentary whisky. *In room:* TV, coffeemaker, hair dryer.

Walton Hotel ✦ *Finds* A real discovery, this little hotel is just a few minutes walk from Princes Street, in a well-restored 200-year-old town house. A complete refurbishment and renovation has maintained the essential Georgian character and elegant features, but have revitalized and modernized the entire hotel. Bedrooms are midsize, cozy, comfortable, and tranquil. In the morning you're served a superior breakfast. Smoking is not permitted on premises.

79 Dundas St., Edinburgh EH3 6SD. ℂ **01315/561137**. Fax 01315/578367. www.waltonhotel.com. Summer £75 ($120) double; off season £45 ($72) double. Rates include breakfast. MC, V. Bus: 23 or 27. **Amenities:** Breakfast lounge. *In room:* TV, beverage maker, hair dryer.

WEST OF THE CENTER
EXPENSIVE

Jarvis Ellersly Country House Hotel ✦ Standing inside walled gardens, this three-story Edwardian country house offers the privacy of a home. It's in a dignified west-end residential section near the Murrayfield rugby grounds, about a 5-minute ride from the center, and is one of Edinburgh's best expensively priced hotels. The well-equipped rooms vary in size and are in either the main house or in a less desirable annex. After recent refurbishments, the hotel is better than ever, and service is first-class.

4 Ellersly Rd., Edinburgh EH12 6HZ. ℂ **01313/376888**. Fax 01313/132543. www.jarvis.co.uk. 57 units. £139 ($209) double; £154 ($231) suite. AE, DC, MC, V. Free parking. Bus: 2, 2A, 21, 26, 31, 36, 36A. Take A-8 4km (2½ miles) west of the city center. **Amenities:** Restaurant; wine cellar; room service; laundry service; valet. *In room:* TV, hair dryer.

SOUTH OF THE CENTER
MODERATE

Nova Hotel *Kids* The Nova, an 1875 Victorian, is situated on a quiet cul-de-sac that's a 10-minute ride from the center, with a view over Brunsfield Links in front and the Pentland Hills in back. It's within walking distance of the Royal Mile and Princes Street. You'll find its guest rooms large and well appointed, with shower-only bathrooms. On the ground floors, guests enjoy the lounge that also operates as a cocktail bar. Two family rooms are roomy enough for six and offer kitchens.

5 Brunsfield Crescent, Edinburgh EH10 4EZ. ⓒ **01314/476437.** Fax 01314/528126. www.novahotel.co.uk. 12 units. £70–£90 ($112–$144) double; £110–£140 ($176–$224) family room for up to 6. AE, MC, V. Bus: 42 or 46. **Amenities:** Bar; lounge. *In room:* TV, coffeemaker, hair dryer.

Teviotdale House ★★ *Value* Some visitors rate this three-story 1848 house— 10 minutes by bus from Princes Street, Waverley Station, and Edinburgh Castle— as the finest B&B in Edinburgh. Elizabeth and Willy Thiebaud's attention to detail has earned them an enviable reputation. The house is completely non-smoking and is furnished with antiques. The three largest can accommodate families with up to four beds. The home-cooked breakfast may be the highlight of your day's dining and can include smoked salmon, kippers, and home-baked bread and scones. It's a great value!

Grange Loan, Edinburgh EH9 2ER. ⓒ/fax **01316/674763.** 7 units. £56–£90 ($90–$144). AE, MC, V. Bus: 42. *In room:* TV, coffeemaker, hair dryer.

Thrums Private Hotel *(Kids* About 1.5km (1 mile) south of Princes Street, Thrums is a pair of connected antique buildings, one a two-story 1820 Georgian and the other a small inn (ca. 1900). This hotel takes its name from J. M. Barrie's fictional name for his hometown of Kirriemuir. Barrie is known to children as the author of *Peter Pan*. The family-friendly hotel contains recently refurbished high-ceilinged guest rooms with firm mattresses and contemporary (in the inn) or reproduction antique (in the Georgian) furnishings. Each unit comes with a small but neatly organized shower-only bathroom. Kids are made especially welcome here and are housed in family rooms with their parents. The bistro-inspired Thrums restaurant serves set-price menus of British food, and there's also a peaceful garden.

14–15 Minto St., Edinburgh EH9 1RQ. ⓒ **01316/675545.** Fax 01316/678707. www.thrumshoteledinburgh.com. 14 units. £75–£95 ($120–$152) double; £95–£125 ($152–$200) family room. Rates include breakfast. MC, V. Free parking. Bus: 3, 7, 8, or 31. **Amenities:** Restaurant; bar. *In room:* TV, coffeemaker, hair dryer.

IN LEITH

The satellite neighborhood of Leith was once run-down, but it's now a hip, up-and-coming area.

EXPENSIVE

The Malmaison ★ *(Finds* This is the most interesting hotel in Edinburgh's dockyard district, a few steps from Leith Water. In the 1990s, it was converted from an 1883 seamen's mission/dorm and is capped by a stately stone clock tower. Its owners have created a hip, unpretentious hotel with a postmodern minimalist decor. The color schemes vary by floor; the purple-and-beige floor has been favored by rock bands, who have stayed here during concert tours. Each average-sized room has a CD player, plus a bathroom with deluxe toiletries and a tub-and-power-shower combo. The amenities and facilities are sparse, but you'll find a high-tech fitness center and a cafe/wine bar favored by locals.

1 Tower Place, Leith, Edinburgh EH6 7DB. ⓒ **01315/556868.** Fax 01314/685002. www.malmaison.com. 60 units. £125–£135 ($200–$216) double; £160 ($256) suite. AE, DC, MC, V. Free parking. Bus: 16 or 22. **Amenities:** Restaurant; bar. *In room:* TV, minibar, coffeemaker, hair dryer, CD player.

4 Where to Dine

Rivaled only by Glasgow, Edinburgh boasts the finest restaurants in Scotland, and the choice is more diverse at the millennium than ever before. Even if you don't care for some of the more exotic regional fare, like *haggis* (spicy intestines), you'll find an array of top French dining rooms along with other foreign fare, especially Indian. And you'll find more and more restaurants catering to vegetarians. But we advise you go native and sample many of the dishes Edinburgh is known for doing best, especially fresh salmon and seafood, game from Scottish fields, and Aberdeen Angus steaks. What's the rage at lunch? Stuffed potatoes (baked potatoes with a variety of stuffings). Many Scots make a lunch out of just one of these.

Some restaurants have sections reserved for nonsmokers and others don't. If smoking and dining (or nonsmoking and dining) are very important to you, inquire when making your reservation.

Note: For the locations of the restaurants below, see the "Edinburgh Accommodations & Dining" map on p. 478–479.

IN THE CENTER: THE NEW TOWN
EXPENSIVE

The Atrium ✦ MODERN SCOTTISH/INTERNATIONAL   Since 1993, this is one of the most emulated restaurants in Edinburgh. No more than 60 diners can be accommodated in the "deliberately moody" atmosphere that's a fusion of Argentinean hacienda and stylish Beverly Hills bistro. Flickering oil lamps create shadows on the dark-colored walls while patrons enjoy dishes prepared by chef Alan Metheison. Although offerings vary according to the inspiration of the chef and his manager, our favorites include grilled salmon or roasted sea bass. The latter comes with Dauphinoise potatoes, baby spinach, charcoal-grilled eggplant, and baby fennel. Whether it's game or lamb from the Scottish Highlands, dishes have taste, style, and flair. The desserts are equally superb, especially the lemon tart with berry soulis and crème fraîche.

10 Cambridge St. (beneath Saltire Court). © **01312/288882.** Reservations recommended. Fixed-price meal £15–£18 ($24–$29) at lunch; main courses £15–£19 ($24–$30) at dinner. AE, DC, MC, V. Mon–Fri noon–2pm and 6:30–10pm; Sat 6:30–10pm. Closed for 1 week at Christmas.

Channings ✦ SCOTTISH/INTERNATIONAL   The main dining room of a an Edwardian charmer of a hotel (p. 477), it offers traditional decor and elegant service from a well-trained staff. The exemplary cuisine is created by head chef Richard Glennie and his first-class team, who let natural flavors shine through and use superior-quality fresh Scottish ingredients. The chef knows, for example, to go to the "Baines of Tarves" for his free-range Aberdeen chickens or to Iain Mellis for his cheese. The lunch menu provides a varied assortment of choices, including roasted monkfish tail on a white bean and smoked bacon cassoulet. For dinner, you might opt for such delights as a saddle of rabbit with prunes, cured ham, and a thyme *jus*; or else a good-tasting turbot with Dauphinoise potatoes, roasted *salsify* (oyster plant), and a light chicken *jus* and parsley oil. The restaurant is proud of its extensive wine list, which incorporates the old standards and newer, more exciting choices.

In addition to the formal dining room, there is a less formal brasserie with a log fireplace and a casual, relaxed atmosphere where you can enjoy bar meals, light lunches, and dinners.

In Channings Hotel, 15 S. Learmonth Gardens. © **01313/152225.** Reservations recommended. Fixed-price lunch £16 ($26) for 2 courses, £19 ($30) for 3 courses. AE, MC, V. Tues–Sat noon–3:30pm and 7–10pm; Sun 7–10pm. Closed Dec 26–29. Bus: 41 or 42.

Cosmo Ristorante ✦ ITALIAN   Even after more than 30 years in business, Cosmo is still one of the most popular Italian restaurants in town, where courtesy, efficiency, and good cooking draw in the crowds. In season, you can ask for mussels as an appetizer, and the soups and pastas are always reliable (the cost and size of your pasta portion are doubled if you order it as a main course). The kitchen is known for its *saltimbocca* (veal with ham) and Italian-inspired preparations of fish. This isn't the greatest Italian dining in Britain, but you'll certainly have a good, filling meal.

58A N. Castle St. ℂ **01312/266743.** Reservations required. Main courses £15–£22 ($23–$35). AE, MC, V. Mon–Fri 12:30–2:15pm; Mon–Sat 7–10:45pm. Bus: 31 or 33.

The Marque ⭐ MODERN SCOTTISH/INTERNATIONAL The Marque is ideally located for the theater and offers reasonably priced pre- and post-theater dinners. Owned and operated by Lara Kearney, John Rutter, and Glyn Stevens, all formerly of the Atrium, this is a fast-growing, popular place. The bold yellow walls and black-and-white chessboard floor give this converted antiques shop a unique, contemporary look. The cuisine is ambitious and seductive. The professionals who run this place know flavor and seek out the finest ingredients at the market. Main courses include breast of duck, halibut roasted in olive oil, chargrilled tuna, and chicken and fois gras terrine with onion jam. The rhubarb crumble with tamarind ice cream or white, dark, and milk chocolate terrine with caramel ice cream is a great way to end an enjoyable meal.

19–21 Causewayside. ℂ **01314/666660.** Reservations recommended. Main courses £12–£17 ($18–$27); set-price lunch and pre- and posttheater dinner £12–£14 ($18–$22) for 2 courses. AE, MC, V. Tues–Thurs 11:45am–2pm and 5:30–10pm; Fri 11:45am–2pm and 5:30–11pm; Sat noon–2pm and 5:30–11pm. Bus: 42.

No. 1 Princes Street ⭐ SCOTTISH/CONTINENTAL This intimate, crimson-colored enclave is the premier restaurant in the Balmoral Hotel. The walls are studded with Scottish memorabilia in formal, yet sporting patterns. This is very much the grand-style hotel dining room, and it offers good food if you don't mind paying high prices. You can sample the likes of pan-seared Isle of Skye monkfish with saffron mussel broth; roulade of Dover sole with langoustine, oyster, and scallop garnish; or grilled filet of Scottish beef served with Bourguignonne sauce. For dessert you can have a variety of sorbets, British cheeses, or something more exotic, such as mulled wine parfait with a cinnamon sauce. There's a separate vegetarian menu and a wide-ranging wine list with celestial tariffs.

In the Balmoral Hotel, 1 Princes St. ℂ **01315/562414.** Reservations recommended. Main courses £20–£23 ($31–$37); fixed-price lunch £15 ($23) for 2 courses; £39 ($62) for 3-course dinner; fixed-price 6-course dinner £53 ($84). AE, DC, MC, V. Sun–Thurs 7–10pm; Fri–Sat 7–10:30pm.

Pompadour Restaurant ⭐⭐ SCOTTISH/FRENCH On the mezzanine of the Caledonian Hotel, the Pompadour is one of Edinburgh's best, serving fine Scottish and French cuisine. The restaurant has been refurbished in a Louis XV decor—after all, it bears the name of his mistress. The chef blends cuisine moderne with traditional menus, and his daily menu reflects the best available from the market, with Scottish salmon, venison, and other game often included. The menu also features fresh produce from local and French markets—items such as goose liver with wild mushrooms, lamb filet with spinach and rosemary, and charlotte of marinated salmon filled with seafood. The wine list is lethally expensive, with bottles from the New World strangely absent.

In the Caledonian Hilton, Princes St. ℂ **01312/228888.** Reservations required. Fixed-price lunch menu £16–£19 ($25–$30); main courses £15–£25 ($24–$40). AE, DC, MC, V. Tues–Fri 12:30–2pm; Tues–Sat 7:30–9:30pm. Bus: 4, 15, or 44.

Oh, Give It a Try!

Haggis, the much-maligned national dish of Scotland, is certainly an acquired taste. But you've come all this way—why not be brave and give it a try? **Macsween of Edinburgh Haggis** is a long-established family business specializing in haggis. Macsween haggis includes lamb, beef, oatmeal, onions, and a special blend of seasonings and spices cooked together. There's also a vegetarian version. Both are sold in vacuum-packed plastic bags that require only reheating in a microwave or regular oven.

You can find this company's product at food stores and supermarkets throughout Edinburgh. Two central distributors are **Peckham's Delicatessen,** 155–159 Bruntsfield Place (© **01312/297054**), open daily from 8am to midnight, and **Jenner's Department Store,** 2 East Princes St. (© **01312/602242**), open Monday through Saturday from 9am to 6pm and Sunday from noon to 5pm.

MODERATE

Café Saint-Honoré FRENCH/SCOTTISH   Between Frederick and Hanover Streets, this is a French-inspired bistro with a dinner format that's much more formal and expensive than its deliberately rapid lunchtime venue. The menu is completely revised each day, based on what's fresh in the market and whatever the chefs feel inspired to cook. An upbeat and usually enthusiastic staff serves a combination of Scottish and French cuisine that includes venison with juniper berries and wild mushrooms, local pheasant in wine and garlic sauce, or lamb kidneys with broad beans inspired by the cuisine of the region around Toulouse. The fish is very fresh.

34 N.W. Thistle St. Lane. © **01312/262211**. Reservations recommended. Main courses £8–£24 ($13–$38) at lunch; fixed-price meal £16–£30 ($26–$48) at dinner. AE, DC, MC, V. Mon–Fri noon–2:15pm; Mon–Fri (pretheater meal) 5:30–7pm; Mon–Sat 7–10pm and sometimes 11pm. Bus: 3, 16, 17, 23, 27, or 31.

Duck's at Le Marché Noir ✮ FRENCH/SCOTTISH   The cuisine here is more stylish, and more attuned to the culinary sophistication of London than many other restaurants in Edinburgh. Set within a wood house whose outside and inside are both decorated in shades of dark green, its handful of dishes honor the traditions of Scotland. (An example is its baked haggis in phyllo pastry on a bed of turnip puree and red-wine sauce.) More modern dishes include seared salmon with leeks, asparagus, zucchini, and a pickled ginger and sesame salad; and roasted rack of lamb with thyme juice and roasted vegetables.

2/4 Eyre Place. © **01315/581608**. Reservations recommended. Dinner main courses £12–£20 ($18–$31). AE, DC, MC, V. Mon–Sat noon–2:30pm and 7–9:30pm. Bus: 23 or 27.

Haldanes Restaurant ✮ SCOTTISH   Set in the cellar of the Albany Hotel building, within a pair of royal blue and gold-tinted dining rooms, Haldanes features the cuisine of George Kelso. During clement weather, the venue moves into the building's verdant garden. Dinners are conducted like meals at a private country house manor, with polite and deferential service. George applies a light touch to dishes he cooks with innovation and style. Menu items include a traditional haggis in phyllo pastry with *tatties* (roasted turnips) and whisky sauce; pan-fried crab cakes with a tomato and spring onion salsa; and a pavé of lamb with mint-flavored herb crust, wild mushrooms, and zucchini. For dessert, try the caramelized lemon tarte with crème fraîche.

39A Albany St. ⓒ 01315/568407. Reservations recommended. Main courses £8.50–£12 ($14–$18). AE, DC, MC, V. Daily noon–1:30pm and 6–9:30pm. Bus: 15.

Restaurant at The Bonham ★★ SCOTTISH/INTERNATIONAL   The setting at one of Edinburgh's most charming restaurants combines the building's 19th-century oak paneling and deep ceiling coves with modern paintings, oversize mirrors, and high-tech lighting. Lunch is a bit simpler than dinner, offering such choices as delightful roast duck with apple-flavored mayonnaise and toasted brioche, followed by navarin of lamb in tomato-garlic sauce with mashed potatoes. Dinner is a tour de force, offering a sophisticated blend of ingredients. For a main course, opt for such delights as baked pave of salmon flavored with a lemon zest or prosciutto-wrapped chicken supreme with a sauce made of lime leaves. Save some room for a small but sublime list of desserts, likely to include a hot orange and caramon soufflé or a dark chocolate fondant.

In The Bonham Hotel, 35 Drumsheugh Gardens. ⓒ 01316/239319. Reservations recommended. Main courses £15–£19 ($24–$30). AE, DC, MC, V. Daily 12:30–2:30pm and 6:30–10pm. Bus: 23 or 27.

The Tower ★★ SEAFOOD/MODERN BRITISH   This is the town's hot new dining ticket set at the top of the Museum of Scotland. The chef uses local ingredients to create some of the capital's tastiest fare. The inventive kitchen will regale you with hearty portions of some of the finest steak and roast beef dishes along with excellent and freshly caught seafood. Dig into an array of oysters, lobsters, and platters with a mixed seafood medley. We still remember fondly the smoked haddock risotto with a poached egg and shavings of Parmesan cheese. A sea bass was perfectly seasoned and grilled; there's even sushi on the menu. Scottish loin of lamb is given a modern twist with a side dish of minted couscous.

In the Museum of Scotland, Chambers St. ⓒ 01312/253003. Reservations required. Lunch main courses £9–£18 ($14–$29). Dinner main courses £14–£25 ($22–$40). AE, DC, MC, V. Daily noon–11pm. Bus: 3, 7, 21, 30, 31, 53, 69, or 80.

INEXPENSIVE

Far Pavilions INDIAN/CONTINENTAL   Established in 1987, this Indian restaurant offers finely tuned service. You might appreciate a drink in the bar

---

ⓘ Tips Tea for Two

If you're looking for a bit of refreshment while sightseeing, try **Clarinda's Tea Room,** 69 Canongate (ⓒ **01315/571888**), for the very British experience of afternoon tea. This cubbyhole of a tearoom is only steps from Holyroodhouse and decorated in the manner you'd expect, with lace tablecloths, bone china, and antique Wedgwood plates on the walls. There are plenty of teas from which to choose, plus a long list of tempting sweets. Homemade soup, lasagna, baked potatoes with cheese, salads, and similar dishes are also offered. It's open Monday through Saturday from 9am to 4:45pm and Sunday from 10am to 4:45pm.

Another choice is **Ryan's Bar,** 2 Hope St. (ⓒ **01312/266669**), near the northwestern corner of the West Princes Street Gardens. It serves tea daily from 10:30am to 1am. If you want a more formal tea ceremony, try the Palm Court at the **Balmoral Hotel,** Princes Street (ⓒ **01315/562414**), serving tea daily from noon to 3pm.

before confronting the long menu with dishes from the former Portuguese colony of Goa and the north Indian province of Punjab. Highly recommended is the house specialty, *murgi masala,* concocted with tandoori chicken that falls off the bone thanks to slow cooking in a garlic-based butter sauce. Menu items include curry dishes influenced by British tastes, as well as authentic platters whose composition is faithful to their original Indian tradition. Most items are suitably pungent and concocted from lamb, seafood, vegetables, and beef.

10 Craighleith Rd., Comely Bank. Ⓒ **01313/323362.** Reservations recommended. Lunch main courses £8–£16 ($13–$26); lunch buffet £6.95 ($11) per person; dinner main courses £8–£16 ($13–$26). AE, MC, V. Mon–Fri noon–2pm; Mon–Sat 5:30pm–midnight. Bus: 19, 39, 55, 81, or X91.

Henderson's Salad Table ★ *Value* VEGETARIAN   This is a Shangri-la for health-food lovers. At this self-service place, you can pick and choose eggs, carrots, grapes, nuts, yogurt, cheese, potatoes, cabbage, watercress—you name it. Hot dishes, such as peppers stuffed with rice and pimiento, are served on request, and a vegetarian twist on the national dish of haggis is usually available. Other well-prepared dishes filled with flavor include vegetable lasagna and a broccoli and cheese crumble. The homemade desserts include a fresh fruit salad or a cake with double-whipped cream and chocolate sauce. The wine cellar offers 30 wines. Live music, ranging from classical to jazz to folk, is played every evening.

94 Hanover St. Ⓒ **01312/252131.** Main courses £4.95–£5.25 ($7.90–$8.40); fixed-price meal at lunch £7.75 ($12); fixed-price meal at dinner £8.50 ($14). AE, MC, V. Mon–Sat 8am–10:30pm. Bus: 23 or 27.

Valvona & Crolla INTERNATIONAL   In 1872, a recent arrival from Italy opened this restaurant, and it's still going strong. It shares space with a delicatessen and food emporium where exotic coffees, Parma ham, Italian cheeses, and breads, as well as takeaway sandwiches and casseroles, are sold. A satellite room, a few steps down from the main shopping area, contains a cafe and luncheon restaurant where food is very fresh and prices refreshingly low. Here, you can order three kinds of breakfasts (continental, Scottish, or vegetarian) for a fixed price of £3.95 ($6.30); or platters of pasta, mixed sausages, and cold cuts; crostini, risottos, and omelets. Don't expect leisurely dining, as the place caters to office workers and shoppers who dash in for midday sustenance, appreciating the informality, low prices, and the freshness of the food.

19 Elm Row. Ⓒ **01315/566066.** Breakfast £3.95–£6.50 ($6.30–$10); pizzas, pastas, or platters £3–£10 ($4.80–$16). AE, DC, MC, V. Cafe with limited food service Mon–Sat 8:30am–5:30pm; full lunch service Mon–Sat noon–2:30pm. Bus: 7, 10, 11, 12, or 14.

Whigham's Wine Cellars SEAFOOD/VEGETARIAN   Whigham's Wine Cellars is in the heart of Edinburgh's financial center. Wine was bottled here in the mid–18th century, and Whigham's used to ship it to the American colonies. Walk across the mellowed stone floors until you find an intimate alcove, where you can make your selection from an assortment of appetizers and *plats du jour* or from the chalkboard specials. The smoked fish (not just salmon) and the fresh oysters from Loch Fyne are exceptional; smoked venison occasionally appears on the menu. A range of international wines is offered.

13 Hope St. Ⓒ **01312/258674.** Reservations recommended. Main courses £6.50–£11 ($10–$18). AE, DC, MC, V. Mon–Thurs noon–midnight; Fri–Sat noon–1am. Bus: 2, 4, or 34.

IN THE CENTER: THE OLD TOWN
MODERATE

Dubh Prais SCOTTISH   Dub Prais (Gaelic for "the black pot") conjures up an image of old-fashioned Scottish recipes bubbling away in a stewpot above a

fireplace. Within dining rooms adorned with stenciled versions of thistles, you'll appreciate the meals prepared by members of the McWilliams family, which composes its menu entirely from Scottish produce and raw ingredients. Menu items are time-tested and not at all experimental, but flavorful nonetheless. Examples include smoked salmon; saddle of venison with juniper sauce; and a supreme of salmon with grapefruit-flavored butter sauce.

123B High St., Royal Mile. ℂ 01315/575732. Reservations recommended. Lunch main courses £6.50–£9.50 ($10–$15); dinner main courses £13–£17 ($20–$26). AE, MC, V. Tues–Fri noon–2pm; Tues–Sat 6–10:30pm. Bus: 11.

Iggs SPANISH/SCOTTISH   Just off the Royal Mile in Old Town, this Victorian-style establishment is the domain of a dynamic chef, Andrew McQueen, who is not afraid to experiment but also seems well grounded in the classics. A dinner here is made more charming by the attention from the staff, clad in black polo shirts. Elegant meals are concocted from the freshest ingredients, often from Scotland. Typical of a dish made from exceptional products with a finely honed technique is the rack of Highland lamb with spring vegetables. If you want to go more exotic, opt for the loin of veal on a truffle and Gruyère risotto given extra flavor by a Madeira sauce. After you think you've had every dessert in the world, along comes a honey-roasted butternut squash cheesecake with a caramel sauce.

15 Jeffrey St. ℂ 01315/578184. Reservations recommended. Main courses £14–£19 ($22–$30); fixed-price lunch £16 ($25) for 3 courses. AE, DC, MC, V. Mon–Sat noon–2:30pm and 6–10:30pm. Bus: 1 or 35.

INEXPENSIVE

Baked Potato Shop *Kids* VEGETARIAN/WHOLE FOOD   This is the least expensive restaurant in a very glamorous neighborhood, and it attracts mobs of office workers every day. It's a great place to take kids as well; they can order flaky baked potatoes with a choice of half a dozen hot fillings along with all sorts of other dishes, including chili and 20 kinds of salads. Many patrons carry their food away. Place your order at the countertop, and it will be served in ecology-conscious recycled cardboard containers. Only free-range eggs, whole foods, and vegetarian cheeses are used. Vegetarian cakes are a specialty.

56 Cockburn St. ℂ 01312/257572. Reservations not accepted. Food items 60p–£3.20 (95¢–$5.10). No credit cards. Daily 9am–9pm (to 10pm in summer). Bus: 5.

Howies *Finds* SCOTTISH   This is an ideal venue for dining if you're antiques-shopping and climbing Victoria Street. This restaurant, which sparked a small chain, has earned its reputation by its use of fresh Scottish produce from vegetables, which are prepared with skill and a certain flair by its kitchen staff. Using the freshest ingredients they can obtain, they produce dishes that are prepared to order. Some of our favorite things are the kitchen's spinach, lemon, and lentil soup, or its parfait of duck liver and smoked bacon with a braised sultana compote. Diners come here in search of such robust dishes as a casserole of Scottish beef with wild mushrooms, shallots, and marjoram, and the chefs will also regale you with their roast duck breast with chargrilled plums and fondant potatoes. Four our finale, we prefer their wonderful selection of Scottish farmhouse cheese served with celery wafers unless you want to dip into their "nursery school" sticky toffee pudding with butterscotch sauce. As desserts go, there's nothing finer than the dark chocolate and Drambuie tart.

10–14 Victoria St. ℂ 01312/251721. Reservations recommended. Fixed-price lunch £7.95–£9.95 ($13–$16); fixed-price dinner £16–£18 ($25–$29) Sun. MC, V. Daily noon–2:30pm and 6–10:30pm. Bus: 1, 34, or 35.

LEITH

In the northern regions of Edinburgh, Leith is the old port town, opening onto the Firth of Forth. Once it was a city in its own right until it (and its harbor facilities) was slowly absorbed into Edinburgh.

EXPENSIVE

Martin Wishart ★★★ MODERN FRENCH   Several gourmet associations claim this is the "Scottish restaurant of the year." The chef/owner Martin Wishart takes it all in stride and continues to improve the quality of his cuisine in a fashionable part of the Leith docklands. With white walls and modern art, the decor is minimalist. The chef knows how to "marry" ingredients, all of which are well chosen for quality and flavor. The menu is short but sweet and always changing, taking advantage of the "best" of any season from sea, air, and field. A gratin of sea bass arrived aromatically with a soft herby crust. Many dishes are simply prepared, the natural flavors coming through. Others show a touch of elegance and fantasy, including partridge breast with black truffle and foie gras or the lobster ravioli with an oyster velouté. After eating the glazed lemon tart with praline ice cream on white raspberry coulis, the day is yours.

54 The Shore, Leith. ✆ 01315/533557. Reservations required. Main courses £19–£24 ($30–$38); set lunch £19 ($30) (3 courses). Tues–Fri noon–2pm; Tues–Thurs 6:30–10pm; Fri–Sat 6:30–10:30pm. Bus: 7 or 10.

MODERATE

Vintner's Room ★ *Finds* FRENCH/SCOTTISH   Join locals and visitors down by the waterfront in Leith. Chances are they are heading to this restaurant. This stone-fronted building was originally constructed around 1650 as a warehouse for barrels of Bordeaux (claret) and port that came in from Europe's mainland. Near the entrance, beneath a venerable ceiling of oaken beams, a wine bar serves platters and drinks beside a large stone fireplace. Most diners, however, head for the small but elegant dining room, illuminated by flickering candles. Here, elaborate Italianate plasterwork decorates a room that functioned 300 years ago as the site of wine auctions. A robust cuisine includes seafood salad with mango mayonnaise, a terrine of pigeon and duck, loin of pork with mustard sauce, and venison in a bitter chocolate sauce.

The Vaults, 87 Giles St., Leith. ✆ 01315/546767. Reservations recommended. Main courses £10–£13 ($16–$21) at lunch; dinner main courses 15–£19 ($23–$30). AE, MC, V. Mon–Sat noon–2pm and 7–10:30pm. Closed 2 weeks at Christmas. Bus: 7 or 10.

IN PRESTONFIELD
EXPENSIVE

Prestonfield House ★★ *Finds* BRITISH   Hidden amidst 23 acres of private parkland and gardens 5km (3 miles) south of Edinburgh's center, this elegant hotel restaurant often hosts locals out to celebrate special occasions. Some kind of manor house has stood here since 1355, but the graceful Dutch-style roof lines of the Jacobean building you see today date from 1687. Highland cattle and peacocks roam the grounds, and inside is an enviable collection of antiques. It's an old-fashioned choice, certainly, but it still offers the same fine quality as always. Menu items include grilled salmon with braised leeks and gazpacho, baked lamb filet in phyllo with tomatoes and wild mushrooms, marinated smoked pigeon with avocado-and-raspberry salad, and venison-and-oyster pie with spring vegetables.

Priestfield Rd., Edinburgh EH16 5UT. ✆ 01316/683346. Reservations preferred. Main courses £15–£20 ($23–$31); table d'hôte menu £19 ($30) lunch. AE, DC, MC, V. Daily noon–2pm and 7–9:30pm. Bus: 2, 14, or 31.

5 Seeing the Sights

SUGGESTED ITINERARY

If You Have 1 Day

Visit **Edinburgh Castle** as soon as it opens in the morning, then walk the **Royal Mile** to the **Palace of Holyroodhouse,** former abode of Mary Queen of Scots. Look out over the city from the vantage point of **Arthur's Seat,** and stroll through **Princes Street Gardens,** capping your day with a walk along the major shopping thoroughfare, Princes Street.

If You Have 2 Days

On the morning of your second day, head for Old Town again, but this time explore its narrow streets, wynds, and closes, and visit the **John Knox House,** the **High Kirk of St. Giles,** and the small museums. After lunch, climb the **Scott Monument** for a good view of Old

Town and the Princes Street Gardens. Spend the rest of the afternoon exploring the **National Gallery of Scotland.**

If You Have 3 Days

Spend Day 3 getting acquainted with the major attractions of New Town, including the **National Museum of Scotland, National Portrait Gallery, Georgian House,** and **Royal Botanic Garden.**

If You Have 4 or 5 Days

On the fourth day, take a trip west to **Stirling Castle** and see some of the dramatic scenery of the Trossachs. On the fifth day you'll feel like a native, so seek out some of the city's minor but interesting attractions, such as the **Camera Obscura,** the **Scotch Whisky Heritage Centre,** and **Dean Village.**

ALONG THE ROYAL MILE

Old Town's **Royal Mile** ✩✩✩ stretches from Edinburgh Castle all the way to the Palace of Holyroodhouse and bears four names along its length: Castlehill, Lawnmarket, High Street, and Canongate. Walking along, you'll see some of the most interesting old structures in the city, with turrets, gables, and towering chimneys. Take bus no. 1, 6, 23, 27, 30, 34, or 36 to reach it.

Edinburgh Castle ✩✩✩   No place in Scotland is filled with as much history, legend, and lore as Edinburgh Castle, one of the highlights of a visit to this little country. It's believed the ancient city grew up on the seat of a dead volcano, Castle Rock. The early history is vague, but it's known that in the 11th century Malcolm III (Canmore) and his Saxon queen, later venerated as St. Margaret, founded a castle on this spot. The only fragment left of their castle—in fact, the oldest structure in Edinburgh—is **St. Margaret's Chapel,** built in the Norman style, the oblong structure dating principally from the 12th century.

You can visit the **State Apartments,** particularly **Queen Mary's Bedroom,** where Mary Queen of Scots gave birth to James VI of Scotland (later James I of England). Scottish Parliaments used to convene in the **Great Hall.** The highlight is the **Crown Chamber,** housing the Honours of Scotland (Scottish Crown Jewels), used at the coronation of James VI, along with the scepter and sword of state of Scotland. The **French Prisons** were put to use in the 18th century, and these great storerooms housed hundreds of Napoleonic soldiers in the early 19th century. Many of them made wall carvings you can see today. Among the batteries of cannons that protected the castle is **Mons Meg,** a 15th-century cannon weighing more than 5 tons.

Castlehill Ⓒ **01312/259846.** Admission £8.50 ($14) adults, £2 ($3.20) children ages 15 and under. Apr–Sept daily 9:30am–5:15pm; Oct–Mar daily 9:30am–4:15pm. Bus: 1 or 6.

Palace of Holyroodhouse ★★ Early in the 16th century, this palace was built by James IV adjacent to an Augustinian abbey David I had established in the 12th century. The nave of the abbey church, now in ruins, still remains, but only the north tower of James's palace is left. Most of what you see was built by Charles II after Scotland and England were united in the 17th century. The palace suffered long periods of neglect, but it basked in glory at the ball thrown by Bonnie Prince Charlie in the mid–18th century, during the peak of his feverish (and doomed) optimism about uniting the Scottish clans in their struggle against the English. Queen Elizabeth II and Prince Philip reside here whenever they visit Edinburgh; when they're not in residence, the palace is open to visitors.

The old wing was the scene of Holyroodhouse's most dramatic incident. Mary Queen of Scots's Italian secretary, David Rizzio, was stabbed 56 times in front of her eyes by her jealous husband, Lord Darnley, and his accomplices. A plaque marks the spot where he died on March 9, 1566. And one of the more curious exhibits is a piece of needlework done by Mary depicting a cat-and-mouse scene (her cousin, Elizabeth I, is the cat).

Highlights of the palace are the oldest surviving section, **King James Tower,** where Mary Queen of Scots lived on the second floor, with Lord Darnley's rooms below. Some of the rich tapestries, paneling, massive fireplaces, and antiques from the 1700s are still in place. The **Throne Room** and other drawing rooms are still used for state occasions. In the rear of the palace is the richly furnished **King's Bedchamber.** The **Picture Gallery** boasts many portraits of Scottish monarchs by Dutch artist Jacob De Witt, who in 1684 signed a contract to turn out one potboiler portrait after another at the rate of one a week for 2 years. However, don't take all the portraits too seriously: Some of these royal figures may have never existed, and the likenesses of some aren't known, so the portraits are from the artist's imagination.

Behind Holyroodhouse begins Edinburgh's largest park, **Holyrood Park.** With rocky crags, a loch, sweeping meadows, and the ruins of a chapel, it's a wee bit of the Scottish countryside in the city. It's a great place for a picnic. If you climb up Holyrood Park you'll come to 250m (823-ft.) high **Arthur's Seat,** from which the view is breathtaking. (The name doesn't refer to King Arthur, as many people assume, but perhaps is a reference to Prince Arthur of Strathclyde or a corruption of *Ard Thor,* the Gaelic for "height of Thor." No one knows for sure.) If you visit on a winter morning, you'll think you're in the heart of the Highlands. Arthur's Seat dates from prehistoric times, and with some difficulty you can trace the remains of a quartet of forts, especially in the Dunsapie Loch and Salisbury Crags district. And you can see clusters of cultivated terraces from the Dark Ages, especially on the east flank of the hill, both above and below Queen's Drive.

Canongate, at the eastern end of the Royal Mile. Ⓒ **01315/567371.** www.royal.gov.uk Admission £7.50 ($12) adults, £6 ($9.60) seniors, £4 ($6.40) children ages 15 and under, £19 ($30) families (up to 2 adults and 2 children). Daily 9:30am–5:15pm. Closed 2 weeks in May and 3 weeks in late June and early July (dates vary). Bus: 1 or 6.

High Kirk of St. Giles Built in 1120, a short walk downhill from Edinburgh Castle, this church is one of the most important architectural landmarks along the Royal Mile. It combines a dark and brooding stone exterior with surprisingly

Edinburgh Attractions

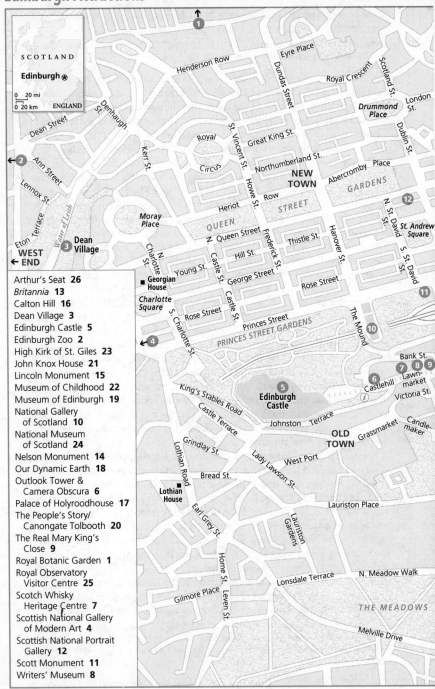

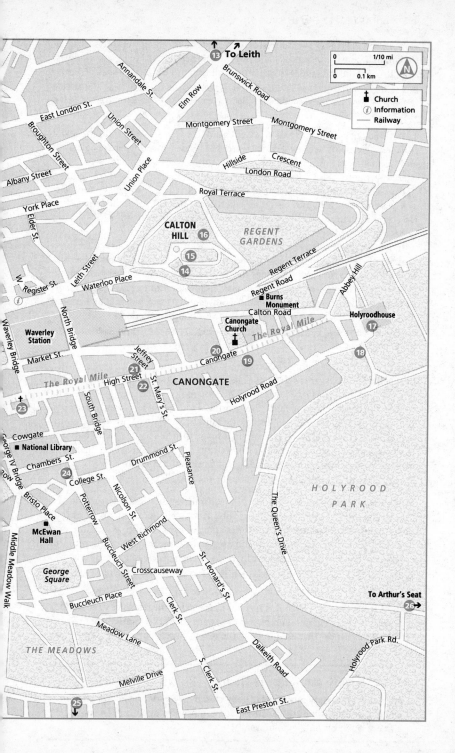

To Leith 13

0   1/10 mi
0   0.1 km

† Church
ⓘ Information
···· Railway

Annandale St.

East London St.

Brunswick Road

Elm Row

Union Street

Broughton Street

Montgomery Street   Montgomery Street

Albany Street

Hillside   Crescent

London Road

Union Place

Royal Terrace

York Place

Elder St.

CALTON
HILL 16

REGENT
GARDENS

15

14

W. Register St.

Leith Street

Waterloo Place

Regent Terrace

Abbey Hill

Regent Road

Burns
Monument

Calton Road

Holyroodhouse

Waverley
Station

North Bridge

Canongate
Church

The Royal Mile

17

Market St.

Jeffrey
Street

20

Canongate

19

18

Waverley Bridge

The Royal Mile

21

High Street

St. Mary's St.

22

CANONGATE

Holyrood Road

South Bridge

† 23

Cowgate

■ National Library

George IV Bridge

Chambers Street

Drummond St.

Pleasance

College St.

24

Bristo Place

Potterrow

Nicolson St.

West Richmond

Buccleuch Street

HOLYROOD

PARK

■
McEwan
Hall

George
Square

Crosscauseway

St. Leonard's St.

The Queen's Drive

Middle Meadow Walk

Buccleuch Place

Clerk St.

Meadow Lane

To Arthur's Seat
26

THE MEADOWS

Melville Drive

S. Clerk St.

Dalkeith Road

Holyrood Park Rd.

25

East Preston St.

graceful and delicate flying buttresses. One of its outstanding features is its **Thistle Chapel,** housing beautiful stalls and notable heraldic stained-glass windows. A group of cathedral guides is available at all times to conduct tours.

High St. (ℂ) 01312/259442. Free admission, but £1 ($1.60) donation suggested. Easter–Sept Mon–Fri 9am–7pm, Sat 9am–5pm, Sun 1–5pm; Oct–Easter Mon–Sat 9am–5pm, Sun 1–5pm. Sun services at 8, 10, and 11:30am, and 6 and 8pm.

The Real Mary King's Close *(Finds)* Beneath the City Chambers on the Royal Mile lies Old town's deepest secret, a warren of hidden streets where people lived and worked for centuries. Opened in 2003, this new attraction allows you to go back into the turbulent days of plague-ridden Edinburgh in the 17th century. Today's visitors can see a number of underground "Closes," originally very narrow walkways with houses on either sides, some dating back centuries. When the Royal Exchange (now the City Chambers) was constructed in 1753, the top floors of the buildings of the Close were torn down, although the lower sections were left standing and used as the foundations of the new building, leaving a number of dark and mysterious passages intact. In April of 2003, guided parties were allowed to visit these dwellings for the first time. Subtle lighting and audio effects add to the experience. You can visit everything from a gravedigger's family stricken with the plague to a grand 16th-century town house. The haunted Shrine room is the best surviving 17th-century house in Scotland.

Writers' Court, off the Royal Mile. (ℂ) 0870/243-0160. Admission £7 ($11) adults, £5 ($8) children, £21 ($34) family ticket. Bus: 1 or 6.

Writers' Museum This 1622 house takes its name from a former owner, Elizabeth, the dowager countess of Stair. Today it's a treasure trove of portraits, relics, and manuscripts relating to three of Scotland's greatest men of letters. The Robert Burns collection includes his writing desk, rare manuscripts, portraits, and many other items. Also on display are some of Sir Walter Scott's possessions, including his pipe, chess set, and original manuscripts. The museum holds one of the most significant Robert Louis Stevenson collections anywhere, including personal belongings, paintings, photographs, and early editions.

In Lady Stair's House, off Lawnmarket. (ℂ) 01315/294901. Free admission. Mon–Sat 10am–4:45pm.

Museum of Childhood The world's first museum devoted solely to the history of childhood stands just opposite John Knox's House. Contents of its four floors range from antique toys to games to exhibits on health, education, and costumes, plus video presentations and an activity area. Because of the youthful crowd it naturally attracts, it probably ranks as the noisiest museum in town.

42 High St. (ℂ) 01315/294142. Free admission. Mon–Sat 10am–5pm; during the Edinburgh Festival, also Sun noon–5pm.

John Knox's House Even if you're not interested in the reformer who founded the Scottish Presbyterian Church, you may want to visit his house, as it's characteristic of the "lands" that used to flank the Royal Mile. All of them are gone now,

---

Tips **A Note on Museum Hours**

Be aware that many museums usually closed on Sunday are open on Sunday during the Edinburgh Festival. Some museums open only in summer also are open on public holidays.

Frommer's Favorite Edinburgh Experiences

Contemplating the City and Environs from Arthur's Seat. At 823 feet (250m) atop Arthur's Seat (which you'll reach by climbing up Holyrood Park), you'll see the Highlands in miniature. The view is magical. Scots congregate here to await the summer solstice.

Visiting Dean Village. About 30m (100 ft.) below the level of the rest of the city, Dean Village is an 800-year-old grain-milling town on the Water of Leith. Go here to soak up local color, and enjoy a summertime stroll on the path by the river; it makes for great people-watching.

Shopping Along Princes Street. This is the main street of Edinburgh, the local equivalent of New York's Fifth Avenue. Flower-filled gardens stretch along the street's whole south side. When not admiring the flowers, you can window-shop and make selections from the country's finest merchandise, everything from kilts to Scottish crystal.

Downing a Pint in an Edinburgh Pub. Sampling a pint of McEwan's real ale or Tennent's lager is a chance to soak up the special atmosphere of Edinburgh. Our favorites are the Abbotsford, Bow Bar, and Kenilworth.

except Knox's house, with its timbered gallery. Inside, you'll see the tempera ceiling in the Oak Room, along with exhibitions of Knox memorabilia.

43–45 High St. ✆ 01315/569579. Admission £2.25 ($3.60) adults, £1.75 ($2.80) seniors and students, 75p ($1.20) children. Mon–Sat 10am–4:30pm.

The People's Story   If you continue walking downhill along Canongate toward Holyroodhouse, you'll see one of the handsomest buildings on the Royal Mile. Built in 1591, the **Canongate Tolbooth** was once the courthouse, prison, and center of municipal affairs for the burgh of Canongate. Now it contains a museum celebrating the social history of the inhabitants of Edinburgh from the late 18th century to the present, with lots of emphasis on the cultural displacements of the Industrial Revolution.

163 Canongate. ✆ 01315/294057. Free admission. Mon–Sat 10am–5pm. Bus: 1.

Museum of Edinburgh   Across from Canongate Tolbooth, the finely restored 16th-century Huntly House mansion is today the city's principal museum of local history. Exhibits run the range from prehistoric times to the present day. Some of the archaeological discoveries date from the Roman occupation some 2,000 years ago. A treasure of the museum is the National Covenant, a petition that demanded religious freedom and one signed by Scotland's Presbyterian leaders in 1638. One of the most touching exhibits relates to the story of "Greyfriars Bobby," a Skye terrier who maintained a vigil by the grave of his dead master for 14 years until the dog's own death. You can see the dog's collar and feeding bowl and the original plaster model for the bronze statue that stands today in Candlemaker Row. Other exhibits include displays illustrating life in the Old Town, going back to the 18th century, and the development of the new town in the mid–18th century. There is also a treasure trove of Scottish silver and glass along with pottery and other grand decorative objects created by Edinburgh's craftspeople.

142 Canongate. ✆ 01315/294143. Free admission. Mon–Sat 10am–5pm; during the Edinburgh Festival, also Sun 2–5pm. Bus: 1.

Finds **For Mr. Hyde Fans**

Near Gladstone's Land is **Brodie's Close,** a stone-floored alleyway. You can wander into the alley for a view of old stone houses that'll make you think you've stepped into a scene from a BBC production of a Dickens novel. It was named in honor of the notorious Deacon Brodie, a respectable councilor by day and a thief by night (he was the inspiration for Robert Louis Stevenson's *The Strange Case of Dr. Jekyll and Mr. Hyde,* although Stevenson set his story in foggy London town, not in Edinburgh). Brodie was hanged in 1788, and the mechanism used for the hangman's scaffolding had previously been improved by Brodie himself—for use on others, of course. Across the street is the most famous pub along the Royal Mile: **Deacon Brodie's Tavern,** 435 Lawnmarket (© **01312/256531).**

Scotch Whisky Heritage Centre   This center is privately funded by a conglomeration of Scotland's biggest distillers. It highlights the economic effect of whisky on both Scotland and the world and illuminates the centuries-old traditions associated with whisky making, showing the science and art of distilling. There's a 7-minute audiovisual show and an electric car ride past 13 sets showing historic moments in the whisky industry. A tour entitling you to sample five whiskies and take away a miniature bottle is £20 ($32) per person.

354 Castlehill. © **01312/200441.** Admission £6.50 ($10) adults, £5.50 ($8.80) seniors, £4.50 ($7.20) students with ID, £3.95 ($6.30) children ages 5–17, free for children ages 4 and under. Daily 10am–5pm.

THE TOP MUSEUMS & MONUMENTS

National Gallery of Scotland ✰✰✰   In the center of Princes Street Gardens, this gallery is small as national galleries go, but the collection was chosen with great care and has been expanded considerably by bequests, gifts, and loans. A recent major acquisition was Giulio Romano's *Vièrge à la Leàgende.* Other important Italian paintings are Verrocchio's *Ruskin Madonna,* Andrea del Sarto's *Portrait of a Man,* Domenichino's *Adoration of the Shepherds,* and Tiepolo's *Finding of Moses.* There are also works by El Greco and Velázquez.

The duke of Sutherland has lent the museum two Raphaels, Titian's two Diana canvases and *Venus Rising from the Sea,* and Nicolas Poussin's *The Seven Sacraments.* On loan from the queen is an early Netherlandish masterpiece historically linked to Edinburgh, Hugo van der Goess's *Trinity Altarpiece.* Notable also are Rubens's *The Feast of Herod* and *The Reconciliation of Jacob and Esau* and Rembrandt's *Woman in Bed,* as well as superb landscapes by Cuyp and Ruisdael. In 1982, the gallery made one of its most prized acquisitions, Pieter Saenredam's *Interior of St. Bavo's Church, Haarlem,* his largest and arguably finest painting.

The most valuable gift to the gallery since its foundation, the Maitland Collection, includes one of Cézanne's *Mont St-Victoire* series, as well as works by Degas, van Gogh, Renoir, Gauguin, and Seurat, among others. In 1980, two rare works were added: an early Monet, *Shipping Scene—Night Effects,* and a stunning landscape, *Niagara Falls, from the American Side,* by 19th-century American painter Frederic Church. You can also see excellent examples of English painting, and the work of Scottish painters is prominent. In the new wing (opened in 1978), Henry Raeburn is at his best in the whimsical *The Rev. Robert Walker Skating on Duddingston Loch.*

2 The Mound. © **01316/246200.** www.nationalgalleries.org. Free admission. Mon–Sat 10am–5pm; Sun noon–5pm (during the festival, Mon–Sat 10am–6pm, Sun 11am–6pm). Bus: 3, 21, or 26.

Britannia: The People's Yacht

In case the queen never invited you to sail aboard her 125m (412-ft.) yacht, there's still a chance to go aboard this world-famous vessel. Launched on April 16, 1953, the luxury yacht was decommissioned December 11, 1997. Today, the *Britannia*—technically a Royal Navy ship—which has sailed more than a million miles, rests at anchor in the port of Leith, 3km (2 miles) from the center of Edinburgh. The gangplank is now lowered for the public, whereas it once was lowered for such world leaders as Mahatma Gandhi, Tony Blair, and Nelson Mandela.

British taxpayers spent £160 million ($256 million) maintaining the yacht throughout most of the 1990s. Even a major refit would have prolonged the vessel's life for only a few more years. Because of budgetary constraints, a decision was made to put it in dry dock. The public reaches the vessel by going through a visitor center designed by Sir Terence Conran. At its centerpiece is the yacht's 12m (41-ft.) tender floating in a pool.

Once onboard, you're guided around all five decks by an audio tour. You can also visit the drawing room and the Royal Apartments, once occupied by the likes of not only the queen but Prince Philip, Prince William, Princess Margaret and a host of other royals. Even the engine room, the galleys, and the captain's cabin can be visited.

All tickets should be booked as far in advance as possible by calling ℂ **01315/555566.** The yacht is open daily except Christmas, with the first tour beginning at 10am, the last tour at 3:30pm. Lasting 90 to 120 minutes, each tour is self-guided with the use of a headset lent to participants. Adults pay £8 ($13), seniors £6 ($9.60), and children ages 5 to 17 £4 ($6.40); those ages 4 and under visit for free. A family ticket, good for two adults and up to two children, is £20 ($32). From Waverley Bridge, take either city bus (Lothian Transport) X50, or else the Guide Friday tour bus, which is marked all over its sides with the word BRITANNIA.

National Museum of Scotland (NMS) ★★★   In 1998, two long-established museums, the Royal Museum of Scotland and the National Museum of Antiquities, were united into this single institution 2 blocks south of the Royal Mile. The museum showcases exhibits in the decorative arts, ethnography, natural history, geology, archaeology, technology, and science. Six modern galleries distill billions of years of Scottish history, a total of 12,000 items ranging from rocks found on the island of South Uist dating back 2.9 billion years to a Hillman Imp, one of the last 500 cars manufactured at the Linwood plant near Glasgow before it closed in 1981. One gallery is devoted to Scotland's role as an independent nation before it merged with the United Kingdom in 1707. One gallery, devoted to industry and empire from 1707 to 1914, includes exhibits on shipbuilding, whisky distilling, the railways, and such textiles as the tartan and paisley.

Chambers St. ℂ **01312/257534.** www.nms.ac.uk. Free admission. Mon and Wed–Sat 10am–5pm; Tues 10am–8pm; Sun noon–5pm. Walk south from Waverley Station for 10 min. to reach Chambers St. or take bus no. 3, 7, 21, 30, 31, 53, 69, or 80.

Scottish National Gallery of Modern Art ★★ Scotland's national collection of 20th-century art occupies a gallery converted from an 1828 school set in 12 acres of grounds a 15-minute walk from the west end of Princes Street. The collection is international in scope and quality despite its modest size. Major sculptures outside include pieces by Henry Moore and Barbara Hepworth. Inside the collection ranges from a fauve Derain and cubist Braque and Picasso to recent works by Paolozzi. English and Scottish art is strongly represented, and you'll find artists from Europe and America, notably Matisse, Mir, Kirchner, Kokoschka, Ernst, Ben Nicholson, Nevelson, Balthus, Lichtenstein, Kitaj, and Hockney. You can study prints and drawings in the Print Room. The licensed cafe sells light refreshments and salads.

Belford Rd. ⓒ 01315/568921. www.nationalgalleries.org. Free admission, except for some temporary exhibits. Mon–Sat 10am–5pm; Sun 10am–5pm. Bus: 13 stops by the gallery but is infrequent; nos. 18, 20, and 41 pass along Queensferry Rd., a 5-minute walk up Queensferry Terrace and Belford Rd. from the gallery.

Scottish National Portrait Gallery Housed in a red-stone Victorian Gothic building by Rowand Anderson, this portrait gallery gives you a chance to see what the famous people of Scottish history looked like. The portraits, several by Ramsay and Raeburn, include everybody from Mary Queen of Scots to Flora Macdonald to Sean Connery.

1 Queen St. ⓒ 01316/246200. www.nationalgalleries.org. Free admission, except for some temporary exhibits. Mon–Sat 10am–5pm; Sun 10am–5pm. Bus: 18, 20, or 41.

Scott Monument ★ Completed in the mid–19th century, the Gothic-inspired Scott Monument is the most famous landmark in Edinburgh. Sir Walter Scott's heroes are carved as small figures in the monument, and you can climb to the top. You can also see the first-ever **floral clock,** which was constructed in 1904, in the West Princes Street Gardens.

In the East Princes St. Gardens. ⓒ 01315/294068. Admission £2.50 ($4). Mar–May and Oct Mon–Sat 9am–6pm, Sun 10am–6pm; June–Sept Mon–Sat 9am–8pm, Sun 10am–6pm; Nov–Feb Mon–Sat 9am–4pm, Sun 10am–4pm. Bus: 1 or 6.

MORE SIGHTS

Our Dynamic Earth ★ *Kids* The Millennium Dome at Greenwich outside London may have been a bust, but the millennium museum for Scotland is still packing in the crowds. Not far from the Palace of Holyroodhouse, Dynamic Earth tells the story of Earth itself in all its diversity. You can push buttons to simulate earthquakes, meteor showers, and views of outer space. You can see replicas of the slimy green primordial soup where life began. Time capsules wind their way back through the eons, and a series of specialized aquariums re-create primordial life forms—and that's not all. There is so much more, ranging from simulated terrains of polar ice caps to tropical rainforests with plenty of creepy crawlies. All 11 galleries sport stunning special effects.

Holyrood Rd. ⓒ 01315/507800. Easter–Oct daily 10am–6pm. Nov–Easter Wed–Sun 10am–5pm. Admission £8.45 ($14), £4.95 ($7.90) students, seniors, and children ages 14 and under. Family ticket £15 ($24).

Outlook Tower & Camera Obscura The 1853 periscope is at the top of the Outlook Tower from which you can view a panorama of the surrounding city. Trained guides point out the landmarks and talk about Edinburgh's fascinating history. In addition, there're several entertaining exhibits, all with an optical theme, and a well-stocked shop selling books, crafts, and compact discs.

Castlehill. ✆ **01312/263709.** Admission £5.75 ($9.20) adults, £4.60 ($7.35) seniors, £3.70 ($5.90) children. Apr–Oct Mon–Fri 9:30am–6pm, Sat–Sun 10am–6pm, until 7:30pm in July and 7pm in Aug; Nov–Mar daily 10am–5pm. Bus: 1 or 6.

Royal Observatory Visitor Centre   On display here are the works of the Scottish National Observatory at home and abroad, featuring the finest images of astronomical objects, Scotland's largest telescope, and antique instruments. There's also a panoramic view of the city from the balcony. An exhibit, *The Universe,* uses photographs, videos, computers, and models to take you on a cosmic whirlwind tour from the beginning of time to the farthest depths of space in a couple of hours.

Blackford Hill. ✆ **01316/688405.** www.roe.ac.uk. Admission £2.60 ($4.15) adults; £1.85 ($2.95) students, seniors, and children ages 5–16; free for children ages 4 and under. Mon–Sat 10am–5pm; Sun noon–5pm. Bus: 40 or 41.

Edinburgh Zoo ★★   This zoo is Scotland's largest animal collection, 10 minutes from Edinburgh's city center on 80 acres of hillside parkland offering unrivaled views from the Pentlands to the Firth of Forth. It contains more than 1,500 animals, including many endangered species: snow leopards, white rhinos, pygmy hippos, and many more. The zoo boasts the largest penguin colony in Europe, with four species, plus the world's largest penguin enclosure. A penguin parade is held daily at 2pm from April to September.

134 Corstorphine Rd. ✆ **01313/349171.** Admission £7.50 ($12) adults, £4.50 ($7.20) seniors, £3.80 ($6.10) children, £20–£27 ($32–$43) families. Apr–Sept daily 9am–6pm; Oct–Mar daily 9am–5pm. Parking £2 ($3.20). Bus: 2, 26, 69, 85, or 86.

THE MONUMENTS ON CALTON HILL

Calton Hill, rising 106m (350 ft.) off Regent Road in the eastern sector, is often credited with giving Edinburgh a look somewhat like that of Athens. It's a hill of monuments; and when some of them were created, they were called "instant ruins" by critics. People visit the hill not only to see its monuments but also to enjoy the **panoramic views** ★★★ of the Firth of Forth and the city spread beneath it. The "Parthenon" was reproduced in part on this location in 1824. The intention of the builders was to honor the brave Scottish dead killed in the

---

Finds   **Dean Village**

Beautiful **Dean Village** ★, in a valley about 30m (100 ft.) below the level of the rest of Edinburgh, is one of the city's most photographed sights. It's a few minutes from the West End, at the end of Bells Brae off Queensferry Street, on the Water of Leith. The settlement dates from the 12th century, and Dean Village's fame grew as a result of its being a grain-milling center.

You can enjoy a celebrated view by looking downstream under the high arches of **Dean Bridge** (1833), designed by Telford. The village's old buildings have been restored and converted into apartments and houses. You don't come here for any one particular site but to stroll around, people-watch, enjoy the village as a whole. You can also walk for miles along the Water of Leith, one of the most tranquil walks in the greater Edinburgh area.

Napoleonic wars. However, the city fathers ran out of money, and the monument (often referred to as "Scotland's shame") was never finished. Other monuments atop the hill include the **Nelson Monument,** containing the relics of the hero of Trafalgar, and the **Lincoln Monument,** which was erected in 1893 in memory of the thousands of American soldiers of Scottish descent who lost their lives in America's Civil War.

GARDENS

At the **Royal Botanic Garden** ★★★, Inverleith Row (© **01315/527171;** www.rbge.org.uk), the main areas of interest are the Exhibition Hall, Alpine House, Demonstration Garden, annual and herbaceous borders (summer only), copse, Woodland Garden, Wild Garden, Arboretum, Peat Garden, Rock Garden, Heath Garden, and Pond. Admission is by voluntary donation. It's open daily: January through February from 10am to 4pm, March from 10am to 6pm, April through September from 10am to 7pm, October from 10am to 6pm, and November through December from 10am to 6pm.

As the New Town grew, the city fathers decided to turn the area below Edinburgh Castle into the **Princes Street Gardens,** now one of the city's main beauty spots. The area was once Nor Loch, a body of water in the city center, but it was drained to make way for a railway line. (When it was still a bog, the great philosopher David Hume fell into it, couldn't remove himself, and called for help from a passing woman. She recognized him, pronounced him an atheist, and wouldn't offer her umbrella to pull him out of the mire until he recited the Lord's Prayer.) The gardens' chief landmark is the Scott Monument, but many find the summer flowers an even bigger attraction.

ORGANIZED TOURS

If you want a quick introduction to the principal attractions in and around Edinburgh, consider one or more of the tours offered by **Lothian Region Transport,** 14 Queen St. (© **01315/556363).** You won't find a cheaper way to hit the highlights. The buses leave from Waverley Bridge, near the Scott Monument. The tours are given from April to late October; a curtailed winter program is also offered.

You can see most of the major sights of Edinburgh, including the Royal Mile, the Palace of Holyroodhouse, Princes Street, and Edinburgh Castle, by double-deck motor coach for £7.50 ($12) for adults, £6 ($9.60) for seniors and students, and £2.50 ($4) for children. This ticket is valid all day on any **LRT Edinburgh Classic Tour bus,** which allows passengers to get on and off at any of the 15 stops along its routes. Buses start from Waverley Bridge every day beginning at 9:40am, departing every 15 minutes in summer and about every 30 minutes in winter, then embark on a circuit of Edinburgh, which if you remain on the bus without ever getting off will take about 1 hour. Commentary is offered along the way.

Tickets for any of these tours can be bought at LRT offices at Waverley Bridge, or at 14 Queen St., or at the tourist information center in Waverley Market. Advance reservations are a good idea. For more information, call © **01315/556363,** 24 hours a day.

6 Shopping

The best buys are in tartans and woolens, along with bone china and Scottish crystal. New Town's **Princes Street** is the main shopping artery. **George Street** and Old Town's **Royal Mile** are also major shopping arteries.

Shopping hours are generally Monday through Saturday from 9am to 5 or 5:30pm and Sunday from 11am to 5pm. Thursdays, many shops remain open to between 7 and 8pm.

BRASS RUBBINGS

Scottish Stone and Brass Rubbing Centre ✯ You may rub any of the brass or stones on display here to create your own wall hangings, or buy them ready made. Those commemorating Robert the Bruce (king of Scotland from 1306–29) are particularly impressive. The brass you choose is covered in white or black paper, silver wax is used to outline the brass, and then you fill it in with different colors of wax. You can visit the center's collection of replicas molded from ancient Pictish stones, rare Scottish brasses, and medieval church brasses. Trinity Apse, Chalmers Close, near the Royal Mile. ✆ 01315/564364. Bus: 1.

CRYSTAL

Edinburgh Crystal ✯ This factory is devoted to handmade crystal glassware. The Visitor Centre (open Mon–Sat 10am–4pm, Sun 11am–4pm) contains the factory shop where the world's largest collection of Edinburgh Crystal (plus inexpensive factory seconds) is on sale. Although Waterford is the more prestigious name, Edinburgh Crystal is a serious competitor, its most popular design being the thistle, symbolizing Scotland. It can be traced back to the 17th century, when the art of glassmaking was brought here by the Venetians. The center also has a gift shop and a coffee shop specializing in home baking.

Thirty-minute tours of the factory to watch glassmakers at work are given Monday through Friday from 10am to 4pm; April through September, weekend tours are given from 10am to 2:30pm. Tours costs £3.50 ($5.60) for adults, £2.50 ($4) for children, £9.50 ($15) for a family ticket. Eastfield, Penicuik (16km/10 miles south of Edinburgh, just off A701 to Peebles). ✆ 01968/675128. Bus: 37, 37A, 62 (Lowland), 64 or 65 (green), 81 or 87 (red) Waverly bus link.

DEPARTMENT STORES & A MALL

Debenham's Old, reliable Debenham's is still the best department store in Edinburgh, with a wide array of Scottish and international merchandise displayed in a marble-covered interior. 109–112 Princes St. ✆ 01312/251320. Bus: 3, 31, or 69.

Jenner's ✯ Everyone in Edinburgh has probably been to Jenner's at least once. Its neo-Gothic facade, opposite the Scott Monument, couldn't be more prominent. The store's array of Scottish and international merchandise is astounding. Jenner's often sells much the same merchandise as Debenham's, but it boasts a wider selection of china and glassware and has a well-known food hall that sells a wide array of homemade products, including heather honey, Dundee marmalade, and a vast selection of Scottish shortbreads and cakes. 48 Princes St. ✆ 01312/252442. Bus: 3, 31, or 69.

Princes Mall There's something for everyone at this tri-level mall. You can browse through some 80 shops selling fashions, accessories, gifts, books, jewelry, beauty products, and a wide selection of Scottish arts and crafts. The Food Court has tempting snacks and the Food Hall top-quality produce. Unique handmade items are sold in the craft center. Next to Waverley Station, Princes St. ✆ 01315/573759. Bus: 3, 31, or 69.

FASHION

Corniche A fashion designer, Nina Grant, operates the most sophisticated boutique in Edinburgh. If it's the latest in Scottish fashion, expect to find it here,

---

Tips **Bring That Passport!**

Take along your passport when you go shopping in case you make a purchase that entitles you to a **VAT** (value-added tax) refund.

---

even "Anglomania kilts" designed by that controversial lady of fashion herself, Vivienne Westwood. Jackie Burke, a relative newcomer to the design world, has made a splash with her fur-trimmed Harris-tweed riding jackets. 2 Jeffrey St. ✆ 01315/563707.

Edinburgh Woollen Mill Shop   One of about 30 such shops throughout the United Kingdom, the Edinburgh Woollen Mill Shop sells good Scottish woolens, knitwear, skirts, and giftware. Note, however, that most of the merchandise is made in England. 139 Princes St. ✆ 01312/263840. Bus: 3, 31, or 69.

Schuh   Schuh has the latest in unique footwear, specializing in the yellow, red, and blue plaid boots made famous by the local rugby team. Expect fierce, funky finds. 6 Frederick St. ✆ 01312/200290.

Shetland Connection   Owner Moira-Ann Leask promotes Shetland Island knitwear, and her shop is packed with sweaters, hats, and gloves in colorful Fair Island designs. She also offers hand-knit mohair, Aran, and Icelandic sweaters. Items range from fine-ply cobweb shawls to chunky ski sweaters in top-quality wool. A large range of Celtic jewelry and gifts makes this shop a top-priority visit. 491 Lawnmarket. ✆ 01312/253525. Bus: 1.

GIFTS

Ness Scotland   Along the Royal Mile, Ness Scotland is filled with whimsical accessories searched out by Gordon MacAulay and Adrienne Wells. They have scoured the country from the Orkney Islands to the Borders for that unique item. Displays are hand-loomed cardigans, tasteful scarves, and an array of other items, including charming Dinky bags made during the long winters on the Isle of Lewis. 367 High St. ✆ 01312/265227.

JEWELRY

Alistir Tait ⭐   This is one of the most charming jewelry stores in Edinburgh, with a reputation for selling Scottish minerals like agates; jewelry fashioned from Scottish gold; garnets, sapphires, and freshwater pearls; estate jewelry in every conceivable style; and even modern pieces. If you didn't realize Scotland was so rich in gemstones, think again. Ask to see the artful depictions of Luckenbooths. Fashioned as pendants, usually as two entwined hearts capped by a royal crest, they're associated with the loves and tragedies of Mary Queen of Scots and often accessorized with a baroque pearl. They come in subtle hues of petal, orange, brown, and (most desirable and rare) purple. 116A Rose St. ✆ 01312/254105. Bus: 3, 31, or 69.

Hamilton & Inches   Since 1866, the prestigious Hamilton & Inches has sold gold and silver jewelry, porcelain and silver, and gift items. You'll find everything you'd want for an upscale wedding present, all sorts of jewelry (including some valuable pieces from estate sales), and two memorable kinds of silver dishes (weighty plates copied from items found in the Spanish Armada wrecks during Elizabeth I's reign and endearingly folkloric quaichs). The *quaichs* originated in the West Highlands as whisky measures crafted from wood or horn and were later gentrified into something like silver porringers or chafing dishes, each with a pair of lugs (ears) fashioned into Celtic or thistle patterns. Also unusual is an exclusive pattern of Hungarian-based Herend china, emblazoned prominently with a Scottish thistle. 87 George St. ℭ 01312/254898. Bus: 41 or 42.

LINENS & BEDS

And So To Bed   The danger of popping into this store is you might make a much larger investment than you'd intended when you see the fine-textured sheets and pillowcases. Most feature Italian and British cotton (not linen), usually in white and cream. (An upscale British brand name is Wendy Woods, Ltd.) There's also a beautiful collection of ornate brass, iron, and wooden beds you can order in several sizes and have shipped anywhere. 30 Dundas St. ℭ 01316/523700. Bus: 23 or 27.

MUSIC

Virgin Megastore   Here you'll find one of the biggest selections of records, CDs, videos, and tapes in Scotland. The shop has a special strength in traditional and Scottish music. The staff is charming and eager to imbue their love of Scottish music to interested visitors. 125 Princes St. ℭ 01312/202230. Bus: 3, 31, or 69.

TARTANS & KILTS

Anta   Some of the most stylish tartans are found at Anta, where "forever plaid" might be the motto. Here Lachian and Anne Stewart, the creative designing team behind Ralph Lauren's home tartan fabrics, present a series of tartans newly invented in unique styles. The woolen blankets with hand-purled fringe are woven on old-style looms. 32 High St. ℭ 01315/578300.

Clan Tartan Centre   This is one of the leading tartan specialists in Edinburgh, regardless of which clan you claim as your own. If you want help in identifying a particular tartan, the staff here will assist you. 70–74 Bangor Rd., Leith. ℭ 01315/535100. Bus: 7 or 10.

Geoffrey (Tailor) Highland Crafts ★   This is the most famous kiltmaker in the Scottish capital. Its customers have included Sean Connery, Charlton Heston, Dr. Ruth Westheimer, members of Scotland's rugby teams, and Mel Gibson (who favors the tartan design Hunting Buchanan and wore his outfit when he received an award from the Scottish government after filming *Braveheart*). Expect a delay of 4 to 8 weeks before your costume can be completed. The company maintains a toll-free number (ℭ 800/566-1467) for anyone who calls from the United States or Canada and wants to be outfitted. The company stocks 200 of Scotland's best-known tartan patterns and is revolutionizing the kilt by establishing a subsidiary called 21st Century Kilts, which makes them in fabrics ranging from denim to leather. 57–59 High St. ℭ 01315/570256. Bus: 1.

James Pringle Woolen Mill   The mill produces a large variety of top-quality wool items, including a range of Scottish knitwear like cashmere sweaters, tartan and tweed ties, travel rugs, tweed hats, and tam o' shanters. In addition, it boasts one of Scotland's best Clan Tartan Centres, with more than 5,000 tartans accessible. A free audiovisual presentation shows the history and development of the tartan. You can visit free, and there's even a free taxi service to the mill from anywhere in Edinburgh (ask at your hotel). 70–74 Bangor Rd., Leith. ℭ 01315/535161. Bus: 7 or 10.

Tartan Gift Shops   If you've ever suspected you might be Scottish, Tartan Gift Shops has a chart indicating the place of origin (in Scotland) of your family name. You'll then be faced with a bewildering array of hunt and dress tartans for men and women, and the high-quality wool is sold by the yard. There's also a line of lambs-wool and cashmere sweaters and all the accessories. 54 High St. © 01315/583187. Bus 1.

7 Edinburgh After Dark

Every year in late August, the **Edinburgh International Festival** brings numerous world-class cultural offerings to the city, but year-round there are plenty of choices, whether you prefer theater, opera, ballet, or other diversions. The waterfront district, featuring many jazz clubs and restaurants, is especially lively in summer, and students flock to the pubs and clubs around Grassmarket. Discos are found off High and Princes streets, and in the city's numerous pubs you can often hear traditional Scottish folk music for the price of a pint.

For a thorough list of entertainment options during your stay, pick up a copy of *The List,* a biweekly entertainment paper available at the tourist office for £1.90 ($3.05). Before you leave home, you might want to check *Time Out's* latest concert, performance, and nightclub listings on the Web at **www.timeout.co.uk**.

FESTIVALS

The highlight of Edinburgh's year—some would say the only time when the real Edinburgh emerges—comes in the last weeks of August during the **Edinburgh International Festival** ★★★. Since 1947, the festival has attracted artists and companies of the highest international standard in all fields of the arts, including music, opera, dance, theater, exhibition, poetry, and prose, and "Auld Reekie" takes on a cosmopolitan air.

During the festival, one of the most exciting spectacles is the Military Tattoo on the floodlit esplanade in front of Edinburgh Castle, high on its rock above the city. Vast audiences watch the precision marching of Scottish regiments and military units from all parts of the world, and of course the stirring skirl of the bagpipes and the swirl of the kilt.

Less predictable in quality but greater in quantity is the **Edinburgh Festival Fringe,** an opportunity for anybody—professional or nonprofessional, an individual, a group of friends, or a whole company of performers—to put on a show wherever they can find an empty stage or street corner. Late-night reviews, outrageous and irreverent contemporary drama, university theater presentations, maybe even a full-length opera—Edinburgh gives them all free rein. A **Film Festival,** a **Jazz Festival,** a **Television Festival,** and a **Book Festival** (every 2nd year) all overlap at varying times during August.

Ticket prices vary from £4 ($6.40) up to about £60 ($96) a seat. Information can be obtained at **Edinburgh International Festival,** The Hub, Castle Hill, Edinburgh EH1 7ND (© **01314/732000**; www.eif.co.uk). The office is open Monday through Friday from 10am to 5pm.

Other sources of event information include **Edinburgh Festival Fringe,** 180 High St., Edinburgh EH1 1BW (© **01312/265257**; www.edfringe.com); **Edinburgh Book Festival,** 137 Dundee St., Edinburgh EH11 1BG (© **01312/ 285444**; www.edbookfest.co.uk); **Edinburgh Film Festival,** 88 Lothian Rd., Edinburgh EH3 9BZ (© **01312/284051**; www.edfilmfest.org.uk); and **Edinburgh Military Tattoo,** 22 Market St., Edinburgh EH1 1QB (© **01312/ 251188**; www.edinburgh-tattoo.co.uk).

THEATER

Edinburgh has a lively theater scene. In 1994, the **Festival Theatre,** 13–29 Nicolson St. (ℂ **01316/621112** for administration, 01315/296000 for tickets during festival times with an additional phone line—ℂ 01314/732000—that's operational during the August festival; www.eft.co.uk; bus: 3, 31, or 33), opened in time for some aspects of the Edinburgh Festival. Set on the eastern edge of Edinburgh, near the old campus of the University of Edinburgh, it has since been called "Britain's de facto Dance House" because of its sprung floor, its enormous stage (the largest in Britain), and its suitability for opera presentations of all kinds. Tickets are £6 to £60 ($9.60–$96).

Another major theater is the **King's Theatre,** 2 Leven St. (ℂ **01315/296000;** bus: 10 or 11), a 1,600-seat Victorian venue offering a wide repertoire of classical entertainment, including ballet, opera, and West End productions. The **Netherbow Arts Centre,** 43 High St. (ℂ **01315/569579;** bus: 1), has been called "informal," and productions here are often experimental and delightful— new Scottish theater at its best.

The resident company of **Royal Lyceum Theatre,** Grindlay Street (ℂ **01312/484848;** www.lyceum.org.uk; bus: 11 or 15), also has an enviable reputation; its presentations range from the works of Shakespeare to new Scottish playwrights. The **Traverse Theatre,** Cambridge Street (ℂ **01312/281404;** bus: 11 or 15), is one of the few theaters in Britain funded solely to present new plays by British writers and first translations into English of international works. In a modern location, it now offers two theaters under one roof: Traverse 1 seats 250 and Traverse 2 seats 100.

BALLET, OPERA & CLASSICAL MUSIC

The **Scottish Ballet** and the **Scottish Opera** perform at the **Playhouse Theatre,** 18–22 Greenside Place (ℂ **0870/606-3424;** bus: 7 or 14), which, with 3,100 seats, is the town's largest theater. The **Scottish Chamber Orchestra** makes its home at the **Queen's Hall,** Clerk Street (ℂ **01316/682019;** bus: 3, 33, or 31), also a major venue for the Edinburgh International Festival.

FOLK MUSIC & CEILIDHS

Folk music is presented in many clubs and pubs in Edinburgh, but these strolling players tend to be somewhat erratic or irregular in their appearances. It's best to read notices in pubs and talk to the tourist office to see where the ceilidhs will be on the night of your visit.

Some hotels regularly feature traditional Scottish music in the evenings. You might check with the **George Hotel,** 19–21 George St. (ℂ **01312/251251;** bus: 3, 31, or 33). **Jamie's Scottish Evening** is presented daily at the King James Hotel on Leith Street (ℂ **01315/560111;** bus: 7 or 14) Tuesday through Sunday at 7pm, costing £44 ($70) for a four-course dinner, wine, and show.

DANCE & ROCK CLUBS

The Cavendish, 3 West Tollcross (ℂ **01312/283252;** bus: 11, 15, or 23), isn't necessarily where you go to hear the next Oasis or Blur, but who knows? The doors open at 10pm and close at 3am. There's a dress code—that is, no tennis shoes or jeans. The bar is open Wednesday through Saturday from 10pm to 3am, with a £6 ($9.60) cover Friday and Saturday.

The glamorous **Club Mercado,** 36–39 Market St. (ℂ **01312/264224;** bus: 1), attracts an 18- to 35-year-old crowd. Once the headquarters of the British Rail's Scottish branch, it hangs suspended over the tracks behind the city's main station. On Friday, the action kicks off with free-admission TFIS, which stands for a somewhat saltier version of "Thank God It's Friday"; it runs from 5 to 10pm and caters to youngish workers who indulge in the cut-price drinks while tapping to the kitsch music. Other special nights alternate—Saturday Viva (a night of eclectic music attracting all sorts from toughs to drag queens) and The Colours of Love (basically a rave featuring the latest house music); both charge £8 to £10 ($13–$16). Sunday's Bubbalicious is student night, charging £5 ($8), and the first Sunday of the month is gay night, charging £5 ($8). Generally, cover runs £3 to £10 ($4.80–$16), and it's open daily from 10:30pm to 3am.

Po Na Na, 43B Frederick St. (© 01312/262224; bus: 80), is a branch of Britain's most successful nightclub chain. The theme is a Moroccan casbah, thanks to wall mosaics, brass lanterns, and artifacts shipped in from Marrakech. You'll dance in the cellar of a transformed 19th-century building, beneath a tented ceiling illuminated with strobes. Expect 25- to 40-year-olds and a highly danceable mix of house and funk. Po Na Na isn't specifically gay but does draw a strong gay following. It's open daily from 10pm to 3am, with a cover running £3 to £5 ($4.80–$8). **Revolution,** 31 Lothian Rd. (© 01312/297670; bus: 11 or 15), is Edinburgh's largest nightclub, popular with an under-25 crowd and with a capacity for 1,500. Mainstream contemporary dance music (plus five bars) attracts the crowds, and there are theme and student nights. Cover is £3 to £10 ($4.80–$16), and it's open Wednesday through Sunday from 10:30pm to 2am.

In the basement of the Dome Bar & Grill, **Whynot,** 14 George St. (© 01316/ 248633; bus: 41 or 42), is a hot new entertainment complex that opened in the former Bank of Scotland building across from the George Inter-Continental Hotel. It has low ceilings with veil-like curtains above the dance floor and lots of seating coves tucked away for privacy. The club swings Friday and Saturday from 10pm to 3am. Friday features mainstream pop, with a £5 ($8) cover, and Saturday features contemporary dance music, with a £7.50 ($12) cover. Behind the main Post Office and Waverley Station is **The Venue,** 15 Calton Rd. (© 01315/ 573073; bus: 26), the principal stage for live music. Some of the biggest bands in the United Kingdom perform here, and other entertainment is by Scottish wannabes. Posters and flyers around town will let you know what's on at any given time. This large hall isn't open unless there's a concert, and admission fees and times are on a per-show basis, so call for details.

PUBS & BARS

Edinburgh's most famous pub, **Café Royal Circle Bar,** 17 W. Register St. (© 01315/561884; bus: 3, 31, or 33), is a long-enduring favorite. One part is now occupied by the Oyster Bar of the Café Royal, but life in the Circle Bar continues at its old pace. The opulent trappings of the Victorian era are still to be seen. Go up to the serving counter, which stands like an island in a sea of drinkers, and place your order.

The Abbotsford, 3 Rose St. (© 01312/255276; bus: 3, 31, or 33), is near the eastern end of Rose Street, a short walk from Princes Street. This pub has served stiff drinks and oceans of beer since it was founded in 1887. Inside, the gaslight era is alive and thriving, thanks to a careful preservation of the original dark paneling, long, battered tables, and an ornate plaster ceiling. The inventories of beer on tap changes about once a week, supplementing a roster of single-malt scotches. Platters of food, priced at from £2.25 to £7.95 ($3.60–$13), are dispensed from the bar. Established in 1806, **Deacon Brodie's Tavern,** 435 Lawnmarket (© 01312/256531; bus: 1), is the neighborhood pub along the

Moments A Wee Dram for Fans of Malt Whisky

It requires a bit of an effort to reach it (take bus 10A, 16, or 17 from Princes St. to Leith), but for fans of malt whisky, the **Scotch Malt Whisky Society** has been called "The Top of the Whisky Pyramid" by distillery-industry maga-zines in Britain. It's on the second floor of a 16th-century warehouse at 87 Giles St., Leith (*©* **01315/543451**), and was originally designed to store Bor-deaux and port wines from France and Portugal. All you can order are sin-gle-malt whiskies, served neat, usually in a dram (unless you want yours watered down with branch water) and selected from a staggering choice of whiskies from more than 100 distilleries throughout Scotland. Hours are Monday through Wednesday from 10am to 5pm, Thursday through Satur-day from 10am to 11pm, and Sunday from 12:30 to 10pm.

Royal Mile. It perpetuates the memory of Deacon Brodie, good citizen by day, robber by night. The tavern and wine cellars contain a restaurant and lounge bar.

GAY BARS & CLUBS

C. C. Bloom's, 23–24 Greenside Place (*©* **01315/569331;** bus: 7 or 14), is one of the most popular gay bars in Edinburgh. The upstairs bar offers drinks and same-sex camaraderie. The downstairs club features dancing to a wide range of music, and one night a week is set aside for karaoke. Attracting a larger female clientele than most other gay bars in Edinburgh is **Planet Out,** 6 Baxters Place (*©* **01315/240061;** bus: 8, 9, or 19). It's mainly a place to sit and enjoy a drink, but once a month there's a theme night with drink specials and activities. Another gay venue is **Habana,** 22 Greenside Place (*©* **01315/581270;** bus: 7 or 14). This pub answers the eternal question of what's under the kilt. Gays enjoy the cafe downstairs or the disco upstairs on Friday and Saturday nights.

8 Side Trips from Edinburgh: The Best of the Lothian Region

Armed with a good map, you can explore the major attractions of the country-side south of the Firth of Forth enveloping Edinburgh in just a day. Most attrac-tions are no more than an hour's drive from Edinburgh. The highlights are **Hopetoun House** of Robert Adam fame and the impressive ruins of **Linlith-gow Palace,** birthplace of Mary Queen of Scots in 1542.

LINLITHGOW & ITS PALACE ⚛

In 1542, Mary Queen of Scots was born in the royal burgh of Linlithgow in West Lothian, 29km (18 miles) west of Edinburgh. You can visit the site of her birth, the roofless Linlithgow Palace. For £6 ($9.60) round-trip, buses and trains arrive daily from Edinburgh after a 20- to 25-minute ride. If you're driving from central Edinburgh, follow A8 toward Glasgow, and then merge with M9, fol-lowing the signs to Linlithgow.

SEEING THE SIGHTS

Linlithgow Palace   Birthplace of Mary Queen of Scots, this was once a favorite residence of Scottish kings and is one of the country's most poignant ruins. Although the palace is roofless, its pink-ocher walls climb five floors and are sup-ported on the lower edge by flying buttresses. It's most dramatic and evocative when floodlit at night. Many of the former royal rooms are still remarkably preserved, so you can get a clear idea of how grand it used to be. The queen's suite was in the north quarter but was rebuilt for the homecoming of James VI (James I of Great Britain) in 1620. In one of the many tragic events associated with Scottish sovereignty, the palace burned to the ground in 1746, along with many of the hopes and dreams of Scottish independence. The Great Hall is on the first floor, and a small display shows some of the more interesting architectural relics.

On A706, on the south shore of Linlithgow Loch, 1km (½ mile) from Linlithgow Station. ✆ **01506/842896.** Admission £3 ($4.80) adults, £2.30 ($3.70) seniors, £1 ($1.60) children. April 1–Sept. 30t daily 9:30am–6:30pm; Oct. 1–March 31 9:30am–4:30pm (last admission 4pm).

St. Michael's Parish Church South of the palace stands the medieval kirk of St. Michael the Archangel, site of worship of many a Scottish monarch since its consecration in 1242. Despite being ravaged by the disciples of John Knox (who then chided his followers for their "excesses") and transformed into a stable by Cromwell, this is one of Scotland's best examples of a parish church.

Adjacent to Linlithgow Palace. ✆ **01506/842188.** Free admission. May–Sept daily 10am–4pm; Oct–Apr Mon–Fri 10:30am–3pm.

Hopetoun House ⭐ Amid beautifully landscaped grounds laid out along the lines of those at Versailles, Hopetoun is Scotland's greatest Robert Adam mansion and a fine example of 18th-century architecture (note its resemblance to Buckingham Palace). It's the seat of the marquess of Linlithgow, whose grandfather and father were the governor-general of Australia and the viceroy of India, respectively. Seven bays extend across the slightly recessed center, and the classical style includes a complicated tympanum, with hood molds, quoins, and straight-headed windows. A rooftop balustrade with urns completes the ensemble. You can wander through splendid reception rooms filled with 18th-century furniture, paintings, statuary, and other artworks and check out the panoramic view of the Firth of Forth from the roof. After touring the house, you can take the nature trail, explore the deer parks, see the Stables Museum, or stroll through the formal gardens. Refreshments are available near the Ballroom Suite.

3km (2 miles) from the Forth Road Bridge near South Queensferry, 16km (10 miles) from Edinburgh off A904. ✆ **01313/312451.** www.hopetounhouse.com. Admission £6 ($9.60) adults, £5 ($8) seniors, £3 ($4.80) children, £16 ($26) families of up to 6. Mar 30–Sept 20 daily 10am–5:30pm (last admission 4:30pm). Closed Sept 21–Mar 29.

DIRLETON: THE PRETTIEST VILLAGE IN SCOTLAND ⭐

Another popular day trip, to a point midway between North Berwick and Gullane, is to the lovely little town of Dirleton. The town plan, drafted in the early 16th century, is essentially unchanged today. Dirleton has two greens shaped like triangles, with a pub opposite Dirleton Castle, placed at right angles to a group of cottages. This is a preservation village and subject to careful control of any development. It's on the Edinburgh–North Berwick road (A198). North Berwick is 8km (5 miles) east and Edinburgh 31km (19 miles) west.

There's no train service to Dirleton. Buses from Edinburgh depart from the St. Andrews Square bus station and include nos. 124 and X5. For information, call ✆ **0800/232323.** Buses from Edinburgh take around 30 minutes and cost £2.65 ($4.25) one-way. If you're driving, take A1 in the direction marked THE SOUTH and DUNBAR; then turn onto A198, following the signs to Dirleton.

SEEING THE SIGHTS

Dirleton Castle ⭐⭐ A rose-tinted 13th-century castle with surrounding gardens, once the seat of the wealthy Anglo-Norman de Vaux family, Dirleton Castle

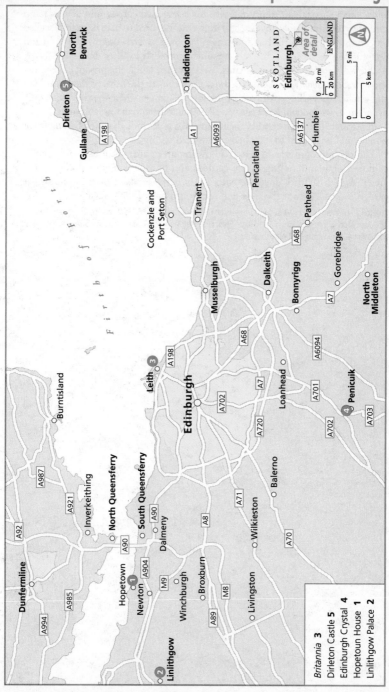

Firth of Forth

North Berwick

Dirleton **5**

Gullane

A198

Haddington

A1

A6093

Pencaitland

A6137

Humbie

Cockenzie and Port Seton

Tranent

Pathead

A68

Dalkeith

Bonnyrigg

Gorebridge

A7

North Middleton

Musselburgh

A68

A198

Leith **3**

Edinburgh

A702

A7

Loanhead

A6094

A701

A702

Penicuik **4**

A703

A720

Balerno

Burntisland

A987

A921

Inverkeithing

North Queensferry

South Queensferry

Dalmeny

A90

A90

Wilkieston

A71

A70

A8

A92

Dunfermline

A985

A994

Hopetown **1**

Newton

A904

M9

Winchburgh

Broxburn

M8

A89

Livingston

Linlithgow **2**

Area of detail

SCOTLAND

Edinburgh

ENGLAND

0   20 mi
0   20 km

5 mi

5 km
0
0

5 km

Britannia **3**

Dirleton Castle **5**

Edinburgh Crystal **4**

Hopetoun House **1**

Linlithgow Palace **2**

looks like a fairy-tale fortification, with towers, arched entries, and an oak ramp similar to the drawbridge that used to protect it. Reputed to have been fully sacked by Cromwell in 1650, the building was in fact only partially destroyed by him and was further torn down by the Nesbitt family, who, after building nearby Archiefield House, desired a romantic ruin on their land. The prison, bakehouse, and storehouses are carved from bedrock. You can see the ruins of the Great Hall and kitchen, as well as what's left of the lord's chamber where the de Vaux family lived: windows and window seats, a wall with a toilet and drains, and other household features. The 16th-century main gate has a hole through which boiling tar or water could be poured to discourage unwanted visitors.

The castle's country garden and a bowling green are still in use, with masses of flowering plants rioting in the gardens and bowlers sometimes seen on the green. A 17th-century dovecote with 1,100 nests stands at the east end of the garden. A small gate at the west end leads onto one of the village greens.

Dirleton, E. Lothian. ⓒ **01620/850330.** Admission £3 ($4.80) adults, £2.50 ($4) seniors, £1 ($1.60) children. Apr–Sept Mon–Sat 9:30am–6pm, Sun 10am–6pm; Oct–Mar Mon–Sat 9:30am–4:30pm, Sun 2–4:30pm (last admission 4pm in winter, 5:30pm in summer).

The Borders & Galloway Regions

The romantic castle ruins and skeletons of Gothic abbeys in the **Borders** region stand as mute reminders of the battles that once raged between England and the proud Scots. For a long time, the "Border Country" was a no-man's-land of plunder and destruction, lying south of the line of the Moorfoot, Pentland, and Lammermuir hill ranges and east of the Annandale Valley and the upper valley of the River Tweed.

The Borders is the land of Sir Walter Scott, master of romantic adventure, who topped the best-seller list in the early 19th century. The remains of the four great mid-12th-century abbeys are here: **Dryburgh** (where Scott is buried), **Melrose, Jedburgh,** and **Kelso.** And because of its abundant sheep-grazing land, the Borders is the home of the cashmere sweater and the tweed suit. Ask at the local tourist office for a "Borders Woollen Trail" brochure, detailing where you can visit woolen mills, shops, and museums and follow the process of weaving from start to finish.

Southwest of the Borders is the often-overlooked **Galloway** region (aka Dumfries and Galloway), a land of unspoiled countryside, fishing harbors, and romantic ruins. Major centers to visit are the ancient city of **Dumfries,** perhaps the best base for touring Galloway, and the artists' colony of **Kirkcudbright,** an ancient burgh filled with color-washed houses. In the far west, **Stranraer** is a major terminal for those making the 56km (35-mile) ferry crossing into Northern Ireland. Among the major sights are Sweetheart Abbey, outside Dumfries, and the Burns Mausoleum at Dumfries. If time remains, explore beautiful **Threave Garden,** outside Castle Douglas.

Edinburgh Airport is about 65km (40 miles) northwest of Selkirk in the Borders and **Glasgow Airport** about 121km (75 miles) north of Dumfries in the Galloway region. Trains from Glasgow run south along the coast, toward Stranraer, intersecting with the rail stations at Ayr and Girvan en route. Another rail line from Glasgow extends due south to Dumfries, depositing and picking up passengers before crossing the English border headed to the English city of Carlisle. In direct contrast, southbound trains from Edinburgh almost always bypass most of the Borders towns en route, making direct, usually nonstop, transits for Berwick, in England. Consequently, to reach most of the Borders towns covered here, you'll probably rely on a rented car or on bus service to Peebles, Selkirk, Melrose, and Kelso, from Edinburgh or Berwick. For train information and schedules, call **National Rail Enquiries** at ⓒ **0845/748-4950.**

If you're coming from England, trains from London's King's Cross Station to Edinburgh's Waverley Station enter Scotland at Berwick-upon-Tweed in 6 hours. From Berwick, a network of local buses runs among the villages and towns. Three rail lines pass through the region from London's

Euston Station en route to Glasgow. Dumfries or Stranraer is the best center if you're traveling by rail in the Uplands. Bus travel isn't recommended for reaching the region, but once you get there, you'll find it a reliable means of public transportation, because many smaller towns have no rail connections.

1 Kelso: Abbey Ruins & Adam Architecture 🎯

71km (44 miles) SE of Edinburgh; 19km (12 miles) NE of Jedburgh; 110km (68 miles) NW of Newcastle-upon-Tyne; 19km (12 miles) E of Melrose; 37km (23 miles) W of Berwick-upon-Tweed

A typical historic border town, Kelso lies at the point where the River Teviot meets the River Tweed. Sir Walter Scott called it "the most beautiful, if not the most romantic, village in Scotland." The settlement that grew up here developed into a town around Kelso Abbey.

Kelso today is a flourishing market town, the center of an agricultural district boasting farming and stock raising. But for visitors, the reasons to come here are the ruined abbey and the nearby palatial Floors Castle (by the great architect William Adam) and Mellerstain (begun by William but finished by his son Robert). The town is also one of the best centers for touring the Borders, because it's near Dryburgh Abbey and Melrose, among other attractions.

ESSENTIALS

GETTING THERE The nearest rail station connection is Berwick-upon-Tweed, from where you can take a bus to Kelso (see below). For information, call ☎ **0845/748-4950.**

From Edinburgh, board the bus to Saint Boswells, with connecting service to Kelso; the full trip lasts about 80 minutes and costs £6 ($9.60) one-way and £11 ($18) round-trip. Phone ☎ **0870/580-8080** for more information. From Berwick to Kelso, there are between six and eight buses a day, depending on the day of the week and the season. Transit costs £4 ($6.40) each way and takes an hour. Because three bus companies make the run, it's best to call the local tourist office at ☎ **01573/223464** for the schedules.

From Edinburgh, take A7 and follow the signs to Hawick; then change to A68, follow the signs to Jedburgh, and take A6089 to Kelso.

VISITOR INFORMATION The **tourist office** is at Town House, The Square (☎ **0870/608-0404**). April through June, it's open Monday through Saturday from 10am to 5pm and Sunday from 10am to 2pm; July and August, hours are Monday through Saturday from 10:30am to 5:30pm and Sunday from 10am to 2pm; September hours are Monday through Saturday from 9:30am to 5pm and Sunday from 10am to 2pm; and October hours are Monday through Saturday from 10am to 4pm and Sunday from 10am to 1pm.

SEEING THE SIGHTS

Floors Castle 🎯 On the banks of the Tweed, the home of the dukes of Roxburghe was designed in 1721 by William Adam and remodeled in the mid–19th century by William Playfair. Part of the castle contains superb French and English furniture, porcelain, tapestries, and paintings by Gainsborough, Reynolds, and Canaletto. You'll also find a licensed restaurant, a coffee shop, and a gift shop, as well as a walled garden and garden center. You might recognize Floors: It was a major backdrop for the Tarzan film *Greystoke.*

Hwy. A697, 3km (2 miles) north of Kelso. ☎ **01573/223333.** Admission £5.75 ($9.20) adults, £4.75 ($7.60) seniors, £3.25 ($5.20) children ages 3–15, free for children ages 2 and under. Apr–Oct daily 11am–4:50pm (last admission 4pm). Closed Nov–Mar. Follow the signs north from Kelso center.

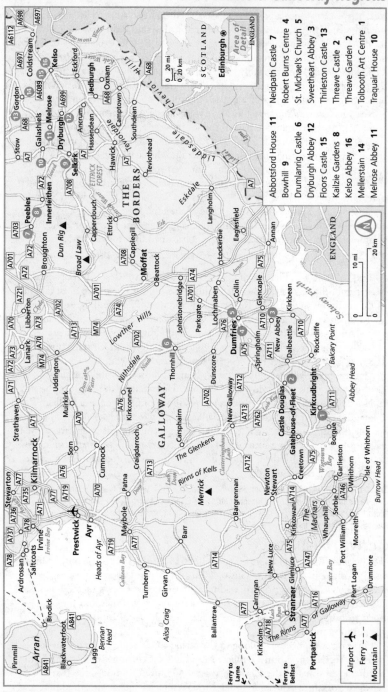

Neidpath Castle **7**
Robert Burns Centre **4**
St. Michael's Church **5**
Sweetheart Abbey **3**
Thirleston Castle **13**
Threave Castle **2**
Threave Garden **2**
Tolbooth Art Centre **1**
Traquair House **10**

Abbotsford House **11**
Bowhill **9**
Drumlanrig Castle **6**
Dryburgh Abbey **12**
Floors Castle **15**
Kailzie Gardens **8**
Kelso Abbey **16**
Mellerstain **14**
Melrose Abbey **11**

SCOTLAND

Edinburgh ✪

Area of
Detail

ENGLAND

20 mi
0   20 km

ENGLAND

10 mi

20 km

Airport ✈
Ferry – – –
Mountain ▲

Kelso Abbey   Once a great ecclesiastical center, Kelso Abbey has lain in ruins since the late 16th century, when it suffered its last and most devastating attack by the English, who ripped off its roofs, burned it, and declared it officially defunct. The lands and remaining buildings were given to the earl of Roxburghe. The oldest (1128) and probably largest of the Border abbeys, it was once one of the richest, collecting revenues and rents from granges, fisheries, mills, and manor houses throughout the region. In 1919, the abbey was given to the nation.

Kelso has had its moments in history, including the crowning of the infant James III. At the entrance is part of the south recessed doorway, where some of the sculpture on the arches is still fairly intact. The massive west transept tower still suggests its original massive construction, and a trio of building sections with round-headed openings remains. The west front and tower are still visible, the whole flanked by buttresses crowned with rounded turrets. A partial cloister here dates from 1933, when it was built as the Roxburghe family vault. Sir Walter Scott knew Kelso Abbey well, as he spent time here studying at Waverley Cottage, which you can see from the abbey's parking area; it was once the Kelso Grammar School, where the famous author learned how to read and write.

Bridge St. Free admission. Apr–Dec Mon–Sat 10am–6:30pm, Sun 2–6:30pm; Jan–Mar by arrangement only.

Mellerstain ★★   Eleven kilometers (7 miles) northwest of Kelso stands Mellerstain, the seat of the earls of Haddington. This is one of the most famous of the mansions designed by Robert Adam and one of Scotland's greatest Georgian residences. William Adam built two wings on the house in 1725, and his more famous son, Robert, designed the main building some 40 years later.

Mellerstain is associated with Lady Grisell Baillie (born Grisell Hume). In 1689, at 13 years of age, this Scottish heroine showed great courage by hiding her father in the village church's crypt, bringing him food and supplies in the dead of night, and facing down the English. Hounded by the English, she fled to Holland but returned in triumph with William of Orange (later William I of England) and later married into the Baillie family, scions of Mellerstain. You can see the interior, with its decorations and ceilings and impressive library, as well as paintings and antique furniture. The garden terrace offers a panoramic view south to the lake, with the Cheviot Hills in the distance. Afternoon tea is served, and souvenir gifts are on sale.

Gordon. Ⓒ 01573/410225. Admission £5.50 ($8.80) adults, £5 ($8) seniors, £3 ($4.80) children. May–Sept Sun–Fri 12:30–5pm; Oct–Apr by arrangement only. From Edinburgh, follow A68 to Earlston, then follow the signs to Mellerstain for another 8km (5 miles); from Kelso, head northwest along A6089 until you see the signposted turn to the left.

ACTIVE PURSUITS

The 18-hole **Roxburghe Golf Course** (Ⓒ **01573/450331**) is the only championship course in the region. This 6,471m (7,111-yard) course was designed by Dave Thomas, one of Britain's leading golf architects. Guests of the hotel (see "Where to Stay & Dine," below) can most easily get tee times, but the course is open to nonmembers as well. Greens fees are £50 ($80) for 18 holes, or £70 ($112) for a full day's play.

Our favorite spot for drinking in the scenic countryside is the nearby village of **Kirk Yeetholm,** 11km (7 miles) southeast of Kelso on B6352. This is the northern terminus of the **Pennine Way,** a 403km (250-mile) hike that begins down in Yorkshire, England. Today Kirk Yeetholm is filled with tired hikers at the end of the trail, but it was once the Gypsy capital of Scotland—until 1883, a Gypsy queen was crowned here. You can see (at least from the outside) the "Gypsy palace," really a tiny cottage in the center of the village.

Another place for walking and hiking is around **Smailholm Tower** (© **01316/ 688800**), on a ridge 13km (8 miles) west of Kelso and 3km (2 miles) south of Mellerstain (see listing, above), signposted off B6404. A so-called peel tower (fortified tower) from the 1500s, it has been restored and rises 18m (60 ft.) above a loch, providing some of the best views of the Borders. October through March, it's open Saturday from 9:30am to 4:30pm and Sunday from 2 to 4:30pm. April through September, it's open daily from 9:30am to 6:30pm, charging £2.20 ($3.50) admission for adults, £1.60 ($2.55) for seniors and students, and 75p ($1.20) for children.

WHERE TO STAY & DINE

For some of the best cuisine in the Borders, refer to Edenwater House below.

Abbey Bank   This sophisticated B&B started out as the home of a local doctor in 1815. Today, it's owned by Douglas McAdam and his wife, Diah, both of whom have lived in Indonesia and Korea. The house is filled with a mix of British and Oriental furniture. Each sunny guest room has streamlined modern furniture. Because of Diah's familiarity with Indonesian cuisine, you'll be offered *nasi goreng,* the national rice-based dish, as well as a traditional Scottish breakfast of bacon, sausage, eggs, and haggis. A greenhouse contains peach vines and many of the seedlings Douglas nurtures during the coldest months. *Note:* Smoking is not permitted in the guest rooms.

The Knowes, Kelso, The Borders TD5 7BH. ©/fax **01573/226550.** www.aboutscotland.com/kelso/abbey bank.html. 5 units. £56 ($90) double. Rates include breakfast. MC, V. *In room:* TV, coffeemaker, no phone.

Cross Keys Hotel   Facing the cobbled main square of the town, the facade of this hotel is done in a stately Georgian style from 1769. Guests here have included Bonnie Prince Charlie and Beatrix Potter. The public areas are comfortable and busy, vaguely inspired by Scottish Art Nouveau master Charles Rennie Mackintosh. The midsize guest rooms are well appointed and have double-glazed windows; each has a shower-only bathroom. The superior rooms are larger and sport sofas; all are nonsmoking. The hotel's cozy Scottish-style bar, The 36, boasts an impressive collection of single-malt whiskies.

36 The Square, Kelso, The Borders TD5 7HL. © **01573/223303.** Fax 01573/225792. www.cross-keys-hotel.co.uk. 28 units. £52–£104 ($83–$166) double. Rates include breakfast. AE, MC, V. **Amenities:** Restaurant; bar. *In room:* TV, coffeemaker, hair dryer (superior rooms only), iron/ironing board.

Edenwater House ★★ *Finds*   This former private manor house opening onto the Edenwater lies in the village of Ednam, 3.2km (2 miles) north of Kelso. It enjoys one of the most tranquil settings in the Borders and is an exceedingly comfortable small private hotel known for its excellent cuisine and personal service. Guests meet each other in the formal and spacious drawing room where a log fire burns on chilly nights. In fair weather they can stroll through the garden and grounds. Bedrooms (all nonsmoking) are large, airy, and beautifully furnished. Units contain a private bathroom, three with tub, one with shower. The food is among the best in the area, but the restaurant is open to nonresidents only for dinner on Friday and Saturday. A fixed-price menu costs £33 ($52).

Ednam (off the B6461), Kelso TD5 7QL. © **01573/224070.** Fax 01573/226615. www.edenwaterhouse.co.uk. 4 units. £70–£90 ($112–$144) double. Rates include full breakfast. MC, V. Closed Jan 1–14. **Amenities:** Restaurant. *In room:* TV, beverage maker, hair dryer, iron.

Ednam House Hotel ★★ The Ednam, on the fringe of Kelso, is a conversion of a 1761 Georgian house often referred to as "that lovely place beside the river." In the oldest section is an unusual collection of antiques, and period furnishings are found throughout. The so-called Principal Rooms— the original master bedrooms of the manor—lie on the third floor and offer a view of the river; less expensive and scenic are those on the first and second floors. The rooms vary in size, but all come with shower or bath and bathrobes.

The Georgian-style Orangerie, a building where oranges were once grown, lies only 9m (30 ft.) from the main house. Often rented to families or groups of friends, it houses two elegantly furnished and most comfortable upstairs bedrooms with a shared living room downstairs overlooking the river. These accommodations are very private and exclusive and feature loads of antiques.

Bridge St., Kelso, The Borders TD5 7HT. ℂ 01573/224168. Fax 01573/226319. www.ednamhouse.com. 32 units. £89–£124 ($142–$198) double. Rates include breakfast. Fishing and golf packages available. MC, V. **Amenities:** Restaurant; nearby golf; babysitting. *In room:* TV, coffeemaker, hair dryer.

Roxburghe Hotel and Golf Course ★★ This late-19th-century castle stands on 200 acres of woodland, lawns, and gardens. It was built as the family home of the Roxburghes, who valued its location on the trout-filled Teviot. In 1982, it was converted into a country hotel: The old stable block contains 6 guest rooms; another 16 are in the main house. All are well appointed; suites and a few doubles have four-poster beds. Amid a subdued but elegant decor, the hotel has four log-burning fireplaces going, even in summer. The hotel also offers a number of leisure and sporting activities, from archery to biking to fishing.

Hwy. A698, Helton, Kelso, The Borders TD5 8JZ. ℂ 01573/450331. Fax 01573/450611. www.roxburghe.net. 22 units. £125–£175 ($200–$280) double, £215 ($344) double with four-poster bed; £265 ($424) suite. Rates include breakfast. AE, DC, MC, V. Take A698 5km (3 miles) southwest of Kelso. **Amenities:** Restaurant; bar; golf course; tennis court; spa; fishing; shooting. *In room:* TV, hair dryer.

A SIDE TRIP TO DRYBURGH ABBEY

Sixteen kilometers (10 miles) west of Kelso and 6km (4 miles) southeast of Melrose (off A68), you'll find the town of **Dryburgh** and its ruined abbey. The adjoining town is **St. Boswells,** an old village on the Selkirk–Kelso road. Near Dryburgh is **Scott's View** ★ (take B6356 north) over the Tweed to Sir Walter's beloved Eildon Hills; it's the most glorious vista in the region.

Dryburgh Abbey ★★ These Gothic ruins are surrounded by gnarled yew trees and cedars of Lebanon, said to have been planted by knights returning from the Crusades. It's still a lovely ruin, and its setting in a loop of the Tweed is memorable. The cloister buildings are relatively intact, but not much remains of the church itself, except a few foundation stones. You can see enough fragments to realize that the architectural style was transitional, between the Romanesque and the pointed early English style. Sir Walter Scott is buried here in a pillared side chapel.

Hwy. A68, Dryburgh, Roxburghshire. ℂ 01835/822381. Admission £3 ($4.80) adults, £2.30 ($3.70) seniors, £1 ($1.60) children ages 5–15, free for children ages 4 and under. Apr–Sept daily 9:30am–6:30pm (July–Aug to 7:30pm); Oct–Mar Mon–Sat 9:30am–4:30pm, Sun 2–4:30pm. Drive south from Dryburgh along B6356 (it's signposted); from Edinburgh take A68 to St. Boswells and turn onto B6404 and then left onto B6356.

ACCOMMODATIONS & DINING

Dryburgh Abbey Hotel ★★ Next to the abbey ruins, this hotel is the best in the area. It was built in 1845 as the home of Lady Grisell Baillie and remained in her family until 1929. It's said to be haunted by the "gray lady," who had an ill-fated affair with a monk that led to his execution and her suicide by drowning.

After restoration, the deteriorated property was the first in the Borders to be awarded five crowns by the Scottish Tourist Board. The accommodations—named for fishing lures—include both deluxe rooms with half-tester or four-poster beds (some have small balconies) and standard abbey- or river-view rooms. The Tower Suites have separate sitting rooms, bathrobes, and abbey or river views.

Hwy. B6404, outside St. Boswells, The Borders TD6 0RQ. © 01835/822261. Fax 01835/823945. www.dry burgh.co.uk. 37 units. £114–£164 ($182–$262) double; £194–£204 ($310–$326) suite for 2. Rates include full Scottish breakfast. AE, MC, V. **Amenities:** Restaurant; bar; heated indoor pool; nearby golf; 24-hr. room service; babysitting; laundry service; nearby fishing. *In room:* TV, coffeemaker, hair dryer, iron/ironing board, trouser press.

2 Melrose

60km (37 miles) SE of Edinburgh; 113km (70 miles) NW of Newcastle-upon-Tyne; 65km (40 miles) W of Berwick-upon-Tweed

Rich in sights, Melrose is one of the highlights of the Borders: It offers one of the most beautiful ruined abbeys in the Borders as well as the region's most widely diversified shopping, and Abbotsford House, former home of Sir Walter Scott, is 3km (2 miles) west. And Melrose is close to the Southern Upland Way, which passes to the north of Melrose. Even if you can take only part of this trail (see chapter 1, "The Best of Britain"), take a day hike on the section along the River Tweed outside Melrose—it's one of the most delightful and scenic walks in Scotland.

ESSENTIALS

GETTING THERE   The nearest rail station is in Berwick-upon-Tweed, where you can catch a bus to Melrose. From Berwick, about five buses per day travel to Melrose; travel time is about 90 minutes. Fares are about £4.55 ($7.30) one-way and £9 ($14) round-trip. Call the tourist office in Berwick-upon-Tweed at © 01289/330733 for bus schedules and © 0845/748-4950 for train schedules.

Many visitors prefer to take the bus into Melrose directly from Edinburgh. Travel time by bus from Edinburgh is 90 minutes, and buses depart every 1½ hours throughout the day. Call © 0870/580-8080 for more information.

Driving from Edinburgh, you can reach Melrose by going southeast along A7 and following the signs to Galashiels. From Kelso, take A699 west to St. Boswells and at the junction with A6091 head northwest.

VISITOR INFORMATION   The tourist office is at **Abbey House,** Abbey Street (© 0870/608-0404). In April, May, and October, it's open Monday through Saturday from 10am to 5pm and Sunday from 10am to 1pm. June and September hours are Monday through Saturday from 10am to 5:30pm and Sunday from 10am to 2pm. July and August, hours are Monday through Saturday from 9:30am to 6:30pm and Sunday from 10am to 6pm.

SEEING THE SIGHTS

Melrose Abbey ★★   These lichen-covered ruins, among the most beautiful in Europe, are all that's left of the ecclesiastical community established by Cistercian monks in 1136. The complex's pure Gothic lines were made famous by Sir Walter Scott, who was instrumental in getting the decayed remains repaired and restored in the early 19th century. In *The Lay of the Last Minstrel,* Scott wrote, "If thou would'st view fair Melrose aright, go visit in the pale moonlight." You can still view its red-sandstone shell, built in the Perpendicular style and filled with elongated windows and carved capitals with delicate tracery. The heart of Robert the Bruce is supposed to be interred in the abbey, but the location is unknown. Look for the beautiful carvings and the tombs of other famous Scotsmen buried in the chancel.

Abbey St. ℭ **01896/822562.** Admission £3.50 ($5.60) adults, £2.50 ($4) seniors, £1.20 ($1.90) children. Apr–Sept daily 9:30am–6:30pm; Oct–Mar Mon–Sat 9:30am–4:30pm, Sun 2–4:30pm.

Abbotsford House ★★   This was the home Sir Walter Scott built and lived in from 1812 until he died. Designed in the Scots baronial style and considered Scott's most enduring monument (after his literary works), it contains many relics, including artifacts and mementos the famous author collected from the Waterloo battlefield. Other exhibits include his clothes and his death mask. Especially interesting is his study, with his writing desk and chair. In 1935, two secret drawers were found in the desk. One of them contained 57 letters, part of the correspondence between Sir Walter and his wife-to-be.

Scott purchased Cartley Hall farmhouse on the banks of the Tweed in 1812. In 1822, he had the old house demolished and replaced it with the building you see today. Scott was one of Britain's earliest souvenir hunters, scouring the land for artifacts associated with the historical characters he rendered into novel form. One of his proudest possessions was a sword given to the duke of Montrose by English king Charles I for his cooperation (some say collaboration) during the struggles between Scotland and England. The sword is proudly displayed near a gun, sword, dagger, and small knife owned by the sworn enemy of the duke, cattle herder Rob Roy, whose exploits were later crafted by Sir Walter Scott into one of his most enduring dramas (you may remember the Liam Neeson film from a few years back). You can see Scott's study, library (with 9,000 rare volumes), drawing room, entrance hall, and armories—even the dining room overlooking the Tweed where he died on September 21, 1832. There are also extensive gardens and grounds to visit, plus the private chapel, added after Scott's death.

Hwy. B6360, Melrose. ℭ **01896/752043.** Admission £4.20 ($6.70) adults, £2.10 ($3.35) children. Mar–Oct Mon–Sat 9:30am–5pm, Sun 2–5pm; Nov–Feb Mon–Sat 9:30am–5pm. Head just off A7, south of the junction with A72, onto B6360, some 4km (2½ miles) southeast of Galashiels.

Thirlestane Castle ★   One of Scotland's most imposing country houses, Thirlestane has been owned by the Lauderdale family since 1218. A T-shaped building, the castle has a keep from around the end of the 16th century and was much altered after Queen Victoria took the throne. The interior is known for its ornamental plaster ceilings, the finest in the country from the Restoration period. In the old nurseries is the Historic Toy Collection, and Border Country Life exhibits depict life in the Borders from prehistoric times to the present.

16km (10 miles) north of Melrose, overlooking Leader Water, about 1km (½-mile) from Lauder. ℭ **01578/ 722430.** www.thirlestanecastle.co.uk. Admission £5.50 ($8.80) adults, £3 ($4.80) children, £15 ($24) families (2 adults and children). May 1–Oct 10 Sun–Fri 10:30am–4:30pm (last admission at 3:30pm). Closed late Oct to Apr. Take A68 to Lauder in Berwickshire, 16km (10 miles) north of Melrose and 45km (28 miles) south of Edinburgh on A68.

Traquair House ★   Dating from the 10th century, this is perhaps Scotland's oldest and most romantic house, rich in associations with Mary Queen of Scots and the Jacobite uprisings. The great house is still lived in by the Stuarts of Traquair. One of the most poignant exhibits is an ornately carved oak cradle in the King's Room, in which Mary rocked her infant son, who later became James VI of Scotland and James I of England. Other treasures here are glass, embroideries, silver, manuscripts, and paintings. Of particular interest is a brew house equipped as it was 2 centuries ago and still used regularly. On the grounds are craft workshops as well as a maze and woodland walks.

Hwy. A72, 26km (16 miles) west of Melrose. (℃ 01896/830323. www.traquair.co.uk. Admission £5.60 ($8.95) adults, £5.30 ($8.50) seniors, £3.10 ($4.95) students and children, £16.50 ($26) families of 5. Easter–May and Sept–Oct Mon–Sat 9:30am–5pm, Sun 2–5pm; June–Aug daily 9:30am–5pm. Closed Nov–Easter.

WHERE TO STAY

Burt's Hotel   Within walking distance of the abbey, this family-run inn dates from 1722. It has a traditional three-story town house design and offers a taste of small-town Scotland. The decor is modern, with an airy and restful feeling. All the guest rooms are well furnished, each equipped with a shower. In the attractive bar, which sports Windsor chairs and a coal-burning fireplace, tasty bar lunches and suppers are served (as well as 90 different single malt whiskies).

Market Square, Melrose, The Borders TD6 9PN. (℃ 01896/822285. Fax 01896/822870. www.burtshotel.co.uk. 20 units. £92–£96 ($147–$154) double. Rates include breakfast. AE, DC, MC, V. Free parking. **Amenities:** Restaurant; bar; room service; laundry service. *In room:* TV, coffeemaker, hair dryer.

Kings Arms Hotel *(Kids)*   One of Melrose's oldest commercial buildings still in use, this 18th-century coaching inn has a three-story stone-and-brick facade that overlooks the pedestrian traffic of the main street. Inside is a series of cozy but slightly dowdy public rooms and half a dozen simple but comfortably furnished small guest rooms, each with a shower. One suite has a kitchen and is large enough for families, and a cottage is available in summer only. The nonsmoking restaurant serves an odd mix of international offerings, including Mexican tacos and enchiladas, Indian curries, British steak pies, and giant Yorkshire puddings.

High St., Melrose, The Borders TD6 9BP. (℃ 01896/822143. Fax 01896/823812. www.kingsarmsmelrose.co.uk. 7 units. £60 ($95) double. MC, V. **Amenities:** Restaurant; bar. *In room:* TV, kitchen (in family suite only), coffeemaker.

Millars of Melrose *(★)*   This well-maintained, family-owned hotel is in the heart of Melrose and easily recognizable by the colorful window boxes adorning its facade in summer. Most accommodations are medium in size and rather functionally but comfortably furnished. The most spacious unit comes with a traditional four-poster bed and a Jacuzzi; honeymooners sometimes stay here and are welcomed in style with a complimentary bottle of champagne, flowers, and chocolates. One room is set aside for use by families. Bathrooms are equipped either with tub or shower.

The split-level dining room offers tasty, reasonably priced meals. Meals are also served in the bar, which boasts a fine assortment of beers, wines, and whiskies.

Market Square, Melrose TD6 9PQ. (℃ 01896/822645. Fax 01896/823474. www.millarshotel.co.uk. 11 units. £85 ($136) double; £90 ($144) family room. Rates include breakfast. MC, V. Follow the A68 into Melrose to the center of town. **Amenities:** Restaurant; bar. *In room:* TV, coffeemaker, hair dryer, trouser press.

Traquair Arms Hotel *(★)*   This is the area's most tranquil retreat for those seeking a country house atmosphere. The small hotel was built as a three-story coaching inn around 1780 and has later Victorian additions. Open fires in the bar lounge and fresh flowers in the dining room create a pleasant ambience. The cozy guest rooms come with comfortable furnishings, well-maintained bathrooms, and views over the valley. The hotel is known for fine pub food; vegetarians and others with special dietary needs can be accommodated. All dishes are freshly prepared by chefs Hugh Anderson and Sara Currie. The hotel is within a 5-minute walk of the River Tweed, and salmon and trout fishing can be arranged.

Traquair Rd., Innerleithen, The Borders EH44 6PD. *©* **01896/830229.** Fax 01896/830260. traquair.arms@ scottishborders.com. 15 units. £72–£80 ($115–$128) double. Rates include breakfast; dinner £18 ($29). AE, MC, V. Take E69 from Melrose for 23km (14 miles). **Amenities:** Restaurant; bar. *In room:* TV, beverage maker.

WHERE TO DINE

Don't miss the pastries at Melrose's best bakery, **Jackie Lunn, Ltd.,** High Street (*©* **01896/822888**).

Two of the town's most likable pubs are the one in the **King's Arms,** High Street (*©* **01896/822143**), where you'll generally find lots of rugby players lifting a pint or two, and the somewhat more sedate one in **Burts Hotel,** The Square (*©* **01896/822285**).

Marmion's Brasserie SCOTTISH   Across from the post office in a 150-year-old building, this tasteful restaurant is a cross between a brasserie and a coffee shop. The kitchen likes to use all-Scottish ingredients. The cheerful staff will offer menu items that frequently change, but might include dishes such as salmon in phyllo with ginger-and-lime sauce; breaded chicken with aged northern Italian Talleggio cheese; swordfish with butter beans, bacon, and sweet onions; exotic ostrich steak in red-wine sauce; and charcoal-grilled steaks done to perfection.

2 Buccleuch St. *©* **01896/822245.** Reservations recommended for dinner. Main courses £3–£11 ($4.80–$18) lunch, £6–£16 ($9.60–$26) dinner. MC, V. Mon–Sat 9am–10pm.

3 Selkirk: At the Heart of Scott Country

65km (40 miles) SE of Edinburgh; 118km (73 miles) SE of Glasgow; 11km (7 miles) S of Galashiels

In the heart of Sir Walter Scott country, Selkirk is a great base if you want to explore many of the region's historic homes, including Bowhill (see below) and Traquair House (see "Melrose," above). Melrose offers more to see and do, but this ancient royal burgh can easily occupy a morning of your time.

Selkirk was the hometown of the African explorer Mungo Park (1771–1806), whose exploits could have made a great Harrison Ford movie. Park was a doctor, but he won fame for exploring the River Niger; he drowned while escaping in a canoe from hostile natives. A statue of him is at the east end of High Street in Mungo Park.

ESSENTIALS

GETTING THERE   Berwick-upon-Tweed is the nearest rail station, where you can get a connecting bus to Selkirk, some of which require a connection in Kelso. The bus ride is just under 2 hours, costing £6 ($9.60) one-way or £12 ($19) round-trip. Call the tourist office in Selkirk at *©* **0870/608-0404** for bus schedules or *©* **0845/748-4950** for rail information.

Buses running between Newcastle-upon-Tyne and Edinburgh make stops at Selkirk. The trip takes about 2½ hours and costs £7 ($11) one-way or £12 ($19) round-trip.

Driving from Edinburgh, head southeast along A7 to Galashiels, then cut southwest along B6360. The trip takes about an hour. To get here from Melrose, take B6360 southwest to Selkirk; it's a 15-minute drive.

VISITOR INFORMATION   A **tourist office** is located at Halliwell's House Museum (*©* **01750/720054**). April, May, and June, it's open Monday through Saturday from 10am to 5pm and Sunday from 10am to noon; July and August, hours are Monday through Saturday from 10am to 5:30pm and Sunday from 10am to 1pm; September hours are Monday through Saturday from 10am to

Finds Where the Literary Greats Found Beauty

In Selkirk, the former royal hunting grounds and forests have given way to textile mills along its riverbanks, but there are many beautiful spots in the nearby countryside—notably **St. Mary's Loch,** 23km (14 miles) southwest. Scottish sailors and fishermen love this bucolic body of water, as did literary greats like Thomas Carlyle and Robert Louis Stevenson. One of the most panoramic stretches of the Southern Upland Way, and one of Scotland's great backpacking trails (see chapter 1, "The Best of Britain"), skirts the east shore of St. Mary's Loch. You can take a day hike on the 13km (8-mile) stretch from the loch to Traquair House (see "Melrose," above).

5pm and Sunday from 10am to noon; October hours are Monday through Saturday from 10am to 4pm and Sunday from 10am to 2pm.

EXPLORING THE AREA

Bowhill ★   This 18th- and 19th-century Border home of the Scotts, the dukes of Buccleuch, contains a rare art collection, French furniture, porcelain, silverware, and mementos of Sir Walter Scott, Queen Victoria, and the duke of Monmouth. Its paintings include works by Canaletto, Claude, Raeburn, Gainsborough, and Reynolds. In the Country Park surrounding the house, you'll find an Adventure Woodland play area, a Victorian kitchen, an audiovisual presentation, a gift shop, and a tearoom/restaurant. Sotheby's "Works of Art" courses are offered at Bowhill.

Hwy. A708, 5km (3 miles) west of Selkirk. ✆ **01750/222-04.** Admission to house £6 ($9.60) adults, £4 ($6.40) seniors, £2 ($3.20) children; admission to Country Park £2 ($3.20). House, July daily 1–5pm; Country Park, Apr–Aug daily 11am–5pm. Closed other months.

WHERE TO STAY & DINE

Heatherlie House Hotel   An imposing stone-and-slate Victorian mansion with steep gables and turrets, this hotel is set on 2 acres of wooded lands and mature gardens, west from the center along the Green and a short walk from Selkirk. The guest rooms are spotlessly maintained and furnished with reproductions of older pieces. The lone single room has no bathroom of its own.

A coal-burning fireplace adds warmth to the lounge, where reasonably priced bar meals are available daily. The high-ceilinged dining room is open for dinners. Golf, fishing, and shooting packages can be arranged. About half a dozen golf courses are a reasonable drive away.

Heatherlie Park, Selkirk, The Borders TD7 5AL. ✆ **01750/721200.** Fax 01750/720005. www.heatherlie. freeserve.co.uk. 7 units, 6 with private bathroom. £70 ($112) double with bathroom. Rates include breakfast. MC, V. **Amenities:** Restaurant; pub. _In room:_ TV, coffeemaker, hair dryer.

4 Peebles

37km (23 miles) S of Edinburgh; 85km (53 miles) SE of Glasgow; 32km (20 miles) W of Melrose

Peebles, a royal burgh and county town, is a market center in the Tweed Valley, noted for its large woolen mills and fine knitwear shopping. Scottish kings used to come here when they hunted in Ettrick Forest, 35km (22 miles) away. It's one of hundreds of forests scattered throughout the Borders and is very pretty, but no more so than forested patches closer to the town.

Peebles is known as a writer's town. It was home to Sir John Buchan (Baron Tweedsmuir, 1875–1940), a Scottish author who later was appointed governor-general of Canada. He's remembered chiefly for the adventure story *Prester John* and was the author of *The Thirty-Nine Steps,* the first of a highly successful series of secret-service thrillers and later a Hitchcock film. Robert Louis Stevenson lived for a time in Peebles and drew on the surrounding countryside in his novel *Kidnapped* (1886).

ESSENTIALS

GETTING THERE   The nearest rail station is in Berwick-upon-Tweed, but bus connections from there into Peebles are quite inconvenient. It's easier to get from Edinburgh to Peebles by a 50-minute bus ride. Bus fares from Edinburgh are around £4.15 ($6.65) one-way. Call ℭ **0845/748-4950** for rail and bus information.

If you're driving, take A703 south from Edinburgh. Continue west along A6091 from Melrose.

VISITOR INFORMATION   The **tourist office** is at the Chamber Institute, 23 High St. (ℭ **0870/608-0404**). From April 1 to June 1, it's open Monday through Saturday from 9am to 5pm and Sunday from 11am to 4pm; from June 2 to June 29, hours are Monday through Saturday from 9am to 5:30pm and Sunday from 10am to 4pm; from June 30 to August 31, hours are Monday through Saturday from 9am to 6pm and Sunday from 10am to 4pm; from September 1 to September 28, hours are Monday through Saturday from 9am to 5:30pm and Sunday from 10am to 4pm; from September 29 to November 1, hours are Monday through Saturday from 9am to 5pm and Sunday from 11am to 4pm; from November 2 to December, hours are Monday through Saturday from 9:30am to 5pm and Sunday from 11am to 3pm; January through March, hours are Monday through Saturday from 9:30am to 4pm and closed on Sunday.

EXPLORING THE TOWNS & THE COUNTRYSIDE

The tourist office (see above) provides pamphlets describing the best walking tours in the region. The £1 ($1.60) pamphlet **"Walks Around Peebles"** describes 20 walks, including one along the Tweed. The **Tweed Walk** begins in the center of Peebles, and—with the twists and turns described in the pamphlet—takes you downstream along the river, then upstream along the opposite bank for a return to Peebles. You can follow the path for segments of 4km (2½ miles), 7km (4½ miles), or 12km (7½ miles). Regardless of the length of your walk, you'll pass the stalwart walls of Neidpath Castle.

Glentress Bicycle Trekking Centre, Glentress, Peebles (ℭ **01721/721736**), is the place to rent a bike. You'll have to leave a refundable deposit of £50 ($80). Daily rates range from £12 ($19) for a half day and £16 ($26) for a full day, and rentals must be arranged in advance. It's open daily April through October from 9am to 7pm (Sat and Sun opens at 10am); November, Wednesday from noon to 10pm and Saturday and Sunday from 10am to 5pm.

Neidpath Castle   Once linked with two of the greatest families in Scotland (the Frasiers and the Hayes), Neidpath, a summer attraction, hasn't been occupied since 1958. Part of the interest here is the way the castle's medieval shell was transformed during the 1600s into a residence, using then-fashionable architectural conceits. Enormous galleries were divided into smaller, cozier spaces, with the exception of the Great Hall, whose statuesque proportions are still visible. The hall's medieval stonework is decorated with 11 batik panels crafted in the mid-1990s by noted artist Monica Hanisch; they depict the life and accomplishments of Mary Queen of Scots. Other displays are Roman and Celtic archaeological remnants and material commemorating the Frasiers and their links to Scottish national pride (members of their family were executed by the English at the same time as William Wallace). Other parts of the museum are devoted to the role the castle has played in the filming of movies such as *The Bruce* (an English film that had the bad luck to be released simultaneously with *Braveheart*), *Merlin, The Quest Begins,* and the courtyard scene in the recent TV miniseries "Joan of Arc," where the heroine was burnt at the stake. Recently filmed here were new British versions of *Hamlet* and *King Lear.*

Tweeddale, on A72, 1.5km (1 mile) west of Peebles. ℂ 01721/720333. Admission £3 ($4.80) adults, £2.50 ($4) seniors, £1 ($1.60) children, £7.50 ($12) families. June 30–Sept 15 and Apr 17–22 Mon–Sat 10:30am–5pm, Sun 12:30–5pm. Closed all other dates.

Kailzie Gardens   These 17 acres of formal walled gardens, dating from 1812, include a rose garden, woodlands, and *burnside* (streamside) walks. Restored during the past 20 years, it provides a stunning array of plants from early spring to late autumn and has a collection of waterfowl and owls. There's also an art gallery, a shop, and a restaurant.

Kailzie on B7062, 4km (2½ miles) southeast of Peebles. ℂ 01721/720007. Admission £2.50 ($4) adults, 75p ($1.20) children; gardens only £1 ($1.60). Daily dawn–dusk.

Dawyck Botanic Garden   This botanical garden, run by the Royal Botanic Garden in Edinburgh, has a large variety of conifers, some exceeding 30m (100 ft.) in height, as well as many species of flowering shrubs. There's also a fine display of early-spring bulbs, plus wood walks rich in wildlife interest.

Hwy. B712, 13km (8 miles) southwest of Peebles. ℂ 01721/760254. Admission £3 ($4.80) adults, £2.50 ($4) seniors and students, £1 ($1.60) children, £7 ($11) families. Mar daily 10am–5pm; Apr–Sept daily 10am–6pm; Oct daily 10am–5pm; and Nov daily 10am–4pm. Local bus marked Biggar.

WHERE TO STAY

You can also rent affordable rooms at the **Horse Shoe Inn** (see "Where to Dine," below).

VERY EXPENSIVE

Cringletie House Hotel ★★★   This imposing 1861 red-sandstone Victorian mansion with towers and turrets is one of the most delightful country-house hotels in the Borders, known for its charming setting and its luxurious rooms. It stands on 28 acres of well-manicured grounds, featuring a superb walled garden that in itself is worth a visit. The tasteful house is immaculately maintained, with public rooms that range from an elegant cocktail lounge to an adjacent conservatory. There's even a small library, plus a large lounge where fellow guests from all over the world meet and chat, and thankfully, there's an elevator. Each of the spacious bedrooms is individually decorated; several units contain their own original fireplaces and a few have four-poster beds. All accommodations open onto views of the extensive grounds. The bathrooms are maintained in state-of-the-art condition and come with luxurious toiletries.

Eddleston, Peebles, The Borders EH45 8PL. ℂ 01721/730233. Fax 01721/730244. www.cringletie.com. 13 units. £120–£140 ($192–$224) double. Rates include breakfast. AE, MC, V. Take A703 for 4km (2½ miles) north of Peebles. **Amenities:** Restaurant; bar; putting green; babysitting; croquet lawn; fishing arranged. *In room:* TV, coffeemaker, hair dryer.

EXPENSIVE/MODERATE

Castle Venlaw Hotel *Kids*　Originally built in 1782 and enlarged in 1854, Castle Venlaw lies among 4 acres of woodlands and offers lovely views of the surrounding countryside. The hotel's round tower and craw-stepped gables are an evocative example of the Scottish baronial style. In early 1999, the hotel was completely redecorated, and the heating system and all bathrooms were replaced and modernized.

Castle Venlaw has 12 spacious and individually decorated rooms—each named for a different malt whisky—that all offer excellent views and a selection of books and magazines. A four-poster room has especially nice views, and the hotel's lone suite has a sitting room with a VCR in addition to the bedroom. In the tower at the top of the castle is a spacious family room with a children's den containing bunk beds, games, TV, and VCR.

Edinburgh Rd., Peebles EH45 8QG. © **01721/720384.** Fax 01721/724066. www.venlaw.co.uk. 13 units. £120–£140 ($192–$224) double; £130–£150 ($208–$240) deluxe; £140–£160 ($224–$256) suite. Rates include breakfast. Children under age 12 staying in parent's room £15 ($24), children ages 13–16 £20 ($32). MC, V. Free parking. Take A703 to Peebles. **Amenities:** Restaurant; bar; room service; laundry service. *In room:* TV, beverage maker.

The Tontine *Finds*　The Tontine has been around since 1807, when it was built as a private club by a group of hunters who sold their friends shares in its ownership. It was constructed by French prisoners of war during the Napoleonic era; later enlargements were made by the Edwardians. Flower boxes adorn its stone lintels, and a stone lion guards the forecourt fountain. The modestly furnished guest rooms are in an angular modern wing built in back of the building's 19th-century core; they come with shower-only bathrooms. The most expensive rooms have river views. The Adam-style dining room is one of the town's architectural gems, with tall fan-topped windows and a minstrels' gallery. The Tweeddale Shoot Bar is cozily rustic.

39 High St., Peebles, The Borders EH45 8AJ. © **01721/720892.** Fax 01721/729732. www.tontinehotel.com. 36 units. £70–£90 ($112–$144) double. Rates include breakfast. Children ages 12 and under stay free in parent's room but pay £5 ($8) for breakfast. AE, DC, MC, V. Free parking. **Amenities:** Restaurant; bar. *In room:* TV, coffeemaker, hair dryer.

INEXPENSIVE

Whitestone House　On the eastern fringe of Peebles, this dignified dark stone house is from 1892. It used to house the pastor of a Presbyterian church that has been demolished and is now the genteel domain of Mrs. Margaret Muir. Its windows overlook a pleasant garden and the glacial deposits of Whitestone Park. The high-ceilinged guest rooms are large and comfortable, evoking life in a quiet private home. Of the two shared bathrooms, one is large and has a shower-and tub-combination, the other only a shower. Mrs. Muir speaks French and German flawlessly, but presides over breakfast with a Scottish brogue.

Innerleithen Rd., Peebles, The Borders EH45 8BD. ©/fax 01721/720337. www.aboutscotland.com/peebles/whitestone.html. 5 units, none with private bathroom. £37–£38 ($59–$61) double. Rates include breakfast. No credit cards. *In room:* TV, radio.

WHERE TO DINE

Horse Shoe Inn SCOTTISH　In the center of the nearby village of Eddleston, this country restaurant serves top-quality beef and steaks. Appetizers include everything from the chef's own paté with oatcakes to smoked Shetland salmon with brown bread. House favorites are steak-and-stout pie, Meldon game pie, and vegetable moussaka. The main focus is the food and drink served in the bar, site of most lunches and dinners. On Friday and Saturday nights and Sunday lunches, the bar is supplemented with a more formal dining room.

The owners, Mr. and Mrs. Hathoway, bought the old school next door and converted it into a guest house with eight rooms at £23 to £45 ($37–$72) per person, depending on the season; the rates include breakfast.

Eddleston. ✆ 01721/730225. Reservations recommended Sat. Main courses £3.50–£17 ($5.60–$27). MC, V. Easter–Oct Mon–Thurs 11am–11pm, Fri–Sun 11am–midnight; Nov–Easter Mon–Thurs 11am–2:30pm and 5:30–11pm, Fri–Sat 11am–2:30pm and 5:30pm–midnight. Take A701 7km (4½ miles) north of Peebles.

PEEBLES AFTER DARK

The town has many options for drinking and dining, and some of the most appealing are in the hotels on the town's edge, even though they may seem rather staid at first glance. On Innerleithen Road, the **Park Hotel** (✆ 01721/720451) and the nearby **Hotel Hydro** (✆ 01721/720602) contain pubs and cocktail lounges.

For an earthier atmosphere, we highly recommend dropping into Peebles's oldest pub, on the ground floor of the **Cross Keys Hotel,** 24 Northgate (✆ 01721/724222), where you'll find 300-year-old smoke-stained panels, a blazing fireplace, and an evocatively crooked bar. Ask the bartender about the resident ghost. Like the Loch Ness monster, she's taken on an almost mythic identity since her last sighting, but the rumor goes that she's the spirit of Sir Walter Scott's former landlady, Marian Ritchie. No one will be shy about telling you his or her theory, especially if you're buying.

5 Moffat

98km (61 miles) S of Edinburgh; 35km (22 miles) NE of Dumfries; 97km (60 miles) SE of Glasgow

A small town at the head of the Annandale Valley, Moffat thrives as a center of a sheep-farming area, symbolized by a statue of a ram on the wide High Street. It's been a holiday resort since the mid–17th century because of the curative properties of its water, and it was here Robert Burns composed the drinking song "O Willie Brewd a Peck o' Maut." Today people visit this town on the banks of the Annan River for its great fishing and golf.

ESSENTIALS

GETTING THERE   The nearest rail station is in Lockerbie, 24km (15 miles) south of Moffat. Call ✆ 0845/748-4950 for train information. Getting to Lockerbie sometimes requires a change of train in Dumfries, so passengers from Edinburgh or Glasgow often transfer to a **National Express** bus at Dumfries for the 35-minute trip straight to Moffat's High Street, which costs £3 ($4.80) one-way. If you are coming from the Lockerbie rail station, though, you can get a National Express bus to Moffat; they run four times a day, and the fare is £4.05 ($6.50) each way. For more bus information, call ✆ 0870/580-8080.

If you're driving from Dumfries, head northeast along A701. From Edinburgh, head south along A701; from Peebles, drive west, following the signs to Glasgow, then turn south on A702 and merge onto M74, following the signs to Moffat.

VISITOR INFORMATION   A tourist office is a 5-minute walk south of the town center, at Unit One, Ledyknowe, off Station Road (✆ 01683/220620). Hours are as follows: from April 1 to June 29, Monday through Saturday from 9:30am to 5pm, Sunday from noon to 4pm; from June 30 to September 14, Monday through Saturday from 9:30am to 6pm, Sunday from noon to 5pm;

Finds **An Angler's Best Friend**

The waters around Moffat teem with salmon, trout, and pike. The best info source about fishing is **Mr. John Jack,** owner/manager of the **Ben Mar Esso Garage,** Station Road (© **01683/220010**), on the town's southern perimeter. He sells fishing permits for £10 to £16 ($16–$26) per day, depending on where you want to fish. The tourist office sells a brochure called *Fishing in Dumfries & Galloway* for £1.50 ($2.40).

---

from September 15 to October 19, Monday through Saturday from 9:30am to 5pm, Sunday from noon to 4pm; and from October 20 to March 31, Monday through Friday from 10am to 5pm, Saturday from 9:30am to 4pm.

EXPLORING THE AREA

The region's most famous course is the **Moffat Golf Course,** Coates Hill (© **01683/220020**), about 1.5km (1 mile) southwest of the town center. Non-members can play if they call in advance. From April to October, a golf pass, valid for a week, allows 7 rounds of golf for £75 ($120) or 10 rounds for £95 ($152). The tourist office has a free brochure called *Golfing in Dumfries & Galloway.*

North of Moffat is lots of panoramic hill scenery. Eight kilometers (5 miles) northwest is a sheer-sided 152m (500-ft.) deep, 3km (2-mile) wide hollow in the hills called the **Devil's Beef Tub,** where cattle thieves *(reivers)* once hid cattle lifted in their raids. This hollow is of interest to geologists because of the way it portrays Ice Age glacial action, and it makes for a good day hike in the quiet countryside. To reach it, walk north from Moffat along the **Annan Water Valley Road,** a rural route with virtually no vehicular traffic. In 6.5km (4 miles), the road will descend a steep slope whose contours form an unusual bowl shape. No signs mark the site, but you'll know it when you get there.

Northeast along Moffat Water, past the 818m (2,696-ft.) high White Coomb, is the **Grey Mare's Tail,** a 61m (200-ft.) hanging waterfall formed by the Tail Burn dropping from Loch Skene; it's part of the National Trust for Scotland.

WHERE TO STAY

You can also find accommodations at **Well View** (see "Where to Dine," below).

Auchen Castle Hotel ✦ About 1.5 km (1 mile) north of the village of Beattock, the area's most luxurious accommodations are at the Auchen, a Victorian mock-castle. It's really a charming country house built in 1849 on the site of Auchen Castle, with terraced gardens and a trout-filled loch. Most of the rooms are spacious. Ask for a room in the main house (which is known as the castle); the others are in the Cedar Lodge, a less desirable annex built in the late 1970s.

Beattock, Dumfriesshire DG10 9SH. © **01683/300407.** Fax 01683/300667. www.auchen-castle-hotel.co.uk. 25 units. £95 ($152) double in main house, £140 ($224) suite breakfast included; £55 ($88) double in Cedar Lodge, breakfast not included, £75 ($120) with breakfast. AE, DC, MC, V. Take A74 for 3km (2 miles) north of Moffat. **Amenities:** Restaurant; bar; room service; laundry service. *In room:* TV, coffeemaker, hair dryer.

Beechwood Country House Hotel *Kids* This is a charming country-house hotel. The Beechwood was the 19th-century headquarters of Miss Thompson's Private Adventure Boarding Establishment and School for Young Ladies. You'll spot its facade of chiseled stone at the end of a narrow rural lane. A tea lawn, smooth as a putting green, is the site for outdoor refreshments on sunny days. The guest rooms have a certain amount of homespun charm; many have been recently renovated. Beds have Egyptian cotton linens and electric blankets to keep you warm on winter nights. Bathrooms were completely refurbished in 2002 and feature deep tubs and Penhaligon toiletries. The hotel has a room set aside for families and has a playpen and provides baby monitors to those traveling with young children.

Harthope Place, Moffat, Dumphriesshire DG10 9HS. ⓒ **01683/220210**. Fax 01683/220889. www.beech woodcountryhousehotel.co.uk. 7 units. £90 ($144) double with breakfast, £138 ($221) double with half board. AE, MC, V. Free parking. **Amenities:** Restaurant; golf, tennis, fishing, and riding arranged. *In room:* TV, coffeemaker, hair dryer.

Moffat House Hotel   The red- and black-stone Moffat House is one of the town's most architecturally noteworthy buildings; it was constructed in 1751 by John Adam. This Best Western affiliate's modernized guest rooms are comfortable and functional, each with a shower and tub bathroom. A few rooms have four-poster beds. Some rooms are equipped for families, others for travelers with disabilities.

Note: The hotel offers some of the best food in town, especially at night, when the chef prepares an international menu.

High St., Moffat, Galloway DG10 9HL. ⓒ **01683/220039**. Fax 01683/221288. www.moffathouse.co.uk. 20 units. £76–£94 ($122–$150) double. Rates include breakfast. AE, DC, MC, V. Free parking. **Amenities:** Restaurant; bar; room service. *In room:* TV, coffeemaker, hair dryer.

Star Hotel   With a 17th-century brick facade, this place bears the quirky fame of being the narrowest free-standing hotel in the United Kingdom—it's only 6m (20 ft.) wide. The guest rooms, last refurbished in 1996, are small and unpretentious, with contemporary furnishings, and bathrooms with either a tub or a shower. The food here is popular; menu items are simple and straightforward but savory. The hotel also rents a 2-bedroom cottage (good for families) for £110 ($176) per night.

44 High St., Moffat, Galloway DG10 9EF. ⓒ **01683/220156**. Fax 01683/221524. www.famousstarhotel.com. 8 units. £56 ($84) double. AE, MC, V. **Amenities:** Restaurant; 2 bars; pool table; babysitting; fishing and golf arranged. *In room:* TV, coffeemaker, hair dryer.

WHERE TO DINE

You can also dine at the restaurants in the hotels above.

Well View ⭑⭑ BRITISH/CONTINENTAL   Come to this hotel restaurant for some of the best food in the region. The setting is mid-Victorian, with Laura Ashley country-cottage charm and views of the kitchen garden. The set-price menus vary almost daily, depending on the season, and may include roasted breast of Perthshire pigeon with red-wine sauce, roasted saddle of venison with gin-and-juniper sauce, or filet of Aberdeen Angus beef with whole-grain mustard sauce.

Upstairs are five guest rooms and a junior suite, with modern furniture and reproduction antiques (including a four-poster bed), Laura Ashley fabrics, free sherry and fresh fruit, TVs, clock radios, tea/coffeemakers, and hair dryers. Depending on the season, doubles are £70 to £102 ($112–$163).

Ballplay Rd., Moffat DG10 9JU. ⓒ **01683/220184**. Fax 01683/220088. www.wellview.co.uk. Reservations recommended. Fixed-price 3-course lunch £15 ($24); fixed-price 6-course dinner £32 ($51). AE, MC, V. Sun–Fri 12:30–1:15pm; daily 7–8:30pm. Take A708 1.2km (¾ mile) east of Moffat.

6 Dumfries: An Ode to Burns

129km (80 miles) SW of Edinburgh; 127km (79 miles) SE of Glasgow; 55km (34 miles) NW of Carlisle

A county town and royal burgh, the Galloway center of Dumfries enjoys associations with national poet Robert Burns and *Peter Pan* author James Barrie. Burns lived in Dumfries from 1791 until his death in 1796 and wrote some of his best-known songs here, including "Auld Lang Syne" and "Ye Banks and Braes of Bonnie Doon." A statue of Burns stands on High Street; you can visit his house, his favorite pub, and his mausoleum. Barrie was a pupil at the academy here and later wrote he got the idea for *Peter Pan* from his games in the nearby garden.

The widest esplanade in Dumfries, **Whitesands,** flanks the edge of the River Nith. It was once the scene of horse and hiring fairs and is a fine place to park your car and explore this provincial town. The town center is reserved for pedestrians, and on the opposite bank of the Nith, the public Deer Park offers a small-scale manicured version of the wild majesty of Scotland. Allow a morning to see the city's major sights, but there's even more to see in the surrounding countryside, including Sweetheart Abbey, Ellisland Farm, and Drumlanrig Castle at Thornhill, which is filled with art, including works by Rembrandt and Leonardo.

ESSENTIALS

GETTING THERE   Seven trains per day make the run from Glasgow's Central Station, taking 1¾ hours. Tickets cost £9.90 ($16) one way but only £10 to £18 ($16–$29) round-trip, depending on time of departure. For 24-hour information, call ℭ **0845/748-4950.**

Stagecoach buses depart from Glasgow (from Buchanan St. Station or Anderston Station); the trip is 2 hours and costs £6.50 ($10) one-way and £10 ($16) round-trip. Buses also run to Dumfries from Edinburgh's St. Andrew's Square. The prices are the same as from Glasgow, but the trip is 3 hours. For bus information, call ℭ **01387/253496.**

If you're driving from Edinburgh, take A701 to Moffat, then continue southwest to Dumfries. From Glasgow, take M74, which becomes A74 before it approaches Moffat. At Moffat, continue southwest along A701.

VISITOR INFORMATION   The **tourist office** is at 64 Whitesands (ℭ **01387/ 253862**), a 2-minute walk from High Street and adjacent to the big parking lots. September through March, it's open Monday through Friday from 10am to 5pm and Saturday from 10am to 4pm; April through August, hours are Monday through Saturday from 10am to 6pm (July and Aug also Sun noon–4pm).

EXPLORING THE TOWN

The 18th-century **St. Michael's Church,** on St. Michael's Street, is the original parish church of Dumfries. Its foundation is ancient—the site was sacred before the advent of Christianity, and a Christian church has stood here for more than 1,300 years. The earliest written records date from 1165 to 1214. The church and the churchyard are interesting to visit because of all their connections with Scottish history, continuing through World War II. You can still see the Burns family pew inside.

In St. Michael's Churchyard, a burial place for at least 900 years, stands the neo-Grecian **Burns Mausoleum.** Built of local sandstone and dripping with literary and patriotic nostalgia, the dome-capped mausoleum is one of the most important pilgrimage sites for Burns fans. The poet is buried here along with his wife, Jean Armour, and five of their children. Burns died in 1796, but his remains weren't moved to the tomb until 1815.

The **Mid Steeple** ✿ on High Street was built in 1707 as municipal buildings, a courthouse, and a prison. The old Scots "ell" measure of almost 1m (37 in.) is carved on the front, and a table of distances includes the mileage to Huntingdon, England, which in the 18th century was the destination for Scottish cattle driven south for the London markets. Today it's used mostly as municipal archives, and its interior is used for government functions.

At Whitesands, the street paralleling the Nith's edge, **four bridges** span the river. The earliest was built by Devorgilla Balliol, widow of John Balliol. Their son, John, was made Scotland's "vassal king" by Edward I of England, the "Hammer of the Scots," who established himself as Scotland's overlord. The bridge (originally with nine arches but now with only six) is still in constant use as a footbridge.

The town's best **shopping** is along the High Street, which is lined with turn-of-the-20th-century facades, and nearby Queensberry Street. **Alternatives,** 73–75 Queensberry St. (© **01387/257467**), is an attractive new-age shop stocking herbal remedies, artful wind chimes, and gift items, especially jewelry inspired by Celtic designs. You'll find men's and women's kilts in dozens of tartan patterns, as well as sweaters, overcoats, hats, and socks, always at realistic prices, at the **Edinburgh Woolen Mill,** 8 Church Place (© **01387/267351**).

If you want to explore the area on two wheels, the **Nithsdale Cycle Centre,** 46 Broon's Rd. (© **01387/254870**), is the place to go. You'll have to leave a 25% deposit; rental rates are £5 ($8) for a half day, £10 ($16) daily, or £35 ($56) weekly. It's open Monday through Saturday from 10am to 5pm.

Burns House   In 1796, Scotland's national poet died in this unpretentious, terraced stone house off St. Michael's Street. Although he only occupied the house during the last 3 years of his life, it contains personal relics and mementos as well as much of the original furniture used by Burns during his creative years.

Burns St. © 01387/255297. Free admission. Apr–Sept Mon–Sat 10am–5pm, Sun 2–5pm; Oct–Mar Tues–Sat 10am–1pm and 2–5pm.

Robert Burns Centre   You'll find this converted 18th-century water mill on the banks of the River Nith. Facilities at the center include an exhibit on the poet, a restaurant, and an audiovisual theater showing films about Burns and the town of Dumfries.

Mill Rd. © 01387/264808. Exhibition free; audiovisual theater £1.50 ($2.40) adults, 75p ($1.20) children, seniors, and students. Apr–Sept Mon–Sat 10am–8pm, Sun 2–5pm; Oct–Mar Tues–Sat 10am–1pm and 2–5pm. From Whitesands, cross the river at Devorgillas Bridge.

Drumlanrig Castle ★   This pink castle, built between 1679 and 1689 in a parkland ringed by wild hills, is the seat of the dukes of Buccleuch and Queensberry. It's home to some outstanding paintings, including a famous Rembrandt, a Leonardo da Vinci, and a Holbein, plus relics related to Bonnie Prince Charlie. There's a playground with amusements for kids and a working crafts center in the old stable yard, and the gardens are gradually being restored to their 1720 magnificence. Meals are served in the old kitchen, hung with gleaming copper.

Thornhill, 5km (3 miles) north of Thornhill off A76 and 26km (16 miles) southwest of A74 at Elvanfoot. © 01848/330248 or 01848/331555. Admission £6 ($9.60) adults, £4 ($6.40) seniors, £2 ($3.20) children, £15 ($24) families. May–Aug Mon–Sat 11am–4pm, Sun noon–4pm. Closed Sept–Apr.

Dumfries Museum   Southwestern Scotland's largest museum occupies a converted 18th-century windmill atop Corbelly Hill. Visit it only if you have extra time and an interest in the region's early geology, history, and archaeology. The museum is rich in collections ranging from early Christian stones to artifacts of 18th-century country life. Some exhibits suggest the site's role as an astronomical observatory in 1836; note the 20cm (8-inch) telescope used to observe Halley's Comet in July 1836. The camera obscura, on the upper floor, provides panoramic views of the town and surrounding countryside.

Church St. ℂ **01387/253374**. www.dumfriesmuseum.demon.co.uk. Museum free; camera obscura £1.50 ($2.40) adults, 75p ($1.20) children and seniors. Museum, Apr–Sept Mon–Sat 10am–5pm, Sun 2–5pm; Oct–Mar Tues–Sat 10am–1pm and 2–5pm. Camera obscura, Apr–Sept Mon–Sat 10am–5pm, Sun 2–5pm. Cross the river at St. Michael's Bridge Rd. and turn right onto Church St.

Ellisland Farm *(Finds)*   From 1788 to 1791, Robert Burns made his last attempt at farming at Ellisland Farm; it was here that he wrote "Tam o' Shanter." After his marriage to Jean Armour, Burns leased the farm from Patrick Miller under the stipulation that he'd assist in erecting the building that's the centerpiece of the homestead. It's still a working farm for sheep and cattle, with many aspects devoted to a museum/shrine honoring Burns and his literary statements. On a circular 400m (¼ mile) trail ("the south trail") adjacent to the banks of the Nith, you can retrace the footsteps of Burns, who walked along it frequently during breaks from his writing.

10km (6 miles) north of Dumfries via A76 (follow the signs to Kilmarnock). ℂ **01387/740426**. Admission £2.50 ($4) adults, £1 ($1.60) children and seniors. Apr–Sept Mon–Sat 10am–5pm, Sun 2–5pm; Oct–Mar Tues–Sat 10am–4pm.

Old Bridge House   Associated with the Burns House (see above), this building dates from 1660, when it replaced a structure that had been on the site since 1431. It was occupied as a private house until as late as 1957 and has been restored and furnished in a style typical of the period between 1850 and 1900, with tons of worthy Victoriana. Devorgillas Bridge itself was constructed in the 16th century.

Mill Rd. at the far end of Devorgillas Bridge. ℂ **01387/256904**. Free admission. Apr–Sept Mon–Sat 10am–5pm, Sun 2–5pm. From Whitesands, cross the river at Devorgillas Bridge.

Sweetheart Abbey *⚜*   The village of New Abbey is dominated by Sweetheart Abbey's red-sandstone ruins. The walls are mostly extant, even though the roof is missing. Devorgilla Balliol founded the abbey in 1273. With the death of her husband, John Balliol the Elder, she became one of Europe's richest women—most of Galloway, as well as estates and castles in England and Normandy, belonged to her. Devorgilla founded Balliol College, Oxford, in her husband's memory. She kept his embalmed heart in a silver-and-ivory casket by her side for 21 years until her death in 1289 at age 80, when she and the casket were buried in front of the abbey altar. The abbey gained the name of "Dulce Cor," Latin for *sweet heart,* a term that has become a part of the English language.

On A710, New Abbey. ℂ **01387/770244** (regional office of Historic Scotland). Admission £3 ($4.80) adults, £2.30 ($3.70) seniors, £1 ($1.60) children under age 16. Apr–Sept daily 9:30am–6:30pm; Oct–Mar Mon, Thurs, Sat 9:30am–4:30pm, Sun 2–4:30pm. Drive 11km (7 miles) southwest from Dumfries on A710 (follow the signs saying SOLWAY FIRTH HERITAGE).

HITTING THE LINKS & CASTING A LINE

Nearby are the **Dumfries & County Golf Club,** Nunfield, Edinburgh Road (ℂ **01387/268918**), about 1.5km (1 mile) north of the town center, and the **Dumfries & Galloway Golf Club,** Laurieston Avenue, Maxwell Town (ℂ **01387/ 253582**), about 1.5km (1 mile) west of the town center. They're available for play by newcomers, but priority tee-off reservations are granted to members.

Galloway's rivers, estuaries, and lakes are particularly rich in salmon and trout. For £1.50 ($2.40), any tourist office here will sell you a copy of the brochure "Fishing in Dumfries & Galloway," listing dozens of fishing sites and giving information about how to get a permit. Some of the best salmon fishing is in the **River Nith,** which flows right through Dumfries. If you want to fish here, you'll have to swallow hard and buy an expensive permit (£50/$80 per day) from the local tourist office. Permits for fishing in local lochs and reservoirs (where you're likely to get brown trout but few if any salmon) may not be as trendy but are a lot less expensive at only £15 ($24).

WHERE TO STAY
EXPENSIVE

Cairndale Hotel & Leisure Club ⭑   This is the finest hotel in Dumfries, easily outdistancing the Station and all other competition. A four-story stone-fronted building from around 1900, the Cairndale is a fine choice with handsome public rooms. It's owned and managed by the Wallace family. Its guest rooms have all been carefully modernized. Executive rooms and suites have queen-size beds, trouser presses, and whirlpool baths. The hotel's leisure facilities are noteworthy, and the restaurant hosts a popular dinner dance on Saturday nights.

132–136 English St., Dumfries, Galloway DG1 2DF. ✆ **01387/254111.** Fax 01387/250555. www.cairndale hotel.co.uk. 91 units. £109–£125 ($174–$200) double; from £149 ($238) suite. Rates include breakfast. AE, DC, MC, V. Free parking. **Amenities:** Restaurant; bar; heated indoor pool; health club; Jacuzzi; solarium; room service; babysitting; laundry service; dry cleaning. *In room:* TV, minibar (only in executive rooms and suites), coffeemaker, hair dryer.

The Station   This is among the most traditional hotels in Dumfries, a few steps from the gingerbread-fringed train station. It was built in 1896 of hewn sandstone, in a design of heavy timbers, polished paneling, and soaring ceilings. The modernized but still somewhat dowdy guest rooms contain comfortable beds and shower-only bathrooms. The four-poster rooms and the suite feature Jacuzzi tubs. A new Garden Room lounge has recently been added, the creation of a Feng Shui consultant hoping to increase the *chi* or "good feeling" of guests.

49 Lovers Walk, Dumfries, Galloway DG1 1LT. ✆ **01387/254316.** Fax 01387/250388. www.stationhotel.co.uk. 32 units. £80–£90 ($128–$144) double; £110 ($176) suite. Rates include breakfast. AE, DC, MC, V. Free parking. **Amenities:** 2 restaurants; 2 bars; golf arranged; room service; babysitting. *In room:* TV, dataport, minibar, coffeemaker, hair dryer, trouser press.

MODERATE

Trigony House Hotel   This pink-sandstone hotel was built around 1895 as the home of a local family. Its name *(trigony)* derives from the shape of the acreage, which looks almost like a perfect isosceles triangle. Today it contains a handful of comfortable but unpretentious high-ceilinged guest rooms, each opening onto countryside views. Adam (the chef of the hotel's restaurant) and Jan Moore are your hosts and will tell you all about the building's occupant during the 1930s: Frances Shakerley lived to be 107 within the walls of this house and thus became famous as the oldest woman in Scotland.

The hotel operates a busy pub and a dinner-only restaurant. Drop into the pub for affordable platters of simple food at lunch or dinner. Meals may include paté of smoked trout, haggis with whisky-flavored cream sauce, salmon filets with lime-and-ginger glaze, and strips of beef with whisky-and-oatmeal sauce.

On the Dumfries–Ayr trunk road, Thornhill, Dumfries, Galloway DG3 5EZ. ✆ **01848/331211.** Fax 01848/ 331303. www.trigonyhotel.co.uk. 8 units. £80–£90 ($128–$144) double. Rates include breakfast. MC, V. From Dumfries, drive 21km (13 miles) north along A76, following the signs to Thornhill. Trigony House is 1.5km (1 mile) south of Thornhill. *In room:* TV, coffeemaker, hair dryer.

WHERE TO DINE

Bruno's ITALIAN   It may seem ironic to recommend an Italian restaurant in the heart of Robert Burns territory, but Bruno's serves some of the best food in town. It's unassuming, but that's part of its charm. The chef's repertoire is familiar—first-rate minestrone, homemade pizza and pasta, veal with ham, and spicy chicken—but everything is done with a certain flair. The pork filet is particularly tender, and the tomato sauce is well spiced and blended. Bruno's special three-course menu is popular.

3 Balmoral Rd. ℂ **01387/255757.** Reservations required Sat–Sun. Main courses £6.50–£16 ($10–$26); fixed-price 3-course dinner £19 ($30); supper pasta menu £9 ($14). MC, V. Wed–Mon 5:30–10pm.

Globe Inn ★ SCOTTISH   This is the traditional favorite. This was Burns's favorite haunt, in business since 1610, and he used an old Scottish expression, *howff* (meaning a small cozy room), to describe his local pub. He was definitely a regular; he had a child with the barmaid, Anna Park. You reach the pub down a narrow flagstone passage off High Street, opposite a Marks & Spencer department store. You can go for a meal (perhaps kipper paté, haggis, mealed herring, or Globe steak pie), or just to have a drink and play a game of dominoes. A little museum is devoted to Burns, and on the windowpanes upstairs you can see verses he scratched with a diamond. Taps include Belhaven, Tennet's Lager, McEwen's 60 and 80 Shilling, Galloway Ale, Stella Lager, and Black Throne Cider.

56 High St. ℂ **01387/252335.** Main courses £4.50–£5.50 ($7.20–$8.80). AE, MC, V. Mon–Thurs 10am–11pm; Fri–Sat 10am–midnight; Sun noon–midnight. Food served Mon–Sat 10–11:30am and noon–3pm.

Hullabaloo SCOTTISH   This is the most unusual restaurant in Dumfries. It's in a renovated grain mill, which you reach by taking a lovely 10-minute stroll across the Nith from the commercial heart of town. Built around 1780 by a prominent engineer, Thomas Sneaton, the mill also shelters a small movie house and the Robert Burns Centre (see above). The offerings are prepared with Scottish ingredients and change with the seasons. A homemade soup of the day is always served along with freshly baked bread, or else you might opt for one of the imaginative salads, including a Thai prawn or else tabbouleh and bean salad. Instead of elaborate main courses, you get various baguettes with such enticements as smoked salmon and cream cheese, or else baked potatoes that are almost meals unto themselves. The aura is one of cafe dining with an emphasis on lighter fare than a major restaurant.

In the Robert Burns Centre, Mill Rd. ℂ **01387/259679.** Reservations recommended. Main courses £2.95–£4.75 ($4.70–$7.60). MC, V. Easter–Sept Mon–Sat 11am–4pm, Tues–Sat 6–10pm, Sun 11am–3pm; Oct–Easter Tues–Sat 11am–4pm and 6–10pm.

DUMFRIES AFTER DARK

The town's most famous pub is the previously recommended **Globe Inn,** 56 High St. (ℂ **01387/252335**), where Robert Burns tipped many a dram. An equally historic pub loaded with local color is **The Hole in the Wall,** 156 High St. (ℂ **01387/252770**), where live music is usually provided by an accordionist. If you want to go dancing, head for either of the town's two discos, **Chancers Nightclub,** 25 Munches St. (ℂ **01387/263170**), or **The Junction,** 36 High St. (ℂ **01387/267262**). The crowd and music at these two clubs change often, depending on the theme for the night, so call ahead to make sure they'll suit you on any given evening.

7 Castle Douglas

26km (16 miles) SW of Dumfries; 158km (98 miles) SW of Edinburgh; 79km (49 miles) SE of Ayr

An old cattle- and sheep-market town, Castle Douglas, at the northern tip of Carlingwark Loch, is near such attractions as Threave Castle, Cardoness Castle,

> **Finds   A Setting for a Sir Walter Scott Novel**
>
> Unique in Scotland, **Orchardton Tower,** 9km (5½ miles) southeast of Castle Douglas off A711, is an example of a round tower house (they were usually built in Ireland). It was constructed around 1450 by John Cairns and later on was purchased by a member of the Maxwell family. The adventures of one family member, Sir Robert Maxwell of Orchardton, a fervent Jacobite captured in the Battle of Culloden, figured in Sir Walter Scott's novel *Guy Mannering.* If you ask the custodian, who lives at the cottage next door, he'll let you see inside for free.
>
> The **Mote of Urr,** 8km (5 miles) northeast of Castle Douglas off B794, is a circular mound enclosed by a deep trench. This is an example of the motte-and-bailey type of defense popular in Norman days.

Kirkcudbright, and Sweetheart Abbey and just southeast of the Galloway Forest Park. On one of the islets in the loch is an ancient lake dwelling known as a *crannog.*

ESSENTIALS

GETTING THERE   The nearest rail station is in Dumfries (see "Dumfries: An Ode to Burns," earlier in this chapter); from there, you can take a bus to Castle Douglas. Call ℂ **0845/748-4950** for rail information.

The **Great Western Bus Co.** runs buses from Dumfries to Castle Douglas every hour throughout the day and early evening; travel time is about 30 minutes and costs £1.80 ($2.70) one-way. Call ℂ **0870/580-8080** for bus information.

If you're driving from Dumfries, head southwest along A75.

VISITOR INFORMATION   A **tourist office** is at the Markethill Car Park (ℂ **01556/502611**). April through October, it's open Monday through Friday from 10am to 6pm, Saturday from 10am to 5pm (July and Aug, also Sun 10am–5pm).

SEEING THE SIGHTS

Threave Castle ⚄   This is the ruined 14th-century stronghold of the Black Douglases. The seven-story tower was built between 1639 and 1690 by Archibald the Grim, lord of Galloway. In 1455, Threave was the last Douglas stronghold to surrender to James II, who employed some of the most advanced armaments of his day (including a cannon similar to Mons Meg, the massive cannon now displayed in Edinburgh Castle) in its subjection. Over the doorway projects the gallows knob from which the Douglases hanged their enemies. In 1640, the castle was captured by the Covenanters (the rebellious group of Scots who questioned the king's right to make laws) and dismantled.

The site is owned by a public group known as Historic Scotland. To reach it, you must walk 1km (½-mile) through farmlands and then take a small boat across the Dee. When you get to the river, you ring a bell signaling the custodian to come and ferry you across. The last sailing is at 6pm. For information, contact Historic Scotland, Longmore House, Salisbury Place, Edinburgh (ℂ **01316/ 688800;** www.historic-scotland.gov.uk).

2.5km (1½ miles) west of Castle Douglas on an islet in the River Dee. Admission (including ferry ride) £2.20 ($3.50) adults, £1.60 ($2.55) seniors, 75p ($1.20) children under 16. Apr–Sept Mon–Sat 9:30am–6:30pm, Sun 2–6:30pm. Closed Oct–Mar.

Threave Garden ★ About 1.5km (1 mile) southeast of Threave Castle, these gardens are built around Threave House, a Scottish baronial mansion constructed during the Victorian era. It's run by the National Trust for Scotland, which uses the complex as a school for gardening and a wildfowl refuge. The garden is at its best in April, when the daffodils bloom, and in June, when rhododendrons and the rock garden are in flower. There's a visitor center and a restaurant.

Off A75 1km (½ mile) west of Castle Douglas. © **01556/502575.** www.nts.org.uk. Admission £5 ($8) adults, £3.75 ($6) children and seniors. Garden, daily 9:30am–5:30pm; visitor center, Mar and Nov–Dec daily 10am–4pm; Apr–Oct daily 9:30am–5:30pm.

EXPLORING THE COUNTRYSIDE

Castle Douglas's location near the northern edge of the estuary of Solway Firth offers panoramic views across the water stretching as far as England's Lake District. If you want to explore the area by bike, rent one at **Ace Cycles,** Church Street in Castle Douglas (© **01556/504542**), open Monday through Saturday from 9am to 12:30pm and 1:30 to 5pm. They rent for £8 to £10 ($13–$16) per day and require a £50 ($80) deposit. Arm yourself with a good map and set out.

WHERE TO STAY

Douglas Arms Originally, a 17th-century coaching inn, this old favorite is up-to-date and modernized even though it lies behind a rather stark two-story facade. The public rooms are bright and cheerful, giving you a toasty feeling on a cold night. The guest rooms were refurbished a few years ago and include shower-only bathrooms.

King St., Castle Douglas, Galloway DG7 1DB. © **01556/502231.** Fax 01556/504000. 24 units. £70 ($111) double. Rates include breakfast. AE, MC, V. **Amenities:** Restaurant; pub. *In room:* TV, coffeemaker, hair dryer.

King's Arms This inn provides reasonably priced accommodations ranging from single rooms to a family room. The guest rooms are touched up every year and in good shape; nine come with shower-only bathrooms (guests in the 10th room get a hallway bathroom with tub reserved solely for their use). The helpful staff will direct you to various activities in the area, including a nine-hole golf course a 45-minute drive away. The sun patio is a great place for tea or coffee or perhaps a sundowner of malt whisky. The cuisine is British with a Scottish emphasis; the range is extensive, featuring local produce, Solway salmon, and Galloway beef.

St. Andrew's St., Castle Douglas, Galloway DG7 1EL. © **01556/502626.** Fax 01556/502097. www.galloway-golf.co.uk. 10 units, 9 with private bathroom. £60 ($96) double with bathroom. Rates include breakfast. MC, V. Free parking. **Amenities:** Restaurant; bar. *In room:* TV, coffeemaker, hair dryer.

Longacre Manor This dignified building lies on about 1½ acres of forest and garden and was constructed in 1927 as the home of a local grain trader. Under the gracious ownership of Elma and Charles Ball, it now offers plush and conservatively furnished large guest rooms, some with four-poster beds. The shower-only bathrooms feature bathrobes and Molton Brown toiletries. The lounge is cozy, and a three-course dinner can be prepared and served in the dining room. The bedrooms and the restaurant are strictly nonsmoking.

Ernespie Rd., Castle Douglas, Galloway DG7 1LE. © **01556/503576.** Fax 01556/503886. www.longacre manor.co.uk. 4 units. £70–£100 ($112–$160) double. Rates include breakfast. MC, V. From the center of Castle Douglas, drive 1km (½ mile) north, following the signs to Dumfries. **Amenities:** Dining room. *In room:* TV, coffeemaker, hair dryer, trouser press.

Urr Valley Country House Hotel ★ *Finds* Reached by a long drive, this country hotel in the scenic Urr Valley is privately owned and set in the midst of

14 acres of lush woodlands and gardens, 1.5km (1 mile) east of the center of Castle Douglas. You're welcomed into a real Scottish macho atmosphere of stag heads and antique rods and reels, along with paneled walls and fireplaces with log fires. Most of the rooms are spacious; a few have four-poster beds and others are designed for families. Two rooms are set aside for nonsmokers.

You can have a drink or enjoy a pub meal in the lounge and bar. In the main restaurant, both French and Scottish cuisine are served, with an emphasis on fresh seafood and local produce such as pheasant and Solway salmon. Dare you try the regional specialty, Scottish haggis?

Ernespie Road, Castle Douglas, Galloway DG7 3JG. © **01556/502188.** Fax 01556/504055. www.scottish-inns.co.uk/UrrValley/index.htm. 19 units. £50–£80 ($80–$128) double; £60–£90 ($96–$144) family room. Rates include breakfast. AE, MC, V. Free parking. Take A75 toward Castle Douglas. **Amenities:** Restaurant; bar. *In room:* TV, coffeemaker, hair dryer.

WHERE TO DINE

Plumed Horse Restaurant SCOTTISH/INTERNATIONAL   Opened in July 1998, this restaurant combines a high-quality cuisine with a relaxed, village atmosphere; it's set the rest of the local competition on its ear. The white linen tablecloths, crystal, silver, and tableware by Villeroy & Boch lends the Plumed Horse an air of elegance. Chef Tony Borthwick changes the menu regularly, but you might find roast Barbary duck breast, crisp filet of salmon, scallop ravioli, and roast monkfish among the choices. Desserts such as pistachio and praline parfait and banana brûlée in butterscotch sauce are favorites. Ingredients used in the meals are often luxurious, including wild mushrooms and foie gras. The restaurant also has an extensive wine and champagne list.

Main St., Crossmichael (5km/3 miles from Castle Douglas). © **01556/670333.** Reservations recommended. Main courses £17–£19 ($27–$30). MC, V. Tues–Sun 12:30–1:30pm and 7–9:30pm (closed on Sat at lunch). Take A713 toward Ayr.

8 Kirkcudbright: An Artists' Colony

174km (108 miles) SW of Edinburgh; 45km (28 miles) SW of Dumfries; 166km (103 miles) S of Glasgow; 81km (50 miles) E of Stranraer; 16km (10 miles) SW of Castle Douglas

The ancient burgh of Kirkcudbright (Kir-*coo*-bree) is at the head of Kirkcudbright Bay on the Dee estuary. Many of this intriguing old town's color-washed houses belong to artists; a lively group of weavers, potters, and painters lives and works in the 18th-century streets and lanes.

What makes Kirkcudbright so enchanting isn't really its sights (although it boasts several) but its artistic life and bohemian flavor. Various festivities take place here in July and August; expect to find anything from marching bagpipe bands to exhibitions of Scottish country dancing to torchlight processions. Activities range from raft racing to nearby walks to a floodlit Tattoo in front of MacLellan's Castle to a puppet festival. Check with the tourist office (see below) about what will be happening when you visit.

ESSENTIALS

GETTING THERE   Kirkcudbright is on the same bus route that serves Castle Douglas from Dumfries, with departures during the day about once per hour. The 40-minute ride from Dumfries is about £4 ($6.40) one-way; a day ticket is £5 ($8). For bus information, call © **0870/580-8080** or the local tourist office.

If you're driving from Castle Douglas, continue along A75 southwest until you come to the junction with A711, which takes you into Kirkcudbright.

VISITOR INFORMATION A **tourist office** is at Harbour Square (© **01557/ 330494**). From April 1 to June 29 and September 15 to October 26, it's open Monday through Saturday from 10am to 5pm and Sunday from 11am to 4:30pm; from June 30 to September 14, hours are Monday through Saturday from 9:30am to 6pm and Sunday from 10am to 5pm.

SEEING THE SIGHTS

In the old town **graveyard** are memorials to Covenanters and to Billy Marshall, the tinker (Gypsy) king who died in 1792 at age 120, reportedly having fathered four children after age 100.

MacLellan's Castle   Dominating the center of town is this castellated castle built in 1582 for the town's provost, Sir Thomas MacLellan. It has been a ruin since 1752, but it's an impressive ruin and worth a visit. A large staircase goes from the cellars on the ground floor to the Banqueting Hall, where a still massive fireplace comes with what was called a "lairds lug" (spy hole). From almost anywhere in town, the jagged fangs of the castle loom overhead.

Off High St. © **01316/688800**. Admission £2 ($3.20) adults, £1.50 ($2.40) seniors, 75p ($1.20) children. Apr–Sept Mon–Sat 9:30am–6:30pm, Sun 2–6pm. Closed Oct–Mar.

Tolbooth Art Centre   The large Tolbooth (1629) has functioned as a prison, the town hall, and a courthouse. In front of it is a 1610 Mercat Cross and inside a memorial to John Paul Jones (1747–92), the gardener's son from Kirkbean who became a slave trader, a privateer, and eventually the father of the American navy. For a time before his emigration, he was imprisoned for murder here. In 1993, Queen Elizabeth inaugurated the building as a gallery displaying paintings by famous local artists. You'll find works by Jessie M. King, Lena Alexander, Robert Sivell, and S. J. Peploe.

High St. © **01557/331556**. Admission £1.50 ($2.40) adults, 75p ($1.20) seniors, students, and children. Apr–June and Aug–Oct Mon–Sat 11am–5pm, Sun 2–5pm; July daily 10am–6pm ; Nov–Mar Mon–Sat 11am–4pm.

Stewartry Museum   Built by the Victorians in 1892 as a showcase for the region's distinctive culture, this museum contains an unusual collection of antiquities, tools, and artworks depicting the history, culture, and sociology of this part of Galloway.

St. Mary St. © **01557/331643**. Free admission. July–Aug daily 10am–6pm; Sept–June Mon–Sat 11am–4pm.

WHERE TO STAY

Baytree House   Named after the enormous bay tree in its back garden, this B&B occupies a Georgian-style house (ca. 1780) whose yellow-painted stone facade faces the main street. The most impressive public room is the drawing salon, a sprawling testimonial to the good life of the 18th century. The midsize guest rooms have been tastefully done in pastels; some contain four-poster beds and/or French windows overlooking the garden. Actor and artist David Hemmings (*Gladiator, Gangs of New York*, among others) has been a guest and some of his works hang in the Pink Room. Hardworking owners Robert Watson and Jackie Callander add a touch of style to your breakfast service.

110 High St., Kirkcudbright, Galloway DG6 4JQ. ©/fax **01557/330824**. www.baytreehouse.net. 3 units. £60–£64 ($96–$102) double. No credit cards. **Amenities:** Breakfast room. *In room:* TV, coffeemaker, hair dryer.

Selkirk Arms   This beloved old favorite—the finest inn in the area—is where Robert Burns stayed when he composed the celebrated "Selkirk Grace."

It was built in the 1770s in a stone-fronted Georgian design with a slate roof. The guest rooms all have standard furniture and garden views. The restaurant/bistro offers a wide range of fresh local produce; bar lunches and suppers are also available. The lounge bar features an array of malt whiskies that would warm Burns's heart.

Old High St., Kirkcudbright, Galloway DG6 4JG. © **01557/330402.** Fax 01557/331639. www.selkirkarms hotel.co.uk. 16 units. £95 ($152) double. Rates include breakfast. Children in parent's room pay only for breakfast. AE, DC, MC, V. Free parking. **Amenities:** Restaurant; bar. *In room:* TV, coffeemaker, hair dryer.

WHERE TO DINE

Auld Alliance Restaurant SCOTTISH/FRENCH   One of the most appealing restaurants in the region is this family-owned and -operated place in an interconnected pair of 1880s buildings constructed with stones from the ruins of Kirkcudbright Castle. The restaurant's cooks are almost obsessed with the freshness of the fish they serve, and the salmon (likely to have been caught several hours before preparation in the Kirkcudbright estuary and its tributary, the Dee) will be full of its legendary flavor. A house specialty is queenies (queen-size scallops from deeper waters than the great scallop).

5 Castle St. © **01557/330569.** Reservations recommended. Main courses £8.50–£15 ($14–$24). MC, V. Apr–Oct daily 6:30–9:30pm. Closed Halloween–Easter.

15

Glasgow & the Strathclyde Region

Glasgow is only 65km (40 miles) west of Edinburgh, but there's an amazing contrast between the two cities. Scotland's economic powerhouse and its largest city (actually Britain's third-largest), up-and-coming Glasgow is now the country's cultural capital and home to half the population. It has long been famous for ironworks and steelworks; the local shipbuilding industry produced the *Queen Mary,* the *Queen Elizabeth,* and other fabled oceanliners.

Once polluted by industry and plagued with some of the worst slums in Europe, Glasgow has been transformed. Urban development and the decision to locate the Scottish Exhibition and Conference Centre here have brought great changes: Industrial grime is being sandblasted away, overcrowding has been reduced, and more open space and less traffic congestion mean cleaner air. Glasgow also boasts a vibrant and even edgy arts scene; it's become one of the cultural capitals of Europe.

The splendor of the city has reemerged. John Betjeman and other critics have hailed Glasgow as "the greatest surviving example of a Victorian city." The planners of the 19th century thought on a grand scale when they designed the terraces and villas west and south of the center.

Glasgow's origins are ancient, making Edinburgh, for all its wealth of history, seem comparatively young. The village that grew up beside a fjord 32km (20 miles) from the mouth of the River Clyde as a medieval ecclesiastical center began its commercial prosperity in the 17th century. As it grew, the city engulfed the smaller medieval towns of Ardrie, Renfrew, Rutherglen, and Paisley.

Glasgow is part of **Strathclyde,** a powerful and populous district whose origins go back to the Middle Ages. Irish chroniclers wrote of the kingdom of Stratha Cluatha some 1,500 years ago, and Strathclyde was known to the Romans, who called its people Damnonii. The old capital, Dumbarton, on its high rock, provided a natural fortress in the days when locals had to defend themselves against enemy tribes.

The fortunes of Strathclyde changed dramatically in the 18th century, when the Clyde estuary became the gateway to the New World. Glasgow merchants grew rich on tobacco and then on cotton. It was Britain's fastest-growing region during the Industrial Revolution, and Glasgow was known as the Second City of the Empire. In 1736, Greenock was the birthplace of James Watt, inventor of the steam engine. Until 1996, Strathclyde functioned as a government entity that included Glasgow, but it's now broken down into several new divisions: the City of Glasgow; Inverclyde, which includes the important industrial center of Greenock; and several others.

Glasgow is a good gateway for exploring **Culzean Castle** and the resorts along the Ayrshire coast, an hour away by frequent train service (see "Side Trips from Glasgow: The Best of the Strathclyde Region," later in this chapter). From Glasgow, you can also tour Loch Lomond, Loch Katrine, and the Trossachs (see chapter 17, "Fife & the Central Highlands"). After a day or so in Glasgow, you can head to Burns country for perhaps another night. Also on Glasgow's doorstep is the scenic estuary of the **Firth of Clyde,** down which you can cruise on a paddle steamer. The Firth of Clyde, with its long sea lochs—Gareloch, Loch Long, Loch Goil, and Holy Loch—is one of the most scenic waterways in the world.

1 Essentials

ARRIVING

BY PLANE The **Glasgow Airport** is at Abbotsinch (© 01418/871111; www. baa.co.uk/main/airports/glasgow), 16km (10 miles) west of the city via M8. You can use the regular Glasgow CityLink bus service to get to the city center. From bus stop no. 2, take bus no. 900 or 901 to the Buchanan Street Bus Station in the center of town. The ride takes about 20 minutes and costs £4 ($6.40). A taxi to the city center costs about £15 ($24). You can reach Edinburgh by taking a bus from Glasgow Airport to Queens Station and then changing to a bus for Edinburgh. The entire journey, including the change, should take about 2 hours and costs £7 ($11) one-way or £12 ($19) round-trip.

Monday through Friday, British Airways runs almost hourly shuttle service from London's Heathrow Airport to Glasgow. The first flight departs London at 7:15am and the last at 8:25pm; service is reduced on weekends, depending on volume. For flight schedules and fares, call British Airways in London at © 0845/779-9977.

From mid-May to October, **American Airlines** (© 800/433-7300; www. aa.com) offers a daily nonstop flight to Glasgow from Chicago; the rest of the year, you'll make at least one transfer. **Northwest Airlines** (© 800/225-2525; www.nwa.com) operates nonstop flights between Boston and Glasgow daily in summer, somewhat less frequently in winter.

British Midland (© 0870/607-0555) flies from Heathrow to Glasgow. **Aer Lingus** (© 800/223-6537, or 01/844-4711 in Ireland; www.aerlingus.ie) flies daily from Dublin to Glasgow.

BY TRAIN Headquarters for British Rail is at Glasgow's Central Station and Queen Street Station. For **National Rail Enquiries,** call © 0845/748-4950. The **Queen Street Station** serves the north and east of Scotland, with trains arriving from Edinburgh every 30 minutes during the day; the one-way trip between the two cities costs £8 ($13) and takes 50 minutes. You'll also be able to travel to such Highland destinations as Inverness and Fort William from here.

The **Central Station** serves southern Scotland, England, and Wales, with trains arriving from London's Euston and King's Cross Stations (call © 0845/748-4950 in London for schedules) frequently throughout the day (trip time is about 5½ hr.). The trains leave Euston Monday through Saturday from 6:20am until 6:25pm, and then the night train departs at 11:40pm, getting into Glasgow at 7:16am. From Glasgow, trains leave for London every hour from 6:15am to 5pm. The night train leaves at 11:55pm. Try to avoid Sunday travel—the frequency of trains is considerably reduced and the duration of the trip lengthened to at least 7 hours because of more stopovers en route.

BY BUS   The **Buchanan Street Bus Station** is 2 blocks north of the Queen Street Station on North Hanover Street (© **0870/608-2608**). **National Express** runs daily coaches from London's Victoria Coach Station to Buchanan frequently throughout the day. Buses from London take 8 hours and 40 minutes to reach Glasgow, depending on the number of stops en route. **Scottish CityLink** (© **08705/505050**) also has frequent bus service to and from Edinburgh, with a one-way ticket costing £3 to £5 ($4.80–$8).

Contact National Express Enquiries at © **0990/808080** for more information.

BY CAR   Glasgow is 65km (40 miles) west of Edinburgh, 356km (221 miles) north of Manchester, and 625km (388 miles) north of London. From England in the south, Glasgow is reached by M74, a continuation of M8 that goes right into the city, making an **S** curve. Call your hotel and find out what exit you should take. M8, another express motorway, links Glasgow and Edinburgh.

Other major routes into the city are A77 northeast from Prestwick and Ayr and A8 from the west (this becomes M8 around the port of Glasgow). A82 comes in from the northwest (the Highlands) on the north bank of the Clyde, and A80 also goes into the city. (This route is the southwestern section of M80 and M9 from Stirling.)

VISITOR INFORMATION

The **Greater Glasgow and Clyde Valley Tourist Board,** 11 George Square (© **01412/044400;** Underground: Buchanan St.), is the country's most helpful office. October through May, it's open Monday through Saturday from 9am to 6pm; June through September hours are daily from 9am to 6pm; August daily from 9am to 8pm.

CITY LAYOUT

The monumental heart of Glasgow—the Victorian City and the Merchant City, along with the Central Station—lies on the north bank of the **River Clyde.** The ancient center has as its core the great Cathedral of St. Kentigern, a perfect example of pre-Reformation Gothic architecture that dates in part to the 12th century. Behind it is the Necropolis, burial ground of many Victorians. Across the square is 1471 Provands Lordship, the city's oldest house. Down **High Street** you'll find the **Tolbooth Steeple** (1626) at Glasgow Cross, and nearer the River Clyde is **Glasgow Green,** Britain's first public park (1662).

From Ingram Street, South Frederick Street will take you to **George Square,** with its many statues, including one dedicated to Sir Walter Scott. This is the center of modern Glasgow.

The **Merchant City,** a compact area of imposing buildings, is the location of the National Trust for Scotland's shop and visitor center at Hutcheson's Hall. The broad pedestrian thoroughfares of Buchanan Street, Argyle Street, and Sauchiehall Street are the heart of the shopping district.

Glasgow's **West End** is just a short taxi journey from the city center, easily accessible from any part of the city and close to M8 and the Clydeside Expressway. An extensive network of local bus routes serves the West End. The Glasgow Underground operates a circular service; by boarding at any station on the system, you can reach the four stations serving the district: Kelvinbridge, Hillhead (the most central), Kelvin Hall, and Partick.

The West End is Britain's finest example of a great Victorian city, and the terraces of the Park Conservation Area rise to afford excellent views. Across Kelvingrove Park is the **Art Gallery and Museum.** Nearby, the tower of **Glasgow**

Tips **Finding an Address**

Glasgow was built in various sections and districts over the years, and massive sections have been torn down—some for slum clearance, others to make way for new highways. Following a consistent street plan can be tough, as squares or terraces can suddenly interrupt a route you're tracing.

House numbers can run in odds or evens and clockwise or counterclockwise, and sometimes Glaswegians don't even use numbers at all. So don't be surprised to see something like "Blackfriars Street" given as an address without a number. Get a detailed map of Glasgow before setting out. Maps aren't available at the tourist center but can be obtained at **John Smith & Son,** 100 Cathedral (© **01415/523377**). Always find the nearest cross street, then look for your location from there. If it's a hotel or restaurant, the sign for the establishment is likely to be more prominent than the number anyway.

University dominates Gilmorehill. Beyond is the **Hunterian Art Gallery,** home to a famous collection of Whistlers. Just a few strides away is **Byres Road,** a street of bars, shops, and restaurants. To the north are the **Botanic Gardens.**

A little more than 5km (3 miles) southwest of the city center is the **Pollok Country Park** and **Pollok Estate.** An extensive network of bus routes passes close by the park area, which is also served by two suburban rail stations. An electric bus service is in operation from the Country Park gates on Pollokshaws Road to Pollok House and the Burrell Collection Gallery. The Burrell Collection is housed in the heavily wooded Pollok Country Park. This museum is Scotland's top tourist attraction, and the focal point of any visit to the South Side. Nearby is the 18th-century Pollok House.

Extensive parklands and greenery characterize the city's southern environs. In addition to the Pollok Country Park and Estate, there's **Haggs Castle Golf Club,** home of the Glasgow Open, and **Bellahouston Park,** scene of the historic papal visit in 1983. En route to the Burrell Collection, you cross by the 148-acre **Queens Park,** honoring Mary Queen of Scots, where panoramic views of the city are possible from the hilltop. Near **Maxwell Park** is the **Haggs Castle Museum,** housed in a 400-year-old building.

THE NEIGHBORHOODS IN BRIEF
See the "Glasgow" map on page 548 to see the locations of the following neighborhoods.

Medieval Glasgow   This is where St. Mungo arrived in 543 and built his little church in what's now the northeastern part of the city. At the top of High Street stands the Cathedral of St. Kentigern and one of Britain's largest Victorian cemeteries. You enter the Necropolis by crossing over the Bridge of Sighs. Old Glasgow's major terminus is the High Street Station near the former site of the University of Glasgow. Glasgow Green, opening onto the River Clyde, has been a public park since 1662. Today vastly restored medieval Glasgow is the best place for strolls.

Along the River Clyde   Once it was said: "The Clyde made Glasgow; Glasgow made the Clyde." Although the city is no longer so dependent on the river, you can still enjoy a stroll along the Clyde Walkway, which stretches from King Albert Bridge, at the western end of Glasgow Green, for 3km (2 miles) downstream to Stohcross, now the site of the Scottish Exhibition and Conference Centre. The river is crossed by several bridges, one named for Queen Victoria and another for her consort, Prince Albert. This is one of the city's grandest walks; on these waters, Glasgow shipped its manufactured goods around the world. However, if your time is limited, you may want to concentrate on the major museums and historic Glasgow instead.

The Merchant City   Glasgow spread west of High Street in the 18th century, largely because of profits made from sugar, cotton, and tobacco in trade with the Americas. The Merchant City extends from Trongate and Argyle Street in the south to George Street in the north. Its major terminus is the Queen Street Station, and the major shopping venue is Argyle Arcade. It's also the site of City Hall

and Strathclyde University and boasts some of Britain's most elegant Georgian and Victorian buildings as well as Greek Revival churches. Tobacco barons once occupied much of the area, but their buildings have been recycled for other uses.

Glasgow Center   Continuing its western progression, the city center of Glasgow is now dominated by the Central Station on Hope Street. This is the major shopping district, including such venues as the Princes Square Shopping Mall. Also here are the Stock Exchange and the Anderston Bus Station (near the Central Station).

The West End   Beyond Charing Cross in the west end are the University of Glasgow and several of the city's major galleries and museums, some of which are in Kelvingrove Park. The West End mixes culture, art, and parks, and is dominated by Glasgow University, with the university structures idyllically placed in various parks. The city itself has more green spaces per resident than any other in Europe. Some of the most important of the city's galleries and museums are here, and 40 acres of the West End are taken up by the Botanic Garden.

2 Getting Around

The best way to explore Glasgow is on foot. The center is laid out on a grid system, which makes map reading relatively easy. However, many of the major attractions, such as the Burrell Collection, are in the environs, and for those you'll need to rely on public transportation.

Remember: Cars drive on the left, so when you cross streets make certain to look both ways.

BY BUS

Glasgow is serviced by **First Glasgow Bus Company.** The buses come in a variety of colors, the lighter ones (blue and yellow) tending to serve the Kelvin Central and Strathclyde rural areas, with the darker ones covering the urban zones. Service is frequent throughout the day, but after 11pm service is greatly curtailed. The major bus station is the **Buchanan Street Bus Station,** Killermont Street (call © **01414/236600** for schedules), 2 blocks north of the Queen Station.

Fares are £2.50 ($4), but you must have exact change. A special round-trip bus ticket for £2.10 ($3.35) operates after 9:30am.

BY UNDERGROUND

Called the "Clockwork Orange" (from the vivid orange of the trains) by Glaswegians, a 15-stop subway services the city. Most Underground trains operate from these stops every 5 minutes, with longer intervals between trains on Sunday and at night. The fare is 90p ($1.45). Service is Monday through Saturday from 6:30am to 10pm and Sunday from 11am to 6pm.

The **Travel Centre** at St. Enoch Square (© **0870/608-2608**), 2 blocks from the Central Station, is open Monday through Saturday from 6:30am to 9:30pm and Sunday from 7am to 9:30pm. Here you can buy an £8 ($13) **Underground pass,** valid for a week's access to all the tube lines of Glasgow, as well as access to all the trains serving routes between Central Station and the southern suburbs, or a £7.80 ($12) **daytripper card,** covering one adult and one child for a day. For details, call © **01413/327133.**

BY TAXI

Taxis are the same excellent ones found in Edinburgh or London. You can hail them on the street or call **TOA Taxis** at © **01414/297070.** Fares are displayed on a meter next to the driver. When a taxi is available on the street, a taxi sign on the roof is lit a bright yellow. Most taxi trips within the city cost £4 to £6 ($6.40–$9.60). The taxi meter starts at £1.80 ($2.90) and increases by 20p (30¢) every 61m (200 ft.), with an extra 10p (15¢) assessed for each additional passenger after the first two. An 80p ($1.30) surcharge is imposed from midnight to 6am. Tip at least 10% of the fare shown on the meter.

BY CAR

Driving around Glasgow is a tricky business, even for locals. You're better off with public transportation. It's a warren of one-way streets, and parking is expensive and difficult to find. Metered parking is available, but you'll need 20p (30¢) coins, entitling you to only 20 minutes. You must watch out for zealous traffic wardens issuing tickets. Some zones are marked PERMIT HOLDERS ONLY—your vehicle will be towed if you have no permit. A yellow line along the curb indicates no parking. Multistory car parks (parking lots), open 24 hours a day, are found at Anderston Cross and Cambridge, George, Mitchell, Oswald, and Waterloo streets.

If you want to rent a car to explore the countryside, it's best to arrange the rental before leaving home (see chapter 3, "Planning Your Trip to Great Britain"). But if you want to rent a car locally, most companies will accept your American or Canadian driver's license. All the major rental agencies are represented at the airport. In addition, **Avis** is at 70 Lancefield St. (© **01412/212827;** bus: 6 or 6A), **Budget** at Glasgow Airport (© **01412/219241;** bus: 38, 45, 48, or 57), and **Europcar** at 38 Anderson Quay (© **01412/488788;** bus: 38, 45, 48, or 57).

BY BICYCLE

Parts of Glasgow are fine for biking, or you might want to rent a bike and explore the surrounding countryside. For what the Scots call cycle hire, go to a well-recommended shop about 1km (½ mile) west of the town center, just off Great Western Road: **Western End Cycles,** 16–18 Chancellor St., in the Hillhead district (© **01413/571344;** Underground: Kelvin Bridge or Hillhead). It rents 21-speed trail and mountain bikes that conform well to the hilly terrain of Glasgow and its surroundings. The cost of £12 ($19) per day must be accompanied by a cash deposit of £100 ($160) or the imprint of a valid credit card.

FAST FACTS: **Glasgow**

American Express   The office is at 115 Hope St. (© **01412/263077;** bus: 38, 45, 48, or 57), open Monday through Friday from 8:30am to 5:30pm and Saturday from 9am to noon (June and July to 4pm Sat).

Business Hours   Most **offices** are open Monday through Friday from 9am to 5 or 5:30pm. Most **banks** are open Monday through Wednesday and Friday from 9:30am to 4pm, Thursday from 9:30am to 5:30pm, and Saturday from 10am to 7pm. Opening times can vary slightly from bank to bank. **Shops** are generally open Monday through Saturday from 10am to 5:30 or 6pm. On Thursday, stores remain open until 7pm.

Currency Exchange   The tourist office and the American Express office (see above) will exchange most major foreign currencies. City-center banks operate *bureaux de change,* and nearly all will cash traveler's checks if you have the proper ID. **Thomas Cook** at the Glasgow Airport (© **0141/632-2396**) operates a bureau de change service daily from 5am to 11pm in summer; off-season hours are Monday through Saturday from 8am to 8pm and Sunday from 8am to 6pm. It operates a larger branch at 15 Gordon St. (© **01412/ 017200;** Underground: Buchanan St.), open Monday through Friday from 9am to 5:30pm.

Dentists   If you have an emergency, go to the Accident and Emergency Department of **Glasgow Dental Hospital & School NHS Trust,** 378 Sauchiehall St. (© **01412/119600;** bus: 57). Its hours are Monday through Friday from 9:15am to 3:15pm and Sunday and public holidays from 10:30am to noon.

Embassies & High Commissions   See "Fast Facts: London," in chapter 4.

Emergencies   Call © **999** in an emergency to summon the police, an ambulance, or firefighters.

Hospitals   The major hospital is the **Royal Infirmary,** 82–86 Castle St. (© **01412/114000;** bus: 2 or 2A).

Hot Lines   Women in crisis may want to call **Women's Aid** at © **01415/ 532022.** Gays and lesbians can call the **Strathclyde Gay and Lesbian Switchboard** at © **01418/470447** daily from 7 to 10pm. The **Rape Crisis Centre** is at © **01413/311990.**

Internet Access   You can send or read e-mail and surf the net at **EasyEverything Internet Café,** 57–61 St. Vincent St. (© **01412/222365**). This outlet offers 400 computers and good rates. Only £1 ($1.60) can buy 40 minutes or even 3 hours, depending on demand. Open daily from 7am to 10:30pm.

Pharmacies   The best is **Boots,** 200 Sauchiehall St. (© **01413/321925;** bus: 57), open Monday through Saturday from 8:30am to 6pm, and Sunday from 11am to 5pm.

Newspapers & Magazines   Published since 1783, the *Herald* is the major newspaper with national, international, and financial news, sports, and cultural listings; the *Evening Times* offers local news.

Police   In a real emergency, call © **999.** For other inquiries, contact police headquarters at © **01415/322000.**

Post Office   The main branch is at 47 St. Vincent's St. ((C) **01412/043689; Underground:** Buchanan St.; bus: 6, 8, or 16). It's open Monday through Friday from 8:30am to 5:45pm and Saturday from 9am to 5:30pm.

Restrooms   They can be found at rail stations, bus stations, air terminals, restaurants, hotels, pubs, and department stores. Glasgow also has a system of public toilets, often marked "wc." Don't hesitate to use them, though they're likely to be closed late in the evening.

Safety   Glasgow is the most dangerous city in Scotland, but it's relatively safe when compared to cities of its size in the United States. Muggings do occur, and often they're related to Glasgow's rather large drug problem. The famed razor gangs of Calton, Bridgeton, and the Gorbals are no longer around to earn the city a reputation for violence, but you should still keep alert.

Weather   Call the Glasgow Weather Centre at (C) **0141/248-3451.**

3 Where to Stay

It's important to reserve your room well in advance (say, 2 months beforehand), especially in late July and August. Glasgow's hotel rates are generally higher than those in Edinburgh, but many business hotels offer bargains on the weekends.

The airport and the downtown branches of Glasgow's tourist office offer an **Advance Reservations Service**—with 2 weeks' notice, you can book a hotel before your arrival by calling (C) **01412/210049.** The 2-week notification is preferred, but the staff will try its best to reserve rooms for walk-ins, although you're taking a chance that nothing will be available. The cost of any booking is £5 ($8).

CENTRAL GLASGOW
VERY EXPENSIVE

Hilton Glasgow Hotel ✰✰✰ *Kids*   Glasgow's government-rated five-star hotel occupies Scotland's tallest building (20 floors). Dignified and modern, it rises in the heart of the city's business district, near the northern end of Argyle Street and Exit 18 (Charing Cross) of M8. The good-sized guest rooms—plush and conservative, and popular with vacationers and business travelers—offer fine views as far as the Clyde dockyards. The three uppermost are the executive floors, which have the enhanced facilities of a semiprivate club. The youthful staff is alert and helpful. Families are especially catered to, and children arriving on the weekend are presented with fun packs, containing drawings, games, bubble bath, and comics.

1 William St., Glasgow G3 8HT. (C) 800/445-8667 in the U.S. and Canada, or 01412/045555. Fax 01412/045004. www.hilton.com. 319 units. £94–£190 ($150–$304) double; £134–£230 ($214–$368) suite. Weekend discounts often available. AE, DC, MC, V. Parking £5 ($8). Bus: 62. **Amenities:** 2 restaurants; bar; lounge; indoor pool; gym; sauna; 24-hr. room service; babysitting; laundry service; dry cleaning. *In room:* A/C, TV, minibar, coffeemaker, hair dryer, iron/ironing board.

Millennium Hotel Glasgow ✰✰✰   Following a £3 million ($5 million) upgrade, this striking landmark, the original Copthorne from 1810, is now better than ever. It stands near Queen Street Station where trains depart for the north of Scotland. As the Copthorne Hotel, this building played a role in world history in 1941. Winston Churchill met in room no. 21 with FDR's envoy, Harry Hopkins. It was a pivotal meeting in which Churchill secured Hopkin's

Glasgow

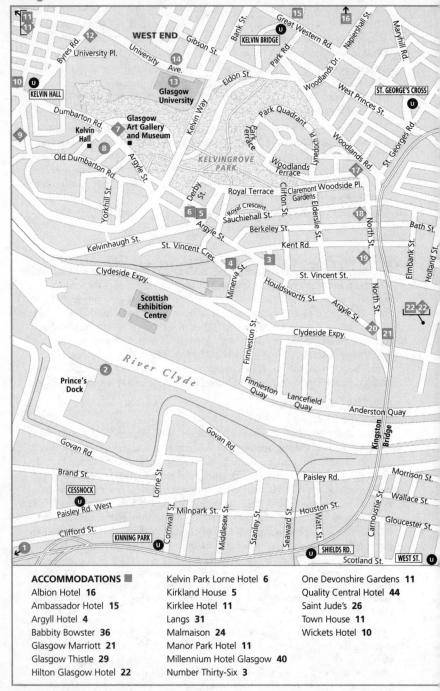

WEST END

Glasgow University

Glasgow Art Gallery and Museum

KELVINGROVE PARK

Kelvin Hall

Scottish Exhibition Centre

Prince's Dock

River Clyde

Kingston Bridge

Stations: KELVIN BRIDGE, ST. GEORGE'S CROSS, KELVIN HALL, CESSNOCK, KINNING PARK, SHIELDS RD., WEST ST.

ACCOMMODATIONS

Albion Hotel **16**
Ambassador Hotel **15**
Argyll Hotel **4**
Babbity Bowster **36**
Glasgow Marriott **21**
Glasgow Thistle **29**
Hilton Glasgow Hotel **22**
Kelvin Park Lorne Hotel **6**
Kirkland House **5**
Kirklee Hotel **11**
Langs **31**
Malmaison **24**
Manor Park Hotel **11**
Millennium Hotel Glasgow **40**
Number Thirty-Six **3**
One Devonshire Gardens **11**
Quality Central Hotel **44**
Saint Jude's **26**
Town House **11**
Wickets Hotel **10**

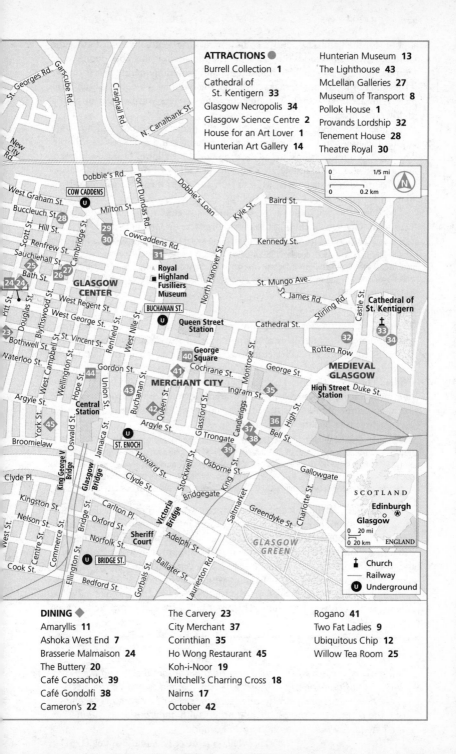

support for the Lend-Lease Bill, a commitment that eventually helped usher the United States into World War II. When its high-ceilinged public rooms were renovated, designers searched out antiques and glistening marble panels to give it the aura of the Victorian era. Even though the building is old, it has been completely modernized with all the amenities and services you'd expect of such a highly rated hotel.

The decor is lighter and more comfortable than ever before. Bedrooms are among the finest in Glasgow, with new furnishings and first-class bathrooms. The best accommodations are at the front of the building facing St. George Square and the less desirable are those in the rear with no view. Millennium Club rooms feature such extras as fresh fruit and bathrobes. One room has been adapted for guests with limited mobility.

The hotel also has some of the best and most elegant drinking and dining facilities in Glasgow, including the classic Brasserie on George Square.

George Square, Glasgow G2 1DS. © **01413/326711.** Fax 01413/324264. www.millenniumhotels.com. 117 units. £198–£350 ($317–$560) double; £258–£410 ($413–$656) suite. AE, DC, MC, V. Parking: £5 ($8). Underground: Buchanan St. **Amenities:** Restaurant; wine bar; cocktail lounge; car rental; room service; babysitting; same-day laundry service; same-day dry cleaning. *In room:* A/C, TV, minibar, dataport, coffee-maker, hair dryer, iron, safe, trouser press.

EXPENSIVE

Glasgow Marriott ⭐ Amid a confusing set of access roads for the highways and commercial boulevards surrounding it, the 13-story Marriott challenges the Hilton as the top business hotel in town. Although we prefer the Hilton, the Marriott is cheaper, and its soaring profile at the Anderston exit of M8 adds a vivid accent to the skyline. The place is big, modern, and chain-hotel efficient. The medium-sized guest rooms have everything you'd expect from an upscale chain, and some offer king-size beds. The hotel has some of the most extensive leisure and fitness facilities in the area.

500 Argyle St., Glasgow G3 8RR. © **800/228-9290** in the U.S. and Canada, or 01412/265577. Fax 01412/217676. www.marriotthotels.com/gladt. 300 units. £69–£125 ($110–$200) double (rates subject to room availability); £100–£145 ($160–$232) suite. AE, DC, MC, V. Free parking. Underground: St. Enoch. **Amenities:** Restaurant; bar; indoor heated pool; gym; spa; sauna; 24-hr. room service; babysitting; laundry service; dry cleaning. *In room:* A/C, TV, minibar, dataport, coffeemaker, hair dryer, iron/ironing board, safe, trouser press.

Langs ⭐ *Finds* If you're looking for Victorian Glasgow, head elsewhere. But if you gravitate to a minimalist Japanese style, check into this trendy and exceedingly contemporary hotel close to the Buchanan Galleries Shopping Mall and the Glasgow Royal Concert Hall. A diverse medley of bedrooms in various shapes, sizes, and configurations await you, but each has a certain flair. Nothing is overly adorned here, yet comfort and style, along with different colors and textures, make every unit a winner. The smallest are the studios, but you can also rent a duplex, a theme suite, or a very large suite. The beautifully kept bathrooms contain such

---

Impressions

[Glasgow is] a place which I shall ever hold in contempt as being filled with a set of unmannerly, low-bred, narrow-minded wretches; the place itself, however, is really pretty, and were the present inhabitants taken out and drowned in the ocean, and others with generous souls put in their stead, it would be an honour to Scotland.

—David Boswell, in a letter to James Boswell (1767)

extras as power showers with body jets. Nothing is evocative of Glasgow in any way. To emphasize the Asian theme all the more, Japanese body treatments are offered in the on-site Oshi Spa.

2 Port Dundas, Tel St., Glasgow G2 3LD. © **01413/331500.** Fax 01413/335700. www.langshotels.com. 100 units. £110–£140 ($176–$224) double; £160–£210 ($256–$336) suite. AE, DC, MC, V. Underground: Queen St. Station. **Amenities:** 2 restaurants; bar; fitness center; spa; sauna; 24-hr. room service; laundry service; dry cleaning. *In room:* TV, minibar, hair dryer, coffeemaker, iron.

Malmaison ★★ *Finds*   This hip hotel beats out all competitors in the best contemporary interior category. The hotel opened in 1994 in a historically important building constructed in the 1830s as a Greek Orthodox church. In 1997, an annex with additional bedrooms was added, designed to preserve the architectural character of the church's exterior. Inside, few of the original details remain; the decor is sleek and ultramodern. Bedrooms vary in size from smallish to average but are chic and well maintained, offering such extras as CD players, two-line phones, specially commissioned art, top-of-the-line toiletries, and power showers in the bathrooms. Breakfast is available but isn't included in the rates.

278 W. George St., Glasgow G2 4LL. © **01415/721000.** Fax 01415/721002. www.malmaison.com. 72 units. £125 ($200) double; from £145 ($232) suite. AE, DC, MC, V. Parking nearby £7 ($11). Bus: 11. **Amenities:** Restaurant; 2 bars; gym; 24-hr. room service; babysitting; laundry service; dry cleaning. *In room:* A/C, TV, dataport, minibar, coffeemaker, hair dryer, iron/ironing board, safe.

MODERATE

Glasgow Thistle *Kids*   The lower floors of this recently refurbished hotel are imbued with a cheerful ambience. The modern structure caters to both business and leisure travelers, and is an option in many of the airlines' vacation packages. The Scottish-themed guest rooms are decently sized. Wheelchair-accessible rooms are available. Guests also have free use of a gym a 5-minute walk away. Kids like the self-service carvery-style breakfast and lunch, one of the best dining values in Glasgow.

36 Cambridge St., Glasgow G2 3HN. © **01413/323311.** Fax 01413/324050. www.thistlehotels.com/ Glasgow. 300 units. £74–£135 ($118–$216) double; from £161 ($258) suite. AE, DC, MC, V. Free parking. Underground: Cowcadden. **Amenities:** Restaurant; bar; gym; indoor heated pool; health club; 24-hr. room service; babysitting; laundry service; dry cleaning. *In room:* A/C (most rooms), TV, minibar (executive rooms only), coffeemaker, hair dryer, iron/ironing board, trouser press.

Quality Central Hotel   This is a creaky old favorite. When it opened in 1883 by the rail station, the Central was the grandest Glasgow had seen, the landmark of the city's most famous street. Now revamped and restored to at least a glimmer of its former glory, the place may be too old-fashioned for some, but traditionalists like it. The baronial wooden staircase leading from the lobby to the upper floors has been stripped and refinished, and sandblasting the facade revealed elaborate Victorian cornices and pilasters. The guest rooms, with an uninspired decor, have televisions that offer Internet access and Sony PlayStation games. The hotel offers special accommodations for families and some rooms are designed for guests with limited mobility.

99 Gordon St., Glasgow G1 3SF. © **01412/219680.** Fax 01412/263948. www.choicehotelseurope.com. 222 units. £90–£105 ($144–$168) double; £140 ($224) suite. AE, DC, MC, V. Parking £9.20 ($15) overnight. Children stay free in room with two paying adults. Underground: Central Station. **Amenities:** Restaurant; 2 bars; coffee shop; indoor pool; gym; Jacuzzi; sauna; 24-hr. room service; laundry service; dry cleaning. *In room:* TV w/pay movies, minibar (some), coffeemaker, hair dryer, iron/ironing board, safe (some).

Saint Jude's   Opened in July 1999, Saint Jude's is hip and modern boutique hotel set inside a Victorian-style building in Glasgow's business district. Centrally located and 15 minutes from the airport, this two-story town house offers well-maintained, comfortable rooms and friendly service. The hotel attracts a young crowd of artists, musicians, writers, and celebs. Saint Jude's is named after the patron saint of sinners, which sets the tone. All rooms have bathrooms (some with showers, some with tubs) and warm, contemporary furnishings.

190 Bath St., Glasgow, G2 4HG. © 01413/528800. Fax 01413/528801. www.saintjudes.com. 6 units. £90–£115 ($144–$184) double; £185 ($296) suite. Rates include continental breakfast and newspaper. AE, MC, V. Metered parking. Underground: Cow Caddens. **Amenities:** Restaurant; bar; room service; laundry service; dry cleaning. *In room:* TV, minibar, coffeemaker, hair dryer, trouser press.

INEXPENSIVE

Babbity Bowster *Value*   In Merchant City, this small but delightful Robert Adam–designed hotel doubles as an art gallery. The guest rooms vary in size but are attractive, with Victorian reproductions and white-lace bedding. All the units come with showers. The hotel attracts students and faculty from Strathclyde University and displays the work of Glaswegian artists (most are for sale). The hotel bar attracts a crowd of regulars, and is a good place for meeting locals. In summer, there's an outdoor barbecue area.

16–18 Blackfriars St., Glasgow G1 1PE. © 01415/525055. Fax 01415/527774. 6 units. £70 ($112) double. Rates include Scottish breakfast. AE, MC, V. Free parking. Underground: Buchanan St. **Amenities:** Restaurant; bar. *In room:* Hair dryer.

Kirkland House   On a quiet street about a 10-minute walk from the Glasgow Art Gallery and Museum, the university, and the Scottish Exhibition Centre, the Kirkland is an impeccably maintained 1832 Victorian crescent house. A mix of antiques and reproductions is used in the large guest rooms, each equipped with a shower-only bathroom. You get a warm welcome from owners Carole and Ewing Divers and their daughter Sally. Ewing is a keen admirer of American swing music and displays a collection of 78-rpm gramophone records, old photographs, and pictures. You're welcome to listen to recordings of Harry James, Benny Goodman, and many others.

42 St. Vincent Crescent, Glasgow G3 8NG. © 01412/483458. Fax 01412/215174. www.kirkland.net43.co.uk/. 5 units. £65 ($104) double; £95 ($152) family room. Rates include continental breakfast. No credit cards. Free parking. Underground: Exhibition Centre. **Amenities:** Room service. *In room:* TV, coffeemaker, hair dryer (available on request).

THE WEST END
VERY EXPENSIVE

One Devonshire Gardens ★★★ *Finds*   This hotel is a gem and a charmer in every way, and attracts many celebrities. It is unquestionably the most glamorous, most elegant, and also the most tranquil hotel in Glasgow. In the Hyndland district just west of the center, the house at no. 1 was built in 1880 as an upper-crust home, but by the early 1980s it had degenerated into a seedy rooming house. In 1986, a designer bought it and made it even more elegant than it was in its heyday. At the ring of the doorbell, a pair of Edwardian chambermaids with frilly aprons and dust bonnets will welcome you. Each of the eight upstairs guest rooms in this building is furnished in period style with impeccable taste and lots of luxurious accessories. The success of building no. 1 led to the acquisition of nos. 2, 3, and 5 bringing the room count to 38. The newer rooms have the same elegant touches and high price tags.

   Note: Its restaurant also serves a finer cuisine than any of the major Glasgow restaurants.

1–3 Devonshire Gardens, Glasgow G12 0UX. ℭ **01413/392001.** Fax 01413/371663. www.onedevonshire gardens.com. 38 units. £125–£185 ($200–$296) double; £345–£475 ($552–$760) suite. AE, DC, MC, V. Free parking. Underground: Hillhead. **Amenities:** 2 restaurants; bar; 24-hr. room service; laundry service; dry cleaning. *In room:* TV, minibar, hair dryer, iron/ironing board, safe.

MODERATE

Kelvin Park Lorne Hotel ☝ *Finds*   In the heart of the residential West End, this is a discreet hotel whose public rooms are in the style of early-1900s Scottish designer Charles Rennie Mackintosh. Although it was built 40 years ago, after his death, its bar (Newberys, honoring Frances Newbery, Mackintosh's mentor) was designed according to Mackintosh's theories. The hotel consists of an early-19th-century building (four floors) and a later five-story structure. The guest rooms were renovated in 1995, resulting in a kind of neutral contemporary comfort; they vary in size, the older ones being noticeably larger. Most of them contain combination tub and showers.

923 Sauchiehall St., Glasgow G3 7TE. ℭ **01413/149955.** Fax 01413/371659. www.regalhotels.co.uk. 100 units. £75 ($120) double; £120 ($192) suite. Children under 12 stay free in parent's room. AE, DC, MC, V. Free parking. Underground: Kelvin Hall. **Amenities:** Restaurant; bar; 24-hr. room service; laundry service; dry cleaning. *In room:* TV, coffeemaker, hair dryer, trouser press.

Manor Park Hotel   This impressive West End town house was a private home when it was built in 1895 in the closing years of Victoria's reign. In 1947 it was converted into a hotel and has been much improved and upgraded since that time. Family-run and licensed for drinks, it offers grand Scottish hospitality from its hosts, Angus and Catherine MacDonald, true Scots to the core, both of whom speak Gaelic. Naturally, with such a Scottish background, they freely use the tartan when decorating. Their home is a blend of modern and traditional furnishings, using beechwood pieces against floral wallpaper. Each accommodation comes with a neat little bathroom with tub or shower.

28 Balshagray Dr., Glasgow G11 7DD. ℭ **01413/392143.** Fax 01413/395842. www.manorparkhotel.com. 10 units. £67–£75 ($107–$120) double. Rates include full breakfast. AE, MC, V. Underground: Partick. **Amenities:** Breakfast room; breakfast-only room service. *In room:* TV, hair dryer, beverage maker, iron.

Town House ☝☝ *Value*   This is one of the most upmarket and charming of the B&Bs of Glasgow. The stone-built Victorian terraced house has been successfully converted to receive guests to its tranquil little cul-de-sac tucked away in the West End, with a tennis club in the back and a rugby club to the front. As a curiosity note, there remains an air-raid shelter in the garden. The place justifiably wins praise from its many repeat visitors. The hospitality, the comfort level, and the atmosphere are first rate. All the large bedrooms have been faithfully restored and fitted with very good furnishings, along with first-rate private bathrooms with showers. Each room is individually decorated, often with many traditional wooden pieces against a decor of blue or yellow. Guests meet in the living room with its many books and coal-burning fireplace.

4 Hughenden Terrace, Glasgow G12 9XR. ℭ **01413/570862.** Fax 01413/399605. www.thetownhouse glasgow.com. 10 units. £72–£84 ($115–$134) double. Rates include Scottish breakfast. MC, V. Underground: Hillhead. **Amenities:** Breakfast room; bar; babysitting; room service; laundry service. *In room:* TV, hair dryer, beverage maker, iron.

Wickets Hotel   Better known for its restaurant and bar than for its comfortable guest rooms, this hotel from the 1890s is an undiscovered West End gem, opposite one of the city's largest cricket grounds (the West of Scotland Cricket Club). The double rooms are pleasantly spacious, each with a brightly cheerful decor; one room is set aside for families. The Conservatory Restaurant is the glamour spot, offering moderately priced regional and continental fare amid old photos of local cricket teams. Adjacent to the restaurant is an open-air beer garden, one of the few in Glasgow. Randall's wine bar sells wine by the glass in an Art Deco setting filled with Erte fashion prints.

52–54 Fortrose St., Glasgow G11 5LP. (℃) **01413/349334.** Fax 01413/349334. www.wicketshotel.co.uk. 11 units. £70 ($112) double; £88 ($141) family room. Rates include Scottish breakfast. AE, MC, V. Free parking. Underground: Partick. **Amenities:** Restaurant; bar; 24-hr. room service; laundry service; dry cleaning. *In room:* TV, coffeemaker, hair dryer, iron.

INEXPENSIVE

Albion Hotel   This unpretentious hotel is formed by connecting two nearly identical beige-sandstone row houses. In the heart of Glasgow's West End, it offers high-ceilinged guest rooms with modern furniture and small refrigerators. All the units contain a shower-only bathroom. If your hotel needs are simple, you're likely to be very happy here.

405–407 N. Woodside Rd., Glasgow G20 6NN. (℃) **01413/398620.** Fax 01413/348159. www.glasgowhotels andapartments.co.uk. 16 units. £49–£60 ($78–$96) double. Rates include breakfast. AE, DC, MC, V. Free parking. Underground: Kelvin Bridge. **Amenities:** Breakfast room; lounge; bar. *In room:* TV, fridge, coffeemaker, hair dryer, safe, trouser press.

Ambassador Hotel ✦ ⓥⓐⓛⓤⓔ   Across from the BBC Studios and the Botanic Gardens, and overlooking the Kelvin River, this small hotel in an Edwardian town house (ca. 1900) is one of the better B&Bs in Glasgow. After a refurbishment in 2002, the hotel is looking quite stylish. Each of the individually decorated and attractively furnished bedrooms has a well-maintained bathroom with tub or shower. The hotel is well situated for exploring the West End, with several art galleries nearby and many good restaurants or brasseries close at hand.

7 Kelvin Dr., Glasgow G20 8QJ. (℃) **01419/461018.** Fax 01419/455377. www.glasgowhotelsandapartments. co.uk. 16 units. £58 ($93) double without breakfast; £66 ($106) double with breakfast. AE, DC, MC, V. Free parking. Underground: Hillhead. **Amenities:** Bar; lounge; ; laundry. *In room:* TV, VCR and DVD players available, coffeemaker, hair dryer, iron/ironing board, safe, trouser press.

Argyll Hotel   This hotel is small but special, housed in a Georgian building near Glasgow University, the Art Gallery and Museum, the Kelvin Hall International Sports Arena, and the Scottish Exhibition Centre. It caters to both business and leisure travelers, and is also popular with women traveling alone. Although completely modernized, it shows a healthy respect for tradition. The guest rooms are comfortable, each equipped with a combination tub and shower. A couple of the rooms are large, and the rest are average size. *Note:* The hotel offers a number of discount packages, including historical- and theater-related offerings.

969–973 Sauchiehall St., Glasgow G3 7TQ. (℃) **01413/373313.** Fax 01413/373283. www.argyllhotelglasgow. co.uk. 38 units. £72 ($115) double. Rates include Scottish breakfast. AE, MC, V. Parking on nearby streets. Underground: Kelvin Hall. Bus: 9, 16, 42, 57, 62, or 64. **Amenities:** Restaurant; bar; room service; babysitting (by prior arrangement); laundry service; dry cleaning. *In room:* TV, coffeemaker, hair dryer, iron/ironing board.

Kirklee Hotel ✦ ⓕⓘⓝⓓⓢ   This red-sandstone Edwardian terraced house is graced with a rose garden that has won several awards. Behind the ornate stained-glass door you'll find public rooms loaded with period furniture and antiques, including a beautiful Edwardian-style lounge. All of the high-ceilinged guest rooms are average size and feature original artwork. All of the bedrooms are nonsmoking. Rosemary and Douglas Rogen will serve you breakfast in your room. The Kirklee is near the university, the Botanic Gardens, and the major art galleries.

11 Kensington Gate, Glasgow G12 9LG. ℂ **01413/345555.** Fax 01413/393828. www.scotland2000.com/ kirklee. 9 units. £68 ($109) double. Rates include Scottish breakfast. MC, V. Parking on nearby streets. Underground: Hillhead. **Amenities:** Lounge. *In room:* TV, coffeemaker, hair dryer, trouser press.

Number Thirty-Six In the heart of the West End, this hotel occupies the two lower floors of a four-story sandstone building that was conceived as an apartment house in 1848. Hardworking entrepreneur John MacKay maintains his high-ceilinged pastel guest rooms (each decorated uniquely) in fine working order. Each is equipped with a tidy shower-only bathroom. Breakfast is the only meal served. The entire hotel is nonsmoking.

36 St. Vincent Crescent, Glasgow G3 8NG. ℂ **01412/482086.** Fax 01412/211477. www.no36.co.uk/html. 5 units. £50–£60 ($80–$96) double. MC, V. Bus: 42, 63, or 64. **Amenities:** Room service (7:30-9am); laundry service. *In room:* A/C, TV, coffeemaker, hair dryer.

4 Where to Dine

The days are long gone when a meal out in Glasgow meant mutton pie and chips. Some of the best Scottish food is offered here (especially lamb from the Highlands, salmon, trout, Aberdeen Angus steaks, and such exotic delights as moor grouse), and there is an ever-increasing number of ethnic restaurants. This still being Britain, however, you'll find the usual fish-and-chip joints, burger outlets, fried chicken eateries, and endless pubs. Many restaurants close on Sunday, and most are shut by 2:30pm, reopening again for dinner around 6pm.

Note: For the locations of the restaurants below, see the "Glasgow" map on pages 548–549.

CENTRAL GLASGOW
VERY EXPENSIVE

Cameron's ★★ MODERN SCOTTISH This is the most glamorous restaurant in one of Glasgow's best hotels, its four sections outfitted like baronial hunting lodges in the wilds of the Highlands. The chef's conservative menu holds few surprises but is a celebration of market-fresh ingredients deftly prepared. Small slip-ups sometimes mar the effect of a dish or two, but we've been dining here since its opening and have always come away pleased. Your best bet is to stay Scottish when ordering. Go with the roasted saddle of venison or seared marlin with Asian-style vegetables and jasmine rice. You can also order a succulent Borders lamb for a main course.

In the Hilton Glasgow Hotel, 1 William St. ℂ **01412/045555.** Reservations recommended. Set-price menu 2-course £28 ($45), 3-course £33 ($53). AE, DC, MC, V. Mon–Fri noon–1:45pm and 7–9:45pm; Sat 7–9:45pm. Bus: 6A, 16, or 62.

Rogano ★★ SEAFOOD Rogano boasts a perfectly preserved Art Deco interior from 1935, when Messrs. Rogers and Anderson combined their talents and names to create a restaurant that has hosted virtually every star of the British film industry. You can enjoy dinner amidst lapis lazuli clocks, etched mirrors, ceiling fans, semicircular banquettes, and potted palms. The menu changes every 2 months but always emphasizes seafood, such as seared sea bream with tomato petals and a sage-flavored court-bouillon. There are at least six varieties of temptingly rich desserts, like coconut-and-pineapple parfait with golden rum syrup. *Note:* A less expensive menu is offered down in the Cafe Rogano, where main courses begin at £9.50 ($15).

11 Exchange Place. ℂ **01412/484055.** Reservations recommended. Main courses £18–£34 ($28–$54); fixed-price lunch £17 ($26). AE, DC, MC, V. Restaurant daily noon–2:30pm and 6:30–10:30pm. Cafe Mon–Thurs noon–11pm, Fri–Sat noon–midnight, Sun noon–11pm. Underground: Buchanan St.

EXPENSIVE

The Buttery ⭐ SCOTTISH   This is the perfect hunter's restaurant, with oak panels, racks of wine bottles, and an air of baronial splendor. The anteroom bar used to be the pulpit of a church, and the waitresses wear high-necked costumes of which Queen Victoria would have approved. Some of the best-tasting items on the menu are sliced sirloin of Scottish beef with pork-and-parsley dumplings, and poached filet of monkfish and scallops in a bacon-flavored sauce with Parmesan.

Adjacent to the Buttery is the **Oyster Bar,** outfitted in church-inspired Victoriana; its menu is shorter and a bit less expensive.

652 Argyle St. ✆ **01412/218188.** Reservations recommended. Set-price menu £32 ($51) (2-course), £36 ($58) (3-course); Oyster Bar lunch main courses £12–£15 ($19–$24). AE, DC, MC, V. Mon–Fri noon–2:30pm; Mon–Sat 6–10:30pm. Underground: St. Enoch.

Nairns ⭐ SCOTTISH/MEDITERRANEAN   This is one of Glasgow's hottest and hippest restaurants, thanks to head chef Derek Blair's cuisine and a style that blends cutting-edge London with traditional Glasgow. In an 18th-century Georgian building, it offers two monochromatic dining rooms where fabric textures are more heavily emphasized than bright colors. Menu items change with the season and the chef's inspiration but are likely to include pan-seared cod in a tapenade crust with herb-laced mashed potatoes or else tender and flavorful filet of Scottish beef with parsley potatoes, white beans, and a savory sauce. Favorite desserts are Chivas whisky parfait with Earl Grey syrup and classic lemon tart.

13 Woodside Crescent. ✆ **01413/530707.** Reservations recommended. Set menu £12–£15 ($19–$24) at lunch, £25–£30 ($39–$47) at dinner. AE, DC, MC, V. Tues–Sat noon–2pm and 6–9:45pm.

MODERATE

Brasserie Malmaison (Kids) SCOTTISH/CONTINENTAL   Located in the hip Hotel Malmaison, converted from a Greek Orthodox church (see above), this restaurant in the crypt, beneath the original vaults, serves well-prepared imaginative food in a masculine, dark decor, with a large bar and wooden banquettes affording privacy. Menu items arrive in generous portions and include grilled entrecote in a sauce with fondant potatoes, or poached filet of halibut with a mussel and saffron chowder. You can also order a perfectly grilled chicken with roasted red-pepper salsa. The chefs serve some of the city's best french fries.

In the Malmaison Hotel, 278 W. George St. ✆ **01415/721000.** Reservations recommended for dinner Thurs–Sun. Brasserie main courses £11–£17 ($17–$26). AE, DC, MC, V. Brasserie daily noon–2:30pm and 5:30–10:30pm. Bus: 11.

Café Cossachok ⭐ (Finds) RUSSIAN   Before the opening of this restaurant near the Tron Theatre, Glasgow was about the last place you'd look for Russian cuisine consumed with lots of vodka. An inviting oasis with its beautiful and authentic Russian decor, including plenty of mahogany pieces and extensive use of the color of red, it's a favorite with a lot of actors appearing at the theater. A little art gallery upstairs is a showcase for Russian art and culture. Every Sunday there is live music with singers performing in both Russian and English.

The chefs concentrate mainly on Russian fare but are also adept at turning out a selection of Armenian, Georgian, and Ukrainian dishes. Come here to feast on all the famous Russian dishes such as borscht, savory blinis, and beef Stroganoff. The beef Stroganoff, for example, is the finest we've had in Scotland, served with fried straw potatoes. Chicken Vladimir is another excellent offering, a breaded breast of chicken with a mushroom sauce resting under a cheese topping, and Zakuski Tzar is a tasty version of home-baked pork flavored with garlic and served with a dip inspired by the kitchen of Georgia.

10 King St., Merchant City. ℂ **01415/530733.** Reservations recommended. Main courses £7–£13 ($11–$21). Pretheater 2-course dinner (5–7pm) £9.95 ($16). MC, V. Tues-Sun 11am–3pm and 6–11pm; Sun 3–11pm. Underground: St. Enoch.

City Merchant SCOTTISH/INTERNATIONAL   In the heart of the city, this restaurant, owned and operated by Tony and Linda Matteo, offers friendly service and an extensive menu that's served throughout the day. The cuisine is more reliable than stunning, but it delivers quite an array of well-prepared fresh food at a good price. One longtime regular told us, "It's a cozy place to eat on a rainy day, and we have a lot of those in Glasgow." Try the roast breast of duck, rack of lamb, or escalope of venison. Also tempting are the fast-seared scallops, a classic smoked haddock, or the filet of salmon. Some of the desserts evoke old-time Scotland, such as a "clootie dumpling," made with flour, spices, and fried fruit and served with home-churned butter.

97–99 Candlebiggs. ℂ **01415/531577.** Reservations recommended. Main courses £8–£25 ($13–$40); fixed-price lunch £10–£12 ($15–$19). AE, DC, MC, V. Mon–Sat noon–10:30pm. Underground: St. Enoch.

Ho Wong Restaurant CANTONESE   Two blocks from the Central Station, Ho Wong is one of the city's finest Chinese restaurants. Jimmy Ho and David Wong opened this remote outpost of their Hong Kong establishment. You can pause for a drink in the cocktail bar, perusing the menu before being shown to your table. The service is obliging. There are at least eight duck dishes on the menu, along with four types of fresh lobster, as well as some "bird's nest" dishes and sizzling platters.

82 York St. ℂ **01412/213550.** Reservations required. Main courses £15–£20 ($24–$32); fixed-price 2-course lunch £8.90 ($14); fixed-price banquet £27 ($43) (5 courses). AE, DC, MC, V. Mon–Sat noon–2pm and 6pm–midnight; Sun 6pm–midnight. Underground: Central Station.

Mitchell's Charing Cross MODERN SCOTTISH   Named for its location near Glasgow's largest library (the Mitchell), this attractively decorated upscale bistro offers Scottish *cuisine moderne.* In a large room lined with plants and sophisticated paintings (usually by Glaswegian artists), you can order from a menu that changes every 2 months. Choices may include salmon, and smoked haddock netted off the Hebridean coast; scallops of Scottish venison; duck; and haggis with fresh *tatties and neeps* (mashed potatoes and turnips) and chive mayonnaise. Even if you miss mealtime here, consider dropping in for a pint or a whisky in the basement bar.

157 North St., Charing Cross. ℂ **01412/044312.** Reservations recommended. Main courses £4–£8 ($6.40–$13) at lunch, £8–£18 ($13–$29) at dinner; fixed-price pretheater supper (5–7pm) £9.95–£11.95 ($16–$19). AE, DC, MC, V. Tues–Fri noon–2:30pm; Tues–Sat 5pm–midnight. Bus: 23 or 57.

October INTERNATIONAL   At the top of the Princes Square shopping district, this bar/restaurant offers a widely diversified cuisine. There are several vegetarian dishes, and one of the best is a type of potato sandwich filled with roasted vegetables. Club sandwiches accompanied by coleslaw or salad are very popular and cost £5.95 ($9.50). Main courses are served from noon to 9pm on Thursday, and for the rest of the week (except Sunday) main courses are served from noon to 5pm and light snacks from 5 to 9pm. There's a wide array of choices—everything from a chicken or shrimp Caesar salad to mussels with white wine, flavored with herbs and garlic. For dessert, try the strawberry brûlée or lemon tart.

The Rooftop, Princes Square, Buchanan St. ℂ **01412/210303.** Reservations recommended. Main courses £5.95–£8.50 ($9.50–$14). AE, MC, V. Mon–Fri noon–9pm; Sat 12:30–4:30pm. Underground: St. Enoch.

(Moments Tea for Two

For tea, a light lunch, or a snack, try the famed **Willow Tea Room,** 217 Sauchiehall St. (© **01413/320521;** Underground: Cowcaddens). When it opened in 1904, the Willow became a sensation because of its Charles Rennie Mackintosh design, and it has been restored to its original condition. Thousands of locals fondly remember coming here as children to enjoy delectable pastries and ice-cream dishes—and it's still a big treat for any kid.

On the ground floor is a well-known jeweler, M. M. Henderson Ltd. The "room de luxe" is in the heart of the building, and it's fashionable to drop in for tea at any time of day. Reservations are recommended, and afternoon tea with pastry is £8.95 ($14). It's open Monday through Saturday from 9am to 4:30pm and Sunday from noon to 3:30pm.

Two Fat Ladies ✦ MODERN BRITISH/SEAFOOD This ranks high on the list of everybody's favorite restaurants, especially for irreverent diners who appreciate the unexpected. The "Two Fat Ladies" refer to the restaurant's street number—a nickname for the number 88 in Scotland's church-sponsored bingo games (there's no connection to the "Two Fat Ladies" of the TV cooking show fame). In honor of the name, owner-chef Calum Matheson displays an impossible-to-miss painting of two voluptuous Venus wannabes near the entrance. The custard-colored decor is minimalist and "post punk." Despite the limited hours (lunch is served on only 2 days), the restaurant packs in crowds for specialties such as scallops wrapped in parma ham with oyster mushroom cream sauce, or a grilled chicken filet salad with apple chutney. The best dessert is the Pavlova (a chewy meringue) with summer berries and Drambuie sauce.

88 Dumbarton Rd. © **01413/391944.** Reservations recommended. Fixed-price lunch £11–£13 ($18–$21); fixed-price pretheater supper (6–7pm) £11–£13 ($18–$21); main courses £14–£17 ($22–$27). MC, V. Mon–Sat noon–3pm; daily 6–10pm. Bus: 16, 42, or 57.

INEXPENSIVE

Cafe Gandolfi (Kids SCOTTISH/MEDITERRANEAN Many university students as well as young professionals will tell you this popular place in Merchant City is their favorite caff—you may sometimes have to wait for a table. A remake of a Victorian pub, it boasts rustic wooden floors, wood benches, and stools. At lunch you should look for chalkboard specials. Vegetarians will find solace here, as will children with fussy tastes. If you don't fill up on soups and salads, try smoked venison with gratin dauphinois or smoked pheasant with an onion tartlet in winter. Of course, whatever you choose should be followed by one of the homemade ice creams, which are the best in the city.

64 Albion St. © **01415/526813.** Reservations recommended on weekends. Main courses £7.50–£16 ($12–$26). MC, V. Mon–Sat 9am–11pm; Sun noon–11pm. Underground: St. Enoch/Cannon St.

The Carvery (Value BRITISH The price of a meal at the Carvery is low considering what you get. In an ambience of brick-lined walls and pinpoint lighting, you can select from one of Glasgow's most amply stocked hot and cold buffets, spread on an altarlike centerpiece. It's augmented with carved roasts and joints produced by uniformed chefs. This is hearty cooking of the type that has delighted Brits for years; it's aimed at filling you up more than following the latest foodie trends.

In the Holiday Inn Glasgow City West, Bothwell St. ℰ **0870/400-9032**. Reservations required. Buffet £17.50 ($28). AE, DC, MC, V. Sun–Fri 6:30–10pm; Sat 5:30–10pm. Underground: Buchanan St.

Corinthian SCOTTISH/INTERNATIONAL   In Lanarkshire House, this restaurant opened 2 years ago and sports a 25-foot illuminated glass dome as its stunning centerpiece. Crystal chandeliers and rococo friezes make for a luxurious atmosphere and a refined dining experience. The menu is attractive and classic, based on the freshest products available in any season. You might, for example, feast on tender lamb brochettes from Highland sheep or salmon caught in Scottish waters. The chef does an enticing grilled tuna along with homemade desserts. In addition to the main restaurant are two bars where you can relax on fine Italian leather sofas while listening to music spun by the local DJ.

191 Ingram St. ℰ **01415/521101.** Reservations recommended. Main courses £12–£16 ($19–$26); fixed-price pretheater dinner (daily 5:30–7pm) £9.75 ($16) for 2 courses, £12.50 ($20) for 3 courses. AE, MC, V. Mon–Sat 11am–3am; Sun noon–3am. Underground: St. Enoch.

THE WEST END
EXPENSIVE

Amaryllis ✹✹✹ SCOTTISH/FRENCH   One Devonshire Gardens is not only one of our favorite hotels in all of Scotland, but its on-site restaurant has blossomed into the finest in Glasgow. The venue re-creates the aura—and the service—of the Edwardian Age. Drinks are served in the elegant drawing room, and you can dine amid Victoriana.

The restaurant has been taken over by Gordon Ramsey, England's most acclaimed chef. Of course, this *enfant terrible* of British cookery is hardly on-site every night, but the actual chef is the talented David Dempsy, who uses only the finest of high-quality ingredients, which he fashions into a fabulous temptation for your palate. Among his heavenly dishes are a pot-roasted rump of lamb with a truffle and potato purée along with braised shallots, a garlic confit, and thyme *jus*. Every dish we've sampled here has been superb, including a creamy risotto flavored with spring onions and fresh herbs and served with Parmesan shavings.

1 Devonshire Garden. ℰ **01413/373434.** Reservations required. Main courses £9–£14 ($14–$22); table d'hôte menu £35 ($56). AE, MC, V. Daily 7–9:30pm. Underground: Partick.

Ubiquitous Chip ✹ SCOTTISH   This restaurant is inside the rough-textured stone walls of a former stable; its glass-covered courtyard boasts masses of climbing vines. Upstairs is a pub where simple platters are served with pints of lager and drams of whisky; they may include chicken, leek, and white-wine casserole or finnan haddies with bacon (but no fish and chips, as you might think from the name). The cooking in the restaurant is bistro style; the lunch menu changes weekly and dinner menu every 2 weeks. Lunch might include free-range chicken, shellfish with crispy seaweed snaps, or wild rabbit, and dinner might feature free-range pigeon with wild mushrooms or whisky-marinated salmon. Vegetarians are catered to at both lunch and dinner.

12 Ashton Lane, off Byres Rd. ℰ **01413/345007.** Reservations recommended. Restaurant fixed-price lunch £22 ($34) for 2 courses, £27 ($42) for 3 courses; fixed-price dinner £33 ($52) for 2 courses, £38 ($60) for 3 courses; bar meals £5–£8 ($8–$13) at lunch, £10–£15 ($16–$24) at dinner. AE, DC, MC, V. Restaurant Mon–Sat noon–2:30pm, daily 5:30–11pm; bar Sun 1–11pm. Underground: Hillhead.

MODERATE

Ashoka West End ✹ INDIAN/PUNJABI   This is a culinary landmark in Glasgow, serving the finest cuisine of the Sub-Continent. Novice chapati chompers and vindaloo veterans alike flock to this restaurant and many Glaswegians learned to "eat Indian" at this very restaurant. The decor is a bit eclectic, involving rugs, brass objects, murals, and greenery.

The dishes are full of flavor with a fragrant and most pleasing aroma when served. You might launch your repast with *Pakora,* which is deep fried chicken, mushrooms, or fish, perhaps a combination of flavors. From here you can go on to order *Jalandhri,* a potent fusion of ginger, garlic, onions, peppers, coconut cream, and fresh herbs served with a choice of chicken, lamb, or mixed vegetables. *Sing Sing Chandni* is a sweet and spicy Cantonese-style dish with crispy peppers, spring onions, and cashew nuts served most often with chicken. Those preferring something less robust should try *Chasni,* a light and smooth creamy sauce served with chicken, lamb, or mixed vegetables.

1284 Argyle St. ⓒ **0800/195-3195.** Reservations required. Main courses £6–£13 ($9.60–$21). AE, DC, MC, V. Wed–Thurs noon–2pm; Fri noon–1am; Sat 5pm–1am; Sun–Thurs 4pm–12:30am. Underground: Kelvin Hall.

INEXPENSIVE
Koh-i-Noor PUNJABI INDIAN   This is one of the city's top Indian restaurants. The family that runs this spacious place comes from the Punjab in Pakistan, and naturally Punjabi specialties like *paratha* and *bhuna* lamb are recommended. The Sunday Indian buffet is one of the great food values of the city; the Indian buffet held on weekdays is another treat. You can also order a three- or four-course business lunch.

235 North St., Charing Cross. ⓒ **01412/211555.** Reservations recommended. Main courses £9–£15 ($14–$24); fixed-price business lunch £4.95 ($7.90) for 3 courses, £6.95 ($11) for 4 courses; Sun–Thurs buffet £11 ($18); Fri–Sat buffet £13 ($21). AE, DC, MC, V. Sun–Thurs noon–midnight; Fri–Sat noon–1am. Underground: St. Georges.

5 Seeing the Sights
THE TOP ATTRACTIONS
The center of Glasgow is **George Square,** dominated by the **City Chambers** Queen Victoria opened in 1888. Of the statues in the square, the most imposing is that of Sir Walter Scott, atop a 24m (80-foot) column. Naturally, you'll find Victoria along with her beloved Albert, plus Robert Burns. The **Banqueting Hall,** lavishly decorated, is open to the public on most weekdays.

Burrell Collection ★★★   This museum houses the mind-boggling treasures left to Glasgow by Sir William Burrell, a wealthy shipowner who had a lifelong passion for art collecting. You can see a vast aggregation of furniture, textiles, ceramics, stained glass, silver, art objects, and pictures (especially 19th-century French art) in the dining room, hall, and drawing room reconstructed from Sir William's home, Hutton Castle at Berwick-upon-Tweed. Ancient artifacts, Asian art, and European decorative arts and paintings are featured. There is a restaurant, and you can roam through the surrounding park, 5km (3 miles) south of Glasgow Bridge.

Pollok Country Park, 2060 Pollokshaws Rd. ⓒ **01412/872550.** Free admission. Mon–Sat 10am–5pm; Sun 11am–5pm. Closed Jan 1 and Dec 25. Bus: 45, 48, or 57.

Glasgow Science Centre ★★★ *(Kids)*   This is Britain's most successful millennium project. On the banks of the River Clyde, it lies in the heart of the city, opposite the Scottish Exhibition and Conference Centre. Opened in 2001, the center is the focal point of Glasgow's drive to become one of Europe's major high-tech locations. In three landmark buildings, the center features the first titanium-clad structures in the United Kingdom, including Scotland's only Space Theatre.

Other features include innovative laboratories, multimedia and science theaters, and interactive exhibits. The overall theme is that of documenting the challenges facing Scotland in the 21st century. The center is also a showcase depicting Glasgow's contribution to science and technology in the past, present, and future. The complex also contains the only 360-degree rotating tower in the world.

Children will love the hands-on activities: They'll be able to make their own soundtrack and animation, do a 3-D head scan and rearrange their own features, or star in their own digital video. At special shows and workshops, you'll see a glass smashed by sound, "catch" shadows, experience a million volts of indoor lighting, see liquid nitrogen, view bacteria that lurk on you, and build a lie detector.

The IMAX Theatre, a first for Glasgow and Scotland, projects a picture that's the size of a five-story tenement block onto the screen. There are some 150 films currently available that take viewers into all kinds of experiences—perhaps to explore the hidden secrets of natural wonders like the Grand Canyon or even the inside of an atom, and certainly the magic of space. The theater charges separate admission: £5.50 ($8.80) for adults or £4 ($6.40) for students and children, with a family ticket ranging from £12 to £16 ($19–$26).

50 Pacific Quay. ℂ **01414/205010.** www.gsc.org.uk. Admission £6.50 ($10) adults; £4.50 ($7.20) students and seniors, £12–£16 ($19–$26) family pass. Daily 10am–6pm. Underground: Buchan St. Station to Cessnock, from which there's a 10-min. walk.

Hunterian Art Gallery ★★ This gallery owns the artistic estate of James McNeill Whistler, including some 60 of his paintings donated by his sister-in-law. It also boasts a Mackintosh collection, including the architect's home (with his own furniture) on three levels, decorated in the original style. The main gallery exhibits 17th- and 18th-century paintings (Rembrandt to Rubens) and 19th- and 20th-century Scottish painters (McTaggart, Scottish Colourists, Gillies, Philipson, and others). Temporary exhibits, selected from Scotland's largest collection of prints, are presented in the print gallery, which also houses a permanent display of printmaking techniques. The outdoor courtyard boasts contemporary sculpture.

University of Glasgow, Hillhead St. ℂ **01413/305431.** www.hunterian.gla.ac.uk. Free admission. Mon–Sat 9:30am–5pm (Mackintosh House closed 12:30–1:30pm). Underground: Hillhead.

Hunterian Museum Opened in 1807, this is Glasgow's oldest museum, in the main Glasgow University buildings 3km (2 miles) west of the heart of the city. The museum is named after William Hunter, its early benefactor, who donated his private collections to get the museum going. The immense collection ranges from dinosaur fossils to coins to relics of the Roman occupation and plunder by the Vikings. The story of Captain Cook's voyages is pieced together in ethnographic material from the South Seas. The museum has a bookstall and an 18th-century-style coffeehouse.

University of Glasgow, Gilmorehill Building. ℂ **01413/304221,** ext. 4221. www.hunterian.gla.ac.uk. Free admission. Mon–Sat 9:30am–5pm. Closed public holidays. Underground: Hillhead.

The Lighthouse *Kids* Also known as **Scotland's Centre for Architecture, Design and the City,** the Lighthouse opened in July 1999. This building was Mackintosh's first public commission and housed the *Glasgow Herald* from 1895. The building is now the site of a seven-story, state-of-the-art exhibition center with a unique blue neon-tracked escalator that leads to four galleries, lecture facilities, education suites, and a cafe.

The Mackintosh Interpretation Centre is the first facility to provide an overview of Mackintosh's art, design, and architecture. The impressive glass timeline wall illustrates his achievements. There are also interaction stations with models, drawings, and computer and video displays.

Visitors can ride the lift up to the Mackintosh Tower and experience a panorama of the city. In addition to exhibitions, the education program offers tours, seminars, films, and workshops for people of all ages.

The Wee People's City is an interactive play area for children 8 years of age and under. The IT Hotspot features Macintosh computers with printing facilities, video conferencing, and a large selection of software for research, training, and hands-on activities.

11 Mitchell Lane. ⓒ 01412/216362. Admission to Lighthouse and Mackintosh Interpretation Center £3 ($4.80) adults, £1.50 ($2.40) seniors, and 80p ($1.30) children. Mon, Wed, Sat 10:30am–5pm; Tues 11am–5pm; Sun noon–5pm. Underground: Buchanan Station.

McLellan Galleries ☆ *Finds*

This used to be an unimportant and little-visited gallery. Today that's all changed. Even though it hardly rivals the Burrell Collection, McLellan came into prominence n 2003 with the closing down of the Glasgow Art Gallery and Museum for a major restoration slated to be completed in 2006. As the Glasgow Art Gallery was the repository of some of the city's greatest art, a decision was made to transfer some of its most important pieces, including oil paintings and sculpture, to the heretofore unimportant McLellan.

The McLellan was already the repository of an impressive collection of Italian works from the 16th and 17th centuries, and it is also a showcase for modern, pop art. Temporary exhibits on loan from the Glasgow Art Gallery include a superb collection of Dutch and Italian Old Masters, featuring Giorgione and Rembrandt. Such international artists as Botticelli are also represented. Perhaps you'll get to see Whistler's *Arrangement in Grey and Black no 2: Portrait of Thomas Carlyle*, the first Whistler work to be hung in a British gallery. Expect a rotating series of art.

270 Sauchiehall St. ⓒ 01413/311854. Free admission. Mon–Thurs and Sat 10am–5pm, Fri–Sun 11am–5pm. Underground: Queen St. Station.

Museum of Transport ☆☆

This museum contains a fascinating collection of all forms of transportation and related technology. Displays include a simulated 1938 Glasgow street with period shopfronts, appropriate vehicles, and a reconstruction of one of the Glasgow Underground stations. An authentic motorcar showroom has a display of mass-produced automobiles. The superb and varied ship models in the Clyde Room reflect the significance of Glasgow and the River Clyde as one of the world's foremost areas of shipbuilding and engineering.

1 Bunhouse Rd., Kelvin Hall. ⓒ 01412/872720. Free admission. Mon–Sat 10am–5pm; Sun and Fri 11am–5pm. Closed Jan 1 and Dec 25. Underground: Kelvin Hall.

Pollok House

The ancestral home of the Maxwells, Pollok House was built around 1750, with additions from 1890 to 1908 designed by Robert Rowand Anderson. The house and its 360 acres of parkland were given to the city of Glasgow in 1966 and are now administered by the National Trust for Scotland. It contains one of the finest collections of Spanish paintings in Britain, with works by El Greco, Goya, and Murillo, among others. There are also displays of silver, ceramics, and glass from the Maxwell family's and the city's collections.

Pollok Country Park, 2060 Pollokshaws Rd. ⓒ 01416/166410. www.nts.org.uk. Free admission Nov 1–Mar 31. Admission Apr–Oct £5 ($8) adult; £3.75 ($6) children, students, and seniors; £14 ($22) family ticket. Daily 10am–5pm. Bus: 57 or 57A.

Tenement House *Finds*   An 1892 building on Garnethill, not far from the main shopping street, Sauchiehall Street, this house has been called a "Glasgow flat that time passed by." Until her death, Agnes Toward was an inveterate hoarder of domestic trivia. For 54 years she lived in this flat and stuffed it with the artifacts of her era, everything from a porcelain jawbox sink to such household aids as Monkey Brand soap. After her death, the property came into the care of the National Trust for Scotland as a virtual museum of a vanished era.

145 Buccleuch St. © **01413/330183.** www.nts.org.uk. Admission £3.50 ($5.60) adults, £2.60 ($4.15) seniors, students, and children. Mar–Oct daily 1–5pm. Underground: Cowcaddens.

MORE ATTRACTIONS

Cathedral of St. Kentigern ★★★   Also known as St. Mungo's, this cathedral was consecrated in 1136, burned down in 1192, and rebuilt soon after; the **Laigh Kirk (lower church),** whose vaulted crypt is said to be the finest in Europe, remains to this day. Visit the **tomb of St. Mungo** in the crypt, where a light always burns. The edifice is mainland Scotland's only complete medieval cathedral from the 12th and 13th centuries. It was once a place of pilgrimage, but 16th-century zeal purged it of all monuments to idolatry.

Highlights of the interior are the 15th-century nave, built later than the choir, with a stone screen (unique in Scotland) showing the seven deadly sins. Both the choir and the lower church are in the mid-1200s First Pointed style. The church, even though a bit austere, is filled with intricate details left by long-ago craftspeople—note the tinctured bosses of the ambulatory vaulting in the back of the main altar. The lower church, reached via a set of steps north of the pulpit, is where Gothic reigns supreme, with an array of pointed arches and piers. Seek out, in particular, the **Chapel of the Virgin,** with its intricate net vaulting and bosses carved with fine detailing. The Blacader Aisle projecting from the south transept was the latest addition to the church, a two-story extension, of which only the lower part was completed in the late Gothic style.

For the best view of the cathedral, cross the Bridge of Sighs into the **Glasgow Necropolis** (© **01412/873961;** bus: 2 or 27), the graveyard containing almost

---

Moments **Frommer's Favorite Glasgow Experiences**

Touring the Burrell Collection. The pièce de resistance of Glasgow (some say of Scotland), this gallery is the city's major attraction. See what good taste and an unlimited budget can acquire in a lifetime.

Following Walkways and Cycle Paths. Greater Glasgow has an array of trails and bike paths cutting through areas of historic interest and scenic beauty, including the Paisley/Irvine Cycle and Walkway, 27km (17 miles) of unused railway line converted to a trail.

Riding the World's Last Seagoing Paddle Steamer. From spring to early fall, the *Waverley* makes day trips to scenic spots on the Firth of Clyde, past docks that once supplied more than half the tonnage of ocean-going ships. Call © **01412/218152** for details.

Shopping Paddy's Market. This daily market by the railway arches on Shipbank Lane gives you the real flavor of the almost-vanished Glaswegian style of street vending.

every type of architecture in the world. Built on a rocky hill and dominated by a statue of John Knox, this fascinating graveyard was opened in 1832. Typical of the mixing of all groups in this tolerant cosmopolitan city, the first person to be buried here was a Jew, Joseph Levi.

Cathedral Square, Castle St. (✆ 01415/526891. Free admission. Apr–Sept Mon–Sat 9:30am–6pm, Sun 1–5pm; Oct–Mar Mon–Sat 9:30am–4pm, Sun 1–4pm. Sun services at 11am and 6:30pm. Underground: Queen St. Station.

House for an Art Lover   This house, which opened in 1996, is based on an unrealized and incomplete 1901 competition entry of Mackintosh. The impressive building—architects Graeme Robertson and John Cane expanded the original designs and added missing details—was brought to life by contemporary artists and craftspeople. The tour begins in the main hall and leads through the dining room, with its lovely gesso panels, and on to the music room, which shows Mackintosh designs at their most inspirational. Finally, you visit the oval boardroom before entering an audiovisual display. Also here are a cafe, a design shop, and a striking parkland setting adjacent to Victorian walled gardens.

Bellahouston Park, Dumbreck Rd. (✆ 01413/534770. Admission £3.50 ($5.60) adults, £2.50 ($4) for children, students, and seniors. Daily 10am–4pm. Underground: Ibrox. Bus: 9A, 39, 54, 59, or 36.

Provands Lordship   Built by Bishop Andrew Muirhead as a residence for churchmen, this is Glasgow's oldest house (1471) and the only pre-Reformation building of interest other than the cathedral. Over the years, it has been a soda shop, the abode of Glasgow's city hangman, and a junk shop before it was turned into a museum. The museum houses 17th- and 18th-century furniture, tapestries, and pictures, as well as the key to Leven Castle in Tayside, where Mary Queen of Scots was imprisoned.

Castle St., across from the Cathedral of St. Kentigern. (✆ 01415/528819. Free admission. Daily 10am–5pm; Sun 11am–5pm. Underground: Buchanan St.

GARDENS & PARKS

Glasgow's **Botanic Gardens,** Great Western Road (✆ **01413/342422;** Underground: Hillhead), covers 40 acres; it's an extensive collection of tropical plants and herb gardens. The garden is acclaimed especially for its spectacular orchids and begonias. It's open daily from 7am to dusk. The greenhouses are open March through October from 10am to 4:45pm and November through February from 10am to 4:15pm. Admission is free.

Linn Park, on Clarkston Road (bus: 24 or 36), is 212 acres of pine and woodland, with many scenic walks along the river. Here you'll find a nature trail, pony rides for children, an old snuff mill, and a children's zoo. The park is open daily from 8am to dusk. **Gleniffer Braes Country Park** (✆ **01418/843794**), Glenfield Road, in Paisley, covers 1,300 acres of woodland and moorland and has picnic areas and an adventure playground. It's open daily from dawn to dusk.

ORGANIZED TOURS

The *Waverley* is the world's last seagoing paddle steamer, and from the last week of June to the end of August (depending on weather conditions), the Paddle Steamer Preservation Society conducts 1-day trips from Anderston Quay in Glasgow to historic and scenic places beyond the Firth of Clyde. As you sail along, you can take in what were once vast shipyards, turning out more than half the earth's tonnage of oceangoing liners. You're allowed to bring your own sandwiches for a picnic aboard, or you can enjoy lunch in the Waverley Restaurant.

Finds Special & Free Events

The **Glasgow International Jazz Festival** opens in the last days of June and usually runs through the first week of July. This festival has attracted some big names in the past, including the late Miles Davis and Dizzy Gillespie. Tickets are available from the Ticket Centre, Candleriggs (✆ **01412/401111**), but some free events are always announced.

On June 10, the **Bearsden** and **Milngavie Highland Games** are held at Burnbray in the small town of Milngavie (pronounced "Mill-guy"), 10km (6 miles) from Glasgow. The games include tug-of-war, wrestling, caber tossing, piping, and Highland dancing and offer a fun day out of the city. Call Cameron Wallace at ✆ **01419/425177** for details.

Boat tours cost £7.95 to £29 ($13–$46). For details, contact **Waverley Excursions,** Waverley Terminal, Anderston Quay, Broomielaw (✆ **01412/218152**).

There's also regular ferry service run by **Caledonian MacBrayne** (✆ **01475/650100**) in Gourock on the banks of the Clyde. The ferry stands close to the station in Gourock, connected to Glasgow Central Station by trains that leave every hour and take 30 to 45 minutes. The ferry service, which can take cars, runs every hour to the attractive seaside resort of Dunoon at the mouth of the Clyde. The journey takes about 20 minutes, and ferries run every hour from 6:20am to 8:20pm, from April to October 16; in winter the service is less frequent and visitors are advised to check beforehand as it's liable to change. The round-trip costs £4.25 ($6.80) adults and £2.50 ($4) seniors and children.

The best Glasgow tours are run by **Scotguide Tourist Services (City Sighting Glasgow)**, operated from 153 Queen Street at George Square, opposite the City Chambers (✆ **01412/040444;** Underground: Buchanan St.). From April 1 to October 31, departures are every 15 minutes from 9:30am to 4pm. The price is £8 ($13) adults, £6 ($9.60) students and seniors, and £3 ($4.80) children under age 7.

6 Shopping

One of the major hunting grounds is **Sauchiehall Street,** Glasgow's fashion center, where many shops and department stores frequently offer good bargains, particularly in woolen goods. About 3 blocks long, this street has been made into a pedestrian mall. **Argyle Street,** which runs by the Central Station, is another major shopping artery.

All dedicated world shoppers know of **Buchanan Street,** a premier pedestrian thoroughfare. This is the location of the famed Fraser's Department Store (see below). From Buchanan Street you can also enter **Princes Square,** an excellent shopping complex with many specialty stores, restaurants, and cafes.

In the heart of Glasgow is the city's latest and most innovative shopping complex, the **St. Enoch Shopping Centre** (Underground: St. Enoch; bus: 16, 41, or 44), whose merchandise is less expensive but a lot less posh than what you'd find at the Princes Square shopping center. You can shop under the biggest glass roof in Europe. The center is to the east of Central Station on St. Enoch Square.

The **Argyll Arcade** is at 30 Buchanan St. (Underground: Buchanan St.). Even if the year of its construction (1827) wasn't set in mosaic tiles above the entrance, you'd still know this is an old collection of shops beneath a curved glass ceiling. The arcade contains what's possibly the largest single concentration of retail **jewelers,** both antique and modern, in Europe, surpassing even Amsterdam. It's considered lucky to purchase a wedding ring here.

Dedicated fashion mavens should take a trip to the **Italian Shopping Centre** (Underground: Buchanan St.), a small complex in the Courtyard, off Ingram Street, where most of the units sell clothes, including Versace, Prada, Gucci, and Armani.

The latest contribution to mall shopping has come in the form of the **Buchanan Galleries** (Underground: Buchanan St.), which connects Sauchiehall, Buchanan, and Argyll streets and was completed in 1999. This plush development includes an enormous **John Lewis department store** and the biggest **Habitat** in Europe—a nirvana for anyone wanting reasonably priced contemporary furniture or accessories.

The Barras, held Saturday and Sunday from 9am to 5pm, takes place about .5km (¼ mile) east of Glasgow Cross. This century-old market has some 800 traders selling their wares in stalls and shops. Not only can you browse for that special treasure, you can also become a part of Glasgow life and be amused by the buskers. **Paddy's Market,** by the rail arches on Shipbank Lane, operates daily if you'd like to see an old-fashioned slice of Glaswegian street vending.

General **shopping hours** are Monday through Saturday from 9am to 5:30 or 6pm, depending on the merchant. On Thursdays, shops stay open to 8pm.

ANTIQUES

Victorian Village This warren of tiny shops stands in a slightly claustrophobic cluster. Much of the merchandise isn't particularly noteworthy, but there are many exceptional pieces if you're willing to go hunting. Several of the owners stock reasonably priced 19th-century articles; others sell old jewelry and clothing, a helter-skelter of artifacts. 93 W. Regent St. (✆ 01413/320808. Bus: 23, 38, 45, 48, or 57.

ART

Compass Gallery This gallery offers refreshingly affordable pieces; you could find something special for as little as £25 ($40), depending on the exhibition. The curators tend to concentrate on local artists, often university students. 178 W. Regent St. (✆ 01412/216370. Bus: 23, 38, 45, 48, or 57.

Cyril Gerber Fine Art One of Glasgow's most respected art galleries veers away from the avant-garde, specializing in British paintings, sculptures, and ceramics crafted between around 1880, and today and Scottish landscapes and cityscapes. Cyril Gerber is a respected art authority with lots of contacts in art circles throughout Britain. Objects begin at around £200 ($320). 148 W. Regent St. (✆ 01412/213095. Bus: 23, 38, 45, 48, or 57.

BOOKS

Borders An impressive bookseller, with premises overlooking Royal Exchange Square, in the heart of Glasgow, this retailer sells books, videos, and music CDs, with a gratifying emphasis on the cultural phenomena (travel, architecture,

---

Tips **Bring That Passport!**

Take along your passport when you go shopping in case you make a purchase that entitles you to a **VAT** (value-added tax) refund.

history, and botany) of Scotland. In some ways, it's a de facto social club as well, hosting contemporary discussion groups about modern fiction, author's readings and signings, piano concerts from emerging musical celebrities, and film discussion groups. There are even once-a-month discussion groups focusing on new works in Italian, Spanish, and German. 98 Buchanan St. © 01412/227700. Underground: Buchanan St.

A DEPARTMENT STORE

Fraser's Department Store   Fraser's is Glasgow's version of Harrods. A soaring Victorian-era glass arcade rises four stories, and inside you'll find everything from clothing to Oriental rugs, from crystal to handmade local artifacts of all kinds. Buchanan St. © 01412/213880. Underground: Buchanan St.

GIFTS & DESIGN

Catherine Shaw   Named after the long-deceased matriarch of the family that runs the place today, Catherine Shaw is a somewhat cramped gift shop that has cups, mugs, postcards, and gift items based on the designs of Charles Rennie Mackintosh. There are also some highly evocative Celtic mugs called *quaichs* (welcoming cups or whisky measures, depending on whom you talk to) and tankards in both pewter and silver. It's a great place for easy-to-pack and somewhat offbeat gifts. Look for another branch at 31 Argyll Arcade (© 01412/219038); entrances to the arcade are on both Argyll and Buchanan streets. 24 Gordon St. © 01412/044762. Underground: Buchanan St.

Mackintosh Shop   This tiny shop prides itself on its stock of books, cards, stationery, coffee and beer mugs, glassware, and sterling-and-enamel jewelry created from the original designs of Mackintosh.

Although the shop doesn't sell furniture, the staff will refer you to a craftsman whose work they recommend: **Bruce Hamilton, Furnituremaker,** 4 Woodcroft Ave., Broomhill (© **01505/322550;** bus: 6, 16, or 44), has been involved in the restoration of many Mackintosh interiors and has produced a worthy group of chairs, sideboards, and wardrobes authentic to Mackintosh's designs. Expect to pay around £250 ($400), not including upholstery fabric, for a copy of the designer's best-known chair (the Mackintosh-Ingram chair); there'll be a delay of at least a month before your furniture is shipped to your home. In the foyer of the Glasgow School of Art, 4 Napier St. © 01413/534526. Underground: Queen St.

National Trust for Scotland Shop   Drop in here for maps, calendars, postcards, pictures, dish towels, bath accessories, and kitchenware. Some of the crockery is in Mackintosh-design styles. The neoclassical building, constructed as a charity and hospice in 1806, is on the site of a larger hospice built in 1641. Hutcheson's Hall, 158 Ingram St. © 01415/528391. Underground: Buchanan St.

KILTS & TARTANS

Hector Russell   Founded in 1881, Hector Russell is Scotland's oldest kiltmaker. This elegant store might be the most prestigious in Scotland. The welcome of the experienced sales staff is genuinely warm-hearted. Crystal and gift items are sold on street level, but the real heart and soul of the place is on the lower level, where you'll find impeccably crafted and reasonably priced tweed jackets, tartan-patterned accessories, waistcoats, and sweaters of top-quality wool for men and women. Men's, women's, and children's hand-stitched kilts are available. 110 Buchanan St. © 01412/210217. Underground: Buchanan St.

PORCELAIN & CRYSTAL

Stockwell Bazaar   This is Glasgow's largest purveyor of porcelain, its four floors bulging with Royal Doulton, Wedgwood, Noritake, and Royal Worcester, plus crystal stemware by many manufacturers. Anything you buy can be insured and shipped to whatever address you specify. 67–77 Glassford St. ✆ **01415/525781.** Underground: St. Enoch.

7 Glasgow After Dark

Glasgow, not Edinburgh, is the cultural center of Scotland, and the city is alive with performances. Before you leave home, check *Time Out*'s latest roundup of who's playing in the clubs and concert halls; it's on the Web at **www.time out.co.uk**. After you've arrived, pick up a copy of *Culture City* or *What's On* at the tourist office or your hotel. Both these monthly publications are free and usually contain complete listings of what's happening in Scotland's largest city. In addition, at most newsstands you can get a free copy of *The List,* published every other week. It details arts and other events for Edinburgh as well as Glasgow.

THE PERFORMING ARTS

OPERA & CLASSICAL MUSIC   The **Theatre Royal,** Hope Street and Cowcaddens Road (✆ **01413/329000;** Underground: Cowcaddens; bus: 23, 48, or 57), is the home of the **Scottish Opera** as well as of the **Scottish Ballet.** The theater also hosts visiting companies from around the world. Called "the most beautiful opera theatre in the kingdom" by the *Daily Telegraph,* it offers splendid Victorian Italian Renaissance plasterwork, glittering chandeliers, and 1,547 comfortable seats, plus spacious bars and buffets on all four levels. However, it's not the decor but the ambitious repertoire that attracts operagoers. Ballet tickets run £3.50 to £30 ($5.60–$48) and opera tickets cost £3.50 to £55 ($5.60–$88). On performance days, the box office is open Monday through Saturday from 10am to 8pm; on nonperformance days, hours are Monday through Saturday from 10am to 6pm.

In winter, the **Royal Scottish National Orchestra** offers Saturday-evening concerts at the **Glasgow Royal Concert Hall,** 2 Sauchiehall St. (✆ **01413/ 326633;** Underground: Buchanan St.). The **BBC Scottish Symphony Orchestra** presents Friday-evening concerts at the **BBC Broadcasting House,** Queen Margaret Drive (Underground: St. Enoch), or at **City Halls,** Albion Street (Underground: St. Enoch). In summer, the Scottish National Orchestra has a short Promenade season (dates and venues are announced in the papers). Tickets can only be purchased at individual venues.

THEATER   Although hardly competition for London, Glasgow's theater scene is certainly the equal of Edinburgh's. Young Scottish playwrights often make their debuts here, and you're likely to see anything from Steinbeck's *The Grapes of Wrath* to Wilde's *Salome* to *Romeo and Juliet* done in Edwardian dress.

The prime symbol of Glasgow's verve remains the **Citizens Theatre,** Gorbals and Ballater streets (✆ **01414/290022;** www.citz.co.uk/default.asp; bus: 12 or 66), founded after World War II by James Bridie, a famous Glaswegian whose plays are still produced on occasion there. It's home to a repertory company, with tickets at £5 to £15 ($8–$24). The box office hours are Monday through Saturday from 9:30am to 6:30pm. The company is usually closed from June to the first week in August.

The **Glasgow Arts Centre,** 12 Washington St. (© **01412/214526;** www.cca-glasgow.com; bus: 2, 4, or 21), always seems to be doing something interesting, including children's productions and other theatrical performances. It's open Monday through Friday from 9:30am to 5pm and 6:30 to 10pm; in summer, it's closed in the evening. The center is funded by the Glasgow Council and performances are free. The **King's Theatre,** 297 Bath St. (© **01412/40111;** bus: 57), offers a wide range of productions, including straight plays, musicals, and comedies. During winter it's noted for its pantomime presentations. Tickets are £6 to £26 ($9.60–$42), and the box office is open Monday through Saturday from 10am to 6pm.

The **Mitchell Theatre,** 6 Granville St. (© **01412/875511;** bus: 57), has earned a reputation for staging small-scale entertainment, ranging from dark drama to dance, as well as conferences and seminars. A small modern theater, it adjoins the well-known Mitchell Library. The theater box office is open when there are performances from 4pm until the show. Ticket prices vary with each production. The **Pavilion Theatre,** 121 Renfield St. (© **01413/321846;** www.paviliontheatre.co.uk; bus: 21, 23, or 38), specializes in modern versions of vaudeville (which, as they'll assure you around here, isn't dead). The Pavilion sells its own tickets for £10 to £25 ($16–$40); they're not available at City Centre. The box office is open Monday through Saturday from 10am to 8pm.

The **Tron Theatre,** 63 Trongate (© **01415/524267;** www.tron.co.uk; Underground: St. Enoch), occupies one of the three oldest buildings in Glasgow, the former Tron Church. The church, with its famous Adam dome and checkered history, has been transformed into a small theater presenting the best of contemporary drama, dance, and music events. The Tron also has a beautifully restored Victorian cafe/bar serving traditional home-cooked meals, including vegetarian dishes and a fine selection of beer and wine. The box office is open Monday through Saturday from 10am to 6pm, over the counter and until 9pm by phone. Tickets are £2 to £15 ($3.20–$24) adults and £1 to £7 ($1.60–$11) children.

THE CLUB SCENE

The 13th Note   This club has moved away from jazz in the past couple of years and now books mainly heavy rock bands on Tuesday, Wednesday, and Thursday nights; country on Monday. On Friday, Saturday, and Sunday, the night is dedicated to ambient and alternative music. Open daily from noon to midnight. 50–60 King St. © 01415/531638. Bus: 21, 23, or 38.

Fury Murry's   Most of the crowd here is made up of students looking for nothing more complicated than a good, sometimes rowdy, time listening to disco music that's upbeat but not ultra-trendy. It's in a cellar, a 2-minute walk from the very central St. Enoch Shopping Centre. There's a very busy bar, a dance floor, and ample opportunities to meet the best and brightest in Scotland's university system. Jeans and T-shirts are the right garb. It's open Thursday through Sunday from 10:30pm to 3:30am. Thursday and Friday feature live bands, and other nights are strictly for dancing or can be reserved for private parties. 96 Maxwell St. © 01412/216511. Cover £2–£6 ($3.20–$9.60). Underground: St. Enoch.

The Garage   A big student crowd tests the limits of the 1,478-person capacity here on weekends. In the downstairs area, surrounded by rough stone walls, you get the impression you're in a castle with a Brit pop and indie soundtrack. Most regulars, however, gravitate to the huge main dance floor, where lots of shiny metal fixtures stand out in contrast to the stone walls. There are three bars downstairs and two upstairs. Open daily from 11pm to 3am. 490 Sauchiehall St. © 01413/321120. Cover £2–£7 ($3.20–$11). Underground: Buchanan St.

Grand Ole Opry   In a sprawling sandstone building 2.5km (1½ miles) south of Glasgow's center, the Grand Ole Opry is the largest club in Europe devoted to country-western music. There's a bar and dancing arena on both levels and a chuck-wagon eatery serving affordable steaks and other such fare on the upper level. Live music is always performed from a large stage at the front. Performers are usually from the United Kingdom, but a handful of artists from the States turn up. Open Friday through Sunday and occasionally Thursday (if demand warrants it) from 6:30pm to 12:30am. 2-4 Govan Rd., Paisley Toll Rd. © 01414/295396. Cover £3–£10 ($4.80–$16). Bus: 23 or 23A.

King Tut's Wah-Wah Hut   This sweaty, crowded rock bar has been in business for nearly a decade. It's a good place to check out the Glasgow music and arts crowd, as well as local bands and the occasional international act. Successful Scottish acts My Bloody Valentine and Teenage Fan Club got their starts here. Open Monday through Saturday from noon to midnight and Sunday from 6pm to midnight. 272 St. Vincent St. © 01412/215279. Cover £4–£10 ($6.40–$16). Bus: 6, 8, 9, or 16.

Nice 'n' Sleazy   This club books live acts Thursday through Sunday. The cover is quite reasonable, but it can get more expensive if you catch a band like the Cranberries, Alice Donut, or Helmet. Holding some 200 patrons, it provides a rare opportunity to catch internationally popular bands in an intimate setting. Upstairs on Sunday and Monday nights, DJs spin an eclectic mix of music for dancing, but most people come for the bands. Open daily from 11:30am to 11:45pm. 421 Sauchiehall St. © 01413/339637. Cover usually £3.50 ($5.60); higher if a big name is playing. Bus: 23 or 48.

Renfrew Ferry   This old car ferry once provided service on the River Clyde. Musical acts are booked infrequently during the year. 42 Clyde Place. © 01698/265511. Cover £6–£20 ($9.60–$32). Bus: 21, 23, 38, 45, 48, or 57.

Victoria's Nightclub   Victoria's prides itself on being the only club in Scotland with cabaret performances. In the heart of town, this building has two floors of high-tech design, with a first-floor dance club and a second-floor cabaret bar/restaurant where singers, comedians, and other artists amuse and titillate their audience. Dress is smart casual, and the crowd tends to be people over age 25, with a bit of money and sophistication. The dance club is open Thursday through Sunday from 10:30pm to 3am and the cabaret is open on Friday and Saturday from 7:30pm to 3am. 98 Sauchiehall St. © 01413/321444. Cover £3–£8 ($4.80–$13) for dance club only, £14–£15 ($22–$24) for dance club, cabaret, and buffet dinner. Underground: Buchanan St.

FAVORITE PUBS

Bon Accord   This amiably battered pub is a longtime favorite. There's an array of hand-pumps—a dozen devoted to real British ales, the rest to beers and stouts from the Czech Republic, Belgium, Germany, Ireland, and Holland. The pub is likely to satisfy your taste in malt whisky as well and offers affordable bar snacks. Open Monday through Saturday from noon to midnight, Sunday from noon to 11pm. 153 North St. © 01412/484427. Bus: 6, 8, or 16.

Cask and Still   Here's the best place for sampling malt whisky. You can taste from a selection of more than 350 single malts, at a variety of strengths (perhaps

not on the same night) and maturities (that is, years spent in casks). Many prefer the malt whisky that has been aged in a sherry cask. There's good bar food at
lunch, including cold meat salads and sandwiches. Open Monday through
Thursday from noon to 11pm, Friday and Saturday from noon to midnight. 154
Hope St. (C) 01413/330980. Bus: 21, 23, or 38.

Corn Exchange   Opposite the Central Station, this place was really the Corn
Exchange in the mid–19th century but now is one of Glasgow's most popular
pubs. Amid dark paneling and high ceilings, you can enjoy a pint of lager up
to 11pm Sunday through Wednesday and until midnight Thursday through
Saturday. Affordable pub grub is served daily from noon to 9pm. 88 Gordon St.
(C) 01412/485380. Bus: 21, 23, or 38.

L'Attaché   One of several traditional Scottish pubs in its neighborhood,
L'Attaché is outfitted with stone floors and rows of decorative barrels. At the self-
service food counter you can order cheap steak pie, lasagna, and salads; at the
bar you can order from an impressive array of single malts. There's a live jazz
band on Saturday afternoons. Open Monday through Saturday from noon to
midnight. 27 Waterloo St. (C) 01412/213210. Bus: 21, 23, or 48.

THE GAY SCENE

There's no strongly visible lesbian bar or nightclub scene in Glasgow. Many
lesbians who attend bars frequent those that cater mainly to males.

   Bennet's, 90 Glassford St. ((C) **01415/525761**) is one of the major gay/
lesbian nightclubs in town. On certain nights (especially Tues) it's the most fun
and crowded gay disco in Scotland. The crowd includes men and women ages
17 to 60, and the music plays on and on, interrupted only by the occasional drag
show. **C. D. Frost,** 8–10 W. George St. ((C) **01413/328005**) is a busy bar catering primarily to a trendy young mixed crowd. It's minimalist chic, with low
lighting. Drag acts are occasionally featured, but it's better known for the
Wednesday-night quiz, kept in check by resident entertainer, "George." The
Court Bar, 69 Hutcheson St. ((C) **01415/522463**), is a small, cozy pub is a popular meeting place for a gay/lesbian crowd to come together for drinks and talk.
The pub gets decidedly more male after 7pm and is a good starting point for a
gay evening on the town. Attracting a slightly older crowd, **Waterloo Bar,** 306
Argyle St. ((C) **01412/217359**), gets most packed during happy hour
(9pm–midnight), when you can make your drink a double for just £2.50 ($4).

8 Side Trips from Glasgow: The Best of the Strathclyde Region

CULZEAN

Some 19km (12 miles) south-southwest of Ayr and 6.5km (4 miles) west of
Maybole on A719 is Culzean Castle. Maidens Bus (no. 60) from the Sandgate
Bus Station in Ayr runs to Culzean six times per day; a 1-day round-trip ticket
is £4.20 ($6.70) for adults and £2 ($3.20) for children.

Culzean Castle   Built by famous Scottish architect Robert Adam at the
end of the 18th century, this clifftop creation is a fine example of his castellated
style, with a view to the south of Alisa Craig, a 334m (1,100-ft.) high rounded
rock 16km (10 miles) offshore, a nesting ground and sanctuary for seabirds.
Culzean (pronounced Cul-*lane*) replaced an earlier Scots tower as the family seat
of the powerful Kennedy clan. In 1945, the castle and grounds were given to the
National Trust for Scotland. It's well worth a visit and is of special interest to

Americans because of General Eisenhower's connection—in 1946, the National Guest Flat was given to the general for life in gratitude for his services as supreme commander of the Allied Forces in World War II. An exhibit of Eisenhower memorabilia, including his North African campaign desk, is sponsored by Scottish Heritage U.S.A, Inc. Culzean stands near the famous golf courses of Turnberry and Troon, a fact that particularly pleased the golf-loving Eisenhower. The tour also includes the celebrated round drawing room, delicately painted ceilings, and outstanding Adam's oval staircase.

Overlooking the Firth of Clyde ℭ **01655/884455.** www.culzeancastle.net. Admission (including entrance to the Country Park below) £9 ($14) adults, £6.50 ($10) seniors and children, £23 ($37) families (2 adults and 2 children). Apr–Oct daily 10:30am–5pm (last admission ½-hr. before closing). Closed Nov–Mar.

Culzean Country Park   Part of the land surrounding the castle includes what in 1969 became the first country park in Scotland. The 600-acre grounds include a walled garden, an aviary, a swan pond, a camellia house, an orangery, an adventure playground, a newly restored 19th-century pagoda, as well as a deer park, miles of woodland paths, and beaches. It has gained an international reputation for its Visitor Centre (Adam's home farm) and related visitor and educational services. Up to 200,000 people visit the country park annually.

On the land surrounding Culzean Castle. ℭ **01655/884400.** Admission included in admission to Culzean Castle. Daily 9am–dusk.

TURNBERRY: WORLD-CLASS GOLF 🏌

On the Firth of Clyde, the little town of Turnberry, south of the castle, was part of the Culzean Estate, owned by the marquess of Ailsa. It began to flourish early in the 20th century, when the Glasgow and South Western Railway developed rail service, golfing facilities, a recognized golfing center, and a first-class hotel.

From the original two 13-hole golf courses, the complex has developed into the two 18-hole courses, Ailsa and Arran, known worldwide as the **Turnberry Hotel Golf courses.** The Ailsa, one of the most exacting courses yet devised, has been the scene of numerous championship tournaments and PGA events. Come here for the prestige, but prepare yourself for the kind of weather a lobster fisherman in Maine might find daunting. (Its par is 70, its SSS 72, and its yardage 6,976/6,348m.) Newer, and usually shunted into the role of also-ran, is the Arran Course. Call ℭ **01655/331000** for details. Guests of the hotel get priority on the Ailsa course. The greens fee of £90 to £105 ($144–$168) for guests, and £130 ($208) (Mon–Fri) or £175 ($280) (weekends) for nonguests includes 18 holes on the Ailsa course and an 18-hole round on the Arran course. Clubs rent for £40 ($64) per round or £55 ($88) per day; caddy service costs £30 ($48) plus tip. If you're not staying here, give them a call in the morning to check on any unclaimed tee times—but it's a long shot.

WHERE TO STAY

Malin Court Hotel   On one of the most scenic strips of the Ayrshire coast, this well-run hotel fronts the Firth of Clyde and the Turnberry golf courses. It is not a great country house, but a serviceable, functional, and welcoming retreat with a blend of informality and comfort. Bedrooms, mostly medium in size, have excellent beds, double glazed windows, and offer such extras as bathrobes and sea views. The staff can arrange hunting, fishing, riding, sailing, and golf.

Turnberry, Ayrshire KA26 9PB. ℭ **01655/331457.** Fax 01655/331072. www.malincourt.co.uk. 18 units. £104–£124 ($166–$198) double. Rates include breakfast. AE, DC, MC, V. Free parking. Take A74 to Ayr exit, then A719 to Turnberry and Maidens. **Amenities:** Restaurant; bar; 24-hr. room service; laundry service; dry cleaning. *In room:* TV, dataport, coffeemaker, hair dryer, iron.

Westin Turnberry Resort ★★★   The 1908 Turnberry, 81km (50 miles) south of Glasgow on A77, is a remarkable and opulent Edwardian property. From afar you can see the hotel's white facade, red-tile roof, and dozens of gables. In World War II, it served as a military hospital but is once again one of Britain's grand hotels. The public rooms contain Waterford crystal chandeliers, Ionic columns, molded ceilings, and well-polished oak paneling. Each suite and guest room is furnished in unique early-1900s style and has a marble-sheathed bathroom. The rooms, which vary in size, open onto views of the lawns, forests, and (in some cases) the Scottish coastline. *Note:* The hotel is home to Scottish golf-pro Colin Montgomery's Links Golf Academy and to the Ailsa Cooking School, which often features internationally renowned chefs.

Maidens Rd., Turnberry, Ayrshire KA26 9LT. ℂ 01655/331000. Fax 01655/331706. www.turnberry.co.uk/hotel/index.html. 221 units. £220–£270 ($352–$432) double; £310–£350 ($496–$560) suite. Rates include Scottish breakfast. AE, DC, MC, V. Free parking. **Amenities:** 3 restaurants; 2 bars; lounge; tennis court; gym; spa; massage; 24-hr. room service; babysitting; laundry service; dry cleaning. *In room:* TV, minibar, coffeemaker, hair dryer, trouser press.

WHERE TO DINE

Cotters Restaurant SCOTTISH   Exemplary service, a scenic location, and good food combine to make a winning combination. Chef Andrea Beach and her team use only the freshest and finest local ingredients. The modern, tasteful decor creates a casual, relaxed atmosphere. The lunch menu offers everything from melon slices to deep-fried haddock in beer batter. For dinner, you might start with melon and peaches glazed with an orange sabayon, or salmon and asparagus terrine with chive butter. For a main course, try the medallions of pork and apple fritter or the baked Ayrshire lamb and chicken mousseline wrapped in phyllo pastry. Desserts are tempting and include a chocolate and hazelnut tart, and a fine selection of cheeses.

In the Malin Court Hotel, Turnberry. ℂ 01655/331457. Reservations recommended. Main courses £5–£13 ($8–$21); table d'hôte £25 ($40). AE, DC, MC, V. Daily 12:30–2pm and 7:30–9pm.

TROON & THE ROYAL TROON GOLF CLUB ★

The resort town of **Troon,** 11km (7 miles) north of Ayr, 50km (31 miles) southwest of Glasgow, and 124km (77 miles) southwest of Edinburgh, looks out across the Firth of Clyde to the Isle of Arran. It's a 20th-century town, its earlier history having gone unrecorded. Troon takes its name from the curiously shaped promontory jutting out into the Clyde estuary on which the old town and the harbor stand. The promontory was called *Trwyn,* the Cymric word for "nose," and later this became Trone and then Troon. A massive statue of *Britannia* stands on the seafront as a memorial to the dead of the two world wars.

Troon offers several golf links, including the **Royal Troon Golf Club,** Craigends Road, Troon, Ayrshire KA10 6EP (ℂ **01292/311555;** www.royaltroon.co.uk). This is a 6,458m (7,097-yard) course (one of the longest in Scotland) with an SSS of 74 and a par of 71. Dignified Georgian and Victorian buildings and the faraway Isle of Arran are visible from fairways, which seem deliberately designed to steer your golf balls into the sea or the dozens of sand traps flanking your shot. The Old Course is the more famous, reserved for men. Nonmembers may play only on certain days. A newer addition, the 5,723m (6,289-yard), par-71 Portland, is open to both men and women and is, by some estimates, even more challenging than the Old Course. The British Open has been played here off and on since 1923 (and will be played here in 2004). The greens fee—£170 ($272) for a day—includes a buffet lunch and two 18-hole sets. For one round of play, a trolley rents for £3 ($4.80) and a caddy £30 ($48); club rental is £25 ($40) per round or £40 ($64) per day.

In summer, visitors find plenty of room on Troon's 3km (2 miles) of **sandy beaches** stretching along both sides of its harbor; the broad sands and shallow waters make it a safe haven. From here you can take steamer trips to Arran and the Kyles of Bute.

Trains from Glasgow's Central Station arrive at the Troon station several times daily (trip time: 40 min.). Call ⓒ **0845/748-4950** for 24-hour information. Trains also connect Ayr with Troon, a 10-minute ride. Buses and trains from Glasgow cost £5.30 ($8.50) each way. From the Ayr bus station, you can reach Troon and other parts of the area by bus, costing £1.90 ($3.05) each way. Call ⓒ **0870/608-2608** for details. From Prestwick, motorists head north along B749.

WHERE TO STAY

Lochgreen House Hotel ★★ Adjacent to the fairways of the Royal Troon Golf Course, one of Scotland's loveliest country-house hotels is set in 30 lush acres of forest and landscaped gardens. The recently expanded property, under the guidance of its owners, Bill and Catherine Costley, opens onto views of the Firth of Clyde and Ailsa Craig. The interior evokes a more elegant bygone time, with detailed cornices, antique furnishings, and elegant oak or cherry paneling. Guests meet and mingle in two luxurious sitting rooms with log fires, or take long walks on the well-landscaped grounds. The spacious and luxurious bedrooms are comfortable and tastefully decorated. Some of the bedrooms were converted from a stable block, but they are equally as luxurious as the older units. Antiques fill the house, enhanced by beautiful and well-chosen fabrics.

Monktonhill Rd. Southwood, Troon, Ayrshire KA10 7EN. ⓒ 01292/313343. Fax 01292/317661. www.costley-hotels.co.uk. 40 units. £130–£160 ($208–$256) double. Rates include breakfast. AE, MC, V. Free parking. Take B749 to Troon. **Amenities:** 2 restaurants; 2 bars; lounge; tennis court; salon; 24-hr. room service; laundry service; dry cleaning. *In room:* TV, coffeemaker, hair dryer, iron/ironing board.

Piersland House Hotel ★ *Finds* This is the most evocative hotel in Scotland in which to have a wee dram of Scotch. Why? The property, located across from Royal Troon, was built more than a century ago by Sir Alexander Walker of the famous Johnnie Walker whisky family. The importation of 17,000 tons of top-soil transformed its marshy surface into a lush 4-acre garden. The highest prices are for a superior twin (a four-poster double) or a cottage suite (with a bedroom, sitting room, and bathroom) adjacent to the hotel. The moderately sized guest rooms have traditional Scottish country-house styling and are themed to various malt whisky distilleries or families. Six rooms have shower-only bathrooms, the rest have tubs and showers.

15 Craigend Rd., Troon, Ayrshire KA10 6HD. ⓒ 01292/314747. Fax 01292/315613. www.piersland.co.uk. 30 units. £124 ($198) double; £140–£170 ($224–$272) suite. Rates include Scottish breakfast. AE, DC, MC, V. Free parking. Drive 3 minutes south of the town center on B749. **Amenities:** Restaurant; bar; lounge; babysitting; 24-hr. room service; laundry service; dry cleaning. *In room:* TV, coffeemaker, hair dryer, trouser press.

WHERE TO DINE

Fairways Restaurant SCOTTISH/INTERNATIONAL This landmark 1890s hotel restaurant stands on the Ayrshire coast overlooking the Royal Troon Golf Course. Fairways can satisfy your hunger pangs with some degree of style. Here you can enjoy traditional Scottish and French cuisine like pillows of smoked Scottish salmon, followed by rosettes of filet of Scottish beef in peppercorn sauce or turbot with langoustines or shrimp.

In the Marine Highland Hotel, 8 Crosbie Rd. © **01292/314444**. Reservations required. Set-price lunch £9.50–£12 ($15–$18); main courses £11–£19 ($18–$30). AE, DC, MC, V. Daily 12:30–2pm and 7–9:30pm.

Lochgreen House Hotel Restaurant ✦ SCOTTISH/FRENCH   Chef Andrew Costley and his skilled team aim to please, tempting you with the finest seafood, game, and prime Scottish beef. The setting of the elegant dining room, with its views of woodlands and gardens, makes the food taste even better. Everything conspires to make this one of the most agreeable culinary stopovers in the region. The service is as flawless as the food. For a main course, sample the seared salmon on branade potatoes with king scallops, bacon, and sauerkraut. Or savor the flavor of roasted breast of chicken with Parmesan tagliatelle and morelle sauce. The wine list roams the world for inspiration, and the desserts are freshly made, often using the fresh fruit of the season.

Monktonhill Rd., Southwood © **01292/313343**. Reservations required. Set-price menu £16 ($26) for a 3-course lunch; £33 ($52) for a 4-course dinner. AE, MC, V. Daily noon–2pm and 7–9pm. Take B749 to Troon.

MacCallums Oyster Bar ✦ SEAFOOD   Right at the harbor adjoining the Seacat Ferry Terminal, this is one of the finest places for fish in the area. Much of the menu is dependent on that day's catch, as the chefs like their seafood served very fresh here. The decor is fairly simple, with wood tables and floors. The setting is among "old men of the sea," boatyards, and Scottish Customs buildings. Big, wide French windows open to a deck, and the atmosphere is rustic, with pictures of yachts and nautical memorabilia. Dig into the seared scallops flavored with a hazelnut-and-coriander flavored butter and served with a rocket salad, or opt for a delectable sole tempura with a sesame stir fry and a sweet chile dressing. For those who don't want fish, the chef will prepare such dishes as roast chicken supreme flavored with bacon-studded cabbage and coming with a grain mustard dressing.

The Harbour. © **01292/319339**. Reservations recommended. Lunch main courses £9.50–£15 ($15–$23). Dinner main courses £11–£13 ($17–$20). MC, V. Tues–Sat noon–2:30pm and 7–9:30pm; Sun noon–3:30pm.

16

Argyll & the Southern Hebrides

The old county of Argyll (in Gaelic, *Earraghaidheal,* "coastland of the Gael") on and off the coast of western Scotland is a rewarding journey. Summers along the coast are usually cool and damp and winters relatively mild but wet, with little snow.

The major center of Gaelic culture for the district is **Oban** ("small bay"), a great port for the Western Isles and the gateway to the Inner Hebrides.

There are several island destinations off the Argyll coast meriting your time. The long **peninsula of Kintyre** separates the islands of the Firth of Clyde from the islands of the Inner Hebrides.

From the Isle of Islay to the Mull of Kintyre, the climate is mild. The land is rich and lush, especially on Arran. The peat deposits on Islay lend flavor to the making of such fine malt whiskies as Lagavulin, Bruichladdick, and Laphroaig. There's a diversity of scenic beauty: hills and glens, fast-rushing streams, and little roads that eventually lead to coastal villages displaying B&B signs in summer. The unspoiled and remote island of Jura is easily reached from Islay.

And the best news for last: These islands, as well as the Kintyre peninsula, are among the best travel bargains in the British Isles.

1 The Isle of Arran: Scotland in Miniature ★★

Brodick: 119km (74 miles) W of Edinburgh; 47km (29 miles) W of Glasgow

At the mouth of the Firth of Clyde, the Isle of Arran is often described as "Scotland in miniature" because of its wild and varied scenery—the glens, moors, lochs, sandy bays, and rocky coasts that have made the country famous. Once you're on Arran, buses will take you to various villages, each with its own character. A coast road, 97km (60 miles) long, runs around the length of the island.

Arran boasts some splendid mountain scenery, notably the conical peak of **Goatfell** in the north, reaching a height of 869m (2,866 ft.), called the "mountain of the winds." Arran is also filled with beautiful glens, especially **Glen Sannox,** in the northeast, and **Glen Rosa,** north of Brodick. Students of geology flock to Arran to study igneous rocks of the Tertiary. Cairns and standing stones at Tormore intrigue archaeologists as well. The island is only 40km (25 miles) long and 16km (10 miles) wide and can be seen in 1 day.

ESSENTIALS
GETTING THERE   High-speed electric trains operate from Glasgow Central direct to Ardrossan Harbour, taking 1 hour and costing £4.70 ($7.50) one-way. For 24-hour rail inquiries, call © **0847/548-4950.** (If you're driving from Glasgow, head southwest along A737 until you reach Ardrossan.) At Ardrossan, you must make a 30-minute ferry crossing to Arran, arriving in Brodick, Arran's main town, on its east coast.

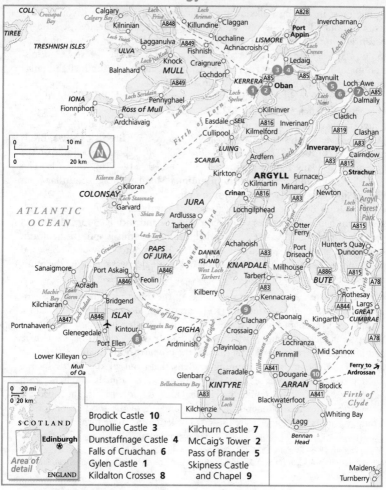

Brodick Castle **10**
Dunollie Castle **3**
Dunstaffnage Castle **4**
Falls of Cruachan **6**
Gylen Castle **1**
Kildalton Crosses **8**

Kilchurn Castle **7**
McCaig's Tower **2**
Pass of Brander **5**
Skipness Castle
and Chapel **9**

In summer, a small ferry runs between Lochranza in the north of Arran across to Claonaig in Argyll, providing a gateway to the Highlands and a visit to Kintyre. There are six boats daily, and the fare is £48 ($76) for a vehicle, plus £8 ($13) per passenger for a return journey. For information about ferry departures (which change seasonally), check with **Caledonian MacBrayne** (© 01457/650100) at the ferry terminal in Gourock.

VISITOR INFORMATION   The **tourist office** is at The Pier, Brodick (© 01770/302140; www.ayrshire-arran.com). June through August, it's open Monday through Saturday from 9am to 7:30pm and Sunday from 10am to 5pm; September through May, hours are Monday through Saturday from 9am to 5pm.

EXPLORING THE ISLAND

After the ferry docks at Brodick, you may want to head for Arran's major sights, **Brodick Castle** and the **Isle of Arran Heritage Museum** (see below).

The most intriguing walks on the island are signposted. But if you're really serious about hiking, buy one of two detailed guides at the tourist office— *Seventy Walks in Arran* for £2.50 ($4) and *My Walks in Arran* for £2.25 ($3.60). While at the office, ask about any guided walks the Forestry Commission might be conducting. They are scheduled frequently in summer and range from 2 to 5 hours, costing £4 to £7 ($6.40–$11).

If you'd prefer to do your exploring on two wheels, stop by **Mr. Bilsland,** The Gift Shop, Brodick (© **01770/302272**). You'll have to show an ID as deposit; rental rates include a helmet and are £5–£10 ($8–$16) daily, £16–£33 ($26–$53) weekly. It's open daily from 9:30am to 6pm. **Brodick Cycles,** Brodick (© **01770/302460**), requires a £5–£25 ($8–$40) deposit, depending on the type of bike. Daily rentals range from £7.50–£10 ($12–$16), with £17–£34 ($27–$54) for a full week. It's open in summer Monday through Saturday from 9am to 6pm and Sunday from 10am to 6pm.

South from Brodick is the village/resort of **Lamlash,** opening onto Lamlash Bay. From here, a ferry takes you over to Holy Island with its 303m (1,000-ft.) peak. A disciple of St. Columba founded a church on this island. In the north, **Lochranza** is a village with unique appeal. It opens onto a bay of pebbles and sand, and in the background lie the ruins of a castle that was reputedly the hunting seat of Robert the Bruce.

Brodick Castle ★★   The historic home of the dukes of Hamilton, this redsandstone castle dates from the 13th century and contains superb silver, antiques, portraits, and objets d'art. Some castle or other has stood on this site since about the 5th century, when the Dalriad Irish, a Celtic tribe, came here and founded their kingdom. The castle is the property of the National Trust for Scotland and boasts award-winning gardens. Laid out in the 1920s by the duchess of Montrose, they're filled with shrubs, trees, perennials, and herbs from Tasmania, New Zealand, Chile, the Himalayas, and northern Britain. Especially noteworthy are the rhododendrons, which are one of the focal points of the Country Park (semi-domesticated forest) bordering the more formal gardens.

2.5km (1½ miles) north of the Brodick pierhead. © **01770/302202**. www.nts.org.uk. Admission to both castle and gardens £7 ($11) adults, £5.30 ($8.50) seniors and students, free for children 5 and under. Castle Apr–Oct daily 9am–4:30pm (to 5pm July–Aug); gardens and Country Park daily 11am–sunset. Bus: Any labeled "Brodick Castle."

Isle of Arran Heritage Museum   A compound of antique structures once used as outbuildings for the nearby castle, this museum provides the best overview of life on Arran from prehistoric times to the present. The most prominent of the buildings is a stone-sided cottage filled with 19th-century memorabilia, costumes, and artifacts, including a working kitchen. Also on site is a

---

⌒*Moments* **Down a Lovely Glen with a Picnic in Hand**

The best way to discover the island's beauty is to stroll around. Right beyond the Isle of Arran Heritage Museum, at the point where String Road divides the island, you can follow the signs to a beauty spot called **Glen Rosa.** This is the island's loveliest glen, and you might want to pick up the makings of a picnic lunch before setting out. Another great walk is to the village of **Corriegills,** which is signposted along A841 south of Brodick. As you stroll, you'll be treated with the finest views of Brodick Bay.

blacksmith's shop and forge, an area containing geological artifacts, and an archive room and small library housing some of the historic records associated with Arran and the castle. Access to the archive room is reserved for bona fide scholars pursuing academic research.

Rosaburn, 2.5km (1½ miles) north of the Brodick ferry piers. (℗ **01770/302636.** www.arranmuseum.co.uk. Admission £2.50 ($4). Apr–Oct Mon–Sat 10am–5pm, Sun 11am–4pm. Bus: Any labeled "Brodick Castle."

WHERE TO STAY
IN BRODICK

Auchrannie Country House Hotel ★★ *Kids*   Acclaimed as the island's finest hotel and restaurant, this Victorian mansion (once the home of the dowager duchess of Hamilton) also features the best resort facilities. In its pristine glory, it stands on 6 acres of landscaped gardens and woods about 1.5km (1 mile) from the Brodick ferry terminal. The restoration here was done with taste and imagination. The guest rooms in the extended new wing are the most comfortable, but all rooms are furnished with taste, using select fabrics and decorative accessories. Family suites (two bedrooms) and four-poster rooms are available.

The property's noteworthy leisure center features an indoor pool, a kids' pool, a playroom, a spa, games room, and sauna. You can enjoy drinks in the cocktail bar or sun lounge before heading for the Garden Restaurant, which offers fixed-price dinners—pricey, but the finest on Arran. The chef is really in his element when preparing West Coast seafood. Nonguests should reserve ahead.

Auchrannie Rd., Brodick, Isle of Arran KA27 8BZ. (℗ **01770/302234.** Fax 01770/302812. www.auchrannie. co.uk. 28 units. £72–£126 ($115–$202) double with breakfast; £116–£168 ($186–$269) double with half board. AE, MC, V. **Amenities:** 2 restaurants; bar; heated indoor pool; Turkish bath; spa; sauna; room service; babysitting; laundry service; solarium. *In room:* TV, minibar, coffeemaker, hair dryer.

Kilmichael Country House Hotel ★★   It was voted Country House Hotel of the Year in a "Taste of Scotland" contest in 1998, and if anything, it's better than ever. The island's most scenically located house, it's said to be the oldest house on the island, perhaps once a stomping ground for Robert the Bruce, complete with some reports of a resident ghost. A combination of the tasteful new and antique is used throughout. The guest rooms are beautiful, as are the bathrooms, which offer luxury toiletries. Some rooms have four-poster beds and Jacuzzis tubs. The aura of gentility is reflected in the log fires and the fresh flowers from the garden. A suite and two other rooms, all with private entrances, are located in a converted 18th-century stables a few yards from the main building. The staff is helpful and welcoming.

The food is also noteworthy, using local produce whenever possible. International dishes are featured, and fine wines and an attention to detail go into the expensive fixed-price menus.

Brodick, Isle of Arran KA27 8BZ. (℗ **01770/302219.** Fax 01770/302068. www.kilmichael.com. 9 units. £150 ($240) double; £190 ($304) suite. Rates include Scottish breakfast. **Amenities:** Restaurant; bar; lounge; room service; laundry service. *In room:* TV, coffeemaker, hair dryer, iron/ironing board (in some).

IN LAMLASH

Glenisle Hotel *Finds*   Across the road from the waterfront, Glenisle could be one of the oldest buildings in the village, but no one knows its age or even the century of its construction. The well-kept gardens of this white-sided B&B, with a view across the bay to the Holy Isle, have flowerbeds and tall old trees. The reception lounge, water-view dining room, and lounge where drinks are available are cheerfully decorated. Each relatively simple but comfortable guest room has flowered curtains, good mattresses, a small but tidy bathroom, and a tasteful decor.

Shore Rd., Lamlash, Isle of Arran KA27 8LS. (C) **01770/600559.** Fax 01770/600966. 13 units. £42 ($67) per person with Scottish breakfast; £108 ($173) double with half board. MC, V. Take the Whiting bus from Brodick. **Amenities:** Restaurant; bar; room service; laundry service. *In room:* TV, coffeemaker, hair dryer, iron/ironing board (in some).

IN KILDONAN

Kildonan Hotel   Built as an inn in 1760, with a section added in 1928, the hotel rises a few steps from the island's best beach. It's in Scottish farmhouse style, with a slate roof, white-painted stone walls, and ample views of seabirds and gray seals basking on the rocks of Pladda Island opposite. The Kildonan is owned by Mr. and Mrs. Acuna. The rooms were upgraded in early 2003 and range from small to midsize. They are traditionally furnished with comfortable beds, and all have private bathrooms with either a tub or shower. Some of the rooms are wheelchair accessible, and there is also a family suite, which rents for £100 ($160) a night.

The spacious dining room serves moderately priced dinners; less formal lunches and dinners are served in the bar. A specialty available in either setting is crab or lobster salad made from shellfish caught by one of the Deighton sons. A crowd of locals is likely to compete in a friendly fashion over the dartboard and billiards tables in the pub.

Kildonan, Isle of Arran, KA27 8SE. (C) 01770/820207. Fax 01770/820320. http://kildonanhotel.com/main.html. 22 units. £75 double. Rates include Scottish breakfast. No credit cards. **Amenities:** Restaurant; bar; room service. *In room:* Hair dryer, no phone.

Kinloch Hotel   This hotel, made from two joined cream-colored Victorian buildings, appears deceptively small from the road. It's actually the largest building in the village of Blackwaterfoot, with a contemporary wing jutting out along the coast. The midsize guest rooms are modestly comfortable and conservative, each with an excellent mattress and a small bathroom. Most of the double rooms have sea views, but the singles tend to look out over the back gardens. A few have four-poster beds. The hotel also offers seven self-contained suites with kitchen facilities, plus five two-bedroom suites with a lounge and a small kitchenette. *Note:* The hotel's website claims the suites on the second floor are new, but they are actually 10 years old.

Blackwaterfoot, Isle of Arran KA27 8ET. (C) **01770/860444.** Fax 01770/860447. www.kinloch-arran.com. 44 units. £68 ($109) per person with half board (Scottish breakfast and dinner); £140 ($224) suite. AE, DC, MC, V. Take the Blackwaterfoot bus from Brodick. **Amenities:** Restaurant; bar; indoor heated pool; sauna; room service; babysitting; laundry service. *In room:* TV, coffeemaker, hair dryer.

WHERE TO DINE
IN BRODICK
The hotels reviewed above also have fine restaurants.

Creelers Seafood Restaurant SCOTTISH   This dining choice lies in a mini-compound of gift shops and bistros created from a 1920s-era farm associated with Brodick Castle and is about 1.5km (1 mile) north of the center of Brodick Village. The most appealing of the places here is Creelers, a family-run enterprise specializing in seafood. The enterprise includes a "smokery" where salmon, scallops, and duck breast are carefully smoked and served almost immediately. You won't go wrong ordering any of the versions of smoked salmon, presented with capers and horseradish or with mushroom-studded risotto. In a cheerful yellow-and-green dining room, you'll find some of the freshest seafood in Scotland, much of it pulled in from local fishing boats that day. Especially appealing are seared Arran scallops with monkfish and pesto, and Scottish lobster with herb-flavored butter sauce.

The Home Farm, Brodick. © **01770/302810.** Reservations recommended. Set-price lunch £9.50–£11 ($15–$17); main courses £8–£14 ($13–$22) at lunch, £12–£20 ($19–$32) at dinner. MC, V. Tues–Sun noon–2:30pm and 6:30–10pm.

IN LAMLASH

Carraig Mhor ✦ CONTINENTAL   Carraig Mhor, in a modernized *pebbledash* (a mortar containing a mixture of pebbles) 1700s cottage in the village center overlooking the water, serves imaginative and beautifully presented dinners. You're welcomed by Austrian-born Peter Albrich and his British wife, Penny. The chef, who has had worldwide experience, makes extensive use of local produce, especially seafood and game. All bread and ice creams, among other offerings, are made on the premises. The menu changes seasonally, and there are separate dining rooms for smokers and nonsmokers.

Lamlash. © **01770/600453.** Reservations recommended. Fixed-price menus £20 ($31) for 2 courses, £25 ($40) for 3 courses. MC, V. Mon–Sat 7–9pm. Closed 2 weeks in Jan and first 2 weeks in Feb. Take the Whiting bus from Brodick.

ARRAN AFTER DARK

Regulars gather in Brodick's pubs to talk, argue, and drink. The **Brodick Bar,** in the center but without a street address (© **01770/302169**), is an old wooden pub open Monday through Saturday from 11am to midnight. Drop in for some real Scottish ale and a bar meal of local seafood (meals are served Mon–Sat noon–2:30pm and 5:30–10pm). Featuring wood-and-leather chairs and walls hung with old photographs and riding gear, **Duncan's Bar,** also in the center but with no street address (© **01770/302531**), keeps the same hours and serves real cask ales and lagers. Meals, available daily from noon to 2pm and 5:30 to 8pm, always include a roast and seafood items.

2 The Kintyre Peninsula ✦

The longest peninsula in Scotland, Kintyre is more than 97km (60 miles) in length, with scenery galore, sleepy villages, and miles of sandy beaches. It's one of the country's most unspoiled areas, owing perhaps to its isolation. Kintyre was ancient Dalriada, the first kingdom of the Scots.

If you drive all the way to the tip of Kintyre, you'll be only 19km (12 miles) from Ireland. Kintyre is joined to the mainland of Scotland by a narrow neck of land near the old port of Tarbert. The largest town on the peninsula is the port of Campbeltown, on the southeastern coast.

AREA ESSENTIALS

GETTING THERE   **Loganair** (© **01418/891111**) makes two scheduled 45-minute flights a day from the Glasgow Airport to Campbeltown, the chief town of Kintyre.

From Glasgow, you can take buses to the peninsula (schedules vary seasonally). The trip takes 4 hours one-way and costs £11 ($17) each way. Inquire at the **Scottish CityLink,** Buchanan Street Bus Station, Glasgow (© **0990/505050**).

Kintyre is virtually an island unto itself, and the most efficient way to travel is by car. From Glasgow, take A82 up to the Loch Lomond side and cut across to Arrochar and go over the "Rest and Be Thankful" route to Inveraray (A83). Then cut down along Loch Fyne to Lochgilphead and continue on A83 south to Tarbert (see below), which can be your gateway to Kintyre. You can take A83 along the western coast or cut east at the junction of B8001 and follow it across the peninsula to B842, which you can take south to Carradale. If your target is Campbeltown, you can reach it by either the western shore (much faster and a better road) or the eastern shore.

TARBERT

A sheltered harbor protects the fishing port and yachting center of Tarbert, on a narrow neck of land at the northern tip of the Kintyre. It's between West Loch Tarbert and the head of herring-filled Loch Fyne and has been called "the world's prettiest fishing port."

Tarbert means "drawboat" in Norse and referred to a place where Vikings dragged their boats across land on rollers from one sea to another. In 1093, King Malcolm of Scotland and King Magnus Barelegs of Norway agreed the Western Isles were to belong to Norway and the mainland to Scotland. An island was defined as anything a Viking ship could sail around, so Magnus proclaimed Kintyre an island by having his dragon ship dragged across the 1.5km (1 mile) of dry land from West Loch Tarbert on the Atlantic to East Loch Tarbert on Loch Fyne. After the Vikings gave way, Kintyre came under the control of the Mac-Donald lordship of the Isles.

SEEING THE SIGHTS

The castle at Tarbert dates from the 13th century and was later extended by Robert the Bruce. The castle ruins, **Bruce Castle,** are on a hillock above the village on the south side of the bay. The oldest part still standing is a keep from the 13th century.

One of the major attractions of the peninsula is the remains of **Skipness Castle and Chapel,** at Skipness along B8001, 16km (10 miles) south of Tarbert, opening onto Loch Fyne. The hamlet was once a Norse village. The ruins of the ancient chapel and 13th-century castle look out onto the Sounds of Kilbrannan and Bute. In its heyday it could control shipping along Loch Fyne. A five-story tower remains.

Before striking out to visit the peninsula, consider stopping at the **Tarbert Heritage Centre** (© **01880/820190**), immediately south of the village. Through various artifacts and exhibits, it traces life on the peninsula that's now largely vanished. Costing £3 ($4.80), it's open daily from 10am to 5pm.

WHERE TO STAY

Stonefield Castle Hotel ★★   The best hotel choice in the area occupies a commanding position on 66 acres of wooded grounds and luxurious gardens 3km (2 miles) outside Tarbert. The Stonefield, with turrets and a steeply pitched roof, was built in the 19th century by the Campbells. The well-appointed guest rooms come in a variety of sizes; smoking is not permitted in any of them. Some family suites are available as well as some four-poster rooms. The hotel's renowned gardens feature plants from all over the world and are one of the world's best repositories for more than 20 species of tree-size Himalayan rhododendrons, which in April are a riot of color. Book well in advance, as Stonefield has a large repeat crowd.

> **Finds** **A Journey to Blood Rock**
>
> **Dunaverty Rock,** a jagged hill marking the extreme southern tip of the Kintyre Peninsula, is located 14km (9 miles) south of Cambeltown and called "Blood Rock" by the locals. It was once the site of a MacDonald stronghold known as Dunaverty Castle, although nothing remains of that structure today. In 1647, it was the scene of a great massacre, where some 300 citizens lost their lives. You can reach it by a local bus (marked SOUTH END) traveling from Campbeltown south about six times a day. Nearby, you'll find a series of isolated, unsupervised **beaches** and the 18-hole **Dunaverty Golf Course** (© 01586/830677).

The kitchen staff does its own baking, and meals feature produce from the hotel's garden.

Tarbert PA29 6YJ. © **01880/820836.** Fax 01880/820929. www.stonefieldcastle.co.uk. 33 units. Sun–Thurs £160–£220 ($256–$352) double; Fri–Sat £190–£220 ($304–$352) double. Rates include half board. AE, MC, V. **Amenities:** Restaurant; bar; room service. *In room:* TV, coffeemaker, hair dryer.

West Loch Hotel　This 18th-century stone inn stands in a rural setting beside A83, 1.5km (1 mile) southwest of town in low-lying flatlands midway between the forest and the loch. This stone inn was built during the 1700s as a staging post for coaches and for farmers driving their cattle to market. Painted white with black trim, it contains two bars and a handful of open fireplaces and woodburning stoves. The small guest rooms are modestly furnished but comfortable, often with views of the estuary. Each has a small bathroom with either tub or shower. The hotel contains a pub and a restaurant specializing in local seafood and game, using only the best local ingredients.

Tarbert PA29 6YF. © **01880/820283.** Fax 01880/820930. 8 units. £60 ($96) double. Rates include Scottish breakfast. MC, V. **Amenities:** Restaurant; 2 bars; limited room service. *In room:* TV, coffeemaker, hair dryer.

WHERE TO DINE

Anchorage Restaurant ✿ *Finds* SCOTTISH/SEAFOOD　The Anchorage remains unpretentious despite its many culinary awards. Housed in a stone harbor-front building that was once a customs house, it's run by Clare Johnson. Her daily menu includes such perfectly crafted seafood dishes as king scallops sautéed with lemon-lime butter and brochette of monkfish with saffron rice. A selection of European wines is available to accompany your fish.

Harbour St., Quayside. © **01880/820881.** Reservations recommended. Main courses £12–£18 ($19–$29). MC, V. Daily 7–10pm. Closed Jan.

SOUTHEND & THE MULL OF KINTYRE

Some 16km (10 miles) south of Campbeltown, the village of Southend stands across from the Mull of Kintyre, and Monday through Saturday three buses a day run here from Campbeltown. It has sandy beaches, a golf course, and views across the sea to the Island of Sanda and to Ireland. Legend has it that footprints on a rock near the ruin of an old chapel mark the spot where St. Columba first set foot on Scottish soil. Other historians suggest the footprints mark the spot where ancient kings were crowned.

About 18km (11 miles) from Campbeltown is the **Mull of Kintyre.** From Southend, you can take a narrow road until you reach the "gap," from where you can walk down to the lighthouse, a distance of 2.5km (1½ miles) before you reach the final point. Expect westerly gales as you go along. This is one of the wildest and most remote parts of the peninsula, and it's this desolation that appeals to visitors. The Mull of Kintyre is only 21km (13 miles) from Ireland. When local resident Paul McCartney made it the subject of a song, hundreds of fans flocked to the area.

3 The Isle of Islay: Queen of the Hebrides $\digamma$

26km (16 miles) W of the Kintyre Peninsula; 1km (¾ mile) SW of Jura

Islay (pronounced "*eye*-lay") is the southernmost island of the Inner Hebrides, separated only by a narrow sound from Jura. At its maximum, Islay is only 32km (20 miles) wide and 40km (25 miles) long. Called the "Queen of the Hebrides," it's a peaceful and unspoiled island of moors, salmon-filled lochs, sandy bays, and wild rocky cliffs—an island of great beauty, ideal for long walks.

ESSENTIALS

GETTING THERE   MacBrayne **steamers** provide daily service to Islay. You leave West Tarbert on the Kintyre Peninsula, arriving in Port Askaig on Islay in about 2 hours. There's also service to Port Ellen. For information about ferry departures, check with Caledonian MacBrayne (② **01880/730253**) at the ferry terminal in Gourock.

VISITOR INFORMATION   The tourist office is at **Bowmore,** The Square (② **01496/810254**). From May to September, it's open Monday through Saturday from 9:30am to 5pm and Sunday from 2 to 5pm; from October to April, hours are Monday through Friday from noon to 4pm.

EXPLORING THE ISLAND

Near **Port Charlotte** are the graves of the U.S. seamen and army troops who lost their lives in 1918 when their carriers, the *Tuscania* and the *Otranto,* were torpedoed off the shores of Islay. There's a memorial tower on the **Mull of Oa,** 13km (8 miles) from Port Ellen. For the greatest **walk** on the island, go along Mull of Oa Road heading toward the signposted solar-powered Carraig Fhada lighthouse, some 2.5km (1½ miles) away. The area is filled with sheer cliffs riddled with caves. Once the Oa peninsula was the haunt of illicit whisky distillers and smugglers.

The island's capital is **Bowmore,** on the coast across from Port Askaig. Here you can see a fascinating Round Church (no corners for the devil to hide in). But the most important town is **Port Ellen** on the south coast, a holiday and golfing resort and Islay's principal port. The 18-hole **Machrie golf course** (② **01496/302310**) is 5km (3 miles) from Port Ellen.

You can see the ancient seat of the lords of the Isles, the ruins of two castles, and several Celtic crosses. The ancient **Kildalton Crosses** are in the Kildalton churchyard, about 12km (7½ miles) northeast of Port Ellen—they're two of the finest Celtic crosses in Scotland. The ruins of the 14th-century fortress **Dunyvaig Castle** are just south of Kildalton.

In the southwestern part of Islay in Port Charlotte, the **Museum of Islay Life** (② **01496/850358**) has a wide collection of island artifacts, ranging from unrecorded times to the present. From Easter to October, the museum is open Monday through Saturday from 10am to 4pm. Admission is £2.60 ($4.15) adults, £1.40 ($2.25) seniors, and £1.20 ($1.90) children. The Portnahaven bus from Bowmore stops here.

TOURING THE DISTILLERIES

The island is noted for its distilleries, which still produce single-malt Highland whiskies by the antiquated pot-still method. Of these, **Laphroaig Distillery,** less than 1.5km (1 mile) along the road from Ardbeg to Port Ellen (© **01496/ 302418**), offers a guided tour Monday through Friday in the morning at 10:15am and in the afternoon at 2:15pm. Admission is free and includes a sample dram. Call for an appointment. **Lagavoulin,** Port Ellen (© **01496/302400**), offers tours Monday through Friday at 10 and 11:30am, and 2:30pm. Admission is £3 ($4.80) per person and comes with a £3 ($4.80) voucher off the price of a bottle of whisky. A sample is included in the tour. A distillery gift shop is open Monday through Friday from 8:30am to noon and 1 to 4:30pm.

Bowmore Distillery, School Street, Bowmore (© **01496/810671**), conducts tours Monday through Friday at 10:30am and 2pm. In summer, there are additional tours during the week at 10am, 11:30am, and 2pm, and Saturday at 10:30am. The admission is £2 ($3.20), which includes a voucher worth £2 ($3.20) off the price of a bottle. Samples are included in the tour. Purchases can be made without taking the tour by stopping at the on-premises gift shop, open Monday through Friday from 9am to 4:30pm and Saturday from 10am to 12:30pm.

Port Askaig is home to two distilleries, **Bunnahabhain** (© **01496/840646**), which offers tours at no charge by appointment and runs a gift shop Monday through Friday from 9am to 4pm, and **Coal Ila** (© **01496/840207**), which runs no tours from October to Easter, but thereafter offers four tours (two morning, two afternoon) a day on Monday, Tuesday, Thursday, and Friday, and two morning tours on Wednesday. Admission is £3 ($4.80). Its gift shop is open to visitors at the end of each tour.

SHOPPING

At Bridgend, you can visit the **Islay Woolen Mill** (© **01496/810563**), for more than a century making a wide range of country tweeds and accessories. It made all the tweeds used in Mel Gibson's movie *Braveheart.* The mill shop, open Monday through Saturday from 10am to 5pm, sells a range of items made with the custom-designed Braveheart tweeds, as well as tasteful Shetland wool ties, mufflers, Jacob mufflers and ties, flat caps, travel rugs, and scarves.

Another good place to find souvenirs is **Port Ellen Pottery,** at Port Ellen (© **01496/302345**), which sells brightly colored goblets, jugs, mugs, and other functional wares daily from 10am to 5pm. Note that the Pottery is very small and doesn't handle shipping on larger purchases.

Moments For Birdies and Ramblers

Loch Gruinart cuts into the northern part of Islay, 11km (7 miles) northeast of Port Charlotte and 13km (8 miles) north of Bowmore. As the winter home for wild geese, it has attracted bird-watchers for decades. In 1984, the 3,000 acres of moors and farmland around the loch were turned into the **Loch Gruinart Nature Reserve.**

This is another place for great walks. Beaches rise out of the falling tides, but they're too cold and rocky for serious swimming. This is a lonely and bleak coastline, but because of that it has a certain kind of beauty, especially as you make your way north along its eastern shoreline. On a clear day you can see the Hebridean islands of Oronsay and Colonsay in the distance.

WHERE TO STAY

Bridgend Hotel ⭐   Victorian spires cap the slate-covered roofs and roses creep up the stone-and-stucco walls of this hotel, part of a complex including a roadside barn and one of the most beautiful flower and vegetable gardens on Islay. This is one of the oldest hotels on the island, with somber charm and country pleasures. Guests enjoy drinks beside the open fireplaces in the Victorian cocktail lounge and the rustic pub, where locals gather after a day in the fields. The midsize guest rooms are comfortably and conservatively furnished, each with a small bathroom with either a tub or shower.

The hotel serves up lots of local produce and many nonguests opt for a moderately priced dinner in the high-ceilinged dining room.

Bridgend, Isle of Islay PA44 7PQ. © **01496/810212.** Fax 01496/810960. www.bridgend-hotel.com. 11 units. £46 ($73) per person; £64 ($102) per person with dinner. Rates include Scottish breakfast. MC, V. **Amenities:** Restaurant; bar; room service; laundry service. *In room:* TV, coffeemaker, hair dryer.

Harbour Inn   Although this establishment is better known for its seafood restaurant (see below), it also offers delightful little bedrooms adjacent to Bowmore Harbour. Family run, the place exudes Hebridean hospitality. Each room is individually decorated in bright colors such as lime or cherry, and the furnishings are mainly wood pieces offset with graceful accessories. Each unit is equipped with a tidy little bathroom with tub or shower. Every room has a theme for its decor, ranging from a Victorian garden aura to a "captain's cabin" in mahogany. Two accommodations are suitable for families. The building dates from the 19th century but it was completely modernized in 2001. The coffee lounge adjacent to the ground-floor dining room, features both specialty coffees and fine views of northern Islay and the Paps of Jura.

The Square, Bowmore, Isle of Islay, Argyll PA43 7JR. © **01496/810330.** Fax 01496/810990. www.harbour-inn.com. 7 units. £95–£105 ($152–$168) double. Rates include full breakfast. AE, MC, V. **Amenities:** Restaurant; bar; fitness center; sauna; babysitting; laundry service. *In room:* TV, beverage maker, hair dryer, iron.

Port Askaig Hotel   On the Sound of Islay overlooking the pier, this island inn dates from the 18th century but was built on the site of an even older inn. It offers island hospitality and Scottish fare and is a favorite of anglers; the bar is popular with local fisherfolk. Bar meals are available for lunch and dinner. The guest rooms are a bit small, but each is furnished in a comfortable though not stylish way, with a little bathroom, some of which contain tub-and-shower combinations, the others showers only.

Hwy. A846 at the ferry crossing to Jura, Port Askaig, Isle of Islay PA46 7RD. © **01496/840245.** Fax 01496/840295. www.portaskaig.co.uk. 8 units. £76–£82 ($122–$131) double. Rates include Scottish breakfast. AE, MC, V. **Amenities:** Restaurant; 2 bars; limited room service. *In room:* TV, coffeemaker, hair dryer.

Port Charlotte Hotel   This 1829 hotel—actually a trio of cottages joined together—stands next to the small sandy beaches of Port Charlotte with views over Loch Indaal. It has been refurbished and immediately won a four-crown rating from the Scottish Tourist Board. The guest rooms are beautiful, most with antiques and Oriental rugs. A small bathroom has been installed in each bedroom. The hotel is wheelchair accessible. Features include a large conservatory, a comfortable lounge, and a public bar.

The hotel is also the best place to dine in the area, with main courses costing £18 to £22 ($29–$35). Typical dishes include sirloin of Islay steak, freshly caught Islay lobster, and grilled filet of Scottish turbot.

Main St., Port Charlotte, Isle of Islay PA48 7TU. (℃ **01496/850360.** Fax 01496/850361. www.portcharlotte hotel.co.uk. 10 units. £59 ($94) single; £100 ($160) double. Rates include Scottish breakfast. MC, V. **Amenities:** Restaurant; bar; limited room service; laundry service. *In room:* TV, coffeemaker, hair dryer.

WHERE TO DINE

You can also dine at one of the hotels above.

The Croft Kitchen BRITISH   On the main highway running through town, this is a low-slung, homey, and utterly unpretentious diner/bistro with a friendly staff. Holding no more than 40 diners at a time and managed by Douglas and Joy Law, it serves wine, beer, and whisky distilled on Islay, along with generous portions of down-home food. You'll find lots of fresh fish and shellfish, as well as soups, fried scallops, roasted Islay venison with rowanberry jelly, and steamed mussels with garlic mayonnaise.

Port Charlotte, Isle of Islay. (℃ **01496/850230.** Sandwiches £3 ($4.80); main courses £9–£12 ($14–$19) at lunch, £10–£16 ($16–$26) at dinner. MC, V. Daily 10am–8:30pm (last order). Closed mid-Oct to mid-Mar.

Harbour Inn Restaurant ⭐ SEAFOOD   Back in 2000 this restaurant won the Automobile Association's seafood restaurant of the year award, and the fish is as fresh and as good as ever. High-quality ingredients are used to produce the Scottish bounty served here that includes not only the best of the catch of the day but some outstanding Scottish lamb and beef dishes as well. Many Scots enjoy this bounty with a locally distilled single malt whisky from Islay itself. We've enjoyed some of the best crab, prawns, and lobster in the Hebrides here. Each dish is prepared to order so be prepared to enjoy the wait. You can begin with a selection of smoked Islay seafood with a savory lemon and garlic mayonnaise, or else a terrine of roe deer with a melon and ginger chutney. For a main course opt for such delights as stir-fried Lagavulin scallops with fresh lime and sprigs of curry plant, or else a bubbling kettle of Islay seafood stew flavored with fennel and served on a bed of linguini with "eggplant spaghetti."

The Square, Bowmore, Isle of Islay, Argyll PA43 7JR. (℃ **01496/810330.** Reservations recommended on weekends. Lunch main courses £6–£10 ($9.60–$16); dinner main courses £12–£20 ($19–$32). AE, MC, V. Daily noon-2:30pm and 6-9pm.

ISLAY AFTER DARK

After work, distillery employees gather at the **Harbour Inn,** Main Street in Bowmore (℃ **01496/810330**), an old pub with stone walls, a fireplace, and wooden floors and furnishings. It's open Monday through Saturday from 11am to 1am and Sunday from noon to 1am. McEwan's beer is served on tap and the pub has a wide selection of single malts. Local seafood is served at lunch and dinner. During the summer, reservations are recommended.

4 The Isle of Jura: Deer Island ⭐

1km (¾ mile) E of Islay

The Isle of Jura is the fourth largest of the Inner Hebrides, 43km (27 miles) long and varying from 3 to 13km (2–8 miles) in breadth. It takes its name from the Norse *jura,* meaning "deer island." The red deer on Jura—at 1.2m high (4 ft.), the largest wild animals roaming Scotland—outnumber the people by about 20 to 1. The hearty islanders number only about 250, and most of them live along the east coast. Jura is relatively little known or explored, and its mountains, soaring cliffs, snug coves, and moors make it an inviting place.

⟨ *Fun Fact* The Gloom & Doom of Orwell's *1984*

George Orwell was quite ill when he lived on Jura in the bitter postwar winters of 1946 and 1947 while working on *1984*. After a close call when he and his adopted son ventured too close to the whirlpool in the Gulf of Corryvreckan—they were saved by local fishermen—he went on to publish his masterpiece in 1949, only to die in London of tuberculosis in 1950.

ESSENTIALS

GETTING THERE From Kennacraig (West Loch, Tarbert) you can go to Port Askaig on Islay (see above) taking one of the **Caledonian MacBrayne ferries** (℃ **01880/730253**). The cost is £59 ($94) for a car and £11 ($17) per passenger each way (4-day return tickets are more economical). From Port Askaig, you can take a second ferry to Feolin on Jura; call **Western Ferries** at ℃ **01496/ 840681.** Car spaces must be booked in advance. The cost for a vehicle is £8 ($13), plus £1.20 ($1.90) for a passenger one-way.

VISITOR INFORMATION The Isle of Islay (see, "The Isle of Islay: Queen of the Hebrides," above) has the nearest tourist information office.

EXPLORING THE ISLAND

Since most of the island is accessible only by foot, wear sturdy walking shoes and bring raingear. The best place for walks is the **Jura House Garden and Grounds** at the southern tip. These grounds were laid out by the Victorians to take advantage of the natural beauty of the region, and you can visit the gardens with their sheltered walks and panoramic views daily from 9am to 5pm. Admission is £3 ($4.80). From June to August, it's also the best place on the island to have tea, but only Saturday and Sunday. Call ℃ **01496/820315** for details.

The capital, **Craighouse,** is hardly more than a hamlet. From Islay, you can take a 5-minute ferry ride to Jura from Port Askaig, docking at the Feolin Ferry berth.

The island's landscape is dominated by the **Paps of Jura,** which reach a peak of 780m (2,571 ft.) at Beinn-an-Oir. An arm of the sea, **Loch Tarbert** nearly divides the island, cutting into it for nearly 10km (6 miles).

The square tower of **Claig Castle,** now in ruins, was the stronghold of the MacDonalds until they were subdued by the Campbells in the 17th century.

WHERE TO STAY & DINE

Jura Hotel ⟨★ *Finds* The island's only hotel is a sprawling gray-walled building near the center of the hamlet (Craighouse lies east of Feolin along the coast). Sections date from the 1600s, but what you see today was built in 1956. The midsize guest rooms are of high quality, with comfortable mattresses and, in most cases, a small bathroom with a tub-and-shower combination. In this remote outpost, you'll get a tranquil night's sleep. Kenya-born Fiona Walton and her husband, Steve, are the managing directors. Affordable meals are served daily at lunch and dinner; the dining room's specialty is Jura-bred venison.

Craighouse, Isle of Jura PA60 7XU. ℃ **01496/820243.** Fax 01496/820249. 18 units, 12 with private bathroom. £80 ($128) double without bathroom; £100 ($160) double with bathroom; £100 ($160) suite. Rates include Scottish breakfast. AE, DC, MC, V. Closed 2 weeks Dec–Jan. **Amenities:** Restaurant; bar; lounge; limited room service. *In room:* Coffeemaker, hair dryer (available at desk), no phone.

5 Loch Awe: Scotland's Longest Loch

159km (99 miles) NW of Edinburgh; 39km (24 miles) E of Oban; 109km (68 miles) NW of Glasgow

Only 1.5km (1 mile) wide in most places and 36km (22 miles) long, Loch Awe is the longest loch in Scotland and acted as a natural freshwater moat protecting the Campbells of Inveraray from their enemies to the north. Along its banks are many reminders of its fortified past. In this area the Forestry Commission has vast forests and signposted trails, and a modern road makes it possible to travel around Loch Awe, so more than ever it's a popular angling center and walking center.

ESSENTIALS

GETTING THERE   The nearest train station is in Oban, where you'd have to take a connecting bus. **Scottish CityLink,** 1 Queens Park Place in Oban (call ✆ 01631/562856 for schedules), has service to Glasgow with stopovers at Loch Awe.

If you're driving from Oban, head east along A85.

VISITOR INFORMATION   Consult the tourist office in Oban (see "Oban: Gateway to the Inner Hebrides," below).

EXPLORING THE AREA

To the east of the top of Loch Awe, **Dalmally** is small, but because of its strategic position it has witnessed a lot of Scottish history. Its 18th-century church is built in an octagonal shape.

A more convenient way to reach it is by taking any of about five boats a day (Mar–Nov) departing from the piers in the village of Loch Awe. The ferries are maintained by the **Loch Awe Steam Packet Company,** Loch Awe Piers (✆ 01838/\200440). Per-person transit across the loch (a 20-min. ride each way) costs £5 ($8) and includes entrance to the ruins of Kilchurn. This steamship company and the **Hotel Ardanaiseig** (see below) are the only sources of info about the castle, which doesn't maintain an on-site staff.

Once you reach the castle, don't expect a guided tour, as the site is likely to be abandoned except for a patrol of goats and sheep, and there's no guardian to enforce strict opening hours. Although it's presently owned by a consortium of five local businessmen, its grass is cut and its masonry maintained by Historic Scotland. You can wander at will through the ruins following a self-guided tour marked by signs.

For reminders of the days when the Campbells of Inveraray held supreme power in the Loch Awe region, there's a ruined **castle** at Fincharn, at the southern end of the loch, and another on the island of Fraoch Eilean. The Isle of

---

Moments Castle of the Once Mighty Campbells

The ruins of **Kilchurn Castle** are at the northern tip of Loch Awe, west of Dalmally, and across from the south bank village of Loch Awe. A stronghold of the Campbells of Glen Orchy in 1440, it's a spectacular ruin with much of the original structure still intact. The ruins have been completely reinforced and balconied so you can now explore them when the weather permits. Access to the ruins is from an unmarked graveled lot. A path leads to the castle's remains, but you may need a pair of boots if the weather is bad.

Inishail has an ancient **chapel and burial ground.** The bulk of **Ben Cruachan,** rising to 1,119m (3,689 ft.), dominates Loch Awe at its northern end and attracts climbers and hikers. On the Ben is the world's second-largest hydro-electric power station, which pumps water from Loch Awe to a reservoir high up on the mountain.

Below the mountain are the **Falls of Cruachan** and the wild **Pass of Brander,** where Robert the Bruce routed the Clan MacDougall in 1308. The Pass of Brander was the scene of many a fierce battle in bygone times, and something of that bloody past seems to brood over the narrow defile. Through it the waters of the Awe flow on their way to Loch Etive. This winding sea loch is 31km (19 miles) long, stretching from Dun Dunstaffnage Bay at Oban to Glen Etive, reaching into the Moor of Rannoch at the foot of the 910m (3,000-ft.) **Buachaille Etive (the Shepherd of Etive),** into which Glencoe also reaches.

WHERE TO STAY & DINE

Hotel Ardanaiseig ★★ Although this gray-stone manorial seat was built in 1834 by a Campbell patriarch, it's designed along 18th-century lines. Its builder also planted some of the rarest trees in Britain, many of them exotic conifers. Today, clusters of fruit trees stand in a walled garden, and the rhododendrons and azaleas are a joy in May and June. Until recently a private home, the hotel has formal sitting rooms graced with big chintzy chairs, fresh flowers, and polished tables. The guest rooms are named for various local mountains and lochs and are uniquely and traditionally furnished with antiques; some have four-poster beds. The price of a room depends on its size, ranging from a small room to a master bedroom with a loch view. The beautifully maintained bathrooms come with either a tub-and-shower combination or a shower only.

Kilchrenan by Taynuilt PA35 1HE. © **800/548-7790** in the U.S., 800/463-7595 in Canada, or 01866/833333. Fax 01866/833222. www.ardanaiseig-hotel.com. 16 units. £82–£186 ($131–$298) double. AE, DC, MC, V. Closed Jan to mid-Feb. Drive 34km (21 miles) south of Oban by following the signs to Taynuilt, then turning onto B845 toward Kilchrenan. Turn left at the Kilchrenan Pub and continue on for 6km (4 miles), following signs into Ardanaiseig. **Amenities:** Restaurant; tennis court. *In room:* TV, coffeemaker, hair dryer.

6 Oban: Gateway to the Inner Hebrides

137km (85 miles) NW of Glasgow; 81km (50 miles) SW of Fort William

One of Scotland's leading coastal resorts, the bustling port of Oban is in a sheltered bay almost landlocked by the island of Kerrera. A busy fishing port in the 18th century, Oban is now heavily dependent on tourism. Because it lacks major attractions of its own, it's often used as a major refueling stop for those exploring the greater west coast of Scotland.

ESSENTIALS

GETTING THERE From Glasgow, the **West Highland** lines run directly to Oban, with departures from Glasgow's Queen Street Station (call © **0845/748-4950** for 24-hr. info). Three trains per day (only two on Sun) make the 3-hour run to Oban, a one-way fare costing £15 ($24).

Frequent coaches depart from Buchanan Station in Glasgow, taking about the same time as the train, although a one-way fare is only £12 ($19). Call **Scottish CityLink** at © **0870/550-5050** in Glasgow or © **01631/563059** in Oban.

If you're driving from Glasgow, head northwest along A82 until reaching Tyndrum, then go west along A85 until you come to Oban.

Fun Fact **Folly? Or Source of Pride?**

Overlooking the town of Oban is an unfinished replica of the Colosseum of Rome, **McCaig's Tower,** built by a banker, John Stuart McCaig, from 1897 to 1900 as a memorial to his family and to create a local work opportunity during an employment slump. Its walls are 61cm (2 ft.) thick and 11m to 12m (37 ft.–40 ft.) high. Set atop **Pulpit Hill,** the tower offers a fine view across the Firth of Lorn and the Sound of Mull. The courtyard within is landscaped, and the tower is floodlit at night. Outsiders have been heard to refer to the tower as "McCaig's Folly," but Obanites are proud of the structure and deplore this term.

VISITOR INFORMATION   The **tourist office** is on Argyll Square (© **01631/ 563122**). From April to mid-June and mid-September to October, it's open Monday through Friday from 9:30am to 5pm and Saturday and Sunday from 10 to 4pm; from mid-June to mid-September, hours are Monday through Saturday from 9am to 8pm and Sunday from 9am to 7pm; and from November to March, it's open Monday through Saturday from 9:30am to 5pm and Sunday from noon to 4pm.

SPECIAL EVENTS   The **Oban Highland Games** are held in August, with massed pipe bands marching through the streets. Ask at the tourist office for details. The **Oban Pipe Band** regularly parades on the main street throughout summer.

EXPLORING THE AREA

To appreciate the coastal scenery of Oban to its fullest, consider renting a bike and cycling around. They're available at **Oban Cycles,** 9 Craigard Rd. (© **01631/562444**).

Near the little granite **Cathedral of the Isles,** 1.5km (1 mile) north of the end of the bay, is the ruin of the 13th-century **Dunollie Castle,** seat of the lords of Lorn, who once owned a third of Scotland.

On the island of Kerrera stands **Gylen Castle,** home of the MacDougalls, dating back to 1587.

You can visit **Dunstaffnage Castle** ★ (© **01631/562465**), 5.5km (3½ miles) north, believed to have been the royal seat of the Dalriadic monarchy in the 8th century. It was probably the site of the Scots court until Kenneth MacAlpin's unification of Scotland, and the transfer of the seat of government to Scone in the 10th century. The present castle was built around 1263. The castle is open April through October from 9am to 6:30pm (until 8pm July–Aug), and November through March from 9:30am to 4:30pm. Admission is £2 ($3.20) adults, £1.40 ($2.25) seniors, and 80p ($1.30) children. You can take a bus from the Oban rail station to Dunbeg, but it's still a 2.5km (1½-mile) walk to the castle.

SHOPPING

Cathness Glass Oban, Railway Pier (© **01631/563386**), is the best place for shopping, but you'll find plenty of gift and souvenir shops around town. At this center, locally produced glass items range from functional dinner- and glassware to purely artistic curios. This firm has one of the most prestigious reputations in Scotland.

Many of the crafts items produced in local crofts and private homes eventually end up at gift shops in Oban, where they're proudly displayed as among the finest of their kind in the West Country. One of the best outlets is **McCaig's Warehouse,** Argyll Square (© **01631/566335**), where the tartan patterns of virtually every clan in Scotland are for sale, either by the meter or in the form of kilts, jackets, traditional Highland garb, or more modern interpretation of traditional fashions.

Celtic-patterned jewelry, made from gold, silver, or platinum, and sometimes studded with semiprecious gems, is featured at **The Gem Box,** Esplanade (© **01631/562180**).

If all other shopping options fail, consider the gift items displayed at the **Oban Tourist Information Office,** Argyll Square (© **01631/563122**). Inventories include tartans, jewelry, woodwork, and glassware, usually crafted into Celtic designs, and books covering the myriad aspects of what to see and do in Scotland.

If you absolutely, positively must have a kilt, a cape, or a full outfit based on your favorite Highland regiment, head for one of the town's two best tailors: **Hector Russell, Kiltmaker,** Argyll Square (© **01631/570240**), and **Geoffrey Tailors,** Argyll Square (© **01631/570557**).

WHERE TO STAY

You may also want to check out the rooms offered at the **Balmoral Hotel** or the **Knipoch Hotel Restaurant** (see "Where to Dine," below).

EXPENSIVE

Manor House Hotel ⚜   This is your best bet for an overnight in Oban. On the outskirts of Oban, opening onto panoramic views of Oban Bay, this 1780 stone house was once owned by the duke of Argyll. Many antiques grace the public rooms. The good-sized guest rooms are filled with tasteful reproductions, and coordinated curtains and bedcovers create a pleasing effect, often in sunsplashed golds and yellows. All have midsize private bathrooms, some with both tub and shower. *Note:* Children under 12 are not welcome as guests.

The restaurant is one of the most satisfying in the area; for more on dining here, see "Where to Dine" below.

Gallanach Rd., Oban PA34 4LS. © 01631/562087. Fax 01631/563053. www.manorhouseoban.com. 11 units. £128–£170 ($205–$272) double. Rates include half board. AE, MC, V. From the south side of Oban, follow the signs for the car ferry but continue past the ferry entrance for about 1km (½ mile). **Amenities:** Restaurant; bar; room service; laundry service. *In room:* TV, coffeemaker, hair dryer.

MODERATE

Alexandra Hotel   On the promenade 1.5km (1 mile) from the train station, the late-1860s stone Alexandra boasts gables and turreted towers and a Regency front veranda. From its public room you can look out onto Oban Bay, and two sun lounges overlook the seafront. The midsize guest rooms are modestly furnished but pleasing, with small bathrooms. Some rooms are specially equipped for those with limited mobility. Most units are rented at the lower rate (see below), except for two spacious bedrooms opening onto dramatic sea views. The restaurant, serving good food, also opens onto the panorama.

Corran Esplanade, Oban PA34 5AA. © 01631/562381. Fax 01631/564497. 77 units . £95–£114 ($152–$182) double. Rates include Scottish breakfast. AE, MC, V. **Amenities:** Restaurant; bar; indoor pool; small gym; steam room; limited room service; laundry service. *In room:* TV, coffeemaker, hair dryer, iron/ironing board (in some).

Columba Hotel   This is one of the most impressive Victorian buildings in Oban. The Columba was built in 1870 by the same McCaig who constructed the hilltop extravaganza known as McCaig's Tower. The location is among the best in town, and the modernized big-windowed dining room offers views of the port. The small guest rooms are unremarkable but well maintained, each with a small bathroom with a tub and shower combination, or just a shower. The restaurant offers a mix of seafood and local produce. Live folk music is sometimes presented in the informal Harbour Inn Bar.

The Esplanade, North Pier, Oban PA34 5QD. © 01631/562183. Fax 01631/564683. 50 units. £75–£95 ($120–$152) double. Rates include breakfast. AE, MC, V. Free parking. The Scottish Midland Bus Company's Ganavan bus passes by. **Amenities:** Restaurant; bar; limited room service. *In room:* TV, coffeemaker, hair dryer.

Dungallan House Hotel ⭐   One of the more upscale inns around Oban is this home (ca. 1870) built for the Campbells. It was used as a hospital during World War I and as a naval office during World War II, but today it is the artfully furnished domain of George and Janice Stewart, who maintain the high-ceilinged proportions and antique furniture with devotion. The guest rooms have been refurbished, each with firm mattresses and quality furnishings. All but two single rooms have small bathrooms, some of which contain a tub-and-shower combination. Breakfasts are served in grand style in the formal dining room; dinners can be arranged, and though priority is granted to guests, nonguests can usually arrange a meal if they phone ahead. Five acres of forest and gardens surround the house, and views stretch out over the Bay of Oban and its islands.

Gallanach Rd., Oban PA34 4PD. © 01631/563799. Fax 01631/566711. www.dungallanhotel-oban.co.uk. 13 units, 11 with private bathroom. £83 ($132) double without bathroom, £120 ($192) double with bathroom. MC, V. Closed Nov–Mar. From Oban's center, drive 1km (½ mile), following the signs to Gallanach. *In room:* TV, no phone.

Dungrianach ⭐ *(Finds)*   It has only a handful of rooms, but if you can get a reservation, this is a little B&B charmer. In Gaelic, the name of the place means "the sunny house on the hill," and the description is apt. It sits in the midst of a wooded area, overlooking Oban Bay and some of the islands of the Inner Hebrides. The location is tranquil and seemingly remote, yet it's only a few minutes' walk from the ferry terminal. The house is impressively furnished with both antiques and reproductions. The owners rent a double and a twin-bedded accommodation, each with a little private bath with shower. Guests meet fellow guests in the living room, which has a collection of books on Scotland and travel literature in general.

Pulpit Hill, Oban, Argyll PA34 4LU. ©/fax 01631/562840. www.dungrianach.com. 2 units. £50 ($80). No credit cards. Free parking. **Amenities:** Breakfast lounge. *In room:* TV, beverage maker, no phone.

INEXPENSIVE

Foxholes ⭐ *(Finds)*   Far from a foxhole, this is actually a spacious country house set in a tranquil glen to the south of Oban. Operated by Barry and Shirley Dowson-Park, it's for those seeking seclusion. The cozy, tasteful, and comfortable bedrooms are painted in soft pastels and furnished traditionally. All rooms open onto panoramic views of the countryside and the hotel's well-maintained gardens. All the bathrooms are in excellent condition, some with a combination tub and shower. In the restaurant, Mrs. Dowson-Park provides traditional, moderately priced Scottish meals. The property is entirely nonsmoking.

Cologin, Lerags, Oban. PA34 4SE. © 01631/564982. www.hoteloban.com. 7 units. £60–£70 ($96–$112) double. Rates include full Scottish breakfast. MC, V. Free parking. Closed Dec–Mar. Take A816 1.8km (3 miles) south of Oban. **Amenities:** Restaurant; bar. *In room:* TV, coffeemaker, hair dryer, no phone.

Glenburnie Hotel   One of Oban's genuinely grand houses is on the seafront esplanade a 5-minute walk west of the town center. Built in 1897 of granite blocks, with elegant ecclesiastical-looking bay windows, it was designed as the surgical hospital and home of a prominent doctor. Today, it's a guesthouse operated by Graeme and Allyson Strachan, who have outfitted the rooms with comfy furniture, much of it antique. Bathrooms are small but tidy, and most have tub-and-shower combinations. The entire hotel is nonsmoking.

The Esplanade, Oban PA34 5AQ. ℂ/fax **01631/562089.** www.glenburnie.co.uk. 14 units. £56–£78 ($90–$125) double. MC, V. Closed Nov–Easter. *In room:* TV, coffeemaker, hair dryer (at the front desk).

Lancaster   Along the seafront on the crescent of the bay, the Lancaster is distinguished by its attractive pseudo-Tudor facade. Its public rooms command views of the islands of Lismore and Kerrera and even the more distant peaks of Mull. The guest rooms are modestly furnished in a somewhat 1960s style, some with complete bathrooms with tub-and-shower combinations (three singles have no private bathroom). There are three rooms set aside for families. This is only one of the two hotels in Oban featuring a heated indoor pool, a sauna, a whirlpool, and a solarium. Its fully licensed dining room offers moderately priced dinners. *Note:* There is no elevator.

Corran Esplanade, Oban PA34 5AD. ℂ/fax **01631/562587.** www.lancasteroban.com. 27 units, 24 with private bathroom. £66 ($106) double with bathroom. Rates include Scottish breakfast. MC, V. **Amenities:** Bar lounge; heated indoor pool; sauna; whirlpool; solarium; room service. *In room:* TV, coffeemaker, hair dryer, no phone.

WHERE TO DINE
EXPENSIVE

Knipoch Hotel Restaurant ★★ SCOTTISH   Oban offers a truly fine restaurant 10km (6 miles) south of town on the shores of Loch Feochan. Jenny and Colin Craig, a mother-and-son team, welcome you to their whitewashed Georgian house (the oldest part dates from 1592) and offer a choice of three dining rooms as well as a daily changing menu of five delectable courses. Salmon and halibut are smoked on the premises, and the menu relies heavily on Scottish produce, including fresh fish. Try the cock-a-leekie soup, followed by Sound of Luing scallops. The wine cellar is excellent, especially in its Bordeaux.

The hotel rents 21 well-furnished rooms, charging £130–£150 ($208–$240) per night in a double, with a suite costing £13 ($21) per person extra. A full Scottish breakfast is included in the rate.

Hwy. A816, Kilninver, Knipoch, by Oban PA34 4QT. ℂ **01852/316251.** Fax 01852/316249. www.knipoch hotel.co.uk. Reservations required. Table d'hôte dinner £34 ($54) for 3 courses, £43 ($68) for 5 courses. AE, DC, MC, V. Daily 7:30–9pm. Closed mid-Dec to mid-Feb. Drive 10km (6 miles) south of Oban on A816.

The Manor House ★ SCOTTISH   Located in the 1780 house built by the duke of Argyll, this formal but not stuffy restaurant overlooks Oban Bay and is one of the finest dining choices along the coast. A traditional Scottish cuisine is served—truly fresh and creative cooking—and the chef uses ingredients of the highest quality. Against a backdrop of Georgian paneling, you can peruse the constantly changing menu. Many visitors to the Highlands opt for venison, and it comes with accompaniments such as black pudding, caramelized root vegetables, and rowanberry glaze. Or try the delicious fresh scallops wrapped in smoked bacon. There are also some selections for vegetarians. You can order such old-fashioned British desserts as sticky toffee pudding with butterscotch sauce, but for something really Scottish, try marinated brambles with whisky custard.

In the Manor House Hotel, Gallanach Rd. ℂ **01631/562087.** Reservations recommended. Main courses £22 ($35); set-price 5-course meal £35 ($56). AE, MC, V. Tues 6:45–9pm; Wed–Sat noon–2pm and 6:45–9pm.

MODERATE

Balmoral Hotel BRITISH   At the top of a granite staircase whose corkscrew shape is an architectural marvel, this is one of the most popular restaurants in town. Filled with a 19th-century kind of charm, it contains Windsor chairs and reproduction Georgian tables crafted from darkly stained wood. Specialties include sliced chateaubriand with mushrooms, Isle of Mull rainbow trout, smoked Tobermory trout, Scottish haggis with cream and whisky, venison casserole, and roast pheasant. Less expensive platters are served in the adjacent bar.

The hotel stands on the eastern extension of the town's main commercial street (George St.), a 4-minute walk from the center. It rents 12 well-furnished rooms with TVs, costing £55–£70 ($88–$112) double, Scottish breakfast included.

Craigard Rd., Oban PA34 5AQ. ℂ 01631/562731. Reservations recommended in midsummer. Main courses £7.20–£17 ($12–$28); bar meals £3.25–£8 ($5.20–$13). AE, DC, MC, V. May to mid-Oct daily noon–2pm and 6–10pm; Mar–Apr and mid-Oct to Dec daily noon–2pm and 6–8pm.

The Gathering BRITISH   Opened in 1882, this imposing building, ringed with verandas, is no longer a private hunting and social club. Today, its ground floor functions as an Irish pub (open Mon–Sat 11am–1am and Sun noon–11pm) and its wood-sheathed upper floor as a well-managed restaurant. Dishes are straightforward but nonetheless tasty and well prepared. Menu items include lots of local produce, fish, and game dishes, such as pheasant, lobster, and lamb. Especially noteworthy are the Highland venison filets with port jelly sauce, loin of saddle of venison with herb-and-port sauce, and local crayfish lightly grilled in garlic butter and served with a fresh salad.

Breadalbane St. ℂ 01631/565421. Reservations recommended. Bar platters £5.50–£14 ($8.80–$22); set-price dinners in restaurant £12–£18 ($19–$29). AE, MC, V. June–Sept daily noon–2pm; year-round dinner daily 5–10pm.

McTavish's Kitchen SCOTTISH   Like its cousin in Fort William, this place is dedicated to preserving the local cuisine. Downstairs is a self-service restaurant offering breakfast, lunch, dinner, and teas with shortbread and scones. Upstairs is the Lairds Bar, and on the ground floor is McTavish's Bar, where bar meals are available all day. The licensed second-floor restaurant has a more ambitious Scottish and continental menu with higher prices, but there are also budget lunches. The fixed-price menu includes an appetizer, a main-course choice that features fresh salmon, and a dessert like strawberries or raspberries (in season). The a la carte menu offers haggis, Loch Fyne kippers (oak-smoked herring), prime Scottish steaks, smoked salmon, venison, and local mussels.

34 George St. ℂ 01631/563064. Main courses £8–£16 ($13–$25); budget 2-course lunch £5 ($8); fixed-price 3-course dinners £7.50–£17 ($12–$27). MC, V. Self-service restaurant daily 9am–9pm; licensed restaurant daily noon–2pm and 6–10:30pm.

OBAN AFTER DARK

From mid-May to the end of September, entertainment is provided at **McTavish's Kitchen** (see above), with Scottish music and Highland dancing by local artists nightly from 8:30 to 10:30pm. Admission is £4 ($6.40) adults and £2 ($3.20) children. Reduced admission for diners is £2 ($3.20) adults and £1.50 ($2.40) children.

You can while away the evening with the locals at the **Oban Inn,** Stafford Street and the Esplanade (ℂ 01631/562484), a popular pub with exposed beams and a flag-covered ceiling. Pints include McEwan's Export, Ale, and Gillespie's Stout. The pub is open daily from 11am to 1am.

Another popular hangout is the town's Irish pub, **O'Donnells,** Breadalbane Street (© **01631/566159**), where you can always expect a warm reception. They serve the ever-popular Guinness and a variety of Irish and Scottish malt whisky. Thursday through Saturday, entertainment is either a live band or a DJ. Over the busy summer, something is scheduled almost every night. Hours are daily from 3pm to 1am.

17

Fife & the Central Highlands

North of the Firth of Forth from Edinburgh, the County of Fife still likes to call itself a kingdom. Even today, its name suggests the romantic episodes and pageantry during the reign of the early Stuart kings, and some 14 of Scotland's 66 royal burghs lay in this shire. And you can visit many of the former royal palaces and castles, either restored or in colorful ruins.

Legendary **Loch Lomond** is the largest and most beautiful of the Scottish lakes. At Balloch in the south, it's a Lowland landscape of gentle hills and islands. But as it moves north, the loch narrows and takes on a stark, dramatic Highland character, with moody cloud formations and rugged, steep hillsides.

The **Trossachs** is the collective name given to that wild Highland area east and northeast of Loch Lomond. Here and along Loch Lomond you find Scotland's finest scenery in moor, mountain, and loch. The area has been famed in history and romance ever since Sir Walter Scott's vivid descriptive passages in "The Lady of the Lake" and *Rob Roy.*

Many sections of the area lie on the doorsteps of Glasgow and Edinburgh; either city can be your gateway to the central Highlands. You can easily reach **Dunfermline** and **St. Andrews** by rail from Edinburgh (St. Andrews also has good bus connections with Edinburgh). By car, the main motorway is M9, the express highway that starts on the western outskirts of Edinburgh and is linked to M80 from Glasgow. M9 passes close to Stirling. M90, reached by crossing the Forth Road Bridge, will take you north into the Fife region. **Stirling** is the region's major rail center, with stops at such places as **Dunblane,** and much of Loch Lomond has rail connections. The towns and some villages have bus service, but you'll find the connections too limited or infrequent. For bus connections, Stirling is the central point.

However, your best bet for discovering the hidden villages and scenic lochside roads of the Trossachs or the fishing villages of East Neuk is renting a car and driving at your own pace.

1 Dunfermline & Its Great Abbey

23km (14 miles) NW of Edinburgh; 63km (39 miles) NE of Glasgow; 84km (52 miles) SW of Dundee

The ancient town of Dunfermline was once the capital of Scotland and is easily reached by the Forth Road Bridge, opened by Elizabeth II in 1964. Scots called their former capital the "auld grey town," and it looms large in their history books. The city is still known for the Dunfermline Abbey and former royal palace (now largely gone). When Scotland reunited with England in 1603, the royal court departed to London, leaving Dunfermline to wither with only its memories. In time, however, the town revived as the center of Scottish linen making, specializing in damask. But by World War I, the market had largely disappeared.

Some of the most interesting sights in Fife are within easy reach of Dunfermline, including one of Scotland's most beautiful villages, Culross. Dunfermline also makes the best base for exploring Loch Leven and Loch Leven Castle.

ESSENTIALS

GETTING THERE Dunfermline is a stop along the main rail route from London via Edinburgh to Dundee, which means it has frequent connections to the Scottish capital. For rail schedules and fares, call ☎ **0870/608-2608.**

From its station at St. Andrews Square in Edinburgh, Scottish **CityLink** (☎ **0990/505050**) operates frequent service to Dunfermline.

If you're driving from Edinburgh, take A90 west, cross the Forth Road Bridge, and follow the signs north to the center of Dunfermline.

VISITOR INFORMATION   A **tourist booth** is at 1 High Street (☎ **01383/ 720999**). It's open Monday through Saturday from 9:30am to 5pm.

SEEING THE SIGHTS

Dunfermline Abbey and Palace ✪   The abbey is on the site of two earlier structures, a Celtic church and an 11th-century house of worship dedicated to the Holy Trinity, under the auspices of Queen Margaret (later St. Margaret). Culdee Church, from the 5th and 6th centuries, was rebuilt in 1072. Traces of both buildings are visible beneath gratings in the floor of the old nave. In 1150, the church was replaced with a large abbey, the nave of which remains, an example of Norman architecture. Later, St. Margaret's shrine, the northwest baptismal porch, the spire on the northwest tower, and the flying buttresses were added. While Dunfermline was the capital of Scotland, 22 royal personages were buried in the abbey. However, the only visible memorial or burial places known are those of Queen Margaret and King Robert the Bruce, whose tomb lies beneath the pulpit.

The once-royal palace of Dunfermline stands adjacent to the abbey. The palace witnessed the birth of Charles I and James I. The last king to reside here was Charles II in 1651. Today only the southwest wall remains of this once gargantuan edifice.

St. Margaret's St. ☎ 01383/739026. Admission £2.20 ($3.50) adults, £1.60 ($2.55) seniors, 75p ($1.20) children. Apr–Sept daily 9:30am–6pm; Oct–Mar Mon–Wed and Sat 9:30am–4pm, Thurs 9:30am–noon, Sun 2–4pm.

Andrew Carnegie Birthplace Museum   In 1835, American industrialist/ philanthropist Andrew Carnegie was born at a site about 182m (300 ft.) down the hill from the abbey. The museum, at the corner of Moodie Street and Priory Lane, comprises the 18th-century weaver's cottage in which he was born and a memorial hall provided by his wife. Displays tell the story of the weaver's son who emigrated to America to become one of the richest men in the world. From the fortune he made in steel, Carnegie gave away more than £244 million ($400 million) before his 1919 death. Dunfermline received the first of the 2,811 free libraries he provided throughout Britain and the United States and also received public baths and Pittencrieff Park and Glen, rich in history and natural charm. A statue in the park honors Carnegie, who once worked as a bobbin boy in a cotton factory.

Moodie St. ☎ 01383/724302. Admission £2 ($3.20) adults, £1 ($1.60) seniors, free for children ages 15 and under. Apr–Oct Mon–Sat 11am–5pm, Sun 2–5pm. Closed Nov–Mar.

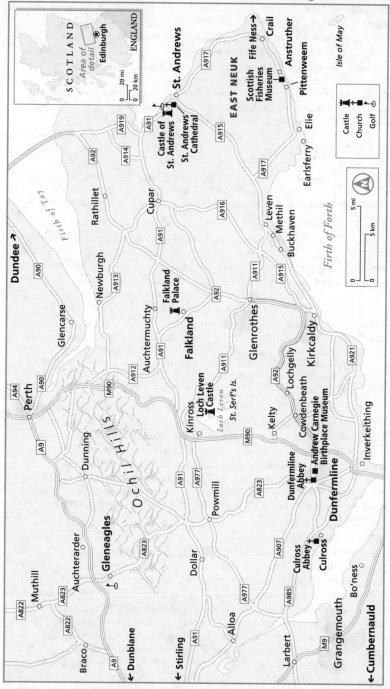

The Kingdom of Fife

SCOTLAND

Area of detail

Edinburgh

ENGLAND

0 20 mi
0 20 km

Castle
Church
Golf

Dundee →

Firth of Tay

A90

A94

Glencarse

Perth

A90

A9

Dunning

Ochil Hills

Auchterarder

Gleneagles

A823

Muthill

A822

A823

Braco

A822

Dunblane ←

Stirling ←

A9

Dollar

A91

Alloa

A977

Powmill

A823

A977

A985

A907

Culross
Culross Abbey

Bo'ness

Grangemouth

Cumbernauld ←

Larbert

M9

Inverkeithing

Dunfermline
Dunfermline Abbey
Andrew Carnegie Birthplace Museum

Cowdenbeath

Kelty

M90

Lochgelly

A92

Kirkcaldy

A921

Glenrothes

A911

A915

Buckhaven

Methil

Leven

A911

Firth of Forth

A915

Earlsferry

Elie

A917

Anstruther
Pittenweem

EAST NEUK

Scottish Fisheries Museum

Crail

Fife Ness →

Isle of May

St. Andrews
Castle of St. Andrews
St. Andrews Cathedral

A91

A919

A914

A917

A915

A916

Cupar

A91

Rathillet

Newburgh

A913

Auchtermuchty

A912

Falkland
Falkland Palace

A91

A92

M90

Kinross
Loch Leven Castle

Loch Leven

St. Serf's Is.

A911

Lochgelly

5 mi
5 km
0
0

N

599

WHERE TO STAY

Davaar House Hotel and Restaurant   This large Georgian-style house lies in a residential neighborhood a 5-minute walk west of the town center. It was built late in the 19th century and boasts distinctive architectural features like a sweeping oak staircase, elaborate cove moldings, and marble mantelpieces. The largest guest rooms, with the loftiest ceilings, are one floor above street level; slightly less grand rooms are two floors above street level. Each is uniquely decorated, with strong colors and pastels, in a traditional Scottish style. All the units contain a shower; some are also equipped with tubs.

The restaurant here is well recommended; it's open only for dinner Monday through Saturday and offers moderate prices and home-style cooking from a talented team of chefs.

126 Grieve St., Dunfermline, Fife KY12 8DW. ✆ **01383/721886.** Fax 01383/623633. www.taste-of-scotland. com/davaar-house-hotel.html. 10 units. £75–£85 ($120–$136) double. Rates include breakfast. MC, V. **Amenities:** Restaurant; limited room service; laundry service. *In room:* TV, coffeemaker, hair dryer (in some).

Keavil House Hotel ★   This tranquil country hotel, only a 30-minute drive from Edinburgh, is set on 12 acres of forested land and gardens and offers lots of leisure facilities. The bedrooms are generous in size and well appointed, each with such amenities as a writing desk and midsize bathrooms (some with tubs). Master bedrooms contain four-poster beds. Several rooms are suitable for families; others are equipped for guests with limited mobility. The hotel offers fine, formal dining in its Conservatory Restaurant (see below) and less formal food in its Armoury Alehouse & Grill.

Main St., Crossford, Dunfermline, Fife KY12 8QW. ✆ **01383/736258.** Fax 01383/621600. www.keavilhouse. co.uk. 47 units. £120–£140 ($192–$224) double; £135–£195 ($216–$312) family suite. AE, DC, MC, V. Closed Dec 31–Jan 1. Free parking. Take A994, 2 miles west of Dunfermline; the hotel is off the main street at the west end of village. **Amenities:** 2 restaurants; bar; indoor heated pool; the finest leisure/health club in the area; Jacuzzi; sauna; steam room; room service; babysitting; laundry service. *In room:* TV, coffeemaker, hair dryer.

King Malcolm Thistle Hotel   The best in town choice for either a meal or a bed is this modern pastel-colored stylish hotel on a roundabout a mile south of Dunfermline on A823. Named after the medieval king of Fife (and later of Scotland), Malcolm Canmore, it was built in 1972 but has been thoroughly revamped since then. The guest rooms are well furnished though rather standardized.

Queensferry Rd., Dunfermline, Fife KY11 5DS. ✆ **01383/722611.** Fax 01383/730865. www.peelhotel.com. 48 units. £120–£160 ($192–$256) double. Children ages 13 and under stay free in parent's room. AE, DC, MC, V. Bus: D3 or D4. **Amenities:** Restaurant; bar; limited room service; laundry service; dry cleaning. *In room:* TV, coffeemaker, hair dryer, trouser press.

WHERE TO DINE

Conservatory Restaurant MODERN SCOTTISH   Some of the best local produce is used deftly here to create true "taste of Scotland" specialties—and that means the best of Scottish beef, locally caught game, and fish from local rivers. Old-time recipes are given a modern twist by the chef. The imaginative dishes are served with flair and originality, appealing to both traditionalists and those with more adventurous tastes. Try the smoked salmon and prawns with salad and Arran mustard dressing, for example, or a real local specialty, a chanterelle and "tattie" scone pocket with a malt vinegar demi-glaze. You can follow with dessert of caramelized heather honey and apple parfait. There's an extensive and well-chosen wine list.

In the Keavil House Hotel, Main St., Crossford. ✆ **01383/736258.** Reservations recommended. Fixed-price 3-course menu £25 ($40), 2-course £20 ($32). AE, DC, MC, V. Daily noon–2pm and 7–9pm. Closed Dec 31–Jan 1.

2 East Neuk's Scenic Fishing Villages ⟨★⟨★

Within half an hour's drive south of St. Andrews, on the eastward-facing peninsula incorporating St. Andrews and Anstruther, is the district of East Neuk, dotted with some of eastern Scotland's most scenic and unspoiled fishing villages.
You can't reach these villages by rail; the nearest stations are Ladybank, Cupar,
and Leuchars, on the main London–Edinburgh–Dundee–Aberdeen line serving
northeast Fife. Buses from St. Andrews connect the villages, but you'll really
want to have your own car here.

If the weather's right, you can cycle among the villages along some of the most
delightful back roads in Fife. Rent a bike at **East Neuk Outdoors,** Cellardyke
Park in Anstruther (✆ **01333/311929**). This outfitter can also fix you up for a
canoe trip.

PITTENWEEM

If you're at Pittenweem in the morning, Monday through Saturday, try to get
caught up in the action at the **fish auction** held under a large shed. The actual
time depends on the tides. Afterward, you can go for a walk through the village
and admire the sturdy stone homes, some of which have been preserved by Scotland's National Trust.

The *weem* in the name of the town means "cave," a reference to **St. Fillan's
Cave** at Cove Wynd (✆ **01333/311495**) in the vicinity of the harbor. This cave
is said to contain the shrine of St. Fillan, a hermit who lived in the 6th century.
Hours are daily from 10am to 5pm, costing £1 ($1.60) admission, free for chil-
dren under 15 years old.

The best way to reach **Anstruther** (see below) is to hike the 2.5km (1½ miles)
over to it, as the road isn't paved. If the day is clear, this is one of the loveliest
walks in eastern Scotland, as you cross Scottish meadows and say hello to a few
lambs. From Pittenweem, follow a signpost directing you to Anstruther. You can
also take the walk in reverse, as most visitors do. In Anstruther, the path begins
at the bottom of West Braes, a small cul-de-sac off the main road in the village.

WHERE TO STAY

The Pittenweem Harbour Guest House   Set directly on the harbor, this
charming stone building was erected around 1910 as a private home. The guest
rooms contain pinewood furniture and comfortable twin beds, each a cozy, no-
frills refuge from the chilly winds and crashing seas. Each unit contains a small,
shower-only bathroom. Because it's run by a local company and not by a family, Harbour is a bit more businesslike than a conventional B&B; in fact, it feels
like a fishing lodge—the staff will direct you to local entrepreneurs who can take
you out for a half-day's fishing or point out spots on the nearby piers and
boardwalks where a rod and reel might attract fish.

14 Mid Shore, Pittenweem, Fife KY10 2NL. ✆ 01333/311273. Fax 01333/310014. www.pittenweem.com.
4 units. £42–£60 ($67–$96) double. Rates include breakfast. Discounts of £8 ($13) per person off nightly rate
Nov–Mar. AE, DC, MC, V. *In room:* TV, coffeemaker, hair dryer.

ANSTRUTHER

Once an important herring-fishing port, **Anstruther** is now a summer resort,
74km (46 miles) northeast of Edinburgh, 55km (34 miles) east of Dunfermline,
6.5km (4 miles) southwest of Crail, and 37km (23 miles) south of Dundee. The
tourist office is on High Street (✆ **01333/311073**); April through September,
it's open Monday through Saturday from 10am to 5pm and Sunday from noon
to 5pm (every Tues, Wed, and Thurs, it closes 1–2pm).

You'll enjoy taking a brisk stroll along the beaches here; it's too chilly for swimming, but it's invigorating and scenic nonetheless. The best nearby is **Billow Ness Beach,** a 10-minute walk east of the center.

The **Scottish Fisheries Museum,** St. Ayles, Harbourhead (© **01333/ 310628;** bus: 95), is down by the harbor. It was expanded in 1999 to include a neighboring building that was an 18th-century tavern and several re-creations of restored fishing boats. Here you can follow the fishermen through every aspect of their industry—from the days of sail to modern times. Associated with the museum but afloat in the harbor is an old herring drifter, *The Reaper,* which you can board to look around. April through October, the museum is open Monday through Saturday from 10am to 5:30pm and Sunday from 11am to 5pm; November through March, hours are Monday through Saturday from 10am to 4:30pm and Sunday from 2 to 4:30pm. Admission is £3.50 ($5.60) adults, £2.50 ($4) seniors/children, and £10 ($16) families. Last admission is one hour before closing time.

From the museum, you can walk to the tiny hamlet of **Cellardyke,** adjoining Anstruther. You'll find many charming stone houses and an ancient harbor where in the year Victoria took the throne (1837), 140 vessels used to put out to sea. You can rent a bike from **East Neuk Outdoors,** Cellardyke Park (© **01333/ 311929**), where rental rates are £12 ($19) daily and £30–£50 ($48–$80) weekly, plus a deposit. It's open daily April through September from 9am to 5pm. Open by appointment only in winter.

The **Isle of May** ⋆, a nature reserve in the Firth of Forth, is accessible by boat from Anstruther. It's a bird observatory and a field station and contains the ruins of a 12th-century chapel as well as an early 19th-century lighthouse.

The **May Princess** (© **01333/310103;** www.isleofmayferry.com) is a 100-passenger boat that departs for the Isle of May from the Lifeboat Station at Anstruther Harbour every day, weather permitting, between mid-April and late September. Tickets for the trip go on sale one hour before departure from a kiosk beside Anstruther Harbour. The 5-hour trip, door-to-door, costs £13 ($21) for adults, £11 ($18) for seniors and students, and £6 ($9.60) for children 3 to 14. Departure times vary with the season, the day of the week, and the vagaries of the weather, so call in advance before planning for the 5-hour trip. Between May and July, expect to see hundreds, even thousands, of puffins, who mate on the Isle of May at that time.

WHERE TO STAY

Craw's Nest Hotel   This black-and-white step-gabled Scottish manse is a popular hotel, with views over the Firth of Forth and May Island. Many extensions were added under the direction of the owners, Mr. and Mrs. Powhan. The midsize guest rooms are handsomely appointed, each with a combination tub and shower. The public areas, including a lounge bar as well as a bustling public bar, are simply decorated and cozy. The food in the dining room is good, and the wine priced reasonably.

Bankwell Rd., Anstruther, Fife KY10 3DA. © 01333/310691. Fax 01333/312216. 50 units. £70–£210 ($112–$336) double. Rates include Scottish breakfast. AE, DC, MC, V. Bus: 915. **Amenities:** Restaurant; bar; limited room service; laundry service; dry cleaning. *In room:* TV, coffeemaker, hair dryer, trouser press.

Smuggler's Inn   This warmly inviting inn evokes memories of smuggling days, with low ceilings, uneven floors, and winding stairs. An inn has stood on this spot since 1300, and in Queen Anne's day it was a well-known tavern. The guest rooms are comfortably furnished. All the units come with showers, two of which have a tub as well. The restaurant serves moderately priced regional cuisine at dinner nightly. Affordable bar lunches are also available.

High St., East Anstruther, Fife KY10 3DQ. (©) **01333/310506.** Fax 01333/312706. 9 units. £50–£60 ($80–$96) double. Rates include Scottish breakfast. MC, V. Bus: 95. **Amenities:** Restaurant; bar; room service; laundry service. *In room:* TV, coffeemaker, hair dryer.

WHERE TO DINE

The Cellar SEAFOOD   Within the solid stone walls of a cellar that dates from 1875 (but possibly from the 16th century), this seafood restaurant is the best in town. It's lit by candlelight, and in winter, by twin fireplaces at opposite ends of the room. The menu offers fresh fish hauled in from nearby waters and cooked with light-textured sauces. The best examples are grilled halibut suprême dredged in breadcrumbs and citrus juices and served with hollandaise sauce; lobster, monkfish, and scallops roasted with herb-and-garlic butter and served on sweet-pepper risotto; and a limited array of meat dishes.

24 East Green, Anstruther. (©) **01333/310378.** Reservations recommended. Fixed-price dinner 2-courses £25 ($39), 3-courses £30 ($47), 4-courses £33 ($52); fixed price lunch 2-courses £16 ($25), 3-courses £19 ($30). AE, DC, MC, V. Wed–Sun 12:30–1:30pm; Tues–Sat 7–9:30pm. Bus: 95.

Haven SCOTTISH   Set within a pair of interconnected 300-year-old fisherman's cottages, this is the only restaurant with a position directly on the harbor of Anstruther. Defining itself as a restaurant with a cocktail lounge (not a pub), it serves simple, wholesome food that's flavorful and utterly unpretentious: pan-fried breaded prawns, halibut filets, Angus steaks, local crabmeat salad, and homemade soups and stews. The upper floor contains one of the town's most popular bars, where the same menu is served. The street level, more formal and sedate, is the site of high teas and evening meals.

1 Shore Rd., Cellardyke, Anstruther. (©) **01333/310574.** Reservations recommended. Main courses £7.95–£14 ($13–$22); high teas (tea, toast, and a meal-sized platter of food) £7.95–£8.35 ($13–$13). MC, V. Mon–Thurs 11am–9pm; Fri–Sun 11am–11pm. Bus: 95; a James Anderson & Co. bus runs every hour from St. Andrews, 13km (8 miles) south, to the door of the restaurant.

AFTER DARK

The **Dreel Tavern,** 16 High St. (© **01333/310727**), was a 16th-century coaching inn but is now a wood-and-stone pub where locals gather to unwind in the evening. Caledonian 80 Shilling and Orkney Dark Island are available on hand pump, along with two guest beers that change weekly. It's open Monday through Saturday from 11am to 11pm and Sunday from noon to 11pm.

ELIE ⊛

With its step-gabled houses and little harbor, Elie, 18km (11 miles) south of Anstruther, is many visitors' favorite village along the coast. Only a 25-minute car ride from Edinburgh, Elie and its close neighbor, Earlsferry, overlook a crescent of gold-sand beach, with more swimming possibilities to be found among sheltered coves. The name Elie is believed to be derived from the *ailie* (island) of Ardross, which now forms part of the harbor and is joined to the mainland by a road. A large stone building, a former granary, at the harbor is a reminder of the days when Elie was a busy trading port. Of all the villages of East Neuk, this one seems more suited to walks and hikes in all directions.

Earlsferry, to the west, got its name from an ancient ferry crossing, which Macduff, the thane of Fife, is supposed to have used in his escape from Macbeth.

East of the harbor stands a stone structure known as the **Lady's Tower,** used by Lady Janet Anstruther, a noted 18th-century beauty, as a bathing cabana. Another member of the Anstruther family, Sir John, added the interesting **bell tower** to the parish church that stands in the center of the village.

Beyond the lighthouse, on a point of land to the east of the harbor, lies **Ruby Bay,** so named because you can find garnets here. Farther along the coast is **Fossil Bay,** where you can find a variety of fossils.

WHERE TO STAY

The Elms *(Value)* Run by Mr. and Mrs. Terras, this 1880 building is on the wide main street behind a conservative stone facade, with a crescent-shaped rose garden in front. The comfortably furnished but small guest rooms contain washbasins, good beds, and showers. Home cooking is a specialty of the house, and dishes include Scottish lamb, Pittenweem haddock, haggis, and Arbroath kippers. A simple dinner is available to nonguests. In the walled flower garden behind the house is a large conservatory for guests' use.

14 Park Place, Elie, Fife KY9 1DH. ℂ/fax **01333/330404**. 6 units. £52 ($83) double. Rates include Scottish breakfast. MC, V. *In room:* TV, hair dryer, coffeemaker.

Rockview Guest House *(Kids)* Next to the Ship Inn (see below), the Rockview overlooks fine sandy beaches around Elie Bay. The small guest rooms are nicely furnished, each with a good bed and shower bathroom. Maintenance is of a high level, and the welcome is warm. A twin-bedded room has a bunk bed for younger children to share with their parents. Family-run, the guesthouse can accommodate about a dozen people. Food and drink are available at the Ship Inn.

The Toft, Elie, Fife KY9 IDT. ℂ **01333/330246**. Fax 01333/330864. www.ship-elie.com. 6 units. May–Oct £50 ($80) double. Rates include breakfast. MC, V. *In room:* TV.

WHERE TO DINE

Ship Inn *⋆* SCOTTISH Even if you're not stopping over in Elie, we suggest you drop in at the Ship (from the center, follow the signs marked HARBOUR) and enjoy a pint of lager or real ale or a whisky from a large selection. The building occupied by this pub with a nautical atmosphere dates from 1778, and a bar has been in business here since 1830. In summer, you can sit outside and look over the water; in colder months, a fireplace burns brightly. On weekends in July and August, a barbecue operates outside. The set menu with daily specials features such items as steak pie, Angus beefsteaks, lasagna, and an abundance of fresh seafood.

The Toft. ℂ **01333/330246**. Main courses £7–£16 ($11–$26). MC, V. Mon–Sat noon–midnight; Sun 12:30–11pm; open to 1am Fri–Sat.

CRAIL *⋆⋆*

The pearl of the East Neuk of Fife, Crail is 81km (50 miles) northeast of Edinburgh, 37km (23 miles) south of Dundee, and 15km (9 miles) south of St. Andrews. It's an artists' colony, and many painters live in cottages around its little harbor. Natural bathing facilities are at Roome Bay, and many **beaches** are nearby. The **Balcomie Golf Course** is one of the oldest in the world and is still in good condition.

The old town grew up along the harbor, and you can still see a lot of fishing cottages clustered here. Crab and lobster boats still set out hoping for a big catch. **Upper Crail** overlooks the harbor and also merits exploration. The **tollbooth** dates from 1598 and is crowned by a belfry. **Marketgate** is lined with trees and flanked by two- and three-floor small houses. Follow the walkway to **Castle Walk,** which offers the most panoramic view of Crail.

To understand the villages of East Neuk better, call at the **Crail Museum & Heritage Centre,** 62 Marketgate (© **01333/450869**), which contains artifacts related to fishing and the former trading links of these tiny villages. Admission is free. June through September, the center is open Monday through Saturday from 10am to 1pm and 2 to 5pm and Sunday from 2 to 5pm. April through May hours are Saturday and Sunday from 2 to 5pm.

WHERE TO STAY

Denburn House   Near the town center, in a historic neighborhood known as Marketgate, this guesthouse occupies a 200-year-old stone-sided building that retains many of its interior architectural features, including the paneling in the lounge and an elaborate staircase. In 1998, most of the interior was tastefully renovated; all the guest rooms were redecorated in a conservative but very pleasing style, each with a shower-only bathroom. In the rear garden is a scattering of lawn furniture and access to the great Scottish outdoors. Everything is very low-key and unpretentious.

1 Marketgate North, Crail, Fife KY10 3TQ. © 01333/450253. www.s-h-systems.co.uk. 6 units. £46–£52 ($74–$83) double. Rates include breakfast. AE, MC, V. **Amenities:** Lounge in summer. *In room:* TV, coffee-maker, hair dryer.

3 St. Andrews: The Birthplace of Golf ✦✦

23km (14 miles) SE of Dundee; 82km (51 miles) NE of Edinburgh

The medieval royal burgh of St. Andrews was once filled with monasteries and ancient houses that didn't survive the pillages of Henry VIII; regrettably, only a few ruins rising in ghostly dignity remain. Most of the town as you'll see it today was built of local stone during the 18th, 19th, and early 20th centuries. This historic sea town in northeast Fife is also known as the seat where the rules of golf in Britain and the world are codified and arbitrated. Golf was played for the first time in the 1400s, probably on the site of St. Andrews's Old Course, and was enjoyed by Mary Queen of Scots here in 1567. Golfers consider this town to be hallowed ground.

ESSENTIALS

GETTING THERE   **BritRail** stops 13km (8 miles) away at the town of Leuchars (rhymes with "euchres") on its London–Edinburgh–Dundee–Aberdeen run to the northeast. About 28 trains per day make the trip. Trip time from Edinburgh to Leuchars is about an hour, and a one-way fare is £8.50 ($14). For information, call © **0845/748-4950.**

Once at Leuchars, you can take a bus the rest of the way to St. Andrews. Bus no. 99 departs about every 20 minutes. Fife Scottish bus no. X24 travels from Glasgow to Glenrothes daily, and from there to St. Andrews. Buses operate daily from 7am to midnight, the trip taking between 2½ and 3 hours. Buses arrive at the St. Andrews Bus Station, Station Road, just off City Road (call © **01334/ 474238** for schedules).

By car from Edinburgh, head northwest along A90 and cross the Forth Road Bridge north. Take A921 to the junction with A915 and continue northeast until you reach St. Andrews.

VISITOR INFORMATION   The **tourist office** is on 70 Market St. (© **01334/ 472021;** www.standrews.com). January through March, November, and December, it's open Monday through Saturday from 9:30am to 5pm; April hours are Monday through Saturday from 9:30am to 5pm and Sunday from 11am to 4pm;

May, June, September, and October, hours are Monday through Saturday from 9:30am to 6pm and Sunday from 11am to 4pm; and July and August, hours are Monday through Saturday from 9:30am to 7pm and Sunday from 10am to 6pm.

HITTING THE LINKS

All six of the St. Andrews courses are fully owned by the municipality and open to the public on a more or less democratic basis—ballots are polled 1 day in advance. This balloting system might be circumvented for players who reserve with the appropriate starters several days or weeks in advance. To play the hallowed Old Course, you must present a current handicap certificate and/or letter of introduction from a bona-fide golf club.

The misty and verdant golf courses are the very symbol of St. Andrews: the famous **Old Course;** the 6,010m (6,604-yard), par-72 **New Course** (opened in 1896); the 6,193m (6,805-yard), par-71 **Jubilee Course** (opened in 1897 in honor of Queen Victoria); the 5,562m (6,112-yard), par-70 **Eden** (opened in 1914); the **Balgove** (a 9-hole course for children's golf training, opened in 1972), and the 4,636m (5,094-yard), par-67 **Strathtyrum** (the newest and most far-flung, an 8-hole course opened in 1993). Encircled by all of them is the world's most prestigious golf club, the **Royal and Ancient Golf Club** (© **01334/ 472112**), founded in St. Andrews in 1754—it remains more or less rigidly closed as a private-membership men's club. The Royal and Ancient traditionally opens its doors to the public only on St. Andrews Day to view its legendary trophy room. This usually, but not always, falls around November 30.

The **Old Course,** Pilmour Cottage (© **01334/466666**), is the world's most legendary temple of golf, one whose difficulty is shaped by nature and the long-ago paths of grazing sheep. Over the centuries, stately buildings have been erected near its start and finish. Aristocrats from virtually everywhere have lent their names and reputations to enhance its glamour, and its nuances have been debated, usually in reverent tones, by golfers in bars and on fairways throughout the world. This fabled par-72 course hosted the 2000 British Open, when golf fans from around the world watched in awe as Tiger Woods became the youngest golfer in history to complete a grand slam (and only the 5th golfer ever to perform the feat). Greens fees are £105 ($168), a caddy costs £38 ($61) plus tip, and clubs rent for £20–£30 ($32–$48) per round. There are no electric carts allowed, and you can rent a trolley on afternoons only between May and September for £3 ($4.80).

Facilities for golfers in St. Andrews are legion—virtually every hotel in town maintains some kind of facility to assist golfers. The most interesting clubhouse in town is **The Links Clubhouse,** West Sand Road (© **01334/466666**). Owned and operated by the St. Andrews Links Trust, and located within 365m (1,200 ft.) of the Old Course's 18th hole, it offers, without charge, lockers, showers, and changing facilities. You can lock up your gear for a day without charge, since lockers are operated with £1 ($1.60) coins, which are refunded when you surrender your key at the end of the day. On-site, there's also a bar and restaurant.

For more details on golf associations and golf tours, see "Special Interest Trips" in chapter 3, "Planning Your Trip to Great Britain."

SEEING THE SIGHTS

Founded in 1411, the **University of St. Andrews** is the oldest in Scotland and the third oldest in Britain and has been called the "Oxbridge" of Scotland. At term time, you can see packs of students in their characteristic red gowns. The university grounds stretch west of the St. Andrews Castle between North Street and the Scores.

The university's most interesting buildings are the tower and church of St. Salvator's College and the courtyard of St. Mary's College, from 1538. An ancient thorn tree, said to have been planted by Mary Queen of Scots, stands near the college's chapel. St. Leonard's College church is also from medieval days. In 1645, the Scottish Parliament met in what was once the University Library and is now a students' reading room. A modern University Library, containing many rare ancient volumes, was opened in 1976.

Castle of St. Andrews ⭐   This ruined 13th-century castle eerily poised at the edge of the sea boasts a bottle dungeon and secret passages. Founded in the early part of the 13th century, it was reconstructed several times and was once a bishop's palace and later a prison for reformers. The bottle dungeon is carved 7m (24 ft.) down into the rock, and both prisoners and food were dropped through it. There's said to be no nastier dungeon in all of Scotland.

Much of the eeriness here concerns the 1546 arrest of religious reformer George Wishart and the show trial that followed. Convicted by a group of Catholic prelates spearheaded by Cardinal Beaton, Wishart was burned at the stake, reputedly while Beaton and his entourage watched from an upper-floor window. Vowing revenge, a group of reformers waited 3 months before gaining access to the castle while disguised as stonemasons. They overpowered the guards (some they killed, some they threw into the castle's moat) and murdered Beaton—and, rather bizarrely, preserved his corpse in salt so they could eventually give it a proper burial. The reformers retained control of the castle for several months, until the Catholic forces of the earl of Arran laid siege. As part of their efforts, the attackers almost completed a tunnel (they called it "a mine"), dug virtually through rock, beneath the castle walls. The (Protestant) defenders, in response, dug a tunnel ("a countermine") of their own, which intersected the first tunnel at a higher elevation, allowing the defenders to drop rocks, boiling oil, or whatever else on the attackers' heads. The resulting underground battle took on epic proportions during the virtually implacable yearlong siege. As part of the tour, you can stumble down the narrow countermine to the place where besieged and besiegers met in this clash.

The Scores (273m/900 ft. northwest of the cathedral). 📞 01334/477196. Admission £3 ($4.80) adults, £2.50 ($4) seniors, £1 ($1.60) children. Combined tickets (castle and cathedral) £4 ($6.40) adults, £3 ($4.80) seniors, £1.25 ($2) children. Apr–Sept daily 9:30am–6:30pm; Oct–Mar daily 9:30am–4:30pm. Last admission 30 min. before closing time.

Holy Trinity Church   Called the Town Kirk, this restored medieval church once stood on the grounds of the now-ruined cathedral (see below). The church was moved to its present site in 1410, considerably altered after the Reformation of 1560, and restored in the early 20th century. You'll find much fine stained glass and carvings inside.

Opposite St. Mary's College, off South St. 📞 01334/474494. Free admission, but call in advance to make sure someone is in attendance. Sat 10am–noon.

Secret Bunker ⭐   Scotland's best-kept secret for 40 years of cold war, this amazing labyrinth, built 30m (100 ft.) below ground and encased in 4½m (15 ft.) of reinforced concrete, is where central government and military commanders would have run the country from if the United Kingdom had been attacked and nuclear war broken out. Built in great secrecy in 1951 to withstand aerial attack, it has a guardhouse entrance designed to look like a traditional Scottish farmhouse. You can visit the BBC studio where emergency broadcasts would have been made and the switchboard room set up to handle 2,800 outside lines. The bunker could allow 300 people to live, work, and sleep in safety while coordinating war efforts, like aboveground retaliation. It also contains two cinemas showing authentic cold war films, an audiovisual theater, a cafe, and a gift shop.

You can wander at will through the underground labyrinth. For some amazing reason, the chapel here has been the site of several local weddings since its decommissioning in 1993.

Underground Nuclear Command Centre, Crown Buildings (near St. Andrews), Fife. (C) 01333/310301. Admission £7.20 ($12) adults, £5.95 ($9.50) seniors, £4.50 ($7.20) children ages 5–16, £22 ($35) families, free for children ages 4 and under. Apr–Oct daily 10am–5pm. From St. Andrews, follow the signs to Anstruther, driving 12km (7½ miles) south. At that point, signs show the way to the bunker.

St. Andrews Cathedral and Priory ✰   Near the Celtic settlement of St. Mary of the Rock, by the sea at the east end of town, is the semi-ruin of St. Andrews Cathedral and Priory. It was founded in 1160 and begun in the Romanesque style; however, the cathedral's construction suffered many setbacks. By the time of its consecration in 1318 in the presence of King Robert the Bruce, it had a Gothic overlay. At the time the largest church in Scotland, the cathedral established St. Andrews as the ecclesiastical capital of the country, but today the ruins can only suggest its former beauty and importance. There's a collection of early Christian and medieval monuments, as well as artifacts discovered on the cathedral site.

Off Pends Rd. (C) 01334/472563. Admission £2 ($3.20) adults, £1.50 ($2.40) seniors, £75 ($1.20) children ages 5–15. Apr–Sept daily 9:30am–5pm; Oct–Mar Mon–Sat 9:30am–4pm, Sun 2–4pm.

SHOPPING

Specializing in Scottish art, **St. Andrews Fine Arts,** 84A Market St. (© **01334/ 474080**), also sells prints, drawings, and watercolors. Paintings for sale were all produced in the national boundaries of Scotland sometime between 1800 and the present. **Renton Oriental Rugs,** 72 South St. (© **01334/476334**), is one of Scotland's leading dealers of Oriental carpets, whether you're seeking antique rugs or reasonably priced reproductions. Rugs range from handmade to machine made and come in many sizes, prices, and styles. At **St. Andrews Pottery Shop,** 4 Church Square (© **01334/477744**), an array of decorative stoneware, ceramics, and enameled jewelry—most of it produced locally—is for sale. **Bonkers,** 80 Market St. (© **01334/473919**), is a typical tourist shop, hawking T-shirts, regional pottery, and other souvenirs, along with cards and stationery.

WHERE TO STAY
VERY EXPENSIVE

Rufflets Country House Hotel ✰   The garden-and-golf crowd loves this cozy 1924 country house set amidst a 10-acre garden. Each good-sized guest room is furnished in a homelike way (often in Queen Anne style), some with canopied or four-poster beds and some with Jacuzzi tubs in the bathrooms. The most modern rooms are in the new wing, but traditionalists request space in the handsome main building. Accommodations specially designed for families and for wheelchair-bound guests are available. Special extras in all the rooms include bathrobes, upscale toiletries, and teddy bears on the beds. Reserve well in advance—Rufflets is very popular with British vacationers.

Even if you aren't staying here, you may want to reserve a table at the garden-style Rufflets Hotel Restaurant, overlooking the award-winning garden. Excellent fresh ingredients are used in the continental and Scottish dishes.

Strathkinness Low Rd., St. Andrews, Fife KY16 9TX. © **01334/472594.** Fax 01334/478703. www.rufflets. co.uk. 22 units. £170–£230 ($272–$368) double. Rates include Scottish breakfast. AE, DC, MC, V. Take B939 2.5km (1½ miles) from St. Andrews. **Amenities:** Restaurant; bar; limited room service; babysitting; laundry service; dry cleaning. *In room:* TV, dataport, coffeemaker, hair dryer, trouser press.

The Rusacks   A grand Victorian pile built in 1887 by Josef Rusack, a German from Silesia who recognized St. Andrews's potential as a golf capital, The Rusacks sits at the edge of the famous 18th hole of Pilmour Links of the Old Course. The hotel's stone walls are capped with neoclassical gables and slate roofs. Inside, chintz picks up the tones from the bouquets of flowers sent in fresh twice a week. Between the panels and Ionic columns of the public rooms, racks of lendable books re-create the atmosphere of a private country-house library. Upstairs, the spacious guest rooms are themed around some of the world's most famous golfers, tournaments, and course hazards (such as the Valley of Sin room). All contain some carved antiques and modern conveniences, but are nothing to equal the St. Andrews Old Course Hotel (see below). Each unit comes with a beautifully maintained private bathroom.

The basement Golf Club has golf-related photos, *trompe-l'oeil* racks of books, Chesterfield sofas, and vested waiters. Here light meals and snacks are served. The Old Course restaurant, overlooking the 18th hole, offers daily specials along with local game, meat, and fish, accompanied by wine from a well-stocked cellar.

Pilmour Links, St. Andrews, Fife KY16 9JQ. © **800/225-5843** in the U.S., or 01334/474321. Fax 01334/ 477896. www.macdonaldhotels.co.uk. 68 units. £110–£189 ($176–$302) double; from £220 ($352) suite. AE, DC, MC, V. **Amenities:** Restaurant; bar; 24-hr. room service; laundry service. *In room:* TV, coffeemaker, hair dryer, safe (in some), trouser press.

St. Andrews Golf Hotel ✸   A combination of greenery, sea mists, and tradition makes this late-Victorian property extremely popular with golfers, despite the fact that many of them confuse it at first glance with the larger and more prestigious St. Andrews Old Course Hotel (see below). About 182m (600 ft.) from the first tee-off of the famous golf course, it was built as a private home and later expanded and transformed into a hotel run by Brian and Maureen Hughes. The comfortable but unstylish midsize guest rooms are individually decorated; some have four-poster beds and others boast sea views. The rooms in the front get the view but also the noise.

Bar lunches are served Monday through Saturday, and table d'hôte dinners are presented nightly in an oak-paneled restaurant with a fireplace.

40 The Scores, St. Andrews, Fife KY16 9AS. © **01334/472611.** Fax 01334/472188. www.standrews-golf. co.uk. 22 units. £160–£200 ($256–$320) double; from £200–£600 ($320–$960) suite. Rates include Scottish breakfast. AE, DC, MC, V. **Amenities:** Restaurant; 2 bars; 24-hr. room service; laundry service; dry cleaning. *In room:* TV, coffeemaker, hair dryer, safe (in some), trouser press.

St. Andrews Old Course Hotel ✸✸✸   Many dedicated golfers choose the St. Andrews Old Course Hotel, close to A91 on the outskirts of town, where it overlooks the 17th fairway, the Road Hole of the Old Course. (Don't let the name mislead you: The hotel isn't related to the links of the same name, and guests here find access to the course just as difficult as it is elsewhere.) Fortified by *finnan haddie* (smoked haddock) and porridge, a real old-fashioned Scottish breakfast, you can face that diabolical stretch of greenery where the Scots have been whacking away since the early 15th century. Some £16 million ($27.2 million) has been spent to transform the place into a world-class hotel (with price tags to match), and the facade was altered to keep it in line with St. Andrews's more traditional buildings; its balconies afford top-view seats at all golf tournaments. The guest rooms and suites have been remodeled and refurbished, offering traditional wooden furniture and state-of-the-art marble bathrooms.

Well-prepared and high-priced international cuisine is served in the Road Hole Grill. In summer, light meals and afternoon tea are served in a casual dining room known as Sands.

Old Station Rd., St. Andrews, Fife KY16 9SP. ℂ 01334/474371. Fax 01334/477668. www.oldcourse hotel.co.uk. 146 units. £225–£375 ($360–$600) double; from £295–£445 ($472–$712) junior suite. Rates include Scottish breakfast. Children under 12 stay free in parent's room. AE, DC, MC, V. **Amenities:** 3 restaurants; 4 bars; indoor pool; health club; spa; whirlpool; steam rooms; 24-hr. room service; babysitting; laundry service; pro shop. *In room:* TV, minibar, coffeemaker, hair dryer, safe (in some).

EXPENSIVE

Peat Inn ☕☕   About 11km (7 miles) from St. Andrews, in the village of Cupar, the Peat is in an inn/post office built in 1760, where beautifully furnished guest rooms and spacious suites are offered, and David Wilson prepares exceptional cuisine in the restaurant. All units are suites that have separate bedrooms and living areas. Most rooms come with shower; some also have a tub. The high-priced restaurant offers local ingredients—even the pigeons come from a St. Andrews farm—and serves lunch and dinner Tuesday through Saturday.

Cupar, Fife KY15 5LH. ℂ 01334/840206. Fax 01334/840530. www.thepeatinn.co.uk/ourhome.htm. 8 units. £145–£155 ($232–$248) suite for 2. Rates include continental breakfast. AE, MC, V. From St. Andrews, drive 11km (7 miles) southwest along A915, then branch onto B940. **Amenities:** Restaurant; bar; limited room service. *In room:* TV, hair dryer (in some).

MODERATE

Inn at Lathones ☕   Once a coaching inn, this 200-year-old manor was thoughtfully restored and provides a reasonable alternative for golfers who can't afford the grand hotels. All of its midsize guest rooms are nicely furnished, with individually controlled heating, and bathrooms with power showers in the bathtubs. Two units have log-burning stoves and Jacuzzis with separate showers. The public rooms reflect Scottish tradition, with open fires and beamed ceilings.

The more formal restaurant is under the guidance of chef Marc Guiburt, who has created a French-inspired continental cuisine using fresh Scottish produce.

By Largoward, St. Andrews, Fife KY9 1JE. ℂ 01334/840494. Fax 01334/840694. www.theinn.co.uk. 14 units. £90–£160 ($144–$256) double. Rates include Scottish breakfast. MC, V. Take A915, 8km (5 miles) southwest of the center of St. Andrews. **Amenities:** Restaurant; bar; limited room service; laundry service. *In room:* TV, coffeemaker, hair dryer.

Russell Hotel   Once a 19th-century private home, the Russell enjoys an ideal location overlooking St. Andrews Bay, a 2-minute walk from the Old Course's first tee. It's well run by Gordon and Fiona de Vries and offers fully equipped though standard guest rooms with tub-only bathrooms (showers in some). Some of the rooms offer sea views. The cozy Victorian pub serves drinks and bar suppers to a loyal local crowd, and the rather unremarkable restaurant offers moderately priced fixed-price dinners nightly.

26 The Scores, St. Andrews, Fife KY16 9AS. ℂ 01334/473447. Fax 01334/478279. www.russellhotelst andrews.co.uk. 11 units. £80–£110 ($128–$176) double. Rates include Scottish breakfast. Children under 12 stay free in parent's room. AE, MC, V. Closed Dec 24–Jan 12. **Amenities:** Restaurant; bar; laundry service. *In room:* TV, coffeemaker, hair dryer.

INEXPENSIVE

Ashleigh House Hotel   This B&B is near the town center built in 1883 as a fever hospital to quarantine patients afflicted with scarlet fever, diphtheria, and other plagues of the day. After World War I, it was transformed into an orphanage and in the late 1980s was converted to a B&B. The trio of thick-walled stone cottages are connected by means of covered passageways. There's a bar with a wide assortment of single malts and a rough-and-ready kind of charm. The guest rooms are outfitted with good beds and flowered upholstery and almost all provide tub or shower bathrooms. One simply furnished bedroom doesn't have a private bathroom; the occupant must use a perfectly adequate corridor bathroom.

37 St. Mary St., St. Andrews, Fife KY16 8AZ. © **01334/475429.** Fax 01334/474383. www.s-h-systems.co.uk/
hotels/ashleigh.html. 10 units, 9 with private bathroom. £50–£70 ($80–$112) double without bathroom,
£60–£110 ($96–$176) double with bathroom. Rates include breakfast. MC, V. **Amenities:** Restaurant; bar;
sauna; solarium. *In room:* TV, coffeemaker, hair dryer.

Bell Craig Guest House   Occupying a century-old stone-fronted house, this B&B is in a historic neighborhood, a 3-minute walk from the Old Course. This guest house has had long practice at housing the parents of students at the nearby university. Sheila Black, the hardworking owner, operates her establishment with decency and pride and makes a point to spruce up each room in a different style at regular intervals. (Our favorite is the one done in tartan.) Each is high-ceilinged, cozy, completely unpretentious, and well scrubbed. Most units contain a shower and tub; two are fitted with a tub only.

8 Murray Park, St. Andrews, Fife KY16. © **01334/472962.** www.bellcraig.co.uk. 6 units. £40–£60 ($64–$96)
double. Rates include breakfast. MC, V. *In room:* TV, coffeemaker, hair dryer.

WHERE TO DINE

Balaka BANGELADESHI/INTERNATIONAL   In the heart of St. Andrews, this Indian and international restaurant has won a number of local culinary awards for its savory cuisine which has done much to wake up the taste buds of the local populace. This restaurant is also a celeb favorite, drawing such luminaries as Sean Connery (Scotland's favorite son), Arnold Palmer, and even the king and queen of Malaysia. Behind a facade of gray Scottish stone, the restaurant lies in a 1-acre garden that is planted with vegetables, flowers, and herbs, each used by the kitchen staff. The Rouf family is exceptionally hospitable and will explain menu items to you as you sit at crisp white tablecloths, smelling the perfumed roses on your table. Mr. Rouf, the owner of the restaurant, is also a keen gardener. Sometimes customers take home a fresh bouquet of coriander from the garden. Not only coriander, but fresh spinach, spring onions, and mint, and other fine ingredients, figure into many of the recipes. Start, perhaps, with samosa, spicy ground beef or a vegetable pastry and follow with such delights as green herb chicken with spring onions, garlic, and freshly chopped coriander with tomato. *Mafbangla* is another justifiably local favorite—Scottish filet of salmon marinated in lime juice and flavored with tumeric, green chile, and other spices.

Alexandra Place. © 01333/474825. Reservations recommended. 2-course lunch £6.95 ($11). Main courses
£7.65–£9.55 ($12–$15). AE, MC, V. Mon-Sat noon-3pm and 5pm-1am.

Grange Inn SCOTTISH/SEAFOOD   An old-fashioned hospitality prevails in this country cottage with its garden, offering a good choice of dishes made from fresh produce. Local beef and lamb always appear on the menu, as do fish and shellfish from the fishing villages of East Neuk. Fruits and herbs come from Cupar. Typical of the dishes served are beef filet with port sauce complemented by wild mushrooms or chicken suprême stuffed with julienne of vegetables and coated with almonds, then served on lemon sauce. A classic opener and an old favorite at the inn is a stew of mussels and onions.

Grange Rd., at Grange (on B959). (© 01334/472670. Reservations recommended. Fixed-price dinner £24 ($38). DC, MC, V. Daily 12:30–2pm and 7–8:45pm. Drive about 2.5km (1½ miles) from St. Andrews on B959.

Ostlers Close ✴ BRITISH/INTERNATIONAL   Sophisticated and intensely concerned with the quality of its cuisine, this charming restaurant occupies a 17th-century building that functioned in the early 20th century as a temperance hotel. Today, in the heart of the hamlet of Cupar, 11km (7 miles) from St. Andrews, it contains a kitchen in what used to be the hotel's stables, with a severely elegant set of dining rooms in the hotel's former public areas. Amanda Graham, co-owner and supervisor of the dining room, is the person you're most likely to meet here, along with a staff serving the cuisine of her husband, Jimmy Graham. Menu items are based on seasonal Scottish produce and are likely to include roasted saddle of roe venison with wild mushroom sauce; a fresh medley of seafood with champagne-flavored butter sauce; and filet of Scottish lamb stuffed with *skirlie*, an old-fashioned but flavorful combination of bacon-flavored oatmeal and herbs. Whenever it's available, opt for the confit of duckling with salted pork and lentils.

25 Bonnygate, in the nearby town of Cupar. (© 01334/655574. Reservations recommended. Main courses £9.50–£14 ($15–$22) at lunch, £16–£19 ($26–$30) at dinner. AE, MC, V. Tues–Sat 7-9:30pm; Sat 12:15-1:30pm. Closed 2 weeks in Apr. From St. Andrews, go along A91 for 11km (7 miles) to the southwest until you reach the village of Cupar.

ST. ANDREWS AFTER DARK

The cultural center of St. Andrews is the **Byre Theatre,** Abbey Street ((© **01334/ 476288**), which features drama ranging from Shakespeare plays to musical comedies. Tickets cost £6 to £14 ($9.60–$22) adults, £5 to £9 ($8–$14) children. Pick up a weekly version of *What's on in Fife* from the local tourist office to find out what's featured.

Victoria, 1A St. Mary's Place ((© **01334/476964**), is the place to catch a live band in St. Andrews. This student-filled pub features folk, rock, and blues acts occasionally, as well as karaoke every Friday. Because of the absence of students over the summer, there's no live music. John Smiths, Beamish Stout, McEwans Lager, 78 Shilling, and 80 Shilling are available on tap. Open Tuesday to Saturday from 10am to 1am; Sunday 11am to midnight; and Monday 10am to midnight.

A pub since 1904, the **Central Bar,** at the corner of Market and College Street ((© **01334/478296**), is an antiquated room with a jukebox, and it may become rowdy during a football or tennis match. The best brews here are Old Peculiar, Theakstons XB, and McEwans Lager. Open Monday through Saturday from 11:30am to 1am.

Chariots, The Scores ((© **01334/472451**), in the Scores Hotel, attracts mainly a local crowd, ranging from 30 to 60 years, who gather in the evening for conversation over a pint. Despite a strong regional tradition of beer brewing, two outsiders, Guinness and Millers, are featured on tap. Open daily from 5pm to midnight.

4 Stirling ✴ ✴

60km (37 miles) NW of Edinburgh; 45km (28 miles) NE of Glasgow

Stirling is dominated by its impressive castle, perched on a 76m (250-ft.) basalt rock formed by the Rivers Forth and Clyde and the relatively small parcel of land

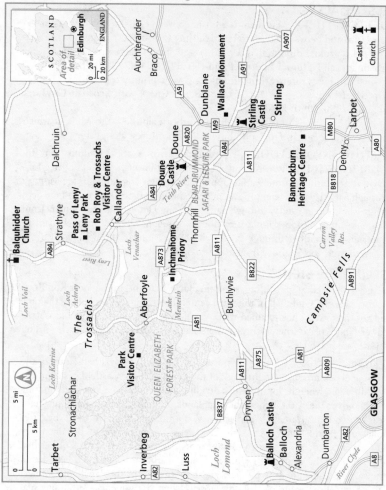

between them. The ancient town of Stirling, on the main east–west route across Scotland, grew up around the castle. It lies in the heart of an area so turbulent in Scottish history it was called the "cockpit of Scotland" (here cockpit refers to the pit where male chickens would be forced to engage in cockfights). A memorable battle fought here was the Battle of Bannockburn in 1314, when Robert I (the Bruce) defeated the army of Edward II of England and gained Scotland its independence.

Ever since the release of Mel Gibson's movie *Braveheart,* world attention has focused on the Scottish national hero William Wallace, a freedom fighter who became known as the "hammer and scourge" of the English. However, *Braveheart* was filmed mostly in Ireland, and the Battle of Stirling Bridge in the movie was played out on a plain with not a bridge in sight.

Stirling is the central crossroads of Scotland, giving easy access by rail and road to all its major towns and cities. If you use it as a base, you'll be only a short distance from many attractions, including Loch Lomond, the Trossachs, and the Highlands.

ESSENTIALS

GETTING THERE   Frequent trains run between Glasgow and Stirling (a 45-min. trip) and between Edinburgh and Stirling (a 60-min. trip). A 1-day round-trip ticket from Edinburgh is £9 ($14) and from Glasgow is £8 ($13). For schedules, call **National Express Enquiries** at ✆ **0845/748-4950.**

Frequent buses run to Stirling from Glasgow (a 40-min. trip). A 1-day round-trip ticket from Glasgow costs £5.30 ($8.50). Check with **Scottish CityLink** (✆ 0870/550-5050) for details.

If you're driving from Glasgow, head northeast along A80 to M80, at which point continue north. From Edinburgh, head northwest along M9.

VISITOR INFORMATION   The **tourist office** is at 41 Dumbarton Rd. (✆ 01786/475019; www.visitscotland.com). April through May, it's open Monday through Saturday from 9am to 5pm; June through August, hours are Monday through Saturday from 9am to 7:30pm and Sunday from 9:30am to 6:30pm; September hours are Monday through Saturday from 9am to 6pm and Sunday from 10am to 5pm; October hours are Monday through Saturday from 9:30am to 5pm; and November through March, it's open Monday through Friday from 10am to 5pm and Saturday from 10am to 4pm.

SEEING THE SIGHTS

To get a real feeling for Stirling, stroll the **Back Walk,** beginning near Rob Roy's statue, near the Guildhall in the town center. Following this trail along the outside of the town's once-fortified walls, you'll find good views, see an old watch-tower (and a place where prisoners were hanged), and eventually reach Stirling Castle (see below).

Stirling Castle ✪✪   There are traces of a 7th-century royal habitation of the Stirling area, and on the right bank of the Forth, Stirling Castle dates from the Middle Ages, when its location on a dividing line between the Lowlands and the Highlands made it the key to the Highlands. The castle became an important seat of two kings, James IV and James V, both of whom added to it, the latter following classic Renaissance style, then relatively unknown in Britain. Mary Queen of Scots lived here as an infant monarch for the first 4 years of her life. After its final defeat in 1746, Bonnie Prince Charlie's army stopped here. Later, the castle became an army barracks and headquarters of the Argyll and Sutherland Highlanders, one of Britain's most celebrated regiments. An audiovisual presentation explains what you're about to see.

In the castle is the **Museum of the Argyll and Sutherland Highlanders** (✆ 01786/475165), presenting an excellent exhibit of colors, pipe banners, and regimental silver, along with medals (some of which go back to the Battle of Waterloo) won by Scottish soldiers for valor. Run by Britain's Ministry of Defense, it functions as a showcase for a military unit.

Upper Castle Hill. ✆ 01786/450000. Admission to castle £7.50 ($12) adults, £5.50 ($8.80) seniors, £2 ($3.20) children ages 6–15, free for children ages 5 and under; free admission to museum. Castle Apr–Sept daily 9:30am–6pm; Oct–Mar daily 9:30am–5pm. Last entry to castle 45 min. before closing time. Museum Mar–Sept Mon–Sat 10am–5:45pm, Sun 11am–4:45pm; Oct–Feb daily 10am–4:15pm.

Church of the Holy Rude ✪   From the early 15th century, the Church of the Holy Rude is said to be the only church in Scotland still in use that has witnessed a coronation. It was 1567 when the 13-month-old James VI—Mary Queen of Scots' son, who eventually became James I of England—was crowned here. John Knox preached the sermon. Constructed with the simplest of building tools more than 600 years ago and built as a reminder of the cross (rude) on which Christ was supposedly crucified, the church is memorable for its rough but evocative stonework and its elaborate 19th-century stained glass—particularly on the south side of the choir. Recent restorations have been carried out in the most tasteful and unobtrusive of styles.

St. John St. ✆ **01786/475275.** Free admission. Mid-Apr to Sept daily 10am–5pm. Closed Oct to mid-Apr.

SHOPPING

Stirling's town center has some interesting shopping. One good hunting ground is the **Thistle Centre** indoor shopping plaza, home of about 65 shops at the junction of Port Street and Murray Place.

The best woolen gift goods are at **R. R. Henderson,** 6–8 Friar St. (✆ **01786/ 473681**), a Highland outfitter selling not only woolen goods like sweaters and scarves but also made-to-order kilts and tartans.

Some of the best shopping is not in Stirling itself but in the outlying area. Take A9 to Larbert and at the roundabout follow A18 west until you see the sign for **Barbara Davidson's Pottery Studio,** Muirhall Farm, at Larbert (✆ **01324/ 554430**), 15km (9 miles) south of Stirling. At this 18th-century farmstead, Barbara Davidson operates a studio and workshop. She's one of Scotland's best-known potters, and a large selection of her functional wares is exhibited and sold here.

East of Stirling, three towns form the **Mill Trail Country:** Alva, Alloa, and Tillicoultry. Many quality textile mills have factory outlets here, offering bargain prices on cotton, woolens, and even cashmere goods. The best selection of sweaters is available in many designs at **Inverallen Handknitters Ltd.,** Alva Industrial Estate, Alva (✆ **01259/762292**). If you're inspired to knit your own creation, head to **Coats Crafts,** Lingsied House, County Durhem (✆ **01325/ 394394**), which manufactures quality hand-knitting and craft yarns.

For more complete details, including any directional information, seasonal closings, or whatever, call or visit the **Mill Trail Visitor Centre,** West Stirling Street at Alva (✆ **01259/769696**), 15km (9 miles) east of the center of Stirling. January through June and September through December, it's open daily from 10am to 5pm; July through August, it's open daily from 9am to 5pm.

WHERE TO STAY
EXPENSIVE

Stirling Highland Hotel ✦   This is Stirling's best hotel. The stylish Highland was installed, after major renovations, in what was once the Old High School, a Victorian building to which everyone in town has an emotional link. The historic atmosphere was treated with respect, and many of the architectural features were kept. Florals, tartans, and solid wood furnishings dominate the public rooms and the guest rooms; the guest rooms, fairly routine, are in a three-story annex. Each unit comes with a shower, and a few are also equipped with tubs. From its position close to Stirling Castle, the hotel enjoys views over the town and surrounding region.

Rather high-priced Scottish cuisine is featured in Scholars Restaurant, and Rizzio's Restaurant serves Italian cuisine.

Spittal St., Stirling, Stirlingshire FK8 1DU. ✆ **01786/272727.** Fax 01786/272829. www.paramount-hotels. co.uk. 96 units. £150–£160 ($240–$256) double. AE, DC, MC, V. **Amenities:** Restaurant; indoor pool; squash courts; gym; Jacuzzi; steam room; solarium; 24-hr. room service; babysitting; laundry service. *In room:* TV, coffeemaker, hair dryer, trouser press.

MODERATE

Golden Lion Hotel About a block downhill from Holyrood Church, the Golden Lion dates back to 1786, when it was a coaching inn, but its sandstone shell was greatly enlarged with the addition of modern wings in 1962. It's now one of the oldest and largest hotels in town and has recently improved and modernized most of its guest rooms. The rooms are simple and easy on the eye, and bathrooms are equipped with either tub or shower.

8–10 King St., Stirling, Stirlingshire FK8 2ND. © **01786/475351.** Fax 01786/472755. www.miltonhotels.com. 67 units. £80–£110 ($128–$176) double. Rates include Scottish breakfast. AE, DC, MC, V. **Amenities:** Restaurant; bar; limited room service; laundry service; dry cleaning. *In room:* TV, coffeemaker, hair dryer, trouser press (in some).

Park Lodge Hotel ✦ This stylish hotel occupies a 19th-century Italianate mansion, across from a city park in a residential neighborhood. Built of stone blocks and slates, it has a Doric portico, Tudor-style chimney pots, a Georgian-era core from 1825, and century-old climbing roses and wisteria. Anne and Georges Marquetty house guests in 10 upstairs rooms and suggest they dine at their elegant restaurant, The Heritage (see below), a 10-minute walk away. Each room contains antique furnishings (no. 6 has a four-poster bed) as well as tub-and-shower combination. You might enjoy tea in a walled garden behind the hotel, with its widely spaced iron benches and terra-cotta statues.

32 Park Terrace, Stirling, Stirlingshire FK8 2JS. © **01786/474862.** Fax 01786/449748. www.parklodge.net. 10 units. £85–£105 ($136–$168) double. Rates include Scottish breakfast. AE, MC, V. Bus: 51 or 52. **Amenities:** Restaurant; bar; room service. *In room:* TV, coffeemaker, hair dryer, trouser press (in some).

Terraces Hotel (Value) Built as a fine Georgian house of sandstone, this hotel stands on a raised terrace in a quiet residential neighborhood. It's one of the best values in town. Each midsize guest room is furnished in a country-house motif of flowered curtains and solidly traditional furniture, with a shower bathroom (some with tubs). One room has a lovely carved four-poster bed. The half-paneled cocktail bar and velvet-upholstered restaurant are popular settings for local parties and wedding receptions. Melville's Restaurant offers both a moderately priced Scottish and a continental menu.

4 Melville Terrace, Stirling, Stirlingshire FK8 2ND. © **01786/472268.** Fax 01786/450314. www.s-h-systems. co.uk/hotels/terraces.html. 17 units. £90 ($144) double. Rates include Scottish breakfast. AE, DC, MC, V. **Amenities:** Restaurant; bar; limited room service; laundry service. *In room:* TV, coffeemaker, hair dryer, trouser press (in some).

INEXPENSIVE

West Plean House ✦ (Value) This working farm is a delight. It not only has a lovely walled garden but also is a great base for taking walks into the surrounding woodland. Your hosts are welcoming and helpful, and they offer extremely good value. Their guest rooms are spacious and well furnished, with an eye to comfort and conveniences, and each is equipped with a shower-only bathroom. Their home-cooked breakfast makes this place a winner.

Denny Rd. (6km/3½ miles from Stirling on A872), Stirling FK7 8HA. © **01786/812208.** Fax 01786/480550. westplean@virgin.net. 3 units. £50–£55 ($80–$88) double. Rates include breakfast. No credit cards. Closed 2 weeks in late Dec. *In room:* TV, coffeemaker, no phone.

WHERE TO DINE

The Heritage ✦ FRENCH/SCOTTISH Culinary sophistication and beautiful decor mark this as one of the best restaurants in the district. Near the center of town, a 5-minute walk east of the rail station, it's on a quiet residential street.

You enter a gentleman's parlor, with somber walls and enviable antiques, to have a drink before descending to the low-ceilinged basement. Amid a French-inspired decor, you'll taste some of the best cuisine in town, prepared with finesse by Georges Marquetty (owner of the Park Lodge Hotel). In his youth he worked as an executive chef in Paris and later spent 12 years in Cincinnati with his British wife, Anne (where he was voted one of the leading chefs of America). His specialties include scallops, scampi and prawns in Pernod sauce; filet of wild venison with port and black-currant sauce; and foie gras with truffles.

Upstairs, nine handsomely furnished doubles, each with a bathroom, TV, and phone, rent for £85 ($136), breakfast included.

At the Park Lodge Hotel. 32 Park Terrace, Stirling, Stirlingshire FK8 2QC. ℰ 01786/473660. Fax 01786/449748. Reservations recommended. Main courses £10–£16 ($16–$26); fixed-price 2-course lunch £10 ($16); fixed-price 3-course dinner £23 ($36). MC, V. Daily noon–2pm and 6:30–9:30pm. Closed Sun in winter.

Hermann's Brasserie AUSTRIAN/SCOTTISH   A reliable favorite, this is an old and traditional town house with high beamed ceilings, pine tables and chairs, and tartan carpeting. Part of the restaurant opens onto a conservatory. You get not only tried-and-true platters of Scottish food here, but a touch of Vienna as well, especially in the golden-brown Wiener schnitzel, served with salad and sautéed potatoes. Scottish Highland venison is a regular feature; the plate here is attractively adorned with a whisky cream sauce. You might start your meal with the most typical of Scottish soups: *Cullen skink,* made with smoked fish and potatoes. Our forever favorite is the fast seared filet of salmon served with a savory sauce laced with pink peppercorns.

58 Broad St. ℰ 01786/450632. Reservations recommended. Main courses £12–£17 ($19–$27). AE, MC, V. Daily noon–2:30pm and 6–9:30pm.

STIRLING AFTER DARK

On the campus of Stirling University, the **Macrobert Arts Centre** (ℰ 01786/466666) offers plays, music, films, and art exhibits. The 497-seat main theater often presents dramas and symphony concerts, and the 140-seat studio theater is used mainly for films. Cinema tickets cost £4 ($6.40) adults and £3 ($4.80) seniors/children, and theater tickets generally run £7–£10 ($11–$16). Admission to most concerts is £10–£13 ($16–$21). Call for current listings.

All that Jazz, 9 Upper Craigs (ℰ 01786/451130), is a lively bar popular with students. Music is usually provided via the stereo, but bands also appear infrequently. The bar serves a good range of single malts and pints of Kronenberg, Beamish Red, and McEwans. The adjoining restaurant serves a mix of Cajun and traditional Scottish fare, including haggis, between 5 and 10pm every evening. The same menu is available throughout the day in the bar, which is open from 11am to midnight; Friday and Saturday from 11am to 1am.

O'Neill's, 11 Maxwell Place (ℰ 01786/459901), is a traditional Irish pub popular with Scottish students. Irish and Scottish folk bands play. To find out who's playing, check the flyers posted in the pub. There's never a cover. Open Sunday through Thursday from noon to midnight and Friday and Saturday from 11am to 1am.

Barnton Bar/Bistro, 3 Barnton St. (ℰ 01786/461698), is an Art Nouveau–style bar with marble-topped tables and high ceilings edged with ornate cornices. It's the center of gay life in Stirling but draws a mixed crowd of students, professionals, and old-timers as well. The Wednesday Quiz Night, where drinkers compete in general-knowledge trivia, is quite popular. There's no cover.

5 Dunblane & Its Grand Cathedral ⍟

11km (7 miles) N of Stirling; 68km (42 miles) NW of Edinburgh; 47km (29 miles) SW of Perth; 53km (33 miles) NE of Glasgow

A small cathedral city on the banks of the Allan Water, Dunblane takes its name from the Celtic Church of St. Blane, which once stood on the site now occupied by the fine 13th-century Gothic cathedral. The cathedral is the main reason to visit; if that doesn't interest you, you'll find more romantic and lovelier places from which to explore the nearby Trossachs and Loch Lomond (say, Callander or Aberfoyle).

ESSENTIALS

GETTING THERE   Trains run between Glasgow and Dunblane with a stopover at Stirling, a one-way fare costing £5.40–£6.70 ($8.65–$11). Rail connections are also possible through Edinburgh via Stirling for £5.60–£7.30 ($8.95–$12) one-way. For 24-hour information, call ℭ **0845/748-4950.**

Buses travel from the Goosecroft Bus Station in Stirling to Dunblane, costing £1.80 ($2.90) each way. Call ℭ **01786/446474** in Stirling for schedules, or contact **First Edinburgh Busline** at ℭ **01324/613777.**

If you're driving from Stirling, continue north along M9 to Dunblane.

VISITOR INFORMATION   A year-round **tourist office** is on Stirling Road (ℭ **01786/824428**). From April 1 to June 1, it's open Monday through Saturday 9am to 5pm; from June 2 to June 29 Monday through Saturday from 9am to 6pm, Sunday from 10am to 4pm; from June 30 to August 31 Monday through Saturday from 9am to 7:30pm, Sunday from 9:30 am to 6:30 pm; from September 1 to September 7 Monday through Saturday from 9am to 7pm and Sunday from 10am to 5pm; from September 8 to September 21 Monday through Saturday from 9am to 6pm, Sunday from 10am to 4pm; from September 22 to October 19 Monday through Saturday from 9:30am to 5pm; from October 20 to March 31 Monday through Friday from 10am to 5pm, Saturday from 10am to 4pm.

SEEING THE SIGHTS

After you visit the cathedral, you can walk and discover the streets around it. They're narrow and twisting and flanked by mellow old town houses, many from the 18th century.

Dunblane Cathedral ⍟⍟   An excellent example of 13th-century Gothic ecclesiastic architecture, this cathedral was spared the ravages of attackers who destroyed other Scottish worship centers. Altered in the 15th century and restored several times in the 19th and 20th centuries, it may have suffered most from neglect subsequent to the Reformation. A Jesse Tree window is in the west end of the building, and of interest are the stalls, the misericords, the pulpit with carved figures of early ecclesiastical figures, and the wooden barrel-vaulted roof with colorful armorials. A Celtic stone from about A.D. 900 is in the north aisle.

Cathedral Close. ℭ **01786/823388.** www.dunblanecathedral.org.uk. Free admission. Apr–Sept Mon–Sat 9:30am–6pm, Sun 1:30–6pm; Oct–Mar Mon–Sat 9:30am–4pm, Sun 2–4pm.

Cathedral Museum   In the 1624 Dean's House, the Cathedral Museum contains articles and papers displaying the story of Dunblane and its ancient cathedral; you can also visit an enclosed garden with a very old (restored) well. A 1687 structure on the grounds contains the library of Bishop Robert Leighton, an outstanding 17th-century churchman; if you're a serious scholar, you'll find a great deal of material on the effects of the troubled times in Scotland, most from before the Industrial Revolution. It's open the same hours as the Cathedral Museum.

On Cathedral Square in the Dean's House. ℂ **01786/823440.** Free admission. May–Sept Mon–Sat 10:30am–4:30pm.

WHERE TO STAY

Cromlix House ★★★   This manor house, built in 1880 as the seat of a family that has owned the surrounding 3,000 acres for the past 500 years, is now the area's most elegant hotel. The owners still live on the estate and derive part of their income from organizing hunting and fishing expeditions in the surrounding moors and forests and on the River Allan. Fishing in three private lakes and hunting is available, as is tennis, and you can walk through the surrounding forests and farmland. It's also a popular spot for weddings.

The manor has an elegant drawing room with big bow windows, and antiques are among the furnishings of both the public rooms and guest rooms. Bouquets of fresh flowers and open fires in cool weather add to the comfort of the place. The individually decorated guest rooms (including eight suites with sitting rooms) are carpeted, and most have Queen Anne furnishings.

Kinbuck, Dunblane FK15 9JT. ℂ **01786/822125.** Fax 01786/825450. www.cromlixhouse.com. 14 units. £225–£260 ($360–$416) double; £285–£320 ($456–$512) suite. AE, DC, MC, V. Closed Jan. Take A9 to B8033; the hotel is 5km (3¼ miles) north of Dunblane just beyond the village of Kinbuck. **Amenities:** Restaurant; bar; laundry service; room service. *In room:* TV, coffeemaker, hair dryer, trouser press (in some).

Kippenross ★ *Finds*   This country manor boasts a richer and more unusual history than many of the region's B&Bs. It was built in 1750 according to the Palladian/neoclassical lines of William Adam, father of Britain's most celebrated neoclassical architect, Robert Adam. Surrounded by 200 acres of parks, lawns, and gardens and artfully landscaped with exotic plantings, it's a perfect example of Scottish country-house living, supervised by the Stirling-Aird family. Two of the guest rooms overlook the sprawling front lawns; the other overlooks the forests at the back. Guests are welcomed into the family's drawing room and to formal breakfasts in the dining room. If any guest wants to stay for dinner and reserves in advance, Susan Stirling-Aird prepares elegant dinners. Guests are invited to bring their own liquor or wine, because the place doesn't have a liquor license. *Note:* Susan's husband, Patrick, is a devoted ornithologist and bird-watcher.

Dunblane FK15 0LQ. ℂ **01786/824048.** Fax 01786/823124. www.aboutscotland.com/stirling/kippenross.html. 3 units. £76 ($122) double. MC, V. From Stirling, drive 8km (5 miles) north, taking A9 toward Perth, then exiting onto B8033 and following the signs to Dunblane. **Amenities:** Dining room. *In room:* Hair dryer (at front desk), no phone.

6 Callander & a Trio of Lochs ★

26km (16 miles) NW of Stirling; 69km (43 miles) N of Glasgow; 84km (52 miles) NW of Edinburgh; 68km (42 miles) W of Perth

In Gaelic, the Trossachs means the "bristled country," an allusion to its luxuriant vegetation. The thickly wooded valley contains three lochs: Venachar, Achray, and Katrine. In summer, the steamer on Loch Katrine offers a fine view of the splendid wooded scenery.

For many, the small town of Callander makes the best base for exploring the Trossachs and Loch Katrine, Loch Achray, and Loch Venachar. For years, motorists—and before them, passengers traveling by bumpy coach—stopped here to rest up on the once-difficult journey between Edinburgh and Oban.

Callander stands at the entrance to the Pass of Leny in the shadow of the Callander Crags. The rivers Teith and Leny meet to the west of the town.

ESSENTIALS

GETTING THERE Stirling (see "Stirling," earlier in this chapter) is the nearest rail link. Once at Stirling, continue the rest of the way to Callander on a First Edinburgh Bus from the Stirling station on Goosecroft Road. Contact the bus station at ℭ **01786/446474** or **First Edinburgh Buses** at ℭ **01324/613777.** A one-way fare is £2.90 ($4.65).

Driving from Stirling, head north along M9, cutting northwest at the junction of A84 to Callander, bypassing Doune.

VISITOR INFORMATION The **Rob Roy & Trossachs Visitor Centre** is at Ancaster Square (ℭ **01877/330342**). It distributes a map pinpointing all the sights. From April 1 to May 31, it's open daily from 10am to 5pm; from June 1 to June 30 daily from 9:30 am to 6pm; from July 1 to August 31 daily from 9am to 6pm; from September 1 to September 30 daily from 10am to 6pm; from October 1 to December 31 daily from 10am to 5pm; from January 1 to March 31 daily from 11am to 3pm. The second floor is home to a permanent **Rob Roy exhibit,** complete with a video presentation about his life and times. Entrance is £3.25 ($5.20) adults, £2.25 ($3.60) seniors and students, £2 ($3.20) children.

EXPLORING THE AREA

In the scenic Leny Hills to the west of Callander beyond the Pass of Leny lie **Leny Park** and **Leny Falls.** At one time all the lands in Leny Park were part of the Leny estate, home of the Buchanan clan for more than 1,000 years. In the wild Leny Glen, a naturalist's paradise, you can see deer grazing. Leny Falls is an impressive sight, near the confluence of the River Leny and the River Teith. In this area you'll see the remains of an abandoned railway; it's a wonderful footpath or cycling path for exploring this scenic area. Rent a bike at **Wheels/Trossachs Backpackers,** on Invertrossachs Road in Callander (ℭ **01877/331100;** www.scotland-info.co.uk; open daily 10am–6pm), which charges £13 ($20) for a full day, £7.50–£10 ($12–$16) for a half day, and from £35 ($56) for a week. It also provides bikers with sleeping rooms for £13 ($20) per night, including continental breakfast, conducts organized walks, and can arrange canoe trips. You must make reservations in advance.

Six and a half kilometers (4 miles) beyond the Pass of Leny lies **Loch Lubnaig** (crooked lake), divided into two reaches by a rock and considered fine fishing waters. Nearby is **Little Leny,** the ancestral burial ground of the Buchanans.

You'll find more falls at **Bracklinn,** 2.5km (1½ miles) northeast of Callander. In a gorge above the town, Bracklinn is one of the most scenic of the local beauty spots.

One of the most interesting sites around Callander is **Balquhidder Church** ⭐, 21km (13 miles) northwest off A84. This is the burial place of Rob Roy MacGregor. The church also has the St. Angus Stone from the 8th century, a 17th-century bell, and some Gaelic Bibles.

A good selection of woolens is at **Callander Woollen Mill,** 12–18 Main St. (ℭ **01877/330273**)—everything from scarves, skirts, and jackets to kilts, trousers, and knitwear. Another outlet for woolen goods, tartans, and woven rugs is the **Trossachs Woollen Mill** (ℭ **01877/330178**), 1.5km (1 mile) north of Callander on A84 in the hamlet of Kilmahog.

The town has an excellent golf course, the wooded and scenic **Callendar Golf Course,** Aveland Road (✆ **01877/330090**). At this 4,664m (5,125-yard) par-66 course, greens fees are £9–£18 ($14–$29) per round or £26 ($42) per day on weekdays, £13–£26 ($21–$42) per round or £31 ($50) per day on Saturdays and Sundays. The trolley charge is included in club rental, which runs £10–£15 ($16–$24) for 18 holes. No caddy service is available. The hilly fairways offer fine views, and the tricky moorland layout demands accurate tee shots.

WHERE TO STAY

Arden House ✿ This stone-sided Victorian B&B is instantly recognizable to several generations of British TV viewers because of its 1970s role as the setting for a BBC series, *Dr. Finlay's Casebook.* (Its setting, the fictional town of Tannochbrae, was modeled after Callander.) Built in 1870 as a vacation home for Lady Willoughby and currently maintained by William Jackson and Ian Mitchell, it offers a soothing rest amid an acre of gardens at the base of a rocky outcropping known as the Callendar Crags. The well-known Bracklinn Falls are a 5-minute walk away. The public areas boast Victorian antiques; the high-ceilinged guest rooms are tasteful and comfortable (the most appealing is the plush Tannochbrae Suite). Each unit comes with a shower; only the suite has a tub bath. Children under 14 are not accepted as guests and smoking is forbidden on premises.

Bracklinn Rd., Callander FK17 8EQ. ✆ 01877/330235. Fax 01877/330235. www.ardenhouse.org.uk. 5 units. £55–£60 ($88–$96) double; £65–£70 ($104–$112) suite. Rates include breakfast. MC, V. From Callander, walk for 5 min. north, following the signs to Bracklinn Falls. *In room:* TV, coffeemaker, no phone.

Highland House Hotel Owned and managed by Robert and Lorna Leckie, who took over in 1998, this Georgian stone building stands on a quiet tree-lined street a few feet from the Teith and a short walk from the Visitor Centre. All the charming guest rooms come with radio alarms and shower-equipped bathrooms (a few with tub). Scottish-style meals are served nightly from 6 to 9pm in the dining room or in simpler versions in the bar. Game casserole, with choice pieces of game in a rich red wine and port gravy, is a house specialty. The lounge offers 20 to 25 brands of malt whiskies, some relatively obscure.

S. Church St. (just off A84, near Ancaster Square), Callander FK17 8BN. ✆ 01877/330269. Fax 01877/339004. www.smoothhound.co.uk/hotels/highl.html. 9 units. £42–£52 ($67–$83) double. Rates include Scottish breakfast. MC, V. **Amenities:** Dining room; lounge; limited room service. *In room:* TV, coffeemaker, trouser press.

Roman Camp ✿✿✿ This is the leading hotel in town. Once a 17th-century hunting lodge with pink walls and small gray-roofed towers, it was built on the site of a Roman camp. Today you drive up a 182m (600-ft.) driveway, with shaggy Highland cattle and sheep grazing on either side. Inside, owners Eric and Marion Brown welcome you into a gracious country house. The dining room was converted in the 1930s from the old kitchen. The ceiling design is based on Scottish painted ceilings of the 16th and 17th centuries. The library, with its ornate plasterwork and richly grained paneling, is an elegant holdover from yesteryear.

Seven of the comfortable guest rooms are on the ground floor, and one is adapted for travelers with limited mobility; all have shower-equipped bathrooms (two with tub). Some rooms are furnished with bed-head crowns, gilt-framed mirrors, and stenciled furnishings; a few have four-posters, and others are contemporary with blond-wood pieces. Suites have separate sitting areas.

Main St., Callander FK17 8BG. ✆ 01877/330003. Fax 01877/331533. www.roman-camp-hotel.co.uk. 14 units. £110–£165 ($176–$264) double; from £180 ($288) suite. Rates include Scottish breakfast. AE, DC, MC, V. As you approach Callander on A84, the entrance to the hotel is signposted between 2 pink cottages on Callander's Main St. **Amenities:** Restaurant; bar; limited room service. *In room:* TV, coffeemaker, hair dryer, trouser press.

WHERE TO DINE

Dalgair Hotel SCOTTISH   This place is best known for its food and wine cellar. The bar, lined in gray bricks, boasts rustic accessories and flickering candles. The menu choices include halibut and Dover or lemon sole, steaks, and game casseroles. Australian, German, and Austrian wine, sold by the glass, gives the place the aura of a wine bar. More formal meals are served after dark in the restaurant, where menu items might include chicken filet in champagne-butter sauce, and preparations of salmon and Angus steaks.

The hotel's eight rooms contain hair dryers, TVs, and tub-and-shower combos. Rooms rent for £55–£75 ($88–$120) double, Scottish breakfast included.

113–115 Main St., Callander FK17 8BQ. (C) 01877/330283. Fax 01877/331114. www.dalgair-house-hotel. co.uk Reservations recommended in restaurant, not necessary in bar. Main courses £8–£14 ($13–$22) in restaurant, £3.50–£6 ($5.60–$9.60) in bar. AE, DC, MC, V. Restaurant daily noon–8:30pm; bar food service daily 11am–8:30pm.

Lade Inn INTERNATIONAL/SCOTTISH   Surrounded by fields and within earshot of the Leny River, the Lade was built as a teahouse, then converted after World War II to a pub and restaurant. The local favorite attracts residents from the surrounding farmlands as well as visitors from afar to enjoy the Highland scenery (which includes Ben Ledi, one of the region's most prominent peaks) and sample the wide range of cask-conditioned ales and cider. If you're hungry, new owners Alan and Frank Roebuck prepare meals of such Scottish standards as rack of lamb, pigeon, venison, steaks, salmon, and trout.

Trossachs Rd. at Kilmahog, Callander FK17 8HD. (C) 01877/330152. Main courses £9.65–£18 ($15–$28). MC, V. Mon–Sat noon–2:30pm and 5:30–9pm; Sun 12:30–9pm. Lies 1.5km (1 mile) north of Callander on A84.

CALLANDER AFTER DARK

The **Bridgend Hotel Pub,** Bridgend ((C) 01877/330130), is an old watering hole that has been done up in matching dusky red wood paneling and carpeting. Tennant brews are available on tap. On Friday and Saturday they have karaoke, and Sunday nights enjoy some live Scottish music. Open Monday through Wednesday from 11:30am to 2:30pm and 5:30pm to midnight; Thursday and Sunday from 11:30am to midnight; and Friday and Saturday from 11:30am to 12:45am. Another old-fashioned bar that's a local favorite is the **Crown Hotel Pub,** 13 Main St. ((C) 01877/330040); it sometimes features live folk music. Otherwise it's a mellow old place for a pint of lager. Open Sunday through Thursday from 11am to 11pm and Friday and Saturday from 11am to 1am.

7 On the Bonnie, Bonnie Banks of Loch Lomond

The largest of Scotland's lochs, **Loch Lomond** ✸✸ was the center of the ancient district of Lennox, in the possession of the branch of the Stewart (Stuart) family to which Lord Darnley (2nd husband of Mary Queen of Scots) belonged. The ruins of Lennox Castle are on Inchmurrin, one of the 30 islands of the loch—one with ecclesiastical ruins, one noted for its yew trees planted by King Robert the Bruce to ensure a suitable supply of wood for the bows of his archers. The loch is fed by at least 10 rivers from west, east, and north and is about 39km (24 miles) long; it stretches 8km (5 miles) at its widest point. On the eastern side is Ben Lomond, which rises to a height of 968m (3,192 ft.).

The song "Loch Lomond" is supposed to have been composed by one of Bonnie Prince Charlie's captured followers on the eve of his execution in Carlisle Jail. The "low road" of the song is the path through the underworld that his spirit

Moments You Take the High Road, and I'll Take the Low Road

Of course, you can also see the loch on foot. One of the great marked footpaths of Scotland, the **West Highland Way** goes along the complete eastern sector of the lovely loch. The footpath actually began at Milngavie outside Glasgow. Serious backpackers often do the entire 153km (95-mile) trail, but you can tackle just sections of it for marvelous day hikes that will allow you to enjoy the scenery along Loch Lomond.

will follow to his native land after death, more quickly than his friends can travel to Scotland by the ordinary high road.

The easiest way to see the famous loch is not by car but by one of the local ships owned by **Sweeney's Cruisers Ltd.,** and based at Sweeney's Shipyard, 26 Balloch Rd., Balloch G83 8LQ (*©* **01389/752376**). Cruises on various boats last for about an hour and in summer depart every hour from 10:30am to 7:30pm (departures in other months are based on demand). At £5.20 ($8.30) per person round-trip, cruises sail from Balloch toward a wooded island, Inchmurrin, year-round home to five families, several vacation chalets, and a summer-only nudist colony. The ship doesn't dock at the island, however.

BALLOCH

At the southern end of Loch Lomond, Balloch is the most touristy of the towns and villages around the lake. It grew up on the River Leven, where the water leaves Loch Lomond and flows south to the Clyde. Today, Balloch is visited chiefly by those wanting to take boat trips on Loch Lomond, which sail in season from Balloch Pier.

EXPLORING THE AREA

The 200-acre **Balloch Castle Country Park** is on the bonnie banks of Loch Lomond, 1.5km (¾ mile) north of Balloch Station. The present **Balloch Castle** (*©* **01389/722199**), replacing one that dated from 1238, was constructed in 1808 for John Buchanan of Ardoch in the castle-Gothic style. Its visitor center explains the history of the property. The site has a walled garden, and the trees and shrubs, especially the rhododendrons and azaleas, reach the zenith of their beauty in late May and early June. You can also visit a Fairy Glen. The park is open all year, daily from 8am to dusk, with no admission charge. From Easter to the end of October, the visitor center is open daily from 10am to 6pm.

Dumbarton District's Countryside Ranger Service is based at Balloch Castle and conducts **guided walks** at various locations around Loch Lomond throughout the summer.

WHERE TO STAY & DINE

Balloch Hotel Called Balloch's grande dame hotel, this is the first hotel to be built in the town. In 1860 it welcomed the Empress Eugénie, wife of Napoleon III, when she toured Scotland (she slept in the Inchmoan Room). It stands beside the river in the center of the village, offering basic, functionally furnished rooms, each with a shower (some with a tub as well).

Balloch Rd., Balloch G83 8LQ. *©* **01389/752579.** Fax 01389/755604. 10 units. £57 ($91) double. Rates include Scottish breakfast. AE, DC, MC, V. **Amenities:** Restaurant; bar; limited room service. *In room:* TV, coffeemaker, hair dryer, trouser press.

Cameron House ★★★ *Kids*   This is one of the great country houses of Scotland, the family home of the Smollets. Its most distinguished son was Tobias Smollet, the 18th-century novelist whose humorous works have been read around the world. Over the years the house has been visited by such illustrious guests as the Emperor of Brazil, Sir Winston Churchill, Princess Margaret, and Earl Mountbatten. Literary celebrities have also shown up at the doorstep, none more famous than Dr. Samuel Johnson and his indefatigable biographer, James Boswell. Dr. Johnson later wrote, "We have had more solid talk in this house than in any other place where we have been."

Today the house has been converted into a top-rated accommodation with one of the best spas in this part of Scotland. The resort also contains some of the finest indoor leisure facilities in the area. The smallest rooms are called "house rooms," with standard rooms being slightly larger and better. Best of all are the spacious suites, furnished with four-poster beds. Much of the furnishings are in the traditional Georgian style, with dark mahogany pieces set against floral bathrooms. Bathrooms are wide ranging: some with tubs, some with showers, and others with a combo.

Children are warmly welcomed and the hotel has a supervised playroom where parents can leave kids for a couple of hours while they relax in the lagoon pool or the spa. The Scottish and French cuisine served in the Georgian Room is among the most refined in this part of Scotland. You can also dine informally in two more restaurants. Many sporting adventures ranging from golf to fishing to private yacht parties can be arranged.

Alexandria, Loch Lomond, G83 8QZ. ℂ **01389/755565.** Fax 01389/759522. www.cameronhouse.co.uk. 96 units. £242–£282 ($387–$451) double; £380–£480 ($608–$768) suite. Rates include full breakfast. AE, DC, MC, V. Take M8 to A82 to Loch Lomand; follow signs to hotel. **Amenities:** 3 restaurants; bar; fitness center; spa; babysitting; 24-hr. room service; laundry service; dry cleaning. *In room:* TV, minibar, hair dryer.

18

Aberdeen & the Tayside & Grampian Regions

The two historic regions of Tayside and Grampian offer a vast array of sightseeing, even though they're relatively small. Tayside, for example, is about 137km (85 miles) east to west and 97km (60 miles) south to north. The regions share the North Sea coast between the Firth of Tay in the south and the Firth of Moray farther north, and the so-called Highland Line separating the Lowlands in the south from the Highlands in the north crosses both. The Grampians, Scotland's highest mountain range, are to the west of this line.

Carved out of the old counties of Perth and Angus, **Tayside** is named for its major river, the 192km (119-mile) long Tay. The region is easy to explore, and its waters offer some of Europe's best salmon and trout fishing. Tayside abounds with heather-clad Highland hills, long blue lochs under forested banks, and miles of walking trails. Perth and Dundee are among Scotland's largest cities. Tayside provided the backdrop for many novels by Sir Walter Scott, including *The Fair Maid of Perth, Waverley,* and *The Abbot.* And its golf courses are world famous, ranging from the trio of 18-hole courses at Gleneagles to the open championships links at Carnoustie.

Grampian boasts Aberdeen, Scotland's third-largest city, and Braemar, site of the most famous of the Highland gatherings. The queen herself comes here for holidays, to stay at Balmoral Castle, her private residence, a tradition dating back to the days of Queen Victoria and her consort, Prince Albert. The very word *Balmoral* seems to evoke images of tartans and bagpipes. As you journey on the scenic roads of Scotland's northeast, you'll pass moorland and peaty lochs, wood glens and rushing rivers, granite-stone villages and ancient castles, and fishing harbors as well as North Sea beach resorts.

1 Aberdeen: The Castle Country ✶✶

209km (130 miles) NE of Edinburgh; 108km (67 miles) N of Dundee

Bordered by fine sandy beaches (delightful if you're a polar bear), Scotland's third city, Aberdeen, is often called the "Granite City," because its buildings are constructed largely of pink or gray granite, hewn from the Rubislaw quarries. The harbor in this seaport is one of the country's largest fishing ports, filled with kipper and deep-sea trawlers, and Aberdeen lies on the banks of the salmon- and trout-filled Don and Dee rivers. Spanning the Don is the **Brig o' Balgownie,** a steep Gothic arch begun in 1285.

Although it hardly compares with Glasgow and Edinburgh, Aberdeen is the center of a vibrant university; it boasts a few marvelous museums and galleries; and it's known for great nightlife and shopping, the best in the northeast. Old

Aberdeen is the seat of one of Scotland's major cathedrals, St. Machars. It's also a good base for exploring the greatest castles of Grampian and the towns and villages along the splendid salmon river, Deeside.

ESSENTIALS

GETTING THERE   Aberdeen is served by a number of airlines, including British Airways, British Midland, Easy Jet, and KLM. For flight information, phone the Aberdeen Airport at ℂ **01224/722331.** The airport is about 11km (7 miles) away from the heart of town and is connected to it by a bus service costing £1.45 ($2.30) one-way. Taxis cost about £12 ($19).

Aberdeen has direct rail links to the major cities of Britain. SuperSaver fares, available by avoiding travel on Friday and Saturday, make the price difference between a one-way fare and a round-trip ticket negligible. Another efficient way of saving on fares by another £10 ($16) is reserving through the booking agency, Apex. For fares in Scotland, call ℂ **0845/755-0033** at least 48 hours in advance. For fares from London, call ℂ **0845/722-5225** at least 1 week in advance. The prices here are for tickets bought on the day of departure, excluding Friday, when prices are higher. Nineteen trains per normal weekday arrive from Edinburgh; a regular one-way ticket costs £17 to £20 ($26–$32). Trip time is about 3½ hours. Some 19 trains per day arrive from Glasgow, costing £32 ($51) one-way or £47 ($74) round-trip. Some 12 trains per day arrive from London as well, with a one-way fare of £70 ($112) and a round-trip fare of only £96 ($153). For rail schedules, call ℂ **0845/748-4950.**

Several bus companies have express routes serving Aberdeen, and many offer special round-trip fares to passengers avoiding travel on Friday or Saturday. Frequent buses arrive from both Glasgow, costing £22 to £25 ($34–$40) round-trip, and from Edinburgh, costing £20 to £25 ($32–$40) round-trip. There are also frequent arrivals from Inverness, a round-trip costing £11 to £13 ($17–$20). For bus schedules in Aberdeen, call ℂ **01224/212266.**

It's also easy to drive to the northeast. From the south, drive via Edinburgh over the Forth and Tay Road bridges and take the coastal road. From the north and west, approach the area from the much improved A9, which links Perth, Inverness, and Wick.

VISITOR INFORMATION   The **Aberdeen Tourist Information Centre** is in St. Nicholas House, Broad Street, Aberdeen, Aberdeenshire AB10 1DE (ℂ **0122/463-2727**). July and August, it's open Monday through Friday from 9am to 7pm, Saturday from 9am to 5pm, and Sunday from 10am to 4pm; April through June and September, hours are Monday through Friday from 9am to 5pm and Saturday from 10am to 2pm; October through March, it's open Monday through Friday from 9am to 5pm and Saturday from 10am to 2pm.

SEEING THE SIGHTS

In old Aberdeen is **Aberdeen University,** a fusion of two colleges. Reached along University Road, **King's College** (ℂ **01224/272137;** bus: 6 or 20) is Great Britain's oldest school of medicine. The college is known for its chapel (ca. 1500) with pre-Reformation carved woodwork, the finest of its kind in Scotland; it's open daily from 9am to 4:30pm, charging no admission. On Broad Street is **Marischal College** (ℂ **01224/273131**), founded in 1593 by Earl Marischal—it's the world's second-biggest granite structure (El Escorial outside Madrid is much larger). King's College was Catholic, but Marischal was Protestant. The main structure is no longer in use, but on-site is the Marischal Museum displaying

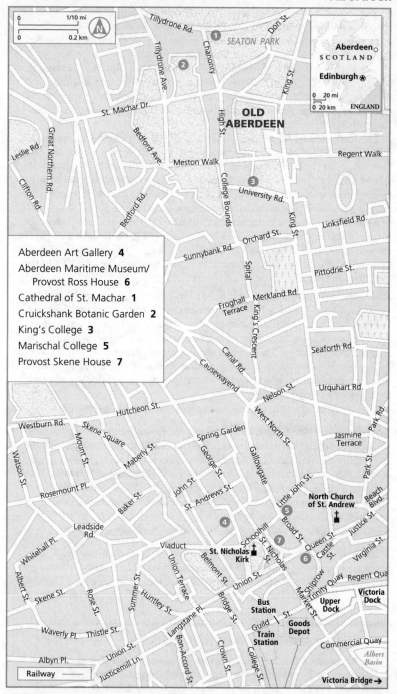

Aberdeen Art Gallery 4

**Aberdeen Maritime Museum/
Provost Ross House 6**

Cathedral of St. Machar 1

Cruickshank Botanic Garden 2

King's College 3

Marischal College 5

Provost Skene House 7

exhibits and photos of the university and the Scottish culture of the Northeast in general; admission is free, and the museum is open Monday through Saturday from 10am to 5pm and Sunday from 2 to 5pm. In 1860, the colleges joined together to form the nucleus of the University of Aberdeen.

Also at the University of Aberdeen, the **Cruickshank Botanic Garden,** St. Machar Drive (© **01224/272704;** bus: 6 or 20), displays alpines, shrubs, and many herbaceous plants, along with rock and water gardens. It's open Monday through Friday from 9am to 5pm; in summer, it's also open Saturday and Sunday from 2 to 5pm. Admission is free.

The **Cathedral of St. Machar,** Chanonry (© **01224/485988** in the morning or 01224/317424 in the afternoon; bus: 1, 2, 3, 4, 5, 6, 7, or 26), was founded in 1131, but the present structure dates from the 15th century. Its splendid heraldic ceiling contains three rows of shields. Be sure to note the magnificent modern stained-glass windows by Douglas Strachan and the pre-Reformation woodwork. The cathedral is open daily from 9am to 5pm.

Alpine Bikes, 66–70 Holburn St. (© **01224/211455**), will rent you a bike so you can go exploring on two wheels. Rates are £12 ($19) daily or £24 ($38) for weekends, with weekly rates of £60 ($96). It's open Sunday from 11am to 5pm, Monday through Wednesday and Friday from 9am to 6pm, and Thursday from 9am to 8pm.

Aberdeen Art Gallery ⭐   Built in 1884 in a neoclassical design by A. Marshall MacKenzie, this building houses one of the most important art collections in Great Britain. It contains 18th-century portraits by Raeburn, Hogarth, Ramsay, and Reynolds and acclaimed 20th-century works by Paul Nash, Ben Nicholson, and Francis Bacon. The exhibits also include excellent Impressionist pieces by Monet, Pissarro, Sisley, and Bonnard as well as a collection of Scottish domestic silver and examples of other decorative arts. Special exhibits and events are frequently offered.

Schoolhill. © 01224/523700. Free admission. Mon–Sat 10am–5pm; Sun 2–5pm. Bus: 20.

Aberdeen Maritime Museum   Using a unique collection of ship models, paintings, artifacts, computer interaction, and exhibits, this museum tells the story of the city's long and fascinating relationship with the sea. A major display on the offshore oil industry features a model of the Murchison oil platform. The complex is housed on four floors, incorporating the 1593 Provost Ross House linked by a modern glass structure to the granite Trinity Church. Windows open onto panoramic views of the harbor.

Shiprow. © 01224/337700. Free admission. Mon–Sat 10am–5pm; Sun noon–3pm. Bus: 20.

Dunnottar Castle   The well-preserved ruins of Dunnottar are on a rocky promontory towering 49m (160 ft.) above the surging sea, and the best way to get here is by a dramatic 30-minute walk from Stonehaven along the cliffs. "Dunnottar speaks with an audible voice," says an old proverb. "Every cave has a record,

---

⎛Value **The Aberdeen Attractions Card**

The **Aberdeen Attractions Card** covers admission to the Toll Booth, the Aberdeen Maritime Museum, and the Provost Skene House and costs £5 ($8) for adults and £3.50 ($5.60) for seniors, students, and children for unlimited visits over a year. You can buy it at any of the three included sights.

every turret a tongue." The ruins include a great square tower and a chapel built in 1392. William Wallace stormed it in 1297 but failed to take it. In 1991, it was the setting for Zeffirelli's film of *Hamlet,* starring Mel Gibson. You can reach Stonehaven from Aberdeen by taking Bluebird Northern bus no. 107, costing £5.40 ($8.65) round-trip, and then walking for 5 minutes. Trains run about every ½-hour from Aberdeen to Stonehaven, costing £5 to £7 ($8–$11) round-trip. Departures are every 30 minutes during the day; the trip takes 30 minutes.

3km (2 miles) south of Stonehaven off A92. ℰ **01569/762173.** Admission £3.50 ($5.60) adults, £2 ($3.20) seniors and students, £1 ($1.60) children. Easter–Oct Mon–Sat 9am–6pm, Sun 2–5pm; Nov–Easter Mon–Fri 9am–3:30pm.

Provost Skene House   This attraction is named for a rich merchant who was Lord Provost of Aberdeen from 1676 to 1685. Off Broad Street, it's a museum with period rooms and artifacts of domestic life. Provost Skene's kitchen has been converted into a cafe.

5 Guestrow, off Broad St. ℰ **01224/641086.** Free admission. Mon–Fri 10am–5pm; Sat 10am–4pm; Sun 1–3pm. Bus: 20.

Toll Booth   Constructed in 1629, this building in the city center was converted into a prison during the reign of Charles II, and the cells as well as talking models of famous prisoners are on display today. Alongside this is a history of crime and punishment at the time and (on a slightly lighter note) a permanent exhibit of Charles II's visit to the city that includes ceremonial costumes. Those interested in municipal development will appreciate the exhibit of maps plotting the growth of Aberdeen from an insignificant village to Scotland's third-largest city.

Castle St. ℰ **01224/621167.** Admission £3 ($4.80) adults, £2 ($3.20) seniors and children, £6 ($9.60) families. Mon–Sat 10am–5pm; Sun 12:30–3:30pm.

SHOPPING

The main shopping districts center on specialty shops on **Chapel** and **Thistle streets** and well-known chains on **George** and **Union streets.** Of interest to collectors, **Colin Wood,** 25 Rose St. (ℰ **01224/643019**), stocks furniture, wall clocks, and grandfather clocks from the 17th to the early 20th centuries. Their specialty, however, is maps from the Elizabethan through the Victorian eras, including a good selection of Jacobean maps. The shop also sells 17th- to early-20th-century prints of northern Scotland. You may also want to browse through the eclectic mix of small bric-a-brac antiques at **Elizabeth Watts Studio,** 69 Thistle St. (ℰ **01224/647232**), where items include glass, brass, antique jewelry, china, silver, and a few small furniture pieces. The shop is actually best known for its china and glass restoration studio.

To trace your Scottish ancestry, go to the **Aberdeen Family History Shop,** 164 King St. (ℰ **01224/646323**), where membership to the Aberdeen and North East Family History Society will cost you £15 ($24) cash, check, or credit card. Once you join, you can go through a vast range of publications kept on hand to help members trace their family histories. You'll find a multitude of gifts at **Nova,** 20 Chapel St. (ℰ **01224/641270**), which stocks china, silver jewelry, rugs, clothing, toys, cards, and gift paper.

Other interesting shops are **Just Scottish,** 4 Upperkirkgate (ℰ **01224/ 621755**), retailers of quality items—all made in Scotland, including ceramics, knitwear, textiles, silver, and jewelry; and **Alex Scott & Co.,** 43 Schoolhill (ℰ **01224/643924**), the town's finest kiltmakers, which also sells quality Scottish gifts and souvenirs, tartans, and traditional clans and crests.

WHERE TO STAY

Because of increasing numbers of tourists and business visitors to the Granite City, Europe's offshore oil capital, hotels are likely to be heavily booked any time of year. If you haven't booked ahead, it's best to go to the **Aberdeen Tourist Information Centre,** St. Nicholas House on Broad Street (*(C)* **01224/632727**). There's a wide range of accommodations available, whether you prefer to stay in a family-run B&B, a guesthouse, or a hotel, and the center's staff can usually find just the right kind of lodging. A £2.50 ($4) service fee is charged. You can also stay at **Ferryhill House** (see "Where to Dine," below).

EXPENSIVE

Ardoe House ✸   Known for its tranquil setting at the end of a winding drive, this Scottish baronial house, graced with soaring turrets, stands on large grounds on the south bank of the River Dee. It was built in 1878 of silver granite and still retains much of its original design, including its carved oak paneling. You can opt for the traditional guest rooms in the old house or the more modern units in the large extension. All units are of decent size.

S. Deeside Rd., Blairs, Aberdeen AB12 5YP. *(C)* **01224/867355.** Fax 01224/860644. www.macdonald hotels.co.uk. 117 units. £160 ($256) double; £200 ($320) suite. Children ages 11 and under stay free in parent's room. AE, DC, MC, V. Free parking. Drive 8km (5 miles) southwest on B9077. **Amenities:** Restaurant; bar; indoor pool; fitness center; room service. *In room:* TV, coffeemaker, hair dryer, iron/ironing board.

Marcliffe at Pitfodels ✸✸✸   On the city's western edge less than ½ hour from the airport, this deluxe hotel is far superior to the Caledonian Thistle and the Ardoe. The traditional three-story manor house was constructed around a courtyard and stands on 6 acres of landscaped grounds. The Oriental rugs, placed on stone floors, and the tartan sofas set the decor note in the public rooms; a scattering of antiques add a graceful note. The rather spacious guest rooms are furnished in Chippendale and reproduction pieces, with armchairs and desks, plus a host of extras such as fresh milk in the minibar.

At breakfast you can sample Aberdeen *rowies,* a local specialty made with butter like a croissant that's been flattened. The conservatory restaurant offers regional dishes like Highland lamb and fresh Scottish salmon, and the more expensive Invery Room is favored by businesspeople entertaining out-of-town guests. In the library lounge, you can choose from more than 130 scotches, 500 wines, and 70 cognacs.

N. Deeside Rd., Aberdeen AB1 9YA. *(C)* **01224/861000.** Fax 01224/868860. www.marcliffe.com. 42 units. £175–£295 ($280–$472) double. AE, DC, MC, V. Free parking. Drive about 1.5km (1 mile) off A90 at the Aberdeen ring road, A93. **Amenities:** 2 restaurants; bar; 24-hr. room service; laundry service; dry cleaning. *In room:* TV, minibar, coffeemaker, hair dryer, iron/ironing board.

Simpsons ✸   This hotel, which opened in 1998, enjoys great popularity. Two traditional granite town houses were joined to offer comfortable accommodations. Rooms are decorated with furniture from Spain and painted in rich, bold colors that create a cool, Mediterranean ambience. Amenities include complimentary use of the health spa.

The hotel bar and brasserie offers a range of moderately priced Scottish and international dishes prepared with the finest of local ingredients.

59 Queens Rd., Aberdeen AB15 4YP. *(C)* **01224/327777.** Fax 01224/327700. www.simpsonshotel.co.uk. 50 units. Sun–Thurs £150–£230 ($240–$368) double; Fri–Sat £150–£240 ($240–$384) double. Rates include breakfast. AE, MC, V. Follow signs for A96 North, and turn right at Queens Rd. Roundabout. **Amenities:** Restaurant; bar; spa; 24-hr. room service; babysitting; laundry service; dry cleaning. *In room:* A/C, TV, minibar, coffeemaker, hair dryer, iron/ironing board.

MODERATE

Caledonian Thistle Hotel ✯ The Caledonian Thistle occupies a grand stone-fronted Victorian in the center of Aberdeen. Recent restorations have added a veneer of Georgian gloss to one of the most elegant series of public rooms in town. The guest rooms are at the top of a 19th-century stairwell, with Corinthian columns and a freestanding atrium. They vary a good deal in size, but all contain double-glazed windows. Each accommodation is comfortably furnished with taste.

10–14 Union Terrace (off Union St.), Aberdeen AB10 1WE. ✆ **01224/640233.** Fax 01224/641627. www. thistlehotels.com. 80 units. £98–£118 ($157–$189) double; from £220 ($352) suite. Children ages 11 and under stay free in parent's room. AE, DC, MC, V. Free parking. Bus: 17. **Amenities:** 2 restaurants; 2 bars; room service; laundry service; dry cleaning. *In room:* TV, minibar, coffeemaker, hair dryer, iron/ironing board.

INEXPENSIVE

Jays Guest House *Value* This is one of the nicest guesthouses in Aberdeen, mainly because of the high standards of the owner, Mrs. Alice Jennings. It's near the university and the Offshore Survival Centre. Everything runs smoothly, and the guest rooms are bright and airy, each newly renovated.

422 King St., Aberdeen AB24 3BR. ✆/fax **01224/638295.** www.jaysguesthouse.co.uk. 10 units. £60–£80 ($96–$128) double. Rates include Scottish breakfast. MC, V. Free parking. Bus: 1, 2, 3, 4, or 7. *In room:* TV, coffeemaker.

Mannofield Hotel Built of silver granite around 1880, this hotel is a Victorian fantasy, with step gables, turrets, spires, bay windows, and a sweeping mahogany-and-teakwood staircase. Owners Bruce and Dorothy Cryle offer a warm Scottish welcome. The nicely sized guest rooms, refurbished in 1998 with paisley curtains and quilts, are equipped with well-maintained shower-only bathrooms.

447 Great Western Rd., Aberdeen AB10 6NL. ✆ **01224/315888.** Fax 01224/208971. 9 units. £64 ($102) double. Rates include Scottish breakfast. AE, DC, MC, V. Free parking. Bus: 18 or 24. **Amenities:** Restaurant; lounge area; room service; babysitting; laundry service; dry cleaning. *In room:* TV, coffeemaker, hair dryer.

Palm Court Set a bit apart from the exact center and a bit more tranquil, this is a highly praised, well-run hotel that is an address Aberdeen citizens give to their friends who are visiting their city. The hotel is known for its good value and fine bedrooms. They're not huge but are comfortably furnished and well decorated in bright pastels. Each comes with a small but tidily kept bathroom with tub or shower. If you don't want to wander the streets of Aberdeen at night, seeking a restaurant, you'll find a good dining room on site, specializing in fine Scottish produce such as salmon.

81 Seafield Rd., Aberdeen AB15 7YX. ✆ **01224/310351.** Fax 01224/312707. 24 units. £60–£99 ($96–$158). AE, MC, V. Rates include full breakfast. **Amenities:** Restaurant; bar; room service; laundry service. *In room:* TV, hair dryer, coffeemaker, iron.

WHERE TO DINE

Elrond's Cafe Bar INTERNATIONAL White marble floors, a long oak-capped bar, evening candlelight, and a garden-inspired decor create the ambience. You can enjoy a full-blown feast here, but no one will mind if you show up just for a drink, a pot of tea, a midday salad or snack. Specialties are burgers, steaks, pastas, fresh fish, lemon chicken supreme, chicken Kiev, and vegetarian dishes. This isn't the world's greatest food, but it's popular nevertheless. Though it's in one of Aberdeen's well-known hotels, the restaurant has a separate entrance onto Union Terrace.

In the Caledonian Thistle Hotel, 10–14 Union Terrace. ✆ 01224/640233. Main courses £7–£15 ($11–$24); pot of tea with pastry £4 ($6.40). AE, DC, MC, V. Mon–Sat 10am–midnight; Sun 10am–11pm. Bus: 16 or 17.

Ferryhill House INTERNATIONAL   In its own park and garden on Aberdeen's southern outskirts, Ferryhill House dates back 250 years. It was built by the region's most successful brick maker/quarry master. It has Georgian detailing, but recent refurbishment has removed many of the original panels and all the ceiling beams. The restaurant boasts one of the region's largest collections of single-malt whiskies—more than 140 brands. There's a fireplace for chilly afternoons and a beer garden for midsummer, as well as a conservatory. Food items include steak or vegetable tempura, chicken dishes like chicken fajita, fried haddock filet, pastas, and chili.

Ferryhill House also rents nine standard guest rooms, with TVs, phones, and hair dryers. Breakfast included, the double rate is £79 ($126) Sunday through Thursday and £52 ($83) Friday and Saturday.

Bon Accord St., Aberdeen AB11 6UA. ℂ **01224/590867.** Fax 01224/586947. Reservations recommended Sat–Sun. Main courses £9.50–£15 ($15–$23). AE, DC, MC, V. Free parking. Bus: 16.

Gerard's ⭐ FRENCH/INTERNATIONAL   Restaurateur Gerard Flecher's popular spot is split into the more formal main dining room and the relaxed Cafe Colmar, which has a separate entrance at the rear of the building. Both eateries have a Gallic atmosphere and French-inspired decor, but the cafe features dishes of a far more international nature. In Gerard's, expect such fare as pan-fried maigrette of duck and Cumberland sausage with five-bean fricassee on cabernet sauvignon jus. In the cafe, dishes include chicken breast filled with creamed lemon cheese in leek-cream sauce. The bar stocks a wide range of single malts and ports, along with French wines unavailable elsewhere in the region.

50 Chapel St. ℂ **01224/639500.** Reservations recommended. Main courses £12–£19 ($19–$30) at lunch, £15–£23 ($24–$36) at dinner; business lunch £13 ($20) for 2 courses, £16 ($26) for 3 courses; fixed-price dinner £23 ($36) for 2 courses, £26 ($42) for 3 courses; cafe main courses £8–£19 ($12–$30) at lunch, £9–£21 ($14–$34) at dinner. AE, DC, MC, V. Restaurant daily noon–2:30pm and 6–10pm. Cafe daily 10am–midnight; meals noon–2:30pm and 5:30–10pm.

Martha's Vineyard Bistro/The Courtyard Restaurant SCOTTISH/ CONTINENTAL   One of the most appealing restaurant compounds in Aberdeen occupies two floors of what was built around 1900 as an extension of the local hospital. Today, a robust- and rustic-looking bistro (Martha's Vineyard) is on the street level and a more substantial and formal-looking restaurant (The Courtyard) upstairs. The menu in the bistro is more formal than you might expect and includes smoked salmon and asparagus salad and gigot of lamb with a compote of leeks in mustard sauce. Upstairs you'll find dishes like local Brie wrapped in smoked salmon or rosemary-flavored loin of Highland venison with wild mushrooms. Dessert in either place might be warm orange pudding with Grand Marnier sauce served with vanilla-ginger ice cream.

Alford Lane. ℂ **01224/213795.** Reservations recommended in The Courtyard, not necessary in Martha's Vineyard. Main courses £5–£12 ($8–$19) bistro, £12–£18 ($18–$29) in restaurant. Mon–Sat noon–2:15pm; Tues–Sat 6–10pm. AE, DC, MC, V. Bus: 1, 2, 3, or 4.

Silver Darling ⭐⭐ FRENCH/SEAFOOD   Silver Darling (a local nickname for herring) is a definite asset to the dining picture in Aberdeen. Occupying a former Customs House at the mouth of the harbor, it spins a culinary fantasy around the freshest catch of the day. You might begin with a savory fish soup, almost Mediterranean in flavor, then go on to one of the barbecued fish dishes. Salmon is the invariable favorite of the more discriminating diners.

Pocra Quay, Footdee. © 01224/576229. Reservations recommended. Main courses £14–£24 ($22–$38); 2-course fixed-price lunch £22 ($34); 3-course fixed-price lunch £26 ($42). AE, DC, MC, V. Mon–Fri noon–2pm and 7–9:30pm; Sat 7–9:30pm; Sun 6–9pm summer only. Closed Dec 23–Jan 8. Bus: 14 or 15.

ABERDEEN AFTER DARK

Tickets to events at most venues are available by calling the **Aberdeen Box Office** at © **01224/641122.** Open Monday through Saturday from 9am to 6:30pm.

THE PERFORMING ARTS The **Aberdeen Arts Centre,** King Street (© **01224/635208**), has a 350-seat theater that is rented to professional and amateur groups hosting everything from poetry readings and plays to musical concerts in various styles. Ticket prices and performance times vary; call for information. Also on the premises is a 60-seat video projection theater that screens world cinema offerings; ticket prices vary depending on what is showing but start at £8 ($13). A large gallery room holds month-long exhibitions of visual art in many different styles and mediums. A cafe/bar, offering light meals and drinks, is open during performance times.

Near Tarves, about 32km (20 miles) from Aberdeen, you'll find **Haddo House** (© **01651/851440**), which hosts operas, ballets, and plays from Easter to October. An early-20th-century hall built of pitch pine, Haddo House is based on the Canadian town halls that Lord Aberdeen saw in his travels abroad. The hall was built for the people of the surrounding area on Aberdeen family land and the present Lady Aberdeen still lives in a house on this property. Follow B9005, 29km (18 miles) north to Tarves, then follow the National Trust and Haddo House signs 3km (2 miles) east to arrive here. Ticket prices range from £7 to £19 ($11–$30). Admittance to the house is £7 ($11) for adults and £5.25 ($8.40) for seniors and children. The house is open daily from 11am to 4:30pm, the shop from 11am to 4:30pm, and the gardens from 9:30am to 4pm. A stylish cafe offers light meals, tea, and other beverages daily, from Easter to October, from 11am to 6pm.

The 19th-century **Music Hall,** Union Street (© **01224/641122**), is an ornately gilded 1,282-seat theater that stages concerts by the Scottish National Orchestra, the Scottish Chamber Orchestra, visiting international orchestras, and pop bands, as well as hosting ceilidhs, crafts fairs, and book sales. Tickets for year-round musical performances average £10 to £30 ($16–$48). The **Aberdeen International Youth Festival** is held annually in this hall in August, and features youth orchestras, choirs, and dance and theater ensembles. Daytime and evening performances are held, and tickets range from £10 to £14 ($16–$22). Contact the Music Hall or the Aberdeen Box Office for more information.

His Majesty's Theatre, Rosemount Viaduct (© **01224/641122**), was designed by Frank Matcham in 1906 and is the only theater in the world build entirely of granite. The interior is late Victorian, and the 1,445-seat theater stages operas, dance performances, dramas, classical concerts, musicals, and comedy shows year-round. Tickets range from £10 to £25 ($16–$40).

A mixed venue is the **Lemon Tree,** 5 W. North St. (© **01224/642230**). Its 150-seat theater stages dance recitals, theatrical productions, and stand-up comedy, with tickets generally priced between £7 and £22 ($11–$35). On Saturday, there's often a matinee at 2 or 3pm, and evening performances are at 7pm. Downstairs, the 500-seat cafe/theater hosts folk, rock, blues, jazz, and comedy acts, with shows starting between 8 and 10pm. On Wednesday the Folk Club is onstage, and other nights have varied offerings. On Sunday afternoon there's free live jazz.

DANCE CLUBS **DeNiro's,** 120 Union St. (© **01224/640641**), has dancing to house music from 10pm until 2am on Friday and Saturday only. The cover charge is £7 ($11), but may vary depending on the guest DJ.

The Pelican, housed in the Hotel Metro, 17 Market St. (© **01224/583275**), offers dancing Thursday through Saturday from 10pm to 2am. The cover charge on Thursday is £4 ($6.40) and Friday and Saturday £6 ($9.60). There's a live band every second Thursday.

The ever-popular **Ministry,** 16 Dee St. (© **01224/211661**), is a sophisticated dance club that features different theme nights throughout the week. On Monday, Moist is a popular student night. On Fridays, guest DJs from England and America take over the sound system, so you might catch New York's hottest DJ of the moment. Cover charges range from £2 to £12 ($3.20–$19) throughout the week, depending on which DJ or band is featured.

A PUB The **Prince of Wales** ⚑, 7 St. Nicholas Lane (© **01224/640597**), in the heart of the shopping district, is the best place in the old city center to go for a pint. Furnished with pews in screened booths, it boasts Aberdeen's longest bar counter. At lunch, it's bustling with regulars who devour chicken in cider sauce or Guinness pie. On tap are such beers as Buchan Gold and Courage Directors. Orkney Dark Island is also sold here.

SIDE TRIPS FROM ABERDEEN: ARCHEOLINK & CASTLE COUNTRY

Aberdeen is at the doorstep of Scotland's "castle country"—some 40 inhabited castles lie within a 64km (40-mile) radius of the city. Here is a selection of the best of them.

Castle Fraser ⚑   One of the most impressive of the fortress-like castles of Mar, Castle Fraser stands in a 25-acre parkland setting. The sixth laird, Michael Fraser, began the structure in 1575, and his son finished it in 1636. Its Great Hall is spectacular, and you can wander around the grounds, which include an 18th-century walled garden.

Sauchen, Inverurie. © **01330/833463**. Admission £5.50 ($8.80) adults, £4 ($6.40) seniors, £1.75 ($2.80) children, free for children ages 4 and under. Easter weekend and Oct Sat–Sun 2–4:45pm; May–June daily 1:30–5pm; July–Aug daily 11am–4:45pm; Sept daily 1:30–5:30pm. Closed Nov–Mar. Head 5km (3 miles) south of Kemnay, 26km (16 miles) west of Aberdeen, off A944.

Kildrummy Castle ⚑   This is the most extensive example of a 13th-century castle in Scotland. Once the ancient seat of the earls of Mar, you can still see the four round towers, the hall, and the chapel from the original structure. The great gatehouse and other remains date from the 16th century. The castle played a major role in Scottish history up to 1715, when it was dismantled.

Hwy. A-97, Kildrummy. © **01975/571331**. Admission £3 ($4.80) adults, £2.25 ($3.60) seniors, £1 ($1.60) children. Easter–Sept daily 9:30am–6:30pm; Oct–Nov daily 9:30am–4pm. Closed Oct–Easter. Take A-97 for 56km (35 miles) west of Aberdeen; it's signposted off A-97, 16km (10 miles) west of Alford.

Fyvie Castle ⚑   The National Trust for Scotland opened this castle to the public in 1986. The oldest part, dating from the 13th century, is the grandest existing example of Scottish baronial architecture. There are five towers, named after Fyvie's five families—the Prestons, Melddrums, Setons, Gordons, and Leiths—who lived here for over 5 centuries. Originally built in a royal hunting forest, Fyvie means "deer hill" in Gaelic. The interior, created by the first Lord Leith of Fyvie, a steel magnate, reflects the opulence of the Edwardian era. His collections contain arms and armor, 16th-century tapestries, and important artworks by Rae-burn, Gainsborough, and Romney. The castle is rich in ghosts, curses, and legends.

Turriff, on the Aberdeen–Banff road. © 01651/891266. Admission £7 ($11) adults, £5.60 ($8.95) seniors and children. Easter–June and Sept daily noon–5pm; July–Aug daily 11am–5pm; Oct Sat–Sun noon–5pm. Closed Nov–Mar. Take A947 for 37km (23 miles) northwest of Aberdeen.

Craigievar Castle ⭐ Structurally unchanged since its completion in 1626, Craigievar Castle is an exceptional tower house where Scottish baronial archi-tecture reached its pinnacle of achievement. It has contemporary plaster ceilings in nearly all its rooms. The castle was continuously lived in by the descendants of the builder, William Forbes, until it came under the care of the National Trust for Scotland in 1963. The family collection of furnishings is complete. Some 6km (4 miles) south of the castle, clearly signposted on a small road leading off A980, near Lumphanan, is **Macbeth's Cairn,** where the historical Macbeth is supposed to have fought his last battle. Built of timber in a rounded format known by historians as "motte and bailey," it's now nothing more than a steep-sided rounded hillock marked with a sign and a flag.

Hwy. A980, 10km (6 miles) south of Alford. © 01339/883635. Admission £7 ($11) adults, £4.50 ($7.20) sen-iors and children. Castle May–Sept daily 1:30–4:45pm. Grounds year-round daily 9:30am–sunset. Head west on A96 to Alford, then south on A980.

2 Tayside & Grampian ⭐⭐⭐

After exploring Edinburgh, you can tour the history-rich regions of Tayside and Grampian. Perth, 70km (44 miles) north of Edinburgh, makes the best "gate-way" to the region.

PERTH ⭐

From its majestic position on the Tay, the ancient city of Perth was the capital of Scotland until the middle of the 15th century. It's here that the Highlands meet the Lowlands. Perth itself has few historic buildings. The main attraction, Scone Place, lies on the outskirts.

ESSENTIALS

GETTING THERE   By Train   ScotRail provides service between Edinburgh and Perth (trip time: 90 min.), with continuing service to Dundee. The trip to Perth costs £9.40 ($15) from Edinburgh; phone © **0845/748-4950** for 24-hour information.

By Bus   Edinburgh and Perth are connected by frequent bus service (trip time: 1½ hr.). The fare is £6.50 ($10). For more information and schedules, check with CityLink (© **0990/505050**).

By Car   To reach Perth from Edinburgh, take A-90 northwest and go across the Forth Road Bridge, continuing north along M-90 (trip time: 1½ hr.).

VISITOR INFORMATION   The **tourist information center** is at Lower City Mills, West Mill St. (© **01738/450600**), and is open April through June daily from 9am to 6pm, July through September daily from 9am to 7pm, Octo-ber daily from 9am to 6pm, and November through March, Monday through Saturday from 10am to 5pm.

SEEING THE SIGHTS

Kirk of St. John the Baptist   This is the main sightseeing attraction of "the fair city." It's believed that the original foundation is from Pictish times. The present choir dates from 1440 and the nave from 1490. In 1559 John Knox preached his famous sermon here attacking idolatry, which caused a turbulent wave of iconoclasm to sweep across the land. In its wake, religious artifacts, stained glass, and organs were destroyed all over Scotland. The church was restored as a World War I memorial in the mid-1920s.

31 St. John Place. © **01738/622241.** Free admission. Mon–Fri 10am–noon and 2–4pm.

Branklyn Garden ★ Once the finest 2 acres of private garden in Scotland, the Branklyn now belongs to the National Trust for Scotland. It has a superb collection of rhododendrons, alpines, and herbaceous and peat-garden plants from all over the world.

116 Dundee Rd. (A-85), in Branklyn. © **01738/625535.** Admission £4.25 ($6.80) adults, £2 ($3.20) children, students, and seniors; family ticket £7.50 ($12). Mar–Oct daily 9:30am–sunset. Closed in winter.

WHERE TO STAY

Dupplin Castle ★★ Only a 1-hour drive from Edinburgh, this modern, severely dignified mansion was built in 1968 by well-known architect Schomber Scott to replace the last of the three castles that had once risen proudly from the site. Surrounded by 30 acres of forest and spectacular gardens (some of its specimens are 250 years old), the site is one of the most beautiful near Perth. Rooms are rented in a spirit of elegance and good manners, and the views from many of them overlook the valley of the River Earn. Meals are served at one large table, dinner-party style, but you must book 24 hours in advance. *Note:* Children under 12 can stay here only if you book the entire castle.

Near Aberdalgie, Perth PH2 0PY. © **01738/623224.** Fax 01738/444140. www.dupplin.co.uk. 7 units. £120–£140 ($192–$224) double. Rates include breakfast. MC, V. From Perth, follow the main highway to Glasgow, turning left onto B-9112 toward Aberdalgie and Forteviot. No children under age 12 accepted for small parties. **Amenities:** Dining room; clay shooting. *In room:* coffeemaker, hair dryer.

Hunting Tower ★ This late-Victorian country house, about a 10-minute drive from the city center, is set on 3½ acres of well-manicured gardens, with a modern wing of rooms added in 1998. Taste and concern went into the interior decoration. Rooms, which vary wildly in size, each have their specific charm. Seven offer spa baths.

Crieff Rd., Perth PH1 3JT. © **01738/583771.** Fax 01738/583777. www.huntingtowerhotel.co.uk 34 units. £90 ($143) double; from £120 ($191) cottage suite. Rates include Scottish breakfast. AE, DC, MC, V. Drive 6km (3½ miles) west on A-85. **Amenities:** Restaurant; bar; room service; laundry service; dry cleaning. *In room:* TV, minibar, coffeemaker, hair dryer, radio.

Parklands Hotel ★ This luxuriously overhauled country-house hotel is in the middle of the city. The beautifully decorated rooms overlook the South Inch Park. All are spacious and well furnished. Light traditional fare is served in a country-house style.

2 St. Leonard's Bank, Perth PH2 8EB. © **01738/622451.** Fax 01738/622046. www.parklandshotelperth.com. 14 units. £89–£115 ($142–$184) double. Rates include breakfast. AE, DC, MC, V. Free parking. **Amenities:** Restaurant; bar; room service; laundry service; dry cleaning. *In room:* TV, coffeemaker, hair dryer.

Sunbank Guest House ★ *Finds* Lying in the vicinity of Branklyn Gardens, this Victorian structure from 1853 is a gray-stone manse with scenic views of the skyline of Perth and the Tay River. Established as a hotel back in the late 1970s, it enjoys repeat business drawn to its handsome and impressively furnished bedrooms. The style is traditional British with light oak furniture and floral pattern wallpaper. Each unit contains a private bathroom, six with a combo tub and shower, the rest with shower only. The private property has its own car park and

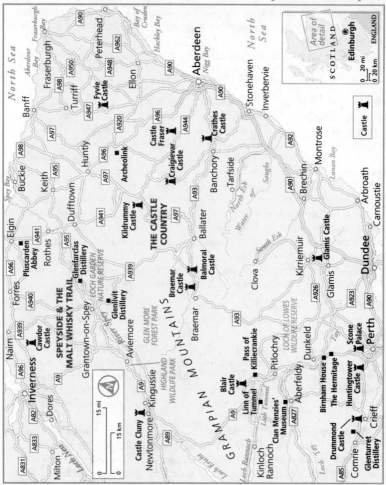

is just a short walk from the center of Perth. The chef and co-owner of the hotel, Remo Ane, has upgraded the restaurant to a point that even nonguests gravitate here for his delicious, well-chosen "Taste of Scotland" menu.

50 Dundee Rd., Perth PH27BA. ℂ **01738/624882.** Fax 01738/442515. www.sunbankhouse.com. 9 units. £80–£90 ($128–$144) double. MC, V. Closed Jan. **Amenities:** Restaurant; bar; room service; babysitting; laundry service. In room: TV, minibar, beverage maker, hair dryer, iron.

WHERE TO DINE

Keracher's Restaurant ✦ SCOTTISH/SEAFOOD   For five generations, the Kerachers have been serving some of the finest seafood in Perth. Chef Andrew Keracher carries on the family tradition by using the freshest ingredients, which are cooked to order. Food is prepared with imagination and panache, but also with a healthy respect for the natural tastes and textures of the produce. Among the main courses on the extensive menu is a "trio of salmon" (with three differ-ence preparations, including smoked), served with a dill-flavored mayonnaise.

Scottish beef is served on a bed of fresh mushrooms with a whole grain mustard cream sauce. For dessert, try the steamed ginger pudding with vanilla ice cream and lime Anglais.

168 South St. (45 min. from Edinburgh on the A90). ℭ01738/449777. Reservations recommended. Main courses £8.90–£16 ($14–$25); set menus £9.90 ($16) for 2 courses, £13 ($21) for 3 courses. MC, V. Tues-Sat noon-2:30pm and 6-10pm. Closed 2 weeks in Jan.

Let's Eat ⭐ BRITISH/INTERNATIONAL   The most visually striking, and most appealing, restaurant in Perth occupies the premises of an 1822 theater and intersperses its tables amid its soaring white columns. There's a particularly cozy lounge, site of a log-burning iron stove and comfortable sofas, where you might want a drink or aperitif before your meal. Menu items, which change frequently, are among the most thoughtful and sophisticated in town. They might include filet of roasted venison with port-wine sauce; or grilled brochettes of monkfish with king prawns, rice, and salad. Also look for handmade black puddings served with "smash" (mashed potatoes), applesauce, and onion gravy. Dessert might be any of several "puddings" that usually live up to their "glorious" billing on the menu. Be careful not to confuse this restaurant with its less grand, less expensive sibling, Let's Eat Again.

77–79 Kinnoul St. ℭ 01738/643377. Reservations recommended. Lunch main courses £8.95–£11 ($14–$17); dinner main courses £9.75–£17 ($16–$26). AE, MC, V. Tues–Sat noon–2pm and 6:30–9:45pm.

A DAY TRIP TO SCONE

Old Scone, 3km (2 miles) from Perth on the River Tay, was the ancient capital of the Picts. On a lump of sandstone called the "Stone of Destiny," the early Scottish monarchs were enthroned. In 1296 Edward I, the "Hammer of the Scots," moved the stone to Westminster Abbey, and for hundreds of years it rested under the chair on which British monarchs were crowned. The Scots have always bitterly resented this theft, and at last, it has been returned to Scotland, to find a permanent home in Edinburgh Castle, where it can be viewed by the public.

The seat of the earls of Mansfield and birthplace of David Douglas of fir-tree fame, **Scone Palace** ⭐⭐, along A-93 (ℭ **01738/552300**), was largely rebuilt in 1802, incorporating the old palace of 1580. Inside is an impressive collection of French furniture, china, ivories, and 16th-century needlework, including bed hangings executed by Mary Queen of Scots. A fine collection of rare conifers is found on the grounds in the Pinetum. Rhododendrons and azaleas grow profusely in the gardens and woodlands around the palace. To reach the palace, head northeast of Perth on A-93. The site is open from April 1 to October 31 only, daily from 9:30am to 5pm. Admission is £6.35 ($10) for adults, £5.50 ($8.80) seniors, £3.75 ($6) for children age 16 years old and under, including entrance to both house and grounds. Admission to the grounds only is £3.25 ($5.20) for adults and £1.80 ($2.90) for children.

WHERE TO STAY & DINE

The Murrayshall ⭐⭐⭐   This elegant country-house hotel is set on 300 acres of parkland. It was completely refurbished in 1987 and reopened as one of the showpieces of Perthshire. Golfers and their families flock here for the excellent, challenging courses. The hotel's public rooms and guest rooms are all traditionally styled, but bedrooms vary in size and comfort. The superior accommodations are the suites and executive rooms, which have the best amenities and views. The less desired standard rooms are also comfortable but lack the character of the others. *Note:* On a windy night in Scotland there is no better place to be than the well-stocked bar with its log fire.

New Scone, Perthshire PH2 7PH. ✆ **01738/551171.** Fax 01738/552595. 41 units. £150–£170 ($240–$272) double; from £180–£200 ($288–$320) suite; £150 ($240) lodge. Rates include Scottish breakfast. AE, DC, MC, V. Take A-94 2.5km (1½ miles) east of New Scone. **Amenities:** Restaurant; 2 bars; 2 golf courses; tennis courts; gym; room service; babysitting; laundry service; dry cleaning. *In room:* TV, hair dryer.

GLENEAGLES

This famous golfing center and sports complex is on a moor between Strathearn and Strath Allan. Gleneagles has four **18-hole golf courses:** King's Course, the longest one; Queen's Course, next in length; Prince's Course, shortest of all; and Glendevon, the newest of the quartet, built in 1980. They're among the best in Scotland, and the sports complex is one of the best-equipped in Europe.

ESSENTIALS
GETTING THERE By Train The 15-minute ride from Perth costs £4 ($6.40). The trip takes 1 hour and 25 minutes from Edinburgh and costs £8.90 ($14). For information, call ✆ **0845/748-4950.**

By Bus The only service departs from Glasgow. The trip takes slightly more than an hour and costs £6 ($9.60). For information and schedules, call ✆ **0870/608-2608.**

By Car Gleneagles is on A-9, about halfway between Perth and Stirling, a short distance from the village of Auchterarder. It lies 88km (55 miles) from Edinburgh and 72km (45 miles) from Glasgow.

VISITOR INFORMATION The year-round tourist center is at 90 High St., Auchterarder (✆ **01764/663450**). It's open November through March Monday through Friday from 10am to 2pm, Saturday from 11am to 3pm; April through June Monday through Saturday from 9:30am to 5:30pm, Sunday from 11am to 4pm; July and August Monday through Saturday from 9am to 7pm, Sunday from 11am to 6pm; and September and October Monday through Saturday from 9:30am to 5:30pm, Sunday from 11am to 4pm.

WHERE TO STAY & DINE
Gleneagles Hotel ★★★   Britain's greatest golf hotel stands on its own 830-acre estate. When it was built in isolated grandeur in 1924, it was Scotland's only five-star hotel. It is a true resort and has tried to keep ahead of the times by offering spa treatments. Public rooms are classical, with pilasters and pillars. Accommodations vary greatly in size. The best and most spacious choices are in the 60 to 90 block series; they have recently been refurbished. The less desirable rooms are called courtyard units; these are a bit small and are equipped with shower-only bathrooms. As for cuisine, the golfers rarely complain, but no one dines here to collect recipes.

Auchterarder PH3 1NF. ✆ **01764/662231.** Fax 01764/662134. www.gleneagles.com. 229 units. £320–£445 ($512–$712) double; from £740 ($1184) suite. Rates include Scottish breakfast. AE, DC, MC, V. Free parking. Take A-9 1½ miles southwest of Auchterarder. **Amenities:** 4 restaurants; 4 bars; 3 pools; health spa; 24-hr. room service; babysitting; laundry service; dry cleaning; hunting excursions. *In room:* TV, minibar, hair dryer, safe.

CRIEFF

From Perth, head west on A-85 for 29km (18 miles) to Crieff. At the edge of the Perthshire Highlands, with good fishing and golf, Crieff makes a pleasant stopover. This small burgh was the seat of the court of the earls of Strathearn until 1747, and the gallows in its marketplace were once used to execute Highland cattle rustlers.

You can take a "day trail" into **Strathearn,** the valley of the River Earn, the very center of Scotland. Here highland mountains meet gentle Lowland slopes, and moorland mingles with rich green pastures. North of Crieff, the road to Aberfeldy passes through the narrow pass of the **Sma' Glen,** a famous spot of beauty, with hills rising on either side to 600m (2,000 ft.).

ESSENTIALS

GETTING THERE **By Train** There's no direct service. The nearest rail stations are at Gleneagles, 14km (9 miles) away, and at Perth, 29km (18 miles) away. Call ℭ **0845/748-4950** for information and schedules.

By Bus Once you arrive in Perth, you'll find regular connecting bus service hourly during the day. For information and schedules, call **Stagecoach** at ℭ **01738/629339.** The bus service from Gleneagles is too poor to recommend.

By Taxi A taxi from Gleneagles will cost from £12 to £15 ($19–$24).

VISITOR INFORMATION The year-round **tourist information office** is in the Town Hall on High Street (ℭ **01764/652578**). It's open November through March, Monday through Friday from 9:30am to 5pm, Saturday from 10am to 2pm; April through June, Monday through Saturday from 9:30am to 5:30pm, Sunday from 11am to 4pm; July and August, Monday through Saturday from 9am to 7pm, Sunday from 11am to 6pm; and September and October, Monday through Saturday from 9:30am to 5:30pm, Sunday from 11am to 4pm.

SEEING THE SIGHTS

Glenturret Distillery Ltd Scotland's oldest distillery, Glenturret was established in 1775 on the banks of the River Turret. Visitors can see the milling of malt, mashing, fermentation, distillation, and cask filling, followed by a free "wee dram" dispensed at the end of the tour. Guided tours take about 25 minutes and leave at frequent intervals—sometimes as often as every 10 minutes when there's a demand for it. This can be followed or preceded by a 20-minute video, *The Water of Life,* that's presented adjacent to a small museum devoted to the implements of the whisky trade.

Hwy. A-85, Glenturret. ℭ **01764/656565.** Guided tours £5.95 ($9.50), £4.95 ($7.90) seniors, £3 ($4.80) children ages 12–17, family ticket £16 ($26), free for children ages 11 and under. Daily 9:30am-5pm. Closed Jan and Dec 25–26. Take A-85 toward Comrie; 1.5km (³⁄₄ mile) from Crieff, turn right at the crossroads; the distillery is .5km (¹⁄₄ mile) up the road.

Drummond Castle Gardens ⭐ The gardens of Drummond Castle, first laid out in the early 17th century by John Drummond, second earl of Perth, are among the finest formal gardens in Europe. There's a panoramic view from the upper terrace, overlooking an example of an early-Victorian parterre in the form of St. Andrew's Cross. The multifaceted sun dial by John Mylne, master mason to Charles I, has been the centerpiece since 1630.

Grimsthorpe, Crieff. ℭ **01764/681257.** Admission £3.50 ($5.60) adults, £2.50 ($4) seniors, £1.50 ($2.40) children. May–Oct daily 2–6pm; Easter weekend 2–6pm. Closed Nov–Apr. Take A-822 for 5km (3 miles) south of Crieff.

PLAYING GOLF

Crieff Golf Club (ℭ **01764/652909**) has two courses—both with panoramic views and excellent facilities. The most challenging is the 18-hole Fern Tower, a par-71 course with three par-5 holes. The Dornock is a 64-par, 9-hole course with three par-3 holes. It's not quite as difficult as the Fern Tower, but a test nonetheless. Greens fees for the Fern Tower are £27 ($43) per round Monday through Friday, and £37 ($59) on weekends. Greens fees for the Dornock are £9 ($14) for 9 holes and £14 ($22) for 18 holes. Carts cost £3 ($4.80) per round. From April to October, the golf club is open from 8am to 11pm; from November to March, hours are Monday through Friday from 9am to 7pm and Saturday and Sunday from 8am to 7:30pm.

WHERE TO STAY & DINE

Murraypark Hotel   This stone-fronted house lies in a residential neighborhood about a 10-minute walk from Crieff's center and close to a golf course. In 1993, a new wing was opened, enlarging the public areas and the number of well-furnished rooms. The property was purchased by new owners in 1999 and has been considerably upgraded, especially its mattresses and the neatly maintained bathrooms. Bedrooms in this former 19-century sea captain's house vary in size and shape, but most open onto views. Although rooms in the new wing are more comfortable, they are hardly as evocative; we still prefer the older wing's traditional Victorian aura.

The hotel's excellent restaurant serves traditional Scottish cuisine in a candlelit dining room.

Connaught Terrace, Crieff PH7 3DJ. ℂ 01764/651670. Fax 01764/655311. www.scotland-hotels.com 19 units. £65–£80 ($104–$128) double or suite. Rates include Scottish breakfast. AE, DC, MC, V. Free parking. **Amenities:** Dining room; bar; room service; babysitting. *In room:* TV, coffeemaker, hair dryer.

ABERFELDY ☆

The "Birks o' Aberfeldy" are among the beauty spots made famous by the poet Robert Burns. Once a Pictish center, this small town makes a fine base for touring Perthshire's glens and lochs. Loch Tay lies 10km (6 miles) to the west; Glen Lyon, 24km (15 miles) west; and Kinloch Rannoch, 29km (18 miles) northwest. The town's shops offer good buys in tweeds and tartans, plus other items of Highland dress.

ESSENTIALS

GETTING THERE   By Train   There's no direct service into Aberfeldy. You can take a train to either Perth or Pitlochry, then continue the rest of the way by bus. Call ℂ 0845/748-4950 for schedules.

By Bus   Connecting buses at either Perth or Pitlochry make the final journey to Aberfeldy. The private bus line **Stagecoach** ℂ 01738/629339) handles much of the bus travel to the smaller towns and villages in the area.

By Car   From Crieff, take A-822 on a winding road north to Aberfeldy. The 48km (30-mile) drive from Perth takes 30 to 45 minutes.

VISITOR INFORMATION   The **tourist office** is at The Square (ℂ 01887/820276; www.perthshire.co.uk). Hours are July and August daily from 9:30am to 6:30pm; April through June, and September and October daily from 9am to 6:30pm, and October through March Monday through Saturday from 9:30am to 5:30pm.

WHERE TO STAY & DINE

Farleyer House Hotel ☆   A tranquil oasis, this hotel of character stands on 70 acres of grounds in the Tay Valley. Although restored and altered over the years, the building dates back to the 1500s. The staff entertains guests as if they were in a private home. The public areas are immaculate and beautifully furnished, and the rooms are well maintained and comfortable.

Hwy. B-846, Aberfeldy PH15 2JE. (© **01887/820332.** Fax 01887/829879. www.farleyer.com. 19 units. £85–£110 ($136–$176) double; £125 ($200) family suite. Rates include breakfast. AE, DC, MC, V. Take B-846 for 3km (2 miles) west of Aberfeldy. **Amenities:** 2 restaurants; 2 bars; room service; babysitting; laundry service; dry cleaning. *In room:* Coffeemaker.

DUNKELD ⚘

A cathedral town, Dunkeld lies in a thickly wooded valley of the Tay River at the edge of the Perthshire Highlands. Once a major ecclesiastical center, it's one of the seats of ancient Scottish history and an important center of the Celtic church.

ESSENTIALS

GETTING THERE   By Train   Trains from Perth arrive every 2 hours and cost £6.20 ($9.90). Travel time by train is 1½ hours. Call © **0345/484950** for information and schedules.

By Bus   Pitlochry-bound buses leaving from Perth make a stopover in Dunkeld, letting you off at the Dunkeld Car Park, which is at the train station (trip time: 50 min.). The cost is £3.75 ($6). Contact **Stagecoach** at © **01738/629339.**

By Car   From Aberfeldy, take A-827 east until you reach the junction of A-9 heading south to Dunkeld.

VISITOR INFORMATION   A **tourist information office** is at The Cross (© **01350/727688**). It's open April through June, Monday through Saturday from 9:30am to 5:30pm and Sunday from 11am to 4pm; from July 1 to September 8, Monday through Saturday from 9:30am to 6:30pm and Sunday from 11am to 5pm; from September 9 to October 27, Monday through Saturday from 9:30am to 5:30pm and Sunday from 11am to 4pm; from October 28 to December, Monday through Saturday from 9:30am to 5:30pm (closed Jan–Mar).

SEEING THE SIGHTS

Founded in A.D. 815, the **Cathedral of Dunkeld** ⚘ was converted from a church to a cathedral in 1127 by David I. It stands on Cathedral Street in a scenic setting along the River Tay. The cathedral was first restored in 1815, and traces of the 12th-century structure remain today. Admission is free, and the cathedral is open May through September Monday through Saturday from 9:30am to 6:30pm, Sunday from 2 to 6:30pm; October through April, Monday through Saturday from 9:30am to 4pm.

The National Trust for Scotland has restored many of the old houses and shops around the marketplace and cathedral. The trust owns 20 houses on High Street and Cathedral Street as well. Many of these houses were constructed in the closing years of the 17th century after the rebuilding of the town following the Battle of Dunkeld. The Trust runs the **Ell Shop,** The Cross (© **01350/727460**), which specializes in Scottish handcrafts. From Easter weekend to December 24, it's open Monday through Saturday from 10am to 5:30pm.

The **Scottish Horse Museum,** The Cross, has exhibits tracing the history of the Scottish Horse Yeomanry, a cavalry force first raised in 1900. The museum is open from Easter to October only, Saturday through Wednesday from 10am to noon and from 1:50 to 5pm. Admission is free.

Shakespeare fans may want to seek out the oak and sycamore in front of the destroyed Birnam House, a mile to the south. This was believed to be a remnant of the **Birnam Wood** in *Macbeth;* you may recall, "Macbeth shall never vanquished be until great Birnam Wood to high Dunsinane Hill shall come against him."

The Hermitage, lying off A-9 about 3km (2 miles) west of Dunkeld, was called a "folly" when it was constructed in 1758 above the wooded gorge of the River Braan. Today it makes for one of the most scenic woodland walks in the area.

PLAYING GOLF

Dunkeld & Birnam, at Dunkeld (✆ **01350/727524**), is touted as the best in the area. The 18-hole course is not too long, but can be quite difficult. It's edged in many areas with bracken, and many a golfer has had to take a drop instead of searching for the errant ball. There are sweeping views of the surrounding environs. Greens fees: Monday through Friday £20 ($32) for 18 holes; Saturday and Sunday £25 ($40) for 18 holes. There are no electric carts; pull carts are available for £4 ($6.40) per round. Hours are daily from 7am to 11pm April through September. October through March, greens fees are reduced to £10 to £11 ($16–$18), and hours are daily from 8am to 4pm. There's no official dress code, although if the starter feels you are not dressed "appropriately" you will be asked to "smarten up" the next time you play the course.

WHERE TO STAY & DINE

Hilton Dunkeld House ★★   The hotel offers the quiet dignity of life in a Scottish country house and is ranked as one of the leading leisure and sports hotels in the area. On the banks of the Tay, the surrounding grounds—280 acres in all— make for a park-like setting. The house is beautifully kept, and rooms come in a wide range of styles, space, and furnishings. In 1999, an annex was converted into an extra wing offering another nine rooms. Salmon and trout fishing are possible right on the grounds, as are an array of other outdoor activities.

Dunkeld PH8 0HX. ✆ **01350/727771.** Fax 01350/728924. www.hilton.com. 97 units. £148–£180 ($237–$288) double; from £220–£240 ($352–$384) suite. Rates include Scottish breakfast. AE, DC, MC, V. **Amenities:** Restaurant; pool; tennis courts; room service; babysitting; laundry service; dry cleaning; fishing. *In room:* TV, minibar, hair dryer.

Kinnaird ★★★   This small hotel rests on a 9,000-acre private estate and offers great warmth, charm, and comfort. Built in 1770 as a hunting lodge, the house has been restored to its previous grandeur. All the beautifully furnished rooms have king-size beds, full private bathrooms, and views. Some rooms overlook the valley of the River Tay; others open onto gardens and woodlands. There are eight cottages on the estate, two of which sleep eight, and the others four.

Kinnaird, Kinnaird Estate, Dunkeld PH8 0LB. ✆ **01796/482440.** Fax 01796/482289. www.kinnairdestate.com. 9 units and 8 estate cottages. £375–£400 ($600–$640) double; £525 ($840) suite; £335–£525 ($536–$840) estate cottages. Rates include dinner and Scottish breakfast. AE, MC, V. Free parking. No children under age 12 accepted in the hotel. **Amenities:** Restaurant; bar; tennis courts; health spa; room service; laundry service; dry cleaning; fishing and hunting excursions. *In room:* TV, hair dryer.

DUNDEE ⊛ & GLAMIS CASTLE ⊛

This royal burgh and old seaport is an industrial city on the north shore of the Firth of Tay. When steamers took over the whaling industry from sailing vessels, Dundee became the leading home port for the ships from the 1860s until World War I. Long known for its jute and flax operations, we think today of the Dundee fruitcakes, marmalades, and jams. This was also the home of the man who invented stick-on postage stamps, James Chalmers. Dundee has a raffish charm and serves well as a base for a trip to Glamis Castle.

Spanning the Firth of Tay is the **Tay Railway Bridge,** opened in 1888. Constructed over the tidal estuary, the bridge is some 3km (2 miles) long, one of the longest in Europe. There's also a road bridge 2km (1¼ miles) long, with four traffic lanes and a walkway in the center.

ESSENTIALS

GETTING THERE **By Train** ScotRail offers frequent service between Perth, Dundee, and Aberdeen. One-way fare from Perth to Dundee is £5 ($8); from Aberdeen, £20 ($31). Phone ℭ **0845/748-4950** for schedules and departure times.

By Bus CityLink buses offer frequent bus service from Edinburgh and Glasgow. Call ℭ **0870/550-5050** for information.

By Car The fastest way to reach Dundee is to cut south back to Perth along A-9 and link up with A-972 going east.

VISITOR INFORMATION The **tourist information office** is at 21 Castle St. (ℭ **01382/527527**. Hours are April through September, Monday through Saturday from 9am to 6pm, Sunday from 10am to 4pm; October through March, Monday through Saturday from 9am to 5pm.

SEEING THE SIGHTS

For a panoramic view of Dundee, the Tay bridges across to Fife, and mountains to the north, go to **Dundee Law,** a 174m (572-ft.) hill just north of the city. The hill is an ancient volcanic plug.

Broughty Castle This 15th-century estuary fort lies about 2.4km (4 miles) east of the city center on the seafront, at Broughty Ferry, a little fishing hamlet and once the terminus for ferries crossing the Firth of Tay before the bridges were built. Besieged by the English in the 16th century and attacked by Cromwell's army under General Monk in the 17th century, it was eventually restored as part of Britain's coastal defenses in 1861. Its gun battery was dismantled in 1956, and it's now a museum with displays on local history, arms and armor, and Dundee's whaling story. The observation area at the top of the castle provides fine views of the Tay estuary and northeast Fife.

Castle Green, Broughty Ferry. ℭ 01382/436916. Free admission. July–Sept Mon 11am–5pm, Tues–Thurs 10am–4pm, Sun 2–4pm; Oct–June Mon 10am–5pm, Tues–Thurs 10am–5pm. Bus: 75 or 76.

HMS *Unicorn* ✯ This 46-gun wooden ship of war commissioned in 1824 by the Royal Navy, now the oldest British-built ship afloat, has been restored and visitors can explore all four decks: the quarterdeck with 32-pound cannonades, the gun deck with its battery of 18-pound cannons and the captain's quarters, the berth deck with officers' cabins and crews' hammocks, and the orlop deck and hold. Various displays portraying life in the sailing navy and the history of the *Unicorn* make this a rewarding visit.

Victoria Dock. ℭ 01382/200900. Admission £3.50 ($5.60) adults, £2.50 ($4) seniors and children; £7.50–£9.50 ($12–$15) family ticket. Easter–Oct daily 10am–5pm; Nov–Easter Wed–Sun 10am–4pm. Bus: 6, 23, or 78.

WHERE TO STAY

Hilton Dundee ✯ This chain hotel helps rejuvenate the once-seedy waterfront of Dundee. Built in a severe modern style, the five-story block takes its name from a famous English tea, which most often accompanies marmalade and

Dundee fruitcakes, the city's two most famous products. Some of the well-furnished rooms overlook the Firth, the river, or the Tay Bridge. Both business and leisure travelers will find solace here in rooms with bright floral upholstery and draperies, blond wood furnishings, and small bathrooms.

Earl Grey Place, Dundee DD1 4DE. (C) **01382/229271.** Fax 01382/200072. www.hilton.com 129 units. £128–£148 ($205–$237) double; from £208 ($333) suite. AE, DC, MC, V. Free parking. Bus: 1A, 1B, or 20. **Amenities:** Restaurant; bar; pool; health spa; room service; laundry service; dry cleaning. *In room:* TV, coffeemaker, hair dryer, trouser press.

Invercarse Hotel   In landscaped gardens overlooking the River Tay, this privately owned hotel lies 5km (3 miles) west of the heart of Dundee. Many prefer it for its fresh air, tranquil location, and Victorian country-house aura. Well-maintained rooms come in a variety of sizes and open onto views across the Tay to the hills of the kingdom of Fife.

371 Perth Rd., Dundee DD2 1PG. (C) **01382/669231.** Fax 01382/644112. 44 units. £90 ($144) double; £100 ($160) suite. Rates include Scottish breakfast. AE, DC, MC, V. Free parking. **Amenities:** Restaurant; bar; room service; laundry service; dry cleaning. *In room:* TV, coffeemaker, hair dryer.

Queen's Hotel ⭐   For the past century and a quarter, this hotel has been a venue for that special occasion in town, be it a wedding or a school reunion. This historic hotel has stayed abreast of the times, but much of its Victorian aura still remains architecturally in spite of modernization. Bedrooms come in a variety of sizes but most of them are quite large, each with a well-kept bathroom. The decorator of the rooms used a rich color palate in the bedrooms, such as classic shades of amber gold or red-wine burgundy. One room is suitable for guests with limited mobility. A local favorite, Nosey Parkers, is a bistro and restaurant, with a Scottish and continental menu supplemented by blackboard specials.

160 Nethergate, Dundee DD1 4DU. (C) **01382/322515.** Fax 01382/202668. www.queenshotel-dundee.com. 52 units. Mon–Thurs £92 ($147) double, £100 ($160) suite; Fri–Sun £62 ($99) double, £82 ($131) suite. Rates include breakfast. Children under 12 stay free. AE, DC, MC, V. **Amenities:** Restaurant; bar; room service; laundry service; dry cleaning. *In room:* TV, hair dryer, beverage maker, iron.

WHERE TO DINE

Jahangir Tandoori INDIAN   Built around an indoor fishpond in a dining room draped with the soft folds of an embroidered tent, this is one of the most exotic restaurants in the region. Meals are prepared with fresh ingredients and cover the gamut of recipes from both north and south India. Some preparations are slow-cooked in clay pots (tandoori) and seasoned to the degree of spiciness you prefer. Both meat and meatless dishes are available.

1 Sessions St. (at the corner of Hawk Hill). (C) **01382/202022.** Reservations recommended. Main courses £10–£15 ($16–$24). AE, MC, V. Daily 5pm–midnight.

A DAY TRIP TO GLAMIS

The little village of Glamis (pronounced without the "i") grew up around **Glamis Castle** ⭐⭐, Castle Office, Glamis ((C) **01307/840393**). Next to Balmoral Castle, visitors to Scotland most want to see Glamis Castle for its link with the crown. For 6 centuries it has been connected to members of the British royal family. The Queen Mother was brought up here; and Princess Margaret was born here, becoming the first royal princess born in Scotland in 3 centuries. The present owner is the queen's great-nephew. The castle contains Duncan's Hall—the Victorians claimed this was where Macbeth murdered King Duncan, but in the play, the murder takes place at Macbeth's castle (Cawdor) near Inverness. In fact, Shakespeare was erroneous, as well—he had Macbeth named Thane of Glamis, but Glamis wasn't made a thaneship (a sphere of influence in medieval Scotland) until years after the play takes place.

The present Glamis Castle dates from the early 15th century, but there're records of a castle having been in existence in the 11th century. The Lyon family has owned Glamis Castle since 1372, and it contains some fine plaster ceilings, furniture, and paintings.

The castle is open to the public, with access to the Royal Apartments and many other rooms, as well as the fine gardens, from the end of March to the end of October only, daily from 10:30am to 5:30pm. Admission to the castle and gardens is £6.70 ($11) adults, £3.50 ($5.60) children, family ticket £18 ($29). If you wish to visit the grounds only, the charge is £3.50 ($5.60) adults, £2.50 ($4) children. Buses run between Dundee and Glamis. The 35-minute ride costs £4 ($6.40) one-way. *Note:* Buses don't run on Sunday, and they don't stop in front of the castle, which lies 1 mile from the bus stop.

WHERE TO STAY

Castleton House Hotel ★ *Finds* This country-house hotel is run with love and care by owners, David Webster and Verity Nicholson, who acquired it in 2000. In cool weather you're greeted by welcoming coal fires in the public lounge; the youthful staff is the most considerate we've encountered in the area. Rooms of various sizes are furnished with reproductions of antiques; the suite features a genuine Regency four-poster bed. Chef Andrew Wilkie presides over the award-winning restaurant, where most of the fruits and vegetables served are grown on the hotel's grounds.

Eassie by Glamis, Forfar, Tayside DD8 1SJ. ✆ **01307/840340.** Fax 01307/840506. www.castletonglamis.co.uk. 6 units. £120 ($192) double. Children ages 10 and under stay free in parent's room. Rates include Scottish breakfast. AE, MC, V. Drive 5km (3 miles) west of Glamis on A-94. **Amenities:** 2 restaurants; bar; room service; laundry service; dry cleaning. *In room:* TV, coffeemaker, hair dryer.

WHERE TO DINE

Strathomore Arms CONTINENTAL/SCOTTISH Try this place near the castle for one of the best lunches in the area. You might begin with the freshly made soup of the day or fresh prawns. Some of the dishes regularly featured might include steak pie or venison. For something a little more exotic there's the Indian chicken breast, marinated in yogurt and spices; and for vegetarians, there's phyllo parcels stuffed with asparagus and cauliflower.

The Square Glamis. ✆ **01307/840248.** Reservations recommended. Main courses £7.50–£19 ($12–$30). AE, MC, V. Daily noon–2pm and 6:30–9pm.

BRAEMAR

In the heart of some of Grampian's most beautiful scenery, Braemar is not only known for its own castle, but it also makes a good center from which to explore Balmoral Castle (see "Ballater & Balmoral Castle," below). In this Highland village, set against a massive backdrop of hills covered with heather in summer, Clunie Water joins the River Dee. The massive **Cairn Toul** towers over Braemar, reaching a height of 1,292m (4,241 ft.).

ESSENTIALS

GETTING THERE **By Train** Take the train to Aberdeen, then continue the rest of the way by bus. For information and schedules, call ✆ **0845/748-4950.**

By Bus Buses run daily from Aberdeen to Braemar 6 times a day (trip time: 2 hr.). One-way fare is £7.20 ($12). The bus and train stations in Aberdeen are next to each other on Guild Street (© **01224/212266** for information about schedules).

By Car   To reach Braemar from Dundee, return west toward Perth, then head north along A-93, following the signs into Braemar. The 70-mile drive will take 70 to 90 minutes.

VISITOR INFORMATION   The year-round **Braemar Tourist Office** is in The Mews, Mar Road (© **01339/742208**). In June, hours are daily from 10am to 6pm; July and August daily from 9am to 7pm, and in September daily from 10am to 1pm and 2 to 6pm. Off-season hours are Monday through Saturday from 10am to 1pm and 2 to 5pm, Sunday from noon to 5pm.

SPECIAL EVENTS   The spectacular **Royal Highland Gathering** takes place annually in late August or early September in the Princess Royal and Duke of Fife Memorial Park. The queen herself often attends the gathering. These ancient games are thought to have been originated by King Malcolm Canmore, a chieftain who ruled much of Scotland at the time of the Norman conquest of England. He selected his hardiest warriors from all the clans for a "keen and fair contest."

Call the tourist office (see "Visitor Information," above) for more information. Braemar is overrun with visitors during the gathering—anyone thinking of attending would be wise to reserve accommodations anywhere within a 32km (20-mile) radius of Braemar no later than early April.

SEEING THE SIGHTS

If you're a royal family–watcher, you might be able to spot members of the family, even the queen, at **Crathie Church,** 14km (9 miles) east of Braemar on A-93 (© **01339/742208**), where they attend Sunday services when in residence. Services are at 11:30am; otherwise the church is open to view April through October, Monday through Saturday from 9:30am to 5:30pm and on Sunday from 2 to 5:30pm.

Nature lovers may want to drive to the **Linn of Dee,** 10km (6 miles) west of Braemar, a narrow chasm on the River Dee, which is a local beauty spot. Other beauty spots include Glen Muick, Loch Muick, and Lochnagar. A **Scottish Wildlife Trust Visitor Centre,** reached by a minor road, is located in this Highland glen, off the South Deeside road. An access road joins B-976 at a point 26km (16 miles) east of Braemar. The tourist office (see above) will give you a map pinpointing these beauty spots.

Braemar Castle ⭐   This romantic 17th-century castle is a fully furnished private residence with architectural grace, scenic charm, and historical interest. The castle has barrel-vaulted ceilings and an underground prison and is known for its remarkable star-shaped defensive curtain wall.

On the Aberdeen-Ballater-Perth Rd. (A-93). © **01339/741219.** Admission £4 ($6.40) adults, £3 ($4.80) seniors and students, £1.50 ($2.40) children age 5–15; free for children age 4 and under. Mon after Easter to Oct, Sat–Thurs 10am–6pm. Closed Nov–Easter. Take A93 .8km (½ mile) northeast of Braemar.

PLAYING GOLF

Braemar Golf Course, at Braemar (© **01339/741618**), is the highest golf course in the country. The second hole green is 380m (1,250 ft.) above sea level—this is the trickiest hole on the course. Pro golf commentator Peter Alliss has deemed it "the hardest par 4 in all of Scotland." Set on a plateau, the hole is bordered on the right by the River Clunie and lined on the left by rough. Greens fees are as follows: Monday through Friday £20 ($32) for 18 holes and £20

($31) for a day ticket; Saturday and Sunday £18 ($28) for 18 holes and £23 ($37) for a day ticket. Pull carts can be rented for £4 ($6.40) per day, and sets of clubs can be borrowed for £7 ($11) per day. The only dress code is "be reasonable." The course is open only April through October daily (call in advance as hours can vary).

WHERE TO STAY & DINE

Braemar Lodge Hotel *Kids*   This hotel, popular with skiers who frequent the nearby Glenshee slopes, is set on 2 acres at the head of Glen Clunie. Bedrooms vary in shape and size, but each is comfortable and well equipped, containing well-maintained bathrooms. Rooms are bright and airy, with soothing color schemes. Two rooms are large enough for families. On cool evenings, you're greeted with log fires. The hotel is on the road to the Glenshee ski slopes near the cottage where Robert Louis Stevenson wrote *Treasure Island*. Three log cabins have been built recently on the grounds. Fully equipped with all modern conveniences, they sleep up to six persons.

6 Glenshee Rd., Braemar AB35 5YQ. ©/fax **01339/741627.** 7 units. £75 ($120) double; £220–£470 ($352–$752) log cabin. Rates include Scottish breakfast. MC, V. Free parking. Closed Nov. **Amenities:** Restaurant; laundry service; dry cleaning. *In room:* TV, hair dryer.

Invercauld Arms Thistle Hotel *⋆*   This is the town's leading inn, with more amenities and greater comfort than Braemar Lodge. The oldest part of this old granite building dates from the 18th century. In cool weather there's a roaring log fire on the hearth. You can go hill walking and see deer, golden eagles, and other wildlife. Fishing and, in winter, skiing are other pursuits in the nearby area. Rooms are comfortably furnished. Although they lack any style or glamour, they serve their purpose well and come in a wide range of sizes. In the pub close by, you'll meet the "ghilles" and "stalkers" (hunting and fishing guides), then return to the hotel for its Scottish and international fare.

Braemar AB35 5YR. © **01339/741605.** Fax 01339/741428. 68 units. £111 ($178) double. Rates include Scottish breakfast. AE, DC, MC, V. Free parking. Bus: 201. **Amenities:** Restaurant; bar; room service; laundry service; dry cleaning. *In room:* TV, coffeemaker, hair dryer.

BALLATER & BALMORAL CASTLE *⋆⋆*

Ballater is a vacation resort center on the Dee River, with the Grampian Mountains in the background. The town still centers on its Station Square, where the royal family used to be photographed as they arrived to spend vacations. The railway is now closed.

ESSENTIALS

GETTING THERE   By Train   Go to Aberdeen and continue the rest of the way by connecting bus. For rail schedules and information, call © **0845/ 748-4950.**

By Bus   Buses run hourly from Aberdeen to Ballater. The bus and train stations in Aberdeen are next to each other on Guild Street (© **01224/212266** for information). Bus no. 201 from Braemar runs to Ballater (trip time: 1¼ hr.). The fare is £4 ($6.40).

By Car   From Braemar, go east along A-93.

VISITOR INFORMATION   The **tourist information office** is at Station Square (© **01339/755306**). Hours are July and August, daily from 10am to 1pm and 2 to 6pm; September and October and May and June, Monday through Saturday from 10am to 1pm and 2 to 5pm, Sunday from 1 to 5pm. Closed November through April.

THE CASTLE

Balmoral Castle   "This dear paradise" is how Queen Victoria described Balmoral Castle, rebuilt in the Scottish baronial style by her beloved Albert and completed in 1855. Today Balmoral, 13km (8 miles) west of Ballater, is still a private residence of the British sovereign, and its principal feature is a 100-foot tower. On the grounds are many memorials to the royal family. In addition to the gardens, there are country walks, pony trekking, souvenir shops, and a refreshment room. Of the actual castle, only the ballroom is open to the public; it houses an exhibition of pictures, porcelain, and works of art.

Balmoral, Ballater. © 01339/742534. Admission £4.50 ($7.20) adults, £3.50 ($5.60) seniors, £1 ($1.60) for children ages 5–16, free for children ages 4 and under. Apr 10–May 3 Mon–Sat 10am–5pm; June 1–Aug 2 daily 10am–5pm. Closed Aug 3–Apr 9. Crathie bus from Aberdeen to the Crathie station; Balmoral Castle is signposted from there (a short walk).

WHERE TO STAY

Hilton Craigendarroch Hotel ★   This hotel, built in the Scottish baronial style, is set amid old trees on a 28-acre estate. Modern comforts have been added, but the owners have tried to maintain a 19th-century aura. The public rooms include a regal oaken staircase and a large sitting room. The fair-size rooms open onto views of the village of Ballater and the River Dee. Each is furnished in individual style, with shower-only bathrooms, and small refrigerators (not minibars). Public facilities are luxurious, especially the study with oak paneling, a log fire, and book-lined shelves.

Braemar Rd., Ballater AB35 5XA. © 01339/755858. Fax 01339/755447. www.hilton.com. 45 units. £115–£135 ($184–$216) double; £190 ($304) suite. Rates include Scottish breakfast. Half board £20 ($32) extra per person. AE, DC, MC, V. **Amenities:** 2 restaurants; 2 bars; tennis courts; solarium; salon; 24-hr. room service; babysitting; laundry service; dry cleaning. *In room:* TV, fridge, hair dryer, trouser press.

Monaltrie Hotel (Kids)   This 1835 hotel is the first in the region and its Arbeen granite finish speaks of its old days as a health spa. Today its clientele come for the live music in its pub and for the savory food served, the most unusual of which is a Thai cuisine. Each of the fair-size guest rooms sports an unobtrusive monochromatic decor and comfortable beds along with a tiled shower-only bathroom. The hotel lies a 3-minute walk east of the center of town.

5 Bridge Sq., Ballater AB35 5QJ. © 01339/755417. Fax 01339/755180. www.monaltriehotel.co.uk. 24 units. £60–£70 ($96–$112) double. Rates include continental breakfast. AE, DC, MC, V. Free parking. **Amenities:** 2 restaurants; bar; children's play area. *In room:* TV, coffeemaker, radio.

WHERE TO DINE

Green Inn SCOTTISH   In the heart of town, once a temperance hotel, this is now one of the finest dining rooms in Ballater, especially for traditional Scottish dishes. The chef places emphasis on local produce, including homegrown vegetables when available. In season, loin of venison is served with a bramble sauce, and you can always count on fresh salmon and the best of Angus beef. Three very simply furnished double rooms are rented here, all with private bathrooms (with shower) and TV. Half board costs £62 ($99) per person.

9 Victoria Rd., Ballater AB35 5QQ. ©/fax 01339/755701. Reservations required. Fixed-price menu £28 ($44) for 2 courses, £33 ($52) for 3 courses. AE, DC, MC, V. Mar–Oct daily 7–9pm; Nov–Feb Tues–Sat 7–9pm.

Oaks Restaurant BRITISH   The most glamorous restaurant in the region, the Oaks is in the century-old mansion that was originally built by the "marmalade kings" of Britain, the Keiller family. (The company's marmalade is still a household word throughout the United Kingdom.) This is the most upscale of the three restaurants in a resort complex that includes hotel rooms, time-share villas, and access to a nearby golf course. To start, try the venison and duck terrine flavored with orange and brandy and served with a warm black conch vinaigrette. Other main courses include roast rack of lamb, breast of Grampian chicken, loin of venison, or filet of Aberdeen Angus beef.

In the Hilton Craigendarroch Hotel, Braemar Rd. ℂ 01339/755858. Reservations strongly recommended. Fixed-price 4-course dinner £33 ($52). AE, DC, MC, V. Daily 7–10:30pm.

SPEYSIDE ✸ & THE MALT WHISKY TRAIL ✸

Much of the Speyside region covered in this section is in the Moray district, on the southern shore of the Moray Firth, a great inlet cutting into the northeastern coast of Scotland. The district stretches in a triangular shape south from the coast to the wild heart of the Cairngorm Mountains near Aviemore. It's a land steeped in history, as its many castles, battle sites, and ancient monuments testify. It's also a good place to fish and, of course, play golf. Golfers can purchase a 5-day ticket from tourist information centers that will allow them to play at more than 11 courses in the area.

One of the best of these courses is **Boat of Garten,** Speyside (ℂ **01479/ 831282**). Relatively difficult, the almost 5,500m (6,000-yard) course is dotted with many bunkers and wooded areas. April through October greens fees are £25 ($40) Monday through Friday, and hours are from 7:30am to 11pm. Saturday greens fees are £32 ($51), and hours are from 10am to 4pm. In winter, call to see if the course is open. Greens fees are then reduced to £15 ($24). Pull-carts can be rented for £4 ($6.40), and electric carts are available for £7 ($11). Dress reasonably; blue jeans are not acceptable.

The valley of the second-largest river in Scotland, the Spey, lies north and south of Aviemore. It's a land of great natural beauty. The Spey is born in the Highlands above Loch Laggan, which lies 64km (40 miles) south of Inverness. Little more than a creek at its inception, it gains in force, fed by the many "burns" that drain water from the surrounding hills. It's one of Scotland's great rivers for salmon fishing, and it runs between the towering Cairngorms on the east and the Monadhliath Mountains on the west. Its major center is Grantown-on-Spey.

The major tourist attraction in the area is the **Malt Whisky Trail,** 113km (70 miles) long, running through the glens of Speyside. Here distilleries, many of which can be visited, are known for their production of *uisge beatha* or "water of life." "Whisky" is its more familiar name.

Half the malt distilleries in the country lie along the River Spey and its tributaries. Here peat smoke and Highland water are used to turn out single-malt (unblended) whisky. There're five malt distilleries in the area: **Glenlivet, Glenfiddich, Glenfarclas, Strathisla,** and **Tamdhu.** Allow about an hour each to visit them.

The best way to reach Speyside from Aberdeen is to take A-96 northwest, signposted Elgin. If you're traveling north on the A-9 road from Perth and Pitlochry, your first stop might be at Dalwhinnie, which has the highest whisky distillery in the world at 575m (1,888 ft.). It's not in the Spey Valley but is at the northeastern end of Loch Ericht, with views of lochs and forests.

KEITH

Keith, 18km (11 miles) northwest of Huntly, grew up because of its strategic location, where the main road and rail routes between Inverness and Aberdeen cross the River Isla. It has an ancient history, but owes its present look to the "town planning" of the late 18th and early 19th centuries. Today it's a major stopover along the Malt Whisky Trail.

The oldest operating distillery in the Scottish Highlands, the **Strathisla Distillery,** on Seafield Avenue (© **01542/783044**), was established in 1786. Hours are from February to mid-March, Monday through Friday from 9:30am to 4pm; from mid-March to November 30, Monday through Saturday from 9:30am to 4pm, Sunday from 12:30 to 4pm; closed December and January. Admission is £5.50 ($8.80) for adults, free for children ages 8 to 18; children ages 7 and under are not admitted. The admission fee includes a £3 ($4.80) voucher redeemable in the distillery shop against a 70cl bottle of whisky. Be warned that tours of this distillery are self-guided.

WHERE TO STAY

Grange House ⭐ This dignified-looking stone house dates from 1815, when it was the manse (home of a minister) for the nearby Church of Scotland, which is still the most prominent building in this tiny hamlet. Doreen Blanche and her husband, Bill, rent two well-decorated and comfortable rooms within their private home. The venue is upscale, charming, and comfortable, with a calm and quiet that's enhanced by the 8 acres of parks and gardens that surrounds this isolated place. Ask the owners to point out the late-Victorian addition, completed in 1898, that greatly enlarged the size of the original house. No smoking indoors.

Grange, near Keith AB55 6RY. © and fax **01542/870206**. www.aboutscotland.com/banff/grangehouse.html. 2 units. £60 ($96) double. Rates include breakfast. No credit cards. From Keith, drive 5km (3 miles) east of town, following the signs to Banff, into the hamlet of Grange. **Amenities:** Dining area; babysitting; laundry service. *In room:* Coffeemaker, hair dryer.

DUFFTOWN

James Duff, the fourth earl of Fife, founded this town in 1817. The four main streets of town converge at the battlemented **clock tower,** which is also the tourist information center. A center of the whisky-distilling industry, Dufftown is surrounded by seven malt distilleries. The family-owned **Glenfiddich Distillery** is on A-941, just north of Dufftown (© **01340/820373**). It's open Monday through Friday from 9:30am to 4:30pm; from Easter to mid-October it's also open on Saturday from 9:30am to 4:30pm and on Sunday from noon to 4:30pm. Guides in kilts show visitors around the plant and explain the process of distilling. A film on the history of distilling is also shown. At the finish of the tour, you're given a dram of malt whisky to sample. The tour is free, but there's a souvenir shop where the owners hope you'll spend a few pounds.

Other sights include **Balvenie Castle,** along A-941 (© **01340/820121**), the ruins of a moated stronghold from the 14th century on the south side of the Glenfiddich Distillery. During her northern campaign against the earl of Huntly, Mary Queen of Scots spent 2 nights here. It's open April through September, daily from 9:30am to 6:30pm. Admission is £1.50 ($2.40) for adults, £1.10 ($1.75) seniors, and 50p (80¢) for children 15 and under.

Mortlach Parish Church in Dufftown is one of the oldest places of Christian worship in the country. It's reputed to have been founded in 566 by St. Moluag. A Pictish cross stands in the graveyard. The present church was reconstructed in 1931 and incorporates portions of an older building.

WHERE TO DINE

Taste of Speyside ✩ SCOTTISH   True to its name, this restaurant in the town center, just off the main square, avidly promotes Speyside cuisine as well as malt whiskies from each of Speyside's 46 distilleries. A platter including a slice of smoked salmon, smoked venison, smoked trout, paté flavored with malt whisky, locally made cheese (cow or goat), salads, and homemade oat cakes is offered at noon and at night. Nourishing soup is made fresh daily and is served with homemade bread. There's also a choice of meat pies, including venison with red wine and herbs or rabbit. For dessert, try Scotch Mist, which contains fresh cream, malt whisky, and crumbled meringue.

10 Balvenie St. ✆ 01340/820860. Reservations recommended in the evening. Main courses £12–£15 ($18–$23); Speyside platter £12 ($19) at lunch, £15 ($24) at dinner. MC, V. Mon–Sat noon–9pm. Closed Nov–Feb.

GRANTOWN-ON-SPEY

This vacation resort, with its gray granite buildings, is 55km (34 miles) southeast of Inverness, in a wooded valley from which it commands views of the Cairngorm Mountains. It's a key center of winter sports in Scotland. Fishers are also attracted to this setting, because the Spey is renowned for its salmon. One of Scotland's many 18th-century planned towns, it was founded on a heather-covered moor in 1765 by Sir James Grant of Grant and became the seat of that ancient family. The town was famous in the 19th century as a Highland tourist center.

From a base here, you can explore the valleys of the Don and Dee, the Cairngorms, and Culloden Moor, scene of the historic battle in 1746, when Bonnie Prince Charlie and his army were defeated.

A year-round **tourist information office** is on High Street (✆ **01479/ 872773**). Hours April through October are daily from 9am to 5pm, Sunday from 10am to 4pm; November through March, Monday through Friday from 9am to 4pm, Saturday from 10am to 4pm.

WHERE TO STAY

Garth Hotel   The elegant, comfortable Garth stands on 4 acres beside the town square. Guests enjoy the use of a spacious upstairs lounge, whose high ceilings, wood-burning stove, and vine-covered veranda make it an attractive place for morning coffee or afternoon tea. The comfortable and handsomely furnished rooms have all the necessary amenities. The extensive and selective meals with a French slant here favor Scottish dishes, with an emphasis on fresh local produce.

The Square, Castle Rd., Grantown-on-Spey, Morayshire PH26 3HN. ✆ 01479/872836. Fax 01479/872116. 17 units. £62 ($99) double. Rates include Scottish breakfast. MC, V. Free parking. **Amenities:** Restaurant; bar; room service. *In room:* TV, coffeemaker, hair dryer.

Tulchan Lodge ✩✩   Built in 1906 to serve as the 23,000-acre Tulchan Estate's fishing and shooting lodge, this is a place for both sports-oriented visitors and travelers who want to experience a place designed with the elegance required by Edward VII; he came here for sports. The lodge offers panoramic views of the Spey Valley, and each room is different in size and furnishings. In the two elegant dining rooms, Scottish and international dishes are served, with only full-board residents accepted.

Advie, Grantown-on-Spey PH26 3PW. ✆ 01807/510200. Fax 01807/510234. www.tulchan.com 13 units. £350–£500 ($560–$800) double. Rates include full board. MC, V. Closed Feb–Mar. Drive 14km (9 miles) northeast of Grantown on B-9102. **Amenities:** 2 dining areas; lounge; tennis court; room service; babysitting; laundry service; dry cleaning; shooting. *In room:* Hair dryer.

WHERE TO DINE

Craggan Mill BRITISH/ITALIAN This licensed restaurant and lounge bar, a 10-minute walk south of the town center, is housed in a restored ruined granite mill whose waterwheel is still visible. The owners offer British or Italian cuisine at attractive prices. Your appetizer might be smoked trout in deference to Scotland, or ravioli, inspired by sunny Italy. Main courses might be breast of chicken with cream or chicken cacciatore, followed by a dessert of rum-raisin ice cream or peach Melba. You've probably had better versions of all the dishes offered here, but what you get isn't bad. A good selection of Italian wines is also offered.

Hwy. A-95 1km (¾ mile) south of Grantown-on-Spey. ℂ 01479/872288. Reservations recommended. Main courses £3.95–£17 ($6.30–$27). MC, V. May–Sept daily noon–2pm and 6–11pm; Oct–Apr Tues–Sun 7–10pm. Closed the first 2 weeks in Nov.

GLENLIVET

As you leave Grantown-on-Spey and head east along A-95, drive to the junction with B-9008; go south and you won't miss the **Glenlivet Distillery.** The location of the **Glenlivet Reception Centre** (ℂ 01542/783220) is 16km (10 miles) north of the nearest town, Tomintoul. Near the River Livet, a Spey tributary, this distillery is one of the most famous in Scotland. It's open from mid-April to October Monday through Saturday from 10am to 4pm, and Sunday from 12:30 to 4pm. July and August, Monday through Saturday from 10am to 4pm and Sunday from 12:30pm to 4pm. Admission is free.

Back on A-95, you can visit the **Glenfarclas Distillery** at Ballindalloch (ℂ 01807/500245), one of the few malt whisky distilleries that's still independent of the giants. Founded in 1836, Glenfarclas is managed by the fifth generation of the Grant family. There's a small craft shop, and each visitor is offered a dram of Glenfarclas Malt Whisky. The admission of £3.50 ($5.60) is for visitors over age 18, and there's a discount of £1 ($1.60) on any purchase of £10 ($16) or more. It's open all year, Monday through Friday from 10am to 5pm; June through September, it's also open Saturday from 10am to 5pm and Sunday from 10am to 4pm.

WHERE TO STAY

Minmore House Hotel ✪ This impressive country house stands on 5 acres of private grounds adjacent to the Glenlivet Distillery. It was the home of the distillery owners before becoming a hotel. The hotel operators have elegantly furnished their drawing room, which opens onto views of the plush Ladder Hills. The well-furnished bedrooms have all the vital amenities, and the oak-paneled lounge bar has an open log fire on chilly nights.

Glenlivet, Ballindalloch AB37 9DB. ℂ 01807/590378. Fax 01807/590472. www.smoothhound.co.uk/hotels/minmore.html. 10 units. £190 ($304) double. Rates include breakfast, afternoon tea, and 4-course dinner. AE, MC, V. Closed Feb. **Amenities:** Dining room; bar; pool. *In room:* Coffeemaker, hair dryer.

KINCRAIG

Kincraig enjoys a scenic spot at the northern end of Loch Insh, overlooking the Spey Valley to the west and the Cairngorm Mountains to the east. Near Kincraig, the most notable sight is the **Highland Wildlife Park** ✪ (ℂ 01540/651270), a natural area of parkland with a collection of wildlife, some of which is extinct elsewhere in Scotland. Herds of European bison, red deer, shaggy Highland cattle, wild horses, St. Kilda Soay sheep, and roe deer range the park. In enclosures are wolves, polecats, wildcats, beavers, badgers, and pine martens.

You can observe protected birds, such as golden eagles and several species of grouse—of special interest is the *capercaillie* (horse of the woods), a large Eurasian grouse native to Scotland's pine forests. There's a visitor center with a gift shop, cafe, and exhibition areas. Ample parking and a picnic site are also available.

You need a car to go through the park; walkers are discouraged and are picked up by park rangers. The park is open every day at 10am. April to October, the last entrance is at 4pm, except during July and August, when the last entrance is at 5pm. From November to March, the last entrance is at 2pm. All people and vehicles are expected to vacate the park within 2 hours of the day's last admission. Admission to the park is £6.50 ($10) for adults, £5.40 ($8.65) for seniors, and £4.35 ($6.95) for children. A family ticket costs £22 ($35).

KINGUSSIE

Your next stop along the Spey might be at the little summer vacation resort and winter ski center of Kingussie (it's pronounced King-*you*-see), just off A-9, the capital of Badenoch, a district known as "the drowned land" because the Spey can flood the valley when the snows of a severe winter melt in the spring.

Kingussie, 188km (117 miles) northwest of Edinburgh, 66km (41 miles) south of Inverness, and 18km (11 miles) southwest of Aviemore, practically adjoins Newtonmore (see below), directly northeast along A-86.

The **Highland Folk Museum** ⚘, Duke Street (② **01540/661307**), was the first folk museum established in Scotland (1934), and its collections are based on the life of the Highlanders. You'll see domestic, agricultural, and industrial items. Open-air exhibits are a turf *kailyard* (kitchen garden), a Lewis "black house," and old vehicles and carts. Traditional events, such as spinning, music making, and handcraft fairs, are held throughout the summer. Admission is £2 ($3.20) for adults, £1 ($1.60) for children and seniors, £15 ($24) for a family ticket. Hours are April through October Monday through Saturday from 10:30am to 4pm.

A summer-only **tourist center** is on King Street (② **01540/661297**). It's open only from April to October, Monday through Saturday from 10am to 1pm and 2 to 6pm, and on Sunday from 10am to 1pm and 2 to 5pm.

WHERE TO STAY

Homewood Lodge ⚘ *Kids*   One of the best B&Bs in the area, this small Highland house offers large, simply furnished doubles and family-size accommodations. In a garden and woodland setting, the house has a sitting room with an open fire. Good traditional local fare is served in the evening (reservations recommended). Summer barbecues are also offered, and children are welcome.

Newtonmore Rd., Kingussie PH21 1HD. ② 01540/661507. www.homewood-lodge-kingussie.co.uk. 4 units. £40 ($64) double. Rates include Scottish breakfast. No credit cards. Free parking. **Amenities:** Dining area; laundry service; dry cleaning. *In room:* TV, coffeemaker, hair dryer, radio.

WHERE TO DINE

The Cross ⚘⚘ SCOTTISH   This chic restaurant comes as a surprise: In an out-of-the-way setting in a remote Highland village, it serves superlative meals that offer a touch of the theatrical as well as fine ingredients. The restaurant stands on 4 acres, with the Gynack Burn running through the grounds. The main building is an old tweed mill. The restaurant has an open-beam ceiling and French doors leading out onto a terrace over the water's edge where al fresco dinners are served. Specialties depend on the availability of produce in the local markets and might include venison Francatelli, or Highland lamb with sorrel.

Nine rooms are rented in a new building. Each room is different in size and style—for example, two rooms have canopied beds, and another has a balcony overlooking the mill pond. Doubles, including half board, cost from £197 ($315). Personal service and attention to detail go into the running of this place, operated by Ruth and Tony Hadley, and Ruth's cooking has put it on the gastronomic map of Scotland.

Tweed Mill Brae, off the Ardbroilach road, Kingussie PH21 1TC. ℰ **01540/661166.** Fax 01540/661080. Reservations recommended. Fixed-price 5-course dinner £41 ($65). MC, V. Wed–Mon 7–9pm. Closed Dec–Feb.

NEWTONMORE

This Highland resort in Speyside is a good center for the Grampian and Monadhliath mountains, and it offers excellent fishing, golf, pony trekking, and hill walking. A track from the village climbs past the Calder River to Loch Dubh and the massive 940m (3,087-ft.) **Carn Ban,** where eagles fly. **Castle Cluny,** ancient seat of the MacPherson chiefs, is 10km (6 miles) west of Newtonmore.

You may want to stop and have a look at **Clan MacPherson House & Museum,** Main Street (ℰ **01540/673332**). Displayed are clan relics and memorials, including the Black Chanter and Green Banner as well as a "charmed sword," and the broken fiddle of the freebooter, James MacPherson—a Scottish Robin Hood. Relics associated with Bonnie Prince Charlie are also here. An annual clan rally is held in August. Admission is free, but donations are accepted. It's open Monday through Saturday from 10am to 5pm, Sunday from 2 to 5pm, but only from April to October.

WHERE TO STAY

Pines Hotel   Built in 1903, this somber-looking house sits on a hill overlooking the Spey Valley and lies just west of the hamlet's center. Your hosts are Colin and Pamela Walker, migrants from Brighton, who charge singles the bargain price of £27 ($43) for a double. All rooms have pleasant views of the Highland countryside and each comes with a small but neat shower-only bathroom. The food is wholesome, straightforward Scottish cuisine, made from fresh ingredients, such as salmon, lamb, venison, and Aberdeen Angus beef. Colin's wife, Pamela, is an expert on desserts and has a particular interest in creating treats for diabetics.

Station Rd., Newtonmore PH20 1AR. ℰ **01540/673271.** 5 units. £50–£53 ($80–$85) double. Rates include Scottish breakfast. MC, V. Free parking. Closed Dec 28–Jan 15. *In room:* TV, coffeemaker, hair dryer.

19

Inverness & the West Highlands

The romantic glens and rugged mountain landscapes of the West Highlands are timeless and pristine. You can see deer grazing only yards from the highway in remote parts and can stop by your own secluded loch to enjoy a picnic or to fish for trout and salmon. The shadow of Macbeth still stalks the land (locals say the 11th-century king was much maligned by Shakespeare). The area's most famous resident, however, is said to live in mysterious Loch Ness: First sighted by St. Columba in the 6th century, "Nessie" has cleverly evaded searchers ever since.

Centuries of invasions, rebellions, and clan feuds are distant memories now. The Highlands aren't as remote as they once were, when many Londoners seriously believed the men of the Highlands had tails! **Fort William** is a major center for the West Highlands, surrounded by wildly beautiful **Lochaber,** the "land of bens, glens, and heroes." Dominating the area is **Ben Nevis,** Britain's highest mountain. This district is the western end of what is known as the **Glen Mor**—the Great Glen, geologically a fissure dividing the northwest of Scotland from the southeast and containing Loch Lochy, Loch Oich, and Loch Ness. The Caledonian Canal, opened in 1847, linked these lochs, the River Ness, and Moray Firth. It provided sailing boats a safe alternative to the stormy route around the north of Scotland. Larger steamships have made the canal commercially out of date, but fishing boats and pleasure steamers still use it. Good roads run the length of the Great Glen, partly following the line of Gen. George Wade's military road. The English general became famous for his road- and bridge-building in Scotland, which did much to open the Highlands to greater access from the south.

Aviemore and the villages and towns of the Spey Valley offer many activities for the visitor. Spey Valley is the doorway to the **Malt Whisky Trail** (see chapter 18, "Aberdeen & the Tayside & Grampian Regions"). Aviemore is the winter sports capital of Britain, and Aviemore Centre offers a multitude of outdoor pursuits: golfing, angling, skiing, and ice skating.

Inverness and legendary Loch Ness are the most popular attractions in the West Highlands and are overcrowded during the summer. They are surrounded by villages and towns that also make good centers to visit—especially if you're driving. If you're dependent on public transportation, make Inverness your base, as it has good rail and bus connections to the rest of Scotland and also to England.

1 Around Loch Linnhe & Loch Leven

South of Fort William is one of the most historic sections of Scotland, a group of settlements around Loch Linnhe and Loch Leven (not the also-famous Loch Leven near Dunfermline). The best-known village is **Glencoe,** site of the

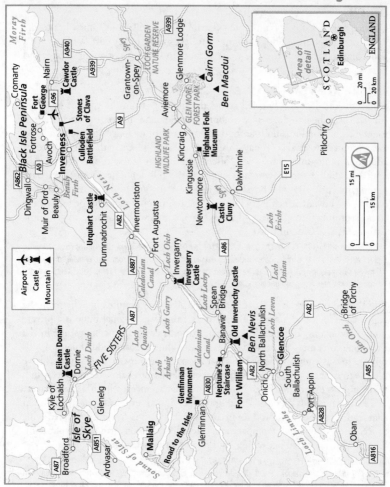

famous 1692 massacre when the Campbells slaughtered the MacDonalds. Glencoe is the most dramatic glen in Scotland, austere in its beauty. Around both lochs are impressive landscapes and moorland, with flora and fauna unique to the western Highlands. Robert Louis Stevenson captured much of the essence of this moorland and wilderness in his novel *Kidnapped.*

The best all-around outfitter for all kinds of sports in the region near Fort William is **Alfresco Adventure,** Onich (*©* **01855/821248**). Nick and Angie Scott rent motorboats, canoes, sailboats, fishing tackle, and more; they're a great source of advice for enjoying the great Highland outdoors. They also offer guided hill walks at £20 ($32) per person for ½ day, and guided canoe trips at £40 ($64) per person for a full day.

As for interesting ½-day drives, consider an excursion from Fort William to Oban. An interesting 1-day excursion would go from Fort William to the Isle of Skye or (even more densely scheduled) from Oban to Mull and on to Iona.

ONICH

On the shores of Loch Linnhe, the charming little village of Onich lies to the north of Ballachulish Bridge, 15km (9 miles) southwest of Fort William. It's a good center if you're taking the western route to Inverness or going to Skye and Fort William.

WHERE TO STAY & DINE

Allt-nan-Ros Hotel   Located across the highway from the edge of the loch, Allt-nan-Ros boasts dozens of elaborate gables and interesting architectural touches. The hotel was built around 1885 as a hunting lodge and weekend get-away for an industrialist. Today, this much-enlarged place, with relatively recent additions built onto either side, offers comfortable guest rooms and a well-managed dining room (which is open to the public). The rooms have dark mahogany furniture and floral-patterned curtains and upholsteries in a style echoing an Edwardian country house. Most rooms offer views of the loch or the stream running through the garden, and each comes with at least a shower (some bathrooms also contain tubs).

Onich, by Fort William PH33 6RY. © 01855/821210. Fax 01855/821462. www.allt-nan-ros.co.uk. 20 units. £99–£120 ($158–$192) double. Rates include breakfast. AE, DC, MC, V. From Fort William, drive 16km (10 miles) south along A82. **Amenities:** Restaurant; bar; room service (7:30am–11pm); babysitting. *In room:* TV, coffeemaker, hair dryer, iron/ironing board.

The Lodge on the Loch Hotel   This 19th-century granite hotel, between the edge of the loch and a semi-forested rocky ridge, was original built as a private home. Today only a handful of the guest rooms (with high ceilings) are in the mansion's core; most are located in a bulky-looking extension added in the 1960s but are just as comfortable as the other rooms. The most expensive rooms have plush extras, such as CD players, bathrobes, and Jacuzzi baths. If the hotel is full, there are two other choices, under the same management, within a short drive.

The restaurant is one of the big draws, serving an expensive set-price dinner that features all-Scottish produce in dishes such as Angus beef filet with red-wine sauce, and various other preparations including salmon, trout, and pheasant. There's also a cocktail bar with a log fire and a fine selection of whiskies.

Onich, by Fort William PH33 6RY. © 01855/821237. Fax 01855/821238. www.freedomglen.co.uk. 16 units. £70–£130 ($112–$208) double. Rates include breakfast and dinner. MC, V. Closed Nov–Mar. From Fort William, drive 24km (15 miles) south of town, following A82 and the signs to Glasgow. **Amenities:** Restaurant; bar; gym; steam room; sauna; massage. *In room:* TV, coffeemaker, hair dryer, iron/ironing board.

GLENCOE: SCENERY & SORROW ★★

Near the spot where Loch Leven joins Loch Linnhe, **Ballachulish Bridge** links the villages of North and South Ballachulish at the entrance to Glencoe. The bridge saves a long drive to the head of the loch if you're coming from the north, but the scenic drive to Kinlochleven lets you come on the celebrated wild Glencoe from the east. Glencoe runs from Rannoch Moor to Loch Leven between majestic mountains, including 1,142m (3,766-ft.) **Bidean nam Bian.** This is an area of massive splendor, with towering peaks and mysterious glens where you can well imagine the fierce battle among the kilted Highlanders to the skirl of the pipes and the beat of the drums.

Known as the "Glen of Weeping," Glencoe is the place where, on February 11, 1692, the Campbells massacred the MacDonalds—men, women, and children—who'd been their hosts for 12 days. Although mass killings weren't uncommon in those times, this one shocked even the Highlanders because it was a breach of hospitality. The **Monument to the Massacre of Glencoe** at Carnoch was erected by the chief of the MacDonald clan. After the incident, the crime of "murder under trust" was introduced into Scottish law as an aggravated form of murder that carried the same penalty as treason.

The glen, much of which now belongs to the National Trust for Scotland, is rich with legend. A tiny lochan is known as the "pool of blood" because by its side some men are said to have quarreled over a piece of cheese and killed each other.

Glen Orchy, to the south, is well worth a visit to see its wild river and photogenic mountain scenery. Glen Orchy is the birthplace of Gaelic bard Duncan Ban MacIntyre, whose masterpiece is the song "In Praise of Ben Doran."

This is great country for hiking and bike rides. In Glencoe village, go to the **Mountain Bike Hire** at the Clachaig Inn (© **01855/811644**), where you can not only rent a bike but also get advice about scenic routes that suit your available time and your ability. The cost is £8–£10 ($13–$16) per ½-day or £12–£15 ($19–$24) per day.

WHERE TO STAY & DINE

You can also choose to base yourself in Fort William (see "Fort William: Gateway to Ben Nevis," below) and explore the Glencoe area on day trips.

Ballachulish Hotel   A country inn of charm and grace, this elegant mansion was burned down in the early 1700s because of the association of its owners with the doomed Stuarts. It was rebuilt in 1764 and retains its lime-washed original stone form, even though it was tastefully expanded in 1997. Your host Greame Robertson is very welcoming. The good-sized guest rooms have flowered wallpaper and a mix of old and new furniture, and each has a view of the loch or forest. The more luxurious bedrooms have complete tub-and-shower bathrooms. There's a billiard room and ample opportunities for long walks beside the loch (maybe one or two of the owners' dogs will join you).

Dinner is a treat here and the chef makes use of fresh ingredients.

Ballachulish PA39 4JX. © **01855/821237.** Fax 01855/821463. www.freedomglen.co.uk. 54 units. £140–£246 ($224–$394) double. Rates include dinner and breakfast. MC, V. Closed Jan. Drive west of Ballachulish for 4km (2½ miles), following A82 until it intersects with A828. Follow the signs to Ballachulish House. **Amenities:** Restaurant; bar. *In room:* TV, coffeemaker, hair dryer (in some), iron/ironing board (in some).

Clachaig Inn   After the bleakness of Glencoe, the trees surrounding this place make it seem like an oasis. It's the only hotel in the glen (look for the signs on the highway), and is reached by a winding gravel-covered road off the main highway. The Daynes family offers Highland hospitality, good food, and an excellent selection of British ales. They rent some contemporary chalets in the back garden, plus several small to midsize guest rooms in the main house. The furnishings are basic and simple, and some singles are without bathrooms. Live folk music brings the place alive on Saturday and Wednesday nights.

Glencoe, Ballachulish PA39 4HX. © **01855/811252.** Fax 01855/811679. www.clachaig.com. 20 units, 18 with private bathroom. £60–£96 ($96–$154) double with bathroom. Rates include Scottish breakfast. MC, V. **Amenities:** Restaurant; bar. *In room:* TV, coffeemaker, hair dryer.

King's House Hotel   The solid walls of this historic inn are from the 1600s, built on a windswept plateau beside A82, 19km (12 miles) southeast of Glencoe village, at the strategic point where Glencoe joins the Glen Etive near a jagged mountain, Buachaille Etive Mor. King's House is one of Scotland's oldest licensed inns, although modernization has changed its interior. Most of the modest but comfortably furnished guest rooms offer sweeping views of majestic scenery and about half of them are equipped with a small, shower-only bathroom. Bedrooms are rather empty of amenities except for a phone. Simple meals are served in the bar; the dining room boasts a selection of fine wines and freshly prepared meals. The hotel is near a ski center with a ski lift, a 30-minute walk from its entrance.

Glencoe PA39 4HZ. ℭ **01855/851259.** Fax 01855/851216. www.kingy.com. 22 units, 12 with private bathroom. £50 ($80) double without bathroom, £56 ($90) double with bathroom. MC, V. You can arrange to be met at the Bridge of Orchy rail station. **Amenities:** Restaurant; bar; coffeemaker; hair dryer.

2 Fort William: Gateway to Ben Nevis ⟨★

214km (133 miles) NW of Edinburgh; 110km (68 miles) S of Inverness; 168km (104 miles) N of Glasgow

Fort William, on the shores of Loch Linnhe, is the best place for an overnight stop between here and Inverness in the northeast. It's a good base for exploring **Ben Nevis** ★★, Scotland's highest mountain, and also for a day trip to Glencoe (see earlier in this chapter).

Fort William stands on the site of a fort built by General Monk in 1655 to help crush any rebellion Highlanders may have been plotting. After several reconstructions, it was finally torn down in 1864 to make way for the railroad. During the notorious Highland Clearances, many starving and evicted people were shipped from here to America. Today Fort William is a bustling town, thriving very well on the summer tourist trade and filled with shops, hotels, and cafes.

ESSENTIALS

GETTING THERE   Fort William is a major stop on the West Highland rail line that begins at the Queen Street Station in Glasgow and ends at Mallaig on the west coast. Three trains a day run this route at a one-way cost of £21 ($34). For schedules, contact the tourist office (see below) or call ℭ **01463/239026** in Inverness.

Four buses run from Glasgow to Fort William per day, taking 3 hours and costing £12 ($20) one-way. Call the **Citilink Bus Station** at ℭ **0870/550-5050** in Glasgow for schedules. If you're driving from Glasgow, head north along A82.

VISITOR INFORMATION   The **tourist office** is at Cameron Centre, Cameron Square (ℭ **01397/703781**). In April and May, it's open Monday through Saturday from 9am to 5pm and Sunday from 10am to 4pm; from June 1 to June 28, hours are Monday through Saturday from 9am to 5:30pm and Sunday from 10am to 4pm; from June 29 to July 26, hours are Monday through Saturday from 9am to 7pm and Sunday from 10am to 6pm; from July 27 to August 16, it's open Monday through Saturday from 9am to 8pm and Sunday from 10am to 6pm; and from August 17 to August 30, hours are Monday through Saturday from 9am to 7pm and Sunday from 10am to 6pm. From August 31 to September 20 hours are Monday through Saturday from 9am to 6pm and Sunday from 10am to 5pm; from September 21 to November 1, hours are Monday through Saturday from 9am to 4pm and Sunday from 10am to 3pm; and from November 2 to March hours are Monday through Saturday from 9am to 5:30pm and Sunday from 10am to 4pm.

SEEING THE SIGHTS

You can reach the ruins of **Old Inverlochy Castle,** scene of a famous battle, by driving 3km (2 miles) north of Fort William on A82. Built in the 13th century, the ruined castle still has round corner towers and a walled courtyard. One of the towers was the keep, the other a water gate. The castle looms in the pages of Scottish history—here in 1645 a small army of Scots defeated government forces, although 1,500 men were lost that day. The former castle was once the stronghold of a clan known as the Comyns, and Inverlochy was the scene of many battles.

Neptune's Staircase, 5km (3 miles) northwest of Fort William off A830 at Banavie, is a series of nine locks that were constructed at the same time as the Caledonian Canal, raising Telford's canal 20m (64 ft.). This "staircase" is one of Scotland's most prominent engineering triumphs of the mid–19th century, when the eastern seacoast at Inverness was connected, via the canal, to the western seacoast at Fort William. This greatly shortened the distance required for goods moving from the North Sea to the Atlantic Ocean and bypassed the treacherous storms that often rage around Scotland's northern tier.

Since much of Fort William is relatively flat, consider biking. The best rentals are at **Off Beat Bikes,** 117 High St. (© **01397/704008**), costing £10 ($16) for ½ day, £15 ($24) for a full day. You need only your ID for the deposit. It's open Monday through Saturday from 9am to 5:30pm and Sunday from 9:30am to 5pm.

In the north end of town, the **Ben Nevis Woolen Mill,** Belford Road (© **01397/704244**), is only a shop, not a functioning woolen mill. Here you'll find a large selection of clothing and accessories: wools, tweeds, tartans, and hand-knit Arran sweaters, and gifts and souvenir items. An on-premises restaurant features regional fare.

Shoppers may also want to check out the **Granite House,** High Street (© **01397/703651**), a family-run business that has been around for a quarter of a century. The owners call themselves "giftmongers" and see their shop as a mini-department store. There's a large selection of Scottish jewelry, with silver pieces in both traditional and contemporary designs and numerous watches. Collectibles like Lilliput Lane china and crystal by Edinburgh, Wedgwood, and Border Fine Arts are found here, and the traditional music department offers more than 1,000 Irish and Scottish music CDs and an array of traditional instruments, including pennywhistles and the *bhodrain* (a large drum struck with a single stick using both ends). The store also carries traditional toys for all ages.

Scottish Crafts & Whisky Centre, 135–139 High St. (© **01397/704406**), is another place with a good mix of the best of all things Scottish: regionally produced jewelry, garden fountains, rugs, and clothing. Whisky connoisseurs will find some limited-edition and very rare bottles stocked, including a 1958 Ben Nevis. Handmade chocolates by Fergusons are also available. **Treasures of the Earth,** Main Street, Corpach (© **01397/772283**), 6.5km (4 miles) west of Fort William along A830, sells crystals, minerals, and polished stones from around the world. They are available loose or set in jewelry, watches, and clocks.

Glenfinnan Monument   At Glenfinnan at the head of Loch Shiel, this monument marks the spot where Bonnie Prince Charlie unfurled his proud red-and-white silk banner on August 19, 1745, in his ill-fated attempt to restore the Stuarts to the British throne. The figure of a kilted Highlander tops the monument. At the visitor center, you can learn of the prince's campaign from Glenfinnan to Derby that ended in his defeat at Culloden.

About 23km (14 miles) west of Fort William, on A830 toward Mallaig. © 01397/722250 for visitor center. Admission to visitor center £1.50 ($2.40). Visitor center mid-May to Aug daily 9:30am–6pm; Sept to early May daily 10am–5pm.

Climbing Britain's Tallest Mountain

In the Central Highlands, **Ben Nevis**, at 1,337m (4,406 ft.), is the tallest mountain in Britain. Although it's not exactly ready to challenge the towering Alps, Ben Nevis can still give hikers a good workout. The pony track to the top is often filled with walkers tackling the difficult 8-hour jaunt. The unpredictable Scottish weather adds to the challenge, requiring you to dress in layers and bring along at least a waterproof jacket. The mean monthly temperature of Ben Nevis falls below freezing; snow has been reported at all times of year, even during the hottest months of July and August. Howling winds are frequent.

Hikers head up for the view, but it's not guaranteed because of weather conditions. On a clear day, you can see the Irish foothills some 193km (120 miles) away, the Hebridean Isle of Rhum 148km (92 miles) away, and the Glencoe peaks (Ben Lawers, Torridon, and the Cairngorms). If you don't want to climb, a cable car can take you to a height of 698m (2,300 ft.) for viewing.

The trail is much rougher but even more beautiful if approached from Glen Nevis, one of the country's most scenic glens. Clear rivers and cascading waterfalls add to the drama of the scenery; meadows and moors seem straight out of Austria.

Before going, discuss the climb with the tourist office in Fort William. The staff can give you advice as well as maps of the area, and they'll pinpoint the best starting places. A signpost to the north of Nevis Bridge points to the path up Ben Nevis. Allow 8½ hours total for the under-16km (10-mile) trip. Take along a windbreaker, sturdy footwear, food, and water.

A word of warning: Sudden weather changes may pose a safety hazard. And that final 303m (1,000 ft.) is really steep terrain, but having gone this far, few can fail the challenge. Some Brits call Ben Nevis the "top of the world." It really isn't. It just feels that way when you finally reach the peak.

West Highland Museum   The collection in this museum sheds light on all aspects of local history, especially the 1745 Jacobite Rising; it also has sections on tartans and folk life. The West Highland museum is in the center of town next to the tourist office.

Cameron Sq. ⓒ **01397/702169.** Admission £2 ($3.20) adults, £1.50 ($2.40) seniors, 50p (80¢) children. June–Sept Mon–Sat 10am–5pm (July–Aug also Sun 2–5pm); Oct–May Mon–Sat 10am–4pm.

WHERE TO STAY

There's no shortage of B&Bs in Fort William; most offer a good view of Loch Linnhe or Ben Nevis. The tourist office can supply you with a list if the selections below don't suit you or are full.

VERY EXPENSIVE

Inverlochy Castle ★★★   This is the premier address in this entire part of Scotland. Inverlochy Castle, against the scenic backdrop of Ben Nevis, hosted Queen Victoria in her day. Back then, it was a newly built (1870) Scottish mansion belonging to Baron Abinger. The monarch claimed in her diary, "I never saw a lovelier or more romantic spot." Now a Relais & Châteaux hotel, the Inverlochy has recently undergone a major refurbishment but has retained its charm as well as its large, friendly staff. Luxurious appointments, antiques, artwork, and crystal, plus a profusion of flowers, create a mood of elegance and refinement. The prices certainly reflect this opulence.

The cuisine here is some of the finest in Scotland (see p 665). Nonguests can dine here if there's room, but reservations are mandatory.

Torlundy, Fort William PH33 6SN. ⓒ **01397/702177.** Fax 01397/702953. www.inverlochycastlehotel.com. 17 units. £395–£435 ($632–$696) double; from £500–£550 ($800–$880) suite. Rates include Scottish breakfast. AE, MC, V. Closed early Jan to late Feb. Free valet parking. Take A82 for 5km (3 miles) northeast of town. **Amenities:** Restaurant; tennis court; game fishing; room service (7am–11pm); babysitting; laundry service. *In room:* TV, hair dryer, iron/ironing board.

EXPENSIVE

Crolinnhe ⭐ *Finds*   Overlooking Loch Linnhe, this impressive 1880 Victorian home—converted to a hotel in 1982—lies only a 10-minute walk from the center of town. It's one of the best and most comfortable B&Bs in the area although small, which means renovations are important. Completely refurbished in 1998, the hotel stands on an acre of handsomely landscaped and manicured gardens in a western suburb. Many of the bedrooms open onto views of the hills beyond, and tables and chairs are placed outside in summer for you to enjoy the view. A blend of antiques and contemporary furnishings grace the main lounge, with its original Victorian fireplace, and the dining room where a traditional Scottish breakfast is served is also beautifully decorated. Bedrooms are furnished as in a luxurious private home, and all come with private bathrooms mainly with tub and shower (one has a shower).

Grange Rd., Fort William PH33 6JF. ⓒ **01397/702709.** Fax 01397/700506. www.crolinnhe.co.uk. 4 units. £80–£110 ($128–$176) double. Rates include full Scottish breakfast. No credit cards. Closed Nov–Mar. **Amenities:** Breakfast room. *In room:* TV, coffeemaker, hair dryer, iron.

MODERATE

The Alexandra Milton Hotel   Across from the rail terminal, the Alexandra boasts the tall gables and formidable granite walls so common in this part of the Highlands. It has been completely modernized, offering pleasant and comfortably furnished guest rooms with shower-and-tub bathrooms. The service and housekeeping standards are good. There are two restaurants and a lounge bar on the premises. The chef makes excellent use of fresh fish, and the wine cellar is amply endowed. The vegetables are simply cooked with enjoyable results. Guests have free use of all the facilities at the nearby Milton Hotel and Leisure Club.

The Parade, Fort William PH33 6AZ. ⓒ **01397/702241.** Fax 01397/705554. www.miltonhotels.com. 97 units. £69–£89 ($110–$142) double. Rates include Scottish breakfast. AE, DC, MC, V. **Amenities:** 2 restaurants; bar; 24-hr. room service; laundry service. *In room:* TV, coffeemaker, hair dryer, iron/ironing board.

Ashburn House ⭐ *Finds*   This luxurious B&B stands on the shore of Loch Linnhe with panoramic views of the Ardgour hills beyond. Standing on its own manicured grounds, the building dates from 1880 and was only turned into a hotel in 1991. Each good-sized room is individually decorated, with six-feet wide, king-size beds. Each comes with a tidily kept private bathroom with shower (one has a tub-and-shower combo). The wood furnishings are both dark and light mahogany, with matching sheets and curtains. A conservatory lounge is for relaxing and absorbing those loch views, and in the corniced Victorian dining room a superb Scottish breakfast with freshly baked scones is served daily.

Achintore Rd., Fort William PH33 6RQ. ℂ **01397/706000.** Fax 01397/702024. www.scotland2000.com/ ashburn. 7 units. £60–£90 ($96–$144). Rates include full breakfast. AE, MC, V. Closed Dec. **Amenities:** Breakfast room; room service (breakfast only); laundry service. *In room:* TV, hair dryer, coffeemaker, iron, no phone.

The Moorings Hotel   One of the most up-to-date hotels in the region, the Moorings was designed in a traditional style in the mid-1970s, with bay and dormer windows and a black-and-white facade. The interior is richly paneled in the Jacobean style. The guest rooms, most of which have undergone recent redecoration, are attractive and modern. Bar lunches and suppers are served in the Mariner Wine Bar, which offers 40 kinds of wine from around the world. More formal meals are served in the Moorings Restaurant, where an even greater selection of wine (more than 200 vintages) accompanies dishes like smoked venison, Scottish oysters, homemade terrines, cullen skink (traditional smoked-haddock soup), and wild salmon in lemon-butter sauce.

Banavie, Fort William PH33 7LY. ℂ **01397/772797.** Fax 01397/772441. www.moorings-hotel.co.uk. 28 units. £100–£110 ($160–$176) double. Rates include Scottish breakfast. AE, DC, MC, V. Drive 5km (3 miles) north of Fort William to the hamlet of Banavie, beside B8004. **Amenities:** Restaurant; bar; room service (noon–11pm). *In room:* TV, coffeemaker, hair dryer, iron/ironing board.

INEXPENSIVE

Croit Anna Hotel   Overlooking Loch Linnhe, the hotel opens onto fine views of the Ardgour Hills and is owned/managed by a corporation called Leisure Plex. All the midsize guest rooms have tidily kept but small shower-and-tub bathrooms. Entertainment is provided on most evenings in season.

Druimarbin, Fort William PH33 6RR. ℂ **01397/702268.** Fax 01397/704099. 95 units. £48–£54 ($77–$86) double with bathroom. Rates include Scottish breakfast. MC, V. Take A82 for 4km (2½ miles) south of town. **Amenities:** Restaurant; 2 bars; lounge; laundry service. *In room:* TV, coffeemaker, hair dryer, iron/ironing board.

Lochview Guest House *Value*   South from the center of Fort William and about a 15-minute walk uphill is this guest house, designed around 1950. The guest rooms are outfitted with comfortable furnishings by Denise and Alan Kirk, who maintain the acre of lawn surrounding their building and protect the view sweeping down over the loch and the rest of the town. Each unit comes with a small bathroom. Other guest houses in town may be older, more historic, and with more dignified architecture—but for the price, Lochview represents good value, and the Kirk family is unfailingly generous. No smoking.

Heathercroft, Argyll Rd., Fort William PH33 6RE. ℂ/fax **01397/703149.** www.lochview.co.uk. 8 units. £44–£54 ($70–$86) double. Rates include breakfast. MC, V. Closed Nov–Mar. *In room:* TV, kitchenette, no phone.

WHERE TO DINE

Crannog Seafood Restaurant ✦ SEAFOOD/INTERNATIONAL   Occupying a converted ticket office and bait store in a quayside setting overlooking Loche Linnhe, this restaurant serves seafood so fresh locals claim "it fairly leaps at you." Much of the fish comes from the owners' own fishing vessels or from their own smokehouse, which turns out smoked salmon, mussels, and trout. Bouillabaisse is a chef's specialty, as are Loch Linnhe prawns and langoustines. A vegetarian dish of the day is invariably featured. Look for the daily specials listed on the chalkboard.

Town Pier. ℂ **01397/705589.** Reservations recommended. Main courses £9–£17 ($14–$27). MC, V. Daily noon–2:30pm and 6–9:30pm. Closed Jan 1–2 and Dec 25–26.

Inverlochy Castle ★★★ *Finds* BRITISH   This is one of the grandest restaurants in Britain (as it should be, at these prices!). The cuisine here has been celebrated ever since Queen Victoria got a sudden attack of the munchies and stopped in "for a good tuck-in." The food, we can only assume, is even better than in her day. You'll dine nowhere better in all of Scotland; your meal will be cooked to order and served on silver platters. The kitchen uses carefully selected local ingredients, including salmon from Spean, crayfish from Loch Linnhe, and produce from the hotel's own farm gardens. Partridge and grouse are offered in season, and roast filet of Aberdeen Angus beef is a classic. The set-price menu has a well-balanced choice, and everything is seasonally adjusted. The chefs also do their own baking, and their specialty, an orange soufflé, may be the best we've ever tasted. Dinner is served in any of three dining rooms, each decorated with period and elaborate furniture presented as gifts to Inverlochy Castle from the king of Norway. The formal service is the finest in the Highlands.

Torlundy, Fort William PH33 6SN. ℂ **01397/702177.** Reservations required. Fixed-price lunch £29 ($46); set-price dinner £52.50 ($84). AE, MC, V. Daily 12:30–1:30pm and 7–9pm. Closed Jan–Feb.

FORT WILLIAM AFTER DARK

Ben Nevis Bar, 103–109 High St. (ℂ **01397/702295**), offers free entertainment by rock, blues, jazz, and folk bands on Thursday and Friday. On tap are McEwan's, Foster's, and Kronenberg lagers, McEwan's 70 Shilling, and Guinness and Gillespie's stouts.

   McTavish's Kitchen, High Street (ℂ **01397/702406**), presents a Scottish show just for tourists. It's fun but corny, featuring tartan-clad dancers, bagpipes, and other traditional instruments every night May through September from 8 to 10pm. You can see the show with or without dinner. A three-course "Taste of Scotland" meal costs £18 ($29). On tap is Tennant's Special and Lager, available for £2.65 ($4.25) per pint. Admission to the show is £4 ($6.40) adults and £2 ($3.20) children; if you're eating, the show only is £2 ($3.20) adults and £1 ($1.60) children.

   Grog & Gruel, 66 High St. (ℂ **01397/705078**), serves up regional cask-conditioned ales. There's an occasional live band, ranging from rock and pop to folk and Scottish music.

3 Aviemore ⟨⟨⟨

208km (129 miles) N of Edinburgh; 47km (29 miles) SE of Inverness; 137km (85 miles) N of Perth

A bit tacky for our tastes, Aviemore, a year-round resort on the Spey, was opened in 1966 in the heart of the Highlands, at the foot of the historic rock of **Craigellachie.** The center of Aviemore itself, with ugly concrete structures, has little of the flavor of Scotland. But visitors flock here not for Aviemore itself—they come because of its accessibility to some of the most beautiful scenery in the Highlands, especially the Cairngorm Mountains, known for their skiing in winter or hiking in summer.

ESSENTIALS

GETTING THERE   Aviemore, on the main Inverness–Edinburgh rail line, is the area's major transportation hub. For rail schedules in Aviemore, call ℂ **01479/810221.** Some eight trains per day pass through from Inverness (trip time: 30–45 min.) at £7.40 ($12) each way. Twelve trains per day also arrive from Glasgow or Edinburgh. Trip time from each city is 3 hours, and a one-way ticket from either is £30 ($48).

Aviemore is on the main Inverness–Edinburgh bus line, with frequent service. The trip from Edinburgh takes about 3 hours (call ☎ **0990/808080** in Edinburgh for schedules) and costs £5 ($8). Frequent buses throughout the day also arrive from Inverness (trip time: 40 min.).

If you're driving from Edinburgh, after crossing the Forth Bridge Road, take M90 to Perth, then continue the rest of the way along A9 into Aviemore.

VISITOR INFORMATION The **Highlands of Scotland Tourist Office** (Aviemore branch) is on Grampian Road (☎ **01479/810363**). June through August, it's open Monday through Friday from 9am to 7pm, Saturday from 9am to 6pm, and Sunday from 10am to 5pm; September through May, hours are Monday through Friday from 9am to 5pm and Saturday and Sunday from 10am to 5pm.

SEEING THE SIGHTS

North of Aviemore, the **Strathspey Railway,** Dalfaber Road (☎ **01479/ 810725;** www.strathspeyrailway.co.uk), is your best bet in Scotland to learn firsthand what it was like to ride the rails in the 19th century. The railway follows the valley of the River Spey between Boat of Garten and Aviemore, a distance of 8km (5 miles). The train is drawn by a coal-burning steam locomotive. The newest locomotive used was made nearly 4 decades ago, the oldest being of 1899 vintage. The trip is meant to re-create the total experience of travel on a Scottish steam railway that once carried wealthy Victorians toward their hunting lodges in North Britain. The round-trip takes about an hour. The rail station at Boat of Garten, where you can board the train, has also been restored.

Round-trip passage costs £12 ($19) first-class or £8.40 ($13) third-class. Schedules change frequently, but from July to the end of August trains make four round-trips daily. From May to June and September, they run 3 times daily, and from March to April and October they run Sunday, Wednesday, and Thursday. There's no regular service in winter; however, special Christmas season trips are made during which Santa Claus makes an appearance. To complete the experience, you can wine and dine aboard on Sunday and Friday in July and August, when a single-seating casual lunch is served; the cost for the fare and meal is £16 ($26). Reservations must be made for the meals. The dining car is a replica of a Pullman parlor car, the Amethyst. For reservations and hours of departure, call ☎ **01479/831692.**

Skiers are attracted to the area any time after October, when snow can be expected. You can rent ski equipment and clothing at the Day Lodge at the main Cairngorm parking area. Weather patterns can change quickly in the Cairngorm massif. Call the number above for a report on the latest weather conditions. To reach the area, take A951, branching off from A9 at Aviemore, then head for the parking area at the Day Lodge.

If you'd like to explore the countryside on two wheels, there are several places to rent bikes. **Speyside Sports,** Main Street (☎ **01479/810656**), rents bikes at £8 ($13) for ½ day, £12 ($19) for a full day, and £43 ($69) for 6 days. **Bothy Bikes,** 81 Grampian Rd. (☎ **01479/810111**), charges £10 ($16) for ½ day, £14 ($22) for a full day, £160 ($256) for 6 days. Discounts begin to apply when you rent for 2 days or more.

The tourist office will give you hiking maps and offer advice, especially about weather conditions depending on the season. One of the best trails is reached by following B9760 to the sign-posted **Glen More Forest Park,** in the vicinity of Loch Morlich.

For the grandest view of the Cairngorm peaks, you can take the **CairnGorm Mountain Railway** (✆ **01479/861261**) to the top. The best views of the Valley of the Spey can be seen from the point where the funicular railway lets you off. At the peak is a visitor's center and restaurant. Wear warm gear as it gets mighty cold at the top, some 914m (3,000 ft.) above sea level. The railway is signposted off B9152. If weather permits, the train runs daily from 8:30am to 4:30pm, costing £7.50 ($12) for adults, £6.50 ($10) or seniors and students, and £5 ($8) for children.

WHERE TO STAY

Aviemore Highlands Hotel   This resort hotel caters to an outdoorsy clientele. It's a labyrinthine complex of wings, staircases, and long halls, which funnel into public rooms with big windows overlooking the countryside. In summer, doors open to reveal flagstone terraces ringed with viburnum and juniper. You can drink in the Illicit Still Bar, which has an antique whisky still and copper-top tables. Sunday is the ever-popular karaoke night. The main restaurant is capped with a soaring ceiling, trussed with beams. The midsize guest rooms are well furnished, and some family rooms are also available. The tidy bathrooms are efficiently organized, each with a shower, and many with a tub bath. Guests can use all the leisure and sports facilities at the Red McGregor.

Aviemore Mountain Resort, Aviemore PH22 1PJ. ✆ **01479/810771.** Fax 01479/811473. www.aviehighlands. demon.co.uk. 103 units. £90–£100 ($144–$160) double. Rates include Scottish breakfast. AE, DC, MC, V. **Amenities:** Restaurant; 2 bars; 24-hr. room service; laundry service. *In room:* TV, coffeemaker, hair dryer.

Corrour House Hotel ★ *(Finds)*   This is an oasis of personality in a sea of impersonal hotels. This isolated granite house was built around 1880 for the mother of the *laird* (baron) of a much-larger manor house about 3km (2 miles) away. The larger of the houses is privately owned and can't be visited. Set on 4 acres of forest and garden, this guesthouse contains simple but comfortable rooms that are attractively decorated, each sporting a shower-only bath. Your hosts are Robin and Sylvia Walton, who will prepare you dinner if you arrange it in advance. Many of their dishes have a true taste of Scotland flavor, including smoked trout and horseradish mousse or Ballindalloch pheasant with a sauce made with red wine, oranges, red currants, and fresh herbs. They also have a selection of more than 100 wines.

On B970, Inverdruie by Aviemore PH22 1QH. ✆ **01479/810220.** Fax 01479/811500. www.corrourhousehotel. co.uk. 8 units. £65–£70 ($104–$112) double. Rates include breakfast and a 5-course dinner. AE, MC, V. Closed mid-Nov to Christmas. From Aviemore, drive 1km (½ mile) east, following the signs to Glenmore. **Amenities:** Restaurant; bar; room service (7am–10pm). *In room:* TV, coffeemaker, hair dryer.

Hilton Aviemore ★ *(Kids)*   This is the resort's best hotel because of its extensive sports and leisure facilities, spread across 65 acres of tree-studded grounds. The midsize guest rooms are spacious and well appointed, with comfortable furnishings and average-sized bathrooms, some with both tub and shower. You have a choice of two dining rooms, although the food is fairly standard. There's often evening entertainment, particularly on weekends. In winter, downhill and cross-country skiing equipment and training are available. The sports and leisure hall also caters to children in its Fun House.

Center of Aviemore PH22 1QN. ✆ **01479/810681.** Fax 01479/811309. www.hilton.com. 88 units. £115 ($184) double; £165 ($264) suite. Half-board rates available for a minimum 2-night stay. AE, DC, MC, V. **Amenities:** Restaurant; bar; pool; sauna; whirlpool; steam bath; salon; 24-hr. room service; babysitting; laundry service. *In room:* TV, coffeemaker, hair dryer, iron/ironing board.

Lynwilg House ⭐ The Victorian solidity of this house is particularly note-worthy in Aviemore, considering the relative modernity of many others of the resort hotels. It was built by the duke of Richmond in the 1880s overlooking the mountains. Today, under the management of Alan and Marjorie Cleary, it retains 4 acres of its original park and gardens, with high-ceilinged guest rooms containing comfortable furnishings, each with a shower-only bathroom. In front of the house is a croquet lawn, and at the bottom of the well-tended garden is a stream where guests like to relax. Most of the produce used in the dining room comes from the garden.

Rte. A9, Aviemore PH22 1PZ. ⓒ **01479/811685**. www.lynwilg.co.uk. 4 units. £60–£70 ($90–$105) double. Rates include breakfast. MC, V. Follow A9 for 2.5km (1½ miles) south of Aviemore's center, following the signs to Perth. **Amenities:** Dining room; room service (7:30am–10:30pm). *In room:* TV, coffeemaker, hair dryer.

WHERE TO DINE

The Bar/The Restaurant SCOTTISH Although the golf course, health club, and leisure facilities of this country club are open only to members, visitors are welcome in the cozy bar and restaurant, which is outfitted in tartan carpets and upholstery, with heavy brocade curtains and views from the big windows. In the bar, where live entertainment is featured nightly, the fare includes venison cutlets or filets, sandwiches, homemade steak pies, fish pies, and any of a variety of malt whiskies. The restaurant serves seafood, such as skewered tiger prawns soaked with butter, as well as grilled Angus steaks, main-course salads, and a limited number of vegetarian dishes.

In the Dalfaber Golf and Country Club, about 1.5km (1 mile) north of the center of Aviemore. ⓒ **01479/ 811244**. Reservations required in the restaurant. Main courses £5.25–£6.95 ($8.40–$11); bar platters £3.50–£5.95 ($5.60–$9.50). MC, V. Restaurant daily 6-9:30pm. Bar daily 11am–11pm.

AVIEMORE AFTER DARK

Crofters, off Grampian Road at the Aviemore Mountain Resort, a 2-minute walk from the center of Aviemore (ⓒ **01479/810771**), has dancing with no cover charge nightly from 10pm to 1am, with guest DJs bringing in their own music and setting the mood. The bar serves Tennant's Lager and Guinness on tap. The private drive leading here is well marked from Grampian Road.

4 Along Loch Ness ⭐⭐

Sir Peter Scott's *Nessitera rhombopteryx,* one of the world's great mysteries, con-tinues to elude her pursuers. The Loch Ness monster, or "Nessie" as she's more familiarly known, has captured the imagination of the world, drawing thousands of visitors yearly to Loch Ness. Half a century ago, A82 was built alongside the banks of the loch's western shores, and since then many more sightings have been claimed.

All types of high-tech underwater contraptions have gone in after the Loch Ness monster, but no one can find her in spite of the photographs and film footage you may have seen in magazines or on TV. Dr. Robert Rines and his associates at the Academy of Applied Science in Massachusetts maintain an all-year watch with sonar-triggered cameras and strobe lights suspended from a raft in Urquhart Bay. However, some people in Inverness aren't keen on collaring the monster, and you can't blame them: An old prophecy predicts a violent end for Inverness if the monster is ever captured.

The loch is 39km (24 miles) long, 1.5km (1 mile) wide, and some 229m (755 ft.) deep. If you'd like to stay along the loch and monster-watch instead of basing yourself at Inverness, we've listed some choices below. Even if the

Moments Spotting Nessie

She's affectionately known as Nessie, but her more formal name is *Nessitera rhombopteryx,* and she has the unflattering appellation of the Loch Ness monster. Is she the beast that never was, or the world's most famous living animal? You decide. Real or imagined, she's Scotland's virtual mascot, and even if she doesn't exist, she's one of the major attractions of the country. Who can drive along the dark waters of Loch Ness without staring at the murky depths and expecting a head or a couple of humps to appear above the water's surface at any minute?

Nessie's lineage is ancient. An appearance in A.D. 565 was recorded by respected 7th-century biographer St. Adamnan, not known as a spinner of tall tales. The claim is that St. Columba was en route along Loch Ness to convert Brude, king of the Picts, to Christianity. The saint ordered a monk to swim across the loch and retrieve a boat. However, as he was in midswim, Nessie attacked. The monk's life was saved only when Columba confronted the sea beast with a sign of the cross and a shouted invocation.

Columba's calming effect on Nessie must have lasted over the centuries, because no attacks have been reported since then. Of course, there was that accident in the 1500s when a chronicle reported that "a terrible beast issuing out of the water early one morning about midsummer knocked down trees and killed three men with its tail." Again, in 1961, 30 hotel guests reported seeing two humps that rose out of the water just before their craft exploded and sank. Bertram Mill has offered £20,000 to have the monster delivered alive to his circus.

Because Scotland is the land not only of Nessie but also whisky, it may be assumed that some of these sightings were hallucinations brought on by the consumption of far too many "wee drams." However, sightings have come from people of impeccable credentials who were stone sober. Nessie seems to like to show herself to monks, perhaps a tradition dating from St. Columba. Several monks at the Fort Augustus Abbey claim to have seen her. A monk who's an organist at Westminster Cathedral reported a sighting in 1973.

Belief in Nessie's existence is so strong that midget yellow submarines and all types of high-tech underwater contraptions have been used in an attempt to track her down. Many photographs exist—most of them faked—usually from the site of the ruins of Urquhart Castle on the loch's shore. Other photographs haven't been so easily explained.

If Nessie does exist, exactly who is she? A sole survivor from prehistoric times? A gigantic sea snake? It has even been suggested she's a cosmic wanderer through time. Chances are you won't see her on your visit, but you can see a fantasy replica of the sea beast at the Official Loch Ness Monster Exhibition at Drumnadrochit.

monster doesn't put in an appearance, you'll enjoy the scenery as you walk along the loch. In summer, from both Fort Augustus and Inverness, you can take boat cruises across Loch Ness.

If you're driving, take A82 between Fort Augustus and Inverness running along Loch Ness. Buses from either Fort Augustus or Inverness also traverse A82, taking you to Drumnadrochit.

DRUMNADROCHIT

The bucolic village of Drumnadrochit is about 1.5km (1 mile) from Loch Ness at the entrance to Glen Urquhart. It's the nearest village to the part of the loch in which sightings of the monster have been reported most frequently.

Although most visitors arrive at Drumnadrochit to see the Loch Ness monster exhibit (see "Seeing the Sights," below), you can also take an offbeat adventure in the great outdoors at the **Highland Riding Centre,** Borlum Farm, Drumnadrochit (© **01456/450220**). This is an 850-acre sheep farm on moorlands overlooking Loch Ness; follow A82 for about 23km (14 miles) west of Inverness and make a reservation in advance. In summer, the stable's 45 horses are booked throughout their working day. Tours depart almost every day, depending on demand; they leave between 9:30am and 4:30pm, last 60 to 120 minutes, and cost £14.50 to £24 ($23–$38).

Wilderness Cycles, The Cottage (© **01456/450223**), will rent you a bike so you can go exploring on your own. Rentals costs £7 ($11) for ½ day, £12 ($19) daily, and £35 to £50 ($56–$80) weekly. It's open daily from 9am to 6pm.

SEEING THE SIGHTS

Official Loch Ness Monster Exhibition This is Drumnadrochit's big attraction, featuring a scale replica of Nessie. It opened in 1980 and has been packing 'em in ever since. You can follow Nessie's story from A.D. 565 to the present in photographs, audio, and video, and you can climb aboard the sonar research vessel *John Murray*. The Exhibition Centre is the most visited place in the Highlands of Scotland, with more than 200,000 visitors annually.

Drumnadrochit. © **01456/450573**. Admission £5.95 ($9.50) adults, £4.50 ($7.20) students, £4.50 ($7.20) seniors, £3.50 ($5.60) children ages 7–16, £15 ($24) families, free for children ages 7 and under. Easter–May daily 9:30am–5pm; June and Sept daily 9am–6pm; July–Aug daily 9am–8pm; Oct daily 9am–5:30pm; Nov–Easter daily 10am–3:30pm.

Urquhart Castle This ruined castle, one of Scotland's largest, is on a promontory overlooking Loch Ness. The chief of Clan Grant owned the castle in 1509, and most of the extensive ruins date from that period. In 1692, the castle was blown up by the Grants to prevent it from becoming a Jacobite stronghold. Rising from crumbling walls, the jagged keep still remains. It's at Urquhart Castle that sightings of the Loch Ness monster are most often reported. There's free off-road parking where you can stand and view the ruins from afar.

Loch Ness along A82. © **01456/450551**. Admission £5.50 ($8.80) adults, £4 ($6.40) seniors, £1.20 ($1.90) children. Apr–Sept daily 9:30am–5:45pm (to 8:30pm July–Aug); Oct–Mar daily 9:30am–3:45pm. Drive 2.5km (1½ miles) southeast of Drumnadrochit on A82.

WHERE TO STAY & DINE

Polmaily House Hotel This is a snug haven in a sea of Loss Ness tourism and over-commercialization. In 1994, John and Sonia Whittington-Davis, third-generation hoteliers, bought this Edwardian inn that re-creates manorial country-house living. The house, on an 18-acre estate with mixed gardens and woodland, is believed to have been built in 1776. The spacious and elegant guest rooms, tastefully filled with antiques, have high ceilings, leaded-glass windows, and flowered wallpaper. All but four rooms come with a shower-tub combination

---

Moments Beauty Spots & Enchanted Glens

The village of Invermoriston, 271km (168 miles) northwest of Edinburgh and 47km (29 miles) south of Inverness, is one of the most beautiful spots along Loch Ness. **Glenmoriston** is one of the loveliest glens in the Highlands. You can take long walks along the riverbanks, with views of Loch Ness. The area is at the junction of the Loch Ness Highway (A82) and the road to the Isle of Skye (A887).

---

bathroom. The restaurant attracts locals as well as hotel guests with dishes like Aberdeen beef and fresh salmon.

Drumnadrochit IV3 6XT. $\textcircled{C}$ **01456/450343.** Fax 01456/450813. 13 units. www.polmaily.co.uk. £100–£144 ($160–$230) double. Rates include Scottish breakfast. MC, V. Drive 3km (2 miles) west of Drumnadrochit on A831. **Amenities:** Restaurant; bar; heated indoor pool; horse-riding; tennis court; croquet lawn; trout pond. *In room:* TV, coffeemaker.

5 Inverness: Capital of the Highlands $\cancel{\star}\cancel{\star}$

251km (156 miles) NW of Edinburgh; 216km (134 miles) NW of Dundee; 216km (134 miles) W of Aberdeen

The capital of the Highlands, Inverness is a royal burgh and seaport at the north end of Great Glen on both sides of the Ness River. For such a historic town, the sights are rather meager, but Inverness is a good center for touring. If your time is limited, confine your visits to Culloden Battlefield, where Bonnie Prince Charlie and his Jacobite army were defeated in 1746; Cawdor Castle of *Macbeth* fame (see "Nairn & Cawdor Castle," later in this chapter), and Black Isle, the most enchanting and scenic peninsula in Scotland. All these attractions would fill a busy day even if you don't have time to walk about the center of Inverness itself.

ESSENTIALS

GETTING THERE Domestic flights from various parts of Britain arrive at the Inverness Airport. Flight time from London's Gatwick to the Inverness/Dalcross Airport is 1¾ hours. Call $\textcircled{C}$ **01667/464000** in Inverness for flight information.

Some five to seven trains per day arrive from Glasgow and Edinburgh (on Sun, two or three trains). The train takes 3½ hours from either city, and a one-way fare from either is £32 ($51). Trains pull into Station Square, off Academy Street in Inverness ($\textcircled{C}$ **0845/748-4950** for schedules).

Scottish CityLink coaches provide service for the area ($\textcircled{C}$ **0870/550-5050** for schedules). Frequent service through the day is possible from either Edinburgh or Glasgow (a 4-hr. trip each way), at a one-way fare of £15 ($24). The bus station is at Farraline Park, off Academy Street ($\textcircled{C}$ **01463/233371**).

Driving from Edinburgh, take M9 north to Perth, then follow along the Great North Road (A9) until you reach Inverness.

VISITOR INFORMATION The Inverness branch of the **Highlands of Scotland Tourist Board** is at Castle Wynd, off Bridge Street ($\textcircled{C}$ **01463/234353**). From October to mid-April, it's open Monday through Friday from 9am to 5pm and Saturday from 10am to 4pm; from mid-April to May, hours are Monday through Friday from 9am to 5pm, Saturday from 9:30am to 5pm, and Sunday from 9:30am to 4pm; June hours are Monday through Friday from 9am to 6pm, Saturday from 9am to 5pm, and Sunday from 9:30am to 5pm;

July and August, it's open Monday through Saturday from 9am to 6pm and Sunday from 9:30am to 5pm; September hours are Monday through Saturday from 9am to 6pm and Sunday from 9:30am to 5pm.

SPECIAL EVENTS   At the **Highland Games** in July, with its sporting competitions and festive balls, the season in Inverness reaches its social peak. For more information and exact dates, consult the tourist office (see above).

SEEING THE SIGHTS

Inverness is one of the oldest inhabited sites in Scotland. On **Craig Phadrig** are the remains of a vitrified fort, believed to date from the 4th century B.C. One of the most important prehistoric monuments in the north, the **Stones of Clava** are about 10km (6 miles) east of Inverness on the road to Nairn. These cairns and standing stones are from the Bronze Age.

The old castle of Inverness stood to the east of the present street Castlehill, and the site still retains the name "Auld Castlehill." David I built the first stone castle in Inverness around 1141, and the **Clock Tower** is all that remains of a fort erected by Cromwell's army between 1652 and 1657. The rebellious Scots blew up the old castle in 1746 to keep it from falling to government troops, and the **present castle** was constructed by the Victorians in the 19th century. Today this landmark houses the laws courts of Inverness and local government offices.

The 16th-century **Abertarff House,** Church Street, is now the headquarters of An Comunn Gaidhealach, the Highland association that preserves the Gaelic language and culture. Opposite the town hall is the **Old Mercat Cross,** with its Stone of the Tubs, said to be the stone on which women rested their washtubs as they ascended from the river. Known as "Clachnacudainn," the lozenge-shaped stone was the spot where local early kings were crowned.

St. Andrew's Cathedral (1866–69), Ardross Street, is the northernmost diocese of the Scottish Episcopal church and a fine example of Victorian architecture, both imposing and richly decorated. Be sure to check out the icons given to Bishop Eden by the czar of Russia. The cathedral is open daily from 9:30am to 6pm. For information, get in touch with the Provost, 15 Ardross St. (© **01334/ 472563**).

If you're interested in bus tours of the Highlands and cruises on Loch Ness, go to **Inverness Traction,** 6 Burnett Rd. (© **01463/239292**). In summer, there are also cruises along the Caledonian Canal from Inverness into Loch Ness.

Shoppers may want to check out a family-owned shrine to Scottish kiltmaking, **Duncan Chisholm & Sons,** 47–53 Castle St. (© **01463/234599**). The tartans of at least 50 of Scotland's largest clans are available in the form of kilts and kilt jackets for men and women. If your heart is set on something more esoteric, the staff can acquire whatever fabric your ancestors would have worn to make up your garment. A section is devoted to Scottish gifts (ties, scarves, yard goods, kilt pins in thistle patterns) and memorabilia. You can visit the on-premises

---

Moments **The Hill of the Fairies**

West of the river rises the wooded hill of **Tomnahurich,** known as the "hill of the fairies." It's now a cemetery from which the views are panoramic. This is the best place to go for a country walk. The boat-shaped hillock is immediately to the southwest of the center. In the Ness are wooded islands, linked to Inverness by suspension bridges and turned into parks.

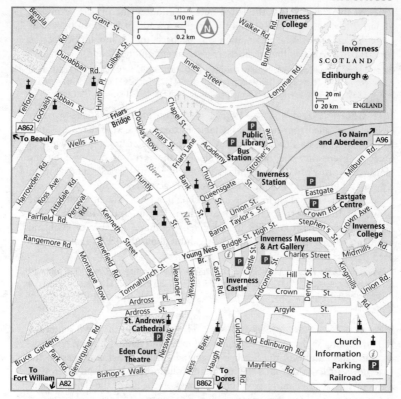

workshop. The town's best jewelry store, with an unusual collection of bangles and bracelets inspired by the decorative traditions of Celtic Scotland, is **D&H Norval,** 88 Church St. (© **01463/232739**). At **Celtic Spirit,** 14 Church St. (© **01463/714796**), the focus is on New Age books and an unusual collection of wind chimes.

Golfers can head about 65km (40 miles) north to hit the links at the renowned **Royal Dornoch Golf Club.** Closer at hand, the 4,960m (5,451-yard) **Torvean Golf Course,** Glen Q Road (© **01463/711434**), offers an 18-hole, par-68 course with greens fees of £16 ($25) Monday through Friday, and £19 ($30) Saturday and Sunday.

Culloden Battlefield   At Culloden Battlefield, Bonnie Prince Charlie and the Jacobite army were finally crushed on April 16, 1746. Leanach Cottage, around which the battle took place, still stands and was inhabited until 1912. A path leads from the **visitor center** through the Field of the English, where 52 men of the duke of Cumberland's forces who died during the battle are said to be buried. Features of interest include the **Graves of the Clans,** communal burial places with simple stones bearing individual clan names; the great **memorial cairn,** erected in 1881; the **Well of the Dead;** and the huge **Cumberland Stone,** from which the victorious "Butcher" Cumberland is said to have reviewed the scene. The battle lasted only 40 minutes; the prince's army lost some 1,200 men out of 5,000, and the king's army 300 of 9,000. In the visitor center is an audiovisual presentation on the background and history of the famous battle. Also on the premises are a restaurant and bookshop.

Culloden Moor, 10km (6 miles) southeast of Inverness. © **01463/790607** for visitor center. Admission to visitor center £5 ($8) adults, £3.75 ($6) seniors and children, £14 ($22) families. Visitor center Apr–June and Sept–Oct daily 9am–6pm; July–Aug daily 9am–7pm; Nov–Dec and Feb–Mar 11am–4pm. Closed Jan.

Fort George/Queen's Own Highlanders Regimental Museum Fort George was called the "most considerable fortress and best situated in Great Britain" in 1748 by Lt. Col. James Wolfe, who went on to fame as Wolfe of Quebec. Built after the Battle of Culloden, the fort was occupied by the Hanoverian army of George II and is still an active army barracks. The rampart, almost 1.5km (1 mile) around, encloses some 42 acres. Dr. Samuel Johnson and James Boswell visited here in 1773 on their Highland trek. The fort contains the admission-free **Queen's Own Highlanders Regimental Museum,** with regimental exhibits from 1778 to today, representing a number of Highland regiments as well as its namesake. A new exhibit about the 1990s Gulf War has been recently added.

On Moray Firth by the village of Ardersier, 18km (11 miles) northeast of Inverness, 13km (8 miles) northwest of Cawdor along B9006. © **01313/108701.** Admission £4.50 ($7.20) adults, £3 ($4.80) seniors, £2.50 ($4) children ages 5–15, free for children ages 4 and under. Apr–Sept daily 10am–6pm; Oct–Mar Mon–Fri 10am–4pm.

Inverness Museum and Art Gallery This museum in the town center is a top attraction, its displays representing the social and natural history, archaeology, art, and culture of the Scottish Highlands, with special emphasis on the Inverness district. Don't miss the important collection of Highland silver, with a reconstructed silversmith's workshop, displays on the life of the clans, a reconstruction of a local taxidermist's workshop, a reconstructed Inverness kitchen of the 1920s, and an art gallery. There's also a permanent exhibit on the story of the Inverness district, from local geology and archaeology to the present. Other facilities are a souvenir shop, a coffee shop, and an information service.

Castle Wynd, off Bridge St. © **01463/237114.** Free admission. Mon–Sat 9am–5pm.

WHERE TO STAY
VERY EXPENSIVE

Culloden House ★★ Culloden House, the most elegant country retreat in the area, is a Georgian mansion with a much-photographed Adam facade. Superbly isolated, with extensive gardens and parkland, it's perfect for a relaxed Highland holiday. At the iron gates to the broad front lawn, a piper in full Highland garb often plays at sundown—the skirl of the bagpipe accompanied by the barking of house dogs. The Prince of Wales and the crown Prince of Japan have stayed here, perfectly at home among the exquisite furnishings and handsome plaster friezes. The cozy yet spacious guest rooms have sylvan views and a history-laden atmosphere and all come with shower-tub combination bathrooms. The hotel maintains traditional ideas of personal service.

Culloden, Inverness IV1 7BZ. © **01463/790461.** Fax 01463/792181. www.cullodenhouse.co.uk. 28 units. £199 ($318) double; £270 ($432) suite. Rates include Scottish breakfast. AE, DC, MC, V. Drive 5km (3 miles) east of Inverness on A96. **Amenities:** Restaurant; bar; 24-hr. room service; tennis court; sauna; laundry service; croquet lawn. *In room:* TV, hair dryer, trouser press.

EXPENSIVE

Bunchrew House Hotel and Restaurant ✮   A fine Scottish mansion on
the shores of Beauly Firth, Bunchrew House is the ancestral home of both the
Fraser and the McKenzie clans. The house, built by Simon Fraser, eighth Lord
Lovat, dates back to 1621 and is set in 15 acres of landscaped gardens. You get
a glimpse of a bygone era when relaxing in the paneled drawing room with roaring log fires in winter. The good-sized guest rooms are individually designed and
decorated; the Lovat Suite has a canopied four-poster bed, and the Wyvis Suite
boasts a half-tester bed. All the bedrooms have showers, and some are equipped
with tubs as well. You can dine in the candlelit restaurant on prime Scottish beef,
fresh lobster, local game and venison, and fresh vegetables.

Bunchrew, Inverness, Inverness-shire IV3 6TA. ✆ **01463/234917.** Fax 01463/710620. www.bunchrew-
inverness.co.uk. 14 units. £150–£200 ($240–$320) suite for 2. Rates include Scottish breakfast. AE, MC, V.
Drive 5km (3 miles) west of Inverness on A862. **Amenities:** Restaurant; bar; room service (7:30am–11pm);
babysitting; laundry service; free fishing on the estate. *In room:* TV, fridge, coffeemaker, hair dryer.

Dunain Park Hotel ✮✮   The Dunain Park stands on 6 acres of gardens and
woods, between Loch Ness and Inverness. This 18th-century house was opened
as a hotel in 1974 and is furnished with fine antiques, china, and clocks, allowing it to retain its atmosphere of a private country house. Although Dunain Park
has won its fame mainly as a restaurant, it does offer guest rooms with a host of
thoughtful details and pretty, soft furnishings, each equipped with a shower or
tub bath.

Dunain Park, Inverness IV3 8JN. ✆ **01463/230512.** Fax 01463/224532. www.dunainparkhotel.co.uk. 13
units. £158 ($253) double; from £200 ($320) suite. Rates include Scottish breakfast. AE, DC, MC, V. Drive 3km
(2 miles) southwest of Inverness on A82. **Amenities:** Restaurant; lounge; indoor heated pool; 24-hr. room
service; laundry service. *In room:* TV, fridge, coffeemaker, hair dryer, iron/ironing board, trouser press.

Inverness Marriott Hotel ✮   Once a private mansion, this hotel is an 18th-
century country house of much charm on 4 acres of woodland gardens adjacent
to an 18-hole golf course. The staff maintains the country-house atmosphere
with an informal and hospitable style. The furnishings throughout are of a high
quality, and all the guest rooms are attractively furnished, each with tub or
shower bath. In the restaurant, the fish dishes are exceptional at dinner. Bar
lunches and snack meals offer a wide choice, including Scottish fare.

A notice in the lobby tells you Robert Burns dined here in 1787, and the
"Charles" who signed the guest register in 1982 was (you guessed it) the Prince
of Wales. His sister, Princess Anne, has also stayed here.

Culcabock Rd., Inverness IV2 3LP. ✆ **01463/237166.** Fax 01463/225208. www.marriott.com. 82 units.
£88–£140 ($141–$224) double; £150–£170 ($240–$272) suite. Rates include Scottish breakfast. Children
ages 13 and under stay free in parent's room. AE, DC, MC, V. Take Kingsmill Rd. 1.5km (1 mile) east of the
center of Inverness. **Amenities:** Restaurant; bar; indoor pool; 3-hole minigolf course; health spa; fitness room;
24-hr. room service; laundry service. *In room:* TV, coffeemaker, hair dryer, iron/ironing board, trouser press.

MODERATE

Culduthel Lodge ✮   Built in 1837, the year Queen Victoria ascended to the
throne, this Georgian mansion of red stone was established as a hotel back in
1985. The property with its pillared portico opens onto the River Ness. The aura
of a country manse is maintained here, made more inviting by the bright log
fires, and the fresh flowers placed about. Located in one of the most desirable
residential areas of Inverness, the lodge lies only a 10-minute walk from the
center of town. Painstakingly restored, the house stands in its own manicured

gardens—a summer sun trap. The elegant drawing room sets the mood, with its big windows, opened onto magnificent vistas. In the dining room the fixed price menu is changed daily and is based mainly on fine cooked and homemade Scottish fare. Each bedroom is individually decorated with dark wood furnishings, and each comes with a well-maintained private bathroom, four with shower, the rest with tub and shower.

14 Culduthel Rd., Inverness IV2 4AG. ©/fax **01463/240089.** www.culduthel.com. 12 units. £80–£110 ($128–$176) double. Rates include full breakfast. MC, V. **Amenities:** Dining room for guests only; room service (7am–midnight). *In room:* TV, coffeemaker, hair dryer, iron.

Glen Mhor Hotel　On the River Ness, this house of gables and bay windows is a hospitable family-run hotel. From many of the individually styled guest rooms you have views of the river, castle, and cathedral; some are suitable for families. Ten rooms are in an annex called the Cottage. Each unit has a well-maintained bathroom, all with a shower, some with shower-tub combinations. In the Riverview Restaurant, specializing in seafood and Scottish dishes, you can enjoy such fine food as salmon caught in the river outside. The wine list is one of the best in the country. There's also a European bistro bar called Nico's.

9–12 Ness Bank, Inverness IV2 4SG. © **01463/234308.** Fax 01463/713170. www.glen-mhor.com. 45 units. £88 ($141) double; from £120 ($192) junior suite. Rates include Scottish breakfast. AE, DC, MC, V. **Amenities:** Restaurant; bistro bar; 24-hr. room service. *In room:* TV, coffeemaker, hair dryer.

Glenmoriston Town House Hotel　★ *Kids*　Glenmoriston Town House, on the River Ness, is a short walk from the town center, and it's the finest townhouse hotel in town. Rooms have been stylish refurbished, are well maintained and individually designed, and come with spacious private bathrooms featuring Molton Brown toiletries and bathrobes. Some accommodations are suitable for use as family units. Guests can enjoy temporary membership at a nearby Squash and Tennis Club. Of the two hotel restaurants, La Terrazza is open daily for lunch, and La Riviera is more formal, specializing in a fine Italian cuisine, with many Tuscan dishes.

20 Ness Bank, Inverness IV2 4SF. © **01463/223777.** Fax 01463/712378. www.glenmoriston.com. 15 units. £115–£135 ($184–$216) double. Rates include full Scottish breakfast. AE, MC, V. Free parking. **Amenities:** 2 restaurants; bar; room service (7am–10pm). *In room:* TV, dataport, coffeemaker.

The Royal Highland Hotel　Constructed in 1859 of somber gray stone and located across from the rail station, Royal Highland was built to celebrate the arrival of rail lines connecting the Highlands, through Inverness, to the rest of Britain. Today, it's an antiques-strewn, slightly faded hotel, despite gradual modernizations and the contemporary decors in about half its guest rooms. You register in a massive lobby, at one end of which is the showiest staircase in Inverness. The rooms, depending on how recently they were remodeled, are either charmingly dowdy or more modern, but always with Scottish traditionalism. The dining room, open only for dinner, retains the elaborate high ceiling of its initial construction and a sense of the Victorian age. Seafood and West Coast shellfish, including a medley of fresh oysters, are house specialties.

18 Academy St., Inverness IV1 1LG. © **01463/231926.** Fax 01463/710705. www.royalhighlandhotel.co.uk. 70 units. £120–£145 ($192–$232) double. Rates include breakfast. AE, DC, MC, V. **Amenities:** Restaurant; 2 bars. *In room:* TV, coffeemaker, hair dryer, iron/ironing board, trouser press.

INEXPENSIVE

Ballifeary House Hotel　*Value*　A well-maintained 1876 Victorian stone villa, with a pleasant garden, Ballifeary House is one of the area's better B&Bs. Mr.

and Mrs. Luscombe, the owners, offer their guests individual attention. The guest rooms, although a bit small, feature Victorian decor and are comfortably furnished. This nonsmoking hotel doesn't accept guests under age 15.

10 Ballifeary Rd., Inverness IV3 5PJ. Ⓒ **01463/235572.** Fax 01463/717583. www.btinternet.com/~ballifhotel. 5 units. £72–£78 ($115–$125) double. Rates include Scottish breakfast. MC, V. *In room:* Coffeemaker, hair dryer, no phone.

Ivybank Guest House   One of the area's better B&Bs, Ivybank (off Castle Rd. about a 10-min. walk north of the town center) was built in 1836 and retains its original fireplaces and an oak-paneled and beamed hall with a rosewood staircase. It has a walled and landscaped garden and comfortably furnished guest rooms. Three of the units contain a shower-only bathroom. Mrs. Catherine Cameron is the gracious hostess, making guests feel at ease and welcome. There's ample parking in the walled garden. Breakfast is the only meal served.

28 Old Edinburgh Rd., Inverness IV2 3HJ. Ⓒ/fax **01463/232796.** 6 units, 3 with private bathroom. £50 ($80) double without bathroom, £55 ($88) double with bathroom. Rates include Scottish breakfast. AE, MC, V. *In room:* TV, coffeemaker, hair dryer.

Trafford Bank   Located in a residential neighborhood about 1km (½ mile) west of Inverness center, this dignified sandstone house was built in 1873 as the manse for the Episcopal bishop of the Inverness cathedral. In 1994, a bishop retired—in a huff—because of the ordination of women in the church. After all those years as a home for the bishops, the manse is now a B&B with five comfortable, dignified guest rooms, and offers a social life revolving around copious Scottish breakfasts. The rooms come with a shower-only bathroom and fresh fruit and flowers on arrival. The owners have worked hard to make their guests' stay pleasant and have built up a loyal North American and British following; they provide complimentary pickup from the bus and train stations as well as the airport. Dinner can be arranged with advance notice.

96 Fairfiled Rd. Ⓒ **01463/241414.** www.traffordbankguesthouse.co.uk. 5 units. £60–£70 ($96–$112) double. Rates include breakfast. AE, MC, V. Bus: 19. From the town center, cross the Ness Bridge and turn right at the first traffic light. *In room:* TV, coffeemaker, hair dryer, iron/ironing board.

WHERE TO DINE
MODERATE

Dickens International Restaurant INTERNATIONAL   On a downtown street next to the oldest house in Inverness, Aberton House, between Bank and Academy streets, this restaurant boasts a decor that has been revamped and updated with furnishings in the style created by Charlie Rennie Mackintosh (1868–1928), Scotland's most famous designer. A wide selection of European, Chinese, and international dishes is offered, including seafood and vegetarian dishes. On the menu are Dickens's own steak, aromatic duck, fresh local salmon, and chateaubriand. Dickens offers the widest choice of side dishes in Inverness, including fried rice, bean sprouts, and cauliflower with cheese.

77–79 Church St. Ⓒ **01463/713111.** Reservations required on weekends. Main courses £9–£12 ($14–$19). AE, DC, MC, V. Mon–Sat noon–2pm and 5:30–11pm.

Kong's Restaurant CHINESE/THAI   Spicy and reasonably priced food await you here. Especially noteworthy is the large array of appetizers, including some dishes from Vietnam. Try the Thai chicken wings or the Szechuan squid before moving on to a wide array of seafood and poultry dishes, along with a selection of pork and beef. The Thai green and red curry dishes are especially flavorful, and the chef's specialties include Peking roast duck and a steamed filet of sole flavored with ginger and spring onions. Vegetarians are well catered to here.

64–66 Academy St. ℂ **01463/237755.** Reservations recommended. Main courses £6–£9 ($9.60–$14); fixed-price menus £12–£21 ($19–$34) per person. AE, MC, V. Mon–Sat noon–2pm; daily 5:30–11pm.

EXPENSIVE

Dunain Park Restaurant ✶ SCOTTISH Ann Nicoll presides over the kitchen here, offering Scottish fare with a French flair, using fresh local ingredients. A game terrine of chicken and guinea fowl is layered with venison and pigeon, and meats are wrapped in bacon and served with a delicious onion confit. Other dishes that may appear on the changing menu are hare-and-pigeon casserole with roasted shallots and wild mushrooms and Shetland salmon baked in sea salt, served with a white-port, lime, and ginger sauce. The restaurant also specializes in Aberdeen Angus steaks. Try one of these desserts from the buffet: crème brûlée, chocolate roulade, or marshmallow pudding.

In the Dunain Park Hotel, Dunain Park. ℂ **01463/230512.** Reservations recommended. Main courses £16–£18 ($26–$29). AE, DC, MC, V. Daily 7–9pm.

Restaurant Riviera BRITISH/ITALIAN Often hosting local family celebrations, this rather staid restaurant occupies the ground floor of an early-20th-century stone-sided hotel on the riverbank near the center of Inverness. At least five chefs labor away in the kitchen. Meals here are part of an entire evening's entertainment, so plan on spending an entire leisurely evening here. Menu items include slices of warm breast of duckling scented with heather-flavored honey and dressed with walnut oil; Scottish beef filet with wild-mushroom polenta, shallots, and Parmesan crackling; and grilled king prawns with roasted tomatoes and pea puree.

In the Glenmoriston Hotel, 20 Ness Bank. ℂ **01463/223777.** Reservations recommended. Main courses £15–£17 ($24–$27); 3-course fixed-price menu £26 ($42). AE, DC, MC, V. Daily noon–2pm and 6:30–9:30pm.

INVERNESS AFTER DARK

It may be the capital of the Highlands, but Inverness is a sprawling small town without much nightlife. You can spend an evening in the town's pubs sampling single-malt whiskies or beers on tap. Although the pubs here may not have the authentic charm of the isolated pubs in more rural areas, you'll still find a lot of Highlander flavor. Try the pub in the **Loch Ness House Hotel,** Glenurquhart Road (ℂ **01463/231248**), on the western periphery of town; **Gellions Pub,** 8–14 Bridge St. (ℂ **01463/233648**); or **Gunsmith's Pub,** 30 Union St. (ℂ **01463/ 710519**). For loud music and dancing, head for either of the town's discos: **Blue,** Rose Street (ℂ **01463/222712**), or **Gs,** 9–21 Castle St. (ℂ **01463/233322**).

6 Nairn & Cawdor Castle ✶

277km (172 miles) N of Edinburgh; 147km (91 miles) NW of Aberdeen; 26km (16 miles) E of Inverness

A favorite family seaside resort on the sheltered Moray Firth, Nairn (from the Gaelic for "Water of Alders") is a royal burgh at the mouth of the Nairn River. Its fishing harbor was constructed in 1820, and golf has been played here since 1672—as it still is today. Most visitors come here on a day trip from Inverness.

ESSENTIALS

GETTING THERE Nairn can be reached by train from the south, with a change at either Aberdeen or Inverness. The service between Inverness and Nairn is frequent and this is the most popular route. For information, check with the Inverness train station at **Station Square** (ℂ **0845/748-4950**).

From Inverness, **Inverness Traction** runs daily buses to Nairn. Call ℂ **0870/ 608-2608** for schedules.

If you're **driving** from Inverness, take A96 east to Nairn.

VISITOR INFORMATION   The **tourist office** is at 62 King St. (ℂ **01667/ 452753**). From April to mid-May, it's open Monday through Saturday from 10am to 5pm; from mid-May to June, hours are Monday through Saturday from 10am to 5pm and Sunday from 11am to 4pm; July and August, hours are Monday through Saturday from 9am to 6pm and Sunday from 10am to 5pm; and September and October, hours are Monday through Saturday from 10am to 5pm.

SEEING THE SIGHTS

Brodie Country, on A96, 5km (3 miles) east of Nairn in Brodie (ℂ **01309/ 641555**), is a family-owned shopping complex with shops carrying a variety of merchandise. Of greatest interest are the regionally produced knitwear, gift items, and foodstuffs; the latter includes smoked meats, jams, mustards, and other condiments. Also on the premises is a fully licensed restaurant serving Scottish cuisine daily from 9:30am to 5pm (to 7pm Thurs), with main courses averaging about £6 ($9.60).

Nairn Antiques, St. Ninian Place (ℂ **01667/453303**), carries a broad range of antiques and a section of upscale crafts and reproductions. Of particular interest are the collections of Scottish pottery, silver, and fine porcelains, but there's also furniture and bric-a-brac from around the world. This is the only shop in the entire north country to stock high-quality Lalique crystal from France.

The Taste of Moray, on the Nairn-Inverness Road, 10km (6 miles) north of Nairn (ℂ **01667/462340;** www.tasteofmoray.co.uk), is all about the pleasures of preparing and consuming Scottish cuisine, with products ranging from quality cookware to regional domestic stoneware. The food hall offers an array of Scottish condiments and smoked meats, and if shopping here makes you hungry, you can step into the adjacent restaurant, serving seafood dishes and steaks, with main courses averaging £5–£25 ($8–$40). Food service is available daily from 10am to 9pm.

The 18-hole **Nairn Dunbar Golf Club,** Loch Loy Road (ℂ **01667/452741**), consists of 6,097m (6,700 yards) of playing area with a par of 72. Greens fees are Sunday through Friday £37 ($59) per round or £50 ($80) per day, and Saturday £45 ($72) per round or £60 ($96) for the day.

Cawdor Castle ✸   To the south of Nairn, you'll encounter 600 years of Highland history at Cawdor Castle, since the early 14th century the home of the thanes of Cawdor. Although the castle was constructed 2 centuries after his time, it has nevertheless been romantically linked to Shakespeare's *Macbeth,* once the thane of Cawdor. The castle has all the architectural elements you'd associate with the Middle Ages: a drawbridge, an ancient tower (this one built around a tree), and fortified walls. Its severity is softened by the handsome gardens, flowers, trees, and rolling lawns. On the grounds are five nature trails through beautiful woodlands, a nine-hole golf course, a putting green, a snack bar, a picnic area, shops, and a licensed restaurant serving hot meals, teas, coffees, and fresh-baked goods all day.

Between Inverness and Nairn on B9090 off A96, Cawdor. ℂ **01667/404615.** www.cawdorcastle.com. Admission £6.10 ($9.75) adults, £5.10 ($8.15) seniors, £3.30 ($5.30) children ages 5–15; children under age 5 free. May to the 2nd Sun in Oct daily 10am–5pm.

20

Cardiff & South Wales

No longer the dreary coal-exporting port as it was so often depicted in the 20th century, **Cardiff,** the capital of Wales, is hot and happening—one of the most attractive cities of Britain to visit. Cardiff (*Caerdydd* in Welsh) is a large seaport built on the tidal estuary of the Taff River.

Enriched by the Industrial Revolution, it eventually declined after World War II with the closing of coal mines, railroads, and factories. The old industrial city long envisioned has been replaced by a progressive, inviting modern port, as exemplified by the new waterfront along Cardiff Bay. Here you'll find renewal at its best, with restaurants, hotels, and a hands-on exhibit, Techniquest.

Cardiff can also be your launching pad for the treasures of South Wales. This area in recent decades has turned a bright, new face to the world and is no longer known for its depressing stories of slag heaps, dreary cottages, and denuded hillsides that were once proudly forested.

In fact, it is imbued with some of the great beauty spots of Britain: the **Brecon Beacons National Park,** 835 sq. km (519 sq. miles) of beauty and pleasure grounds with nature reserves; **Gower Peninsula,** an area of outstanding natural beauty stretching for 23km (14 miles) from the Mumbles to Worms Head in the West; and, finally, **Pembrokeshire Coast National Park,** one of the smallest national parks of Britain (only 362 sq. km/225 sq. miles) but an area acclaimed for its coastal scenery.

On the western side of Cardiff, the city of **Swansea** on Swansea Bay of the Bristol Channel, seems a natural starting place for a visit to Southwest Wales. After a sojourn in the immediate vicinity of the port city, the beautiful peninsula of **Gower,** Swansea's neighbor, draws you westward. You'll see where Dylan Thomas, the country's outstanding 20th-century poet, was born, and then move on to the west to Laugharne, where the poet lived, wrote, and is buried.

Swansea is on the western edge of West Glamorgan county. When the counties of Wales were realigned and consolidated in 1973, Pembrokeshire and Carmarthenshire, familiar names in Welsh history, became part of Dyfed County, an even older designation for the area they occupy. In this southwestern corner of the country, you'll be introduced to the land of St. David and Celtic crosses, of craggy coastlines and the cromlechs marking the burial places of prehistoric humans.

In addition to Swansea, you'll find two more excellent bases outside Cardiff—**Tenby,** one of the most famous coastal resorts of Wales, its charm and character dating from the Middle Ages, plus **St. Davids,** a tiny cathedral city, birthplace of the patron saint of Wales.

Two major attractions that you may want to seek out even on a rushed visit are **Pembroke Castle,** oldest castle in West Wales, and seat of the earls of Pembroke, and **Tintern Abbey,** in the Wye Valley, founded in 1131, once one of the richest and most important monastic houses of Wales.

The northern periphery of South Wales is actually called **Mid Wales,** but because Wales is such a small country, this region is grouped in this section for the convenience of touring. All its attractions can easily be explored while you are based in South Wales or you can transfer there for overnight visits.

The scenery of Mid Wales is rich and varied. Wide beaches and craggy promontories, from which you can see all the way to Ireland over Cardigan Bay and the Irish sea, outline the western reaches. Forests, foothills, moors, mountains, and gently rolling meadowlands are all part of this beautiful section of the principality. For a long time it was impossible—well, almost—to drive from the Welsh–English border to the sea in much of this area, as its parts were linked only by the old drovers' tracks across the Cambrian Mountains, along which farmers took their sheep and cattle to the markets. The interior, much of it heavily wooded and with deep river valleys and ravines, holds tranquil little farms, villages, and traces of religious centers and mining enterprises.

1 Cardiff ⟨★

249km (155 miles) W of London; 177km (110 miles) SW of Birmingham; 64km (40 miles) SE of Swansea.

If you remember Cardiff's dull, industrial reputation from yesteryear, you may not want to fit the capital of Wales into your already busy schedule. But to omit it would be a shame, because it has blossomed into one of the most inviting cities of Britain, and is an ideal base for exploring its own attractions, plus the major scenic beauty spots of South Wales.

You can visit it for its castles and museums. The National Museum of Wales is the treasure trove of the principality—from paintings to silver, from ceramics to dinosaur skeletons—and the Welsh Folk Museum, on 100 acres of parkland, is one of Europe's leading open-air museums. A trio of castles is a worthy sightseeing goal, including Cardiff Castle, an extravaganza of whimsy, color, and rich architectural detail—built on the site of a Roman fort. Caerphilly Castle is an imposing moated fortress whose massive water defenses form the second largest castle area in Britain, and Castell Coch is a fairy-tale castle with pepperpot turrets and round towers. On the outskirts, Llandaff Cathedral is built on the site of a religious community from the 16th century.

In spite of its industrial reputation from long ago, Cardiff today is also visited for its parks and gardens, notably Dyffryn Gardens, 560 acres of landscaped botanical wonder, and Roath Park, east of the center, with facilities for boating and fishing on a 32-acre site. There's a lot going here, especially in summer. Winter visits tend to be duller.

ESSENTIALS

GETTING THERE   In recent years, Cardiff has greatly expanded its air facilities, and flights now wing in from across Europe. Airlines that service **Cardiff International Airport** (✆ **01446/711111**) include **British Airways** (✆ **0845/ 773-3377**), which offers flights to Brussels, Paris, Belfast and points throughout southern Ireland, and Scotland; **KLM** (✆ **0870/575-0900**), which offers transfers, through Amsterdam, to points around the world. **Ryan Air** (✆ **0871/ 246-0000**) flies to Dublin and points throughout Britain that include Newcastle, Edinburgh, and Aberdeen. Surprisingly, there is no direct air service between Cardiff and London, but airport officials think that during the lifetime of this edition, service will be offered several times a week between Cardiff and

London's Stanstead Airport by a relatively new airline, **Air Wales** (© 0870/ 777-3131).

The **Cardiff Bus Service** operates bus no. X91, which travels between the airport and the railway station at hourly intervals daily from 9am to 10pm. Cost of a one-way trip is £3 ($4.80).

Trains arrive in Cardiff at the Central Station on Wood Street, in back of the bus station. Trains from London pull in at the rate of one every hour during the day; the trip takes 2 hours. Trains also arrive every hour from Glasgow and Edinburgh going via Crewe; trip time is 7 hours. For rail information and schedules, call © 0845/748-4950. For bus and motor routes into Cardiff, refer to the "Getting There" section of chapter 3, "Planning Your Trip to Great Britain."

VISITOR INFORMATION   For information about Cardiff and its environs, the **Cardiff Visitors Centre** is at 16 Wood St. (© 029/2022-7281), in the heart of the city. Between November and March, it's open Monday and Wednesday through Saturday from 9am to 5pm; Tuesday from 10am to 5pm; and Sunday from 10am to 2pm. Between April and October, it maintains the same hours noted above but closes at 6pm Monday through Saturday, and has Sunday hours of 10am to 4pm. A branch office at Cardiff Bay, the Tube, Harbour Dr. (© 029/ 2046-3833), lying 2.5km (1½ miles) to the south, is open daily from 10:30am to 6pm.

CITY LAYOUT

Cardiff Castle, on Castle Street, is in the center of Cardiff, one of the most architecturally distinguished cities of Britain. It is the city's major landmark. To get your bearings and for the best overview, climb the clock tower at the castle, where you'll see all the major shopping streets of central Cardiff, as well as the River Taff, the Sophia Gardens Cricket Ground, and the Arms Park Rugby Stadium.

To its northeast is **Cathays Park,** developed in the early 1900s as a Civic Centre. Don't take the word "park" too seriously. It's a complex of white stone structures that include the University College, the National Museum of Wales, and the City Hall, all placed along gardens and streets. The Law Courts and Welsh Office (seat of the government) are also located here. The tourist office (see above) arranges walking tours of the Civic Centre in summer only.

Tree-lined avenues line the center, and these include the main commercial and shopping areas of the capital. The most important is **St. David's Shopping Centre,** which is a big, bustling shopping mall that takes in St. David's Hall, one of the best of the new concert halls of Europe. The main shopping streets of Cardiff are **Working Street, The Hayes, St. Mary Street,** and **Queen Street.**

In all, it's "A proper fine Towne," in the words of Christopher Saxton, a cartographer of the 1600s.

FINDING AN ADDRESS

Street numbering—or lack of it—can be confusing. Odd numbers ascend in order as you go along, and even numbers follow the same pattern on the opposite side of the street. The only problem is that many establishments do not use street numbers, only street names. They may have been assigned a number by the city, but they don't post it on their building or use it in their letterheads in correspondence. Even though the street may run for several blocks, no number may appear. If it's a place of public business, look for the sign. You might also, when attempting to find an address, ask for the nearest cross street. That way, you'll be able to find the building you're looking for much quicker.

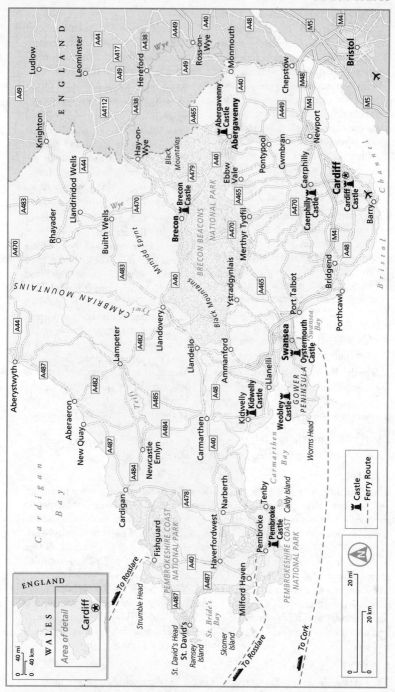

NEIGHBORHOODS IN BRIEF

Central Cardiff   Its centerpiece is Cardiff Castle on Castle Street, lying in Bute Park, which is only one section of the city's hundreds of acres of parkland. Two blocks east is the Civic Centre, and surrounding the complex are tree-lined avenues that embrace the major business and shopping streets of Cardiff, including Queens Street. Another major landmark is St. David's Shopping Centre, with its focal point at St. David's Hall.

Llandaff   Before becoming part of Cardiff, Llandaff, 3.2km (2 miles) from the center, was a city in its own right. Buses travel here or you can reach it by crossing Llandaff Fields. It's still a somewhat sleepy village, with many Victorian homes and inns. On its village green, a path leads to its major attraction, Llandaff Cathedral, dating from the 12th century.

Roath Park   This park covers some 100 acres in Cardiff, with rose gardens and many rare plants resting in greenhouses. A memorial here honors Captain Robert Falcon Scott (1868–1912), the Antarctic hero who sailed from Cardiff on an ill-fated expedition to the South Pole.

Welsh Folk Museum   Just 6.4km (4 miles) west of Llandaff, this museum is a virtual neighborhood unto itself at St. Fagan's. It covers 100 acres of parkland and gardens and is the major attraction of the city.

Cardiff Bay   What about Tiger Bay, one asks? After all, it's the most famous and notorious section of Cardiff. Books and tall tales have been written or told of the seafaring men (and their women) who lived in this squalid, seamy dockland area. Today it's Cardiff Bay, and the Tiger Bay of legend is gone. A rather mixed community of various races, it is rather respectable today. Because the coal trade isn't what it used to be, the restored Cardiff Bay area pursues other interests, as reflected by its many banking and shipping offices. It is also the home of the new Techniquest (see below).

GETTING AROUND   If you don't have a car, you must depend on taxis, buses, or your trusty feet to get around in Cardiff.

BY BUS

There's fairly good bus service, even to the sights in the environs. Your hotel staff will usually be able to help you plan a day's outing. Note that prices of bus routes vary with the time of day and according to the number of zones you want to travel in. One-way travel within zone 1 (the commercial heart of the city) costs between 75p ($1.20) and £1.25 ($2) per person. One-way travel across all four zones of the city (a very large metropolitan area, taking in far-flung suburbs) costs between £1.50 and £1.75 ($2.40–$2.80) per person.

For bus routes, go to **BWS Caerdydd,** Wood Street (*©* **0870/608-2608**), which is the office of Cardiff City Transport. Across from the bus station, it is open Monday and Friday from 8am to 5:30pm, and Tuesday through Thursday and on Saturday from 8:30am to 5:30pm. Bus service on Sunday morning tends to be infrequent, and service stops completely every night at 11pm.

BY TAXI

Taxis are usually easy to find, especially in the busy shopping areas, and most cab fares within Cardiff range from £4 to £8 ($6.40–$13) each. The most prominent taxi ranks are at the rail and bus station and at St. David's Hall. Or you can

Cardiff

ATTRACTIONS ●

Barry Island Pleasure Park **15**
Bute Park **17**
Caerphilly Castle **18**
Cardiff Bay's Inner Harbour **5**
Cardiff Castle **10**
Cardiff City Hall **22**
Castell Coch **16**
Cathays Park **20**
Dyffryn Gardens **7**
Llandaff Cathedral **12**
Millennium Stadium **8**
National Museum of Wales **21**
Roath Park **3**
St. Fagans Castle **15**
Techniquest **5**
Welsh Folk Museum **15**

ACCOMMODATIONS ■

The Abbey Hotel **14**
Angel Hotel **9**
The Big Sleep Hotel **2**
Cardiff Bay **5**
Egerton Grey Country House Hotel **7**
Jurys Cardiff **1**
Llanerch Vineyard **15**
Lincoln Hotel **13**
New House Country **18**
St. David's Hotel & Spa **4**
Town House **11**

DINING ◆

Armless Dragon **19**
Champers **6**
DaCastaldo **15**
Gilby's Restaurant **15**
Harry Ramsden's **5**
La Brasserie **6**
Le Gallois **15**
Le Monde **6**
Woods Brasserie **8**

have your hotel or the place where you've dined call you a taxi. Wonder of wonders, the meter starts ticking only when you get into the vehicle, not when it leaves the station, as is the case in most U.K. cities. For service call **Capital Cabs** at © **029/2077-7777, Black Cabs** at © **029/2034-3343,** or **Premier Cabs** at © **029/2055-5555,** all operating 24 hours a day.

BY CAR

You'll find driving around Cardiff awkward and congested, so you're better off skipping the experience. You will, however, need a car to get the most out of a day trip. If you're touring Britain by car, arrangements should be made before you leave home (see chapter 3 for information on renting a car in Great Britain). Impulse renters in Cardiff can go to **Avis** at 1422 Tudor St. (© **029/2034-2111**), or **Hertz** at 9 Central Sq. (© **029/2022-4548**).

PARKING

Metered parking is available. You'll need the right change and also to watch out for traffic wardens who issue tickets. Cardiff also offers pay and display parking, whereby you purchase a ticket and display it on your dashboard. Parking this way costs 80p ($1.30) giving you the right to the space for 1 to 5 hours, depending on what part of the city you're in. Some zones are marked PERMIT HOLDERS ONLY. Don't park there unless you have a permit as a local resident—your vehicle will be towed if you do. A yellow line along the curb indicates "no parking." Public car parks are available at certain major centers in Cardiff, including multistory car parks on Quay Street, Bridge Street, and Hills Street.

BY BICYCLE

Much of Cardiff, including its surrounding area, has a terrain suitable for bike riding. For rentals go to **Taff Trail Cycle Hire,** Caravan Park, Pontcanna Fields (off Sophia Close; © **029/2039-6362**). It's open March through October daily from 9:30am to 7pm. Prices depend on the type of bike rented. Here you'll be directed to the scenic Taff Trail, starting at the Pierhead at Cardiff Bay. You can follow this mapped trail for as many miles as your endurance dictates.

BY FOOT

This is the best way to explore Cardiff, but be careful. Many Americans have accidents because they look the wrong way when crossing a street—remember that *cars drive on the left.* Always look both ways before stepping off a curb. Cardiff is relatively flat and easy to explore; however, many of its major attractions lie in outlying areas, which can be reached by public bus.

BY ORGANIZED TOUR

One of the most efficient ways to see Cardiff and the attractions within its central core involves joining up with one of the open-top bus tours conducted by **Guide Friday** (© **01789/294466** for information about its services in Cardiff and throughout the United Kingdom, or **02920/384291** for information specifically about its services within Cardiff). Tours follow a clearly signposted itinerary that begins at Platform no. F1 at the Cardiff Bus Station, between April and October, daily from 10am to 4pm; they cover a route that incorporates the most visible monuments of Cardiff. Participants can get on or get off the bus at any of the designated stops, returning for the next bus to carry them on to the next monument. Adults pay £7 ($11), seniors and students £5 ($8), children 5-15 £2.50 ($4), family ticket £17 ($26).

FAST FACTS: Cardiff

American Express An office is at 3 Queen St. (☎ 029/2066-5843).

Area Code The area code for Cardiff is **029**.

Currency Exchange Banks can change your traveler's checks, and you'll find them scattered strategically throughout the city. Two of the most visible include **Barclay's**, 121 Queen St. (☎ 029/2042-6600), and **Lloyd's**, 31 Queen St. (☎ 029/2038-2727).

Dentist For dental emergencies, contact **Dr. P.A. James Dental Surgeon**, 112 Newport Rd. (☎ 029/2048-6231).

Doctor For medical emergencies, dial **999** and ask for an ambulance. Doctors are on 24-hour call service. A full list of doctors is posted at all post offices, or else visitors can ask at their hotel desk.

Drugstores To get a prescription filled, go to **Boots the Chemist**. There are outlets all over town. The main dispensing service is at 5 Wood St. (☎ 029/2023-1291), open Monday through Friday from 8:30am to 6pm, Saturday from 9am to 5:30pm, and Sunday only from 11am to 5pm.

Emergencies To summon police or call firefighters, dial **999**, the same number used to call an ambulance.

Hospitals The most visible and best-accessorized hospital in Cardiff is the **University Hospital of Wales** (also known as **The Heath Hospital**), Heath Park (☎ 029/2074-7747).

Hot Lines **The Samaritans** (☎ 029/2034-4022) ensure that a 24-hour hot line is staffed and receptive to problems that include virtually anything, including questions about abuse, rape, extreme poverty, homelessness, or substance abuse. For emergencies involving possible intervention by the police, fire department, or an ambulance, call **999**.

Internet Access To stay in touch, you can go to the **Internet Exchange**, 8 Church St. (☎ 029/2023-6048), which is by St. John's Church. It charges £4 ($6.40) per hour for use of its facilities. Open Monday through Thursday from 9am to 9pm, Friday and Saturday from 9am to 8pm, and Sunday from 11am to 7pm.

Maps Detailed maps can be obtained for free from the **Cardiff Visitors Centre** at 16 Wood St. (☎ 029/2022-7281). Also, see "Visitor Information" above.

Police In an emergency, dial **999**. Otherwise, contact the **Central Cardiff Police Station**, Cathays Parks (☎ 029/2022-2211).

Post Office The main post office is at 2 Hill St. (☎ 029/2022-7305), open Monday to Friday 9am to 5:30pm and Saturday from 9am to 1pm.

EXPLORING THE TOWN

The Welsh capital has many interesting things to see, from antiquities to something as modern as Epstein's controversial carving *Christ in Majesty* at Llandaff Cathedral. If you're in Cardiff for only a short time, try to see the major sights described below.

Fun Fact **Did you know . . . ?**

- Cardiff is Europe's youngest capital city; the status was awarded in 1956 by Queen Elizabeth II.
- The most famous and notorious section of Cardiff, Tiger Bay, subject of legend and lore, no longer exists.
- Cardiff's city center, one of the most attractive in Britain, is called "the Welsh Washington."
- Five centuries after the fact, Cardiff City Hall erected a marble statue to the Welsh political comet and independence fighter, Owain Glyndwr, even though he'd sacked the town.
- Because of its architecture, Cardiff, along with Glasgow, ranks as one of the greatest Victorian cities of Britain.

THE TOP ATTRACTIONS

Cardiff Bay's Inner Harbour ✸   Allow 2 hours to visit this redeveloped area of the old dockland of Tiger Bay, lying 2.5km to 3.2km (1½–2 miles) south of the town center. The salty old sea dogs of yesteryear who used to hang out here between sails wouldn't recognize the place today. No longer tawdry, it bustles with shops, restaurants, pubs, and attractions.

In the 19th century, when the area was called Tiger Bay, it became notorious among sailors around the world. The setting for many a novel, Tiger Bay meant poverty, crime, and violence. Today, the panoramic view of the harbor is worth the visit alone, as are the scenic promenades along the bay and even a science center (see below).

Drop in at the **Cardiff Bay Visitor Centre,** The Tube, Harbour Dr. (© 029/2046-3833), to pick up any information about the area. Admission is free, and it is open daily from 9:30am to 5pm, standing next to the Welsh Industrial and Maritime Museum.

The chief attraction here is **Techniquest** ✸ (© 029/2047-5475), Britain's leading science discovery center. Here you can enjoy 160 hands-on exhibits, and you can visit both a Science Theatre and Planetarium. The attraction was founded in 1986 with the aim of developing people's understanding of science and technology. Some 100,000 people—both young and old—visit it annually. Admission is £6.50 ($10) for adults, £4.50 ($7.20) for children ages 5 to 16 (free for children ages 4 and under), or £18 ($29) for a family ticket. Open Monday through Friday from 9:30am to 4:30pm, Saturday and Sunday from 10:30am to 5pm.

Cardiff Castle ✸   Some 1,900 years of history are embodied in this castle located in the heart of the city. The Romans first built a forum on this site, and you can see the remains of massive 10-foot-thick stone walls. The Normans constructed a castle on what was left of the Roman fort, and much of the Norman work still exists, added to by medieval lords. It came under assault in the Anglo-Welsh wars and was besieged during the English civil war. The third marquess of Bute, by then the owner, had it restored in the 19th century by Victorian architect William Burges, who transformed the interior into the extravaganza of whimsy, color, and rich architectural detail you see today. The Welsh Regimental

Museum and the First Queen's Dragoon Guards Regimental Museum are also here. Admission includes the full conducted tour.

Castle St. ⓒ **029/2087-8100**. www.cardiffcastle.com. Admission £5.50 ($8.80) adults, £3.30 ($5.30) children, students, and seniors. Mar–Oct daily 9:30am–5pm; Nov–Feb daily 9:30am–3:30pm. Bus: 32 or 62.

Cardiff City Hall   A 59m (194-ft.) clock tower and dome topped by a fierce Welsh dragon are among the hallmarks of the Cardiff City Hall. The outstanding feature of this magnificent building of white Portland stone is the Marble Hall on the second floor. Here you'll find columns of Siena marble and a series of statues of Welsh heroes, each surveying the scene from marble plinths. Each statue was carved from Serraveza marble by a different sculptor. Most of the heroes are cultural rather than military figures. Among them is King Hywel, a 10th-century ruler who was the first codifier of law for the Welsh. He was also an early women's rights sympathizer, and his laws put women on a par with men. Other statues are of St. David, patron saint of Wales; Owen Glyndwr; and Harri Tewdwr, who as Henry VII founded the Tudor dynasty. Try also to see the council chamber, a room of gleaming polished paneling with tiers of comfortable-looking crimson seats for the council members.

Civic Centre, North Rd. ⓒ **029/2087-2000**. Free admission. Mon–Sat 9am–6pm. Bus: 32 or 62.

National Museum of Wales ⚡   This imposing white, classic building with a columned entrance and a large cupola houses eclectic art and science collections. Along with City Hall, it stands at the Civic Centre. The diverse exhibits here focus on natural science, industry, archaeology, and geology, plus there are extensive collections of silver, china, and glass (some dating from 1250). The emphasis is on the story of Wales from earliest times. There are also modern and classic sculptures and works from old masters and modern artists from Rembrandt to Kokoschka.

Much of the museum's ambience comes from the openness and light that fills the main entrance and hall below the high ceiling. From the floor of the rotunda, the visitor can look up to the mezzanine gallery that girdles the main hall. The exhibits are at the head of the impressive staircase from the main hall. Also on this level is the French Impressionist collection—our favorite part of the museum—which includes Monet's *Waterlilies,* Renoir's *Parisian Girl,* and Manet's haunting *The Rabbit.* Here you can also see Rodin's bronze couple *The Kiss,* and paintings by Rubens, Cézanne, Augustus John, and Brangwyn. A well-stocked bookstore is situated off the main hall.

Cathays Park in the Civic Centre. ⓒ **029/2039-7951**. www.nmgw.ac.uk. Free admission except for special exhibitions (prices vary). Tues–Sun 10am–5pm. Closed some public holidays. Bus: 32 or 62.

Llandaff Cathedral ⚡   This cathedral is in the tiny city of Llandaff, which stood just outside the western boundary of Cardiff until 1922 when it was made a part of the capital. It still retains its village atmosphere, with modern shops in old half-timbered buildings. The cathedral stands in a green hollow at a place where religious history goes back 1,400 years. It began as a religious community founded by St. Teilo in the 6th century, with many churches under its aegis scattered throughout South Wales. A 10th-century Celtic cross is all that's left of the pre-Norman church. Among relics of the Norman church erected on-site is a fine arch behind the high altar. The west front, built in the 13th century, is one of the best medieval works of art in Wales. Cromwell's army used the cathedral as a beer house and post office; then in 1941 a German bomb severely damaged the building. Postwar reconstruction gave the cathedral two fine new features: the Welsh Regiment Chapel and Sir Jacob Epstein's soaring sculpture *Christ in Majesty.* Epstein's striking work, which dominates the interior of the structure, has elicited mixed reactions from viewers. The ruin of the 800-year-old Bishop's Palace has been made into a peaceful public garden. Call for times of services.

Cathedral Rd. © 029/2056-3848. Free admission (donations requested). Daily 7am–7pm. Bus: 25, 26, 27, 28, 29, 30, 31, 32, 33, or 62.

Caerphilly Castle ★★   About 13km (8 miles) north of Cardiff is this imposing moated fortress built partly on the site of a Roman fort. It was constructed by Earl Gilbert de Clare, Lord of Glamorgan, as protection against invasion by the Welsh prince Llewelyn ap Gwynedd in the 13th century. The massive water defenses of the castle form the second-largest castle area in Britain. You will note the leaning tower as you approach the castle, a result of efforts by Cromwell to blow up the towers. Perhaps you'll see the castle ghost, the Green Lady. She is supposed to be the spirit of a French princess who loved a handsome Welsh prince. When her husband, the Norman lord of Caerphilly, learned of the matter, he sent her into exile, but her ghost is still supposed to be here, lamenting her lost love. You should come here mainly to see the impressive layout of the castle, with its defenses and great gatehouse, along with a fortified dam separating the outer moat from the inner moat. Wander also into the Great Hall. What you don't get is a luxurious interior filled with fascinating paintings or antiques.

On the A469 at Caerphilly. © 029/2088-3143. www.caerphillycastle.org. Admission £2.50 ($4) adults, £2 ($3.20) children ages 15 and under. Mid-Mar to mid-Oct daily 9:30am–6pm; off season daily 9:30am–4pm. Bus: 26 from Cardiff leaves for Caerphilly every hour during the day. Caerphilly train with several departures daily from Central Station in Cardiff.

Castell Coch ★   Known as "The Red Castle," this fairy-tale structure stands on a wooded hillside 5 miles northwest of Cardiff. Its pepper-pot turrets and round towers were the work of the third marquess of Bute and his imaginative and whimsical architect, William Burges designed this castle in the 19th century while he oversaw the interior restoration of Cardiff Castle. This one was constructed on the ruins of a medieval fort and contains a fantasy of morals, painted vaulted ceilings, and beautiful friezes. There's even a gloomy dungeon, with a flight of stone steps leading down to it.

Signposted off the A470 at Tongwynlais. © 029/2081-0101. Admission £3 ($4.80) adults, £2.50 ($4) children, students, and seniors. Family ticket £8.50 ($14). Mid-Mar to mid-Oct daily 9am–6:30pm; off season daily 9:15am–4pm. Bus: 26.

Welsh Folk Museum ★★   One of the most interesting places to visit in all of Wales is this museum, which provides a glimpse of Welsh life in centuries past. In the wooded parkland of an Elizabethan mansion, you can visit a treasury of ancient buildings that have been brought from their original sites all over the country and re-erected, in some cases even restored to their former use. In this superb collection of traditional buildings, widely distributed over the 100 acres of parkland, you can see a 15th-century Tudor farmhouse furnished in the fashion of its day, cottages, a tollhouse, a schoolhouse, a chapel, and a cockpit. You'll also see a woolen mill and a flour mill from long ago put back into use so that people of the present can see how such work was done back in the days before electricity, steam power, or other modern conveniences. A wood turner and a cooper (barrel maker) are also at work, using the tools and materials of another age.

Besides the open-air museum, you can also visit the handsome headquarters building of the Welsh Folk Museum with its wealth include costumes, agricultural farm equipment used to till Welsh fields centuries ago, and articles of material culture, from Welsh dressers and cooking utensils to love spoons and early-day toys.

Also on the grounds is **St. Fagans Castle,** the 16th-century mansion that was given to the National Museum of Wales by the earl of Plymouth as a center for the folk museum. The mansion house, built inside the curtain wall of a Norman castle, with its formal gardens, has been refurbished and restored to the way it was at the end of the 18th century.

St. Fagans. © 029/2057-3500. www.nmgw.ac.uk/mwl. Free admission. Daily 10am–5pm. Bus: 32 leaving from the bus station in Cardiff every hour during the day.

PARKS & GARDENS
Cardiff has been called a city of parks, with some 2,700 acres of well-designed parklands. **Bute Park,** in the heart of the city, spreads its green swath along the River Taff for the pleasure of residents and visitors.

Of special interest, **Roath Park,** Lake Road West (© 029/2075-5328), is east of the city center, offering facilities for boating and fishing on its 32-acre lake, as well as tennis courts and bowling greens. Rose and dahlia gardens, a subtropical greenhouse, a children's play area, and an island bird sanctuary add to the pleasures found here. The lighthouse clock tower in the lake is a memorial to Captain Scott. Admission is free, and it's open daily from 10:30am to 1pm and 2 to 4:30pm. Bus: 32 or 62.

Close to 5km (3 miles) from Cardiff, **Dyffryn Gardens,** St. Nicholas (© 029/ 2059-3328), stands in a secluded valley in the Vale of Glamorgan. This park of 50 acres contains a landscaped botanical garden. Herbaceous borders, a rose garden, a rock garden, and the largest heather garden in Wales are found here, along with an extensive arboretum. Grass walks invite you for long, leisurely strolls through the grounds. A palm house, an orchid house, a cactus and succulent house along with seasonal display houses of potted plants are also on view. Admission is £3 ($4.80) for adults or £2 ($3.20) for students and children. A family ticket goes for £6.50 ($10). From May to August it is open daily from 10am to 6pm. It is also open daily from 10am to 5pm in April, September, and October.

ESPECIALLY FOR KIDS
Many of the attractions already mentioned are of interest to both adults and children. These include **Cardiff Castle, Castell Coch,** the **Welsh Folk Museum,** and the **Welsh Industrial and Maritime Museum.** Another park of particular interest to children is **Roath Park.**

A final seasonal attraction is **Barry Island Pleasure Park,** Friars Road (© 01446/732844). The place is fun for kids, and there are plenty of rides and adventure games for the family, even a log flume to enjoy. Tickets for the various rides can be purchased at the kiosk at the park, although there is no admission charge to the park itself. It is open June through September daily from noon to 10pm. Drive 6 miles west of Cardiff along the coast, taking Exit 22 from the M4. From Cardiff Station, Barry-bound trains leave several times a day.

OUTDOOR ACTIVITIES
Built at the cost of £100 million ($160 million), the 70,000-seat **Millennium Stadium** (© 0870/558-2852) is only the second sports arena in the whole of Europe to have a retractable roof. This is the home of Welsh rugby, the national sport. The location is right in the city center on the banks of the River Taf just to the south of Cardiff Castle. The location is Cardiff Arms Park, but you can

hardly miss it. When a game isn't in progress, the stadium can be toured daily from 10am to 5pm. Adults pay £5 ($8) and children £2.50 ($4). A family ticket goes for £15 ($24). Ticket prices vary according to the event.

In the heart of Cardiff, the **Wales National Ice Rink,** Hayes Bridge Road (© **029/2039-7198**), encourages every skater from ice hockey buffs to speed skaters. The Cardiff Devils, one of Britain's leading ice hockey teams, are based at this rink. Admission is £6 ($9.60). The rink is closed Monday and Tuesday but open otherwise; hours are subject to change however, so call before heading here.

SHOPPING

Whether you're looking for gifts to take home, hunting for souvenirs, or just browsing, you'll like the shops of Cardiff. They are many and varied, ranging from a multiplicity of offerings in a modern shopping precinct, **St. David's Centre**—a stone's throw from the castle—to the stalls of a covered market. Bus: 2, 3, 7, 8, or 9. Shops are usually open Monday through Friday from 9am to 5pm, to 9pm on Thursday.

The **main shopping streets** are St. Mary, High, Castle, Duke, and Queen, plus the Hayes. Most of this area has been made into a pedestrian mall, with trees, shrubs, and gracious Edwardian arcades. These arcades, a dozen in all, are the most famous shopping precincts in all of Wales. The best known is the **Castle Arcade,** constructed in 1887. The interior has a fascinating first-floor wooden gallery with a wooden second floor overhanging it. Dating from 1858, the **Royal Arcade** is the oldest of the city's shopping arcades. Look for the original Victorian storefronts at nos. 29, 30, and 32. The **Morgan Arcade** from 1896 is the best preserved. Note the first-floor Venetian windows and the original slender wooden storefronts such as nos. 23 and 24. All in all, the arcades stretch to a length of 797m (2,655 ft.) in the city.

In the St. David's Shopping Centre is a branch of **Marks & Spencer,** 72 Queen St. (© **029/2037-8211**), one of the country's oldest branches of a major chain store, offering clothing with emphasis on British-made goods. A food section contains a range of high-quality specialty items. This is the anchor store in the enclosed center, which has shops opening off wide walkways.

David Morgan, 26 The Hayes (© **029/2022-1011**), is the largest independent department store in Wales, launched by the son of an impoverished tenant farmer in early Victorian times. The present store dates from 1879, offering a wide array of Welsh gifts and souvenirs for the visitors, along with such substantial merchandise as clothing for the locals. It offers restaurants, a coffee shop, a snack bar, and a beauty salon. Bus: 1 or 2.

The best Welsh craft shop in the center is **Castle Welsh Crafts,** 1 Castle St. (© **029/2034-3038**), opposite the castle entrance. Mailing service is available, and VAT-refund forms are available for overseas visitors.

Markets are held at several sites. The **Central Indoor Market** on St. Mary Street is open Monday through Friday. The **Outdoor Fruit and Vegetable Market,** St. David Street and Mary Ann Street, is open Monday through Saturday. On Bessemer Road, an **open-air market** is held on Sunday morning.

For a novel shopping jaunt, visit **Jacob Antique Centre,** Penarth Road (© **029/2039-0939**), to see what's for sale from Grandmother Welsh's attic. Perhaps a Victorian fireplace, 19th-century jewelry, antique brass or hardware, pocket watches, and certainly furnishings mainly from Victoria's heyday. Bus: 2 or 3.

Close to St. David's Centre, the **Capitol Shopping Centre** along Queen Street is another place to shop for bargains or special gifts. In the complex is one of Britain's best men's stores, **Austin Reed,** 13–14 The Capitol (© **029/ 2022-8357**). Bus: 70, 78, 80, or 82.

With pop music playing in the background, you can also visit **Ciro Citterio,** 71–73 Queen St. (© **029/2039-7096**), which has one of the largest selections of men's shoes and suits in Wales. Bus: 50, 51, 52, 70, 71, or 72. Women find that **Jaeger,** 12 Queen St., The Capitol (© **029/2022-6898**), carries quality apparel made of high-quality fabrics. Bus: 50, 51, 52, 70, 71, or 72.

At the **Martin Tinney Gallery,** 6 Windsor Place (© **029/2064-1410**), a short distance from the Cardiff rail station, you'll find the region's best commercial galleries. Finally, **Craft in the Bay,** 57 Bute St., Cardiff Bay (© **029/ 2048-4611**), features the largest selection of handmade quality crafts in Wales—baskets, pottery, jewelry, hand-crafted furniture, ceramics, and the like.

WHERE TO STAY
EXPENSIVE

Egerton Grey Country House Hotel ⭐ *Kids* Sixteen kilometers (10 miles) west of the city, this elegant country-house hotel lies in a bucolic setting in the Vale of Glamorgan. The house dates from the 17th century and has been carefully restored, and it's filled with antiques and well-chosen accessories, including paintings and porcelain. In nippy weather you can warm yourself by the open fires. Standing amidst 7 acres of gardens, it faces the sea in the hamlet of Porthkerry, within easy driving distance of the Brecon Beacons and Gower Peninsula. It was once a rectory and private residence but was opened as a small luxurious house in 1988. All the rooms are spacious and exceedingly comfortable; some have four-poster beds. The suites offer beautiful coastal views. Guests can enjoy the library or a magnificent Edwardian drawing room, and can dine in the first-class mahogany-paneled restaurant. *Note:* Children over 10 years of age are welcome at the hotel, which has plenty of grounds where kids can run and play.

Porthkerry, near Barry and Cardiff, Vale of Glamorgan, CF62 3BZ. © **01446/711666.** Fax 01446/711690. www.egertongrey.co.uk. 10 units. £115 ($184) double; £130 ($208) suite. AE, MC. Free parking. From junction 33 of M4 follow signs to the airport, bypassing Barry and turning left at the small roundabout, signposted Porthkerry. After about 457m (500 yards), turn left again at the signpost to the hotel. **Amenities:** Restaurant; room service; babysitting; laundry service. *In room:* TV, coffeemaker, hair dryer, trouser press.

St. David's Hotel & Spa ⭐⭐⭐ *Finds* We'd rate this as hotel of the year for Wales. A strikingly contemporary structure, it dwarfs the competition, rising along the new waterfront development. A seven-story atrium towers above the lobby, an unusual sight for a Welsh hotel. An immediate hit, it is the first five-star hotel to arrive in Wales and is the only one in South Wales that qualifies as one of the Leading Hotels of the World. You get the highest level of service in South Wales, the ultimate in comfort, and the best leisure facilities. St. David's is especially known for its extensive spa and beauty facilities. Roomy and beautifully furnished bedrooms offer floor-to-ceiling windows and open onto private balconies with panoramic sweeps of the bay. The marble bathrooms are state of the art and offer Italian toiletries and bathrobes. A superb modern European cuisine is presented nightly in the hotel's restaurant.

Havannah St., Cardiff Bay, Cardiff CF10 5SD. © **029/2031-3018.** Fax 029/2048-7056. www.rfhotels.com. 136 units. £200 ($320) double; from £260 ($416) suite. AE, DC, MC, V. Parking £4.20 ($6.70). **Amenities:** Restaurant; bar; indoor pool; health club; spa; Jacuzzi; sauna; room service; babysitting; laundry service; dry cleaning. *In room:* A/C, TV, coffeemaker, hair dryer, safe.

MODERATE

Angel Hotel ⭐ This elegant Victorian hotel across from Cardiff Castle and has regained some of its old prestige following a restoration in 2000. When it was first built, it was *the* place to stay in South Wales. Over the years it has attracted everybody from Garbo to the Beatles to every prime minister of Britain. There is no way it will ever regain its old supremacy, as greater hotels such as Cardiff Bay and St. David's Hotel & Spa have long surpassed it, but the Angel is still there and still good—a world of neo-Doric decor, *trompe-l'oeil* ceilings, Waterford crystal chandeliers, and hand-stippled faux-marble columns. As befits a hotel of this age, rooms come in a wide variety of styles and sizes ranging from standard (the smallest) to deluxe (spacious and superior in every way).

Castle St., Cardiff, CF10 1SZ. (℃) **029/2064-9200.** Fax 029/2039-6212. www.paramount-hotels.co.uk/angx.html. 102 units. £88–£180 ($141–$288) double; £150–£200 ($240–$320) suite. AE, DC, MC, V. Free parking. **Amenities:** Restaurant; bar and lounge; 24-hr. room service; babysitting. *In room:* A/C, TV, coffeemaker, hair dryer, iron/ironing board.

Cardiff Bay ⭐⭐ Not the equal of St. David's Hotel & Spa, which is in a class by itself, this is our runner-up in the area. It too lies in the heart of the waterfront development and has already become a new Cardiff landmark. It combines modern, cruiseliner-style architecture with a restored, part-Victorian warehouse, and it does so dramatically with a maritime theme. Appropriately, the color schemes are aquamarine. Adding yet another atrium to the city's hotels, it uses glass elevators in the style pioneered by the Hyatt chain. Bedrooms are spacious and beautifully furnished with comfort in mind. Some family rooms are available, and some accommodations are reserved for nonsmokers. Bathrooms are roomy and superbly equipped.

Schooner Way, Atlantic Wharf, Cardiff Bay, Cardiff CF10 4RT. (℃) **029/2047-5000.** Fax 029/2048-1491. www.hanover-international.com. 156 units. £85–£150 ($136–$240) double; from £150 ($240) suite. AE, DC, MC, V. **Amenities:** 2 restaurants; 2 bars; pool; health club; spa; Jacuzzi; sauna. *In room:* A/C, TV, dataport, coffeemaker, hair dryer.

Jurys Cardiff ⭐ *Kids* Adjacent to the Cardiff International Arena, this refurbished hotel is stylish and classic, ideal for both business travelers and vacationers. There's a vibrant spirit about the place that attracts us. Spacious and well-furnished bedrooms are grouped around a central atrium, which gives access to the hotel's fashionable public rooms. The accommodations are among the city's finest, with some of the best amenities. Some units are suitable for both nonsmokers and persons with disabilities. A few family rooms are available, and children are given a very hospitable welcome.

Mary Ann St., Cardiff CF10 2JH. (℃) **029/2034-1441.** Fax 029/2022-3742. www.jurysdoyle.com. £80–£210 ($128–$336) double. Rates include breakfast. AE, DC, MC, V. **Amenities:** Restaurant; Irish-themed bar; 24-hr. room service; babysitting; laundry service; dry cleaning. *In room:* TV, coffeemaker, hair dryer, safe, trouser press.

New House Country ⭐ On the fringe of Cardiff this elegant Georgian mansion is our choice for a tranquil retreat from the city. Opening onto panoramic views—on a clear day you can see the North Devon Coast—the hotel is imbued with an inviting country-house flavor, as evoked by open fires, exquisite furnishings, and beautifully restored bedrooms. The individually designed bedrooms, many with four-poster beds, are spacious and comfortable. Although traditional, there is modern luxury here. Bathrooms are roomy and sumptuous, with deluxe toiletries. Most of the bedrooms are in a large annex, and rooms here are as good as those in the main building. Three are large enough for families, and three units are also set aside for nonsmokers.

Thornhill, Cardiff CF14 9UA. © **800/528-1234** in the U.S., or 029/2052-0280. Fax 029/2052-0324. www. newhousehotel.com. 36 units. £115 ($184) double; £135 ($216) suite. AE, DC, MC, V. Free parking. **Amenities:** Restaurant; bar; lounge; room service. *In room:* A/C (in some), TV, coffeemaker, hair dryer, iron/ironing board.

INEXPENSIVE

The Abbey Hotel   Built in 1898 as a home for a wealthy sea captain and his family, this house retains many of its original features and is one of the better and more reasonably priced B&Bs. Richard Burton once attended elocution lessons in the public lounge back when the hotel was a private school. Bedrooms are small but comfortably furnished, often in a "Great Aunt" style, and have shower-only bathrooms. A few have four-posters, and many have VCRs. Breakfast is the only meal served, but the staff can recommend one of the many restaurants nearby.

149–51 Cathedral Rd., Cardiff CF11 9PJ. © **029/2039-0896.** Fax 029/2023-8311. 28 units (shower only). £50–£90 ($80–$144) double; £75–£100 ($120–$160) triple. Rates include continental breakfast. MC, V. Free parking. Bus: 25. *In room:* TV, VCR (some), coffeemaker, hair dryer (in some).

The Big Sleep Hotel ⊀ *(Value)*   What are pictures of the actor John Malkovich doing scattered throughout this hotel? The actor, who made a career out of playing "evil bastards," is one of the major shareholders. And his hotel has been named one of *Conde Nast Traveller's* "coolest places to stay." A rather dull office tower built in the 1960s has been successfully transformed into a hotel with a certain chic minimalism but with most affordable prices. Each of the midsize bedrooms is individually decorated with contemporary pieces, a rather smart styling. Family rooms and rooms for those with limited mobility are available. The best rooms are the "New on Ninth" and cost more. All accommodations come with a new bathroom that's well maintained. If there's a downside, it's that some of the bedrooms overlook the rail tracks nearby, a rather noisy location.

Bute Terrace, Cardiff CF 2FE. © **029/2063-6363.** Fax 029/2063-6364. www.thebigsleephotel.com. 81 units. Mon–Thurs £58–£89 ($93–$142) double; Fri–Sun £53 ($85) double. Suite £99–£135 ($158–$216) all week. Rates include breakfast. AE, DC, MC, V. **Amenities:** Breakfast room; bar. *In room:* TV, coffeemaker, hair dryer, iron.

Lincoln Hotel *(Kids)*   This Victorian house provides a cozy and reasonably priced nest along popular Cathedral Road. The majestic home was created in 1900 by joining together two older residences, resulting in a superb and completely restored hotel. Surprisingly the hotel is named for Abraham Lincoln, not the English cathedral city of Lincoln. The four-poster units exude romance, but there are also modern facilities. Rooms are spacious, with well-kept bathrooms, and furnishings offer both style and comfort. Several family rooms are available. Smoking is not permitted in the guest rooms. You can meet your fellow guests in the snug sitting room.

118 Cathedral Rd., Cardiff CF11 9LQ. © **029/2039-5558.** Fax 029/2023-0537. www.lincolnhotel.co.uk. 18 units. £75–£90 ($120–$144) double, £85–£120 ($136–$192) double with 4-poster. Rates include breakfast. AE, DC, MC, V. Free parking. **Amenities:** Bar; room service; laundry service. *In room:* TV, coffeemaker, hair dryer, trouser press.

Llanerch Vineyard ⊀ *(Finds)*   If you don't have time to explore Wales in depth and have to settle for only a visit to Cardiff, you can sample country life by driving 16km (10 miles) west of the city to live here on a 21-acre estate in a country farmhouse dating from 1848. In a Vale of Glamorgan vineyard, you are far removed from the bustle of Cardiff in this attractive and tranquil setting. The bedrooms are midsize and furnished for the most part with pine pieces, a country comfortable decor with small bathrooms, mostly with tub and shower (the rest with shower only). Several nonsmoking studio suites have recently been installed in some of the property's old winery buildings; extras in these rooms include refrigerators and microwaves. Two cottages set in an old stable block are equipped with kitchens, VCRs, and CD players, and are large enough for families.

You can explore the grounds at leisure going through forest and vineyards, and you can also check with the owners about setting up a wine tasting from the Welsh vineyards. You'll be rare among your friends as an expert on Welsh wines. The owners, Peter and Diana Andrews, share their farm and home with you, and, although it has an old-fashioned aura, it's been thoughtfully modernized. The farmhouse has been selected as one of the "Great Little Places" in Wales and has been featured on programs for the BBC. Although no dinner is served, there are many pubs and restaurants within a short drive of the hotel.

Hensol, Pendoylan, Vale of Clamorgan CF72 8GG. ℂ **01443/225877.** Fax 01443/225546. www.llanerch-vineyard.co.uk. 11 units. £50–£75 ($80–$120) double. Rates include continental breakfast. MC, V. **Amenities:** Breakfast room; coin-operated laundry; vineyard. *In room:* TV, coffeemaker, hair dryer, iron.

Town House ✦ *Value*　This is the best B&B in Cardiff, preferable even to the neighboring Lincoln. A classic Victorian town house, it lies in the shadow of the great Norman castle and has been completely restored and tastefully decorated. Its original architectural details are still here, including the mosaic-tiled floors in the elegantly decorated hallway, the stained-glass windows so beloved of Victorians, and even the original fireplaces in the public lounge and dining area. A cosmopolitan guest house, it attracts guests from San Francisco to Sydney. The roomy bedrooms are immaculately furnished and have excellent bathrooms. The location is a 10-minute walk from the city center. The entire property is non-smoking.

70 Cathedral Rd., Cardiff CF11 9LL. ℂ **029/2023-9399.** Fax 029/2022-3214. www.thetownhousecardiff.co.uk. 8 units. £53–£63 ($84–$100) double. Rates include breakfast. AE, MC, V. Free parking. Bus: 32. **Amenities:** Breakfast room. *In room:* TV, coffeemaker, hair dryer.

WHERE TO DINE
EXPENSIVE
Le Gallois ✦ CONTINENTAL　For the flavors of the Mediterranean, this restaurant is without peer in Cardiff. It even surpasses the nearby Le Cassoulet. The chef and patron, Padrig Jones, served under the enfant terrible of English chefs, the famous Marco Pierre White, and Jones learned his lessons well, scoring some knockout dishes from his own culinary imagination as well. In a stylish, contemporary atmosphere, this family-run favorite is two-tiered with clean, bold lines. Fashion and technique are evident in the salt-marsh Welsh rump of lamb with fondant potatoes, marinated Provençale vegetables, and a tomato and fresh basil jus. The fish dishes are also a delight, especially the steamed sea bass with crab and a chile salsa we recently sampled.

6–10 Romilly Crescent, Canton. ℂ **029/2034-1264.** Fixed lunch £13–£27 ($21–$43); set dinner £22–£32 ($35–$51). AE, MC, V. Tues–Sat noon–2:30pm and 6:30–10:30pm.

MODERATE
Da Castaldo ✦ *Kids* ITALIAN　Chefs here serve the best Italian cuisine in the Welsh capital. Lying in a warren of Edwardian streets west of Cathedral Road, this popular bistro specializes in robust Italian classics. Its specialty is *pasta al fagioli*, the popular bean and pasta dish of southern Italy. Some Welsh families

come here at least once every other week just to feast off this delectable and savory offering. Many other specialties beloved by the citizens of Naples are also served here including transparently thin-crusted individual pizzas. The cookery is careful and precise, and always filled with flavor. For dessert we reluctantly said no to the tiramisu, settling for a perfect *pannacotta*. You could even make a meal of the two dozen cheeses served here nightly.

5 Romilly Crescent, Canton. ℭ 029/2022-1905. Reservations required. Main courses £12–£15 ($19–$24). DC, MC, V. Tues–Fri noon–2pm and 7–10pm. Closed 2 weeks in Aug.

Gilby's Restaurant SEAFOOD/WELSH   Near the Culverhouse Cross roundabout, two old converted farm buildings are now the venue for some of the finest viands in and around Cardiff. It's a lively place, popular with punters, who come here mainly for seafood, such as fresh lobster and oysters caught on nearby shores, along with crab from Pembroke. A young team in the kitchen turns out one tempting dish after another, including roast rack of salt-marsh rump of lamb with butternut squash and chanterelles. Our guest raved over the risotto of scallops with saffron, as we enjoyed a perfectly cooked sea bass baked with aromatic fennel only to have a regular tell us we should have opted for the poached smoked haddock on a bed of fresh spinach. For dessert, who could say no to the lemon tart with a side dish of amaretto-spiked pistachio ice cream?

Old Port Rd., Culverhouse Cross. ℭ 029/2067-0800. Reservations recommended. Main courses £8.95–£25 ($14–$40); set lunch Tues–Sat £11 ($18), Sun £9.95–£17 ($16–$27); set dinner Tues–Fri £15 ($24). AE, MC, V. Tues–Sat noon to 2:30pm (until 3:30pm Sun) and 6–10pm. From M4 133 follow signs for Airport/Cardiff West; take A4050 Barry/Bairport Rd., turning right at the first roundabout.

Woods Brasserie MODERN BRITISH/CONTINENTAL   In the old Pilotage Building down by the dock, this is a haven of modernity, serving not only the best of Britain, but dishes inspired by the cuisines of the Pacific Rim and the Mediterranean. Martyn Peters roams the world for inspiration and finds it in such spicy and savory combinations as Asian griddled chicken salad with a little Mexican guacamole on the side. He is addicted to Asian flavorings, such as a sweet chile sauce used to perk up pork tenderloin (ginger and garlic help, too). Aberdeen Angus filet, tender and juicy, is marvelously combined with a Gorgonzola polenta. Wales temptingly turns up on the menu in a rump of Welsh salt-march lamb with a red onion tart. Some of the wines come all the way from Australia.

Pilotage Building, Stuart S., Cardiff Bay. ℭ 029/2049-2400. Reservations required. Main courses £9.50–£22 ($15–$35). AE, DC, MC, V. Tues–Sat noon–2pm and 7–10pm; Sun 11:30am–3pm.

INEXPENSIVE

Armless Dragon WELSH   A mile north of the center in a busy suburb, this popular restaurant occupies a 19th-century stone core and is known for its simple, unpretentious, and nutritious food. The kitchen hires skilled chefs whose suppliers offer the best in Welsh produce and meats. The cooks are strong on their "taste of Wales" dishes, as exemplified by such delights as deep-fried laverballs coated in sunflower and sesame seeds, Brecon lamb brochettes, and a delicious mussel quiche. The place attracts both students and the family trade. One of our favorite dishes is roast Monmouthshire pork with a cockle and coriander sauce. Save room for their ginger cake with rhubarb compote.

97 Wyeverne Rd. ℭ 029/2038-2357. Reservations recommended. Main courses £10–£17 ($16–$26); set lunch £8–£10 ($13–$16). MC, V. Tues–Fri noon–2pm; Tues–Sat 7–10pm. Closed Dec 25–26.

Harry Ramsden's SEAFOOD   This member of a chain, at least according to its devotees, serves the best fish and chips in Wales. Until we get to sampling hundreds of others, we'll have to let the claim remain. Under crystal chandeliers, with nostalgic pictures displayed, this is both a place for traditional British cuisine, mainly seafood, as well as entertainment. Begin perhaps with a prawn cocktail. You can opt for fish platters, such as a 14-ounce batter-fried haddock with chips. If you finish the whole thing, you can have any dessert you want for free. You can also try such other main dishes as chargrilled chicken with fresh vegetables. At a table opening onto a view of Cardiff Bay, you can sample such traditional favorite desserts as a bread-and-butter pudding. On certain nights (programs vary) there is live entertainment such as jazz bands, making the whole night festive.

Landsea House, Stuart St. © **029/2046-3334**. Reservations recommended. Main courses £6.80–£13 ($11–$21). AE, DC, MC, V. Daily noon–9pm.

La Brasserie, Champers, Le Monde *Kids* CONTINENTAL Benigno Martinez enjoys one of the best dining formulas in the capital—a three-in-one winner—a wine bar, a brasserie, and a Spanish bodega. A bustling, informal atmosphere prevails, and much of young Cardiff turns up here nightly, beginning with the bar food in Champers, which in this case means the tastiest tapas in town. La Brasserie was originally built as a warehouse in the 19th century. You order your drinks from a wood-topped bar and food from an attendant, who waits behind a well-stocked display case. The establishment serves 50 kinds of wine. Opt for the spit-roasted suckling pig or a platter of fresh oysters. Game, including grouse, woodcock, and partridge is featured in season. Le Monde concentrates on fresh fish, including a delectable Marseilles-style fish soup and sea bass baked in rock salt. Of course, the regulars always seem to gravitate to the whole lemon sole. Something new and novel? Opt for the ostrich kebabs. At Champers you get a lively Spanish atmosphere with a cuisine to match. If your family, including the kids, wants real food instead of a Big Mac, this is an appealing choice because of its variety, quality, and reasonable prices.

60 St. Mary St. © **029/2023-4134**. www.le-monde.co.uk/champers.htm. Reservations not needed. Main courses £9–£24 ($14–$38); set-price lunch £7.20–£8.50 ($12–$14). Mon–Sat noon–2:30pm and 7pm–12:15am. Closed Dec 15–26. MC, V.

CARDIFF AFTER DARK

There's no Soho in Cardiff, but you can find many interesting places to go after dark.

St. David's Hall (see below) is one of Britain's leading centers of music, offering an extensive program, including visits by international conductors, soloists, and orchestras. Top rock and pop artists also appear there. The most outstanding local troupe is the **Welsh National Opera,** which *Punch* magazine acclaimed as "the world's best opera company."

For information abut After Dark diversions, pick up a brochure from the Cardiff tourist office *(Cardiff 2004)*, revised annually. In it you'll see a selective rundown of the city's most worthwhile entertainment.

THE PERFORMING ARTS

The most innovative space for musical presentations in Britain—outside London, that is—is **St. David's Hall** (or Neuadd Dewi Sant in Welsh), The Hayes (© **029/2087-8444;** www.newtheatrecardiff.co.uk). Designed in an octagonal format of shimmering glass and roughly textured concrete, it is the most comprehensive forum for the arts in Wales. A number of world-class orchestras appear regularly, along with popular music stars—everybody from Tina Turner to Welsh-born Tom Jones. Dance, films, and classical ballet, among other events, are also presented.

The hall maintains an information desk for the sale of tickets throughout the day. It also has dining facilities, plus a changing exhibition of art. Prince Charles laid the hall's cornerstone, and the Queen Mother officially opened the arts center in 1983. The top-notch acoustics are attributed to its interior arrangements of a series of interlinked sloping terraces, any of which can be opened or closed for seating depending on the size of the audience.

Instant confirmed bookings for events can be made by phone with a Visa or MasterCard daily from 10am to 6 or 8pm, depending on the concert schedule. The box office is open Monday through Saturday from 10am to 8pm (but only until 6pm on days when there's no performance). On Sunday, hours are from 10am to either 6pm or until 1 hour before the start of a scheduled performance. Ticket prices depend on the event. Bus: 1 or 2.

A charming Edwardian building from 1906, the **New Theatre,** Park Place (© **029/2087-8889;** www.newtheatrecardiff.co.uk), is the city's second cultural venue, seating 1,000 patrons for major productions of drama, ballet, contemporary dance, and pantomime. As of this writing, it is also the home of the Welsh National Opera, although this troupe may one day move to a newer building. Many theatergoers often enjoy shows here before they head for London's West End. The box office is open Monday through Saturday from 10am to 8pm. If there's no performance scheduled, the ticket office closes at 6pm. Most tickets generally cost from £7 to £24 ($11–$38). Bus: 70, 78, 80, or 82.

Cardiff's main repertory theater, **Sherman Theatre,** Senghennydd Road (© **029/2064-6900;** www.shermantheatre.co.uk), is on the campus of the University of Wales. It has two auditoriums—the Main Theatre and the more intimate Arena Theatre. More than 600 performances a year are staged here, including drama, dance, and Welsh folkloric performances. The box office is open Monday through Saturday from 10am to 8pm (until 6pm if no performance is scheduled). The cost for most tickets is £9 ($14) for adults or £6 ($9.60) for students and children. Bus: 70, 78, 80, or 82.

Finally, **Chapter,** Market Road, in Canton (© **029/2030-4400;** www.chapter. org), is an arts center complete with a theater; two movie facilities; three galleries and artists' studios; video, photography, and silk-screen workshops; a dance studio; a book shop; two bars; and a restaurant. Its box office is open Monday through Friday from 11am to 8:30pm, Saturday from 2 to 8:30pm, and Sunday from 3 to 8:30pm. Take bus no. 17, 18, or 31.

DANCE CLUBS

Try **The Clwb Ifor Bach (The Welsh Club)** at 11 Womanby St. (© **029/2023-2199**), reached by turning left on the road from Castle Street. On most nights this is a rocking venue. Bus: 50, 51, 52, 70, 71, or 72. Its competitor, which is a bit more fun on most nights, is **Blah Blah's,** 114 St. Mary St. (© **029/2034-45110**), which stays open later than most places in the center—that is, until 1am, late by Welsh standards. This is one of the city's most popular clubs, attracting crowds in the 20-to-35 age range (as does The Welsh Club) to its split-level floor.

PUBS & BARS

A local favorite, **Angel Tavern,** in the Angel Hotel, Castle Street (© **029/2064-9200**), is still charming after all these years. Ales are drawn by hand-pumps from the cellars of this traditional tavern, walled with red brick, its ceiling supported by heavy wooden beams. Facing Cardiff Castle, it is on the corner of Castle and Westgate streets. Bars meals are served at lunch—not in the actual tavern but in the street-level cocktail lounge of the hotel. Take bus no. 1 or 2.

Another traditional favorite is **The Park Vaults,** in The Thistle Hotel, Park Lane (℃ **029/2038-3471**), a cozy pub and bistro format. Stained-glass windows evoke Victorian nostalgia. You can also come here for a pub dinner. Bus: 1 or 2.

More modern and attracting a younger crowd, **Bar 38,** Stuart Street, Mermaid Quay (℃ **029/2049-4375**), is a two-story bar that serves some of the best mixed drinks in town—from champagne cocktails to red wine. Bus: 8.

A hangout for rugby fans, **City Arms,** 10 Quay St. (corner of Quay and Womanby sts.; ℃ **029/2022-5258**), attracts sports enthusiasts, and is the most likely venue for any pop star or celebrity likely to be visiting Wales. Bus: 50, 51, 52, 70, 71, or 72.

GAY CLUBS

If you're dreaming of gay love with a Welsh accent, head for **Exit Club,** 48 Charles St. (℃ **029/2064-0101**), a hot spot which is usually crowded and cruisy. Its precincts accommodate the young Richard Burton or Dylan Thomas types of the 21st century. Surveying the dance floor of heavy drinking hot guys, one patron claimed, "You want to get 'em before they're too pissed." There's no cover before 9:30pm; after that hour, you pay from £2 to £3 ($3.20–$4.80). Open Monday through Saturday from 6pm to 1am, Sunday from 6pm to 2am.

2 Abergavenny

262km (163 miles) W of London; 78km (49 miles) NE of Swansea; 49km (31 miles) NE of Cardiff

This flourishing market town of nearly 10,000 people is called "the Gateway to Wales," and it's certainly the gateway to the Brecon Beacons, which lie to the west. The Welsh word *aber* means the mouth of a river, and Abergavenny lies at the mouth of the River Gavenny, where it joins the River Usk. The town is in a valley with mountains and hills spread around it. Humankind has found this a good, sometimes safe place to live for some 5,000 years, as revealed by archaeological finds from the late Neolithic Age. The Romans established one of their forts here; centuries later a Norman castle was built nearby.

Try to be in Abergavenny on a market day. On Tuesday and Friday you can shop among stalls carrying a wide selection of goods, ranging from antiques, food, and clothing to furniture and junk. On Tuesday there is a livestock market.

Abergavenny is renowned as a center for outdoor holiday activities, including pony trekking, hill walking and climbing, golfing, hang gliding, and fishing. A Leisure Centre provides for indoor sports. The tourist office (see below) keeps an up-to-date list of activities available at any season.

ESSENTIALS

GETTING THERE   The town is linked by rail to both Shrewsbury and Hereford (in England) and to Newport, a distance of 31km (19 miles) to the southwest, in Wales. From Newport, rail connections are made to Cardiff, Bristol, and London. The Abergavenny Rail Station is on Station Road, off Monmouth Road. It usually takes 2½ hours if you're arriving from London. For rail information and schedules, call ℃ **0845/748-4950.**

The no. 20 **National Welsh Bus** from Hereford arrives four times per day. Bus no. 21 arrives six times per day from Brecon, and bus nos. 20 and 21 arrive at the rate of 12 per day from Newport (from which connections are made to Cardiff). For information, call © **0870/608-2608.**

From Hereford, take the A465 southwest, and from Cardiff take the M4 motorway east toward London, but cut north along the A4042 toward Abergavenny.

VISITOR INFORMATION   The town's Civic Society has laid out a **Town Trail,** listing buildings and other points of interest.

From Easter to September, for information about Abergavenny and its environs, get in touch with the **tourist information center,** Swan Meadows, Monmouth Road (© **01873/857588).** Open April through October daily from 10am to 6pm; November through March daily from 9:30am to 4:30pm.

SEEING THE SIGHTS

Only fragments of the 12th-century **Abergavenny Castle,** on Castle Street, remain, but a gruesome segment of its history is remembered. An early owner of the fortress, the Norman knight William de Braose, angered at the slaying of his brother-in-law by Welsh lords of Gwent, invited a group of them to dinner and had them murdered as they sat unarmed at his table. Visitors today fare better in visiting. Admission is free, and it's open daily from dawn to dusk.

The **Abergavenny Museum,** Castle Street (© **01873/854282),** is in a house attached to the 19th-century hunting lodge on the castle grounds. The museum contains archaeological artifacts, farming tools, and a fascinating collection of old prints and pictures. A Welsh farmhouse kitchen and the contents of an old saddler's shop are on display. Admission is £1 ($1.60) for adults, 75p ($1.20) for seniors and students, free for children. Open March through October Monday through Saturday from 11am to 1pm and 2 to 5pm, Sunday from 2 to 5pm. November through February, Monday through Saturday from 11am to 1pm and 2 to 4pm.

St. Mary's Parish Church, Monk Street, is all that's left of a 12th-century Benedictine priory church. Little remains of the original Norman structure, as the building was redone from the 13th to the 15th century. It is believed that Cromwell's troops, which were billeted in Abergavenny for a while during the siege of Raglan Castle, did some damage to the church and its tombs. In the Herbert Chapel are a number of sarcophagi of lords of Abergavenny and family members, with requisite effigies on top. The oldest brass memorial in the church records a death in 1587. The 15th-century Jesse Tree in the Lewis Chapel is an unusual, 10-foot-long wood carving portraying Christ's family tree growing out of the body of Jesse, father of David. There is also a Norman font, as well as some 14th-century oak choir stalls. In spite of vandalism that has been committed in the church throughout the centuries, the building is kept open most days for worship and inspection. The hours will be found in the porch or at the parking lot hut. For information, call the vicarage (© **01873/853168).**

WHERE TO STAY

Bear 🐾 *Value*   This 15th-century coaching inn is hailed for its evocative atmosphere, bedrooms, and cuisine—a winning combination. About 8km (5 miles) northwest of Abergavenny in a charming little town, the hotel grew in fame back in the days when stagecoaches from London would pull in here. On chilly nights, a blazing log fire is waiting to greet you. The place has been upgraded to keep up with modern times, but the old character has been respected—for example, some units with four-posters also have Jacuzzi baths. In summer a secluded outdoor garden is the place to sit and watch a Welsh twilight. A recent addition is a range of newly installed superior bedrooms bordering a courtyard.

This annex was designed in the style of an old Tudor manse. Or you can opt for the individually furnished bedrooms in the main building, which come in a variety of styles. The standard rooms, the least desirable, are at the front of the hotel, and have showers, whereas the deluxe and executive rooms are larger and have shower-bath combos or Jacuzzis with separate shower stalls. The restaurant is always winning awards either for best hotel pub grub in Great Britain or else AA rosettes for a "taste of Wales." Fresh local produce and home-grown herbs are used—try the Welsh lamb or salmon from the Usk and Wye Rivers.

High Street, Crickhowell, Powys NP8 1BW. ℂ 01873/810408. Fax 01873/811696. www.bearhotel.co.uk. 36 units. £72–£92 ($115–$147) double; £135 ($216) suite. Rates include breakfast. AE, MC, V. On A40 between Abergavenny and Brecon. **Amenities:** Restaurant; bar. *In room:* TV, coffeemaker, hair dryer.

Llansantffraed Court ★★ You'll have to drive 16km (10 miles) from Abergavenny to reach it, but this hotel is worth the journey. As you head up the drive an impressive redbrick country house in William and Mary style comes into view. It's set on extensive and well-kept grounds with a small lake, everything opening onto distant views of the Brecon Beacons. The midsize bedrooms are comfortably furnished and some offer panoramic views of the surrounding mountains. Some of the accommodations contain four-posters, and a number of units are set aside for nonsmokers. The dining room, serving Welsh and French cuisine, is decorated with oak beams and oil paintings and has an outdoor terrace.

Llanvihangel Gobion, Abergavenny NP7 9BA. ℂ 01873/840678. Fax 01873/840674. www.llch.co.uk. 21 units. £92–£102 ($147–$163) double. Rates include breakfast. AE, DC, MC, V. At A465/A40 Abergavenny intersection take B4598 signposted to Usk. Continue toward Raglan until you see the hotel. **Amenities:** Restaurant; bar; room service. *In room:* TV, minibar, coffeemaker.

Pantrhiwgoch Hotel Sandwiched between the River Usk and the Sugar Loaf mountain, this privately run hotel dates from the 16th century, containing an annex housing the well-equipped and pleasantly furnished bedrooms. Not architecturally grand, it looks much like a roadside inn; however, all but a trio of its accommodations offer river or mountain views, and many have balconies. Bathrooms are neat and tidy. Two stretches of the river are available for guests who want to fish for trout or salmon.

Brecon Road, Abergavenny, NP8 1EP. ℂ 01873/810550. Fax 01873/811880. www.pantrhiwgoch.co.uk. 18 units. £73 ($117) double. Rates include breakfast. AE, MC, V. Free parking. Lies 3 miles northwest of Abergavenny on A40. **Amenities:** Restaurant; bar. *In room:* TV.

WHERE TO DINE

Walnut Tree Inn ★ WELSH/ITALIAN This popular restaurant wins praise all over the British Isles—and rightly so. Franco and Ann Taruschio, the owners, borrow freely from Franco's native Italy but also have a keen appreciation and respect for native Welsh produce. Franco brought to Wales an 18th-century recipe for lasagna, and we highly recommend it. With Parma ham, porcini, black truffles, and an aromatic Parmesan cheese, how can it fail? Try a platter of *fruits de mer,* a bounty of the sea, including langoustines, whelks, mussels, oysters, and crab. Game is also a feature, including a burgundy-colored wood pigeon with a strong gamey taste, its outdoors flavor enhanced with a serving of fresh mushrooms. Even the spaghetti tastes different here—it comes in a sauce of cockles. There is an overwhelming array of two dozen desserts, from elderberry sorbet to the best tiramisu in South Wales.

Llandewi Skirrid. ℂ 01873/852797. Reservations recommended. Main courses £11–£21 ($18–$34); cover £1 ($1.60). MC, V. Tues–Sat 7–10:30pm. Closed 2 weeks at Christmas. Take B4521 4.8km (3 miles) northeast of Abergavenny.

SIDE TRIPS FROM ABERGAVENNY
TINTERN ABBEY

The famous Wye Valley winds north from Chepstow, passing by the Lancaut Peninsula at the foot of the Windcliffe, a 243m (800-ft.) hill with striking views over the Severn estuary and the English border as far as the south part of the Cotswolds. About 1.6km (1 mile) or so farther north, you come to the little village of Tintern.

Now in magnificent ruins, **Tintern Abbey** ★★ (© **01291/689251**) is in the exact center of this riverside village and is the focal point of the town. The Cistercian abbey is one of the greatest monastic ruins of Wales, and it was only the second Cistercian foundation in Britain and the first in Wales. The abbey was founded in 1131 and was active until the dissolution of the monasteries by King Henry VIII. Most of the standing structure dates from the 13th century, when the abbey was almost entirely rebuilt. It became one of the richest and most important monastic houses in Wales. Wordsworth was one of the first to appreciate the serene beauty of the abbey remains, as his poetry attests. There is ample parking quite near the entrance, and refreshments are available nearby.

Admission is £2.50 ($4) for adults, and £2 ($3.20) for children. Open April through May and October daily from 9:30am to 5pm; June through September daily from 9:30am to 6pm; November through March Monday through Saturday from 9:30am to 4pm and Sunday from 11am to 4pm.

To get here from Abergavenny, take the A40 east to Monmouth, from which you can connect with the A466 south along the trail of Offa's Dyke to Tintern.

3 Brecon & Brecon Beacons National Park

275km (171 miles) W of London; 64km (40 miles) N of Cardiff

This busy little market town is the main base for touring Brecon Beacons National Park. Brecon, situated where the Usk and Honddu rivers meet, is the center of a farming section.

The Romans thought the area was a good place for a military encampment to discourage the Celts, and they built a fort, **Y Gaer,** in A.D. 75, about 4km (2½ miles) west of the present town. To get to Y Gaer, you walk across private farm fields. You can look around for no admission charge.

Brecon Castle, built in 1093, is practically nonexistent, but it was militarily important when Llewelyn the Great and later Owain Glyndwr were battling against outsiders who wanted sovereignty in Wales. However, at the close of the Civil War after Cromwell's visitations, the people of Brecon, tired of centuries of strife, pulled the castle down. All that's left is a section of wall joined to the Castle Hotel and the Ely Tower, named for the bishop of Ely imprisoned there by Richard III. Access to the ruins is without charge, and there's no time limit on when it can be viewed. Oddly, it lies on the grounds of the Castle of Brecon Hotel and requires a transit through the hotel lobby to view it.

Of special interest is the fortified red sandstone priory church of St. John the Evangelist, with its massive tower, now the **Cathedral of Swansea and Brecon,** Priory Hill (© **01874/623857**). It stands high above the River Honddu. The oldest parts of the cathedral date from the 12th century. It's open daily from 8am to 6:30pm and admission is free.

ESSENTIALS

GETTING THERE   Go from Cardiff to Merthy Tydfil, then take one of the **Stagecoach Red and White Buses** (© **0870/608-2608**) for information) on through the park to the town of Brecon, which is the last stop on the bus line. Monday through Saturday there are five buses making the connection, but there are only three on Sunday. Stagecoach also maintains three buses per day between Swansea and Brecon. Travel time is about 90 minutes. From Cardiff, motorists can head north along A470.

VISITOR INFORMATION The **Brecon Tourist Information Office** is in the Cattle Market Car Park (© **01874/622485**). Open daily from 10am to 6pm.

SEEING THE SIGHTS
BRECON BEACONS NATIONAL PARK ★★★

Brecon Beacons National Park comprises 835 sq. km (519 sq. miles) of land from the Black Mountains in the west. National parks in the British Isles are maintained differently from those in the United States. Here people own land, live, and work within the park boundaries, though the landscape is safeguarded, and access to the park area is provided.

The park takes its name from the mountain range in the center of the park area. Pen y Fan, the highest peak in the range, rises to nearly 914m (3,000 ft.). The park contains sandstone moors covered with bracken, and limestone crags with wooded gorges. Vast stretches of open common land lie in pastoral country. Farming is the main industry of the park. You can enjoy drives over the mountains, but walking or pony trekking are the best ways to explore the park.

There are nature reserves, a mountain center, and 51km (32 miles) of canal. The limestone area contains Britain's deepest cave system. A number of ancient monuments and historic buildings lie within the park boundaries.

For information regarding the park and its facilities, call one of the **National Park Information Centres,** the main one being at Wharton Mount, Glamorgan Street, in Brecon (© **01874/624437**). Other information numbers include © **01873/853254** in Abergavenny, and © **01550/720693** in Llandovery.

The park's southern boundary is only 40km (25 miles) from Cardiff, 23km (14 miles) from Swansea, and 16km (10 miles) from Newport. Abergavenny lies on the eastern boundary.

Run by the Brecon Beacons National Park Committee, the **Mountain Centre,** near Libanus (© **01874/623366**), 8km (5 miles) southwest of Brecon, offers a good point from which to begin your tour of the park. There is a spacious lounge, displays explaining the major points of interest, talks and films, an informative staff, a picnic area, a refreshments buffet, and toilets. Wheelchairs have access to all parts of the building.

The center is open daily, except Christmas Day, from 9:30am; the buffet is open from 10:30am (10am July and Aug). Closing times vary according to the time of year. The center shuts its doors at 5pm in March, June, September, and October; at 6pm in July and August; and at 4:30pm from November to February. Closing is ½ hour later on Saturday, Sunday, and bank holidays from April to June and in September. The buffet closing time varies, so check when you go to the center.

Over the millennia, the force of flowing water has carved underground caverns through the extensive limestone regions in the southwestern portions of the Brecon Beacons National Park. Experienced cavers can explore many of these by making arrangements with one of the caving clubs, through the national park information centers. However, only the **Dan-yr-Ogof Showcaves,** Abercraf (© **01639/730801**), are open to the general public, including children.

Midway between Brecon and Swansea on the A4067, this is the largest showcave complex in Western Europe. Visitors are able to follow dry, firm walkways to see stalagmite and stalactite formations under floodlights. Tours through Dan-yr-Ogof, Cathedral Cave, Bone Cave, and the Dinosaur Park last about 2½ hours. The complex is open from Easter to the end of October, daily from 10am to 5pm. The charge is £7.50 ($12) for adults and £4 ($6.40) for children (accompanied children under age 4 are admitted free). There is a restaurant, craft shop, museum, dry-ski slope, and information center at the caves.

The caves are near the **Craig-y-Nos Country Park,** about 16km (10 miles) south of Sennybridge, a property that was once the "home sweet home" of the famous singer Adelina Patti. For more information about the park, call ℂ **01639/ 730395.** It's open daily from 10am to dusk, the time varying with the seasons. There is no charge for admission.

WHERE TO STAY & DINE
EXPENSIVE
Llangoed Hall ★★★ Sir Bernard Ashley, widower of Laura Ashley, presides over one of the great country houses of Wales. In the Wye Valley, 18km (11 miles) northeast of Brecon, the house opens onto panoramic views of the Black Mountains. The Welsh Parliament, so it is said, stood on this site 1,400 years ago. A former Jacobean manor house, it was redesigned by the celebrated architect Cloug Williams-Ellis, in 1912, who had wanted to create the aura of a great Edwardian country house party. Sir Bernard has gone even beyond the Edwardians in this fantasy, creating grand luxury with the help of floor-to-ceiling Laura Ashley fabrics, of course—that and his own personal art collection. The individually decorated bedrooms and suites are spacious and elegant, as are the bathrooms, with Laura Ashley fabrics at every turn. All offer extras such a fresh fruit, sherry, and a small selection of books. A library in the south wing is the only surviving part of the original Jacobean mansion that stood on this spot in 1632.

Llyswen, Brecons, Powys LD3 0YP. ℂ 01874/754525. Fax 01874/754545. www.llangoedhall.com. 23 units. £160 ($256) double; £320 ($512) suite. Rates include breakfast. AE, DC, MC, V. On A470, 3.2km (2 miles) northwest of Llyswen. **Amenities:** Restaurant; 2 tennis courts; room service; laundry service; dry cleaning; fishing. *In room:* TV, coffeemaker, hair dryer.

MODERATE
Castle of Brecon   This early-19th-century coaching inn has kept abreast of the times and remains one of the best, most comfortable, and reasonable places to stay within the town of Brecon itself. It may be in the town center, but it still opens onto views of the Usk Valley and the Brecon Beacons National Park. The hotel lies near the ruined castle and has been considerably improved and renovated. It's certainly far better than it was in 1820, when it started receiving wayfarers from around the world. The small bedrooms have been modernized and conservatively furnished; they're comfortable but hardly stylish. The best rooms are the Beacon View rooms facing south with views toward the mountains. The shower-only bathrooms are small. Twelve of the units are in a lackluster annex, serviceable but not a lot more, and four accommodations are large enough to fit families comfortably.

Castle Square, Brecon, Pwys LD3 9DB. ℂ 800/528-1234 in the U.S., or 01874/624611. Fax 01874/623737. www.breconcastle.co.uk. 45 units. £69–£98 ($110–$157) double. AE, DC, MC, V. Free parking. **Amenities:** Restaurant; 2 bars; separate lounge for guests; room service. *In room:* TV, coffeemaker.

Felin Fach Griffin ★ *Finds*   This is an exceptional discovery for Wales, much of it looking as if you'd wandered back through a time capsule. Old-fashioned though it may look, it is absolutely comfortable and up-to-date. Crisp white linen and soft goosedown pillows top ornate beds placed on stripped floorboards, and will make you want to linger in bed long into the morning. Bedrooms are beautifully maintained, quietly elegant, and three have four-poster beds. Each comes with a small, immaculate bathroom.

Felin Facvh (A470, directly east of Brecon), Powys LD3 OUB. ℂ **01874/620111.** Fax 01874/620120. www.eatdrinksleep.ltd.uk. 7 units. £86–£93 ($137–$148). Rates include full breakfast. MC, V. **Amenities:** Restaurant; bar; room service. *In room:* Beverage maker, hair dryer, iron.

Griffin Inn ★ *Value*   Though hardly in the league of Llangoed, this little oasis is infinitely more affordable. Outside Brecon, it was originally constructed in the 15th century as a cider house. Today it's an inn popular with fishermen who come hoping to get lucky while casting into the River Wye. Behind its ivy-covered facade, four generations of the Stockton family have received guests into their tidy bedrooms, offering them good pub grub as well. The inn itself is one of the oldest in the Upper Wye Valley, and lake fishing, pony trekking, and hiking are part of the summer fun in the Brecon Beacons. A few years ago the Griffin was voted "Britain's Pub of the Year," so drinking is still big here and the food is popular with locals. But we gravitate to the small to midsize bedrooms and their somewhat cramped baths, soaking up the atmosphere of old beams and exposed stonework.

Llyswen, near Brecon, Powys LD3 OUR. ℂ **01874/754241.** Fax 01874/754592. £70 ($112) double. MC, V. Lies 16km (10 miles) northeast of Brecon at the junction of A4079 and A470. **Amenities:** Restaurant. *In room:* TV, coffeemaker.

Nant Ddu Lodge ★ *Kids*   This is your best bet for staying in the heart of the Brecon Beacons National Park—in fact, in 1999, AAA voted it "best Welsh hotel of the year." Originally built as a shooting lodge during the 19th century for Lord Tredegar, its name translates as "Black Stream," but that is hardly meant to suggest pollution, as its situation is idyllic for walking, climbing, fishing, and escaping from urban pressures. Though unified with a common hunter's theme, each of the small to midsize bedrooms is different from its neighbor and equipped with VCRs and tiny bathrooms. The superior rooms offer extras such as bathrobes and wide-screen TVs; a few have four-poster beds. There are panoramic views of the mountains from all the bedrooms. Family rooms with sofa beds are available. The hotel opened a brand-new spa in 2003, and it offers all the latest equipment and treatments.

Cwm Taf, Brecon, CF Powys CF48 2HY. ℂ **01685/379111.** Fax 01685/377088. www.nant-ddu-lodge.co.uk. 28 units. £80–£100 ($127–$159) double. AE, MC, V. Free parking. Beside the A470, 8km (5 miles) north of Merthyr Tydfil and 19km (12 miles) south of Brecon. **Amenities:** Bistro; bar; indoor heated pool; room service; health club; spa; sauna. *In room:* TV, coffeemaker, hair dryer, trouser press.

Three Cocks Hotel ★ *Value*   This 15th-century inn, surrounded by the countryside of the Brecon Beacons, is one of the best-known little inns of Wales. It deserves its fame. As you pass through the tiny hamlet of Three Cocks, don't blink, or you might miss the inn. The place is really small but has a certain charm. It's a stone building, which over the years has incorporated the trunk of a live tree into one of its walls. The inn and its elegant restaurant are operated by Mr. and Mrs. Michael Winstone, who extend very cordial hospitality to their guests. Downstairs is an elegant paneled drawing room, and upstairs are midsize bedrooms that have modern furnishings and well-kept bathrooms. Throughout the inn is richly furnished with antiques, Oriental rugs, and oil paintings, with log fires burning on chilly nights. There's no TV in the rooms, but you can find one in a separate sitting room.

Three Cocks, Brecon, Powys LD3 0SL. (℃ **01497/847215.** Fax 01497/847339. www.threecockshotel.com. 7 units. £69 ($110) double. Rates include Welsh breakfast. MC, V. Free parking. On A438 18km (11 miles) northeast of Brecon and 6.4km (4 miles) southwest of Hay-on-Wye. **Amenities:** Restaurant. *In room:* No phone.

INEXPENSIVE

Canter Selyf ⭐ *(Finds*   One of the historic properties of Brecon, this town house dates from the 17th century. Close to St. Mary's Church, this Georgian house is one of the most convenient locations in town. When viewed only from the front, the property looks rather small, but it's a nice spread, complete with a large walled garden enclosed by a Norman wall. Much of the 17th century architecture remains inside, although subsequent additions were made in the following century. The bedrooms still have their former beamed ceilings, cast-iron beds, and Georgian fireplaces, along with private bathrooms with showers. Guests meet fellow guests in the formal sitting room. Smoking is not permitted.

5 Lion St., Brecon, Powys LD3 7AU. (℃ **01874/622904.** Fax 01874/622315. www.cantreselyf.co.uk. 3 units. £45–£65 ($72–$104) double. Rates include full breakfast. No credit cards. Closed Dec. **Amenities:** Restaurant; bar; room service; laundry service. *In room:* TV, beverage maker, hair dryer, iron.

4 Swansea & Gower Peninsula ⭐

307km (191 miles) W of London; 64km (40 miles) W of Cardiff; 131km (82 miles) W of Bristol

Vikings, Normans, English, Welsh, industry, seaport activity, holiday magic, and cultural prominence—all have combined to make the Swansea of today. It's tough, bold, and fun. Parks abound, and the tender loving care bestowed on them has caused Swansea to be a winner of the "Wales in Bloom" award year after year.

Swansea entered recorded history some 800 years ago, bearing a Viking name believed derived from "Sweyn's ey," or Sweyn's island. The Sweyn in question may well have been Sweyn Forkbeard, king of Denmark (987–1014), known to have been active in the Bristol Channel. Normans founded the marcher lordship of Gower, with its capital at Swansea, and a small trading community grew up here, as sea-going business, including coal exportation, became important through the Middle Ages. In the early 18th century at the town at the mouth of the River Tawe (Swansea's Welsh name is Abertawe), copperworks began to be built, and soon it was the copper capital of the world, as well as a leading European center for zinc refining, tin plating, steel making, and many chemical activities.

This "ugly, lovely city," as native son Dylan Thomas described it, has today pretty well obliterated the ugliness. Devastation of the town center by German air raids during World War II led to complete rebuilding. Traditional industries in the Lower Swansea Valley have vanished, leaving economic woes and an industrial wasteland. Reclamation and redevelopment, however, have long been underway. The leveling of old mine tips and slag heaps and the planting of trees in their stead points to a more attractive Swansea for both today and tomorrow. Clean industries are coming in, but they are being placed out in wooded areas and suitable industrial parks, and they do not cast a pall over the city. Nonetheless, if your time clock allows for only one of the major cities of South Wales, make it Cardiff.

ESSENTIALS

GETTING THERE   Trains arrive from both Cardiff and from London every 60 minutes throughout the day. The trip takes about an hour from Cardiff, about 3 hours from London. The Swansea Railway Station is on High Street. For reservations and information, call ℂ **0845/748-4950.**

National Express Coaches (ℂ **0870/583-8383**) arrive in Swansea about once an hour from London, Manchester, Birmingham, and Cardiff. From Cardiff, motorists can continue west along the M4.

VISITOR INFORMATION   The **City of Swansea Information Centre,** Plymouth Street (ℂ **01792/468321**), is open year-round, Monday through Saturday from 9:30am to 5:30pm. Between June and September, it's also open every Sunday from 9:30am to 5:30pm. Its services are duplicated within Swansea's historic suburb of Mumbles at the **Mumbles Tourist Information Centre,** Dunns Lake (ℂ **01792/361302**), open only from March to October, daily from 9:30am to 5:30pm.

GETTING AROUND   Swansea is serviced by a good bus network, buses leaving from the Quadrant Bus Station, at the Quadrant Shopping Centre. Bus nos. 4 and 4A link the train station at 35 High St. and the bus station. For bus schedules and information, call ℂ **0870/608-2608.** Because distances are usually short, consider calling a taxi—either **Cab Charge** (ℂ **01792/474747**) or **A.A. Taxis** at (ℂ **01792/360600**).

SEEING THE SIGHTS

In a once-dirty waterfront area, a **Maritime Quarter** has emerged. Lying between the city center and the seafront, it is centered on the historic South Dock and its Half Tide Basin and is complete with urban villages and a modern marina on the Swansea Yacht Haven. Open spaces, a promenade, and a sea wall round out the scene.

A statue of Dylan Thomas stands in the Maritime Quarter, and the **Dylan Thomas Theatre** is nearby at 7 Gloucester Place (ℂ **01792/473238**). Many different types of plays are presented here (look for listings in local newspapers), not just works by Dylan Thomas. The poet was born in the Uplands, a residential area of Swansea, at 5 Cwmdonkin Drive, a steep street off Walter Road. You can walk in **Cwmdonkin Park** close by, which the poet made famous in his writings.

Swansea is one of the few cities to have a beach within walking distance of the center. A **promenade** leads all the way to Oystermouth, 6.4km (4 miles) away, although you can drive the route on the A4067. Along the way you pass a rugby and cricket ground and the entrance to the city's largest park, Singleton. About halfway down the bay is a nine-hole golf course and a well-equipped resort beach, in an area known as Blackpill. It includes the entrances to the city's country park, Clyne Valley, and the Clyne Gardens. Before long you come to the villages of Westcross and Norton, and then comes Oystermouth, which has a Norman castle renowned for its imposing position on a headland commanding a view of the bay and Swansea.

Five miles south of Swansea, across Swansea Bay, lies **The Mumbles** ⭐. It has been compared to the Bay of Naples because of its shape and beauty, especially after dark. This former fishing village has two faces (both pleasing): By day it has a tranquil atmosphere, but when the sun goes down Mumbles bursts into action and becomes a nightlife center, with crowded pubs, clubs, and restaurants.

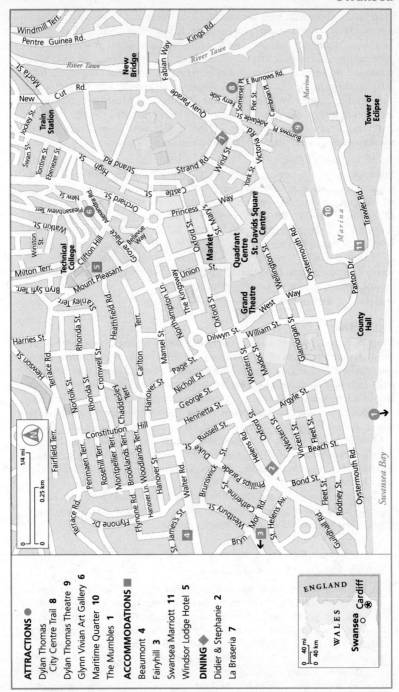

Swansea

ATTRACTIONS ●
Dylan Thomas
City Centre Trail **8**
Dylan Thomas Theatre **9**
Glynn Vivian Art Gallery **6**
Maritime Quarter **10**
The Mumbles **1**

ACCOMMODATIONS ■
Beaumont **4**
Fairyhill **3**
Swansea Marriott **11**
Windsor Lodge Hotel **5**

DINING ◆
Didier & Stephanie **2**
La Braseria **7**

ENGLAND

WALES

Swansea Cardiff ⊛

0 — 40 mi
0 — 40 km

N

0 ─ 1/4 mi
0 ─ 0.25 km

Windmill Terr.
Pentre Guinea Rd.
Morfa St.
New
Cut Rd.
River Tawe
New Bridge
Fabian Way
Kings Rd.
River Tawe
Quay Parade
Ferry Side
Somerset Pl. E Burrows Rd.
Adelaide St.
Pier St.
Cambrian Pl.
Marina
Burrows Pl.
Tower of Eclipse
Train Station
Jockey St.
Swan St.
Tontine St.
Ebenezer St.
High St.
Strand Rd
New St.
Orchard St.
Castle St.
Strand Rd.
Wind St.
York St.
Victoria Rd
Alexandra Rd.
Pleasantview Terr.
Watkin St.
Winston St.
Bellevue Way
Grove Place
Clifton Hill
Princess Way
Oxford St.
St. Mary's
Market St.
St Davids Square
Quadrant Centre
St. Davids Square Centre
Marina
Technical College
Milton Terr.
Bryn Syfi Terr.
Mount Pleasant
Stanley Terr.
Heathfield Rd.
Northampton Ln.
The Kingsway
Union St.
Grand Theatre
West Way
Wellington St.
Oystermouth Rd.
Paxton Dr.
Trawler Rd.
Harries St.
Terrace Rd
Rhonda St.
Carlton Terr.
Mansel St.
Hanover St.
Dilwyn St.
Oxford St.
William St.
Madoc St.
Western St.
Glamorgan St.
County Hall
Hewson St.
Norfolk St.
Rhonda St.
Cromwell St.
Chaddesley Terr.
Page St.
Nicholl St.
George St.
Henrietta St.
Russell St.
Helens Rd
Oxford St.
Western St.
Vincent St.
Fleet St.
Argyle St.
Beach St.
Swansea Bay
Fairfield Terr.
Penmaen Terr.
Rosehill Terr.
Montpellier Terr.
Brooklands Terr.
Woodlands Terr.
Constitution Hill
Hanover Ln.
Hanover St.
Duke St.
Walter Rd.
Phillips Parade
Bond St.
Fleet St.
Rodney St.
Oystermouth Rd.
Terrace Rd.
Ffynone Rd.
Ffynone Dr.
St. James's St.
Westbury St.
Brunswick St.
Catherine St.
St. Helens Av.
Bryn Mor
Guildhall Rd.

1 **2** **3** **4** **5** **6** **7** **8** **9** **10** **11**

Mumbles has been attracting tourists since Victorian times, when the handsome pier was built, as in most British sea towns. It protrudes 274m (900 ft.) from Mumbles Head into the bay and affords sweeping views. Away from the seafront, tiny fishermen's cottages can be seen built into the limestone rock. Souvenirs and examples of local crafts can be found in shops that cling to the hillside. Yachting, swimming, fishing, beach games, and bowling are enjoyed here.

Note: The popular **Swansea Maritime & Industrial Museum** has closed to make room for the new National Waterfront Museum, slated to open in 2005. For information on the progress of the new museum's construction, see **www.swansea.gov.uk/culture/Museums/maritime.htm**.

Glynn Vivian Art Gallery ⋆   Founded in 1911, although little known, this gallery is one of the treasure troves of art in Wales. It was created by Richard Glynn Vivian, scion of a copper industrialist family. An inveterate traveler and art collector, he wanted to pass on his treasures to the world. The special reason to visit is to see the 20th-century collection of Welsh artists, including Ceri Richards, Josef Herman, and Evan Walters. We are especially fond of Alfred Janes's penetrating portrait of Dylan Thomas from 1964. There are also displays of elegant porcelain and pottery, both European and Asian. On-site is an unusual gift shop with a selection of original works by Welsh artists, including ceramics, glass, and jewelry.

Alexandra Rd. © **01792/655006.** Free admission. Tues–Sun 10am–5pm.

SHOPPING

Swansea shopping is dominated by the **Quadrant Shopping Centre,** behind the main bus station. Rows of covered malls are lined with shops and big-name stores. The center is connected to the **Swansea Market,** where rows of open stalls have sold food for centuries. Some of the local delicacies include fresh laverbread, now available in cans so you can take some home. Here you can also find cockles, fish both local and exotic, meats, dairy products, eggs, and poultry, as well as fresh fruits and vegetables. The market deals in hardware also.

Outside the heart of the city's **shopping area,** running parallel to the centers, is Oxford Street, and above are Union Street, Portland Street, and the Kingsway, also packed with interesting stores. Princess Way runs along the end of Kingsway and Oxford Street.

Top-quality gift shops and crafts abound, not just in the city center but in Gower. The Mumbles is also a popular area for souvenirs and gifts; local artisans display their wares amid a village atmosphere.

Finds **For Dylan Thomas Junkies**

At the Swansea tourist office pick up a free copy of the *Swansea Bay Guide,* which will take you along the Dylan Thomas Uplands Trail and past some of the bulbous-nosed poet's favorite haunts. Drop in to the **Dylan Thomas City Centre** on Somerset Place (© **01792/463980**), which is the National Literature Centre for Wales. Admission is free; it's open Tuesday through Sunday from 10am to 4:30pm. Exhibitions and photographs bring you closer to this legendary figure, one of the great lyric poets of the 20th century, a man who descended tragically into chronic alcoholism. A video on the artist suggests he was not the ladies' man he pretended to be with his drinking cronies.

WHERE TO STAY

Beaumont   In its moderate-price bracket, this is the town's leading choice, lying only a short walk from the town center and a 10-minute taxi ride from the rail depot. A family-run hotel, it looks like a large private village, and its public rooms are done with traditional styling and old-fashioned warmth, evoking the comforts of a middle-class Welsh home. The midsize bedrooms have been furnished with comfort and style in mind, and the bathrooms with bath or shower are well organized with tidy cubicles. The executive rooms are larger and have sunken tubs in the tiled bathrooms; some have four-poster beds. There is a conservatory-style restaurant for home-cooked Welsh, Italian, and French fare.

72–73 Walter Rd., Swansea SA1 4QA. ℂ **01792/643956.** Fax 01792/643044. www.beaumonthotel.co.uk. 18 units. £70–£90 ($112–$144) double. AE, DC, MC, V. Free parking. **Amenities:** Restaurant; bar. *In room:* TV, coffeemaker, trouser press.

Fairyhill ⍟   Sometimes the most fun in Swansea is leaving it. If you want to escape from the world, head to this stone-built 18th-century manor set on 25 acres of wooded grounds that also hold a lake and a fishing stream. It's an ideal base for exploring not only Swansea but also the little populated Gower Peninsula that juts out into the British Channel west of Swansea and offers a good deal of natural beauty. After passing through a sumptuously appointed lounge, you are directed to one of the individually styled bedrooms—most often medium-sized with a snug but efficient bathroom. Crackling log fires and deep-cushioned sofas create the aura of a cozy, snug country house. A real "taste of Wales" emerges from the menu. *Note:* Children under 8 are not accepted as guests.

Reynoldston SA3 1BS. ℂ **01792/390139.** Fax 01792/391358. www.fairyhill.net. 8 units. £120–£245 ($192–$392). Rates include breakfast. AE, MC, V. Outside Reynoldston off the A4118 from Swansea (18km/11 miles) away. **Amenities:** Restaurant. *In room:* TV, coffeemaker.

Swansea Marriott ⍟⍟   This is the town's premier choice—the best amenities, the most dramatic location, and the most luxurious bedrooms. The four-story structure lies on the marina, opening onto panoramic views over the bay. By Swansea standards, it is large and bustling, attracting an equal mix of business clients and tourists. The hotel offers spacious bedrooms and roomy baths, each immaculate and comfortable.

Maritime Quarter, Swansea SA1 3SS. ℂ **800/228-9290** in the U.S. or Canada; 01792/642020. Fax 01792/ 650345. www.marriott.com. 117 units. £100–£144 ($160–$230) double. Rates include breakfast. AE, DC, MC, V. Free parking. **Amenities:** Restaurant; bar; indoor pool; health club; Jacuzzi; sauna; room service; laundry service. *In room:* A/C, TV, minibar, coffeemaker, hair dryer, iron/ironing board, trouser press.

Windsor Lodge Hotel   Architecturally undistinguished, this is a nonetheless welcoming family-run hotel, close to the town center. It offers good value and cozy bedrooms with decent furnishings and tidy bathrooms for the night. The building itself is 2 centuries old and has been sheltering wayfarers to Swansea for decades. You never know who is likely to turn up. We once encountered former President Jimmy Carter and Mrs. Carter leaving the inn after having enjoyed a lunch here. Your hosts, Pam and Ron Rumble, maintain medium-sized bedrooms that are well cared for and provide a good night's sleep. The decoration is modern, and the location is about 5-minute walk to the train station.

Mount Pleasant, Swansea SA1 6EG. ℂ **01792/642158.** Fax 01792/648996. www.windsor-lodge.co.uk. 19 units. £55–£70 ($88–$112) double. Rates include breakfast. AE, DC, MC, V. **Amenities:** Restaurant; bar. *In room:* TV, coffeemaker.

WHERE TO DINE

La Braseria SPANISH   No, this is not Madrid, although this Spanish bodega (in Swansea, of all places) evokes sunny Spain, lying only a 5-minute walk from the train station. It's a marvelous change of pace when you've had too many leeks and too much Welsh lamb. The food, prepared daily from fresh ingredients, complements the list of Spanish wines and champagne. This is not the place for "lager louts." Come here for the town's best chargrilled meats. Tossed on that grill is everything from tender suckling pig to great chunks of beef, even ostrich. Flavors are straightforward here, as the cooks don't like to mess up their grills with a lot of sauces. Likewise, they prepare the catch of the day in the same way, be it shark, bass, or snapper. Specific choices change according to the seasons, the availability of ingredients, and the inspirations of the chefs. In addition to items from the grill, you might opt for a savory kettle of mussels.

28 Wind St. © 01792/469683. Reservations recommended. Main courses £5–£18 ($8–$29); set 2-course lunch £7.50 ($12). AE, DC, MC, V. Mon–Sat noon–2:30pm and 7–11:30pm.

Didier & Stephanie ★ *Value* CONTINENTAL/WELSH   This eatery despite is known for its good food and good value. The restaurant lies about a 3-minute walk west of the center in a fully renovated Victorian house.

Didier and Stephanie are to be lauded for their search for market-fresh ingredients and their deft preparation in the kitchen. Their inspiration is ever changing but reflected by such dishes as a velvet smooth and tasty pumpkin soup, an unusual dish for Wales. Some of their dishes, such as pigs' trotters or fish mousse with black pudding, may sound inappropriate but are in fact amazing concoctions filled with delicacy and flavor. Of course, they are not always experimental, and are equally good when preparing long-standing favorites such as salmon in a creamy saffron sauce or boeuf bourguignon.

56 St. Helen's Rd. © 01792/655603. Reservations recommended. Main courses £11–£13 ($17–$21); 2- to 3-course fixed-price lunch £7.20–£9.20 ($12–$15). Tues–Sat noon–2pm and 7–9pm. AE, MC, V.

SWANSEA AFTER DARK

Long gone are the days when Swansea's nocturnal entertainment consisted of a handful of battered pubs with a jukebox blaring out pre-Beatles tunes. Since the 1990s gentrification of many areas of Swansea's central core, there has been an explosion of nightlife options, many of them focusing on the city's nightlife-related pride and joy—Wind (it rhymes with "wined and dined") Street. The best way to explore the place involves popping in and out of any of the pubs, bars, and shops that appeal to you along this cobble-covered thoroughfare, especially on evenings when the City Council has blocked off traffic, transforming it into a pedestrian-only walkway that—on weekend evenings—becomes very crowded.

(*Fun Fact*   Brain Food

One night in May 1988, Ed Witten, one of the world's leading mathematicians, was dining at **Didier & Stephanie.** For years the American had searched without success for a mathematical explanation of the make-up of knots. Suddenly jotting down a formula on a napkin, he rose to his feet and triumphantly announced, "I've done it! I've cracked the Theory of Knots."

Some of our favorites include **The Bank Statement,** 57–58 Wind St. (© 01792/455477), a pub and restaurant contained within the grandly ornate premises of what was built as a bank during the Victorian age. Nearby is the **Goose & Granite,** 2 Wind St. (© 01792/630941), where a 19th-century storefront serves up copious portions of pub grub, platters, and foaming mugfuls of local ale. More self-consciously trendy, evoking a hip bar in faraway London, is the **No Sign Wine Bar,** 56 Wind St. (© 01792/465300), where you're likely to see members of the local TV news team, off-duty, sampling whatever French, Chilean, or Californian vintage happens to be uncorked at the moment.

Other streets, each nearby, but none as densely packed as Wind Street with bars and restaurants, also have goodly numbers of nightlife offerings. **O'Brian's Exchange Bar,** 10 The Strand (© 01792/645345), and **Fagin's,** 63 The Kings Way (© 01792/481951), each offers glimpses of Ireland, with live music and generous amounts of Celtic *joie de vivre.* **The Potters Wheel,** 86–88 The Kings Way (© 01792/465113), a member of the same chain as the above-mentioned Bank Statement, offers food and drink in a setting that's nostalgically evocative of turn-of-the-20th-century Wales. Business deals by day, and the occasional romantic dialogue by night, tend to be consummated within. **The Hanbury,** 43 The Kings Way (© 01792/641824), has food that is a cut above what you might expect within most workaday pubs.

In addition to the **Dylan Thomas Theatre** (see above), Swansea has a cultural side as well. **The Grand Theatre,** Singleton Street (© 01792/475715), adjacent to the Quadrant Shopping Centre, is a Victorian theater that has been refurbished and redeveloped into a multimillion-pound theater complex. The venue hosts international opera, ballet, and theater companies, plus one-night stands that often feature internationally known entertainers. It also has its own schools of song and dance.

SIDE TRIPS FROM SWANSEA
GOWER PENINSULA ⊛
The first area in Britain designated "an area of outstanding natural beauty," Gower is a broad peninsula stretching about 22km (14 miles) from the Mumbles to Worms Head in the west. This attraction begins 6.4km (4 miles) west of Swansea on A4067. The coastline of Gower starts at Bracelet Bay, just around the corner from the Mumbles. You can drive—at least to some parts of the peninsula—but the best way to see its sometimes-rugged, sometimes-flat coast is to walk, even for short distances if you don't have time to make the complete circuit.

There are many and varied beaches on Gower: **Caswell Bay,** with its acres of smooth, golden sand and safe swimming; **Langland,** a family attraction with facilities for golf, swimming, tennis, and surfing; and **Rotherslade,** which at high tide features some of the largest waves around the peninsula crashing onto the shore. Secluded **Pwil-du** is a place to sunbathe in solitude, despite the crowds elsewhere along the coast, and there are numerous other small coves tucked away beneath the cliffs. **Oxwich Bay** is one of the largest on the peninsula, with 4.8km (3 miles) of uninterrupted sand, where you can enjoy beach games, picnics, water-skiing, and sailing. Windsurfing is popular at Oxwich too. Oxwich village, at one end of the bay, is a typical Gower hamlet of cottages and tree-lined lanes. There is a nature reserve here that is home to some rare orchid species.

After the commercial and often-crowded Oxwich beach, you may be happy to see **Slade,** which has to be approached on foot down a steep set of steps. The spotless beach is usually wind-free. Around the next corner, you'll find the villages of **Horton** and **Port Eynon,** with a long, curving beach backed by sand dunes. Refreshments are available on the beach, and the two villages offer nighttime entertainment.

From Port Eynon, a spectacular 7.2km (4½-mile) cliff walk, leads past Culver Hole, Paviland Cave, Mewslade, and Fall Bay to Worms Head and Rhossilli. The **Paviland Caves** can be explored. It was here that human remains have been found dating back 100,000 years. **Worms Head** is a twisted outcrop of rock shaped into the form that sometimes, depending on the tides, looks like a prehistoric worm sticking its head up out of the water. **Rhossilli** is a long, sweeping bay and a beach reached from the treeless village of Rhossilli, with a church and houses perched 61m (200 ft.) up on the clifftops. This is an international center for hang gliding. Halfway along the beach at Llangennith is the most popular surfing site on the peninsula. Rolling dunes connect it with Broughton Bay and Whitford Sands, and eventually you come to **Penclawdd,** a little village where a centuries-old cockle industry still thrives. If the tide is right, you can see the pickers with their rakes and buckets gleaning the tiny crustaceans from the flats.

Although the coastal attractions are Gower's biggest lure, there are pleasant farms, attractive country roads, and places of interest inland. **Parc le Breos (Giant's Grave)** burial chamber, almost in the center of the peninsula, close to Parkmill on the A4118, is an ancient legacy from Stone Age people. The remains of at least four people were found there. A central passage and four chambers are in a cairn about 21m (70 ft.) long. **Pennard Castle** has suffered under ravages of weather and time, but from the north you can see the curtain wall almost intact. It can be visited for free.

Weobley Castle, Llawrhidian (© **01792/390012**), on North Gower, is actually a fortified house rather than a castle. There was no space for a garrison, and the rooms were for domestic purposes. On the northern edge of bare upland country, it overlooks the Llanrhidian marshes and the Loughor estuary. There are substantial remains of this 13th- and 14th-century stronghold, and the view is panoramic. Weobley is off the Llanrhidian-Cheriton road, 11km (7 miles) west of Gowerton. Open April through September daily from 9:30am to 6pm, November through March daily from 9:30am to 4pm. Entrance costs £2 ($3.20) for adults or £1.50 ($2.40) for children ages 16 and under and students.

Even though it is protected from development, Gower has been invaded by caravans (mobile homes), recreational vehicles, beach huts, retirement homes, and bungalows. Nevertheless, you can still find solitude in secluded bays and especially in the center of the peninsula, along the Cefn Bryn ridge or on Rhossilli Down. From the top of **Cefn Bryn,** 185m (609 ft.) above sea level, you can see the entire peninsula and far beyond on clear days. By taking the Green Road, which runs the length of the ridge from Penmaen, you'll find a path about 1km (½ mile) east of Reynoldston which leads to **Arthur's Stone,** a circular burial chamber. The mound of earth that once covered it has been weathered away, but you can see the huge capstone that protected the burial place. From Rhossilli Down, at 192m (632 ft.), the English coast comes into view. Here also are megalithic tombs, cairns, and barrows.

LAUGHARNE: MEMORIES OF DYLAN THOMAS

Laugharne (pronounced *Larne*), 24km (15 miles) east of Tenby, is a hamlet looking out over broad waters. This ancient township on the estuary fed by the River

Taf (not be confused with the River Taff in Cardiff) and the River Cywyn, was for centuries a bone of contention between Welsh, English, Cromwellians, and royal supporters. However, it did not come into the limelight of public attention until after the death of its adopted son, Swansea-born Dylan Thomas, and his acclaim as one of the great poets of the 20th century.

Head west from Swansea along the A4070, which becomes the A484 signposted north to Carmarthen. Once in Carmarthen, continue west along the A40 to St. Clears where you cut southeast along the A4066 to Laugharne.

Seeing the Sights

Dylan Thomas Boathouse ⍟, along a little path named Dylan's Walk, is the waterside house where the author lived with his wife, Caitlin, and their children until his death in 1953 during a visit to America. In the boathouse, a white-painted little three-story structure wedged between the hill and the estuary, you can see the family's rooms, photographs, interpretive panels on his life and works, an audio and audiovisual presentation that portrays him reading some of his work, a small art gallery, a book and record shop, and a little tearoom where you can have tea and Welsh cakes while you listen to the poet's voice and look out over the tranquil waters of the wide estuary.

On the way along the path, before you come to the boathouse, there's a little shack where this untidy wretch of a man wrote many of his minor masterpieces. You can't enter it, but you can look through an opening and see his built-in plank desk. Wadded-up scraps of paper on the floor give the feeling that he may have just stepped out to visit a favorite pub. The boathouse is open from April to the first week of November, daily from 10am to 5:30pm (last entrance). Admission is £2.50 ($4) for adults, £1.50 ($2.40) for children. For more information, call © **01994/427420.**

The poet is buried in the churchyard near the **Parish Church of St. Martin,** which you pass as you drive into town. A simple wooden cross marks his grave. A visit to the church is worthwhile. It dates from the 14th century and is entered through a lych-gate (iron gate), with the entrance to the church guarded by ancient yew trees. Memorial stones and carvings are among the interesting things to see.

Laugharne Castle, a handsome ruin called the home of the "Last Prince of Wales," sits on the estuary at the edge of the town. A castle here, Aber Corran, was first mentioned in 1113, believed to have been built by the great Welsh leader Rhys ap Gruffydd. The present romantic ruins date from Tudor times. Dylan Thomas described the then ivy-mantled castle as a "castle brown as owls."

Where to Dine

Stable Door Restaurant ⍟ INTERNATIONAL/BRITISH   A stable block in days gone by, this is the finest dining choice in the area, serving meals with taste and flair. Recently restored by its owner, Wendy Joy, it operates behind walls that were originally built in the 14th century to house horses Edward I brought from England during the construction of a nearby castle. Later, Oliver Cromwell's forces shot cannon into it when the masters of the castle switched their loyalties back to the Royalist side. Today, it's the most likable and enjoyable restaurant in the area, serving a menu of fresh ingredients that is varied and artfully prepared. On a windy day, we blew in here with the wind to sample the homemade soup of the day with freshly baked bread, although the Stilton, walnut, and port paté looked equally tempting. The menu suggests that the chef has traveled and gained inspiration from many countries. From Greece comes an authentic moussaka, and from Hungary a savory paprika pork with baby mushrooms and sour cream. The Thai vegetable and creamed-coconut curry delighted our party, and was followed by a white- and dark-chocolate layered terrine.

Market Lane. ℂ 01994/427777. Reservations recommended. Main courses £8–£14 ($13–$22). AE, MC, V. Wed–Sat 7–10pm; Sun 12:30–2pm.

A MUSEUM

National Botanic Museum ⚘ Lying 32km (20 miles) northwest of Swansea, this mammoth project of the millennium is the first modern botanic garden in Britain dedicated to science, education, and leisure. A project costing £45 million ($72 million), this 568-acre Regency estate was developed by financier William Paxton in the late 18th century, with walled gardens, lakes, and cascades. Its centerpiece is a magnificent Great Glasshouse, the largest single span greenhouse in the world, blending in naturally with the rolling and bucolic Tywi Valley. The greenhouse is dedicated to threatened Mediterranean climates of the world, and its interior includes a ravine, rock faces, bridges, and waterfalls. Laboratories on the property mean that this garden of Wales is fast becoming the European pacesetter in conservation and reproductive biology.

Middleton Hall, Llanarthne. ℂ 01558/668768. Admission £6.95 ($11) adults, £3.50 ($5.60) children, £18 ($28) family ticket. May–Aug daily 10am–6pm; Sept–Oct daily 10am–5:30pm; Nov–Dec daily 10am–4:30pm.

5 Pembrokeshire Coast National Park ⚘

This national park is the smallest of Britain's national parks. It's unique in that it extends over cliff and beaches whereas most parks encompass mountains or hill country. The coastline takes in 180 miles (290km) of sheer rugged beauty, with towering cliffs and turbulent waters. **Tenby** (see below) is the chief resort for exploring the park, but the town of Pembroke itself and St. Davids also make worthy stopovers.

TENBY ⚘

The leading resort in Pembrokeshire, Tenby is packed with vacationers during the summer months, but it has a charm and character dating from medieval times, which makes it an interesting place to visit at any time of year. The location is 4.8km (3 miles) south of Saundersfoot and 43km (27 miles) southwest of Carmarthen.

The main southern rail line through Tenby is run by Wales on West Rail Service (for information and reservations ℂ **0845/748-4950**). Trains run from Swansea seven times a day Monday through Friday and four times a day on Saturday and Sunday.

For information, go to the **Tourist Information Office** at the Croft (ℂ **01834/ 842402**). It is open November through March Monday through Saturday from 10am to 4pm; April and May daily from 10am to 5pm; June through September daily from 10am to 5:30pm (until 9pm in July and Aug), and in October Monday through Saturday from 10am to 5pm.

SEEING THE SIGHTS

There was already a Welsh village here when the Normans built **Tenby Castle,** now in ruins. Today the castle attracts interest because of its location on the headland overlooking the town and harbor. The town walls had four gates, one of which, the West Gate, known as Five Arches, remains. The west wall is in good condition. Tenby was also a target during the Civil War.

Tenby Museum and Art Gallery, Castle Hill (© **01834/842800**), is housed near the ruins of Tenby Castle. Exhibits cover the geology, archaeology, and natural history of the district, as well as the history of Tenby from the 12th century. In the art gallery you'll see works by Augustus and Gwen John, and Charles Norris, a local artist of the early 19th century. Open April through October daily from 10am to 5pm; November through March Monday through Friday from 10am to 5pm. Admission costs £2 ($3.20) for adults or £1 ($1.60) for children.

Tudor Merchant's House, Quay Hill (© **01834/842279**), is a beautifully furnished medieval dwelling of the 15th century with a fine Flemish chimney. On three interior walls, paintings with designs similar to Flemish weaving patterns were discovered under years of whitewash. Open April through September Thursday through Tuesday from 10am to 5pm, except on Sunday, when it's open from 1 to 5pm. Admission costs £2 ($3.20) for adults or £1 ($1.60) for children under age 16.

Tenby's parish church, **St. Mary's,** dates from the 13th century and is the largest parish church in Wales. Giraldus Cambrensis (Gerald the Welshman), a great religious leader of the 13th century, was the first rector. Charging no admission, it is open daily from 8am to 6pm.

In the bay just 3.2km (2 miles) south of Tenby, little **Caldy Island** ✪ has long been a Roman Catholic venue. A Celtic monastic cell is believed to have been here, and today it is farmed by Cistercian monks, whose abbey is the island's outstanding attraction. From the 12th century until the dissolution of the monasteries by Henry VIII, a Benedictine priory was here. For the next few centuries, lay people living on the island farmed and quarried limestone until, in 1906, English Benedictines established a community here.

The Benedictines left solid evidence of their occupation: the refectory, gatehouse, and the priory's lodging, which is now used as a guesthouse. In 1929, the Cistercian order took over the island, and today they produce perfume, chocolate, and dairy products, all sold locally. Only male visitors are allowed to enter the monastery, but anyone can visit St. David's Church, the Old Priory, and St. Illtud's Church, with a leaning stone spire. Inside St. Illtud's is a 6th-century Ogham stone, a relic of the time when monks from Ireland came here to establish their religious house. The writing on the Ogham stones was Celtic, which was then translated into Latin by the monks.

Allow about 2 hours for a visit. Access to the island is via a boat that runs only between Easter and late September Monday through Friday from 10am to 4pm. In July and August boats run on Saturday. The vessels depart every 20 minutes; the crossing also takes 20 minutes. A round-trip passage costs £7 ($11) per person, regardless of age. For information about all aspects of the island, including boat access, call © **01834/844453**.

WHERE TO STAY & DINE

Fourcroft Hotel   This is our favorite hotel within the town itself, though we prefer the greater elegance and secluded location of Penally Abbey (see below). On the cliffs above Tenby's sheltered North Beach, the hotel lies a 5-minute walk from the medieval walled town center. Fourcroft forms part of a landmarked Georgian terrace, built more than 150 years ago as summer homes for Londoners. Obviously you'll prefer the front bedrooms, which are generally more spacious and open onto a view of the sea. All the rooms, however, have modern comfort, ranging from midsize to spacious, with roomy, well-kept bathrooms. Guests can use a private garden walk leading to the beach. Other amenities include a human-sized chess set, a snooker table, a children's playground, and a restaurant and lounge offering views of the sea.

North Beach, Tenby, Pembrokeshire SA70 8AP. (C) **01834/842886.** Fax 01834/842888. www.fourcroft-hotel. co.uk. 48 units. £74–£84 ($118–$134) double. AE, DC, MC, V. Limited free parking for 6 cars. **Amenities:** Restaurant; bar; outdoor heated pool; fitness center; Jacuzzi; sauna; room service. *In room:* TV, coffeemaker, hair dryer.

Penally Abbey ✦ This country-house hotel—the finest lodging in the area—opens onto a gracious, timeless world. The house is 2 centuries old, but parts of its foundation date back to the 6th century, when a monastery was established here. Today the flowering garden partially conceals the ruins of St. Deniol's Chapel and a Flemish chimney of a long-ago homestead. The wide-open sea and the still-functioning Cistercian monastery on Caldey Island contribute to the panoramic sweep from the terraces. The house is built of Pembrokeshire stone, containing ogee-headed doors, large square windows, and Gothic-inspired architectural details. The spacious bedrooms are full of character, often enhanced by a four-poster bed. Superior period furnishings are used, and the medium-sized bathrooms are immaculately kept. We prefer the rooms in the family house to the newer ones in the annex. There's a dining room of candlelit elegance, serving Welsh and continental cuisine.

Penally, Tenby, Pembrokeshire SA70 7PY. (C) **01834/843033.** Fax 01834/844714. www.penally-abbey.com. 12 units. £126–£146 ($201–$234) double. Discounts for children sharing parent's room. AE, MC, V. 2 miles southwest of town by A4139. **Amenities:** Restaurant; heated indoor pool. *In room:* TV, coffeemaker, hair dryer.

PEMBROKE

At a point 51km (32 miles) southwest of Carmarthen and 405km (252 miles) west of London, the ancient borough of Pembroke is the most English town in South Wales. It was never really a typical Welsh town, because the Normans and the English had such a strong hold on it. It was settled by English and Flemish people, and its first language was always English. It is visited for two reasons today—to see Pembroke Castle, one of the most impressive in South Wales, and to use it as a base for exploring the national park.

Pembroke received its charter about 1090 from King Henry I and was built around Pembroke Castle, a great fortress set on a rocky spur above the town. The town walls formed the castle's outer ward, and the entire complex, a 14-mile-wide medieval defense system, can still be viewed as a fortified town, with the castle as its hub.

ESSENTIALS

GETTING THERE Most trains coming to Pembroke require transfers in Swansea, an hour's travel away. From Swansea, there are six trains per day, and from Swansea, trains fan out to many other points within Britain. For railway information, call (C) **0845/748-4950.**

There are bus connections into Pembroke from Tenby about every hour throughout the day Monday through Saturday, with limited service on Sunday. For bus information about service from Wales into Pembroke, call (C) **0870/608-2608.** For information about long-distance bus transit from London or big cities of the English Midlands, call **National Express** at (C) **0870/580-8080.**

VISITOR INFORMATION Pembroke maintains a tourist information office—Pembroke Visitor Centre, Commons Road ((C) **01646/622388**)—that's open only between Easter and October, daily from 10am to 5:30pm. The rest of the year, people should contact the year-round tourist office in Haverfordwest:

The **Tourist Information Centre,** 19 Old Bridge, Haverfordwest (✆ **01437/ 763110**). Between November and Easter, it's open Monday through Saturday from 10am to 4pm. From Easter to October, it's open daily from 10am to 5:30pm.

VISITING THE CASTLE

Pembroke Castle ★★   With its massive keep and walls, the castle still looks formidable, although little inside it remains. It is the oldest castle in West Wales, and for more than 300 years it was the seat of the earls of Pembroke. It was founded by the Montgomerys in 1093, and work began on the fine masonry a century later with the circular great tower, or keep. Dominating the castle, the tower stands 22m (75 ft.) high and is the finest of its type in Britain. Home to such great leaders as Earl William Marshal, regent to Henry III, and to the early Tudors, the castle was also the birthplace of Henry VII ("Harri Tewdwr"). During the Civil War, the castle was held in turn for both Parliament and the king. Cromwell arrived in person to start the siege that led to its final surrender. A vast cavern underneath the castle, called the Wogan, is where food and water were stored. The water defenses of the fortress can still be traced in a millpond on the north and in marshes on the south, outside the walls, as well as in the River Pembroke over which it looms.

Main St. ✆ **01646/681510.** www.pembrokecastle.co.uk/home.htm. Admission £3 ($4.80) for adults, £2 ($3.20) students and children. Apr–Sept daily 9:30am–6pm; Mar and Oct daily 10am–5pm; Nov–Feb daily 10am–4pm.

WHERE TO STAY

Coach House Hotel   Built along traditional lines after World War II (though the facade dates back to medieval times), this family-room hotel is the best place for lodgings within the town itself, although the Court (see below) at Lamphey is far more elegant. Bedrooms are small to midsize, each comfortably furnished with a little shower-only bathroom. Set on the main thoroughfare of Pembroke, the hotel has a classic facade of black and white. View it mainly as an overnight stopover and don't expect a lot of style.

116 Main Street, Pembroke, Pembrokeshire SA71 4HN. ✆ **01646/684602.** Fax 01646/687456. 14 units. £70 ($112) double. Rates include breakfast. AE, MC, V. Free parking. **Amenities:** Restaurant; bar; laundry service. *In room:* TV, coffeemaker, hair dryer (available at reception).

Lamphey Court Hotel ★   This impressive Georgian mansion set on several acres of landscaped gardens adds a touch of class to the area. This Best Western affiliate is by far the finest place for lodging and dining in the area. Both the public rooms and the bedrooms have a certain grandeur. Many units are spacious enough for family suites. You can stay in the house where the units are more traditional or in an 11-room annex where accommodations may not have tradition but are quite luxurious as well. Local produce is cooked to perfection in the formal restaurant. Bar food is also available.

Lamphey, Pembrokeshire SA71 5NT. ✆ **800/528-1234** in the U.S., or 01646/672273. Fax 01646/672480. www.lampheycourt.co.uk. 37 units. £58–£80 ($93–$128) double. Rates include breakfast. AE, DC, MC, V. Take A477 to Pembroke, turning left at Village Milton (Lamphey is signposted from there). **Amenities:** Restaurant; bar; heated indoor pool; night-lit tennis court; health club; Jacuzzi; sauna; solarium; room service; babysitting. *In room:* TV, coffeemaker, hair dryer, trouser press.

WHERE TO DINE

Left Bank CLASSICAL FRENCH   Other than the hotels, this is the only truly good independent restaurant in the area. Right in the heart of town, it was converted from an old bank that went belly up. Invitingly informal with a sympathetic staff, it has a limited menu but one with fine selection of temptations. Seasonal produce from the Welsh countryside is emphasized. The restaurant offers dishes for vegetarians and a separate area for nonsmokers. The restaurant sits on the left bank of the Cleddau River. Peruse the menu while relaxing in a brasserie-like decor. Tired of the Welsh lamb we saw passing by, we opted for a splendid filet of perfectly cooked Welsh Black beef, which was made all the more inviting with parsnip "crisps" and a well-flavored sauce. Save room for the velvety chocolate mousse with a raspberry sorbet—it's perfect.

63 Main St. ℂ **01646/622333.** Reservations recommended. Fixed-price dinners £22–£26 ($35–$42); lunch main courses around £7 ($11). AE, DC, MC, V. Tues–Sat noon–2:30pm and 7–9:30pm. Closed Dec 24–26 and 2 weeks in Jan.

ST. DAVIDS ✦✦

St. Davids and its environs are in a part of the Pembrokeshire Coast National Park that had inhabitants far back in Paleolithic and Mesolithic times. About 5,000 years ago, New Stone Age (Neolithic) farmers arrived and made their homes here. They didn't leave many traces, but their tombs, or cromlechs, have survived. Many lie on or near St. Davids Head, on Newport Bay, and in the Preseli foothills. Many people believe that the massive blue or foreign stones at Stonehenge came from the Preseli hills more 4,000 years ago. Bronze Age cairns have also been found in the Preseli region.

Iron Age Celts came here, bringing with them from Gaul the beginnings of the Welsh and Gaelic languages. Near St. Davids, walls built during that era are still in use around fields. The Romans ignored this part of Wales, and contacts with Ireland, where fellow Celts lived, were strong. Irish tribes settled in Dyfed in the 3rd and 4th centuries, and then the monastic movement in the early Christian church was brought by Irish and spread by Welsh missionaries, when a vigorous Christian community was established on the St. Davids Peninsula.

The coming of the Normans did not really affect this section of Wales, and Welsh is still widely spoken here. In Tudor times and later, village seafaring came in, taking the mining output of coal, silver, and lead out of small village ports. All this has changed of course, and today the coastal area is a popular holiday territory, with beaches, boating, fishing, and other leisure pursuits taking over.

There's a tremendous allure to one of Britain's most visited surf beaches, **Whitesands** ✦, which is located 3.2km (2 miles) northwest of St. Davids. From June to early September, lifeguards are on duty. Access to this windswept beach is free, but there's a £1.50 ($2.40) charge for parking. Whitesands is noted for some of the consistently best surf waves in Britain. As such, it's the site of surfing exhibitions, where participants arrive from as far away as Huntington Beach, California.

The tiny cathedral city of St. Davids is the birthplace of the patron saint of Wales. The countryside around it is centuries away from the hurry of modern times. The cathedral lies in a grassy hollow of the River Alun, chosen by St. David for its small monastic community because the site was hidden from approach by attackers from land and from sea, yet it was conveniently only a mile from the waters of St. Bride's Bay.

Dewi Sant (later St. David), son of a Welsh chieftain and a Welsh woman named Non, was a Celtic religious leader in the 6th century. The little church he and his monks built where the present cathedral stands was burned down in 645, rebuilt, sacked and burned by the Danes in 1078, and then burned again

---

⌐ Fun Fact   Sizing Up a City

The designation of St. Davids, which appears to be little more than a village, as a city may puzzle Americans, but in Britain only a place that contains a cathedral is called a city. Therefore, a huge metropolis may actually be defined as a town.

---

in 1088. After that, a Norman cathedral was built, its organization changing from the Celtic monastic to diocesan type. The stone village of St. Davids grew up on the hill around the secluded church.

St. Davids lies 74km (46 miles) west of Carmarthen and 428km (266 miles) west of London. Motorists take the A487 to reach St. Davids from Haverfordwest, 24km (15 miles) away. **Richard Brothers** (© 01239/613756) runs buses from Haverfordwest to St. Davids every hour; a one-way ticket costs only £3 or £4 ($4.80–$6.40) round-trip. Haverfordwest is the nearest rail station.

For information, the tourist office is at **The Grove** (© 01437/720392), open from Easter to October from 9:30am to 5:30pm daily. From November to Easter, open Monday through Saturday from 10am to 4pm.

SEEING THE SIGHTS

With its ornately carved roof and a Norman nave, **St. Davids Cathedral** ★★, Cathedral Close (© 01437/721885; www.stdavidscathedral.org.uk), is a magnificent example of medieval religious architecture. Its reliquary contains what are supposed to be the bones of St. David. The nave, a product of 3 centuries of craftsmanship, is a place of medieval beauty. The choir stalls, from the late 15th century, have witty, even light-hearted misericord carvings (those on the hinged seats in the stalls). Visitors are welcome at the cathedral, open Monday through Saturday from 8am to 6pm, Sunday from 12:45 to 5:45pm. Donations are accepted to help with the upkeep of the building.

Associated with the cathedral, the ruins of **Bishop's Palace,** Cathedral Close (© 01437/720517), stands across the meadow and river, with the gatehouse, battlements and curtain walls showing how even such a place needed fortification in medieval days. An outstanding sight is the elegant arcaded parapet that runs along both main walls. You can visit the palace ruins; note especially the fine piscina at the east end of the chapel's south wall. The site is open March and April daily from 9:30am to 5pm; May through September daily from 9:30am to 6pm; and October through February Monday through Saturday from 9:30am to 4pm and Sunday from noon to 2pm. Admission is £2 ($3.20) for adults or £1 ($1.60) for children.

The cathedral is no longer Roman Catholic, nor is it Church of England. It is a member of the Church of Wales. When St. David was canonized in the 12th century, the pope declared that two pilgrimages to St. Davids were worth one to Rome, and three pilgrimages equaled one to Jerusalem. You can make such a pilgrimage today; although the pope's promise may not have been honored since the days of Henry VIII, we can promise you an interesting and educational tour of St. Davids peninsula.

Porth Clais, at the mouth of the River Alun about 1.6km (1 mile) south from St. Davids, was the seaport used by travelers to Ireland and elsewhere for centuries before and after the birth of Christ, and then by pilgrims making their way to St. Davids. In medieval days it became a coal port, and lime kilns were used to reduce limestone to slaked lime for use on fields, in building, and for household purposes. The restored lime kilns can be seen.

A little eastward around the bay on a headland is **St. Non's Chapel,** now in ruins, supposedly built on the spot where St. David was born. It is dedicated to his mother. St. Non's Well is there also, reportedly in full flow. Its waters were said to have healing properties in the past. The site can be viewed 24 hours a day without charge.

WHERE TO STAY

Ramsey House *Value*   The town's best bargain lies 1km (½ mile) from the cathedral on the road to Porthclais. An adults-only establishment, it stands amid manicured gardens and looks very much like the private house it is. Just 1km (½ mile) from the house, you can reach the Pembrokeshire Coast Path that takes you along some of the most panoramic coastal scenery in Wales. Mac and Sandra Thompson are on hand to greet you, showing you one of their immaculately kept midsize bedrooms, each with a cozy and efficient private bathroom. We prefer the second-floor rooms because of their views, either of the sea, cathedral, or open country. For those who don't like stairs, there are ground-floor rooms. An entirely nonsmoking establishment, the hotel serves the best Welsh breakfast in town.

Lower Moor, St. Davids, Pembrokeshire SA62 6RP. ℂ 01437/720321. Fax 01437/720025. www.ramseyhouse. co.uk. 7 units. £96–£104 ($154–$166) double. Rates include breakfast and dinner. MC, V. Free parking. **Amenities:** "Taste of Wales" menu. *In room:* TV, coffeemaker, hair dryer.

Warpool Court Hotel ⚹   This hotel, a 5-minute walk from the heart of the city, is the town's premier address, far outdistancing all competitors. A country house overlooking the sea, it is privately owned and set amid secluded gardens of great natural beauty. The vine-covered structure overlooks one of the most beautiful coastal stretches in Wales. Originally the cathedral choir school, it has been successfully transformed into a hotel with a courteous staff. Most of the rooms are midsize to spacious, and some are large enough for families. The more expensive rooms offer sea views. Asa Williams, who lived here early in the 20th century, decorated some 3,000 tiles, which are positioned throughout the house—some are embellished with Celtic illuminations. The hotel's restaurant offers exceptional cuisine and a varied menu, though seafood is the specialty.

Southwest 1km (½ mile) by Port Clais Rd., St. Davids, Dyfed SA62 6BN. ℂ 01437/720300. Fax 01437/ 720676. www.warpoolcourthotel.com. 25 units. £79–£99 ($126–$158) per person. Rates include breakfast. AE, DC, MC, V. Free parking. **Amenities:** Restaurant; bar; covered heated swimming pool (Easter–October only); 2 tennis courts; health club; sauna; game room; babysitting. *In room:* TV, coffeemaker, hair dryer.

WHERE TO DINE

Morgan's Brasserie ⚹ WELSH/CONTINENTAL   Unless you dine at one of the inns, this is by far the best independent restaurant in town, and has been since it opened back in 1993. Peruse the menu while admiring the art collection on the walls. The chef is known for making use of local produce and market-fresh ingredients. The fresh fish is rushed here from the Pembrokeshire coast after it lands at the nearby port of Milford Haven. Blackboard menus display the catch of the day. Meat-eaters will also find the most reliable Welsh spring lamb or "black steaks" from the countryside, even game in season. Our party found the roast Gressingham duck supreme worth the trip here. All dishes are cooked to order and specially prepared to bring out the best flavor.

20 Nun St. ℂ 01437/720508. Reservations required. Main courses £13–£17 ($21–$27). AE, MC, V. Mon–Sat 7–9pm. Closed Jan–Feb.

21

North Wales

North Wales is a rewarding target for those willing to seek it out. Distinctly different from England, it is linguistically and culturally different from most of Britain and is known for its beauty spots, a land of mountains and lakes interspersed with castles. The most powerful of the Welsh princes held sway here, and the land remains staunchly nationalistic even to this day. British families flock to the coastal resorts on holidays, especially in July and August, whereas others prefer to seek out the footpaths of Snowdonia National Park.

Mountain peaks and steep wooded slopes, spectacular estuaries and rugged cliffs brooding over secluded coves, lakes, little rivers, and valleys with tiny towns looking as if they were carved out of granite—all these join to make up **Snowdonia National Park.** The park, with slate mines, moors, heavy forests, mountain lakes, grain fields, and pastures, swift-moving rivers, and sandy beaches, takes its name from Snowdon, at 1,085m (3,560 ft.) the highest peak in Wales and England. Most of the Snowdonia area is in the County of Gwynedd, once the ancient Welsh kingdom of that name. Its prince, Owen ap Gwynedd, never agreed to let himself be reduced to the status of baron under the English kings. Because his terrain

was mountainous and wild, it helped him stave off an invasion by forces accustomed to fighting on flat land.

The rocky, majestic crags of Snowdonia National Park are rivaled by the mighty walls and soaring towers of **Caernarfon Castle**, the best example of castle-building in medieval Wales. Caernarfon (formerly spelled Caernarvon) and its neighbors, Anglesey and the Lleyn Peninsula, reaching out from its northwest and west, are all part of the County of Gwynedd. Legends of holy islands and druidical mysteries flourished among the Celtic peoples who lived in this area in long-ago centuries.

Many of the native-born people of this region are of blood stock little changed over the centuries. Most are bilingual, with English as their second tongue, and signs are usually in both languages.

The County of Clwyd, which occupies northeastern Wales, has miles of sandy beaches along the north coast; highland ranges, peat bogs, and deep valleys lush with greenery in the center; coal country to the southeast; and industry, agriculture, and sheep farming in the section nearest the estuary of the River Dee and the English border. What is now Clwyd (by order of Parliament since 1973) was before that time Denbighshire and Flintshire.

1 Harlech

363km (226 miles) W of London; 40km (25 miles) SW of Betws-y-Coed; 43km (27 miles) S of Caernarfon

Views from Harlech of Snowdon, Tremadog Bay, Cader Idris, and the Lleyn Peninsula are splendid today, and they give an understanding as to why this was the setting for the strong fortification at Harlech Castle (see below). The waters of Tremadog Bay lapped around the foot of the cliffs at one time, adding to the protection of the little town that grew up around the castle. Today the area formerly underwater is filled in and is the site of the well-known Royal St. David's 18-hole championship golf course.

ESSENTIALS

GETTING THERE The **Cambrian Coast Line** runs eight trains a day into Harlech from Shrewbury, the nearest large rail junction in England, with easy connections to London. Service is more frequent in the summer. For rail information and schedules, call **0845/748-4950.**

Arriva buses (© **0870/608-2608**) service Harlech from links along the coast. In Wales, after passing through the town of Machynlleth, head north along A487 until you come to the junction with A496, at which point you go northwest to Harlech.

VISITOR INFORMATION Tourist information is dispensed from **Gwynedd House,** High Street (© **01766/780658**), open from Easter to late October daily from 10am to 6pm. The rest of the year, information is available in the town of Doltgellau at Ty Meirion, Eldon Square (© **01341/422888**), 32km (20 miles) from Harlech. This office is open Thursday through Monday from 10am to 5pm.

SEEING THE SIGHTS

Harlech Castle ★★ Built in 1283, this castle stands on a rocky promontory that once looked down on the sea, which added to its protection. The strong defense of this castle for the Lancastrians in the Wars of the Roses failed, but it did inspire the famous marching song "Men of Harlech." The main feature of the castle is its gatehouse. Visitors can climb 143 steps to the top. You can also take a walk along the walls. Harlech Castle is on the A496 9.6km (6 miles) south of Harlech. Allow about an hour for a visit.

Along the A496. © 01766/780552. www.castlewales.com/harlech.html. Admission £3 ($4.80) adults, £2 ($3.20) children under age 16. Mar–Oct daily 9:30am–5pm; Nov–Feb daily 9:30am–4pm.

Old Llanfair Quarry Slate Caverns A working slate mine until just before World War II, this is the most evocative sight for some of that *How Green Was My Valley* scenery. This quarry, unlike most of the North Wales slate mines and quarries, is only a short distance from the sea. Visitors can take guided tours through the mine caverns and tunnels. The underground temperature seldom rises above 50° Fahrenheit (10°C), so visitors should wear warm clothing. Allow 45 minutes to an hour.

Llanfair. © 01766/780247. Admission £3.50 ($5.60) adults, £2.40 ($3.85) children ages 15 and under. Take the A496 .8km (1 mile) south of Harlech.

WHERE TO STAY & DINE

Castle Cottage Living here is about as close as you can get to residing at the castle itself. Just off High Street, it lies only 91m (100 yards) from Harlech Castle. A Welsh version of a *restaurant avec chambres,* this cozy inn is known more for its excellent cuisine than for its bedrooms, but it makes for a snug overnight as well. The rooms are a bit small but are well appointed and carefully decorated; the doubles come with small bathrooms.

As far as amenities go, there's the restaurant, and that's about it. But the 16th-century beamed dining room exemplifies old-fashioned atmosphere. Its modern

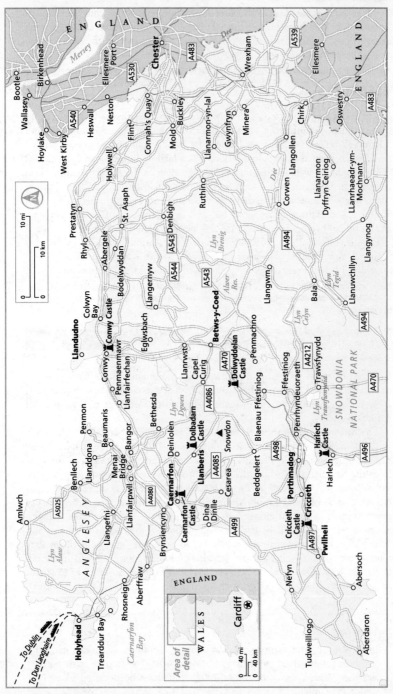

725

Welsh cooking is based on fresh seasonal produce, with which chef Patron Glyn Roberts does wonders in his kitchen. Perhaps you'll skip the Welsh haggis with bashed *neeps* (turnips) with whisky gravy and opt instead for the herb-crusted rack of lamb with a red-wine sauce.

Pen Llech, Harlech, Gwynedd LL46 2YL. ℭ **01766/780476.** Fax 01766/780479. www.castlecottageharlech. co.uk. 9 units, 4 with bathroom. £65 ($104) double. MC, V. Rates include breakfast. Free parking. **Amenities:** Restaurant. *In room:* No phone.

Hotel Maes-y-Neuadd ⭐⭐ The core of this charmer—a 14th-century manor house—stands on 8 acres of beautifully tended grounds and parkland 5.6km (3½ miles) northeast of Harlech by B4573. The country house atmosphere is augmented by personal service and a mellow ambience of oak-beamed ceilings, granite walls, and the inevitable inglenook fireplace. Medium-sized units are in the main house with four slightly lackluster units in an adjoining coach house. Rooms are imaginatively decorated and well furnished, often with antiques, and bathrooms are small but well kept. If you want real atmosphere, ask for one of two bedrooms that are cozy nests straight out of the 14th century.

Even if you're not a guest, call for a dinner reservation, as the food is worthy, prepared by a talented chef from fresh produce. The Welsh farmhouse cheeses are a delight. Fresh vegetables are gathered in season from the inn's garden.

Talsarnau, Gwynedd, LL47 6YA. ℭ **01766/780200.** Fax 01766/780211. www.neuadd.com. 16 units. £199–£255 ($318–$408) double. Rates include breakfast and dinner. AE, DC, MC, V. **Amenities:** Restaurant; bar. *In room:* TV.

2 Llanberis

376km (234 miles) W of London; 11 km (7 miles) SE of Caernarfon

The starting point for going up Snowdon by mountain railway, Llanberis nestles between Lake Padarn and Lake Peris. Views of outstanding beauty greet your eyes, and there are several man-made sights worth seeing, as well as some of nature's wonders.

The **Snowdon Mountain Railway** ⭐ runs from Llanberis to within a few yards of the top of the Snowdon peak at about 1,085m (3,560 ft.). The only rack-and-pinion train in Britain, it is also the steepest train ride, and the view from the top platform, where the train stops, is one of the most panoramic in the country. It's possible to see some 160km (100 miles) away into Ireland, especially the peeks of the Wicklow Mountain chain, on the clearest and brightest of days. Another "great little train," in the region is the Llanberis Lake Railway, which takes you along Lake Padarn. The purpose of the trains in this area and in the Vale of Ffestiniog to the south was to bring the "gray gold" from slate caverns for shipping all over the world. For information and schedules, call ℭ **01286/870223.** Trains run between May and October, costing £17 ($27) for adults round-trip or £12 ($19) for children under age 15.

Fun Fact **A Taste for Trains**

Restoration of the century-old Snowdon Mountain Railway was carried out with funds raised by Britain's National Trust. The largest contributor was the Welsh-born actor, Sir Anthony Hopkins, who donated some £1 million ($1.6 million) to the effort, much of it earned playing the infamous cannibal Hannibal Lector in the movies.

Padarn Country Park, open daily until dusk, has marked footpaths that will take you past the Vivian Quarry, with its dramatic slate cliffs and deep pools, through galleries where slate was worked, and to lookouts from which the Snowdon range and the lakes can be viewed. The entrance to these 700 acres of countryside are signposted from High Street and begin .8km (½ mile) north of the town center.

Craft workshops and a woodcraft center are open at the park, where you can watch artisans work in clay, copper, slate, and wood. One workman specializes in Celtic folk harps, including miniature models and do-it-yourself kits.

Dolbadarn Castle ruins overlook Lake (Llyn) Padarn in the Llanberis pass, .8km (½ mile) east of Llanberis, a relic of the time when the pass was used by the conquering armies. It is notable for its location and a mortared masonry tower that still stands. You can take a look around the meager ruins for free.

GETTING THERE   There's no railway station in Llanberis, but the nearest rail station is at Bangor, 14km (9 miles) north of Llanberis. From Bangor, there's at least one bus an hour, which departs in front of Bangor's railway station. For information on buses into Llanberis, contact the **Arriva Bus Company** (© **0870/608-2608** for information and reservations). Because of the many stops en route, buses take about 40 minutes each way.

Two buses per hour make the run between Llanberis and Caernarfon, Monday through Saturday only. Bus timetables are available from the **Caernarfon Tourist Information Office,** Castle Ditch, 1 Castle Street, in Caernarfon (© **01286/672232**), or at the Llanberis Tourist Information Office, 41A High St., in Llanberis (© **01286/870765**). Motorists from Caernarfon head southeast along the A4086.

VISITOR INFORMATION   The **Llanberis Tourist Information Office** (see address above) is open from Easter to the end of October daily from 10am to 6pm. The rest of the year, it's open Wednesday, Friday, Saturday, and Sunday from 9:30am to 4:30pm.

SEEING THE SIGHTS

Half a mile north of the center of Llanberis in Padarn Country Park (see above), the **Welsh State Museum** (© **01286/870630**), offers a minor museum in the workshops of Dinorwic slate quarry, one of the largest in Britain until it closed in 1969. Slate-mining communities were intensely Welsh, nonconformist in religion, and radical in politics, as films shown here reveal. The exhibitions, which should take no more than 30 minutes of your time, are mainly of interest to those who have a particular interest in this aspect of Welsh life of long ago. Admission is free. It's open from Easter to October daily from 10am to 5pm; off season daily from 10am to 4pm. Take the A4086 at the start of the lake railway and Padarn Country Park.

Electric Mountain Visitor Centre, along the A4086 (© **01286/870636**), is a scientific-looking observation center, functioning as the meeting point between the public and one of the most technologically advanced power stations in Wales. Set about .4km (¼ mile) north of Llanberis, it incorporates a hydroelectric system harnessing the waters of a pair of nearby lakes, whose turbines and channels are concealed deep within the mountains so as not to spoil the natural beauty of the nationally protected site. Entrance to the visitor center is free. Hours of visitation between April and September are daily from 9:30am to 5pm, October through March daily from 10:30am to 4:30pm. Once you get here, if a staff member isn't busy with other tasks, you can take a tour of the turbines for a fee of £5 ($8) for adults, £2.50 ($4) for children under age 15.

WHERE TO STAY

Lakeview Hotel   This hotel is appropriately named, its bedrooms opening onto a panorama of the vast lake, with the dramatic landscapes of Snowdon as a backdrop. The hotel has been much improved in both its public and private rooms. The public lounge is a good place to sit and read a book as it has real country-inn character. The bedrooms for the most part are midsize and are comfortably furnished, with small bathrooms that contain shower units.

Tan-y-Pant, Llanberis, Gwynedd LL55 4EL. *©* **01286/870422.** Fax 01286/872591. www.lakeviewhotel.co.uk. 10 units. £55–£62 ($88–$99) double. Rates include breakfast. AE, MC, V. Free parking. Lies 1 mile from Llanberis on A4086 toward Caernarfon. **Amenities:** Restaurant; bar. *In room:* TV, coffeemaker.

Royal Victoria Hotel   Although it's a venue for local weddings and social functions and is a bit stuffy, this is nonetheless the most prestigious address in town. Its accommodations are better and more inviting than Lakeview, although Lakeview is more informal and friendlier. Royal Victoria is long established at the foothills of Snowdon, between Padarn and Peris Lakes, a bucolic setting. The bedrooms in general are spacious and have been recently modernized, with comfortable and endurable furniture and well-maintained private baths. Four rooms are set aside for families. The place bustles with activity, often providing live entertainment at night or arranging mountain treks during the day.

Llanberis, Gwynedd, LL55 4TY. *©* **01286/870253.** Fax 01286/870149. www.royal-victoria-hotel.co.uk. 111 units. £60 ($96) double. Discounts available for children under 15 staying in parent's room. AE, DC, MC, V. Free parking. **Amenities:** Restaurant; large dining room with a conservatory opening onto the lakes; bar; room service. *In room:* TV, coffeemaker, hair dryer.

WHERE TO DINE

Y Bistro ✦ TRADITIONAL WELSH   When it comes to food, this is the only hot ticket in town. Nothing else matters—there's not even a good inn here. For more than 2 decades, we've been popping in here to see what the Robertses (Nerys and Danny) are offering on their "taste of Wales" menu, and we've never been disappointed. Nerys has appeared on numerous British TV shows about cuisine and has won many deserved accolades for her cooking skills. The place is so Welsh that it even offers wines from Wales, although you should stick to the French and Spanish vintages. Excellent use is made of local produce. Here's a chance to learn some Welsh when ordering. *Eog peris* is a delectable locally smoked salmon in a creamy sauce; *ffryth* is a chilled melon flavored with orange zest and Cointreau, a delightful way to launch yourself in such game dishes as a perfectly roasted and herb-seasoned pheasant or succulent pigeon breasts. Try the tasty appetizer, lamb ribs flavored with honey, mint, and rosemary. The Welsh wine tastes better when cooked with grapes to make a sauce to flavor the melt-in-your-mouth pork tenderloins.

43–45 High St. *©* **01286/871278.** Reservations required. Main courses £13–£15 ($21–$24); fixed-price menu (including ½ liter of wine) £17 ($27). MC, V. Mon–Sat 7:30–10pm. Closed Mon–Tues in winter.

3 Betws-y-Coed ✦

363km (226 miles) W of London; 70km (44 miles) SE of Holyhead

This idyllic Snowdonia village, with tumbling rivers, waterfalls, and mountains, is nestled in the tree-lined valley of the River Conwy. It has an antique church with a Norman font; old bridges, stone houses, and hotels on rocky outcrops; and woodland paths.

Although crowded in summer, this town is one of the best centers for exploring North Wales. It's mainly a one-street town, but you get the feel that you're in the great outdoors far removed from England's polluted cities of the Midlands. There's an alpine feeling about the place.

The town is known for its eight bridges, of which our favorite is the Waterloo Bridge at the village's southern end, the construction of Telford in 1815 in cast iron. There's also a suspension bridge near St. Michael's Church. If you walk upon it, it sways in the wind but seems perfectly safe. The most regal bridge is Pont-y-Pair, "the bridge of the cauldron," bounding the Llugwy River to the north. In fact, walking across the bridges of Betws-y-Coed and taking in the views is one of the main reasons to come here.

ESSENTIALS
GETTING THERE   The **Conwy Valley** line between Llandudno and Blaenau Ffestiniog passes through Betws-y-Coed with six trains daily Monday through Saturday (only two trains on Sun). For rail information and schedules, call © **0845/748-4950.**

The **Arriva** bus company services Betws-y-Coed from both Llandudno and Porthmadog. For schedules, call © **01492/592111.**

Motorists from Llandudno can take A470 south.

VISITOR INFORMATION   For information about the town and Snowdonia National Park, head for the **local tourist office** at Holyhead Road in the town center (© **01690/710426**). It's open from Easter to October daily from 10am to 6pm; off season daily from 9:30am to 4:30pm.

SEEING THE SIGHTS
If time is short, we'd skip the minor sights of town—that is, after you've walked over those bridges—and head instead for one of the beauty spots of Wales, the **Swallow Falls** ☆ and **Miners Bridge.** Take the A5 for 3.2km (2 miles) to the west of Betws-y-Coed. The Swallow Falls is one of the most mystical and evocative—also one of the most powerful—in Wales. It's composed of a series of waterfalls strung together, creating a mist. Miners Bridge is a wooden footbridge impregnated with pitch for preservation and dating from the late 18th century. It's not a conventional flat bridge, but rather it's a steeply inclined "staircase"-style bridge, with elevation much higher on one end than on the other. The Miners Bridge doesn't charge anything to visit—and, as such, many walkers opt for a brisk ½-hour riverfront walk from the center of Betws-y-Coed, with the bridge as their final destination. You'll pay £1 ($1.60) to see the falls, however. There's no guardian—just drop a coin into a tollbooth, and visit anytime you want, night or day.

Again, and only if you have time, there are two more evocative places to visit in the area. One is **Dolwyddelan Castle** at the hamlet of Dolwyddelan (© **01690/750366**).

Standing lonely on a ridge, this castle was the birthplace of Llewlyn the Great, according to tradition. It was certainly his royal residence. Restored to its present condition in the 19th century, the castle's remains look out on the rugged grandeur of Moel Siabod peak. A medieval road from the Vale of Conwy ran just below the west tower, which made this a strategic site for a castle to control passage. About a mile from Dolwyddelan, the castle is accessible by a rough track off the A470 to the southwest of Betws-y-Coed, on the road to Blaenau Ffestiniog. To enter, adults pay £2 ($3.20); children under age 16 £1 ($1.60) (free for those age 4 and under). Open April through October daily from 9:30am to 6:30pm; off season Monday to Saturday from 9:30am to 4pm, Sunday from 11am to 4pm.

One of the premier literary sights of Wales, **Ty Mawr,** Wybrnant, Penmachno (© **01690/760213**), lies 11km (7 miles) southeast of Betws-y-Coed. From the town head southwest for 5.6km (3½ miles), going west of Penmachno along B4406 the rest of the way. At the head of the little valley of Gwybernant, this cottage is where Bishop William Morgan was born in the 16th century. He was the first person to translate the Bible into Welsh, and his translation is viewed even today as a masterpiece and the foundation of modern Welsh literature. It's an isolated stone-walled cottage with a slate roof that you might pass by unless you knew its pedigree. Between April and September, it's open Thursday through Sunday from noon to 5pm. In October it is open only Thursday, Friday, and Sunday from noon to 4pm. Admission is £2 ($3.20) for adults and £1 ($1.60) for children.

WHERE TO STAY & DINE
EXPENSIVE

Tan-y-Foel Country House Hotel ★★★ *Finds* A 16th-century manor house, this gem is the best hotel in the area, opening onto a panoramic sweep of Conwy Valley, with Snowdonia looming in the background. Stay here if you can, forsaking all other places. Vibrant fabrics and modern paintings bring you into the 21st century, but the atmosphere is still yesterday. Two miles north of town, it is set on 8 acres of woodlands and pastures. Charm and grace prevail in the public and private bedrooms. The latter are moderate to spacious, each individually furnished with immaculate little bathrooms. Two rooms are in an annex and have less charm. All units are nonsmoking. We prefer one of the four bedrooms opening onto the front of the hotel, as they offer the best views.

The hotel cuisine here is better than all its competitors. Owner/chef Janet Pitman has even gone on the BBC to tell Britain the secret of making her Celtic pancakes with Carmarthen ham, pork, and apple puree.

Capel Garmon, near Betws-y-Coed, LL26 0RE. © **01690/710507.** Fax 01690/710681. www.tyfhotel.co.uk. 7 units. £182–£232 ($291–$371) double. Rates include breakfast. AE, DC, MC, V. No children age 7 and under accepted. From Betws-y-Coed, take A5 onto A470, heading north to Llanrwst, turning at the signpost for Capel Garmon. **Amenities:** Restaurant. *In room:* TV, iron/ironing board.

MODERATE

Henllys Hotel (The Old Courthouse) ★★ This is a good, centrally located best bet for those who like B&B style luxury but want the amenities of a small inn as well. Once a Victorian magistrates' court, the hotel and has been successfully converted and set in lovely gardens along the river, just a 3-minute walk from the city center. You can dine in the antique courtroom where prisoners were sentenced long ago, have a lager in the police station bar, and sleep either in the judge's chambers or the "handcuff room." Bedrooms range from small to spacious, and each has been cleverly converted, offering much comfort from the new mattresses to the nicely appointed bathrooms, with a choice of tub or shower. At this nonsmoking establishment, some rooms are suitable for persons with disabilities. Try to avoid the smallest room in the house, originally a single cell reserved "for a ruffian." It still has bars on the door.

In the cozy, galleried dining room, Barbara Valadini is known in town for her fine and imaginative Welsh fare.

Old Church Rd., Betws-y-Coed, LL24 0AL. © **01690/710534.** Fax 01690/710884. www.guesthouse-snowdonia.co.uk. 8 units. £63–£66 ($101–$106) double. MC, V. Free parking. *In room:* TV, coffeemaker, hair dryer (on request), iron (on request).

The Park Hill Hotel ⭐   About a 5-minute walk west of town, this small Victorian hotel is surrounded by secluded gardens and opens onto panoramic views of the Conwy and Llugwy valleys. For such a small hotel, it offers some exceptional recreational facilities (see below) and is also known for its justly praised cuisine. Your hosts, Jaap and Ghislaine Buis, run a good little inn, with moderately sized bedrooms and small but well-kept bathrooms. Front rooms are preferable to those on the side. Furnishings are traditional, and one room is graced with a four-poster.

Llanwst Rd., Betws-y-Coed, Gwynedd LL24 0HD. © **01690/710540.** Fax 01690/710540. www.park-hill-hotel.co.uk. 9 units. £54–£78 ($86–$125) double. MC, V. Free parking. No children under age 6. **Amenities:** Bar; indoor heated pool; whirlpool; sauna. *In room:* TV, coffeemaker, no phone.

Ty Gwyn ⭐   This is one of the most charming hotels and pubs in town. You could ask Teddy Roosevelt, if he were still around. Much has changed since the American president stayed here in the late 1800s, but much is still the same as well. Laden with carved beams and local artifacts, Ty Gwyn is low slung, sitting on the opposite side of Waterloo Bridge from the rest of town. Inside it's a world of old prints and chintz, time-darkened beams, and copper pans. Originally it was a coaching inn from the 16th century, drawing horsemen traveling between London and the ferryboats to Ireland. The rooms, often small, are still comfortably furnished, often with a four-poster or a half-tester bed (ca. 1800). Most rooms have a shower only, though two have a tub-shower combo. The best unit has a "health spa" tub, small lounge, and private balcony. The four rooms without private bathrooms share two small bathrooms equipped with a shower only; the rooms themselves have wash basins with hot and cold running water.

Along the A5, Betws-y-Coed, Gwynedd LL24 0PSG. © **01690/710383.** www.tygwynhotel.co.uk. 13 units, 9 with bathroom. £36 ($58) double without bathroom, £60 ($96) double with bathroom; £80 ($128) four-poster room. Children under 12 stay free in same room with two paying adults. AE, MC, V. Free parking. **Amenities:** Restaurant; pub. *In room:* TV, coffeemaker, no phone.

4 The Lleyn Peninsula ⭐⭐

Separating Cardigan Bay and its northern arm, Tremadog Bay, from Caernarfon Bay, the gentle western Lleyn Peninsula thrusts out alone into the Irish Sea. It's bounded by the mountains of Snowdonia on the east and by the sea. Having little communication with the outside world before the coming of railroads and highways, the peninsula has a large Welsh-speaking population, although most people also have English as a second language, made necessary by the influx of people coming here to retire, to do business, or just to take holidays.

The peninsula takes its name from an Irish tribe, the Celtic Legine or Laigin, who didn't have very far to go from home to invade the country of fellow Celts. They were followed by missionaries and pilgrims in the Christian era. The distance from Ireland is so short that when you stand on National Trust property high on a cliff above St. Mary's Well you can often see the Wicklow Mountains of Ireland with the naked eye.

The Lleyn Peninsula has beaches, hills, farmland, moorland, villages nestled in the hollows, trees, heather, gorse, and country lanes. There are traces of hill forts here, and you can find standing stones, monastery ruins, pilgrim trails, holy wells (four of them), and nonconformist chapels. Sportsmen find fishing, golf, watersports, and rough shooting.

For information on the peninsula, get in touch with the **Tourist Information Centre, Y Maes,** Pwllheli (© **01758/613000**).

The two best towns on the peninsula are Porthmadog and Criccieth (see below).

Pwllheli, lying 13km (8 miles) to the west of Criccieth, is the principal transportation hub of the peninsula, with daily buses arriving from London. Buses also pull in here every hour from Bangor. You may not want to linger in Pwllheli, but take a connecting bus to either Porthmadog or Criccieth, which, as mentioned, make better centers.

BritRail's Cambrian Coast line, which begins at Aberystwth, with a change of trains at Machynlleth, will take you to both Porthmadog and Criccieth. Call BritRail at © **0845/748-4950** for more information about rail connections.

PORTHMADOG

The estuary of the River Glaslyn has long been the scene of shipping and fishing activity, emptying as it does into Tremadoc Bay and thence into Cardigan Bay.

This is the main town east of the Lleyn Peninsula. It grew up as a slate-shipping port on the coast near the mouth of the River Glaslyn. T. E. Lawrence (Lawrence of Arabia) was born in Tremadog, close by.

The town was named after a "Celtification" of the English name of its builder, William Madocks, a mining mogul who built the town from scratch between 1808 and 1811. The harbor that later figured so prominently in the town's history was custom-built between 1821 and 1825. In the 1870s, there were as many as 1,000 vessels a year that pulled into harbor here to haul away slate. At its peak in 1873, 116,000 tons of Blaenau slate were shaped from this harbor to points throughout the empire and the world.

The location is 428km (266 miles) west of London and 32km (20 miles) south of Caernarfon. The **Wales Information Centre,** High Street (© **01766/512981**), is open daily from Easter to October from 10am to 6pm. Off-season hours are Thursday through Tuesday from 10am to 5pm.

SEEING THE SIGHTS

The view of the mountains of Snowdonia from Porthmadog Cob, the embankment, is panoramic. Porthmadog is the coastal terminal of the Ffestiniog Railway, and a small museum may be visited at the station. From the town there's access to beaches at Borth-y-Gest and Black Rock Sands, where cars may be driven onto the beach. Other than the scenery, attractions are not exceptional.

The production of traditional tapestries and tweeds can be observed at the small **Brynkir Woollen Mill,** Golan, Garndolbenmaen (© **01766/530236**), in a beautiful rural setting. The products are available for sale at this mill shop. Admission is free, and it is open Monday through Friday from 9am to 4:30pm. Head out the A487 for 5.6km (3½ miles) from Porthmadog.

NEARBY ATTRACTIONS

Penrhyndeudraeth, "the headland of the two beaches," is a tiny and uninspired town known mainly for having on its outskirts the Italianate village of **Portmeirion** ✦, set on its own wooded peninsula overlooking Tremadog Bay. Here, the late Sir Clough Williams-Ellis built a village of pastel-colored structures resembling Portofino or Sorrento in a landscape of sea and mountains. The village contains shops as well as miles of paths through the woods. White sandy beaches border it. This charming folly is privately owned and open daily from 9:30am to 5:30pm. Entrance is £4.50 ($7.20); a family ticket costs £11 ($18).

WHERE TO STAY & DINE

Hotel Portmeirion ★★★ *Finds*   There's nothing else like it in Wales. Sir Clough Williams-Ellis set out to build an idyllic village on a romantic coast, and he succeeded. Standing amid one of the finest scenic settings in Wales, this hotel already existed as an early Victorian villa before it was converted into an evocative hotel in 1926. The hotel was partially reconstructed after its destruction by fire in 1981.

Writers such as H. G. Wells and George Bernard Shaw became habitués, Noël Coward wrote *Blithe Spirit* here in 1941, and the cult TV classic, *The Prisoner,* was filmed here in the late '60s. The hotel overlooks Cardigan Bay from its own private peninsula. The decor inside is exotic: fabrics from Kashmir, paintings from Rajasthan, tiles from Delft, and wallpaper from New York. Many of the rooms have half-tester or four-poster beds. About a dozen units are in the main house, the rest in a cluster of "village houses." In the main house, some rooms are cramped, whereas accommodations in the cluster of houses outside are often more spacious. Four accommodations are designated for families or small groups traveling together. The best sea views are from the rooms in the main house, however. Bathrooms are sumptuous.

At the highly praised restaurant, chefs use local produce as a foundation of daily changing menus. The modern Welsh cuisine has many Mediterranean influences. Call for a dinner reservation even if you're not a guest—the experience is worth it.

Portmeirion, Gwynedd, LL48 6ET (off A487, signposted from Minffordd, 2 miles west of Portmeirion). ✆ 01766/770000. Fax 01766/771331. www.portmeirion.com. 37 units. £125–£187 ($200–$299) double; from £235 ($376) suite. AE, DC, MC, V. **Amenities:** 2 restaurants; pool; tennis court; limited room service; babysitting. *In room:* TV, coffeemaker, hair dryer.

CRICCIETH

Now in ruins, **Criccieth Castle** (✆ **01766/522227**), built as a native Welsh stronghold, is on a grassy headland and offers a commanding view of Tremadog Bay. During its years as an active fortress it changed hands, Welsh to English and back and forth, until it was finally sacked and burned in 1404 by Owain Glyndwr, never to rise again as a fortification. The castle houses an interesting exhibition on the theme of the native castles of Welsh princes. On a fine day, from its heights you can see westward to the tip of the peninsula, north and east to Snowdonia, and far down the bay to the south. Admission costs £2.80 ($4.50) for adults or £2 ($3.20) for students and children ages 5 to 16 (children ages 4 and under free). A family ticket goes for £7 ($11). Open April and May daily from 9:30am to 6pm, June through September daily from 9:30am to 6pm. The castle's exhibition center is closed the rest of the year, but you can still head here to enjoy the panoramic view.

About 1¾ miles west of Criccieth in Llanystumdwy, you can visit **Highgate,** the boyhood home of David Lloyd George, prime minister of Britain in the 1914–18 war years, and also the **Lloyd George Memorial Museum** (✆ **01766/522071**), designed by Sir Clough Williams-Ellis of Portmeirion fame. The museum outlines the statesman's life, and the main displays illustrate his political career and include a collection of "freedom" caskets, a "talking head" portrayed by Philip Madoc, the actor, with excerpts of three of Lloyd George's famous speeches, and an audiovisual display. Admission is £4 ($6.40) for adults,

£3 ($4.80) for children, or £8.50 ($14) for a family ticket. From April to June it is open Monday through Saturday from 10:30am to 5pm; July through September daily from 10:30am to 5pm; and October Monday through Friday from 11am to 4pm. Lloyd George's grave is nearby on the banks of the swift-running River Dwyfor, shaded by large oak trees. The name of the hamlet, Llanystumdwy, means "the church at the bend of the River Dwyfor."

St. Cybi's Well, Llangybi, is 6.4km (4 miles) northwest of Criccieth on a minor road. Of 6th-century origin, only two chambers remain of the holy well, although in the mid–18th century a bathhouse was built to surround the font. You can visit it free.

North of the well is the site of a small Iron Age hill fort. **Tourist information** about the Criccieth area is available from Porthmadog (see above).

WHERE TO STAY & DINE

Bron Eifion Country House Hotel ★★ On 5 acres of well-manicured gardens, this baronial mansion is the finest and most elegant place to stay in the area. This tranquil Welsh country estate lies close to the Snowdonia National Park and makes a good base for exploring the area. The interior looks like it would make a good place to stage an Agatha Christie murder mystery. Alan and Carole Thompson are warm and gracious hosts. You'll surely be impressed by their grand stairway and the minstrels' gallery, with its lofty timbered roof. Rooms are spacious and traditionally furnished; some have four-poster beds. Bathrooms are good-sized and well kept. You can wander the lovingly tended gardens evoking the south of France. There's a candlelit restaurant in old conservatory overlooking the floodlit gardens. A special flambé menu is a highlight.

Criccieth, Gwynedd, LL52 0SA. ℂ 800/528-1234 in the U.S., or 01766/522385. Fax 01766/522003. www.broneifion.co.uk. 19 units. £116–£148 ($186–$237) double. MC, V. Lies .8km (½ mile) outside Criccieth on A497 signposted Pwllheli. **Amenities:** Restaurant; room service; babysitting; laundry service. *In room:* TV, coffeemaker, hair dryer, trouser press.

The Lion Hotel *Kids* This former private home from the 19th century lies in the town's most enviable spot: beside the village green behind a painted stone facade. The lager-drinking pubbers of town head here at sundown, and it's a lively, cozy nest for an overnight stop and some good Welsh cookery. Rooms are homelike and often small but comfortably furnished with tidy housekeeping and somewhat cramped bathrooms, most often with shower. There are a few rooms designed to accommodate guests with limited mobility. Families are especially welcome here, as the hotel sets aside separate bedrooms for them, and offers early dinners for children. The inn also has such devices as "baby-listening" facilities along with cots and high chairs that are provided.

In addition to staying in the main building, you can also find lodgings in the Castle Cottage, offering a dozen well-furnished bedrooms. Half of these accommodations open onto panoramic views of the castle.

Y Maes, Criccieth, Gwynedd LA52 LL52. ℂ 01766/522460. Fax 01766/523075. www.lionhotelcriccieth.co.uk. 46 units. £58–£60 ($93–$96) double. Rates include breakfast. AE, DC, MC, V. **Amenities:** Restaurant; pub. *In room:* TV, coffeemaker.

5 Caernarfon ★★★

400km (249 miles) W of London; 100km (68 miles) W of Chester; 48km (30 miles) SE of Holyhead; 14km (9 miles) SW of Bangor.

In the 13th century, when King Edward I of England had defeated the Welsh after long and bitter fighting, he felt the need for a castle in this area as part of his network of fortresses in the still-rebellious country. He ordered its construction on the site of an old Norman castle at the western end of the Menai Strait, where the River Seiont flows into the sea, a place from which his sentinels could command a view of the land around all the way to the mountains and far out across the bay to the Irish Sea. Based either on his first-hand observations (historians believed he might have visited Constantinople during his involvement in the Crusades) or based on ancient drawings of Constantinople procured by his architect, the Savoy-born James St. George, the walls were patterned after the fortifications surrounding ancient Byzantium. Most of the walls of the 13th-century town still stand, although growth outside the walls has been inevitable.

The main reason to flock here today is to see the castle. After that, you will have seen the best of Caernarfon and can press on to another town for the night, or else stay at one of the local inns. The downside? Tourist buses overrun the place in summer. Other than the castle, there is nothing in the town that needs to take up too much of your time.

ESSENTIALS
GETTING THERE   There's no railway station in Caernarfon; the nearest connection is through Bangor to which Caernarfon is linked by bus.

Buses run between Caernarfon and Bangor, a 25-minute ride, every 10 minutes throughout the day. Bus timetables are available either by calling the tourist office (see below), or by dialing © **0870/608-2608.**

From Bangor, head southwest along the A487; from Porthmadog (see above) head north along the A487.

The **Caernarfon Tourist Information Centre** is at Oriel Pendeitsh, 1 Castle St. (© **01286/672232**). From November to April, it's open Thursday through Tuesday from 9:30am to 4:30pm; the rest of the year, it's open daily from 10am to 6pm.

SEEING THE SIGHTS
Every Saturday, a market is held in **Castle Square,** where there's a statue of David Lloyd George, prime minister of Great Britain between 1916 and 1922, who is generally credited, along with King George V, for leading the United Kingdom through the rigors of World War I. He's also credited with introducing what's defined today as Britain's national health care system. Born in Manchester, he was reared on the nearby Lleyn Peninsula, and was later instrumental in preserving the remnants of the town's famous castle (see below).

The nearest thing Wales ever had to a royal palace is **Caernarfon Castle** ✮✮✮, described by Dr. Samuel Johnson after a visit in 1774 as "an edifice of stupendous majesty and strength." Legend has it that after the birth, in 1301, of the son of Edward I in this castle, he showed the infant boy to the Welsh, calling him "the native-born prince who can speak no English." Since that time the title "Prince of Wales" has belonged to every male heir-apparent to the English throne. The eyes of the world were on Caernarfon in 1969 when it was the scene of the investiture of Charles as Prince of Wales.

The castle is open to visitors. Although in some places only the shell of the wall remains, some rooms and stone and wooden steps remain so that you can climb up into it. Eagle Tower has an exhibition on the ground floor showing the history of the fortress and of the town around it. In the northeast are exhibits on the princes of Wales. You can also visit the **Regimental Museum of the Royal Welch Fusiliers** (the regiment retains the Olde English spelling of the word "Welsh"), which occupies all three floors of Queen's Tower and contains many items of interest relating to the regiment and its military history. In 2000, millions of pounds were spent on the renovation and enlargement of this historic castle, with additional exhibition space for the museum set up within the Chamberlain Tower. It is the castle as a whole that's of interest—not one special exhibition or hall. Allow 1½ hours.

Between late May and the end of September, the castle is open daily from 9:30am to 6pm. From Easter to late May, and during all of October, it's open daily from 9:30am to 5pm. From November to Easter, it's open Monday through Saturday from 9:30am to 4pm and Sunday from 11am to 4pm. Admission costs £4.50 ($7.20) for adults, and £3.50 ($5.60) for students and children under age 16. For more information, call © **01286/677617.**

Today the town's quays are less animated than they were during the heyday of the region's slate mining, when boats lined up to haul roofing tiles off to points as far away as London, the United States, the mainland of Europe, and India. In the mid-1990s, a full-service marina, with about 60 slips, was built to accommodate the increasing numbers of yachts and pleasure craft that moor here when not in use. The population of the town today is between 10,000 and 11,000 year-round occupants.

The Romans recognized the strategic importance of northwest Wales and maintained a fort at **Segontium** for some 3 centuries. Excavations on the outskirts of Caernarfon on the A4085 have disclosed foundations of barracks, bathhouses, and other structural remains. Finds from the excavations are displayed in the **museum** (© **01286/675625**) on the site. Open from Easter to late October, Monday through Saturday from 10am to 5pm, Sunday from 2 to 5pm; from November to Easter, it's open Monday through Saturday from 10am to 4pm, Sunday from 2 to 4pm. Admission is free. Some archaeologists and historians think that native Britons may have been displaced from the site, which was one of their strongholds at the time of the Roman invasion. There are no outstanding relics here; allow about 30 minutes to walk about.

WHERE TO STAY

Celtic Royal Hotel ✦ Carved out of a 19th-century grand hotel shell, and massively enlarged, this is the blockbuster and leading choice in town. Its uniformed, well-trained staff grew accustomed long ago to groups of visitors pulling in by motorcoach to see the famous castle, just a 3-minute walk away. The hotel's current look derives from a 1996 face-lift and radical enlargement of what had become a dowdy and outmoded "grand hotel" built in 1843. Today, most of the antique original vestiges lie within the hotel's lobby, with bedrooms and dining facilities placed within modern, three-story wings that contain all of the conveniences you'd expect from a first-class property. The midsize bedrooms are blandly uncontroversial, outfitted in pastels with comfortable furnishings and small bathrooms with shower units. Several rooms have been outfitted for those with limited mobility.

The restaurant is for formal dining, but the Irish Pub, site of nightly live music and a convivial hub, is more fun.

Bangor St., Caernarfon, Gwynedd LL55 1AY. © **01286/674477.** Fax 01286/674139. www.celtic-royal.co.uk. 110 units. £100 ($160) double. Rates include breakfast. AE, MC, V. Free parking. **Amenities:** Restaurant; bar; leisure center with pool; gym; steam room; sauna; 24-hr. room service. *In room:* TV w/pay movies, coffeemaker.

Gwesty Seiont Manor ✦✦ *(Kids)* In the tranquil Welsh countryside, this is one of the best bases for exploring Snowdonia National Park. It can also be an excellent base for visiting the Isle of Anglesey. With a slight exaggeration, the owners proclaim, "We're a Pandora's box of wondrous treasures." Constructed from the original farmstead of a Georgian manor house, the hotel has been tastefully converted into a honeycomb of spacious rooms, each with good-sized bathrooms and all with views over 150 acres of parkland. Eight bedrooms are set aside for nonsmokers. Come here for seclusion, a sense of style, and some of the best leisure facilities in the area. It's also a great family favorite. Several bedrooms are set aside for families and offer VCRs and a selection of children's videos.

The hotel restaurant's award-winning chefs concentrate on local produce when available. We still remember that fresh sea bass with spinach and red pesto sauce.

Llanrug, Caernarfon LL55 2AQ. ✆ **01286/673366.** Fax 01286/672840. www.arcadianhotels.co.uk. 28 units. £165 ($264) double. Rates include breakfast. AE, MC, V. From Caernarfon head east on A4086 for 3.2km (2 miles). **Amenities:** Restaurant; pool; gym; sauna; solarium; room service; babysitting; laundry service. *In room:* TV, coffeemaker, hair dryer.

Stables ★ *Kids* Those who don't like living in a stable should rethink their prejudice. This unusual hotel was constructed around stone stables that were famous locally many years ago for horse breeding. Some of the trained horses here eventually ended up helping fight South Africa's Boer War. Today those stables have been considerably enlarged with modern wings and slate roofs whose materials and angles match those of the original core. Most of the good-sized and comfortably furnished accommodations with commodious private baths are in an L-shaped annex whose innermost corner shelters a swimming pool. Several of the bedrooms have four-poster beds, which we find more desirable; a trio of rooms are rented to families. Just in case you're interested, guests may bring their own horses to the stables here.

Atmospheric dining and drinking facilities have been installed in the oldest part of the original stables. A few of the stall doors have been retained, along with the exposed beams and trusses of the roofline.

Llanwnda, near Caernarfon. Gwynedd LL55 2UF. ✆ **01286/830711.** Fax 01286/830413. www. caernarfon.com/stables.html. 23 units. £59 ($94) double. Rates include breakfast. MC, V. Free parking. From Caernarfon, follow the B4366 9.6km (6 miles) east, and follow signs to Bethel. **Amenities:** Restaurant; pub; room service; babysitting. *In room:* TV, coffeemaker.

Ty'n Rhos Country House Hotel & Restaurant ★★ This is the most charming, best furnished, and most appealing country-house hotel in the neighborhood of Caernarfon. It's the centerpiece of 72 acres of land, some of which is devoted to well-maintained forests and gardens, the remainder of which is leased out to tenant farmers for grazing of sheep and cattle. Maintained as a perky family-owned business by several generations of the Kettle family, it originated in the 19th century as a farmhouse, although the antiques-laden, chintz-draped version you'll see today is a far cry from its original humble origins. Log fires blaze in the rustic-looking lounge, a dining room (see below) attracts nonguests from the region, and couples looking for a romantic interlude in the Merry Old Wales of long ago have been known to disappear into the bedrooms for weekends. Guests enjoy bird-watching walks around the private lake, and strolls on the footpaths that meander across the sprawling property. The midsize and nonsmoking bedrooms are attractively furnished with tidily kept bathrooms adjoining. All units have a complete bathroom, except two, which have showers instead of tubs. One room is equipped for guests in wheelchairs. The lounge with its slate inglenook fireplace offers an impressive collection of whiskies.

Llanddeiniolen LL55 3AE. ✆ **01248/670489.** Fax 01248/670079. www.tynrhos.co.uk. 14 units. £70–£90 ($112–$144) double. Rates include breakfast. AE, MC, V. Free parking. From Caernarfon, take the B4366 for 9.6km (6 miles) east, following the signs to Bethel. **Amenities:** Restaurant; bar; room service; croquet. *In room:* TV, dataport, coffeemaker, hair dryer.

WHERE TO DINE

Ty'n Rhos Country Hotel & Restaurant CONTINENTAL   The most endearing restaurant in the vicinity of Caernarfon occupies the elegant premises of what was originally built in the 1800s as a simple farmhouse, and which was intensely gentrified by the resident owners. Meals are served with views out toward manicured gardens and inward to the sight and scents of at least one blazing log fireplace. This is good country cooking without pretensions. Fresh produce is served, and the cuisine is strong on flavors but not overpoweringly so. The menu changes, but we've particularly enjoyed such dishes as Welsh lamb sausage with creamy potatoes served with a sweet-onion sauce, just like your Welsh grandmother used to make. Rack of lamb also appears in a more modern version infused with a fresh rosemary sauce with a lemon-flavored couscous serving as an added delight. The creamy leeks with saffron sauce overpower the grilled sea bass, however. Save room for that glazed lemon tart with nutmeg custard and homegrown rhubarb as an accompaniment.

Llanddeiniolen (for directions, see above). ✆ **01248/670489.** Reservations recommended. Fixed-price dinners £19 ($30). AE, MC, V. Daily 6:30–8:15pm.

6 The Isle of Anglesey ⋆⋆⋆⋆

The Welsh name of this island is Mon (the Romans called it Mona), and it is called Mon, Mam Cymru, or Anglesey, Mother of Wales. If this is true, we must say that the child doesn't much resemble the mother. The scenery differs totally from that of the mainland, with low-lying farmland interrupted here and there by rocky outcrops. The landscape is dotted with single-story whitewashed cottages, and the rolling green fields stretch down to the sea—all against a backdrop of the mountains of Snowdonia across the Menai Strait, which divides this island from the rest of Wales.

Visitors cross the strait by one of the two bridges built by celebrated engineers of the 19th century; the **Menai Suspension Bridge,** designed by Thomas Telford and completed in 1826, and the **Britannia Bridge,** originally a railroad bridge, which was the work of Robert Stephenson. The Britannia, a neighbor of the suspension bridge, had to be rebuilt after a devastating fire that destroyed its pitch and timberwork; it now carries both trains and cars on two different levels. The bridges are about a mile west of Bangor on the mainland.

Many people have passed through Anglesey on the train that operates between London and Holyhead, for a ferry journey to Ireland. A stopover for a day in Anglesey is recommended. Neolithic tombs of Stone Age settlers have been found on the island, as have Iron Age artifacts. The Romans left artifacts behind, as did the early Christians who settled here.

The coming of steamers and then of the railroad brought Victorian-era visitors. However, if you're not really sold on antiquity, there's a lot to do on Anglesey that is totally in tune with today. Yachting, sea fishing, and leisure centers that offer swimming, squash, and other activities are within easy reach wherever you stay. Golf, tennis, nature walks, pony trekking, canoeing—whatever—are offered in the daytime, and in the evening you can wine, dine, even dance to the latest music.

To find out about activities on the island, call or write for a brochure from the **Wales Tourist Board Information Centre,** Railway Station Site, Llanfairpwll-gwyngyllgogerychwyrndrobwllllantysiliogogogoch, Isle of Anglesey (© **01248/ 713177**). Open April through October Monday through Saturday from 9:30am to 5:30pm and Sunday from 10am to 5pm; November through March, Monday through Friday from 9:30am to 1pm and 1:30 to 5pm, and Sunday from 10am to 5pm.

The island has good bus service. For information about bus service on the island, call **Arriva Cymru** at © **0870/608-2608.** The major route (bus no. 4) runs between Bangor and Holyhead via Llangefni. Buses operate at the rate of two per hour during the day Monday through Saturday, but on Sunday service is curtailed to six buses. Bus no. 56 goes from Bangor to Beaumaris every 30 minutes during the day Monday through Saturday; on Sunday, only two buses make the run. All buses cross the Menai Bridge at the town of Menai Bridge (see below).

Menai Bridge   The small town of Menai Bridge, 4km (2½ miles) west of Bangor, has several points of interest. Take a stroll westward along the Belgian Promenade, a walk constructed along the strait during World War II by Belgian refugees. You can go under the bridge, past some standing stones which were recently erected and Coed Cyrnol, a pinewood, to **Church Island.** The island's 14th-century **Church of St. Tysilio** was originally founded in the 7th century by St. Tysilio, son of the royal house of Powys and grandson of St. Pabo. St. Pabo is believed to have been a northern British chief who sought asylum on Anglesey. There is no phone to call for information, and hours are erratic.

Menai Bridge is the site every October 24 of the **Ffair-y-Borth fair,** which has been held here since the 16th century. Today it's really a flea market, not worth a trip unless you're in the area.

This is an excellent place from which to view the Menai Strait sailing regatta in August each year.

For information, the little **tourist office** (© **01248/713177**) lies on High Street in the Pringle Sweater Shop. Its hours are irregular, depending on volunteers.

WHERE TO STAY & DINE

Gazelle   This former posting inn beside the Menai Straits is your top choice for a combined hotel, restaurant, and pub in the area. If you're arriving late in the day, it can be your overnight stopover and gateway to Anglesey, which you can explore the next day. Three miles from the center of Menai Bridge, beside the road signposted to Beaumaris, the hotel's quayside pub has panoramic views of both the waterfront and the mountains. It's the best place to meet locals and visitors, the latter of whom often have yachts moored nearby. The inn is attractively decorated; old Welsh dressers and time-blackened settles give the place character. Bedrooms are small to moderate in size, each simply decorated but comfortable. Bathrooms are just adequate for the function—nothing more. Some guests have to use the bathrooms in the hallways.

Substantial bar meals are served as well as full dinners in the restaurant. Solid Welsh fare includes fresh fish and local lamb. The Gazelle has the best food in the area, so try to dine here even if you're not staying as a guest.

Glyn Garth, Menai Bridge, Isle of Anglesey LL59 5PD. © 01248/713364. Fax 01248/713167. 8 units, 5 with bathrooms. £62 ($99) double. MC, V. 3.2km (2 miles) northeast of Menai Bridge along A545. Amenities: Restaurant; limited room service; babysitting. *In room:* TV, coffeemaker.

LLANFAIR PG (LLANFAIRPWLLGWYNGYLLGOGERYCHWYRN-DROBWLLLLANTYSILIOGOGOGOCH)

Practically a suburb of Menai Bridge is a village to the west that has been heard of all over the world. Its fame is its name: Llanfairpwllgwyngyllgogerychwyrn-drobwllllantysiliogogogoch, or something like that. It means "St. Mary's Church in the Hollow of the White Hazel near a Rapid Whirlpool and the Church of St. Tysilio near the Red Cave." The thought has been voiced that perhaps the name was invented as a tourist attraction. You can get the longest train platform ticket in the world from the station here, giving the full name. On maps and most references it is usually called "Llanfair PG" to differentiate it from several other Llanfairs in Wales. The first Women's Institute in Britain was founded here in 1915.

You're sure to see the **Marquess of Anglesey's column,** standing 27m (90 ft.) high on a mount 76m (250 ft.) above sea level. It has a statue of the marquess on top, to which visitors can climb (115 steps up a spiral staircase). The marquess lost a leg while he was second in command to the duke of Wellington at Waterloo and was thereafter called "One Leg" ("Ty Coch" in Welsh).

SEEING THE SIGHTS
PLASNEWYDD

A mile southwest of the village with the long name, on the A4080, from a turn off the A5 almost opposite the Marquess of Anglesey Column, is **PlasNewydd, Llanfairpwll** ✦✦ (✆ **01248/714795;** www.nationaltrust.org.uk), standing on the shores of the Menai Straits. It was the home of the seventh marquess of Anglesey, but is now owned by the National Trust. An ancient manor house, it was converted between 1783 and 1809 into a splendid mansion in the Gothic and neoclassical styles. Its Gothic Hall features a gallery and elaborate fan vaulting. In the long dining room, see the magnificent *trompe-l'oeil* mural by Rex Whistler. A military museum houses relics and uniforms of the Battle of Waterloo where the first marquess of Anglesey lost his leg. The beautiful woodland garden and lawns are worth visiting. The mansion is open to visitors. The gardens are open daily from 11am to 5:30pm from April to November, whereas the home can be visited only Saturday through Wednesday from noon to 5pm, also from April to November. A combined ticket for both the house and garden costs £5 ($8) for adults and £3 ($4.80) for children under age 16.

WHERE TO STAY

Carreg Bran Country Hotel Set at the edge of the village, within a 10-minute walk from the center, this hotel dates from the late 1800s, when it was a privately owned manor house. Today, much-altered and enlarged from its original design, it sports a white-painted brick facade and a modern wing that contains the simple but efficient and well-scrubbed small to midsize bedrooms, with little bathrooms containing shower stalls. Seven units are rented to nonsmokers. This is the only conventional hotel in town, providing more rooms than any of its smaller and less accessorized competitors. Since the building's transformation into a hotel occurred during the mid-1970s, some of the infrastructure might seem a bit dated, but overall, it provides comfortable and safe lodgings.

Church Lane. Llanfair PG, Anglesey LL61 5YH. ✆ **800/528-1234** in the U.S., or 01248/714224. Fax 01248/715983 www.carregbran.uk.com. 29 units. £69 ($110) double. Rates include breakfast. AE, DC, MC, V. **Amenities:** Restaurant; pub; cocktail lounge. *In room:* TV, coffeemaker.

WHERE TO DINE

Penrohos Arms BRITISH/WELSH   In the town with the long name, this is your best bet for pub grub for the night. It's especially inviting after you've climbed the Anglesey monument and are ready for a cold beer. You can't miss it, as it lies in the center of the village opposite the famous rail station of the village with the impossible name. The food is typical and standard, but it's made from fresh ingredients. If you like steak with mushrooms, fried seafood, or sausage and mashed potatoes, this is for you.

The pub also lets four bedrooms, each comfortable and costing £35 ($56) double, with breakfast included. Expect a TV and a small cubicle with a shower and toilet. Rooms have a chintz-filled decor inspired by Laura Ashley, but no phones. Views from the bedroom windows overlook the peaks of Snowdonia.

Holyhead Rd. Llanfair PG, Angelsey, LL61 5YQ. © **01248/714620.** Reservations not needed. Main courses £6.25–£13 ($10–$21); lunch platters £2.25–£4 ($3.60–$6.40). DC, MC, V. Mon–Sat 11am–9pm; Sun noon–2pm and 6–9pm.

7 Holyhead & Holy Island

550km (342 miles) NW of London; 346km (215 miles) NW of Cardiff; 305km (190 miles) N of Swansea

The largest town on Anglesey, Holyhead (it's pronounced Holly-head—don't ask us why) is not actually on Anglesey at all but on Holy Island. However, the two islands have long been linked. Packet boats between Holyhead and Ireland were recorded as far back at 1573.

The harbor of Holyhead was reconstructed in 1880 and now serves as a terminal for container-bearing ships.

People have come to this far point of northern Wales for a long, long time by water. Celtic invaders, early Christian missionaries, Romans, Vikings—whoever—have made their way here and in many cases stayed on for centuries.

ESSENTIALS

GETTING THERE   Holyhead is the terminus of the **North Wales Coast** rail line. Trains arrive hourly during the day from Cardiff, Bangor, Llandudno, Chester, Birmingham, and London. For information and schedules, call © **0845/748-4950. Arriva** buses pull into Holyhead from Bangor every 30 minutes during the day. There is no station here, buses arriving along both London Road and Market Street. For information and schedules, call © **0845/604-0500.**

A causeway carries motorists across on the A5, which has come all the way from London, and a Four Mile Bridge on B4545 also links Holy Island to Anglesey.

Two unrelated ferryboat companies operate service between Holyhead and the Irish port of Dun Laoghaire, a railway and highway junction close to Dublin. (Some of them continue on even into Dublin harbor.) Both companies run both conventional ferryboat service (transit time 3½ hours each way, with two departures daily). Both types of conveyance are suitable for both passengers and cars, although the catamarans cannot carry freight. Transit costs £20 ($32) round-trip on the conventional ferryboats; £30 ($48) round-trip on the catamarans for passengers traveling and returning on the same days. For more information, contact either the **Stena Line** (© **0870/570-7070;** www.stenaline.co.uk) or **Irish Ferries** (© **0870/532-9129;** www.irishferries.ie).

VISITOR INFORMATION   Information is available at the **Kiosk,** Stena Line, Terminal 1 (© **01407/762622**), open daily in summer from 8:30am to

6pm. From October to March hours are from 10am to 4:30pm Monday through Saturday.

SEEING THE SIGHTS

Holyhead Mountain 🎯 is the highest point in Anglesey, at 216m (710 ft.). From the rocky height you can see the Isle of Man, the Mourne Mountains in Ireland, Snowdonia, and Cumbria on a clear day. The summit is the site of an ancient hill fort and the ruins of an Irish settlement from the 2nd to the 4th century A.D. The towering cliffs of North and South Stack are home to thousands of sea birds, and gray seals breed in the caves below. At the southern point of the mountain, **South Stack** is an automatic lighthouse built in 1808. It's 27m (91 ft.) high (60m/197 ft. above mean high water) and can be seen for 32km (20 miles). It's noted for its antique walls, its strategic position, and a state-of-the-art light beam. Open March through September daily from 8am to 6pm, charging £4 ($6.40) for adults or £3 ($4.80) for children under age 16. For information, contact the **Royal Society for the Protection of Birds** at ✆ **01407/763043.**

On Friday and Saturday, **general markets** are held in Holyhead.

St. Cybi's Church, Market Street (no phone), near the town center, is on the site of a 6th-century church; a Roman fort from the 3rd century also stood here. The site is open daily from 8am to 6pm; admission is free. For information, contact the tourist office (see above).

WHERE TO STAY & DINE

Boathouse Hotel If you decide to overnight before taking a ferry in the morning, this, the town's finest inn, is just a few minutes' walk away from the terminal. It lies in a stellar position looking out over the water and the Holyhead Mountains, which can be seen through the bedroom windows. The midsize bedrooms are pleasantly and comfortably furnished, and the bathrooms, though small, are spick-and-span, with shower units. Most of the accommodations are nonsmoking, and one unit is large enough for families.

Newry Promenade, Newry Beach, Holyhead LL65 1YF. ✆ **01407/762094.** Fax 01407/764898. www.boathouse-hotel.co.uk. 17 units. £65–£70 ($104–$112) double. Rates include breakfast. AE, MC, V. **Amenities:** Bar lounge with food service; room service. *In room:* TV, coffeemaker.

Bull Hotel *Kids* A bustling hotel, the long-popular Bull stands right at the approach to Holyhead. We'd give its competitor, the Boathouse, a slight edge, but the Bull is almost as good. We prefer the more comfortable midsize rooms in the main building, as opposed to the newer and more sterile ones in the annex, but both are comfortable, containing tidy bathrooms with showers. Four rooms are large enough for families. Because of its popular bars, the Bull is much patronized by the locals.

London Rd. Valley, Holyhead LL65 3DP. ✆ **01407/740351.** Fax 01407/742328. 14 units. £55 ($87) double. Rates include breakfast. AE, DC, MC, V. **Amenities:** 2 bars serving food. *In room:* TV, coffeemaker.

8 Conwy 🎯

387km (241 miles) NW of London; 59km (37 miles) E of Holyhead; 35km (22 miles) NE of Caernarfon

Unlike Llandudno, its 19th-century neighbor, Conwy is an ancient town. With its mighty medieval castle and complete town walls, this is a richly historic place.

The Conwy estuary is crossed by three **bridges** that lead to Conwy. The handsome suspension bridge was built in 1826 by Thomas Telford, bridge-builder extraordinaire. It looks as if it runs right into the castle, but it doesn't. It's closed to vehicular traffic now, but you can walk across it for free and marvel at how it served as the main entrance to the town for so long, with its narrow lanes and the sure bottleneck at the castle end. It replaced the ferry that was previously the only means of crossing the river. An exhibit of Telford's work is in the tollhouse. You can also see Robert Stephenson's tubular railroad bridge built in 1848, and the modern arched road bridge, completed in 1958.

St. Mary's, the parish church, stands inside the town walls on the site of 12th-century Cistercian abbey. In it are a Byzantine processional cross, a beautiful Tudor cross, and a 15th-century screen of fine workmanship. Look at the churchyard, which contains a grave associated with William Wordsworth's poem "We Are Seven."

ESSENTIALS

GETTING THERE   Trains run between Conwy and Llandudno, Bangor, and Holyhead, with easy connections to the rest of Wales. Llandudno is only a 4-minute ride away. For schedules and information, call ✆ **0845/604-0500.**

Arriva buses from Bangor heading for Llandudno pass through Conwy every 20 minutes during the day. Call ✆ **0870/608-2608** for schedules and more information. Motorists from England head west along the North Wales coastline on A548.

VISITOR INFORMATION   The local tourist board at the **Conwy Castle Visitor Centre,** Castle Street (✆ **01492/592248**), dispenses information from Easter to October daily from 9:30am to 4pm; the rest of the year, Friday, Saturday, and Monday from 11am to 4pm.

SEEING THE SIGHTS

Aberconwyu House   This is the only remaining medieval merchant's house in Conwy, a town that used to have hundreds of them. Dating from the 14th century, this structure is even older than Plas Mawr. Owned by the National Trust, the building houses an exhibition depicting the life of Conwy from Roman times. It includes a re-created 18th-century kitchen and a mussel-fishing corner, with the traditional instruments still used by the industry.

Castle St. and High St. ✆ 01492/592246. Admission £2.20 ($3.50) adults, £1.10 ($1.75) children under age 16, £5.50 ($8.80) family ticket. Mar 29–Nov 2 Wed–Mon 11am–5pm.

Conwy Castle ★★   The town centers around Conwy Castle. Edward I had this masterpiece of medieval architecture built after he conquered the last native prince of Wales, Llewelyn. The English king put up massive castles to convince the Welsh that he was the supreme authority. The castle follows the contours of a narrow strip of rock, the eight towers commanding the estuary of the River Conwy. The town wall that protected the borough, chartered by Edward in 1284, is almost intact, with 21 flanking towers and three twin-towered gateways. Visitors to the town can walk the walls. This is one castle you can't possibly miss seeing, as the road runs almost close enough for you to touch the walls in place. Allow an hour to visit.

Castle St. ✆ 01492/592358. www.castlewales.com/conwy.html. Admission £3.50 ($5.60) adults, £3 ($4.80) children under 16. Apr–May and Oct daily 9:30am–5pm; June–Sept daily 9:30am–6pm; Nov–Mar Mon–Sat 9:30am–4pm, Sun 11am–4pm. Closed Dec 24–26, Jan 1.

Plas Mawr   Built between 1576 and 1585 for the Welsh merchant Robert Wynn, this is one of the finest surviving examples in Britain of an Elizabethan-era town house. Although there are many excellent examples of Elizabethan manors still standing, there aren't that many town houses. Restored today, the house is noted for its plasterwork ceilings. A short visit should take only 20 minutes.

High St. Ⓒ **01492/580167.** www.conwy.com/plasmawr.html. Admission £4 ($6.40) adults, £3 ($4.80) children. Apr–May and Sept Tues–Sun 9:30am–5pm; June–Aug Tues–Sun 9:30am–6pm; Oct Tues–Sun 9:30am–4pm.

Smallest House in Britain   Listed in the *Guinness Book of World Records* as the "smallest" house, this building is on the quayside. It looks as if someone had a narrow space between two other structures and decided to utilize it by building the tiny house, which measures something like 3m (10 ft.) long by 1.8m (6 ft.) wide. Its outdoor privy at the rear is now gone.

The Quay. Ⓒ **01492/593484.** Admission 50p (80¢) adults, 30p (50¢) children. Apr–June and Sept to mid-Oct daily 10am–6pm; July–Aug daily 10am–9:30pm.

WHERE TO STAY & DINE

Groes Inn 🌟🌟   Oozing with four centuries of atmosphere and old-fashioned charm, this is for nostalgia buffs, as it dates back to 1573 and was the first licensed house in Wales. Although it has expanded over the years, the original core is still here, evoked by log fires, antiques, and open-beamed, time-blackened ceilings. For history buffs, it's the finest choice in the area. The accommodations are in a separate house away from the noise of the pub, and each midsize unit is comfortably furnished and equipped with a modernized bathroom. Rooms open onto bucolic views of sheep grazing in the fields and of rolling hills. The best units have balconies or private terraces. One room has a four-poster bed and another is set up for guests in wheelchairs. Stop in for a lager or a pub dinner of hearty, home-cooked food.

Tyn-y-Groes, Conwy. LL32 8TN. Ⓒ **01492/650545.** Fax 01492/650855. www.groesinn.com. 14 units. £85–£135 ($136–$216) double. AE, DC, MC, V. Lies 3 miles south of Conwy on B5106. **Amenities:** Restaurant; pub. *In room:* TV, coffeemaker, hair dryer.

The Old Rectory 🌟   The Welsh motto for the house, *Hardd Hafan Hedd,* means a beautiful haven of peace—and so it is. From its hillside perch, with terraced gardens, the inn sweeps across the Conwy Estuary for a view of Conwy Castle and the Snowdonia mountain range. Once the Tudor home of the rectors of the parish for centuries, it is furnished with paintings and antiques. A night here is like entering a bygone era. Each good-sized bedroom has its own charm and style; a few have four-poster or half-tester beds. Comfort is foremost, from the sleep-inducing bed to the well-maintained private bath.

Wendy Vaughan is a grand chef, producing high-quality and creative dishes that have delicacy, a light touch, and artistic presentation. Call for a reservation. The Conwy salmon is a winner, and hormone-free meats are served, including succulent mountain Welsh lamb.

Llansanffraid, Glan Conwy, Conwy LL28 5LF. Ⓒ **01492/580611.** Fax 01492/584555. www.oldrectorycountry house.co.uk. 6 units. £52–£72 ($83–$115) double. Take the A470 4.8km (3 miles) from Conwy; Old Rectory .8km (½ mile) south from A55/A470 junction on the left. No children under age 5. **Amenities:** Restaurant; bar. *In room:* TV, coffeemaker.

9 Llandudno 🌟

243 miles NW of London; 43 miles E of Holyhead

This Victorian seaside resort—the largest in Wales—nestles in a crescent between the giant headlands of the **Great Orme** and the **Little Orme,** which received their names from early Vikings who thought they resembled sea

Llandudno

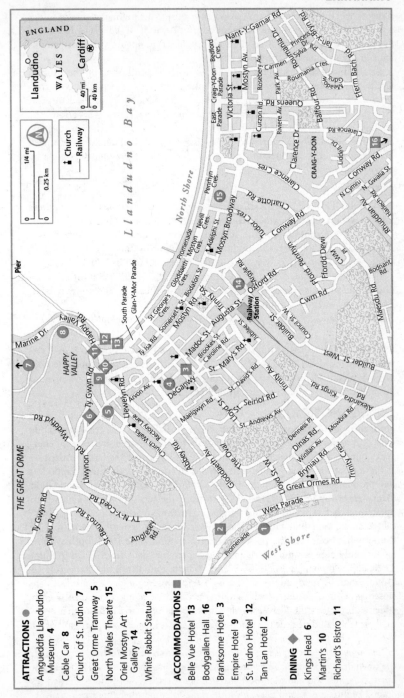

ATTRACTIONS ●
Amgueddfa Llandudno
  Museum **4**
Cable Car **8**
Church of St. Tudno **7**
Great Orme Tramway **5**
North Wales Theatre **15**
Oriel Mostyn Art
  Gallery **14**
White Rabbit Statue **1**

ACCOMMODATIONS ■
Belle Vue Hotel **13**
Bodygallen Hall **16**
Branksome Hotel **3**
Empire Hotel **9**
St. Tudno Hotel **12**
Tan Lan Hotel **2**

DINING ◆
Kings Head **6**
Martin's **10**
Richard's Bistro **11**

serpents when their bases were shrouded in mist. This premier resort of Wales has two beaches, one on the northern edge of town, flanking a boardwalk and the Irish Sea, and the other on the west side of town, opening onto the mountains of Snowdonia and the Conwy Estuary.

Llandudno is a resort that was built beginning around 1850 by the Mostyn family, after whom many local roads, avenues, and sites are named. It was conceived as a means to cash in on the already-proven proclivity of the British of Queen Victoria's day—particularly the great middle classes—to go to the seashore in summer. It is built in a typically Victorian way with a promenade along the beach. The Victorian elegance and tradition of Llandudno has been maintained in the architecture of its buildings, but there the days-gone-by atmosphere stops.

ESSENTIALS

GETTING THERE   **BritRail** operates about six trains a day from London's Euston Station, many of which require changes of equipment in either Crewe or Chester, and in some cases, both. Overall, with waiting time included, it takes about 2½ hours to reach Llandudno from London by train. For information about this or any other railway schedule in Wales, call ℂ **0845/604-0500.**

During the day, the **Arriva Bus Company** (ℂ **0870/608-2608** for information about any bus timetable in Wales) maintains buses to and from Bangor. They depart every 60 minutes.

From England, take the M6 to the M56, then head across North Wales along the A55.

VISITORS INFORMATION   The **Llandudno Tourist Information Centre,** 1–2 Chapel St. (ℂ **01492/876413**) is open between April and October every day from 10am to 6pm. From November to March, it's open Monday to Wednesday, Friday, and Saturday from 9:30am to 4:30pm.

SEEING THE SIGHTS

From the summit of the **Great Orme** ⚡ (206m/679 feet) you get a panoramic view of the North Wales coast. You can walk up to the top if you're really energetic, but we advise other means. At Happy Valley, exotic sheltered gardens lie at the foot of the Great Orme, near the pier at the west end of the Llandudno Bay promenade. Take either the **Cable Car** (ℂ **01492/877205**) or the **Great Orme Tramway** (ℂ **01492/574237**) to reach the top. The Cable Car, which operates with a series of counterweights equivalent to what's used to haul the cable cars of San Francisco, is the longest cable-car system in Britain. The tramway has been carrying passengers to the summit since 1902. Both systems operate only between mid-April and mid-September, daily from 10am to 6pm. The Cable Car charges £6.20 ($9.90) per person, round-trip; the Tram costs £4 ($6.40) round-trip for adults, £2.80 ($4.50) for children under age 14. Both are closed in winter, during which period you can drive along a spectacular cliff-edge road, the Marine Drive, which winds uphill in a circular route that eventually reaches a point near the summit of the Great Orme. Cars pay a toll of £1 ($1.60) each.

Just above the Marine Drive is the ancient **Church of St. Tudno,** from which the town derives its name. The present stone building dates to the 12th century, but the church was founded 600 years earlier. Between April and October, it's open 24 hours a day, and between June and September there are open-air worship services every Sunday at 11am. For more information about the church and its services, or to gain entrance during other times of the year, contact the Reverend P. Cousins at © **01492/876624.**

At the end of the north-shore promenade, one of Britain's finest Victorian piers was built jutting 699m (2,295 ft.) out into the bay at the base of the Great Orme, with an ornate covered pavilion at the end. You can find entertainment, food, fishing, or just relaxation on the pier. The north-shore beach is busy in summer, with traditional British seaside activities, including donkey rides, Punch and Judy shows, boat trips, and a children's funland across the promenade.

The seafront's most visible public monument is the **North Wales Theatre,** The Promenade (© **01492/872000**). Built in the early 1990s, it had what amounted to the longest stage in Britain, until the more recent construction of a theater in Bournemouth surpassed it by a mere 6 inches (15cm). Throughout the year, it's the venue for a changing roster of entertainment that includes everything from opera to rock 'n' roll concerts. Recent performances have included *Phantom of the Opera on Ice.*

The west shore is more tranquil, with its sandy beach on the shore of Conwy Bay where the estuary broadens out to join the Irish Sea. Along its promenade is the **White Rabbit Statue,** which commemorates the link of *Alice in Wonderland* with Llandudno. The real Alice Liddell was the daughter of Henry Liddell, dean of Christ Church, Oxford, who had honeymooned here with Alice's mother. They established a summer home here. Lewis Carroll (Charles Dodgson) was a house guest of the Liddells. Fond of children, he spent many hours with Alice, spinning stories for her enjoyment. It is almost certain that she was the inspiration for his classic tales.

Oriel Mostyn Art Gallery, 12 Vaughan St. (© **01492/879201**), has a series of free temporary exhibitions as well as some evening events. There is a design and crafts shop here. It is open Monday through Saturday from 10am to 5pm.

Amgueddfa Llandudno Museum, 17–19 Gloddaeth St. (© **01492/ 876517**), displays development of Llandudno as a seaside resort. Period rooms are open to viewers. It is open Monday through Saturday from 10am to 12:45pm and again from 2pm, closing at 5pm from May to August and at 4pm the rest of the year. Admission is £1.50 ($2.40) for adults, 75p ($1.20) for children, £3.50 ($5.60) family ticket.

WHERE TO STAY

Martins (see "Where to Dine," below) also rents rooms.

VERY EXPENSIVE

Bodysgallen Hall ★★★ *(Finds)*   This is the finest address in the north of Wales, a dramatic 17th-century country house set in 200 acres of parkland and manicured gardens. It would be the only suitable address for the novelist Henry James, were he alive today. Skillfully restored, it offers architectural merit combined with 21st-century comfort. The hall has a 13th-century tower hat was a lookout post for Conwy Castle, 2.5km (1½ miles) away. You can still climb it today for a panoramic view. Each of the spacious and elegantly furnished bedrooms evokes a certain period in their styles and colors; some have four-poster beds. Bathrooms are large and state of the art. Some of the units, as good as those in the main house, are in converted cottages. Wherever you wander, the past is evoked with wood-paneled walls, oil paintings, and open fires.

One snippy British food critic felt that after 2 days the menu in the restaurant becomes monotonous. We once based here for a week, however, and found infinite variety in game, including pigeon and venison, and local fare such as smoked salmon and Welsh rabbit, even Welsh veal in an old-fashioned honey and mead sauce. Call for a reservation if staying elsewhere; it's a memorable culinary experience, in cuisine, atmosphere, and service.

2 miles southeast along A470 from Llandudno, Llandudno LL30 IRS. © **800/260-8338** in the U.S., or 01492/584466. Fax 01492/582519. www.bodysgallen.com. 35 units. £165–£270 ($265–$432) double. MC, V. Free parking. No children under age 8. **Amenities:** Restaurant; bar; indoor pool; tennis court; health club; spa; laundry service. *In room:* TV/VCR, dataport, fridge, hair dryer.

EXPENSIVE

Empire Hotel ★★★ In an ocean of tacky hotels, this one is a winner, the best within the town itself, equaled only by the more deluxe Bodysgallen Hall outside. It is, in fact, one of the best hotels in North Wales. Off the Promenade, near the Great Orme cable car, it looks down on the pier and Happy Valley, about 274m (300 yards) away. Family managed, it is furnished with antiques and fine paintings in the Victorian tradition. Bedrooms are medium-sized to spacious—luxuriously furnished with excellent marble bathrooms, which are impeccably kept. A Victorian annex, known as "Number 72," contains eight of the establishment's finest rooms, filled with Victorian antiques, French linen, touches of silk, and a bathtub-cum-Jacuzzi. We prefer these to the accommodations in the main building. You get luxury and style throughout, and not a lot of attitude. The public areas carry out the Victorian theme, and are known for their collection of Russell Flint prints.

The award-winning Watkins restaurant presents an excellent fixed-price menu changed daily and based whenever possible on local produce.

Church Walks, Llandudno, Conwy LL30 2HE. © **01492/860555.** Fax 01492/860791. www.empirehotel. co.uk. 58 units. £60–£100 ($96–$160) double; £110 ($176) suite, AE, DC, MC, V. Free parking. **Amenities:** Restaurant; bar; 2 pools; solarium; sauna; room service; laundry service; beauty treatments; live entertainment. *In room:* TV, coffeemaker, hair dryer.

St. Tudno Hotel ★★ For fans of *Alice in Wonderland*, this is the only place to stay in town. Alice Liddell, immortalized by Lewis Carroll in *Alice in Wonderland*, checked in here at the age of 8 on her first visit to Llandudno in 1861. It's a charming Victorian terraced seafront hotel that escapes the tacky curse of many of its neighbors. The hotel has kept abreast of the times—you won't fall down the rabbit hole if checking in here. We'd rank this as one of the top seafront hotels in North Wales. Richly decorated inside, it is opulent and luxurious, with first-class service. Martin and Janette Bland offer a beautiful product with individually designed bedrooms that come in a variety of sizes. Rooms in the rear have slightly less glamour but are more tranquil and a lot cheaper. Traditionalists prefer to check into the Alice Suite. Public rooms evoke the Victorian era.

If you're not a guest, call for a dinner reservation, as St. Tudno offers some of the area's finest dining. Local seafood gets prominently featured (try the Conwy mussel risotto with saffron). The Welsh specials have flair—not the usual drab British resort food. Chefs aren't faint-hearted about tossing alcohol into the skillets to enhance flavor.

North Promenade, Llandudno, Gwynedd LL30 2LP. © **01492/874411.** Fax 01492/860407. www.st-tudno. co.uk. 18 units. £180–£205 ($288–$328) double; £320 ($512) Alice Suite. Rates include breakfast. AE, MC, V. Free parking. **Amenities:** Restaurant; bar; heated indoor pool; room service; babysitting. *In room:* TV, coffeemaker, hair dryer.

MODERATE

Tan Lan Hotel ★ *Value* This is your best for the night if you're seeking good value accommodations on the tranquil west shore of Llandudno near the White

Rabbit Memorial. It lies under the Great Orme, and its owners offer cozy lodgings and a warm welcome. The rooms upstairs are a bit quieter, but all are medium-sized and brightly decorated and well-furnished, with firm mattresses and small but adequate bathrooms that are kept immaculately clean. A trio of units are big enough for families and children get a warm welcome. All bedrooms are nonsmoking. Owners Kerry and Peter Saunders are a font of information about touring in the area.

The dining room, decorated in the best tradition of the English play *Separate Tables*, is known for a varied menu—nothing too experimental, however.

Great Orme's Rd., West Shore, Llandudno, Conwy LL30 2AR. © **01492/860221.** Fax 01492/870219. www. tanlanhotel.co.uk. 17 units. £46–£54 ($74–$86) double. Rates include breakfast. MC, V. Free parking. **Amenities:** Restaurant; bar; 2 lounges; garden for drinks. *In room:* TV, coffeemaker, hair dryer.

INEXPENSIVE

Belle Vue Hotel   This hotel is one of the best examples of Victorian architecture in a town filled with worthy competitors. Set adjacent to the boardwalk, its elaborately gabled and bow-windowed facade overlooks the seafront and the busy activities that take place there, especially in midsummer. Inside, a high-ceilinged, engagingly old-fashioned series of only slightly dowdy public rooms lead toward equivalently proportioned bedrooms. Many of them contain formal, slightly fussy furniture that's offset by the large dimensions and the sense of late-19th-century nostalgia. The well-maintained bathrooms, however, are modern.

26 North Parade, Llandudno LL30 2LP. © **01492/879547.** Fax 01492/870001. www.thebellevuehotel.co.uk. 13 units. £60–£72 ($96–$115) double. Rates include breakfast. MC, V. **Amenities:** Restaurant; bar; sun terrace. *In room:* TV, coffeemaker.

Branksome Hotel   Serviceable and unpretentious, and set midway between the town's "two shores," this hotel offers reasonably priced accommodations within a setting (ca. 1910) that was radically enlarged and upgraded in 1997, when private bathrooms were added to each of the simple, no-nonsense bedrooms. Despite a location near the heart of town, the establishment's bar and restaurant are patronized almost exclusively by residents of the hotel, usually "commercial gents" (traveling salesmen) during winter, and holiday beachgoers during July and August, rather than by local townspeople. There's some kind of live entertainment in the bar every night, either a pianist or perhaps a father-daughter musical duet, and a small dance floor. The small to midsize rooms are well furnished, sporting tiny but tidy bathrooms equipped with shower stalls.

62 Lloyd St. Llandudno, Gwynedd LL30 2YP. ©/fax **01492/875989.** 51 units. £48–£56 ($77–$90) double. Rates include breakfast. DC, MC, V. Free parking. **Amenities:** Restaurant. *In room:* TV, coffeemaker.

WHERE TO DINE

Kings Head ✿ BRITISH/INTERNATIONAL   This is the oldest and most evocative pub in town, with a 300-year-old pedigree, a prominent logo that features every Brit's favorite royal, Henry VIII, and bottle-glass windows. This place used to welcome scores of miners, and in their memory, instead of a ploughman's lunch of bread and cheese, it offers a miner's platter (essentially the same, we find.) All arriving patrons enter the establishment by passing through the pub, then remain for either a pint or two, or settle down for a meal that's available either within the pub, or within a separate dining room. Lunches are simpler than dinners and feature standard but not exceptional dishes, such an excellent—and always popular—version of steak and ale pie. Dinners are more elaborate, with fresh fish, such as sea bass enlivened by a lemon-flavored butter sauce; and hearty meat dishes, such a tender and flavor-filled filet steak with pepper sauce.

Old Rd. Ⓒ **01492/877993.** Reservations not necessary. Lunch platters £3–£6 ($4.80–$9.60); dinner main courses £6.25–£13 ($10–$20). DC, MC, V. Food service daily noon–2:30pm; Mon–Sat 6–8:30pm; Sun 2:30–10:30pm. Bar Mon–Sat 11am–11pm; Sun noon–10:30pm.

Richard's Bistro ⚔ WELSH/CONTINENTAL   Martin's has a slight edge, but Richard Hendey's cuisine and friendly service have him a faithful list of habitués nightly. In his basement bistro, a short walk from the pier, he spins his own culinary magic in the kitchen, turning out satisfying meals that are full of flavor. From the carnivore to the vegetarian, he aims to please, and does so admirably well. Not for the faint of heart, his perfectly roasted Welsh lamb comes with its own sautéed kidneys, everything bound together in a red-wine and grainy mustard sauce. A blackboard announces the seafood specials of the day, and generally these dishes are your best bet. His chargrilled filet of gray mullet with a white-wine sauce properly showcases this chef's talents. Everything is handled with admirable ease. Once you see the toffee apple cheesecake with caramel sauce float by, you'll somehow manage to make room for it.

7 Church Walks. Ⓒ **01492/877924.** Reservations required. Main courses £13–£16 ($20–$26). AE, MC, V. Daily 6–10pm.

Appendix:
Great Britain in Depth

1 British History 101

FROM MURKY BEGINNINGS TO ROMAN OCCUPATION Britain was probably split off from the continent of Europe some 8 millennia ago by continental drift and other natural forces. The early inhabitants, the Iberians, were later to be identified with stories of fairies, brownies, and "little people." These are the people whose ingenuity and enterprise are believed to have created Stonehenge, but despite that great and mysterious monument, little is known about them.

They were replaced by the iron-wielding Celts, whose massive invasions around 500 B.C. drove the Iberians back to the Scottish Highlands and Welsh mountains, where some of their descendants still live today.

In 54 B.C. Julius Caesar invaded England, but the Romans did not become established here until A.D. 43. They went as far as Caledonia (now Scotland), where they gave up, leaving that land to "the painted ones," or the warring Picts. The wall built by Emperor Hadrian across the north of England marked the northernmost reaches of the Roman Empire. During almost four centuries of occupation, the Romans built roads, villas, towns, walls, and fortresses; they farmed the land and introduced first their pagan religions then Christianity. Agriculture and trade flourished.

In Wales the Romans built roads to outlying fortresses at Carmarthen, Llandovery, and other sites, but they stuck to the lowlands and did not set

Dateline

- 54 B.C. Julius Caesar invades England.
- A.D. 43 Romans conquer England.
- 410 Jutes, Angles, and Saxons form small kingdoms in England.
- 500–1066 Anglo-Saxon kingdoms fight off Viking warriors.
- 1066 William, duke of Normandy, invades England, defeats Harold II at the Battle of Hastings.
- 1154 Henry II, first of the Plantagenets, launches their rule (which lasts until 1399).
- 1215 King John signs the Magna Carta at Runnymede.
- 1266 The Hebrides and the coast of western Scotland are released from Norse control.
- 1272 Edward I of England embarks on an aggressive campaign to conquer both Wales and Scotland but is deflected by Robert the Bruce among others.
- 1301 Edward I proclaims his oldest son (later Edward II) Prince of Wales, a title still held by all male heirs to the throne.
- 1337 Hundred Years' War between France and England begins.
- 1485 Battle of Bosworth Field ends the War of the Roses between the Houses of York and Lancaster; Henry VII, a Welshman, launches the Tudor dynasty.
- 1534 Henry VIII brings the Reformation to Britain and dissolves the monasteries.
- 1558 The accession of Elizabeth I ushers in an era of exploration and a renaissance in science and learning.
- 1588 Spanish Armada defeated.
- 1561 Mary Queen of Scots returns to Scotland from France.

continues

out to subdue the natives of this wild country who took to the hills and mountains. Some of the hill forts established by the Iron Age Celts were still the homes of their descendants, and some of these were very near Roman forts. Remains of many of the hill forts may be seen today.

FROM ANGLO-SAXON RULE TO THE NORMAN CONQUEST

When the Roman legions withdrew, around A.D. 410, they left the country open to waves of invasions by Jutes, Angles, and Saxons, who established themselves in small kingdoms throughout the former Roman colony. From the 8th through the 11th centuries, the Anglo-Saxons contended with Danish raiders for control of the land.

By the time of the Norman conquest, the Saxon kingdoms were united under an elected king, Edward the Confessor. His successor was to rule less than a year before the Norman invasion.

The date 1066 is familiar to every British schoolchild. It marked an epic event, the only successful military invasion of Britain in history, and one of the country's great turning points: King Harold, the last Anglo-Saxon king, was defeated at the Battle of Hastings, and William of Normandy—aka William the Conqueror—was crowned William I.

One of William's first acts was to order a survey of the land he had conquered, assessing all property in the nation for tax purposes. This survey was called the *Domesday Book,* or "Book of Doom," as some pegged it. The resulting document was completed around 1086 and has been a fertile sourcebook for British historians ever since.

Norman rule had an enormous impact. The Norman barons were given great grants of lands and built Norman-style castles and strongholds throughout the country. French was the language of the court for centuries—few people

- 1603 Mary's son, James VI of Scotland, becomes James I of England, thus uniting the crowns of England and Scotland.
- 1620 Pilgrims sail from Plymouth on the Mayflower to found a colony in the New World.
- 1629 Charles I dissolves Parliament, ruling alone.
- 1642–49 Civil War between Royalists and Parliamentarians; the Parliamentarians win.
- 1649 Charles I beheaded, and Britain is a republic.
- 1653 Oliver Cromwell becomes Lord Protector.
- 1660 Charles II restored to the throne with limited power.
- 1665–**66** Great Plague and Great Fire decimate London.
- 1688 James II, a Catholic, is deposed, and William and Mary come to the throne, signing a bill of rights.
- 1727 George I, the first of the Hanoverians, assumes the throne.
- 1746 Bonnie Prince Charlie's attempt to reclaim his grandfather's throne ends in defeat at the Battle of Culloden, destroying hopes for a Stuart restoration.
- 1756–63 In the Seven Years' War, Britain wins Canada from France.
- 1775–83 Britain loses its American colonies.
- 1795–1815 The Napoleonic Wars lead, finally, to the Battle of Waterloo and the defeat of Napoleon.
- 1837 Queen Victoria begins her reign as Britain reaches the zenith of its empire.
- 1901 Victoria dies, and Edward VII becomes king.
- 1914–18 Britain enters World War I and emerges victorious on the Allied side.
- 1936 Edward VIII abdicates to marry an American divorcée.
- 1939–45 In World War II, Britain stands alone against Hitler from the fall of France in 1940 until America enters the war in 1941. Dunkirk is evacuated in 1940; bombs rattle London during the Blitz.
- 1945 Germany surrenders. Churchill is defeated; the Labor government

realize that heroes such as Richard the Lionheart probably spoke little or no English.

While Europe's feudal system was coming to full flower and the Normans were reshaping England, Scotland was preoccupied with the territorial battles of clan allegiance and the attempt to define its borders with England. Cultural assimilation with England continued under David I (1081–1153), who made land grants to many Anglo-Norman families, providing Scotland with a feudal aristocracy and bringing in such ancient names as Fraser, Seton, and Lindsay. He also embarked on one of the most lavish building sprees in Scottish history, erecting many abbeys, including Jedburgh, Kelso, Melrose, and Dryburgh. You can still see these abbeys or their ruins. This extravagance, although giving modern visitors lots of photogenic medieval monuments, almost bankrupted his treasury.

FROM THE RULE OF HENRY II TO THE MAGNA CARTA   In 1154 Henry II, the first of the Plantagenets, was crowned (reigned 1154–89). This remarkable character in English history ruled a vast empire—not only most of Britain but Normandy, Anjou, Brittany, and Aquitaine in France.

Henry was a man of powerful physique, both charming and terrifying. He reformed the courts and introduced the system of common law, which still operates in moderated form in England today, and also influenced the American legal system. But Henry is best remembered for ordering the infamous murder of Thomas à Becket, archbishop of Canterbury. Henry, at odds with his archbishop, exclaimed, "Who will rid me of this turbulent priest?" His knights, overhearing and taking him at his word, murdered Thomas in front of the high altar in Canterbury Cathedral.

Henry's wife, Eleanor of Aquitaine, the most famous woman of her time,

introduces the welfare state and begins to dismantle the empire.

- **1952** Queen Elizabeth II ascends the throne.
- **1973** Britain joins the European Union. The discovery of North Sea oil revitalizes the Scottish economy.
- **1979** Margaret Thatcher becomes prime minister.
- **1982** Britain defeats Argentina in the Falklands War.
- **1990** Thatcher is ousted; John Major becomes prime minister.
- **1992** The Royals are jolted by fire at Windsor Castle and the marital troubles of two of the princes. Britain joins the European Single Market. Deep recession signals the end of the booming 1980s.
- **1994** Britain is linked to the Continent by rail via the Channel Tunnel or Chunnel. Tony Blair elected Labour Party leader.
- **1996** The IRA breaks a 17-month cease-fire with a truck bomb at the Docklands that claims two lives. Prince Charles and Princess Diana divorce. The government concedes a possible link between mad-cow disease and a fatal brain ailment afflicting humans; British beef imports face banishment globally.
- **1997** The Labour Party ends 18 years of Conservative Party rule with a landslide election victory and Tony Blair becomes Prime Minister. The tragic death of Diana, princess of Wales, prompts worldwide outpouring of grief. A sheep is cloned for the first time.
- **1999** Britain rushed toward the 21st century with the Millennium Dome at Greenwich; Queen Elizabeth I opens a new Scottish Parliament for the first time in 300 years.
- **2000** London "presides" over millennium celebration, and hereditary peers in the House of Lords get the boot from Blair.
- **2001** A foot-and-mouth disease epidemic brings devastation to the British economy.
- **2003** Britain joins an Allied front with the U.S. to topple the dictatorship of Saddam Hussein in Iraq.

was no less colorful. She accompanied her first husband, Louis VII of France, on the Second Crusade, and it was rumored that she had a romantic affair at that time with the Saracen leader, Saladin. Domestic and political life did not run smoothly, however, and Henry and Eleanor and their sons were often at odds. The pair have been the subject of many plays and films, including *The Lion in Winter, Becket,* and T. S. Eliot's *Murder in the Cathedral.*

Two of their sons were crowned kings of England. Richard the Lionheart actually spent most of his life outside England, on crusades, or in France. King John was forced by his nobles to sign the Magna Carta at Runnymede, in 1215—another date well known to English schoolchildren.

The Magna Carta guaranteed that the king was subject to the rule of law and gave certain rights to the king's subjects, beginning a process that eventually led to the development of parliamentary democracy as it is known in Britain today, a process that had enormous influence on the American colonies many years later. The Magna Carta became known as the cornerstone of British liberties, though it only granted liberties to the barons. It took the rebellion of Simon de Montfort half a century later to introduce the notion that the boroughs and burghers should also have a voice and representation.

The restless Welsh joined the Scots in invading England, and by the time the previously mentioned Plantagenet dynasty arose (1154), the ancient Welsh kingdom of Gwynedd (composed mainly of the northwestern section of the country) had a powerful force under Owen ap Gwynedd. Rulers of the three other Welsh kingdoms became subjects of King Henry II and were made barons. Owen agreed to do homage to Henry, but only if he was made a prince, a title he was not given by the king. Subsequent to this, however, Llewelyn the Great, as ruler of Gwynedd and with the consent of King Henry III, claimed the title of Prince of Wales in 1267.

King Edward I, in his desire to rule over an undivided nation, built the ring of castles most familiar to today's visitors and from 1277 to 1282 sent troops to subdue Wales. In that year the last native Prince of Wales, Llewelyn II, was killed in a minor skirmish near Builth Wells (the site of his fatal encounter and where his burial place can be visited). In 1301 Edward proclaimed his oldest son, later King Edward II, Prince of Wales, a title held ever since by all male heirs to the British throne.

Major changes were also sweeping across Scotland. In 1266, after about a century of Norse control, the foggy and windswept Western Isles were returned to Scotland following the Battle of Largs. Despite nominal allegiance to the Scottish monarch, this region's inhabitants quickly organized themselves around the Donald (or MacDonald) clan, which for nearly 100 years was one of the most powerful and ruled its territory almost as an independent state. The honorary title of their patriarch, Lord of the Isles, is still one of the formal titles used on state occasions by Britain's Prince of Wales.

In the meantime, real trouble was brewing in the south. Edward I, the ambitious king of England (also known as Longshanks and then the Hammer of the Scots), yearned to rule over an undivided nation incorporating England, Scotland, and Wales. Successful at first, he set up John de Balliol as a vassal king to do homage to him for Scotland. Many of Scotland's legendary heroes lived during this period: Sir William Wallace (1270–1305), who drove the English out of Perth and Stirling; Sir James Douglas (the Black Douglas; 1286–1330), who terrorized the English borders; and Robert the Bruce (1274–1329), who finally succeeded in freeing Scotland from England. Crowned Robert I at Scone in

1306, Robert the Bruce defeated Edward II of England decisively at the 1314 Battle of Bannockburn. Scotland's independence was formally recognized in the 1328 Treaty of Northampton, inaugurating a heady but short-lived separation from England.

THE BLACK DEATH & THE WARS OF THE ROSES   In 1348, the Black Death ravaged Great Britain and by the end of the century, the region's population had fallen from 4 million to 2 million.

Through these decades of struggle and conflict, Wales simmered. The cause of national independence was still strong.

"A scrambling and unquiet time," Shakespeare called the reign of King Henry IV (1399–1413), and so it was, with the Welsh doing their part to make it so. Owain Glyndwr, connected by blood to many of the royal lines of Wales and declared Prince of Wales by members of his own family, embarked on a campaign of pillage and devastation against English-held towns and castles. His banner was a red dragon on a white background, the prototype of today's Welsh flag, a red dragon on a green-and-white ground. Glyndwr succeeded in laying waste much of his country and gaining control of most of it. Some strong English nobles, notably Mortimer and Percy, joined his cause, and by the end of 1403 Glyndwr held the country except for Pembroke Castle—an English and Flemish stronghold—and the largest castles in the north. Parliaments were held at Machynlleth and at Harlech, which Glyndwr had designated as his capital. France sent military aid, and the Welsh leader even planned the future of England and Wales under the aegis of himself, Marcher Earl Mortimer, and Percy, earl of Northumberland.

From 1405, however, Glyndwr's forces lost ground and soon thereafter the country was regained by the English king. Although a new king, Henry V, offered him and his followers a pardon in 1413, Glyndwr refused it and vanished from the stage of history.

England was embattled on other fronts as well, suffering through the Hundred Years' War. By 1371, England had lost much of its land on French soil. Henry V, immortalized by Shakespeare, revived England's claims to France, and his victory at Agincourt was notable for making obsolete the forms of medieval chivalry and warfare.

After Henry's death in 1422, disputes arose among successors to the crown that resulted in a long period of civil strife, the Wars of the Roses, between the Yorkists, who used a white rose as their symbol, and the Lancastrians with their red rose. The last Yorkist king was Richard III, who got bad press from Shakespeare, but who is defended to this day as a hero by the people of the city of York. Richard was defeated at Bosworth Field, and the victory introduced England into its first Tudor, the shrewd and wily Henry VII. By a twist of fate, Henry Tudor was a Welshman.

Scotland in the 15th century was also changing. In 1468, the Orkneys and the Shetlands, Norse to the core, were brought into the Scottish web of power as part of the marriage dowry of the Norse princess Margaret to James III. This acquisition was the last successful expansion of Scottish sovereignty during the period when Scottish power and independence were at their zenith. It was at this time the Scots entered with the French into an alliance that was to have far-reaching effects. The line of Stuart (or Stewart) kings, so named because the family had become powerful as stewards of the English king, were generally accepted as the least troublesome of a series of potential evils. Real power, however, lay with Scotland's great lords, patriarchs of the famous clans. Jealous of both their bloodlines and their territories, they could rarely agree on anything other than their common distrust of England.

THE TUDORS TAKE THE THRONE   The Tudors were unlike the kings who had ruled before them. They introduced a strong central monarchy with far-reaching powers. The system worked well under the first three strong and capable Tudor monarchs, but began to break down later when the Stuarts came to the throne.

Henry VIII is surely the most notorious Tudor monarch. Imperious and flamboyant, a colossus among English royalty, he slammed shut the door on the Middle Ages and introduced the Renaissance to England. He is best known, of course, for his treatment of his six wives and the unfortunate fates that befell five of them.

When his first wife, Catherine of Aragon, failed to produce an heir, and his ambitious mistress, Anne Boleyn, became pregnant, he tried to annul his marriage, but the pope refused, and Catherine contested the action. Defying the power of Rome, Henry had his marriage with Catherine declared invalid and secretly married Anne Boleyn in 1533.

The events that followed had profound consequences and introduced the religious controversy that was to dominate English politics for the next four centuries. Henry's break with the Roman Catholic Church and the formation of the Church of England, with himself as supreme head, was a turning point in British history. It led eventually to the dissolution of the monasteries, civil unrest, and much social dislocation. The confiscation of the church's land and possessions brought untold wealth into the king's coffers, wealth that was distributed to a new aristocracy that supported the monarch. In one sweeping gesture, Henry destroyed the ecclesiastical culture of the Middle Ages. Among those executed for refusing to cooperate with Henry's changes was Sir Thomas More, humanist, international man of letters, and author of *Utopia*.

Anne Boleyn eventually bore Henry a daughter, the future Elizabeth I, but failed to produce a male heir. She was brought to trial on a trumped-up charge of adultery and beheaded; in 1536, Henry married Jane Seymour, who died giving birth to Edward VI. For his next wife, he looked farther afield and chose Anne of Cleves from a flattering portrait, but she proved disappointing—he called her "The Great Flanders Mare." He divorced her the same year and next picked a pretty young woman from his court, Catherine Howard. She was also beheaded on a charge of adultery but, unlike Anne Boleyn, was probably guilty. Finally, he married an older woman, Catherine Parr, in 1543. She survived him.

Henry's heir, sickly Edward VI (reigned 1547–53), did not live long. He died of consumption—or, as rumor has it, overmedication. He was succeeded by his sister, Mary I (reigned 1553–58), and the trouble Henry had stirred up with the break with Rome came home to roost for the first time. Mary restored the Roman Catholic faith, and her persecution of the adherents of the Church of England earned her the name of "Bloody Mary." Some 300 Protestants were executed, many burned alive at the stake. She made an unpopular and unhappy marriage to Philip of Spain; despite her bloody reputation, her life was a sad one.

Elizabeth I (reigned 1558–1603) came next to the throne, ushering in an era of peace and prosperity, exploration, and a renaissance in science and learning. An entire age was named after her: the Elizabethan age. She was the last great and grand monarch to rule England, and her passion and magnetism were said to match her father's. Through her era marched Drake, Raleigh, Frobisher, Grenville, Shakespeare, Spenser, Byrd, and Hilliard. During her reign, she had to face the appalling precedent of ordering the execution of a fellow sovereign,

Mary Queen of Scots. Her diplomatic skills kept war at bay until 1588, when at the apogee of her reign, the Spanish Armada was defeated. She is forever remembered as "Good Queen Bess."

THE REFORMATION   The passions of the Reformation burst on an already turbulent Scottish scene in the person of John Knox, a devoted disciple of the Geneva Protestant John Calvin and a bitter enemy of both the Catholic Church and the Anglican Church. Knox became famous for the screaming insults he heaped on ardently Catholic Queen Mary and for his absolute lack of a sense of humor. His polemics were famous—in his struggle against Queen Mary, he wrote his *First Blast of the Trumpet Against the Monstrous Regiment of Women.* His was a peculiar mixture of piety, conservatism, strict morality, and intellectual independence that's still a pronounced feature of the Scottish character.

Knox's teachings helped shape the democratic form of Scottish government and set the Scottish church's austere moral tone for generations to come. He focused on practical considerations as well as religious ones: church administration and funding, and the relationship between church and state. Foremost among the tenets were provisions for a self-governing congregation and pure allegiance to the word of God as contained in meticulous translations of the Old and New Testaments.

On Knox's 1562 death, his work was continued by Scottish-born, Geneva-trained Andrew Melville, who hated ecclesiastical tyranny even more (if that were possible) than Knox himself. Melville reorganized the Scottish universities and emphasized classical studies and the study of the Bible in its original Hebrew and Greek. Under his leadership emerged a clearly defined Scottish Presbyterian Church whose elected leaders were responsible for practical as well as spiritual matters.

Later, the Church of Scotland's almost obsessive insistence on self-government led to endless conflicts, first with the Scottish and then, after unification, with the British monarchs.

MARY QUEEN OF SCOTS   When Mary Stuart, Queen of Scots (1542–87), took up her rule, she was a Roman Catholic of French upbringing trying to govern an unruly land to which she was a relative newcomer. Daughter of Scotland's James V and France's Mary of Guise, she became queen when she was only 6 days old. She was sent to be educated in France and at age 15 married the heir to the French throne; she returned to Scotland only after his death. Mary then set out on two roads that were anathema to the Scots—to make herself absolute monarch in the French style and to impose Roman Catholicism. The first alienated the lords who held the real power, and the second made her the enemy of John Knox and the Calvinists. After a series of disastrous political and romantic alliances and endless abortive episodes of often indiscreet intrigue, her life was ended by the headsman's ax in England. The execution order was reluctantly issued by her cousin, Elizabeth I, who considered Mary's presence an incitement to civil unrest and a threat to the stability of the English throne.

The power of the great lords of Scotland was broken only in 1603, when Mary's son, James VI of Scotland, assumed the throne of England as James I, Elizabeth's heir. James succeeded where his doomed mother had failed. He was the first of the Stuarts to occupy the English throne, and his coronation effectively united England and Scotland.

CIVIL WAR ERUPTS   The Stuarts held the throne through a century of civil war and religious dissension, but they were not as capable as the Tudors in walking the line between the demands of a strong centralized monarchy and the rights increasingly demanded by the representatives of the people in Parliament.

Charles I, attracted by the French idea of the divine right of the king, considered himself above the law, a mistake the Tudors had never made (Elizabeth, in particular, was clever and careful in her dealings with Parliament). Charles's position was a fatal response to the Puritans and other dissenters who sought far more power. In 1629, Charles dissolved Parliament, determined to rule without it.

Civil War followed, and the victory went to the Roundheads under Oliver Cromwell. Charles I was put on trial and was led to his execution, stepping onto the scaffold through the window of his gloriously decorated Banqueting House. His once-proud head rolled on the ground.

Oliver Cromwell, the melancholy, unambitious, clumsy farmer, became Britain's first and only virtual dictator. He saw his soldiers as God's faithful servants, and promised them rewards in heaven. The people, however, did not take kindly to this form of government, and after Cromwell's death, Charles II, the dead king's son, returned and was crowned in 1660, but he was given greatly limited powers.

THE REIGN OF WILLIAM AND MARY   The reign of Charles II was the beginning of a dreadful decade that saw London decimated by the Great Plague and destroyed by the Great Fire.

His successor, James II, attempted to return the country to Catholicism; this attempt so frightened the powers that be that Catholics were for a long time deprived of their civil rights. James was deposed in the "Glorious Revolution" of 1688 and succeeded by his daughter Mary (1662–94) and William of Orange (1650–1702). (William of Orange was the grandson of Charles I, the tyrannical king whom Cromwell helped depose.) This secured a Protestant succession that has continued to this day. These tolerant and levelheaded monarchs signed a bill of rights, establishing the principle that the monarch reigns not by divine right but by the will of Parliament. William outlived his wife, reigning until 1702.

THE JACOBITES   This change of thrones and dynasties did not play out well in Scotland. When the English Parliament stripped James II of his crown and imported those Protestant monarchs, William and Mary, from Holland, the exiled ex-king and then his son James Edward (the Old Pretender) became focal points for Scottish unrest. The Jacobites (the name comes from *Jacobus,* the Latin form of James) attempted unsuccessfully in 1715 to place the Old Pretender on the English throne and restore the Stuart line. Although James died in exile, his son Charles Edward (the Young Pretender), better known as Bonnie Prince Charlie, carried on his father's dream. Charismatic but with an alcohol-induced instability, he was the central figure of the 1745 Jacobite uprising.

Although the revolt was initially promising because of the many Scottish adherents who crossed religious lines to rally to the cause, the Jacobite forces were crushed at the Battle of Culloden, near Inverness, by a numerically superior English army led by the duke of Cumberland. Many supporters of the Pretender's cause were killed in battle, some were executed, and others fled to the United States and other safe havens. Fearing a rebirth of similar types of Scottish nationalism, the clan system was rigorously suppressed, clans that supported the Jacobite cause lost their lands, and, until 1782, the wearing of Highland dress was made illegal.

The Young Pretender himself was smuggled unglamorously out of Scotland, assisted by a resident of the obscure Hebridean island of South Uist, Flora MacDonald. One of the era's most visible Scottish heroines, she has ever since provided fodder for the Scottish sense of romance. The Bonnie Prince dissipated himself in Paris and Rome, and the hopes of an independent Scotland were buried.

FROM QUEEN ANNE TO THE NAPOLEONIC WARS   Queen Anne, sister of Mary of Orange and another daughter of James II, ruled from 1702 until her own death in 1714. The last of the Stuarts, Anne marked her reign with the most significant event, the 1707 Act of Union with Scotland. She outlived all her children, leaving her throne without an heir.

Upon the death of Anne, England looked for a Protestant prince to succeed her, and chose George of Hanover who reigned from 1714–27. Chosen because he was the great-grandson of James I, the king spoke only German and spent as little time in England as possible. Beginning with this "distant cousin" to the throne, the reign of George I marked the beginning of the 174-year rule of the Hanoverians who preceded Victoria.

George I left the running of the government to the English politicians and created the office of Prime Minister. Under the Hanoverians, the powers of Parliament were extended, and the constitutional monarchy developed into what it is today.

The American colonies were lost under the Hanoverian George III, but other British possessions were expanded: Canada was won from the French in the Seven Years' War (1756–63), British control over India was affirmed, and Captain Cook claimed Australia and New Zealand for England. The British became embroiled in the Napoleonic Wars (1795–1815), achieving two of their greatest victories and acquiring two of their greatest heroes: Nelson at Trafalgar and Wellington at Waterloo.

THE INDUSTRIAL REVOLUTION & THE REIGN OF VICTORIA   The mid- to late 18th century saw the beginnings of the Industrial Revolution. This event changed the lives of the laboring class, created a wealthy middle class, and transformed Britain from a rural, agricultural society into an urban, industrial economy. Britain was now a world-class financial and military power. Male suffrage was extended, though women were disenfranchised for the rest of the century.

Queen Victoria's reign (1837–1901) coincided with the height of the Industrial Revolution. When she ascended the throne, the monarchy as an institution was in considerable doubt, but her 64-year reign, the longest tenure in British history, was an incomparable success.

The Victorian era was shaped by the growing power of the bourgeoisie, the queen and her consort's personal moral stance, and the perceived moral responsibilities of managing a vast empire. During this time, the first trade unions were formed, a public (state) school system was developed, and railroads were built.

Victoria never recovered from the death of her German husband, Albert. He died from typhoid fever in 1861, and the queen never remarried. Although she had many children, she found them tiresome, but she was a pillar of family values nonetheless. One historian said her greatest asset was her relative ordinariness.

Middle-class values ruled Victorian Britain and were embodied by the queen. The racy England of the past went underground. Our present-day view of England is still influenced by the attitudes of the Victorian era, and we tend to forget that English society in earlier centuries was famous for its rowdiness, sexual license, and spicy scandal.

Victoria's son Edward VII (reigned 1901–10) was a playboy who had waited too long in the wings. He is famous for mistresses, especially Lillie Langtry, and his love of elaborate dinners. During his brief reign, he, too, had an era named after him: the Edwardian age. Under Edward, the country entered the 20th century at the height of its imperial power, and at home the advent of the motorcar and the telephone radically changed social life, and the women's suffrage movement began.

World War I marked the end of an era. It had been assumed that peace, progress, prosperity, empire, and even social improvement would continue indefinitely. World War I and the troubled decades of social unrest, political uncertainty, and the rise of Nazism and fascism put an end to these expectations.

THE WINDS OF WAR   World War II began in 1939, and soon thereafter Britain found a new and inspiring leader, Winston Churchill. Churchill led the nation during its "finest hour." From the time the Germans took France, Britain stood alone against Hitler. The evacuation of Dunkirk in 1940, the Blitz of London, and the Battle of Britain were dark hours for the British people, and Churchill is remembered for urging them to hold on to their courage. Once the British forces were joined by their American allies, the tide finally turned, culminating in the D-Day invasion of German-occupied Normandy. These bloody events are still remembered by many with pride, and with nostalgia for the era when Britain was still a great world power.

The years following World War II brought many changes. Britain began to lose its grip on an empire (India became independent in 1947), and the Labour government, which came into power in 1945, established the welfare state and brought profound social change to Britain.

QUEEN ELIZABETH RULES TO THE PRESENT DAY   On the death of the "wartime king," George VI, Queen Elizabeth II ascended the throne in 1953. Her reign has seen the erosion of Britain's once-mighty industrial power.

Political power has seesawed back and forth between the Conservative and Labour Parties. Margaret Thatcher, who became prime minister in 1979, seriously eroded the welfare state and was ambivalent toward the European Union. Her popularity soared during the successful Falklands War, when Britain seemed to recover some of its military glory for a brief time.

Although the queen has remained steadfast and punctiliously performed her ceremonial duties, in the year 1992, which Queen Elizabeth labeled an *annus horribilis,* a devastating fire swept through Windsor Castle, the marriages of several of her children crumbled, and the queen agreed to pay taxes for the first time. Prince Charles and Princess Diana agreed to a separation, and there were ominous rumblings about the future of the House of Windsor. (The princess died in 1997 in a car accident in Paris.) By 1994 and 1995, Britain's economy was improving after several glum years, but Conservative prime minister John Major, heir to Margaret Thatcher's legacy, was coming under increasing criticism.

The Irish Republican Army (IRA), reputedly enraged at the slow pace of peace talks, relaunched its reign of terror across London in February 1996, planting a massive bomb that ripped through a building in London's Docklands, injuring more than 100 people and killing 2. Shattered, too, was the 17-month cease-fire by the IRA, which brought hope that peace was at least possible.

Headlines about the IRA bombing gave way to another big bomb: the end of the marriage of Princess Diana and Prince Charles. The wedding of the century became the divorce of the century. The lurid tabloids had been right all along about this unhappy pair. But details of the $26 million divorce settlement didn't satisfy the curious: Scrutiny of Prince Charles's relationship with Camilla Parker-Bowles, as well as gossip about Princess Diana's love life, continued in the press.

But in 1997, everyone's attention shifted to the parliamentary election. John Major's support had been steadily eroding since the early 1990s, but the public's confidence in him seemed to hit an all-time low with his handling of the mad-cow disease crisis.

The political limelight now rested on the young Labour Leader Tony Blair. His media-savvy personality obviously registered with the British electorate. On May 1, 1997, the Labour Party ended 18 years of Conservative rule with a landslide election victory. At age 44, Blair became Britain's youngest prime minister in 185 years, following in the wake of the largest Labour triumph since Winston Churchill was swept out of office at the end of World War II.

The national election results gave Blair a victory over the Nationalist Party of Scotland. Labour, however, failed to win outright control of the Scottish Parliament; but Blair said he felt the results represented an endorsement of his reform of British politics. Nine seats short of a majority in the new 129-seat Parliament (the first legislature Scotland has had since its 1707 union with England), Labour was obliged to enlist the centrist Liberal Democrats in a coalition, a form of governance not seen in Britain since World War II.

The new Scottish legislature has authority to pursue such matters as health, education, public transportation, and public housing. Unlike the new Welsh Parliament, the Scottish Parliament will also have taxing powers and can make laws. The main Parliament, of course, will remain in London, where Scotland will be widely represented. The country will bow to the greater will of Britain in matters like foreign policy, national defense, and economic and fiscal policies and may one day become part of euro-land, the new umbrella of single-currency countries (France, Germany, Italy, and so on). So far, Britain has decided to stick with the pound sterling as its time-honored form of currency.

Blair continues to lead Britain on a program of constitutional reform without parallel in this century. Critics fear that Blair will one day preside over a "disunited" Britain, with Scotland breaking away, and Northern Ireland forming a self-government.

Of course, the future of the monarchy still remains a hot topic of discussion in Britain. There is little support for doing away with the monarchy in Britain today in spite of wide criticism of the royal family's behavior in the wake of Diana's death. Apparently, if polls are to be believed, some three-quarters of the British populace want the monarchy to continue. Prince Charles is even making a comeback with the British public and has appeared in public—to the delight of the paparazzi—with his longtime mistress, Camilla Parker-Bowles. At the very least the monarchy is good for the tourist trade, on which Britain is increasingly dependent. And what would the tabloids do without it?

Tony Blair continues to shake up the House of Lords—that is, in expelling the hereditary peers from the 1,200-member chamber. For the first time in their political careers, members of the House of Lords may have to face the unthinkable—an election.

After promising beginnings, the 21st century got off to a bad start in Britain. In the wake of mad-cow disease flare-ups, the country was swept by a foot-and-mouth disease epidemic that disrupted the country's agriculture, already suffering from mad-cow disease, and threatened one of the major sources of British livelihoods, its burgeoning tourist industry. Billions of pounds in tourism were lost before order was returned.

2 Pies, Pudding & Pints: The Lowdown on British Cuisine

The late British humorist George Mikes wrote that "the Continentals have good food; the English have good table manners." But the British no longer deserve their reputation for soggy cabbage and tasteless dishes. Contemporary

London—and the country as a whole—boasts many fine restaurants and sophisticated cuisine.

There's a lot more to British food today than the traditional roast, which has been celebrated since long before the days of Henry VIII. Of course, parsnip soup is still served, but now it's likely to be graced with a dollop of walnut salsa verde. In contemporary England, the chef of the early millennium has taken on celebrity status. The creator of breast of Gressingham duck topped with deep-fried seaweed and served with a passion-fruit sauce is honored the way rock stars were in the 1970s. Some restaurants are so popular that they are demanding reservations 2 weeks in advance, if not more.

If you want to see what Britain is eating today, just drop in at Harvey Nichol's Fifth Floor in London's Knightsbridge for its dazzling display of produce from all over the globe.

The new buzzword for British cuisine is *magpie,* meaning borrowing ideas from global travels, taking them home, but improving on the original.

Be aware that many of the trendiest, most innovative restaurants are mind-blowingly expensive, especially in London. We've pointed out some innovative but affordable choices in this book, but if you're really trying to save on dining costs, you'll no doubt find yourself falling back on the traditional pub favorites (or better still, turning to an increasingly good selection of ethnic restaurants).

EATING OUT IN ENGLAND   On any pub menu you're likely to encounter such dishes as the **Cornish pasty** and **shepherd's pie.** The first, traditionally made from Sunday-meal leftovers and taken by West Country fishers for Monday lunch, consists of chopped potatoes, carrots, and onions mixed together with seasoning and put into a pastry envelope. The second is a deep dish of chopped cooked beef mixed with onions and seasoning, covered with a layer of mashed potatoes, and served hot. Another version is cottage pie, which is minced beef covered with potatoes and also served hot. Of course, these beef dishes are subject to availability. In addition to a pasty, Cornwall also gives us **Stargazy pie**—a deep-dish fish pie with a crisp crust covering a creamy concoction of freshly caught herring and vegetables.

The most common pub meal, though, is the **ploughman's lunch,** traditional farm-worker's fare, consisting of a good chunk of local cheese, a hunk of homemade crusty white or brown bread, some butter, and a pickled onion or two, washed down with ale. You'll now find such variations as paté and chutney occasionally replacing the onions and cheese. Or you might find **Lancashire hot pot,** a stew of mutton, potatoes, kidneys, and onions (sometimes carrots). This concoction was originally put into a deep dish and set on the edge of the stove to cook slowly while the workers spent the day at the local mill.

Among appetizers, called **starters** in Britain, the most typical are potted shrimp (small buttered shrimp preserved in a jar), prawn cocktail, and smoked salmon. You might also be served paté or *fish pie,* which is very light fish paté. Most menus will feature a variety of soups, including cock-a-leekie (chicken soup flavored with leeks), perhaps a game soup that has been doused with sherry, and many others.

Among the best-known traditional British meals is **roast beef** and **Yorkshire pudding** (the pudding is made with a flour base and cooked under the roast, allowing the fat from the meat to drop onto it). The beef could easily be a large sirloin (rolled loin), which, so the story goes, was named by James I when he was a guest at Houghton Tower, Lancashire. "Arise, Sir Loin," he cried, as he knighted the leg of beef before him with his dagger. (Again, because of the mad-cow crisis, beef dishes may not be available or advisable.) Another dish that makes use of a flour base is toad-in-the-hole, in which sausages are cooked in batter. Game, especially pheasant and grouse, is also a staple on British tables.

On any menu, you'll find **fresh seafood:** cod, haddock, herring, plaice, and Dover sole, the aristocrat of flatfish. Cod and haddock are used in making British **fish and chips** (chips are fried potatoes or thick french fries), which the true Briton covers with salt and vinegar. If you like **oysters,** try some of the famous Colchester variety. Every region of England has its seafood specialties. On the west coast, you'll find a not-to-be-missed delicacy: **Morecambe Bay shrimp.**

The British call desserts *sweets,* although some people still refer to any dessert as **pudding. Trifle** is the most famous English dessert, consisting of sponge cake soaked in brandy or sherry, coated with fruit or jam, and topped with cream custard. A **fool,** such as gooseberry fool, is a light cream dessert whipped up from seasonal fruits. Regional sweets include the **northern flitting dumpling** (dates, walnuts, and syrup mixed with other ingredients and made into a pudding that is easily sliced and carried along when you're "flitting" from place to place). Similarly, **hasty pudding,** a Newcastle dish, is supposed to have been invented by people in a hurry to avoid the bailiff. It consists of stale bread, to which some dried fruit and milk are added before it is put into the oven.

Cheese is traditionally served after dessert as a savory. There are many regional cheeses, the best known being cheddar, a good, solid, mature cheese. Others are the semi-smooth Caerphilly, from a beautiful part of Wales, and Stilton, a blue-veined crumbly cheese that's often enjoyed with a glass of port.

IN SCOTLAND: FROM ANGUS TO HAGGIS   For most of the 20th century, restaurants in Scotland were known mainly for their modest prices, watery overcooked vegetables, and boiled meats. But you need no longer expect a diet of oats, fried fish, and greasy chips—in the past 25 or so years there has been a significant improvement in Scottish cookery. There was a time that the Scot going out for dinner would head for the nearest hotel, but independent restaurants are now opening everywhere, often by newly arrived immigrants, along with bistros and wine bars.

More and more restaurants are offering "taste of Scotland" menus of traditional dishes prepared with the freshest local ingredients, a culinary program initiated by the Scottish Tourist Board. Scotland's culinary strength is in its fresh raw ingredients, ranging from seafood, beef, and game to vegetables and native fruits.

One of Scotland's best-known dishes is pedigree **Aberdeen Angus beef.** In fact, the famous ye olde roast beef of England often came from Scotland. Scottish **lamb** is known for its tender, tasty meat. A true connoisseur can taste the difference in lamb by its grazing grounds, ranging from the coarse pastureland and seaweed of the Shetlands to the heather-clad hills of the mainland.

Game plays an important role in the Scottish diet, from woodcock, red deer, and grouse to the rabbit and hare in the crofter's kitchen. And **fish** in this land of seas, rivers, and lochs is a mainstay, from salmon to the pink-fleshed brown trout to the modest herring that's transformed into the elegant kipper (the best are the Loch Fyne kippers). Scottish smoked salmon is, of course, a delicacy known worldwide.

The good news is that the word *eclectic* now describes many restaurants in Scotland. To cite only an example or two, fresh salads often are given a Thai kick with lime leaves and chile, and stir-fry and chargrill are standard features. Scots today eat better than ever in their history. Robert Burns would be shocked at some of the new taste sensations creative chefs are devising. But he would be happy to learn that alcohol—especially whisky—is still a favored ingredient in many dishes and sauces.

Of course, it takes a wise chef to leave well enough alone, and many Scottish cooks know the simplest dishes have never lost their appeal, especially if that means Lismore oysters or Loch Etive mussels. The Scots have always been good bakers, and many small tearooms still bake their own scones, buttery shortbread, and fruity breads. Heather honey is justly celebrated, and jams make use of Scotland's abundant harvest of soft fruit. Scottish raspberries, for example, are said to be among the finest in the world.

You'll most definitely want to try some of Scotland's excellent **cheeses.** The mild or mature cheddars are the best known. A famous hard cheese, Dunlop, comes from the Orkney Islands as well as Arran and Islay. One of the best-known cheeses from the Highlands is Caboc, creamy and rich, formed into cork shapes and rolled in pinhead oatmeal. Many varieties of cottage cheese are flavored with herbs, chives, or garlic.

And, yes, **haggis** is still Scotland's national dish—it's perhaps more symbolic than gustatory. One wit described this dish as a "castrated bagpipe." Regardless of what you might be told facetiously, haggis isn't a bird. Therefore, you should turn down invitations (usually offered in pubs) to go on a midnight haggis hunt. Cooked in a sheep's paunch (nowadays more likely a plastic bag), it's made with bits and pieces of the lung, liver, and heart of sheep mixed with suet and spices, along with onions and oatmeal. Haggis is often accompanied by single-malt whisky—then again, what isn't?

A TASTE OF WALES   The food you'll be served in Wales is often indistinguishable from that you would have in Britain or Scotland, but there are a number of specialties you should try that you won't find elsewhere. **A Taste of Wales** restaurant program has been established whereby travelers can enjoy traditional Welsh cuisine. A symbol, an iron bakestone or griddle bearing the words "Blas ar Gymru—A Taste of Wales," indicates that a restaurant, pub, cafe, hotel, guest house, or farmhouse offers traditional and contemporary Welsh food, as well as other choices.

The **leek** is one of the national emblems of Wales, and is used in a number of dishes. The selection of the leek for this national honor is lost in the dim past, although associated with St. David, patron saint of Wales. Today the leek is worn on St. David's Day, March 1, a national holiday.

Among dishes in which the leek is used is **cawl mamgu,** a rich soup or stew. The most commonly used recipe calls for lamb or mutton, turnips (the Welsh call them Swedes), carrots, potatoes, parsnips, onions, and leeks. At home the broth is often served first with bread, the meat and vegetables being used as a main course. In some sections of the country, home-cured bacon is the meat used, brewed up with finely chopped vegetables. The **leek pastie,** usually made in the shape of a little leek, is a popular appetizer or side dish.

The potato became a dietary staple of Wales in the 18th century. **Anglesey** eggs feature potatoes and leeks as well as cheese. **Punchnep** is a combination of potatoes and turnips served with heavy cream. **Teisen nionod,** or onion cake, is a tasty, slow-baked potato-and-onion dish.

Most people are familiar with **Welsh rarebit** (or rabbit, if you prefer), but another cheese dish you should try that is not found elsewhere is **Glamorgan**

sausage, a meatless concoction of onion, cheese, breadcrumbs, and seasonings, shaped like sausages, dipped in breadcrumbs, and fried. Another good dish, **skirettes,** is served at the Skirrid Inn near Abergavenny. This is a sort of mashed-potato pancake with a difference. The difference is supplied by grated walnuts, prawns, hard-boiled eggs, onion, cheddar cheese, and spices. It's all given a breadcrumb coating and baked or deep-fried.

Faggots used to be made of meat fragments left over after pig slaughter, wrapped in membrane that covers the pig's abdominal organs, and shaped like sausages. Today it's all a little more palatable sounding, being made of liver, bacon, onions, breadcrumbs, and sage, cooked and served cold.

Rabbit, chicken, turkey, duckling, game, even pheasant appear on the menus, and a rabbit casserole is offered in some restaurants as a Taste of Wales, so popular is the meat. Special dishes include a **poacher's pie** (containing beef, rabbit, chicken, and game) and **Welsh salt duck,** which rivals any offered on Asian menus. Predominant on the list of what to eat while in Wales are freshwater fish and seafood. **Trout and salmon** prevail among the products of rivers and lakes, tumbling practically from the fisherman's creel to your plate, with a little detour through the kitchen. Perhaps you'll get to taste a rare salmon, the **gwyniad,** which is found only in Bala Lake. Baked trout with bacon is a favorite.

From the ocean and coastal waters come crabs, lobsters, sewin (sea trout), crayfish, mackerel, herring, Pollack, bass, hake, ling, whiting, and flat fish, as well as cockles, limpets, scallops, and mussels. The Romans were great cockle eaters, as revealed by huge mounds of the shells found in excavating the sites occupied by the long-ago conquerors. You might enjoy the **cockle-and-bacon pie** offered on some menus, or Gower scallops and bacon. Mussel stew and mussel and queenie (scallop) cawl, which is like a bouillabaisse, are popular dishes.

The Welsh word for bread is *bara.* At least once, you should try **laverbread (bara lawr),** which has probably been part of the Welsh diet since prehistoric times. It's made of laver weed, a parchmentlike seaweed, which is boiled and mixed with oatmeal, shaped into laverbread cakes, and fried like pancakes. It's full of vitamins and minerals. You'll find it on all Taste of Wales menus, so take a nibble at least. **Bara ceirch,** a flat oatcake, is rolled very thin and cooked on a griddle. A rich currant bread, **bara brith,** is found all over the country, although the ingredients may vary. It's baked in a loaf, and some cooks use raisins and candied citrus peel along with the currants.

Perhaps you'll get a chance to sample **Welsh cakes** made with currants. You may want to buy some at Dylan Thomas's boathouse at Laugharne and munch them with your tea as you look across the wide estuary where the poet had much the same view as his Iron Age predecessors. **Oat biscuits** are another treat, much like the oatmeal cookies you may have had back home. Desserts (*puddings* they're called here, whatever their form) seem to be mainly **fruit crumbles—** blackberry, apple, what have you—topped with custard and/or thick cream.

BRITISH BREAKFASTS & AFTERNOON TEA   Britain is famous for its enormous breakfast of bacon, eggs, grilled tomato, and fried bread. Some places have replaced this cholesterol festival with a continental breakfast, but you'll still find the traditional morning meal available.

Kipper, or smoked herring, is also a popular breakfast dish. The finest come from the Isle of Man, Whitby, or Loch Fyne, in Scotland. The herrings are split open, placed over oak chips, and slowly cooked to produce a nice pale-brown smoked fish.

Many people still enjoy afternoon tea, which may consist of a simple cup of tea or a formal tea that starts with tiny crustless sandwiches filled with cucumber or watercress and proceeds through scones, crumpets with jam, or clotted cream, followed by cakes and tarts—all accompanied by a proper pot of tea.

In the country, including Wales and Scotland, tea shops abound, and in Devon, Cornwall, and the West Country you'll find the best cream teas; they consist of scones spread with jam and thick, clotted Devonshire cream. It's a delicious treat, indeed. People in Britain drink an average of four cups of tea a day, although many younger people prefer coffee.

WHAT TO WASH IT ALL DOWN WITH   British pubs serve a variety of cocktails, but their stock-in-trade is beer: brown beer, or bitter; blond beer, or lager; and very dark beer, or stout. The standard draft beer is much stronger than American beer and is served "with the chill off" because it doesn't taste good cold. Lager is always chilled, whereas stout can be served either way. Beer is always served straight from the tap, in two sizes: half pint (8 oz.) and pint (16 oz.).

One of the most significant changes in British drinking habits has been the popularity of wine bars, and you will find many to try, including some that turn into discos late at night. Britain isn't known for its wine, although it does produce some medium-sweet fruity whites. Its cider, though, is famous—and mighty potent in contrast to the American variety.

Whisky (spelled without the *e*) refers to scotch. Canadian and Irish whiskey (spelled with the *e*) are also available, but only the best-stocked bars have American bourbon and rye.

"It's the only liquor fit for a gentleman to drink in the morning if he can have the good fortune to come by it . . . or after dinner either." Thus wrote Sir Walter Scott of the drink of his country—**scotch whisky.** Of course, if you're here or almost anywhere in Britain or Europe, you don't have to identify it as *scotch* whisky when you order. That's what you'll get. In fact, in some parts of Scotland, England, and Wales, they look at you oddly if you order scotch as you would in the States.

The true difference in the scotch whiskies you may have become accustomed to seeing on bars or shelves of liquor stores at home is whether they're blends or single-malt whiskies. Many connoisseurs prefer single malts, whose tastes depend on their points of origin: Highlands, Lowlands, Islay, or Campbeltown on Kintyre. These are usually seen as sipping whiskies, not to be mixed with water (well, maybe soda) and not to be served with ice. Many have come to be used as after-dinner drinks, served in a snifter like cognac.

The blended scotches came into being both because the single malts were for a long time too harsh for delicate palates and because they were expensive and time-consuming to produce. A shortcut was developed: The clear and almost tasteless alcohol produced in the traditional way could be mixed with such ingredients as American corn, Finnish barley, Glasgow city tap water, and caramel coloring with a certain percentage of malt whiskies that flavored the entire bottle. Whichever you prefer, both the single malts and the blends must be made within the borders of Scotland and then aged for at least 3 years before they can legally be called scotch whisky.

The British tend to drink everything at a warmer temperature than Americans are used to. So if you like ice in your soda, be sure to ask for lots of it, or you're likely to end up with a measly, quickly melting cube or two.

Index

HIT THE ROAD WITH FROMMER'S DRIVING TOURS!

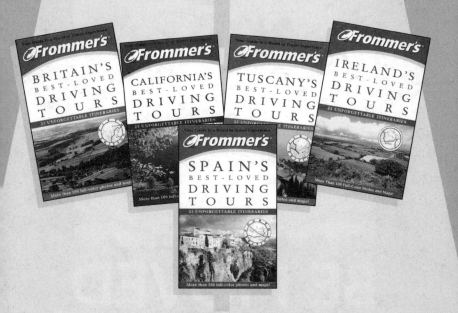

BE MOVED

 London's Transport Museum

Covent Garden Piazza

www.ltmuseum.co.uk
24 hr info (020) 7565 7299

FROMMER'S® COMPLETE TRAVEL GUIDES

Alaska
Alaska Cruises & Ports of Call
Amsterdam
Argentina & Chile
Arizona
Atlanta
Australia
Austria
Bahamas
Barcelona, Madrid & Seville
Beijing
Belgium, Holland & Luxembourg
Bermuda
Boston
Brazil
British Columbia & the Canadian Rockies
Brussels & Bruges
Budapest & the Best of Hungary
California
Canada
Cancún, Cozumel & the Yucatán
Cape Cod, Nantucket & Martha's Vineyard
Caribbean
Caribbean Cruises & Ports of Call
Caribbean Ports of Call
Carolinas & Georgia
Chicago
China
Colorado
Costa Rica
Cuba
Denmark
Denver, Boulder & Colorado Springs
England
Europe
European Cruises & Ports of Call

Florida
France
Germany
Great Britain
Greece
Greek Islands
Hawaii
Hong Kong
Honolulu, Waikiki & Oahu
Ireland
Israel
Italy
Jamaica
Japan
Las Vegas
London
Los Angeles
Maryland & Delaware
Maui
Mexico
Montana & Wyoming
Montréal & Québec City
Munich & the Bavarian Alps
Nashville & Memphis
New England
New Mexico
New Orleans
New York City
New Zealand
Northern Italy
Norway
Nova Scotia, New Brunswick & Prince Edward Island
Oregon
Paris
Peru
Philadelphia & the Amish Country
Portugal

Prague & the Best of the Czech Republic
Provence & the Riviera
Puerto Rico
Rome
San Antonio & Austin
San Diego
San Francisco
Santa Fe, Taos & Albuquerque
Scandinavia
Scotland
Seattle & Portland
Shanghai
Sicily
Singapore & Malaysia
South Africa
South America
South Florida
South Pacific
Southeast Asia
Spain
Sweden
Switzerland
Texas
Thailand
Tokyo
Toronto
Tuscany & Umbria
USA
Utah
Vancouver & Victoria
Vermont, New Hampshire & Maine
Vienna & the Danube Valley
Virgin Islands
Virginia
Walt Disney World® & Orlando
Washington, D.C.
Washington State

FROMMER'S® DOLLAR-A-DAY GUIDES

Australia from $50 a Day
California from $70 a Day
England from $75 a Day
Europe from $70 a Day
Florida from $70 a Day
Hawaii from $80 a Day

Ireland from $60 a Day
Italy from $70 a Day
London from $85 a Day
New York from $90 a Day
Paris from $80 a Day

San Francisco from $70 a Day
Washington, D.C. from $80 a Day
Portable London from $85 a Day
Portable New York City from $90 a Day

FROMMER'S® PORTABLE GUIDES

Acapulco, Ixtapa & Zihuatanejo
Amsterdam
Aruba
Australia's Great Barrier Reef
Bahamas
Berlin
Big Island of Hawaii
Boston
California Wine Country
Cancún
Cayman Islands
Charleston
Chicago
Disneyland®
Dublin
Florence

Frankfurt
Hong Kong
Houston
Las Vegas
Las Vegas for Non-Gamblers
London
Los Angeles
Los Cabos & Baja
Maine Coast
Maui
Miami
Nantucket & Martha's Vineyard
New Orleans
New York City
Paris
Phoenix & Scottsdale

Portland
Puerto Rico
Puerto Vallarta, Manzanillo & Guadalajara
Rio de Janeiro
San Diego
San Francisco
Savannah
Seattle
Sydney
Tampa & St. Petersburg
Vancouver
Venice
Virgin Islands
Washington, D.C.

FROMMER'S® NATIONAL PARK GUIDES

Banff & Jasper
Family Vacations in the National Parks

Grand Canyon
National Parks of the American West
Rocky Mountain

Yellowstone & Grand Teton
Yosemite & Sequoia/Kings Canyon
Zion & Bryce Canyon

FROMMER'S® MEMORABLE WALKS

Chicago	New York	San Francisco
London	Paris	

FROMMER'S® WITH KIDS GUIDES

Chicago	Ottawa	Vancouver
Las Vegas	San Francisco	Washington, D.C.
New York City	Toronto	

SUZY GERSHMAN'S BORN TO SHOP GUIDES

Born to Shop: France	Born to Shop: Italy	Born to Shop: New York
Born to Shop: Hong Kong, Shanghai & Beijing	Born to Shop: London	Born to Shop: Paris

FROMMER'S® IRREVERENT GUIDES

Amsterdam	Los Angeles	San Francisco
Boston	Manhattan	Seattle & Portland
Chicago	New Orleans	Vancouver
Las Vegas	Paris	Walt Disney World®
London	Rome	Washington, D.C.

FROMMER'S® BEST-LOVED DRIVING TOURS

Britain	Germany	Northern Italy
California	Ireland	Scotland
Florida	Italy	Spain
France	New England	Tuscany & Umbria

HANGING OUT™ GUIDES

Hanging Out in England	Hanging Out in France	Hanging Out in Italy
Hanging Out in Europe	Hanging Out in Ireland	Hanging Out in Spain

THE UNOFFICIAL GUIDES®

Bed & Breakfasts and Country Inns in:	Southwest & South Central Plains	Mexio's Best Beach Resorts
California	U.S.A.	Mid-Atlantic with Kids
Great Lakes States	Beyond Disney	Mini Las Vegas
Mid-Atlantic	Branson, Missouri	Mini-Mickey
New England	California with Kids	New England & New York with Kids
Northwest	Central Italy	New Orleans
Rockies	Chicago	New York City
Southeast	Cruises	Paris
Southwest	Disneyland®	San Francisco
Best RV & Tent Campgrounds in:	Florida with Kids	Skiing & Snowboarding in the West
California & the West	Golf Vacations in the Eastern U.S.	Southeast with Kids
Florida & the Southeast	Great Smoky & Blue Ridge Region	Walt Disney World®
Great Lakes States	Inside Disney	Walt Disney World® for Grown-ups
Mid-Atlantic	Hawaii	Walt Disney World® with Kids
Northeast	Las Vegas	Washington, D.C.
Northwest & Central Plains	London	World's Best Diving Vacations
	Maui	

SPECIAL-INTEREST TITLES

Frommer's Adventure Guide to Australia & New Zealand	Frommer's France's Best Bed & Breakfasts and Country Inns
Frommer's Adventure Guide to Central America	Frommer's Gay & Lesbian Europe
Frommer's Adventure Guide to India & Pakistan	Frommer's Italy's Best Bed & Breakfasts and Country Inns
Frommer's Adventure Guide to South America	Frommer's Road Atlas Britain
Frommer's Adventure Guide to Southeast Asia	Frommer's Road Atlas Europe
Frommer's Adventure Guide to Southern Africa	Frommer's Road Atlas France
Frommer's Britain's Best Bed & Breakfasts and Country Inns	The New York Times' Guide to Unforgettable Weekends
Frommer's Caribbean Hideaways	Places Rated Almanac
Frommer's Exploring America by RV	Retirement Places Rated
Frommer's Fly Safe, Fly Smart	Rome Past & Present

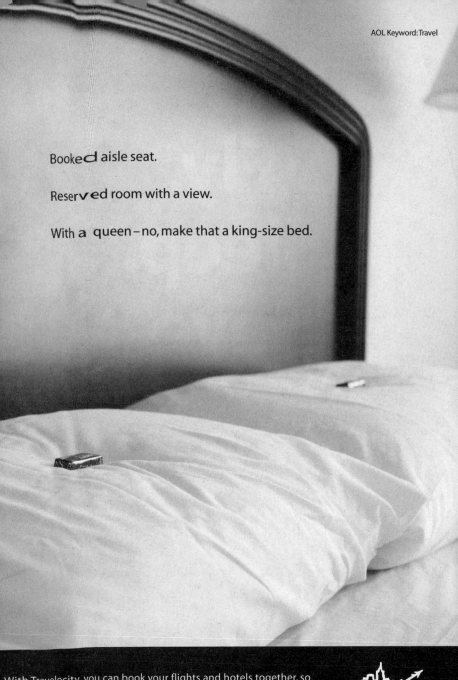